it's as simple as 1, 2, 3.

3 Self Study Options

Realizing that every candidate's needs are different, **Bisk CPA Review** offers a variety of products to help you pass the CPA Exam. Choose the formats that best suit your learning style.

Mix and match or call **1-888-CPA-BISK** about our many cost saving packages. And don't forget there are **Special Discount Coupons** at the back of this textbook!

Bisk Audio Tutor — *Study on the Go!*

a) Listen to them in the car and gain **10-15 hours of study time each week.**

b) Packed with nearly 40 hours of vital exam information. Easy to follow format includes an index to help you locate specific topics of interest quickly and easily.

c) Available on CD or cassette by individual exam section or as a 4 volume set.

d) Great reinforcers! The audio lectures work hand in hand with other **Bisk CPA Review** materials.

e) Digitally recorded, featuring America's best CPA instructors.

f) **Bisk CPA Review** originated CPA Review audio more than 30 years ago and still sets the industry standard!

Hot•Spot™ Video Series — *Targeted Training!*

a) Your choice of 32 topic-specific videos, each packed with valuable exam tips plus viewer's guides with complete notes *(call for a complete listing of titles).*

b) Weak in a specific area? Order just the titles you need!

c) The perfect complement to round out those rough spots before the exam.

Intensive Video Series—*Cram for the Exam!*

a) The only video cram course available today - specially designed for the weeks right before the exam.

b) Guidance from America's leading CPA Review instructors - Bob Monette and Ivan Fox, who have more than 50 years of combined teaching experience and the unique ability to analyze, simplify and explain exam topics so that you will pass.

c) Tips, tricks and techniques from our lively experts who teach problem-solving tips and helpful memory aids with an engaging style and humor.

d) The videos will refresh your memory on subjects you covered previously and will clarify topics you didn't quite grasp the first time you studied them.

e) Exclusive "how-to" advice. Targets only the information you must know to pass - so you won't waste valuable time. Our experts will tell you what to study, what not to study and how to most effectively prepare for the exam.

f) Available by individual exam section or as a complete 4 section set; with helpful viewer guides that let you follow along with minimal note-taking.

For Free Demos, Information or to Order: Call or Click Today!

1-888-CPA-BISK • www.cpaexam.com/book31

Our promise to you...

- **You will pass because** we offer a wide variety of products and packages, from our structured approach on the Internet to our multimedia, self-study programs that include software, videos, audiotapes and books – *to ensure that each customer's individual learning needs will be met.*
- **You will pass because** we produce our materials in our own state-of-the art production facility – *to ensure that each program is of the highest quality.*
- **You will pass because** we strive to maintain a winning combination of quality products, personalized customer service and exceptional value – *because in our business your success truly is our success.*
- And, finally, **you will pass because** our products feature America's Best CPA Review instructors – *Nathan Bisk, Ivan Fox and Bob Monette, who have over 75 years of combined exam preparation experience.*

Watch, Listen, and Learn from America's Best CPA Review Instructors

Publisher and Editor-in-Chief

NATHAN M. BISK, JD, CPA (FL)
Publisher and Editor-in-Chief of **Bisk CPA Review**. He is recognized as the leading expert in the nation on the CPA Exam and is well known as the "dean" of CPA Review. He is both an attorney and a CPA in the State of Florida, and has written and taught CPA Review, accounting, auditing, taxation and business law programs since 1971. Mr. Bisk is also the originator of video, audio, software, CD-ROM and Internet continuing education programs for accountants and attorneys.

IVAN FOX, JD, LLM – currently serves as Professor of Law at Pace University, where he formerly served as Chair of the Law Department. He is a recipient of the Outstanding Teaching Award, and author of the bestselling business law text, *Business Law & the Legal Environment*. With more than 30 years of CPA exam preparation experience, Dr. Fox is known as the "dean" of CPA Law Review and is one of the expert instructors on Bisk's family of CPA Review products.

ROBERT L. MONETTE, JD, CPA (PA) – is nationally recognized as an expert on the CPA Exam, and currently runs the largest live CPA Review in Philadelphia. His background also includes teaching CPA Review in Boston, New York and New Jersey, where he has helped tens-of-thousands of candidates become CPAs. Mr. Monette is one of the expert instructors on Bisk's family of CPA Review products.

We Passed . . . So Can You!

In addition to Gold Medal winners, Paul K. Ito and Stephanie H. Seiberg, (see inside front cover) here are a few more success stories

"Thanks to Bisk I was able to pass the CPA Exam! I had taken Becker CPA Review four years ago without any success. Their teaching style was not my learning style. With Bisk, I was able to learn at my own pace. The Hot-Spot video series was a great way to start my studying. I also used them as a final review. I have been suggesting Bisk to everyone I know that is taking the CPA Exam. Thanks again for all your help!" – ***Michelle Roseberry, Ohio.***

"I am writing this letter from the heart, because I really feel that you helped me so much. I worked hard, but without your books I would not have been able to accomplish what I did – which is pass the CPA Exam! Thank you so very much for the greatest exam preparation materials I have ever used." – ***Kirill Denisin, Washington, D.C.***

"By using your CD-ROM series, I was able to focus on and retain the most important points in all four testing areas. I passed all four parts in one sitting!" – ***Patsy Blackman, Texas***

"As I researched CPA review courses, I didn't want a strict classroom schedule or to have to learn at someone else's designated pace. With Bisk's Online Review I was able to squeeze study time in when it was convenient for me, and I could focus on the areas that I needed to study more. Bisk CPA Review worked wonders for me – I passed all four sections in my first attempt." – ***Leah Burggraf, California.***

1-888-CPA-BISK or 1-800-874-7599

Internet www.cpaexam.com/book31 • Email info@cpaexam.com • Fax 1-800-345-8273

CPA

Comprehensive Exam Review

Auditing

Nathan M. Bisk, J.D., C.P.A.

ACKNOWLEDGEMENTS

CONTRIBUTING EDITORS

Joseph K. Beach
J.D., C.P.A.
Merritt & Tenney, L.L.P.

Lowell S. Broom
D.B.A., C.P.A.
University of Alabama at Birmingham

J. Ralph Byington
Ph.D., C.P.A.
Georgia Southern University

Ivan Fox
J.D., LL.M.
Pace University

Marilyn F. Hunt
M.A., C.P.A.
University of Central Florida

Anne Keaty
J.D.
University of Louisiana at Lafayette

Kathryn M. Means
Ph.D., C.P.A.
Florida Atlantic University

Janet E. Mercincavage
M.B.A., C.P.A.
King's College

Robert L. Monette
J.D., C.P.A.
Bisk CPA Review

Paul Munter
Ph.D., C.P.A.
University of Miami

Thomas A. Ratcliffe
Ph.D., C.P.A.
Troy State University

James P. Sanford
J.D., C.P.A.
Grand Valley State University

C. William Thomas
M.B.A., Ph.D., C.P.A.
Baylor University

Mark A. Turner
D.B.A., C.P.A., C.M.A.
Stephen F. Austin State University

We wish to thank the **American Institute of Certified Public Accountants** and other organizations for permission to reprint or adapt the following copyright © materials:

1. Uniform CPA Examination Questions and Unofficial Answers, Copyright © American Institute of Certified Public Accountants, Inc., Harborside Financial Center, 201 Plaza Three, Jersey City, NJ 07311-3881.

2. Accounting Research Bulletins, APB Opinions, Audit and Accounting Guides, Auditing Procedure Studies, Risk Alerts, Statements of Position, and Code of Professional Conduct, Copyright © American Institute of Certified Public Accountants, Inc., Harborside Financial Center, 201 Plaza Three, Jersey City, NJ 07311-3881.

3. FASB Statements, Interpretations, Technical Bulletins, and Statements of Financial Accounting Concepts , Copyright © Financial Accounting Standards Board, 401 Merrit 7, P.O. Box 5116, Norwalk, CT 06856.

4. GASB Statements, Interpretations, and Technical Bulletins, Copyright © Governmental Accounting Standards Board, 401 Merritt 7, P.O. Box 5116, Norwalk CT 06856-5116.

5. Statements on Auditing Standards, Statements on Standards for Consulting Services, Statements on Responsibilities in Personal Financial Planning Practice, Statements on Standards for Accounting and Review Services, Statements on Quality Control Standards, Statements on Standards for Attestation Engagements, and Statements on Responsibilities in Tax Practice, Copyright © American Institute of Certified Public Accountants, Inc., Harborside Financial Center, 201 Plaza Three, Jersey City, NJ 07311-3881.

6. ISB Standards, Copyright © Independence Standards Board, 6th Floor, 1211 Avenue of the Americas, New York, NY 10036-8775

THIRTY-FIRST EDITION

PREFACE

Our texts provide comprehensive, complete coverage of all the topics tested on all four sections of the CPA Examination, including **Business Law & Professional Responsibilities, Financial Accounting & Reporting, Accounting & Reporting,** and **Auditing**. Used effectively, our materials will enable you to achieve maximum preparedness for the Uniform CPA Examination. Here is a brief summary of the **features** and **benefits** that our texts will provide for you:

1. **Information on the Closed Exam . . .** Beginning with the May 1996 Exam, the Uniform CPA Examination is non-disclosed. See Appendix B for a full discussion of this issue. This edition contains up-to-date coverage, including complete coverage of all exam changes. This edition also includes all the latest pronouncements of the AICPA and FASB, the current tax rates, governmental and nonprofit accounting, and other topics that are tested on the CPA exam. Our coverage is based on the most recent **AICPA Content Specification Outlines for the Uniform CPA Exam.**

2. **Separate and Complete Volumes . . .** Each volume includes text, multiple choice and other objective questions with solutions, plus essays and problems where appropriate for that section of the CPA exam. There is no need to refer to any other volume.

3. **More than 2,600 Pages of Text . . .** Including a selection of more than 3,200 recent CPA Examination questions, problems, and essays with Unofficial Answers. Solving these questions and problems under test conditions with immediate verification of results instills confidence and reinforces our **SOLUTIONS APPROACH™** to solving exam questions.

4. **Complete Coverage . . .** No extra materials required. We discuss and explain all important AICPA, FASB, GASB, and ISB pronouncements, including all significant ARBs, APBs, SASs, SSARs, SFACs, and FASB materials. We also cite and identify all authoritative sources including the dates of all AICPA Questions and Unofficial Answers covered in our materials.

5. **Detailed Summaries . . .** We set forth the significant testable concepts in each CPA exam topic. These highly readable summaries are written in complete sentences using an outline format to facilitate rapid and complete comprehension. The summaries isolate and emphasize topics historically tested by the CPA examiners.

6. **Emphasis on "How to Answer Questions" and "How to Take the Exam" . . .** We teach you to solve problem, essay, and objective questions using our unique and famous **SOLUTIONS APPROACH™**.

7. **Discussion and Development of . . .** AICPA grading procedures, grader orientation strategies, examination confidence, and examination success.

8. **Unique Objective Question Coverage and Unofficial Answers Updated . . .** We explain ***why*** the multiple choice alternatives are either right or wrong. Plus, we clearly indicate the changes that need to be made in the Unofficial Answers to correctly reflect current business and tax laws and AICPA, FASB, GASB, and other authoritative pronouncements.

9. **Writing Skills . . .** Financial Accounting & Reporting, Auditing, and Business Law & Professional Responsibilities contain a section to help you brush up on your writing skills for the CPA exam.

10. **Indexes . . .** We have included a comprehensively compiled index for easy topic reference in all four sections.

11. **Trend Analysis of Recent Exams . . .** We include short summaries of all essays and problems given on the most recent exams, to assist you in accurately pinpointing topics tested most frequently.

12. **Diagnostic Exam to Test Your Present Level of Knowledge . . .** And we include a **Final Exam** to test your exam preparedness under actual exam conditions. These testing materials are designed to help you single out for concentrated study the exam topic areas in which you are dangerously deficient.

Our materials are designed for the candidate who has previously studied accounting. Therefore, the rate at which a candidate studies and learns (not merely reads) our material will depend on a candidate's background and aptitude. Candidates who have been out of school for a period of years might need more time to study than recent graduates. The point to remember is that all the material you will need to know to pass the exam is here. All you need to do is apply yourself and learn this material at a rate that is appropriate to your situation. **As a final thought**, keep in mind that test confidence gained through disciplined preparation equals success.

OUR EDITORIAL BOARD INCLUDES THE NATION'S LEADING CPAs, ATTORNEYS AND EDUCATORS!

The Only CPA Review Texts Developed By Full-Time Experts.

Publisher and Editor-in-Chief

NATHAN M. BISK, J.D., C.P.A. (FL), is both an attorney and a CPA in the State of Florida. He is a graduate of Franklin and Marshall College and the University of Florida College of Law. He is a member of the Florida Institute of CPAs, AICPA, American Accounting Association, National Association of Accountants, Association of Gov't. Accountants, American Association of Attorney-CPAs, Florida Bar, and American Bar Association. His background includes public accounting experience at both Ernst & Young and Arthur Andersen & Co. He is a graduate of the 2-year JET program of Merrill Lynch, Pierce, Fenner & Smith, Inc. Mr. Bisk has written and taught CPA Review, accounting, auditing, taxation, and business law programs since 1970. He has been a pioneer in the development, writing, and production of audio, video, and software Continuing Education programs for accountants and attorneys.

Contributing Editor

IVAN FOX, J.D., LL.M., currently serves as a professor of law at Pace University, where he formerly served as Chair of the Law Department. He is a recipient of the Outstanding Teaching Award, and author of the country's best-selling business law text entitled, *Business Law & the Legal Environment*. With more than 20 years of CPA exam preparation experience, Mr. Fox is known as the "Dean" of CPA Law Review and is one of the expert instructors on Bisk Education's Hot•Spots CPA Review video series.

Consulting Editor

MARILYN F. HUNT, M.A., C.P.A. (FL), is an accounting instructor at the University of Central Florida, where she has been CPA Review Program Coordinator for more than 15 years. Ms. Hunt is a contributing editor for *The Internal Auditor* magazine and is an author and reviewer for various accounting and CPA Review texts. In addition, she regularly writes questions for the Certified Internal Auditor Examination. Ms. Hunt has conducted CPE programs for the AICPA, the Associated Regional Accounting Firms, the IMA, the Florida Institute of Certified Public Accountants, DisneyWorld, Blue Cross/Blue Shield, and many local and national CPA firms. Her background includes public accounting experience with Price Waterhouse.

Contributing Editor

PAUL MUNTER, Ph.D., C.P.A. (CO and TX), is a KPMG Peat Marwick Accounting Scholar, Professor of Accounting and Chair of the Department of Accounting at the University of Miami. Before joining the faculty at UM, Dr. Munter served as professor of accounting at Texas Tech University for 11 years. He has extensively published articles on financial accounting and auditing matters in journals such as the *Journal of Accountancy, CPA Journal, Management Accounting, Accounting Review, Today's CPA,* and *Practical Accountant*. Dr. Munter is a member of the IMA's national teaching faculty and was honored by the Texas Society of CPAs as its first Outstanding Discussion Leader. In addition, he was selected as the Outstanding Educator of the Year by the Florida Institute of CPAs. Dr. Munter also teaches CPE courses for accountants in public accounting and industry.

Contributing Editor

ROBERT L. MONETTE, J.D., C.P.A. (PA), is nationally recognized as an expert on the CPA exam, and currently runs the largest live CPA Review in Philadelphia. His background also includes teaching CPA Review in Boston, New York, and New Jersey, where he has helped tens-of-thousands of candidates become CPAs. Mr. Monette is one of the expert instructors on Bisk Education's Hot•Spots CPA Review video series.

Consulting Editor

DONALD C. ALEXANDER, LL.B., LL.D., is a partner with the law firm of Akin, Gump, Strauss, Hauer and Feld. He has served as Commissioner of the Internal Revenue Service, and currently serves as Director of the United States Chamber of Commerce and Chair of the Commissioner's Exempt Organizations Advisory Group. Mr. Alexander is an active member of the Tax Advisory Group of the American Law Institute, and is a nationally recognized author of more than 30 articles on federal tax subjects.

YOU WILL LEARN FROM OUR OUTSTANDING EXPERTS . . . WITHOUT LEAVING YOUR HOME OR OFFICE.

Consulting Editor

MORTIMER M. CAPLIN, LL.B., J.S.D., LL.D., is a senior partner with the Washington D.C. law firm of Caplin and Drysdale. He served as Commissioner of the Internal Revenue Service and as a member of the President's Task Force on Taxation. He received the Alexander Hamilton Award (the highest award conferred by the Secretary of the Treasury) for outstanding and unusual leadership during service as a U.S. Commissioner of Internal Revenue. For more than 25 years, Mr. Caplin has been in private practice with his present law firm, and has served as adjunct professor for the University of Virginia Law School. He is a nationally acclaimed author of numerous articles on tax and corporate matters.

Consulting Editor

RICHARD M. FELDHEIM, M.B.A., J.D., LL.M., C.P.A. (NY), is a New York CPA as well as an attorney in New York and Arizona. He holds a Masters in Tax Law from New York University Law School. Mr. Feldheim is a member of the New York State Society of CPAs, AICPA, New York State Bar Association, Association of the Bar of the City of New York, Arizona Bar, and American Bar Association. His background includes practice as both a CPA with Price Waterhouse & Co. and as a Senior Partner with the Arizona law firm of Wentworth & Lundin. He has lectured for the AICPA, the Practicing Law Institute, Seton Hall University, and the University of Arizona.

Consulting Editor

WILLIAM J. MEURER, CPA (FL), is former Managing Partner for both the overall operations in Central Florida and the Florida Audit and Business Advisory Services sector of Arthur Andersen LLP. During his 35-year career with the firm, Mr. Meurer developed expertise in several industries, including high technology, financial services, real estate, retailing/distribution, manufacturing, hospitality, professional services, and cable television. A graduate of Regis University, he is a member of both the American Institute of CPAs and the Florida Society of CPAs.

Consulting Editor

THOMAS A. RATCLIFFE, Ph.D., C.P.A. (TX), is Dean of the Sorrell College of Business Administration and Eminent Scholar in Accounting and Finance at Troy State University. He has published more than 100 technical works in accounting and auditing and serves as consultant to several CPA firms. He received the Alabama Society of CPAs Outstanding Discussion Leader Award for six years (this award is now named the Thomas A. Ratcliffe Outstanding Discussion Leader Award) and the 1991 Outstanding Accounting Educator Award. Dr. Ratcliffe is 2001-2002 President of the Alabama Society of CPAs, serves on several committees, and is a past Council Representative. He was the 1991 President of the Southeast Alabama Chapter.

Consulting Editor

C. WILLIAM THOMAS, M.B.A., Ph.D., C.P.A. (TX), currently serves as J.E. Bush Professor and former Chair of the Department of Accounting and Business Law at Baylor University. He is a member of the AICPA, the Texas Society of CPAs, the Central Texas Chapter of CPAs, and the American Accounting Association, where he is past Chair for the Southwestern Regional Audit Section. Professor Thomas is a nationally known author and has extensive experience in Auditing CPA Review. In addition, he has received recognition for special audit education and curriculum projects he developed for Coopers & Lybrand. His background includes public accounting experience with KPMG Peat Marwick.

CHANGE ALERT

SAS 93, *Omnibus Statement on Auditing Standards—2000,* is discussed in Chapters 32 and 39.

SAS 93 amends SAS 58, *Reports on Audited Financial Statements*, to require that a practitioner identify the country of GAAS and GAAP referred to in a practitioner's report. Two different acceptable sets of phrases are illustrated in the standard: "U.S. generally accepted accounting principles" and "U.S. generally accepted auditing standards" as well as "accounting principles generally accepted in the United States of America" and "auditing standards generally accepted in the United States of America."

SAS 93 amends SAS 84, *Communications Between Predecessor and Successor Auditors*, to explicitly include, within the definition of *predecessor auditor*, any auditor who is engaged to perform, but does not complete, an audit.

Both of these parts of SAS 93 are effective for audits of financial statements for periods ending on or after June 1, 2001, with earlier application permitted.

SAS 93 retracts SAS 75, *Engagements to Apply Agreed-Upon Procedures to Specified Elements, Accounts, or Items of a Financial Statement*. SSAE 10, *Attestation Standards: Revision and Recodification*, among other provisions, removes the requirement for a written assertion in connection with agreed-upon procedures engagements. The withdrawal of SAS 75 is concurrent with the effective date of SSAE 10, *Attestation Standards: Revision and Recodification*. This part of SAS 93 is effective for engagements for which the subject matter or assertion is as of, or for a period ending on or after, June 1, 2001, with earlier application permitted.

AUDITING

VOLUME III of IV

TABLE OF CONTENTS

The editors recommend that candidates remain cognizant of the depth of coverage of a topic and their proficiency with it when studying for the exam. Make informed decisions about your study plan by reading the information in the **Getting Started** and **Practical Advice** sections of this volume.

QUICK TEXT REFERENCE

The editors strongly recommend that candidates read the entire **Getting Started**, **Practical Advice**, and **Accounting for 5%** sections of this volume, unless they have already read these sections in the *Financial Accounting & Reporting* or *Business Law and Professional Responsibilities* volumes. The references on this page are only intended for conveniently relocating selected parts of the volume. Add items to this list that you find yourself revisiting frequently.

FOREWORD: GETTING STARTED

STEP ONE: READ PART ONE OF THE PRACTICAL ADVICE SECTION

Part One of the **Practical Advice** section (Appendix B) is designed to familiarize you with the CPA Examination. Included in **Practical Advice** are general comments about the exam, a schedule of exam dates, addresses and numbers of state boards of accountancy, and attributes required for exam success.

STEP TWO: TAKE THE DIAGNOSTIC EXAMS

The diagnostic exam in this foreword is designed to help you determine your strong and weak areas. This in turn will help you design your personalized training plan so that you spend more time in your weak areas and do not waste precious study time in areas where you are already strong. You can take the exams using either the books or CPA Review Software for Windows™. The books provide you with a worksheet that makes self-diagnosis fast and easy. CPA Review Software for Windows will automatically score your exams for you and give you a personalized analysis of your strong and weak areas.

NOTE: If you took a previous CPA exam and passed some but not all the sections, also analyze these exam sections to help you determine where you need to concentrate your efforts this time.

NOTE: If you purchase a package that includes software, you will also want to go through all of the software tutorials prior to beginning intensive study. They are each only a few minutes long, but they are loaded with valuable information. There is simply no better way to prepare yourself to study.

STEP THREE: DEVELOP A PERSONALIZED TRAINING PLAN

Based on the results from your diagnostic exams, develop your personalized training plan. If you are taking the exam for the first time, and you are the "average" CPA candidate, we recommend that you train for 20 weeks at a minimum of 20 hours per week. This level of intensity should increase during the final four weeks of your training and peak at a minimum of 40 hours the final week before the exam. Designed to complete your study program, our Intensive Video Series is a concentrated and effective "cram course" that targets the information you must know to pass. The videos will refresh your memory on subjects you covered weeks earlier and clarify topics you haven't yet fully grasped.

If you took the exam previously and did not condition (you still have to take all four sections), and you are the "average" CPA candidate, we recommend that you train for 12 weeks at a minimum of 20 hours per week. Again, this level of intensity should increase during the final four weeks of your training and peak during the final week before the exam. If you have conditioned (you have to take three or less sections), you can adjust these guidelines accordingly.

You may wonder what we mean by an "average" candidate. We are referring to a candidate who is just finishing or has just finished his or her academic training, attended a school that has a solid accounting curriculum, and received above average grades in accounting and business law courses. (An "average" candidate's native language is English.) Remember, "average" is a benchmark. Many candidates are not "average," so adjust your training plan accordingly.

TIME AVAILABILITY

	MON	TUES	WED	THURS	FRI	SAT	SUN
1:00 AM							
2:00 AM							
3:00 AM							
4:00 AM							
5:00 AM							
6:00 AM							
7:00 AM							
8:00 AM							
9:00 AM							
10:00 AM							
11:00 AM							
12:00 PM							
1:00 PM							
2:00 PM							
3:00 PM							
4:00 PM							
5:00 PM							
6:00 PM							
7:00 PM							
8:00 PM							
9:00 PM							
10:00 PM							
11:00 PM							
12:00 AM							

How to Find 20 Hours a Week to Study

The typical CPA candidate is a very busy individual. He or she goes to school and/or works full or part time. Some candidates have additional responsibilities such as a spouse, children, a house to take care of—the list can go on and on. Consequently, your first reaction may be, "I don't have 20 hours a week to devote to training for the CPA exam." Using the chart on the previous page, we will show you how to "find" the time that you need to develop your training schedule.

1. Keeping in mind what you would consider to be a typical week, first mark out in black the time that you know you won't be able to study. For example, mark an "X" in each block which represents time that you normally sleep, have a class, work, or have some other type of commitment. Be realistic.

2. Next, in a different color, put a "C" in each block that represents commute time, an "M" in each block that represents when you normally eat, and an "E" in each block that represents when you exercise.

3. Now pick one hour each day to relax and give your mind a break. Write "BREAK" in one block for each day. Do not skip this step. By taking a break, you will study more efficiently and effectively.

4. In a third color, write "STUDY" in the remaining blocks. Count the "STUDY" blocks. Are there 20? If not, count your "C", "M", and "E" blocks; if needed, these blocks of time can be used to gain additional study time by using Bisk Education CPA Review audio tapes and videotapes. For example, our audios are ideal for candidates on the go, you can listen to them whenever you're in the car or exercising and gain valuable study time each week.

5. If you still do not have 20 "STUDY" blocks, and you scored 70% or more on your diagnostic exams, you may still be able to pass the exam even with your limited study time. If, however, you scored less than 70% on your diagnostic exams, you have 2 options: (1) re-prioritize and make a block that has an "X" in it available study time; or (2) concentrate on conditioning (passing some but not all of the sections) instead of on passing the entire exam. Before you choose to condition, check with your state board about the details. A drastic solution is to skip the managerial portion of the ARE section of the exam if you are extremely pressed. Ordinarily, we do not recommend this strategy.

How to Allocate Your 20 Weeks

Develop your overall training plan. We outline a recommended training plan based on 20 hours per week and 20 weeks of study. The time allocated to each topic was based on the length of the chapter, the difficulty of the material, and how heavily the topic is tested on the exam (refer to the exam specifications and our frequency analysis found in the **Practical Advice** section of your book). Keep in mind that this plan is for the "average" CPA candidate. You should customize this plan based on the results of your diagnostic exams and level of knowledge in each area tested. **Warning:** When studying, be careful not to fall into the trap of spending too much time on an area that is rarely tested on the exam. **NOTE:** For each week listed below there are corresponding Hot•Spot videos and audio tapes for more in-depth study. Call 1-888-CPA-BISK.

Recommended Training Plan (all 4 sections)*

		Hours
Week 1:	READ **GETTING STARTED** AND **PRACTICAL ADVICE** SECTIONS	1
	TAKE DIAGNOSTIC EXAMS	10
	GET ORGANIZED	2
	READ **ACCOUNTING FOR 5%** SECTION	1
	CHAPTER 1—OVERVIEW OF FINANCIAL ACCOUNTING & REPORTING	2
	CHAPTER 2—CASH, SHORT-TERM INVESTMENTS & RECEIVABLES	4

* Candidates should make modifications to suit their individual circumstances. For instance, this training plan repeats Chapter 21. Candidates may not need to return to Chapter 21, particularly those who took a governmental accounting course.

		Hours
WEEK 2:	CHAPTER 2—CASH, SHORT-TERM INVESTMENTS & RECEIVABLES	3
	CHAPTER 3—INVENTORIES	5
	CHAPTER 4—PROPERTY, PLANT & EQUIPMENT	5
	CHAPTER 5—INTANGIBLES, R&D COSTS & OTHER ASSETS	4
	CHAPTER 6—BONDS	3
WEEK 3:	WEEKLY REVIEW OF WEEKS 1 - 2	2
	CHAPTER 6—BONDS	2
	CHAPTER 7—LIABILITIES	6
	CHAPTER 8—LEASES	5
	CHAPTER 9—PENSIONS & OTHER POSTRETIREMENT BENEFITS	5
WEEK 4:	WEEKLY REVIEW OF WEEKS 1 - 3	1
	CHAPTER 10—OWNERS' EQUITY	7
	CHAPTER 31—STANDARDS & RELATED TOPICS	4
	CHAPTER 32—PLANNING	6
	CHAPTER 33—INTERNAL CONTROL: GENERAL	2
WEEK 5:	WEEKLY REVIEW OF WEEKS 1 - 4	2
	CHAPTER 33—INTERNAL CONTROL: GENERAL	4
	CHAPTER 34—INTERNAL CONTROL: TRANSACTION CYCLES	4
	CHAPTERS 35—EVIDENCE & PROCEDURES	6
	CHAPTERS 36—AUDIT PROGRAMS	4
WEEK 6:	WEEKLY REVIEW OF WEEKS 1 - 5	2
	CHAPTER 11—REPORTING THE RESULTS OF OPERATIONS	11
	CHAPTER 37—AUDIT SAMPLING PROCEDURES	3
	CHAPTER 38—AUDITING EDP SYSTEMS	4
WEEK 7:	WEEKLY REVIEW OF WEEKS 1 - 6	1
	CHAPTER 12—REVENUE & EXPENSE RECOGNITION: SPECIAL AREAS	6
	CHAPTER 39—REPORTS ON AUDITED FINANCIAL STMTS	9
	CHAPTER 40—OTHER TYPES OF REPORTS	4
WEEK 8:	WEEKLY REVIEW OF WEEKS 1 - 7	2
	CHAPTER 13—ACCOUNTING FOR INCOME TAXES	5
	CHAPTER 14—STATEMENT OF CASH FLOWS	7
	CHAPTER 15—FINANCIAL STATEMENT ANALYSIS & EPS	4
	CHAPTER 40—OTHER TYPES OF REPORTS	2
WEEK 9:	WEEKLY REVIEW OF WEEKS 1 - 8	2
	CHAPTER 16—FINANCIAL REPORTING & CHANGING PRICES	2
	CHAPTER 17—FOREIGN OPERATIONS	3
	CHAPTER 18—PARTNERSHIPS & PERSONAL F/S	3
	CHAPTER 19—INVESTMENTS IN EQUITY SECURITIES	3
	CHAPTER 41—OTHER PROFESSIONAL SERVICES	7
WEEK 10:	WEEKLY REVIEW OF WEEKS 1 - 9	2
	OVERALL REVIEW OF AUDITING	3
	CHAPTER 20—CONSOLIDATED F/S	12
	CHAPTER 21—GOVERNMENTAL OVERVIEW	3

		Hours
WEEK 11:	OVERALL REVIEW OF FINANCIAL ACCOUNTING & REPORTING	6
	CHAPTER 22—GOVERNMENTAL FUNDS & ACCOUNT GROUPS	7
	CHAPTER 42—ACCOUNTANT'S PROFESSIONAL RESPONSIBILITIES	3
	CHAPTER 43—ACCOUNTANT'S LEGAL RESPONSIBILITIES	4
WEEK 12:	WEEKLY REVIEW OF WEEKS 1 - 11	4
	CHAPTER 21—GOVERNMENTAL OVERVIEW	3
	CHAPTER 23—NONPROFIT ACCOUNTING	7
	CHAPTER 44—CONTRACTS	6
WEEK 13:	WEEKLY REVIEW OF WEEKS 1 - 12	4
	CHAPTER 24—DECISION MAKING	4
	CHAPTER 25—COST ACCOUNTING	4
	CHAPTER 44—CONTRACTS	2
	CHAPTER 45—SALES	6
WEEK 14:	WEEKLY REVIEW OF WEEKS 1 - 13	3
	CHAPTER 27—DECISION MAKING	1
	CHAPTER 26—PLANNING & CONTROL	5
	CHAPTER 28—FEDERAL TAXATION: PROPERTY	5
	CHAPTER 46—NEGOTIABLE INSTRUMENTS	3
	CHAPTER 47—SECURED TRANSACTIONS & DOCUMENTS OF TITLE	3
WEEK 15:	WEEKLY REVIEW OF WEEKS 1 - 14	3
	CHAPTER 27—FEDERAL TAXATION: INDIVIDUALS	10
	CHAPTER 48—BANKRUPTCY	4
	CHAPTER 49—DEBTORS, CREDITORS & GUARANTORS	3
WEEK 16:	WEEKLY REVIEW OF WEEKS 1 - 15	3+
	CHAPTER 29—FEDERAL TAXATION: CORPORATIONS	10
	CHAPTER 50—AGENCY	3
	CHAPTER 51—PARTNERSHIPS	4
WEEK 17:	WEEKLY REVIEW OF WEEKS 1 - 16	4+
	CHAPTER 30—FEDERAL TAXATION: PARTNERSHIPS & OTHER TOPICS	10
	CHAPTER 52—CORPORATIONS	3
	CHAPTER 53—ESTATES & TRUSTS	3
WEEK 18:	WEEKLY REVIEW OF WEEKS 1 - 17	2+
	CHAPTER 54—EMPLOYMENT & ENVIRONMENTAL REGULATION	2
	CHAPTER 55—FEDERAL SECURITIES REGULATION	4
	CHAPTER 56—REAL & PERSONAL PROPERTY	4
	CHAPTER 57—FIRE & CASUALTY INSURANCE	1
	OVERALL REVIEW OF ACCOUNTING & REPORTING	4
	OVERALL REVIEW OF BUSINESS LAW & PROFESSIONAL RESPONS.	3
WEEK 19:	REVIEW AREAS IN WHICH YOU STILL FEEL WEAK	20+
WEEK 20:	TAKE FINAL EXAMS UNDER EXAM CONDITIONS	10
	DO FINAL REVIEWS	10+

YOUR PERSONALIZED TRAINING PLAN:

WEEK	TASK	DIAGNOSTIC SCORE	EST. HOURS	DATE COMPLETE	CHAPTER SCORE	FINAL SCORE
1						
2						
3						
4						
5						
6						
7						
8						
9						

WEEK	TASK	DIAGNOSTIC SCORE	EST. HOURS	DATE COMPLETE	CHAPTER SCORE	FINAL SCORE
10						
11						
12						
13						
14						
15						
16						
17						

WEEK	TASK	DIAGNOSTIC SCORE	EST. HOURS	DATE COMPLETE	CHAPTER SCORE	FINAL SCORE
18						
19						
20						

STEP FOUR: READ THE REST OF THE PRACTICAL ADVICE SECTION

Part Two of the **Practical Advice** section of the book will familiarize you with how the CPA examination is graded and tell you how you can earn extra points on the exam simply by knowing what the grader is going to seek. In addition, in Part Three we explain our Solutions Approach™, an approach that will help you maximize your grade. In Part Four, we discuss examination strategies. In Part Five, we provide information on the AICPA exam content specifications and point distribution.

STEP FIVE: INTEGRATE YOUR REVIEW MATERIALS

In this step, we demonstrate how to integrate the Bisk Education CPA Review products to optimize the effectiveness of your training plan. Find and read the section that corresponds to the package that you purchased. (To facilitate easy reference to your package guidance, you may want to strike through the sections corresponding to other packages.)

VIDEOTAPES

The videotapes are designed to supplement all of the study packages. Note how we recommend using the audiotapes in the following review plans. These recommendations also apply to the videotape programs. FYI: The videotapes have similar content as the online video lectures, but they are not exactly the same. Each of the Hot•Spot™ videotapes concentrates on a few topics. Use them to help you study the areas that are most troubling for you. Each of the Intensive videotapes are designed for a final, intensive review, after a candidate has already done considerable work. If time permits, use the Intensive tapes at both the very beginning (for an overview) and set them aside until the final review in week 19. They contain concise, informative lectures, as well as CPA exam tips, tricks, and techniques that will help you to learn the material needed to pass the exam.

Online Package: Books, Video Lectures, and CPA Software for Windows

This is our most comprehensive review package. This combination provides the personal advice, discipline, and camaraderie of a classroom setting with the convenience of self-study. It is intended for those candidates who want to make sure that they pass the exam the **first** time. By using this package, you are eligible to qualify for Bisk Education's money-back guarantee. Contact a customer representative for details on the components of this package. Contact your online faculty advisor if you have questions about integrating your materials after viewing the web site guidance. The editors strongly recommend that candidates working full-time take a maximum of 2 sections per six-week session.

Books, Audiotapes, and CPA Review Software for Windows

This is our most comprehensive self-study review package. This combination is designed expressly for the serious CPA candidate. It is intended for those candidates who want to make sure that they pass the exam the **first** time (or *this* time, if you have already taken the exam). In addition, by using this package, you are eligible to qualify for Bisk Education's money-back guarantee.

How to Use This Package:

1. First take the diagnostic exams using CPA Review Software for Windows™. CPA Review Software for Windows™ automatically scores your exams and tells you what your strong and weak areas are.

In chapters where you are strong (i.e., you scored 65% or better on the diagnostic exam):

2. Answer the objective questions using CPA Review Software for Windows™.

3. Read the subsections of the chapter that correspond to your weak areas.

4. Listen to the audiotape for topics covered in this chapter to reinforce your weak areas and review your strong areas.

5. Now, using CPA Review Software for Windows™, answer the objective questions that you previously answered incorrectly. If you answer 70% or more of the questions correctly, you are ready to move to the next chapter. If you answer less than 70% of the questions correctly, handle this chapter as if you scored less than 65% on the diagnostic exam.

6. Answer the related essay questions.

In chapters where you are weak (i.e., you scored less than 65% on the diagnostic exam):

2. Read the chapter in the book.

3. Listen to the audiotape lectures on topics covered in the chapter.

4. Re-read the subsections of the chapter that correspond to your weak subtopics.

5. Using CPA Review Software for Windows™, answer the objective questions for this chapter. If you answer 70% or more of the questions correctly, you are ready to move on to the next chapter. If you get less than 70% of the questions correct, review the subtopics where you are weak. Then answer the questions that you previously answered incorrectly. If you still do not get at least 70% correct, check the exam specification and frequency charts in the Practical Advice section to find out how heavily the area is tested. If this is an area that is heavily tested, continue reviewing the material and answering multiple choice questions until you can answer at least 70% correctly. Allocate more time than you originally budgeted, if necessary. If this is not a heavily tested area, move on, but make a note to come back to this area later as time allows.

6. Answer the related essay questions.

BOOKS AND CPA REVIEW SOFTWARE FOR WINDOWS™

This combination allows you to use the books to review the material and CPA Review Software for Windows™ to practice exam questions. You can also use the books to practice exam questions when you do not have access to a computer. In addition, by using this package, you are eligible to qualify for Bisk Education's money-back guarantee.

How to Use This Package:

1. Take the diagnostic exams using CPA Review Software for Windows™. CPA Review Software for Windows automatically scores your exams and tells you what your strong and weak areas are.

In chapters where you are strong (i.e., you scored 65% or better on the diagnostic exam):

2. Answer the objective questions using CPA Review Software for Windows™.

3. Read the subsections of the chapter that correspond to your weak areas.

4. Now using CPA Review Software for Windows™, answer the objective questions that you previously answered incorrectly. If you answer 70% or more of the questions correctly, you are ready to move on to the next chapter. If you answer less than 70% of the questions correctly, handle this chapter as if you scored less than 65% on the diagnostic exam.

5. Answer the related essay questions.

In chapters where you are weak (i.e., you scored less than 65% on the diagnostic exam):

2. Read the chapter in the book.

3. Using CPA Review Software for Windows™, answer the objective questions for this chapter. If you answer 70% or more of the questions correctly, you are ready to move on to the next chapter. If you get less than 70% of the questions correct, review the subtopics where you are weak. Then answer the questions that you previously answered incorrectly. If you still do not get at least 70% correct, check the exam specification and frequency charts in the Practical Advice section to find out how heavily the area is tested. If this is an area that is heavily tested, continue reviewing the material and answering multiple choice questions until you can answer at least 70% correctly. Allocate more time than you originally budgeted, if necessary. If this is not a heavily tested area, move on, but make a note to come back to this area later as time allows.

4. Answer the related essay questions.

BOOKS AND AUDIOTAPES

This combination is designed for the candidate who does not have access to a computer to study, who spends time commuting or doing other activities that could take valuable time away from studying, and for those who like to reinforce what they read by listening to a lecture on tape.

How to Use This Package:

1. Take the diagnostic exams found in your book. Using the worksheets provided, score your exams to determine your strong and weak areas.

In chapters where you are strong (i.e., you scored 65% or better on the diagnostic exam):

2. Do the objective questions for that chapter. Using the worksheet provided, analyze your strong and weak areas.
3. Read the subsections of the chapter that correspond to your weak subtopics.
4. At this point, listen to the audiotape on topics covered in this chapter to reinforce weak areas and review strong areas.
5. Answer the objective questions that you previously answered incorrectly. If you answer 70% or more of the questions correctly, you are ready to move on to the next chapter. If you answer less than 70% of the questions correctly, handle this chapter as if you scored 65% or less on the diagnostic exam.
6. Answer at least one essay question (if there are any) and review any other essay questions and solutions.

In chapters where you are weak (i.e., you scored less than 65% on the diagnostic exam):

2. First read the chapter in the book.
3. Now listen to the audiotape lectures covering topics in this chapter.
4. Re-read the subsections of the chapter that correspond to your weak subtopics.
5. Do the objective questions and score yourself using the worksheet provided. If you answer 70% or more of the questions correctly, you are ready to move on to the next chapter. If you answer less than 70% of the questions correctly, review the subtopics that are still giving you trouble. Then answer the questions that you have previously answered incorrectly. If you still do not get at least 70% of the questions correct, check the exam specification and frequency charts in the Practical Advice section to find out how heavily this area is tested. If this is an area that is heavily tested, continue reviewing the material and answering questions until you can answer at least 70% of them correctly. Allocate more time than you originally budgeted for if necessary. If this area is not heavily tested, move on, but make a note to come back to this topic later as time allows.
6. Answer at least one essay question (if there are any) and review any other essay questions and solutions.

STEP SIX: USE THESE HELPFUL HINTS AS YOU STUDY

- SPEND YOUR WEEKLY REVIEW TIME EFFECTIVELY. DURING EACH WEEKLY REVIEW:

  Answer the objective questions that you previously answered incorrectly or merely guessed correctly.

  Read through your notes.

  Pick one essay question or problem to work. (Do not wait until the end of your 20 weeks to attempt the essay questions.) Read the other essay and problem questions and solutions.

  Go through your flashcards.

- DO NOT MARK THE OBJECTIVE QUESTION ANSWERS IN THE BOOK.

  Do not circle the answer to objective questions in the book. You should work every multiple-choice question at least twice and you do not want to influence your later answers by knowing how you previously answered the question.

- MARK THE OBJECTIVE QUESTIONS THAT YOU ANSWER INCORRECTLY OR MERELY GUESS CORRECTLY.

  This way you know to answer this question again at a later time.

- MAKE NOTES AS YOU STUDY

  Make notes and/or highlight when you read the chapters in the book. When possible, make notes when you listen to the tapes. You will find these very useful for weekly reviews and your final review.

- MAKE FLASHCARDS

  Make flashcards for topics that are heavily tested on the exam or that are giving you trouble. By making your own flashcards, you can tailor them to your individual learning style and problem areas. You will find these very useful for weekly reviews and your final review. Replace flashcards of information you know with new material as you progress through your study plan. Keep these handy and review them when you are waiting in line or on hold. This will turn nonproductive time into valuable study time. Review your complete set during the last two weeks before the exam.

- EFFECTIVELY USE THE VIDEOTAPES

  Watch the videotapes in an environment without distractions. Be prepared to take notes and answer questions just as if you were attending a live class. Frequently, the instructors will have you stop the tape to work a question on your own. This means a 2-hour tape may take 2½ hours or more to view.

- EFFECTIVELY USE THE AUDIOTAPES

  Use these tapes to turn nonproductive time into valuable study time. For example, play the tapes when you are commuting, exercising, getting ready for school or work, doing laundry, etc. The tapes will help you to memorize and retain key concepts. They will also reinforce what you have read in the books. Get in the habit of listening to the tapes whenever you have a chance. The more times that you listen to each tape, the more familiar you will become with the material and the easier it will be for you to recall it during the exam.

STEP SEVEN: IMPLEMENT YOUR TRAINING PLAN

This is it! You are primed and ready. You have decided which training tools will work best for you and you know how to use them. As you implement your personalized training plan, keep yourself focused. Your goal is to obtain a grade of 75 or better on each section and, thus, pass the CPA exam. Therefore, you should concentrate on learning new material and reviewing old material only to the extent that it helps you reach this goal. Also, keep in mind that now is not the time to hone your procrastination skills. Utilize the personalized training plan that you developed in step three so that you do not fall behind schedule. Adjust it when necessary if you need more time in one chapter or less time in another. Refer to the AICPA content specification and the frequency analysis to make sure that the adjustment is warranted. Above all else, remember that passing the exam is an **attainable** goal. Good luck!

DIAGNOSTIC EXAMINATION

PROBLEM 1 MULTIPLE CHOICE QUESTIONS (120 to 150 minutes)

1. The third general standard states that due care is to be exercised in the performance of an audit. This standard is ordinarily interpreted to require
a. Thorough review of the existing safeguards over access to assets and records.
b. Limited review of the indications of employee fraud and illegal acts.
c. Objective review of the adequacy of the technical training and proficiency of firm personnel.
d. Critical review of the judgment exercised at every level of supervision.
(5/95, Aud., #23, 5641)

2. One of a CPA firm's basic objectives is to provide professional services that conform with professional standards. Reasonable assurance of achieving this basic objective is provided through
a. A system of quality control.
b. A system of peer review.
c. Continuing professional education.
d. Compliance with generally accepted reporting standards. (11/92, Aud., #3)

3. When auditing an entity's financial statements in accordance with Government Auditing Standards (the Yellow Book), an auditor is required to report on

I. Recommendations for actions to improve operations.
II. The scope of the auditor's tests of compliance with laws and regulations.

a. I only
b. II only
c. Both I and II
d. Neither I nor II (R/00, Aud., #19, 6944)

4. A successor auditor most likely would make specific inquiries of the predecessor auditor regarding
a. Specialized accounting principles of the client's industry.
b. The competency of the client's internal audit staff.
c. The uncertainty inherent in applying sampling procedures.
d. Disagreements with management as to auditing procedures. (5/95, Aud., #2, 5620)

5. An auditor should design the written audit program so that
a. All material transactions will be selected for substantive testing.
b. Substantive tests prior to the balance sheet date will be minimized.
c. The audit procedures selected will achieve specific audit objectives.
d. Each account balance will be tested under either tests of controls or tests of transactions.
(5/95, Aud., #16, 5634)

6. Which of the following procedures would an auditor most likely include in the initial planning of a financial statement audit?
a. Obtaining a written representation letter from the client's management.
b. Examining documents to detect illegal acts having a material effect on the financial statements.
c. Considering whether the client's accounting estimates are reasonable in the circumstances.
d. Determining the extent of involvement of the client's internal auditors. (11/94, Aud., #1)

7. An auditor who discovers that a client's employees paid small bribes to municipal officials most likely would withdraw from the engagement if
a. The payments violated the client's policies regarding the prevention of illegal acts.
b. The client receives financial assistance from a federal government agency.
c. Documentation that is necessary to prove that the bribes were paid does not exist.
d. Management fails to take the appropriate remedial action. (R/00, Aud., #6, 6931)

8. When considering internal control, an auditor should be aware of the concept of reasonable assurance, which recognizes that
a. Internal control policies and procedures may be ineffective due to mistakes in judgment and personal carelessness.
b. Adequate safeguards over access to assets and records should permit an entity to maintain proper accountability.
c. Establishing and maintaining internal control is an important responsibility of management.
d. The cost of an entity's internal control should **not** exceed the benefits expected to be derived.
(5/95, Aud., #26, amended)

9. Which of the following are considered control environment factors?

	Detection risk	Personnel policies and practices
a.	Yes	Yes
b.	Yes	No
c.	No	Yes
d.	No	No

(11/94, Aud., #29)

10. Assessing control risk at below the maximum level most likely would involve

a. Performing more extensive substantive tests with larger sample sizes than originally planned.
b. Reducing inherent risk for most of the assertions relevant to significant account balances.
c. Changing the timing of substantive tests by omitting interim-date testing and performing the tests at year end.
d. Identifying specific internal control policies and procedures relevant to specific assertions.

(11/95, Aud., #22, amended, 5969)

11. After obtaining an understanding of internal control and assessing control risk, an auditor decided to perform tests of controls. The auditor most likely decided that

a. It would be efficient to perform tests of controls that would result in a reduction in planned substantive tests.
b. Additional evidence to support a further reduction in control risk is **not** available.
c. An increase in the assessed level of control risk is justified for certain financial statement assertions.
d. There were many internal control weaknesses that could allow errors to enter the accounting system. (5/95, Aud., #33, amended)

12. Control risk should be assessed in terms of

a. Specific control activities.
b. Types of potential fraud.
c. Financial statement assertions.
d. Control environment factors.

(5/95, Aud., #27, amended, 5645)

13. On the basis of audit evidence gathered and evaluated, an auditor decides to increase the assessed level of control risk from that originally planned. To achieve an overall audit risk level that is substantially the same as the planned audit risk level, the auditor would

a. Decrease substantive testing.
b. Decrease detection risk.
c. Increase inherent risk.
d. Increase materiality levels.

(11/94, Aud., #10, 5083)

14. The objective of tests of details of transactions performed as tests of controls is to

a. Monitor the design and use of entity documents such as prenumbered shipping forms.
b. Determine whether internal control structure policies and procedures have been placed in operation.
c. Detect material misstatements in the account balances of the financial statements.
d. Evaluate whether internal control procedures operated effectively.(11/94, Aud., #42, amended)

15. When an auditor assesses control risk at the maximum level, the auditor is required to document the auditor's

	Understanding of the entity's accounting system	*Basis for concluding that control risk is at the maximum level*
a.	No	No
b.	No	Yes
c.	Yes	No
d.	Yes	Yes

(5/95, Aud., #29, 5647)

16. Which of the following procedures would an auditor most likely perform to test controls relating to management's assertion about the completeness of cash receipts for cash sales at a retail outlet?

a. Observe the consistency of the employees' use of cash registers and tapes.
b. Inquire about employees' access to recorded but undeposited cash.
c. Trace the deposits in the cash receipts journal to the cash balance in the general ledger.
d. Compare the cash balance in the general ledger with the bank confirmation request.

(11/97, Aud., #15, 6578)

17. Which of the following controls most likely would be effective in offsetting the tendency of sales personnel to maximize sales volume at the expense of high bad debt write-offs?

a. Employees responsible for authorizing sales and bad debt write-offs are denied access to cash.
b. Shipping documents and sales invoices are matched by an employee who does **not** have authority to write off bad debts.
c. Employees involved in the credit-granting function are separated from the sales function.
d. Subsidiary accounts receivable records are reconciled to the control account by an employee independent of the authorization of credit. (5/92, Aud., #45)

18. The objectives of internal control for a production cycle are to provide assurance that transactions are properly executed and recorded, and that
a. Independent internal verification of activity reports is established.
b. Transfers to finished goods are documented by a completed production report and a quality control report.
c. Production orders are prenumbered and signed by a supervisor.
d. Custody of work in process and of finished goods is properly maintained.
(11/90, Aud., #52, amended)

19. The purpose of segregating the duties of hiring personnel and distributing payroll checks is to separate the
a. Authorization of transactions from the custody of related assets.
b. Operational responsibility from the record keeping responsibility.
c. Human resources function from the controllership function.
d. Administrative controls from the internal accounting controls. (11/91, Aud., #40)

20. For effective internal control, the accounts payable department generally should
a. Stamp, perforate, or otherwise cancel supporting documentation after payment is mailed.
b. Ascertain that each requisition is approved as to price, quantity, and quality by an authorized employee.
c. Obliterate the quantity ordered on the receiving department copy of the purchase order.
d. Establish the agreement of the vendor's invoice with the receiving report and purchase order.
(11/95, Aud., #30, 5977)

21. Which of the following controls would an entity most likely use in safeguarding against the loss of marketable securities?
a. An independent trust company that has **no** direct contact with the employees who have record keeping responsibilities has possession of the securities.
b. The internal auditor verifies the marketable securities in the entity's safe each year on the balance sheet date.
c. The independent auditor traces all purchases and sales of marketable securities through the subsidiary ledgers to the general ledger.
d. A designated member of the board of directors controls the securities in a bank safe-deposit box. (11/92, Aud., #22)

22. Which of the following types of audit evidence is the most persuasive?
a. Prenumbered client purchase order forms
b. Client work sheets supporting cost allocations
c. Bank statements obtained from the client
d. Client representation letter (5/95, Aud., #39)

23. Which of the following statements is generally correct about the competence of evidential matter?
a. The more effective the internal control, the more assurance it provides about the reliability of the accounting data and financial statements.
b. Competence of evidential matter refers to the amount of corroborative evidence obtained.
c. Information obtained indirectly from independent outside sources is more persuasive than the auditor's direct personal knowledge obtained through observation and inspection.
d. Competence of evidential matter refers to the audit evidence obtained from outside the entity.
(5/92, Aud., #16, amended)

24. In testing the existence assertion for an asset, an auditor ordinarily works from the
a. Financial statements to the potentially unrecorded items.
b. Potentially unrecorded items to the financial statements.
c. Accounting records to the supporting evidence.
d. Supporting evidence to the accounting records.
(11/90, Aud., #17)

25. During an audit an internal auditor may provide direct assistance to an independent CPA in

	Obtaining an understanding of the internal control	Performing tests of controls	Performing substantive tests
a.	No	No	No
b.	Yes	No	No
c.	Yes	Yes	No
d.	Yes	Yes	Yes

(5/95, Aud., #60, amended)

26. For all audits of financial statements made in accordance with generally accepted auditing standards, the use of analytical procedures is required to some extent

	In the planning stage	As a substantive test	In the review stage
a.	Yes	No	Yes
b.	No	Yes	No
c.	No	Yes	Yes
d.	Yes	No	No

(11/90, Aud., #22)

27. An entity's income statements were misstated due to the recording of journal entries that involved debits and credits to an unusual combination of expense and revenue accounts. The auditor most likely could have detected this irregularity by

a. Tracing a sample of journal entries to the general ledger.
b. Evaluating the effectiveness of the internal control policies and procedures.
c. Investigating the reconciliations between controlling accounts and subsidiary records.
d. Performing analytical procedures designed to disclose differences from expectations.

(11/94, Aud., #14, amended)

28. To which of the following matters would materiality limits **not** apply in obtaining written management representations?

a. The availability of minutes of stockholders' and directors' meetings
b. Losses from purchase commitments at prices in excess of market value
c. The disclosure of compensating balance arrangements involving related parties
d. Reductions of obsolete inventory to net realizable value (5/95, Aud., #66)

29. For which of the following matters should an auditor obtain written management representations?

a. Management's cost-benefit justifications for not correcting internal control weaknesses.
b. Management's knowledge of future plans that may affect the price of the entity's stock
c. Management's compliance with contractual agreements that may affect the price of the entity's stock.
d. Management's acknowledgment of its responsibility for employees' violations of laws.

(5/99, Aud., #25, 6841)

30. In using the work of a specialist, an auditor may refer to the specialist in the auditor's report if, as a result of the specialist's findings, the auditor

a. Becomes aware of conditions causing substantial doubt about the entity's ability to continue as a going concern.
b. Desires to disclose the specialist's findings, which imply that a more thorough audit was performed.
c. Is able to corroborate another specialist's earlier findings that were consistent with management's representations.
d. Discovers significant deficiencies in the design of the entity's internal control that management does **not** correct.

(5/95, Aud., amended, #62, 5680)

31. The primary reason an auditor requests letters of inquiry be sent to a client's attorneys is to provide the auditor with

a. The probable outcome of asserted claims and pending or threatened litigation.
b. Corroboration of the information furnished by management about litigation, claims, and assessments.
c. The attorneys' opinions of the client's historical experiences in recent similar litigation.
d. A description and evaluation of litigation, claims, and assessments that existed at the balance sheet date. (11/94, Aud., #66, 5139)

32. In performing a count of negotiable securities, an auditor records the details of the count on a security count worksheet. What other information is usually included on this worksheet?

a. An acknowledgment by a client representative that the securities were returned intact
b. An analysis of realized gains and losses from the sale of securities during the year
c. An evaluation of the client's internal control concerning physical access to the securities
d. A description of the client's procedures that prevent the negotiation of securities by just one person (R/00, Aud., #12, 6937)

33. When auditing related party transactions, an auditor places primary emphasis on

a. Ascertaining the rights and obligations of the related parties.
b. Confirming the existence of the related parties.
c. Verifying the valuation of the related party transactions.
d. Evaluating the disclosure of the related party transactions. (5/95, Aud., #68, 5686)

34. Which of the following strategies most likely could improve the response rate of the confirmation of accounts receivable?

a. Including a list of items or invoices that constitute the account balance
b. Restricting the selection of accounts to be confirmed to those customers with relatively large balances
c. Requesting customers to respond to the confirmation requests directly to the auditor by fax or e-mail
d. Notifying the recipients that second requests will be mailed if they fail to respond in a timely manner (R/00, Aud., #11, 6936)

35. An internal auditor's work would most likely affect the nature, timing, and extent of an independent CPA's auditing procedures when the internal auditor's work relates to assertions about the

a. Existence of contingencies.
b. Valuation of intangible assets.
c. Existence of fixed asset additions.
d. Valuation of related party transactions.

(5/95, Aud., #59)

36. Under which of the following circumstances would the use of the blank form of confirmations of accounts receivable most likely be preferable to positive confirmations?

a. The recipients are likely to sign the confirmations without devoting proper attention to them.
b. Subsequent cash receipts are unusually difficult to verify.
c. Analytical procedures indicate that few exceptions are expected.
d. The combined assessed level of inherent risk and control risk is low. (11/98, Aud., #23, 6714)

37. An auditor traced a sample of purchase orders and the related receiving reports to the purchases journal and the cash disbursements journal. The purpose of this substantive audit procedure most likely was to

a. Identify unusually large purchases that should be investigated further.
b. Verify that cash disbursements were for goods actually received.
c. Determine that purchases were properly recorded.
d. Test whether payments were for goods actually ordered. (11/95, Aud., #48, 5995)

38. An auditor vouched data for a sample of employees in a payroll register to approved clock card data to provide assurance that

a. Payments to employees are computed at authorized rates.
b. Employees work the number of hours for which they are paid.
c. Segregation of duties exists between the preparation and distribution of the payroll.
d. Internal controls relating to unclaimed payroll checks are operating effectively.

(5/95, Aud., #37, 5655)

39. The risk of incorrect acceptance and the likelihood of assessing control risk too low relate to the

a. Allowable risk of tolerable misstatement.
b. Preliminary estimates of materiality levels.
c. Efficiency of the audit.
d. Effectiveness of the audit.

(11/95, Aud., #19, 5966)

40. An advantage of statistical sampling over nonstatistical sampling is that statistical sampling helps an auditor to

a. Eliminate the risk of nonsampling errors.
b. Reduce the level of audit risk and materiality to a relatively low amount.
c. Measure the sufficiency of the evidential matter obtained.
d. Minimize the failure to detect errors and fraud.

(11/95, Aud., #44, amended, 5991)

41. For which of the following audit tests would an auditor most likely use attribute sampling?

a. Selecting accounts receivable for confirmation of account balances
b. Inspecting employee time cards for proper approval by supervisors
c. Making an independent estimate of the amount of a LIFO inventory
d. Examining invoices in support of the valuation of fixed asset additions (5/96, Aud., #4, 6236)

42. A retail entity uses electronic data interchange (EDI) in executing and recording most of its purchase transactions. The entity's auditor recognizes that the documentation of the transactions will be retained for only a short period of time. To compensate for this limitation, the auditor most likely would

a. Increase the sample of EDI transactions to be selected for cutoff tests
b. Perform tests several times during the year, rather than only at year end
c. Plan to make a 100% count of the entity's inventory at or near the year end
d. Decrease the assessed level of control risk for the existence or occurrence assertion

(R/00, Aud., #9, 6934)

43. A customer intended to order 100 units of product Z96014, but incorrectly ordered nonexistent product Z96015. Which of the following controls most likely would detect this error?

a. Check digit verification.
b. Record count.
c. Hash total.
d. Redundant data check. (5/98, Aud., #5)

44. A client is concerned that a power outage or disaster could impair the computer hardware's ability to function as designed. The client desires off-site backup hardware facilities that are fully configured and ready to operate within several hours. The client most likely should consider a

a. Cold site.
b. Cool site.
c. Warm site.
d. Hot site. (5/98, Aud., #6)

45. In which of the following situations would an auditor ordinarily choose between expressing a qualified opinion or an adverse opinion?

a. The auditor did **not** observe the entity's physical inventory and is unable to become satisfied about its balance by other auditing procedures.
b. Conditions that cause the auditor to have substantial doubt about the entity's ability to continue as a going concern are inadequately disclosed.
c. There has been a change in accounting principles that has a material effect on the comparability of the entity's financial statements.
d. The auditor is unable to apply necessary procedures concerning an investor's share of an investee's earnings recognized on the equity method. (R/00, Aud., #17, 6942)

46. Pell, CPA, decides to serve as principal auditor in the audit of the financial statements of Tech Consolidated, Inc. Smith, CPA, audits one of Tech's subsidiaries. In which situation(s) should Pell make reference to Smith's audit?

I. Pell reviews Smith's working papers and assumes responsibility for Smith's work, but expresses a qualified opinion on Tech's financial statements.
II. Pell is unable to review Smith's working papers; however, Pell's inquiries indicate that Smith has an excellent reputation for professional competence and integrity.

a. I only
b. II only
c. Both I and II
d. Neither I nor II (5/97, Aud., #5, 6394)

47. For which of the following events would an auditor issue a report that omits any reference to consistency?

a. A change in the method of accounting for inventories
b. A change from an accounting principle that is not generally accepted to one that is generally accepted
c. A change in the useful life used to calculate the provision for depreciation expense
d. Management's lack of reasonable justification for a change in accounting principle (11/96, Aud., #15, 6367)

48. On February 25, a CPA issued an auditor's report expressing an unqualified opinion on financial statements for the year ended January 31. On March 2, the CPA learned that on February 11 the entity incurred a material loss on an uncollectible trade receivable as a result of the deteriorating financial condition of the entity's principal customer that led to the customer's bankruptcy. Management then refused to adjust the financial statements for this subsequent event. The CPA determined that the information is reliable and that there are creditors currently relying on the financial statements. The CPA's next course of action most likely would be to

a. Notify the entity's creditors that the financial statements and the related auditor's report should **no** longer be relied on.
b. Notify each member of the entity's board of directors about management's refusal to adjust the financial statements.
c. Issue revised financial statements and distribute them to each creditor known to be relying on the financial statements.
d. Issue a revised auditor's report and distribute it to each creditor known to be relying on the financial statements. (R/99, Aud., #32, 6848)

49. Which of the following events occurring after the issuance of an auditor's report most likely would cause the auditor to make further inquiries about the previously issued financial statements?

a. An uninsured natural disaster occurs that may affect the entity's ability to continue as a going concern.
b. A contingency is resolved that had been disclosed in the audited financial statements.
c. New information is discovered concerning undisclosed lease transactions of the audited period.
d. A subsidiary is sold that accounts for 25% of the entity's consolidated net income. (11/95, Aud., #85, 6032)

50. When an independent CPA assists in preparing the financial statements of a publicly held entity, but has **not** audited or reviewed them, the CPA should issue a disclaimer of opinion. In such situations, the CPA has **no** responsibility to apply any procedures beyond

a. Ascertaining whether the financial statements are in conformity with generally accepted accounting principles.
b. Determining whether management has elected to omit substantially all required disclosures.
c. Documenting that internal control is **not** being relied on.
d. Reading the financial statements for obvious material misstatements. (5/92, Aud., #2, amended)

51. An auditor concludes that there is substantial doubt about an entity's ability to continue as a going concern for a reasonable period of time. If the entity's financial statements adequately disclose its financial difficulties, the auditor's report is required to include an explanatory paragraph that specifically uses the phrase(s)

	"Reasonable period of time, not to exceed one year"	*"Going concern"*
a.	Yes	Yes
b.	Yes	No
c.	No	Yes
d.	No	No

(5/98, Aud., #14, 6631)

52. An auditor is engaged to report on selected financial data that are included in a client-prepared document containing audited financial statements. Under these circumstances, the report on the selected data should

a. Be limited to data derived from the audited financial statements.
b. Be distributed only to senior management and the board of directors.
c. State that the presentation is a comprehensive basis of accounting other than GAAP.
d. Indicate that the data are **not** fairly stated in all material respects. (11/95, Aud., #87, 6034)

53. Which of the following statements is correct concerning letters for underwriters, commonly referred to as comfort letters?

a. Letters for underwriters are required by the Securities Act of 1933 for the initial public sale of registered securities.
b. Letters for underwriters typically give negative assurance on unaudited interim financial information.
c. Letters for underwriters usually are included in the registration statement accompanying a prospectus.
d. Letters for underwriters ordinarily update auditors' opinions on the prior year's financial statements. (5/95, Aud., #86, 5704)

54. The objective of a review of interim financial information of a public entity is to provide an accountant with a basis for reporting whether

a. Material modifications should be made to conform with generally accepted accounting principles.
b. A reasonable basis exists for expressing an updated opinion regarding the financial statements that were previously audited.
c. Condensed financial statements or pro forma financial information should be included in a registration statement.
d. The financial statements are presented fairly in accordance with generally accepted accounting principles. (5/95, Aud., #83, 5701)

55. During an engagement to review the financial statements of a nonpublic entity, an accountant becomes aware that several leases that should be capitalized are not capitalized. The accountant considers these leases to be material to the financial statements. The accountant decides to modify the standard review report because management will not capitalize the leases. Under these circumstances, the accountant should

a. Issue an adverse opinion because of the departure from GAAP.
b. Express **no** assurance of any kind on the entity's financial statements.
c. Emphasize that the financial statements are for limited use only.
d. Disclose the departure from GAAP in a separate paragraph of the accountant's report.

(5/96, Aud., #7, 6239)

56. When providing limited assurance that the financial statements of a nonpublic entity require **no** material modifications to be in accordance with generally accepted accounting principles, the accountant should

a. Assess the risk that a material misstatement could occur in a financial statement assertion.
b. Confirm with the entity's lawyer that material loss contingencies are disclosed.
c. Understand the accounting principles of the industry in which the entity operates.
d. Develop audit programs to determine whether the entity's financial statements are fairly presented.

(5/95, Aud., #58)

57. Which of the following procedures would an accountant **least** likely perform during an engagement to review the financial statements of a nonpublic entity?

a. Observing the safeguards over access to and use of assets and records
b. Comparing the financial statements with anticipated results in budgets and forecasts
c. Inquiring of management about actions taken at the board of directors' meetings
d. Studying the relationships of financial statement elements expected to conform to predictable patterns (11/94, Aud., #74)

58. Financial statements of a nonpublic entity that have been reviewed by an accountant should be accompanied by a report stating that a review

a. Provides only limited assurance that the financial statements are fairly presented.
b. Includes examining, on a test basis, information that is the representation of management.
c. Consists principally of inquiries of company personnel and analytical procedures applied to financial data.
d. Does **not** contemplate obtaining corroborating evidential matter or applying certain other procedures ordinarily performed during an audit. (11/95, Aud., #79)

59. An entity engaged a CPA to determine whether the client's web sites meet defined criteria for standard business practices and controls over transaction integrity and information protection. In performing this engagement, the CPA should comply with the provisions of

a. Statements on Assurance Standards.
b. Statements on Standards for Attestation Engagements.
c. Statements on Standards for Management Consulting Services.
d. Statements on Auditing Standards (R/99, Aud., #3, 6819)

60. Which of the following is a conceptual difference between the attestation standards and generally accepted auditing standards?

a. The attestation standards provide a framework for the attest function beyond historical financial statements.
b. The requirement that the practitioner be independent in mental attitude is omitted from the attestation standards.
c. The attestation standards do **not** permit an attest engagement to be part of a business acquisition study or a feasibility study.
d. **None** of the standards of field work in generally accepted auditing standards are included in the attestation standards. (5/94, Aud., #10)

OTHER OBJECTIVE FORMAT QUESTIONS

PROBLEM 2 (15 to 25 minutes)

Bond, CPA, is considering audit risk at the financial statement level in planning the audit of Toxic Waste Disposal (TWD) Company's financial statements for the year ended December 31, 20X6. TWD is a privately-owned entity that contracts with municipal governments to remove environmental wastes. Audit risk at the financial statement level is influenced by the risk of material misstatements, which may be indicated by a combination of factors related to management, the industry, and the entity.

Based only on the information above, indicate whether each of the following factors **(Items 1 through 15)** would most likely increase audit risk (I), decrease audit risk (D), or have **no** effect on audit risk (N).

Company profile:

1. This was the first year TWD operated at a profit since 20X4 because the municipalities received increased federal and state funding for environmental purposes.

2. TWD's Board of Directors is controlled by Mead, the majority stockholder, who also acts as the chief executive officer.

3. The internal auditor reports to the controller and the controller reports to Mead.

4. The accounting department has experienced a high rate of turnover of key personnel.

5. TWD's bank has a loan officer who meets regularly with TWD's CEO and controller to monitor TWD's financial performance.

6. TWD's employees are paid biweekly.

7. Bond has audited TWD for five years.

Recent developments:

8. During 20X6, TWD changed its method of preparing its financial statements from the cash basis to generally accepted accounting principles.

9. During 20X6, TWD sold one half of its controlling interest in United Equipment Leasing (UEL) Co. TWD retained significant interest in UEL.

10. During 20X6, litigation filed against TWD in 20X1 alleging that TWD discharged pollutants into state waterways was dropped by the state. Loss contingency disclosures that TWD included in prior years' financial statements are being removed for the 20X6 financial statements.

11. During December, TWD signed a contract to lease disposal equipment from an entity owned by Mead's parents. This related party transaction is not disclosed in TWD's notes to its financial statements.

12. During December, TWD completed a barter transaction with a municipality. TWD removed waste from a municipally-owned site and acquired title to another contaminated site at below market price. TWD intends to service this new site in 20X7.

13. During December, TWD increased its casualty insurance coverage on several pieces of sophisticated machinery from historical cost to replacement cost.

14. Inquiries about the substantial increase in revenue TWD recorded in the fourth quarter of 20X6 disclosed a new policy. TWD guaranteed to several municipalities that it would refund the federal and state funding paid to TWD if any municipality fails federal or state site clean-up inspection in 20X7.

15. An initial public offering of TWD's stock is planned for late 20X7. (5/94, Aud., #3, amended)

PROBLEM 3 (15 to 25 minutes)

ITEMS 1 THROUGH 15 represent a series of unrelated statements, questions, excerpts, and comments taken from various parts of an auditor's working paper file. Below the items is a list of the likely sources of the statements, questions, excerpts, and comments. Select, as the best answer for each item, the most likely source. Select only one source for each item. A source may be selected once, more than once, or not at all.

1. There are no material transactions that have not been properly recorded in the accounting records underlying the financial statements.

2. In connection with an audit of our financial statements, management has prepared, and furnished to our auditors, a description and evaluation of certain contingencies.

3. Provision has been made for any material loss to be sustained in the fulfillment of, or from the inability to fulfill, any sales commitments.

4. Fees for our services are based on our regular per diem rates, plus travel and other out-of-pocket expenses.

5. The objective of our audit is to express an unqualified opinion on the financial statements, although it is possible that facts or circumstances encountered may preclude us from expressing an unqualified opinion.

6. There has been no fraud involving employees that could have a material effect on the financial statements.

7. Are you aware of any facts or circumstances that may indicate a lack of integrity by any member of senior management?

8. If a difference of opinion on a practice problem existed between engagement personnel and a specialist or other consultant, was the difference resolved in accordance with firm policy and appropriately documented?

9. Although we have not conducted a comprehensive, detailed search of our records, no other deposit or loan accounts have come to our attention except as noted below.

10. At the conclusion of our audit, we will request certain written representations from you about the financial statements and related matters.

11. We have no plans or intentions that may materially affect the carrying value or classification of assets and liabilities.

12. As discussed in Note 14 to the financial statements, the Company has had numerous dealings with businesses controlled by, and people who are related to, the officers of the company.

13. There were unreasonable delays by management in permitting the commencement of the audit and in providing needed information.

14. If this statement is not correct, please write promptly, using the enclosed envelope, and give details of any differences directly to our auditors.

15. The Company has suffered recurring losses from operations and has a net capital deficiency that raises substantial doubt about its ability to continue as a going concern.

List of Sources	
(A)	Partner's engagement review program.
(B)	Communication with predecessor auditor.
(C)	Auditor's engagement letter.
(D)	Management representation letter.
(E)	Standard financial institution confirmation request.
(F)	Auditor's communication with the audit committee.
(G)	Auditor's report.
(H)	Letter for underwriters.
(I)	Audit inquiry letter to legal counsel.
(J)	Accounts receivable confirmation.

(11/95, Aud., #91-#105, amended)

ESSAY QUESTIONS

ESSAY 4 (15 to 25 minutes)

Post, CPA, accepted an engagement to audit the financial statements of General Co., a new client. General is a publicly held retailing entity that recently replaced its operating management. In the course of applying auditing procedures, Post discovered that General's financial statements may be materially misstated due to the existence of possible fraud.

REQUIRED:

a. Describe Post's responsibilities in the circumstances described above.

b. Describe Post's responsibilities for reporting on General's financial statements and other communications if Post is precluded from applying necessary procedures in searching for fraud.

c. Describe Post's responsibilities for reporting on General's financial statements and other communications if Post concludes that General's financial statements are materially affected by fraud.

d. Describe the circumstances in which Post may have a duty to disclose possible fraud to third parties outside General's management and its audit committee. (5/93, Aud., #4, amended)

ESSAY 5 (15 to 25 minutes)

An auditor is required to obtain a sufficient understanding of each of the components of an entity's internal control. This is necessary to plan the audit of the entity's financial statements and to assess control risk.

REQUIRED:

a. For what purposes should an auditor's understanding of internal control components be used in planning an audit?

b. What is required for an auditor to assess control risk at below the maximum level?

c. What should an auditor consider when seeking a further reduction in the planned assessed level of control risk?

d. What are an auditor's documentation requirements concerning an entity's internal control and the assessed level of control risk? (11/92, Aud., #4)

ANSWERS TO MULTIPLE CHOICE QUESTIONS

1. d	6. d	11. a	16. a	21. a	26. a	31. b	36. a	41. b	46. b	51. c	56. c
2. a	7. d	12. c	17. c	22. c	27. d	32. a	37. c	42. b	47. c	52. a	57. a
3. b	8. d	13. b	18. d	23. a	28. a	33. d	38. b	43. a	48. b	53. b	58. c
4. d	9. c	14. d	19. a	24. c	29. c	34. a	39. d	44. d	49. c	54. a	59. b
5. c	10. d	15. c	20. d	25. d	30. a	35. c	40. c	45. b	50. d	55. d	60. a

PERFORMANCE BY TOPICS

Diagnostic exam questions corresponding to each chapter of the Auditing text are listed below. To assess your preparedness for the CPA exam, record the number and percentage of questions you correctly answered in each topic area. The point distribution of the multiple choice questions (not counting the other objective format or essay questions) approximates that of the exam. The numbers in parenthesis in the performance by topics diagnostic chart refer to an explanation of a question in the referenced chapters. (The question in the chapter may not be the same question as in the diagnostic exam.)

Chapter 31: Standards & Related Topics

Question #	Correct √
1 (3)	
2 (5)	
3 (15)	
# Questions	3
# Correct	
% Correct	

Chapter 32: Planning

Question #	Correct √
4 (6)	
5 (13)	
6 (40)	
7 (24)	
# Questions	4
# Correct	
% Correct	

Chapter 33: Internal Control: General

Question #	Correct √
8 (2)	
9 (8)	
10 (20)	
11 (21)	
12 (23)	
13 (25)	
14 (31)	
15 (32)	
# Questions	8
# Correct	
% Correct	

Chapter 34: Internal Control: Transaction Cycles

Question #	Correct √
16 (8)	
17 (6)	
18 (25)	
19 (28)	
20 (13)	
21 (40)	
# Questions	6
# Correct	
% Correct	

Chapter 35: Evidence & Procedures

Question #	Correct √
22 (4)	
23 (7)	
24 (9)	
25 (21)	
26 (64)	
27 (13)	
28 (26)	
29 (27)	
30 (39)	
31 (43)	
32 (50)	
33 (58)	
# Questions	12
# Correct	
% Correct	

Chapter 36: Audit Programs

Question #	Correct √
34 (14)	
35 (22)	
36 (15)	
37 (38)	
38 (43)	
# Questions	5
# Correct	
% Correct	

Chapter 37: Audit Sampling

Question #	Correct √
39 (4)	
40 (8)	
41 (19)	
# Questions	3
# Correct	
% Correct	

Chapter 38: Auditing EDP Systems

Question #	Correct √
42 (9)	
43 (28)	
44 (58)	
# Questions	3
# Correct	
% Correct	

Chapter 39: Reports on Audited Financial Statements

Question #	Correct √
45 (13)	
46 (25)	
47 (31)	
48 (62)	
49 (67)	
50 (76)	
51 (80)	
# Questions	7
# Correct	
% Correct	

Chapter 40: Other Types of Reports

Question #	Correct √
52 (7)	
53 (10)	
54 (15)	
# Questions	3
# Correct	
% Correct	

Chapter 41: Other Professional Services

Question #	Correct √
55 (22)	
56 (19)	
57 (49)	
58 (23)	
59 (30)	
60 (32)	
# Questions	6
# Correct	
% Correct	

OTHER OBJECTIVE FORMAT QUESTION SOLUTIONS

PROBLEM 2 AUDIT RISK (Explanations for these answers are found in Chapter 32, Problem 32-3.)

1.	D	4.	I	7.	D	10.	D	13.	N
2.	I	5.	D	8.	I	11.	I	14.	I
3.	I	6.	N	9.	I	12.	I	15.	I

PROBLEM 3 WORKING PAPERS (Explanations for these answers are found in Chapter 35, Problem 35-3.)

1.	D	4.	C	7.	B	10.	C	13.	F
2.	I	5.	C	8.	A	11.	D	14.	J
3.	D	6.	D	9.	E	12.	G	15.	G

EXPLANATIONS TO SPECIFIC QUESTIONS

We strongly recommend that candidates **not** spend much time on the answers to specific questions that they answered incorrectly on the diagnostic exam, particularly at the beginning of their review. Instead, study the related chapter. After studying the appropriate chapter(s), question-specific explanations will be more understandable.

ESSAY SOLUTIONS

SOLUTION 4 REPORTING FRAUD

a. If Post discovers that General's financial statements may be materially misstated due to the **existence of fraud**, Post should consider the **implications** for other aspects of the audit and discuss the matter and approach to further investigation with an **appropriate level of management that is at least one level above those involved** with the fraud. Post should also attempt to obtain sufficient competent evidential matter to determine whether, in fact, material fraud does exist and, if so, its effect. Post may suggest that General consult with its legal counsel on matters concerning questions of law.

b. If Post is precluded from applying necessary procedures, Post should **disclaim or qualify** an opinion on the financial statements and **communicate** these findings to General's **audit committee** or its **board of directors**.

c. If Post concludes that General's financial statements **are materially affected** by fraud, Post should insist that **the financial statements be revised** and, if they are not, express a **qualified or** an **adverse** opinion on the financial statements, disclosing all the substantive reasons for such an opinion. Additionally, Post should adequately inform General's audit committee or its board of directors about the fraud.

d. Post may have a duty to disclose possible fraud to **third parties** outside General's management and its audit committee in the following circumstances:

- When General reports an **auditor change** under the appropriate securities law.
- When a **successor auditor appropriately makes inquiries** of a predecessor auditor.
- When responding to a **subpoena**.
- When **communicating with a funding or other specified agency**, as required for entities that receive financial assistance from a government agency.

SOLUTION 5 UNDERSTANDING OF INTERNAL CONTROL

a. In **planning** an audit, an auditor's understanding of the internal control structure elements should be used to **identify** the types of **potential misstatements** that could occur, to consider the factors affecting the risk of material misstatement, and to influence the design of substantive tests.

b. An auditor obtains an **understanding of the design** of relevant internal control policies and procedures and whether they have been **placed in operation**. Assessing control risk at **below the maximum** level further involves **identifying specific policies and procedures** relevant to specific assertions that are **likely to prevent or detect material misstatements** in those assertions. It also involves performing **tests of controls** to evaluate the operating design and effectiveness of such policies and procedures.

c. When seeking a **further reduction** in the assessed level of **control risk**, an auditor should consider whether **additional evidential matter** sufficient to support a further reduction is **likely to be available**, and whether it would be **efficient to perform tests** of controls to obtain that evidential matter.

d. An auditor should **document the understanding** of an entity's internal control components obtained to plan the audit. The auditor also should **document** the **basis for the auditor's conclusion** about the **assessed level of control risk**. If control risk is assessed at the maximum level, the auditor should **document that conclusion**, but it is **not required to document the basis** for that conclusion. However, if the assessed level of control risk is **below the maximum** level, the auditor should **document the basis for the conclusion that the effectiveness** of the design and operation **of internal control** policies and procedures **supports that assessed level.**

CHAPTER 31

STANDARDS & RELATED TOPICS

EXAM COVERAGE: The Evaluate Client and Plan Engagement portion of the Auditing section of the CPA exam is designated by the examiners to be 40 percent of the section's point value. Historically, exam coverage of the topics in this chapter hovers at 1 to 4 percent of the Auditing section. More information about the point value of various topics is included in the **Practical Advice** section of this volume.

CHAPTER 31

STANDARDS & RELATED TOPICS

I. An Overview of the Audit Function

A. Responsibilities

The independent auditor is responsible for rendering an opinion on the organization's financial statements in accordance with generally accepted auditing standards. The objective of the audit is the expression of an opinion as to whether, in all material respects, the financial position, results of operations, and cash flows are presented fairly in conformity with generally accepted accounting principles. The auditor's responsibility to express an opinion on the financial statements is explicitly stated in the introductory paragraph of the auditor's report.

1. **Management** Management is responsible for the contents of financial statements, even if the statements are prepared and/or audited by CPAs. Financial statements are the representation of management of the effects of transactions and events that have affected the organization's financial position and results of operations. Management is also responsible for establishing and maintaining effective internal control and for developing accounting policies.

2. **Users** Financial statement users should recognize that the accounting process necessitates the use of estimates and evaluations that affect the fairness of the financial statements. They should also understand the meaning and significance of the auditor's report.

B. Nature of the Audit Function

To independently accumulate and evaluate evidence of an economic entity for the purpose of reporting on the degree of correspondence between information produced and established criteria (e.g., generally accepted accounting principles).

Exhibit 1 ♦ Comparison of Financial Accounting and Auditing

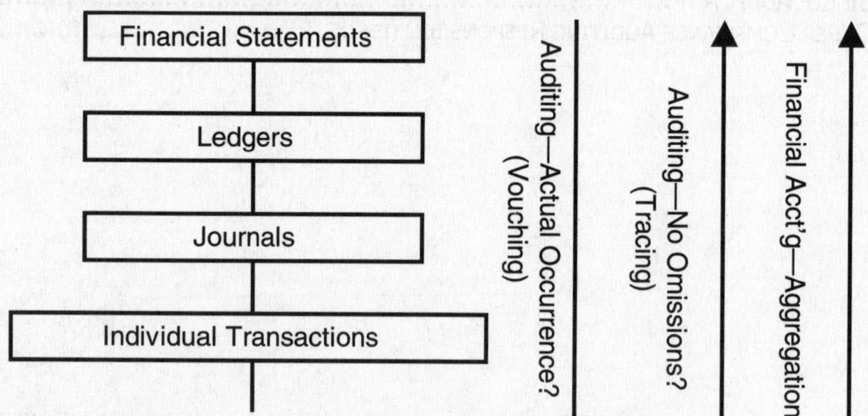

Note that financial accounting is a **process of aggregation**. Individual transactions are first recorded in journals; subsequently, the data in journals are classified in ledgers; and finally, the data in ledgers are summarized in the financial statements.

1. **VOUCHING** Did the transactions summarized in the financial statements actually occur? The auditor makes this determination by vouching items from the financial statements back to the accounts and ultimately to the original transaction documents. This is a downward process in Exhibit 1.

2. **TRACING** Have all transactions that occurred during the period been properly recorded in the accounts and summarized in the financial statements? (Are the financial statements complete?) The auditor makes this determination by tracing items from original transaction documents to the accounts and ultimately to the financial statements. This is an upward process in Exhibit 1.

C. STEPS IN THE AUDIT PROCESS

1. **PLAN THE AUDIT** The auditor must plan the audit to obtain sufficient, competent evidential matter about the financial statement assertions. Planning involves obtaining an understanding of the industry and significant transactions of the client, an assessment of the risk of errors and fraud occurring, and an understanding of the entity's internal control. Additionally, planning will involve a preliminary assessment of audit risk and materiality. The planning should be documented in both a planning memorandum and in a detailed audit program.

   a. **UNDERSTAND THE CLIENT** The auditor becomes familiar with the industry in which the client operates and the client's organization and accounting system. Based on this initial understanding, the auditor determines whether to accept the client.

   b. **ENGAGEMENT LETTER** An engagement letter is issued outlining the nature of the audit, the responsibilities of the client for the financial statements, and the meaning of the auditor's report. Both the auditor and the client sign the engagement letter.

2. **REVIEW THE INTERNAL CONTROL**

3. **EVALUATE THE INTERNAL CONTROL** The auditor makes a preliminary assessment of control risk.

4. **EVIDENCE** Consider evidence to justify further reduction of control risk.

5. **DETERMINE THE FINAL ASSESSED LEVEL OF CONTROL RISK** This helps the auditor determine the **N**ature, **E**xtent, and **T**iming of substantive tests.

6. **SUBSTANTIVE TESTS** The auditor uses the knowledge provided by the understanding of internal control and the assessed level of control risk in determining the nature, timing, and extent of substantive tests for financial statement assertions. Substantive tests consist of tests of details of transactions and balances, and analytical procedures. After all substantive tests have been performed, the auditor analyzes the accumulated evidence to decide whether an audit opinion can be reached.

7. **AUDIT REPORT** The audit report describes the scope of the audit and states the auditor's conclusion regarding the fairness of the financial statements, including the related disclosures. Consistency in application of accounting principles is implied in the standard auditor's report unless otherwise indicated by the auditor. The audit report should also include any reservations the auditor has regarding the financial statements.

D. DEFINITIONS

1. **FINANCIAL STATEMENT AUDIT** This is the audit discussed above and throughout the remainder of the text unless otherwise indicated. Its objective is to express an opinion on the fairness, in all material respects, with which the financial statements present the

organization's financial position, results of operations, and cash flows in conformity with generally accepted accounting principles (GAAP).

2. **Compliance Audit** The purpose of this type of audit is to evaluate an organization's compliance with a defined set of specifications. Common examples include Internal Revenue Service audits to determine whether a taxpayer has complied with applicable provisions of the Internal Revenue Code; audits of governmental units to verify their compliance with applicable state and federal regulations; and verification audits by a CPA to determine a client's compliance with the provisions of a bond or loan indenture.

3. **Operational Audit** These audits, usually performed by internal auditors, evaluate the efficiency and effectiveness of some part of an organization in achieving its specific goals vis-à-vis the general goals of an organization. This type of audit involves an evaluation of operating procedures and methods, and usually requires the auditor to issue a report to management recommending ways to improve efficiency and/or effectiveness. A common example would be a review by government auditors (e.g., General Accounting Office auditors) to determine the effectiveness and continued utility of specific government-funded programs. This type of audit is not usually concerned with financial information.

4. **Independent Auditors** These are external auditors (i.e., outside of the organization being audited) who provide an independent, professionally competent evaluation of the financial statements of a client. Additionally, independent CPAs are actively engaged in tax services, consulting services, and other types of financial services for their clients. Consistent with their external audit and advisory responsibilities, CPAs are certified and licensed by the individual states in which they practice, and many belong to the American Institute of Certified Public Accountants (AICPA). The terms "CPA" and "auditor" are frequently used interchangeably. In this text, unless otherwise indicated, the term "auditor" signifies a CPA who is independent of the client.

Exhibit 2 ♦ Important Characteristics of Audits and Auditors

Independence	Auditors represent neither the financial statement preparers (management) nor the financial statement users (investors, creditors, etc.).
Materiality	An audit is directed toward the discovery of material misstatements or omissions in the financial statements. Materiality involves professional judgment and is influenced by the auditor's perception of the needs of a reasonable person relying on the financial statements.
Selective Testing	Auditors base their opinions on selective testing; they rarely examine all of the items in an individual account or in the financial statements.
Audit Risk	Since auditors base their opinions on selective testing, there is always a risk that material misstatements or omissions in the financial statements will not be detected. Therefore, an auditor's report provides assurance (not a guarantee) as to whether the financial statements adhere to the established criteria. Even if the auditor examines 100 percent of an account, the audit still is subject to audit risk.
Overall Opinion	The auditor's opinion relates to the financial statements as a whole rather than individual items within the financial statements.
Presentation	An audit is concerned with financial statement presentation; it is not concerned with the effectiveness of management, or the advisability of investing in the organization.

5. **Internal Auditors** Internal auditors work full time for the organization or entity. Some internal auditors perform financial statement audits, while others perform compliance or

operational audits. Since internal auditors are not independent in the same sense as a CPA, they cannot issue an audit report for stockholders or other interested outside parties.

6. **Organizational Independence** For an internal audit function to be effective, it is important that it be directed to a level of the organization that is above the level being audited. For example, if the internal auditors are based at corporate headquarters and report to the audit committee of the board of directors, the internal audit function would be organizationally independent from a particular plant audited by the internal audit staff.

7. **Governmental Auditors** These are auditors who work for the federal, state, or local government. Two of the most commonly mentioned are the following:

   a. **General Accounting Office (GAO) Auditors** GAO auditors conduct audits for Congress. While they do a considerable number of compliance audits, they also perform an increasing amount of operational-type audit work.

   b. **Internal Revenue Agents** These are auditors who conduct compliance audits for the Internal Revenue Service.

8. **Audit Committees** These are special committees formed by the audit client's board of directors to act as a liaison between the board and the independent auditor. Also, they are formed to reinforce the auditor's independence in relation to client management. The following are some of the committee's normal functions:

   a. Select the independent auditor and negotiate appropriate fees.

   b. Review the auditor's overall audit plan.

   c. Review relevant company policies and procedures.

   d. Review the results of the audit and discuss the auditor's management letter.

   e. Consider matters that the auditor believes should be brought to the attention of the shareholders or directors.

II. Generally Accepted Auditing Standards (AU 150)

A. Auditing Procedures vs. Auditing Standards

1. Procedures relate to the acts to be performed; for example, the confirmation of a predetermined number of accounts receivable. The auditing procedures used will vary from engagement to engagement.

2. Standards deal with measures of the quality of performance of the auditing procedures and the objectives the procedures are to attain. These include both professional qualities and audit judgment. The auditing standards will not vary from engagement to engagement.

B. Observations on GAAS

CPAs must comply with GAAS.

1. The concepts of **materiality** and **audit risk** underlie the application of GAAS, especially the standards of field work and reporting. Materiality and audit risk need to be considered when determining the nature, timing, and extent of audit procedures to be performed, as well as evaluating the results of those procedures.

   a. Materiality is used to determine the effect of misstatements, individually and in the aggregate, on the financial statements taken as a whole. Materiality involves professional judgment of the auditor made in light of the surrounding circumstances, involving both quantitative and qualitative considerations, and the auditor's perception of the needs of a reasonable person relying on the financial statements.

b. Audit risk is the risk that the auditor may unknowingly fail to modify his or her opinion on financial statements that are materially misstated. Audit risk is reflected in the auditor's report with the statement that the auditor obtained reasonable assurance that the financial statements are free of material misstatements. Audit risk should also be considered at the account and class of transactions level, taking into consideration inherent risk, control risk, and detection risk factors.

2. GAAS are applicable to all services covered by the Statements on Auditing Standards, to the extent that they are relevant. They deal with measures of the quality of performance of the auditor.

GENERALLY ACCEPTED AUDITING STANDARDS

T Training
I Independence
P Performance

S Supervision and Planning
I Internal Control
E Evidence

A Accounting = U.S. GAAP
C Consistency
D Disclosure
E Expressing an Opinion

C. **GENERAL STANDARDS (TIP)**
The general standards are personal in nature. They relate to the qualifications of the auditor and the quality of the work performed.

1. **TECHNICAL TRAINING AND PROFICIENCY** The audit is to be performed by a person or persons having adequate technical training and proficiency as an auditor.

2. **INDEPENDENCE** In all matters relating to the assignment, an independence in mental attitude is to be maintained by the auditor or auditors.

3. **DUE PROFESSIONAL CARE** Due professional care is to be exercised in the performance of the audit and the preparation of the report.

D. **STANDARDS OF FIELD WORK (SIE)**

1. **ADEQUATE PLANNING AND SUPERVISION** The work is to be adequately planned and assistants, if any, are to be properly supervised.

2. **UNDERSTANDING OF INTERNAL CONTROL** A sufficient understanding of internal control is to be obtained to plan the audit and to determine the nature, timing, and extent of tests to be performed.

3. **Sufficient Competent Evidential Matter** Sufficient competent evidential matter is to be obtained through inspection, observation, inquiries, and confirmations to afford a reasonable basis for an opinion regarding the financial statements under audit.

E. Standards of Reporting (ACDE)

1. **Accounting in Conformity With U.S. GAAP** The report shall state whether the financial statements are presented in conformity with U.S. generally accepted accounting principles.

2. **Consistency** The report shall identify those circumstances in which such principles have not been consistently observed in the current period in relation to the preceding period.

3. **Adequate Informative Disclosure** Informative disclosures in the financial statements are to be regarded as reasonably adequate unless otherwise stated in the report.

4. **Expression of an Opinion** The report shall contain either an expression of opinion regarding the financial statements, taken as a whole, or an assertion to the effect that an opinion cannot be expressed. When an overall opinion cannot be expressed, the reasons should be stated. In all cases where an auditor's name is associated with financial statements, the report should contain a clear-cut indication of the character of the auditor's work, if any, and the degree of responsibility the auditor is taking.

III. The General Standards

A. Training and Proficiency of the Independent Auditor (AU 210)

The auditor holds him- or herself out as being proficient in accounting and auditing. This requires academic training and professional experience. Training is an ongoing process that includes remaining current with new developments taking place in business and in the accounting profession.

Exhibit 3 ♦ The First General Standard

> "The audit is to be performed by a person or persons having adequate technical training and proficiency as an auditor."

B. Independence (AU 220)

The attitude implied by independence is that of judicial impartiality or fairness toward clients and others who rely upon the independent auditor's report. The auditor's objective is to ensure that the general public maintains confidence in the independence of the auditor. Independence in attitude also implies the auditor is without bias towards the client. Our discussion of the AICPA Code of Professional Conduct includes an in-depth discussion of the area of independence (see the *Business Law and Professional Responsibilities* volume).

- ISBS 1 is applicable to any auditor intending to be considered an independent accountant with regard to an entity according to the security acts administered by the SEC (the Acts). Annually, an independent accountant must perform three duties.

    a. The auditor must disclose, in writing, to the audit committee (or equivalent), all relationships between the auditor and its related entities and the client entity and its related entities that, in the auditor's judgment, may be considered to bear on independence.

    b. The auditor must confirm in writing that, in the auditor's judgment, it is independent of the client entity according to the Acts.

    c. The auditor must discuss the auditor's independence with the audit committee.

EXHIBIT 4 ♦ THE SECOND GENERAL STANDARD

> "In all matters relating to the assignment, an independence in mental attitude is to be maintained by the auditor or auditors."

C. DUE CARE IN THE PERFORMANCE OF WORK (AU 230)

Each person within an independent auditor's organization has the responsibility to exercise due care and to adhere to the standards of field work and reporting. This responsibility necessitates critical review by supervisors of the work done and judgment exercised by those assisting in the audit.

EXHIBIT 5 ♦ THE THIRD GENERAL STANDARD

> "Due professional care is to be exercised in the performance of the audit and the preparation of the report."

1. **FRAUD** An auditor commits a type of fraud if he or she alleges possessing the degree of skill commonly possessed by other auditors when the auditor actually does not possess such skill.

2. **NOT INFALLIBLE** Due care does not guarantee infallibility in either performance or in matters of pure judgment.

IV. QUALITY CONTROL STANDARDS

A. RELATIONSHIP OF GAAS AND QUALITY CONTROL STANDARDS

GAAS relates to the conduct of individual audit engagements. Quality control standards relate to the conduct of a CPA firm's audit practice as a whole. Since a firm's audit practice is composed of individual audit engagements, GAAS and quality control standards are related, and the latter may affect the conduct of individual audit engagements as well as the firm's audit practice as a whole.

1. **STANDARDS** Individual CPAs and firms of CPAs must comply with GAAS in the conduct of their audit practice. Firms should establish quality control policies and procedures that provide reasonable assurance of conforming with GAAS in the conduct of their audit engagements.

2. **QUALITY CONTROL** The nature and extent of the quality control policies and procedures depend on such factors as the firm's size, the degree of operating autonomy that its personnel and its practice offices are allowed, the nature of its practice, its organization, and appropriate cost-benefit considerations.

B. SYSTEM OF QUALITY CONTROL (SQCS 2, 4)

SQCS 2 applies to quality control for all auditing, accounting, review, compilation, and agreed-upon procedure services for which professional standards have been established. It does not prescribe provisions for other areas of a firm's practice, such as tax services and management consulting services except to the extent they are part of applicable services. Firms that are members of the AICPA Division for CPA Firms must adhere to quality control standards promulgated by the Institute. All members of the AICPA may be called upon to justify departures.

1. **DEFINITIONS**

   a. **OBJECTIVE** The reason for having a system of quality control is to give the firm reasonable assurance that it is meeting its responsibility to provide professional services that conform with professional standards.

b. **FIRM** "A proprietorship, partnership, or professional corporation or association engaged in the practice of public accounting, including individual partners or shareholders thereof."

c. **PROFESSIONAL STANDARDS** Relate to the professional qualities and performance of individual members of the AICPA. These include AICPA Rules of Conduct, Auditing Standards Board Pronouncements, and pronouncements of the Accounting and Review Services Committee.

d. **PERSONNEL** Unless stated otherwise, *personnel* includes all of a firm's professionals who perform auditing and accounting and review services. This includes proprietors, partners, principals, and stockholders or officers of professional corporations, and their professional employees.

e. **SYSTEM OF QUALITY CONTROL** A system of quality control includes the organizational structure of the firm and the policies adopted and procedures established to provide reasonable assurance that the firm is meeting its responsibility to provide professional services that conform with professional standards. Because the organizational structure, policies, and nature of practice will vary from firm to firm, the system should be appropriately comprehensive and suitably designed (i.e., each firm will not have the same system of quality control).

(1) **LIMITATIONS** There are inherent limitations in any system of quality control that can reduce its effectiveness (for example, variance in individual performance and understanding of professional requirements).

(2) **FOREIGN OFFICES** A U.S. firm should have a system of quality control that provides reasonable assurance that work performed by its foreign offices or by its domestic or foreign affiliates or correspondents meets U.S. professional standards.

f. **RESPONSIBILITIES** Responsibilities for the Quality Control system design and maintenance should be assigned to personnel as needed to effectively implement the quality control policies and procedures. All firm personnel are responsible for compliance with the policies and procedures.

g. **COMMUNICATION** The quality control policies and procedures should be communicated to personnel in a way that will provide reasonable assurance that they will understand the policies and procedures.

h. **DOCUMENTATION** While having written policies and procedures usually enhances the communication, it is not necessarily true that the effectiveness of a firm's system of quality control will be harmed if it is not written. Factors such as the size, structure, and nature of practice of the firm are determining factors in assessing the need to document and, if it is required, the extent of documentation. Usually, it would be expected that a large firm would have more documentation than a small firm and that a multi-office firm's documentation would be more extensive than a single-office firm.

2. **ELEMENTS OF QUALITY CONTROL** Each of the following interrelated elements should be included in quality control policies and procedures:

a. **INDEPENDENCE, INTEGRITY, AND OBJECTIVITY** Policies and procedures should be established to provide reasonable assurance that personnel maintain independence (in fact and appearance) as required, discharge all professional responsibilities with integrity, and maintain objectivity in performing professional responsibilities.

b. **PERSONNEL MANAGEMENT** Personnel management includes hiring, assigning personnel to engagements, professional development, and advancement decisions. The efficiency of the quality control system depends on the characteristics of personnel that perform, supervise, and review work. Usually, less direct supervision is needed when personnel assigned to a specific engagement are more able and more experienced.

(1) **Hiring** Policies and procedures for hiring should be established to provide reasonable assurance that those persons hired possess the appropriate characteristics to enable them to perform their work competently.

(2) **Assignment of Personnel to Engagements** Policies and procedures for assigning personnel to engagements should be established to provide reasonable assurance that the work will be performed by those who possess the appropriate degree of technical training and proficiency. It is important to consider the nature and extent of supervision that will be required. As a general rule, the need for supervision decreases as more able and experienced personnel are assigned to the engagement.

(3) **Professional Development** Policies and procedures for professional development should be established to provide reasonable assurance that the personnel will have the knowledge that is required to fulfill those responsibilities assigned and to progress within the firm.

(4) **Advancement** Policies and procedures for advancing personnel should be established to provide reasonable assurance that those advanced within the firm will be qualified to perform their new responsibilities and that those meeting stated criteria are assigned increased degrees of responsibilities. Qualifications that personnel selected for advancement should possess include character, motivation, intelligence, and judgment.

QUALITY CONTROL

I Independence, Integrity, & Objectivity
M Monitoring

A Acceptance & Continuance of Clients
P Personnel Management
E Engagement Performance

I'M APE Over Quality Control!

QUALITY CONTROL: PERSONNEL MANAGEMENT

H Hiring
E Assignment of Personnel to Engagements
A Advancement
D Professional Development

c. **Acceptance and Continuance of Clients and Engagements** Policies and procedures should be established for making the decision as to whether or not to accept or continue a client (to minimize the chance of being associated with a client whose management lacks integrity). For example, the auditor should inquire of third parties (i.e., bankers and attorneys) about the prospective clients. SQCS 2 requires policies to ensure obtaining an (oral or written) understanding with the client concerning the nature, scope, and limitations of provided services. Quality control policies should also ensure that the firm appropriately considers the risks associated with providing services in the specific engagement and undertakes only engagements that the firm can reasonably expect to complete with professional competence.

d. **ENGAGEMENT PERFORMANCE** Engagement performance includes all steps of the design and performance of an engagement. Policies should provide reasonable assurance that work meets applicable professional standards, regulatory requirements, and the firm's standards of quality **plus** that personnel consult appropriate authoritative literature or other sources as needed. SQCS 4 requires QC policies and procedures to address, where applicable, the concurring partner review requirements applicable to SEC engagements required by membership in the SEC Practice Section of the AICPA.

e. **MONITORING** Monitoring is an ongoing evaluation of each of the other elements of quality control to ensure that they are effectively designed and applied.

3. **DOCUMENTATION OF COMPLIANCE WITH QUALITY CONTROL POLICIES AND PROCEDURES** Documentation concerning compliance with quality control policies and procedures should be retained for a sufficient period of time for monitoring and peer reviews. The form and content of documentation is a matter of judgment and depends on several factors.

C. PRACTITIONER-IN-CHARGE (SQCS 5)

SQCS 5 expands on the policies and procedures related to personnel management discussed in SQCS 2. SQCS 5 requires policies to be adequate to provide a firm with reasonable assurance that a PIC possesses the competencies appropriate to the circumstances of particular engagements, i.e., those competencies necessary to fulfill a PIC's engagement responsibilities. When establishing policies and procedures related to the competencies of the PIC, a firm may need to consider other quality control policies and procedures.

1. **PRACTITIONER-IN-CHARGE** A practitioner-in-charge of an attest engagement (PIC) is the individual signing (or authorizing another to sign) the accountant's report in connection with accounting, auditing, and attestation engagements. A PIC is responsible for supervising these engagements.

2. **COMPETENCIES** Competencies are knowledge, skills, and abilities that enable a PIC to perform engagements. A firm must determine necessary competencies for particular engagements. Competencies are measured in qualitative, rather than quantitative, terms. Ordinarily, a PIC obtains required competencies through experience in public accounting practice. Relevant industry, governmental, and academic experience also may provide a PIC with competencies. A PIC may supplement experience with continuing professional education (CPE) and consultation.

3. **EXTENT** The nature and extent of competencies required for a particular engagement are dependent on the attributes of an individual client, industry, and type of service. For instance, different competencies are necessary for the following services: compiling versus reviewing or auditing financial statements; financial service entities, governmental entities, employer benefit plan entities versus entities in other industries; public versus nonpublic companies; an engagement to examine management's assertion about the effectiveness of an entity's internal control over financial reporting versus an engagement to examine investment performance statistics.

4. **SCOPE** While necessary competencies are broad in scope and varied in nature, they ordinarily include: understanding of quality control and the code of professional conduct; understanding of the service to be performed; technical proficiency; familiarity with the industry; professional judgment; and understanding the entity's information technology

systems. Obtaining one competency may be related to gaining another, as competencies are interrelated.

5. **Uniform Accountancy Act** A firm's compliance with SQCS 5 is intended to meet and exceed the requirements of the Uniform Accountancy Act (UAA). CPAs are required to meet the legal requirements of the applicable licensing jurisdiction governing public accounting, which may incorporate parts of the UAA.

D. Monitoring (SQCS 3)

When monitoring quality control, the effects of the firm's management philosophy and the environment in which the firm and its clients operate should be considered. Monitoring involves an ongoing consideration of the: (1) relevance and adequacy of the policies and procedures, (2) appropriateness of guidance materials and practice aids, (3) effectiveness of professional development activities, and (4) compliance with the policies and procedures.

1. **Inspection Procedures** Inspection procedures include the evaluation of the adequacy of, personnel's comprehension of, and compliance with the firm's QC policies and procedures. The extent, nature and need for inspection procedures depends on the existence and effectiveness of the monitoring procedures. Inspection procedures include

   a. Review of engagement work papers, reports, and clients' financial statements

   b. Annual summaries of findings from inspection processes and consideration of systemic causes of findings

   c. Determination of corrective actions or improvements for the specific engagements involved

   d. Communication of findings to appropriate firm management

   e. Timely consideration of findings by appropriate firm management

2. **Pre-issuance or Post-issuance Review of Selected Engagements** Personnel performing or supervising a review to be used as an inspection procedure should not be directly associated with the engagement performance. Sufficiently comprehensive pre-issuance or post-issuance review procedures may constitute inspection procedures if findings indicating the need for improvement or modification are summarized and communicated to management personnel responsible for monitoring the QC system. The management personnel must consider any systematic cause of these finding on a timely basis and implement, communicate, and monitor appropriate changes. Pre-issuance or post-issuance review of engagements by the person with final responsibility for the engagement does **not** constitute a monitoring procedure.

3. **Evaluation** Analysis and evaluation of new pronouncements, results of independence confirmations, professional development activities, acceptance/continuance decisions, and personnel interview. Determination of improvements and corrections to be made to the system

4. **Communication** Communication of any weakness in, lack of understanding of, or compliance with the quality control system to the appropriate management personnel.

5. **Follow-up** Timely modifications by appropriate personnel.

6. **Small Firms** In firms with a limited number of management-level personnel, monitoring procedures may need to be performed by people who are responsible for compliance with QC procedures. Post-issuance review of engagements by the person with final responsibility for the engagement may constitute a monitoring procedure in small firms. Small firms may prefer to engage a qualified outside individual to perform inspection procedures.

7. **Peer Review** A peer review does **not** substitute for *monitoring* procedures. However, a firm's QC policies and procedures may provide that a peer review may substitute for some of its *inspection* procedures for the applicable period.

V. Government Auditing

A. Compliance Auditing Considerations in Governmental Audits (SAS 74)

The auditor should design the audit to provide reasonable assurance that the financial statements are free of material misstatements resulting from violations of laws and regulations that have a direct and material effect on the determination of financial statement amounts.

1. **Applicability** SAS 74 is applicable when an auditor is engaged to audit a government entity and engaged to test and report on compliance with laws and regulations under *Government Auditing Standards* (the Yellow Book) or in other circumstances involving governmental financial assistance, such as single (or organization-wide) audits or program-specific audits under certain federal or state audit regulations.

2. **Auditor's Understanding** The auditor should obtain an understanding of the possible effects of laws and regulations that are generally recognized by auditors to have a direct and material effect on the determination of amounts in an entity's financial statements.

3. **Management's Identification** The auditor should assess whether management has identified laws and regulations that have a direct and material effect on the determination of amounts in the entity's financial statements.

4. **Procedures** The auditor may perform the following procedures in assessing such laws and regulations and in obtaining an understanding of their possible effects on the financial statements:

   a. Consider knowledge obtained in prior years' audits.

   b. Discuss laws and regulations with the entity's chief financial officer, legal counsel, or grant administrators.

   c. Obtain written management representations regarding the completeness of management's identification.

   d. Review any directly related agreements, such as those related to grants and loans.

   e. Review the minutes of meetings of the governing board of a governmental entity being audited for the enactment of laws and regulations that have a direct and material effect on the determination of amounts in that entity's financial statements.

   f. Inquire of the appropriate audit oversight organization about the laws and regulations applicable to entities within its jurisdiction, including statutes and uniform reporting requirements.

   g. Review information about compliance requirements and state and local policies and procedures.

5. **Misstatements** *Government Auditing Standards* require the auditor to design the audit to provide reasonable assurance of detecting material misstatements resulting from noncompliance with provisions of contracts or grant agreements that have a direct and material effect on the financial statements. For financial audits, *Government Auditing Standards* prescribes fieldwork and reporting standards beyond those required by GAAS. The general standards of *Government Auditing Standards* relate to qualifications of the staff, independence, due professional care, and quality control.

6. **Characteristics** These audits generally have the following common elements. The auditor

   a. Conducts the audit in accordance with GAAS and *Government Auditing Standards.*

   b. Includes obtaining and documenting an understanding of internal control established to ensure compliance with the laws and regulations applicable to the federal award in the auditor's consideration of internal control. In some instances, federal audit regulations mandate a "test of controls" to evaluate the effectiveness of the design and operation of the policies and procedures in preventing or detecting material noncompliance.

   c. Issues a report on the consideration of internal control.

   d. Determines and reports on whether the federal award has been administered in accordance with applicable laws and regulations (compliance requirements).

7. **Financial Assistance Recipients** A recipient of federal award may be subject to a single (or organization-wide) audit or to a program-specific audit. In planning the audit, the auditor should determine and consider the specific federal audit requirements applicable to the engagement, including the issuance of additional reports.

8. **Evaluation** In evaluating whether an entity has complied with laws and regulations that, if not complied with, could have a material effect on each major federal award program, the auditor should consider the effect of identified instances of noncompliance on each such program. In doing so, the auditor should consider

   a. The frequency of noncompliance identified in the audit

   b. The adequacy of the primary recipient's system of monitoring subrecipients and the possible effect on the program of any noncompliance identified by the primary recipient or the auditors of the subrecipients

   c. Whether any instances of noncompliance identified in the audit resulted in "questioned costs," and if so, whether questioned costs are material to the program

B. Single Audit Act

OMB Circular A-133, *Audits of States, Local Governments, and Nonprofit Organizations*, sets forth requirements for audits in accordance with the Single Audit Act and the Single Audit Act Amendments of 1996.

1. **Thresholds** Thresholds are based on the amount of federal awards expended by a non-federal entity (as opposed to receipts).

   a. Entities that expend total federal awards equal to or in excess of $300,000 in a fiscal year require an audit performed in accordance with the Single Audit Act and OMB Circular A-133. Those expending $300,000 or more, but receiving awards under only one program have the option of having an audit performed in accordance with A-133 or having an audit made of the one program.

   b. Institutions expending less than $300,000 per year in federal awards are exempt from federal audit requirements, but records must be available for review by appropriate officials of the grantor agency or sub-granting agency.

2. **Compliance Reporting** Compliance should be tested for those requirements that relate to the allowability of program expenditures as well as the eligibility of the individual or groups to which federal award is provided. The auditor should test and report on the following matters pertaining to compliance with laws and regulations:

a. Laws and regulations that may have a material effect on the financial statements

b. General requirements applicable to federal financial assistance

c. Specific requirements that may have a material effect on each major program, as defined by the Single Audit Act

d. Certain laws and regulations applicable to nonmajor federal award programs

3. **Compliance Requirements** OMB Circular A-133 identifies compliance requirements. For each federal program, the auditor reports whether there are audit findings for each of 14 types of compliance requirements and the total amount of questioned costs.

   a. **Activities Allowed or Not Allowed** Specifies the types of goods or services entities may purchase with financial assistance.

   b. **Allowable Costs/Cost Principles** Prescribes the direct and indirect costs allowable to federal reimbursement.

   c. **Cash Management** Requires recipients of federal award to minimize the time lapsed between receipt and disbursement of that assistance.

   d. **Davis-Bacon Act** Requires that laborers working on federally financed construction projects be paid a wage not less than the prevailing regional wage established by the Secretary of Labor.

   e. **Eligibility** Specifies the characteristics of individuals or groups to whom entities may give financial assistance.

   f. **Equipment and Real Property Management**

   g. **Matching, Level of Effort, or Earmarking** Specifies amounts entities should contribute from their own resources toward projects for which financial assistance is provided.

   h. **Period of Availability of Federal Funds**

   i. **Procurement, Suspension, and Debarment**

   j. **Program Income**

   k. **Relocation Assistance and Real Property Acquisition** Prescribes how real property should be acquired with federal award and how recipients must help relocate people displaced when that property is acquired.

   l. **Reporting** Specifies reports entities must file in addition to those required by the general requirements.

   m. **Subrecipient Monitoring**

   n. **Special Tests and Provisions** Other provisions for which federal agencies have determined noncompliance could materially affect the program (for example, some programs require recipients to hold public hearings on the proposed use of federal awards; other programs set a deadline for the expenditure of federal awards).

4. **Management Responsibilities** Management is required to prepare a schedule of major and nonmajor federal award programs.

5. **MATERIALITY** In auditing an entity's compliance with requirements governing each major federal award program in accordance with the Single Audit Act, the auditor considers materiality in relation to each program. (This differs from audits in accordance with GAAS.)

6. **RISK** OMB Circular A-133 prescribes a risk-based approach to determine major programs, requiring the auditor to consider a combination of materiality, internal control, and other factors in determining whether a program must be tested as major. It also allows federal agencies to designate certain programs as major, requiring the auditor to test them as major, even though they may not satisfy the risk-based criteria. The auditor must perform procedures that assess inherent and control risk and restrict detection risk. The auditor must obtain an understanding of internal control over federal programs sufficient to plan the audit to support a low assessed level of control risk for major programs.

   a. **INHERENT RISK** In assessing inherent risk, the auditor considers the results of any procedures performed as part of the audit of the financial statements, and of any tests of compliance with the general requirements.

   b. **DETECTION RISK** In determining an acceptable level of detection risk, the auditor considers the level to which he or she seeks to restrict audit risk related to the major federal award program and the assessed levels of inherent risk and control risk.

   c. **CLUSTER OF PROGRAMS** A cluster of programs as a group of closely related programs that share common compliance requirements. The auditor must consider a cluster of programs as one program for determining major programs, with some exceptions.

7. **CONSISTENCY WITH FINANCIAL STATEMENTS** Auditors must determine whether financial reports and claims for advances and reimbursement contain information supported by the records from which the basic financial statements were prepared, and that amounts claimed or used for matching purposes were determined in accordance with OMB Circulars A-87 and A-102.

8. **NONCOMPLIANCE** To properly evaluate the effects of questioned costs on the opinion on compliance, the best estimate of total costs questioned for each major federal award program is considered, not just those questioned costs that were specifically identified. The auditor must report any instances of noncompliance found and resulting questioned costs.

9. **SUBRECIPIENTS** In a single year, if a primary recipient passes $25,000 or more of federal award through to a subrecipient, that primary recipient becomes responsible for determining that the assistance is spent in accordance with applicable laws and regulations. The primary recipient should

   a. Determine that subrecipients met the audit requirements of OMB Circular A-133, if applicable.

   b. Determine if the assistance was spent in accordance with applicable laws and regulations.

   c. Ensure that corrective action is taken within six months after receipt of a report that identifies instances of noncompliance.

   d. Consider the need for an adjustment to the records of the primary recipient.

   e. Require each subrecipient to permit independent auditors to have access to their records and financial statements as necessary to comply with OMB Circular A-133.

10. **NONMAJOR PROGRAMS** The Single Audit Act requires that "transactions selected from federal assistance programs, other than major federal assistance programs,...shall be tested for compliance with federal laws and regulations that apply to such transactions."

11. **Reporting** The auditor must summarize the results of the audit concerning internal control, financial statements, and compliance with laws and regulations. The audit report must be issued within 9 months after the entity's year-end.

  a. Auditees and recipient entities must complete their respective parts of a data collection form. This form states whether the audit was completed in accordance with Circular A-133 and provides information about the entity, its federal programs, and the results of the audit.

  b. Auditors must report findings and questioned costs in a single schedule, using prescribed criteria for reporting. The schedule of findings and questioned costs must include a summary of the auditor's results, the auditor's findings relating to the financial statements, and findings and questioned costs for federal awards.

  c. Recipient entities must prepare a summary schedule of prior audit findings. Auditees must report the status of all audit findings included in the prior audit's schedule of findings and questioned costs relative to federal awards.

12. **Conflict of Interest** The same auditor may not prepare the indirect cost proposal or cost allocation plan when indirect costs exceed $1,000,000 in the prior year. (The auditor should not audit his or her own work.)

C. **Other Compliance Auditing Responsibilities**

1. **Program-Specific Audits** The Single Audit Act and OMB Circular A-133 permit certain recipients of federal awards to have *program-specific* audits. When engaged to conduct such an audit, the auditor should first obtain an understanding of the audit requirements for that particular program from an agreement with the grantor agency, from an audit guide published by the grantor agency, or through contact with the grantor agency.

2. **Compliance Testing** An auditor may be engaged to test and report on compliance with laws and regulations other than those previously discussed.

  a. **Procedures** Auditors should consider performing the following procedures:

    (1) Inquire of management about additional compliance auditing requirements applicable to the entity.

    (2) Inquire of the office of the state or local auditor or other appropriate audit oversight organization about audit requirements applicable to the entity.

    (3) Review information about governmental audit requirements available from state societies of CPAs or associations of governments.

  b. **Noncompliance** When the audit of an entity's compliance with requirements governing a major federal award program detects noncompliance with those requirements that the auditor believes have a material effect on the program, the auditor should express a qualified or adverse opinion.

Auditing Coverage

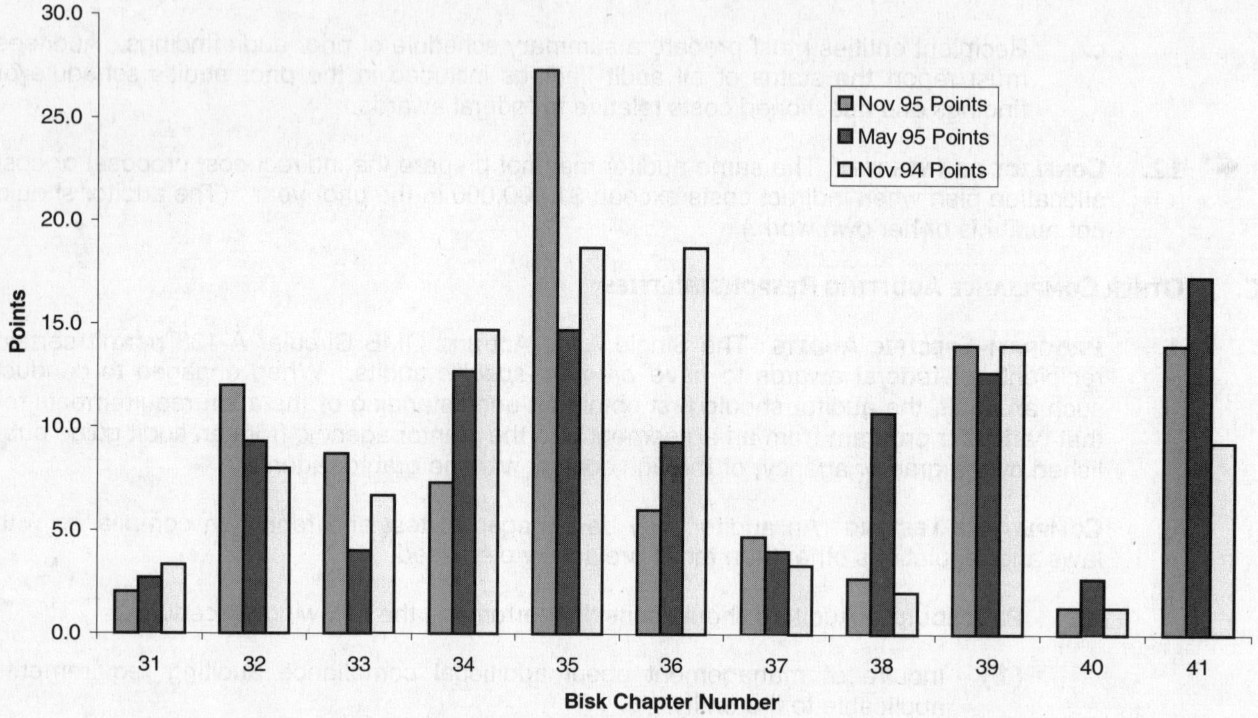

November 1995 was the last fully disclosed examination. (Please bear in mind that the content specifications changed slightly since the November 1995 exam.)

Note that the heavily-tested areas remain the same, but the emphasis may shift on any one exam.

See the **Practical Advice** appendix for more information.

CHAPTER 31—STANDARDS & RELATED TOPICS

PROBLEM 31-1 MULTIPLE CHOICE QUESTIONS (40 to 50 minutes)

1. Which of the following best describes what is meant by the term generally accepted auditing standards?
a. Procedures to be used to gather evidence to support financial statements
b. Measures of the quality of the auditor's performance
c. Pronouncements issued by the Auditing Standards Board
d. Rules acknowledged by the accounting profession because of their universal application
(11/91, Aud., #9, 9400)

2. Which of the following statements is correct concerning an auditor's responsibilities regarding financial statements?
a. Making suggestions that are adopted about the form and content of an entity's financial statements impairs an auditor's independence.
b. An auditor may draft an entity's financial statements based on information from management's accounting system.
c. The fair presentation of audited financial statements in conformity with GAAP is an implicit part of the auditor's responsibilities.
d. An auditor's responsibilities for audited financial statements are **not** confined to the expression of the auditor's opinion. (11/94, Aud., #19, 5092)

3. The third general standard states that due care is to be exercised in the performance of an audit. This standard is ordinarily interpreted to require
a. Thorough review of the existing safeguards over access to assets and records.
b. Limited review of the indications of employee fraud and illegal acts.
c. Objective review of the adequacy of the technical training and proficiency of firm personnel.
d. Critical review of the judgment exercised at every level of supervision.
(5/95, Aud., #23, 5641)

4. A CPA wishes to determine how various publicly-held companies have complied with the disclosure requirements of a new financial accounting standard. Which of the following information sources would the CPA most likely consult for this information?
a. SEC Statement 10-K Guide
b. AICPA Accounting Trends and Techniques
c. SEC Quality Control Review
d. AICPA Codification of Statements on Auditing Standards (R/00, Aud., #1, amended, 6926)

5. One of a CPA firm's basic objectives is to provide professional services that conform with professional standards. Reasonable assurance of achieving this basic objective is provided through
a. A system of quality control.
b. A system of peer review.
c. Continuing professional education.
d. Compliance with generally accepted reporting standards. (11/92, Aud., #3, 2937)

6. In assessing whether to accept a client for an audit engagement, a CPA should consider the

	Client's business risk	CPA's business risk
a.	Yes	Yes
b.	Yes	No
c.	No	Yes
d.	No	No

(R/99, Aud., #5, 6821)

7. The primary purpose of establishing quality control policies and procedures for deciding whether to accept a new client is to
a. Enable the CPA firm to attest to the reliability of the client.
b. Satisfy the CPA firm's duty to the public concerning the acceptance of new clients.
c. Minimize the likelihood of association with clients whose management lacks integrity.
d. Anticipate before performing any field work whether an unqualified opinion can be expressed.
(11/94, Aud., #24, 5097)

8. After field work audit procedures are completed, a partner of the CPA firm who has not been involved in the audit performs a second or wrap-up working paper review. This second review usually focuses on
a. The fair presentation of the financial statements in conformity with GAAP.
b. Fraud involving the client's management and its employees.
c. The materiality of the adjusting entries proposed by the audit staff.
d. The communication of internal control weaknesses to the client's audit committee.
(11/94, Aud., #5, amended, 5078)

9. Although the scope of audits of recipients of federal financial assistance in accordance with federal audit regulations varies, these audits generally have which of the following elements in common?

a. The auditor is to determine whether the federal financial assistance has been administered in accordance with applicable laws and regulations.
b. The materiality levels are lower and are determined by the government entities that provided the federal financial assistance to the recipient.
c. The auditor should obtain written management representations that the recipient's internal auditors will report their findings objectively without fear of political repercussion.
d. The auditor is required to express both positive and negative assurance that illegal acts that could have a material effect on the recipient's financial statements are disclosed to the inspector general. (5/98, Aud., #1, 6618)

10. In reporting under Government Auditing Standards, an auditor most likely would be required to report a falsification of accounting records directly to a federal inspector general when the falsification is

a. Discovered after the auditor's report has been made available to the federal inspector general and to the public.
b. Reported by the auditor to the audit committee as a significant deficiency in internal control.
c. Voluntarily disclosed to the auditor by low-level personnel as a result of the auditor's inquiries.
d. Communicated by the auditor to the auditee and the auditee fails to make a required report of the matter. (R/99, Aud., #31, 6847)

11. An auditor was engaged to conduct a performance audit of a governmental entity in accordance with *Government Auditing Standards.* These standards do **not** require, as part of this auditor's report

a. A statement of the audit objectives and a description of the audit scope.
b. Indications or instances of illegal acts that could result in criminal prosecution discovered during the audit.
c. The pertinent views of the entity's responsible officials concerning the auditor's findings.
d. A concurrent opinion on the financial statements taken as a whole. (11/94, Aud., #90, 5163)

12. Which of the following is a documentation requirement that an auditor should follow when auditing in accordance with *Government Auditing Standards?*

a. The auditor should obtain written representations from management acknowledging responsibility for correcting instances of fraud, abuse, and waste.
b. The auditor's working papers should contain sufficient information so that supplementary oral explanations are **not** required.
c. The auditor's working papers should contain a caveat that all instances of material errors and fraud may **not** be identified.
d. The auditor should document the procedures that assure discovery of all illegal acts and contingent liabilities resulting from noncompliance. (11/93, Aud., #44, amended, 4281)

13. An auditor notes reportable conditions in a financial statement audit conducted in accordance with *Government Auditing Standards.* In reporting on internal control, the auditor should state that

a. Expressing an opinion on the entity's financial statements provides **no** assurance on internal control.
b. The auditor obtained an understanding of the design of relevant policies and procedures, and determined whether they have been placed in operation.
c. The specified government funding or legislative body is responsible for reviewing internal control as a condition of continued funding.
d. The auditor has **not** determined whether any of the reportable conditions described in the report are so severe as to be material weaknesses. (5/94, Aud., #85, amended, 4750)

14. When auditing an entity's financial statements in accordance with *Government Auditing Standards* (the Yellow Book), an auditor is required to report on

I. Noteworthy accomplishments of the program
II. The scope of the auditor's testing of internal controls

a. I only
b. II only
c. Both I and II
d. Neither I nor II (R/00, Aud., #18, 6943)

15. When auditing an entity's financial statements in accordance with *Government Auditing Standards* (the Yellow Book), an auditor is required to report on

I. Recommendations for actions to improve operations.
II. The scope of the auditor's tests of compliance with laws and regulations.

a. I only
b. II only
c. Both I and II
d. Neither I nor II (R/00, Aud., #19, 6944)

16. Wolf is auditing an entity's compliance with requirements governing a major federal financial assistance program in accordance with *Government Auditing Standards.* Wolf detected noncompliance with requirements that have a material effect on the program. Wolf's report on compliance should express

a. No assurance on the compliance tests.
b. An adverse or disclaimer of opinion.
c. A qualified or adverse opinion.
d. Reasonable assurance on the compliance tests.

(11/94, Aud., #85, amended, 5158)

17. In performing a financial statement audit in accordance with *Government Auditing Standards,* an auditor is required to report on the entity's compliance with laws and regulations. This report should

a. State that compliance with laws and regulations is the responsibility of the entity's management.
b. Describe the laws and regulations that the entity must comply with.
c. Provide an opinion on overall compliance with laws and regulations.
d. Indicate that the auditor does **not** possess legal skills and **cannot** make legal judgments.

(11/93, Aud., #58, 4295)

18. Hill, CPA, is auditing the financial statements of Helping Hand, a not-for-profit organization that receives financial assistance from governmental agencies. To detect misstatements in Helping Hand's financial statements resulting from violations of laws and regulations, Hill should focus on violations that

a. Could result in criminal prosecution against the organization.
b. Involve reportable conditions to be communicated to the organization's trustees and the funding agencies.
c. Have a direct and material effect on the amounts in the organization's financial statements.
d. Demonstrate the existence of material weaknesses in the organization's internal control.

(11/92, Aud., #56, amended, 2990)

19. Tell, CPA, is auditing the financial statements of Youth Services Co. (YSC), a not-for-profit organization, in accordance with *Government Auditing Standards.* Tell's report on YSC's compliance with laws and regulations is required to contain statements of

	Positive assurance	*Negative assurance*
a.	Yes	Yes
b.	Yes	No
c.	No	Yes
d.	No	No

(5/93, Aud., #60, 3956)

20. In auditing compliance with requirements governing major federal financial assistance programs under the Single Audit Act, the auditor's consideration of materiality differs from materiality under generally accepted auditing standards. Under the Single Audit Act, materiality is

a. Calculated in relation to the financial statements taken as a whole.
b. Determined separately for each major federal financial assistance program.
c. Decided in conjunction with the auditor's risk assessment.
d. Ignored, because all account balances, regardless of size, are fully tested.

(11/95, Aud., #89, 6036)

PROBLEM 31-2 ADDITIONAL MULTIPLE CHOICE QUESTIONS (32 to 40 minutes)

21. Which of the following elements underlies the application of generally accepted auditing standards, particularly the standards of field work and reporting?

a. Internal control
b. Corroborating evidence
c. Materiality and audit risk
d. Quality control (Editors, 0015)

22. An auditor strives to achieve independence in appearance in order to

a. Maintain public confidence in the profession.
b. Become independent in fact.
c. Maintain an unbiased mental attitude.
d. Comply with the generally accepted auditing standards of field work. (Editors, 0020)

23. A CPA firm evaluates its personnel advancement experience to ascertain whether individuals meeting stated criteria are assigned increased degrees of responsibility. This is evidence of the firm's adherence to which of the following prescribed standards?

a. Quality control
b. Human resources
c. Acceptance and continuance of clients
d. Independence (Editors, 9401)

24. The nature and extent of a CPA firm's quality control policies and procedures depend on

	The CPA firm's size	*The nature of the CPA firm's practice*	*Cost-benefit considerations*
a.	Yes	Yes	Yes
b.	Yes	Yes	No
c.	Yes	No	Yes
d.	No	Yes	Yes

(5/95, Aud., #5, 5623)

25. Which of the following are elements of a CPA firm's quality control that should be considered in establishing its quality control policies and procedures?

	Advancement	*Professional Development*	*Hiring*
a.	Yes	Yes	No
b.	Yes	Yes	Yes
c.	No	No	Yes
d.	Yes	No	Yes

(Editors, 0009)

26. A CPA firm's quality control procedures pertaining to the acceptance of a prospective audit client would most likely include

a. Consideration of whether internal control is sufficiently effective to permit a reduction in the extent of required substantive tests.
b. Consideration of whether sufficient competent evidential matter may be obtained to afford a reasonable basis for an opinion.
c. Inquiry of third parties, such as the prospective client's bankers and attorneys, about information regarding the prospective client and its management.
d. Inquiry of management as to whether disagreements between the predecessor auditor and the prospective client were resolved satisfactorily. (Editors, 0014)

27. Which of the following is an element of a CPA firm's quality control system that should be considered in establishing its quality control policies and procedures?

a. Complying with laws and regulations
b. Using statistical sampling techniques
c. Assigning personnel to engagements
d. Considering audit risk and materiality (5/94, Aud., #15, 4680)

28. Because of the pervasive effects of laws and regulations on the financial statements of governmental units, an auditor should obtain written management representations acknowledging that management has

a. Identified and disclosed all laws and regulations that have a direct and material effect on its financial statements.
b. Implemented internal control policies and procedures designed to detect all illegal acts.
c. Expressed both positive and negative assurance to the auditor that the entity complied with all laws and regulations.
d. Employed internal auditors who can report their findings, opinions, and conclusions objectively without fear of political repercussion.

(5/94, Aud., #84, 4749)

29. A governmental audit may extend beyond an audit leading to the expression of an opinion on the fairness of financial presentation to include

	Program results	*Compliance*	*Economy & efficiency*
a.	Yes	No	Yes
b.	Yes	Yes	Yes
c.	No	Yes	Yes
d.	Yes	Yes	No

(Editors, 0019)

30. In auditing a not-for-profit entity that receives governmental financial assistance, the auditor has a responsibility to

a. Issue a separate report that describes the expected benefits and related costs of the auditor's suggested changes to the entity's internal control.
b. Render an opinion concerning the entity's continued eligibility for the governmental financial assistance.
c. Notify the governmental agency providing the financial assistance that the audit is **not** designed to provide any assurance of detecting errors and fraud.
d. Assess whether management has identified laws and regulations that have a direct and material effect on the entity's financial statements.

(11/95, Aud., #88, amended, 6035)

31. Which of the following bodies promulgates standards for audits of federal financial assistance recipients?
a. Governmental Accounting Standards Board
b. Financial Accounting Standards Board
c. Governmental Auditing Standards Board
d. General Accounting Office (Editors, 9402)

32. Reporting on internal control under *Government Auditing Standards* differs from reporting under generally accepted auditing standards in that *Government Auditing Standards* requires a
a. Statement of positive assurance that internal control procedures designed to detect material errors and fraud were tested.
b. Written report describing each reportable condition observed including identification of those considered material weaknesses.
c. Statement of negative assurance that internal control procedures **not** tested have an immaterial effect on the entity's financial statements.
d. Written report describing the entity's internal control procedures specifically designed to prevent fraud, abuse, and illegal acts.
(5/93, Aud., #24, amended, 3920)

33. In reporting on compliance with laws and regulations during a financial statement audit in accordance with *Government Auditing Standards*, an auditor should include in the auditor's report
a. A statement of assurance that all controls over fraud and illegal acts were tested.
b. Material instances of fraud and illegal acts that were discovered.
c. The materiality criteria used by the auditor in considering whether instances of noncompliance were significant.
d. An opinion on whether compliance with laws and regulations affected the entity's goals and objectives. (5/95, Aud., #89, 5707)

34. Which of the following statements is a standard applicable to financial statement audits in accordance with *Government Auditing Standards* (the Yellow Book)?
a. An auditor should report on the scope of the auditor's testing of compliance with laws and regulations.
b. An auditor should assess whether the entity has reportable measures of economy and efficiency that are valid and reliable.
c. An auditor should report recommendations for actions to correct problems and improve operations.
d. An auditor should determine the extent to which the entity's programs achieve the desired results. (R/99, Aud., #28, 6844)

35. Which of the following statements is a standard applicable to financial statement audits in accordance with *Government Auditing Standards* (the Yellow Book)?
a. An auditor should report on the scope of the auditor's testing of internal controls.
b. All instances of abuse, waste, and mismanagement should be reported to the audit committee.
c. An auditor should report the views of responsible officials concerning the auditor's findings.
d. Internal control activities designed to detect or prevent fraud should be reported to the inspector general. (R/99, Aud., #29, 6845)

36. In an audit in accordance with *Government Auditing Standards*, an auditor is required to report on the auditor's tests of the entity's compliance with applicable laws and regulations. This requirement is satisfied by designing the audit to provide
a. Positive assurance that the internal control policies and procedures tested by the auditor are operating as prescribed.
b. Reasonable assurance of detecting misstatements that are material to the financial statements.
c. Negative assurance that reportable conditions communicated during the audit do **not** prevent the auditor from expressing an opinion.
d. Limited assurance that the internal controls designed by management will prevent or detect errors, fraud, and illegal acts.
(5/92, Aud., #32, amended, 2785)

ESSAY QUESTIONS

Essay 31-3 (15 to 25 minutes)

Cook, CPA, has been engaged to audit the financial statements of General Department Stores Inc., a continuing audit client, which is a chain of medium-sized retail stores. General's fiscal year will end on June 30, 20X1, and General's management has asked Cook to issue the auditor's report by August 1, 20X1. Cook will not have sufficient time to perform all of the necessary field work in July, but will have time to perform most of the field work as of an interim date, April 30. For the accounts to be tested at the interim date, Cook will also perform substantive tests covering the transactions of the final two months of the year. This will be necessary to extend Cook's conclusions to the balance sheet date.

REQUIRED:

a. Describe the factors Cook should consider before applying principal substantive tests to General's balance sheet accounts at April 30.

b. For accounts tested at April 30, describe how Cook should design the substantive tests covering the balances as of June 30, 20X1, and the transactions of the final two months of the year.

(11/92, Aud., #5, amended)

ESSAY 31-4 (15 to 25 minutes)

Feiler, the sole owner of a small hardware business, has been told that the business should have financial statements reported on by an independent CPA. Feiler, having some bookkeeping experience, has personally prepared the company's financial statements and does not understand why such statements should be audited by a CPA. Feiler discussed the matter with Farber, a CPA, and asked Farber to explain why an audit is considered important.

REQUIRED:

a. Describe the objectives of an independent audit.

b. Identify ten ways in which an independent audit may be beneficial to Feiler. (5/87, Aud., #3, 3005)

ESSAY 31-5 (15 to 25 minutes)

Toxic Waste Disposal Co., Inc. (TWD) is a nonprofit organization that receives grants and fees from various state and municipal governments as well as grants from several federal government agencies.

TWD engaged Hall & Hall, CPAs, to audit its financial statements for the year ended July 31, 20X1, in accordance with *Government Auditing Standards*. Accordingly, the auditors' reports are to be submitted by TWD to the granting government agencies, which make the reports available for public inspection.

The auditors' separate report on compliance with laws and regulations that was drafted by a staff accountant of Hall & Hall at the completion of the engagement contained the statements below. It was submitted to the engagement partner who reviewed matters thoroughly and properly concluded that no material instances of noncompliance were identified.

1. A statement that the audit was conducted in accordance with generally accepted auditing standards and with *Government Auditing Standards* issued by the Comptroller General of the United States.
2. A statement that the auditors' procedures included tests of compliance.
3. A statement that the standards require the auditors to plan and to perform the audit to detect all instances of noncompliance with applicable laws and regulations.
4. A statement that management is responsible for compliance with laws, regulations, contracts, and grants.
5. A statement that the auditors' objective was to provide an opinion on compliance with the provisions of laws and regulations equivalent to that to be expressed on the financial statements.
6. A statement of positive assurance that the results of the tests indicate that, with respect to the items tested, the entity complied, in all material respects, with the provisions of laws, regulations, contracts, and grants.
7. A statement of negative assurance that, with respect to items tested, nothing came to the auditors' attention that caused the auditors to believe that the entity had not complied, in all material respects, with the provisions of laws, regulations, contracts, and grants.
8. A statement that the report is intended only for the information of the specific legislative or regulatory bodies, and that this restriction is intended to limit the distribution of the report.

REQUIRED:

For each of the above statements, indicate whether each is an appropriate or inappropriate element within the report on compliance with laws and regulations. If a statement is **not** appropriate, explain why. (11/91, Aud., #2, amended)

SOLUTION 31-1 MULTIPLE CHOICE ANSWERS

GAAS

1. (b) AU 150.01 states, "Auditing standards ...concern themselves not only with the auditor's professional qualities but also with the judgment exercised by him [or her] in the performance of the audit." Auditing standards are issued by the Auditing Standards Board, but that does not describe what is meant by generally accepted auditing standards. Auditing procedures relate to the acts to be performed during an audit. The standards deal with measures of the quality of the performance of the procedures; they are not a strict set of rules.

2. (b) AU 110.02 states, "The...auditor may make suggestions about the form and content of the financial statements or draft them, in whole or in part, based on information from management's accounting system." The fair presentation of the financial statements in conformity with GAAP is management's responsibility (AU 110.02). The auditor's responsibility is to express an opinion on the financial statements (AU 110.02).

3. (d) The third general standard states, "Due professional care is to be exercised in the performance of the audit and the preparation of the report," and "The exercise of due care requires critical review at every level of supervision of the work done and the judgment exercised by those assisting in the audit." Safeguards over assets and records and review of indications of fraud and illegal acts are internal control issues specific to one audit. Objective review of the adequacy of the training and proficiency of personnel is a quality control issue.

4. (b) As indicated by its title, AICPA *Accounting Trends and Techniques* focuses on accounting and implementation. The other publications establish standards and guidelines, as opposed to reporting implementation. Statements on Auditing Standards provide guidance for auditing, not accounting.

QUALITY CONTROL

5. (a) SQCS 2 states, "A *system of quality control* is broadly defined as a process to provide the firm with reasonable assurance that personnel comply with applicable professional standards...." A peer review provides information on whether a CPA firm is following an appropriate quality control system and would not by itself provide reasonable assurance that a CPA firm is providing professional services that conform with professional standards. Continuing professional education is only one of the policies and procedures concerned with the professional development element of quality control. Compliance with generally accepted reporting standards is only one part of the basic objective of providing professional services that conform with professional standards.

6. (a) QC 20.15 requires qualify control procedures to assure that a firm "... undertakes only those engagements that ...[it can execute]...with competence...[and]...appropriately considers the risks associated with providing professional services in the particular circumstances."

7. (c) SQCS 2 states, "...policies and procedures should provide the firm with reasonable assurance that the likelihood of association with a client whose management lacks integrity is minimized." A CPA firm does not perform any attestation engagements regarding the reliability of a client, only assertions made by the client. The CPA firm's duty to the public is established in the AICPA's Rules of Conduct. Answer (d) is not required before the acceptance of a new client; the opinions rendered are based upon the results of procedures performed.

8. (a) The secondary review partner usually focuses on the fair presentation of the financial statements in accordance with GAAP. Answers (b), (c), and (d) are usually done by staff directly involved in the audit.

GAS—RESPONSIBILITIES

9. (a) The auditor must design the audit to provide reasonable assurance that the financial statements are free of material misstatements resulting from violations of law and regulations that have a direct and material effect on the determination of financial statement amounts. Materiality levels are determined by the auditor in relation to an entity's federal programs. An auditor generally does not obtain representations regarding internal auditors' reports. An auditor usually does not express assurance on disclosures to an inspector general.

10. (d) Generally, the auditor need report a falsification of accounting records only to the audit committee (or equivalent). GAS ¶5.22 states, "...If auditors have communicated such irregularities or illegal acts to the auditee, and it fails to report them, then the auditors should communicate their awareness of that failure to the auditee's governing body. If the auditee does not make the require

report as soon as practicable after the auditors' communication with its governing body, then the auditors should report the irregularities or illegal acts directly to the external party specified...."

11. (d) *Governmental Auditing Standards* do not require an opinion on the financial statements taken as a whole, when the engagement is a *performance* audit. GAS does require a statement of the audit scope, indications of illegal acts discovered during the audit, and the views of the responsible officials concerning the auditor's findings in the auditor's report.

12. (b) Included in the field work standards of supplemental working paper requirements for financial audits is the statement that working papers should contain sufficient information so that supplementary oral explanations are not required. Written representations from management are not required. An audit does not ensure that all illegal acts and contingent liabilities resulting from noncompliance will be discovered by the auditor. The auditor's workpapers should include positive statements about the procedures applied and the results of those procedures; thus, there is no requirement that the working papers contain a caveat statement.

GAS—INTERNAL CONTROL

13. (b) AU 801.10(g) presents this requirement. Other requirements for the auditor's report on internal control in these circumstances are in AU 801.10. None of the items listed in (a), (c), and (d) are on the list.

14. (b) AU 801.10 states that Government Auditing Standards require a written report on the consideration of internal control in all audits; whereas GAAS require communication only when the auditor has noted reportable conditions. Reporting on program accomplishments is not required of the auditor.

GAS—COMPLIANCE

15. (b) In an audit in accordance with Governmental Auditing Standards, an auditor is required to report on the auditor's test of the entity's compliance with applicable laws and regulations. Among the basic elements of such a report is a statement that the standards require that the auditor plan and perform the audit to obtain reasonable assurance about whether the financial statements are free of material misstatement (AU 801.06). Recommendations for actions to improve operations are a beneficial side-benefit of an audit, but are not required.

16. (c) When an auditor detects noncompliance with requirements that have a material effect on a program, the auditor should express a qualified or adverse opinion. A disclaimer is appropriate only when an audit has not been done. Reasonable assurance on tests is implicit, not explicit.

17. (a) The basic elements of a report on compliance should include a statement that management is responsible for compliance with laws, regulations, contracts, and grants.

18. (c) AU 801.08 (concerning nonprofit organizations and business enterprises that receive federal financial assistance) states, "These standards...include designing the audit to detect material misstatements of financial statements resulting from violations of laws and regulations that have a direct and material effect on the determination of financial statement amounts...." Answers (a), (b), and (d) do not represent the focus that is stated in AU 801.08.

19. (a) Reports on compliance with laws and regulations should contain positive assurance consisting of a statement by the auditor that the tested items were in compliance with applicable laws and regulations, and negative assurance stating that nothing came to the auditor's attention as a result of specified procedures that caused him or her to believe the untested items were not in compliance with applicable laws and regulation, as indicated in the *Government Auditing Standards* (the Yellow Book).

20. (b) According to AU 801.17, in auditing an entity's compliance with requirements governing each major federal financial assistance program in accordance with the Single Audit Act, the auditor considers materiality in relation to each program.

SOLUTION 31-2 ADDITIONAL MULTIPLE CHOICE ANSWERS

GAAS

21. (c) AU 150.03 states, "*Materiality* and *audit risk* underlie the application of all the standards, particularly the standards of field work and reporting."

22. (a) AU 220.03 states, "It is of utmost importance to the profession that the general public maintain confidence in the independence of independent auditors. Public confidence would be impaired by evidence that independence was actually lacking, and it might also be impaired by the existence of circumstances which reasonable people might believe likely to influence independence."

QUALITY CONTROL

23. (a) The evaluation of personnel advancement provides evidence of adherence to the broad category of Quality Control Standards (QC 20.13). Answers (c) and (d) are two of the elements of those standards per SQCS 2. Answer (b) is not, by itself, a standard or an element of the Quality Control Standards.

24. (a) AU 161.02 states, "The nature and extent of a firm's quality control policies and procedures depend on factors such as its size,...the nature of its practice,...and appropriate cost-benefit considerations." Answers (b), (c), and (d) are considerations in determining the nature and extent of a CPA firm's quality control policies and procedures.

25. (b) A firm shall consider each of the elements of quality control, to the extent applicable to its practice, in establishing its quality control policies and procedures. SQCS 2 includes advancement, hiring, and professional development decisions as part of the personnel management element of quality control decisions.

26. (c) QC 20.14 states, "Policies and procedures should be established for deciding whether to accept or continue a client relationship and whether to perform a specific engagement for that client. Such policies and procedures should provide the firm with reasonable assurance that the likelihood of association with a client whose management lacks integrity is minimized...." The CPA firm should inquire of the *predecessor auditor* as to whether disagreements were resolved satisfactorily. (AU 315) Answers (a) and (b) are audit steps that would occur *after* accepting the client.

27. (c) SQCS 2 states, "The quality control policies and procedures...should encompass ...personal management...." Answer (a) is irrelevant. Answers (b) and (d) would be associated with auditing requirements and procedures.

GAS

28. (a) AU 333.04 presents and discusses the items which should be included in management's representations. The items in (b), (c) and (d) are not listed in AU 333.04 as items which should be in the representation.

29. (b) The first standard on government auditing states that the full scope of an audit should include a review and evaluation of the following three elements of a comprehensive audit:

Financial and Compliance—This element is designed to determine whether the agency audited is (1) exercising appropriate controls over its assets, liabilities, receipts, and expenditures; (2) maintaining the appropriate records of such items; and (3) rendering accurate and useful reports in much the same manner as a traditional financial audit.
Economy and Efficiency—This element is a review of how efficiently and economically resources are used.
Program Results—This element is a review to determine whether the desired results of the program are being effectively achieved.

30. (d) According to AU 801.07, the auditor, when auditing a nonprofit organization that receives governmental financial assistance should "assess whether management has identified laws and regulations that have a direct and material effect...on the entity's financial statements."

31. (d) The standards for audits of federally assisted programs may be found in the publication of the U.S. General Accounting Office (GAO) entitled *Standards for Audit of Governmental Organizations, Programs, Activities, and Functions.* The Governmental Accounting Standards Board (GASB) establishes financial accounting principles for state and local government entities. The Financial Accounting Standards Board (FASB) establishes GAAP. The Governmental Auditing Standards Board does not exist.

32. (b) AU 801.10 states that *Government Auditing Standards* requires a written report on the consideration of internal control in all audits; whereas GAAS require communication only when

the auditor has noted reportable conditions. The auditor is not required to report on the description of the entity's internal control procedures. The auditor should not issue the representations in answer (c) or give positive assurance because of the potential for misinterpretation of the limited degree of assurance associated with the auditor's issuing a written report representing that no reportable conditions were noted.

33. (b) GAS §5.18 states, "When auditors conclude, based on evidence obtained, that an irregularity [fraud] or illegal act either has occurred or is likely to have occurred, they should report relevant information. Auditors need not report information about an irregularity or illegal act that is clearly inconsequential. Thus, auditors should present in a report the same irregularities and illegal acts that they report to audit committees under AICPA standards." (The footnote to GAS §5.18 cautions the auditor to take care not to imply that they have made a determination of illegality when they disclose matters that have led them to conclude that an illegal act is likely to have occurred, as the determination of illegality may have to await final decision by a court of law.) Per GAS §5.17, "Auditors should report the scope of their testing of compliance with laws and regulations and of internal controls...[and] whether or not the tests they performed provided sufficient evidence to support an opinion on compliance or internal controls." There is no requirement that *all* controls be tested. Answer (c) is the second best answer; GAS §5.19 requires the auditor to place their findings in proper perspective and identify at least the condition, criteria, and possible asserted effect of noncompliance. Answer (d) is not required in a financial statement audit.

34. (a) The auditor must report on the scope of tests of compliance with laws and regulations. An auditor may report recommendations to correct problems and improve operations, but this is not the purpose of an audit. The auditor expresses an opinion on whether the information is correct; users of the report determine whether the measures of economy and efficiency are valid and reliable as well as the extent to which programs achieve the desired results.

35. (a) The auditor must summarize the audit results concerning internal control, financial statements, and compliance with laws and regulations. Immaterial amounts are not necessarily reported to the audit committee. Officials may report their own views—it is not the auditor's duty to do so. A report on all internal control activities designed to detect or prevent fraud is far more than need be reported to the inspector general or other parties.

36. (b) In an audit in accordance with *Governmental Auditing Standards,* an auditor is required to report on the auditor's test of the entity's compliance with applicable laws and regulations. Among the basic elements of such a report is a statement that the standards require that the auditor plan and perform the audit to obtain reasonable assurance about whether the financial statements are free of material misstatement (AU 801.06).

PERFORMANCE BY SUBTOPICS

Each category below parallels a subtopic covered in Chapter 31. Record the number and percentage of questions you correctly answered in each subtopic area.

GAAS

Question #	Correct √
1	
2	
3	
4	
# Questions	4
# Correct	
% Correct	

Quality Control

Question #	Correct √
5	
6	
7	
8	
# Questions	4
# Correct	
% Correct	

GAS—Responsibilities

Question #	Correct √
9	
10	
11	
12	
# Questions	4
# Correct	
% Correct	

GAS—Internal Control

Question #	Correct √
13	
14	
# Questions	2
# Correct	
% Correct	

GAS—Compliance

Question #	Correct √
15	
16	
17	
18	
19	
20	
# Questions	6
# Correct	
% Correct	

ESSAY SOLUTIONS

Solution 31-3 Steps in the Audit Process

a. Before applying principal substantive tests to balance sheet accounts at April 30, 20X1, the interim date, Cook should assess the difficulty in controlling **incremental audit risk.** Cook should consider whether

- Cook's experience with the **reliability** of the **accounting records** and **management's integrity** has been good;
- Rapidly changing **business conditions** or circumstances may predispose General's management to misstate the financial statements in the remaining period;
- The **year-end balances** of accounts selected for interim testing will be **predictable;**
- General's procedures for **analyzing and adjusting** its interim balances and for reestablishing **proper accounting cutoffs** will be appropriate;
- General's accounting system will provide **sufficient information** about year-end balances and transactions in the final two months of the year to permit investigation of **unusual transactions, significant fluctuations,** and **changes in balance compositions** that may occur between the interim and balance sheet dates;
- The **cost** of the substantive tests necessary to cover the final two months of the year and provide the appropriate audit assurance at year end is **substantial**.

Assessing control risk at **below the maximum** would **not be required** to extend the audit conclusions from the interim date to the year end; however, if Cook assesses control risk **at the maximum** during the final two months, Cook should consider whether the **effectiveness** of the **substantive tests** to cover that period will be **impaired**.

b. Cook should **design the substantive tests** so that the **assurance** from those tests and the tests to be applied as of the **interim date,** and any assurance provided from the assessed level of **control risk,** achieve the **audit objectives at year end.** Such tests should include the **comparison** of **year-end information** with comparable **interim information** to identify and investigate unusual amounts. Other **analytical procedures and/or substantive tests** should be performed to **extend Cook's conclusions** relative to the assertions tested at the **interim date to the balance sheet date.**

Solution 31-4 Objectives & Benefits of an Independent Audit

a. Farber should explain to Feiler that an independent audit is an **audit** of the financial statements in accordance with certain **generally accepted auditing standards**. The objective of an ordinary audit is **to render an opinion on the fairness, in all material respects,** with which the financial statements **present financial position, results of operations, and cash flows in conformity with generally accepted accounting principles**. The auditor, after an objective **evidence-gathering audit,** expresses an opinion and "bears witness" to the fair presentation of financial statements. An independent expert is needed to lend **credibility** to the financial statements. It would not be meaningful for a company to report on itself without the **attestation of an independent party** because the company, itself, might not be **objective**.

b. Farber should inform Feiler of the following ways in which an independent audit can be beneficial:

1. To serve as a basis for the **extension of credit**.
2. To supply credit rating agencies with required information.
3. To serve as a basis for preparation of **tax returns.**
4. To **establish amounts of losses** from fire, theft, burglary, and so forth.
5. To **determine amounts receivable or payable** under
   a. Agreements for bonuses based on profits.
   b. **Contracts** for sharing expenses.
   c. Cost-plus contracts.
6. To provide data for proposed changes in financial structure or to supply proper financial data in the event of a proposed **sale or merger**.
7. To serve as a **basis for changes** in accounting or recording practices.
8. To serve as a basis for action in **bankruptcy** and insolvency cases.
9. To determine proper execution of **trust agreements.**
10. To furnish **estates** with information in order to obtain proper settlements and avoid costly litigation.
11. To provide a review of many aspects of the organization's activities and procedures.
12. To establish and/or improve **internal control** policies and procedures.
13. To provide important aid in case of **tax audits, court actions**, and so forth.

14. To **discourage employees from planning errors,** fraud, and so forth, by making them aware of auditor presence.
15. To provide **industry-wide comparisons.**
16. To provide a realistic look at **inventories.**
17. To review adequacy of **insurance coverage.**
18. To provide the **professional knowledge** of an external auditor, which is generally superior to the client's bookkeeping experience.

SOLUTION 31-5 GOVERNMENT AUDIT REPORTS

1. Statement 1 is **appropriate.**
2. Statement 2 is **appropriate.**
3. Statement 3 is **not appropriate** because the auditors are **required** to **plan** and **perform** the audit to **provide reasonable assurance** of **detecting instances** of **noncompliance** having a **direct** and **material effect** on the financial statements, **not all instances** of noncompliance.
4. Statement 4 is **appropriate.**
5. Statement 5 is **not appropriate** because **rendering an opinion** is a **higher level of reporting** than the **positive** and **negative assurance** required by Government Auditing Standards.
6. Statement 6 is **appropriate.**
7. Statement 7 is **not appropriate** because **negative assurance** applies to **items not tested.**
8. Statement 8 is **not appropriate** because *Government Auditing Standards* require that, unless restricted by law or regulation, copies of the reports should be made **available for public inspection.**

Wondering how to find 20 hours a week for study time?

In the Bisk Education video, *How to Pass the CPA Exam*, Bob Monette shares the method he used to find 20 hours a week to study while working 40 hours a week. (Ask a customer service representative about a copy of this demo video.) Notice how this plan leaves most of the weekend free, ensuring time for you to take care of yourself, spend time with your family, meet with friends, and in general, take care of your other commitments.

Lunch hours, Monday through Friday	5 hours
Three hours, after work, Monday through Thursday	12 hours
Three hours, Saturday morning	3 hours
Sunday, total break from studying	0 hours
Weekly total	20 hours

This plan may work for you, or it may not. Consider Bob's plan and adapt it to your situation. For example, perhaps you prefer to study an hour before work Tuesday through Thursday, and relax on Saturday as well as Sunday.

Also consider how you use time. Listening to audio tapes could transform a hour of radio listening into an hour of study time. Do you have a 30-minute commute to and from work? That could add up to 5 hours in a work week. Do you jog three times a week? That could be study time as well as exercise time.

Remember, with the techniques and information in your material,

A passing score is well within reach!

CHANGE ALERT

SAS 93, *Omnibus Statement on Auditing Standards—2000,* is discussed in Chapters 32 and 39.

SAS 93 amends SAS 58, *Reports on Audited Financial Statements*, to require that a practitioner identify the country of GAAS and GAAP referred to in a practitioner's report. Two different acceptable sets of phrases are illustrated in the standard: "U.S. generally accepted accounting principles" and "U.S. generally accepted auditing standards" as well as "accounting principles generally accepted in the United States of America" and "auditing standards generally accepted in the United States of America."

SAS 93 amends SAS 84, *Communications Between Predecessor and Successor Auditors*, to explicitly include, within the definition of *predecessor auditor*, any auditor who is engaged to perform, but does not complete, an audit.

EXAM COVERAGE: The Evaluate Client and Plan Engagement portion of the Auditing section of the CPA exam is designated by the examiners to be 40 percent of the section's point value. Historically, exam coverage of the topics in this chapter is 10 to 15 percent of the Auditing section. More information about the point value of various topics is included in the **Practical Advice** section of this volume.

CHAPTER 32

PLANNING

CHAPTER 32

PLANNING

I. Relationship Between the Auditor's Appointment and Planning (AU 310, SAS 45)

A. Audit Plan

Once the auditor understands the general environment for the audit, a tentative audit plan is developed. Next, the auditor gains an understanding of the client's internal control. When the auditor gains an understanding of the internal control and decides that the client is auditable, the tentative audit plan is revised and a **written audit program** is developed to guide the auditor through the audit. (SAS 77 requires a **written** audit plan.) The program aids the auditor in the satisfaction of the first standard of field work by showing that the field work was planned. The audit program also communicates the plan to assistants.

Exhibit 1 ♦ The First Standard of Field Work

> "The work is to be adequately planned, and assistants, if any, are to be properly supervised."

B. *Establishing an Understanding With the Client* (SAS 83, 89)

SAS 83 amends SAS 1, *Relationship Between the Auditor's Appointment and Planning.*

1. **Guidance** The practitioner must establish an understanding with the client for each engagement with respect to the engagement services, including the objectives and limitations of the engagement as well as the practitioner's and management's responsibilities. The practitioner must document the understanding in the work papers. A practitioner may **not** accept an engagement if the understanding with the client has **not** been established.

2. **Required Elements in an Understanding With an Audit Client**

    a. The objective of the audit is the expression of an opinion on the financial statements.

    b. Management's responsibilities include the entity's financial statements; establishing and maintaining internal control; identification and compliance with applicable laws and regulations; making all financial records and related information available to the auditor, and adjusting the financial statements to correct material misstatements and for affirming to the auditor in the representation letter that the effects of any uncorrected misstatements aggregated by the auditor during the current engagement and pertaining to the latest period presented are immaterial, both individually and in the aggregate, to the financial statements taken as a whole. (SAS 89 adds this last requirement.) Management will provide the auditor with a letter confirming its representations at the conclusion of the audit.

    c. The auditor is responsible for conducting the audit in accordance with GAAS and making communications required by GAAS. An audit includes obtaining an understanding of internal control, but is not designed to provide assurance on internal control. However, the auditor is responsible for communicating reportable conditions, if the auditor becomes aware of any.

3. **Optional Elements in an Understanding With an Audit Client** The understanding with a client may also include other matters; for instance, arrangements concerning engagement performance, involvement of specialists or internal auditors, predecessor auditors, fees, billing, auditor liability, and access to the auditor's work papers.

C. Engagement Letter

Helps ensure that the auditor and the client clearly understand the services the auditor is engaged to perform. It will usually include reference to (1) the periods covered; (2) assurance that the audit will be performed in accordance with GAAS, but a specific opinion is not guaranteed; (3) any assistance to be rendered by client personnel; (4) management's responsibility for preparing the financial statements; (5) fee basis; (6) and other matters the auditor feels need to be included, such as other services. (**NOTE**: Engagement letters are not required by GAAS but are recommended.)

1. **Addressee** Usually the **audit committee**, the board of directors, or the chief executive officer of the client.

2. **Client Response** The client is asked to indicate its agreement with the letter by signing a copy and returning it to the auditor.

Exhibit 2 ♦ Sample Engagement Letter

(CPA Company Name)
[Date]

Audit Committee
Anonymous Company Inc.
Route 32
Nowhere, New York 10000

This will confirm our understanding of the arrangements for our audit of the financial statements of Anonymous Company Inc., for the year ending (date).

We will audit the Company's balance sheet at (date), and the related statements of income, retained earnings, and cash flows for the year then ended, for the purpose of expressing an opinion on them. The financial statements are the responsibility of the Company's management. Our responsibility is to express an opinion on the financial statements based on our audit.

We will conduct our audit in accordance with generally accepted auditing standards. Those standards require that we plan and perform the audit to obtain reasonable assurance about whether the financial statements are free of material misstatement. An audit includes examining, on a test basis, evidence supporting the amounts and disclosures in the financial statements. An audit also includes assessing the accounting principles used and significant estimates made by management, as well as evaluating the overall financial statement presentation. We believe that our audit will provide a reasonable basis for our opinion.

Our procedures will include tests of documentary evidence supporting the transactions recorded in the accounts, tests of the physical existence of inventories, and direct confirmation of receivables and certain other assets and liabilities by correspondence with selected customers, creditors, legal counsel, and banks. At the conclusion of our audit, we will request certain written representations from you about the financial statements and matters related thereto.

Our audit is subject to the inherent risk that material errors and irregularities, including fraud or defalcations, if they exist, will not be detected. However, we will inform you of irregularities that come to our attention, unless they are inconsequential.

If you intend to publish or otherwise reproduce the financial statements and make reference to our firm, you agree to provide us with printers' proofs or masters for our review and approval before printing. You also agree to provide us with a copy of the final reproduced material for our approval before it is distributed.

(continued on next page)

We will review the Company's federal and state (identify states) income tax returns for the fiscal year ended (date). These returns, we understand, will be prepared by the controller.

Further, we will be available during the year to consult with you on the tax effects of any proposed transactions or contemplated changes in business policies.

Our fee for these services will be at our regular per diem rates, plus travel and other out-of-pocket costs. Invoices will be rendered every two weeks and are payable on presentation.

We are pleased to have this opportunity to serve you.

If this letter correctly expresses your understanding, please sign the enclosed copy where indicated and return it to us.*

Very truly yours,

(CPA Name, Signature, and Title)

APPROVED:
By: ....
Date: ....

* Some accountants prefer not to obtain an acknowledgment, in which case their letter would omit the paragraph beginning, "If this letter..." and the spaces for the acknowledgment. The first paragraph of their letter might begin as follows: "This letter sets forth our understanding of the terms and objectives of our audit...."

D. Auditor Appointment

1. **Early** An early appointment is advantageous. This allows proper planning of the audit so that the work may be performed effectively and efficiently.

2. **Near Year End** Before accepting an engagement near or after the close of the accounting period, the auditor should consider whether it will be possible to obtain evidence sufficient to support an unqualified opinion. If that is not possible, the auditor should discuss, with the potential client, the possible scope limitation and the necessity for issuing a qualified opinion or disclaimer of opinion.

II. Communications Between Predecessor and Successor Auditors (AU 315, SAS 84, 93)

A. Overview

AU §315 provides guidance relating to communications between the predecessor and successor auditors when a change in auditors has taken place or is in process.

1. **Predecessor Auditor** An auditor who has resigned or has been terminated. An auditor who previously reported on financial statements that a client wants re-audited is also a predecessor auditor. A CPA who performed a review or compilation is not a predecessor auditor for the purposes of SAS 84. Generally, SAS 84 does not apply when the two fiscal periods immediately preceding the current fiscal period were not audited. SAS 93 amends SAS 84 to explicitly include, as a predecessor auditor, any auditor who is engaged to perform, but does not complete, an audit.

2. **Successor Auditor** An auditor who has (perhaps provisionally) accepted an engagement or has been asked to make a proposal for an engagement.

3. **Re-audit** An engagement to audit and report on financial statements that have previously been audited and reported on by another auditor.

B. COMMUNICATIONS

The successor has the responsibility to initiate communication. Either written or oral communication is permissible. The information communicated should be kept confidential, regardless of whether or not the successor accepts the engagement.

1. **BEFORE THE SUCCESSOR ACCEPTS THE ENGAGEMENT** The successor auditor should attempt certain communications **before** accepting the engagement.

   a. **PERMISSION** Since the AICPA Code of Professional Conduct precludes an auditor from disclosing confidential information unless the client gives permission, the successor must ask the prospective client to authorize the predecessor to respond promptly and fully to the successor's questions. If a prospective client refuses to permit the predecessor to respond or limits the response, the successor auditor should inquire as to the reasons and consider the implications of that refusal in deciding whether to accept that engagement.

   b. **INQUIRY** These communications would include specific questions regarding facts that bear on (1) the integrity of management; (2) disagreements between the predecessor and management on accounting principles, auditing procedures, or other significant matters; (3) the predecessor's understanding about why there was a change in auditors; and (4) predecessor communications to audit committees (or similar authorities) regarding internal control related matters, illegal acts by clients, and fraud. These inquiries should relate to matters the successor feels will help in deciding whether to accept the engagement.

   c. **RESPONSE** The predecessor should respond promptly and fully. If the predecessor decides not to respond fully (due to unusual circumstances such as impending litigation), the predecessor should indicate that a limited response is being given. The successor should consider the implications of receiving a limited response in deciding whether or not to accept the engagement.

2. **REVIEW OF WORK PAPERS** Other communications prior to, or subsequent to, acceptance of the engagement are concerned with assisting the successor with the audit, such as evaluations of consistency in applying accounting principles, inquiries into audit areas that required an inordinate amount of time, and problems that arose because of the condition of accounting systems or records.

3. **REVISION** During the course of the audit, it is possible that the successor may become aware of information that leads to a belief that the financial statements reported on by the predecessor may require revision. The successor should ask the client to arrange a meeting with the client, the predecessor, and the successor to resolve the matter. If the client refuses or if the successor is not satisfied, the auditor should consider consulting an attorney.

C. RELEASE OF WORK PAPERS

Ultimately, the predecessor determines what work papers the successor may review or copy. A predecessor may not care to release work papers containing matters pertaining to pending litigation or potentially fraudulent client representations.

1. **SIGNED STATEMENT** The predecessor auditor may request a signed statement acknowledging the successor's responsibility to keep the information confidential and consenting to use the work papers solely for purposes of planning the successor's audit. The predecessor may request the successor to consent not to comment on the performance of the predecessor's audit, not to provide expert testimony on the quality of the predecessor's audit, and not to use the work papers as evidential material in the successor's audit.

2. **USE** The successor auditor uses the predecessor's work papers as a start for obtaining confidence in the beginning balances. (The predecessor's work does not replace the need

for some testing.) This can encompass a review of virtually all of the predecessor's work papers. The successor should **not** make any reference to the predecessor's work as a basis for the successor's own opinion. The nature, extent, and timing of audit procedures, as well as the opinion the successor auditor reaches, are solely that auditor's responsibility.

III. Planning and Supervision (AU 311, SAS 22)

A. Planning

Planning involves the development of an overall strategy for the expected conduct and scope of the audit. The nature, extent, and timing of the audit are functions of the size and complexity of the entity, the auditor's experience with the entity, and the auditor's knowledge of the entity's business.

1. **Considerations in Planning** The auditor should consider (a) relevant matters relating to the entity's business and the industry in which it operates; (b) the entity's accounting policies and procedures; (c) planned assessed level of control risk; (d) preliminary estimates of materiality levels; (e) any financial statement items that are likely to require adjustment; (f) any conditions that may necessitate modifying or extending audit tests (e.g., material errors or fraud or related party transactions); (g) the types of audit reports (e.g., a special report, a report on statements to be filed with the SEC, etc.); and (h) the methods used by the entity to process significant transactions.

2. **Procedures in Planning** Procedures that the auditor may consider in planning the audit usually involve a review of client records and discussions with personnel of the client and the audit team. Examples of these procedures include: (a) the review of the auditor's correspondence files, prior year's working papers, permanent files, copies of financial statements, and previous audit reports; (b) discussion with firm personnel who are responsible for providing nonaudit services to the client; (c) inquiry concerning current business developments affecting the entity; (d) reading the interim financial statements for the current year; (e) discussing the type, scope, and timing of the audit with the entity's management, the audit committee, or the board of directors; (f) considering accounting and auditing pronouncements that apply; (g) coordinating the assistance of the entity's personnel in data preparation; (h) determining how, if at all, consultants, specialists, and internal auditors will be used; (i) establishing a time schedule for the engagement; and (j) establishing and coordinating staffing requirements.

3. **Written Audit Program** A written audit program, setting forth the necessary audit procedures in reasonable detail, is **required**. Its form and degree of detail will vary from engagement to engagement, and modification of the audit program may be necessary if circumstances change during the audit.

4. **Knowledge of the Client's Business** The auditor must understand the client's business (i.e., the auditor must understand the **events**, **transactions**, and **practices** that may significantly affect the financial statements). This understanding helps to (a) identify areas that may need special consideration; (b) comprehend the accounting systems; (c) evaluate the reasonableness of estimates; (d) evaluate the reasonableness of representations made by management; and (e) evaluate the appropriateness of the accounting principles used and the adequacy of disclosures. Knowledge of the client's business includes a knowledge of matters relating to its nature, organization, and operating characteristics (e.g., the type of business, types of products and services, locations, and related parties).

5. **Knowledge of the Industry** The auditor should consider relevant matters affecting the industry in which the client operates. These would include (a) economic conditions, (b) government regulations, (c) changes in technology, (d) industry accounting practices, (e) competitive conditions, and (f) available industry trends and ratios.

6. **Computer Usage** The extent to which computer processing is used and its complexity may influence the nature, timing, and extent of audit procedures. If specialized skills are needed to evaluate the effect of computer processing on the audit, the auditor should use a

specialist. If the use of such a professional is planned, the auditor should have sufficient computer-related knowledge to communicate the objectives, evaluate whether the specified procedures will meet the auditor's objectives, and evaluate the results of the procedures.

B. SUPERVISION
Involves directing assistants in accomplishing the audit objectives and subsequently determining whether those objectives were accomplished. The extent of supervision required will vary from situation to situation, depending on the complexity of the subject matter and the qualifications of the persons performing the work.

1. **ASSISTANTS** Audit firm personnel who perform technical aspects of the engagement but who do not have final responsibility for the audit.

2. **AUDITOR** The professional responsible for the engagement. The auditor is in charge of field work. If there are assistants, the auditor supervises them. The auditor provides the written audit program and oral instructions to the assistants.

3. **INFORM ASSISTANTS** The auditor should inform assistants of their responsibilities and the objectives of the audit procedures they are to perform in sufficient detail. The assistants should be instructed to bring significant accounting and auditing questions to the auditor's attention.

4. **REVIEW ASSISTANTS' WORK** The auditor should review the work of each assistant to be sure it was adequately performed and that the results obtained are consistent with the conclusions presented in the audit report.

5. **DISAGREEMENTS** Both the auditor and the assistants should be aware of the procedures to be followed when differences of opinion arise on accounting and auditing issues. The procedures should allow assistants to document their disagreements with the conclusions reached if, after appropriate consultation, assistants believe it necessary to disassociate themselves from the issue's resolution. The basis for the resolution should also be documented.

IV. AUDIT RISK AND MATERIALITY IN CONDUCTING AN AUDIT (AU 312, SAS 47)

A. NATURE OF AUDIT RISK
Audit risk is the risk that an auditor may unknowingly fail to modify the opinion on financial statements that are materially misstated. The existence of audit risk is **acknowledged** in the auditor's standard report in that the auditor obtained "reasonable assurance" that the financial statements are free of material misstatement. Audit risk and materiality should be considered in planning the audit and evaluating the results of audit procedures for determining whether the financial statements taken as a whole are presented fairly.

B. NATURE OF MATERIALITY
The concept of materiality recognizes that some matters affect the fair presentation of financial statements, while others do not. Materiality judgments involve both **quantitative** and **qualitative** considerations. For example, an illegal payment that is immaterial in amount could be material if there is a reasonable possibility that it could lead to a material contingent liability or a material loss of revenue or if users might find such a payment significant.

Misapplies GAAP
or
Omits necessary information
or
Departs from fact

} = **MISSTATEMENT**

1. **Material Misstatements** Material misstatements are errors or fraud that cause the financial statements to not be presented fairly in conformity with GAAP. They result from misapplications of GAAP, omissions of necessary information, or departures from fact.

2. **Assessment** In assessing materiality, misstatements should be considered both individually and in the aggregate. A material misstatement means either an individual misstatement or the aggregate of misstatements that cause a material misstatement of the financial statements. When judging the materiality of misstatements, the auditor must consider their nature and amount in relation to the nature and amount of items in the financial statements. Materiality depends on the circumstances.

3. **Professional Judgment** The auditor's assessment of materiality is a matter of professional judgment. In making this assessment, the auditor should consider the needs of a reasonable person who will rely on the financial statements. A material misstatement is one that would change or influence the judgment of a reasonable person relying on the information contained in the financial statements.

C. Financial Statement Level

1. **Preliminary Judgment** In planning the audit, the auditor must make a preliminary judgment about the acceptable level of audit risk and materiality.

2. **Audit Risk** The auditor should plan the audit so that audit risk will be reduced to a low level. The auditor's assessment of audit risk may be in quantitative or nonquantitative terms.

3. **Level of Misstatement** Materiality levels include an overall level for each financial statement. However, in planning audit procedures, the auditor should consider materiality in terms of the smallest aggregate level of misstatements that could be considered material to any one of the financial statements.

4. **Designing Procedures** The auditor ordinarily designs audit procedures to detect misstatements that are quantitatively material. It is generally impractical to design audit procedures to detect qualitatively material misstatements. However, the auditor should be alert for qualitatively material misstatements during the course of the audit.

5. **Change in Risk** A decrease in the acceptable level of audit risk in an account balance or class of transactions or a decrease in the amount of misstatements that the auditor believes could be material would require the auditor to increase the extent and/or effectiveness of the applicable auditing procedures, thereby increasing the likelihood that smaller misstatements would be found.

6. **Change in Materiality** The auditor's assessment of materiality may change as the audit progresses. Thus, materiality levels considered in evaluating audit findings may differ from those used for planning purposes. If significantly lower materiality levels become appropriate in evaluating audit findings, the auditor should reevaluate the sufficiency of the audit procedures performed.

7. **Prior Experience** In planning the audit, the auditor should consider the nature, cause, and extent of misstatements found in audits of prior periods' financial statements.

D. Individual-Account-Balance or Class-of-Transaction Level

1. **Risk/Materiality Relationship** There is an inverse relationship between audit risk and materiality considerations. A decrease in either the acceptable level of audit risk or the perceived materiality level of an account balance or class of transactions would require the auditor to do one or more of the following:

   a. Select a more effective auditing procedure (nature).

b. Perform auditing procedures closer to the balance sheet date (timing).

c. Increase the extent of a particular auditing procedure (extent).

EXHIBIT 3 ♦ RISK RELATIONSHIPS

Inherent Risk and Control Risk	Acceptable Level of Detection Risk	Substantive Tests
Increase	Decrease	Increase
Decrease	Increase	Decrease

NOTE: A change in substantive tests means to alter the nature, timing, or extent of such tests.

2. **MATERIALITY** In planning audit procedures for a specific account balance or class of transactions, the auditor should design procedures to detect misstatements that, if aggregated with other misstatements, could be material to the financial statements taken as a whole. The maximum amount of misstatement in any balance or class that could exist without causing a material misstatement of the financial statements may or may not be explicitly stated.

3. **LEVEL OF AUDIT RISK** The audit risk at the individual account-balance or class-of-transactions level should be low enough that an opinion can be expressed on the financial statements. Thus, audit risk should be considered in determining the scope of auditing procedures for the balance or class.

4. **COMPONENTS** At the account-balance or class-of-transactions level, there are three components of audit risk. The relationship between audit risk and its three components is expressed in the following model:

$$AR = IR \times CR \times DR$$

where: AR = Audit risk, IR = Inherent risk, CR = Control risk, DR = Detection risk

a. **INHERENT RISK** The susceptibility of an assertion to a material misstatement, assuming that there are no related internal control policies or procedures. The risk that misstatement is greater for some assertions than for others. For example, cash is more susceptible to theft than an inventory of coal. External factors also influence inherent risk. For example, technological developments might make a particular product obsolete, thereby causing an overstatement of inventory.

b. **CONTROL RISK** The risk that a material misstatement that could occur in an assertion will not be prevented or detected on a timely basis by the **entity's** internal control policies or procedures. This risk is a function of the effectiveness of the design and operation of such policies and procedures. Some control risk will always exist because of the limitations of any entity's internal control.

c. **DETECTION RISK** The risk that the **auditor** will not detect a material misstatement that exists in an assertion. Detection risk is a function of the effectiveness of an auditing procedure and of its application by the auditor. It arises partly from uncertainties that exist when the auditor examines less than 100 percent of an account balance or class of transactions. Other uncertainties are present even when 100 percent of the balance or class is examined. For example, the auditor might select an inappropriate procedure, misapply an appropriate procedure, or misinterpret the audit results.

(1) Detection risk should bear an inverse relationship to inherent and control risk. The less the inherent and control risk the auditor believes exists, the greater the detection risk that can be accepted.

(2) Inherent risk and control risk differ from detection risk in that they exist independently of the audit, whereas detection risk relates to the auditor's procedures and can be altered by adjusting the nature, timing, and extent of substantive procedures. Thus, the auditor **assesses** inherent risk and control risk. Detection risk is a function of the nature, timing, and extent of audit procedures, and, as such, may be changed by the auditor.

5. **MEASUREMENT OF RISK** The components of audit risk may be assessed quantitatively or nonquantitatively.

   a. **INHERENT RISK** The assessment of inherent risk is a matter of professional judgment. Factors that should be considered include those peculiar to the account balance or class of transaction, as well as those pervasive to the financial statements taken as a whole. The effort required to evaluate the inherent risk for a balance or class may exceed the potential reduction in audit procedures that might be derived from such an evaluation. If this is the case, the auditor should assess inherent risk at its maximum level.

   b. **CONTROL RISK** Professional judgment is also required in the assessment of control risk. The auditor's assessment is based on the sufficiency of evidential matter obtained to support the effectiveness of internal control policies or procedures. If the auditor believes such policies or procedures are unlikely to be effective, or if evaluating them would be inefficient, control risk for that assertion is assessed at the maximum level.

6. **DOCUMENTATION OF BASIS** If the auditor assesses inherent and/or control risk at less than the maximum, there should be an appropriate basis for the assessment. The basis must be documented. The auditor might choose to use materials such as flowcharts, questionnaires, checklists, or narratives to document the basis.

7. **DETECTION RISK** The detection risk that an auditor can accept is based on the maximum acceptable level of audit risk and the assessed levels of inherent and control risks. As the assessments of inherent and control risks decrease, the auditor can accept a greater level of detection risk. However, the auditor **cannot** rely completely on assessments of inherent and control risks to the exclusion of performing substantive tests.

8. **CHANGE IN ASSESSMENT** The auditor's assessments regarding the levels of inherent and control risks may change as the audit progresses, causing the preliminary judgment concerning materiality to be altered. In such cases, the auditor should reevaluate the planned auditing procedures to be applied.

E. EVALUATING AUDIT FINDINGS

1. **AGGREGATE MISSTATEMENTS** The auditor should aggregate uncorrected misstatements in a way that enables the auditor to consider whether they materially misstate the financial statements taken as a whole. Misstatements may be aggregated in relation to individual amounts, subtotals, or totals in the financial statements. The aggregation of misstatements in account balances or classes of transactions should include all likely misstatements and known misstatements (i.e., misstatements specifically identified).

2. **LIKELY MISSTATEMENTS** Likely misstatements are those that the auditor has projected from the sample results to the population.

3. **ACCOUNTING ESTIMATES** The risk of material misstatement of the financial statements is generally greater when accounting estimates are involved because of the inherent subjectivity in estimating future events. An estimated amount supported by audit evidence may differ from the estimated amount included in the financial statements. If the difference is reasonable, it would not be considered a likely misstatement. However, if the difference is unreasonable, the auditor should treat the difference as a likely misstatement and aggregate it with other likely misstatements.

   - In some cases, individual accounting estimates may be reasonable, but the cumulative effect of such estimates may cause a misstatement of the financial statements. Thus, the auditor must consider the aggregate effect of accounting estimates.

4. **PRIOR IMMATERIAL MISSTATEMENTS** In prior periods, likely misstatements may not have been corrected because they did not materially misstate the financial statements. Those misstatements might affect the current financial statements. If likely misstatements from prior periods, aggregated with likely misstatements arising in the current period, cause a material misstatement of the current period's financial statements, the misstatements from prior periods should be included in the auditor's audit evaluation.

5. **UNCORRECTED MISSTATEMENTS** If the aggregation of likely misstatements causes the financial statements to be materially misstated, the auditor should request management to correct the material misstatement. If the material misstatement is not corrected, the auditor should issue a qualified or adverse opinion on the financial statements. If the auditor concludes that the aggregation of likely misstatements does not cause the financial statements to be materially misstated, the auditor should recognize that they could still be materially misstated due to further misstatement remaining undetected. This risk is usually reduced by appropriately specifying the acceptable level of detection risk.

V. SUBSTANTIVE TESTS PRIOR TO THE BALANCE SHEET DATE (AU 313, SAS 45)

A. OBJECTIVES

Audit testing at an interim date allows the auditor to obtain an early consideration of significant matters that may affect the year-end financial statements. The potential for increased audit risk becomes greater as the interim period is lengthened.

1. **PROCEDURES THAT CAN BE PERFORMED PRIOR TO YEAR-END** Planning the audit, obtaining an understanding of internal control, assessing control risk, and applying substantive tests to transactions.

2. **DANGERS** Substantive tests used to cover the period subsequent to the interim test date should be designed so that this potentially increased audit risk can be controlled.

B. FACTORS TO CONSIDER

The auditor should assess the difficulty in controlling the incremental audit risk that may result from the performance of substantive tests at an interim date. This assessment also involves a consideration of the costs of the substantive tests that are necessary to provide the appropriate audit assurance over the period from the interim date to the balance-sheet date.

1. **ASSESSING CONTROL RISK AT THE MAXIMUM** If the auditor assesses control risk at the maximum level for the period from the interim period tests to the balance-sheet date, the auditor should consider whether the effectiveness of the substantive tests covering the period will be impaired. If so, additional audit assurance should be sought or the account should be tested at the balance-sheet date.

2. **RAPIDLY CHANGING BUSINESS CONDITIONS** The auditor should consider whether the post-interim-date substantive tests would be effective in controlling the incremental audit risk associated with misstated financial statements due to rapidly changing business conditions.

3. **Predictability of the Amount, Relative Significance, and Composition of Account Balance** The auditor should consider the appropriateness of the client's procedures for analyzing and adjusting the accounts at interim dates and for establishing proper cutoffs.

C. **Extending Audit Conclusions to the Balance Sheet Date**

1. **Substantive Tests Design** The substantive tests for the post-interim-date period should be designed so that the audit assurance obtained from the tests, combined with the assurances obtained from the substantive tests performed at the interim date and from the assurance provided from the assessed level of control risk, will achieve the overall audit objectives at the balance-sheet date. Analytical procedures and other substantive tests should provide a reasonable basis for extending the conclusions reached at the interim date to the balance-sheet date.

2. **Misstatements at Interim Dates** The existence of misstatements at the interim date may cause the auditor to modify the nature, timing, or extent of the planned substantive tests to be performed for the post-interim-date period, or the auditor may have to reperform certain procedures at the balance-sheet date.

D. **Coordinating the Timing of Auditing Procedures**

In deciding how related procedures are to be coordinated, the auditor should consider (1) coordinating the work of related parties, (2) coordinating the testing of interrelated accounts and cutoffs, and (3) asserting temporary control over certain negotiable assets, and testing such assets simultaneously with other related items such as cash on hand and in banks.

VI. Consideration of Fraud in a Financial Statement Audit (AU 316, SAS 82)

A. **Characteristics of Fraud**

Fraud is differentiated from error by the intent that causes the misstatement in the financial statements. A pressure or incentive to commit fraud and a perceived opportunity to commit fraud are often present when either type of fraud is committed, although the specifics may be different. Misstatements due to *fraudulent financial reporting* are misstatements or omissions intended to deceive financial statement users. Misstatements due to *misappropriation of assets* occur when financial statements are not in conformity with GAAP due to asset theft.

1. **Responsibilities** Management has the responsibility for preventing and detecting fraud. The auditor must include evidence of the fraud risk evaluation in the work papers. When risk factors are present, the documentation must include the factors identified and the auditor's response.

2. **Detection** Fraud is usually concealed (through false documents, including forgery, or collusion between employees or third parties). An audit conducted in accordance with GAAS usually does not include authentication of documentation. The existence of risk factors or other circumstances may cue the auditor to the potential for the presence of fraud. Due to the hidden nature of fraud and the requirement to use professional judgment in regard to fraud risk factors and other circumstances, even an audit executed in accordance with GAAS may not detect a material misstatement caused by fraud. Nevertheless, in an audit conducted in accordance with GAAS, the auditor is expected to discover errors or fraud that are material to the financial statements.

B. **Auditor Assessment**

Audit risk includes the risk of material misstatements because of fraud. The auditor must evaluate the risk of material misstatement due to fraud in particular and consider that evaluation in designing the audit. As part of this evaluation, the auditor must question management on its knowledge of actual fraud and assess the significance of fraud risk factors.

1. **RISK FACTORS OF FRAUD DUE TO FRAUDULENT FINANCIAL REPORTING**

   a. **MANAGEMENT ATTRIBUTES AND THE CONTROL ENVIRONMENT** Examples of this are motivation to engage in fraudulent financial reporting, a failure to support a proper stand regarding internal control, non-financial managers' extreme involvement in the choice of accounting principles or estimates, high turnover of senior management or counsel, strained relationship between management and auditors, and a history of allegations or violations of laws and regulations.

   b. **INDUSTRY CONDITIONS** Examples of this are new requirements that might impair the financial health of the entity, extreme competition or market maturity along with declining margins, declining industry, and rapid technological changes.

   c. **OPERATING CHARACTERISTICS AND FINANCIAL STABILITY** Examples of this are poor cash flows while reporting earnings growth, pressure to obtain capital to remain competitive, valuations based on estimates that are subjective or uncertain or subject to fluctuations, significant related-party transactions, unusual or complex transactions that involve "substance over form" considerations, operations in tax-haven jurisdictions or complex organizational structure or ownership without apparent business purpose, growth or profitability outside of industry parameters, high exposure to interest rate changes, marginal debt-carrying ability, unrealistic incentive programs, possibility of bankruptcy or hostile takeover, and poor financial condition when management has personally guaranteed sizable debts for the entity.

2. **RISK FACTORS OF FRAUD DUE TO MISAPPROPRIATION OF ASSETS** The auditor's evaluation of risk factors presented by the lack of controls are colored by the susceptibility of assets to misappropriation. The auditor is not required to search for information regarding employees' financial stress or strained employee-employer relationships, but may become aware of such information (pending layoffs, employee dissatisfaction, behavior or lifestyle changes, personal financial pressures, etc.). In this case, the auditor should factor this information into the assessment of the risk of material misstatement due to misappropriation of assets.

   a. **SUSCEPTIBILITY OF ASSETS TO MISAPPROPRIATION** Examples include large amounts of cash; inventory and fixed asset attributes, such as small size, large value, high demand, ready marketability, or lack of ownership identification; or readily convertible assets. **NOTE:** These risk factors are equivalent to the auditor's assessment of inherent risk as previously discussed in the audit risk model.

   b. **CONTROLS** Examples include ineffective, inadequate, or absent controls, such as supervision or monitoring; job applicant screening for employees; asset record-keeping; segregation of duties; approval and authorization for transactions; physical safeguards over assets; timely documentation for transactions; and mandatory vacations for key control employees. **NOTE:** These risk factors are equivalent to the auditor's assessment of control risk as previously discussed in the audit risk model.

3. **EVALUATION OF RISK FACTORS** The evaluation of fraud risk is a cumulative process including assessment of individual and combined risk factors. Auditors must use professional judgment when evaluating risk as fraud risk factors do not combine into an effective predictive model. The particular attributes of an entity influence the consideration of risk factors. The auditor can use the knowledge gained during consideration of internal control, including a program to prevent or detect fraud, to assess whether there are specific conditions that mitigate or exacerbate fraud risk. Fraud risk factors may be identified during the planning or fieldwork of an audit. For example, the auditor may discover conflicting or missing evidence or have a problematic relationship with the client.

C. **RESPONDING TO THE RESULTS OF FRAUD ASSESSMENT**

Although fraud risk factors are present, the auditor may conclude that procedures otherwise planned remain sufficient.

1. **OVERALL CONSIDERATION** Judgments about fraud risk may increase the auditors professional skepticism; the extent of supervision or qualifications of persons performing the audit work; the auditor's consideration of the application of accounting principles; and the auditor's consideration of internal controls and management's ability to override controls. The auditor may need to modify the nature, extent, and timing of audit procedures to obtain sufficient evidence.

2. **SPECIFIC CONSIDERATIONS** The auditor might perform certain tests on an unannounced basis; request that inventory be counted at a date close to year-end; alter the audit approach from the previous year; review the entity's adjusting entries in detail; examine the sources of financial resources and the possibility of related parties for significant and unusual transactions; perform more detailed analytical procedures; interview employees in an area where fraud risk is high; discuss fraud risk with auditors auditing other divisions; and perform additional procedures with regard to specialist's work.

3. **FRAUDULENT FINANCIAL REPORTING** The auditor's response to the possibility of misstatements arising from fraudulent financial reporting include more extensive tests. In the case of improper revenue recognition, the auditor may confirm relevant contract terms with customers. In the case of incorrect inventory quantities, the auditor may identify locations or items for specific attention during the physical inventory count, observe inventory counts on an unannounced basis, or examine items in a physical count more rigorously.

4. **MISAPPROPRIATION OF ASSETS** Generally, the audit response to risk from misappropriation of assets involves increased examination of related control activities, account balances and classes of transactions. The use of analytical procedures at a high level of precision may also be appropriate.

D. CONCLUSIONS

At the end of the audit, the auditor evaluates whether the results of audit procedures affect the evaluation of fraud risk made during audit planning. The evaluation of fraud risk is an ongoing, cumulative process that is primarily a qualitative matter based on the auditor's judgment. The auditor considers whether identified misstatements are indicative of fraud.

1. **PROCEDURES** If the auditor determines that misstatements might be due to fraud, and either has determined that the effect is material or is unable to evaluate whether the effect is material, the auditor should consider the implications for other audit aspects; discuss the matter with a level of management at least one level above those involved and with senior management; attempt to determine whether fraud has occurred by obtaining additional evidence, and if so, its effect on the financial statements; and suggest that management consult with legal counsel, if appropriate.

2. **WITHDRAWAL** The fraud risk assessment may cause the auditor to consider withdrawing from the engagement and communicating the reasons for withdrawal to the audit committee.

E. COMMUNICATIONS

If the auditor determines that fraud may exist, the appropriate level of management must be informed, even if the matter may be insignificant. The auditor must consider whether risk factors that have ongoing control implications represent reportable conditions relating to internal control.

1. **AUDIT COMMITTEE** The auditor must directly inform the audit committee (or equivalent) regarding fraud possibly concerning senior management or causing a material misstatement of the financial statements.

2. **EXTERNAL PARTIES** The auditor may be required to disclose information regarding potential fraud to outside parties. The auditor may wish to consult with legal counsel before discussing findings with outside parties. In the following circumstances, an auditor may need to disclose information:

a. When legal and regulatory compliance requirements exist. (When the entity reports an auditor change under securities law on Form 8-K.)

b. To a successor auditor making inquiries in accordance with SAS 84, *Communications Between Predecessor and Successor Auditors*.

c. In response to a subpoena.

d. To a funding agency or other specified agency in accordance with requirements for the audits of entities that receive financial assistance from a governmental agency.

VII. Illegal Acts by Clients (AU 317, SAS 54)

A. Illegal Acts

Illegal acts are defined as violations of laws or governmental regulations by management or employees acting on behalf of the company. Illegal acts by clients do not include personal misconduct by the entity's personnel unrelated to their business activities. Generally, the auditor leaves the determination of the legality of an act to an expert qualified to practice law or to a court of law. The auditor's experience and knowledge of the client and its industry may provide a basis for recognition of acts that may be illegal. In applying audit procedures, the auditor may encounter information (or "red flags") that may raise a question concerning possible illegal acts, such as the following:

1. Unauthorized or improperly recorded transactions
2. Investigation by a governmental agency
3. Large payments for unspecified services to consultants
4. Excessive sales commissions or agents' fees
5. Unusually large cash payments
6. Unexplained payments to government officials or employees
7. Failure to file tax returns
8. Forced to discontinue operations in a foreign country

B. Relation to Financial Statements

Generally, the further removed an illegal act is from the events and transactions reflected in the financial statements, the less likely the auditor is to become aware of the act. The auditor normally considers only those laws and regulations having a **direct and material** effect on the financial statement amounts. The auditor is **required** to consider illegal acts that could have a direct and material effect on the financial statements (e.g., violations of tax law) and consider that in the design of substantive tests.

1. An entity may be affected by many laws or regulations relating more to its operating aspects than to the financial statements. An auditor ordinarily does not have sufficient basis for recognizing possible violations of laws and regulations (for example, shipping regulations for tractor-trailers or maritime vessels).

2. The auditor may not become aware of illegal acts that could have an indirect effect on the financial statements unless the client discloses such information, or there is evidence of a governmental agency investigation or enforcement proceeding in the records normally inspected in an audit. Examples would include price fixing, equal employment violations, and occupational safety and health violations.

C. PROCEDURES

Normally, an audit conducted in accordance with GAAS does not include procedures specifically designed to detect illegal acts not having a **direct and material** effect on the financial statements. During the course of an audit, however, other audit procedures may bring illegal acts to the auditor's attention. Such procedures may include the following: reading minutes; inquiring of client's management and legal counsel concerning litigation, claims, and assessments; and performing substantive tests of details of transactions or balances. The auditor should also make inquiries of management concerning the client's compliance with laws and regulations, and the client's policies to prevent illegal acts. The auditor should obtain written representations from management concerning the absence of violations or possible violations of laws or regulations whose effects must be considered for disclosure in the financial statements or as a basis for recording a loss contingency.

1. **POSSIBLE ILLEGAL ACT** If a possible illegal act has occurred, the auditor should obtain an understanding of the act, the circumstances under which it occurred, and sufficient information to evaluate its effect on the financial statements. The auditor may wish to consult with the client's legal counsel or other specialists regarding the possible illegal act and its effects, and additional procedures may be applied, if necessary, to obtain further understanding of the acts.

2. **ADDITIONAL PROCEDURES** Additional audit procedures may include the following:

   a. Examining supporting documents, such as invoices, canceled checks, and agreements, and comparing them with accounting records

   b. Confirming significant information concerning the matter with the other party to the transaction or with intermediaries, such as banks or lawyers

   c. Determining whether the transaction has been properly authorized

   d. Considering whether other similar transactions or events may have occurred, and applying procedures to identify them

D. FINANCIAL STATEMENT EFFECT

When an illegal act has occurred, the auditor should consider both the quantitative and qualitative materiality of the act on the financial statements as well as the implications for other aspects of the audit, such as the reliability of representations of management. The illegal act may involve contingent liabilities that must be disclosed. The auditor should consider whether material revenue or earnings are derived from transactions involving illegal acts, or if illegal acts create significant unusual risks associated with material revenue or earnings.

E. AUDIT COMMITTEE

The auditor should ascertain that the audit committee, or those with equivalent authority, are adequately informed about illegal acts that come to the auditor's attention. The communication should describe the act, the circumstances, and the effect on the financial statements. The communication may be written or oral. If oral, the communication should be documented. The auditor need not communicate inconsequential matters.

F. AUDITOR'S REPORT

If the client refuses to accept the auditor's report as modified, the auditor should withdraw from the engagement and indicate the reasons for doing so in writing to the audit committee or board of directors.

1. **NOT DISCLOSED** If the auditor concludes that an illegal act having a material effect on the financial statements has occurred, and the act has not been properly accounted for or disclosed, the auditor should express a qualified opinion or an adverse opinion, depending on the materiality.

2. **Scope Limitation** If the auditor is precluded by the client from obtaining sufficient evidential matter to determine whether an illegal act that could be material has, or is likely to have, occurred, (i.e., a scope limitation), the auditor should disclaim an opinion on the financial statements.

G. **Other Considerations**
The auditor may decide that withdrawal is necessary when the client does not take remedial action that the auditor considers necessary, even when the illegal act is not material to the financial statements.

1. **Management Integrity** The auditor should consider the implications of an illegal act in relation to other aspects of the audit, particularly the reliability of management representations.

2. **Outside Parties** The auditor may wish to consult with legal counsel before discussing illegal acts with outside parties. Disclosure of illegal acts to outside parties may be necessary in certain circumstances, such as

    a. When the entity reports an auditor change under the appropriate securities law on Form 8-K. Also see Private Securities Litigation Reform Act of 1995.

    b. To an auditor making inquiries in accordance with SAS 84, *Communications Between Predecessor and Successor Auditors.*

    c. In response to a subpoena.

    d. To a funding agency or other specified agency in accordance with requirements for the audits of entities that receive governmental financial assistance.

3. **Private Securities Litigation Reform Act of 1995** Auditors must include procedures to (1) detect illegal acts that would have a direct and material effect on the financial statements, (2) identify related party transactions that would have a material effect on the financial statements, and (3) evaluate an issuer's ability to continue as a going concern.

    a. **Reports to Entity** An auditor who becomes aware of possible illegal activities shall inform the entity's management and assure that the audit committee or the board of directors is adequately informed. If the auditor concludes that the illegal act has a material effect on the financial statements and management has not taken appropriate remedial actions, and departure from a standard report seems reasonable, the auditor shall directly report this to the board of directors.

    b. **Reporting to SEC** The entity is required to notify the SEC no later than 1 business day after receipt of such report. If the entity fails to notify the SEC within 1 business day, the auditor must resign from the engagement and/or report to the SEC within 1 business day.

H. **Responsibilities in Other Circumstances**
An auditor may accept an engagement that entails, by agreement with the client, a greater responsibility for detecting illegal acts than a typical audit. For example, an auditor may be engaged to test and report on compliance with specific government regulations.

VIII. Communication With Audit Committees (AU 380, SAS 61, 89, 90)

A. **Audit Committee**
Those responsible for oversight of the financial reporting process. The auditor is responsible for ensuring that the audit committee receives any additional information regarding the scope and results of the audit that may assist the audit committee in overseeing the financial reporting process. The communication is not required to be made before issuance of the report. The

communication may be oral or written. Oral communication should be documented by the auditor. Written communication should specify that it is intended solely for the audit committee, board of directors, or management, if appropriate.

B. Matters to be Communicated

1. **Service Provided** The auditor should communicate (a) the level of responsibility assumed under GAAS, and (b) that the audit should provide reasonable, rather than absolute, assurance about the financial statements.

2. **General Information** The auditor should inform the audit committee of

   - Significant matters related to internal control.
   - Selection of or changes in significant accounting policies.
   - Management's process in making accounting estimates.
   - Adjustments arising from the audit that could have a significant impact on the financial statements.
   - Any disagreements, whether or not resolved, with management about matters that, individually or in the aggregate, could have a significant impact on the financial statements.
   - Any serious difficulties encountered in dealing with management related to the performance of the audit.
   - Responsibility for other information in documents containing financial statements.
   - Any consultations management had with other accountants about accounting and auditing matters.
   - Any major issues discussed regarding initial or recurring retention of the auditor.
   - Uncorrected misstatements aggregated by the auditor during the current engagement and pertaining to the latest period presented that were determined by management to be immaterial, both individually and in the aggregate, to the financial statements taken as a whole. (SAS 89 adds this requirement. Communication of immaterial amounts does not constitute a communication pursuant to SAS 54.)

3. **Reportable Conditions** The auditor must also communicate reportable conditions and material weaknesses noted during an audit. It is not necessary to repeat the communication of recurring matters each year, although the auditor should determine if changes in the composition of the audit committee warrant repetition of previously communicated matters.

4. **Independence** The auditor must discuss the auditor's independence annually.

5. **Quality of Principles and Estimates** SAS 90 requires an auditor to discuss the auditor's judgments about the quality of an SEC company's accounting principles and underlying estimates in the financial statements with the SEC client's audit committee, generally with management present.

CHAPTER 32—PLANNING

PROBLEM 32-1 MULTIPLE CHOICE QUESTIONS (60 to 75 minutes)

1. An auditor is required to establish an understanding with a client regarding the services to be performed for each engagement. This understanding generally includes
a. Management's responsibility for errors and the illegal activities of employees that may cause material misstatement.
b. The auditor's responsibility for ensuring that the audit committee is aware of any reportable conditions that come to the auditor's attention.
c. Management's responsibility for providing the auditor with an assessment of the risk of material misstatement due to fraud.
d. The auditor's responsibility for determining preliminary judgments about materiality and audit risk factors. (R/99, Aud., #6, 6822)

2. An auditor obtains knowledge about a new client's business and its industry to
a. Make constructive suggestions concerning improvements to the client's internal control.
b. Develop an attitude of professional skepticism concerning management's financial statement assertions.
c. Evaluate whether the aggregation of known misstatements causes the financial statements taken as a whole to be materially misstated.
d. Understand the events and transactions that may have an effect on the client's financial statements. (5/94, Aud., #4, amended, 4669)

3. Which of the following procedures would an auditor most likely include in the planning phase of a financial statement audit?
a. Obtain an understanding of the entity's risk assessment process
b. Identify specific internal control activities designed to prevent fraud
c. Evaluate the reasonableness of the entity's accounting estimates
d. Perform cutoff tests of the entity's sales and purchases (11/98, Aud., #18, 6709)

4. Which of the following factors most likely would lead a CPA to conclude that a potential audit engagement should be rejected?
a. The details of most recorded transactions are not available after a specified period of time.
b. Internal control activities requiring the segregation of duties are subject to management override.
c. It is unlikely that sufficient competent evidence is available to support an opinion on the financial statements.
d. Management has a reputation for consulting with several accounting firms about significant accounting issues. (R/00, Aud., #2, 6927)

5. Ordinarily, the predecessor auditor permits the successor auditor to review the predecessor's working paper analyses relating to

	Contingencies	*Balance sheet accounts*
a.	Yes	Yes
b.	Yes	No
c.	No	Yes
d.	No	No

(11/98, Aud., #19, 6710)

6. A successor auditor most likely would make specific inquiries of the predecessor auditor regarding
a. Specialized accounting principles of the client's industry.
b. The competency of the client's internal audit staff.
c. The uncertainty inherent in applying sampling procedures.
d. Disagreements with management as to auditing procedures. (5/95, Aud., #2, 5620)

7. In auditing the financial statements of Star Corp., Land discovered information leading Land to believe that Star's prior year's financial statements, which were audited by Tell, require substantial revisions. Under these circumstances, Land should
a. Notify Star's audit committee and stockholders that the prior year's financial statements **cannot** be relied on.
b. Request Star to arrange a meeting among the three parties to resolve the matter.
c. Notify Tell about the information and make inquiries about the integrity of Star's management.
d. Request Star to reissue the prior year's financial statements with the appropriate revisions.
(5/95, Aud., #18, amended, 5636)

8. Which of the following procedures would an auditor most likely perform in planning a financial statement audit?
a. Inquiring of the client's legal counsel concerning pending litigation.
b. Comparing the financial statements to anticipated results.
c. Searching for unauthorized transactions that may aid in detecting unrecorded liabilities.
d. Examining computer generated exception reports to verify the effectiveness of internal controls. (5/95, Aud., #4, amended, 5622)

9. The audit program usually **cannot** be finalized until the
a. Consideration of the entity's internal control has been completed.
b. Engagement letter has been signed by the auditor and the client.
c. Search for unrecorded liabilities has been performed and documented.
d. Reportable conditions have been communicated to the audit committee of the board of directors. (5/95, Aud., #17, amended, 5635)

10. In developing a preliminary audit strategy, an auditor should consider
a. Whether the allowance for sampling risk exceeds the achieved upper precision limit.
b. Findings from substantive tests performed at interim dates.
c. Whether the inquiry of the client's attorney identifies any litigation, claims, or assessments **not** disclosed in the financial statements.
d. The planned assessed level of control risk. (11/91, Aud., #8, 2276)

11. The element of the audit planning process most likely to be agreed upon with the client before implementation of the audit strategy is the determination of the
a. Evidence to be gathered to provide a sufficient basis for the auditor's opinion.
b. Procedures to be undertaken to discover litigation, claims, and assessments.
c. Pending legal matters to be included in the inquiry of the client's attorney.
d. Timing of inventory observation procedures to be performed. (5/95, Aud., #1, 5619)

12. The audit work performed by each assistant should be reviewed to determine whether it was adequately performed and to evaluate whether the
a. Audit procedures performed are approved in the professional standards.
b. Auditor's system of quality control has been maintained at a high level.
c. Results are consistent with the conclusions to be presented in the auditor's report.
d. Audit has been performed by persons having adequate technical training and proficiency as auditors. (11/91, Aud., #5, amended, 2273)

13. An auditor should design the written audit program so that
a. All material transactions will be selected for substantive testing.
b. Substantive tests prior to the balance sheet date will be minimized.
c. The audit procedures selected will achieve specific audit objectives.
d. Each account balance will be tested under either tests of controls or tests of transactions. (5/95, Aud., #16, 5634)

14. The in-charge auditor most likely would have a supervisory responsibility to explain to the staff assistants
a. That immaterial fraud is **not** to be reported to the client's audit committee.
b. How the results of various auditing procedures performed by the assistants should be evaluated.
c. Why certain documents are being transferred from the current file to the permanent file.
d. What benefits may be attained by the assistant's adherence to established time budgets. (5/95, Aud., #7, amended, 5625)

15. Which of the following statements is **not** correct about materiality?
a. The concept of materiality recognizes that some matters are important for fair presentation of financial statements in conformity with GAAP, while other matters are **not** important.
b. An auditor considers materiality for planning purposes in terms of the largest aggregate level of misstatements that could be material to any one of the financial statements.
c. An auditor's consideration of materiality is influenced by the auditor's perception of the needs of a reasonable person who will rely on the financial statements.
d. Materiality judgments are made in light of surrounding circumstances and necessarily involve both quantitative and qualitative judgments. (11/94, Aud., #11, amended, 5084)

16. Which of the following would an auditor most likely use in determining the auditor's preliminary judgment about materiality?
a. The results of the initial assessment of control risk.
b. The anticipated sample size for planned substantive tests.
c. The entity's financial statements of the prior year.
d. The assertions that are embodied in the financial statements. (11/97, Aud., #10, 6573)

17. Holding other planning considerations equal, a decrease in the amount of misstatements in a class of transactions that an auditor could tolerate most likely would cause the auditor to
a. Apply the planned substantive tests prior to the balance sheet date.
b. Perform the planned auditing procedures closer to the balance sheet date.
c. Increase the assessed level of control risk for relevant financial statement assertions.
d. Decrease the extent of auditing procedures to be applied to the class of transactions. (11/97, Aud., #11, 6574)

18. Which of the following procedures would an auditor **least** likely perform before the balance sheet date?
a. Confirmation of accounts payable
b. Observation of merchandise inventory
c. Assessment of control risk
d. Identification of related parties (5/95, Aud., #73, 5691)

19. Because an audit in accordance with generally accepted auditing standards is influenced by the possibility of material misstatements, the auditor should conduct the audit with an attitude of
a. Objective judgment.
b. Conservative advocacy.
c. Professional responsiveness.
d. Professional skepticism. (Editors, 0213)

20. Which of the following statements describes why a properly designed and executed audit may **not** detect a material misstatement in the financial statements resulting from fraud?
a. Audit procedures that are effective for detecting an unintentional misstatement may be ineffective for an intentional misstatement that is concealed through collusion.
b. An audit is designed to provide reasonable assurance of detecting material errors, but there is **no** similar responsibility concerning fraud.
c. The factors considered in assessing control risk indicated an increased risk of intentional misstatements, but only a low risk of unintentional errors in the financial statements.
d. The auditor did **not** consider factors influencing audit risk for account balances that have effects pervasive to the financial statements taken as a whole. (11/91, Aud., #10, amended, 2278)

21. Which of the following statements reflects an auditor's responsibility for detecting errors and fraud?
a. An auditor is responsible for detecting employee errors and simple fraud, but **not** for discovering fraud involving employee collusion or management override.
b. An auditor should plan the audit to detect errors and fraud that is caused by departures from GAAP.
c. An auditor is **not** responsible for detecting errors and fraud unless the application of GAAS would result in such detection.
d. An auditor should design the audit to provide reasonable assurance of detecting errors and fraud that is material to the financial statements. (5/95, Aud., #15, amended, 5633)

22. Disclosure of possible fraud to parties other than a client's senior management and its audit committee ordinarily is not part of an auditor's responsibility. However, to which of the following outside parties may a duty to disclose that possible fraud exists?

	To the SEC when the client reports an auditor change	*To a successor auditor when the successor makes appropriate inquiries*	*To a funding agency from which the client receives governmental financial assistance*
a.	Yes	Yes	No
b.	Yes	No	Yes
c.	No	Yes	Yes
d.	Yes	Yes	Yes

(5/90, Aud., #55, amended, 0163)

23. Which of the following factors most likely would heighten an auditor's concern about the risk of fraudulent financial reporting?
a. Inability to generate cash flows from operations while reporting substantial earnings growth
b. Management's lack of interest in increasing the entity's stock trend
c. Large amounts of liquid assets that are easily convertible into cash
d. Inability to borrow necessary capital without granting debt covenants (R/00, Aud., #5, 6930)

24. An auditor who discovers that a client's employees paid small bribes to municipal officials most likely would withdraw from the engagement if

a. The payments violated the client's policies regarding the prevention of illegal acts.
b. The client receives financial assistance from a federal government agency.
c. Documentation that is necessary to prove that the bribes were paid does not exist.
d. Management fails to take the appropriate remedial action. (R/00, Aud., #6, 6931)

25. When an auditor becomes aware of a possible illegal act by a client, the auditor should obtain an understanding of the nature of the act to

a. Evaluate the effect on the financial statements.
b. Determine the reliability of management's representations.
c. Consider whether other similar acts may have occurred.
d. Recommend remedial actions to the audit committee. (11/92, Aud., #4, 2938)

26. If information comes to an auditor's attention that implies the existence of possible illegal acts that could have a material, but indirect effect on the financial statements, the auditor should next

a. Apply audit procedures specifically directed to ascertaining whether an illegal act has occurred.
b. Seek the advice of an informed expert qualified to practice law as to possible contingent liabilities.
c. Discuss the evidence with the client's audit committee, or others with equivalent authority and responsibility.
d. Report the matter to an appropriate level of management at least one level above those involved. (Editors, 0172)

27. Which of the following relatively small misstatements most likely could have a material effect on an entity's financial statements?

a. An illegal payment to a foreign official that was **not** recorded.
b. A piece of obsolete office equipment that was **not** retired.
c. A petty cash fund disbursement that was **not** properly authorized.
d. An uncollectible account receivable that was **not** written off. (5/95, Aud., #9, 5627)

28. Which of the following information discovered during an audit most likely would raise a question concerning possible illegal acts?

a. Related party transactions, although properly disclosed, were pervasive during the year.
b. The entity prepared several large checks payable to cash during the year.
c. Material internal control weaknesses previously reported to management were **not** corrected
d. The entity was a campaign contributor to several local political candidates during the year. (11/97, Aud., #13, 6576)

29. An auditor would **least** likely initiate a discussion with a client's audit committee concerning

a. The methods used to account for significant unusual transactions.
b. The maximum dollar amount of misstatements that could exist without causing the financial statements to be materially misstated.
c. Indications of fraud and illegal acts committed by a corporate officer that were discovered by the auditor.
d. Disagreements with management as to accounting principles that were resolved during the current year's audit. (5/95, Aud., #19, 5637)

30. Under the Private Securities Litigation Reform Act of 1995, Baker, CPA, reported certain uncorrected illegal acts to Supermart's board of directors. Baker believed that failure to take remedial action would warrant a qualified audit opinion because the illegal acts had a material effect on Supermart's financial statements. Supermart failed to take appropriate remedial action and the board of directors refused to inform the SEC that it had received such notification from Baker. Under these circumstances, Baker is required to

a. Resign from the audit engagement within ten business days.
b. Deliver a report concerning the illegal acts to the SEC within one business day.
c. Notify the stockholders that the financial statements are materially misstated.
d. Withhold an audit opinion until Supermart takes appropriate remedial action. (R/99, Aud., #4, 6820)

PROBLEM 32-2 ADDITIONAL MULTIPLE CHOICE QUESTIONS (50 63 minutes)

31. In planning an audit of a new client, an auditor most likely would consider the methods used to process accounting information because such methods
a. Influence the design of internal control.
b. Affect the auditor's preliminary judgment about materiality levels.
c. Assist in evaluating the planned audit objectives.
d. Determine the auditor's acceptable level of audit risk. (11/94, Aud., #7, amended, 5080)

32. During the initial planning phase of an audit, a CPA most likely would
a. Identify specific internal control activities that are likely to prevent fraud.
b. Evaluate the reasonableness of the client's accounting estimates.
c. Discuss the timing of the audit procedure with the client's management.
d. Inquire of the client's attorney as to whether any unrecorded claims are probable of assertion. (5/98, Aud., #2, 6619)

33. Before accepting an engagement to audit a new client, a CPA is required to obtain
a. An understanding of the prospective client's industry and business.
b. The prospective client's signature to the engagement letter.
c. A preliminary understanding of the prospective client's control environment.
d. The prospective client's consent to make inquiries of the predecessor auditor, if any. (5/97, Aud., #2, 6391)

34. Which of the following statements would least likely appear in an auditor's engagement letter?
a. Fees for our services are based on our regular per diem rates, plus travel and other out-of-pocket expenses.
b. During the course of our audit we may observe opportunities for economy in, or improved controls over, your operations.
c. Our engagement is subject to the risk that material errors or irregularities, including fraud and defalcations, if they exist, will **not** be detected.
d. After performing our preliminary analytical procedures we will discuss with you the other procedures we consider necessary to complete the engagement. (5/95, Aud., #3, 5621)

35. Which of the following factors most likely would cause a CPA to decide not to accept a new audit engagement?
a. The CPA's lack of understanding of the prospective client's internal auditor's computer-assisted audit techniques
b. Management's disregard of its responsibility to maintain an adequate internal control environment
c. The CPA's inability to determine whether related party transactions were consummated on terms equivalent to arm's-length transactions
d. Management's refusal to permit the CPA to perform substantive tests before the year end (R/00, Aud., #3, 6928)

36. Which of the following matters generally is included in an auditor's engagement letter?
a. Management's responsibility for the entity's compliance with laws and regulations
b. The factors to be considered in setting preliminary judgments about materiality
c. Management's vicarious liability for illegal acts committed by its employees
d. The auditor's responsibility to search for significant internal control deficiencies (R/00, Aud., #4, 6929)

37. A successor auditor should request the new client to authorize the predecessor auditor to allow a review of the predecessor's

	Engagement letter	*Working papers*
a.	Yes	Yes
b.	Yes	No
c.	No	Yes
d.	No	No

(11/96, Aud., #9, 6361)

38. Before accepting an audit engagement, a successor auditor should make specific inquiries of the predecessor auditor regarding the predecessor's
a. Awareness of the consistency in the application of generally accepted accounting principles between periods.
b. Evaluation of all matters of continuing accounting significance.
c. Understanding as to the reasons for the change of auditors.
d. Opinion of any subsequent events occurring since the predecessor's audit report was issued. (Editors, 0207)

39. Would the following factors ordinarily be considered in planning an audit engagement's personnel requirements?

	Opportunities for on-the-job training	*Continuity and periodic rotation of personnel*
a.	Yes	Yes
b.	Yes	No
c.	No	Yes
d.	No	No

(5/95, Aud., #6, 5624)

40. Which of the following procedures would an auditor most likely include in the initial planning of a financial statement audit?

a. Obtaining a written representation letter from the client's management.
b. Examining documents to detect illegal acts having a material effect on the financial statements.
c. Considering whether the client's accounting estimates are reasonable in the circumstances.
d. Determining the extent of involvement of the client's internal auditors. (11/94, Aud., #1, 5074)

41. The senior auditor responsible for coordinating the field work usually schedules a pre-audit conference with the audit team primarily to

a. Give guidance to the staff regarding both technical and personnel aspects of the audit.
b. Provide an opportunity to document staff disagreements regarding technical issues.
c. Establish the need for using the work of specialists and internal auditors.
d. Discuss staff suggestions concerning the establishment and maintenance of time budgets. (11/94, Aud., #4, amended, 5077)

42. Audit programs should be designed so that

a. Most of the required procedures can be performed as interim work.
b. Inherent risk is assessed at a sufficiently low level.
c. The auditor can make constructive suggestions to management.
d. The audit evidence gathered supports the auditor's conclusions. (11/94, Aud., #16, 5089)

43. A difference of opinion regarding the results of a sample cannot be resolved between the assistant who performed the auditing procedures and the in-charge auditor. The assistant should

a. Accept the judgment of the more experienced in-charge auditor.
b. Refuse to perform any further work on the engagement.
c. Document the disagreement and ask to be disassociated from the resolution of the matter.
d. Notify the client that a serious audit problem exists. (Editors, 0209)

44. Which of the following would an auditor most likely use in determining the auditor's preliminary judgment about materiality?

a. The anticipated sample size of the planned substantive tests.
b. The entity's annualized interim financial statements.
c. The results of the internal control questionnaire.
d. The contents of the management representation letter. (5/95, Aud., #11, 5629)

45. The risk that an auditor will conclude, based on substantive tests, that a material error does **not** exist in an account balance when, in fact, such error does exist is referred to as

a. Sampling risk.
b. Detection risk.
c. Nonsampling risk.
d. Inherent risk. (11/91, Aud., #7, 2275)

46. Which of the following audit risk components may be assessed in nonquantitative terms?

	Control risk	*Detection risk*	*Inherent risk*
a.	Yes	Yes	No
b.	Yes	No	Yes
c.	Yes	Yes	Yes
d.	No	Yes	Yes

(5/95, Aud., #10, 5628)

47. Inherent risk and control risk differ from detection risk in that inherent risk and control risk are

a. Functions of the client and its environment, while detection risk is **not**.
b. Changed at the auditor's discretion, while detection risk is **not**.
c. Considered at the individual account-balance level, while detection risk is **not**.
d. Elements of audit risk, while detection risk is **not**. (Editors, 2810)

48. Which of the following circumstances most likely would cause an auditor to consider whether material misstatements due to fraud exist in an entity's financial statements?
a. Differences are discovered during the client's annual physical inventory count.
b. Reportable conditions previously communicated have **not** been corrected.
c. Clerical errors are listed on a monthly computer-generated exception report.
d. Supporting records that should be readily available are frequently **not** produced when requested. (11/91, Aud., #12, amended, 2280)

49. Which of the following factors most likely would cause a CPA **not** to accept a new audit engagement?
a. The prospective client's unwillingness to permit inquiry of its legal counsel.
b. The inability to review the predecessor auditor's working papers.
c. The CPA's lack of understanding of the prospective client's operations and industry.
d. The indications that management has **not** investigated employees in key positions before hiring them. (11/96, Aud., #10, 6362)

50. Morris, CPA, suspects that a pervasive scheme of illegal bribes exists throughout the operations of Worldwide Import-Export Inc., a new audit client. Morris notified the audit committee and Worldwide's legal counsel, but neither could assist Morris in determining whether the amounts involved were material to the financial statements or whether senior management was involved in the scheme. Under these circumstances, Morris should
a. Express an unqualified opinion with a separate explanatory paragraph.
b. Disclaim an opinion on the financial statements.
c. Express an adverse opinion of the financial statements.
d. Issue a special report regarding the illegal bribes. (5/90, Aud., #57, 0165)

ITEMS 51 AND 52 are based on the following:

During the annual audit of Ajax Corp., a publicly held company, Jones, CPA, a continuing auditor, determined that illegal political contributions had been made during each of the past seven years, including the year under audit. Jones notified the board of directors about the illegal contributions, but they refused to take any action because the amounts involved were immaterial to the financial statements.

51. Jones should reconsider the intended degree of reliance to be placed on the
a. Letter of audit inquiry to the client's attorney.
b. Prior years' audit programs.
c. Management representation letter.
d. Preliminary judgment about materiality levels. (11/94, Aud., #12, 5085)

52. Since management took no action, Jones should
a. Report the illegal contributions to the Securities and Exchange Commission.
b. Issue an "except for" qualified opinion or an adverse opinion.
c. Disregard the political contributions since the board of directors were notified and the amounts involved were immaterial.
d. Consider withdrawing from the engagement or dissociating from any future relationship with Ajax Corp. (Editors, 9403)

53. An auditor would most likely question whether a client has committed illegal acts if the client has
a. Been forced to discontinue operations in a foreign country.
b. Been an annual donor to a local political candidate.
c. Disclosed several subsequent events involving foreign operations in the notes to the financial statements.
d. Failed to correct material weaknesses in internal control that were reported after the prior year's audit. (Editors, 0189)

54. Jones, CPA, is auditing the financial statements of XYZ Retailing Inc. What assurance does Jones provide that direct effect illegal acts that are material to XYZ's financial statements, and illegal acts that have a material, but indirect effect on the financial statements will be detected?

	Direct effect illegal acts	*Indirect effect illegal acts*
a.	Reasonable	None
b.	Reasonable	Limited
c.	Limited	None
d.	Limited	Limited

(5/94, Aud., #6, amended, 4671)

55. In identifying matters for communication with an entity's audit committee, an auditor most likely would ask management whether

a. The turnover in the accounting department was unusually high.
b. It consulted with another CPA firm about accounting matters.
c. There were any subsequent events of which the auditor was unaware.
d. It agreed with the auditor's assessed level of control risk. (5/96, Aud., #6, 6238)

OTHER OBJECTIVE FORMAT QUESTION

Problem 32-3 (15 to 25 minutes)

Bond, CPA, is considering audit risk at the financial statement level in planning the audit of Toxic Waste Disposal (TWD) Company's financial statements for the year ended December 31, 20X2. TWD is a privately-owned entity that contracts with municipal governments to remove environmental wastes. Audit risk at the financial statement level is influenced by the risk of material misstatements, which may be indicated by a combination of factors related to management, the industry, and the entity.

Based only on the information above, indicate whether each of the 15 following factors would most likely increase audit risk (I), decrease audit risk (D), or have **no** effect on audit risk (N).

Company profile

1. This was the first year TWD operated at a profit since 20X0 because the municipalities received increased federal and state funding for environmental purposes.
2. TWD's Board of Directors is controlled by Mead, the majority stockholder, who also acts as the chief executive officer.
3. The internal auditor reports to the controller and the controller reports to Mead.
4. The accounting department has experienced a high rate of turnover of key personnel.
5. TWD's bank has a loan officer who meets regularly with TWD's CEO and controller to monitor TWD's financial performance.
6. TWD's employees are paid biweekly.
7. Bond has audited TWD for five years.

Recent developments

8. During 20X2, TWD changed its method of preparing its financial statements from the cash basis to generally accepted accounting principles.
9. During 20X2, TWD sold one half of its controlling interest in United Equipment Leasing (UEL) Co. TWD retained significant interest in UEL.
10. During 20X2, litigation filed against TWD in 1995 alleging that TWD discharged pollutants into state waterways was dropped by the state. Loss contingency disclosures that TWD included in prior years' financial statements are being removed for the 20X2 financial statements.
11. During December, TWD signed a contract to lease disposal equipment from an entity owned by Mead's parents. This related party transaction is not disclosed in TWD's notes to its financial statements.
12. During December, TWD completed a barter transaction with a municipality. TWD removed waste from a municipally-owned site and acquired title to another contaminated site at below market price. TWD intends to service this new site in 20X3.
13. During December, TWD increased its casualty insurance coverage on several pieces of sophisticated machinery from historical cost to replacement cost.
14. Inquiries about the substantial increase in revenue TWD recorded in the fourth quarter of 2000 disclosed a new policy. TWD guaranteed to several municipalities that it would refund the federal and state funding paid to TWD if any municipality fails federal or state site clean-up inspection in 20X3.
15. An initial public offering of TWD's stock is planned for late 20X3.

(5/94, Aud., #3, amended, 4905-4919)

ESSAY QUESTIONS

ESSAY 32-4 (15 to 25 minutes)

Dodd, CPA, audited Adams Company's financial statements for the year ended December 31, 20X0. On November 1, 20X1, Adams notified Dodd that it was changing auditors and that Dodd's services were being terminated. On November 5, 20X1, Adams invited Hall, CPA, to make a proposal for an engagement to audit its financial statements for the year ended December 31, 20X1.

REQUIRED:

a. What procedures concerning Dodd should Hall perform before accepting the engagement?

b. What additional procedures should Hall consider performing during the planning phase of this audit (after acceptance of the engagement) that would **not** be performed during the audit of a continuing client? (11/90, Aud., #2, amended, 3023)

ESSAY 32-5 (15 to 25 minutes)

5. On October 13, 20X3, Park, CPA, was engaged to audit the financial statements of Discount Computer Company (DCC) for the year ending December 31, 20X3. DCC purchases used computers and computer parts, refurbishes whatever is salvageable, and sells the refurbished items. DCC is a new client whose common stock was first offered to the public in 20X0. DCC received an unqualified opinion on its financial statements in each of the prior three years. In accepting the engagement, Park completed all the appropriate client-acceptance procedures, which included assessing the integrity of management, communicating with the predecessor auditor, and preparing an engagement letter. Park instructed Ford, the engagement's audit team leader, to draft a planning checklist that would assist Park in preparing the six-person audit team for the field work that is scheduled to begin on December 17, 20X3. On October 25, 20X3, Ford prepared the planning checklist below.

REQUIRED:

Describe the additional considerations that should be addressed in Ford's planning checklist. Presume that the elements of Ford's planning checklist already drafted are correct.

PLANNING CHECKLIST FOR THE DISCOUNT COMPUTER COMPANY (DCC) ENGAGEMENT:

I. Understanding the assignment

In planning the audit, has the audit team considered:

- DCC's accounting policies and procedures?
- Financial statement items likely to require adjustment?
- The nature of the reports expected to be rendered?
- The coordination and cooperation of DCC's employees in data preparation and the time required for DCC's employees to perform these functions?
- The effects of accounting and auditing pronouncements, particularly new ones?

In planning the audit, has the audit team discussed:

- The general scope and timing of the audit work with DCC's management, board of directors, or audit committee?
- The extent of involvement of consultants, other independent auditors, specialists, and internal auditors?
- The methods of audit sampling to be applied by the audit team on the engagement?

II. Assigning personnel to the engagement

Has a time budget been prepared for approval by Park, the engagement partner?

Has an engagement staffing schedule been approved by Park, the engagement partner?

Have the following factors been considered in achieving a balance of personnel requirements and skills, and individual development:

- Engagement size and complexity?
- Personnel available?
- Special expertise required?
- Timing of the work to be performed?
- Opportunities for on-the-job training?

Have annual independence questionnaires been reviewed for all audit team members to assure that those individuals assigned to the engagement are independent?

III. Knowledge of the entity's business

Has the audit team obtained an overall understanding of DCC's operations by reviewing:

- The predecessor auditor's prior year's working papers, permanent file, auditors report, and DCC's prior years' financial statements?
- Interim financial statements or reports for the current year, including filings with regulatory agencies?
- Recent management/reportable conditions letters?
- DCC's correspondence file?

Has the audit team obtained knowledge of DCC's organization and operating characteristics?

Has the audit team discussed matters that may affect the audit with firm personnel responsible for non-audit services to DCC?

Has the audit team obtained a knowledge of matters affecting the industry in which DCC operates, including:

- Economic conditions?
- Current business developments?
- Government regulations?
- Changes in technology?
- Specialized industry accounting practices?
- Competitive conditions?
- Financial trends and ratios?

IV. Illegal acts

Have the following matters been considered in assessing the risk that DCC has not complied with laws and regulations that have a direct and material effect on the financial statements:

- DCC's policy relative to the prevention of illegal acts?
- Management's understanding of the requirements of laws and regulations pertinent to its business?
- Internal control components designed to give management reasonable assurance that DCC complies with those laws and regulations?

(R/00, Aud., #5, amended, 6965)

ESSAY 32-6 (20 to 25 minutes)

Kent, CPA is the engagement partner on the financial statement audit of Super Computer Services Co. (SCS) for the year ended April 30, 20X1. On May 6, 20X1, Smith, the senior auditor assigned to the engagement, had the following conversation with Kent concerning the planning phase of the audit:

Kent: Do you have all the audit programs updated yet for the SCS engagement?

Smith: Mostly, I still have work to do on the fraud risk assessment.

Kent: Why? Our "errors and irregularities" program from last year is still OK. It's passed peer review several times. Besides, we don't have specific duties regarding fraud. If we find it, we'll deal with it then.

Smith: I don't think so. That new CEO, Mint, has almost no salary, mostly bonuses and stock options. Doesn't that concern you?

Kent: No, Mint's employment contract was approved by the Board of Directors just three months ago. It was passed unanimously.

Smith: I guess so, but Mint told those stock analysts that SCS's earnings would increase 30% next year. Can Mint deliver numbers like that?

Kent: Who knows? We're auditing the 20X1 financial statements, not 20X2. Mint will probably amend that forecast every month between now and next May.

Smith: Sure, but all this may change our other audit programs.

Kent: No, it won't. The programs are fine as is. If you find fraud in any of your tests, just let me know. Maybe we'll have to extend the tests. Or maybe we'll just report it to the audit committee.

Smith: What would they do? Green is the audit committee's chair, and remember, Green hired Mint. They've been best friends for years. Besides, Mint is calling all the shots now. Brown, the old CEO, is still on the Board, but Brown's never around. Brown's even been skipping the Board meetings. Nobody in management or on the Board would stand up to Mint.

Kent: That's nothing new. Brown was like that years ago. Brown caused frequent disputes with Jones, CPA, the predecessor auditor. Three years ago, Jones told Brown how ineffective the internal audit department was then. Next thing you know, Jones is out and I'm in. Why bother? I'm just as happy that those understaffed internal auditors don't get in our way. Just remember, the bottom line is...are the financial statements fairly presented? And they always have been. We don't provide any assurances about fraud. That's management's job.

Smith: But what about the lack of segregation of duties in the cash disbursements department? That clerk could write a check for anything.

Kent: Sure. That's a reportable condition every year and probably will be again this year. But we're talking cost-effectiveness here, not fraud. We just have to do lots of testing on cash disbursements and report it again.

Smith: What about the big layoffs coming up next month? It's more than a rumor. Even the employees know it's going to happen, and they're real uptight about it.

Kent: I know, it's the worst kept secret at SCS, but we don't have to consider that now. Even if it happens, it will only improve next year's financial results. Brown should have let these people go years ago. Let's face it, how else can Mint even come close to the 30% earnings increase next year?

REQUIRED:

a. Describe the fraud risk factors that are indicated in the accompanying dialogue.

b. Describe Kent's misconceptions regarding the consideration of fraud in the audit of SCS's financial statements that are contained in the dialogue above **and** explain why each is a misconception.

c. Describe an auditor's working paper documentation requirements regarding the assessment of the risk of material misstatement due to fraud.

(5/98, Aud., #2, amended, 6635-6637)

ESSAY 32-7 (25 to 35 minutes)

Smith, CPA, is the supervising partner of the financial statement audit of Digit Sales Co., a publicly-held entity that files reports with the SEC. Hall, the senior auditor assigned to the engagement, had the following conversation with Smith at the end of the field work:

Smith: Don't you think that Digit's board of directors would be surprised with those huge inventory adjustments that we had Digit book last week?

Hall: I guess so, but what about that new assistant controller, Green? What incompetence!

Smith: Well, I suppose Green has a bit to learn about GAAP, but I was really upset when Dodd, the controller, contacted that other CPA firm about the contingent liability I wanted booked.

Hall: Which one was that?

Smith: You know, the employment discrimination suit filed by the union.

Hall: Oh, now I remember. Digit's going to lose that one big time.

Smith: Right! You know it. I know it. The lawyer knows it. Even Dodd knows it, but it wasn't booked until the other CPAs agreed with me.

Hall: Well, the important thing is that they did book it. I was more upset about their two-week delay in having the financial statements completed on time.

Smith: I know it cost us a lot of time, but Dodd was never late on that before. Maybe I should change the dates on next year's engagement letter rather than complain to the board.

Hall: How about that large receivable?

Smith: What a joke! Dodd wouldn't write that overdue account off and Digit doesn't even sell that model anymore. At least Green was on our side.

Hall: They never did collect a penny on that account.

Smith: I heard that the customer finally filed for bankruptcy last month.

Hall: At least Dodd finally booked the write-off after that poorly-timed vacation.

Smith: I suppose so, but I still can't believe that Dodd took two weeks off near the end of our field work.

Hall: Actually, that was great. With Dodd gone, Green booked that inventory adjustment without much of a battle.

Smith: Sure, but we couldn't finish the field work until Dodd signed the rep letter and booked that receivable write-off. The report was late and it caused me grief with our managing partner.

Hall: But that's not fair. It wasn't our fault. The bottom line is they got a clean opinion and this job is history.

Smith: Not really. We haven't communicated with the audit committee yet.

Hall: What do we have to tell them? They got an unqualified opinion...and remember, there were only a few reportable conditions. I'm out of here.

REQUIRED:

a. From the discussion above, what specific matters is Smith **required** to communicate to Digit's audit committee? Do **not** include matters that are **not required** to be communicated under GAAS.

b. What other matters (omitted from the discussion above) is Smith **required** to communicate to Digit's audit committee under GAAS?

(11/96, Aud., #3, amended, 6386)

SOLUTION 32-1 MULTIPLE CHOICE ANSWERS

APPOINTMENT & PLANNING

1. (b) AU 310.06 states that an understanding with the client regarding a financial statement audit generally includes that "...the auditor is responsible for ensuring that the audit committee or others with equivalent authority or responsibility are aware of any reportable conditions which come to his or her attention."

2. (d) AU 311.06 states that the auditor should obtain a level of knowledge of the entity's business that will enable him or her to plan and perform the audit in accordance with GAAS...and this knowledge should enable him or her to obtain an understanding of the events and transactions that may have a significant effect on the financial statements. Answer (a) would be a possible result of obtaining an understanding of the internal control structure of the client. Answers (b) and (c) would be required of the auditor regardless of the business and industry knowledge obtained about the client.

3. (a) Gaining an understanding of internal control is the first of these four procedures to be performed in an audit. The entity's risk assessment process is part of its internal control. The auditor identifies specific activities designed to prevent fraud when considering relying on internal control. The other two options are substantive tests of evidence.

4. (c) If sufficient competent evidence is not available to support an opinion, an audit cannot be performed. In many online systems, most routine transaction details are not available after a specified period of time. Internal control is usually subject to management override. Consultation with several accounting firms reflects management's concern over proper accounting and reporting.

PREDECESSOR & SUCCESSOR AUDITORS

5. (a) The successor auditor uses the predecessor's work papers as a start for obtaining confidence in beginning balances. This can encompass a review of virtually all of the predecessor's work papers.

6. (d) AU 315.06 states, "[The successor auditor's] inquiries should include specific questions regarding, among other things, facts that might bear on the integrity of management; on disagreements with management as to accounting principles, auditing procedures, or other similarly significant matters; and on the predecessor's understanding as to the reasons for the change of auditors." The auditor would use other sources for learning specialized accounting principles of the client's industry and the inherent uncertainty in applying sampling procedures. The competency of the client's internal audit staff should be an evaluation of the current auditor.

7. (b) AU 315.10 states that if during an audit, the successor auditor "becomes aware of information that leads [the auditor] to believe the financial statements reported on by the predecessor auditor may require revision, [the successor auditor] should request his [or her] client to arrange a meeting among the three parties to resolve the matter. If the client refuses or if the successor is not satisfied with the result, the successor auditor should consult with an attorney in determining an appropriate course of action."

PLANNING & SUPERVISION

8. (b) AU 329.06 states, "The purpose of applying analytical procedures [for example, comparing recorded amounts to anticipated results] is to assist the auditor in planning the nature, timing, and extent of auditing procedures that will be used to obtain evidential matter for account balances." Inquiry of the client's legal counsel is an audit procedure that would be performed near the end of the audit engagement. AU 319.21 states that the auditor is not required to obtain knowledge about operating effectiveness as part of the understanding of internal control. Answer (c) is a substantive audit procedure that would be performed near the end of the audit engagement to support management's assertion of completeness.

9. (a) Consideration of the entity's internal control is part of the planning of the audit. An engagement letter is recommended, but not

required, by GAAS. Reportable conditions are usually communicated to the audit committee during the audit (as they become known) or at the end. The search for unrecorded liabilities is part of the performance of the audit program.

10. (d) When the auditor is developing a preliminary audit strategy, the auditor has not performed sampling, interim tests, nor inquiry of the client's attorney. In planning the audit, the auditor should consider, among other matters, the planned assessed level of control risk (AU 311.03).

11. (d) "Procedures that an auditor may consider in planning the audit usually involve review of his [or her] records relating to the entity and discussion with other firm personnel and personnel of the entity." An example of these procedures would be the establishment of the timing of the audit work (AU 311.04). The other answers would be considered subsequent to the planning process.

12. (c) AU 311.13 states, "The work performed by each assistant should be reviewed to determine whether it was adequately performed and to evaluate whether the results are consistent with the conclusions to be presented in the auditor's report."

13. (c) The auditor should prepare a written set of audit programs. Such written audit programs should detail the specific audit procedures that are necessary to accomplish the objectives of the audit (AU 311.05). All material transactions and all account balances are not required to be tested in all circumstances. Minimizing substantive tests prior to the balance sheet date is not required.

14. (b) AU 311 states that the auditor should inform assistants of their responsibilities and the objective of the audit procedures they are to perform in sufficient detail so that they understand what they are doing. Assistants should be informed of matters that affect the procedures the assistants perform, such as the nature of the client's business. The in-charge auditor should instruct assistants to bring to his or her attention significant questions raised during the audit so the in-charge auditor can assess their significance. As the auditor would most likely report to the client's audit committee, the in-charge auditor would not need to outline to assistants what would be included in that report. Answers (c) and (d) are less vital duties than audit procedure evaluation.

AUDIT RISK & MATERIALITY

15. (b) AU 312.03 states that the concept of materiality recognizes that some matters affect the fair presentation of financial statements, while others do not. Materiality judgments involve both quantitative and qualitative considerations. In making the assessment of materiality, an auditor should consider the needs of a reasonable person who would rely on the financial statements.

16. (c) The assertions in the prior year (audited) financial statements are the most likely determining factor. The current year financial statements may have considerable under- or overstatements. Materiality impacts the preliminary level of control risk and anticipated sample size for planned substantive tests, rather than the reverse.

17. (b) If an auditor must decrease detection risk, the auditor should change the nature, extent, or timing of audit procedures. Performing procedures closer to the balance sheet date allows less opportunity for misstatements due to roll-forward adjustments to the auditor's preliminary work. The increase in the assessed level of control risk is a cause of decrease in the amount of misstatements that an auditor can tolerate. A decrease in the amount of misstatements would increase, not decrease, the extent of auditing procedures.

SUBSTANTIVE TESTS PRIOR TO BALANCE SHEET DATE

18. (a) While the confirmation of accounts *receivable* and the other answer options are common audit procedures, confirmation of accounts *payable* is an extended procedure and usually occurs under unusual conditions. AU 330.07 states, "The greater the combined level of risk, the greater the assurance that the auditor needs from substantive tests related to a financial statement assertion....In these situations, the auditor might use confirmation procedures rather than or in conjunction with tests directed toward documents or parties within the entity." In a low risk situation, review of post balance sheet date payments to vendors may adequately substantiate the accounts payable balance.

ERRORS & FRAUD

19. (d) AU 316.07 states, "Due professional care requires the auditor to exercise professional skepticism. Professional skepticism is an attitude that includes a questioning mind and a critical assessment of audit evidence."

20. (a) AU 316.10 states that because of the characteristics of fraud, "even a properly designed and planned audit may not detect a material misstatement resulting from fraud." Audit procedures that are effective for detecting unintentional misstatements may be ineffective for intentional misstatements concealed through collusion.

21. (d) AU 110.02 states, "The auditor has a responsibility to plan and perform the audit to obtain reasonable assurance about whether the financial statements are free of material misstatements, whether caused by error or fraud."

22. (d) AU 316.40 states, "Disclosure of possible fraud to parties other than the client's senior management and its audit committee ordinarily is not part of the auditor's responsibility, and ordinarily would be precluded by the auditor's ethical or legal obligation of confidentiality unless the matter is reflected in the auditor's report. The auditor should recognize, however, that in the following circumstances a duty to disclose outside the client may exist: (a) [when the entity reports an auditor change under the appropriate securities law on Form 8-K due to the possible fraud or pursuant to the Private Securities Litigation Reform Act of 1995 relating to an illegal act that has a material effect of the financial statements], (b) to a successor auditor when the successor makes inquiries in accordance with [AU 315]..., (c) in response to a subpoena, and (d) to a funding agency or other specified agency in accordance with requirements for the audits of entities that receive governmental financial assistance."

23. (a) It is unusual to have no increase in cash flows from operations when reporting earnings growth. A lack of interest in increasing stock trends would reduce the risk of fraudulent reporting. Plentiful liquid assets are characteristic of an financially secure entity. The management of a financially secure entity has little motivation for fraudulent reporting. Debt covenants are common practice in some industries; the existence of a covenant may reduce risk as there is increased scrutiny of budgets and other financial information.

Illegal Acts by Clients

24. (d) If management fails to take appropriate remedial action when informed of illegal acts, management's integrity and representations may be questionable. The auditor should consider withdrawal if illegal payments do not violate the client's policies. If the client receives financial assistance from the government, the discovery of illegal acts may increase the auditor's reporting responsibilities. It is not in employees' interests to document their illegal acts, so it would not be surprising that documentation might not exist.

25. (a) AU 317.10 states, "When the auditor becomes aware of information concerning a possible illegal act, the auditor should obtain an understanding of the nature of the act, the circumstances in which it occurred, and sufficient other information to evaluate the effect on the financial statements." Obtaining an understanding of the act will not necessarily affect the reliability of management's representations (AU 317.12). Consideration of whether other similar acts may have occurred is an additional procedure used, if necessary, by the auditor to obtain further understanding of the nature of the acts. It would not be considered until after the auditor determined the effect of the act on the financial statements (AU 317.11). While the occurrence of illegal acts will be communicated to the audit committee, the auditor will not necessarily recommend remedial actions.

26. (a) AU 317.07 states, "If specific information comes to the auditor's attention that provides evidence concerning the existence of possible illegal acts that could have a material indirect effect on the financial statements, the auditor should apply audit procedures specifically directed to ascertaining whether an illegal act has occurred." Only after determining that an illegal act has occurred would the auditor contemplate the steps in the alternatives.

27. (a) AU 317.16 states, "The auditor should consider the implications of an illegal act in relation to other aspects of the audit, particularly the reliability of representations of management." A relatively small misstatement of unretired fixed assets, improperly authorized petty cash fund disbursement, or uncollectible account receivable that was not written off have less impact on the financial statements taken as a whole and, by themselves, do not tend to place doubt on the integrity of management.

28. (b) Large cash payments are unusual in normal, legal business practice. Cash transactions have the attribute of anonymity, which is useful for hiding illegal acts. Properly disclosed related party transactions and contributions to several local candidates, in and of themselves, do not suggest the occurrence of illegal acts. Internal control procedures are subject to cost/benefit constraints. An entity may appropriately decide that a major weakness is too costly to alleviate.

COMMUNICATIONS WITH AUDIT COMMITTEE

29. (b) While the amount of misstatements that would be material may be discussed with the audit committee, the auditor *must* report the methods used to account for significant unusual transactions (AU 380.07) and disagreements with management, whether or not satisfactorily resolved (AU 380.11). The auditor also has the responsibility to report reportable conditions and material weaknesses. Indications of fraud and illegal acts are listed as examples of material weaknesses in AU 325.21.

30. (b) An auditor who becomes aware of possible illegal activities shall inform the entity's management. If the auditor concludes that the illegal act has a material effect on the financial statements and management has not taken appropriate remedial actions, and departure from a standard report seems reasonable, the auditor shall directly report this to the board of directors. The entity is required to notify the SEC no later than 1 business day after receipt of such report. If the entity fails to notify the SEC within 1 business day, the auditor must resign from the engagement and/or report to the SEC within 1 business day.

SOLUTION 32-2 ADDITIONAL MULTIPLE CHOICE ANSWERS

APPOINTMENT & PLANNING

31. (a) The auditor should obtain sufficient knowledge about the accounting system because the methods influence the design of internal control. Materiality levels, audit objectives, and an auditor's acceptable level of audit risk are independent of the methods used to process accounting information.

32. (c) In the planning phase of an audit a CPA most likely would coordinate with client personnel, requiring a discussion of the timing of audit procedures, such as a physical count of inventory. An auditor would identify specific internal control activities that are likely to prevent fraud during the review of internal control or when fraud factors are discovered. An auditor would evaluate the reasonableness of a client's accounting estimates and inquire of a client's attorney regarding unrecorded claims when collecting evidence.

33. (d) If a prospective client refuses to permit a predecessor auditor to respond to a successor's questions, the successor auditor should inquire as to the reasons and consider the implications of that refusal in deciding whether to accept that engagement. Obtaining an understanding of the client's industry and business may be done after accepting an engagement to audit a client. The client's signature on an engagement letter is never *required* by GAAS. A preliminary understanding of the client's control environment is obtained after the engagement is accepted.

34. (d) AAM 3130.01 states, "In an engagement letter, the firm and the client indicate their mutual understanding and agree to the nature and terms of the engagement." Answer (a) would be included as part of the terms of the engagement. Answer (b) would be included to indicate the nature of the services the client could expect in the engagement. Answer (c) would be included to establish the mutual understanding of some of the limitations inherent in an audit due to less than 100% testing of all accounts. The auditor would usually not outline to the client the specific procedures to be performed during the audit.

35. (b) Management's carelessness regarding an adequate internal control environment may make it improbable that an auditor will be able to collect sufficient evidential matter to form an opinion. An auditor need not understand the internal auditor's techniques, particularly before accepting an engagement. The auditor merely needs to determine if related party transactions are properly disclosed, not whether they occur similarly to arm's-length transactions. Performing substantive tests at year-end is adequate if all records are available.

36. (a) The engagement letter helps to ensure that the auditor and client both clearly understand the services the auditor is engaged to perform. Management's responsibilities are a large part of the understanding the auditor and client must reach; the engagement letter documents this understanding. The auditor sets materiality without consulting, or generally even officially informing, management. Management's liability for employee acts is irrelevant to the engagement terms. An auditor is not responsible to search for internal control deficiencies.

PREDECESSOR & SUCCESSOR AUDITORS

37. (c) AU §315 states that prior to acceptance of the engagement, the successor auditor should make specific and reasonable inquiries of the predecessor regarding matters that the successor believes will assist in determining whether to accept the engagement. This information should be in the

predecessor's working papers. Review of an engagement letter is unlikely to be of much use to a successor auditor, as the predecessor likely uses a similar letter for all audit clients.

38. (c) AU 315.06 states, "The successor auditor should make specific and reasonable inquiries of the predecessor regarding matters that the successor believes will assist him [or her] in determining whether to accept the engagement. His [or her] inquiries should include specific questions regarding, among other things, facts that might bear on the integrity of management; on disagreements with management as to accounting principles, auditing procedures, or other similarly significant matters; and on the predecessor's understanding as to the reasons for the change of auditors."

PLANNING & SUPERVISION

39. (a) The auditor uses professional judgment in planning an audit engagement's personnel requirements; the auditor has final responsibility and may delegate portions of the audit functions to other firm personnel, referred to in the code as "assistants." Opportunities for on-the-job training as well as continuity and periodic rotation of personnel are all valid factors the auditor may consider in this task.

40. (d) Of the procedures listed, an auditor is most likely to determine the extent of involvement of the client's internal auditors in the initial planning of a financial statement audit. A written representation letter from the client's management is usually obtained at the end of an audit, not the beginning. Examining documents and considering the reasonableness of estimates are procedures that are done during the audit.

41. (a) In a pre-audit conference, a senior auditor would most likely discuss the technical and personnel aspects of a job. Feedback from the staff would occur later. Establishing the need for specialists and the use of internal auditors is done during the planning stage. Answer (b) is done during field work.

42. (d) The primary purpose of the audit is to gather sufficient evidence to support the auditor's conclusions. The design of the audit program has no effect on inherent risk. Procedures *may* be performed prior to the balance sheet date only if the effectiveness of interim work is not likely to be impaired. Suggestions to management are secondary considerations in an audit.

43. (c) AU 9311.37 states, "...each assistant has a professional responsibility to bring to the attention of the appropriate individuals in the firm, disagreements or concerns the assistant might have....In addition, each assistant should have a right to document his [or her] disagreement if he [or she] believes it is necessary to disassociate himself [or herself] from the resolution of the matter."

AUDIT RISK & MATERIALITY

44. (b) Materiality considerations for planning purposes are generally based on the financial statements to be audited. Alternatively, the auditor may base the assessment of materiality on the entity's annualized interim financial statements (AU 312.14). The anticipated sample size of the planned tests and the internal control questionnaire are, if anything, dependent on materiality, not vice versa. The contents of the management representation letter (with a date the same as the auditor's report) are not always known during the planning stages of the audit.

45. (b) AU 312.20 states, "Detection risk is the risk that the auditor will not detect a material misstatement that exists in an assertion....Inherent risk is the susceptibility of an assertion to a material misstatement assuming that there are no related internal control structure policies or procedures." "Sampling risk arises from the possibility that, when a test of controls or a substantive test is restricted to a sample, the auditor's conclusions may be different from the conclusions he [or she] would reach if the test were applied in the same way to all items in the account balance or class of transactions." (AU 350.10) "Nonsampling risk includes all the aspects of audit risk that are not due to sampling." (AU 350.11)

46. (c) All three components of audit risk (inherent, control, and detection) may be assessed quantitatively or nonquantitatively (AU 312.21).

47. (a) Inherent risk is the susceptibility of an assertion to a material misstatement, assuming that there are no related internal control policies and procedures. Control risk is the risk that a material misstatement that could occur in an assertion will not be prevented or detected on a timely basis by the entity's internal control policies or procedures. Detection risk is the risk that the auditor will not detect a material misstatement that exists in an assertion. Thus, inherent risk and control risk are functions of the client and its environment while detection risk is not. Inherent risk, control risk, and detection risk are all a part of audit risk (AU 312.20). Inherent risk and control risk differ from detection

risk in that they exist independently of the audit of financial statements, whereas detection risk relates to the auditor's procedures and can be changed at his or her discretion (AU 312.21). All of the elements of audit risk (inherent, control, and detection risk) should be considered at the individual account-balance or class-of-transactions level because such consideration directly assists the auditor in determining the scope of auditing procedures for the balance or class of related assertions (AU 312.19).

Errors & Fraud

48. (d) AU 316.25 states, "The assessment of the risk of material misstatement due to fraud is a cumulative process that includes a consideration of risk factors individually and in combination...other conditions may be identified during fieldwork that change or support a judgment regarding the assessment...." One of the examples given of such a circumstance is when unusual delays by the entity occur in providing requested information. Another is when the client denies access to records, certain employees, facilities, customers, etc. from whom audit evidence might be sought.

49. (a) The refusal of a client to allow necessary communications with a lawyer is a scope limitation that usually results in a disclaimer of opinion. Requesting permission to obtain information from a predecessor is a necessary step in an audit. However, the predecessor may deny access to some or all working papers. The CPA may acquire an understanding of a client's operations and industry after the audit engagement has been accepted. There is no requirement that management investigate key employees before hiring them. (Internal controls are subject to cost benefit restraints.)

Illegal Acts by Clients

50. (b) When the auditor is unable to conclude whether the financial statements are materially misstated due to an illegal act, he or she should disclaim an opinion or issue a qualified opinion on the financial statements.

51. (c) AU 317.16 states, "The auditor should consider the implications of an illegal act in relation to other aspects of the audit, particularly the reliability of representations of management."

52. (d) AU 317.22 states, "...the auditor may conclude that withdrawal is necessary when the client does not take the remedial action that the auditor considers necessary in the circumstances even when the illegal act is not material to the financial statements."

53. (a) Forced discontinuance of operations in a foreign country may indicate illegal acts. Annual donations to a local politician generally are not illegal. Management may elect not to correct material weaknesses if the cost of correction would exceed the benefit. Disclosure of subsequent events generally would not cause the auditor to question whether illegal acts have occurred.

54. (a) AU 316.05 states that the auditor should assess the risk that errors and fraud may cause the financial statements to contain a material misstatement, and based on that assessment, the auditor should design the audit to provide reasonable assurance of detecting errors and fraud that are material to the financial statements. AU 317.07 states, "Because of the characteristics of illegal acts...[having material but indirect effects on the financial statements]...an audit made in accordance with generally accepted auditing standards provides no assurance that [indirect] illegal acts...will be disclosed."

Communications With Audit Committee

55. (b) AU 380.12 states, "In some cases, management may decide to consult with other accountants about auditing and accounting matters. When the auditor is aware that such consultation has occurred, he [or she] should discuss with the audit committee his [or her] views about significant matters that were the subject of such consultation." The rate of turnover being too high is a judgment of the auditor. The question of subsequent events would not be discussed when an auditor is identifying matters for communication with an entity's audit committee. Management's agreement with the auditor's assessed level of control risk is irrelevant.

PERFORMANCE BY SUBTOPICS

Each category below parallels a subtopic covered in Chapter 32. Record the number and percentage of questions you correctly answered in each subtopic area.

Appointment & Planning

Question #	Correct √
1	
2	
3	
4	
# Questions	4
# Correct	
% Correct	

Predecessor & Successor Auditors

Question #	Correct √
5	
6	
7	
# Questions	3
# Correct	
% Correct	

Planning & Supervision

Question #	Correct √
8	
9	
10	
11	
12	
13	
14	
# Questions	7
# Correct	
% Correct	

Audit Risk & Materiality

Question #	Correct √
15	
16	
17	
# Questions	3
# Correct	
% Correct	

Substantive Tests Prior to Balance Sheet Date

Question #	Correct √
18	
# Questions	1
# Correct	
% Correct	

Errors & Fraud

Question #	Correct √
19	
20	
21	
22	
23	
# Questions	5
# Correct	
% Correct	

Illegal Acts by Clients

Question #	Correct √
24	
25	
26	
27	
28	
# Questions	5
# Correct	
% Correct	

Communications With Audit Committee

Question #	Correct √
29	
30	
# Questions	2
# Correct	
% Correct	

OTHER OBJECTIVE FORMAT QUESTION SOLUTION

PROBLEM 32-3 AUDIT RISK

1. D The organization's ability to continue as a going concern decreases audit risk.

2. I Audit risk is increased when management operating and financial decisions are dominated by one person.

3. I Audit risk is increased when the internal auditors report to the person they are evaluating (i.e., controller).

4. I High turnover of accounting personnel increases the potential for errors due to poorly trained personnel and, thus, increases audit risk.

5. D The monitoring of financial performance decreases audit risk.

6. N The pay period has no effect on audit risk since it has no effect on the possibility for error or fraud.

7. D Audit risk is decreased due to familiarity with the audit history, client industry, and client procedures.

8. I Changing accounting methods increases audit risk due to the complicated accounting issues involved.

9. I The retention of a significant interest, while losing decision-making powers in the operations of the company, results in increased audit risk.

10. D The settlement of a contingency reduces audit risk.

11. I Related party transactions increase audit risk.

12. I Difficult-to-audit transactions, such as the barter transaction, increase audit risk.

13. N The increase in casualty insurance coverage has no effect on the possibility of errors and fraud and, therefore, does not effect audit risk.

14. I The guarantee represents a loss contingency which could result in revenue not being realized. Therefore, audit risk is increased.

15. I The impending initial public offering could cause an unduly aggressive attitude toward financial reporting and an emphasis on meeting earnings projections in an effort to improve the financial results. Therefore, audit risk is increased.

ESSAY SOLUTIONS

SOLUTION 32-4 NEW CLIENT PROCEDURES

a. The procedures Hall should perform before accepting the engagement include the following:

1. Hall should explain to Adams the need to make an **inquiry of Dodd** and should **request permission** to do so.
2. Hall should ask Adams to authorize Dodd to respond fully to Hall's inquiries.
3. If Adams **refuses** to permit Dodd to respond or limits Dodd's response, Hall should **inquire as to the reasons** and **consider** the implications in deciding **whether to accept the engagement.**
4. Hall should make **specific and reasonable inquiries** of Dodd regarding matters Hall believes will assist in determining whether to accept the engagement, including specific questions regarding

- Facts that might bear on the **integrity of management.**
- **Disagreements with management** as to accounting principles, auditing procedures, or other similarly significant matters.
- Dodd's understanding as to the **reasons for the change** of auditors.

5. If Hall receives a **limited response**, Hall should **consider its implications** in deciding whether to accept the engagement.

b. The additional procedures Hall should consider performing during the planning phase of this audit that would not be performed during the audit of a continuing client may include the following:

1. Hall may apply appropriate **auditing procedures** to the account balances at the **beginning of the audit period** and, possibly, to transactions in prior periods.
2. Hall may make **specific inquiries** of Dodd regarding matters Hall believes may affect the conduct of the audit, such as

- Audit areas that have required an inordinate amount of time.
- Audit problems that arose from the condition of the accounting system and records.

3. Hall may request Adams to authorize Dodd to allow a **review of Dodd's working papers.**
4. Hall should **document compliance** with **firm policy** regarding acceptance of a new client.
5. Hall should start obtaining the **documentation** needed to create a **permanent working paper file.**

SOLUTION 32-5 PLANNING & SUPERVISION

The following are the additional considerations that Ford should have addressed in the planning checklist:

Ford omitted the necessary reference to preparing a **written audit program** that should set forth in reasonable detail the audit procedures that are necessary to accomplish the objectives of the audit.

Ford did not include "**minutes of meetings of DCC's stockholders and its board of directors**" among the documents that the audit team should review to obtain an understanding of DDC's business.

Ford omitted the necessary reference to obtaining an **understanding of internal control** or its components **sufficient to plan the audit** of DCC's financial statements.

Ford did not address the auditor's requirement to consider audit risk and materiality. In planning the audit, Park will use judgment as to the **appropriately low level** of **audit risk** and **preliminary judgment** about **materiality**, but Ford omitted any reference to these two concepts in the draft of the planning checklist.

Ford did not address the auditor's requirement to **assess fraud risk**. This assessment of the risk of material misstatement due to fraud is necessary in designing the audit procedures to be performed.

Ford omitted any consideration of the methods that DCC uses to **process accounting information**.

Finally, Ford did not include any questions or comments regarding the auditor's requirement to **perform analytical procedures** during the planning stage of the audit.

SOLUTION 32-6 FRAUD

a. There are many fraud risk factors that are indicated in the dialogue. Among the fraud risk factors are the following:

- A significant portion of Mint's compensation is represented by **bonuses and stock options**. Although this arrangement has been approved by SCS's Board of Directors, this may be a motivation for Mint, the new CEO, to engage in fraudulent financial reporting.

- Mint's statement to the stock analysts that SCS's earnings would increase 30% next year may be both an **unduly aggressive and unrealistic forecast**. That forecast may tempt Mint to intentionally misstate certain ending balances this year that would increase the profitability of the next year.

- SCS's audit committee may not be **sufficiently objective** because Green, the chair of the audit committee, hired Mint, the new CEO, and they have been best friends for years

- **One individual**, Mint, appears to **dominate management** without any compensating controls. Mint seems to be making all the important decisions without any apparent input from other members of management or resistance from the Board of Directors.

- There were frequent disputes between Brown, the prior CEO, who like Mint apparently dominated management and the Board of Directors, and Jones, the predecessor auditor. This fact may indicate that an **environment** exists in which management will be reluctant to make any changes that Kent suggests.

- Management seems to be satisfied with an understaffed and ineffective internal audit department. This situation displays an **inappropriate attitude** regarding the internal control environment.

- Management has failed to properly monitor and correct a significant deficiency in its internal control—the lack of segregation of duties in cash disbursements. This **disregard for the control environment** is also a risk factor.

- Information about anticipated future layoffs has spread among the employees. This information may cause an increase in the risk of material misstatement arising from the misappropriation of assets by **dissatisfied employees**.

b. Kent has many misconceptions regarding the consideration of fraud in the audit of SCS's financial statements that are contained in the dialogue. Among Kent's misconceptions are the following:

- Kent states that an auditor does not have specific duties regarding fraud. In fact, an auditor has a responsibility to **specifically assess** the risk of material misstatement due to fraud and to **consider that assessment** in designing the audit procedures to be performed.

- Kent is not concerned about Mint's employment contract. Kent should be concerned about a CEO's contract that is based primarily on **bonuses and stock options** because such an arrangement may indicate a **motivation** for management to engage in fraudulent financial reporting.

- Kent does not think that Mint's forecast for 20X2 has an effect on the financial statement audit for 20X1. However, Kent should consider the possibility that Mint may **intentionally misstate** the 20X1 ending balances to increase the reported profit in 20X2.

- Kent believes that the audit programs are fine as is. Actually, Kent should **modify** the audit programs because of the many risk factors that are present in the SCS audit.

- Kent is not concerned that the internal audit department is ineffective and understaffed. In fact, Kent should be concerned that SCS has **permitted this situation to continue** because it represents a risk factor relating to misstatements arising from fraudulent financial reporting and/or the misappropriation of assets.

- Kent states that an auditor provides no assurances about fraud because that's management's job. In fact, an auditor has a responsibility to **plan and perform** an audit to obtain **reasonable assurance** about whether the financial statements are free of material misstatement, **whether caused by error or fraud**.

- Kent is not concerned that the prior year's reportable condition has not been corrected. However, Kent should be concerned that the **lack of segregation of duties** in the cash disbursements department represents a risk factor relating to misstatements arising from the misappropriation of assets.

- Kent does not believe that the rumors about big layoffs in the next month have an effect on audit planning. In planning the audit, Kent should consider this risk factor because it may cause an increase in the risk of material misstatement arising from the misappropriation of assets by **dissatisfied employees**.

c. In planning a financial statement audit, the auditor should **document** in the working papers evidence of the performance of the assessment of the **risk of material misstatement due to fraud**. Where risk factors are identified, the documentation should include those **risk factors identified** and the **auditor's response** to those risk factors, individually or in combination. In addition, during the performance of the audit, the auditor may identify fraud risk factors or other conditions that cause the auditor to believe that an **additional response** is required. The auditor should document such risk factors or other conditions, and any further response that the auditor concludes is appropriate.

SOLUTION 32-7 AUDIT COMMITTEE

a. Smith should inform Digit's audit committee about the inventory **adjustments arising from the audit**. These adjustments probably have a significant effect on the financial statements and should be included amount the required matters to be communicated to the audit committee.

Dodd's consultation with another CPA firm concerning the previously unrecorded contingent liability should also be discussed with the audit committee. Smith should make the audit committee aware of Smith's views about any **significant matters that were the subject of that consultation.**

Smith should also inform the audit committee of any **serious difficulties encountered in dealing with management** related to the performance of the audit. Specifically, the two-week delay in completing the financial statements and the unavailability of Dodd, the controller, near the end of the field work should be reported to the audit committee.

Smith's **disagreement** with Dodd over the write-off of the overdue account receivable, **even though satisfactorily resolved**, should also be discussed with the audit committee.

Finally, the **reportable conditions** that Smith became aware of during the audit should be communicated to the audit committee.

b. In order for Digit's audit committee to understand the nature of the assurance that an audit provides, Smith should communicate the **level of responsibility assumed under generally accepted auditing standards**. The audit committee should understand that an audit is designed to obtain **reasonable, rather than absolute, assurance** about the financial statements.

Smith should also determine that Digit's audit committee is informed about the initial selection of and changes in **significant accounting policies and their application**. The audit committee would be interested in the methods Digit uses to account for **significant unusual transactions** and accounting policies in controversial or emerging areas for which there is no authoritative guidance or consensus.

The audit committee should also be informed about the **accounting estimates** that are based upon management's judgments, the processes used to formulate particularly sensitive estimates, and the basis for Smith's conclusions regarding the reasonableness of those estimates.

Additionally, Smith should discuss with the audit committee Smith's responsibility for **other information in documents containing audited financial statements**, such as the "Management's Discussion and Analysis of Financial Condition and Results of Operations" that is presented in the annual report to shareholders. Smith should also discuss any procedures performed and the results.

Smith should also discuss with the audit committee any **major issues** that were discussed with management in connection with the recurring retention of Smith's CPA firm, including discussions regarding the application of accounting principles and auditing standards.

Finally, Smith should be assured that the audit committee is informed about any **fraud** and **illegal acts** that Smith becomes aware of during the audit unless those matters are clearly inconsequential. However, if senior management is involved in fraud or an illegal act, Smith should communicate directly with the audit committee.

VIDEOTAPE CROSS REFERENCE

The videotapes are designed to supplement all of our study packages. They contain concise, informative lectures, as well as CPA exam tips, tricks, and techniques to help you learn the material needed to pass the exam. The **HotSpots™** videotapes concentrate on particular topics. Use them to study the areas that are most troubling for you. Each one of the **Intensive** video programs covers one of the four exam sections. The **Intensive** videotapes are designed for final, intensive review, after you already have done considerable work. Alternatively, the **Intensive** videotapes may be used as both a preview and a final review. Please see the information in the **Getting Started** section of this volume for a discussion on integrating videos into your study plan. This information is accurate as we go to press, but it is subject to change without notice.

Video Title	Text Chapters	Approx. Time
HotSpots™ Assets	2, 4, 5	4:15
HotSpots™ Inventory	3	2:25
HotSpots™ Bonds & Other Liabilities	6, 7	4:00
HotSpots™ Leases & Pensions	8, 9	2:50
HotSpots™ Owners' Equity	10	2:50
HotSpots™ Revenue Recognition & Income Statement Presentation	11, 12	3:00
HotSpots™ FASB 109: Accounting for Income Taxes	13	2:00
HotSpots™ FASB 95: Statement of Cash Flows	14	2:00
HotSpots™ EPS & Everything Else	15 - 18	3:00
HotSpots™ Consolidations	19, 20	5:00
HotSpots™ Governmental & Nonprofit Accounting	21 - 23	5:40
HotSpots™ Cost & Managerial Accounting	24 - 26	3:20
HotSpots™ General Taxation	27, 29	3:00
HotSpots™ Individual Taxation	27	3:00
HotSpots™ Property Taxation	28	2:30
HotSpots™ Corporate Taxation	29	3:20
HotSpots™ Partnerships & Other Tax Topics	30	3:00
HotSpots™ Audit Planning & Standards	31, 32	3:05
HotSpots™ Internal Control	33, 34	2:10
HotSpots™ Audit Evidence	35, 36	2:25
HotSpots™ EDP Auditing & Statistical Sampling	37, 38	2:50
HotSpots™ Standard Audit Reports	39	2:55
HotSpots™ Other Reports, Reviews & Compilations	40, 41	1:50
HotSpots™ Contracts	44	2:35
HotSpots™ Sales	45	2:00
HotSpots™ Commercial Paper & Documents of Title	46	2:00
HotSpots™ Secured Transactions	47	1:10
HotSpots™ Bankruptcy & Suretyship	48, 49	1:30
HotSpots™ Business Organizations	50 - 53	2:15
HotSpots™ Government Regulation of Business	54, 55	1:20
HotSpots™ Real Property, Personal Property & Insurance	56, 57	1:45
HotSpots™ Professional & Legal Responsibilities	42, 43	1:30

Intensive Video Review	FARE	ARE	AUD	BLPR	Total
Text Chapters	1 - 20	21 - 30	31 - 41	42 - 57	
Approximate Time	6:00	6:00	3:30	3:30	19:00

CHAPTER 33

INTERNAL CONTROL: GENERAL

EXAM COVERAGE: The Plan the Engagement and Obtain and Document Information portions of the Auditing section of the CPA exam are designated by the examiners to be 40 and 35 percent of the section's point value, respectively. Historically, exam coverage of the topics in Chapters 33 and 34 fluctuates from 15 to 26 percent of the Auditing section. More information about the point value of various topics is included in the **Practical Advice** section of this volume.

CHAPTER 33

INTERNAL CONTROL: GENERAL

I. OVERVIEW

A. DEFINITION

SAS 78 defines internal control as a *process* designed to provide reasonable assurance that entity objectives will be achieved. SAS 78 establishes three categories of objectives: "reliability of financial reporting, effectiveness and efficiency of operations, and compliance with applicable laws and regulations."

EXHIBIT 1 ♦ THE SECOND STANDARD OF FIELD WORK

> "A sufficient understanding of internal control is to be obtained to plan the audit and to determine the nature, timing, and extent of tests to be performed."

1. An entity's management and other personnel bring about the entity's internal control.

2. There is a direct association between *objectives* and *components* of internal control. Objectives are the goals an entity endeavors to accomplish. Components are the requirements to accomplish the objectives.

3. The primary function of internal control is to provide assurance that errors and fraud may be discovered with reasonable promptness. The fundamental concept behind internal control is the segregation of duties in order to eliminate incompatible functions. Incompatible functions place a person in the position to both perpetrate and conceal errors or fraud in the normal course of his or her duties. Therefore, a well designed plan of organization separates the duties of **authorization**, **recordkeeping**, and **custody** of the assets. Specific internal controls may be relevant to an entire organization or to any of its divisions.

B. GENERAL CONSIDERATIONS

1. **PERSPECTIVE** The classification of internal control into five components establishes a framework for evaluation of an entity's internal control, but it is not necessarily how the entity implements internal control. The auditor's main concern is the effect a specific control has on financial statement assertions rather than its relationship to a particular component. An entity's internal control components should be considered in the context of the following:

BASIC INFLUENCES ON INTERNAL CONTROL	
M	Methods of information processing
O	Organization and ownership characteristics
D	Diversity and complexity of its operations
E	Entity's size
R	Regulatory and legal requirements
N	Nature of its business

   a. Its methods of processing information.

   b. Its organization and ownership characteristics.

   c. The diversity and complexity of its operations.

d. Its size. Small and midsize companies may use less formal means to accomplish internal control objectives than large entities.

e. Its applicable legal and regulatory requirements.

f. The nature of its business.

2. **Responsibility** The responsibility for establishing and maintaining internal control is management's.

3. **Inherent Limitations** Inherent limitations exist with respect to the effectiveness of an entity's internal control. The best designed and operated system of internal control can provide only reasonable assurance regarding accomplishment of control objectives.

   a. **Errors (Inadvertent)** Mistakes may occur in the application of certain policies and procedures due to **misunderstanding** of instructions or personal **carelessness**.

   b. **Fraud (Intentional)** Policies and procedures that require segregation of duties could be circumvented by **collusion** or by management **override**. The corporate culture may inhibit fraud (or irregularities) by management, but cannot absolutely deter them. The control environment may mitigate or heighten the probability of fraud. Examples of adverse factors are the existence of management incentives tied to performance, change in ownership or control, and unexpected industry developments.

4. **Cost-Benefit Restraints** The cost of an entity's internal control should not exceed the benefits derived. The precise measurement of costs and benefits usually is not possible; hence, management makes both **quantitative** and **qualitative** estimates and judgments in evaluating the cost-benefit relationship.

C. **Components of Internal Control**

The Components of Internal Control Fight CRIME

C	**C**ontrol Activities
R	**R**isk Assessment
I	**I**nformation & Communication
M	**M**onitoring
E	Control **E**nvironment

1. **Control Activities** Control activities are those policies and procedures established to provide reasonable assurance that management decisions are executed, providing for actions to address risks to attainment of objectives. Control activities may have various objectives and are found at several levels. Control activities relevant to an audit are categorized as practices that related to

   a. Performance reviews

   b. Information processing

   c. Physical controls

   d. Segregation of duties

2. **Risk Assessment** Risk assessment is an **entity's** (not an auditor's) location, evaluation, and management of risk. For example, risk assessment addresses the possibility of unrecorded transactions or errors in material estimates. Risk is impacted by changes in the

operating environment such as new personnel, new or revised information systems, rapid growth, new technology, new product lines or activities, corporate restructuring, and new accounting pronouncements. Foreign operations often add new types of risk.

3. **Information & Communication** This refers to the identification, retention, and transfer of information in a timely manner enabling personnel to execute their responsibilities.

   a. **Information** Information quality impacts management's capacity to make decisions to direct the entity's activities and prepare financial statements. The information system of concern to the auditor, including the accounting system, is composed of the procedures and records established to record, process, summarize, and report transactions and maintain accountability for the corresponding assets, liabilities, and equity.

   b. **Communication** Communication includes establishing individual duties and responsibilities relating to internal control and making them known to involved personnel.

4. **Monitoring** Monitoring is a process that evaluates the quality of internal control design and execution over time. Monitoring also includes initiating appropriate corrective actions. The process is achieved through separate evaluations or ongoing activities. Customer complaints and other external communication may indicate areas of concern.

   a. Monitoring is a responsibility of management. Management must monitor internal control to consider whether it is being implemented as planned and that it is appropriately modified as changes occur. Internal auditors, or personnel with similar duties, may contribute to monitoring.

   b. Monitoring is necessary, due to the tendency of internal control to break down over time.

5. **Control Environment** The control environment establishes the overall attitude, awareness, and actions of the board of directors, management, owners, employees, and others concerning the importance of control and its emphasis in the entity. The control environment represents the collective effect of various factors on establishing, enhancing, or mitigating the effectiveness of specific policies and procedures. Such factors include the following:

   a. Management's philosophy and operating style

   b. The entity's organizational structure

   c. The functioning of the board of directors and its committees, particularly the audit committee

   d. Methods of assigning authority and responsibility

   e. Management's commitment to competence

   f. Personnel policies and practices

   g. Integrity and ethical values

II. Consideration of Internal Control in Planning the Audit

A. Summary of the Consideration of Internal Control

Exhibit 2 ♦ Consideration of Internal Control in Planning The Audit

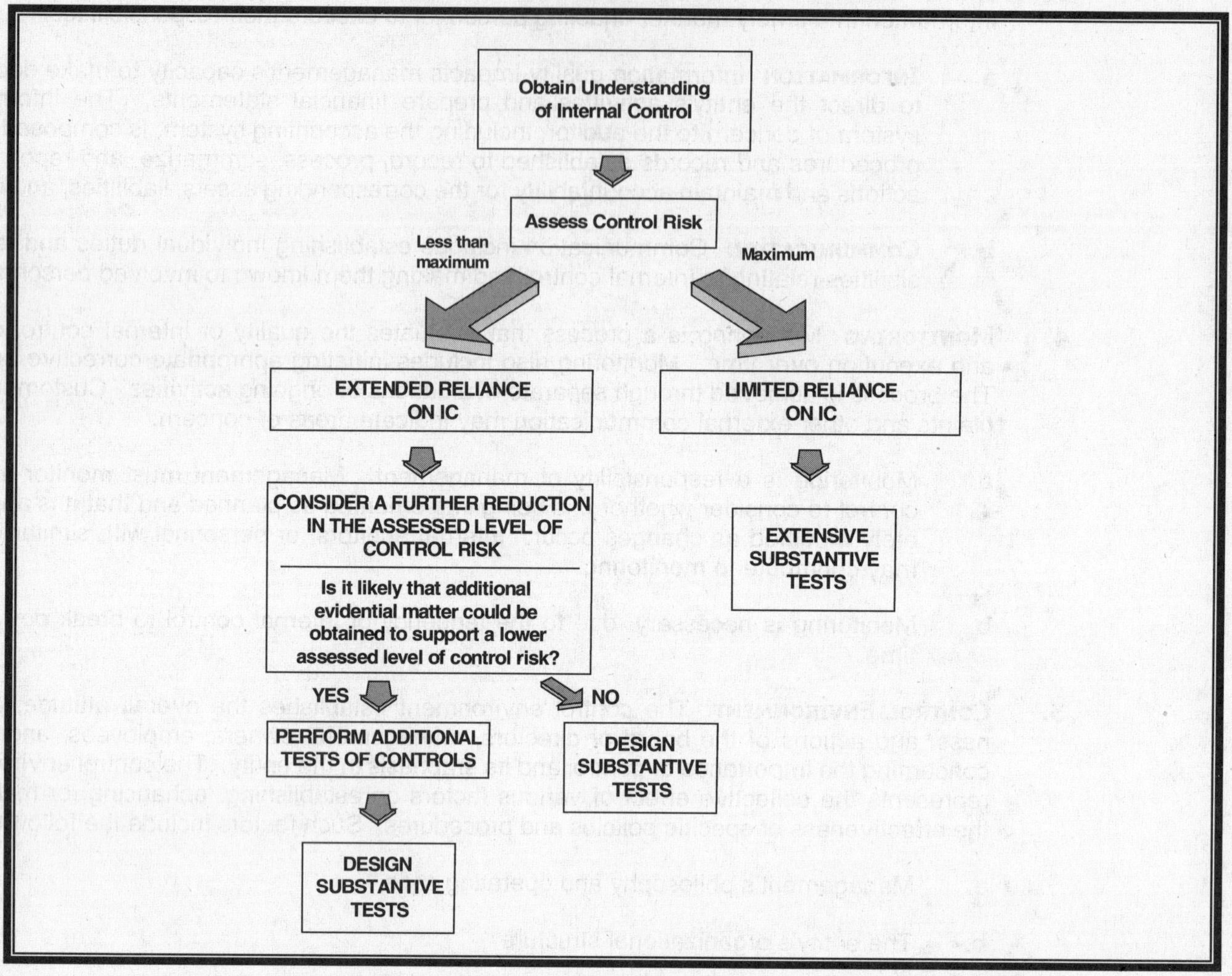

1. Obtain an understanding of the design of relevant internal control components and whether or not they have been placed in operation. The understanding should include all five components of internal control.

2. Document the understanding of internal control obtained to **plan** the audit.

3. Assess the control risk by (a) considering the misstatements that could occur in financial statement assertions, (b) identifying policies and procedures relevant to specific assertions, and (c) performing tests of controls to evaluate the effectiveness of the design and operation of policies and procedures in preventing or detecting material misstatements in assertions. In some cases, the procedures used to obtain an understanding of internal control and to assess control risk may be performed concurrently.

4. After obtaining an understanding of internal control and assessing control risk, the auditor may desire a further reduction in the assessed level of control risk for certain assertions. In such cases, the auditor considers whether sufficient evidential matter exists to support a further reduction and whether the performance of the additional tests would be efficient.

5. Document the basis for conclusions about the assessed level of control risk for financial statement assertions, if the auditor chooses to assess control risk at **below** the maximum level. Otherwise, the auditor need document only the **understanding** of internal control and the fact that control risk is assessed **at** the maximum level.

6. Auditors use their understanding of internal control and from assessed level of control risk in designing the nature, extent, and timing (NET) of substantive tests for assertions.

B. Understanding of Internal Control

The auditor's understanding of internal control should either heighten or mitigate the auditor's concern about the risk of material misstatements.

1. In making a judgment about the understanding of internal control necessary to plan the audit, the auditor should consider his or her assessment of inherent risk, judgments about materiality, and the complexity and sophistication of the entity's operations and systems.

2. In planning the audit, knowledge about internal control should be used to (a) identify types of misstatements that could occur, (b) consider factors that affect the risk of material misstatement, and (c) design substantive tests.

3. A control being placed in operation is different from the control's operating effectiveness. Operation is concerned with the control being used. Operating effectiveness is concerned with how the policy or procedure was applied, the consistency with which it was applied, and by whom. The auditor is **not** required to obtain knowledge about operating effectiveness as part of the understanding of internal control.

4. The auditability of the entity's financial statements may come into question as the auditor obtains the understanding of internal control. Doubts as to the integrity of management or the sufficiency of evidential matter may cause the auditor to conclude that an audit cannot be completed. The entity's records may also cause concern regarding that sufficient competent evidential matter will be available to support an opinion on the financial statements.

5. The explicit addition of **service organizations** to the audit planning requirement clarifies the auditor's responsibility to understand all controls relevant to a financial statement audit. SAS 88 states that the auditor's understanding of internal control may encompass controls placed in operation by service organizations whose services are part of the entity's information system as well as by the entity.

C. Understanding of the Components of Internal Control

In all audits, the auditor must obtain an understanding of the five components of internal control to allow for adequate planning of the audit. The understanding should include knowledge about the design of relevant controls and whether they have been **placed** in operation.

1. **Control Environment** The auditor should obtain sufficient knowledge of the control environment to understand management's and the board of directors' attitude, awareness, and actions concerning the control environment. The auditor should concentrate on the substance and collective impact of management's controls **rather** than the form, because appropriate controls may exist but not be enforced.

2. **Risk Assessment** The auditor obtains sufficient familiarity of the client's risk assessment process to discern how management evaluates risks relevant to financial reporting objectives and elect actions to settle those risks. This includes identification, calculation of impact, appraisal of the potential for occurrence, and connection to financial reporting. An entity's perspective when assessing risk differs from the auditor's evaluation of audit risk. The entity seeks to identify, evaluate, and manage risk that impact the entity objectives. The auditor evaluates inherent and control risk to assess the potential for material misstatement of the financial statements. The understanding of risk assessment essential to plan an audit for an organization operating in a relatively stable environment may be limited.

3. **Control Activities** The auditor becomes familiar with control activities relevant to the audit. The process of obtaining an understanding of control activities usually overlaps with obtaining knowledge of other components. The understanding gained regarding the existence of control activities while considering other components will indicate if additional understanding of control activities is warranted. Audit planning does **not** demand knowledge of control activities related to **every** account balance, transaction class, or disclosure component in the financial statements.

4. **Information & Communication** The auditor should obtain sufficient understanding of the process the entity employs to communicate duties, responsibilities, and material matters pertaining to financial reporting. The auditor should obtain sufficient knowledge about the information system pertaining to financial reporting to understand the following.

   a. The classes of transactions in the entity's operations that are significant to the financial statements.

   b. How those transactions are initiated.

   c. The accounting records, supporting information, and specific accounts in the financial statements involved in the processing and reporting of transactions.

   d. The accounting processing involved from the initiation of a transaction to its inclusion in the financial statements, including electronic means used to process, maintain, and access information.

   e. The financial reporting process used to prepare the entity's financial statements, including significant accounting estimates and disclosures.

5. **Monitoring** The auditor must obtain sufficient understanding of the major types of activities the entity employs to monitor internal control pertaining to financial reporting, including the manner that those activities are used to take appropriate corrective actions. The understanding of monitoring essential to plan an audit for a simple and small entity may be limited.

D. Relevance

The auditor need consider only the objectives and related controls relevant to the audit. It may not be essential for the auditor to obtain an understanding of internal control relevant to all of an entity's divisions and operations for an audit. Not all categories of objectives and related controls are relevant to a financial statement audit. Internal control components may be relevant to the entire entity or to only a portion of its divisions or operations.

1. **Relevant Controls** Controls including those that pertain to the entity's ability to produce financial statements for external use in accordance with generally accepted accounting principles (GAAP) or an other comprehensive basis of accounting (OCBOA).

2. **Overlapping Controls** Internal control over safeguarding assets to reduce unauthorized procurement and disposition of assets may involve controls related to both financial reporting and operations objectives. Use of a lockbox system for collecting payments or passwords for restricted access to payroll records may be relevant to the audit. Controls reducing the waste of raw material in production usually are irrelevant to the audit.

3. **Partially Relevant Controls** Controls pertaining to data the auditor uses to apply or evaluate auditing procedures. For example, an auditor may use production statistics in analytical procedures. Also, controls related to compliance with tax laws determining income tax provision may have a direct and material effect on the financial statements.

4. **Irrelevant Controls** Controls concerned with adherence to health and safety regulations or the effectiveness, economy, and efficiency of certain management decision-making

processes (the appropriate price to charge for its products, etc). These relate to operational aspects of the client's business and are not ordinarily related to a financial statement audit.

E. PROCEDURES TO OBTAIN UNDERSTANDING

The nature and extent of procedures performed generally vary with the size and complexity of the entity, the entity's documentation, previous experience with the entity, and the nature of the particular control. The auditor also considers his or her assessments of inherent risk, judgments about materiality, and the complexity and sophistication of the entity's operations and systems. Ordinarily, the procedures used to obtain sufficient knowledge of the design of the relevant policies, procedures, and records pertaining to each of the five internal control components and whether they have been placed in operation would include

1. Prior experience with the entity;
2. Inquiries of appropriate management, supervisory, and staff personnel;
3. Inspection of entity documents and records;
4. Observation of entity activities and operations.

F. DOCUMENTATION OF UNDERSTANDING

The auditor should document the understanding of the entity's internal control components obtained to plan the audit. The form and extent of documentation is influenced by the size and complexity of the entity, as well as the nature of the entity's internal control. For a large, complex entity, this may include flowcharts, questionnaires, or decision tables. For a small, simple entity, a memorandum may be sufficient.

III. CONSIDERATION OF INTERNAL CONTROL IN ASSESSING CONTROL RISK

A. RISK OF MATERIAL MISSTATEMENT

The risk of material misstatement in financial statement assertions consists of the following:

1. **INHERENT RISK** The **susceptibility** of an assertion to misstatement, assuming no related internal control.
2. **CONTROL RISK** The risk that a material misstatement could occur and not be detected on a timely basis by the **entity's** internal control.
3. **DETECTION RISK** The risk that the **auditor** will fail to detect an existing material misstatement.

B. ASSESSING CONTROL RISK

Assessing control risk is the process of evaluating the effectiveness of an entity's internal control policies and procedures in preventing or detecting material misstatements in the financial statements. Control risk should be assessed in terms of financial statement assertions. After obtaining an understanding of internal control, the auditor may assess control risk as follows:

1. At the maximum level for some or all assertions because the auditor believes policies and procedures are unlikely to pertain to an assertion, are unlikely to be effective, or because evaluating their effectiveness would be inefficient. The auditor assesses control risk at the maximum when there is a high probability that a material misstatement that could occur in an assertion will not be prevented or detected on a timely basis by an entity's internal control.

2. Below the maximum level, which involves the following:

   a. Identifying specific internal control policies and procedures relevant to specific assertions that are likely to prevent or detect material misstatement in those assertions.

b. Performing tests of controls to evaluate the effectiveness of such policies and procedures.

C. **IDENTIFYING INTERNAL CONTROLS**
Identifying internal control policies and procedures relevant to specific financial statement assertions involves the consideration of whether the policies and procedures have either a pervasive effect on many assertions or a specific effect on an individual assertion. Another consideration is whether the policies and procedures can be either directly or indirectly related to an assertion. The more indirect the relationship, the less effective that policy or procedure may be in reducing control risk for that assertion.

D. **TESTS OF CONTROLS**
Procedures directed toward either of the following:

1. The effectiveness of the design of an internal control policy or procedure is concerned with whether that policy or procedure is suitably designed to prevent or detect material misstatements in specific financial statement assertions. Tests to obtain such evidential matter ordinarily include the following:

   a. Inquiries of appropriate entity personnel

   b. Inspection of documents and reports

   c. Observation of the application of specific internal control policies and procedures

2. The operating effectiveness of an internal control policy or procedure is concerned with how the policy or procedure was applied, the consistency with which it was applied during the audit period, and by whom it was applied. These tests ordinarily include procedures such as the following:

   a. Inquiries of appropriate entity personnel

   b. Inspection of documents and reports

   c. Observation of the application of specific internal control policies and procedures

   d. Reperformance of the application of the policy or procedure by the auditor

E. **ASSESSED LEVEL OF CONTROL RISK**
The assessed level of control risk is the conclusion reached as a result of evaluating control risk. In determining the evidential matter necessary to support a specific assessed level of control risk at below the maximum level, the auditor should consider the characteristics of evidential matter about control risk. Generally, the lower the assessed level of control risk, the greater the assurance the evidential matter must provide that internal control policies and procedures relevant to an assertion are designed and operating effectively.

1. The auditor uses the assessed level of control risk (together with the assessed level of inherent risk) to determine the acceptable level of detection risk for financial statement assertions.

2. The auditor then uses the acceptable level of detection risk to determine the nature, timing, and extent of the auditing procedures (i.e., substantive tests) to be used to detect material misstatements in the financial statement assertions.

F. **Documentation of the Assessed Level of Control Risk**

1. For those financial statement assertions where control risk is assessed at the maximum level, the auditor should document the conclusion that control risk is at the maximum level but need **not** document the **basis** for that conclusion.

2. For those assertions where the assessed level of control risk is **below** the maximum level, the auditor should document that conclusion **and** the basis for the conclusion that the effectiveness of the design and operation of internal control policies and procedures supports that assessed level.

IV. Relationship of Understanding to Assessing Control Risk

A. Concurrent Performance

Obtaining an understanding of internal control and assessing control risk may be performed concurrently in an audit. For example, the auditor's procedures to obtain an understanding of internal control may, in some circumstances, also provide evidential matter sufficient to support an assessed level of control risk that is below the maximum level. Procedures are not sufficient to support an assessed level of control risk below the maximum level if they do not provide sufficient evidential matter to evaluate the effectiveness of both the design and operating effectiveness of a policy or procedure relevant to an assertion.

B. Further Reduction in the Assessed Level of Control Risk

After obtaining the understanding of internal control and assessing control risk, the auditor may decide to seek a further reduction in the assessed level of control risk for certain assertions.

1. In such cases, the auditor considers whether additional evidential matter sufficient to support a further reduction is likely to be available, and whether it would be efficient to perform tests of controls to obtain that evidential matter. The results of the procedures performed to obtain the understanding of internal control, as well as information obtained from other sources, help the auditor's evaluation.

2. For those assertions for which the auditor performs additional tests of controls, the auditor determines the assessed level of control risk that the results of those tests will support. This assessed level of control risk is used in determining the appropriate detection risk to accept for those assertions and, accordingly, in determining the nature, timing, and extent of substantive tests for such assertions.

V. Evidential Matter to Support the Assessed Level of Control Risk

A. Sufficiency

When the auditor assesses control risk at below the maximum level, the auditor should obtain sufficient evidential matter to support that assessed level. The sufficiency of the evidential matter is based on the auditor's judgment. The type of evidential matter, its source, its timeliness, and the existence of other evidential matter related to the conclusions to which it leads, all bear on the degree of assurance evidential matter provides. These characteristics influence the nature, timing, and extent of the tests of controls that the auditor applies to obtain evidential matter about control risk. The auditor selects such tests from a variety of techniques such as inquiry, observation, inspection, and reperformance of a policy or procedure that pertains to an assertion. No one specific test of controls is always necessary, applicable, or equally effective in every circumstance.

1. **Type** The nature of the particular policies and procedures that pertain to an assertion influences the type of evidential matter that is available to evaluate the effectiveness of the design or operation of those policies and procedures.

2. **Source** Generally, evidential matter about the effectiveness of the design and operation of policies and procedures obtained directly by the auditor, such as through observation, provides more assurance than evidential matter obtained indirectly or by inference, such as

through inquiry. Inquiry alone generally will not provide sufficient evidential matter to support a conclusion about the effectiveness of the design or operation of a specific control procedure.

3. **TIMELINESS** The timeliness of evidential matter concerns when it was obtained and the portion of the audit period to which it applies. In evaluating the degree of assurance that is provided by evidential matter, the auditor should consider that the evidential matter obtained by some tests of controls, such as observation, pertains only to the point in time at which the auditing procedure was applied. Consequently, such evidential matter may be insufficient to evaluate the effectiveness of the design or operation of internal control policies and procedures for periods not subjected to such tests. In such circumstances, the auditor may decide to supplement these tests with other tests of controls that are capable of providing evidential matter about the entire audit period.

   a. Evidential matter about the effective design or operation of internal control policies and procedures that was obtained in **prior audits** may be considered by the auditor in assessing control risk in the current period. The auditor should consider that the longer the time elapsed since the performance of tests of controls to obtain evidential matter about control risk, the less assurance it may provide. When considering evidential matter obtained from prior audits, the auditor should obtain evidential matter in the current period about whether changes have occurred in internal control subsequent to the prior audits, as well as the nature and extent of any such changes.

   b. When the auditor obtains evidential matter about the design or operation of internal control policies and procedures during an **interim period**, the auditor should determine what additional evidential matter should be obtained for the remaining period. The auditor should obtain evidential matter about the nature and extent of any significant changes in internal control, including its policies, procedures, and personnel, that occur subsequent to the interim period.

B. **INTERRELATIONSHIP**

The auditor should consider the combined effect of various types of evidential matter relating to the same assertion in evaluating the degree of assurance that evidential matter provides. In some circumstances, a single type of evidential matter may not be sufficient to evaluate the effective design or operation of an internal control policy or procedure. For example, because an observation is pertinent only at the point in time at which it is made, the auditor may supplement the observation with inquiries.

1. When evaluating the degree of assurance provided by evidential matter, the auditor should consider the interrelationship of the five components of internal control.

2. Generally, when various types of evidential matter support the same conclusion about the design or operation of an internal control policy or procedure, the degree of assurance provided increases. Conversely, if various types of evidential matter lead to different conclusions, the assurance provided decreases.

3. An audit of financial statements is a cumulative process; as the auditor assesses control risk, the information obtained may cause the auditor to modify the nature, timing, or extent of the other planned tests of controls for assessing control risk. In addition, information may come to the auditor's attention as a result of performing substantive tests or from other sources during the audit that differs significantly from the information on which the planned tests of controls for assessing control risk were based. In such circumstances, the auditor may need to reevaluate the planned substantive procedures, based on a revised consideration of the assessed level of control risk for all or some of the financial statement assertions.

VI. CORRELATION OF CONTROL RISK WITH DETECTION RISK

A. INVERSE RELATIONSHIP

After considering the level to which the auditor seeks to restrict the risk of a material misstatement in the financial statements and the assessed levels of inherent risk and control risk, the auditor performs substantive tests to restrict detection risk to an acceptable level. As the assessed level of control risk decreases, the acceptable level of detection risk increases. Accordingly, the auditor may alter the nature, timing, and extent of the substantive tests performed.

EXHIBIT 3 ♦ CORRELATION OF CONTROL RISK WITH DETECTION RISK

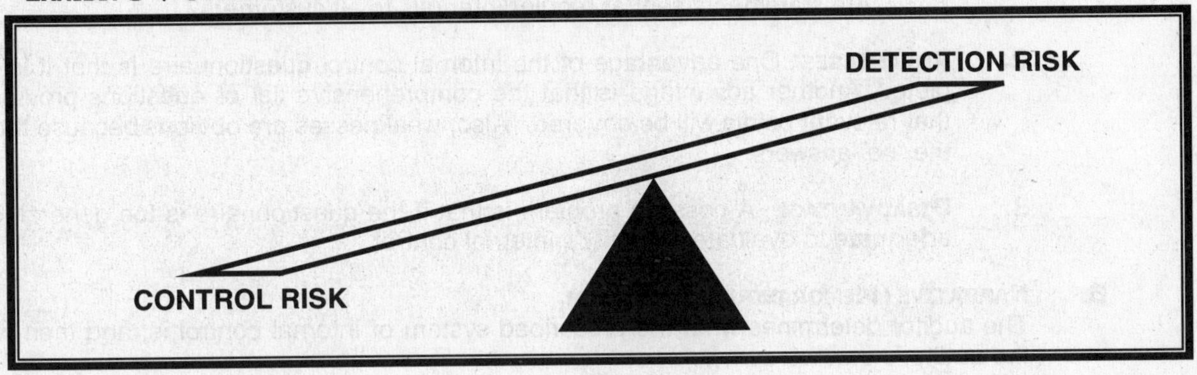

B. REQUIREMENTS FOR PERFORMING SUBSTANTIVE TESTS

The assessed level of control risk cannot be sufficiently low to eliminate the need to perform any substantive tests. Consequently, regardless of the assessed level of control risk, the auditor should perform substantive tests for **significant** account balances and transaction classes.

C. TYPES OF SUBSTANTIVE TESTS

The substantive tests that the auditor performs consist of tests of details of transactions and balances, and analytical procedures. In assessing control risk, the auditor also may use tests of details of transactions as tests of controls. The objective of tests of transactions performed as substantive tests is to detect material misstatements in the financial statements. The objective of tests of details of transactions, performed as tests of controls, is to evaluate whether an internal control policy or procedure operated effectively. Although these objectives are different, both may be accomplished concurrently through performance of a test of details on the same transaction.

VII. TOOLS FOR OBTAINING AND DOCUMENTING AN UNDERSTANDING OF INTERNAL CONTROL

A. QUESTIONNAIRE APPROACH

An internal control questionnaire is simply an enumeration of the matters to be investigated in the auditor's consideration of internal control. It should be designed by persons who are fully conversant with the problems of internal control and who have **experience** in the kind of structure being reviewed.

1. **SAMPLE QUESTIONS** While the size and scope of internal control questionnaires will vary, some possible questions for an accounts receivable system are as follows:

   a. Are the following functions performed by employees other than accounts receivable bookkeepers?

      (1) Handling cash and maintaining cash records

      (2) Opening incoming mail

      (3) Credit and collection

      (4) Review and mailing of statements to customers

b. Are the accounts receivable ledgers unavailable to the cashier?

c. Are the subsidiary ledgers regularly balanced with the control accounts?

d. Are the subsidiary ledgers occasionally balanced with the control accounts by someone other than the accounts receivable bookkeepers?

e. Are aged trial balances of accounts receivable regularly prepared and submitted for executive approval?

f. Are statements sent at regular intervals to all customers?

2. **ADVANTAGES** One advantage of the internal control questionnaire is that it is easy to complete. Another advantage is that the comprehensive list of questions provides assurance that relevant points will be covered. Also, weaknesses are obvious because they are usually the "no" answers.

3. **DISADVANTAGE** A possible problem is that if the questionnaire is too general, it may not be **adequate** to evaluate an entity's internal control.

B. NARRATIVE (MEMORANDUM) APPROACH

The auditor determines what the prescribed system of internal control is, and then writes it out in the auditor's own words.

1. **ADVANTAGES** The narrative is **tailor-made** for each engagement. Another advantage is that it requires a **detailed analysis** of the client's internal control since the auditor must thoroughly understand the structure in order to describe it.

2. **DISADVANTAGES** The narrative approach is very **time consuming**. It does not have built-in safeguards to prevent the auditor from **overlooking** some aspect of internal control—weaknesses are not always obvious and may not be detected by this approach.

C. FLOWCHART APPROACH

An internal control flowchart is a **graphic** representation of a portion of a company's internal control. It shows the segregation of functions, document flows, controls, etc.

1. **ADVANTAGES** The internal control flowchart is a graphic representation of a series of sequential processes. It shows the steps required and the flow of documents from person to person in carrying out the functions depicted. Therefore, the tendency to overlook the controls existing between functions or departments is **minimized**. Another advantage is that the flowchart **clearly** communicates the structure. The use of a flowchart is especially useful in the evaluation of electronic data processing systems because it avoids much of the terminology that would be present in a narrative. Finally, constructing a flowchart requires the auditor to completely understand the structure.

2. **DISADVANTAGE** It may be more time consuming to construct a flowchart rather than to fill out an internal control questionnaire.

EXHIBIT 4 ♦ COMMON FLOWCHART SYMBOLS

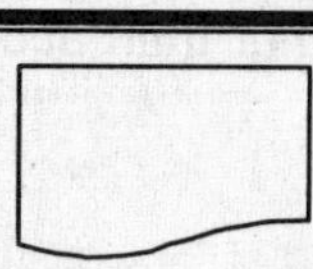

DOCUMENT: Paper documents and reports of all kinds, e.g., sales invoices, purchase orders, employee paychecks, and computer-prepared error listings.

COMPUTER OPERATION/PROCESS: Execute defined operations resulting in some change in the information or the determination of flow direction, e.g., checking customer's credit limit.

(continued on next page)

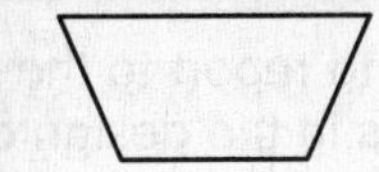
MANUAL OPERATION: Off-line process that is performed manually, e.g., preparing a three-part sales invoice or manually posting to customer accounts.

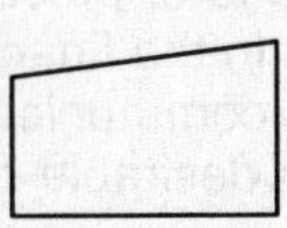
MANUAL INPUT: Represents input entered manually at the time of processing, e.g., using a keyboard.

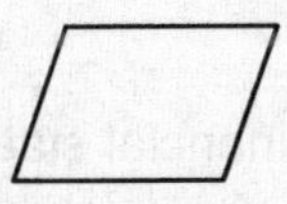
INPUT/OUTPUT: General input/output symbol, e.g., general ledger, can be used regardless of the type of medium or data.

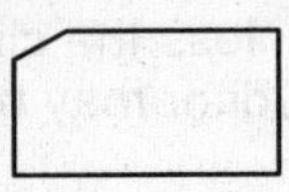
PUNCHED CARD: Input/output function in which the medium is a punched card, e.g., payroll earnings card.

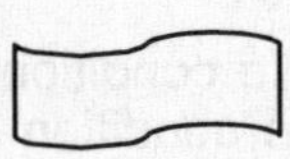
PUNCHED TAPE: Input/output function in which the medium is punched tape.

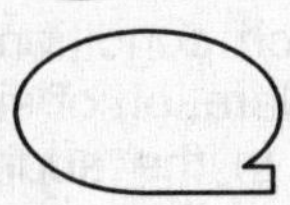
MAGNETIC TAPE: Input/output function in which the medium is magnetic tape, e.g., master payroll data file.

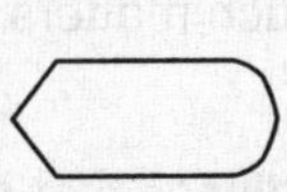
DISPLAY: Input/output device in which the information is displayed at the time of processing for human use, e.g., display customer number.

ON-LINE STORAGE: Storage that is connected to and under the control of the computer, e.g., disk, drum, magnetic tape, etc.

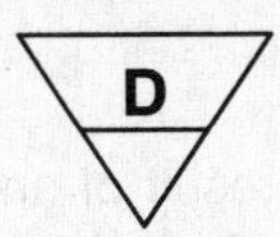

OFF-LINE STORAGE: Any off-line storage of information regardless of the medium on which the information is recorded. This includes filing documents such as sales invoices and purchase orders. An "A" signifies an alphabetic file, an "N" is for a numeric file, and a "D" indicates a file organized by date.

OFF-PAGE CONNECTOR: Designates entry to or exit from a page. For example, it can be used to indicate sending a copy of an invoice to a customer.

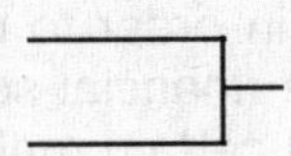
ANNOTATION: Provides additional information.

DECISION: Determines next action. Used in program flowcharts, e.g., is A = B?

VIII. Communication of Internal Control Related Matters Noted in an Audit (AU 325, SAS 60)

A. Audit Committee

Communication regarding internal control related matters should be directed to the audit committee or directed to individuals with a level of authority and responsibility equivalent to an audit committee such as the board of directors, the board of trustees, or others who may have engaged the auditor. It is then common for these reports to be made available to management.

B. Reportable Conditions

Reportable conditions are those matters that the auditor is **required** to report to the audit committee. They represent, in the auditor's judgment, significant deficiencies in the design or operation of the internal control that could adversely affect the entity's ability to record, process, summarize, and report financial data consistent with the assertions of management in the financial statements. The auditor may identify conditions that are not reportable but decide to communicate such matters for the benefit of management. These constructive suggestions are a desirable by-product of an audit.

C. Identifying Reportable Conditions

The auditor's objective in an audit is to form an opinion on the entity's financial statements.

1. It is **not** the auditor's duty to search for reportable conditions unless the client has specifically requested that the auditor be alert to such matters. The auditor may notice reportable conditions as a consequence of performing audit procedures.

2. In some cases, management may be aware of certain reportable conditions due to a conscious decision to accept the degree of risk associated with the condition as a result of a cost-benefit analysis. The auditor does not need to report such conditions, provided the audit committee has acknowledged its understanding and consideration of such deficiencies and the associated risks. Changes in management, changes in the audit committee, or passage of time might make it appropriate and timely to report such matters.

D. Agreed-Upon Criteria

Clients may request the auditor to be alert to matters and to report conditions that go beyond those in a normal audit. The auditor is not precluded from reporting matters that are viewed to be of value to management in the absence of any specific request to do so. Agreed-upon arrangements between the auditor and the client to report conditions noted may include for example, the reporting of matters of less significance than would normally be reported.

E. Reporting Form and Content

Conditions determined by the auditor to be reportable or that are the result of an agreement with the client should be reported to the audit committee, preferably in writing. If the communication is oral, that fact should be documented in the workpapers.

Exhibit 5 ♦ Excerpt From a Report Regarding Reportable Conditions

> In planning and performing our audit of the financial statements of the ABC Corporation for the year ended December 31, 20XX, we considered its internal control in order to determine our auditing procedures for the purpose of expressing our opinion on the financial statements and not to provide assurance on the internal control. However, we noted certain matters involving the internal control and its operation that we consider to be reportable conditions under standards established by the American Institute of Certified Public Accountants. Reportable conditions involve matters coming to our attention relating to significant deficiencies in the design or operation of the internal control that, in our judgment, could adversely affect the organization's ability to record, process, summarize, and report financial data consistent with the assertions of management in the financial statements.
>
> [Include paragraph(s) to describe the reportable conditions noted.]
>
> This report is intended solely for the information and use of the audit committee (board of directors, board of trustees, or owners in owner-managed enterprises), management, and others within the organization (or specified regulatory agency or other specified third party).

1. Any report issued on reportable conditions should

a. Indicate that the purpose of the audit was to report on the financial statements and not to provide assurance on internal control.

b. Include the definition of reportable conditions.

c. State that the report is solely for the information and use of the audit committee, management, and others within the organization.

d. Identify reportable conditions noted.

2. In some instances, the auditor may decide to include statements regarding inherent limitations of the internal control in general, and the specific extent and nature of the auditor's consideration of the internal control.

3. Because of the potential for misinterpretation of the limited degree of assurance associated with the auditor issuing a written report representing that no reportable conditions were noted during an audit, the auditor should **not** issue such representations.

4. Timely communication of reportable conditions may be important. The auditor may communicate significant matters during the course of an audit rather than at the conclusion based upon the relative significance of the matters and the urgency of corrective follow-up action.

F. MATERIAL WEAKNESSES

A material weakness is a reportable condition in which the design or operation of a specific internal control component does not reduce to a relatively low level the risk that errors or fraud in amounts that would be material in relation to the financial statements may occur and not be detected within a timely period by employees in the normal course of performing their assigned functions. The auditor is not required to separately identify material weaknesses from reportable conditions but the auditor may choose to do so or the client may request that it be done.

IX. FOREIGN CORRUPT PRACTICES ACT OF 1977

A. ANTIBRIBERY PROVISIONS

The Act makes it illegal for any U.S. business engaged in interstate commerce to offer a bribe to a foreign official. **Companies** are subject to a fine of up to $1,000,000, while **individuals** are subject to a maximum fine of $10,000 and/or up to 5 years imprisonment.

B. RECORDKEEPING AND INTERNAL CONTROL

The Act requires entities to maintain books, records, and accounts which accurately reflect the transactions and dispositions of the assets of the entity. Entities must also maintain a system of accounting control sufficient to provide reasonable assurance that (1) transactions are executed in accordance with management's authorization, (2) transactions are properly recorded in conformity with GAAP, (3) access to assets is restricted only to those authorized by management, and (4) the recorded accountability for assets is periodically compared to, and reconciled with, the existing assets.

C. REPORTING

The Act does **not** require the auditor to issue a special report on internal control.

Wondering how you can prepare for essay questions?

Some candidates who are otherwise confident about the exam are overwhelmed by essay questions. The following tips are designed to help you increase your confidence when presented with questions requiring free-form answers.

Review the **Accounting for 5%** appendix. This appendix has an example of what the AICPA labels as "ideal" and "good" solutions. Notice that the gap between "ideal" and "good" is larger than the gap between "good" and "poor." This works to your benefit.

As you progress through your study plan, answer an essay from each major topic; waiting until the last month leaves you little time to prepare for essays. The more uncomfortable that you are with essays, the more important this becomes. Bear in mind, you might not realize that you are uncomfortable with essays, if you don't try answering some of them.

Once you grade your essay in comparison to the unofficial solution, reflect on the question. Assigning a point value is probably the least important part of answering the question. Any mistakes or omissions are solid learning opportunities. Additional information about essay techniques is in the **Practical Advice** appendix. Also, some Hot*Spot videos spend time on essay-answering techniques explicitly. In the Auditing section, these videos are *Internal Control* and *Audit Evidence*.

Read through the essay questions (with their related unofficial solutions) of essay questions you will not be answering within the next few days. This provides a good review of the material you have just covered, as well as acquainting you with the types of questions and the length of the expected responses.

Once you know the content, you will be able to prepare a response regardless of the question format. However, exam time is limited, and you don't want the pressure of time considerations to distract you from providing your best answer to a question. To reduce the pressure, remember that you must earn 75 points to pass—it doesn't matter which answer format that you use to earn those 75 points. Practice more essay questions that cover topics that have high point value; be prepared to answer an essay question in any topic area.

Remember, with the techniques and information in your material,

A passing score is well within reach!

CHAPTER 33—INTERNAL CONTROL: GENERAL

PROBLEM 33-1 MULTIPLE CHOICE QUESTIONS (80 to 100 minutes)

1. Which of the following most likely would **not** be considered an inherent limitation of the potential effectiveness of an entity's internal control?
a. Incompatible duties
b. Management override
c. Mistakes in judgment
d. Collusion among employees
(5/94, Aud., #22, amended, 4687)

2. When considering internal control, an auditor should be aware of the concept of reasonable assurance, which recognizes that
a. Internal control policies and procedures may be ineffective due to mistakes in judgment and personal carelessness.
b. Adequate safeguards over access to assets and records should permit an entity to maintain proper accountability.
c. Establishing and maintaining internal control is an important responsibility of management.
d. The cost of an entity's internal control should **not** exceed the benefits expected to be derived.
(5/95, Aud., #26, amended, 5644)

3. Management's attitude toward aggressive financial reporting and its emphasis on meeting projected profit goals most likely would significantly influence an entity's control environment when
a. External policies established by parties outside the entity affect it's accounting practices.
b. Management is dominated by one individual who is also a shareholder.
c. Internal auditors have direct access to the board of directors and the entity's management.
d. The audit committee is active in overseeing the entity's financial reporting policies.
(5/97, Aud., #1, 6390)

4. Which of the following auditor concerns most likely could be so serious that the auditor concludes that a financial statement audit **cannot** be conducted?
a. The entity has **no** formal written code of conduct.
b. The integrity of the entity's management is suspect.
c. Procedures requiring segregation of duties are subject to management override.
d. Management fails to modify prescribed controls for changes in conditions.
(11/95, Aud., #4, 5953)

5. Which of the following is a management control method that most likely could improve management's ability to supervise company activities effectively?
a. Monitoring compliance with internal control requirements imposed by regulatory bodies
b. Limiting direct access to assets by physical segregation and protective devices
c. Establishing budgets and forecasts to identify variances from expectations
d. Supporting employees with the resources necessary to discharge their responsibilities
(11/95, Aud., #6, 5955)

6. Which of the following is **not** a component of an entity's internal control?
a. Control risk
b. Control activities
c. The information and communication
d. The control environment (Editors, 0086)

7. When obtaining an understanding of an entity's internal control procedures, an auditor should concentrate on the substance of the procedures rather than their form because
a. The procedures may be operating effectively but may **not** be documented.
b. Management may implement procedures whose costs exceed their benefits.
c. The procedures may be so inappropriate that **no** reliance is contemplated by the auditor.
d. Management may establish appropriate procedures but **not** enforce compliance with them.
(5/94, Aud., #21, amended, 4686)

8. Which of the following are considered control environment factors?

	Detection risk	*Personnel policies and practices*
a.	Yes	Yes
b.	Yes	No
c.	No	Yes
d.	No	No

(11/94, Aud., #29, 5102)

9. In obtaining an understanding of an entity's internal control, an auditor is required to obtain knowledge about the

	Operating effectiveness of policies and procedures	*Design of policies and procedures*
a.	Yes	Yes
b.	No	Yes
c.	Yes	No
d.	No	No

(5/93, Aud., #12, amended, 3908)

10. An auditor should obtain sufficient knowledge of an entity's accounting system to understand the
a. Safeguards used to limit access to computer facilities.
b. Process used to prepare significant accounting estimates.
c. Procedures used to assure proper authorization of transactions.
d. Policies used to detect the concealment of fraud.
(5/94, Aud., #20, amended, 4685)

11. An auditor uses the knowledge provided by the understanding of internal control and the final assessed level of control risk primarily to determine the nature, timing, and extent of the
a. Tests of controls.
b. Compliance tests.
c. Attribute tests.
d. Substantive tests. (Editors, 0054)

12. An auditor would most likely be concerned with internal control policies and procedures that provide reasonable assurance about the
a. Methods of assigning production tasks to employees.
b. Appropriate prices the entity should charge for its products.
c. Efficiency of management's decision-making process.
d. Entity's ability to process and summarize financial data. (Editors, 2303)

13. In planning an audit, the auditor's knowledge about the design of relevant internal control policies and procedures should be used to
a. Identify the types of potential misstatements that could occur.
b. Assess the operational efficiency of internal control.
c. Determine whether controls have been circumvented by collusion.
d. Document the assessed level of control risk.
(11/95, Aud., #2, amended, 5951)

14. In obtaining an understanding of an entity's internal control in a financial statement audit, an auditor is **not** obligated to
a. Determine whether the control procedures have been placed in operation.
b. Perform procedures to understand the design of the internal control policies.
c. Document the understanding of the entity's internal control.
d. Search for significant deficiencies in the operation of the internal control.
(11/93, Aud., #19, amended, 4256)

15. In his or her consideration of an entity's internal control, the auditor is basically concerned that the controls provide reasonable assurance that
a. Operational efficiency has been achieved in accordance with management plans.
b. Errors and fraud have been prevented or detected.
c. Management **cannot** override the controls.
d. Controls have **not** been circumvented by collusion. (Editors, 9405)

16. Regardless of the assessed level of control risk, an auditor would perform some
a. Tests of controls to determine the effectiveness of internal control policies.
b. Analytical procedures to verify the design of internal control procedures.
c. Substantive tests to restrict detection risk for significant transaction classes.
d. Dual-purpose tests to evaluate both the risk of monetary misstatement and preliminary control risk. (11/93, Aud., #23, 4260)

17. In planning an audit of certain accounts, an auditor may conclude that specific procedures used to obtain an understanding of an entity's internal control need **not** be included because of the auditor's judgments about materiality and assessments of
a. Control risk.
b. Detection risk.
c. Sampling risk.
d. Inherent risk. (11/90, Aud., #44, amended, 0056)

18. In assessing control risk, an auditor ordinarily selects from a variety of techniques, including
a. Inquiry and analytical procedures.
b. Reperformance and observation.
c. Comparison and confirmation.
d. Inspection and verification.
(11/95, Aud., #18, 5965)

19. An auditor assesses control risk because it
a. Is relevant to the auditor's understanding of the control environment.
b. Provides assurance that the auditor's materiality levels are appropriate.
c. Indicates to the auditor where inherent risk may be the greatest.
d. Affects the level of detection risk that the auditor may accept. (11/95, Aud., #21, 5968)

20. Assessing control risk at below the maximum level most likely would involve
a. Performing more extensive substantive tests with larger sample sizes than originally planned.
b. Reducing inherent risk for most of the assertions relevant to significant account balances.
c. Changing the timing of substantive tests by omitting interim-date testing and performing the tests at year end.
d. Identifying specific internal control policies and procedures relevant to specific assertions.
(11/95, Aud., #22, amended, 5969)

21. After obtaining an understanding of internal control and assessing control risk, an auditor decided to perform tests of controls. The auditor most likely decided that
a. It would be efficient to perform tests of controls that would result in a reduction in planned substantive tests.
b. Additional evidence to support a further reduction in control risk is **not** available.
c. An increase in the assessed level of control risk is justified for certain financial statement assertions.
d. There were many internal control weaknesses that could allow errors to enter the accounting system. (5/95, Aud., #33, amended, 5651)

22. An auditor may decide to assess control risk at the maximum level for certain assertions because the auditor believes
a. Control policies and procedures are unlikely to pertain to the assertions.
b. The entity's control environment, monitoring, and control activities are interrelated.
c. Sufficient evidential matter to support the assertions is likely to be available.
d. More emphasis on tests of controls than substantive tests is warranted.
(11/93, Aud., #21, amended, 4258)

23. Control risk should be assessed in terms of
a. Specific control activities.
b. Types of potential fraud.
c. Financial statement assertions.
d. Control environment factors.
(5/95, Aud., #27, amended, 5645)

24. After assessing control risk at below the maximum level, an auditor desires to seek a further reduction in the assessed level of control risk. At this time, the auditor would consider whether
a. It would be efficient to obtain an understanding of the entity's accounting system.
b. The entity's internal control policies and procedures have been placed in operation.
c. The entity's internal control policies and procedures pertain to any financial statement assertions.
d. Additional evidential matter sufficient to support a further reduction is likely to be available.
(11/95, Aud., #23, amended, 5970)

25. On the basis of audit evidence gathered and evaluated, an auditor decides to increase the assessed level of control risk from that originally planned. To achieve an overall audit risk level that is substantially the same as the planned audit risk level, the auditor would
a. Decrease substantive testing.
b. Decrease detection risk.
c. Increase inherent risk.
d. Increase materiality levels.
(11/94, Aud., #10, 5083)

26. Inherent risk and control risk differ from detection risk in that they
a. Arise from the misapplication of auditing procedures.
b. May be assessed in either quantitative or nonquantitative terms.
c. Exist independently of the financial statement audit.
d. Can be changed at the auditor's discretion.
(11/94, Aud., #8, 5081)

27. The acceptable level of detection risk is inversely related to the
a. Assurance provided by substantive tests.
b. Risk of misapplying auditing procedures.
c. Preliminary judgment about materiality levels.
d. Risk of failing to discover material misstatements.
(5/91, Aud., #26, 0044)

28. As the acceptable level of detection risk increases, an auditor may change the
a. Assessed level of control risk from below the maximum to the maximum level.
b. Assurance provided by tests of controls by using a larger sample size than planned.
c. Timing of substantive tests from year-end to an interim date.
d. Nature of substantive tests from a less effective to a more effective procedure.
(11/92, Aud., #10, 2944)

29. Which of the following procedures most likely would provide an auditor with evidence about whether an entity's internal control activities are suitably designed to prevent or detect material misstatements?

a. Reperforming the activities for a sample of transactions
b. Performing analytical procedures using data aggregated at a high level
c. Vouching a sample of transactions directly related to the activities
d. Observing the entity's personnel applying the activities (5/97, Aud., #4, 6393)

30. In addition to evaluating the frequency of deviations in tests of controls, an auditor should also consider certain qualitative aspects of the deviations. The auditor most likely would give broader consideration to the implications of a deviation if it was

a. The only deviation discovered in the sample.
b. Identical to a deviation discovered during the prior year's audit.
c. Caused by an employee's misunderstanding of instructions.
d. Initially concealed by a forged document. (11/95, Aud., #26, 5973)

31. The objective of tests of details of transactions performed as tests of controls is to

a. Monitor the design and use of entity documents such as prenumbered shipping forms.
b. Determine whether internal control structure policies and procedures have been placed in operation.
c. Detect material misstatements in the account balances of the financial statements.
d. Evaluate whether internal control procedures operated effectively. (11/94, Aud., #42, amended, 5115)

32. When an auditor assesses control risk at the maximum level, the auditor is required to document the auditor's

	Understanding of the entity's accounting system	Basis for concluding that control risk is at the maximum level
a.	No	No
b.	No	Yes
c.	Yes	No
d.	Yes	Yes

(5/95, Aud., #29, 5647)

33. When assessing control risk below the maximum level, an auditor is required to document the auditor's

	Understanding of the entity's control environment	Basis for concluding that control risk is below the maximum level
a.	Yes	No
b.	No	Yes
c.	Yes	Yes
d.	No	No

(11/95, Aud., #24, 5971)

34. Which of the following statements is correct concerning reportable conditions in an audit?

a. An auditor is required to search for reportable conditions during an audit.
b. All reportable conditions are also considered to be material weaknesses.
c. An auditor may communicate reportable conditions during an audit or after the audit's completion.
d. An auditor may report that **no** reportable conditions were noted during an audit. (5/95, Aud., #38, 5656)

35. Which of the following statements is correct concerning an auditor's required communication of reportable conditions?

a. A reportable condition previously communicated during the prior year's audit that remains uncorrected causes a scope limitation.
b. An auditor should perform tests of controls on reportable conditions before communicating them to the client.
c. An auditor's report on reportable conditions should include a restriction on the use of the report.
d. An auditor should communicate reportable conditions after tests of controls, but before commencing substantive tests. (11/94, Aud., #45, 5118)

36. An auditor most likely would be responsible for communicating significant deficiencies in the design of the internal control

a. To the Securities and Exchange Commission when the client is a publicly held entity.
b. To shareholders with significant influence (more than 20% equity ownership) when the reportable conditions are deemed to be material weaknesses.
c. To court-appointed creditors' committee when the client is operating under Chapter 11 of the Federal Bankruptcy Code.
d. To specific legislative and regulatory bodies when reporting under *Government Auditing Standards*. (5/95, Aud., #76, amended, 5694)

37. The development of constructive suggestions to a client for improvements in its internal control is
a. A requirement of the auditor's consideration of internal control.
b. As important as establishing a basis for assessing the level of control risk below the maximum.
c. Addressed by the auditor only during a special engagement.
d. A desirable by-product of an audit engagement. (Editors, 0083)

38. A previously communicated reportable condition that has not been corrected, ordinarily should be communicated again if
a. The deficiency has a material effect on the auditor's assessment of control risk.
b. The entity accepts that degree of risk because of cost-benefit considerations.
c. The weakness could adversely affect the entity's ability to report financial data.
d. There has been major turnover in upper-level management and the board of directors. (5/91, Aud., #35, 0052)

39. In general, a material internal control weakness may be defined as a condition in which material errors or fraud may occur and not be detected within a timely period by
a. Outside consultants who issue a special-purpose report on internal control.
b. Employees in the normal course of performing their assigned functions.
c. Management when reviewing interim financial statements and reconciling account balances.
d. An independent auditor during the testing of controls phase of the consideration of internal control. (Editors, 9409)

40. Which of the following representations should **not** be included in a report on internal control related matters noted in an audit?
a. The auditor's consideration of the internal control would **not** necessarily disclose all reportable conditions that exist.
b. There are **no** significant deficiencies in the design or operation of the internal control.
c. Corrective follow-up action is recommended due to the relative significance of material weaknesses discovered during the audit.
d. Reportable conditions related to the internal control design exist, but **none** is deemed to be a material weakness. (Editors, 2957)

PROBLEM 33-2 ADDITIONAL MULTIPLE CHOICE QUESTIONS (26 to 33 minutes)

41. The overall attitude and awareness of an entity's board of directors concerning the importance of internal control usually is reflected in its
a. Computer-based controls.
b. System of segregation of duties.
c. Control environment.
d. Safeguards over access to assets. (5/95, Aud., #25, amended, 5643)

42. Management philosophy and operating style most likely would have a significant influence on an entity's control environment when
a. The internal auditor reports directly to management.
b. Management is dominated by one individual.
c. Accurate management job descriptions delineate specific duties.
d. The audit committee actively oversees the financial reporting process. (11/95, Aud., #5, 5954)

43. The primary objective of procedures performed to obtain an understanding of internal control is to provide an auditor with
a. Knowledge necessary for audit planning.
b. An evaluation of the consistency of application of management's policies.
c. A basis for modifying tests of controls.
d. Evidential matter to use in assessing inherent risk. (5/95, Aud., #24, amended, 5642)

44. In an audit of financial statements, an auditor's primary consideration regarding an internal control policy or procedure is whether the policy or procedure
a. Reflects management's philosophy and operating style.
b. Affects management's financial statement assertions.
c. Provides adequate safeguards over access to assets.
d. Enhances management's decision-making processes. (11/94, Aud., #28, 5101)

45. An auditor uses the assessed level of control risk to

a. Evaluate the effectiveness of the entity's internal control policies and procedures.
b. Identify transactions and account balances where inherent risk is at the maximum.
c. Indicate whether materiality thresholds for planning and evaluation purposes are sufficiently high.
d. Determine the acceptable level of detection risk for financial statement assertions.

(5/94, Aud., #24, 4689)

46. Which of the following statements is correct concerning an auditor's assessment of control risk?

a. Assessing control risk may be performed concurrently during an audit with obtaining an understanding of the entity's internal control.
b. Evidence about the operation of control procedures in prior audits may **not** be considered during the current year's assessment of control risk.
c. The basis for an auditor's conclusions about the assessed level of control risk need **not** be documented unless control risk is assessed at the maximum level.
d. The lower the assessed level of control risk, the less assurance the evidence must provide that the control procedures are operating effectively.

(11/95, Aud., #20, amended, 5967)

47. The ultimate purpose of assessing control risk is to contribute to the auditor's evaluation of the risk that

a. Tests of controls may fail to identify procedures relevant to assertions.
b. Material misstatements may exist in the financial statements.
c. Specified controls requiring segregation of duties may be circumvented by collusion.
d. Entity policies may be overridden by senior management. (11/94, Aud., #30, 5103)

48. Which of the following types of evidence would an auditor most likely examine to determine whether internal control policies and procedures are operating as designed?

a. Gross margin information regarding the client's industry
b. Confirmations of receivables verifying account balances
c. Client records documenting the use of EDP programs
d. Anticipated results documented in budgets or forecasts (11/95, Aud., #11, amended, 5958)

49. Audit evidence concerning segregation of duties ordinarily is best obtained by

a. Performing tests of transactions that corroborate management's financial statement assertions.
b. Observing the employees as they apply control procedures.
c. Obtaining a flowchart of activities performed by available personnel.
d. Developing audit objectives that reduce control risk. (5/93, Aud., #10, 3906)

50. A letter issued on reportable conditions relating to an entity's internal control observed during an audit of financial statements should include a

a. Restriction on the use of the report.
b. Description of tests performed to search for material weaknesses.
c. Statement of compliance with applicable laws and regulations.
d. Paragraph describing management's evaluation of the effectiveness of the control structure.

(5/93, Aud., #23, amended, 3919)

51. An auditor's letter issued on reportable conditions relating to an entity's internal control observed during a financial statement audit should

a. Include a brief description of the tests of controls performed in searching for reportable conditions and material weaknesses.
b. Indicate that the audit's purpose was to report on the financial statements and **not** to provide assurance on the internal control.
c. Include a paragraph describing management's assertion concerning the effectiveness of internal control.
d. Indicate that the reportable conditions should be disclosed in the annual report to the entity's shareholders. (11/95, Aud., #35, amended, 5982)

52. An auditor's communication of internal control related matters noted in an audit usually should be addressed to the

a. Audit committee.
b. Director of internal auditing.
c. Chief financial officer.
d. Chief accounting officer. (Editors, 0050)

53. Reportable conditions are matters that come to an auditor's attention that should be communicated to an entity's audit committee because they represent

a. Disclosures of information that significantly contradict the auditor's going concern assumption.
b. Material fraud or illegal acts perpetrated by high-level management.
c. Significant deficiencies in the design or operation of internal control.
d. Manipulation or falsification of accounting records or documents from which financial statements are prepared. (11/94, Aud., #44, amended, 5117)

OTHER OBJECTIVE FORMAT QUESTION

PROBLEM 33-3 (15 TO 25 MINUTES)

Field, CPA, is auditing the financial statements of Miller Mailorder, Inc. (MMI) for the year ended January 31, 20X1. Field has compiled a list of possible errors and fraud that may result in the misstatement of MMI's financial statements, and a corresponding list of internal control procedures that, if properly designed and implemented, could assist MMI in preventing or detecting the errors and fraud.

REQUIRED:

For each possible error and fraud numbered **1 THROUGH 15**, select one internal control procedure from the answer list that, if properly designed and implemented, most likely could assist MMI in preventing or detecting the errors and fraud. Each response in the list of internal control procedures may be selected once, more than once, or not at all.

Possible Errors and Fraud

1. Invoices for goods sold are posted to incorrect customer accounts. (5724)
2. Goods ordered by customers are shipped, but are not billed to anyone. (5725)
3. Invoices are sent for shipped goods, but are not recorded in the sales journal. (5726)
4. Invoices are sent for shipped goods and are recorded in the sales journal, but are not posted to any customer account. (5727)
5. Credit sales are made to individuals with unsatisfactory credit ratings. (5728)
6. Goods are removed from inventory for unauthorized orders. (5729)
7. Goods shipped to customers do not agree with goods ordered by customers. (5730)
8. Invoices are sent to allies in a fraudulent scheme and sales are recorded for fictitious transactions. (5731)
9. Customers' checks are received for less than the customers' full account balances, but the customers' full account balances are credited. (5732)
10. Customers' checks are misappropriated before being forwarded to the cashier for deposit. (5733)
11. Customers' checks are credited to incorrect customer accounts. (5734)
12. Different customer accounts are each credited for the same cash receipt. (5735)
13. Customers' checks are properly credited to customer accounts and are properly deposited, but errors are made in recording receipts in the cash receipts journal. (5736)
14. Customers' checks are misappropriated after being forwarded to the cashier for deposit. (5737)

15. Invalid transactions granting credit for sales returns are recorded. (5738)

Internal Control Procedures

A. Shipping clerks compare goods received from the warehouse with the details on the shipping documents.

B. Approved sales orders are required for goods to be released from the warehouse.

C. Monthly statements are mailed to all customers with outstanding balances.

D. Shipping clerks compare goods received from the warehouse with approved sales orders.

E. Customer orders are compared with the inventory master file to determine whether items ordered are in stock.

F. Daily sales summaries are compared with control totals of invoices.

G. Shipping documents are compared with sales invoices when goods are shipped.

H. Sales invoices are compared with the master price file.

I. Customer orders are compared with an approved customer list.

J. Sales orders are prepared for each customer order.

K. Control amounts posted to the accounts receivable ledger are compared with control totals of invoices.

L. Sales invoices are compared with shipping documents and approved customer orders before invoices are mailed.

M. Prenumbered credit memos are used for granting credit for goods returned.

N. Goods returned for credit are approved by the supervisor of the sales department.

O. Remittance advices are separated from the checks in the mailroom and forwarded to the accounting department.

P. Total amounts posted to the accounts receivable ledger from remittance advices are compared with the validated bank deposit slip.

Q. The cashier examines each check for proper endorsement.

R. Validated deposit slips are compared with the cashier's daily cash summaries.

S. An employee, other than the bookkeeper, periodically prepares a bank reconciliation.

T. Sales returns are approved by the same employee who issues receiving reports evidencing actual return of goods.

(5/95, Aud., #3, amended, 5724-5738)

ESSAY QUESTIONS

ESSAY 33-4 (15 TO 20 MINUTES)

Smith, CPA, has been engaged to audit the financial statements of Reed, Inc., a publicly held retailing company. Before assessing control risk, Smith is required to obtain an understanding of Reed's control environment.

REQUIRED:

a. Identify additional control environment factors (excluding the factor illustrated in the example below) that establish, enhance, or mitigate the effectiveness of specific policies and procedures.

b. For the control environment factors identified in a., describe the components that could be of interest to the auditor.

Use the following format:

Management Philosophy and Operating Style

Management philosophy and operating style characteristics may include the following: management's approach to taking and monitoring business risks; management's attitudes and actions toward financial reporting; and management's emphasis on meeting budget, profit, and other financial and operating goals.

(11/91, Aud., #3)

ESSAY 33-5 (15 TO 25 MINUTES)

An auditor is required to obtain a sufficient understanding of each of the components of an entity's internal control. This is necessary to plan the audit of the entity's financial statements and to assess control risk.

REQUIRED:

a. For what purposes should an auditor's understanding of internal control components be used in planning an audit?

b. What is required for an auditor to assess control risk at below the maximum level?

c. What should an auditor consider when seeking a further reduction in the planned assessed level of control risk?

d. What are an auditor's documentation requirements concerning an entity's internal control and the assessed level of control risk? (11/92, Aud., #4)

ESSAY 33-6 (15 TO 25 MINUTES)

Green, CPA, is considering audit risk at the financial statement level in planning the audit of National Federal Bank (NFB) Company's financial statements for the year ended December 31, 20X1. Audit risk at the financial statement level is influenced by the risk of material misstatements, which may be indicated by a combination of factors related to management, the industry, and the entity. In assessing such factors, Green has gathered the following information concerning NFB's environment.

Company profile:

NFB is a federally insured bank that has been consistently more profitable than the industry average by marketing mortgages on properties in a prosperous rural area, which has experienced considerable growth in recent years. NFB packages its mortgages and sells them to large mortgage investment trusts. Despite recent volatility of interest rates, NFB has been able to continue selling its mortgages as a source of new lendable funds.

NFB's board of directors is controlled by Smith, the majority stockholder, who also acts as the chief executive officer. Management at the bank's branch offices has authority for directing and controlling NFB's operations and is compensated based on branch profitability. The internal auditor reports directly to Harris, a minority shareholder, who also acts as chairman of the board's audit committee.

The accounting department has experienced little turnover in personnel during the five years Green has audited NFB. NFB's formula consistently underestimates the allowance for loan losses, but its controller has always been receptive to Green's suggestions to increase the allowance during each engagement.

Recent developments:

During 20X1, NFB opened a branch office in a suburban town thirty miles from its principal place of business. Although this branch is not yet profitable due to competition from several well-established regional banks, management believes that the branch will be profitable by 20X3.

Also, during 20X1, NFB increased the efficiency of its accounting operations by installing a new, sophisticated computer system.

REQUIRED:

Based only on the information above, describe the factors that most likely would have an effect on the risk of material misstatements. Indicate whether each factor increases or decreases the risk. Use the format illustrated below.

Environmental factor	Effect on risk of material misstatements
Branch management has authority for directing and controlling operations	Increase

(5/91, Aud., #5, amended)

ESSAY 33-7 (25 TO 35 MINUTES)

Recently there has been a significant number of highly publicized cases of alleged or actual management fraud involving the misstatement of financial statements. Although most client managements possess unquestioned integrity, a very small number, given sufficient incentive and opportunity, may be predisposed to fraudulently misstate reported financial condition and operating results.

a. What distinguishes management fraud from a defalcation?

b. What are an auditor's responsibilities under generally accepted auditing standards to detect management fraud?

c. What are the characteristics of management fraud that an auditor should consider to fulfill the auditor's responsibilities under generally accepted auditing standards related to detecting management fraud?

d. Three factors that heighten an auditor's concern about the existence of management fraud include (1) an intended public placement of securities in the near future, (2) management remuneration dependent on operating results, and (3) a weak internal control environment evidenced by lack of concern for basic controls and disregard of the auditor's recommendations. What other factors should heighten an auditor's concern about the existence of management fraud? (11/95, Aud., #4)

ESSAY 33-8 (15 TO 25 MINUTES)

During the course of an audit made in accordance with generally accepted auditing standards, an auditor may become aware of matters relating to the client's internal control that may be of interest to the client's audit committee or to individuals with an equivalent level of authority and responsibility, such as the board of directors, the board of trustees, or the owner in an owner-managed enterprise.

REQUIRED:

a. What are meant by the terms "reportable conditions" and "material weaknesses"?

b. What are an auditor's responsibilities in identifying and reporting these matters?

(5/90, Aud., #3, amended, 3012)

SOLUTION 33-1 MULTIPLE CHOICE ANSWERS

GENERAL CONSIDERATIONS

1\. (a) AU 319.16 states that the potential effectiveness of an entity's internal control is subject to inherent limitations such as mistakes in judgment. Policies and procedures that require segregation of duties can be circumvented by collusion among employees and by management override.

2\. (d) AU 319.17 states, "The cost of an entity's internal control should not exceed the benefits...expected to be derived."

COMPONENTS

3\. (b) The control environment reflects the overall attitude, awareness, and actions of the board of directors, management, owners and others concerning the importance of control and its emphasis in the entity. If management is dominated by one individual who is also a shareholder, aggressive reporting and the achievement of profit goals may be overemphasized to the detriment of proper reporting. Answers (a), (c), and (d) represent examples of positive control environment influences.

4\. (b) AU 319.22 states, "Concerns about the integrity of the entity's management may be so serious as to cause the auditor to conclude that the risk of management misrepresentations in the financial statements is such that an audit cannot be conducted." Answers (a), (c), and (d) should be considered by the auditor but are not necessarily serious enough to cause an auditability question.

5\. (c) AU 319.84 (8), includes the use of budgets and forecasts as management control activities. Answer (a) is discussed under external influences. Answer (b) is a control procedure. Answer (d) is part of personnel policies and procedures.

6\. (a) AU 319.07 states that internal control consists of five interrelated components: the control environment, control activities, risk assessment, information and communication, and monitoring. Control risk is one of the three components of audit risk (AU 312.46).

7\. (d) AU 319.26 states, "The auditor should obtain sufficient knowledge of the control environment to understand management's and the board of directors' attitude, awareness, and actions concerning the control environment, considering both the substance of controls and their collective effect. The auditor should concentrate on the substance of controls rather than their form because controls may be established but not acted upon." Depending on the size of the entity, written policies, such as formal credit policies, may not be necessary. Answer (c) would require alternative audit procedures be performed to compensate for the lack of internal control because this would be a result of understanding the substance of a procedure rather than its form, and answer (b) would not affect the auditor's assessment of the performance of control procedures.

8\. (c) AU 319.25 states, "The control environment sets the tone of an organization, influencing the control consciousness of its people." Factors include management's philosophy and operating style, personnel policies and practices, etc. Detection risk is an element of audit risk and is a factor used by the auditor in determining overall audit risk. Detection risk is a factor in determining audit risk, not a factor of the control environment.

UNDERSTANDING OF INTERNAL CONTROL

9. (b) AU 319.21 does not require the auditor to obtain knowledge about operating effectiveness as part of the understanding of internal control. AU 319.19 states that the auditor's understanding of the entity's internal control should include knowledge about the design of relevant controls and whether they have been placed in operation by the entity.

10. (b) AU 319.34 states, "The information system relevant to financial reporting objectives, which includes the accounting system, consists of the methods and records established to record, process, summarize, and report an entity's transactions...and to maintain accountability...." Answers (a), (c), and (d) are all examples of control procedures.

11. (d) AU 319.05 states, "The auditor uses the knowledge provided by the understanding of internal control and the assessed level of control risk in determining the nature, timing, and extent of substantive tests for financial statement assertions."

12. (d) AU 319.10 states, "Generally, controls that are relevant to an audit pertain to the entity's objective of preparing financial statements for external purposes...."

13. (a) AU 319.19 states, "[The auditor's] knowledge should be used to identify types of potential misstatements, consider factors that affect the risk of material misstatements, and design substantive tests." AU 319.12 states "Controls concerning...the effectiveness and efficiency of... processes...ordinarily do not relate to a financial statement audit." Answer (c) refers to an inherent limitation (AU 319.16). AU 319.05 states, "The auditor uses the knowledge provided by the understanding of internal control and the assessed level of control risk in determining the nature, timing, and extent of substantive tests for financial statement assertions."

14. (d) AU 319.02 states that the auditor should obtain an understanding of internal control sufficient to plan the audit by performing procedures to understand the design of controls relevant to an audit of financial statements, and whether they have been placed in operation. AU 319.44 states, "The auditor should document the understanding of the entity's internal control obtained to plan the audit." The auditor is not obligated to search for significant deficiencies in the operation of internal control in obtaining an understanding of the entity's internal control.

15. (b) A function of internal control is to provide assurance that errors and fraud may be discovered with reasonable promptness. AU 319.12 states, "Controls concerning the effectiveness and efficiency of processes...ordinarily do not relate to a financial statement audit." Internal controls will not provide reasonable assurance that collusion or management intervention has not occurred.

ASSESSMENT OF CONTROL RISK

16. (c) AU 319.81 states, "Ordinarily the assessed level of control risk cannot be sufficiently low to eliminate the need to perform any substantive tests to restrict detection risk for all of the assertions relevant to significant...transaction classes." Tests of controls are used in assessing the level of control risk. Analytical procedures are required to be used in the planning stage of the audit. However, they would not be performed to verify the design of internal control procedures. A dual purpose test is a sample that is designed to both assess control risk and to provide substantive testing as to whether a recorded balance or amount is correct, and is not a required procedure.

17. (b) According to AU 319.53, in assessing control risk, an auditor selects from tests such as inquiry, observation, inspection, and reperformance of a policy or procedure that pertains to an assertion. Answers (a), (c), and (d) contain substantive tests.

18. (d) AU 319.23 states, "In making a judgment about the understanding of the internal control necessary to plan the audit,...the auditor considers his or her assessments of inherent risk, judgments about materiality, and the complexity and sophistication of the entity's operations and systems."

19. (d) AU 319.80 states, "As the assessed level of control risk decreases, the acceptable level of detection risk increases." Understanding the control environment and inherent risk come before control risk assessment. Auditor materiality judgments are inputs to the process.

20. (d) AU 319.48 states, "Assessing control risk at below the maximum level involves identifying specific internal control policies and procedures relevant to specific assertions that are likely to prevent or detect material misstatements in those assertions...." Inherent risk is assessed separately and before control risk. According to AU 313.05, changing the timing of substantive tests by omitting interim-date testing and performing the tests at year end is a procedure that is either not affected or would go in the opposite direction.

21. (a) AU 319.61 and .62 state that after obtaining an understanding of internal control, the auditor considers if it is efficient to perform tests of controls that would result in a reduction in planned substantive tests. If evidence is not available, tests of controls are not performed. As the assessed level of control risk increases, the auditor is less likely to test controls. If the auditor is aware of many internal control weaknesses, the assessed level of control risk will be high, and controls will not be tested.

22. (a) AU 319.47 states, "The auditor may assess control risk at the maximum level for some or all assertions because he or she believes policies and procedures are unlikely to pertain to an assertion, are unlikely to be effective, or because evaluating their effectiveness would be inefficient." Answer (b) is a true statement, but, it would not be valid reasoning for assessing control risk at the maximum. Answer (d) is incorrect because the opposite would be true when assessing control risk at the maximum. This situation would apply when control risk is assessed at below the maximum.

23. (c) AU 319.47 states, "Control risk should be assessed in terms of financial statement assertions."

24. (d) After the auditor obtains an understanding of the entity's internal control and assesses control risk, the auditor may want to seek a further reduction in the assessed level of control risk for certain assertions. In such a case, the auditor considers whether additional evidential matter is available to support a further reduction. AU 319.62 states, "The auditor weighs the increase in audit effort associated with the additional tests of controls that is necessary to obtain...[additional] evidential matter [that supports a further reduction in the assessed level of control risk for an assertion] against the resulting decrease in audit effort associated with the reduced substantive tests." Answers (b) and (c) would have occurred prior to the auditor's initial control risk assessment.

RISK RELATIONSHIPS

25. (b) Detection risk has an inverse relationship to control risk. Therefore, if an auditor decides to *increase* the assessed level of control risk from the originally planned level, in order to achieve an equivalent overall level of risk, the detection risk must be *decreased*.

26. (c) Inherent risk and control risk are present whether or not an audit is done. Detection risk is the risk that a material misstatement is present, and it is not detected during the audit. All three components of audit risk may be assessed in quantitative or qualitative terms. None of these types of risk arise from the misapplication of auditing standards; they are present in any audit. Inherent risk and control risk cannot be changed at the auditor's discretion; the auditor can only change the *assessment* of the level of inherent and control risk.

27. (a) AU 319.55 states, "The auditor uses the acceptable level of detection risk to determine the nature, timing and extent of the auditing procedures to be used to detect material misstatements in the financial statements in the financial statement assertions. Auditing procedures designed to detect such misstatements are referred to in this section as substantive tests." AU 319.56 states, "As the acceptable level of detection risk decreases, the assurance provided from substantive tests should increase." The risk of misapplying audit procedures is a part of detection risk. The acceptable level of detection risk is unrelated to the preliminary judgment about materiality levels. The risk of failing to discover material misstatements during an audit is detection risk.

28. (c) AU 319.80 states, "As the assessed level of control risk decreases, the acceptable level of detection risk increases. Accordingly, the auditor may alter the nature, timing, and extent of the substantive tests performed." The auditor would change the extent of substantive tests, such as using a larger sample size than planned when the acceptable level of detection risk decreases (AU 319.56). The auditor would change the nature of substantive tests from a less effective to a more effective procedure when the acceptable level of detection risk decreases (AU 319.56).

TESTS OF CONTROLS

29. (d) Observing the entity's personnel applying the activities provides evidence about the implementation of internal control activities. Entity personnel may have trouble implementing poorly designed activities. The procedures in the other answer options might detect misstatements, but would not provide much information about internal control.

30. (d) According to AU 350.42, evidence that a deviation was covered up in a fraudulent manner would require the auditor to consider the implications of the deviation more closely. Answers (a), (b), and (c) give no causes for added concern.

31. (d) AU 319.58 states, "The objective of tests of controls is to provide the auditor with evidential matter to use in assessing control risk" AU 319.47 states, "Assessing control risk is the process of evaluating the effectiveness of an entity's internal control." Answer (a) would be a substantive test rather than a test of controls. Determining whether internal control policies and procedures have been placed in operation is the objective of obtaining a sufficient understanding of each of the five components in an entity's internal control. Answer (c) is the objective of tests of details of transactions performed as substantive tests.

Documentation

32. (c) AU 319.44 states that the auditor must document the understanding of the components of internal control regardless of the level of assessed control risk. The information system includes the accounting system per AU 319.34 When control risk is assessed at the maximum level, the auditor documents the conclusion that control risk is at the maximum level, but is not required to document the basis for the conclusion (AU 319.57).

33. (c) According to AU 319.57, the auditor is required to document the understanding of the entity's internal control and the basis for concluding that control risk is below the maximum level. The control environment is one component of internal control.

Audit Committee

34. (c) AU 325.18 states that reportable conditions may be communicated during the course of the audit or after its completion. AU 325.04 states, "The auditor is not obligated to search for reportable conditions." AU 325.15 specifies which reportable conditions might be considered material weaknesses. AU 325.17 *prohibits* an auditor from reporting that no reportable conditions were noted.

35. (c) AU 325.11 states that any report issued on reportable conditions should include the definition of reportable conditions, indicate that the purpose of the audit was to report on the financial statements and not to provide assurance on internal control, and include a restriction on distribution. The restriction in the report should state that the communication is intended solely for the information and the use of the audit committee, management, and others within the organization. Reportable conditions do not create scope limitations, and management may have made a conscious decision, of which the audit committee is aware, to accept the degree of risk related to the reportable condition due to cost or other considerations. It is the responsibility of management to make the decision concerning costs to be incurred and related benefits of any corrective measures. The auditor's objective in an audit of financial statements is to form an opinion on the entity's financial statements taken as a whole. AU 325.04 states, "The auditor is not obligated to search for reportable conditions." AU 325.18 states, "Because timely communication may be important, the auditor may choose to communicate significant matters during the course of the audit, rather than after the audit is concluded." The auditor is not required to perform tests of controls on reportable conditions; however, performing tests of controls in an audit may reveal reportable conditions. The decision on whether an interim communication should be issued would be influenced by the significance of the matters noted and the urgency of corrective follow-up action, not in which stage of the audit the auditor is.

36. (d) The Yellow Book, *GAO Government Auditing Standards*, 5.21-.23 states that GAGAS require auditors to report fraud directly to parties outside the auditee if the management of the auditee fails to take remedial steps or does not report the irregularity as soon as practicable to the appropriate entity. GAS 5.25 states that laws, regulations, or policies may require the auditor to report indications of certain types of fraud to proper authorities under some circumstances.

37. (d) The auditor is *required* to report to the audit committee all "reportable conditions" (i.e. matters coming to the auditor's attention that, in his or her judgment, should be reported because they represent significant deficiencies in the design or operation of internal control). The auditor may also choose to communicate, for the benefit of management, matters which would not fit the definition of reportable conditions (i.e., constructive suggestions) (AU 325.01-.03). Constructive suggestions would be a desirable by-product of the audit. They need not be limited to special engagements, nor are they required during the consideration of internal control.

38. (d) AU 325.06 states, "Periodically, the auditor should consider whether, because of changes in management, the audit committee, or simply because of the passage of time, it is appropriate and timely to report [the existence of reportable conditions already known]." Answers (a) and (c) may affect the auditor's judgment about necessary audit procedures, but they would not require the communication of a previously communicated reportable condition. There is no point in communicating a reportable condition again if the entity is aware of and accepts the degree of risk associated with the condition.

39. (b) AU 325.15 states, "A material weakness in internal control...is a reportable condition in which the design or operation of the specified internal control...[components do] not reduce to a relatively low level the risk that errors or fraud in amounts that would be material in relation to the financial statements being audited may occur and not be detected within a timely period by employees in the normal course of performing their assigned functions."

40. (b) AU 325.17 states, "Because of the potential for misinterpretation of the limited degree of assurance associated with the auditor issuing a written report representing that no reportable conditions were noted during an audit, the auditor should not issue such representations." *Significant deficiencies* are reportable conditions about which the report does not guarantee do not exist. Answers (a), (c), and (d) are all examples of items that could be included in a report on internal control related matters noted in an audit.

SOLUTION 33-2 ADDITIONAL MULTIPLE CHOICE ANSWERS

COMPONENTS

41. (c) AU 319.25 states, "The auditor should obtain sufficient knowledge of the control environment to understand...the board of directors' attitude, awareness, and actions concerning the control environment." In its discussion of the control environment, AU 319.84(3) states, "An entity's control consciousness is influenced significantly by the entity's board of directors or audit committee." Computer-based controls, the system of segregation of duties, and safeguards over access to assets are day-to-day details with which board members are unlikely to have as much influence (unless they are also officers).

42. (b) AU 319.84(3) states, "Management philosophy and operating style encompass a broad range of characteristics..." that have a significant influence on the control environment, particularly when management is dominated by one or a few individuals. (Also AU 316.10) Answers (a), (c), and (d) are aspects of other control environment factors.

UNDERSTANDING OF INTERNAL CONTROL

43. (a) The second standard of field work is, "An understanding of internal control is to be obtained sufficient to plan the audit...." The other choices are intermediate considerations.

44. (b) AU 319.14 states, "The auditor's primary consideration is whether a specific control affects financial statement assertions, rather than its classification into any particular category." Management's philosophy and operating style are elements of the control environment that would influence policies and procedures, but are not the primary consideration. Answer (c) represents physical control over assets, but would not be a control policy applicable to liabilities and is therefore not a primary consideration of general policies and procedures. Control policies should *reflect* management's decision-making processes. Sufficient financial and substantive information would help *enhance* management's decision-making processes.

ASSESSMENT OF CONTROL RISK

45. (d) AU 319.55 states, "The auditor uses the assessed level of control risk...to determine the acceptable level of detection risk for financial statement assertions." The effectiveness of control policies and procedures are evaluated by the actual tests of control. Answer (b) is not an objective of assessing control risk. Answer (c) is not a direct result of assessing control risk but a result of performing tests of controls.

46. (a) AU 319.58 states that obtaining an understanding of internal control and assessing control risk may be performed concurrently in an audit. AU 319.71 states, "Evidential matter about the effective design or operation of controls that was obtained in prior audits may be considered by the auditor in assessing control risk in the current audit." According to AU 319.57, when the auditor assesses control risk below the maximum level, the auditor is required to document the auditor's understanding of the entity's control environment and basis for concluding that control risk is below the maximum level. The lower the assessed level of control risk, the *more* assurance the evidence must provide that the control procedures are operating effectively. (AU 319.64, .65)

47. (b) AU 319.79 states, "The ultimate purpose of assessing control risk is to contribute to the auditor's evaluation of the risk that material misstatements exist in the financial statements." Tests of controls are performed on procedures after making a preliminary assessment of control risk and when it is likely and potentially efficient to obtain a lower assessed level of control risk. Thus, tests of controls are not performed to identify procedures, but rather to test procedures relevant to assertions. Answers

(c) and (d) are resulting by-products of assessing control risk and performing tests of controls.

TESTS OF CONTROLS

48. (c) When a client has documentation regarding the use of EDP programs, it is an effective internal control. Answer (b) is a substantive test. Answers (a) and (d) are analytical procedures.

49. (b) AU 326.19 states that the persuasiveness of evidential matter depends upon the circumstances under which it is obtained and the independent auditor's direct personal knowledge, obtained through physical examination, observation, computation, and inspection, is more persuasive than information obtained indirectly. Performing tests of transactions tests segregation of duties from the past which may not be operating currently. A flowchart reflects the ideal operating conditions of the company, established at a point in time, which may not be representative of the actual processing procedures being performed. Audit objectives cannot in themselves reduce control risk.

AUDIT COMMITTEE

50. (a) AU 325.10 states, "The report on reportable conditions should state that the communication is intended solely for the information and use of the audit committee, management, and others within the organization." Answers (b) and (c) should not be included in the letter. The auditor bases the nature, extent, and timing of his or her substantive tests on the operating effectiveness of the controls. Management's evaluation of internal control is not reported on by the auditor.

51. (b) According to AU 325.11, "Any report issued on reportable conditions [relating to an entity's internal control] should [1] indicate that the purpose of the audit was to report on the financial statements and not to provide assurance on the internal control structure, [2] include the definition of reportable conditions, and [3] include the restriction on distribution as discussed in paragraph .10." AU 325.10 provides that the report "is intended solely for the information and the use of the audit committee, management, and others within the organization," and, in some circumstances, specified regulatory authorities as appropriate (AU 325.10). A brief description of the tests of controls performed is not required. Reportable conditions are not required to be disclosed in the annual report to the shareholders. A paragraph describing management's assertion concerning the effectiveness of internal control is not required.

52. (a) AU 325.01 states, "It is contemplated that the communication [of internal control matters] would generally be to the audit committee or to individuals with a level of authority and responsibility equivalent to an audit committee in organizations that do not have one, such as the board of directors, the board of trustees, an owner in an owner-managed enterprise, or others who may have engaged the auditor." In some situations, the auditor may report to the director of internal auditing, chief financial officer or chief accounting officer, but whenever possible, communication should be made with the audit committee.

53. (c) AU 325.02 states that reportable conditions are matters coming to the auditor's attention that, in his or her judgment, should be communicated to the audit committee because they represent significant deficiencies in the design or operation of internal control, which could adversely affect the organization's ability to record and process, financial data consistent with the assertions of management in the financial statements. Reportable conditions do not necessarily indicate an inability for the entity to continue as a going concern. Answer (b) and (d) represent employee fraud or illegal acts.

PERFORMANCE BY SUBTOPICS

Each category below parallels a subtopic covered in Chapter 33. Record the number and percentage of questions you correctly answered in each subtopic area.

General Considerations

Question #	Correct √
1	
2	
# Questions	2
# Correct	
% Correct	

Components

Question #	Correct √
3	
4	
5	
6	
7	
8	
# Questions	6
# Correct	
% Correct	

Understanding of Internal Control

Question #	Correct √
9	
10	
11	
12	
13	
14	
15	
# Questions	7
# Correct	
% Correct	

Assessment of Control Risk

Question #	Correct √
16	
17	
18	
19	
20	
21	
22	
23	
24	
# Questions	9
# Correct	
% Correct	

Risk Relationships

Question #	Correct √
25	
26	
27	
28	
# Questions	4
# Correct	
% Correct	

Tests of Controls

Question #	Correct √
29	
30	
31	
# Questions	3
# Correct	
% Correct	

Documentation

Question #	Correct √
32	
33	
# Questions	2
# Correct	
% Correct	

Audit Committee

Question #	Correct √
34	
35	
36	
37	
38	
39	
40	
# Questions	7
# Correct	
% Correct	

OTHER OBJECTIVE FORMAT QUESTION SOLUTION

SOLUTION 33-3 ERRORS & FRAUD

1. C The error of posting a customer's invoice to the wrong account would be detected when a monthly statement was received, indicating a balance due, when no payment is owed.

2. G Before goods are shipped from the warehouse, an employee should determine that a valid sales invoice exists that matches the shipping documents and actual shipment being made. This would prevent shipments being made that did not result from a customer order.

3. F To prevent having unrecorded sales, the company should make a comparison each day of the total sales invoices with the daily sales summaries. This comparison would detect differences between the total sales made and recorded.

4. K Unrecorded accounts receivable would be prevented by comparing the control total of sales invoices to the control total amount posted to the accounts receivable ledger. Any differences would indicate possible errors in the recording function and require a reconciliation, which would detect unposted customer sales.

5. I Requiring employees to use an approved customer list before making credit sales to customers would prevent the company from allowing sales to be made to uncreditworthy customers.

6. B An internal control procedure that would prevent goods being removed from the warehouse when a bona fide sale does not exist would be the requirement that an approved sales order be received in the warehouse before the goods could be released from the warehouse.

7. D The company should implement an internal control procedure to prevent shipping Customer A's order to Customer B. A control procedure to prevent such errors would be to have the shipping

clerk compare the order received from the warehouse and prepared for shipping to the approved customer sales order.

8. L The company would be able to prevent a fraudulent sales scheme where sales were recorded for fictitious transactions if certain control procedures were in place. For example, requiring an employee not in the sales department to compare customer sales invoices to shipping documents and approved customer orders before invoices were recorded and sent would prevent other than bona fide sales transactions from being recorded.

9. P The company would be able to detect errors in postings to customer accounts by placing certain control procedures in place. For example, by comparing the validated bank deposit slip total to the accounts receivable posting total for the day, a difference in the amount posted from the remittance advice to the accounts receivable ledger and the amount of checks actually received and deposited would be discovered.

10. C Mailing monthly statements to all customers with outstanding balances would most likely detect if customers' checks are misappropriated before being forwarded to the cashier for deposit. The customers would be billed for invoices already paid and would let MMI know.

11. C The company should implement control procedures to detect errors in postings to customer accounts. For example, mailing monthly statements to all customers with outstanding balances would detect posting errors as customers who had paid their accounts (but receive statements indicating a balance due) would most likely call the company to report the error in their account balance status.

12. P By comparing the accounts receivable postings to the validated deposit slip total, the difference resulting from posting one cash receipt remittance advice amount to two accounts in the accounts receivable ledger would be detected.

13. S Errors made in recording receipts in the cash receipts journal would most likely be detected if bank reconciliations are periodically prepared as the deposit amounts on the bank statements would be compared to the receipts as listed in the cash receipts journal. For internal control purposes, the person preparing the bank reconciliation should be someone other than the bookkeeper who is preparing the cash receipts journal.

14. P The company should implement control procedures to prevent customer checks from being misappropriated before being deposited by the cashier. One procedure to have in place would require comparing the total amount posted to the accounts receivable ledger from the remittance advice to the validated deposit slip. Differences may indicate misappropriation of customer checks because they were not deposited or were deposited to accounts other than the company's operating account or possibly a bank account unrelated to the company.

15. N To prevent invalid transactions granting credit for sales returns from being recorded, internal control procedures should be implemented to require proper authorization of any sales returns. Authorization by the supervisor of the sales department would be appropriate, especially as the sales supervisor's goals are generally higher sales results, and thus, he or she would not likely have a motivation for approving invalid sales returns.

ESSAY SOLUTIONS

SOLUTION 33-4 CONTROL ENVIRONMENT

The control environment factors (excluding the factor illustrated in the example) that establish, enhance, or mitigate the effectiveness of specific policies and procedures, and their components are

Organizational Structure

An entity's organizational structure provides the **overall framework** for planning, directing, and controlling operations. An organizational structure includes consideration of the form and nature of an entity's **organizational units**, including the **data processing organization**, and **related management** functions and **reporting relationships**. In addition, the organizational structure should **assign authority and responsibility** within the entity in an appropriate manner.

Audit Committee/Board of Directors

An effective audit committee takes an **active role** in **overseeing** an entity's accounting and financial **reporting policies and practices**. The committee should **assist the board** of directors in fulfilling its **fiduciary and accountability responsibilities** and should help maintain a direct line of communication between the board and the entity's external and internal auditors.

Methods of Assigning Authority and Responsibility

These methods affect the understanding of reporting relationships and responsibilities established within the entity. Methods of assigning authority and responsibility include consideration of

- **Entity policy regarding** such matters as **acceptable business practices**, conflicts of interest, and **codes of conduct**.
- Assignment of responsibility and delegation of authority to deal with such matters as organizational goals and objectives, operating functions, and regulatory requirements.
- Employee **job descriptions** delineating specific duties, reporting relationships, and constraints.
- **Computer systems documentation** indicating the procedures for authorizing transactions and approving system changes.

Internal Audit Function

The internal audit function is established within an entity to **examine and evaluate the adequacy** and **effectiveness of other internal control policies and procedures**. Establishing an effective internal audit function includes consideration of its **authority** and **reporting relationships**, the **qualifications** of its staff, and its **resources**.

Management Control Methods

These methods affect management's direct control over the exercise of authority delegated to others and its ability to effectively supervise overall company activities. Management control methods include consideration of

- **Establishing planning and reporting systems** that set forth management's plans and the results of actual performance. Such systems may include **business planning; budgeting**, forecasting, and profit planning; and responsibility accounting.
- Establishing **methods that identify** the status of **actual performance and exceptions from planned performance**, as well as communicating them to the appropriate levels of management.
- Using such methods at appropriate management levels to **investigate variances from expectations** and to take appropriate and timely **corrective action**.
- Establishing and **monitoring** policies **for** developing and **modifying accounting systems** and **control procedures**, including the development, modification, and use of any related computer programs and data files.

Personnel Policies and Practices

These polices and practices affect an entity's ability to employ sufficient competent personnel to accomplish its goals and objectives. **Personnel policies** and practices include consideration of an entity's policies and procedures for **hiring, training, evaluating, promoting**, and **compensating** employees, and giving them the resources necessary to **discharge** their assigned responsibilities.

External Influences

These are influences established and exercised by parties outside an entity that affect an entity's operations and practices. They include monitoring and **compliance requirements** imposed by legislative and regulatory bodies, such as examinations by bank regulatory agencies. They also include review and **follow-up by parties outside the entity** concerning entity actions. External influences are ordinarily outside an entity's authority. Such influences, however, may **heighten management's consciousness** of and attitude towards the conduct and reporting of an entity's operations and may also prompt management to establish specific internal control policies or procedures.

SOLUTION 33-5 UNDERSTANDING OF INTERNAL CONTROL

a. In **planning** an audit, an auditor's understanding of the internal control structure elements should be used to **identify** the types of **potential misstatements** that could occur, to consider the factors affecting the risk of material misstatement, and to influence the design of substantive tests.

b. An auditor obtains an **understanding of the design** of relevant internal control policies and procedures and whether they have been **placed in operation**. Assessing control risk at **below the maximum** level further involves **identifying specific policies and procedures** relevant to specific assertions that are **likely to prevent or detect material misstatements** in those assertions. It also involves performing **tests of controls** to evaluate the operating design and effectiveness of such policies and procedures.

c. When seeking a **further reduction** in the assessed level of **control risk**, an auditor should consider whether **additional evidential matter** sufficient to support a further reduction is **likely to be available**, and whether it would be **efficient to perform tests** of controls to obtain that evidential matter.

d. An auditor should **document the understanding** of an entity's internal control components obtained to plan the audit. The auditor also should **document** the **basis for the auditor's conclusion** about the **assessed level of control risk**. If control risk is assessed at the **maximum level**, the auditor should **document that conclusion**, but it is **not required to document the basis** for that conclusion. However, if the assessed level of control risk is **below the maximum** level, the auditor should **document the basis for the conclusion that the effectiveness** of the design and operation **of internal control** policies and procedures **supports that assessed level**.

SOLUTION 33-6 MATERIAL MISSTATEMENT

The factors most likely to have an effect on the risk of material misstatements and their resulting effect include the following:

Environmental factor	Effect on risk of material misstatements
Governmental regulation over the banking industry is extensive.	Decrease
NFB operates profitably in a growing prosperous area.	Decrease
Overall **demand for the industry's product** is high.	Decrease
Interest rates have been **volatile** recently	Increase
The **availability of funds** for additional mortgages is **promising**.	Decrease
The **principal shareholder** is also the **chief executive officer** and controls the board of directors.	Increase
Branch **management is compensated based on branch profitability**.	Increase
The **internal auditor reports directly to the chairman of the board's audit committee**, a minority shareholder.	Decrease
The **accounting department** has experienced **little turnover** in personnel recently.	Decrease
NFB is a **continuing audit client**.	Decrease
Management **fails to establish proper procedures** to provide reasonable assurance of reliable **accounting estimates.**	Increase
Management has been receptive to Green's **suggestions** relating to accounting adjustments.	Decrease
NFB recently **opened a new branch** office that is **not yet profitable**.	Increase
NFB recently installed a **new sophisticated computer system**.	Increase

SOLUTION 33-7 MANAGEMENT FRAUD

a. Management fraud is the **deliberate falsification** or alteration of accounting records or documents committed by management to **intentionally** render the financial statements **misleading.** A defalcation is the misappropriation of an entity's assets by an employee through **embezzlement**, the **falsification** of documents, or **violation** of policy.

b. Under GAAS an auditor is **responsible to assess the risk** that management fraud may cause the financial statements to be materially misstated. Based on that assessment, the **auditor should design the audit to provide reasonable assurance** of detecting management fraud that is material to the financial statements.

c. The characteristics of management fraud that an auditor should consider include the **materiality of** the effect on the financial statements, the level of **management** involved, the **extent and skillfulness of any concealment**, the **relationship to established control procedures**, and **the specific financial statements affected**.

d. Among the other factors that should heighten an auditor's concern about the existence of management fraud are the following:

- **Potential sale** of the entity.
- Undertaking an aggressive acquisition program **using the entity's stock as consideration**.
- Indications that the entity will fall short of meeting **earnings or sales forecasts.**
- Indications of **financial distress** such as insufficient working capital, high debt, slow collection of receivables, or other going concern problems.
- **Unfavorable industry conditions.**
- The existence of **related party transactions**.
- A CEO who **dominates the board of directors.**

SOLUTION 33-8 REPORTABLE CONDITIONS/ MATERIAL WEAKNESSES

a. Reportable conditions are matters that come to an auditor's attention, which, in the auditor's judgment, should be **communicated to the client's audit committee or** its **equivalent** because they represent significant deficiencies in the design or operation of the entity's internal control, which could **adversely affect the organization's ability to record, process, summarize, and report** financial data consistent with the assertions of management in the financial statements.

Material weaknesses are reportable conditions in which the **design or operation** of specific internal control elements do not reduce, to a relatively low level, the **risk that errors or fraud** in amounts that would be **material** in relation to the financial statements being audited **may occur and not be detected** within a **timely period by employees** in the normal course of performing their assigned functions.

b. An auditor is required to identify reportable conditions that come to the auditor's attention in the normal course of an audit, but is not obligated to search for reportable conditions. The auditor uses judgment as to which matters are reportable conditions. Provided the audit committee has acknowledged its understanding and consideration of such deficiencies and the associated risks, the auditor may decide certain matters do not need to be reported unless, because of changes in management or the audit committee, or because of the passage of time, it is appropriate to do so.

Conditions noted by the auditor that are considered reportable **should be reported, preferably in writing**. If information is communicated orally, the auditor should **document the communication**. The report should state that the communication is intended solely for the information and use of the audit committee, management, and others within the organization.

The auditor **may identify and communicate separately** those **reportable conditions the auditor considers to be material weaknesses**, but **may not state that no reportable conditions were noted** during the audit. Reportable conditions may be communicated during the course of the audit rather than after the audit is concluded, depending on the relative significance of the matters noted and the urgency of corrective follow-up action.

Wondering how to allocate your study time?

In your excitement to answer multiple choice questions, don't forget that the examiners ask questions in other formats!

The first pass through a chapter:

1. Strive to answer **all** the multiple choice and other objective format questions.

2. Choose one or more of the essay questions to answer.

When you review the chapter later:

1. Answer **at least** those objective questions that you did not understand the first time. (If you had a lucky guess, did you really understand?)

2. Select a new essay question to answer.

When you review the chapter for the final time (for some chapters, the second time may **be** the final time):

1. Only review the notes you would review just before the exam. For a whole exam section, this should take less than five minutes. Answer the questions "cold turkey" (without reviewing the text materials just before answering questions).

2. Answer **at least** those objective questions that you did not understand the first time.

3. Select a new essay question to answer.

Remember, with the techniques and information in your material,

A passing score is well within reach!

STUDY TIP

On past CPA exams, candidates have been asked to prepare various segments of an internal control questionnaire in the essay section, or answer objective questions identifying audit procedures that most effectively provide audit evidence of internal control policies and procedures. We structure a section of this chapter as the actual questionnaire would appear, starting with the objectives of internal control accompanied by the questions which identify controls to meet the objectives. It is not necessary that you memorize this information, but you should be familiar with the thought processes involved. The editors also strongly suggest candidates familiarize themselves with the policies and procedures within transaction cycles.

CHAPTER 34

INTERNAL CONTROL: TRANSACTION CYCLES

EXAM COVERAGE: The Plan the Engagement and Obtain and Document Information portions of the Auditing section of the CPA exam are designated by the examiners to be 40 and 35 percent of the section's point value, respectively. Historically, exam coverage of the topics in Chapters 33 and 34 fluctuates from 15 to 26 percent of the Auditing section. More information about the point value of various topics is included in the **Practical Advice** section of this volume.

CHAPTER 34

INTERNAL CONTROL: TRANSACTION CYCLES

I. Internal Control Objectives and Procedures for Specific Transaction Cycles

A. Objectives of Internal Control

A well designed internal control should ensure five objectives.

1. **Authorization** The starting point for establishing accounting control of transactions is appropriate authorization. Obtaining reasonable assurance of appropriate general or specific authorization requires independent evidence that authorizations are issued by persons acting within the scope of their authority and that transactions conform with the terms of the authorizations.

2. **Validity** Controls should provide reasonable assurance relative to the validity or existence of assets and liabilities at a given date and whether recorded transactions have occurred during a given period.

3. **Proper Recording** The objective of internal control with respect to the proper recording of transactions encompasses several sub-objectives. These include the following:

   a. **Completeness** Transactions are not omitted from the accounting records.

   b. **Valuation** Transactions are to be recorded at the actual amounts at which they transpired.

   c. **Classification** Transactions are to be classified in the appropriate accounts.

   d. **Timing** Transactions are to be recorded in the accounting period in which they occurred. Additionally, they are to be recorded as promptly as practicable when recording is necessary to maintain accountability.

4. **Accountability and Comparison** The accountability objective of internal control is to assure the availability of information necessary to follow assets from the time of their acquisition until their disposition. This requires maintaining records for accountability of assets and periodic comparison of these records with the related assets. The purpose of comparing recorded accountability with assets is to determine whether the actual assets agree with the recorded accountability. Consequently, it is closely related to the above discussion of proper recording of transactions.

5. **Protection and Limited Access** Controls should provide adequate protection of assets. Such protection is facilitated through segregation of incompatible functions and requires that access to assets be limited to authorized personnel. Access to assets includes both direct physical access and indirect access through documents that authorize use or disposition of assets.

B. Source Documents and Accounting Records

To determine the correct test of an internal control or to identify an internal control weakness, you must understand how source documents and accounting records relate to each other and what type of internal controls should exist.

1. Remember that the authorization of a transaction, its recordkeeping, and the custody of the related asset should all be separated. If any person or department was responsible for more

than one of these functions, an internal control weakness would exist. For example, in the payroll function

a. The personnel department should authorize pay rates (authorization).

b. The timekeeping department should prepare attendance and timekeeping data (recordkeeping).

c. The payroll department prepares the payroll (recordkeeping).

d. The treasurer's department prepares the payroll checks and distributes them to employees (custody).

2. Source documents should be pre-numbered and controlled so that they can all be accounted for.

3. Subsidiary ledgers should be reconciled to general ledgers.

4. When considering a question about testing an internal control, first determine what is being asked.

a. Tracing from a source document to the recorded entry tests the completeness assertion by looking for understatements.

b. Vouching from a recorded entry to the source document tests the existence assertion by looking for overstatements.

C. Transaction Cycles

Internal control objectives can be analyzed based on specific business activities or logical groups of transactions. Groupings of similar transactions or functions of an entity are known as transaction cycles. Dividing the audit into transaction cycles is known as the **cycle approach**. The cycle approach combines similar transactions with the ledger balances that result from those transactions. This is more efficient than treating each account balance as a separate segment. Although classification is somewhat arbitrary, the following is representative of the cycles of most businesses:

1. Sales, Receivables, and Cash Receipts Cycle

2. Purchases, Payables, and Cash Disbursements Cycle

3. Inventory and Production Cycle

4. Personnel and Payroll Cycle

5. Property, Plant, and Equipment Cycle

D. Policies and Procedures Within the Transaction Cycles

This section examines the five transaction cycles more closely by relating specific internal control policies and procedures within the cycles to the objectives of internal control. Additionally, for each control, an audit test of controls is suggested to evaluate the effectiveness of the policies and procedures.

1. Sales, Receivables, and Cash Receipts Cycle

Objective	Internal Control	Test of Controls
Authorization	Credit approval occurs before shipment is authorized.	Examine appropriate document for approval.
	Existence of a cash discount policy.	Discuss policy with management. Review sales orders for evidence of compliance.
	Approval of cash discounts and adjustments.	Examine remittance advices for proper approval.
	Sales prices are from authorized price list or executed contract.	Compare sales invoice prices to appropriate price list or contract.
Validity	Prenumbered sales invoices.	Account for numerical sequence of sales invoices.
	Sales are supported by authorized shipping documents and approved customer orders.	Examine supporting bills of lading and customer orders.
	Monthly statements are mailed to customers.	Observe mailing of statements.
	Independent follow-up of customer complaints.	Examine customer correspondence files.
	Separation of the functions of cash handling and recordkeeping.	Observation. Discuss with management and review employee job descriptions.
	Shipment is acknowledged by shipping department.	Examine acknowledgment on sales order copy.
Proper Recording	Shipping documents are prenumbered (Completeness).	Accounting for numerical sequence of shipping documents. Trace documents to recording of sales and accounts receivable subsidiary ledger.
	A chart of accounts is used and is adequate (Classification).	Review adequacy and use of proper accounts. Examine sales documents to determine if sales transactions are properly classified.
	Cash receipts are recorded immediately and deposited on a daily basis. (Timing).	Observation. Trace totals to duplicate deposit slips.
	Sales invoices and credit memoranda are prenumbered (Completeness).	Account for numerical sequence of sales invoices and credit memoranda.

Objective	Internal Control	Test of Controls
Proper Recording (con't.)	Internal verification of invoice preparation and posting (Valuation, Completeness, Classification).	Observation. Discuss policy with management.
Accountability and Comparison	Independent reconciliation of bank statements.	Observation. Review bank reconciliation.
	Cash register totals are verified by persons not having access to cash or cash records.	Examine documentation of verification.
	Cash receipts are recorded immediately to establish accountability.	Observe the cash receiving process.
	A list of checks is prepared as the mail is opened.	Observation. Compare check listing total to duplicate deposit slip.
Protection and Limited Access	Persons receiving or otherwise handling cash are bonded.	Discuss with management. Review appropriate documentation of bonding.
	Checks are immediately endorsed.	Observation.
	Separation of cash handling and recordkeeping functions.	Observation. Discuss with management and review employee job descriptions.

2. Purchases, Payables, and Cash Disbursements Cycle

Objective	Internal Control	Test of Controls
Authorization	Appropriate approval is required for all purchases.	Examine supporting documentation for indication of approval (purchase requisition and order).
	Payment approval required before check signing.	Observation. Examine documentation for indication of approval.
	Authorized signatures on checks. Two signatures on large checks.	Select a sample of large disbursements from the cash disbursements journal and examine the correlating canceled checks for two signatures.
Validity	Purchases are supported by purchases requisition, purchase order, receiving report, and vendor invoice.	Examine supporting documentation of vouchers.
	Documentation is canceled to prevent reuse.	Examine documentation for indication of cancellation.

Objective	Internal Control	Test of Controls
Validity (con't.)	Receiving reports are prenumbered.	Account for numerical sequence of receiving reports.
	Receiving reports are required before approval of invoice for payment.	Discuss policy with management. Observation. Compare payment approval and receiving report dates.
Proper Recording	Vouchers are prenumbered (Completeness).	Account for numerical sequence of vouchers.
	Internal verification of vendor invoice amounts and calculations. (Valuation).	Examine invoice copy for indication of clerical accuracy verification.
	Transactions are recorded as soon as possible after receiving goods. (Timing).	Compare purchase journal dates to receiving report and invoice dates. (Observation).
	Purchase orders are prenumbered (Completeness).	Account for numerical sequence of purchase orders.
	A chart of accounts is used and is adequate (Classification).	Review adequacy and use of proper accounts. Examine sales documents to determine if sales transactions are properly classified.
Accountability and Comparison	Independent reconciliation of bank statement.	Observation. Review bank reconciliation.
	Checks are signed only with appropriate support, by the treasurer, and the treasurer mails the checks.	Observation. Examine canceled check signatures.
	Monthly suppliers' statements are compared to accounts payable.	Examine statements for indication of agreement.
	Receiving department examines quantity and quality of merchandise upon receipt.	Examine copies of receiving reports and purchase orders for indication of goods received.
	Accountability is established for unused and voided checks.	Discuss policy with management.
Protection and Limited Access	Separation of functions between accounts payable and custody of signed checks.	Observation. Review employee job descriptions.
	Checks are prenumbered.	Account for numerical sequence of checks.
	Mechanical check protector is used.	Examine check copies for evidence of check protector use.

Objective	Internal Control	Test of Controls
Protection and Limited Access (con't.)	Separation of purchasing department functions from receiving and recordkeeping.	Observation. Review employee job descriptions.
	Physical control of unused checks is properly and securely maintained.	Observation. Discuss policy with management.

3. Inventory and Production Cycle

Objective	Internal Control	Test of Controls
Authorization	Movement of inventory items is authorized by requisitions.	Examine requisitions for indication of approval. Inquire of client personnel.
	Inventory purchases are appropriately authorized.	Select a sample of recorded purchases and vouch to documents authorizing purchase.
	Write-offs and write-downs of obsolete inventory are appropriately authorized.	Examine appropriate documentation for indication of authorization.
Validity	Receiving prepares prenumbered receiving reports.	Account for numerical sequence of receiving reports.
	Payment for inventory is approved only after verification of quantity and prices of vendor invoice.	Examine documentation for indication of verification.
Proper Recording	Merchandise receiving reports are matched with vendor invoices (Valuation, Completeness).	Examine vendor invoice copy for indication of agreement with receiving report.
	Purchase orders are prenumbered (Completeness).	Account for numerical sequence of purchase orders.
	Shipping or transfer reports are prenumbered (Completeness).	Account for numerical sequence of reports.
	Movement of inventory items is accounted for on a timely basis by authorized requisitions (Timing, Completeness, Classification).	Compare dates recorded for shipping reports of transferor with receiving report and requisition data of receiving department.
	Clerical accuracy of vendor invoices is checked prior to payment (Valuation).	Examine invoice for indication of accuracy check.

Objective	Internal Control	Test of Controls
Accountability and Comparison	Receiving department indicates inventory received on prenumbered receiving reports as to description and quantity.	Examine receiving reports.
	Perpetual inventory records maintained for large dollar value items.	Review inventory records. Discuss policy with management.
	Periodic comparison made between inventory records and physical inventory.	Review inventory records for indication of agreement with physical count.
Protection and Limited Access	Inventory is stored under the control of a custodian. Access is limited.	Observation. Discuss procedures with management and custodian.
	Inventory purchasers and handlers are bonded.	Review appropriate documentation of bonding.
	Inventory records are maintained separate from the functions of shipping, receiving, and custody.	Observation.
	Physical safeguards against theft and fire exist.	Examine physical safeguards.
	Insurance coverage on inventory is adequate.	Review insurance policies.

4. **PERSONNEL AND PAYROLL CYCLE**

Objective	Internal Control	Test of Controls
Authorization	Employment is authorized before hiring.	Review hiring policies and verify the hiring authorization of a sample of employees.
	Payment rates (including commissions and bonuses) and hours to be worked are authorized at the appropriate levels.	Examine approval for rates or union contracts and approval for hours to be worked.
	Deduction authorizations are obtained for each payroll deduction.	Review personnel file for authorizations.
	Personnel department authorizes all changes to payroll master file.	Review change authorizations for sample of changes made during the year.
	Authorized signature(s) is/are required on payroll checks.	Examine payroll checks for evidence of appropriate signature(s).
Validity	Time clock is used to record time worked by employees.	Observation.

Objective	Internal Control	Test of Controls
Validity (con't.)	Department head or foreman approves and signs time cards.	Examine time cards for indication of approval.
	A paymaster (with no other payroll responsibilities) distributes payroll checks.	Observation. Discuss policy with management.
	Personnel department keeps personnel files on each employee.	Review personnel files.
	Terminations are properly documented.	Review personnel files.
Proper Recording	Accounting procedures require recording payroll transactions as timely as possible (Timing).	Compare time card dates with recording date and paycheck dates for proper timing.
	Job time tickets are reconciled to time clock cards.	Examine job time tickets for indication of reconciliation and/or approval.
	An adequate chart of accounts is maintained including appropriate payroll accounts (Classification).	Review adequacy and use of proper accounts.
	Calculation and amounts of payroll are internally verified. (Completeness, Valuation).	Examine indication of internal verification.
	Account classification of payroll-related transactions is internally verified (Classification).	Review reconciliation of monthly payroll with labor distribution.
Accountability and Comparison	Independent reconciliation of bank statement for imprest payroll account.	Observation. Review reconciliation of bank statement.
	Unclaimed payroll checks are returned to a person responsible for their custody (e.g., internal audit).	Discuss policy with management. Observe distribution of paychecks. Inquire of client personnel.
	Accountability is established for unused and voided payroll account checks.	Discuss policy with management and personnel responsible for check accountability (Observation).
Protection and Limited Access	Separation of personnel, payroll, and timekeeping functions.	Observation. Discuss functions with management.
	Use of a separate imprest payroll account.	Review separate documentation such as bank statements.
	Payroll checks are prenumbered.	Account for numerical sequence of payroll checks.

Objective	Internal Control	Test of Controls
Protection and Limited Access (con't.)	Treasurer signs payroll checks.	Observation. Examine canceled payroll checks.

5. Property, Plant, and Equipment Cycle

Objective	Internal Control	Test of Controls
Authorization	Authorization is required for all purchases over a certain amount.	Discuss policy with management. Review documentation of a sample of large purchases for indication of approval.
Validity	Major purchases require authorization by the board of directors.	Examine documentation of major purchases for approval by board. Review minutes of board meetings.
	Movements or sales of equipment have prior approval.	Examine appropriate documentation for existence of approval.
	Abandonments are reported to accounting department by foremen.	Discuss abandonment policy with management and foremen.
	Purchases are supported by appropriate authorizations, purchase order, receiving report, and vendor invoice.	Examine acquisition files for supporting documentation.
	Policies exist for classification of fixed assets, including a policy for expensing or capitalizing items (Classification).	Examine written policies. Vouch a selected sample of capitalized and expenses disbursements for compliance with policies.
	Policies exist for asset life estimations and depreciation tables used (Valuation, Timing).	Review written policies. Discuss with management. Vouch a sample of items for compliance with policies.
	Depreciation charges are recorded in subsidiary ledgers and amounts are internally verified periodically (Valuation, Completeness).	Examination subsidiary ledgers for appropriate depreciation charges and evidence of internal verification.
	Accounting procedures require timely recording of purchases and associated depreciation (Timing).	Compare receiving report dates, invoice dates, and recording dates for appropriate timing.
Accountability and Comparison	Subsidiary ledgers exist and are used.	Verify the existence of subsidiary ledgers and review entry detail for appropriateness.
	The responsibility for small tools is assigned to individual foremen.	Review tool responsibility with management and foremen. Examine the internal verification of the existence of tools.

Objective	*Internal Control*	*Test of Controls*
Accountability and Comparison (con't.)	Internal verification is performed to examine existence and condition of fixed assets on a periodic basis.	Discuss policy with internal audit. Examine records for indication of verification.
Protection and Limited Access	Equipment has identification numbers to protect against loss.	Examine assets for existence of identification numbers.
	Insurance coverage on property, plant, and equipment is adequate.	Review insurance policies for adequacy of coverage.
	Physical safeguards are available for protection of assets from fire and theft (e.g., fire extinguishers, burglar alarms, etc.).	Examine physical safeguards for adequacy.

II. GENERAL INTERNAL CONTROL QUESTIONNAIRES

A. CONTROL ENVIRONMENT

This questionnaire's objective is to determine if responsibilities are defined and authority is assigned to specific individuals to permit identification of whether persons are acting within the scope of their authority.

Management Philosophy and Operating Style

1. Does management have clear objectives in terms of budget, profit, and other financial and operating goals?

2. Are policies

   a. Clearly written?

   b. Communicated throughout the entity?

   c. Actively monitored?

3. Does management adequately consider the effects of taking business risks?

Organizational Structure

1. Is the organization of the entity clearly defined in terms of lines of authority and responsibility?

2. Does the entity have a current organization chart?

3. Are policies and procedures for authorization of transactions established at adequately high levels?

Audit Committee

1. Does the board of directors have an audit committee?

2. Does the audit committee take an active role in overseeing the entity's accounting and financial reporting policies and practices?

3. Does the audit committee

a. Hold regular meetings?

b. Appoint members with adequate qualifications?

c. Adequately assist the board in meeting its fiduciary responsibilities?

d. Assist the board in maintaining a direct line of communication with the internal and external auditors?

Methods of Assigning Authority and Responsibility

1. Does the entity have code of conduct and conflict of interest requirements?

2. Are employees given job descriptions which delineate specific duties, reporting relationships, and constraints?

3. Has the entity developed computer systems documentation which indicates procedures for authorizing transactions and approving systems changes?

Management Control Methods

1. Are there regular meetings of the board of directors and are minutes of such meetings prepared on a timely basis?

2. Does the entity have in place planning and reporting systems that

   a. Identify variances from planned performance?

   b. Communicate variances to the appropriate management level?

   c. Adequately investigate variances?

   d. Allow management to take appropriate and timely corrective action?

3. Has the company established a records retention policy and made arrangements for the storage of the information?

Internal Audit Function

1. Does the entity have an internal audit function?

2. If the entity has an internal audit function

   a. Is the internal auditor independent of the activities he or she audits?

   b. Is the internal audit function adequately staffed?

   c. Does the internal auditor document internal control and perform tests of controls?

   d. Does the internal auditor perform substantive tests of the details of transactions and account balances?

   e. Does the internal auditor document the planning and execution of his or her work?

   f. Does the internal auditor render written reports on his or her findings and conclusions?

   g. Are the internal auditor's reports submitted to the board or to a similar committee?

3. Does management take timely action to correct conditions reported by the internal auditor?

Personnel Policies and Procedures

1. Are employees adequately trained?

2. Is performance systematically evaluated?

3. Does the entity dismiss employees on a timely basis for critical violations of control policies?

4. Are employees in positions of trust bonded?

5. Are employees required to take mandatory vacations?

6. Is access to records limited to authorized persons?

B. ACCOUNTING SYSTEM

This questionnaire's objective is to determine if accounting policies and procedures are determined in accordance with management's authorization.

- Access to the accounting and financial records is limited to minimize opportunity for errors and fraud and provide reasonable protection from physical hazards.
- Accounting entries are initiated and approved in accordance with management's authorization.
- Accounting entries are appropriately accumulated, classified, and summarized.
- The general ledger and related records permit preparation of financial statements in conformity with GAAP.
- Financial statements with related disclosures are prepared and released in accordance with management's authorization.
- Individuals at appropriate levels consider reliable information in making estimates and judgments required for preparation of the financial statements and related disclosures.

General Accounting

1. Does the entity have adequate written statements and explanations of its accounting policies and procedures, such as

a. Chart of accounts?

b. Assignment of responsibilities and delegation of authority?

c. Explanations of documentation and approval requirements for various types of transactions and journal entries?

2. Is access to the general ledger and related records restricted to those who are assigned general ledger responsibilities?

3. Is appropriate insurance coverage maintained (such as loss of records coverage and fidelity bonding of employees in positions of trust) in accordance with management's authorization?

4. Are all journal entries reviewed and approved?

5. Are all journal entries explained and supported?

6. Are individuals who review and approve journal entries independent of initiation of the entries they are authorized to approve?

Preparation of Financial Statements

1. Are the general ledger accounts arranged in orderly groupings which are conducive to efficient statement preparation?

2. Are there adequate instructions and procedures for

   a. Assignment of specific preparation and review responsibilities?

   b. Accumulation of information on intercompany transactions?

   c. Accumulation of information for footnote disclosure?

3. Are estimates and adjustments to provide valuation allowances reviewed and approved by appropriate levels in the organization independent of the persons originating the estimates and adjustments?

4. Are procedures adequate for the review and comparison of working papers to source data and comparison of elimination and reclassification entries to those made in prior periods?

5. Are financial statements subjected to overall review and comparisons with the prior period and budgeted amounts by appropriate levels of management?

C. Universal Procedures

Several internal control policies and procedures are common to most, if not all, transaction cycles. Listed in the Appendix at the end of this chapter are general internal control questions that can be asked for most of the transaction cycles indicated. These questions are presented in this format to help you become familiar with the general questions. Specific internal control questions applicable to the individual transaction cycles are included under the transaction cycle titles in the Appendix of this chapter. Questions should generally be worded to require a yes or no answer.

III. Transaction Cycle Internal Control Questionnaires

A. Revenues and Receivables

This questionnaire's objectives are to determine if the types of goods and services provided, the manner in which they will be provided, and the customers to which they will be provided are in accordance with management's authorization.

- The prices and other terms of sales are established in accordance with management's authorization.
- Credit terms and limits are established.
- Goods delivered and services provided are based on orders which have been approved.
- Deliveries of goods and services result in preparation of accurate and timely billings.
- Sales related deductions and adjustments are made in accordance with management's authorization.

1. Are sales orders approved before shipment?

2. Do approved sales orders record the terms of sales in detail?

3. Are unfilled sales commitments periodically reviewed?

4. Is current information on prices, discounts, sales taxes, freight, warranties, and returned goods clearly communicated to the sales and billing personnel (i.e. approved sales catalogs, manuals, and price lists)?

5. Is the credit of prospective customers investigated before it is extended to them?

6. Is there a periodic review of credit limits?

7. Are shipping documents prepared for all shipments?

8. Are goods shipped based on documented sales orders which have been approved?

9. Are shipping documents subjected to

a. Timely communication to persons who physically perform the shipping function?

b. Timely communication to persons who perform the billing function?

10. Are quantities of goods shipped verified, by double counting or comparison with counts by common carriers?

11. Are shipping documents compared with billings to determine that all goods shipped are billed and accounted for?

12. Are sales invoices prepared for all shipments of goods?

13. Are sales invoices

a. Matched with approved sales orders?

b. Matched with shipping documents?

14. Are credit memos

a. Pre-numbered and accounted for?

b. Matched with applicable receiving reports for returns?

c. Approved by a responsible employee independent of the person preparing the credit memo?

15. Are monthly statements reviewed and mailed by a responsible employee who is independent of the accounts receivable and cash functions?

16. Is an aging schedule of past due accounts prepared monthly?

17. Is there documentation of review and analysis of accounts receivable balances for determining valuation allowances and any specific balances to be written-off?

18. Are valuation allowances and write-offs approved?

B. Cash Receipts

This questionnaire's objectives are to determine if access to cash receipts records, accounts receivable records, and billing and shipping records is controlled to prevent the taking of unrecorded cash receipts or abstraction of recorded cash receipts.

- Detailed transaction and account balance records are reconciled with control accounts and bank statements at least monthly for the timely detection and correction of errors.
- All cash receipts are recorded at the correct amounts in the period in which received and are properly classified and summarized.

1. Does the person who opens the mail

a. Place restrictive endorsements on all checks received so they are for deposit only?

b. List all remittances and prepare totals daily?

c. Forward all remittances to the person who prepares and makes a daily bank deposit?

2. Are currency receipts forwarded daily to the person who prepares the daily bank deposit?

3. Is a summary listing of daily currency receipts forwarded to a person independent of physical handling of remittances and accounts receivable?

4. Are each day's receipts deposited intact daily?

5. Are all employees who handle receipts adequately bonded?

6. Does company policy prohibit the cashing of any accommodation checks (payroll, personal) out of collections?

7. Are bank chargebacks received directly from the bank and investigated by a person independent of the physical handling of collections and posting of accounts receivable subsidiary ledgers?

8. Are entries to the cash receipts journal compared with

a. Duplicate deposit slips authenticated by the bank?

b. Deposits per the bank statement?

c. Listings prepared when the mail is opened?

9. Is information from remittance documentation adequate for the accurate posting of credits to individual accounts receivable subsidiary records or accounts such as investment income, rents, and sales of property?

10. Are details of collections posted to subsidiary accounts receivable records by a person independent of the general ledger functions, physical handling of collections, and receipt and investigation of bank chargebacks?

C. PURCHASES AND ACCOUNTS PAYABLE

This questionnaire's objectives are to determine if the types of goods and services to be obtained, the manner in which they are obtained, the vendors from which they are obtained, the quantities to be obtained, and the prices and terms initiated and executed are in accordance with management's authorization.

- Adjustments to vendor accounts and account distributions are made in accordance with management's authorization.
- All goods and services received are accurately accounted for on a timely basis.
- Only authorized goods and services are accepted and paid for.
- Amounts payable for goods and services received are accurately recorded at the correct amounts in the appropriate period and properly classified.
- Access to purchasing, receiving, and accounts payable records is controlled to prevent or detect duplicate or improper payments.

1. Are written purchase orders used for all commitments and do those orders include the vendor description, quantity, quality, price, terms, and delivery requirements for the goods or services ordered?

2. Is there a record of open purchase commitments?

3. Are open purchase orders periodically reviewed and investigated?

4. Are goods received inspected for condition and independently counted, for comparison with the applicable purchase order?

5. Are receiving reports prepared promptly for all goods received?

6. Do receiving reports provide for recording of

a. Description, quantity, and acceptability of goods?

b. Date on which the goods or services are received?

c. Signature of the individual approving the receipt?

7. Are receiving reports subjected to

a. Accounting for all receiving reports used?

b. Copies distributed for timely matching with purchase orders and vendor invoices?

8. Is control established over all invoices received?

9. Are duplicate invoices stamped or destroyed as a precaution against duplicate payment?

10. Are vendors' invoices, prior to payment, compared in detail to purchase orders and receiving reports?

11. Are all available discounts taken?

12. Are there procedures for periodic review and investigation of unprocessed invoices, unmatched purchase orders and receiving reports to provide for follow-up and proper accruals and to result in a proper cutoff for financial reporting purposes?

13. Are vendors' statements reviewed for, and proper follow-up made of, overdue items?

D. PAYROLL

This questionnaire's objectives are to determine if employees are hired and retained only at rates and benefits determined by management's authorization.

- Payroll withholdings and deductions are based on evidence of appropriate authorization.
- Compensation is made only to company employees at authorized rates and for services rendered.
- Gross pay, withholdings, deductions, and net pay are correctly computed using authorized rates and properly authorized withholding exemptions and deductions.
- Payroll costs and related liabilities are correctly accumulated, classified, and summarized in the accounts in the proper period.
- Comparisons are made of personnel, payroll, and work records at reasonable intervals for timely detection and correction of errors.
- Net pay and related withholdings and deductions are remitted to the appropriate employees when due.
- Functions are assigned so that no single individual is in a position to both perpetrate and conceal errors and fraud in the normal course of their duties.
- Access to personnel and payroll records is limited.

1. Are all new hires, rates of pay and changes thereto, changes in position, and terminations based on written authorizations by management's criteria?

2. Are appropriate written authorizations obtained from employees for all payroll deductions and withholding exemptions?

3. Are personnel files maintained on individual employees which include appropriate written authorizations for rates of pay, payroll deductions, and withholding exemptions?

4. Are methods for determining premium pay rates for matters such as overtime, night shift work, and employee benefits determined in accordance with management's authorizations?

5. Do employees who perform the payroll processing function receive timely notification of wage and salary rate changes, new hires, changes in position, terminations, and changes in authorized deductions and withholding exemptions?

6. Is there an adequate chart of accounts for determining account distributions for wages and related taxes and controlling liabilities for payroll deductions and taxes withheld?

7. Are clerical operations in the preparation of payrolls verified by re-performance or reconciliation with independent controls over source data?

8. Are piece rate records reconciled with production records, or salesmen's commission records reconciled with recorded sales, or total production hours reconciled with production statistics?

9. Are payroll checks drawn on a separate imprest account, and are deposits equal to the amount of net pay?

10. Is responsibility for custody and follow-up of unclaimed wages assigned to a responsible person independent of personnel, payroll processing, and cash disbursement functions?

11. Are procedures adequate to result in timely and accurate preparation and filing of payroll tax returns and payment of accumulated withholdings and related accrued taxes?

12. Are personnel and payroll records reasonably safeguarded (locked file cabinets, work areas with limited access)?

E. CASH DISBURSEMENTS

This questionnaire's objectives are to determine if functions are assigned so that no single individual is in a position to both perpetrate and conceal errors or fraud in the normal course of their duties.

- Disbursements are made only for expenditures incurred in accordance with management's authorization.
- Adjustments to cash accounts are made only in accordance with management's authorizations.
- Disbursements are recorded at correct amounts in the appropriate period and are properly classified in the accounts.
- Access to cash and disbursement records is restricted to minimize opportunities for irregular or erroneous disbursements.
- Comparison of detail records, control accounts, and bank statements are made at reasonable intervals for detection and appropriate disposition of errors or fraud.

1. Are bank accounts and check signers authorized by the board of directors?

2. Are approved supporting documents presented with the checks to the check signer?

3. Is a mechanical check protector used to inscribe amounts on checks to protect against alteration?

4. Are supporting documents for checks canceled to avoid reuse?

5. Are signed checks independently mailed directly after signing without being returned to persons involved in the invoice processing and check preparation functions?

6. Are all voided checks retained and mutilated?

7. Are there written policies that prohibit making checks payable to cash or bearer, and signing blank checks?

8. Are dual signatures required for large disbursements, and are the signers independent of one another?

9. If a check-signing machine is used, are the keys, signature plate, and operation of the signing machine under control at all times of the official whose signature is on the plate? Are employees who have custody of them independent of voucher and check preparation functions, and are they denied access to blank checks?

10. If cash funds are maintained on the premises, they should be kept on an imprest basis; and

- **a.** Are they kept in a safe place?
- **b.** Are they reasonable in amount?
- **c.** Are they controlled by one custodian?
- **d.** Are disbursements supported by vouchers?
- **e.** Are vouchers approved with management's authorization?
- **f.** Are cash funds on a surprise basis counted by someone other than the custodian?
- **g.** Is the custodian independent of cash receipts?
- **h.** Does the custodian have no access to accounting records?
- **i.** Are reimbursements of the cash fund remitted by checks made payable to the order of the custodian?

11. Are old outstanding checks investigated, controlled, and their proper disposition arranged?

F. INVENTORY AND COST OF SALES

This questionnaire's objectives are to determine if all production activity and accounting therefor is determined in accordance with management's general or specific authorizations.

- Resources obtained and used in the production process and completed results are accurately recorded on a timely basis.
- Transfer of finished products to customers and other dispositions such as sales of scrap are accurately recorded.
- Inventory, production costs, and costs of sales are accumulated and classified in the accounts to maintain accountability for costs and permit preparation of statements in conformity with GAAP.
- Inventory is protected from unauthorized use or removal.
- Recorded balances of inventory are substantiated and evaluated at reasonable intervals by comparison with quantities on hand.

1. Are production goals and schedules based on accompanying sales forecasts?

2. Are methods and materials to be used based upon product engineering plans and specifications?

3. Does the company have budgeted inventory levels and predetermined reorder points authorized by management?

4. Does the company have policies for identification and disposition of excess or obsolete inventory?

5. Are all adjustments to inventory and cost of sales made in accordance with management's authorizations?

6. Are all dispositions of obsolete or excess inventory approved?

7. Does the chart of accounts provide adequate general ledger control accounts and subsidiary detail for the accumulation and classification of costs of materials, direct labor, and overhead?

8. Is access to the detailed inventory records and control accounts limited to persons responsible for their maintenance, oversight, and internal audit?

9. Are there physical safeguards against theft, fire, and flooding?

10. Is insurance coverage of the inventory maintained and reviewed periodically for adequacy?

11. Do detailed written inventory procedures and instructions exist that have been approved and are they adequately communicated to the persons who perform the physical counts?

12. Are inventory physical counts performed by persons whose duties do not include the physical custody and detailed record keeping of inventory or maintenance of control accounts?

13. Are differences in physical counts and detailed records investigated?

14. Are adjustments of the inventory detail records and control accounts given prior approval by management?

15. Are dispositions of obsolete or excess inventories made in accordance with criteria authorized by management?

G. Property and Equipment

This questionnaire's objectives are to determine if additions and related accumulation of depreciation retirements, and dispositions of property and equipment are made in accordance with management's authorization.

- Transactions involving property and equipment and depreciation are accurately recorded, accumulated, and classified in detail and in control accounts to maintain accountability for the assets.
- Property and equipment is reasonably safeguarded from loss.

1. Are work order forms approved by management for property additions?

2. Are contracts and agreements signed by individuals in accordance with appropriately documented designation by the board of directors?

3. Are detailed records maintained for property and equipment indicating a description of the assets; their location, cost, acquisition date, date of service, depreciable life; and method of depreciation used?

4. Is property and equipment insured and coverage reviewed periodically for additions, disposals, and adequacy?

5. Is there a written capitalization/expense policy for property and equipment purchases?

H. Stockholders' Equity and Capital Accounts

This questionnaire's objectives are to determine if capital transactions are authorized and approved in conformity with the entity's governing document (corporate charter, partnership agreement).

- Transactions and obligations are promptly and accurately recorded.
- Access to records, agreements, and negotiable documents is permitted only in accordance with management's authorization.
- Records, agreements, and documents are subjected to adequate physical safeguards and custodial procedures.
- Dividends are disbursed accurately and in conformity with decisions of the board of directors.

1. Are authorizations and approvals for specific capital transactions appropriately recorded?

2. Are two officials authorized by the board required to sign and countersign stock certificates?

3. Are all stock certificates prepared and approved before issuance within management's authorization?

4. Are appropriate control records maintained for each class of stock on information such as number of shares authorized, issued and outstanding, and the number of shares subject to options, warrants, and conversion privileges?

5. Are timely detailed records maintained on specific stock certificates issued and outstanding for each class of capital stock and the identity of holders of record and the number of shares for each certificate?

6. Are detailed stock certificate records reconciled at reasonable intervals with the control records and the general ledger?

7. Are reconciliations of detailed records with the control records and general ledger performed by persons independent of custody of unissued stock certificates, maintenance of the detailed records, and cash functions?

8. Are unissued stock certificates, reacquired certificates and detailed stockholder records subject to reasonable physical safeguards?

9. Are stock certificates pre-numbered so that all certificates (unissued, issued, and retired) may be accounted for?

10. Are retired stock certificates examined for proper endorsement and effectively canceled by a person whose duties do not include maintenance of the detailed stockholder records?

11. Are treasury stock certificates registered in the name of the company and recorded to be readily distinguished from other outstanding shares?

12. Are dividends declared recorded in the minutes of the board of directors meetings?

13. Do procedures result in an accurate cutoff and accurate listing of stockholders as of the record date?

14. Are total dividends disbursed reconciled to total outstanding shares as of the record date?

APPENDIX: GENERAL INTERNAL CONTROL QUESTIONS

General Control Questions	Cash Receipts	Cash Disbursements	Payroll
1. Are forms used that are prenumbered?	Prenumbered Receipts, Cash Register tapes by date	Prenumbered Checks	Prenumbered Payroll Checks
2. Is adequate control maintained of unissued forms to prevent misuse?	Unused Blank Receipts controlled	Unused Blank Checks controlled	Unused Blank Payroll Checks controlled
3. Are policies and procedures in place for the authorization of transactions?	Remittance listing prepared by designated mail opener.	Check signers authorized by board of directors. Authorization for bank accounts to be maintained.	Payroll approved in writing by responsible employee prior to issuance of paychecks.
4. Is approval of transaction obtained prior to processing?	Comparison of remittance listing and validated deposit slip before processing.	Invoice matched to approved receiving report and approved purchase order. Disbursements and bank transfers approved.	Supervisor reviews and approves time cards.
5. Is a proper segregation of duties maintained to reduce potential errors and fraud?	Employee responsible for preparing remittance lists independent of billing, cash disbursement, and general ledger functions. Employee making deposit independent of cash disbursement, billing, and general ledger functions.	Employee performing bank reconciliation independent of invoice processing, cash disbursements, cash receipts, petty cash, and general ledger functions.	Payroll checks signed by treasurer. Payroll checks distributed by person independent of personnel, payroll preparation, time-keeping, and check preparation.
6. Are all prenumbered forms accounted for?	Detail Cash Receipts Journal	Outstanding check list maintained.	Payroll Journal, Outstanding check list maintained.
7. Is a detailed record of transactions maintained?	Cash Receipts Journal	Check Register, Cash Disbursements Journal	Payroll Journal
8. Are periodic (monthly, annual) reconciliations made between source documents, quantities on hand, subsidiary ledgers, and the general ledger?	Trace cash receipts journal total to bank statement and/or validated deposit slips.	Bank reconciliations, Cash Disbursements Journal reconciled to general ledger.	Time card hours reconciled to job time tickets.
9. Is access to assets and/or accounting records limited?	Mail received by same person daily who is independent of cash, billings, general ledger and shipping functions.	Bank statement received directly by person who will reconcile.	Payroll records and Personnel files kept in locked file cabinets.
10. Are transactions and source documents checked for clerical accuracy?	Remittance list footed and agreed to validated deposit slip.	Checks compared to approved invoice and supporting documents before signing. Discounts, if available, have been taken.	Time card totals checked by supervisor.
11. Is there a proper cut-off of transactions for accurate reporting?	Bank reconciliations are prepared and approved on a timely basis.	Bank reconciliations are prepared and approved on a timely basis.	Bank reconciliations are prepared and approved on a timely basis.

Inventory	Cost of Sales	Fixed Assets	Accounts Receivable	Accounts Payable
Prenumbered: Shipping Documents, Purchase Orders, Receiving Reports	Prenumbered Inventory Requisitions	Prenumbered Purchase Orders	Prenumbered Invoices	Prenumbered Vouchers
Unused Purchase Orders, Receiving Reports, Shipping Documents controlled.	Unused Inventory Requisitions controlled.	Unused Purchased Orders controlled	Unused Invoices controlled	Unused Vouchers controlled
Purchases made in accordance with vendor acceptability. Customer Acceptance/Terms of Sale, credit clearance all preestablished.	Pre-established overhead rates, requisition processing controls	Additions/Retirements have authorization in Board of Directors meeting minutes.	Invoices prepared from approved shipping reports and matching vendor purchase orders.	Authorization by Board of Directors for large purchases (contracts).
Approved purchase order, Approved inventory requisitions, sales orders approved before shipment	Inventory requisitions, overhead rate changes and personnel rate changes are properly approved.	Approval of additions and retirements in writing; Board minutes, manager approval.	Approval noted on invoice.	Invoices and supporting documents approved before payment.
Credit, Sales, Shipping, Billing, Collections, receiving, and general accounting all independent of one another.	Authority to approve inventory requisitions assigned to employees independent of physical custody, and maintenance of inventory records and inventory control accounts.	Responsibility for physical custody assigned to employees independent of maintaining detailed property records and general ledger functions.	Individual responsible for accounts receivable function is independent of cash and general ledger functions.	Vendors' invoices processed by employee independent of purchasing, receiving, shipping, and cash functions.
Purchase Orders, Shipping Documents, Receiving Reports	Work Orders, Inventory Requisitions	Physical asset identification plates numbered consecutively	Numbered sales invoices properly filed.	Numbered vouchers and Purchase Orders maintained in open, pending, or paid files.
Shipment Log, Receiving Log, Purchases Journal	Work-in-Process and Finished Goods journals	Detailed listing of fixed assets maintained	Sales Invoice Register	Purchases Journal and Accounts Payable Subsidiary Ledger maintained
Inventory physically counted annually. Inventory detail records and control accounts reconciled to physical count. Perpetual records reconciled to general ledger and physical counts.	Cost accounting system reconciled to general ledger.	Detailed records of assets compared to actual property and equipment on hand, and reconciled to general ledger.	Accounts receivable subsidiary ledger reconciled to general ledger control account.	Accounts payable subsidiary ledger reconciled with general ledger control account.
Finished goods and merchandise are restricted so that withdrawals are based on approved sales orders.	Releases from storage of raw materials and supplies based upon approved requisitions.	Physical controls such as fences, burglar alarms, fire alarms, security guards, and requisitioning procedures for the use of portable equipment.	Passwords used on computer system limiting data entry to designated individuals.	Passwords used on computer system limiting data entry to designated individuals.
Receiving Reports, Shipping Documents, Purchase Orders	Inventory Requisitions checked	Invoices compared to approved purchase order and totals including taxes and freight are checked for reasonableness.	Sales Invoices	Vendors' Invoices
Inventory received included, goods on consignment included, goods sold but not shipped excluded from inventory totals.	See Inventory	Cash receipts and disbursements checked and compared to bank reconciliation for cut-off.	Shipping documents and related billings compared for proper cut-off.	Receiving reports or service dates and vendor invoices compared prior to recording.

Wondering how to allocate your study time?

Now that you have had a chance to become familiar with the text format, you may want to skim the **Getting Started, Practical Advice,** and **Accounting for 5%** sections of the book again. These provide helpful information on:

- how to integrate materials so they work best for you;
- answering all question types;
- the heavily tested topics on exams;
- how to use your time wisely; and
- exam taking techniques that will earn extra points!

Remember, with the techniques and information in your material,

A passing score is well within reach!

CHAPTER 34—INTERNAL CONTROL: TRANSACTION CYCLES

PROBLEM 34-1 MULTIPLE CHOICE QUESTIONS (80 to 100 minutes)

1. Proper segregation of functional responsibilities in an effective internal control structure calls for separation of the functions of
a. Authorization, payment, and recording.
b. Authorization, recording, and custody.
c. Custody, execution, and reporting.
d. Authorization, execution, and payment.
(Editors, 0092)

2. Proper segregation of duties reduces the opportunities to allow persons to be in positions to both
a. Journalize entries and prepare financial statements.
b. Record cash receipts and cash disbursements.
c. Establish internal controls and authorize transactions.
d. Perpetuate and conceal errors and fraud.
(11/94, Aud., #26, amended, 5099)

3. Which of the following procedures most likely would **not** be an internal control procedure designed to reduce the risk of errors in the billing process?
a. Comparing control totals for shipping documents with corresponding totals for sales invoices
b. Using computer programmed controls on the pricing and mathematical accuracy of sales invoices
c. Matching shipping documents with approved sales orders before invoice preparation
d. Reconciling the control totals for sales invoices with the accounts receivable subsidiary ledger
(11/94, Aud., #36, 5109)

4. Sound internal control procedures dictate that immediately upon receiving checks from customers by mail, a responsible employee should
a. Add the checks to the daily cash summary.
b. Verify that each check is supported by a prenumbered sales invoice.
c. Prepare a duplicate listing of checks received.
d. Record the checks in the cash receipts journal.
(5/95, Aud., #30, 5648)

5. Proper authorization of write-offs of uncollectible accounts should be approved in which of the following departments?
a. Accounts receivable
b. Credit
c. Accounts payable
d. Treasurer
(11/94, Aud., #35, 5108)

6. Which of the following controls most likely would be effective in offsetting the tendency of sales personnel to maximize sales volume at the expense of high bad debt write-offs?
a. Employees responsible for authorizing sales and bad debt write-offs are denied access to cash.
b. Shipping documents and sales invoices are matched by an employee who does **not** have authority to write off bad debts.
c. Employees involved in the credit-granting function are separated from the sales function.
d. Subsidiary accounts receivable records are reconciled to the control account by an employee independent of the authorization of credit.
(5/92, Aud., #45, 2798)

7. Which of the following internal controls most likely would reduce the risk of diversion of customer receipts by an entity's employees?
a. A bank lockbox system
b. Prenumbered remittance advices
c. Monthly bank reconciliations
d. Daily deposit of cash receipts
(11/95, Aud., #12, 5959)

8. Which of the following procedures would an auditor most likely perform to test controls relating to management's assertion about the completeness of cash receipts for cash sales at a retail outlet?
a. Observe the consistency of the employees' use of cash registers and tapes.
b. Inquire about employees' access to recorded but undeposited cash.
c. Trace the deposits in the cash receipts journal to the cash balance in the general ledger.
d. Compare the cash balance in the general ledger with the bank confirmation request.
(11/97, Aud., #15, 6578)

9. An auditor observes the mailing of monthly statements to a client's customers and reviews evidence of follow-up on errors reported by the customers. This test of controls most likely is performed to support management's financial statement assertion(s) of

	Presentation and disclosure	*Existence or occurrence*
a.	Yes	Yes
b.	Yes	No
c.	No	Yes
d.	No	No

(5/96, Aud., #5, 6237)

10. Tracing shipping documents to prenumbered sales invoices provides evidence that
a. No duplicate shipments or billings occurred.
b. Shipments to customers were properly invoiced.
c. All goods ordered by customers were shipped.
d. All prenumbered sales invoices were accounted for. (5/95, Aud., #32, 5650)

11. In assessing control risk for purchases, an auditor vouches a sample of entries in the voucher register to the supporting documents. Which assertion would this test of controls most likely support?
a. Completeness
b. Existence or occurrence
c. Valuation or allocation
d. Rights and obligations (11/94, Aud., #39, 5112)

12. Which of the following internal control procedures is **not** usually performed in the vouchers payable department?
a. Matching the vendor's invoice with the related receiving report
b. Approving vouchers for payment by having an authorized employee sign the vouchers
c. Indicating the asset and expense accounts to be debited
d. Accounting for unused prenumbered purchase orders and receiving reports

(11/94, Aud., #40, 5113)

13. For effective internal control, the accounts payable department generally should
a. Stamp, perforate, or otherwise cancel supporting documentation after payment is mailed.
b. Ascertain that each requisition is approved as to price, quantity, and quality by an authorized employee.
c. Obliterate the quantity ordered on the receiving department copy of the purchase order.
d. Establish the agreement of the vendor's invoice with the receiving report and purchase order.

(11/95, Aud., #30, 5977)

14. In testing controls over cash disbursements, an auditor most likely would determine that the person who signs checks also
a. Reviews the monthly bank reconciliation.
b. Returns the checks to accounts payable.
c. Is denied access to the supporting documents.
d. Is responsible for mailing the checks.

(11/95, Aud., #29, 5976)

15. Which of the following questions would most likely be included in an internal control questionnaire concerning the completeness assertion for purchases?
a. Is an authorized purchase order required before the receiving department can accept a shipment or the vouchers payable department can record a voucher?
b. Are purchase requisitions prenumbered and independently matched with vendor invoices?
c. Is the unpaid voucher file periodically reconciled with inventory records by an employee who does **not** have access to purchase requisitions?
d. Are purchase orders, receiving reports, and vouchers prenumbered and periodically accounted for? (5/92, Aud., #46, 2799)

16. When the shipping department returns non-conforming goods to a vendor, the purchasing department should send to the accounting department the
a. Unpaid voucher.
b. Debit memo.
c. Vendor invoice.
d. Credit memo. (11/92, Aud., #16, 2950)

17. To provide assurance that each voucher is submitted and paid only once, an auditor most likely would examine a sample of paid vouchers and determine whether each voucher is
a. Supported by a vendor's invoice.
b. Stamped "paid" by the check signer.
c. Prenumbered and accounted for.
d. Approved for authorized purchases.

(5/95, Aud., #34, 5652)

18. An entity's internal control requires for every check request that there be an approved voucher, supported by a prenumbered purchase order and a prenumbered receiving report. To determine whether checks are being issued for unauthorized expenditures, an auditor most likely would select items for testing from the population of all
a. Purchase orders.
b. Canceled checks.
c. Receiving reports.
d. Approved vouchers.

(11/92, Aud., #17, amended, 2951)

19. Which of the following questions would an auditor most likely include on an internal control questionnaire for notes payable?
a. Are assets that collateralize notes payable critically needed for the entity's continued existence?
b. Are two or more authorized signatures required on checks that repay notes payable?
c. Are the proceeds from notes payable used for the purchase of noncurrent assets?
d. Are direct borrowings on notes payable authorized by the board of directors?
(11/93, Aud., #32, 4269)

20. The authority to accept incoming goods in receiving should be based on a(an)
a. Vendor's invoice.
b. Materials requisition.
c. Bill of lading.
d. Approved purchase order.
(5/93, Aud., #17, 3913)

21. An auditor generally tests the segregation of duties related to inventory by
a. Personal inquiry and observation.
b. Test counts and cutoff procedures.
c. Analytical procedures and invoice recomputation.
d. Document inspection and reconciliation.
(5/95, Aud., #31, 5649)

22. Sound internal control procedures dictate that defective merchandise returned by customers should be presented initially to the
a. Accounts receivable supervisor.
b. Receiving clerk.
c. Shipping department supervisor.
d. Sales clerk. (5/93, Aud., #20, 3916)

23. Which of the following internal control procedures most likely would prevent direct labor hours from being charged to manufacturing overhead?
a. Periodic independent counts of work in process for comparison to recorded amounts
b. Comparison of daily journal entries with approved production orders
c. Use of time tickets to record actual labor worked on production orders
d. Reconciliation of work-in-process inventory with periodic cost budgets (5/94, Aud., #32, 4697)

24. Which of the following internal control procedures most likely would be used to maintain accurate inventory records?
a. Perpetual inventory records are periodically compared with the current cost of individual inventory items
b. A just-in-time inventory ordering system keeps inventory levels to a desired minimum
c. Requisitions, receiving reports, and purchase orders are independently matched before payment is approved
d. Periodic inventory counts are used to adjust the perpetual inventory records
(5/94, Aud., #33, 4698)

25. The objectives of the internal control for a production cycle are to provide assurance that transactions are properly executed and recorded, and that
a. Production orders are prenumbered and signed by a supervisor.
b. Custody of work in process and of finished goods is properly maintained.
c. Independent internal verification of activity reports is established.
d. Transfers to finished goods are documented by a completed production report and a quality control report. (11/93, Aud., #28, amended, 4265)

26. In obtaining an understanding of a manufacturing entity's internal control concerning inventory balances, an auditor most likely would
a. Analyze the liquidity and turnover ratios of the inventory.
b. Perform analytical procedures designed to identify cost variances.
c. Review the entity's descriptions of inventory policies and procedures.
d. Perform test counts of inventory during the entity's physical count.
(11/95, Aud., #32, amended, 5979)

27. An auditor most likely would assess control risk at the maximum if the payroll department supervisor is responsible for
a. Examining authorization forms for new employees.
b. Comparing payroll registers with original batch transmittal data.
c. Authorizing payroll rate changes for all employees.
d. Hiring all subordinate payroll department employees. (5/94, Aud., #29, 4694)

28. The purpose of segregating the duties of hiring personnel and distributing payroll checks is to separate the
a. Human resources function from the controllership function.
b. Administrative controls from the internal accounting controls.
c. Authorization of transactions from the custody of related assets.
d. Operational responsibility from the record-keeping responsibility. (11/93, Aud., #30, 4267)

29. Which of the following is a control procedure that most likely could help prevent employee payroll fraud?
a. The personnel department promptly sends employee termination notices to the payroll supervisor
b. Employees who distribute payroll checks forward unclaimed payroll checks to the absent employees' supervisors
c. Salary rates resulting from new hires are approved by the payroll supervisor
d. Total hours used for determination of gross pay are calculated by the payroll supervisor (11/95, Aud., #15, 5962)

30. In determining the effectiveness of an entity's policies and procedures relating to the existence or occurrence assertion for payroll transactions, an auditor most likely would inquire about and
a. Observe the segregation of duties concerning personnel responsibilities and payroll disbursement.
b. Inspect evidence of accounting for prenumbered payroll checks.
c. Recompute the payroll deductions for employee fringe benefits.
d. Verify the preparation of the monthly payroll account bank reconciliation. (11/95, Aud., #31, 5978)

31. Which of the following circumstances most likely would cause an auditor to suspect an employee payroll fraud scheme?
a. There are significant unexplained variances between standard and actual labor cost.
b. Payroll checks are disbursed by the same employee each payday.
c. Employee time cards are approved by individual departmental supervisors.
d. A separate payroll bank account is maintained on an impress basis. (11/95, Aud., #50, 5997)

32. Which of the following flowcharts indicates that new equipment transactions and the old equipment file have been used to prepare equipment labels, prepare a printed equipment journal, and generate a new equipment file?

a.
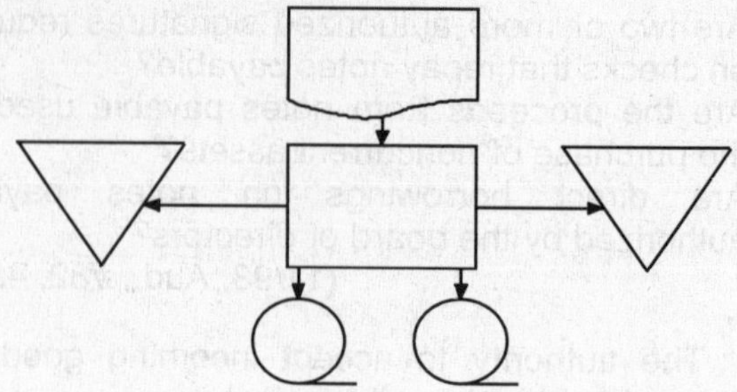

b.
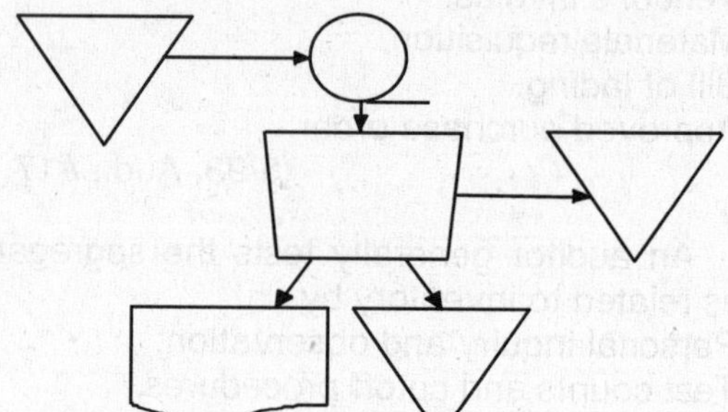

c.
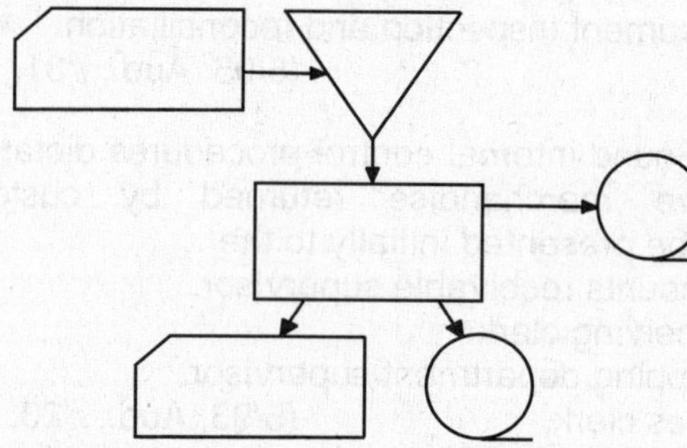

d.
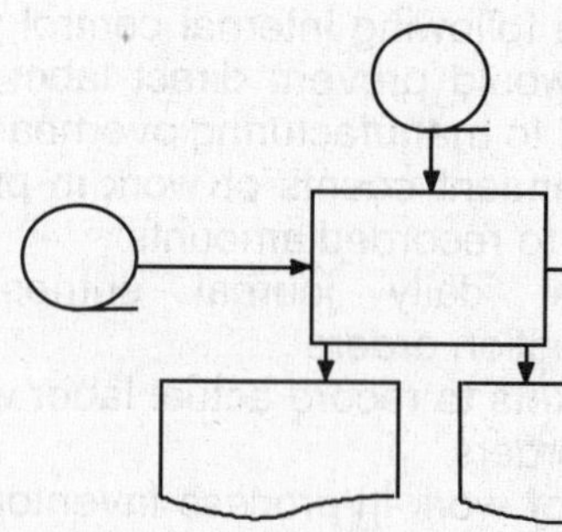

(Editors, 9408)

33. Which of the following questions would an auditor **least** likely include on an internal control questionnaire concerning the initiation and execution of equipment transactions?
a. Are requests for major repairs approved at a higher level than the department initiating the request?
b. Are prenumbered purchase orders used for equipment and periodically accounted for?
c. Are requests for purchases of equipment reviewed for consideration of soliciting competitive bids?
d. Are procedures in place to monitor and properly restrict access to equipment?
(11/94, Aud., #41, 5114)

34. Equipment acquisitions that are misclassified as maintenance expense most likely would be detected by an internal control procedure that provides for
a. Segregation of duties of employees in the accounts payable department.
b. Authorization by the board of directors of significant equipment acquisitions.
c. Investigation of variances within a formal budgeting system.
d. Independent verification of invoices for disbursements recorded as equipment acquisitions.
(11/93, Aud., #34, amended, 4271)

35. Which of the following internal control procedures most likely would justify a reduced assessed level of control risk concerning plant and equipment acquisitions?
a. Periodic physical inspection of plant and equipment by the internal audit staff
b. Comparison of current-year plant and equipment account balances with prior-year actual balances
c. The review of prenumbered purchase orders to detect unrecorded trade-ins
d. Approval of periodic depreciation entries by a supervisor independent of the accounting department
(5/93, Aud., #21, 3917)

36. A weakness in internal control over recording retirements of equipment may cause an auditor to
a. Trace additions to the "other assets" account to search for equipment that is still on hand but **no** longer being used.
b. Select certain items of equipment from the accounting records and locate them in the plant.
c. Review the subsidiary ledger to ascertain whether depreciation was taken on each item of equipment during the year.
d. Inspect certain items of equipment in the plant and trace those items to the accounting records.
(Editors, 0081)

37. When an entity uses a trust company as custodian of its marketable securities, the possibility of concealing fraud most likely would be reduced if the
a. Trust company has **no** direct contact with the entity employees responsible for maintaining investment accounting records.
b. Securities are registered in the name of the trust company, rather than the entity itself.
c. Interest and dividend checks are mailed directly to an entity employee who is authorized to sell securities.
d. Trust company places the securities in a bank safe-deposit vault under the custodian's exclusive control.
(5/94, Aud., #34, 4699)

38. Which of the following controls would a company most likely use to safeguard marketable securities when an independent trust agent is **not** employed?
a. The investment committee of the board of directors periodically reviews the investment decisions delegated to the treasurer.
b. Two company officials have joint control of marketable securities, which are kept in a bank safe-deposit box.
c. The internal auditor and the controller independently trace all purchases and sales of marketable securities from the subsidiary ledgers to the general ledger.
d. The chairman of the board verifies the marketable securities which are kept in a bank safe-deposit box, each year on the balance sheet date.
(11/95, Aud., #16, 5963)

39. Which of the following procedures most likely would give the greatest assurance that securities held as investments are safeguarded?
a. There is no access to securities between the year-end and the date of the auditor's security count.
b. Proceeds from the sale of investments are received by an employee who does not have access to securities.
c. Investment acquisitions are authorized by a member of the Board of Directors before execution.
d. Access to securities requires the signatures and presence of two designated officials.
(5/93, Aud., #22, 3918)

40. Which of the following controls would an entity most likely use in safeguarding against the loss of marketable securities?
a. An independent trust company that has **no** direct contact with the employees who have record keeping responsibilities has possession of the securities.
b. The internal auditor verifies the marketable securities in the entity's safe each year on the balance sheet date.
c. The independent auditor traces all purchases and sales of marketable securities through the subsidiary ledgers to the general ledger.
d. A designated member of the board of directors controls the securities in a bank safe-deposit box. (11/92, Aud., #22, 2956)

PROBLEM 34-2 ADDITIONAL MULTIPLE CHOICE QUESTIONS (20 to 25 minutes)

41. Which of the following fraudulent activities most likely could be perpetrated due to the lack of effective internal controls in the revenue cycle?
a. Fictitious transactions may be recorded that cause an understatement of revenues and an overstatement of receivables.
b. Claims received from customers for goods returned may be intentionally recorded in other customers' accounts.
c. Authorization of credit memos by personnel who receive cash may permit the misappropriation of cash.
d. The failure to prepare shipping documents may cause an overstatement of inventory balances. (11/97, Aud., #14, 6577)

42. Which of the following procedures concerning accounts receivable would an auditor most likely perform to obtain evidential matter in support of an assessed level of control risk below the maximum level?
a. Observing an entity's employee prepare the schedule of past due accounts receivable
b. Sending confirmation requests to an entity's principal customers to verify the existence of accounts receivable
c. Inspecting an entity's analysis of accounts receivable for unusual balances
d. Comparing an entity's uncollectible accounts expense to actual uncollectible accounts receivable (5/96, Aud., #2, 6234)

43. Employers bond employees who handle cash receipts because fidelity bonds reduce the possibility of employing dishonest individuals and
a. Protect employees who make unintentional errors from possible monetary damages resulting from their errors.
b. Deter dishonesty by making employees aware that insurance companies may investigate and prosecute dishonest acts.
c. Facilitate an independent monitoring of the receiving and depositing of cash receipts.
d. Force employees in positions of trust to take periodic vacations and rotate their assigned duties. (5/90, Aud., #35, 0073)

44. For the most effective internal control, monthly bank statements should be received directly from the banks and reviewed by the
a. Cash disbursements accountant.
b. Cash receipts accountant.
c. Controller.
d. Internal auditor. (Editors, 0111)

45. Mailing disbursement checks and remittance advices should be controlled by the employee who
a. Matches the receiving reports, purchase orders, and vendors' invoices.
b. Signs the checks last.
c. Prepares the daily voucher summary.
d. Agrees the check register to the daily check summary. (5/93, Aud., #18, 3914)

46. Which of the following controls would be most effective in assuring that recorded purchases are free of material errors?
a. The receiving department compares the quantity ordered on purchase orders with the quantity received on receiving reports
b. Vendors' invoices are compared with purchase orders by an employee who is independent of the receiving department
c. Receiving reports require the signature of the individual who authorized the purchase
d. Purchase orders, receiving reports, and vendors' invoices are independently matched in preparing vouchers (11/90, Aud., #51, 9406)

47. Independent internal verification of inventory occurs when employees who
a. Issue raw materials obtain material requisitions for each issue and prepare daily totals of materials issued.
b. Compare records of goods on hand with physical quantities do **not** maintain the records or have custody of the inventory.
c. Are independent of issuing production orders update records from completed job cost sheets and production cost reports on a timely basis.
d. Obtain receipts for the transfer of completed work to finished goods prepare a completed production report. (Editors, 0089)

48. Which of the following internal control procedures is **not** usually performed in the treasurer's department?
a. Verifying the accuracy of checks and vouchers
b. Controlling the mailing of checks to vendors
c. Approving vendors' invoices for payment
d. Canceling payment vouchers when paid (11/93, Aud., #27, 4264)

49. Which of the following most likely would be an internal control procedure designed to detect errors and fraud concerning the custody of inventory?
a. Periodic reconciliation of work in process with job cost sheets
b. Segregation of functions between general accounting and cost accounting
c. Independent comparisons of finished goods records with counts of goods on hand
d. Approval of inventory journal entries by the storekeeper (5/91, Aud., #29, amended, 9407)

50. Which of the following departments most likely would approve changes in pay rates and deductions from employee salaries?
a. Personnel
b. Treasurer
c. Controller
d. Payroll (11/93, Aud., #31, 4268)

ESSAY QUESTIONS

ESSAY 34-3 (15 to 25 minutes)

Flowchart 34-3 depicts the activities relating to the sales, shipping, billing, and collecting processes used by Newton Hardware, Inc.

REQUIRED:

Identify the weaknesses in internal control relating to the activities of (a) the warehouse clerk, (b) bookkeeper A, and (c) the collection clerk. Do no identify weaknesses relating to the sales clerk or bookkeepers B and C. Do not discuss recommendations concerning the correction of these weaknesses. (5/88, Aud., #4)

FLOWCHART 34-3 (RELATES TO ESSAY 34-3)

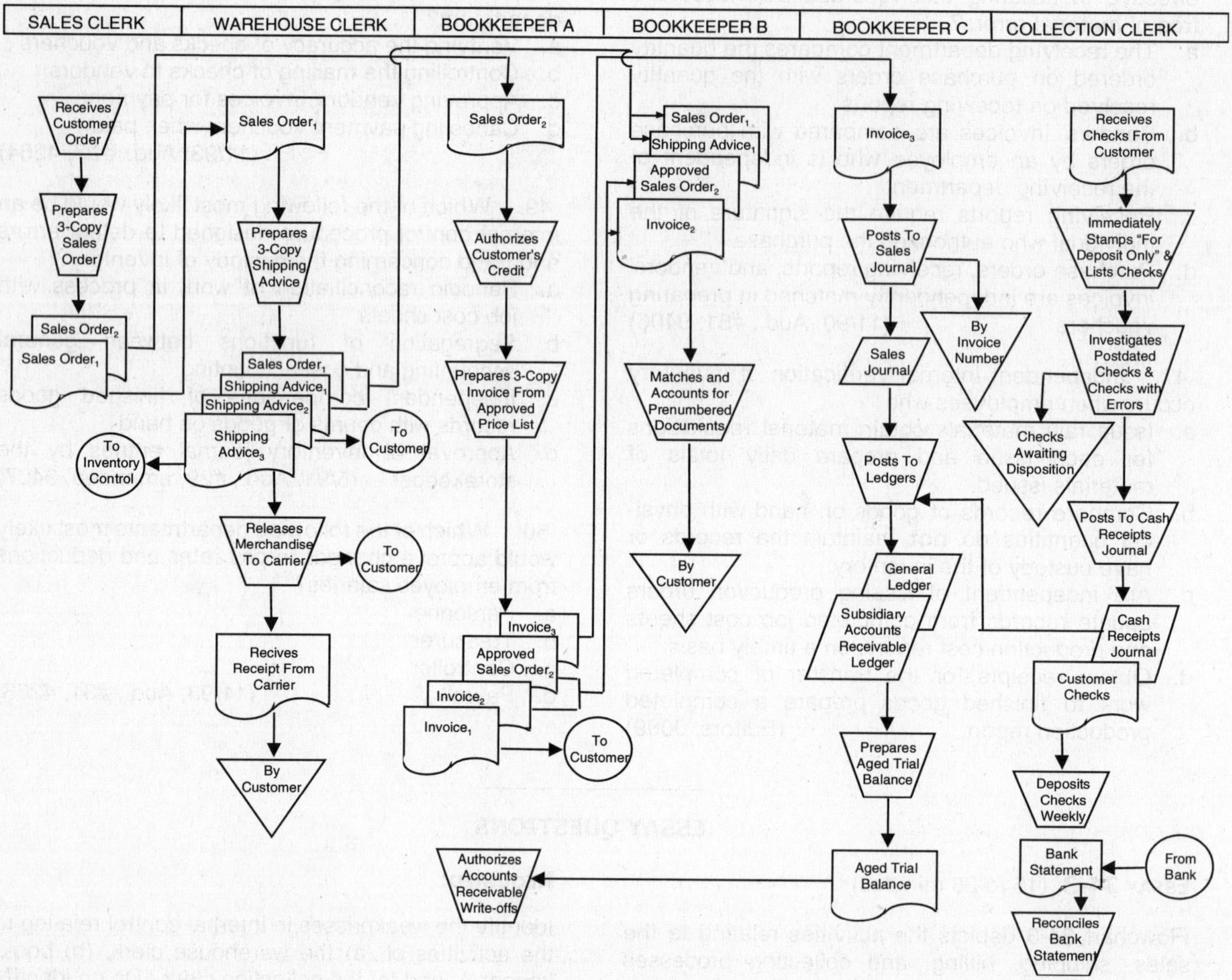

ESSAY 34-4 (15 to 25 minutes)

An auditor's working papers include the narrative description below of the cash receipts and billing portions of Southwest Medical Center's internal control. Southwest is a healthcare provider that is owned by a partnership of five physicians. It employs 11 physicians, including the five owners, 20 nurses, five laboratory and X-ray technicians, and four clerical workers. The clerical workers perform such tasks as reception, correspondence, cash receipts, billing, accounts receivable, bank deposits, and appointment scheduling. These clerical workers are referred to in the narrative as "office manager," "clerk #1," "clerk #2," and "clerk #3." Assume that the narrative is a complete description of the system.

REQUIRED:

a. Using only the information in the narrative, describe the strengths in Southwest's internal control that an auditor most likely could consider in assessing control risk below the maximum level.

b. Using only the information in the narrative, describe the weaknesses in Southwest's internal control that could permit material misstatements to occur in the financial statements. In addition, for each weakness, identify one internal control activity that most likely could help correct that weakness.

Use the following format for requirement b.:

Weaknesses	Internal control activities

NARRATIVE

About two-thirds of Southwest's patients receive medical services only after insurance coverage is verified by the office manager and communicated to the clerks. Most of the other patients pay for services by cash or check when services are rendered, although the office manager extends credit on a case-by-case basis to about 5% of the patients.

When services are rendered, the attending physician prepares a prenumbered service slip for each patient and gives the slip to clerk #1 for pricing. Clerk #1 completes the slip and gives the completed slip to clerk #2 and a copy to the patient.

Using the information on the completed slip, clerk #2 performs one of the following three procedures for each patient.

- Clerk #2 files an insurance claim and records a receivable from the insurance company if the office manager has verified the patient's coverage; or
- Clerk #2 posts a receivable from the patient on clerk #2's PC if the office manager has approved the patient's credit; or
- Clerk #2 receives cash or a check from the patient as the patient leaves the medical center, and clerk #2 records the cash receipt.

At the end of each day, clerk #2 prepares a revenue summary.

Clerk #1 performs correspondence functions and opens the incoming mail. Clerk #1 gives checks from insurance companies and patients to clerk #2 for deposit. Clerk #2 posts the receipt of patients' checks on clerk #2's PC patient receivable records and insurance companies' checks to the receivables from the applicable insurance companies. Clerk #1 gives mail requiring correspondence to clerk #3.

Clerk #2 stamps all checks "for deposit only" and each day prepares a list of checks and cash to be deposited in the bank. (This list also includes the cash and checks personally given to clerk #2 by patients.) Clerk #2 keeps a copy of the deposit list and gives the original to clerk #3.

Clerk #3 personally makes the daily bank deposit and maintains a file of the daily bank deposits. Clerk #3 also performs appointment scheduling for all of the doctors and various correspondence functions. Clerk #3 also maintains a list of patients whose insurance coverage the office manager has verified.

When insurance claims or patient receivables are not settled within 60 days, clerk #2 notifies the office manager. The office manager personally inspects the details of each instance of nonpayment. The office manager converts insurance claims that have been rejected by insurance companies into patient receivables. Clerk #2 records these patient receivables on clerk #2's PC and deletes these receivables from the applicable insurance companies. Clerk #2 deletes the patient receivables that appear to be uncollectible from clerk #2's PC when authorized by the office manager. Clerk #2 prepares a list of patients with uncollectible balances and gives a copy of the list to clerk #3, who will not allow these patients to make appointments for future services.

Once a month an outside accountant posts clerk #2's daily revenue summaries to the general ledger, prepares a monthly trial balance and monthly financial statements, accounts for the prenumbered service slips, files payroll forms and tax returns, and reconciles the monthly bank statements to the general ledger. This accountant reports directly to the physician who is the managing partner.

All four clerical employees perform their tasks on PCs that are connected through a local area network. Each PC is accessible with a password that is known only to the individual employee and the managing partner. Southwest uses a standard software package that was acquired from a software company and that cannot be modified by Southwest's employees. None of the clerical employees have access to Southwest's check-writing capabilities.

(11/98, Aud., #3)

ESSAY 34-5 (15 to 25 minutes)

Flowchart 34-5 depicts the activities relating to the purchasing, receiving, and accounts payable departments of Model Company, Inc.

REQUIRED:

Based only on the flowchart, describe the internal control procedures (strengths) that most likely would provide reasonable assurance that specific internal control objectives for the financial statement assertions regarding purchases and accounts payable will be achieved. Do **not** describe weaknesses in internal control. (5/91, Aud., #4)

FLOWCHART 34-5 (RELATES TO ESSAY 34-5)

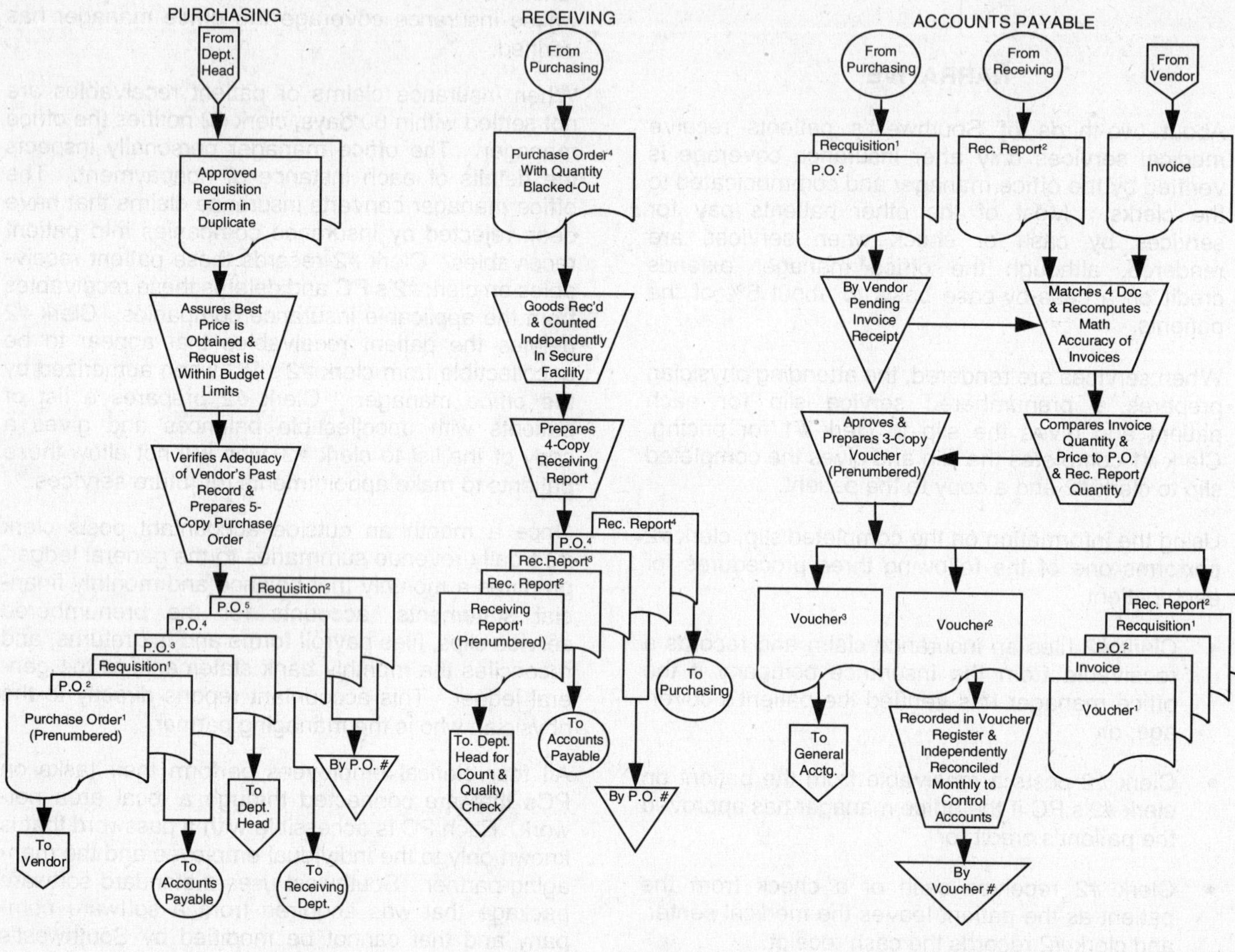

ESSAY 34-6 (15 to 25 minutes)

Butler, CPA, has been engaged to audit the financial statements of Young Computer Outlets, Inc., a new client. Young is a privately-owned chain of retail stores that sells a variety of computer software and video products. Young uses an in-house payroll department at its corporate headquarters to compute payroll data, and to prepare and distribute payroll checks to its 300 salaried employees. Butler is preparing an internal control questionnaire to assist in obtaining an understanding of Young's internal control and in assessing control risk.

REQUIRED:

Prepare a "Payroll" segment of Butler's internal control questionnaire that would assist in obtaining an understanding of Young's internal control and in assessing control risk. Do **not** prepare questions relating to cash payrolls, EDP applications, payments based on hourly rates, piecework, commissions, employee benefits (pensions, health care, vacations, etc.), or payroll tax accruals other than withholdings.

Use the format in the following example:

Question	*Yes*	*No*
Are paychecks prenumbered and accounted for?		

(5/93, Aud., #3)

ESSAY 34-7 (15 to 20 minutes)

Harris, CPA, has accepted an engagement to audit the financial statements of Grant Manufacturing Co., a new client. Grant has an adequate control environment and a reasonable segregation of duties. Harris is about to assess control risk for the assertions related to Grant's property and equipment.

REQUIRED:

Describe the key internal control policies and procedures related to Grant's property, equipment and related transactions (additions, transfers, major maintenance and repairs, retirements, and dispositions) that Harris may consider in assessing control risk. (5/92, Aud., #3)

SOLUTION 34-1 MULTIPLE CHOICE ANSWERS

SEGREGATION OF DUTIES

1. (b) Incompatible functions are those that place any person in a position to both perpetrate and conceal errors or fraud in the normal course of his or her duties. Therefore, a well-designed plan of organization separates the duties of *authorization*, *recordkeeping*, and *custody* of assets.

2. (d) AU 319.84(9) states, "Control activities…pertain[ing] to…segregation of duties is intended to reduce the opportunities to allow any person to be in a position to both perpetrate and conceal errors or irregularities [fraud] in the normal course of his or her duties." Answers (a), (b), and (c) are incompatible functions that could result in errors or fraud by the person with these responsibilities.

REVENUE CYCLE

3. (d) Answers (a), (b), and (c) are all controls applicable to the billing process. Answer (d) is a control used *after* the billing process.

4. (c) By immediately recording the receipt of the checks, the employee is providing evidence of the existence of cash. While each of the procedures in answers (a), (b), and (d) should be performed, preparing a duplicate listing of the checks is of immediate concern.

5. (d) The treasury department is independent of the recordkeeping and custodial functions for the accounts receivable. Incompatible functions are those that place any person in a position to both perpetrate and conceal errors or fraud in the normal course of his or her duties. Therefore, a well-designed plan of organization separates the duties of *authorization*, *recordkeeping*, and *custody* of assets. Answer (a) would not separate the authorization and recordkeeping functions. The authorization for approval of credit and write-off of accounts by the same department could allow for an employee defalcation scheme. Answer (c) is incorrect because this department would not have adequate information to make such a recommendation and could result in the concealment of errors or fraud.

6. (c) The most effective control in offsetting the tendency of sales personnel to maximize sales volume at the expense of high bad debt write-offs would be the segregation of duties of those employees involved in the credit-granting function and those employees in the sales function. If this segregation of duties exists, those employees in the credit-granting function should help to screen those potential customers likely to result in high bad-debt write-offs.

7. (a) A bank lockbox system assures accountability control as cash enters the client's cash receipts system. Answers (b), (c), and (d) are cash receipt controls imposed after cash is captured in the system.

8. (a) Assertions about completeness are tested by testing whether or not all cash is recorded. If employees consistently use cash registers and tapes, it is likely that all cash is recorded. Inquiry about employees' access to undeposited recorded cash, comparing the cash receipts journal to the general ledger, and comparing the cash balance in the general ledger with the bank confirmation request, tests assertions about only *recorded* cash.

9. (c) AU 326.04 states, "Assertions about existence or occurrence deal with whether assets or liabilities of the entity existed at a given date and

whether recorded transactions have occurred during a given period." The receipt by a customer of a monthly statement with errors could generate inquiries as to invoices for unreceived goods or the absence of the posting of payments. AU 326.08 states, "Assertions about presentation and disclosure deal with whether particular components of the financial statements are properly classified, described, and disclosed." The observation of the mailing of monthly statements would not provide much evidence to support presentation and disclosure assertions.

10. (b) Tracing from the source document (shipping document) to the recorded item (invoice) provides evidence of completeness. That is, all shipments should be invoiced. To test for answer (a), the auditor vouches from the sales invoices back to the shipping documents, sales orders, and customer orders. To test for answer (c), the auditor traces forward from the customer order to the sales order to the shipping documents. To test for answer (d), the auditor accounts for a sequence of invoice numbers.

Disbursements Cycle

11. (b) AU 326.04 states, "Assertions about existence or occurrence deal with whether assets or liabilities of the entity exist at a given date and whether recorded transactions have occurred during a given period." Thus, management asserts that the purchases reported are the result of transactions occurring through a given date. This would be tested by vouching entries from the voucher register to the supporting documentation. Answer (a) tests the opposite, vouching from the source documents to the financial statement amounts. Assertions about valuation and allocation would be tested by comparing the costs to purchase invoices received from outside vendors. Assertions about rights and obligations are focused more on asset and liability accounts and would be tested primarily by confirmation procedures.

12. (d) Accounting for unused purchase orders and receiving reports by the same department does not provide sufficient segregation of duties for the authorization, custody, and reporting functions of an effective internal control system. The lack of segregation of these items could result in an employee defalcation scheme. Answers (a), (b), and (c) each represent a procedure that is usually performed in the vouchers payable department.

13. (d) The agreement of the documents will verify that the goods were ordered (purchase order), received (receiving report), and the company has been billed (vendor's invoice). The individual signing the checks, not accounts payable, should stamp, perforate, or otherwise cancel the supporting documentation. The purchasing department, not accounting, is involved with the approval of purchase requisitions and blanking out the quantity ordered on the receiving department copy of the purchase order.

14. (d) A control for cash disbursements is for the person who signs the checks to compare them to supporting documents, cancel the documents, and to also mail them. The person who signs the checks should have access to the supporting documents in order to validate their legitimacy. Reconciliation of the monthly bank statement is a control that should be done by a person independent of cash transactions. The checks should not be returned or given to anyone who has responsibility in the cash disbursement process.

15. (d) AU 326.05 states, "Assertions about completeness deal with whether all transactions and accounts that should be presented in the financial statements are so included." One step in assuring this would be the periodic reconciliation of prenumbered purchase orders, receiving reports, and vouchers.

16. (b) When the shipping department returns nonconforming goods to a vendor the purchasing department should send to the accounting department the debit memo. This enables the accounting department to make the appropriate adjustment to the vendor's account. Answers (a) and (c) are incorrect because the accounting department would have no use for the unpaid voucher and the vendor invoice. Answer (d) is incorrect because a credit memo would be provided by the vendor, not by the purchasing department.

17. (b) By immediately stamping "paid" on the paid voucher, the check signer prevents the voucher from being paid again. While each of the items in answers (a), (c), and (d) is a recommended practice, none prevent the voucher from being paid again.

18. (b) When the internal control dictates that each check be accompanied by an approved voucher, and supported by a prenumbered purchase order and a prenumbered receiving report, the auditor would select items for testing from the population of all the canceled checks. If the auditor were to consider populations made up of all purchase orders, receiving reports, or approved vouchers, those canceled checks which were issued without such supporting documentation would not be discovered.

19. (d) Approved borrowings by the board of directors indicate that transactions must be approved before the recording and custody functions can take place. This is also performed by a party independent of the recording and custody functions.

20. (d) A good system of internal control will include the segregation of duties, such as the comparison of an approved purchase order to items received. Answers (a) and (c) represent documentation included with the order as it is received, without any indication of authorization. Answer (b) represents a form used when goods and materials are taken from the inventory supply to be used or shipped.

INVENTORY & PRODUCTION CYCLE

21. (a) To test for appropriate segregation of duties, the auditor makes inquiries and conducts observations. The procedures in answers (b), (c), and (d) are not applicable to testing for segregation of duties.

22. (b) For sound internal controls, all receipts for goods, including returned goods or materials, should be handled by the receiving clerk. Receiving reports should be prepared for all items received. Those employees who have recording responsibilities should not also be given custody of the related assets.

23. (c) Use of time tickets indicates the amount of actual labor employed during the day on a given job. An internal control procedure requiring the use of charging the actual time to the job in progress would help prevent mistakes in the recording of direct and indirect labor. Answers (a) and (d) would indicate variances after improperly charging direct labor to factory overhead, but would not be good preventative measures. Answer (b) would have no effect on identifying misposted direct labor.

24. (d) AU 326.04 states "Assertions about existence or occurrence deal with whether assets or liabilities of the entity exist at a given date and whether recorded transactions have occurred during a given period." In this question, periodically comparing goods on hand with perpetual inventory records would assist in identifying any potential errors. Answer (a) addresses the valuation of the inventory. Answer (b) would not identify variances in actual inventory on hand compared to the recorded amounts. Answer (c) represents examples of controls necessary for the proper segregation of duties in purchasing inventory.

25. (b) Controlling the access to assets is an important objective of proper inventory control. Answers (a), (c), and (d) are procedures for satisfying inventory control objectives—not actual internal control objectives.

26. (c) To obtain an understanding of a manufacturer's internal control concerning inventory balances, an auditor would review the entity's descriptions of inventory policies and procedures. Analyzing inventory ratios, performing cost variance analytical procedures, and performing inventory test counts are substantive procedures.

PERSONNEL & PAYROLL CYCLE

27. (c) Incompatible functions are those that place any person in a position to both perpetrate and conceal errors or fraud in the normal course of his or her duties. Therefore, a well-designed plan of organization separates the duties of authorization, record keeping, and custody of assets. Answers (a) and (d) are similar in that they would place the functions of authorization and custody or personal bias under the control of one person. General accounting should perform the processing of payroll.

28. (c) Incompatible functions are those that place any person in a position to both perpetrate and conceal errors or fraud in the normal course of his or her duties. Therefore, a well-designed plan of organization separates the duties of authorization, recordkeeping, and custody of assets.

29. (a) By promptly notifying the payroll supervisor of employee terminations the personnel department would avoid a terminated employee from continuing to be paid. Unclaimed payroll checks should be forwarded to the Treasurer's office. Salary rates should be controlled in the personnel office. Total hours should be determined and approved prior to getting to the payroll department. Although answers (c) and (d) are good controls, they would not prevent employee payroll fraud.

30. (a) Observing the segregation of duties concerning personnel responsibilities and payroll disbursement is a common audit procedure relating to the existence or occurrence assertion for payroll transactions. Inspecting evidence of accounting for prenumbered payroll checks would provide evidence related to the completeness assertion. Recomputing the payroll deductions for employee fringe benefits would provide evidence related to the valuation and the rights and obligations assertions. An auditor would likely review payroll checks and bank reconciliations to determine that all checks were cashed as part of obtaining evidence for the existence or

occurrence assertion and not just verify the preparation of the monthly payroll account bank reconciliation.

31. (a) Significant unexplained variances between standard and actual labor cost could cause an auditor to suspect a payroll fraud scheme. Payroll checks disbursed by the same employee each payday (as long as that person has no other payroll responsibilities), employee time cards being approved by individual departmental supervisors, and a separate payroll bank account maintained on an imprest basis are proper internal control procedures.

PP&E Cycle

32. (d) The requirement is to find the flowchart which indicates two forms of input (new transactions and the old file) being processed to generate three forms of output (labels, printed journal, and a new file). Answer (a) shows only one input with four forms of output. Answer (b) represents a manual process while the facts given indicate that a printed journal is to be generated. Answer (c) shows a punched card as one of the output functions when labels, a printed journal, and a new file should be represented in the output.

33. (d) The procedures in place to monitor and properly restrict access to equipment would more likely be *observed* by the auditor than be part of a questionnaire, as this is very important. Answer (a) represents the authorization function of the control structure, which would be included on the internal control questionnaire. Answer (b) represents a procedure to test the accounting and recording function of the control structure, which the auditor would include in the internal control questionnaire. Requests for competitive bids reduce the possibility of an individual's personal gain at the expense of the business in unusual and material transactions.

34. (c) The investigation of variances within a formal budgeting system would identify any unusual and unanticipated fluctuations in the repairs and maintenance accounts when asset acquisitions are incorrectly recorded there. While the segregation of duties is necessary for good internal controls; however, answer (a) would not ensure that equipment acquisitions were not misclassified. Answer (b) is a good internal control, but would not ensure that equipment purchases were properly recorded because these invoices only represent those acquisitions which are already properly recorded as fixed assets. Answer (d) would not prevent the recording of the acquisition to the repairs and maintenance accounts, nor would it serve to identify misclassifications.

35. (a) The internal control procedure of the periodic inspection of physical equipment to what is recorded by the internal auditor (who does not actively participate in the acquisition or disposal process) would allow for a reduction in the scope of the auditor's tests of asset acquisitions. The comparison of account balances and entries is an analytical procedure that would highlight unusual and unanticipated fluctuations; however, it would not indicate acquisitions which were not approved. The review of prenumbered purchase orders would indicate trade-ins or retirements of fixed assets in exchange for new assets; thus, there would be no change in the quantity of fixed assets on hand.

36. (b) The auditor may test the internal control over the recording of retirements by tracing certain items of equipment from the accounting records and locating them in the plant to make sure that they have not been retired. The "other assets" account has nothing to do with the recording of retired assets. Tracing from the plant assets to the books does not consider assets which may appear on the books even though they have been retired. The depreciation of equipment has nothing to do with whether or not the equipment has been retired.

Investing Cycle

37. (a) The fact that only the trust company has access to the securities should prevent unauthorized entity personnel with record keeping responsibility from conspiring or colluding to misappropriate the securities. Trust company employees or management could potentially sell or otherwise mismanage the assets. Answers (c) and (d) put the custody and record keeping functions in the hands of one individual or party which could result in unauthorized transactions of the securities.

38. (b) A bank safe-deposit box with two company officials in control of the asset provides strong physical control over the securities. Answers (a) and (c) would not safeguard the physical marketable security. Answer (d) does not provide for dual control throughout the year, as is preferred.

39. (d) Custody of investment securities is usually maintained on the company premises or assigned to an outside agent such as a brokerage house. Good internal controls dictate that at least two officers should sign for and be present to access these investments to prevent unauthorized sales. Answer (a) provides no guarantee that unauthorized access to the investments during the time period indicated did not occur. Answers (b) and (c) are good internal controls, but do not address the physical control of the assets.

40. (a) Of the choices given, the strongest internal control in safeguarding against the loss of marketable securities would be the use of an independent trust company that has no direct contact with the employees who have record keeping responsibilities. The fact that only the trust company has access to the securities should prevent unauthorized entity personnel with record keeping responsibility from conspiring or colluding to misappropriate the securities. In determining appropriate controls in safeguarding an asset against loss, the auditor would start with those controls involving access to the asset in question. Neither verifying the securities in the safe nor tracing all purchases and sales provides evidence as to who has access to, or custody of, the marketable securities. Allowing just one person access to an asset enables the individual to take the asset without being discovered.

SOLUTION 34-2 ADDITIONAL MULTIPLE CHOICE ANSWERS

REVENUE CYCLE

41. (c) One of the most effective means of detecting or preventing fraud is the segregation of duties involving authorization, custody, and recordkeeping. Authorization of credit memos by personnel who receive cash (custody) is not segregation of duties. The recording of fictitious transactions and failure to prepare shipping documents resulting in an overstatement of inventory would likely be discovered during reconciliations. Return claims applied to inappropriate accounts would likely be discovered by customers when monthly statements are issued.

42. (a) Observation of an entity's preparation of a schedule provides evidence on internal control. Confirmation requests, inspection of an analysis of accounts receivables, or comparison of an entity's uncollectible accounts expense to actual uncollectible accounts receivables are all forms of evidence to support the information provided by management.

43. (b) In addition to indemnification in case of loss, fidelity bonds provide a psychological deterrent to employees considering defalcations. The insurance company's investigation before an employee is bonded tends to discourage those with intentions of committing defalcations from accepting jobs requiring bonds. A further deterrent is the employee's knowledge that the insurance company will prosecute in an effort to recover a material loss, whereas the employer might be persuaded to forego prosecution.

44. (d) Internal verifications of cash balances should generally be made monthly. Recorded cash on hand and petty cash balances should be compared with cash counts, and recorded bank balances should be reconciled to balances shown on bank statements. These verifications should be made by personnel who are not otherwise involved in executing or recording cash transactions to maintain a segregation of functions. The cash receipts accountant, the cash disbursements accountant, and the controller should not reconcile the monthly statements as they are involved in the executing or recording of cash transactions.

DISBURSEMENTS CYCLE

45. (b) Good internal controls require that the person who last signs the checks keep control of them until they are mailed. Answers (a), (c), and (d) do not provide sufficient segregation of duties for the authorization, custodial, and reporting functions of an effective internal control system.

46. (d) The most effective controls over recorded purchases occur when supporting forms such as purchase orders, receiving reports, and vendor invoices are compared independently for agreement. For good control, the receiving department should not know the quantity ordered. Answer (b) is a step in the right direction, but does not encompass as many independent comparisons as does answer (d). Answer (c) is an example of incompatible functions. The assets should not be checked in and recorded by the same person who authorized their purchase.

47. (b) Incompatible functions are those that place any person in a position to both perpetrate and conceal errors or fraud in the normal course of his or her duties. A well-designed plan of organization separates the duties of *authorization*, *recordkeeping*, and *custody* of assets. Answers (a) and (d) do not separate custody and recordkeeping. Answer (c) does not provide verification of inventory.

48. (c) Incompatible functions are those that place any person in a position to both perpetrate and conceal errors or fraud in the normal course of his or her duties. Therefore, a well-designed plan of organization separates the duties of authorization, record keeping, and custody of assets. The treasurer would generally perform the other procedures.

INVENTORY & PRODUCTION CYCLE

49. (c) An independent comparison of finished goods records with counts of goods on hand is designed to detect errors and fraud concerning custody of the inventory as it provides an independent reconciliation of the two amounts. Answers (a) and (b) do not consider the inventory itself nor the custody of the inventory. The storekeeper should not have both access and authorization.

PERSONNEL & PAYROLL CYCLE

50. (a) The authorization of a transaction, its recordkeeping, and the custody of the related asset should all be separated. In a payroll function, the treasurer's department prepares and distributes payroll checks to employees (custody), the controller reviews the payroll, and the payroll department prepares the payroll (recordkeeping).

PERFORMANCE BY SUBTOPICS

Each category below parallels a subtopic covered in Chapter 34. Record the number and percentage of questions you correctly answered in each subtopic area.

Segregation of Duties

Question #	Correct √
1	
2	
# Questions	2
# Correct	
% Correct	

Revenue Cycle

Question #	Correct √
3	
4	
5	
6	
7	
8	
9	
10	
# Questions	8
# Correct	
% Correct	

Disbursements Cycle

Question #	Correct √
11	
12	
13	
14	
15	
16	
17	
18	
19	
20	
# Questions	10
# Correct	
% Correct	

Inventory & Production Cycle

Question #	Correct √
21	
22	
23	
24	
25	
26	
# Questions	6
# Correct	
% Correct	

Personnel & Payroll Cycle

Question #	Correct √
27	
28	
29	
30	
31	
# Questions	5
# Correct	
% Correct	

PP&E Cycle

Question #	Correct √
32	
33	
34	
35	
36	
# Questions	5
# Correct	
% Correct	

Investing Cycle

Question #	Correct √
37	
38	
39	
40	
# Questions	4
# Correct	
% Correct	

ESSAY SOLUTIONS

SOLUTION 34-3 FLOWCHART OF REVENUE CYCLE

The weaknesses in Newton Hardware's internal controls include these:

Warehouse Clerk

- **Initiates posting to inventory records** by preparation of shipping advice.
- **Releases merchandise** to customers **before** proper **approvals** of customers' credit.
- Does **not retain a copy of the shipping advice** for comparison with receipt from carrier.

Bookkeeper A

- **Authorizes customers' credit and prepares source documents** for posting to customers' accounts.
- **Prepares invoices without notice** that the merchandise was actually shipped and the date it was shipped.
- **Authorizes write-offs** of customer accounts receivable and authorizes **customers' credit.**

Collection Clerk

- **Receives directly** and **records** customers' checks.
- **Does not deliver checks** excluded from the deposit to an employee independent of the bank deposit for review and disposition.
- Initiates posting of receipts to subsidiary accounts receivable ledger and has **initial access to cash receipts.**
- Does **not deposit** cash receipts **promptly.**
- **Reconciles bank statement** and has initial access to cash receipts.

SOLUTION 34-4 REVENUE CYCLE

a. There are many strengths in Southwest's internal control that an auditor most likely could consider in assessing control risk below the maximum level. Among the strengths are the following:

- Insurance **coverage for patients is verified** and communicated to the clerks by the office manager before medical services are rendered.
- The physician who renders the medical services documents the services on a **prenumbered service slip** that is used for recording revenue and as a receipt for the patient.
- Patients with uncollectible balances are prevented from making future appointments or receiving additional services because **the clerk** (clerk #3) **who makes appointments receives a list of patients with uncollectible balances.**
- **Prenumbered service slips are accounted for on a monthly basis** by the outside accountant who is independent of the revenue generating and revenue recording functions.
- The **bank reconciliation is prepared monthly** by the outside accountant who is independent of the revenue generating and revenue recording functions.
- **Computer passwords** are only known to the individual employees and the managing partner who has no duties in the revenue recording functions.
- Computer **software cannot be modified** by Southwest's employees.
- None of the employees who perform duties in the revenue generating and revenue recording areas have **access to check-writing capabilities.**

---

b. There are many weaknesses in Southwest's internal control that could permit material misstatements to occur in the financial statements. The following are the weaknesses and the internal control activities that most likely could help correct the weaknesses:

Weaknesses	*Internal control activities*
The office manager does not extend credit on the basis of a formal credit search, established credit limits, or any objective criteria.	**Objective credit limits** should be established and a formal credit search should be performed.
The office manager approves the extension of credit to patients and also approves the write-off of uncollectible patient receivables.	The **approval of credit and the write-off of patient receivables should be segregated**. One of the partners should be assigned the task of deciding which patient receivables should be written off.
There is no independent verification of clerk #1's pricing procedures.	The **verification of clerk #1's pricing procedures** should be assigned to another employee, such as clerk #3.

Weaknesses	*Internal control activities*
Clerk #2 performs numerous **incompatible functions**. For example, clerk #2: • **Receives cash and check directly from patients**; • **Receives check through the mail** from patients and insurance companies; • Prepares the **daily revenue summary**; • Prepares the daily bank deposit; • Maintains the accounts receivable records and **can add or delete information on the PC without proper authorization**; • Notifies the office manager when insurance claims and patient receivables are **not settled within 60 days**; and • Prepares the **list of patients with uncollectible balances**.	• The preparation of the daily revenue summary and the daily bank deposit should be assigned to an employee who does not receive cash directly from patients and check from patients and insurance companies. • The checks received through the mail should be stamped by clerk #1 who opens the mail and the remittance advices or copies of the checks or a list of the checks should be given to clerk #2. • The recording of accounts receivable and the deleting of uncollectible accounts should be assigned to an employee who does not have access to cash and checks. • The office manager should be notified by an employee who does not maintain the accounts receivable records when insurance claims and patient receivables are not settled within 60 days. • The preparation of the list of patients with uncollectible balances should be assigned to an employee who does not maintain the accounts receivable records.
No aged trial balance of patient receivables is prepared and reconciled to the general ledger.	An aged trial balance of patient receivables should be prepared and reconciled to the general ledger by someone other than clerk #2, such as the outside accountant, and reviewed by one of the partners.
Rejected insurance claims are **automatically converted to patient receivables without any follow-up** or investigation. In addition, there is no investigation of other unsettled insurance claims that are over 60 days.	Rejected insurance claims and other unsettled insurance claims over 60 days should be reviewed by one of the partners, and formal follow-up procedures to discover why claims were rejected or are unsettled should be implemented.
Uncollectible patient receivables are not determined on the basis of established objective criteria. In addition, there is no follow-up on uncollectible accounts, such as the use of phone calls, letters, or collection agencies.	**Objective write-off criteria** should be established and **follow-up procedures** should be implemented such as the use of phone calls, letters, and collection agencies.

Solution 34-5 Disbursements Cycle

The internal control procedures that most likely would provide reasonable assurance that specific control objectives for the financial statement assertions regarding purchases and accounts payable will be achieved are:

1. Proper **authorization of requisitions** by department head is required before purchase orders are prepared.
2. Purchasing department assures that **requisitions are within budget limits** before purchase orders are prepared.
3. The adequacy of each **vendor's** past record as a supplier is **verified**.
4. Secure facilities **limit access** to the goods during the receiving activity.
5. Receiving department makes a **blind count** of the goods received, independently of any other department.

6. The requisitioning department head **independently verifies** the quantity and quality of the goods received.

7. **Requisitions, purchase orders**, and **receiving reports** are **matched with vendor invoices** as to quantity and price.

8. Accounts payable department **recomputes** the **mathematical accuracy** of each **invoice**.

9. The **voucher register** is **independently reconciled** to the **control accounts monthly**.

10. All **supporting documentation is required** for payment and is made available to the treasurer.

11. The purchasing, receiving, and accounts payable **functions are segregated**.

SOLUTION 34-6 PAYROLL CYCLE

Young Computer Outlets, Inc.
Payroll
Internal Control Questionnaire

Question	*Yes*	*No*
1. Are **payroll changes** (hires, separations, salary changes, overtime, bonuses, promotions, etc.) properly **authorized and approved**?		
2. Are discretionary payroll **deductions and withholdings authorized** in writing by employees?		
3. Are the employees who perform each of the following payroll functions **independent** of the other five functions? • **personnel and approval of payroll changes** • **preparation** of payroll data • **approval** of payroll • **signing** of paychecks • **distribution** of paychecks • **reconciliation** of payroll account		
4. Are changes in standard data on which payroll is based (hires, separations, salary changes, promotions, deduction and withholding changes, etc.) **promptly input** to the system to process the payroll?		
5. Is gross pay determined by using **authorized salary rates and time and attendance records**?		
6. Is there a **suitable chart of accounts** and/or established guidelines for determining salary account distribution and for recording payroll withholding liabilities?		
7. Are **clerical operations** in payroll preparation **verified**?		
8. Is **payroll preparation and recording reviewed** by supervisors or internal audit personnel?		
9. Are **payrolls approved** by a responsible official **before** payroll checks are **issued**?		
10. Are payrolls disbursed through an **imprest account**?		
11. Is the payroll **bank account reconciled monthly** to the general ledger?		
12. Are payroll **bank reconciliations** properly **approved** and differences promptly followed up?		
13. Is the custody and follow-up of **unclaimed salary checks** assigned to a responsible official?		
14. Are **differences reported by employees followed up on a timely basis** by persons not involved in payroll preparation?		
15. Are there **procedures** (e.g., tickler files) to assure **proper and timely payment of withholdings** to appropriate bodies and to file required information returns?		
16. Are employee **compensation records reconciled to control accounts**?		
17. Is **access** to personnel and payroll records, checks, forms, signature plates, etc. **limited**?		

SOLUTION 34-7 PP&E CYCLE

The key internal control policies and procedures related to Grant's property, equipment, and related transactions that Harris may consider in assessing control risk include the following:

- Advance **approval** in accordance with management's criteria is required for property and equipment transactions.
- Approval authority for transactions above an established dollar value is required at a higher level, such as the board of directors.
- Property and equipment transactions are **adequately documented**.
- There are **written policies covering capitalizing expenditures**, classifying **leases**, and determining estimated **useful lives**, salvage values, and methods of depreciation and amortization.
- There are adequate policies and procedures to determine whether property and equipment are received and properly recorded, such as a system that matches purchase orders, receiving reports, and vendors' invoices.
- There are adequate procedures to determine whether **dispositions** of property and equipment are **properly accounted for** and proceeds, if any, are received in accordance with management's authorization.
- A property and equipment **subsidiary ledger is maintained** showing additions, retirements, and depreciation, and the ledger is periodically reconciled.
- Property and equipment is **physically inspected** and **reconciled** at reasonable intervals with independently maintained property and equipment records.
- An **annual budget** is prepared and monitored to forecast and **control acquisitions and retirements** of property and equipment.
- Reporting procedures assure prompt **identification and analysis of variances** between **authorized expenditures and actual costs**.
- Property and equipment is protected by adequate **safeguards**.
- Property and equipment is **insured** in accordance with management's authorization.
- Documents evidencing **title and property rights** are periodically **compared with** the detailed property records.
- The **entity employs internal auditors** to test whether the internal control structure policies and procedures are operating effectively.

CHAPTER 35

EVIDENCE & PROCEDURES

EXAM COVERAGE: The Obtain and Document Information portion of the Auditing section of the CPA exam is designated by the examiners to be 35 percent of the section's point value. Historically, exam coverage of the topics in Chapters 35 and 36 fluctuates from 18 to 28 percent of the Auditing section. More information about the point value of various topics is included in the **Practical Advice** section of this volume.

CHAPTER 35

EVIDENCE & PROCEDURES

I. Evidential Matter (AU 326, SAS 31)

A. The Third Standard of Field Work

Exhibit 1 ♦ The Third Standard of Field Work

> "Sufficient competent evidential matter is to be obtained through inspection, observation, inquiries, and confirmations to afford a reasonable basis for an opinion regarding the financial statements under audit."

1. This broad standard encompasses many steps in the audit process. The consideration of internal control provides evidential matter that has an important effect on the nature, timing, and extent of the auditor's substantive testing. Therefore, the auditor's consideration of the client's internal control and the results of the auditor's substantive testing together comprise evidential matter that must be both sufficient and competent in order to provide the auditor with a reasonable basis to form an opinion (or to disclaim an opinion) on the financial statements.

2. The **sufficiency** and **competence** of evidential matter are subjective issues to be decided by the auditor on the basis of his or her judgment. The evidential matter is obtained through two general classes of substantive tests: (a) tests of details of transactions and balances and (b) analytical procedures applied to financial information. Reliance on substantive tests will vary with the assessed level of control risk. Therefore, an auditor may compensate for a weakness in internal control by increasing the substantive tests.

B. Nature of Assertions

Assertions are representations made by management and embodied in the financial statements being audited. There are five broad categories of assertions.

C	Completeness
O	Obligations and Rights
V	Valuation or Allocation
E	Existence or Occurrence
S	Statement Presentation & Disclosure

1. **Completeness** Deals with whether all accounts and all transactions that should be presented in the financial statements are included and whether all transactions that should be recorded in the accounts actually are.

2. **Obligations and Rights** Concerns whether, at a given date, recorded assets indeed represent rights of the entity and liabilities represent obligations.

3. **Valuation or Allocation** Deals with whether assets and liabilities are properly valued and whether revenues and expenses are allocated appropriately between periods.

4. **Existence or Occurrence** Deals with whether assets or liabilities exist as of a financial statement date and whether recorded transactions did occur during a reporting period.

5. **Statement Presentation and Disclosure** Concerns the proper classification, description, and disclosure in the financial statements (including footnotes).

C. USE OF ASSERTIONS IN DEVELOPING AUDIT OBJECTIVES AND DESIGNING SUBSTANTIVE TESTS

1. **AUDIT OBJECTIVES** In obtaining evidential matter in support of financial statement assertions, the auditor should develop specific audit objectives. These objectives should take into consideration the specific circumstances of the entity, including the nature of its economic activity, the accounting practices of the particular industry, and the unique aspects of the entity.

EXHIBIT 2 ♦ OBTAINING EVIDENTIAL MATTER

Management's Assertions	→	*Specific Audit Objectives*	→	*Audit Procedures*

2. **SUBSTANTIVE TESTS** Once the specific audit objectives have been identified, the auditor must design specific substantive tests to attain those objectives. The design of substantive test procedures is based on considerations such as the following:

    a. The risk of material misstatement of the financial statements, including the assessed levels of control risk, and the expected effectiveness and efficiency of such tests

    b. The nature and materiality of the items being tested

    c. The kinds and competence of available evidential matter

    d. The nature of the audit objective to be achieved

D. NATURE OF EVIDENTIAL MATTER

Evidential matter supporting financial statement assertions consists of the underlying accounting data and all corroborating information available to the auditor.

1. **UNDERLYING ACCOUNTING DATA** Includes books of original entry, subsidiary ledgers, supporting schedules, etc. By **itself**, accounting data does **not** constitute sufficient evidential matter; yet, it provides a necessary step in translating the raw economic events into financial statements. As such, the propriety and accuracy of accounting data must be ascertained as a prerequisite to forming an opinion on the financial statements. The auditor tests the underlying accounting data by analysis and review, by retracing the procedural steps in the accounting process, by recalculation and redevelopment of allocations and schedules, and by reconciling related types of information.

2. **CORROBORATING EVIDENTIAL MATTER** Includes documents such as checks, invoices, contracts, and minutes of meetings; confirmations and other written representations; and information obtained by the auditor from observation, inquiry, inspection, physical examination, and other appropriate sources.

E. COMPETENCE OF EVIDENTIAL MATTER

Competent evidence is both **valid** and **relevant**. The validity of evidential matter is highly dependent upon the circumstances under which it is obtained. Subject to exceptions for certain specific circumstances, however, the following generalizations can be made (AU 326.19):

1. **INDEPENDENT** "When evidential matter can be obtained from **independent** sources outside an entity, it provides greater assurance of reliability for the purposes of an independent audit than that secured solely within the entity."

2. **INTERNAL CONTROL** "The more **effective** the internal control structure, the more assurance it provides about the reliability of the accounting data and financial statements."

3. **DIRECT** "The independent auditor's **direct** personal knowledge, obtained through physical examination, observation, computation, and inspection, is more persuasive than information obtained indirectly."

F. SUFFICIENCY OF EVIDENTIAL MATTER

1. **OBJECTIVE** The independent auditor's objective is to obtain sufficient evidential matter to provide a reasonable basis for forming an opinion on the financial statements.

   a. The amounts and kinds of evidence needed are a matter of professional judgment. In exercising this judgment, the auditor considers both the materiality of the item in question and the inherent risk of the item.

   b. In most cases, it will be necessary to rely on evidence that is **persuasive** rather than *convincing.* An auditor is seldom convinced beyond all doubt with respect to all of the financial statements being audited. Remember, audit risk is reduced to a low level; it cannot be reduced to zero.

2. **TIME AND COST CONSTRAINTS** Professional judgment is required to determine whether the evidence obtained is sufficient to form an opinion. Audit risk and cost/benefit relationships may be considered in deciding whether to obtain a particular kind of evidence. *The degree of difficulty and expense involved in testing a particular item, however, is not, by itself, a valid basis for omitting the test.*

G. EVALUATION OF EVIDENTIAL MATTER

The basis for evaluation is whether specific audit objectives have been achieved. The search for evidential matter should be thorough and its analysis should be unbiased. If the audit evidence does not provide a basis for an opinion relative to any assertion of material significance, the auditor must obtain sufficient competent evidential matter. Failure to do so will result in a qualified opinion or a disclaimer of opinion due to scope limitation.

H. IMPACT OF INFORMATION TECHNOLOGY (SAS 94)

Information systems have a prominent impact on business processes, on the initiation and processing of accounting trânsactions, and, therefore, on auditing. The impact of information technology is discussed further in Chapter 38, *Auditing EDP Systems.*

II. INTERNAL AUDIT FUNCTION (AU 322, SAS 65)

A. INTERNAL AUDITORS

An external auditor will usually perform financial audits to enable him or her to attest to the fairness of an entity's financial statements. Internal auditors may also perform financial audits as well as procedural and operational audits beyond the scope of the external audit. Therefore, a comprehensive **internal** audit program may be more **detailed** and cover more **areas** than an independent auditor's program. SAS 65 provides the auditor with guidance on the work of internal auditors.

1. **EXTERNAL AUDITOR** The auditor maintains **independence** from the *entity* to fulfill the responsibility to obtain sufficient competent evidential matter to provide a reasonable basis for the opinion of the entity's financial statements.

2. **INTERNAL AUDITOR** Internal auditors maintain **objectivity** with respect to the *activity* being audited to fulfill the responsibility for providing analyses, evaluations, recommendations, and other information to the entity's management and board of directors or to others with equivalent authority.

B. INTERNAL AUDIT

When obtaining an understanding of internal control, the auditor should obtain an understanding of the internal audit function sufficient to identify those internal audit activities that are relevant to planning the audit.

1. **Procedures** The auditor ordinarily should make inquiries of appropriate management and internal audit personnel about the internal auditors' (a) organizational status within the entity; (b) application of professional standards; (c) audit plan, including the nature, timing, and extent of audit work; (d) access to records; and (e) whether there are limitations on the scope of their activities.

2. **Relevance** Internal audit activities **relevant** to an audit of the entity's financial statements are those that provide evidence about the design and effectiveness of **internal control** policies and procedures that pertain to the entity's ability to record, process, summarize, and report financial data consistent with the assertions embodied in the financial statements, or that provide direct evidence about **potential misstatements** of such data. The following procedures help the auditor assess the relevancy of internal audit activities: (a) considering knowledge from prior-year audits, (b) reviewing how the internal auditors allocate their audit resources to financial or operating areas in response to their risk assessment process, and (c) obtaining detailed information about the scope of internal audit activities.

3. **Consideration of Internal Auditors' Work** The auditor may conclude that some of the internal auditors' activities are **relevant** to the audit and that it would be efficient to consider how the internal auditors' work might affect the nature, timing, and extent of audit procedures. In that case, the auditor should assess the **competence** and **objectivity** of the internal audit in light of the intended effect of the internal auditors' work on the audit.

   a. **Competence of Internal Auditors**

      (1) Education level and professional experience

      (2) Professional certification and continuing education

      (3) Evaluation of internal auditors' performance

      (4) Supervision and review of internal auditors' activities

      (5) Quality of working paper documentation, reports, and recommendations

   b. **Objectivity of Internal Auditors**

      (1) The organizational status of the internal auditor

      (2) What organizational level does the internal auditor report to (the higher, the more objective)

      (3) Amount of access to the board of directors or audit committee

      (4) Whether the board of directors, the audit committee, or the owner-manager oversees employment of the internal auditors

      (5) Policies to maintain internal auditor's objectivity about areas audited

C. **Coordination With Internal Auditors**
Work is coordinated by (1) holding periodic meetings, (2) scheduling audit work, (3) arranging access to internal auditors' working papers, (4) reviewing audit reports, and (5) discussing possible audit issues.

D. **Effectiveness of the Internal Auditors' Work**
Involves determining whether the scope of work is appropriate; audit programs are adequate; working papers adequately document work performed, including evidence of supervision and review; conclusions are appropriate; and reports are consistent with the results of the work performed.

E. DIRECT ASSISTANCE
If the internal auditors provide direct assistance, the auditor should inform the internal auditors of their responsibilities, the objectives of the procedures, and matters that may affect the nature, timing, and extent of audit procedures.

1. **SUPERVISION** The external auditor should assess the internal auditors' competence and objectivity, and supervise, review, evaluate, and test the work performed. The external auditor should test the internal auditors' work by examining some of the controls, transactions, or balances that the internal auditors examined, or similar evidence not actually examined by the internal auditors.

2. **GUIDANCE** The internal auditor should also be informed of the need to bring all significant accounting and auditing issues identified to the external auditor's attention.

III. MANAGEMENT REPRESENTATIONS (AU 333, SAS 85)

A. WRITTEN REPRESENTATIONS
In order to comply with GAAS, the auditor must obtain certain written representations from management. These are part of evidential matter, but are not a substitute for the application of auditing procedures. Written representations (1) confirm the oral representations that were given to the auditor during the engagement, (2) serve as documentation of the continuing appropriateness of the representations, and (3) reduce the chance of misunderstanding between the auditor and the client.

1. **CORROBORATION** The auditor frequently performs auditing procedures in order to corroborate the substance of the written representations. In some cases, however, there cannot be any corroboration.

2. **RELIANCE** It is reasonable for the auditor to rely on the written representations of management unless audit procedures provide evidential matter that indicates otherwise. However, the auditor must maintain an appropriate level of professional skepticism.

3. **IMPACT** In cases where management representations are contradicted by other audit evidence, the auditor should investigate the circumstances and consider the reliability of the representations being made. Based on the circumstances, the auditor should consider whether reliance on management's representations relating to other aspects of the financial statements is appropriate and justified.

4. **AFFIRMATION** SAS 89 requires that representations include management's responsibility for corrections of misstatements noted by the auditor in the current and previous engagements. If management believes that certain items are not misstatements, management's belief may be acknowledged by adding to the representation, for example, "We do not agree that items XX and XY constitute misstatements because [description of reasons]." (See paragraph 11 in Exhibit 3.)

B. REQUIREMENTS
Written representations from management must be obtained for all financial statements and periods covered by the auditor's report. For example, when comparative financial statements are presented, the written representations obtained at the completion of the most recent audit should address all periods being presented. Representations specifically required for all audits are noted in the sample representation letter in Exhibit 3.

1. **ADAPT** The specific written representations obtained by the auditor depend on the circumstances of the particular engagement and the nature and basis of the financial statement presentation (e.g., whether the financial statements are based on GAAP or OCBOA). The representation letter ordinarily is tailored to include additional appropriate representations from management relating to matters specific to the entity's business or industry.

2. **DURATION** If current management was not present during all periods covered by the auditor's report, the auditor still should obtain written representations from current management on all such periods.

3. **SUBSIDIARY** If the independent auditor performs an audit of the financial statements of a subsidiary, but does not audit those of the parent company, he or she may want to obtain representations from management of the parent company concerning matters that may affect the subsidiary (for instance, the parent company's intention to provide continuing financial support to the subsidiary).

C. **MATERIALITY**
Management's representations may be limited to matters that are considered either individually or collectively material to the financial statements, provided management and the auditor have reached an understanding on materiality for this purpose. Materiality may be different for different representations. A discussion of materiality may be included explicitly in the representation letter, in either qualitative or quantitative terms. Materiality considerations would not apply to those representations that are not directly related to amounts included in the financial statements. In addition, because of the possible effects of fraud on other aspects of the audit, materiality would not apply with respect to management or those employees who have significant roles in internal control.

D. **FORM OF REPRESENTATIONS**

1. **ADDRESS** The written representations should be addressed to the auditor.

2. **DATES** The representations should be made as of a date no earlier than the date of the auditor's report. If the auditor *dual dates* his or her report, the auditor should consider whether obtaining additional representations relating to the subsequent event is appropriate.

3. **SIGNATURES** The letter should be signed by those members of management with overall responsibility for financial and operating matters whom the auditor believes are responsible for and knowledgeable about (directly or through others in the organization) the matters covered by the representations. Such members of management normally include the chief executive officer and chief financial officer (or others with equivalent positions in the entity). In certain circumstances, the auditor may want to obtain written representations from other individuals. For example, he or she may want to obtain written representations about the completeness of the minutes of the meetings of stockholders, directors, and committees of directors from the person responsible for keeping such minutes.

E. **UPDATING REPRESENTATION LETTER**
The updating management representation letter should state (1) whether any information has come to management's attention that would cause member of management to believe that any of the previous representations should be modified, and (2) whether any events have occurred subsequent to the balance sheet date of the latest financial statements reported on by the auditor that would require adjustment to or disclosure in those financial statements. An auditor should obtain updating representation letters from management in the following circumstances.

1. **REISSUANCE** When a predecessor auditor is requested by a former client to reissue (or consent to the reuse of) his or her report on the financial statements of a prior period, and those financial statements are to be presented on a comparative basis with audited financial statements of a subsequent period.

2. **SEC FILINGS** When performing subsequent events procedures in connection with filings under the Securities Act of 1933.

F. **SCOPE LIMITATION**
Management's refusal to furnish written representations constitutes a limitation on the scope of the audit sufficient to preclude an unqualified opinion and ordinarily is sufficient to cause an auditor to disclaim an opinion on the financial statements or withdraw from the engagement. Further, the

auditor should consider the effects of the refusal on his or her ability to rely on other management representations.

1. **Qualified Opinion** Based on the nature of the representations not obtained or the circumstances of the refusal, the auditor may conclude that a qualified opinion is appropriate.

2. **Other Procedures** If the auditor is precluded from performing procedures that he or she considers necessary in the circumstances with respect to a matter that is material to the financial statements, even though management has given representations concerning the matter, there is a limitation on the scope of the audit. In this case, the auditor should qualify his or her opinion or disclaim an opinion.

Exhibit 3 ♦ Sample Representation Letter

(Date of Auditor's Report)

To (Independent Auditor)

We are providing this letter in connection with your audit(s) of the [*identification of financial statements*] of [*name of entity*] as of [*dates*] and for the [*periods*] for the purpose of expressing an opinion as to whether the [*consolidated*] financial statements present fairly, in all material respects, the financial position, results of operations, and cash flows of [*name of entity*] in conformity with generally accepted accounting principles [or OCBOA]. We confirm that we are responsible for the fair presentation in the [*consolidated*] financial statements of financial position, results of operations, and cash flows in conformity with generally accepted accounting principles [or OCBOA]. [**NOTE:** The last sentence in this paragraph is required on all audits per SAS 85.]

Certain representations in this letter are described as being limited to matters that are material. Items are considered material, regardless of size, if they involve an omission or misstatement of accounting information that, in the light of surrounding circumstances, makes it probable that the judgment of a reasonable person relying on the information would be changed or influenced by the omission or misstatement.

[**NOTE:** Items 1 through 10 and the last paragraph are required on all audits per SAS 85.]

We confirm, to the best of our knowledge and belief, [*as of (date of auditor's report),*] the following representations made to you during your audit(s).

1. The financial statements referred to above are presented fairly in conformity with generally accepted accounting principles [or OCBOA].

2. We have made available to you all—

   - Financial records and related data.
   - Minutes of the meetings of stockholders, directors, and committees of directors, or summaries of actions of recent meetings for which minutes have not yet been prepared.

3. There have been no communications from regulatory agencies concerning noncompliance with or deficiencies in financial reporting practices.

4. There are no material transactions that have not been properly recorded in the accounting records underlying the financial statements.

5. There has been no—

   - Fraud involving management or employees who have significant roles in internal control.
   - Fraud involving others that could have a material effect on the financial statements.

6. The company has no plans or intentions that materially may affect the carrying value or classification of assets and liabilities.

(continued on next page)

7. The following have been recorded properly or disclosed in the financial statements:
   - Related-party transactions, including sales, purchases, loans, transfers, leasing arrangements, and guarantees, and amounts receivable from or payable to related parties.
   - Guarantees, whether written or oral, under which the company is contingently liable.
   - Significant estimates and material concentrations known to management that are required to be disclosed in accordance with the SOP 94-6, Disclosure of Certain Significant Risks and Uncertainties.

8. There are no—
   - Violations or possible violations of laws or regulations where the effects should be considered for disclosure in the financial statements or as a basis for recording a loss contingency.
   - Unasserted claims or assessments that our lawyer has advised us are probable of assertion and must be disclosed in accordance with FASB Statement No. 5, Accounting for Contingencies.
   - Other liabilities or gain or loss contingencies that are required to be accrued or disclosed by FASB Statement No. 5.

9. The company has satisfactory title to all owned assets, and there are no liens or encumbrances on such assets nor has any asset been pledged as collateral.

10. The company has complied with all aspects of contractual agreements that would have a material effect on the financial statements in the event of noncompliance.

11. Management's belief that the effects of any uncorrected financial statement misstatements aggregated by the auditor during the current engagement and pertaining to the latest period presented are immaterial, both individually and in the aggregate, to the financial statements taken as a whole. [A summary of such items should be included in or attached to the letter.]

To the best of our knowledge and belief, no events have occurred subsequent to the balance sheet date and through the date of this letter that would require adjustment to or disclosure in the aforementioned financial statements.

[Name and Title of Chief Executive Officer] *[Name and Title of Chief Financial Officer]*

IV. ANALYTICAL PROCEDURES (AU 329, SAS 56)

A. OVERVIEW

Procedures consist of evaluations of financial information made by a study of **plausible relationships** among both financial and nonfinancial data. The procedures range from simple comparisons to complex models. To utilize analytical procedures, the auditor must understand financial relationships and have knowledge of the client and its industry.

1. PURPOSE

a. To assist the auditor in **planning** the nature, timing, and extent of substantive tests. (This is **required** by GAAS.) Analytical procedures should focus on enhancing the auditor's understanding of the client's business and the transactions and events that have occurred since the last audit date, and identifying areas that may represent specific risks relevant to the audit.

b. As a substantive test to obtain evidential matter about particular assertions related to account balances or classes of transactions. (**Not** required by GAAS, but commonly used.)

c. As an overall **review** of the financial information in the final review stage of the audit. (This is also **required** by GAAS.)

2. **Expectations** Analytical procedures involve comparisons of recorded amounts, or ratios developed from recorded amounts, to expectations developed by the auditor. The auditor develops expectations by identifying relationships that are reasonably expected to exist from understanding the client and the industry in which the client operates. The following are examples of sources of information for developing expectations.

   a. Financial information for comparable prior periods giving consideration to known changes

   b. Anticipated results; for example, forecasts including extrapolations from interim data

   c. Relationships among elements of financial information within the period

   d. Information regarding the industry in which the client operates; for example, gross margin information

   e. Relationships of financial information with relevant nonfinancial information

3. **Benford's Law** Application of Benford's Law is an example of a complex analytical procedure. Benford's Law is a numerical probability theory establishing the frequency of the appearance of digits in naturally occurring sets of numbers. A common assumption is that in a sample of numbers from any population, all numbers have an equal probability of appearing. Many people do not create convincing dummy data sets because they are unaware of the unequal probability of the appearance of numbers 1 through 9. Benford's Law predicts the following approximate frequencies of occurrence as first digits: 1, 30%; 2, 18%; 3, 12%; 4, 10%; 5, 8%; 6, 7%; 7, 6%; 8, 5%; and 9, 4%. (The law predicts more, but that level of detail is beyond this discussion.) Large and varied populations of numbers adhere more closely to the distribution predicted by Benford's Law than small samples.

   Exhibit 4 ♦ Benford's Law

   > A manager's ceiling for invoice approval is $5,000. Anomalies in the occurrence of 5, 6, 7, 8, and 9 as first digits would be expected. A higher than expected level of occurrence of 4 as a first digit (i.e., invoices at $4,001 to $4,999) suggest that purchases were intentionally divided into component parts to avoid higher level approval procedures. If 4 occurs more frequently than expected, the manager's spending warrants further scrutiny.

   a. Seemingly divergent sets of numbers (such as utility bills of a given region, numbers on a newspaper page, and sport statistics) all adhere to Benford's Law. Computer software based on Benford's Law is a powerful device for detecting financial errors (including those due to software bugs), as well as fraud.

   b. False positives do occur. Also, innocent anomalies can be created by "unnatural" external factors. Thresholds and ceilings are some factors that may cause anomalies. For instance, an HMO's fee schedule can create clustering, and hence, non-compliant number repetition, in a medical office's billing.

B. **Used in Overall Review**
Analytical procedures are used in the overall review stage to assist the auditor in *assessing conclusions reached* and in *evaluating the overall financial statement presentation.* The overall

review would generally include reading the financial statements and notes and considering the adequacy of evidence gathered in response to unusual or unexpected balances identified in planning the audit or in the course of the audit, and unusual or unexpected balances or relationships that were not previously identified. The results of an overall review may indicate that additional evidence may be needed. Also, use of analytical procedures in the overall review helps the auditor in the going concern assessment.

C. USED AS SUBSTANTIVE TESTS

The auditor's reliance on substantive tests to achieve an audit objective related to a particular assertion (representation by management) may be derived from *tests of details*, from *analytical procedures*, or from a combination of *both*.

1. **EFFECTIVENESS AND EFFICIENCY** The expected effectiveness and efficiency of an analytical procedure in identifying potential misstatements depends on, among other things, the nature of the assertion, the plausibility and predictability of the relationship, the availability and reliability of the data used to develop the expectation, and the precision of the expectation. For example, the auditor may use inventory turnover figures to evaluate inventory salability.

2. **SIGNIFICANT DIFFERENCES** In planning the analytical procedures as a substantive test, the auditor should consider the amount of difference from the expectation that can be accepted without further investigation. The auditor should evaluate significant unexpected differences. If an explanation for the difference cannot be obtained, the auditor should obtain sufficient evidence about the assertion by performing other audit procedures to determine whether the difference is likely to be a misstatement.

D. PLAUSIBILITY AND PREDICTABILITY

A basic premise underlying the application of analytical procedures is that plausible relationships among data may reasonably be expected to exist and continue in the absence of known conditions to the contrary.

1. Relationships are more predictable in a stable environment, while relationships in a dynamic environment lose predictability.

2. Relationships involving income statement accounts are usually more predictable than those involving only balance sheet accounts because income statement accounts represent transactions over a period, while balance sheet accounts represent amounts as of a point in time.

E. RELIABILITY

The reliability of the data used by the auditor to develop expectations should be appropriate for the desired level of assurance from the analytical procedures. The auditor should assess the reliability of the data by considering the source of the data and the conditions under which it was gathered. The following factors influence the auditor's consideration of the reliability of data for purposes of achieving audit objectives.

1. Whether the data was obtained from independent sources outside the entity or from sources within the entity

2. Whether sources within the entity were independent of those who are responsible for the amount being audited

3. Whether the data was developed under a reliable system with adequate controls

4. Whether the data was subjected to audit testing in the current or prior year

5. Whether the expectations were developed using data from a variety of sources

F. **PRECISION**
The expectation should be precise enough to provide the desired level of assurance that differences that may be potential material misstatements, individually or when aggregated with other misstatements, would be identified for the auditor to investigate. The auditor's identification and consideration of factors that significantly affect the amount being audited and the level of detail of data used to develop expectations affect the precision of the expectations. Greater detail of data increases reliability of expectations. For example, using monthly amounts will generally be more effective than annual amounts.

V. USING THE WORK OF A SPECIALIST (AU 336, SAS 73)

A. DEFINITION
A specialist is a person (or firm) possessing special skill or knowledge in a particular field other than accounting or auditing. Specialists include, but are not limited to, actuaries, appraisers, engineers, environmental consultants, and geologists. Additionally, SAS 73 applies to attorneys engaged as specialists in situations other than to provide services to a client concerning litigation, claims, or assessments.

B. DECISION TO USE A SPECIALIST'S WORK
The auditor is not expected to have the expertise of a person trained for, or qualified to engage in, the practice of another profession or occupation. An auditor may encounter complex or subjective matters that may require special skill or knowledge and require using the work of a specialist to obtain competent evidential matter. Examples of the types of matters that may decide the auditor to consider using the work of a specialist include

1. Valuation (i.e., special-purpose inventories, high-technology materials or equipment, pharmaceutical products, complex financial instruments, real estate, restricted securities, works of art, and environmental contingencies).

2. Determination of quantities or amounts derived by using specialized techniques or methods (i.e., actuarial determinations for employee benefits obligations and disclosures, and determination of insurance loss reserves).

3. Interpretation of technical requirements, regulations, or agreements (i.e., the potential significance of contracts or other legal documents, or legal title to property).

C. SELECTION
The auditor should evaluate the professional qualifications of the specialist to determine that the specialist possesses the necessary skill or knowledge in the particular field.

1. **CONSIDERATIONS**

   a. The professional certification, license, or other recognition of competence

   b. The reputation and standing of the specialist in the views of peers and others

   c. The specialist's experience in the type of work under consideration

2. **ENGAGED BY MANAGEMENT** Management may engage or employ a specialist and the auditor may use that specialist's work as evidential matter in performing substantive tests to evaluate material financial statement assertions. Alternatively, management may engage a specialist employed by the auditor's firm to provide advisory services.

3. **ENGAGED BY AUDITOR** The auditor may engage a specialist and use that specialist's work as evidential matter in performing substantive tests to evaluate material financial statement assertions.

D. **UNDERSTANDING THE WORK**
The auditor should obtain an understanding of the nature of the work performed or to be performed by the specialist. This understanding should cover the following:

1. **OBJECTIVES AND SCOPE OF THE SPECIALIST'S WORK**

2. **SPECIALIST'S RELATIONSHIP TO THE CLIENT** The auditor should evaluate circumstances that might impair the objectivity of the specialist. Such circumstances include situations in which the client has the ability (through employment, family relationship, or otherwise) to directly or indirectly control or significantly influence the specialist.

   a. **NO RELATIONSHIP WITH THE CLIENT** The specialist's work will usually provide the auditor with greater assurance when there is no relationship.

   b. **RELATIONSHIP WITH THE CLIENT** The auditor should assess the risk that the specialist's objectivity might be impaired. If the relationship might impair the specialist's objectivity, the auditor should perform additional procedures or engage another specialist.

3. **METHODS USED** The appropriateness and reasonableness of methods and assumptions used and their application are the responsibility of the specialist.

   a. The auditor should obtain an understanding to determine whether the findings are suitable for corroborating the assertions in the financial statements. The auditor should consider whether the specialist's findings support the related assertions in the financial statements and make appropriate tests of data provided to the specialist.

   b. Ordinarily, the auditor would use the work of the specialist unless the auditor's procedures lead him or her to believe that the findings are unreasonable, in which case, he or she should apply additional procedures.

4. **COMPARISON OF METHODS OR ASSUMPTIONS USED WITH THOSE USED IN THE PRECEDING PERIOD**

5. **APPROPRIATENESS** The appropriateness of using the specialist's work for the intended purpose.

6. **FORM AND CONTENT OF THE SPECIALIST'S FINDINGS**

E. **AUDITOR'S CONCLUSIONS**
If the auditor determines that the specialist's findings support the related assertions in the financial statements, he or she may reasonably conclude that sufficient competent evidential matter has been obtained.

1. **INDETERMINATE** If there is a material difference between the specialist's findings and the assertions in the financial statements, the auditor should apply additional procedures. If the auditor is unable to resolve the matter, the auditor should obtain the opinion of another specialist, unless it appears that the matter cannot be resolved. A matter that has not been resolved will ordinarily cause the auditor to qualify the opinion or disclaim an opinion.

2. **DISAGREEMENT** The auditor may conclude that the assertions in the financial statements are not in conformity with GAAP. In that event, the auditor expresses a qualified or adverse opinion.

F. **EFFECT ON THE AUDITOR'S REPORT**
Normally, the auditor should not refer to the work or findings of the specialist. Such a reference might be misunderstood to be a qualification of the auditor's opinion or a division of responsibility, neither of which is intended. Further, there may be an inference that the auditor making such

reference performed a more thorough audit than an auditor not making such reference. Reporting alternatives are

1. **Unqualified Opinion, Standard Report** No reference to the specialist.

2. **Unqualified Opinion, Explanatory Paragraph Added to Report** Refer to specialist in explanatory paragraph **only** if doing so will help clarify the reason for the explanatory paragraph.

3. **Qualified or Disclaimer of Opinion** Scope limitation, the auditor is unable to obtain sufficient, competent evidential matter—No reference to the specialist.

4. **Qualified or Adverse Opinion** Auditor concludes there is a departure from GAAP—Refer to specialist in explanatory paragraph **only** if doing so will help clarify the reason for the qualification or adverse opinion.

VI. Inquiry of a Client's Lawyer (AU 337, SAS 12)

A. Accounting

Management has the responsibility to adopt policies and procedures that will identify, evaluate, and account for litigation, claims, and assessments as a basis for the preparation of financial statements in conformity with GAAP.

B. Auditing

The auditor should obtain evidential matter relating to (1) the existence of conditions or circumstances that indicate a possible loss from litigation, claims, and assessments, (2) the period in which the underlying cause for legal action occurred, (3) the probability of an unfavorable outcome, and (4) the amount or range of the potential loss.

1. **Procedures** Management is the primary source of information. The auditor should

   a. Inquire of, and discuss with, management the client's policies and procedures for identifying, evaluating, and accounting for litigation, claims, and assessments.

   b. Obtain from management a description and evaluation of litigation, claims, and assessments that existed at the balance sheet date and during the time until management furnishes the information. Further, the auditor should obtain assurance in writing, that the client disclosed all such matters that are required to be disclosed by SFAS 5, *Accounting for Contingencies*.

   c. Examine appropriate documents in the possession of the client that relate to these contingencies, including correspondence and invoices from lawyers.

   d. Obtain assurance from management, ordinarily in writing, that it has disclosed all unasserted claims the lawyer feels are probable of assertion and that must be disclosed in accordance with SFAS 5.

      (1) **Inform Lawyer** With the **client's permission**, the auditor should inform the lawyer that the client has given the auditor this assurance.

      (2) **Other Audit Procedures** The auditor will find that some of the regular audit procedures (e.g., reading the minutes of the board of directors meetings, sending bank confirmations, reading contracts and loan agreements, and inspecting documents for guarantees by the client) may also disclose possible litigation, claims, and assessments.

2. **Letter of Audit Inquiry to a Client's Lawyer** The auditor should request client management to send a letter of inquiry to those lawyers consulted by management concerning

litigation, claims, and assessments (however, the letter should be physically mailed by the auditor). This serves to corroborate the information furnished by management. Additionally, this corroboration may be provided by information from inside legal counsel. However, such information is not a substitute for information that outside counsel refuses to furnish.

EXHIBIT 5 ♦ SAMPLE INQUIRY LETTER TO LEGAL COUNSEL

In connection with an audit of our financial statements at (balance sheet date) and for the (period) then ended, management of the Company has prepared, and furnished to our auditors (name and address of auditors), a description and evaluation of certain contingencies, including those set forth below involving matters with respect to which you have been engaged and to which you have devoted substantive attention on behalf of the Company in the form of legal consultation or representation. These contingencies are regarded by management of the Company as material for this purpose (management may indicate a materiality limit if an understanding has been reached with the auditor). Your response should include matters that existed at (balance sheet date) and during the period from that date to the date of your response.

Pending or Threatened Litigation *(excluding unasserted claims)*

[Ordinarily the information would include the following: (1) the nature of the litigation, (2) the progress of the case to date, (3) how management is responding or intends to respond to the litigation (for example, to contest the case vigorously or to seek an out-of-court settlement), and (4) an evaluation of the likelihood of an unfavorable outcome and an estimate, if one can be made, of the amount or range of potential loss.] Please furnish to our auditors such explanation, if any, that you consider necessary to supplement the foregoing information, including an explanation of those matters as to which your views may differ from those stated and an identification of the omission of any pending or threatened litigation, claims, and assessments or a statement that the list of such matters is complete.

Unasserted Claims and Assessments *(considered by management to be probable of assertion, and that, if asserted, would have at least a reasonable possibility of an unfavorable outcome)*

[Ordinarily management's information would include the following: (1) the nature of the matter, (2) how management intends to respond if the claim is asserted, and (3) an evaluation of the likelihood of an unfavorable outcome and an estimate, if one can be made, of the amount or range of potential loss.] Please furnish to our auditors such explanation, if any, that you consider necessary to supplement the foregoing information, including an explanation of those matters as to which your views may differ from those stated.

We understand that whenever, in the course of performing legal services for us with respect to a matter recognized to involve an unasserted possible claim or assessment that may call for financial statement disclosure, if you have formed a professional conclusion that we should disclose or consider disclosure concerning such possible claim or assessment, as a matter of professional responsibility to us, you will so advise us and will consult with us concerning the question of such disclosure and the applicable requirements of Statement of Financial Accounting Standards No. 5. Please specifically confirm to our auditors that our understanding is correct.

Please specifically identify the nature of and reasons for any limitation on your response.

[The auditor may request the client to inquire about additional matters, for example, unpaid or unbilled charges or specified information on certain contractually assumed obligations of the company, such as guarantees of indebtedness of others.]

a. **CONTENTS** Some of the matters that should be covered in a letter of audit inquiry include the following:

(1) Identification of the company, subsidiaries, and audit date.

(2) A management-prepared list and evaluation of pending or threatened litigation, claims, and assessments with which the lawyer has been substantially involved (if management prefers, they may request the lawyer to prepare the list). The lawyer is asked either to furnish the following information or to comment as to where the lawyer's views differ from management's.

(a) A **description** of the matter, **progress** to date, and the **action** the company plans to take

(b) An evaluation of the likelihood of an unfavorable outcome and, if possible, an estimate of the amount or range of potential loss

(c) An identification of any missing items or a statement that the list is complete

(3) A management-prepared list describing and evaluating unasserted claims and assessments that management considers are probable of assertion and that have at least a reasonable probability of unfavorable outcome. For example, due to client negligence, a customer may have suffered a serious injury. It is possible the client may expect a lawsuit and may have consulted the lawyer in that regard. The lawyer is requested to comment on those areas where the lawyer's views differ from those of management.

(4) A statement that management understands that it will be notified by the lawyer when an unasserted claim or assessment requiring financial disclosure per SFAS 5 comes to the attention of the lawyer. The communication includes a request that the lawyer confirm this understanding.

(5) A request that the lawyer specifically indicate the nature of, and the reason for, any **limitations** on the response.

b. **MATERIALITY** No inquiry needs to be made concerning matters not considered material as long as the auditor specifies a materiality amount in the letter.

c. **CONFERENCE** If the client's lawyers provide the auditor with the information in a conference, the auditor should **document** the information received.

d. **CHANGE OF LAWYERS** If there has been a change or resignation of lawyers, the auditor should consider the need to inquire of the reasons for the change. Lawyers may be required to resign when clients fail to follow their advice on matters of disclosure.

3. **LAWYER'S RESPONSE LIMITED** The lawyer may limit the response to those matters that the lawyer had been substantially involved with and that are considered to be material (provided the lawyer and the auditor have agreed on what will be considered material). The refusal of a lawyer to furnish the information requested in an inquiry letter is a **limitation** on the scope of the audit that is sufficient to preclude an unqualified opinion if not satisfactorily resolved.

4. **OTHER LIMITATIONS ON A LAWYER'S RESPONSE** Due to the inherent uncertainties present, the lawyer may feel unable to respond to the likelihood of an unfavorable outcome and/or to the amount or range of potential loss on one or more items. The auditor is then faced with an uncertainty that will be resolved in the future but that cannot be reasonably estimated at the

present time. If the effect on the financial statements could be material, the auditor may add an explanatory paragraph to the report to emphasize the uncertainty.

5. **COMMUNICATIONS PROHIBITED** The refusal of a client to allow necessary communications with a lawyer is a scope limitation that usually results in a disclaimer of opinion.

C. DATES

The client's letter should specify the date by which the lawyer's response should be sent to the auditor and should also request the lawyer to specify the effective date of the response. The latest date of the period covered by the lawyer's response (the "effective date") should be as close as possible to the date of the auditor's completion of field work. If the lawyer's response does not specify an effective date, the auditor can assume it is the date of the response.

VII. WORKING PAPERS (AU 339, SAS 41)

A. REQUIREMENT

The auditor is **required** to prepare and maintain working papers that are designed to meet the circumstances of a particular engagement.

1. **DOCUMENTATION** Working papers document the work that the auditor has done and the conclusions that have been reached concerning significant matters. They provide the **principal support** for the auditor's report, including the auditor's representation regarding observance of the standards of field work, which is implicit in the reference in the report to GAAS.

2. **SUPERVISION** Working papers aid the auditor in the conduct and supervision of the audit.

B. FUNCTION AND NATURE

Working papers are records kept by the auditor of the (1) procedures applied, (2) tests performed, (3) information obtained, and (4) pertinent conclusions reached in the engagement. Working papers may be data stored on tapes, films, or other media.

1. **EXAMPLES** Audit programs, analyses, memoranda, letters of confirmation and representation, abstracts of company documents, schedules and entity or auditor commentaries.

2. **TYPES OF FILES**

   a. Current files contain evidence of the entity's current account balances (e.g., bank reconciliations or recomputation of depreciation expense).

   b. Permanent files contain items of continuing interest (e.g., articles of incorporation, a pension plan contract, a flowchart of internal controls).

3. **QUANTITY, TYPE, AND CONTENT** The quantity, type, and content of working papers for a particular engagement are a matter of judgment. The working papers should be sufficient to show that the accounting records agree or reconcile with the financial statements or other information reported on and that the applicable standards of field work have been observed. The auditor's judgment may be affected by the following factors:

   a. The nature of the engagement

   b. The nature of the auditor's report

   c. The nature of the financial statements, schedules, or other information

   d. The nature and condition of the client's records

   e. The assessed level of control risk

   f. The needs in the particular circumstances for supervision and review of the work

4. **MINIMUM** Working papers ordinarily include documentation showing that

   a. The work has been adequately planned and supervised, indicating observance of the first standard of field work. SAS 77 requires a written audit program.

   b. A sufficient consideration of internal control has been performed to plan the audit and to determine the nature, timing, and extent of tests to be performed.

   c. The audit evidence obtained, the auditing procedures applied, and the testing performed have provided sufficient, competent evidential matter to afford a reasonable basis for an opinion, thereby indicating observance of the third standard of field work.

5. **ORGANIZATION** Detailed audit working papers are subdivided and grouped by financial statement accounts, which are filed in order of appearance in the financial statements. Working papers for each asset, liability, and equity account begin with a lead schedule summarizing the account's balance per the general ledger, and then show adjusting and reclassification entries, and the final balance per audit. The lead schedule also includes the auditor's conclusions about whether the account is fairly stated.

C. OWNERSHIP AND CUSTODY

Working papers are the property of the auditor. Some states have statutes that designate the auditor as the owner of the working papers. The auditor's rights of ownership are subject to ethical limitations relating to the confidential relationship with clients.

1. **REFERENCE** Certain auditor's working papers may sometimes serve as a useful reference source for the client, but the working papers should not be regarded as a part of, or a substitute for, the client's accounting records.

2. **SECURITY** The auditor should adopt reasonable procedures for safe custody of the working papers and should retain them for a period sufficient to meet the needs of the practice and to satisfy any legal requirements of records retention.

VIII. RELATED PARTIES (AU 334, SAS 45)

A. DEFINITION

Related parties include (1) the reporting entity; (2) its affiliates; (3) principal owners (owner of record or known beneficial owner of more than 10 percent of the voting interests), management, and members of their immediate families; (4) equity-method investees; (5) trusts for the benefit of employees, such as pension or profit-sharing trusts that are managed by, or under the trusteeship of, management; and (6) any other party that can exercise significant influence over the reporting entity, or over which the reporting entity can exercise significant influence. Examples of related party transactions include parent-subsidiary transactions and transactions among subsidiaries of a common parent. Transactions between related parties are considered related party transactions even if they are not given accounting recognition (e.g., a parent providing free services to a subsidiary).

B. ACCOUNTING CONSIDERATIONS

Related party transactions should be adequately and properly disclosed in conformity with GAAP. Recognition should be given to their **economic substance** rather than merely their legal form. Transactions that may indicate the existence of related party transactions include the following:

1. **LOANS** Borrowing or lending money **without** charging interest or at an interest rate significantly different from current market rates or making loans without scheduled repayment terms

2. **SALES** Selling real estate at a price considerably different from its appraised value or exchanging property for similar property in a nonmonetary transaction

C. **AUDIT PROCEDURES**

The auditor should be aware of the possible existence of such transactions and of any common ownership or management control relationships and may decide there is a need for additional procedures to determine their existence in certain cases. The auditor should be aware that business structure and operating style are occasionally *deliberately designed to obscure* related party transactions. The auditor should gain an understanding of management and the business in order to evaluate the possible existence of related party transactions. Related party transactions should **not** be assumed to be outside of the normal course of business unless there is applicable evidence.

1. **EXAMPLES OF MOTIVATING CONDITIONS**

   a. Lack of sufficient working capital or credit to continue in business.

   b. An urgent desire for a favorable earnings record to support the company's stock price.

   c. An overly optimistic earnings forecast.

   d. Significant litigation, especially between stockholders and management.

   e. Excess capacity or a declining industry with a large number of business failures.

   f. Dependence on a single (or a relatively few) products, customers, or transactions for the ongoing success of the business.

   g. Significant dangers of obsolescence because of being in a high technology industry.

2. **DETERMINING THE EXISTENCE OF RELATED PARTIES** The auditor will want to audit material transactions between related parties and the client. To determine the existence of less obvious relationships, the auditor may apply one or more specific procedures, such as

   a. Evaluation of the company's procedures for identifying and properly accounting for related party transactions.

   b. Request of appropriate management personnel the names of all related parties and inquire whether any transaction occurred with these parties during the period (should be documented in the management representation letter).

   c. Review the workpapers from prior years for the names of known related parties. Inquire of the predecessor, principal, or other auditors of related parties as to their knowledge of existing relationships.

   d. Determine the names of all pensions and trusts established for the benefit of employees and the names of their officers and trustees. They will be considered related parties if managed by or under the trusteeship of the client's management.

   e. Review SEC filings, etc., for the names of related parties and for other businesses in which officers and directors occupy directorship or management positions. Review stockholder listings of closely held companies to identify principal stockholders.

   f. Review the period's material investment transactions to determine if any related party transactions were created.

3. **IDENTIFYING MATERIAL RELATED PARTY TRANSACTIONS** The following procedures may help the auditor identify material transactions with known related parties or that may indicate previously undetermined relationships.

   a. Provide the names of related parties to the audit staff so they can watch for transactions with those parties.

b. Review the minutes of the board of directors' meetings (and other executive or operating committees) to see if any material transactions were authorized or discussed.

c. Review invoices from law firms that have performed regular or special services.

d. Review "conflict-of-interests" statements obtained by the company from its management.

e. Review the extent and nature of transactions with major customers, suppliers, etc. Review loans receivable and payable confirmations to see if any are guaranteed by parties that may be considered related parties.

f. Consider whether nonmonetary transactions, such as free accounting or management expertise, are being provided but not recorded.

g. Review the accounting records for large, unusual, or nonrecurring transactions or balances. Special attention should be paid to transactions that are recognized at or near the end of the reporting period.

h. Review confirmations of compensating balance arrangements.

4. **Examining Identified Related Party Transactions** Once related party transactions have been identified, the auditor should apply whatever procedures considered necessary to obtain reasonable satisfaction as to their purpose, nature, and effect on the financial statements. In extending inquiry beyond the range of management, the auditor should

a. Obtain an understanding of the business purpose of the transaction.

(1) Examine pertinent documents such as invoices, contracts, and receiving and shipping documents.

(2) Determine whether appropriate officials, such as the board of directors, have approved the transaction.

(3) Test the amounts to be disclosed (or considered to be disclosed) in the financial statements for reasonableness.

(4) Consider having intercompany balances audited on the same date. The auditors would then exchange relevant information.

(5) Inspect or confirm the transferability and value of collateral.

b. Perform additional procedures needed to fully understand the particular transaction.

(1) Confirm the amounts and terms of the transactions (including guarantees) with the other parties.

(2) Inspect evidence that is in the possession of the other party (or parties) to the transaction.

(3) Confirm or discuss significant information with such intermediaries as banks, guarantors, or attorneys.

(4) If there is reason to believe that transactions lacking substance were conducted with any unfamiliar customers, businesses, etc., the auditor should refer to trade journals, credit agencies, etc., to verify the lack of substance.

(5) Obtain information on the financial capability of the other party (parties) with respect to material uncollected balances, guarantees, and other obligations.

D. DISCLOSURE

The auditor must evaluate the competence and sufficiency of evidence concerning related parties. This evaluation involves **all** the information available so that, using professional judgment, the auditor can determine the adequacy of the related party disclosures.

1. **DIFFICULTY** Unless a transaction with a related party is of a routine nature, it is generally **not** possible to determine whether a particular transaction would have taken place had the parties not been related. As a result, it is quite difficult to determine if the terms were equivalent to those that prevail in arm's-length transactions.

2. **REPRESENTATION** If the financial statements contain a representation that a material transaction was carried out at *arm's-length bargaining* and the *representation is unsubstantiated by management*, the auditor should, depending upon the materiality of the unsubstantiated representations, express a *qualified or adverse opinion* because of a departure from GAAP.

CHAPTER 35—EVIDENCE & PROCEDURES

PROBLEM 35-1 MULTIPLE CHOICE QUESTIONS (120 TO 150 minutes)

1. Which of the following circumstances most likely would cause an auditor to consider whether material misstatements exist in an entity's financial statements?
   a. Management places little emphasis on meeting earnings projections.
   b. The board of directors makes all major financing decisions.
   c. Reportable conditions previously communicated to management are **not** corrected.
   d. Transactions selected for testing are **not** supported by proper documentation.

   (11/94, Aud., #13, 5086)

2. Which of the following factors would **least** influence an auditor's consideration of the reliability of data for purposes of analytical procedures?
   a. Whether the data were processed in an EDP system or in a manual accounting system.
   b. Whether sources within the entity were independent of those who are responsible for the amount being audited.
   c. Whether the data were subjected to audit testing in the current or prior year.
   d. Whether the data were obtained from independent sources outside the entity or from sources within the entity. (5/90, Aud., #2, 0151)

3. Which of the following procedures would provide the most reliable audit evidence?
   a. Inquiries of the client's internal audit staff held in private
   b. Inspection of prenumbered client purchase orders filed in the vouchers payable department
   c. Analytical procedures performed by the auditor on the entity's trial balance
   d. Inspection of bank statements obtained directly from the client's financial institution

   (5/93, Aud., #26, 3922)

4. Which of the following types of audit evidence is the most persuasive?
   a. Prenumbered client purchase order forms
   b. Client work sheets supporting cost allocations
   c. Bank statements obtained from the client
   d. Management representation letter

   (5/95, Aud., #39, amended, 5657)

5. Which of the following statements concerning audit evidence is correct?
   a. To be competent, audit evidence should be either persuasive or relevant, but need **not** be both.
   b. The measure of the validity of audit evidence lies in the auditor's judgment.
   c. The difficulty and expense of obtaining audit evidence concerning an account balance is a valid basis for omitting the test.
   d. A client's accounting data can be sufficient audit evidence to support the financial statements.

   (11/93, Aud., #36, 4273)

6. In designing written audit programs, an auditor should establish specific audit objectives that relate primarily to the
   a. Timing of audit procedures.
   b. Cost-benefit of gathering evidence.
   c. Selected audit techniques.
   d. Financial statement assertions.

   (5/94, Aud., #8, 4673)

7. Which of the following presumptions is correct about the reliability of evidential matter?
   a. Information obtained indirectly from outside sources is the most reliable evidential matter.
   b. To be reliable, evidential matter should be convincing rather than persuasive.
   c. Reliability of evidential matter refers to the amount of corroborative evidence obtained.
   d. An effective internal control structure provides more assurance about the reliability of evidential matter. (11/94, Aud., #47, 5120)

8. An auditor may achieve audit objectives related to particular assertions by
   a. Performing analytical procedures.
   b. Adhering to a system of quality control.
   c. Preparing auditor working papers.
   d. Increasing the level of detection risk.

   (11/95, Aud., #38, 5985)

9. In testing the existence assertion for an asset, an auditor ordinarily works from the
   a. Financial statements to the potentially unrecorded items.
   b. Potentially unrecorded items to the financial statements.
   c. Accounting records to the supporting evidence.
   d. Supporting evidence to the accounting records.

   (11/90, Aud., #17, 0136)

10. In determining whether transactions have been recorded, the direction of the audit testing should be from the
a. General ledger balances.
b. Adjusted trial balance.
c. Original source documents.
d. General journal entries. (5/95, Aud., #57, 5675)

11. The objective of tests of details of transactions performed as substantive tests is to
a. Comply with generally accepted auditing standards.
b. Attain assurance about the reliability of the accounting system.
c. Detect material misstatements in the financial statements.
d. Evaluate whether management's policies and procedures operated effectively. (11/95, Aud., #51, 5998)

12. The primary source of information to be reported about litigation, claims, and assessments is the
a. Client's lawyer.
b. Court records.
c. Client's management.
d. Independent auditor. (11/93, Aud., #39, 4276)

13. An entity's income statements were misstated due to the recording of journal entries that involved debits and credits to an unusual combination of expense and revenue accounts. The auditor most likely could have detected this misstatement by
a. Tracing a sample of journal entries to the general ledger.
b. Evaluating the effectiveness of internal control policies and procedures.
c. Investigating the reconciliations between controlling accounts and subsidiary records.
d. Performing analytical procedures designed to disclose differences from expectations. (11/94, Aud., #14, amended, 5087)

14. A client uses a suspense account for unresolved questions whose final accounting has not been determined. If a balance remains in the suspense account at year end, the auditor would be most concerned about
a. Suspense debits that management believes will benefit future operations.
b. Suspense debits that the auditor verifies will have realizable value to the client.
c. Suspense credits that management believes should be classified as "Current liability."
d. Suspense credits that the auditor determines to be customer deposits. (11/96, Aud., #13, 6365)

15. Which of the following procedures would an auditor most likely perform in obtaining evidence about subsequent events?
a. Determine that changes in employee pay rates after year end were properly authorized.
b. Recompute depreciation charges for plant assets sold after year end.
c. Investigate changes in long-term debt occurring after year end.
d. Inquire about payroll checks that were recorded before year end but cashed after year end. (5/95, Aud., #65, amended, 5683)

16. Which of the following procedures would an auditor most likely perform in auditing the statement of cash flows?
a. Compare the amounts included in the statement of cash flows to similar amounts in the prior year's statement of cash flows.
b. Reconcile the cutoff bank statements to verify the accuracy of the year-end bank balances.
c. Vouch all bank transfers for the last week of the year and first week of the subsequent year.
d. Reconcile the amounts included in the statement of cash flows to the other financial statements' balances and amounts. (5/95, Aud., #56, 5674)

17. In assessing the objectivity of internal auditors, an independent auditor should
a. Evaluate the quality control program in effect for the internal auditors.
b. Examine documentary evidence of the work performed by the internal auditors.
c. Test a sample of the transactions and balances that the internal auditors examined.
d. Determine the organizational level to which the internal auditors report. (11/95, Aud., #1, 5950)

18. The work of internal auditors may affect the independent auditor's

I. Procedures performed in obtaining an understanding of internal control.
II. Procedures performed in assessing the risk of material misstatement.
III. Substantive procedures performed in gathering direct evidence.

a. I and II only
b. I and III only
c. II and III only
d. I, II, and III (11/95, Aud., #53, amended, 6000)

19. For which of the following judgments may an independent auditor share responsibility with an entity's internal auditor who is assessed to be both competent and objective?

	Assessment of inherent risk	*Assessment of control risk*
a.	Yes	Yes
b.	Yes	No
c.	No	Yes
d.	No	No

(5/96, Aud., #3, 6235)

20. In assessing the competence and objectivity of an entity's internal auditor, an independent auditor **least** likely would consider information obtained from
a. Discussions with management personnel.
b. External quality reviews of the internal auditor's activities.
c. Previous experience with the internal auditor.
d. The results of analytical procedures. (11/94, Aud., #68, 5141)

21. During an audit an internal auditor may provide direct assistance to an independent CPA in

	Obtaining an understanding of internal control	*Performing tests of controls*	*Performing substantive tests*
a.	No	No	No
b.	Yes	No	No
c.	Yes	Yes	No
d.	Yes	Yes	Yes

(5/95, Aud., #60, amended, 5678)

22. In assessing the competence of an internal auditor, an independent CPA most likely would obtain information about the
a. Quality of the internal auditor's working paper documentation.
b. Organization's commitment to integrity and ethical values.
c. Influence of management on the scope of the internal auditor's duties.
d. Organizational level to which the internal auditor reports. (R/99, Aud., #16, 6832)

23. A written management representation letter most likely would be an auditor's best source of corroborative information of a client's plans to
a. Settle an outstanding lawsuit for an amount less than the accrued loss contingency.
b. Make a public offering of its common stock.
c. Terminate an employee pension plan.
d. Discontinue a line of business. (Editors, 0183)

24. A purpose of a management representation letter is to reduce
a. Audit risk to an aggregate level of misstatement that could be considered material.
b. An auditor's responsibility to detect material misstatements only to the extent that the letter is relied on.
c. The possibility of a misunderstanding concerning management's responsibility for the financial statements.
d. The scope of an auditor's procedures concerning related party transactions and subsequent events. (5/93, Aud., #32, 3928)

25. When considering the use of management's written representations as audit evidence about the completeness assertion, an auditor should understand that such representations
a. Complement, but do not replace, substantive tests designed to support the assertion.
b. Constitute sufficient evidence to support the assertion when considered in combination with the assessment of control risk.
c. Replace the assessment of control risk as evidence to support the assertion.
d. Are not part of the evidential matter considered to support the assertion. (Editors, 0218)

26. To which of the following matters would materiality limits **not** apply in obtaining written management representations?
a. The availability of minutes of stockholders' and directors' meetings
b. Losses from purchase commitments at prices in excess of market value
c. The disclosure of compensating balance arrangements involving related parties
d. Reductions of obsolete inventory to net realizable value (5/95, Aud., #66, 5684)

27. For which of the following matters should an auditor obtain written management representations?
a. Management's cost-benefit justifications for not correcting internal control weaknesses.
b. Management's knowledge of future plans that may affect the price of the entity's stock
c. Management's compliance with contractual agreements that may affect the price of the entity's stock.
d. Management's acknowledgment of its responsibility for employees' violations of laws. (R/99, Aud., #25, 6841)

28. Key Co. plans to present comparative financial statements for the years ended December 31, 2000, and 2001, respectively. Smith, CPA, audited Key's financial statements for both years and plans to report on the comparative financial statements on May 1, 2002. Key's current management team was not present until January 1, 2001. What period of time should be covered by Key's management representation letter?
a. January 1, 2000, through December 31, 2001.
b. January 1, 2000, through May 1, 2002.
c. January 1, 2001, through December 31, 2001.
d. January 1, 2001, through May 1, 2002.
(R/99, Aud., #26, amended, 6842)

29. A scope limitation sufficient to preclude an unqualified opinion always will result when management
a. Prevents the auditor from reviewing the working papers of the predecessor auditor
b. Engages the auditor after the year-end physical inventory is completed
c. Requests that certain material accounts receivable not be confirmed
d. Refuses to acknowledge its responsibility for the fair presentation of the financial statements in conformity with GAAP (R/00, Aud., #16, 6941)

30. An auditor's analytical procedures performed during the overall review stage indicated that the client's accounts receivable had doubled since the end of the prior year. However, the allowance for doubtful accounts as a percentage of accounts receivable remained about the same. Which of the following client explanations most likely would satisfy the auditor?
a. The client liberalized its credit standards in the current year and sold much more merchandise to customers with poor credit ratings.
b. Twice as many accounts receivable were written off in the prior year than in the current year.
c. A greater percentage of accounts receivable were currently listed in the "more than 90 days overdue" category than in the prior year.
d. The client opened a second retail outlet in the current year and its credit sales approximately equaled the older, established outlet.
(R/00, Aud., #15, 6940)

31. Which of the following ratios would an engagement partner most likely calculate when reviewing the balance sheet in the overall review stage of an audit?
a. Quick assets/current assets
b. Accounts receivable/inventory
c. Interest payable/interest receivable
d. Total debt/total assets (11/96, Aud., #14, 6366)

32. Which of the following nonfinancial information would an auditor most likely consider in performing analytical procedures during the planning phase of an audit?
a. Turnover of personnel in the accounting department
b. Objectively of audit committee members
c. Square footage of selling space
d. Management's plans to repurchase stock
(5/97, Aud., #3, 6392)

33. Which of the following comparisons would an auditor most likely make in evaluating an entity's costs and expenses?
a. The current year's accounts receivable with the prior year's accounts receivable.
b. The current year's payroll expense with the prior year's payroll expense.
c. The budgeted current year's sales with the prior year's sales.
d. The budgeted current year's warranty expense with the current year's contingent liabilities.
(11/97, Aud., #17, 6580)

34. Which of the following would **not** be considered an analytical procedure?
a. Estimating payroll expense by multiplying the number of employees by the average hourly wage rate and the total hours worked
b. Projecting an error rate by comparing the results of a statistical sample with the actual population characteristics
c. Computing accounts receivable turnover by dividing credit sales by the average net receivables
d. Developing the expected current-year sales based on the sales trend of the prior five years
(5/95, Aud., #48, 5666)

35. An auditor's analytical procedures most likely would be facilitated if the entity
a. Segregates obsolete inventory before the physical inventory count.
b. Uses a standard cost system that produces variance reports.
c. Corrects material weaknesses in internal control before the beginning of the audit.
d. Develops its data from sources solely within the entity. (11/95, Aud., #41, 5988)

36. Analytical procedures used in planning an audit should focus on
a. Reducing the scope of tests of controls and substantive tests.
b. Providing assurance that potential material misstatements will be identified.
c. Enhancing the auditor's understanding of the client's business.
d. Assessing the adequacy of the available evidential matter. (5/95, Aud., #8, 5626)

37. An auditor's decision either to apply analytical procedures as substantive tests or to perform tests of transactions and account balances usually is determined by the
a. Availability of data aggregated at a high level.
b. Auditor's familiarity with industry trends.
c. Timing of tests performed after the balance sheet date.
d. Relative effectiveness and efficiency of the tests. (11/92, Aud., #31, amended, 2965)

38. Which of the following statements is correct concerning an auditor's use of the work of a specialist?
a. The auditor need **not** obtain an understanding of the methods and assumptions used by the specialist.
b. The auditor may **not** use the work of a specialist in matters material to the fair presentation of the financial statements.
c. The reasonableness of the specialist's assumptions and their applications are strictly the auditor's responsibility.
d. The work of a specialist who has a contractual relationship with the client may be acceptable under certain circumstances. (11/95, Aud., #54, 6001)

39. In using the work of a specialist, an auditor may refer to the specialist in the auditor's report if, as a result of the specialist's findings, the auditor
a. Becomes aware of conditions causing substantial doubt about the entity's ability to continue as a going concern.
b. Desires to disclose the specialist's findings, which imply that a more thorough audit was performed.
c. Is able to corroborate another specialist's earlier findings that were consistent with management's representations.
d. Discovers significant deficiencies in the design of the entity's internal control that management does **not** correct. (5/95, Aud., #62, amended, 5680)

40. The refusal of a client's attorney to provide information requested in an inquiry letter generally is considered
a. Grounds for an adverse opinion.
b. A limitation on the scope of the audit.
c. Reason to withdraw from the engagement.
d. Equivalent to a reportable condition. (5/95, Aud., #63, 5681)

41. A lawyer's response to an auditor's inquiry concerning litigation, claims, and assessments may be limited to matters that are considered individually or collectively material to the client's financial statements. Which parties should reach an understanding on the limits of materiality for this purpose?
a. The auditor and the client's management.
b. The client's audit committee and the lawyer.
c. The client's management and the lawyer.
d. The lawyer and the auditor. (R/99, Aud., #24, 6840)

42. The scope of an audit is **not** restricted when an attorney's response to an auditor as a result of a client's letter of audit inquiry limits the response to
a. Matters to which the attorney has given substantive attention in the form of legal representation.
b. An evaluation of the likelihood of an unfavorable outcome of the matters disclosed by the entity.
c. The attorney's opinion of the entity's historical experience in recent similar litigation.
d. The probable outcome of asserted claims and pending or threatened litigation. (11/90, Aud., #19, 0138)

43. The primary reason an auditor requests letters of inquiry be sent to a client's attorneys is to provide the auditor with
a. The probable outcome of asserted claims and pending or threatened litigation.
b. Corroboration of the information furnished by management about litigation, claims, and assessments.
c. The attorneys' opinions of the client's historical experiences in recent similar litigation.
d. A description and evaluation of litigation, claims, and assessments that existed at the balance sheet date. (11/94, Aud., #66, 5139)

44. Which of the following is an audit procedure that an auditor most likely would perform concerning litigation, claims, and assessments?
a. Request the client's lawyer to evaluate whether the client's pending litigation, claims, and assessments indicate a going concern problem
b. Examine the legal documents in the client's lawyer's possession concerning litigation, claims, and assessments to which the lawyer has devoted substantive attention
c. Discuss with management its policies and procedures adopted for evaluating and accounting for litigation, claims, and assessments
d. Confirm directly with the client's lawyer that all litigation, claims, and assessments have been recorded or disclosed in the financial statements (11/95, Aud., #55, 6002)

45. Which of the following sets of information does an auditor usually confirm on one form?
a. Accounts payable and purchase commitments
b. Cash in bank and collateral for loans
c. Inventory on consignment and contingent liabilities
d. Accounts receivable and accrued interest receivable (11/95, Aud., #40, 5987)

46. Which of the following is required documentation in an audit in accordance with generally accepted auditing standards?
a. A written engagement letter formalizing the level of service to be rendered.
b. A flowchart depicting the segregation of duties and authorization of transactions.
c. A written audit program describing the necessary procedures to be performed.
d. A memorandum setting forth the scope of the audit. (11/91, Aud., #53, 2321)

47. In creating lead schedules for an audit engagement, a CPA often uses automated workpaper software. What client information is needed to begin this process?
a. Interim financial information such as third quarter sales, net income, and inventory and receivables balances.
b. Specialized journal information such as the invoice and purchase order numbers of the last few sales and purchases of the year.
c. General ledger information such as account numbers, prior-year account balances, and current-year unadjusted information.
d. Adjusting entry information such as deferrals and accruals, and reclassification journal entries. (5/98, Aud., #11, 6628)

48. The permanent (continuing) file of an auditor's working papers most likely would include copies of the
a. Lead schedules.
b. Attorney's letters.
c. Bank statements.
d. Debt agreements. (11/95, Aud., #60, 6007)

49. Which of the following documentation is **not** required for an audit in accordance with generally accepted auditing standards?
a. A written audit program setting forth the procedures necessary to accomplish the audit's objectives
b. An indication that the accounting records agree or reconcile with the financial statements
c. A client engagement letter that summarizes the timing and details of the auditor's planned field work
d. The basis for the auditor's conclusions when the assessed level of control risk is below the maximum level (11/94, Aud., #15, 5088)

50. In performing a count of negotiable securities, an auditor records the details of the count on a security count worksheet. What other information is usually included on this worksheet?
a. An acknowledgment by a client representative that the securities were returned intact
b. An analysis of realized gains and losses from the sale of securities during the year
c. An evaluation of the client's internal control concerning physical access to the securities
d. A description of the client's procedures that prevent the negotiation of securities by just one person (R/00, Aud., #12, 6937)

51. Which of the following factors would **least** likely affect the quantity and content of an auditor's working papers?
a. The condition of the client's records
b. The assessed level of control risk
c. The nature of the auditor's report
d. The content of the representation letter (11/94, Aud., #73, 5146)

52. "There have been no communications from regulatory agencies concerning noncompliance with, or deficiencies in, financial reporting practices that could have a material effect on the financial statements." The foregoing passage is most likely from a
a. Report on internal control.
b. Special report.
c. Management representation letter.
d. Letter for underwriters. (5/97, Aud., #8, 6397)

53. The audit working paper that reflects the major components of an amount reported in the financial statements is the
a. Interbank transfer schedule.
b. Carryforward schedule.
c. Supporting schedule.
d. Lead schedule. (11/91, Aud., #52, 2320)

54. An auditor ordinarily uses a working trial balance resembling the financial statements without footnotes, but containing columns for
a. Cash flow increases and decreases.
b. Audit objectives and assertions.
c. Reclassifications and adjustments.
d. Reconciliations and tickmarks. (11/94, Aud., #72, 5145)

55. An auditor's working papers serve mainly to
a. Provide the principal support for the auditor's report.
b. Satisfy the auditor's responsibilities concerning the Code of Professional Conduct.
c. Monitor the effectiveness of the CPA firm's quality control procedures.
d. Document the level of independence maintained by the auditor. (5/95, Aud., #71, 5689)

56. An auditor most likely would modify an unqualified opinion if the entity's financial statements include a footnote on related party transactions
a. Disclosing loans to related parties at interest rates significantly below prevailing market rates.
b. Describing an exchange of real estate for similar property in a nonmonetary related party transaction.
c. Stating that a particular related party transaction occurred on terms equivalent to those that would have prevailed in an arm's-length transaction.
d. Presenting the dollar-volume of related party transactions and the effects of any change in the method of establishing terms from prior periods. (5/93, Aud., #44, 3940)

57. Which of the following auditing procedures most likely would assist an auditor in identifying related party transactions?
a. Inspecting correspondence with lawyers for evidence of unreported contingent liabilities
b. Vouching accounting records for recurring transactions recorded just after the balance sheet date
c. Reviewing confirmations of loans receivable and payable for indications of guarantees
d. Performing analytical procedures for indications of possible financial difficulties (11/95, Aud., #58, 6005)

58. When auditing related party transactions, an auditor places primary emphasis on
a. Ascertaining the rights and obligations of the related parties.
b. Confirming the existence of the related parties.
c. Verifying the valuation of the related party transactions.
d. Evaluating the disclosure of the related party transactions. (5/95, Aud., #68, 5686)

59. An auditor searching for related party transactions should obtain an understanding of each subsidiary's relationship to the total entity because
a. The business structure may be deliberately designed to obscure related party transactions.
b. Intercompany transactions may have been consummated on terms equivalent to arm's-length transactions.
c. This may reveal whether particular transactions would have taken place if the parties had **not** been related.
d. This may permit the audit of intercompany account balances to be performed as of concurrent dates. (Editors, 0185)

60. After determining that a related party transaction has, in fact, occurred, an auditor should
a. Add a separate paragraph to the auditor's standard report to explain the transaction.
b. Perform analytical procedures to verify whether similar transactions occurred, but were **not** recorded.
c. Obtain an understanding of the business purpose of the transaction.
d. Substantiate that the transaction was consummated on terms equivalent to an arm's-length transaction. (11/94, Aud., #69, 5142)

PROBLEM 35-2 ADDITIONAL MULTIPLE CHOICE QUESTIONS (30 TO 38 minutes)

61. Miller Retailing, Inc., maintains a staff of three full-time internal auditors who report directly to the controller. In planning to use the internal auditors to provide assistance in performing the audit, the independent auditor most likely will

a. Place limited reliance on the work performed by the internal auditors.
b. Decrease the extent of the tests of controls needed to support the assessed level of detection risk.
c. Increase the extent of the procedures needed to reduce control risk to an acceptable level.
d. Avoid using the work performed by the internal auditors. (5/90, Aud., #28, 0157)

62. Which of the following matters would an auditor most likely include in a management representation letter?

a. Communications with the audit committee concerning weaknesses in internal control
b. The completeness and availability of minutes of stockholders' and directors' meetings
c. Plans to acquire or merge with other entities in the subsequent year
d. Management's acknowledgment of its responsibility for the detection of employee fraud (11/95, Aud., #57, amended, 6004)

63. The date of the management representation letter should coincide with the date of the

a. Balance sheet.
b. Latest interim financial information.
c. Auditor's report.
d. Latest related party transaction. (5/95, Aud., #67, 5685)

64. For all audits of financial statements made in accordance with generally accepted auditing standards, the use of analytical procedures is required to some extent

	In the planning stage	*As a substantive test*	*In the review stage*
a.	Yes	No	Yes
b.	No	Yes	No
c.	No	Yes	Yes
d.	Yes	No	No

(11/90, Aud., #22, 0141)

65. Analytical procedures used in the overall review stage of an audit generally include

a. Gathering evidence concerning account balances that have **not** changed from the prior year.
b. Retesting control procedures that appeared to be ineffective during the assessment of control risk.
c. Considering unusual or unexpected account balances that were **not** previously identified.
d. Performing tests of transactions to corroborate management's financial statement assertions. (5/95, Aud., #47, 5665)

66. Which of the following comparisons would be most useful to an auditor in evaluating the results of an entity's operations?

a. Prior year accounts payable to current year accounts payable
b. Prior year payroll expense to budgeted current year payroll expense
c. Current year revenue to budgeted current year revenue
d. Current year warranty expense to current year contingent liabilities (5/91, Aud., #5, 0125)

67. Which of the following tends to be most predictable for purposes of analytical procedures applied as substantive tests?

a. Data subject to audit testing in the prior year
b. Transactions subject to management discretion
c. Relationships involving income statement accounts
d. Relationships involving balance sheet accounts (5/92, Aud., #20, amended, 2773)

68. An auditor compares 2000 revenues and expenses with those of the prior year and investigates all changes exceeding 10%. By this procedure the auditor would be most likely to learn that

a. An increase in property tax rates has not been recognized in the client's accrual.
b. The client changed its capitalization policy for small tools in 2000.
c. Fourth quarter payroll taxes were not paid.
d. The 2000 provision for uncollectible accounts is inadequate because of worsening economic conditions. (Editors, 9410)

69. Analytical procedures performed in the overall review stage of an audit suggest that several accounts have unexpected relationships. The results of these procedures most likely would indicate that

a. Fraud exists among the relevant account balances.
b. Internal control activities are **not** operating effectively.
c. Additional tests of details are required.
d. The communication with the audit committee should be revised.

(5/97, Aud., #9, amended, 6398)

70. The objective of performing analytical procedures in planning an audit is to identify the existence of

a. Unusual transactions and events.
b. Illegal acts that went undetected because of internal control weaknesses.
c. Related party transactions.
d. Recorded transactions that were **not** properly authorized. (5/94, Aud., #5, 4670)

71. Which of the following statements extracted from a client's lawyer's letter concerning litigation, claims, and assessments most likely would cause the auditor to request clarification?

a. "I believe that the possible liability to the company is nominal in amount."
b. "I believe that the action can be settled for less than the damages claimed."
c. "I believe that the plaintiff's case against the company is without merit."
d. "I believe that the company will be able to defend this action successfully."(11/96, Aud., #12, 6364)

72. A client's lawyer is unable to form a conclusion about the likelihood of an unfavorable outcome of pending litigation because of inherent uncertainties. If the litigation's effect on the client's financial statements could be material, the auditor most likely would

a. Issue a qualified opinion in the auditor's report because of the lawyer's scope limitation.
b. Withdraw from the engagement because of the lack of information furnished by the lawyer.
c. Disclaim an opinion on the financial statements because of the materiality of the litigation's effect.
d. Add an explanatory paragraph to the auditor's report because of the uncertainty.

(5/95, Aud., #64, 5682)

73. Which of the following statements ordinarily is correct concerning the content of working papers?

a. Whenever possible, the auditor's staff should prepare schedules and analyses rather than the entity's employees.
b. It is preferable to have negative figures indicated in red figures instead of parentheses to emphasize amounts being subtracted.
c. It is appropriate to use calculator tapes with names or explanations on the tapes rather than writing separate lists onto working paper.
d. The analysis of asset accounts and their related expense or income accounts should **not** appear on the same working paper.

(5/92, Aud., #24, 2777)

74. "There are no violations or possible violations of laws or regulations whose effects should be considered for disclosure in the financial statements or as a basis for recording a loss contingency." The foregoing passage most likely is from a (an)

a. Client engagement letter.
b. Report on compliance with laws and regulations.
c. Management representation letter.
d. Attestation report on an entity's internal control.

(11/94, Aud., #64, amended, 5137)

75. Which of the following most likely would indicate the existence of related parties?

a. Writing down obsolete inventory just before year end
b. Failing to correct previously identified internal control structure deficiencies
c. Depending on a single product for the success of the entity
d. Borrowing money at an interest rate significantly below the market rate (11/92, Aud., #40, 2974)

OTHER OBJECTIVE FORMAT QUESTIONS

Problem 35-3 (15 to 20 minutes)

Items 1 through 19 represent a series of unrelated statements, questions, excerpts, and comments taken from various parts of an auditor's working paper file. Select the most likely source from the list of sources. Select only one source for each item. A source may be selected once, more than once, or not at all.

List of Sources

A. Practitioner's report on management's assertion about an entity's compliance with specified requirements

B. Auditor's communications on reportable conditions

C. Audit inquiry letter to legal counsel

D. Lawyer's response to audit inquiry letter

E. Audit committee's communication to the auditor

F. Auditor's communication to the audit committee (other than with respect to reportable conditions)

G. Report on the application of accounting principles

H. Auditor's engagement letter

I. Letter for underwriters

J. Accounts receivable confirmation request

K. Request for bank cutoff statement

L. Explanatory paragraph of an auditor's report on financial statements

M. Partner's engagement review notes

N. Management representation letter

O. Successor auditor's communication with predecessor auditor

P. Predecessor auditor's communication with successor auditor

1. During our audit we discovered evidence of the company's failure to safeguard inventory from loss, damage, and misappropriation.

2. The company considers the decline in value of equity securities classified as available-for-sale to be temporary.

3. Was the difference of opinion on the accrued pension liabilities that existed between the engagement personnel and the actuarial specialist resolved in accordance with firm policy and appropriately documented?

4. Our audit is designed to provide reasonable assurance of detecting misstatements that, in our judgment, could have a material effect on the financial statements taken as a whole. Consequently, our audit will not necessarily detect all misstatements that exist due to error, fraudulent financial reporting, or misappropriation of assets.

5. There have been no communications from regulatory agencies concerning noncompliance with or deficiencies in financial reporting practices.

6. Nothing came to our attention that caused us to believe that at October 31, 2000, there was any change in the capital stock, increase in long-term debt, or decrease in consolidated net current assets or stockholders' equity as compared with the amounts shown in the September 30, 2000 unaudited condensed consolidated balance sheet.

7. It is our opinion that the possible liability to the company in this proceeding is nominal in amount.

8. As discussed in Note 4 to the financial statements, the company experienced a net loss for the year ended July 31, 2000, and is currently in default under substantially all of its debt agreements. In addition, on September 25, 2000, the company filed a prenegotiated voluntary petition for relief under Chapter 11 of the U.S. Bankruptcy Code. These matters raise substantial doubt about the company's ability to continue as a going concern.

9. During the year under audit, we were advised that management consulted with Better & Best, CPAs. The purpose of this consultation was to obtain another CPA firm's opinion concerning the company's recognition of certain revenue that we believe should be deferred to future periods. Better & Best's opinion was consistent with our opinion, so management did not recognize the revenue in the current year.

10. The company believes that all material expenditures that have been deferred to future periods will be recoverable.

11. Our use of professional judgment and the assessment of audit risk and materiality for the purpose of our audit mean that matters may have existed that would have been assessed differently by you. We make no representation as to the sufficiency or appropriateness of the information in our working papers for your purposes.

12. Indicate in the space provided below whether this information agrees with your records. If there are exceptions, please provide any information that will assist the auditor in reconciling the difference.

13. Blank checks are maintained in an unlocked cabinet along with the check-signing machine. Blank checks and the check-signing machine should be locked in separate locations to prevent the embezzlement of funds.

14. Our audit cannot be relied upon to disclose significant deficiencies in the design or operation of internal control. Nevertheless, we will communicate to you all reportable conditions and potential areas for improvement that we become aware of during the course of our audit.

15. The timetable set by management to complete our audit was unreasonable considering the failure of the company's personnel to complete schedules on a timely basis and delays in providing necessary information.

16. Several employees have disabled the anti-virus detection software on their PCs because the software slows the processing of data and occasionally rings false alarms. The company should obtain anti-virus software that runs continuously at all system entry points and that cannot be disabled by unauthorized personnel.

17. In connection with an audit of our financial statements, management has prepared, and furnished to our auditors, a description and evaluation of certain contingencies.

18. The company has no plans or intentions that may materially affect the carrying value or classification of assets and liabilities.

19. In planning the sampling application, was appropriate consideration given to the relationship of the sample to the audit objective and to preliminary judgments about materiality levels?

(R/00, Aud., #2, 6946-6964)

PROBLEM 35-4 (15 to 25 minutes)

Analytical procedures are evaluations of financial information made by a study of plausible relationships among financial and nonfinancial data. Understanding and evaluating such relationships are essential to the audit process. The following financial statements were prepared by Holiday Manufacturing Co. for the year ended December 31, 20X1. Also presented are various financial statement ratios for Holiday as calculated from the prior year's financial statements. Sales represent net credit sales. The total assets and the receivables and inventory balances at December 31, 20X1, were the same as at December 31, 20X0.

Holiday Manufacturing Co.
Balance Sheet
December 31, 20X1

Assets		Liabilities and Capital	
Cash	$ 240,000	Accounts payable	$ 160,000
Receivables	400,000	Notes payable	100,000
Inventory	600,000	Other current liabilities	140,000
Total current assets	$1,240,000	Total current liabilities	$ 400,000
Plant and equipment—net	760,000	Long-term debt	350,000
		Common stock	750,000
		Retained earnings	500,000
Total assets	$2,000,000	Total liabilities and capital	$2,000,000

Holiday Manufacturing Co.
Income Statement
Year Ended December 31, 20X1

Sales		$3,000,000
Cost of goods sold		
Material	$800,000	
Labor	700,000	
Overhead	300,000	1,800,000
Gross margin		$1,200,000
Selling expenses	$240,000	
General and administrative expenses	300,000	540,000
Operating income		$ 660,000
Less interest expense		40,000
Income before taxes		$ 620,000
Less federal income taxes		220,000
Net income		$ 400,000

REQUIRED:

a. **ITEMS 1 THROUGH 9** represent financial ratios that the auditor calculated during the prior year's audit. For each ratio, calculate the current year's ratio from the financial statements presented and select the answer from List A. Calculations should be rounded, if necessary, to the same number of places as the prior year's ratios. Answers on the list may be selected once, more than once, or not at all.

Ratio	*20X1*	*20X0*
1. Current ratio		2.5
2. Quick ratio		1.3
3. Accounts receivable turnover		5.5
4. Inventory turnover		2.5
5. Total asset turnover		1.2
6. Gross margin percentage		35%
7. Net operating margin percentage		25%
8. Times interest earned		10.3
9. Total debt to equity percentage		50%

List A: Ratio Calculations

A. 0.6	H. 3.1	O. 13%
B. 0.7	I. 4.5	P. 22%
C. 1.0	J. 5.0	Q. 28%
D. 1.5	K. 7.5	R. 33%
E. 1.6	L. 10.0	S. 38%
F 2.0	M. 15.5	T. 40%
G. 3.0	N. 16.5	U. 60%
		V. 67%

(5/96, Aud., #2a, amended, 6241-6256, 6290-6295)

b. **ITEMS 10 THROUGH 15** represent an auditor's observed changes in certain financial statement ratios or amounts from the prior year's ratios or amounts. For each observed change, select the most likely explanation or explanations from List B. Select only the number of explanations as indicated. The observed changes are not related to the calculations in requirement a. and are independent of each other. Answers on the list may be selected once, more than once, or not at all.

Auditor's Observed Changes

10. Inventory turnover increased substantially from the prior year. (3 explanations) (6250, 6251, 6252)

11. Accounts receivable turnover decreased substantially from the prior year. (3 explanations) (6253, 6254, 6255)

12. Allowance for doubtful accounts increased from the prior year, but allowance for doubtful accounts as a percentage of accounts receivable decreased from the prior year. (3 explanations) (6256, 6290, 6291)

13. Long-term debt increased from the prior year, but interest expense increased a larger-than proportionate amount than long-term debt. (1 explanation) (6292)

14. Operating income increased from the prior year although the entity was less profitable than in the prior year. (2 explanations) (6293, 6294)

15. Gross margin percentage was unchanged from the prior year although gross margin increased from the prior year. (1 explanation)

List B: Explanations

A. Items shipped on consignment during the last month of the year were recorded as sales.

B. A significant number of credit memos for returned merchandise that were issued during the last month of the year were not recorded.

C. Year-end purchases of inventory were overstated by incorrectly including items received in the first month of the subsequent year.

D. Year-end purchases of inventory were understated by incorrectly excluding items received before the year end.

E. A larger percentage of sales occurred during the last month of the year, as compared to the prior year.

F. A smaller percentage of sales occurred during the last month of the year, as compared to the prior year.

G. The same percentage of sales occurred during the last month of the year, as compared to the prior year.

H. Sales increased at the same percentage as cost of goods sold, as compared to the prior year.

I. Sales increased at a greater percentage than cost of goods sold increased, as compared to the prior year.

J. Sales increased at a lower percentage than cost of goods sold increased, as compared to the prior year.

K. Interest expense decreased, as compared to the prior year.

L. The effective income tax rate increased, as compared to the prior year.

M. The effective income tax rate decreased, as compared to the prior year.

N. Short-term borrowing was refinanced on a long-term basis at the same interest rate.

O. Short-term borrowing was refinanced on a long-term basis at lower interest rates.

P. Short-term borrowing was refinanced on a long-term basis at higher interest rates.
(5/96, Aud., #2b, amended)

ESSAY QUESTIONS

ESSAY 35-5 (25 to 35 minutes)

Most of an auditor's work in forming an opinion on financial statements consists of obtaining and evaluating evidential matter concerning the financial statement assertions.

a. What is the definition of "financial statement assertions?" **Do not list the assertions.**

b. What is the relationship between audit objectives and financial statement assertions?

c. What should an auditor consider in developing the audit objectives of a particular engagement?

d. What is the relationship between audit objectives and audit procedures?

e. What are an auditor's primary considerations when selecting particular substantive tests to achieve audit objectives? (11/95, Aud., #5)

ESSAY 35-6 (15 to 25 minutes)

Hart, an assistant accountant with the firm of Better & Best, CPAs, is auditing the financial statements of Tech Consolidated Industries, Inc. The firm's audit program calls for the preparation of a written management representation letter.

REQUIRED:

a. 1. In an audit of financial statements, in what circumstances is the auditor required to obtain a management representation letter?

2. What are the purposes of obtaining the letter?

b. 1. To whom should the representation letter be addressed and as of what date should it be dated?

2. Who should sign the letter and what would be the effect of their refusal to sign the letter?

c. In what respects may an auditor's other responsibilities be relieved by obtaining a management representation letter? (11/93, Aud., #4)

ESSAY 35-7 (15 TO 25 minutes)

Analytical procedures consist of evaluations of financial information made by a study of plausible relationships among both financial and nonfinancial data. They range from simple comparisons to the use of complex models involving many relationships and elements of data. They involve comparisons of recorded amounts, or ratios developed from recorded amounts, to expectations developed by the auditors.

REQUIRED:

a. Describe the broad purposes of analytical procedures.

b. Identify the sources of information from which an auditor develops expectations.

c. Describe the factors that influence an auditor's consideration of the reliability of data for purposes of achieving audit objectives.

(11/89, Aud., #3, 3026)

ESSAY 35-8 (15 TO 25 minutes)

Kent, CPA, is engaged in the audit of Davidson Corp.'s financial statements for the year ended December 31, 20X1. Kent is about to commence auditing Davidson's employee pension expense, but Kent's preliminary inquiries concerning Davidson's defined benefit pension plan lead Kent to believe that some of the actuarial computations and assumptions are so complex that they are beyond the competence ordinarily required of an auditor. Kent is considering engaging Park, an actuary, to assist with this portion of the audit.

REQUIRED:

a. What are the factors Kent should consider in the process of selecting Park?

b. What are the matters that should be understood among Kent, Park, and Davidson's management as to the nature of the work to be performed by Park?

c. May Kent refer to Park in the auditor's report if Kent decides to issue an unqualified opinion? Why?

d. May Kent refer to Park in the auditor's report if Kent decides to issue other than an unqualified opinion as a result of Park's findings? Why?

(5/90, Aud., #5, amended)

ESSAY 35-9 (15 TO 25 minutes)

Cole & Cole, CPAs, are auditing the financial statements of Consolidated Industries Co. for the year ended December 31, 20X4. On April 2, 20X5, an inquiry letter to J. J. Young, Consolidated's outside attorney, was drafted to corroborate the information furnished to Cole by management concerning pending and threatened litigation, claims, and assessments, and unasserted claims and assessments. On May 6, 20X5, C. R. Brown, Consolidated's Chief Financial Officer, gave Cole a draft of the inquiry letter below for Cole's review before mailing it to Young.

REQUIRED:

Describe the omissions, ambiguities, and inappropriate statements and terminology in Brown's letter below.

May 6, 20X5

J. J. Young, Attorney at Law
123 Main Street
Anytown, USA

Dear J. J. Young:

In connection with an audit of our financial statements at December 31, 20X4, and for the year then ended, management of the Company has prepared, and furnished to our auditors, Cole & Cole, CPAs, 456 Broadway, Anytown, USA, a description and evaluation of certain contingencies, including those set forth below involving matters with respect to which you have been engaged and to which you have devoted substantive attention on behalf of the Company in the form of legal consultation or representation. Your response should include matters that existed at December 31, 20X4. Because of the confidentiality of all these matters, your response may be limited.

In November 20X4, an action was brought against the Company by an outside salesman alleging breach of contract for sales commissions and pleading a second cause of action for an accounting with respect to claims for fees and commissions. The causes of action claim damages of $300,000, but the Company believes it has meritorious defenses to the claims. The possible exposure of the Company to a successful judgment on behalf of the plaintiff is slight. In July 20X0, an action was brought against the Company by Industrial Manufacturing Co. (Industrial) alleging patent infringement and seeking damages of $20,000,000. The action in U. S. District Court resulted in a decision on October 16, 20X4, holding that the Company infringed seven Industrial patents and awarded damages of $14,000,000. The

Company vigorously denies these allegations and has filed an appeal with the U. S. Court of Appeals for the Federal Circuit. The appeal process is expected to take approximately two years, but there is some chance that Industrial may ultimately prevail.

Please furnish to our auditors such explanation, if any, that you consider necessary to supplement the foregoing information, including an explanation of those matters as to which your views may differ from those stated and an identification of the omission of any pending or threatened litigation, claims, and assessments or a statement that the list of such matters is complete. Your response may be quoted or referred to in the financial statements without further correspondence with you.

You also consulted on various other matters considered pending or threatened litigation. However, you may not comment on these matters because publicizing them may alert potential plaintiffs to the strengths of their cases. In addition, various other matters probable of assertion that have some chance of an unfavorable outcome, as of December 31, 20X4, are unasserted claims and assessments.

C. R. Brown
Chief Financial Officer (5/93, Aud., #5, amended)

ESSAY 35-10 (15 TO 25 minutes)

Temple, CPA, is auditing the financial statements of Ford Lumber Yards, Inc. a privately held corporation with 300 employees and five stockholders, three of whom are active in management. Ford has been in business for many years, but has never had its financial statements audited. Temple suspects that the substance of some of Ford's business transactions differ from their form because of the pervasiveness of related party relationships and transactions in the local building supplies industry.

REQUIRED:

Describe the audit procedures Temple should apply to identify related party relationships and transactions.

(11/88, Aud., #2)

ESSAY 35-11 (15 TO 25 minutes)

Young, CPA, is considering the procedures to be applied concerning a client's loss contingencies relating to litigation, claims, and assessments.

REQUIRED:

What substantive audit procedures should Young apply when testing for loss contingencies relating to litigation, claims, and assessments?

(5/88, Aud., #3, 3033)

SOLUTION 35-1 MULTIPLE CHOICE ANSWERS

NATURE OF EVIDENTIAL MATTER

1. (d) The auditor would most likely consider whether material misstatements exist when transactions selected for testing are not supported by proper documentation. Reduced emphasis on meeting earnings projections would be a factor *decreasing* the likelihood of overstatements of earnings and assets (the most frequent misstatement). Having the board of directors making all major financing decisions would decrease the incentive for management to use questionable reporting by reducing the amount of management's responsibility. Reportable conditions previously communicated to management may not have been corrected because of an unfavorable cost-benefit relationship.

2. (a) AU 329.16 states, "The following factors influence the auditor's consideration of the reliability of data for purposes of achieving audit objectives: Whether the data was obtained from independent sources outside the entity or from sources within the entity; Whether sources within the entity were independent of those who are responsible for the amount being audited; Whether the data was developed under a reliable system with adequate controls; Whether the data was subjected to audit testing in the current or prior year; Whether the expectations were developed using data from a variety of sources." Whether the data were processed in an EDP system or in a manual accounting system would generally not influence the auditor's consideration of the reliability of data for purposes of analytical procedures.

3. (d) AU 326.19 states that the validity of evidential matter in auditing is more reliable when the evidential matter can be obtained from independent sources outside the entity; it provides greater assurance of reliability for the purposes of an independent audit than evidential matter secured solely within the entity. Answers (a), (b), and (c) are all examples of auditing procedures performed on information obtained from within the entity.

4. (c) Despite the bank statements being handled by the client, they originate outside the entity and are therefore the most persuasive of the choices. Both purchase orders and work sheets originate within the client. A management representation letter only documents the client's oral representations.

5. (b) AU 326.02 states that the measure of the validity of evidential matter for audit purposes lies in the judgment of the auditor. AU 326.19 states that for evidence to be competent, it must be both valid and relevant. AU 326.22 states that the matter of difficulty and expense involved in testing a particular item is not in itself a valid basis for omitting the test. AU 326.15 states that by itself, accounting data cannot be considered sufficient support for financial statements.

6. (d) AU 326.09 states that the auditor develops specific audit objectives for obtaining evidential matter in support of financial statement assertions. Answers (a), (b), and (c) are all considerations of the substantive and analytical procedures necessary to satisfy the audit objectives.

7. (d) AU 326.19 states, "The more effective the internal control structure, the more assurance it provides about the reliability of the accounting data and financial statements," and, "When evidential matter can be obtained from independent sources outside an entity, it provides greater assurance of reliability for the purposes of an independent audit. Information obtained directly, not indirectly, from outside sources would provide the most reliable evidence." AU 326.20 states, "In a great majority of cases, the auditor finds it necessary to rely on evidence that is persuasive rather than convincing." An auditor typically works within economic limits; an opinion, to be economically useful, must be expressed within a reasonable length of time and at a reasonable cost (AU 326.21). Thus, the amount and kinds of evidential matter required to support an informed opinion are matters for the auditor to determine exercising professional judgment.

Evidential Matter

8. (a) AU 329.04 states that one of the uses of analytical procedures is as a substantive test to obtain evidential matter about particular assertions. In the process of achieving objectives, auditors adhere to a system of quality control, prepare working papers, and may possibly increase the level of detection risk; however, none of these actually cause the auditor to achieve audit objectives.

9. (c) In testing the existence assertion for an asset, the auditor would start with the accounting records themselves to determine that the assets recorded on the client's books do exist. Further evidence of the asset existence would then be found in the supporting evidence.

10. (c) To determine whether transactions have been recorded (completeness), audit procedures include tracing from supporting documentation to accounting records. Testing from the general ledger balances, the adjusted trial balance, and general journal entries (vouching) would all provide evidence of existence (occurrence).

11. (c) According to AU 326.11, in selecting particular substantive tests to achieve the audit objectives developed, an auditor considers, among other things, the risk of material misstatement of the financial statements. Omitting a test of details of transactions in some situations would not be a violation of auditing standards. Attaining assurance about the reliability of the accounting system and evaluating whether management's policies and procedures operated effectively are involved in assessing control risk.

12. (c) AU 337.05 states that since the events or conditions that should be considered in the accounting for, and reporting of, litigation, claims, and assessments are matters within the direct knowledge, and often control, of management of an entity, that management is the primary source of information about such matters. Although a letter of audit inquiry to the client's lawyer is the auditor's primary means of obtaining *corroboration* of the information furnished by management concerning litigation, claims, and assessments, it is not the primary means of obtaining that information.

13. (d) Performing analytical procedures designed to disclose differences from expectations would be the most likely way to detect unusual entries. Evaluating the effectiveness of the internal control would not ordinarily detect journal entries with unusual combinations of accounts. Investigating the reconciliations between controlling accounts and subsidiary records would mostly expose the auditor to only typical, recurring journal entries. Tracing a sample of journal entries to the general ledger would most likely not be among the early work of an audit, and thus, the unusual entries would most likely be detected before this step.

14. (a) Suspense debits that management believes will benefit future operations are assets. The auditor is most concerned that assets are not overstated and that liabilities are not understated.

Suspense debits that the auditor verifies will have realizable value to the client are, insofar as the auditor knows, correct. Thus, for these items, there would be no overstatement. The other two answer options contain items that, if incorrect, would overstate *liabilities*.

15. (c) Per AU 560.12, the "auditor should perform other auditing procedures with respect to the period after the balance-sheet date for the purpose of ascertaining the occurrence of subsequent events that may require adjustment or disclosure..." including [AU 560.12 (b)(ii)] investigating changes in long-term debt after year end. Other auditing procedures are applied to transactions occurring after the balance-sheet date (AU 560.11) for the purpose of assurance that proper cutoffs have been made, and for the purpose of obtaining information to aid in the evaluation of the assets and liabilities as of the balance-sheet date. Answer (a) is a test of internal control.

16. (d) A reconciliation between the amounts included in the cash flow statement and other financial statements would be a procedure the auditor would perform because the cash flow statement amounts are a result of the transactions reflected in and the changes in balances on the other financial statements. Relationships between current year and prior year amounts due do not necessarily exist as can be expected on the balance sheet and income statement. This procedure would provide more audit evidence in the overall review stage of the audit for the balance sheet and income statement. Answer (b) is an audit procedure an auditor would perform in auditing the cash balance on the balance sheet. Answer (c) is a procedure the auditor would perform in auditing the cash balance for the balance sheet presentation.

INTERNAL AUDITORS

17. (d) AU 322.10 states, "When assessing the internal auditor's objectivity, the auditor should obtain...information...about...the organizational status of the internal auditor...including the organizational level to which the internal auditor reports." Answers (a), (b), and (c) would give an indication as to competency, not objectivity.

18. (d) According to AU 322.12, "The internal auditors' work may affect the nature, timing, and extent of the audit, including: procedures the auditor performs when obtaining an understanding of the entity's internal control structure; procedures the auditor performs when assessing risk; and substantive procedures the auditor performs."

19. (d) AU 322.19 states, "The responsibility to report on the financial statements rests solely with the [independent] auditor. Because the auditor has the ultimate responsibility to express an opinion on the financial statements, judgments about assessments of inherent and control risks, the materiality of misstatements, the sufficiency of test performed, the evaluation of significant accounting estimates, and other matters affecting the auditor's report should always be those of the auditor."

20. (d) Answers (a), (b), and (c) are all specifically mentioned in AU 322.11 as items the auditor considers in assessing the internal auditor's competence and objectivity.

21. (d) According to AU 322.27, "In performing an audit, the auditor may request direct assistance from the internal auditors...[including] assist-[ance]...in obtaining an understanding of...internal control...or in performing tests of controls or substantive tests..."

22. (a) The quality of internal auditors' working paper documentation reflects on their competence. The other answers are concerned with the internal auditors' objectivity.

MANAGEMENT REPRESENTATIONS

23. (d) AU 333.03 states, "In some cases involving written representations, the corroborating information that can be obtained by the application of auditing procedures other than inquiry is limited. When a client plans to discontinue a line of business, for example, the auditor may not be able to obtain information through other auditing procedures to corroborate the plan or intent. Accordingly, the auditor should obtain a written representation to provide confirmation of management's intent." Plans to terminate an employee pension plan, make a stock offering, or settle a lawsuit for an amount less than the accrued loss contingency would usually be seen in the minutes of the board meetings.

24. (c) AU 333.02 states that written representations from management ordinarily "reduce the possibility of misunderstanding concerning the matters that are the subject of the representations" (i.e., the financial statements). The auditor does not reduce audit risk or the scope of audit procedures performed based on the representations made in the management representation letter. A representation letter does not reduce the auditor's responsibility to detect material misstatements in the audit.

25. (a) AU 333.02 states, "During an audit, management makes many representations to the auditor, both oral and written, in response to specific inquiries or through the financial statements. Such representations from management are part of the evidential matter the independent auditor obtains, but they are *not a substitute* for the application of those auditing procedures necessary to afford a reasonable basis for his [or her] opinion on the financial statements. Written representations from management ordinarily confirm oral representations given to the auditor, indicate and document the continuing appropriateness of such representations, and reduce the possibility of misunderstanding concerning the matters that are the subject of the representations."

26. (a) According to AU 333.05, management's representations may be limited to matters that are considered material. Materiality limitations would not apply to those representations that are not directly related to amounts included in the financial statements, such as the availability of minutes of stockholders' and directors' meetings. Answers (b), (c), and (d) relate directly to amounts included in the financial statements and thus the materiality limits would apply.

27. (c) AU 333.06(p) lists non-compliance with contractual agreements that may affect the financial statements as a matter ordinarily included in management representations. Management's justifications for not correcting internal control weaknesses are primarily of concern to the audit committee, not the auditor. Generally, the auditor is not concerned with forecasts of the entity's stock price. Management is unlikely to acknowledge any responsibility for employees' violations of laws—merely responsibility for having reasonable internal controls in place.

28. (b) AU 333.05 states, "...if comparative financial statements are reported on, the written representations obtained at the completion of the most recent audit should address all periods being reported on." AU 333.09 states, "...the representations should be made as of a date no earlier than the date of the auditor's report." AU 333.10 states, "If current management was not present during all periods covered by the auditor's report, the auditor should nevertheless obtain written representations from current management on all such periods."

29. (d) An unqualified opinion requires written management representations. Alternative procedures may be used when the client prevents the auditor from reviewing the predecessor's working papers, engages the auditor after the year-end physical inventory is completed, or requests that certain material A/R not be confirmed.

ANALYTICS

30. (d) Increased sales to comparable clients would double accounts receivable (A/R) without a change in the allowance for doubtful accounts as a percentage of A/R. The client should increase this percentage if it has more customers with poor credit ratings. With no other changes, if twice as many A/R were written off previously or if more A/R are old, it suggests the current write-offs are inadequate.

31. (d) The overall review of the audit is concerned with the big picture. The other answer options are analytical procedures that are likely performed during earlier stages, or not at all.

32. (c) Analytical procedures are concerned with plausible mathematical relationships among numbers. The square footage of selling space might be used to compared retail revenues and expenses to industry figures and prior year performance. Personnel turnover and objectivity of audit committee members are concerned with the control environment. Management plans are considered when evaluating the control environment, valuation, and disclosure.

33. (b) Analytics involve evaluations of information made by a study of plausible relationships. The relationship between two consecutive years' payroll expenses is more closely related than warranty expense and contingent liabilities. A/R and sales are not the primary accounts likely to be examined in evaluating an entity's costs and expenses.

34. (b) Analytical procedures consist of evaluations of financial information made by a study of plausible relationships among both financial and nonfinancial data. Projecting an error rate is not an evaluation of financial information.

35. (b) AU 329.06 states, "The objective of the procedures is to identify such things as the existence of unusual transactions and events, and amounts, ratios, and trends that might indicate matters that have financial statement and audit planning ramifications." The use of a standard cost system that produces variance reports allows the auditor an opportunity to compare the output from the standard cost system with the financial information presented by management. Segregating obsolete inventory before the physical inventory count would likely facilitate inventory auditing procedures, but not necessarily the analytical procedures. According to AU 329.16, "The auditor should assess the reliability of the data by considering the source of the data and the conditions under which it was gathered." Strong internal control and independent sources of data enhance the reliability of data used in analytical procedures.

36. (c) AU 329.06 states, "The purpose of applying analytical procedures in planning the audit is to assist in planning the nature, timing, and extent of auditing procedures that will be used to obtain evidential matter for specific account balances or classes of transactions. To accomplish this, the analytical procedures used in planning the audit should focus on enhancing the auditor's understanding of the client's business and the transactions and events that have occurred since the last audit date...." Consideration of reductions in the scope of test of controls and substantive tests occurs after the auditor understands the client's business. The audit as a whole provides reasonable assurance that potential material misstatements will be identified. Assessing the adequacy of available evidential matter can occur only after examination of evidential matter, not in the planning stage.

37. (d) AU 329.09 states, "The auditor's reliance on substantive tests to achieve an audit objective related to a particular assertion may be derived from tests of details, from analytical procedures, or from a combination of both. The decision about which procedure or procedures to use to achieve a particular audit objective is based on the auditor's judgment on the expected effectiveness and efficiency of the available procedures." An auditor's decision whether to apply analytical procedures or to perform tests of transactions and account balances is not solely determined by the availability of data aggregated at a high level, the timing of tests performed after the balance sheet date, or the auditor's familiarity with industry trends.

USING THE WORK OF A SPECIALIST

38. (d) According to AU 336.11, "When a specialist does not have a relationship with the client, the specialist's work usually will provide the auditor with greater assurance of reliability. However, the work of a specialist having a relationship to the client may be acceptable under certain circumstances." AU 336.12 states, "The appropriateness and reasonableness of methods and assumptions used and their application are the responsibility of the specialist. The auditor should obtain an understanding of the methods or assumptions used by the specialist,... [and] evaluate whether the specialist's findings support the related assertions in the financial statements." AU 336.06 states, "...an auditor may encounter complex or subjective matters potentially material to the financial statements. Such matters may require special skill or knowledge and that in the auditor's judgment require using the work of a specialist..."

39. (a) AU 336.16 states, "The auditor may, as a result of the report or findings of the specialist, decide to add explanatory language to his or her standard report or depart from an unqualified opinion. Reference to and identification of the specialist may be made in the auditor's report if the auditor believes such reference will facilitate an understanding of the reason for the explanatory paragraph or the departure from the unqualified opinion." If, as a result of the use of the specialist, the auditor concludes that conditions exist that cause substantial doubt about the entity's ability to continue as a going concern and the auditor believes a reference to the specialists will facilitate an understanding of the reason for the reference to this conclusion, the auditor may refer to the specialist in the auditor's report. Disclosure of the specialist's findings, implying that a more thorough audit was performed is not appropriate. (AU 336.15) If a specialist's findings are consistent with management's representations and corroborate another specialist's earlier findings, there would be no need to disclose the findings of the specialist for the reasons above. Internal control is generally not a matter that would require the use of a specialist, as described in AU 336.07.

INQUIRY OF A CLIENT'S LAWYER

40. (b) According to AU 337.13, "A lawyer's refusal to furnish the information requested in an inquiry letter...would be a limitation on the scope of the audit sufficient to preclude an unqualified opinion." The auditor would need to use alternate procedures to obtain evidence to satisfy the auditor on litigation or potential litigation issues before issuing an unqualified opinion. Such a refusal *and the results of other procedures* may result in the auditor determining to issue an adverse opinion, or to withdraw from the engagement, or to include disclosures in the financial statements or report to management and/or the audit committee.

41. (d) AU 337.12 states, "...a lawyer's response may be limited to matters that are considered individually or collectively material to the financial statements provided the lawyer and auditor have reached an understanding on the limits of materiality for this purpose." This is a question where the instruction to select the best answer is important to bear in mind as, one could argue that all responses are correct. (The last sentence of AU 337.09 states, "Inquiry need not be made concerning matters that are not considered material, provided the client and the auditor have reached an understanding on the limits of materiality for this purpose.")

42. (a) AU 337.12 states, "A lawyer may appropriately limit his response to matters to which he [or she] has given substantive attention in the form of legal consultation or representation." Answers (b) and (d) are addressed in AU 337.13 where it indicates these are sufficient to cause a scope limitation. Answer (c) is also incorrect, as it may lead the auditor to conclude that the financial statements are affected by an uncertainty which is not susceptible to a reasonable estimate (AU 337.14).

43. (b) AU 337.08 states that the letter of inquiry to the client's attorney is the primary means the auditor has to obtain corroboration of information furnished by management concerning litigation, claims, and assessments. The terms mentioned in answers (a) and (c) might be covered by the attorney, but are not the primary reasons the auditor makes the request. The items in answer (d) are normally furnished by management (or management may request that the attorney prepare the description and evaluation); they are not the primary reason that the auditor sends a letter of inquiry.

44. (c) AU 337.05 states, "Since the events that should be considered in the financial accounting for and reporting of litigation, claims, and assessments are matters within the direct knowledge and, often, control of management of an entity, management is the primary source of information about such matters. Accordingly, the independent auditor's procedures should include [inquiry and discussion] with management [concerning] the policies and procedures adopted for identifying, evaluating, and accounting for litigation, claims, and assessments." AU 337.08 states, "A letter of audit inquiry to the client's lawyer is the auditor's primary means of obtaining corroboration of the information furnished by management concerning litigation, claims, and assessments." However, the lawyer does not evaluate the client's ability to continue as a going concern or whether all litigation, claims, and assessments have been recorded or disclosed in the financial statements. Examination of the legal documents in the client's lawyer's possession would be an unusual procedure.

Work Papers

45. (b) A standard confirmation request sent to a financial institution at which the client has both a checking or savings account and a loan would include requests on one form regarding the cash balance and the loan balance and, in addition, a description of the collateral for the loan. While confirmation of accounts receivable is a generally accepted auditing procedure (AU 330.34), confirmation of accounts payable is not. It is generally used only in cases of suspected fraud, sloppy or missing records, or suspected understatements. The entity holding inventory on consignment generally would not have information related to contingent liabilities. Accrued interest receivable would most likely be related to notes receivable rather than accounts receivable.

46. (c) The auditor should prepare a written set of audit programs after considering the nature, extent, and timing of the work to be performed. Such written audit programs should detail the specific audit procedures that are necessary to accomplish the objectives of the audit. Audit programs may change as the audit progresses, to account for changed conditions (AU 311.05).

47. (c) Lead schedules generally summarize information, such as a summary of all cash accounts with debits and credits summarized into major categories and information about beginning and ending balances.

48. (d) AU 339.02 states, "Working papers serve mainly to provide the principal support for the auditor's report...[and to] aid the auditor in the conduct and supervision of the audit." Permanent files contain items of continuing interest, such as debt agreements, flowcharts of internal controls, and articles of incorporation. The other items are of temporary interest only.

49. (c) Engagement letters are a matter of sound business practice, rather than a professional requirement. AU 311.05 states that a written audit program establishing auditing procedures to accomplish the audit's objectives is necessary. AU 326.14 states that the basic accounting data and all corroborating information support the financial statements. Without an indication that the accounting records agree or reconcile with the financial statements, the auditor cannot express an opinion upon them. AU 319.57 states the basis for the auditor's conclusions is required to be documented when the assessed level of control risk is below the maximum level.

50. (a) A physical count of assets that could be readily stolen (negotiable securities or gems, for instance) should include acknowledgement that the assets are again in the client's custody, if they are handled by the auditor. Sold securities would not be counted, so an analysis of realized gains and losses is not closely related to a count. An evaluation of the internal control policies concerning physical access and negotiation generally would be documented with other internal control evaluations, not with substantive tests.

51. (d) The matters noted in answers (a), (b), and (c) would all have a significant impact on the quantity and content of the auditor's working papers. While the content of the representation letter may affect the quantity and content of the auditor's working papers, the effect is minimal.

52. (c) This is from the illustrative client representation letter in AU §333A.05. A report on internal control or another special report would generally not discuss communications from other entities. Letters for underwriters concentrate on financial statements, not internal control.

53. (d) Detailed audit working papers are subdivided and grouped by financial statement accounts, which in turn are filed in order of appearance in the financial statements. Working papers for each asset, liability, and equity account begin with a lead schedule summarizing the account's balance per the general ledger, and then showing adjusting and reclassification entries, and the final balance per audit. The lead schedule also includes the auditor's conclusion about whether the account is fairly stated.

54. (c) Worksheets contain reclassification and adjustments columns. The items in answers (a), (b), and (d) are included in the audit workpapers, but are not included in the working trial balance.

55. (a) AU 339.02 states, "Working papers serve mainly to provide the principal support for the auditor's report…[and to] aid the auditor in the conduct and supervision of the audit."

Related Parties

56. (c) AU 334.12 states, "Except for routine transactions, it will generally not be possible to determine whether a particular transaction would have taken place if the parties had not been related, or assuming it would have taken place, what the terms and manner of settlement would have been. Accordingly, it is difficult to substantiate representations that a transaction was consummated on terms equivalent to those that prevail in arm's-length transactions. If such a representation is included in the financial statements and the auditor believes that the representation is unsubstantiated by management, he [or she] should express a qualified or adverse opinion because of a departure from [GAAP], depending on materiality." The disclosure of loans below market value is additional support for items included in the financial statements. Describing the exchange of real estate or presenting the dollar volume of related party transactions and any changes in the method of establishing terms from prior periods are all typical disclosure items that should be included in the financial statements for them to be in conformity with GAAP.

57. (c) Loans receivable and payable would be more likely to be guaranteed by related parties than the other listed transactions are to involve related parties. The procedures in answer (a) might reveal related party transactions, but as a by-product. Answers (b) and (d) are more part of a search for unrecorded liabilities and doubts about the entity's ability to continue as a going concern.

58. (d) According to AU 334.02, an auditor places primary emphasis on the adequacy of disclosure when auditing related party transactions. Answers (a), (b), and (c) are among the possible audit procedures used to evaluate the adequacy of related party disclosure.

59. (a) When searching for related party transactions, the auditor should obtain an understanding of each subsidiary's relationship to the total entity because "…business structure and operating style are occasionally deliberately designed to obscure related party transactions." (AU 334.05) Answers (b), (c), and (d) are not reasons for an auditor to obtain an understanding of each subsidiary's relationship to the total entity.

60. (c) AU 334.09 notes that after identifying related party transactions, the auditor should obtain an understanding of the business purpose of the transactions. The other answers are all procedures that may be performed later.

Solution 35-2 ADDITIONAL MULTIPLE CHOICE ANSWERS

Internal Auditors

61. (a) If the independent auditor decides that the work performed by internal auditors may have a bearing on his or her own procedures, he or she should assess the competence and objectivity of internal auditors and evaluate their work. AU 322.10 states, "When assessing the internal auditor's objectivity, the auditor should [determine]…the organizational status of the internal auditor responsible for the internal audit function, including: whether the internal auditor reports to an officer of sufficient status to ensure broad audit coverage and adequate consideration of, and action on, the findings and recommendations of the internal auditors; whether the internal auditor has direct access and reports regularly to the board of directors, the audit

committee, or the owner-manager; and whether the board of directors, the audit committee, or the owner-manager oversees employment decisions related to the internal auditor." In this case, the independent auditor would only place limited reliance on the work of the internal auditors because the internal auditors report to the corporate controller and may be reluctant to report weaknesses in the controller's activities.

MANAGEMENT REPRESENTATIONS

62. (b) A management representation letter is from the audited entity's management to the auditor. AU 333.04 lists the third item to be included in a management representation letter as the completeness and availability of minutes of stockholders' and directors' meetings. Communications with the audit committee would be verbal or in a letter addressed to the audit committee from the auditor. Plans to acquire or merge with other entities in the subsequent year would most likely be included in the minutes of stockholders' and directors' meetings. Management's acknowledgment of responsibility for the detection of *employee* fraud is not *explicitly* stated in the representation letter.

63. (c) According to AU 333.09, the management representation letter should be dated as of the date of the auditor's report.

ANALYTICS

64. (a) AU 329.04 indicates that analytical procedures are to be used to some extent in all audits in the planning of the audit and in the final review stages. The use of analytical procedures as a substantive test is not mandated, but can be "more effective or efficient than tests of details for achieving substantive audit objectives."

65. (c) AU 329.22 states, "The objective of analytical procedures used in the overall review stage of the audit is to assist the auditor in assessing the conclusions reached and in the evaluation of the overall financial statement presentation.... The overall review would generally include reading the financial statements and notes and considering...unusual or unexpected balances or relationships that were not previously identified." The other options are activities to be done before the overall review stage.

66. (c) A comparison of current year revenue to budgeted current year revenue would provide an evaluation of the entity's expected results for the year. Comparisons between prior year amounts and current year amounts are not as likely to provide useful information about current year results. Also, the study of accounts payable, payroll expense, warranty expense and contingent liabilities would not, by themselves, provide sufficient evidence to evaluate an entity's results of operations.

67. (c) AU 329.14 states, "Relationships involving income statement accounts tend to be more predictable than relationships involving only balance sheet accounts since income statement accounts represent transactions over a period of time, whereas balance sheet accounts represent amounts as of a point in time. Relationships involving transactions subject to management discretion are sometimes less predictable."

68. (b) A comparison of revenues and expenses with those of the prior year is likely to reveal a change in the capitalization policy for small tools. For instance, if tools costing less than $25 were formerly expensed and the policy is changed to $100, this is likely to show a substantial increase in the amount of tools expensed during the period. Answer (c) concerns a liability account, Payroll Taxes Payable, not a revenue or expense account. Failure to recognize the property tax increase would make the account balances comparable and so the auditor would *not* investigate.

69. (c) Unexpected relationships discovered through analytical procedures indicate additional investigation is appropriate. To assume that fraud exists in the relevant accounts or to revise communications with the audit committee without further investigation would be an over-reaction. Analytics are a substantive test, not a test of internal control.

70. (a) AU 329.06 states "the objective of the procedures is to identify such things as the existence of unusual transactions and events..." Answers (b), (c), and (d) would not necessarily be discovered in the performance of analytical procedures, but would more likely be discovered in the performance of substantive tests.

INQUIRY OF A CLIENT'S LAWYER

71. (b) The response in answer (b) is vague and would probably need clarification. The other answer options indicate that the audit client probably doesn't have any material liability concerning the matters discussed.

72. (d) According to AU 337.14, when a client's lawyer is unable to form a conclusion about the likelihood of an unfavorable outcome of pending litigation because of inherent uncertainties and the effect on the financial statements could be material,

the auditor will ordinarily conclude that an explanatory paragraph should be added to the report.

WORK PAPERS

73. (c) Among the examples of timesaving considerations in workpaper content listed in the AICPA Audit and Accounting Manual is that the auditor should consider using adding machine tape instead of separate lists, and may enter names or explanations on the tapes where appropriate (AAM 6300.03).

74. (c) AU 333A.05 provides an example of a sample management representation letter and the types of assertions that should be made. Among these assertions is *that no violations or possible violations of laws or regulations whose effects should be considered for disclosure in the financial statements or as a basis for recording a loss contingency.*

RELATED PARTIES

75. (d) AU 334.03 states, "Transactions that because of their nature may be indicative of the existence of related parties include: (a) *Borrowing or lending on an interest-free basis or at a rate of interest significantly above or below market rates prevailing at the time of the transaction*; (b) selling real estate at a price that differs significantly from its appraised value; (c) exchanging property for similar property in a nonmonetary transaction; (d) making loans with no scheduled terms for when or how the funds will be repaid."

PERFORMANCE BY SUBTOPICS

Each category below parallels a subtopic covered in Chapter 35. Record the number and percentage of questions you correctly answered in each subtopic area.

Nature of Evidential Matter

Question #	Correct √
1	
2	
3	
4	
5	
6	
7	

\# Questions 7

\# Correct ____
% Correct ____

Evidential Matter

Question #	Correct √
8	
9	
10	
11	
12	
13	
14	
15	
16	

\# Questions 9

\# Correct ____
% Correct ____

Internal Auditors

Question #	Correct √
17	
18	
19	
20	
21	
22	

\# Questions 6

\# Correct ____
% Correct ____

Management Representations

Question #	Correct √
23	
24	
25	
26	
27	
28	
29	

\# Questions 7

\# Correct ____
% Correct ____

Analytics

Question #	Correct √
30	
31	
32	
33	
34	
35	
36	
37	

\# Questions 8

\# Correct ____
% Correct ____

Using the Work of a Specialist

Question #	Correct √
38	
39	

\# Questions 2

\# Correct ____
% Correct ____

Inquiry of a Client's Lawyer

Question #	Correct √
40	
41	
42	
43	
44	

\# Questions 5

\# Correct ____
% Correct ____

Work Papers

Question #	Correct √
45	
46	
47	
48	
49	
50	
51	
52	
53	
54	
55	

\# Questions 11

\# Correct ____
% Correct ____

Related Parties

Question #	Correct √
56	
57	
58	
59	
60	

\# Questions 5

\# Correct ____
% Correct ____

OTHER OBJECTIVE FORMAT QUESTION SOLUTIONS

SOLUTION 35-3 WORKING PAPERS

1. B

The auditor's report to the audit committee regarding reportable conditions includes a description of the conditions noted.

2. N

Management is a knowledgeable source of the company's viewpoint, beliefs, intentions, and occurrence of events.

3. M

An auditor's review notes include reminders of select conditions to allow a double check to ensure that all matters are resolved appropriately.

4. H

Appropriate places for disclaimers are the engagement letter and post-engagement reports. The statement speaks of the audit in the future ("Consequently, our audit will not…") from the perspective of the auditor.

5. N

Management is a knowledgeable source of the company's viewpoint, beliefs, intentions, and occurrence of events.

6. I

Letters to underwriters may contain negative assurance, which is used in few instances, certainly not in a report on reportable conditions. A practitioner's report on a management assertion would not be discussing stockholder's equity in relation to previous unaudited financial statements; it would discuss the practitioner's work in relation to management's assertion.

7. D

An opinion regarding liability related to a proceeding is usually from a lawyer in response to an audit inquiry letter. The management representation letter usually has a less specific statement of all possible liabilities being included in the financial statements as appropriate. These are the two parties most likely to be knowledgeable about proceedings related to the client.

8. L

The phrases *substantial doubt* and *ability to continue as a going concern* are required in the auditor's report when there is a going concern uncertainty.

9. F

The auditor's communication to the audit committee should include any disagreements, whether or not resolved, with management about matters that, individually or in the aggregate, could have a significant impact on the financial statements.

10. N

Management is a knowledgeable source of the company's viewpoint, beliefs, intentions, and occurrence of events.

11. P

The client, a CPA performing a review, and a successor auditor are most likely to be the external viewers of work papers. Typically, each successor will try to view a predecessor's work papers, but the opposite will be rare. A client is the most atypical user of the three. Further, there is no answer option with a communication regarding the client or reviewer viewing the work papers.

12. J

A confirmation request seeks an indication of agreement between provided information with another's records. The language in this statement is more suitable to an accounts receivable confirmation (a relatively straight-forward matter of matching amounts) than an inquiry of legal counsel (a relatively complex matter requiring the judgment by counsel, and thus a more complex letter of inquiry).

13. B

The auditor's report to the audit committee regarding reportable conditions includes a description of the conditions noted.

14. H

The statement speaks of the future ("…we will communicate to you….") from the perspective of the auditor. It is most likely that an auditor would send this message to management. The appropriate place for this disclaimer is in the engagement letter.

15. F

The auditor's communication to the audit committee should include any serious difficulties encountered in dealing with management related to the performance of the audit.

16. B

The auditor's report to the audit committee regarding reportable conditions includes a description of the conditions noted.

17. C

This statement is from the entity's management ("our financial statements") to a party (other than the auditor) who is knowledgeable about the company's contingent liabilities. In connection with audits, lawyers frequently are asked to provide their opinion of contingent liabilities related to the services that they provide to clients.

18. N

Management is a knowledgeable source of the company's viewpoint, beliefs, intentions, and occurrence of events.

19. M

An auditor's review notes include reminders to check on issues where mistakes have a relatively high probability of being made.

Solution 35-4 Analytical Procedures

1. H

The current ratio is total current assets divided by total current liabilities. ($1,240,000 / $400,000 = 3.1)

2. E

The quick (or acid-test) ratio is cash plus marketable securities plus net receivables divided by current liabilities. [($240,000 + $400,000) / $400,000 = 1.6]

3. K

Accounts receivable turnover is net credit sales divided by average net receivables. {$3,000,000 / [($400,000 + $400,000) / 2] = 7.5}

4. G

Inventory turnover is cost of goods sold divided by average inventory. {$1,800,000 / [($600,000 + $600,000) / 2] = 3.0}

5. D

Total asset turnover is sales divided by total assets. ($3,000,000 / $2,000.000 = 1.5)

6. T

Gross margin percentage is the gross margin divided by sales, expressed as a percentage. ($1,200,000 / $3,000,000 = 0.4 = 40%)

7. P

Net operating margin percentage is operating income divided by sales, expressed as a percentage. ($660,000 / $3,000,000 = .22 = 22%)

8. N

Times interest earned is income before income taxes and interest charges divided by interest charges. [($400,000 + $220,000 + $40,000) / $40,000 = 16.5]

9. U

Total debt to equity percentage is total liabilities divided by owners' equity, expressed as a percentage. [($400,000 + $350,000) / ($750,000 + $500,000) = 0.6 = 60%]

10. A, B, D

Inventory turnover is cost of goods sold divided by average inventory. When cost of goods sold is overstated, this ratio will increase. Due to recording consignment items shipped during the last month as sales, the cost of goods sold is overstated. Due to not recording a significant number of credit memos for returned merchandise, the cost of goods sold is overstated. When average inventory is understated, this ratio will increase. Due to the incorrect understatement of inventory from the exclusion of inventory received before year-end, average inventory is understated.

11. A, B, E

Accounts receivable turnover is net credit sales divided by average net receivables. This ratio will decrease when net credit sales decreases or average net receivables increases. Due to recording consignment items shipped during the last month as sales, sales and accounts receivable are both overstated by the same amount. However, proportionately, accounts receivables increases more than net credit sales, decreasing the ratio. Due to not recording a significant number of credit memos for returned merchandise, sales and accounts receivable are disproportionately overstated. A larger percentage of sales occurring during the last month of the year, as compared to the prior year, increases the amount in accounts receivable. This increases average accounts receivable, as compared to last year, without increasing sales, as compared to last year.

12. A, B, E

The allowance for doubtful accounts as a percentage of accounts receivable will decrease when the allowance for doubtful accounts decreases proportionately less than the accounts receivable does or when accounts receivable increases. Due to recording consignment items shipped during the last month as sales, accounts receivable is overstated. Due to not recording a significant number of credit memos for returned merchandise, accounts receivable is overstated. However, these occurrences do not impact the allowance for doubtful accounts. A larger percentage of sales occurring during the last month of the year, as compared to the prior year, increases the amount in accounts receivable. This increases average accounts receivable, as compared to last year, without increasing the allowance for doubtful accounts, as compared to last year.

13. P

The rate of interest paid will increase the proportionate amount of interest expense even with the same amount of debt.

14. L, P

Operating income does not include interest or income tax expense; the rates for these apparently increased.

15. H

Percentages measure proportional changes. The items being compared must have changed proportionately if the percentage did not change.

ESSAY SOLUTIONS

SOLUTION 35-5 ASSERTIONS

a. Financial statement assertions are **representations by management** that are embodied in financial statement components.

b. In obtaining **evidential matter in support of financial statement assertions**, an auditor develops specific audit objectives in the light of those assertions.

c. In developing the audit objectives of a particular engagement, an auditor should consider the **specific circumstances** of the entity, including the **nature of its economic activity** and the accounting **practices unique to its industry**.

d. There is not necessarily a one-to-one relationship between audit objectives and procedures. Some **auditing procedures may relate to more than one objective.** On the other hand, a **combination of auditing procedures may be needed to achieve a single objective.** The procedures adopted should be **adequate** to achieve the audit objectives.

e. In selecting particular substantive tests to achieve audit objectives, an auditor considers, among other things, the **risk of material misstatement** in the financial statements, including the assessed levels of control risk, and the expected effectiveness and efficiency of such tests. An auditor's considerations also include the **nature and materiality of the items being tested**, the **kinds and competence of available evidential matter**, and the **nature of the audit objective** to be achieved.

SOLUTION 35-6 MANAGEMENT REPRESENTATIONS

a. 1. An auditor is required to obtain a written management representation letter as part of **every audit performed in accordance with generally accepted auditing standards**.

2. The purposes of obtaining a written management representation letter are to:

- **Confirm the oral representations** given to the auditor.
- Indicate and document the **continuing appropriateness** of management's representations.
- **Reduce the possibility of misunderstanding** concerning the matters that are the subject of the representations.
- Complement the other auditing procedures by **corroborating the information discovered** in performing those procedures.
- Obtain evidence concerning **management's future plans and intentions**, e.g., when refinancing debt or discontinuing a line of business.

b. 1. The representation letter should be addressed **to the auditor** and dated as of **the date of the auditor's report**.

2. The letter should be signed by **members of management** whom the auditor believes are **responsible for and knowledgeable**, directly or through others in the organization, about the matters covered by the representation. Their refusal to sign the letter would constitute a **limitation on the scope** of the audit sufficient to preclude an unqualified opinion and affect the auditor's ability to **rely on other management representations**.

c. Obtaining a management representation letter does **not relieve an auditor** of any other responsibility for planning or performing an audit. Accordingly, an auditor should still perform all the usual tests to corroborate representations made by management.

SOLUTION 35-7 ANALYTICAL PROCEDURES

a. Analytical procedures are used for these broad purposes:

- To assist the auditor in **planning the nature, timing, and extent** of other auditing procedures.
- As a **substantive test** to obtain **evidential matter** about particular **assertions** related to account balances or classes of transactions.
- As an **overall review** of the financial information in the final review stage of the audit.

b. An auditor's expectations are developed from the following sources of information:

- Financial information for **comparable prior periods** giving consideration to known changes.
- **Anticipated results**—for example, budgets, forecasts, and extrapolations.
- **Relationships** among elements of financial information **within the period**.
- **Information regarding the industry** in which the client operates.
- **Relationships** of financial information **with** relevant **nonfinancial information**.

c. The factors that influence an auditor's consideration of the reliability of data for purposes of achieving audit objectives are whether the

- Data were **obtained from independent sources** outside the entity or from sources within the entity.
- **Sources within the entity were independent** of those who are responsible for the amount being audited.
- Data were **developed under a reliable system** with adequate controls.
- Data were **subjected to audit testing** in the current or prior year.
- Expectations were developed using data from a variety of sources.

SOLUTION 35-8 SPECIALIST

a. The factors Kent should consider in the process of selecting Park include

- **Park's professional certification**, license, or other recognition of Park's competence.
- **Park's reputation** and standing in the view of **Park's peers** and others familiar with Park's capability or performance.
- **Park's relationship**, if any, to Davidson Corporation.

b. The understanding among Kent, Park, and Davidson's management as to the nature of the work to be performed by Park should cover

- The **objectives and scope** of Park's work.
- Park's representations as to Park's relationship, if any, to Davidson.
- The **methods** or **assumptions** to be **used**.
- A comparison of the methods or assumptions to be used with those used in the preceding period.
- Park's **understanding** of Kent's **corroborative use of Park's findings**.
- The form and content of Park's report that would enable Kent to evaluate Park's findings.

c. Kent **may refer to Park in the auditor's report** if Kent decides to issue an unqualified opinion, only if it will facilitate an understanding of the reason for an explanatory paragraph.

d. Kent **may refer** to Park in the auditor's report **if** Kent decides to **issue other than an unqualified opinion** as a result of Park's findings. Reference is permitted if it will facilitate an understanding of the reason for the modification.

SOLUTION 35-9 LEGAL INQUIRY LETTER FOR LITIGATION, CLAIMS, AND ASSESSMENTS

The omissions, ambiguities, and inappropriate statements and terminology in Brown's letter are as follows:

1. The **action** that Consolidated **intends to take** concerning each suit (for example, to contest the matter vigorously, to seek an out-of-court settlement, or to an appeal an adverse decision) is omitted.

2. A **description of the progress** of each case to date is omitted.

3. An **evaluation** of the **likelihood of an unfavorable outcome** of each case is omitted.

4. An **estimate**, if one can be made, of the **amount or range of potential loss** of each case is omitted.

5. The various **other pending or threatened litigation** on which Young was consulted is not identified and included.

6. The **unasserted claims and assessments** probable of assertion that have a reasonable possibility of an unfavorable outcome are not identified.

7. Consolidated's understanding of Young's responsibility to advise Consolidated concerning the **disclosure of unasserted possible claims or assessments** is omitted.

8. **Materiality** (or the limits of materiality) is not addressed.

9. The reference to a **limitation** on Young's response **due to confidentiality is inappropriate**.

10. Young is not requested to identify the nature of and **reasons for any limited response**.

11. **Young is not requested to include matters that existed after December 31, 20X4**, up to the date of Young's response.

12. The **date** by which Young's **response is needed** is not indicated.

13. The reference to Young's response possibly being quoted or referred to in the financial statements is inappropriate.

14. **Vague terminology** such as "slight" and "some chance" is included where "remote" and "possible" are more appropriate.

15. There is **no inquiry about** any unpaid or **unbilled charges**, services, or disbursements.

SOLUTION 35-10 RELATED PARTY TRANSACTIONS

The audit procedures Temple should apply to identify Ford's related party relationships and transactions include the following:

- Evaluate the company's procedures for **identifying and properly reporting** related party relationships and transactions.
- **Request** from management the **names of all related parties** and inquire whether there were any transactions with these parties during the period.
- **Review tax returns** and filings with other regulatory agencies for the names of related parties.
- Determine the **names of all pension plans** and other trusts and the names of their officers and trustees.
- Review **stock certificate book** to identify the stockholders.
- Review material investment transactions to determine whether the investments created related party relationships.
- Review the **minutes of board of directors' meetings**.
- Review **conflict-of-interest statements** obtained by the company from its management.
- Review the extent and nature of business transacted with major customers, suppliers, borrowers, and lenders.
- Consider whether transactions are occurring, but are not being given proper accounting recognition, e.g., personal use of company vehicles, interest-free loans, etc.
- Review accounting records for **large, unusual, or nonrecurring transactions** or balances, paying particular attention to transactions recognized at or near the end of the reporting period.
- **Review confirmations of compensating balance arrangements** for indications that balances are or were maintained for or by related parties.
- Review **invoices from law firms** that have performed services for the company for indications of the existence of related party relationships or transactions.
- Review **confirmations of loans receivable and payable** for indications of **guarantees**, and determine their nature and the relationships, if any, of the guarantors to the reporting entity.

SOLUTION 35-11 LOSS CONTINGENCY

The substantive audit procedures that Young should apply when testing for loss contingencies relating to litigation, claims, and assessments include the following:

- **Read minutes** of meetings of stockholders, directors, and committees.
- **Read contracts, loan agreements, leases**, and other documents.
- Read **correspondence with taxing** and other governmental **agencies**.
- Read **correspondence with insurance** and bonding **companies**.
- Read confirmation replies for information concerning guarantees.

- **Discuss with management** the entity's **policies and procedures** for identifying, evaluating, and accounting for litigation, claims, and assessments.
- **Obtain from management** or inside general counsel a **description and evaluation of litigation, claims, and assessments.**
- Obtain **written assurance from management** that the financial statements include all accruals and disclosures required by Statement of Financial Accounting Standards No. 5.
- **Examine documents** in the client's possession concerning litigation, claims, or assessments, including correspondence from lawyers.

Obtain an analysis of **professional fee expenses and review supporting invoices** for indications of contingencies.

- Request the client's management to prepare for transmittal a **letter of inquiry to** those **lawyers** consulted by the client concerning litigation, claims, and assessments.
- Compare the lawyer's response to the items in the letter of inquiry to the description and evaluation of litigation, claims, and assessments obtained from management.
- Determine that the financial statements include **proper accruals and disclosures** of the contingencies.

Wondering how you can prepare for OOAF questions?

Some candidates who are otherwise confident about the exam are overwhelmed by other objective answer format (OOAF or OOF) questions. The following tips are designed to help you increase your confidence when presented with these lengthy questions.

As you progress through your study plan, answer an OOAF question from each major topic; waiting until the last month leaves you little time to prepare for this question type. The more uncomfortable that you are with OOAF questions, the more important this becomes. You might not realize that you are uncomfortable with OOAF questions, if you don't try answering some of them.

After answering an OOAF question (using the suggested time limit) and checking your answers, reflect on the question. If you had trouble with some aspect, evaluate whether you need to review the material, refine your answering technique, or merely gain confidence with this format.

- Did you feel pressured for time? If you in fact didn't have enough time, this may indicate you need to review the text again. As you become more familiar with the material, your speed will increase. A shortage of time may also indicate a need to consider techniques to answering OOAF questions. Specific information about OOAF question answering techniques is in the **Practical Advice** appendix.

- If you felt pressured for time, but actually had time to finish the question, answer several more OOAF questions using the suggested time limit. This experience will help you learn not to be intimidated by this format.

Once you know the content, you will be able to prepare a response regardless of the question format. Exam time is limited and you don't want the pressure of time considerations to distract you from providing your best answer to questions. To reduce the pressure, remember that you must earn 75 points to pass—the answer format that you use to earn those 75 points doesn't matter. Practice more OOAF questions that cover topics that have high point value; be prepared to answer an OOAF question in any topic area.

Remember, with the techniques and information in your material,

A passing score is well within reach!

CHAPTER 36

AUDIT PROGRAMS

EXAM COVERAGE: The Obtain and Document Information portion of the Auditing section of the CPA exam is designated by the examiners to be 35 percent of the section's point value. Historically, exam coverage of the topics in Chapters 35 and 36 fluctuates from 18 to 28 percent of the Auditing section. More information about the point value of various topics is included in the **Practical Advice** section of this volume.

CHAPTER 36

AUDIT PROGRAMS

I. Overview

A. Audit Program

A list of audit procedures comprehensive enough to enable the gathering of evidence indicating the satisfaction of the audit objectives of the particular account(s). The program should be concise and understandable so that anyone examining the working papers can evaluate the work performed.

B. Substantive Testing

Substantive testing involves procedures that are designed to determine the accuracy of the dollar amounts reported in the financial statements. Substantive testing entails analytical procedures and tests of details—either tests of transactions or tests of balances.

SUBSTANTIVE TESTS

- **C** Confirm
- **O** Observe
- **R** Retrace (Trace)
- **V** Vouch
- **A** Analytics
- **I** Inquire
- **R** Recompute

1. **Tests of Transactions** These tests are performed to determine whether the entity's transactions are correctly recorded and summarized in the accounting records. Many of these tests can be performed simultaneously with the tests of controls of internal control (i.e., dual-purpose tests).

2. **Tests of Balances** These tests are primarily concerned with monetary misstatements in the account balances. Tests of balances can be distinguished from tests of transactions because the tests of balances relate to individual accounts, whereas the tests of transactions relate to the different transaction cycles.

C. Considerations

AUDIT OBJECTIVES

- **C** Classification / Disclosure
- **C** Cutoff / Completeness
- **O** Ownership / Obligation
- **V** Valuation / Accuracy
- **E** Existance / Occurence

1. **Audit Objectives** Consider the objectives of the audit of the specific account. In other words, what does the auditor want to determine through the audit procedures? There are several objectives that must be addressed in the audit of each account.

2. **Internal Control** Visualize and understand the accounting system, control environment, and control procedures that are designed into internal control. A good technique is to visualize the physical flow of the goods and the resulting accounting entries and records.

3. **Audit Evidence** Determine which of the forms of audit evidence are applicable in the particular situation. Audit evidence must be both **valid** and **relevant**.

4. **Audit Procedures** Determine the types of audit procedures that will be required to obtain the audit evidence.

a. **INTERIM TESTS VS. YEAR-END TESTS** Some tests, including tests of controls, can be done during the year, rather than at year-end. Therefore, the audit program may be broken into two parts, one dealing with interim procedures and the other with year-end procedures. Note that interim work consists primarily of procedural work.

b. **COST/BENEFIT ANALYSIS** The audit procedures must be justifiable in terms of their cost/benefit relationship. This will include consideration of (1) the materiality of the account being audited, (2) the materiality of possible misstatements, and (3) the audit risk associated with the account. For example, certain items such as cash have a much greater risk associated with them than accounts such as land. In general, the more material an account and its possible misstatements, the higher the audit risk and the more extensive the audit procedures should be.

AUDIT OBJECTIVES
(Alternative Mnemonic)

C Transactions must be properly **classified**.
A Data must be **accurate** in amount.
V Transactions must be properly **valued**.
E Items of interest must actually **exist**.
T Transactions must be recorded on a **timely** basis.
O Assets and liabilities must be **owned/ owed** by the client.
D Financial statements must properly **disclose** the outcome of transactions.
C All transactions must be recorded—**completeness.**

EXHIBIT 1 ♦ MANAGEMENT ASSERTIONS AND AUDIT OBJECTIVES

Definition	Management Assertion	Audit Objective
All Transactions Recorded	Completeness	Completeness
Assets and Liabilities "Owned" and "Owed"	Obligations and Rights	Ownership/Authorization
Accuracy of Amounts in Financial Statements	Valuation or Allocation	1. Estimates are reasonable and realistic 2. Good cutoff obtained 3. Mechanical accuracy reliable
Recorded Transactions Exist	Existence	Validity
Reporting Standards—GAAP, Consistency, Disclosure	Statement Presentation and Disclosure	1. Adequate disclosure 2. G/L classification reasonable

D. **REVIEW OF AUDIT EVIDENCE**

1. **CALCULATIONS BY THE AUDITOR** For example, the auditor may recompute a tax liability or depreciation. In addition to *verifying* the amount in the financial records, this procedure also contributes to the auditor's *understanding* of the summarization of the data in the financial statements.

2. **ANALYTICAL PROCEDURES** The interrelationships among the various data are investigated to provide evidence of reasonable presentation in the financial statements. For example, the auditor may examine the ratio of interest expense to long-term debt, the ratio of accounts receivable to sales, and the gross profit ratios for a period of several years. Alternatively, the auditor may match several associated accounts and audit the data simultaneously (e.g., purchases and accounts payable, accounts receivable and sales).

> **REVIEW OF AUDIT EVIDENCE**
>
> **C** Calculations by the auditor
> **A** Analytical procedures
> **D** Documents (authoritative)
> **S** Subsequent events
> **C** Client statements
> **R** Records (subsidiary)
> **I** Internal control
> **P** Physical evidence
> **T** Third party statements

3. **AUTHORITATIVE DOCUMENTS** Documents such as vendor's invoices, time cards, receiving reports, and purchase orders provide support for recording transactions in journals and are used to authorize transactions.

   a. **PREPARATION** In general, documents prepared by third parties are a better form of evidence than those prepared by the client.

   b. **CIRCULATION** In general, documents used by third parties are a better form of evidence than those used only by the client.

   c. **INTERNAL CONTROL** Authoritative documents prepared under strong internal control are generally considered better evidence than those prepared under weak internal control.

4. **SUBSEQUENT EVENTS** The occurrence of events subsequent to the financial statement date is especially important evidence regarding cut-off work on year-end balances. An important use of subsequent evidence is the search for unrecorded liabilities. In analyzing the cash disbursements made after the year-end, the auditor is looking for items that were a liability at year-end but that were not recorded and disclosed in the financial statements.

> **PROCEDURES FOR DISCOVERING SUBSEQUENT EVENTS**
>
> **M** Management Representation Letter
> **I** Inquiry
> **R** Read Minutes / Interim Financial Statements
> **A** Asset / Liability Valuation
> **C** Cutoff
> **L** Legal Letters

5. **CLIENT'S STATEMENTS** The auditor frequently must rely on statements made by the client. The client's explanations must be evaluated as to the treatment of various items and as to the reasoning that supports certain judgmental decisions.

6. **SUBSIDIARY RECORDS** Subsidiary records add to the evidential matter supporting the financial statement generation process. Subsidiary ledgers for accounts receivable, inventory, and fixed assets are examples of the types of evidence the auditor evaluates.

7. **INTERNAL CONTROL** Can be thought of as a form of audit evidence since the auditor considers internal control in reaching conclusions concerning the fairness of the financial statements. The strength of internal control affects the nature, timing, and extent of the procedures that will be performed. Therefore, under strong internal control, the auditor may require *less* audit evidence than under weak internal control.

8. **PHYSICAL EVIDENCE** Examples include counting cash, counting inventory, and observing fixed assets such as buildings and machines.

9. **THIRD PARTY STATEMENTS** Statements by third parties are strong types of evidence since they are prepared by independent parties. Examples include accounts receivable confirmations, confirmations from insurance brokers concerning the status of various insurance policies, confirmations of the number of shares outstanding from registrars, and confirmations of account balances by banks.

II. STANDARDIZED AUDIT PROCEDURES

Many past CPA Exams have contained essay questions in which the candidate was required to develop an audit program for a particular account or transaction cycle. Composing an audit program is greatly simplified if the candidate has knowledge of the key terms used in describing audit procedures.

A. OBTAIN AN UNDERSTANDING OF RELEVANT INTERNAL CONTROLS AND ASSESS CONTROL RISK

In order to ascertain the nature, timing, and extent of substantive tests to be applied.

B. GENERAL AUDIT PROCEDURES

The following are frequently used audit procedures. Because they are in general form, each procedure in an audit program should specify the account balance or transaction to which it applies (e.g., vouch sales journal entries to the bills of lading).

1. Consider internal control, assess control risk.
2. Evaluate whether transactions are properly recorded in conformity with GAAP.
3. Reconcile detail records and data with the general ledger.
4. Confirm and observe for proper segregation of duties and actual practice.
5. Test posting from the journals to the ledgers.
6. Compare an account's beginning balance with the ending balance from the previous period.
7. Scan the accounts for unusual items.
8. Investigate unusual items.
9. Test for proper authorizations.
10. Vouch (i.e., examine) source documents.
11. Inquire about significant accounts and events.
12. Test for adequate disclosures.
13. Foot and cross-foot.
14. Test for interrelationships between certain accounts and between certain amounts (i.e., perform analytical procedures).
15. Recalculate significant figures.

16. Review cut-off dates.
17. Examine subsequent events.
18. Make inquiries of client personnel.
19. Obtain written representations from management.
20. Read the minutes of the Board of Directors' meetings and committee meetings of the Board.
21. Make inquiries of client's attorney.

STANDARDIZED AUDIT PROCEDURES

T	**TRACING**	Follow transaction from supporting documentation to accounting records.
R	**RECONCILE**	Account for difference between two amounts.
A	**ANALYZE**	Search for unexpected trends or the lack of expected deviations.
F	**FOOT**	Recompute column totals within financial statements and individual accounts.
I	**INSPECT**	Physically confirm the existence of assets such as stock certificates.
C	**CONFIRM**	Confirmation of certain account balances with third parties.
C	**CONSIDER**	Internal control.
I	**INQUIRE**	Make inquiries of client management and employees.
V	**VOUCHING**	Examine documentation that supports entries in the accounting records.
I	**INVESTIGATE**	Look for cause of detected fraud discovered in testing.
C	**COUNT**	Physical count of inventories on hand and fixed assets owned.
S	**SUBSEQUENT EVENTS**	Events occurring after the year-end that may have an effect on the financial statements.

C. Guidelines for Tracing or Vouching

Exam questions frequently require determination of the purpose of tracing or vouching given documents through the accounting process.

1. **Tracing From Source Documents to Ledgers** Provides evidence of **completeness** (i.e., all transactions are recorded and the ledger accounts are not understated). This is indicated by the upward arrow in Exhibit 2.

2. **Vouching From Ledgers to Source Documents** Provides evidence of **existence** (i.e., all transactions summarized in the ledgers actually occurred, the ledgers contain no unsupported entries, and ledger balances are not overstated). This is indicated by the downward arrow in Exhibit 2.

EXHIBIT 2 ♦ GUIDELINES FOR TRACING OR VOUCHING

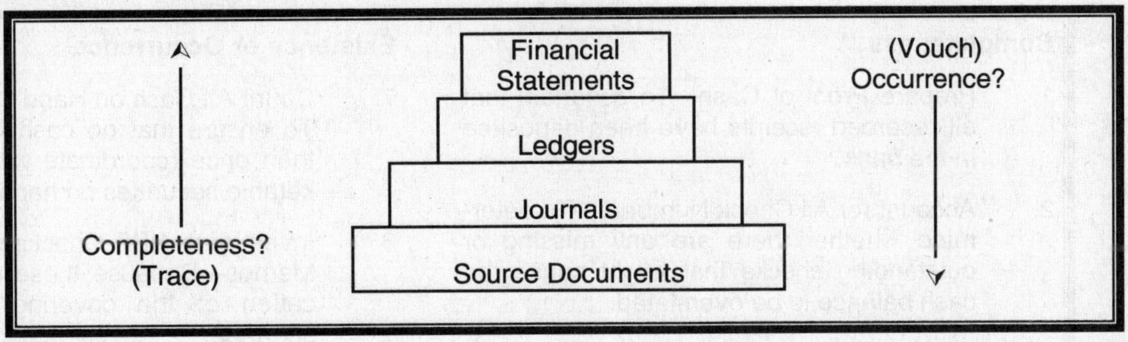

III. AUDIT PROGRAMS

A. CASH

The audit procedures in Exhibit 3 are generally performed during the audit of cash accounts to obtain supporting evidence of the objectives.

EXAMPLE 1 ♦ KITING

> Allen Richards is the bookkeeper for Diversified Inc. Diversified has two bank accounts—one in the First Federal Bank and another in the Fourth National Bank. On a hot tip from Allen's investment broker, Allen writes himself a $5,000 check on the First Federal account, makes no entry, and purchases stock in STCG Inc. Shortly thereafter, STCG Inc. is subjected to SEC investigation and all trading in its stock is frozen. As the end of the year nears, Allen's predicament remains unchanged. To cover the defalcation, Allen writes a $5,000 check on the Fourth National account on December 31 and deposits it in the First Federal account on the same day. Furthermore, he makes no entry in the cash disbursements journal and fails to list the check as outstanding on the year-end bank reconciliation. Since the check will not show up as a decrease in the Fourth National account until it clears, that account will still reflect the same account balance without the check deduction, and the First Bank will reflect the $5,000 deposited as of December 31. The money "appears" to be in both accounts, when in reality, only due to the delay in transaction posting, it is not.

1. **KITING** This is the practice whereby an employee who is embezzling funds makes a transfer of funds from a bank account in one bank to a bank account in another bank near the end of the period. The transfer is effected through the use of a check and, therefore, does not show up as a withdrawal from the first bank until the check clears. It is listed as a deposit in transit on the receiving bank's books but not as an outstanding check on the disbursing bank's books. As a result, the overall cash balance is temporarily overstated at the balance sheet date and the embezzlement is not detected.

2. **AUDIT OBJECTIVES' FOCUS** To ensure (a) there are adequate internal control policies and procedures over cash, (b) all cash that should be in the custody of the client is (existence), (c) all of the cash in custody of the client is properly recorded (completeness), and (d) the cash in the custody of the client is properly disclosed in the financial statements.

3. **SUBFUNCTIONS** Subfunctions for cash include (a) accounts receivable, (b) accounts payable, (c) cash sales, and (d) general ledger accounting.

EXHIBIT 3 ♦ SAMPLE PROGRAM FOR CASH

Completeness

1. Prepare Proof of Cash—To ascertain that all recorded receipts have been deposited in the bank.
2. Account for All Check Numbers—To determine whether there are any missing or outstanding checks that might cause the cash balance to be overstated.
3. Obtain and Review or Prepare a Year-End Bank Reconciliation—To accurately determine the client's actual cash position at the close of the period.
4. Obtain a Bank Cutoff Statement Directly From the Bank—To ascertain whether the items on the year-end reconciliation have cleared the bank and, therefore, were valid. Bank cutoff statements are generally requested for one to two weeks after year end. After finishing this procedure, the cutoff bank statement is given to the client. This procedure is useful for detecting kiting between account balances

Obligations and Rights

5. Investigate Any Checks Made to Cash or Bearer—To determine the propriety of the disbursement.

Valuation or Allocation

6. Trace a Sample of Entries in the Cash Receipts Journal to the A/R Subsidiary Ledger, Duplicate Deposit Ticket, and General Ledger—In order to determine whether the cash is accurately stated.

Existence or Occurrence

7. Count All Cash on Hand Simultaneously—To ensure that no cash is counted more than once (coordinate with count of marketable securities on hand).

8 Investigate NSF Checks and Other Debit Memos—Because these may be an indication of the covering up of a cash shortage.

9. Prepare a Schedule of Bank Transfers—Around year-end to help detect kiting.
10. Confirm the Existence of Year-End Bank Balances—Of the following:
    a. Amounts on deposit
    b. Direct liabilities
    c. Contingent liabilities on notes discounted
    d. Other direct or contingent liabilities
    e. Other security agreements

Statement Presentation and Disclosure

11. Determine If Any Cash Is Restricted—So that the restricted balance is properly classified on the balance sheet, and requirements of compensating balance agreements are properly disclosed

B. ACCOUNTS RECEIVABLE AND SALES

The procedures (and the purpose behind each procedure) in Exhibit 4 are generally performed during the audit of accounts receivable and sales to obtain supporting evidence of the objectives.

1. **AUDIT OBJECTIVES' FOCUS** To ascertain: (a) adequate internal control policies and procedures exist; (b) all sales and receivables that should be recorded are properly recorded (completeness); (c) only sales and receivables that should be recorded are recorded (existence); and (d) accounts receivable are presented at approximate realizable value.

2. **SUBFUNCTIONS** After the audit objectives for an audit area are specified, they should be broken into subfunctions. For accounts receivable and sales, possible subfunctions include (a) credit granting, (b) billing, (c) shipping, (d) cash receipts, (e) detailed ledger bookkeeping, and (f) general ledger accounting.

3. BROAD OUTLINE OF AN AUDIT PROGRAM FOR ACCOUNTS RECEIVABLE AND SALES

a. INTERIM WORK Possibilities include (1) obtaining understanding of the internal control (may include walking through a transaction, inquiry, and observation), and (2) performing tests of control as to operating effectiveness.

b. YEAR-END WORK: SALES (1) Analytical procedures (including ratio and trend analysis), (2) review sales cutoff and consignment sales, and (3) review sales returns and allowances and sales discounts.

c. YEAR-END WORK: ACCOUNTS RECEIVABLE (1) Review aged trial balance, (2) confirm accounts receivable by positive and/or negative confirmations, and (3) review bad debts allowance and expense.

4. CONFIRMATION OF ACCOUNTS RECEIVABLE (AU 330, SAS 67) Confirmation of accounts receivable is a generally accepted auditing procedure (although not a standard). Therefore, if the procedure is not performed, the auditor must document the reason.

a. AUDITOR'S RESPONSIBILITY Confirmation requests should always be mailed by the auditor. In addition, the auditor's firm should receive all requests directly. These procedures diminish the possibility that the confirmation requests could be altered by the client, either during the mailing process or upon receipt.

b. SUBJECT OF CONFIRMATION Confirmations may deal with the **account balance** or with **individual items**. The latter are useful when the customer may not be in a position to confirm the total account balance owed to the client. This occurs frequently when sales or contracts are made with governmental agencies.

c. EXTENT AND METHOD OF CONFIRMATION The extent and method of confirmation is determined by the auditor after considering (a) the effectiveness of internal control; (b) the possibility of disputes, inaccuracies, and fraud in the accounts; (c) the expected degree of **cooperation** by the debtor; (d) the probability that the debtor will be **able** to confirm the amounts involved; and (e) the **materiality** of the amounts involved. A combination of the two forms may be appropriate, with the positive form used for large balances and the negative form for small balances.

d. POSITIVE FORM OF CONFIRMATION REQUEST Requests a response concerning whether or not the customer is in agreement with the client's records. A positive request may also be **blank**, requesting the recipient to indicate balances and furnish other information. The positive form is **preferable** when individual account balances are relatively large or when there is reason to believe that a substantial number of the accounts may be disputed or that errors and/or fraud exist.

- Nonresponse—Generally requires the use of follow-up requests such as additional mailings or telephone calls. In cases where there is still no response to requests dealing with significant accounts, alternative procedures should be used to obtain adequate evidence. These additional procedures may involve the examination of documents such as subsequent cash receipts, sales invoices, and shipping documents.

e. NEGATIVE FORM OF CONFIRMATION REQUEST Requests a response only in cases where the customer disagrees with the stated balance. The negative form is useful when the assessed level of control risk is low, when a large number of small balances are involved, and when the auditor has no reason to believe the persons receiving the requests are unlikely to give them consideration.

- Nonresponse—An inherent weakness in the negative form is that a nonresponse does not necessarily mean that the balance is accurate. Rather, a nonresponse may have nothing to do with the correctness or incorrectness of the balance. The response form may simply have not been returned by the debtor or may have been lost enroute from the debtor to the auditor.

5. **LAPPING** This is one of the most common types of fraud. It involves the delay in the recording of a cash receipt in order to cover up an existing shortage in the actual cash on hand. Lapping is made possible through either bad internal control (i.e., having the same employee handle both the cash and the accounts receivable records) or collusion. In order to detect a lapping scheme, the auditor must compare the name, amounts, and dates shown on the customers' remittance advices with entries in the cash receipts journal and the related deposit slips.

EXAMPLE 2 ♦ LAPPING

> Georgia Thomas is the bookkeeper for Farley Fabrics (a retail cloth distributor), and her duties consist of receiving the checks from the customers and recording the payments in the A/R subsidiary ledger. On January 8th, Georgia hears the president talk about a one-time purchase of a unique fabric by Colin's Casuals. She also hears that Colin's is going to make a $640 purchase. The next day, Colin's Casuals submits its order for that $640 of fabric. With all of this in mind, Georgia embezzles $640 of that day's payments received from Mama's Moo Moos and Jabba's Jammies (both of whom are regular customers of Farley). Georgia makes no entries in the accounts. Five days later, Colin's Casuals pays its bill, and Georgia credits the payments to Mama's and Jabba's accounts. Colin does no more business with Farley and, at the end of the year, Georgia writes off Colin's receivable as uncollectible.

EXHIBIT 4 ♦ SAMPLE PROGRAM FOR A/R AND SALES

Completeness

1. Compare a Sample of Shipping Documents to the Related Sales Invoices—For the purpose of discovering orders that have been shipped but not billed. (Cutoff tests should be performed both at the confirmation date and balance sheet date, if different.)
2. Reconcile a Sample of Cash Register Tapes and Sales Tickets With the Sales Journals—So that evidence is gathered that shows that all sales have been recorded—and recorded accurately.
3. Perform Analytical Procedures—For example, a gross profit test, to determine that all sales have been recorded and classified correctly. Investigate any unexpected fluctuations.

Obligations and Rights

4. Review Sales Discount Procedures and Documentation—To determine that discounts were granted only for payments received within the discount period.
5. Vouch Debits in Individual A/R Accounts to Sales Invoices—In order to determine whether the sale actually occurred.
6. Review Sales and Receipts Occurring Near Year-End—In order to ascertain that such transactions were recorded in the proper time period and were valid transactions.

(continued on next page)

Valuation or Allocation

7. Test Foot the Sales Journal and Reconcile With Postings to the General Ledger—To find out if the sales figures were brought forward accurately.

8. Vouch Debit Entries in the Allowance for Doubtful Accounts to the Individual Accounts and Original Write-Off Authorizations—So that it can be determined that such write-offs were properly reflected in the accounts and were authorized.

9. Prepare or Obtain an Aged A/R Schedule—(a) To help identify accounts that should be written off, (b) to determine the reasonableness of the bad-debt expense and allowance for doubtful accounts, and (c) to aid the confirmation of A/R.

10. Investigate Any Unusual Items, Transactions, or Amounts—To determine the substance behind, and treatment of, such items, transactions, and amounts.

11. Recalculate and Review Bad-Debt Expense and Allowance—For reasonableness of expense and adequacy of the allowance.

12. Examine cash receipts after the balance sheet date to provide evidence of collectibility at the balance sheet date.

Existence or Occurrence

13. Examine All Aspects of a Sample of Sales Transactions—In order to determine whether the internal control procedures are being applied properly (i.e., perform tests of controls directed toward operating effectiveness). This procedure includes the following:

a. Comparing the sales invoice with the customer's purchase order

b. Checking for proper credit approval

c. Comparing prices on sales invoice with those on price list. Ascertaining the propriety of discounts granted to purchasers

d. Recomputing extensions and footings

e. Checking the recording in the sales journal and the posting of the sale in the A/R subsidiary ledger

14. Confirm A/R on a Test Basis—To verify the existence and accuracy of the account balances and that the receivables are the rights of the company.

Statement Presentation and Disclosure

15. Review Loan Agreements—For pledging of accounts and agreements, for any factoring of accounts, and for disclosure purposes.

C. INVENTORY

The audit procedures in Exhibit 5 are typically performed during the audit of the inventory account to obtain supporting evidence of the objectives.

1. **AUDIT OBJECTIVES' FOCUS** To ascertain (a) the inventory exists and the client owns it (existence and rights), (b) it is priced correctly, (c) the quantities shown are reasonable (rights), (d) the computations used to arrive at the inventory dollar amounts are accurate (valuation), and (e) there is adequate disclosure in the financial statements.

2. **SUBFUNCTIONS** Subfunctions for inventory include (a) purchasing, (b) receiving, (c) storing, (d) processing, (e) shipping, (f) detailed bookkeeping, and (g) general ledger accounting.

3. **EVIDENCE FOR INVENTORIES (AU 331)** The observation of the taking of the inventory is a generally accepted auditing procedure (although not a standard). Therefore, if an observation is not performed, the auditor must document the reason.

   a. **PERIODIC INVENTORY** When the client determines its inventory quantities entirely by means of a physical count at or near the balance sheet date, the auditor ordinarily must be present at the count. The auditor should use suitable observations, tests, and inquiries to become satisfied that the method of accounting for inventory is effective and that the client's claims as to the quantities and physical condition are reliable.

b. **Perpetual Inventory System** When a good perpetual inventory system is maintained in which the client periodically compares the inventory records with the physical counts, the auditor should observe the counting and comparing. However, this can be done either during the period (assuming an adequate system of internal control over inventory and the assessed level of control risk is low) or at or after the end of the period.

c. **Advanced Methods** Some companies have developed highly effective inventory methods (using statistical sampling) that make annual counts of each item of inventory unnecessary. In these cases, the auditor must be present at such partial countings as considered necessary. The auditor must also be satisfied that the inventory method will produce results that are comparable to those that would be obtained by an annual count of physical inventory. If the inventory plan is based on statistical sampling, the auditor must be satisfied that the plan has statistical validity and is properly applied, and that the resulting precision and reliability are statistically reasonable.

d. **Sufficient Audit Evidence** Tests of the accounting records are not sufficient evidence as to current inventories. Rather, the auditor will always have to make or observe some physical counts of the inventory, apply appropriate tests to the intervening transactions, and review any client counts and procedures relating to the physical inventory.

e. **Auditor Has Not Audited Prior Inventories** When auditing financial statements covering the current period and one or more periods for which the auditor has not observed or made some physical counts of prior inventories, the auditor must be satisfied as to the prior period's inventory with appropriate tests. These tests might include tests of prior transactions, review of prior record counts, and gross profit tests. An example of this type of situation would be the first audit of a new client who has opening inventory.

f. **Inventories Held in Public Warehouses** In some cases, inventories will be held in public warehouses or by other outside custodians. In these situations, direct written confirmation from the custodian is acceptable when the inventory is not material. When the amounts are substantial, relative to current or total assets, the auditor should undertake one or more of the following procedures: (a) test the owner's control procedures for investigating the warehouse and evaluating its performance; (b) obtain an independent accountant's report on the warehouse's control procedures relevant to custody of goods and, if applicable, pledging of receipts, or apply alternative procedures at the warehouse to gain reasonable assurance that information received from the warehouse is reliable; (c) observe physical counts wherever reasonable and practicable; and finally (d) obtain confirmations from lenders in cases where warehouse receipts have been pledged as collateral.

g. **Outside Inventory-Taking Firm (AU 9508)** Some companies (e.g., retail stores, hospitals, and automobile dealers) use outside firms of nonaccountants who specialize in the taking of physical inventories to count, list, price, and subsequently compute the total dollar amount of the inventory. While the use of an outside firm will ordinarily reduce the work, it is not, by itself, a satisfactory substitute for the auditor's observation or taking of physical counts. In this situation, the auditor's primary concern will be to evaluate the effectiveness of the outside firm's procedures. Therefore, the auditor would (a) examine its inventory program, (b) observe its procedures and controls, (c) make or observe some physical counts of the inventory, (d) recompute calculations of the submitted inventory on a test basis, and (e) apply appropriate tests to the intervening transactions.

EXHIBIT 5 ♦ SAMPLE PROGRAM FOR INVENTORY

Completeness

1. Account for the Numerical Sequence of Inventory Purchase Requisitions—To ascertain that none are missing, thereby helping to assure that no unauthorized purchases were made.
2. Trace a Sample of Receiving Reports for Inventory to the Perpetual Inventory Records—To determine that all shipments were properly reflected in the accounts. (This cutoff test must be performed at the inventory observation date and at the balance sheet date, if different.)
3. Perform Analytical Procedures on Cost of Goods Sold—To determine if significant fluctuations exist that would necessitate audit investigation; perform procedures to test turnover and compare gross margin of current year with that of prior year to test for overstatement or understatement.
4. Account for Inventory Tags and Count Sheets—To verify the inventory has completely been accounted for.
5. Trace Test Counts of Inventory Items From the Floor to the Client's Inventory Listing—To ensure all items of inventory have been counted and included in the total inventory balance.

Obligations and Rights

6. Vouch a Sample of Inventory Requisitions to Customer or Department Order—So that evidence is obtained that all requisitions are valid.
7. Review Purchase and Sales Cutoffs—To ascertain that ending inventory is properly valued and that the inventory transactions are recorded in the proper time period.
8. Review Inventory on Consignment (as both consignee and consignor)—To determine the inventory actually owned by the client.
9. Confirm Inventory Held at Public Warehouses and With Third Parties—To identify other inventory actually owned by the client.

Valuation or Allocation

10. Test Pricing Method Used by the Client—So that the proper inventory value is attained.
11. Apply Lower-of-Cost-or-Market Rule—So that the proper inventory value and any losses are recognized and disclosed.
12. Perform analytical procedures such as, gross profit percentage calculations, inventory turnover ratios, and number of days sales in inventory ratio analysis.

    In addition, inventory audit procedures for a manufacturing client could include the following:

13. Test Cost Accumulation Process—So that the ending inventory and cost-of-goods-sold are properly valued.
14. Review the Overhead Allocations and Rates—For accuracy when compared with actual experience.
15. Vouch a Sample of Additions to Perpetual Inventory to Supporting Receiving Reports—To assure that the recorded inventory was actually received.

Existence or Occurrence

16. Physical Inventory: Review the Client's Plan for Taking the Physical Inventory—In order to determine whether the necessary information will be obtained.
17. Physical Inventory: Observe the Physical Count—To become satisfied that the counting methods are effective and the client's representations are reliable.
18. Physical Inventory: Trace Client's Physical Counts to Perpetual Records and Inventory Sheets—In order to test the accuracy of the perpetual records.
19. Physical Inventory: Vouch the Validity of the Perpetual Records and Inventory Sheets Against the Physical Count—In order to determine that items in the perpetual records exist and quantities are correct.
20. Physical Inventory: Test Inventory Sheet and Perpetual Record Computation for Clerical Accuracy—Thereby helping to ascertain that the inventory is properly valued and quantities are correct.

(continued on next page)

21. Physical Inventory: Make Random Test Counts—To assure that the counts made by the client are accurate. Test counts of inventory items should also be traced to client's inventory sheets and to client's final inventory compilation report.

Statement Presentation and Disclosure

22. Review Purchase and Sales Commitments—To determine whether there is a need to accrue a loss and disclose its relevant facts.

23. Determine Whether Any Inventory Has Been Pledged—To assure that such facts are properly disclosed in the financial statements.

D. Fixed Assets

The procedures in Exhibit 6 are normally performed during the audit of fixed assets to obtain supporting evidence of the objectives.

1. **Audit Objectives' Focus** To (a) ascertain the adequacy of internal control policies and procedures over fixed assets, (b) verify the existence and ownership of the fixed assets, and (c) ascertain the adequacy of valuation and disclosure of the fixed assets in the financial statements.

2. **Subfunctions** Subfunctions for fixed assets include (a) depreciation, (b) financing, (c) detailed ledger bookkeeping, and (4) general ledger accounting.

Exhibit 6 ♦ Sample Program For Fixed Assets

Completeness

1. Trace—From fixed assets to the plant and equipment subsidiary ledger—To determine that the assets are recorded.

2. Obtain or Prepare an Analysis of the Repair and Maintenance Expense Account—To consider if any items should be classified as capital expenditures.

3. Review Rental Revenue and Property Tax Expense—By obtaining a map of rented and leased property. This procedure will help determine the accuracy of the rental revenue and tax expense accounts by exposing all the client's real property, thereby enabling a thorough evaluation.

Obligations and Rights

4. Verify the Client's Ownership of the Assets—By examining titles to the fixed assets.

5. Review Lease Agreements—For determining whether assets should be capitalized.

Valuation or Allocation

6. Reconcile the Plant and Equipment Subsidiary Ledger With the General Ledger — To determine that the accounting for the plant and equipment transactions was consistent.

7. Recalculate—The accounting for retirements of fixed assets.

8. Review Depreciation Methods—For consistency with prior periods.

9. Review Useful Lives—For appropriateness and consistency with prior periods.

10. Recalculate—Depreciation computations.

Existence or Occurrence

11. Vouch—From the plant and equipment subsidiary ledger to the fixed assets—To determine that the assets actually exist.

12. Vouch Acquisitions—To purchase orders or contracts approved by appropriate personnel.

Statement Presentation and Disclosure

13. Review Loan Agreements—To verify any loans collateralized by property or equipment for proper disclosure.

E. INVESTMENTS

The audit procedures in Exhibit 7 are generally performed during the audit of long-term investments to obtain supporting evidence of the objectives.

1. **AUDIT OBJECTIVES' FOCUS** To (a) ascertain the adequacy of internal control policies and procedures over long-term investments; (b) ascertain whether the investments are accounted for in conformity with GAAP; (c) ascertain the adequacy of financial statement disclosure of such investments; (d) determine whether a loss in value of such investments should be considered as temporary or permanent; and (e) obtain evidence as to the existence of securities by inspection and/or confirmation.

2. **SUBFUNCTIONS** Subfunctions for long-term investments include (a) financing, (b) cash, (c) detailed ledger bookkeeping, and (d) general ledger accounting.

3. **EVIDENCE FOR LONG-TERM INVESTMENTS (AU 332.04-.05)** The auditor is concerned with gathering sufficient competent evidence pertaining to the existence, ownership, and cost of long-term investments, as well as their carrying amounts, or valuation, on the balance sheet.

   a. Evidence of the existence, ownership, and cost of long-term investments can be obtained from the accounting records and documents of the investor. In the case of securities, such evidence can be corroborated through inspection or, when appropriate, confirmation from an independent custodian. In the case of loans, bonds, and similar debt obligations, evidence should be corroborated through written confirmation from the debtor or trustee.

   b. Evidence of the carrying amount of long-term investments and income and losses attributable to such investments can be obtained from the following sources:

      (1) **AUDITED FINANCIAL STATEMENTS** Generally provide sufficient evidential matter, when the statements have been audited by an independent auditor, regarding equity in underlying net assets and results of operation of investee, as well as corroboration of investments in bonds and other debt instruments.

      (2) **UNAUDITED FINANCIAL STATEMENTS** Provide insufficient information. The investor's auditor may utilize the investee's auditor to apply auditing procedures to unaudited statements, thereby obtaining sufficient evidence.

      (3) **MARKET QUOTATIONS** If the market is reasonably broad and active, such quotations ordinarily constitute sufficient competent evidence as to the current market value of unrestricted securities.

      (4) **PUBLISHED DIVIDEND RECORDS** These provide the strongest evidence supporting dividends earned on marketable equity securities.

EXHIBIT 7 ♦ SAMPLE PROGRAM FOR INVESTMENTS

Completeness

1. Obtain or Prepare an Account Analysis for the Long-Term Investment and Related Revenue or Loss Accounts—This procedure allows the auditor to
   a. Establish the accuracy of the individual debits and credits occurring during the year, and
   b. Prove the validity of the year-end balance in the accounts.
2. Perform Analytical Procedures—By comparing dividends, interest and other investment income with those of prior years to ascertain the reasonableness of the completeness of recorded investment income. Calculate the percentage of accrued investment income to total investments and estimate total accrued income based on current investments.

Obligations and Rights

3. Verify Purchases and Sales of Securities During the Year and For a Short Period Subsequent to the Balance Sheet Date—This procedure allows the auditor to determine whether all of the securities are accounted for in the accounting records.

Valuation or Allocation

4. Investigate Method of Accounting for Equity Securities—To determine whether such securities should be accounted for under the SFAS 115, SFAS 124, SFAS 133, or the equity method.
5. Determine FMV of Securities on Balance Sheet Date—This procedure provides evidence as to the proper carrying amount of debt and equity securities accounted for under SFAS 115, SFAS 124, or SFAS 133, and may also be necessary for disclosure purposes.
6. Verify the Interest Earned on Bonds—By recomputing the interest earned on the basis of the face amount, interest rate, and period held.
7. Examine Financial Statements of Investee Companies—To determine gains and losses from investments in equity securities, as well as the carrying amounts of securities accounted for under the equity method.
8. Test calculations of premium and discount amortization for accuracy.
9. Impairment—The auditor must consider management's evaluation relating to the existence of an other-than-temporary impairment.

Existence or Occurrence

10. Inspection—Inspect securities on hand and compare serial numbers with those shown in previous year's working papers. This procedure will help identify any undisclosed sales or purchases of investments. (Coordinate with cash count to prevent substitution.)
11. Obtain Confirmation of Securities From Third-Party Custodian—In order to provide evidence as to the existence of such investments.

Statement Presentation and Disclosure

12. Examine Financial Presentation of Long-Term Investments—To determine whether GAAP is followed.
13. Inquiry—Inquire of management and review loan documents as to possible pledging of securities for appropriate disclosure purposes.
14. Evaluate—The auditor should evaluate whether management's stated intent to buy and hold an investment is supported by actual activities and the entity's ability to do so.

4. **THE EQUITY METHOD OF ACCOUNTING (AU 332.06-.15)** APB Opinion 18 requires the use of the equity method by an investor whose investment in voting stock gives it the ability to exercise significant influence over operating and financial policies of the investee. If the investor owns 50 percent or more of the investee's voting stock, the ability to exercise significant influence is presumed to exist. The auditor must be satisfied as to the correctness of the accounting method adopted by the investor (i.e., cost or equity method).

5. **CLASSIFICATION** SAS 94, *Derivative Instruments, Hedging Activities, and Auditing Investments in Securities*, revises guidance on auditing investments to conform to SFAS 115, 124, and 133. The auditor must determine whether investments are accounted for in conformity with GAAP. Some investments require cost or equity methods of accounting. Some entities follow specialized industry accounting policies. The auditor normally obtains written management representations concerning the proper classification of securities. The procedures that auditors perform to obtain evidential matter concerning investments varies depending on the types of investments involved and the assessment of audit risk for a particular engagement.

6. **VALUATION** The auditor should be aware that GAAP requires the use of several possible methods including cost, equity, or fair value. For the vast majority of instruments, GAAP calls for the fair value valuation model. Also, GAAP may call for recognition of gains and/or losses prior to realization.

   (a) The accounting model will differ depending on the type of security, the nature of the transaction, management's objectives related to the security, and the type of entity. For derivatives, the accounting for the unrealized gain or loss will depend upon whether hedge accounting is appropriate and, if so, the type of hedge. For marketable securities accounted for in accordance with the provisions of SFAS 115, the accounting will depend upon management's investment intention (e.g., trading, available-for-sale, held-to-maturity).

   (b) When quoted prices are not readily available, a significant amount of judgment will be needed to properly evaluate the sufficiency of the evidential matter for the valuation assertion. For securities which are not subject to mark-to-market accounting, there is the additional issue of determining whether an impairment loss exists which should be recognized. This involves judgment since the auditor is compelled to make a determination as to whether a loss is considered to be other than temporary which necessitates an estimation of the outcome of future events.

F. ACCOUNTS PAYABLE, PURCHASES, AND OTHER LIABILITIES

The audit procedures in Exhibit 8 are commonly performed during the audit of the A/P, purchasing, and other liabilities accounts to obtain supporting evidence of the objectives.

1. **AUDIT OBJECTIVES' FOCUS** To ensure: (a) there are adequate internal control policies and procedures over payables and purchases; (b) all transactions that should be recorded are recorded (completeness); (c) those transactions that are recorded are recorded properly (valuation); and (d) the financial statement presentation is adequate (disclosure and obligation).

2. **SUBFUNCTIONS** Subfunctions for payables and purchases include (a) purchasing, (b) receiving, (c) payment, (d) detailed ledger bookkeeping, and (e) general ledger accounting.

EXHIBIT 8 ♦ SAMPLE PROGRAM FOR SHORT-TERM LIABILITIES

Completeness

1. Perform Search for Unrecorded Liabilities—To ascertain that all payables have been recorded in the proper period. This search is performed, at the balance sheet date, in the following areas:
   a. Unmatched invoices and unbilled receiving reports
   b. Significant payments subsequent to the end of the period may indicate liabilities that existed at the end of the period
   c. Invoices received after the end of the period may have been for goods received at or before the end of the period
   d. Customer deposits recorded as credits to A/R
   e. Unbilled professional fees at the end of the period under audit
   f. Perform inventory receiving cutoff test
2. Perform Analytical Procedures—To assess the reasonableness of balances. Compare the average number of days purchases in accounts payable at the end of the current year to prior years. Compare purchases divided by payables to payables divided by total current liabilities for the current and prior years. Compare payables and purchases to budgeted or forecasted amounts.

Obligations and Rights

3. Vouch—The paid check and invoice from the vendor to the receiving report to determine if any payments were made for goods that were not received.
4. Review the Cutoff of Purchases, Returns, and Disbursements—To determine that transactions are recorded in the proper periods.

Valuation or Allocation

5. Obtain a listing of A/P and reconcile with general ledger A/P balance.
6. Recalculate the Extensions and Footings on Customer Invoices—To determine whether such invoices were accurately priced and computed.
7. Trace Vendor Invoices to Voucher Register and Checks to Check Register—To determine that all payables and related disbursements have been properly recorded.
8. Foot Voucher Register and Trace to General Ledger—To substantiate the entries in the general ledger.
9. Reclassify debit balances as receivables and review for collectibility.
10. Recalculate Other (Accrued) Liabilities—To test computations for reasonableness and consistent treatment when compared to prior years. Examples include property and income taxes, commissions, profit-sharing and pension plans, and warranties.

Existence or Occurrence

11. Vouch Purchase Requisitions of a Sample of Purchase Orders—To determine if any unrequested purchases were made.
12. Confirm—Accounts payable balances with vendors, although not a generally accepted auditing procedure, confirm in cases of suspected fraud, sloppy or missing records, or suspected understatements.
13. Inspect copies of notes and other agreements.

Statement Presentation and Disclosure

14. Review Purchase Commitments—To determine whether there are any losses to be accrued and/or disclosed.

G. PAYROLL

The audit procedures in Exhibit 9 are usually performed during the audit of the payroll accounts to obtain supporting evidence of the objectives.

1. **AUDIT OBJECTIVES' FOCUS** To (a) ascertain the adequacy of internal control over payroll, (b) verify that all employees included in the payroll actually exist and work for the client (existence), (c) verify the accuracy of the payroll computations (valuation), and (d) ascertain the adequacy of disclosure in the financial statements.

2. **SUBFUNCTIONS** Subfunctions for payroll include (a) personnel, (b) production, (c) detailed ledger bookkeeping, and (d) general ledger accounting.

EXHIBIT 9 ♦ SAMPLE PROGRAM FOR PAYROLL

Completeness

1. Review Time Reports and Piecework or Commission Records—To determine that such reports and records agree with production records.

Obligations and Rights

2. Verify Payroll Deductions—To ascertain that they are computed accurately and that they agree with withholding authorizations.
3. Review Accounting for Unclaimed Wages—To ascertain that they are being properly classified.
4. Examine Payroll Cutoff—To determine that wages were reported in the proper time period.
5. Analyze Officers' Compensation—To determine that salaries agree with contracts, minutes of directors' meeting, or other authorization.

Valuation or Allocation

6. Recompute Payroll Register—To determine its accuracy.
7. Vouch Items From the Payroll Register to Employee Time Cards—To verify employees worked the number of hours for which pay was computed.
8. Observe the Use of the Time Clocks by the Employees—To be assured that each employee punches only one time card.
9. Compare Payroll Expenses With Prior Periods and Investigate Differences—So as to determine the accuracy and validity of the expense.
10. Perform Analytical Procedures—To determine reasonableness of balances. Calculate ratios to determine whether accounts relate to each other in the manner expected. If relationships vary significantly from expected results, additional substantive tests of account balances may be necessary.
11. Review the results of audits of related pension and profit-sharing plans.

Existence or Occurrence

12. Review Payroll Checks and Bank Reconciliations—To determine that all checks were cashed.
13. Review the Payroll Register—To determine if all payroll transactions were recorded.
14. Examine Personnel Records—To determine that a name, salary rate, and job position all exist for each employee on the payroll.
15. On a Surprise Basis, Observe the Distribution of the Paychecks—To determine that every name on the company payroll is that of a bona fide employee presently working.

Statement Presentation and Disclosure

16. Review Related Tax Expense and Liability, Unemployment Insurance, and Other Payroll Deduction Accounts—To determine accuracy and proper classification in the financial statements.

H. Long-Term Liabilities

The audit procedures in Exhibit 10 are normally performed during the audit of long-term liabilities to obtain supporting evidence of the objectives.

1. **Audit Objectives' Focus** To (a) ascertain the adequacy of internal control policies and procedures over long-term liabilities; (b) verify that all long-term liabilities are recorded properly (existence and obligation); (c) verify that interest expense is correctly computed and that other contractual obligations are satisfied (valuation); and (d) ascertain the adequacy of disclosure of long-term liabilities in the financial statements.

2. **Subfunctions** Subfunctions for long-term liabilities include (a) financing, (b) fixed assets, (c) cash, (d) detailed ledger bookkeeping, and (e) general ledger accounting.

Exhibit 10 ♦ Sample Program For Long-Term Liabilities

Completeness

1. Obtain or Prepare an Account Analysis for the Long-Term Debt, Discount, Premium, and Related Interest Accounts—This procedure allows the auditor to
   a. Verify the payment or other disposition of the debt listed as outstanding at the beginning of the period.
   b. Establish the accuracy of the individual debits and credits occurring during the year.
   c. Prove the validity of the year-end balance in the accounts.
2. Perform Analytical Procedures—By comparing current amortization amounts to prior actual and current budgeted amounts. Compare current interest costs to prior actual and current budgeted amounts. Compare current and noncurrent debt obligations to prior actual and current budgeted amounts.
3. Review bank confirmation for indication of loans and other commitments, including any unrecorded debt.

Obligations and Rights

4. Review Cutoff—To determine that transactions recorded at the end of the year are recorded in the proper period.

Valuation or Allocation

5. Verify Interest Computations and Amortization of Premiums and/or Discounts—To determine whether such amounts were properly and accurately disclosed. This procedure also aids in the discovery of undisclosed liabilities.

Existence or Occurrence

6. Confirm with the creditor the transactions of the period and compliance with the contractual provisions. This procedure provides evidence that the transactions actually occurred and that the transactions were properly carried out (e.g., deposits into a sinking fund).

Statement Presentation and Disclosure

7. Review the Contractual Provisions and Supporting Documents of Long-Term Debt—To determine that details of the debt instruments correspond to those in the account analysis and that such details are accurately disclosed in the financial statements. Supporting documents include note and loan agreements, bond indentures, and lease agreements.

I. Stockholders' Equity

The audit procedures in Exhibit 11 are normally performed during the audit of stockholders' equity to obtain supporting evidence of the objectives.

1. **Audit Objectives' Focus** To (a) ascertain the adequacy of internal control over stock transactions, stock certificates, and receipts payments; (b) verify that the transactions are properly authorized and comply with applicable regulations; (c) verify that the transactions are recorded in conformity with GAAP; and (d) ascertain the adequacy of *disclosure* of stockholders' equity in the financial statements.

2. **Subfunctions** Subfunctions for stockholders' equity include (a) financing, (b) cash, (c) detailed ledger bookkeeping, and (d) general ledger accounting.

Exhibit 11 ♦ Sample Program For Stockholders' Equity

Completeness

1. Obtain or Prepare an Account Analysis for All Accounts—To outline the historical picture of corporate capital and any changes to corporate capital.
2. Account for All Certificate Numbers—To determine that no unauthorized securities were issued during the period.
3. Perform Analytical Procedures—By computing the return on stockholders' equity, the book value per share, and the dividend payout ratio and comparing them to those of prior years. Compare current year dividend amounts and balances for common and preferred stock and additional paid-in capital to those of prior years.

Obligations and Rights

4. Vouch All Retirements of Securities—To ascertain that no certificates were fraudulently reissued.
5. Review Compliance With Stock Option Plans and Other Restrictions on Capital Stocks—This procedure allows the auditor to do the following:
   a. Determine the adequacy of disclosure with respect to these arrangements.
   b. Verify the number of shares issued during the year through conversion or exercise of convertible stocks and bonds, stock options, and stock warrants.
   c. Ascertain whether the shares held in reserve exceed the shares authorized but unissued.
   d. Determine that the call provisions of preferred stock are accurately carried out.
6. Review Minutes of Board of Directors' Meetings—To verify that stock and dividend transactions have been properly authorized.

Valuation or Allocation

7. Account for All Proceeds From Security Issues—To determine whether the transactions were accounted for in accordance with underwriting contracts, state stock issuance permits, and SEC registration statements.
8. Analyze Treasury Stock Transactions—To determine that such transactions were properly authorized and recorded in conformity with GAAP.
9. Reconcile Subsidiary Ledger With General Ledger Control Account—To establish the amount of outstanding stock and to rule out the possibility of an overissuance of shares.
10. Reconcile Dividend Distributions and Verify Dividend Calculations—To ascertain the accurate dividend amount and to discover any declared, but yet unpaid, dividends.

Existence or Occurrence

11. Confirm Shares Outstanding With Registrar—To ascertain whether the corporate records are accurate and that stock is issued in accordance with the authorization of the board of directors and the articles of incorporation.

Statement Presentation and Disclosure

12. Analyze the Retained Earnings Account—To determine whether it is accurately disclosed in the financial statements, and determine the amount of any restrictions on retained earnings that result from loans, other agreements, or state law.
13. Analyze Prior-Period Adjustments—To ascertain whether they are valid and are treated properly in the financial statements and determine the amount of any restrictions on retained earnings that result from loans, other agreements, or state law.

J. ACCOUNTING ESTIMATES (AU 342)

1. **AUDIT OBJECTIVES' FOCUS** To ensure (a) all accounting estimates that could be material to the financial statements have been developed, (b) the estimates are reasonable, and (c) the estimates are in conformity with GAAP and are properly disclosed.

   a. Accounting estimates are used when the measurement of some amounts or the valuations of some accounts is uncertain pending the outcome of future events.

   b. Estimates are also used when relevant data concerning events that have already occurred cannot be accumulated on a timely, cost-effective basis.

2. **DEVELOPING ACCOUNTING ESTIMATES** Management is responsible for establishing the process for preparing accounting estimates. Generally this consists of the following:

   a. Identifying situations that require accounting estimates

   b. Identifying relevant factors

   c. Accumulating relevant, sufficient, and reliable data on which to base the estimate

   d. Developing assumptions based on management's judgment of the most likely circumstances and events

   e. Determining estimated amounts based on the assumptions

   f. Determining the estimate is presented in conformity with applicable accounting principles and that disclosure is adequate

3. **INTERNAL CONTROL** Internal control may reduce the risk of material misstatements of accounting estimates. Some relevant features of internal control include the following:

   a. Management communication of the need for proper accounting estimates

   b. Accumulation of relevant, sufficient, and reliable data on which to base an accounting estimate

   c. Preparation of estimates by qualified personnel

   d. Adequate review and approval of accounting estimates by appropriate levels of authority

   e. Comparison of prior accounting estimates with subsequent results to assess the reliability of the process used to develop estimates

   f. Consideration by management of whether the resulting accounting estimate is consistent with the operational plans of the entity

4. **SAMPLE AUDIT PROCEDURES**

   a. To determine whether management has identified all accounting estimates that could be material to the financial statements, the auditor should evaluate information regarding the following: changes made or planned in the entity's business; changes in the method of accumulating information; litigation, claims, and assessments; minutes of meetings; and regulatory or examination reports.

b. The auditor must evaluate the reasonableness of accounting estimates, and consider them with an attitude of professional skepticism. The auditor should understand how management develops estimates. The auditor should develop an independent expectation of the estimate based on knowledge of the entity and its industry. The historical experience of the entity in making past estimates should be considered.

c. Management's process of developing accounting estimates should be reviewed and tested. The auditor should consider performing the following procedures:

(1) Identify controls over the preparation of accounting estimates and supporting data that may be useful in the evaluation.

(2) Identify the sources of data and factors that management used and consider whether such data and factors are relevant, reliable, and sufficient for the purpose.

(3) Evaluate whether the assumptions are consistent with each other, the supporting data, historical data, and industry data.

(4) Consider whether changes in business or industry may cause other factors to become significant.

(5) Consider whether there are additional factors that should be evaluated.

(6) Evaluate historical data used to develop assumptions to assess whether data is comparable and consistent with data of the period being audited.

WEB SITES

(Each address has www. as a prefix except WY.)

AK	dced.state.ak.us/occ/pcpa.htm	MT	discoveringmontana.com/dli/bsd
AL	asbpa.state.al.us	NE	nol.org/home/BPA
AZ	accountancy.state.az.us	NV	accountancy.state.nv.us
AR	state.ar.us/asbpa	NH	state.nh.us/accountancy
CA	dca.ca.gov/cba	NC	state.nc.us/cpabd
DC	dcra.org/acct/newboa.shtm	ND	state.nd.us/ndsba
FL	myflorida.com	OK	sta.ok.us/~oab
GU	guam.net/gov/gba	OR	boa.state.or.us/boa.html
ID	state.id.us/boa	SD	state.sd.us/dcr/accountancy
IL	illinois-cpa-exam.com/cpa.htm	TX	tsbpa.state.tx.us
KY	state.ky.us/agencies/boa	UT	commerce.state.ut.us
MD	dllr.state.md.us/license/occprof/account.html	VI	usvi.org/dlca/liscensing/cpa.html
		WV	state.wv.us/wvboa/
MN	boa.state.mn.us	WY	cpaboard.state.wy.us
MS	msbpa.state.ms.us		

These sites are subject to change without notice. Bisk Education assumes no responsibility with regard to address accuracy.

EXAMINATION SERVICES

CPA Examination Services, a division of the National Association of State Boards of Accountancy (NASBA), administers the examination for 25 states. Contact CPA Examination Services at (800) CPA-EXAM (272-3926), (615) 880-4250, or www.nasba.org.

CO	CT	DE	GA	HI	IA	IN	KS	LA	MA	ME	MI	
MO	NJ	NM	NY	OH	PA	PR	RI	SC	TN	VA	VT	WA

Continental Testing Services at (800) 717-1201 administers the examination for WI.

See the **Practical Advice** appendix for more information.

CHAPTER 36—AUDIT PROGRAMS

PROBLEM 36-1 MULTIPLE CHOICE QUESTIONS (100 to 125 minutes)

1. The primary purpose of sending a standard confirmation request to financial institutions with which the client has done business during the year is to
a. Detect kiting activities that may otherwise **not** be discovered.
b. Corroborate information regarding deposit and loan balances.
c. Provide the data necessary to prepare a proof of cash.
d. Request information about contingent liabilities and secured transactions.
(5/93, Aud., #34, 3930)

2. The usefulness of the standard bank confirmation request may be limited because the bank employee who completes the form may
a. Not believe that the bank is obligated to verify confidential information to a third party.
b. Sign and return the form without inspecting the accuracy of the client's bank reconciliation.
c. Not have access to the client's cutoff bank statement.
d. Be unaware of all the financial relationships that the bank has with the client.
(11/95, Aud., #45, 5992)

3. The best primary evidence regarding year-end bank balances is documented in the
a. Standard bank confirmations.
b. Interbank transfer schedule.
c. Bank reconciliations.
d. Bank deposit lead schedule. (Editors, 0146)

4. Which of the following cash transfers results in a misstatement of cash at December 31, 20X1?

Bank Transfer Schedule

	Disbursement		Receipt	
Transfer	Recorded in books	Paid by bank	Recorded in books	Received by bank
a.	12/31/X1	01/04/X2	12/31/X1	12/31/X1
b.	01/04/X2	01/05/X2	12/31/X1	01/04/X2
c.	12/31/X1	01/05/X2	12/31/X1	01/04/X2
d.	01/04/X2	01/11/X2	01/04/X2	01/04/X2

(Editors, 0200)

5. In evaluating the adequacy of the allowance for doubtful accounts, an auditor most likely reviews the entity's aging of receivables to support management's financial statement assertion of
a. Existence or occurrence.
b. Valuation or allocation.
c. Completeness.
d. Rights and obligations. (5/93, Aud., #29, 3925)

6. An auditor's purpose in reviewing credit ratings of customers with delinquent accounts receivable most likely is to obtain evidence concerning management's assertions about
a. Valuation or allocation.
b. Presentation and disclosure.
c. Existence or occurrence.
d. Rights and obligations. (11/94, Aud., #50, 5123)

7. An auditor selects a sample from the file of shipping documents to determine whether invoices were prepared. This test is performed to satisfy the audit objective of
a. Accuracy.
b. Completeness.
c. Existence.
d. Control. (Editors, 9411)

8. An auditor suspects that a client's cashier is misappropriating cash receipts for personal use by lapping customer checks received in the mail. In attempting to uncover this embezzlement scheme, the auditor most likely would compare the
a. Dates checks are deposited per bank statements with the dates remittance credits are recorded.
b. Daily cash summaries with the sums of the cash receipts journal entries.
c. Individual bank deposit slips with the details of the monthly bank statements.
d. Dates uncollectible accounts are authorized to be written off with the dates the write-offs are actually recorded. (11/95, Aud., #28, 5975)

9. An auditor most likely would limit substantive audit tests of sales transactions when control risk is assessed as low for the existence or occurrence assertion concerning sales transactions and the auditor has already gathered evidence supporting
a. Opening and closing inventory balances.
b. Cash receipts and accounts receivable.
c. Shipping and receiving activities.
d. Cutoffs of sales and purchases.
(11/95, Aud., #46, 5993)

10. Which of the following audit procedures would an auditor most likely perform to test controls relating to management's assertion concerning the completeness of sales transactions?
a. Verify that extensions and footings on the entity's sales invoices and monthly customer statements have been recomputed
b. Inspect the entity's reports of prenumbered shipping documents that have **not** been recorded in the sales journal
c. Compare the invoiced prices on prenumbered sales invoices to the entity's authorized price list
d. Inquire about the entity's credit granting policies and the consistent application of credit checks (5/94, Aud., #27, 4692)

11. Which of the following most likely would be detected by an auditor's review of a client's sales cut-off?
a. Shipments lacking sales invoices and shipping documents
b. Excessive write-offs of accounts receivable
c. Unrecorded sales at year end
d. Lapping of year-end accounts receivable (5/92, Aud., #25, 2778)

12. Which of the following internal control procedures most likely would deter lapping of collections from customers?
a. Independent internal verification of dates of entry in the cash receipts journal with dates of daily cash summaries
b. Authorization of write-offs of uncollectible accounts by a supervisor independent of credit approval
c. Segregation of duties between receiving cash and posting the accounts receivable ledger
d. Supervisory comparison of the daily cash summary with the sum of the cash receipts journal entries (5/93, Aud., #14, 3910)

13. In auditing accounts receivable, the negative form of confirmation request most likely would be used when
a. The total recorded amount of accounts receivable is immaterial to the financial statements taken as a whole.
b. Response rates in prior years to properly designed positive confirmation requests were inadequate.
c. Recipients are likely to return positive confirmation requests without verifying the accuracy of the information.
d. The combined assessed level of inherent risk and control risk relative to accounts receivable is low. (11/97, Aud., #19, 6582)

14. Which of the following strategies most likely could improve the response rate of the confirmation of accounts receivable?
a. Including a list of items or invoices that constitute the account balance
b. Restricting the selection of accounts to be confirmed to those customers with relatively large balances
c. Requesting customers to respond to the confirmation requests directly to the auditor by fax or e-mail
d. Notifying the recipients that second requests will be mailed if they fail to respond in a timely manner (R/00, Aud., #11, 6936)

15. Under which of the following circumstances would the use of the blank form of confirmations of accounts receivable most likely be preferable to positive confirmations?
a. The recipients are likely to sign the confirmations without devoting proper attention to them.
b. Subsequent cash receipts are unusually difficult to verify.
c. Analytical procedures indicate that few exceptions are expected.
d. The combined assessed level of inherent risk and control risk is low. (11/98, Aud., #23, 6714)

16. When an auditor does **not** receive replies to positive requests for year-end accounts receivable confirmations, the auditor most likely would
a. Inspect the allowance account to verify whether the accounts were subsequently written off.
b. Increase the assessed level of detection risk for the valuation and completeness assertions.
c. Ask the client to contact the customers to request that the confirmations be returned.
d. Increase the assessed level of inherent risk for the revenue cycle. (5/95, Aud., #46, 5664)

17. In confirming accounts receivable, an auditor decided to confirm customers' account balances rather than individual invoices. Which of the following most likely would be included with the client's confirmation letter?
a. An auditor-prepared letter explaining that a nonresponse may cause an inference that the account balance is correct.
b. A client-prepared letter reminding the customer that a nonresponse will cause a second request to be sent.
c. An auditor-prepared letter requesting the customer to supply missing and incorrect information directly to the auditor.
d. A client-prepared statement of account showing the details of the customer's account balance. (R/99, Aud., #18, 6834)

18. Which of the following statements would an auditor most likely add to the negative form of confirmation of accounts receivable to encourage timely consideration by the recipients?

a. "This is **not** a request for payment; remittances should **not** be sent to our auditors in the enclosed envelope."
b. "Report any differences on the enclosed statement directly to our auditors; **no** reply is necessary if this amount agrees with your records."
c. "If you do **not** report an differences within 15 days, it will be assumed that this statement is correct."
d. "The following invoices have been selected for confirmation and represent amounts that are overdue." (R/99, Aud., #19, 6835)

19. To measure how effectively an entity employs its resources, an auditor calculates inventory turnover by dividing average inventory into

a. Net sales.
b. Cost of goods sold.
c. Operating income.
d. Gross sales. (11/95, Aud., #42, 5989)

20. While observing a client's annual physical inventory, an auditor recorded test counts for several items and noticed that certain test counts were higher than the recorded quantities in the client's perpetual records. This situation could be the result of the client's failure to record

a. Purchase discounts.
b. Purchase returns.
c. Sales.
d. Sales returns. (5/95, Aud., #52, 5670)

21. When auditing inventories, an auditor would **least** likely verify that

a. The financial statement presentation of inventories is appropriate.
b. Damaged goods and obsolete items have been properly accounted for.
c. All inventory owned by the client is on hand at the time of the count.
d. The client has used proper inventory pricing. (5/93, Aud., #28, 9412)

22. Which of the following auditing procedures most likely would provide assurance about a manufacturing entity's inventory valuation?

a. Testing the entity's computation of standard overhead rates
b. Obtaining confirmation of inventories pledged under loan agreements
c. Reviewing shipping and receiving cutoff procedures for inventories
d. Tracing test counts to the entity's inventory listing (11/94, Aud., #48, 5121)

23. A client maintains perpetual inventory records in both quantities and dollars. If the assessed level of control risk is high, an auditor would probably

a. Increase the extent of tests of controls of the inventory cycle.
b. Request the client to schedule the physical inventory count at the end of the year.
c. Insist that the client perform physical counts of inventory items several times during the year.
d. Apply gross profit tests to ascertain the reasonableness of the physical counts. (11/94, Aud., #58, 5131)

24. Which of the following audit procedures probably would provide the most reliable evidence concerning the entity's assertion of rights and obligations related to inventories?

a. Inspect the open purchase order file for significant commitments that should be considered for disclosure
b. Inspect agreements to determine whether any inventory is pledged as collateral or subject to any liens
c. Select the last few shipping advices used before the physical count and determine whether the shipments were recorded as sales
d. Trace test counts noted during the entity's physical count to the entity's summarization of quantities (5/92, Aud., #17, amended, 2770)

25. An auditor most likely would inspect loan agreements under which an entity's inventories are pledged to support management's financial statement assertion of

a. Presentation and disclosure.
b. Valuation or allocation.
c. Existence or occurrence.
d. Completeness. (5/95, Aud., #40, 5658)

26. An auditor selected items for test counts while observing a client's physical inventory. The auditor then traced the test counts to the client's inventory listing. This procedure most likely obtained evidence concerning management's assertion of

a. Rights and obligations.
b. Completeness.
c. Existence or occurrence.
d. Valuation. (5/94, Aud., #41, 4706)

27. To gain assurance that all inventory items in a client's inventory listing schedule are valid, an auditor most likely would trace

a. Inventory tags noted during the auditor's observation to items listed in the inventory listing schedule.
b. Inventory tags noted during the auditor's observation to items listed in receiving reports and vendors' invoices.
c. Items listed in the inventory listing schedule to inventory tags and the auditor's recorded count sheets.
d. Items listed in receiving reports and vendors' invoices to the inventory listing schedule.

(5/95, Aud., #53, 5671)

28. An auditor analyzes repairs and maintenance accounts primarily to obtain evidence in support of the audit assertion that all

a. Noncapitalizable expenditures for repairs and maintenance have been recorded in the proper period.
b. Expenditures for property and equipment have been recorded in the proper period.
c. Noncapitalizable expenditures for repairs and maintenance have been properly charged to expense.
d. Expenditures for property and equipment have **not** been charged to expense.

(11/94, Aud., #62, 5135)

29. In testing plant and equipment balances, an auditor may inspect new additions listed on the analysis of plant and equipment. This procedure is designed to obtain evidence concerning management's assertions of

	Existence or occurrence	*Presentation and disclosure*
a.	Yes	Yes
b.	Yes	No
c.	No	Yes
d.	No	No

(5/97, Aud., #7, 6396)

30. Which of the following explanations most likely would satisfy an auditor who questions management about significant debits to the accumulated depreciation accounts?

a. The estimated remaining useful lives of plant assets were revised upward
b. Plant assets were retired during the year
c. The prior year's depreciation expense was erroneously understated
d. Overhead allocations were revised at year end

(11/95, Aud., #49, 5996)

31. Determining that proper amounts of depreciation are expensed provides assurance about management's assertions of valuation or allocation and

a. Presentation and disclosure.
b. Completeness.
c. Rights and obligations.
d. Existence or occurrence.

(11/94, Aud., #51, 5124)

32. In confirming with an outside agent, such as a financial institution, that the agent is holding investment securities in the client's name, an auditor most likely gathers evidence in support of management's financial statement assertions of existence or occurrence and

a. Valuation or allocation.
b. Rights and obligations.
c. Completeness.
d. Presentation and disclosure.

(5/95, Aud., #44, 5662)

33. An auditor usually tests the reasonableness of dividend income from investments in publicly-held companies by computing the amounts that should have been received by referring to

a. Dividend record books produced by investment advisory services.
b. Stock indentures published by corporate transfer agents.
c. Stock ledgers maintained by independent registrars.
d. Annual audited financial statements issued by the investee companies.

(11/96, Aud., #11, 6363)

34. In testing long-term investments, an auditor ordinarily would use analytical procedures to ascertain the reasonableness of the

a. Completeness of recorded investment income.
b. Classification between current and noncurrent portfolios.
c. Valuation of marketable equity securities.
d. Existence of unrealized gains or losses in the portfolio.

(5/93, Aud., #31, 3927)

35. In establishing the existence and ownership of a long-term investment in the form of publicly-traded stock, an auditor should inspect the securities or

a. Correspond with the investee company to verify the number of shares owned.
b. Inspect the audited financial statements of the investee company.
c. Confirm the number of shares owned that are held by an independent custodian.
d. Determine that the investment is carried at the fair market value.

(11/94, Aud., #49, amended, 5122)

36. Which of the following is a substantive test that an auditor most likely would perform to verify the existence and valuation of recorded accounts payable?
a. Investigating the open purchase order file to ascertain that prenumbered purchase orders are used and accounted for
b. Receiving the client's mail, unopened, for a reasonable period of time after the year end to search for unrecorded vendor's invoices
c. Vouching selected entries in the accounts payable subsidiary ledger to purchase orders and receiving reports
d. Confirming accounts payable balances with known suppliers who have zero balances
(5/93, Aud., #36, 3932)

37. Which of the following procedures would an auditor most likely perform in searching for unrecorded liabilities?
a. Trace a sample of accounts payable entries recorded just before year end to the unmatched receiving report file
b. Compare a sample of purchase orders issued just after year end with the year-end accounts payable trial balance
c. Vouch a sample of cash disbursements recorded just after year end to receiving reports and vendor invoices
d. Scan the cash disbursements entries recorded just before year end for indications of unusual transactions (11/95, Aud., #47, 5994)

38. An auditor traced a sample of purchase orders and the related receiving reports to the purchases journal and the cash disbursements journal. The purpose of this substantive audit procedure most likely was to
a. Identify unusually large purchases that should be investigated further.
b. Verify that cash disbursements were for goods actually received.
c. Determine that purchases were properly recorded.
d. Test whether payments were for goods actually ordered. (11/95, Aud., #48, 5995)

39. To determine whether accounts payable are complete, an auditor performs a test to verify that all merchandise received is recorded. The population of documents for this test consists of all
a. Payment vouchers.
b. Receiving reports.
c. Purchase requisitions.
d. Vendor's invoices. (11/93, Aud., #26, 4263)

40. Cutoff tests designed to detect purchases made before the end of the year that have been recorded in the subsequent year most likely would provide assurance about management's assertion of
a. Valuation or allocation.
b. Existence or occurrence.
c. Completeness.
d. Presentation and disclosure.
(5/95, Aud., #42, 5660)

41. When control risk is assessed as low for assertions related to payroll, substantive tests of payroll balances most likely would be limited to applying analytical procedures and
a. Observing the distribution of paychecks.
b. Footing and crossfooting the payroll register.
c. Inspecting payroll tax returns.
d. Recalculating payroll accruals.
(5/95, Aud., #54, 5672)

42. An auditor most likely would extend substantive tests of payroll when
a. Payroll is extensively audited by the state government.
b. Payroll expense is substantially higher than in the prior year.
c. Overpayments are discovered in performing tests of details.
d. Employees complain to management about too much overtime. (5/94, Aud., #49, 4714)

43. An auditor vouched data for a sample of employees in a payroll register to approved clock card data to provide assurance that
a. Payments to employees are computed at authorized rates.
b. Employees work the number of hours for which they are paid.
c. Segregation of duties exists between the preparation and distribution of the payroll.
d. Internal controls relating to unclaimed payroll checks are operating effectively.
(5/95, Aud., #37, 5655)

44. In auditing long-term bonds payable, an auditor most likely would
a. Perform analytical procedures on the bond premium and discount accounts.
b. Examine documentation of assets purchased with bond proceeds for liens.
c. Compare interest expense with the bond payable amount for reasonableness.
d. Confirm the existence of individual bondholders at year-end. (11/94, Aud., #60, 5133)

45. In auditing a client's retained earnings account, an auditor should determine whether there are any restrictions on retained earnings that result from loans, agreements, or state law. This procedure is designed to corroborate management's financial statement assertion of
a. Valuation or allocation.
b. Existence or occurrence.
c. Presentation and disclosure.
d. Rights and obligations. (11/98, Aud., #22, 6713)

46. An auditor usually obtains evidence of stockholders' equity transactions by reviewing the entity's
a. Minutes of board of directors meetings.
b. Transfer agent's records.
c. Canceled stock certificates
d. Treasury stock certificate book.
(R/99, Aud., #21, 6837)

47. The primary responsibility of a bank acting as registrar of capital stock is to
a. Ascertain that dividends declared do **not** exceed the statutory amount allowable in the state of incorporation.
b. Account for stock certificates by comparing the total shares outstanding to the total in the shareholders subsidiary ledger.
c. Act as an independent third party between the board of directors and outside investors concerning mergers, acquisitions, and the sale of treasury stock.
d. Verify that stock is issued in accordance with the authorization of the board of directors and the articles of incorporation. (5/91, Aud., #32, 0133)

48. In auditing intangible assets, an auditor most likely would review or recompute amortization and determine whether the amortization period is reasonable in support of management's financial statement assertion of
a. Valuation or allocation.
b. Existence or occurrence.
c. Completeness.
d. Rights and obligations. (5/95, Aud., #41, 5659)

49. Which of the following procedures would an auditor ordinarily perform first in evaluating management's accounting estimates for reasonableness?
a. Develop independent expectations of management's estimates
b. Consider the appropriateness of the key factors or assumptions used in preparing the estimates
c. Test the calculations used by management in developing the estimates
d. Obtain an understanding of how management developed its estimates (5/95, Aud., #69, 5687)

50. In evaluating the reasonableness of an entity's accounting estimates, an auditor normally would be concerned about assumptions that are
a. Susceptible to bias.
b. Consistent with prior periods.
c. Insensitive to variations.
d. Similar to industry guidelines.
(5/97, Aud., #6, 6395)

PROBLEM 36-2 ADDITIONAL MULTIPLE CHOICE QUESTIONS (30 to 38 minutes)

51. An auditor most likely would review an entity's periodic accounting for the numerical sequence of shipping documents and invoices to support management's financial statement assertion of
a. Existence or occurrence.
b. Rights and obligations.
c. Valuation or allocation.
d. Completeness. (5/93, Aud., #27, 3923)

52. To reduce the risks associated with accepting fax responses to requests for confirmations of accounts receivable, an auditor most likely would
a. Examine the shipping documents that provide evidence for the existence assertion.
b. Verify the sources and contents of the faxes in telephone calls to the senders.
c. Consider the faxes to be nonresponses and evaluate them as unadjusted differences.
d. Inspect the faxes for forgeries or alterations and consider them to be acceptable if none are noted. (11/97, Aud., #18, 6581)

53. To reduce the risks associated with accepting e-mail responses to requests for confirmation of accounts receivable, an auditor most likely would
a. Request the senders to mail the original forms to the auditor.
b. Examine subsequent cash receipts for the accounts in question.
c. Consider the e-mail responses to the confirmations to be exceptions.
d. Mail second requests to the e-mail respondents.
(5/98, Aud., #12, 6629)

54. Hemp, CPA, is auditing the financial statements of a small rural municipality. The receivable balances represent residents' delinquent real estate taxes. Internal control at the municipality is weak. To determine the existence of the accounts receivable balances at the balance sheet date, Hemp would most likely

a. Send positive confirmation requests.
b. Send negative confirmation requests.
c. Inspect the internal records such as copies of the tax invoices that were mailed to the residents.
d. Examine evidence of subsequent cash receipts.

(Editors, 0178)

55. The confirmation of customers' accounts receivable rarely provides reliable evidence about the completeness assertion because

a. Many customers merely sign and return the confirmation without verifying its details.
b. Recipients usually respond only if they disagree with the information on the request.
c. Customers may **not** be inclined to report understatement errors in their accounts.
d. Auditors typically select many accounts with low recorded balances to be confirmed.

(11/95, Aud., #39, 5986)

56. Which of the following statements is correct concerning the use of negative confirmation requests?

a. Unreturned negative confirmation requests rarely provide significant explicit evidence.
b. Negative confirmation requests are effective when detection risk is low.
c. Unreturned negative confirmation requests indicate that alternative procedures are necessary.
d. Negative confirmation requests are effective when understatements of account balances are suspected.

(5/95, Aud., #45, 5663)

57. An auditor most likely would make inquiries of production and sales personnel concerning possible obsolete or slow-moving inventory to support management's financial statement assertion of

a. Valuation or allocation.
b. Rights and obligations.
c. Existence or occurrence.
d. Presentation and disclosure.

(5/95, Aud., #43, 5661)

58. When there are numerous property and equipment transactions during the year, an auditor who plans to assess control risk at a low level usually performs

a. Analytical procedures for property and equipment balances at the end of the year.
b. Analytical procedures for current year property and equipment transactions.
c. Tests of controls and limited tests of current year property and equipment transactions.
d. Tests of controls and extensive tests of property and equipment balances at the end of the year.

(11/95, Aud., #27, amended, 5974)

59. A weakness of internal control over recording retirements of equipment may cause an auditor to

a. Inspect certain items of equipment in the plant and trace those items to the accounting records.
b. Review the subsidiary ledger to ascertain whether depreciation was taken on each item of equipment during the year.
c. Trace additions to the "other assets" account to search for equipment that is still on hand but **no** longer being used.
d. Select certain items of equipment from the accounting records and locate them in the plant.

(11/95, Aud., #34, 5981)

60. To satisfy the valuation assertion when auditing an investment accounted for by the equity method, an auditor most likely would

a. Inspect the stock certificates evidencing the investment.
b. Examine the audited financial statements of the investee company.
c. Review the broker's advice or canceled check for the investment's acquisition.
d. Obtain market quotations from financial newspapers or periodicals. (11/91, Aud., #44, 2312)

61. In auditing accounts payable, an auditor's procedures most likely would focus primarily on management's assertion of

a. Existence or occurrence.
b. Presentation and disclosure.
c. Completeness.
d. Valuation or allocation. (11/93, Aud., #37, 4274)

62. Cooper, CPA, performs a test to determine whether all merchandise for which the client was billed was received. The population for this test consists of all

a. Merchandise received.
b. Vendors' invoices.
c. Receiving reports.
d. Canceled checks.

(Editors, 0195)

63. When using confirmations to provide evidence about the completeness assertion for accounts payable, the appropriate population most likely would be
a. Vendors with whom the entity has previously done business.
b. Amounts recorded in the accounts payable subsidiary ledger.
c. Payees of checks drawn in the month after the year end.
d. Invoices filed in the entity's open invoice file.
(11/94, Aud., #53, 5126)

64. An auditor's program to examine long-term debt most likely would include steps that require
a. Comparing the carrying amount of the debt to its year-end market value.
b. Correlating interest expense recorded for the period with outstanding debt.
c. Verifying the existence of the holders of the debt by direct confirmation.
d. Inspecting the accounts payable subsidiary ledger for unrecorded long-term debt.
(5/91, Aud., #8, 0127)

65. In performing tests concerning the granting of stock options, an auditor should
a. Confirm the transaction with the Secretary of State in the state of incorporation.
b. Verify the existence of option holders in the entity's payroll records or stock ledgers.
c. Determine that sufficient treasury stock is available to cover any new stock issued.
d. Trace the authorization for the transaction to a vote of the board of directors.
(11/94, Aud., #61, 5134)

OTHER OBJECTIVE FORMAT QUESTIONS

PROBLEM 36-3 (15 to 25 minutes)

Items 1 through 12 represent possible errors and fraud that an auditor suspects are present. The accompanying *List of Auditing Procedures* represents procedures that the auditor would consider performing to gather evidence concerning possible errors and fraud. For each item, select one or two procedures, as indicated, that the auditor most likely would perform to gather evidence in support of that item. The procedures on the list may be selected once, more than once, or not at all.

Possible Errors and Fraud

1. The auditor suspects that a kiting scheme exists because an accounting department employee who can issue and record checks seems to be leading an unusually luxurious lifestyle. (Select only 1 procedure)

2. The auditor suspects that the controller wrote several checks and recorded the cash disbursements just before the year end but did not mail the checks until after the first week of the subsequent year. (Select only 1 procedure)

3. The entity borrowed funds from a financial institution. Although the transaction was properly recorded, the auditor suspects that the loan created a lien on the entity's real estate that is not disclosed in its financial statements. (Select only 1 procedure)

4. The auditor discovered an unusually large receivable from one of the entity's new customers. The auditor suspects that the receivable may be fictitious because the auditor has never heard of the customer and because the auditor's initial attempt to confirm the receivable has been ignored by the customer. (Select only 2 procedures)

5. The auditor suspects that fictitious employees have been placed on the payroll by the entity's payroll supervisor, who has access to payroll records and to the paychecks. (Select only 1 procedure)

6. The auditor suspects that selected employees of the entity received unauthorized raises from the entity's payroll supervisor, who has access to payroll records. (Select only 1 procedure)

7. The entity's cash receipts of the first few days of the subsequent year were properly deposited in its general operating account after the year end. However, the auditor suspects that the entity recorded the cash receipts in its books during the last week of the year under audit. (Select only 1 procedure)

8. The auditor suspects that vouchers were prepared and processed by an accounting department employee for merchandise that was

neither ordered nor received by the entity. (Select only 1 procedure)

9. The details of invoices for equipment repairs were not clearly identified or explained to the accounting department employees. The auditor suspects that the bookkeeper incorrectly recorded the repairs as fixed assets.

10. The auditor suspects that a lapping scheme exists because an accounting department employee who has access to cash receipts also maintains the accounts receivable ledger and refuses to take any vacation or sick days. (Select only 2 procedures)

11. The auditor suspects that the entity is inappropriately increasing the cash reported on its balance sheet by drawing a check on one account and not recording it as an outstanding check on that account, and simultaneously recording it as a deposit in a second account. (Select only 1 procedure)

12. The auditor suspects that the entity's controller has overstated sales and accounts receivable by recording fictitious sales to regular customers in the entity's books. (Select only 2 procedures)

(5/97, Aud., #2, amended, 6399-6413)

List of Auditing Procedures

A. Compare the details of the cash receipts journal entries with the details of the corresponding daily deposit slips.

B. Scan the debits to the fixed asset accounts and vouch selected amounts to vendors' invoices and management authorization.

C. Perform analytical procedures that compare documented authorized pay rates to the entity's budget and forecast.

D. Obtain the cutoff bank statement and compare the cleared checks to the year-end bank reconciliation.

E. Prepare a bank transfer schedule.

F. Inspect the entity's deeds to its real estate.

G. Make inquiries of the entity's attorney concerning the details of real estate transactions.

H. Confirm the terms of borrowing arrangements with the lender.

I. Examine selected equipment repair orders and supporting documentation to determine the propriety of the charges.

J. Send requests to confirm the entity's accounts receivable on a surprise basis at an interim date.

K. Send a second request for confirmation of the receivable to the customer and make inquiries of a reputable credit agency concerning the customer's creditworthiness.

L. Examine the entity's shipping documents to verify that the merchandise that produced the receivable was actually sent to the customer.

M. Inspect the entity's correspondence files for indications of customer disputes or for evidence that certain shipments were on consignment.

N. Perform edit checks of data on the payroll transaction tapes.

O. Inspect payroll check endorsements for similar handwriting.

P. Observe payroll check distribution on a surprise basis.

Q. Vouch data in the payroll register to documented authorized pay rates in the human resources department's files.

R. Reconcile the payroll checking account and determine if there were unusual time lags between the issuance and payment of payroll checks.

S. Inspect the file of prenumbered vouchers for consecutive numbering and proper approval by an appropriate employee.

T. Determine that the details of selected prenumbered vouchers match the related vendor's invoices.

U. Examine the supporting purchase orders and receiving reports for selected paid vouchers.

PROBLEM 36-4 (10 to 15 minutes)

ITEMS 1 THROUGH 10 represent tick marks (symbols) that indicate procedures performed or comments documented in auditing the *Long-term Debt* account of American Manufacturers, Inc.

American Manufacturers, Inc.
Long-Term Debt
October 31, 20X1

	Lender	Interest rate	Payment terms	Collateral	Balance 10/31/X0	Current year borrowings	Current year reductions	Balance 10/31/X1	Interest paid to	Accrued interest payable 10/31/X1	Comments
▲	First National Bank	10%	Interest only on last day of each quarter; principal due in full on 9/30/X3.	Manufacturing equipment	500,000 ■	200,000 ◆ 3/31/X1	(100,000) ✪ 6/30/X1	600,000 √	9/30/X1	5,000 ✖	[1]
▲	Second State Bank	9%	$10,000 principal plus interest due on the 1st of each month; due in full on 1/1/X4.	First mortgage on production facilities	380,000 ■	0	(110,000) ✚	270,000 √ ★	9/30/X1	2,025 ✖	[2]
▲	Third Savings & Loan	12%	$5,000 principal plus interest due on the 15th of each month; due in full on 10/15/X3.	Second mortgage on production facilities	180,000 ■	0	(60,000)	120,000 ✱★	10/15/X1	600	[3]
▲	A. Clark, majority stockholder	0%	Due in full 10/31/X3.	Unsecured	700,000 ■	0	(200,000) 10/28/X1	500,000 √		0	[4]
					1,760,000	200,000	(470,000)	1,490,000 ●		7,625 ●	

[1] First National confirms that interest payments are current and agrees with account balance.
[2] Monthly payment for $12,025 was mailed on 11/3/X1; Second State agrees with account balance.
[3] Third Savings & Loan claims 10/15/X1 payment wasn't received as of 11/5/X1; adjusting entry proposed to increase accrued interest payable.
[4] Borrowed additional $200,000 from Clark on 11/5/X1; need to investigate reborrowing just after year end and consider imputed interest on 0% stockholder loan.

List of procedures/comments—Long-Term Debt	
A. Confirmed, without exception.	H. Agreed to canceled check and board of directors' authorization.
B. Confirmed, with exception.	I. Agreed interest rate, terms, and collateral to note & loan agreement.
C. Traced amount to prior year's working papers.	J. Agreed to loan agreement, validated bank deposit ticket, and board of directors' authorization.
D. Traced amount to current year's trial balance and general ledger.	K. Reclassification entry proposed for current portion of long-term debt.
E. Does not recompute correctly.	
F. Tested reasonableness of calculations.	
G. Agreed to canceled checks and lender's monthly statements.	

Items to be Answered	
1. ▲	6. √
2. ■	7. ★
3. ◆	8. ✱
4. ✪	9. ●
5. ✚	10. ✖

American Manufacturers, Inc.
Property, Plant, & Equipment and Accumulated Depreciation
October 31, 20X1

Property, Plant, & Equipment

Account	Balance 10/31/X0		Additions		Disposals		Other		Balance 10/31/X1	
Land	650,000	➤	70,000	↕	0		0		720,000	→
Buildings	3,270,000	➤	230,000	✓	0		(30,000)	⊗	3,470,000	→
Equipment	1,750,000	➤	90,000	∠	(12,000)	↔	0		1,828,000	→
Fixtures	850,000	➤	200,000	✓	0		30,000	⊗	1,080,000	→
	6,520,000		590,000		(12,000)		0		7,098,000	

Accumulated Depreciation

Account	Depreciation Rate	Depreciation Method	Balance 10/31/X0		Provision		Disposal	Balance 10/31/X1	
Land									
Buildings	5%	S/L	1,144,500	➤	168,500	↲	0	1,313,000	→
Equipment	10%	S/L	700,000	➤	179,500	↲	(12,000)	867,500	→
Fixtures	15%	S/L	510,000	➤	144,750	↲	0	654,750	→
			2,354,500		492,750		(12,000)	2,835,250	

List of procedures/comments Property, Plant, & Equipment and Accumulated Depreciation

A. Does not recompute correctly.
B. Tested reasonableness of calculation.
C. Traced amount to current year's trial balance and general ledger.
D. Reclassification entry for fixtures erroneously recorded as buildings.
E. Reclassification entry for buildings erroneously recorded as fixtures.
F. Traced amount to prior year's working papers.
G. Sold six fully-depreciated computers to employees; no audit procedures necessary.
H. Confirmed, with exception.
I. Confirmed, without exception.
J. Examined supporting vendors' invoices, canceled checks, asset subsidiary ledger and board of directors' minutes of meetings authorizing transactions.
K. Examined supporting work orders and engineers' reports, canceled checks, asset subsidiary ledger, and board of directors' minutes of meetings authorizing transactions.
L. Examined supporting deed and purchase contract, canceled checks, asset subsidiary ledger, and board of directors' minutes of meeting authorizing transactions.

Items to be Answered

11. ➤	12. ↕	13. ✓	14. ∠
15. ↔	16. ⊗	17. →	18. ↲

Required:

Select, from the accompanying lists of procedures/comments, the procedure/comment that the auditor most likely performed/documented at each point of the audit where a tick mark was made on the working papers. Select only one procedure/comment for each item. A procedure/comment may be selected once or not at all. Assume that the working papers foot and crossfoot.

Items 11 through 18 represent tick marks (symbols) that indicate procedures performed or comments documented in auditing the Property, plant, and equipment and Accumulated depreciation accounts of American Manufacturers, Inc. During the year under audit, American Manufacturers purchased new computers directly from wholesalers and constructed an addition to one of its buildings. The company's employees also refurbished the fixtures of several older buildings.

(11/97, Aud., amended, #2)

PROBLEM 36-5 (3 to 5 minutes)

The information below was taken from the bank transfer schedule prepared during the audit of Fox Co.'s financial statements for the year ended December 31, 20X1. All checks are dated and issued on December 30, 20X1.

Check	Bank Accounts		Disbursement Date		Receipt Date	
No.	From	To	Per Books	Per Bank	Per Books	Per Bank
1	National	Federal	Dec. 30	Jan. 4	Dec. 30	Jan. 3
2	County	State	Jan. 3	Jan. 2	Dec. 30	Dec. 31
3	Federal	American	Dec. 31	Jan. 3	Jan. 2	Jan. 2
4	State	Republic	Jan. 2	Jan. 2	Jan. 2	Dec. 31

1. Which two checks might indicate kiting? (5/92, Aud., #26, amended, 2779)

2. Which two checks illustrate deposits/transfers in transit at December 31, 20X1? (5/92, Aud., #27, amended, 2780)

ESSAY QUESTIONS

ESSAY 36-6 (15 to 25 minutes)

MLG Company's auditor received directly from the banks, confirmations and cutoff statements with related checks and deposit tickets for MLG's three general-purpose bank accounts. The auditor determined that internal control over cash was satisfactory and control risk could be assessed at below the maximum level. The proper cutoff of external cash receipts and disbursements was established. No bank accounts were opened or closed during the year.

REQUIRED:

Prepare the audit program of substantive procedures to verify MLG's bank balances. Ignore any other cash accounts. (11/87, Aud., #3)

ESSAY 36-7 (25 to 35 minutes)

King, CPA, is auditing the financial statements of Cycle Co., an entity that has receivables from customers, which have arisen from the sale of goods in the normal course of business. King is aware that the confirmation of accounts receivable is generally accepted auditing procedure.

REQUIRED:

a. Under what circumstances could King justify omitting the confirmation of Cycle's accounts receivable?

b. In designing confirmation requests, what factors are likely to affect King's assessment of the reliability of confirmations that King sends?

c. What alternative procedures would King consider performing when replies to positive confirmation requests are **not** received? (5/94, Aud., #5, 4973)

ESSAY 36-8 (25 to 35 minutes)

Miller, CPA, is engaged to audit the financial statements of Superior Wholesaling for the year ended December 31, 20X1. Miller obtained and documented an understanding of Superior's internal control relating to accounts receivable and assessed control risk relating to accounts receivable at the maximum level. Miller requested and obtained from Superior an aged accounts receivable schedule listing the total amount owed by each customer as of December 31, 20X1, and sent positive confirmation requests to a sample of the customers. Subsequently, Miller tested the accuracy of the aged accounts receivable schedule. Miller has asked Adler, the staff assistant assigned to the engagement, to follow up on the eight returned confirmations* that appear on the following two pages. Assume that each confirmation is material if the potential misstatement is projected to the population.

REQUIRED:

a. Describe the procedure(s), if any, that Adler should perform to resolve each of the eight confirmations that were returned. Assume that Superior will record any necessary adjusting entries and that Adler will verify that they are appropriate.

b. Assume that Miller sent second requests for accounts receivable balances initially selected for confirmation for which no responses were received. Describe the alternative substantive procedures that Miller should consider applying to the accounts receivable selected for confirmation for which no responses were received to Miller's second requests. Assume that these accounts receivable in the aggregate, when projected as misstatements to the population, would affect Miller's decision about whether the financial statements are materially misstated.

c. In addition to performing the confirmation procedures and alternative procedures described in requirements **a.** and **b.** and the procedures described in the first paragraph above, what additional substantive procedures should Miller consider performing to complete the audit of Superior's accounts receivable and related allowances? Assume that all accounts receivable are trade receivables.

(5/97, Aud., #3, 6414-6416)

Superior Wholesaling, Inc
123 Commercial Blvd.
Anytown, USA

January 15, 20X2

Atom Co.
362 Main Street — *Confirm # 11*
Anytown, USA

Dear *C. L. Adams*:

Our auditor, Miller, CPA, is currently auditing our financial statements. To facilitate this audit, please confirm the balance due us as of December 31, 20X1, which is shown on our records as *$15,000*. Indicate in the space below whether this is in agreement with your records. If there are exceptions, please provide any information that will assist the auditor in reconciling the difference.

Please mail your reply directly to Miller, CPA. A stamped, self-addressed envelope is enclosed for your convenience.

Sincerely

J. Blake

J. Blake, Controller
Superior Wholesaling, Inc.

To Miller, CPA:

The amount shown above is correct as of December 31, 20X1, except as follows:

Yes, we ordered $15,000 worth of merchandise from Superior in November. However, we mailed Superior a check for $15,000 on 12/18/X1

Name *C. L. Adams* Position *Accounting Mgr.*
Date *1/22/X2*

Note to files: Blake indicates that the check was received and deposited on 12/28/X1, but posted to the wrong customer's account.

C. Miller

Superior Wholesaling, Inc
123 Commercial Blvd.
Anytown, USA

January 15, 20X2

Baker Co.
18 Lakeview Drive — *Confirm # 28*
Central City, USA

Dear *S. Brown*: ... *$25,000*. ...

To Miller, CPA:

The amount shown above is correct as of December 31, 20X1, except as follows:

Sure we ordered $25,000 of merchandise on Oct. 10, 20X1, but Superior was out-of-stock until recently. They back-ordered the goods and we finally received them on Jan. 6, 20X2.

Name *S. Brown* Position *A/P Supervisor*
Date *Jan. 18, 20X2*

Superior Wholesaling, Inc
123 Commercial Blvd.
Anytown, USA

January 15, 20X2

Clark Retailing
35 Lincoln Avenue — *Confirm # 34*
Jackson, USA

Dear *J. P. Cummings*: ... *$32,000*. ...

To Miller, CPA:

The amount shown above is correct as of December 31, 20X1, except as follows:

We received $24,000 of goods on consignment from Superior on 12/10/X1, but they're not sold yet!

Name *J. Cummings* Position *President*
Date *1/19/X2*

* To conserve paper, the portion of the confirmation form after the greeting and ending with "J. Blake, Controller, Superior Wholesaling, Inc." is abbreviated for seven confirmations. In the illustration, the editors replaced this repetitive material with the balance to be confirmed by Superior Wholesaling's customers. Aside from this value, this section of these forms did not differ from confirmation #11.

Superior Wholesaling, Inc
123 Commercial Blvd.
Anytown, USA

January 15, 20X2

Delta Outlet Stores, Inc.
Sunshine Mall. *Confirm # 41*
River City, USA

Dear *R. Dunn*: ... *$45,000*. ...

To Miller, CPA:

The amount shown above is correct as of December 31, 20X1, except as follows:

No way! Superior promised these goods in 10 days on Dec. 2nd. When we didn't receive them, I canceled the order on Dec. 12th. General Wholesaling shipped us similar goods overnight!

Name *R. Dunn* Position *General Manager*
Date *Jan. 18th*

Superior Wholesaling, Inc
123 Commercial Blvd.
Anytown, USA

January 15, 20X2

Eagle Distributors
2700 Ocean Shore Blvd. *Confirm # 58*
Ocean City, USA

Dear *I. Eagle*: ... *$59,000*. ...

To Miller, CPA:

The amount shown above is correct as of December 31, 20X1, except as follows:

I use an accounts payable voucher system by individual invoice. I can't verify $59,000, but Superior is one of my regular suppliers. I am sure I probably owe them something

Name *I. Eagle* Position *Accounting Mgr.*
Date *1-20-X2*

Superior Wholesaling, Inc
123 Commercial Blvd.
Anytown, USA

January 15, 20X2

Franklin Co.
17 United Street *Confirm # 67*
Industry City, USA

Dear *S. Brown*: ... *$65,000*. ...

To Miller, CPA:

The amount shown above is correct as of December 31, 20X1, except as follows:

Name Position
Date

Note to files: This confirmation was returned by the postal service as "return to sender—no such address at this location."

C. Miller

Superior Wholesaling, Inc
123 Commercial Blvd.
Anytown, USA

January 15, 20X2

Grove Retailing
3838 Curtis Blvd. *Confirm # 71*
Union Center, USA

Dear *H. Gates*: ... *$75,000*. ...

To Miller, CPA:

The amount shown above is correct as of December 31, 20X1, except as follows:

Our records show that a check for $75,000 was mailed on 12/27/X1

Name *H. Gates* Position *Controller*
Date *1/22/X2*

Questions 36-38

Superior Wholesaling, Inc
123 Commercial Blvd.
Anytown, USA

January 15, 20X2

Hall Enterprises, Inc.
55 Green St. *Confirm # 86*
Grant City, USA

Dear *K. Hines*: ... *$80,000*. ...

To Miller, CPA:

The amount shown above is correct as of December 31, 20X1, except as follows:

Mailed that check for full amount on 1-3-X2, merchandise was only received on 12-23-X1.

Name *K. Hines* Position *Accountant*
Date

ESSAY 36-9 (15 to 25 minutes)

The purpose of all auditing procedures is to gather sufficient competent evidence for an auditor to form an opinion regarding the financial statements taken as a whole.

REQUIRED:

a. In addition to the example below, identify and describe five means or techniques of gathering audit evidence used to evaluate a client's inventory balance.

Technique	Description
Observation	An auditor watches the performance of some function, such as a client's annual inventory count.

b. Identify the five general assertions regarding a client's inventory balance and describe one **different** substantive auditing procedure for each assertion.

Use the format illustrated below.

Assertion	Substantive Auditing Procedure

(11/88, Aud., #5)

ESSAY 36-10 (15 to 25 minutes)

Larkin, CPA, has been engaged to audit the financial statements of Vernon Distributors, Inc., a continuing audit client, for the year ended September 30, 20X1. After obtaining an understanding of Vernon's internal control, Larkin assessed control risk at the maximum level for all financial statement assertions concerning investments. Larkin determined that Vernon is unable to exercise significant influence over any investee and none are related parties.

Larkin obtained from Vernon detailed analyses of its investments in domestic securities showing:

- The classification between trading, available-for-sale, and held-to-maturity portfolios;
- A description of each security, including the interest rate and maturity date of bonds and par value and dividend rate on stocks;
- A notation of the location of each security, either in the Treasurer's safe or held by an independent custodian;
- The number of shares of stock or face amount of bonds held at the beginning and end of the year;
- The beginning and ending balances at cost and at market, and the unamortized premium or discount on bonds;
- Additions to and sales from the portfolios for the year, including date, number of shares, face amount of bonds, cost, proceeds, and realized gain or loss;
- Valuation allowances at the beginning and end of the year and changes therein;
- Accrued investment income for each investment at the beginning and end of the year, and income earned and collected during the year.

Larkin then prepared the following partial audit program of substantive auditing procedures:

1. Foot and crossfoot the analyses.
2. Trace the ending totals to the general ledger and financial statements.
3. Trace the beginning balances to the prior year's working papers.
4. Obtain positive confirmation as of the balance sheet date of the investments held by any independent custodian.
5. Determine that income from investments has been properly recorded as accrued or collected by reference to published sources, by computation, and by tracing to recorded amounts.

6. For investments in nonpublic entities, compare carrying value to information in the most recently available audited financial statements.
7. Determine that all transfers between trading and available-for-sale portfolios have been properly authorized and recorded.
8. Determine that any other-than-temporary decline in the price of an investment has been properly recorded.

REQUIRED:

a. Identify the primary financial statement assertion relative to investments that would be addressed by each of the procedures #4 through #8 and describe the primary audit objective of performing those procedures. Use the format illustrated below.

Primary Assertion	Objective

b. Describe three additional substantive auditing procedures Larkin should consider in auditing Vernon's investments. (11/91, Aud., #4, amended)

ESSAY 36-11 (25 to 35 minutes)

Cook, CPA, is auditing the financial statements of DollarMart, a local retailer of clothes, appliances, sporting goods, and electronics. During prior years' audits of DollarMart, Cook noticed that management was less concerned about the timely recording of expenses and liabilities than revenues and assets. As a result, very little of DollarMart's internal control resources were expended in assuring an accurate and timely recording of accounts payable. Cook also believes that DollarMart's management may be motivated to delay recording its liabilities at year end, so Cook is approaching the search for unrecorded liabilities with caution.

REQUIRED:

a. What substantive auditing procedures would Cook most likely consider performing in searching for DollarMart's unrecorded liabilities?

b. How would the nature, timing, and extent of Cook's substantive auditing procedures most likely be affected by DollarMart's deficient control environment? (5/96, Aud., #3, 6296)

ESSAY 3-12 (15 to 25 minutes)

Bell, CPA, was engaged to audit the financial statements of Kent Company, a continuing audit client. Bell is about to audit Kent's Payroll transactions. Kent uses an in-house payroll department to compute payroll data, and prepare and distribute payroll checks.

During the planning process, Bell determined that the inherent risk of overstatement of payroll expense is high. In addition, Bell obtained an understanding of internal control and assessed control risk at the maximum level for payroll-related assertions.

REQUIRED:

Describe the audit procedures Bell should consider performing in the audit of Kent's payroll transactions to address the risk of overstatement. Do **not** discuss Kent's internal control structure. (11/89, Aud., #2, amended)

ESSAY 36-13 (15 to 25 minutes)

Jones, CPA, the continuing auditor of Sussex, Inc., is beginning the audit of the common stock and treasury stock accounts. Jones has decided to assess control risk at the maximum level.

Sussex has no par, has no stated value common stock, and acts as its own registrar and transfer agent. During the past year Sussex both issued and reacquired shares of its own common stock, some of which the company still owned at year-end. Additional common stock transactions occurred among the shareholders during the year.

Common stock transactions can be traced to individual shareholders' accounts in a subsidiary ledger and to a stock certificate book. The company has not paid any cash or stock dividends. There are no other classes of stock, stock rights, warrants, or option plans.

REQUIRED:

What substantive audit procedures should Jones apply in examining the common stock and treasury stock accounts? (5/86, Aud., #2)

SOLUTION 36-1 MULTIPLE CHOICE ANSWERS

CASH

1. (b) AU 326.19 states that for audit evidence to be competent, it must be both valid and relevant. When evidential matter can be obtained from independent sources outside an entity, it provides greater assurance of reliability for the purposes of an independent audit than that secured solely within the entity. Answers (a), (c), and (d) represent audit procedures that may be performed and evidence that can be obtained as a by-product of receiving the standard confirmation; however, they do not represent the primary purpose for obtaining the confirmation.

2. (d) AU 330.14 states, "The AICPA Standard Form to Confirm Account Balance Information With Financial Institutions is designed to substantiate information that is stated on the confirmation request; the form is not designed to provide assurance that information about accounts not listed on the form will be reported." The bank employee completing the form may be unaware of all the financial relationships that the client has with the bank and the request may not ask specifically about all the financial relationships, thus the usefulness of the confirmation in providing evidence for financial statement assertions may be limited. Responding to bank confirmation requests is a normal activity for a bank. It would be unlikely that a bank employee would not believe that the bank is obligated to verify confidential information to the third party, especially as the confirmation request is signed by the client authorizing the bank to release the information to the auditor. The bank would not have access to the client's bank reconciliation and thus would not inspect its accuracy. The bank does have access to the client's cutoff bank statements, but that information is not used by the bank to confirm year end balances.

3. (a) The bank confirmations provide the best primary evidence of the year-end bank balance. In an audit engagement, the best evidence is from an independent third party. If financial statements are being compiled rather than audited, no confirmation is required and the bank reconciliation would provide the primary evidence. A bank deposit lead schedule is not primary evidence by itself.

4. (b) This bank transfer results in an overstatement of cash at December 31. The receipt of the transfer was recorded in the books on December 31, thus increasing that bank account's cash balance on that date. However, the disbursement of the transfer was not recorded in the books until January 4; thus, that bank account's cash balance was not decreased until after the financial statement date. The bank transfers indicated in answers (a), (c), and (d) do not result in a misstatement of cash. The books recorded the disbursement and receipt of each of these bank transfers in the same fiscal year.

A/R & SALES

5. (b) AU 326.07 states, "Valuation and allocation deal with whether asset, liability, revenue, and expense components have been included in the financial statements at appropriate amounts." An example would be management's assertion that trade accounts receivable included in the balance sheet are stated at net realizable value. Answer (a) deals with whether assets or liabilities of the entity exist at a given date and whether recorded transactions have occurred during a given period. Answer (c) deals with whether all transactions and accounts that should be presented in the financial statements are so included. Answer (d) deals with whether assets are the rights of the entity and liabilities are the obligations of the entity at a given date.

6. (a) AU 326.07 states that assertions about valuation deal with whether assets (among other components) are included in financial statements at appropriate amounts. An auditor's primary purpose in reviewing credit ratings of customers with delinquent accounts receivable is to obtain evidence relating to valuation. If the valuation account is too low, net accounts receivable would be too high, and the assets would, therefore, be overstated.

7. (b) This test is performed to satisfy the audit objective of completeness. The primary purpose of this objective is to establish whether all transactions that should have been recorded by the client are included in the accounts.

8. (a) Lapping involves the theft of one customer's payment and subsequently crediting the customer with payment made by another customer. Future remittances may be deposited but would be credited to the account from which funds were stolen, thus comparison of remittance dates would detect the scheme. Answers (b), (c), and (d) occur after the theft and would not show differences to pursue.

9. (b) When the auditor has already gathered evidence supporting cash receipts and accounts receivable, the same evidence would support sales. Thus, having already gathered this evidence and having assessed control risk as low for the existence

or occurrence assertion regarding sales transactions, the auditor most likely would conclude that he or she has substantial evidence for sales and would limit substantive tests of sales transactions. Evidence supporting opening and closing inventory balances, shipping and receiving activities, and cut-offs of sales and purchases would give only limited information regarding sales.

10. (b) AU 326.05 states, "Assertions about completeness deal with whether all transactions and accounts that should be presented in the financial statements are so included." Periodically accounting for the numerical sequence of documents and invoices helps ensure that all entries affecting those accounts have been recognized and posted. Answer (a) is a clerical test for accuracy. Answer (c) relates to management's assertion of accuracy and valuation. Answer (d) is a test of controls for authorization of credit prior to the sale being approved.

11. (c) In general, cut-off tests are used to detect unrecorded transactions at the end of the period. In this question, the auditor would most likely detect unrecorded sales for the year by reviewing a sales cut-off to determine that sales were recorded in the period in which title to the goods passed to the customer. Such a review would not reveal shipments lacking invoices, excessive write-offs of accounts receivable, or lapping of year-end accounts receivable.

12. (c) Answer (c) identifies the segregation of custody and reporting as important internal controls. Authorization of write-offs by a supervisor is a good control but would not in itself prevent an employee from misappropriating accounts receivable collections because the supervisor is unfamiliar with the accounts, as indicated in the question, and would, therefore, not be aware of customers who are delinquent in their payments. Answers (a) and (d) are examples of good internal controls but would not by themselves uncover a lapping of collections scheme.

A/R Confirmations

13. (d) Negative confirmations are used when the auditor can tolerate a high level of detection risk, i.e., when inherent risk and control risk are low. Negative confirmations provide less persuasive evidence than positive confirmations. (The auditor is unable to determine if a lack of response is due to customer agreement or lack of delivery of the request for confirmation, etc.) If the total recorded amount of A/R is immaterial to the financial statement taken as a whole, confirmations of any kind would be unlikely. If response rates in prior year were inadequate, the auditor may consider other procedures, but not a type of confirmation for which response rates cannot be determined. If recipients are likely to return positive confirmations requests without verifying the accuracy of the information, it is unlikely they would have greater inclination to verify the accuracy of the information for a negative one.

14. (a) Providing additional information may make the task of confirming debts appear easier to the client's customers' employees, resulting in a response getting prepared and approved, rather than indefinitely waiting in a stack for a supervisor to examine and then approve. Customers with large balances may have the worse response rate. The use of fax or e-mail may impact the response time, but probably not the response rate. The threat of a second request will probably have no more positive impact than the first request had, and may annoy the client's customers.

15. (a) Blank A/R confirmations request that the customers supply the amount owed, if any. By having the customers provide the information, the auditor increases the likelihood that customers did examine their records. Positive confirmations have the amount that the customers owe provided by the client, typically invoice-by-invoice. The invoice-by-invoice form simplifies verifying subsequent cash receipts as compared to a single sum owed. Negative confirmations request the customer to return the confirmation, with corrections, only if their records differ. They usually are used if the combined assessed level of inherent risk and control risk is low, i.e., if few exceptions are expected.

16. (c) Nonresponse to positive requests for accounts receivable confirmations generally requires the use of follow-up requests, such as additional mailings or telephone calls. It is appropriate that the auditor ask the client to contact the customers. In cases where there is still no response to requests dealing with significant accounts, alternative procedures should be used to obtain adequate evidence, as discussed in AU 330.31 and .32. These additional procedures may involve the examination of documents such as subsequent cash receipts, sales invoices, and shipping documents. While nonresponse increases risks associated with the audit, it is the auditor's responsibility to apply alternative procedures to keep the risks within acceptable levels.

17. (d) The client prepares account confirmation requests. To maintain customer goodwill, an indication that a non-response will cause a second request should be avoided. A non-response to a positive confirmation request generates further inquires, **not** an assumption that a balance is correct.

18. (c) Answer (c) clearly states the consequences of the client's customer's actions and informs the customer of the deadline. Answer (b) omits any indication of a deadline. While informing the client's customers that the confirmation request is not a payment request may be included in the letter, it only informs the client's customers what not to do—rather than the desired action. Amounts on A/R confirmation requests represent all owed amounts, not just those that are overdue.

INVENTORY

19. (b) The formula for inventory turnover is cost of goods sold divided by average inventory. Cost of goods sold includes only inventory related expenses and thus is the best value to use to compare to average inventory to calculate inventory turnover. Net sales, operating income, and gross sales are all based on the prices charged the customers, not the actual costs to the company for the goods that were sold, and thus are not as closely related to the costs associated with inventory.

20. (d) Physical counts of inventory items higher than the recorded quantities in perpetual inventory records could be the result of the failure to record sales returns in the books when sales return items were returned to inventory. Failure to record purchase discounts would have nothing to do with the recorded *quantities* in the records. Failure to record purchase returns and sales would result in the physical counts being *lower* than the quantities in the perpetual records.

21. (c) When auditing inventory, the auditor needs to obtain evidence supporting management's assertions of presentation and disclosure, answer (a), and valuation, answers (b) and (d). It would not be unusual for the client to have inventory out on consignment or held in a warehouse beyond the client's premises. Also, some of the inventory items could be in transit at the inventory date. The auditor needs to obtain confirmation or perform other auditing procedures to support management's assertions as to the existence and valuation of these assets, but the assets would not necessarily need to be on hand.

22. (a) The procedure in answer (a) helps provide assurance about valuation of inventory. The procedures in answers (b), (c), and (d) provide assurance regarding existence.

23. (b) Normally, when perpetual inventory records are well-kept and physical count comparisons are made on a regular basis, an auditor may perform inventory observation during or after the end of the period being audited. An auditor would probably request that the physical inventory count be done at year-end, if the auditor does not have much confidence in the ability of the present internal controls to detect errors when control risk is high.

24. (b) Inspecting agreements to determine whether any inventory is pledged as collateral or subject to any liens would provide the accountant with evidence concerning the assertions about rights and obligations which deal with whether assets are the rights of the entity and liabilities are the obligations of the entity at a given date.

25. (a) The account scrutinized in this question is inventory (not loans payable). The valuation, existence, and completeness of the inventory are not in question. The inventory is collateral for the loan; disclosure is the issue.

26. (b) AU 326.05 states, "Assertions about completeness deal with whether all transactions and accounts that should be presented in the financial statements are so included." For example, management asserts that all purchases of goods and services are recorded and included in the financial statements. By tracing from the inventory floor to the records, the auditor is checking for completeness. Answer (a) would deal with the rights to the inventory which would be evidenced by vendor invoices. Answer (c) would be tested by vouching or going from the inventory list to the floor to identify the assets are in existence. Answer (d) deals with extending the counts at the proper amount in the financial statements which would be tested by multiplying the inventory count of an item by its cost based on a vendor's invoice.

27. (c) To gain assurance that all items in a client's inventory listing schedule are valid, an auditor most likely would trace items listed in the listing schedule to inventory tags and the auditor's recorded count sheets. To trace the inventory tags to the listing schedule and to trace items listed in receiving reports and vendors' invoices to the listing schedule would provide assurance that all the inventory items are on the schedule, but would not give assurance that all of the items on the schedule are valid; some items on the schedule may not exist. Tracing tags to receiving reports and vendors' invoices does not involve the inventory listing schedule and thus does not provide any assurances related to the listing schedule.

FIXED ASSETS

28. (d) The repairs and maintenance expense accounts are analyzed by an auditor in obtaining evidence regarding the completeness of fixed assets, since there is the possibility that items were expensed that should have been capitalized.

29. (b) Inspecting plant and equipment will provide evidence concerning its existence. However, just because an asset is physically present in a plant doesn't mean that it is correctly presented in the financial statements. For example, an asset may be leased, not owned.

30. (b) When plant assets are retired, the accumulated depreciation account is debited for the amount of depreciation that has been recorded for those assets, which could be a satisfactory explanation for significant debits to this account. When the estimated remaining useful life of a plant asset is revised upward, the calculation for current and future depreciation is revised to reflect the new estimate of remaining useful life; accumulated depreciation is not affected. If the prior year's depreciation expense was erroneously understated, a correction would require a credit, not a debit, to accumulated depreciation. Revisions in overhead allocations would not affect the accumulated depreciation accounts.

31. (a) Since recording depreciation is necessary for the financial statements to conform with GAAP, after valuation and allocation, the secondary purpose of determining that the proper amount of depreciation was expensed is presentation and disclosure.

INVESTMENTS

32. (b) In accordance with AU 332.04, an auditor confirms with an outside agent that the agent is holding investment securities in the client's name on deposit, pledged, or in safekeeping to support assertions pertaining to the existence, ownership and cost (not valuation). Ownership assertions include rights and obligations. The auditor would check valuation with a listing of market values, as not all agents undertake to value the securities that they hold. Completeness would not be confirmed, as an entity might have more than one agent or have some securities in transit. Presentation and disclosure would depend, in part, on the nature of the securities, not that they are being held.

33. (a) Investment advisory services have an interest in having accurate records of dividends and are ordinarily independent of the audit client. Stock indentures and stock ledgers may not have dividend records. Annual audited investee financial statements may not be timely available.

34. (a) Analytical tests as a source of information for developing expectations include analysis of the relationships among elements of financial information within the period. Answers (b), (c), and (d) represent management's assertions of disclosure, valuation and existence which would be verified by substantive tests applied to the respective accounts.

35. (c) AU 332.04 states, "Evidential matter pertaining to the existence, ownership, and cost of long-term investments includes accounting records and documents of the investor relating to their acquisition." In the case of investments in the form of securities (such as stocks, bonds, and notes), this evidential matter should be corroborated by inspection of the securities, or by written confirmation from an independent custodian of securities on deposit, pledged, or in safekeeping. Shares owned and signed over to new owners or purchased from other investors would not always be made known to the issuing company on a timely basis. Inspecting the financial statements of the investee company would not indicate the number of shares owned and who the owners are. Per SFAS 115, investment securities are to be reported at market value, not the lower of cost or market.

A/P, PURCHASES & OTHER LIABILITIES

36. (c) In order to verify the existence and valuation of the accounts payable account, the auditor should go to the source documents. These would include purchase orders and receiving reports. Answer (a) pertains to the completeness assertion and whether or not management has included all obligations in the account. Answer (b) is not a standard auditing procedure but deals with determining whether management has included all obligations for the rights and obligations assertions in the account. Answer (d) also pertains to determining whether or not there are any unrecorded obligations of the company not recorded in the account.

37. (c) In searching for unrecorded liabilities, the auditor would most likely vouch a sample of cash disbursements recorded just after year end to receiving reports and vendor invoices to ascertain that payables had been recorded in the proper period. Tracing a sample of accounts payable entries recorded **just after** (not just before) year end to the year-end unmatched receiving report file, comparing a sample of purchase orders issued **just before** (not just after) year end with the year end accounts payable, and scanning the cash

disbursements entries recorded **just after** (not just before) year end for indications of unusual transactions may also aid in the detection of unrecorded liabilities.

38. (c) Tracing a sample of purchase orders and the related receiving reports to the purchases journal and the cash disbursements journal provides evidence to determine that purchases were properly recorded. Although during this audit procedure the auditor might identify unusually large purchases that should be investigated further, this would not be the prevailing purpose of this substantive audit procedure. To verify that cash disbursements were for goods actually received would require vouching from the cash disbursements journal to the receiving reports. To test whether payments were for goods actually ordered would require vouching from the cash disbursements journal to the purchase orders.

39. (b) To verify that all merchandise received is recorded, the auditor would trace from the receiving reports to the related records. Payment vouchers, purchase requisitions, and vendor's invoices would not provide evidence that the related merchandise was actually received.

40. (c) AU 326.05 states, "Assertions about completeness deal with whether all transactions and accounts that should be presented in the financial statements are so included. For example, management asserts that all purchases of goods and services are recorded and are included in the financial statements." AU 326.10 states, "There is not necessarily a one-to-one relationship between audit objectives and procedures. Some auditing procedures may relate to more than one objective." The primary focus of cutoff tests is completeness.

PAYROLL

41. (d) Substantive tests of payroll balances when control risk is assessed as low most likely would be limited to applying analytical procedures and recalculating payroll accruals to assure the accuracy of the payroll liabilities. Observing the distribution of paychecks, recomputing the payroll register and inspecting payroll tax returns would be of greater importance if control risk related to payroll was assessed as high. In such case, these procedures would be required to assure the accuracy, and other assertions, related to payroll accounts.

42. (c) Most of the auditor's work in forming his or her opinion on financial statements consists of obtaining and evaluating evidential matter concerning the assertions in such financial statements. The auditor's objective is to obtain sufficient competent evidential matter to provide him or her with a reasonable basis for forming an opinion. The amount and kinds of evidential matter required to support an informed opinion are matters for the auditor to determine based upon his or her professional judgment. Answer (a) would not indicate the need for additional substantive testing because the auditor uses his or her own judgment based upon the evidence obtained from his or her own tests. Answer (b) could be the result of nonaccounting factors, such as opening up of a new branch, or hiring additional employees for new contracts received. Answer (d) could be a reason supporting an increase in payroll from one year to the next, but would not indicate the need for additional testing.

43. (b) To test for the appropriate number of hours worked, the auditor examines clock card data. To test for answer (a), the auditor checks personnel records. To test for answers (c) and (d), the auditor uses inquiries and observation.

LONG-TERM LIABILITIES

44. (c) One of the audit objectives of long-term liabilities is to verify that interest expense is correctly computed and that other contractual obligations are satisfied. The auditor would most likely compare interest expense with the bond payable to see if it is reasonable, and thereby test valuation. This could also aid discovery of undisclosed liabilities.

STOCKHOLDERS' EQUITY

45. (c) Restrictions on retained earnings should be disclosed in the financial statements. Restrictions would not impact the valuation, allocation, existence, or occurrence of retained earnings. Rights and obligations generally refer to assets and liabilities, not retained earnings.

46. (a) One of the auditor's objectives in the examination of owners' equity is to determine that all transactions during the year affecting owners' equity accounts were properly authorized and recorded. In the case of a corporation, changes in capital stock accounts should receive formal advance approval by the *board of directors*. A transfer agent's records show detail about the owners of the stock, and do not focus on the total outstanding. Canceled stock certificates and a treasury stock certificate book are less reliable than the minutes, as they would be updated only after the transaction is complete.

47. (d) The primary responsibility of a registrar of capital stock is to verify that securities are properly issued, recorded, and transferred.

Accounting Estimates

48. (a) Amortization allocates the cost of the intangible to the periods in which the benefit is received and yields an appropriate valuation of the intangible in those periods. Amortization is not relevant to the existence or occurrence, completeness, or rights and obligations assertions.

49. (d) AU 342.10 states, "In evaluating reasonableness, the auditor should obtain an understanding of how management developed the [accounting] estimate." Based on that understanding, the auditor should use at least one of several approaches which include reviewing and testing the process used by management to develop the estimate and developing an independent expectation of the estimate. An auditor would consider the appropriateness of the key factors or assumptions used in preparing the estimates (AU 342.11).

50. (a) Assumptions that are susceptible to bias provide an opportunity for the overstatement of assets and income and understatement of liabilities. Assumptions that meet the criteria of the other answers offer less scope for creative accounting.

Solution 36-2 ADDITIONAL MULTIPLE CHOICE ANSWERS

A/R & Sales

51. (d) AU 326.05 states, "Assertions about completeness deal with whether all transactions and accounts that should be presented in the financial statements are so included." Periodically accounting for the numerical sequence of documents and invoices helps ensure that all entries affecting those accounts have been recognized and posted. Answer (a) deals with whether assets or liabilities of the entity exist at a given date and whether recorded transactions have occurred during a given period. Answer (b) deals with whether assets are the rights of the entity and liabilities are the obligations of the entity at a given date. Answer (c) deals with whether asset, liability, revenue, and expense components have been included in the financial statements at appropriate amounts.

A/R Confirmations

52. (b) Verifying the sources and contents of the faxes in telephone calls to sources is relatively easy and quick. It also provides a direct check on the external faxes. Internal shipping documents do not provide evidence as persuasive as the external faxes. The connection from fax to shipping document would also take time and effort to research. Considering faxes as non-responses and evaluating them as unadjusted differences is unreasonably harsh. Additional procedures would be required to conclude that A/R is overvalued. The inspection of faxes for forgeries or alterations is unlikely to be as easy and quick as phone conversations.

53. (a) The original forms are the (signed) evidence that the auditor first sought. A/R confirmations are more timely and complete evidence than subsequent cash receipts. Accounts may not be paid rapidly or in single payments. Considering e-mail responses as exceptions is unreasonably harsh. Second requests generally would gain the same response as the first requests.

54. (a) The positive (confirmation) form is preferable when individual account balances are relatively large or when there is reason to believe that there may be a substantial number of accounts in dispute or with errors or fraud. In this case, errors or fraud are likely since internal controls are weak. Negative confirmations are used when the assessed level of control risk is low. With weak internal controls, the auditor needs to obtain third party verification.

55. (c) The A/R and sales audit objective related to the completeness assertion is to ascertain that **all** sales and receivables that should be recorded are properly recorded. Customers may not be inclined to report understatement errors in their accounts, and thus not all the sales and receivables that should be recorded are necessarily recorded. It is not as likely that customers will merely sign and return the confirmation without verifying its details; the accounts they are verifying represent liabilities to them. It is more likely that the customers will not return forms. A nonresponse could mean that the intended recipient did not receive the request, has misplaced or not processed the request, or has returned the request but it was delayed or lost in transit. Auditors typically confirm few accounts with low recorded balances and a high percentage of accounts with large balances.

56. (a) AU 330.22 states that unreturned negative confirmations do not provide explicit evidence. AU 330.20 notes that negative confirmations may be effective when three criteria are met; one of

the criteria is that the combined assessed level of inherent and control risk is low. AU 330.31 notes that for unreturned positive confirmations, alternative procedures are used. The auditor would be more likely to use positive confirmations, which provide more persuasive evidence, if understatements are suspected.

INVENTORY

57. (a) The cost of obsolete or slow-moving inventory may have to be written down; this affects the valuation assertion. Rights, obligations, existence, occurrence, presentation, and disclosure are not affected by obsolete or slow-moving items.

FIXED ASSETS

58. (c) AU 319.81 states, "...ordinarily the assessed level of control risk cannot be sufficiently low to eliminate the need to perform any substantive tests significant to restrict detection risk for all of the assertions relevant to account balances and transaction classes." AU 319.80 states, "As the assessed level of control risk decreases, the acceptable level of detection risk increases. Accordingly, the auditor may alter the...extent of substantive tests performed." With a low level of control risk, minimal substantive testing is required. Answer (d) is the opposite, indicating extensive tests. Answers (a) and (b) do not include test of controls as would be required for a lower control risk assessment.

59. (d) A weakness in internal control over recording retirements of equipment most likely would result in assets that have been retired continuing to be carried in the accounting records. Tracing from the records to the actual assets would be an audit procedure designed to detect such errors. Tracing equipment in the plant to the accounting records would only provide evidence about equipment not yet retired. Depreciation is applied to assets carried on the books and thus depreciation would continue to be taken on retired equipment erroneously still on the books. A review of depreciation would not of itself indicate that certain equipment had been retired. Additions to the "other assets" account would be newly acquired other assets rather than retired equipment and would not likely give any evidence about retired equipment.

INVESTMENTS

60. (b) The valuation assertion for an investment accounted for by the equity method can generally be satisfied by referring to the audited financial statements of the investee company.

A/P, PURCHASES & OTHER LIABILITIES

61. (c) AU 326.05 states, "Assertions about completeness deal with whether all transactions and accounts that should be presented in the financial statements are so included." Because liabilities have the inherent risk of being understated, substantive tests and tests of controls are directed towards determining that all liabilities of the company as of the balance sheet date are properly included.

62. (b) The objective of the auditor's test is to determine whether all merchandise for which the client was billed was received. The population for this test consists of all vendor's invoices (bills for merchandise). The auditor would select a sample of vendor's invoices and then trace them to supporting receiving reports to assure that the merchandise for which the client was billed was received.

63. (a) In performing a search for unrecorded liabilities, one procedure performed is to send requests of confirmation of zero liabilities to previous vendors. These liabilities would be tend to be unrecorded, if they did exist. Requesting confirmations of payees of checks drawn just after year-end provides evidence of timing, not completeness.

LONG-TERM LIABILITIES

64. (b) An auditor's program to examine long-term debt should include a step where the auditor reconciles interest expense with debt outstanding during the year (period). This step would provide information as to the completeness and valuation of the account balance. The auditor is not concerned with the year-end market value of the debt. The auditor would not verify the existence of the holders of the debt by direct confirmation. Outstanding balances, terms, and conditions are confirmed with the credit grantor or independent trustee. The search for unrecorded liabilities would generally be made by scanning cash disbursements made in the period following the balance sheet date. Also, the accounts payable subsidiary ledger would not likely provide evidence as to long-term liabilities.

STOCKHOLDER'S EQUITY

65. (d) One of the primary objectives in testing related to Stockholder's Equity and Capital accounts is to verify that capital transactions are appropriately authorized and approved. The granting of stock options would require board of director approval because it could affect the number of shares outstanding.

PERFORMANCE BY SUBTOPICS

Each category below parallels a subtopic covered in Chapter 36. Record the number and percentage of questions you correctly answered in each subtopic area.

Cash

Question #	Correct √
1	
2	
3	
4	
# Questions	4
# Correct	
% Correct	

A/R & Sales

Question #	Correct √
5	
6	
7	
8	
9	
10	
11	
12	
# Questions	8
# Correct	
% Correct	

A/R Confirmations

Question #	Correct √
13	
14	
15	
16	
17	
18	
# Questions	6
# Correct	
% Correct	

Inventory

Question #	Correct √
19	
20	
21	
22	
23	
24	
25	
26	
27	
# Questions	9
# Correct	
% Correct	

Fixed Assets

Question #	Correct √
28	
29	
30	
31	
# Questions	4
# Correct	
% Correct	

Investments

Question #	Correct √
32	
33	
34	
35	
# Questions	4
# Correct	
% Correct	

A/P, Purchases & Other Liabilities

Question #	Correct √
36	
37	
38	
39	
40	
# Questions	5
# Correct	
% Correct	

Payroll

Question #	Correct √
41	
42	
43	
# Questions	3
# Correct	
% Correct	

Long-Term Liabilities

Question #	Correct √
44	
# Questions	1
# Correct	
% Correct	

Stockholders' Equity

Question #	Correct √
45	
46	
47	
# Questions	3
# Correct	
% Correct	

Accounting Estimates

Question #	Correct √
48	
49	
50	
# Questions	3
# Correct	
% Correct	

OTHER OBJECTIVE FORMAT QUESTION SOLUTIONS

PROBLEM 36-3 AUDIT PROCEDURES

1. E Preparing a bank transfer schedule would permit the auditor to determine whether a kiting scheme exists.

2. D Obtaining a cutoff bank statement and comparing the cleared checks to the year-end bank reconciliation would provide some evidence that checks were not mailed until after the first week of the subsequent year.

3. H Confirming loan terms with a lender would reveal that lender's lien on the real estate.

4. K,L Sending a second confirmation request and making inquiries of a reputable credit agency would provide evidence of the customer's existence and credit worthiness. Examining the shipping documents assists the auditor to determine whether merchandise was actually shipped to the customer.

5. P A surprise observation of the distribution of payroll checks would provide evidence that the new employees exist and are currently working.

6. Q Vouching data in the payroll register to authorized pay rates in the human resource files would permit the auditor to determine whether rate increases are properly authorized.

7. A Comparing the details of the cash receipts journal entries with the corresponding daily deposit slips would permit the auditor to determine whether the receipts were properly recorded.

8. U Examining the purchase orders and receiving reports for selected vouchers would permit

the auditor to determine whether the merchandise was ordered and received by the entity.

9. B Vouching fixed asset accounts debits to the vendors' invoices would permit the auditor to determine whether equipment repairs had been misclassified as fixed assets.

10. A, J Comparing the details of cash receipts journal entries with the corresponding daily deposit slips and confirming the entity's accounts receivable on a surprise basis would permit the auditor to determine whether a lapping scheme exists.

11. E Preparing a bank transfer schedule would permit the auditor to determine whether cash is being inappropriately increased by drawing an unrecorded check on one account and simultaneously recording a deposit in a second account.

12. J, L Confirming the entity's accounts receivable on a surprise basis would permit the auditor to determine whether sales to those customers were genuine. Examining the shipping documents would permit the auditor to determine whether merchandise was actually shipped to those customers.

Solution 36-4 Audit Procedures

1. I A mark next to the lenders' names is most likely to indicate that the information in the next 3 columns is accurate. This mark is unlikely to relate to a dollar balance as it is not positioned closely to any numbers.

2. C Material beginning balances are generally traced to the prior year's working papers.

3. J Increased borrowings should be processed with the board of directors' authorization, should correspond to the loan agreement, and their disposition should be traceable. These are all items of interest to an auditor.

4. H As the loan to First National Bank has the principal due in 20X3, any payment before that date would have specific authorization by board of directors. The auditor would also likely examine the canceled check(s) associated with this transfer.

5. G The repayments did not agree to the BOD authorization. [Assume the board of directors (BOD) authorized payment of the full $120,000 ($10,000 x 12 months), based on the terms of the loan.] Confirmation of receipt of the $110,000 is obtained from the monthly statement that the bank issues. The auditor would also likely examine the canceled check(s) associated with this transfer.

6. A The comments column shows that two of the three lenders with this mark in the ending balance column agrees with the account balance. The third doesn't show a dispute about the amount. The lender without this mark does have a comment about a dispute.

7. K This mark is next to the two loans that have required payments of due in the next year.

8. B This mark is next to the one loan that has a dispute between the lender and the audit client.

9. D The total long-term debt and the total accrued interest payable are likely to be entire, separate accounts in the trial balance and general ledger. It is reasonable to trace accounts to the current year financial statements (via the trial balance etc.) after examining them.

10. F It is normal for the auditor to recompute interest accruals and check the reasonableness of the client's interest accrual.

11. F Material beginning balances are generally traced to the prior year's working papers.

12. L Documentation for additions to PP&E is generally examined in an audit. Deeds and purchase contracts would be appropriate documents to examine for a land purchase.

13. K Documentation for additions to PP&E is generally examined in an audit. Work orders and engineers' reports would be appropriate documents to examine for constructed assets.

14. J Documentation for additions to PP&E is generally examined in an audit. Vendors' invoices would be appropriate documents to examine for purchased assets.

15. G As the disposals are fully depreciated and of relatively small amount, procedures may not be necessary.

16. D An amount is removed from buildings and added to fixtures, but the net for PP&E is zero.

17. C The individual categories of PP&E and accumulated depreciation are likely to be entire, separate accounts in the trial balance and general ledger. It is reasonable to trace accounts to the current year financial statements (via the trial balance etc.) after auditing them.

18. B The provision for accumulated depreciation can be easily checked against the PP&E accounts, as the rate and method for each category is known.

SOLUTION 36-5 CASH

1. 2, 4

The term kiting refers to the practice of transferring cash between or among various bank accounts, with recording of the cash receipt (deposit) being made on a timely basis, while the recording of the disbursement (withdrawal) is delayed. Thus, for a period of time, the amount of the check could appear in two different accounts simultaneously. In this question, note that the *receipt* of check #2 was recorded (per the books) at 12/30, while the disbursement was not recorded (per the books) until 1/3. Also, note that check #4 (written from State Bank) was received by the bank on 12/31 but was not recorded on the Fox Co.'s books until 1/2.

2. 1, 3

Deposits/transfers in transit refer to checks which have been recorded on the entity's books but have not yet cleared the bank. In this question, note that checks #1 and #3 were disbursed (per books) at the end of December, but were not received by the bank until early January.

ESSAY SOLUTIONS

SOLUTION 36-6 CASH

The auditor should:

- **Review answers to questions on confirmation requests** to determine proper recognition in accounting records and the necessity for financial statement disclosure.
- Make inquiries as to compensating balances and restrictions.
- **Obtain copies** of the **bank reconciliations** as of the balance sheet date, and
- **Trace** the adjusted book balances to the general ledger balances.
- Compare the bank balances to the opening balances on the cutoff bank statements.
- Compare the bank balances to the balances on the confirmations.
- Trace amounts of **deposits in transit** to the cutoff bank statements and ascertain whether the **time lags** are reasonable.
- Verify the **clerical accuracy** of the reconciliations.
- Obtain explanation for **unusual reconciling items**, including checks drawn to "bearer," "cash," and related parties.
- Trace checks dated prior to the **end of the period** that were returned with the cutoff statements to the **list of outstanding checks**.
- **Investigate outstanding checks** that did not clear with the cutoff bank statements.
- **Examine a sample of checks** for payee, amount, date, authorized signatures, and endorsements to determine any irregularities from company policy or accounting records.
- **Prepare a bank transfer schedule** from a review of the cash receipts and disbursements journals, bank statements, and related paid checks for the last few days before and the first few days after the year-end, and
- Review the schedule to determine that the deposit and disbursement of each transfer is **recorded in the proper period.**
- Trace incomplete transfers to the schedule of outstanding checks and deposits in transit.

SOLUTION 36-7 ACCOUNTS RECEIVABLE

a. Although there is a presumption that King will request the confirmation of Cycle's accounts receivable, King could justify omitting this procedure if Cycle's accounts receivable are **immaterial to its financial statements**. King could also justify omitting this procedure if the **expected response rates** to properly designed confirmation requests **will be inadequate**, or if **responses will be unreliable**. In these circumstances, King may determine that the use of confirmations would be **ineffective**.

Additionally, King could justify omitting the confirmation of Cycle's accounts receivable if King's **combined assessed level of inherent** and **control risk** is low and the **assessed level, in conjunction** with the **evidence** expected to be **provided by analytical procedures** or other **substantive tests of details**, is **sufficient to reduce audit risk** to an **acceptably low level** for the applicable financial assertions.

b. Among the factors likely to affect the **reliability of confirmations** that King sends is King's decision in choosing the confirmation form. Some positive forms **request agreement or disagreement with information stated** on the form; other positive forms, known as **blank forms**, request the respondent to **fill in the balance or furnish other information**; **negative forms request** a response **only if there is disagreement** with the information stated on the request.

King's prior experience with Cycle or similar clients is also likely to affect reliability because King probably would have **prior knowledge** of the **expected confirmation response rates**, inaccurate **information on prior years' confirmations**, and **misstatements identified during prior audits**.

The **nature of the information** being confirmed may affect the **competence of the evidence** obtained as well as the response rate. For example, Cycle's **customers' accounting systems** may permit confirmation of individual transactions, but not account balances, or vice versa.

Additionally, King's sending of each confirmation request to the **proper respondent** will likely provide meaningful and competent evidence. Each request should be sent to a person who King believes is **knowledgeable about the information** to be confirmed.

c. The nature of the alternative procedures King would apply when replies to positive confirmation request are not received varies according to the account and assertion in question. Possible alternative procedures include **examining subsequent cash receipts**, and **matching** such **receipts with the actual items being paid**. King would also consider **inspecting Cycle's shipping documents or invoices**, or Cycle's **customers' purchase orders** on file. **Inspecting correspondence** between Cycle and its customers could provide additional evidence. King may also establish the existence of Cycle's customers by **reference to credit sources** such as Dun & Bradstreet.

SOLUTION 36-8 ACCOUNTS RECEIVABLE

a. Confirmation #11—Atom. Adler should determine that Superior received and deposited Atom's check on December 28, 20X1, by **examining supporting documentation**, e.g., the entry in the cash receipts journal and either Superior's deposit ticket or its bank statement. Adler should also determine the account to which the check was recorded and **why** it was not credited to Atom's account.

Confirmation #28—Baker. Adler should **examine the terms of the sale and the shipping documents**, especially whether the sale/shipment was to be FOB shipping point or FOB destination and the date the goods were shipped to Baker, to **verify** when the **criteria for revenue recognition were met**.

Confirmation #34—Clark. Adler should read Superior's correspondence files for evidence concerning the **terms of the shipment** to Clark to determine whether the criteria for revenue recognition were met.

Confirmation #41—Delta. Adler should **investigate** whether the merchandise was ever shipped to Delta and, if so, whether the sale was ever consummated, or whether the merchandise was returned, or whether Superior expects it to be returned.

Confirmation #58—Eagle. Adler should send a **second request** to Eagle providing the individual invoice numbers and amounts or attaching copies of the individual unpaid invoices that Eagle's accounts payable voucher system can verify. In the alternative, Adler should examine shipping documents and subsequent cash receipts.

Confirmation #67—Franklin. Adler should determine Franklin's correct address and send a **second request**.

Confirmation #71—Grove. Adler should **determine when the check was received** and where it was recorded by examining Superior's cash receipts records, bank statements, and accounts receivable detail.

Confirmation #86—Hall. No additional procedures are necessary to resolve this confirmation request, although Adler may want to **trace the cash receipt** to verify that Hall's check was actually received, deposited, and credited to Hall's account in January 20X2.

b. When replies to positive confirmation requests have not been received, Miller should apply alternative substantive procedures to the non-responding accounts receivable. Miller most likely would **examine subsequent cash receipts** for the accounts that have been paid. This would include matching such receipts with the actual items being paid. In addition, especially for receivables that have not been paid, Miller should **inspect shipping documents** or other client documentation (e.g. sales invoices, customers' purchase orders, etc.) that may provide evidence for the existence assertion. Miller should also consider **reading any correspondence in Superior's files** that may indicate disagreements with its customers about the amounts billed or the terms of the sales. In addition, Miller may consider **contacting a reputable credit agency** to verify the existence of customers who are new to the client or who Miller may be unfamiliar with.

c. The additional substantive procedures that Miller should consider performing to complete the audit of Superior's accounts receivable and related allowances include the following:

- **Test the cut-off** of sales, cash receipts, and sales returns and allowances.
- Evaluate the reasonableness of all allowances against receivables.
- **Perform analytical procedures** for accounts receivable, such as sales returns and allowances to sales, bad debt expense to net credit sales, accounts receivable turnover, and days' sales in receivables.
- **Determine that** Superior's revenue recognition **policies are appropriate**, including policies for consignment sales.
- **Review activity after the balance sheet date** for unusual transactions, such as large sales returns.
- Determine whether any accounts receivable are **pledged or factored**.

Determine that the **presentation and disclosure** of accounts receivable and related allowances are in conformity with generally accepted accounting principles.

SOLUTION 36-9 INVENTORY

a. The means or techniques of gathering audit evidence, in addition to the example, are as follows:

Technique	Description
Inquiry	An auditor **questions** client personnel about events and conditions, such as obsolete inventory.
Confirmation	An auditor obtains **acknowledgments** in writing from third parties of transactions or balances, such as inventory in public warehouses or on consignment.
Calculation or Recomputation	An auditor **recomputes** certain amounts, such as the multiplication of quantity times price to determine inventory amounts.
Analysis	An auditor **combines amounts in meaningful ways** to allow the application of audit judgment, such as the determination of whether a proper inventory cutoff was performed.
Inspection	An auditor **examines** documents relating to transactions and balances, such as shipping and receiving records to establish ownership of inventory.
Comparison	An auditor **relates two or more amounts**, such as inventory cost in perpetual inventory records to costs as shown on vendor invoices as part of the evaluation of whether inventory is priced at the lower of cost or market.

b. Substantive auditing procedures that would satisfy the five general assertions regarding a client's inventory balance include the following: (one different procedure required for each assertion)

Assertion	Substantive Auditing Procedure
1. Existence or Occurrence	• **Observe physical inventory** counts. • **Obtain confirmation** of inventories at locations outside the entity. • Test inventory transactions between a preliminary physical inventory date and the balance sheet date. • **Review perpetual inventory records**, production records, and purchasing records for indications of current activity. • **Compare inventories** with a current sales catalog and subsequent sales and delivery reports. • Use the work of specialists to **corroborate the nature of specialized products**.
2. Completeness	• **Observe physical inventory counts.** • Apply **analytical procedures** to the relationship of inventory balances to recent purchasing, production, and sales activities. • Test shipping and receiving cutoff procedures. • **Obtain confirmation** of inventories at locations outside the entity. • **Trace test counts** recorded during the physical inventory observation to the inventory listing. • **Account for all inventory tags** and count sheets used in recording the physical inventory counts. • Test the clerical accuracy of inventory listings. • Reconcile physical counts to perpetual records and general ledger balances and investigate significant fluctuations.
3. Rights and Obligations	• **Observe** physical inventory counts. • Obtain **confirmation of inventory** at **locations outside the entity**. • Examine **paid vendors' invoices, consignment agreements**, and **contracts**. • Test **shipping and receiving cutoff** procedures.
4. Valuation or Allocation	• Examine **paid vendors' invoices.** • Review **direct labor rates.** • **Test the computation** of standard overhead rates. • Examine **analyses** of purchasing and manufacturing **standard cost variances.** • Examine an **analysis of inventory turnover.** • Review **industry experience and trends.** • Apply analytical procedures to the relationship of **inventory balances to anticipated sales volume.** • **Tour** the plant. • Inquire of production and sales personnel concerning possible **excess or obsolete inventory** items. • Obtain **current market value** quotations. • Review current market value quotations.

	• Examine **sales after year-end and open purchase order** commitments.
5. Presentation Disclosure	• **Review drafts** of the financial and statements. • Compare the **disclosures** made in the financial statements to the requirements of generally accepted accounting principles. • Obtain confirmation of **inventories pledged under loan agreements.**

SOLUTION 36-10 INVESTMENTS

a.

Primary Assertion	Objective
4. **Existence or occurrence**	To determine that the custodian **holds the securities** as identified in the confirmation.
5 **Completeness**	To determine that **all income and related collections** from the investments are properly **recorded.**
6. **Valuation or allocation**	To determine that the **market or other value** of the investments is **fairly stated.**
7. **Presentation and disclosure**	To determine that the financial statement **presentation and disclosure** of investments is in **conformity** with generally accepted accounting principles **consistently applied.**
8. **Valuation or allocation**	To determine that the **market or other value** of the investments is **fairly stated** and the **loss** is properly **recognized and recorded.**

b. Larkin should consider applying the following additional substantive auditing procedures in auditing Vernon's investments:

- **Inspect** securities on hand in the presence of the custodian.
- **Examine supporting evidence** (broker's advices, etc.) for transactions between the balance sheet date and the inspection date.
- Obtain **confirmation** from the issuers or trustees for investments in nonpublic entities.
- **Examine** contractual **terms** of debt securities and preferred stock.
- Determine that sales and purchases were properly **approved** by the Board of Directors or its designee.
- **Examine** broker's advices in support of transactions or **confirm transactions** with broker.
- Determine that **gains and losses** on dispositions have been **properly computed.**
- **Trace** payments for purchases to canceled checks, and proceeds from sales to entries in the cash receipts journal.
- Determine that the **amortization** of premium and discount on bonds has been **properly computed.**
- **Determine** that **market value** for trading, available-for-sale, and held-to-maturity portfolios has been properly computed by tracing quoted market prices to competent published or other sources.
- **Compute the unrealized** gains and losses on trading, available-for-sale, and held-to-maturity portfolios for marketable equity securities.
- Determine that the unrealized **gains and losses** on the trading and available-for-sale portfolios have been **properly classified** in the income statement, and the unrealized gains and losses on the held-to-maturity portfolio have been properly classified in the equity section of the balance sheet.
- **Ascertain whether** any investments are **pledged** as collateral or encumbered by liens, and, if so, are properly **disclosed.**

SOLUTION 36-11 ACCOUNTS PAYABLE

a. In searching for DollarMart's unrecorded liabilities, Cook most likely would **review** DollarMart's **cash disbursements journal near the conclusion of field work for checks written after year end** and examine the supporting documentation, such as receiving reports and vendors' invoices, for selected disbursements to determine that the related accounts payable were properly recorded and to **verify the cutoff** of DollarMart's receipt of inventory. Alternatively, Cook could review DollarMart's voucher register for selected transactions similarly recorded shortly after year end and examine the supporting detail to identify items that should have been recorded at the balance sheet date, but were not.

Cook most likely would consider examining files of receiving reports and comparing them to recorded accounts payable entries. This would assist Cook in **searching for significant merchandise received before year end** to verify DollarMart's schedule of merchandise received but not yet billed. Cook may also consider **inspecting** DollarMart's files of **unprocessed vendors' invoices**, vendors' statements, and outstanding purchase orders, and comparing them with the receiving records and accounts payable entries for unrecorded liabilities.

Although confirmations are usually not the best source of evidence for unrecorded accounts payable, Cook may consider confirming selected **accounts payable** with vendors, including regular suppliers showing small or zero balances at year end.

Cook most likely would consider performing **analytical procedures** such as comparing gross margin, purchases, or certain expense account balances with those of the prior year to identify any large changes that should be investigated because they may represent unrecorded liabilities.

Additionally, Cook may tailor the **management representation letter** to impress upon DollarMart the need to be concerned about unrecorded accounts payable.

b. Cook most likely would perform more **substantive auditing procedures** at year end because of DollarMart's deficient control environment. For example, Cook would be more likely to confirm DollarMart's accounts payable. Tests would most likely be performed **further into the subsequent year** and at a **lower dollar value or materiality level** than otherwise.

SOLUTION 36-12 PAYROLL

Bell should consider performing the following procedures in the audit of Kent's payroll transactions:

Select a **sample of payments to employees** from the **payroll register** and compare each selected transaction to the related documents and records examining

- Evidence in support of **authorization of rate** of pay.
- Evidence in support of **time** on which compensation was based, such as approved **time cards or attendance records**.
- Evidence in support of proper **authorization** of payroll **withholdings**.
- Evidence in support of payments, such as **canceled payroll checks**.
- Evidence in support of **account distribution**.
- The **clerical accuracy** of the transaction.
- The entry to the employee's records used to summarize employee compensation for payroll reporting purposes.

Obtain the **payroll register** for a selected period and

- Test the **arithmetical accuracy** of the payroll register.
- Determine whether **payroll** was **approved** in accordance with management's prescribed procedures.
- Trace totals per the register to postings in the general ledger.
- Observe the distribution of payroll checks.
- Review the accounting for unclaimed wages.
- Observe a sample of employees in the performance of their duties.
- Perform analytical procedures.

SOLUTION 36-13 EQUITY

The substantive audit procedures that Jones should apply in examining the common stock and treasury stock accounts are as follows:

- **Review the corporate charter** to verify details of the common stock such as authorized shares, par value, etc.
- **Obtain** or prepare an **analysis of changes** in common stock and treasury stock accounts.
- Compare opening balances with prior year's working papers.
- **Foot the total shares outstanding** in the stockholders' ledger and stock certificate book.
- Determine **authorization for common stock issuances** and **treasury stock transactions** by inspecting the minutes of the board of directors' meetings.
- **Verify capital stock issuances** by examining supporting documentation and tracing entries into the records.
- **Verify treasury stock transactions** by examining supporting documentation and tracing entries into the records.
- Examine all certificates canceled during the year.
- Inspect all treasury stock certificates owned by the client.
- **Reconcile** the details of the individual certificates in the stock certificate book with the individual shareholders' accounts in the stockholders' ledger.
- **Compare** the totals in the stockholders' ledger and the stock certificate book to the balance sheet presentation.
- Recompute the weighted average number of shares outstanding.
- **Compare** the **financial statement presentation** and disclosure with generally accepted accounting principles.
- Determine the existence of, and proper accounting for, common stock and treasury stock **transactions occurring since year-end.**
- **Obtain written representations** concerning common and treasury stock in the client representation letter.

CHAPTER 37

AUDIT SAMPLING

EXAM COVERAGE: The Obtain and Document Information portion of the Auditing section of the CPA exam is designated by the examiners to be 35 percent of the section's point value. Historically, exam coverage of the topics in Chapter 37 hovers at 3 to 5 percent of the Auditing section. More information about the point value of various topics is included in the **Practical Advice** section of this volume.

CHAPTER 37

AUDIT SAMPLING

I. Overview

A. Definition

Audit sampling is defined by SAS 39 as the application of an audit procedure to less than 100% of the items within an account balance or class of transactions (the audit population) with the intent of drawing conclusions about the population based on the results of the sample.

1. **Effective** The underlying principle of sampling is that the results of a sample yield information about the population from which the sample was taken. Sampling, therefore, can be looked upon as an **effective** and **efficient** method of gathering audit evidence.

2. **Efficient** Absent sampling, an auditor would examine every item comprising an account balance or every transaction occurring within a class of transactions. The cost would (a) be prohibitive due to the amount of time required to perform the examination and (b) far outweigh the benefit obtained. Sampling provides the auditor with a means of obtaining information, but at a much lower cost.

B. Types of Sampling

1. **Attributes Sampling** In the auditor's consideration of internal control, tests are performed on the client's internal control policies and procedures in order to determine the degree to which the client's employees have complied (i.e., tests of controls). These tests involve the determination of the rate of occurrence of some characteristic (i.e., attribute), in a population. The attribute of interest is frequently a deviation from the particular control procedure. Thus, the auditor takes a sample from the population, computes the deviation rate in the sample, and draws conclusions about the true population deviation rate.

2. **Variables Sampling** In performing the tests of details of transactions and account balances (i.e., substantive tests), the auditor is concerned with the dollar amounts reported in the financial statements. Thus, the auditor draws a sample from the population of interest, determines the proper dollar value of the items sampled, and makes inferences, based upon projection of the sample results to the population, about the fairness of the amounts reported in the financial statements.

3. **Dual-Purpose Sampling** In some circumstances, the auditor may design a test that will be used for dual purposes—tests of controls and substantive testing. A **dual-purpose sample** is a sample that is designed to both assess control risk and to provide a substantive objective.

   a. **Preliminary Risk Assessment** Because the auditor will have begun substantive procedures before determining whether the tests of controls support the initial assessment of control risk, an auditor planning to use a dual-purpose sample would have made a preliminary assessment that there is an acceptably low risk that the rate of deviations in the population exceeds the maximum acceptable rate without altering the assessment of control risk.

   b. **Objectives** To assess control risk and to test whether the recorded monetary amounts of a transaction are correct.

   c. **Low Risk Factor** Generally, the auditor who plans to use this type of sample believes that there is an acceptably low risk that the rate of deviations from prescribed internal control policies and procedures in the population is greater than the tolerable rate.

d. **SIZE** The size of the sample should be the larger of the samples that would have been designed for the two separate purposes.

C. GUIDANCE

SAS 39 provides guidelines on the use of sampling in an audit. The Third Standard of Field Work requires sufficient competent evidential matter to be obtained through inspection, observation, inquiries, and confirmations to afford a reasonable basis for an opinion on the financial statements. The use of audit sampling relates to this standard.

1. **DESCRIPTION** Audit sampling is the application of an audit procedure to less than 100% of the items within an account balance or class of transactions for the purpose of evaluating some characteristic of the balance or class. There are two general approaches to audit sampling: statistical and nonstatistical. Both require the auditor to use professional judgment.

2. **SUFFICIENCY** The sufficiency of evidential matter is determined by the size and design of an audit sample (among other factors).

   a. **SIZE** Depends on both the objectives and efficiency of the sample.

   b. **DESIGN** Relates to the efficiency of the sample; for example, one sample is more efficient than another if it achieves the same objectives with a smaller sample size.

3. **COMPETENCE** The competence of evidential matter is determined by auditor judgment—not the design and evaluation of an audit sample.

D. UNCERTAINTY AND AUDIT SAMPLING

The concept of a "reasonable basis for an opinion" suggests some degree of uncertainty or audit risk. The theory of sampling is well established in auditing practice because it is unusual to find instances where 100 percent of the items need to be examined for each account balance and class of transactions.

1. **CIRCUMSTANCES** There are some situations in which the surrounding factors do **not** justify the acceptance of any amount of sampling risk, and, therefore, **all** related data is examined.

2. **AUDIT RISK** The uncertainty inherent in applying audit procedures is referred to as audit risk. Using professional judgment, the auditor evaluates numerous factors to assess inherent risk and control risk, and performs substantive tests to reduce detection risk to an appropriate level.

   a. **SAMPLING RISK** Sampling risk results from the possibility that if a test is restricted to a sample, the conclusions reached may be different than the conclusions that may result if the entire population is examined. The smaller the sample size is, the greater the sampling risk becomes, thus sampling risk varies inversely with sample size.

   b. **NONSAMPLING RISK** Nonsampling risk includes all aspects of audit risk not due to sampling. Nonsampling risk can be reduced by adequate planning and supervision of audit work, and adherence to quality control standards. For example:

      (1) Incorrect audit procedures for a given objective

      (2) Nonrecognition of misstatements, making the procedure ineffective

E. ASSESSING SAMPLING RISK

The judgment of the auditor should be used to assess sampling risk.

1. **Tests of Internal Control** The auditor is concerned with two aspects of sampling risk while performing **tests of controls.**

   a. **Risk of Assessing Control Risk Too Low** The risk that the assessed level of control risk based on the sample is less than the true operating effectiveness of the internal control policy or procedure.

   b. **Risk of Assessing Control Risk Too High** The risk that the assessed level of control risk based on the sample is greater than the true operating effectiveness of the internal control policy or procedure.

Exhibit 1 ♦ Risk For Tests of Control Procedures

Auditor's Assessment of Control Risk Is	Client's Control Risk Is: Less Than Maximum	Client's Control Risk Is: Maximum
Less than Maximum Level	Correct Decision (1)	Incorrect Decision (2)
Maximum Level	Incorrect Decision (3)	Correct Decision (4)

(2) Assessing Control Risk Too Low (effectiveness)
(3) Assessing Control Risk Too High (efficiency)

2. **Substantive Tests of Details** The auditor is concerned with two aspects of sampling risk while performing **substantive tests.**

Exhibit 2 ♦ Risk For Substantive Tests

Indication of Sample Results	Client's Book Value Is: Fairly Stated	Client's Book Value Is: Not Fairly Stated
Accept Book Value	Correct Decision (5)	Incorrect Decision (6)
Reject Book Value	Incorrect Decision (7)	Correct Decision (8)

(6) Incorrect Acceptance (effectiveness)
(7) Incorrect Rejection (efficiency)

   a. **Risk of Incorrect Acceptance (Beta Risk)** The risk that the sample supports the conclusion that the recorded account balance is not materially misstated when it is, in fact, materially misstated.

   b. **Risk of Incorrect Rejection (Alpha Risk)** The risk that the sample supports the conclusion that the recorded account balance is materially misstated when, in fact, it is not materially misstated.

3. **Types of Risk** The risk of incorrect rejection and the risk of assessing control risk too high on internal control relate to the efficiency of the audit. Thus, if the auditor assesses control risk too high, additional substantive tests will be performed beyond what is necessary. The risk of incorrect acceptance and the risk of assessing control risk too low on internal control relate to the effectiveness of the audit in the detection of existing material misstatements. This could potentially result in materially misstated financial statements from not expanding substantive audit tests to a necessary level.

F. Sample Selection

Items for sampling should be chosen in such a way that the sample can be representative of the population. The auditor should ensure that all items have an opportunity to be selected. The following are commonly used selection procedures: haphazard sampling, random sampling, systematic sampling, stratified sampling, block sampling, and probability-proportional-to-size sampling. Note that block sampling does not meet the requirements for a representative sample.

G. Sampling in Tests of Internal Controls

1. **Planning a Sample** The auditor should take the following into consideration:

    a. The relationship of the sample to the objective of the test of controls. For many tests of controls, such as those concerning segregation of duties, sampling does not apply.

    b. The maximum, or tolerable, rate of deviations from prescribed internal control policies and procedures that would support the auditor's planned assessed level of control risk. The tolerable rate is assessed by considering the relationship of procedural deviations to (1) the planned assessed level of control risk and (2) the degree of assurance desired by the auditor related to the evidential matter in the sample.

    c. The auditor's allowable risk of assessing control risk too low. When the degree of assurance desired by the sample is high, the auditor should allow for a low level of sampling risk (that is, the risk of assessing control risk too low).

    d. Characteristics of the population, that is, the items comprising the account balance or class of transactions of interest. To determine sample size for a test of controls, the auditor should consider (1) the tolerable rate of deviation from the internal control policies or procedures being tested, (2) the likely rate of deviations, and (3) the allowable risk of assessing control risk too low.

2. **Professional Judgment** The auditor must apply professional judgment in determining these factors in order to determine the sample size.

3. **Performance and Evaluation** In performing audit procedures on items included in a sample and in evaluating sample results, the auditor should repeat the same steps that are outlined for substantive testing. However, in tests of controls, if the accountant is unable to perform all tests, it is considered a **deviation**. If the auditor concludes that the sample results do not support the planned assessed level of control risk for an assertion, the auditor should reevaluate the nature, timing, and extent of substantive procedures based on a revised consideration of the assessed level of control risk.

H. Sampling in Substantive Tests of Details

The extent of substantive tests required to obtain sufficient evidential matter under the Third Standard should vary with the auditor's assessed level of control risk.

1. **Planning a Sample** The auditor should consider the audit objectives to be achieved and decide on the procedure to be applied that will achieve those objectives. The auditor should consider the following:

a. **RELATIONSHIP** Relationship of the sample to the relevant audit objectives. The population being sampled should be appropriate for the audit objective.

b. **MATERIALITY** Preliminary judgments of materiality levels.

c. **ALLOWABLE RISK** Auditor's allowable risk of incorrect acceptance.

d. **CHARACTERISTICS** Characteristics of the population, that is, the items comprising the account balance or class of transactions of interest. The auditor may be able to reduce the needed sample size by separating the population into relatively homogenous groups on the basis of some characteristic related to the specific audit objective. (For example, dividing accounts receivable into several groups based on the size of the individual account balances.)

e. **TOLERABLE MISSTATEMENT** How much monetary misstatement in the related account balance may exist without causing the financial statements to be materially misstated. This is called the tolerable misstatement or tolerable error for the sample.

2. **PROFESSIONAL JUDGMENT** The required sample size is also influenced by (a) the auditor's assessment of the tolerable misstatement, (b) the allowable risk of incorrect acceptance, and (c) the characteristics of the population.

3. **PERFORMANCE** Procedures that are appropriate to the particular audit objective should be applied to each sample item. If certain selected sample items **cannot** be examined, the auditor's treatment of these unexpected items will depend upon their effect on the auditor's evaluation of the sample. If the auditor's evaluation of the sample results would not be altered by considering those unexamined items to be misstated, it is not necessary to examine the items. However, if considering those unexamined items to be misstated would lead to a conclusion that the balance or class contains material misstatements, the auditor should consider alternative procedures, and should consider whether the inability to examine the items has implications in relation to the auditor's assessed level of control risk or degree of reliance on management representations. Note that this applies to substantive testing, not to tests of controls.

4. **EVALUATION** The auditor compares total projected misstatement with the tolerable misstatement.

   a. The auditor's judgment is a necessary factor in this evaluation for both statistical and nonstatistical sampling.

   b. In addition to the evaluation of the frequency and amounts of monetary misstatements, consideration should be given to the *qualitative aspects of the misstatements*. Specifically, the auditor considers the nature and cause of the misstatement and the possible relationship of the misstatement to other phases of the audit.

   c. When the auditor evaluates whether the financial statements taken as a whole may be materially misstated, projected misstatement results for all audit sampling applications, and all known misstatements from nonsampling applications should be considered in the aggregate along with other relevant audit evidence.

I. AUDIT RISK

1. **AUDIT MODEL** The appendix to SAS 39, *Audit Sampling*, provides a model that expresses the general relationship of audit risk to the extent of necessary substantive tests of details. Because the acceptable level of audit risk is a matter of professional judgment, the model is not intended to be a mathematical formula including all factors that may influence the determination of individual risk components. However, the model may be useful for planning appropriate risk levels for audit procedures to achieve the desired audit risk.

EXHIBIT 3 ♦ AUDIT RISK MODEL

AR = IR x CR x AP x TD.

AR = The allowable **audit risk** that monetary misstatements equal to tolerable misstatements might remain undetected for the account balance or class of transactions and related assertions after the auditor has completed all audit procedures deemed necessary.

IR = **Inherent risk** is the susceptibility of an assertion to a material misstatement assuming there are no related internal control policies or procedures.

CR = **Control risk** is the risk that material misstatements that could occur in an assertion will not be prevented or detected on a timely basis by the entity's internal control policies and procedures. If the auditor believes that internal control policies and procedures would prevent or detect misstatements equal to tolerable misstatements about half the time, the auditor would assess this risk as 50 percent.

AP = The auditor's assessment of the risk that **analytical procedures** and other relevant substantive tests would fail to detect misstatements that could occur in an assertion equal to tolerable misstatement, given that such misstatements occur and are not detected by internal control.

TD = The allowable risk of incorrect acceptance for the substantive test of details, given that misstatements equal to tolerable misstatement occur in an assertion and are not detected by the internal controls or analytical procedures and other relevant substantive tests.

2. **SUBJECTIVE ASSESSMENTS** The auditor can mathematically compute TD if the auditor first assigns an acceptable audit risk (AR) and subjectively quantifies the judgment risks (IR and AP). To compute TD, the model must be restated as TD = AR/(IR x CR x AP).

EXAMPLE 1 ♦ USE OF THE AUDIT RISK MODEL

Assume the auditor is planning a sampling application to test a client's accounts receivable voucher register. If AR = .05 and IR = 1.0 and the auditor has subjectively assessed CR and AP equal to 50% and 30%, respectively, then the auditor can use the model to compute an appropriate level of risk of incorrect acceptance (sampling risk).

TD = AR/(IR x CR x AP)
TD = .05/(1.0 x .5 x .3)
TD = .33 (or 33%)

II. CLASSICAL SAMPLE SELECTION METHODS

A. JUDGMENTAL (HAPHAZARD) SAMPLING

The auditor uses professional judgment to decide how many and which items should be included in the sample. (i.e., the items included in the sample are selected without any conscious bias and without any special reason for including or omitting items from the sample).

1. **DESCRIPTION** It does **not** consist of sampling units selected in a careless manner; rather, the sample is selected in a manner the auditor expects to be representative of the population. For example, the auditor decides to select 100 accounts from a population of 1,000 accounts based on the auditor's judgment as to how many and which specific accounts should be included in the sample.

2. **USE** While haphazard sampling is useful for nonstatistical sampling, it is not used for statistical sampling because it does not allow measurement of the probability of selecting the combination of sampling units.

B. RANDOM NUMBER SAMPLING

The auditor may select a random sample by matching random numbers generated by a computer or selected from a random number table with, for example, document numbers. With this method, every item in the population has the same probability of being selected as every other item in the population, and every sample has the same probability of being selected as every other sample of the same size.

1. **REPLACEMENT** With random number and other sample selection methods, the auditor may sample with or without replacement (i.e., with or without replacing an item in the population after its value or attribute has been selected). Sampling with replacement may result in the appearance of a particular item in the sample more than once. In practice, auditors generally choose the without replacement approach.

2. **USE** This approach is useful for both statistical and nonstatistical sampling.

C. SYSTEMATIC SAMPLING

For this method, the auditor determines a uniform interval by dividing the number of physical units in the population by the sample size. A random number is selected as a starting point for the first interval, and one item is selected throughout the population at each of the uniform intervals from the starting point (every nth item). For example, if the auditor wishes to select 100 items from a population of 20,000 items, the uniform interval is every 200th item. First the auditor selects a random starting point (a random number from 1 to 200) and then selects every 200th item from the random start, including the random start item.

1. **DESCRIPTION** Because a random start is used, the systematic method provides a sample that allows every sampling unit in the population an equal chance of being selected. If the population is arranged randomly, systematic selection is essentially the same as random number selection. However, unlike random number sampling, this method may not always give every possible combination of sampling units the same probability of being selected. For example, a population of employees on a payroll for a construction company might be organized by teams, each team consisting of a crew leader and nine other workers. A selection of every tenth employee will either list every crew leader or no crew leaders, depending on the random start. No combination would include both crew leaders and other employees. In these circumstances, the auditor may consider using a different sample selection method such as random selection or making a systematic selection with multiple starts. For example, in the case related to payroll cited above, the auditor could use an interval of 50 rather than 10. This would require that the auditor select 5 different random starting points and move through the population 5 different times.

2. **USE** This method is useful for both statistical and nonstatistical sampling.

D. STRATIFIED SAMPLING

The population is divided into groups, called strata, according to some common characteristic, and then random sampling is applied to each stratum. For example, the auditor may divide the client's accounts receivable into three strata—those with balances of $2,000 and above, those with balances between $500 and $2,000, and those with balances of $500 and below. The auditor might positively confirm the whole population of accounts with balances of $2,000 and above, positively confirm a random sample of the accounts with balances between $500 and $2,000, and negatively confirm a random sample of those accounts with balances of $500 and below. The primary objective of stratified sampling is to *decrease the effect of variance in the total population* thereby *reducing sample size.*

1. **DESCRIPTION** The mean-per-unit method is a classical variables sampling technique that uses the sample average to project the total population dollar value by multiplying the sample average by the number of items in the population. A smaller sample size can be obtained by stratifying a highly variable population into segments. These segments will then have a minimum of variability within segments and variability between segments will be eliminated. As a result, the total sample size of all combined segments will be less. This is

accomplished without a loss of reliability or precision. Therefore, stratified MPU sampling may be more efficient than unstratified MPU because it usually produces an estimate having the desired level of precision, with a smaller sample size.

2. **USE** This approach can be used for both statistical and nonstatistical sampling. It is particularly useful in **reducing the overall sample size** when the auditor is using the MPU approach on populations that include sampling units (such as individual customer receivable balances) that have a wide range of dollar values.

E. BLOCK SAMPLING

A block sample consists of selecting contiguous transactions. For example, a block sample from a population of all vouchers processed for the year 20X1 might be all vouchers processed on February 3, May 17, and July 19, 20X1. This sample includes only three sampling units out of 250 business days because the sampling unit, in this case, is a period of time rather than an individual transaction. A sample with so few blocks is generally not adequate to reach a reasonable audit conclusion. Although a block sample might be designed with enough blocks to minimize this limitation, using such samples might be inefficient. If an auditor decides to use a block sample, special care should be exercised to control sampling risk in designing that sample. Block sampling should not be used with statistical sampling approaches. Block sampling is often used to evaluate changes in control procedures by examining all transactions at that time.

III. STATISTICAL SAMPLING

A. BASIC CONCEPT

Statistical sampling is based on the assumption that, within a given confidence level and allowance for sampling risk, a randomly selected sample of items from a population will reflect the same characteristics that occur in the population. Therefore, auditors may draw valid conclusions based on data derived from a relatively small sample of the total population. The distinguishing feature of statistical sampling methods as opposed to nonstatistical methods is that the user is able to provide a mathematical measurement of the degree of uncertainty that results from examining only part of a population. That is, statistical sampling allows an auditor to measure sampling risk.

B. SIMILARITIES

Both statistical and nonstatistical sampling involve examining less than the whole body of data to express a conclusion about the total body of data. Both methods involve audit judgment in planning and performing a sampling procedure and evaluating the results of the sample. Both provide sufficient, competent, evidential matter. Also, the audit procedures involved in examining the selected items in a sample generally do not depend on the sampling approach used.

C. BENEFITS

The auditor must choose between statistical and nonstatistical sampling. This choice is primarily a cost/benefit consideration. Because either nonstatistical or statistical sampling can provide sufficient evidential matter, the auditor chooses between them after considering their relative cost and effectiveness in the circumstances. Statistical sampling helps the auditor to (1) design an efficient sample, (2) measure the sufficiency of the evidential matter obtained, and (3) evaluate the sample results. If audit sampling, either nonstatistical or statistical, is used, some sampling risk is always present. One benefit of statistical sampling is that it uses the laws of probability to measure sampling risk. Another benefit of statistical sampling is that it provides a model for determining sample size while explicitly recognizing relevant factors such as the risk of assessing control risk too low, tolerable misstatement, and the expected population deviation rate. With nonstatistical sampling, on the other hand, the auditor implicitly recognizes the relevant factors while determining the sample size based on his or her own judgment and experience.

D. COSTS

Statistical sampling might involve additional costs for (1) training auditors, (2) designing individual samples to meet the statistical requirements, and (3) selecting the items to be examined. For example, if the individual balances comprising an account balance to be tested are not maintained in an organized pattern, it might not be cost effective for an auditor to select items in a way that would satisfy the requirements of a properly designed statistical sample.

E. DISTINGUISHING FEATURE
A properly designed nonstatistical sampling application can provide results that are as effective as those from a properly designed statistical sampling application. The one difference is that statistical sampling allows the sampling risk associated with the sampling procedure to be quantified.

F. SELECTING A SAMPLING APPROACH
Statistical or nonstatistical approaches can provide sufficient evidential matter.

1. **SELECTION** Because either can provide sufficient evidential matter, the auditor chooses between statistical or nonstatistical sampling after considering their relative cost and effectiveness in the specific situation.

2. **ADVANTAGES** Statistical sampling helps to (a) design efficient samples, (b) measure the sufficiency of evidential matter, and (c) evaluate sample results.

IV. ATTRIBUTES SAMPLING

A. OPERATING EFFECTIVENESS OF INTERNAL CONTROL POLICIES AND PROCEDURES
The attribute of interest is normally a control procedure. For example, the auditor may be concerned with estimating the percentage of purchase orders that do not have proper authorization.

1. In performing tests of controls, the auditor is frequently interested in determining the rate of deviation from prescribed internal control policies and procedures. The sampling plan generally used in this situation is **attribute sampling**.

   Tests of Controls → Attribute Sampling → Deviation Rate

2. A weakness in internal control does not necessarily mean that there will be a misstatement in the financial statements. If a material misstatement occurs **and** is not detected by internal controls or substantive tests, only then will the financial statements be misstated.

3. The auditor should determine the maximum rate of deviations from the prescribed internal control policy and procedure that he or she would be willing to accept without altering the planned assessed level of control risk. This is referred to as the tolerable rate.

B. METHODS

1. **ATTRIBUTE ESTIMATION METHOD** A sample is selected and its attribute error rate is determined. This rate serves as an estimate of the error rate in the population and allows the auditor to make statistical statements about the population attribute error rate.

2. **ACCEPTANCE SAMPLING METHOD** A special case of estimation of attributes. An acceptance sampling table, which utilizes the population size, sample size, and number of errors found in the sample, is used to make a statistical statement that the error rate in the population is not greater than a specified error rate. For example, based on sample results, an auditor may obtain 95 percent confidence that the actual error rate in the population does not exceed 8 percent.

3. **SEQUENTIAL SAMPLING** The sample is selected in several steps, with each step conditional on the results of previous steps.

4. **DISCOVERY SAMPLING METHOD** A special case of acceptance sampling. The objective is to attain a specified level of confidence that if the error rate in the population is at least a certain percentage the sample will include at least one instance of failure to comply with the control procedure being audited. For example, discovery sampling can be used to determine how large a sample needs to be for the auditor to have 95 percent confidence that, if

the error rate in the population is 1 percent or higher, the auditor's sample will include at least one example of an error. What if a sample of the determined size is selected and no error found? The auditor then has 95 percent confidence that the error rate in the population is less than 1 percent.

- Discovery sampling is frequently used when the auditor expects an **extremely low error rate**, usually zero. It is often used in testing for critical problems such as forgery. If a forgery is found, the auditor would discontinue sampling and investigate further.

C. Steps

The following general steps are appropriate for attributes sampling in tests of controls with prescribed internal control procedures.

1. **Determine the Objective** In a compliance test of control procedures, the objective is to compare the actual deviation rate to the tolerable rate. It should be remembered that the purpose of the test is to provide reasonable assurance that internal controls are operating in an effective manner.

2. **Determine the Tolerable Rate** This is the maximum rate of deviations from the prescribed internal control procedure (i.e., maximum misstatement rate) that the auditor is willing to accept without altering the assessment of control risk on the particular internal control procedure and is a judgmental decision. Therefore, the tolerable rate is a function of both the expected level of control risk and the degree of assurance desired. Thus, an increase in the tolerable rate would allow a reduction in sample size. If, after performing the sampling application, the auditor finds that the rate of deviations from the prescribed control procedure is close to or exceeds the tolerable rate, the auditor normally would decide that there is an unacceptably high risk that the deviation rate for the population exceeds the tolerable rate. In such cases, the auditor should consider modifying the assessed level of control risk.

3. **Determine the Confidence (Reliability) Level** This is a judgmental decision that quantifies the level of sampling risk the auditor is willing to accept. The auditor's willingness to accept sampling risk is determined, to a large extent, by the nature of the other tests that the auditor intends to perform that would complement the test of controls.

4. **Determine the Expected Population Deviation Rate** This is the expected rate of occurrence of deviations from the prescribed internal control procedure (i.e., the expected error rate). The expected population deviation rate should not exceed the tolerable rate. If prior to testing, the auditor believes that the actual deviation rate is higher than the tolerable rate, the auditor generally omits testing of that control procedure and either seeks to obtain assurance by testing other relevant internal control policies and procedures, or assesses control risk at the maximum level for the related financial statement assertion. The auditor estimates the expected population deviation rate, considering such factors as results of the prior years' tests and the overall control environment. Prior years' results should be considered in light of changes in the entity's internal control and changes in personnel.

5. **Consider the Effect of Population Size** When a sample is small in relation to the population, the population size has little or no effect on the determination of an appropriate sample size. If the sample size is greater than 10 percent of the population size, which is rarely the case, a finite population correction factor may be used. However, the finite population correction factor tends to decrease the sample size. Therefore, most auditors ignore the factor because any error in sample size that results will be on the conservative side. **NOTE**: The finite population correction factor is not given in this text because it has not been asked on past exams.

6. **Determine the Method of Selecting the Sample** The sample should be representative of the population, and all items should have a chance of being selected. The various methods for selecting samples are discussed in Section III.

7. **Compute the Sample Size** Sample sizes can be computed by the use of formulas, computer software, and, most often, sample size tables. Consideration should be given to the following when determining sample size:

   a. **Assessing Control Risk Too Low** As discussed earlier, there is an inverse relationship between the risk of assessing control risk too low and sample size.

   b. **Tolerable Deviation Rate** The maximum rate of deviation from a prescribed control policy or procedure that the auditor is willing to accept without modifying the planned level of control risk.

Exhibit 4 ♦ Sample Size When Other Factors Are Changed

Increase in Population	Effect on Sample Size
	Slight increase for increased populations, generally little or no effect
Tolerable rate	Decrease
Expected deviation rate	Increase
Sample Size	**Increase in**
Decrease	Risk of assessing control risk too low

NOTE: This is frequently tested on the CPA exam.

Table 1 ♦ Tolerable Rate

5% Risk of Assessing Control Risk Too Low
(with number of expected errors in parentheses)

Expected Population Deviation Rate	2%	3%	4%	5%	6%	7%	8%	9%	10%	15%	20%
0.00%	149(0)	99(0)	74(0)	59(0)	49(0)	42(0)	36(0)	32(0)	29(0)	19(0)	14(0)
.25	236(1)	157(1)	117(1)	93(1)	78(1)	66(1)	58(1)	51(1)	46(1)	30(1)	22(1)
.50	*	157(1)	117(1)	93(1)	78(1)	66(1)	58(1)	51(1)	46(1)	30(1)	22(1)
.75	*	208(2)	117(1)	93(1)	78(1)	66(1)	58(1)	51(1)	46(1)	30(1)	22(1)
1.00	*	*	156(2)	93(1)	78(1)	66(1)	58(1)	51(1)	46(1)	30(1)	22(1)
1.25	*	*	156(2)	124(2)	78(1)	66(1)	58(1)	51(1)	46(1)	30(1)	22(1)
1.50	*	*	192(3)	124(2)	103(2)	66(1)	58(1)	51(1)	46(1)	30(1)	22(1)
1.75	*	*	227(4)	153(3)	103(2)	88(2)	77(2)	51(1)	46(1)	30(1)	22(1)
2.00	*	*	*	181(4)	127(3)	88(2)	77(2)	68(2)	46(1)	30(1)	22(1)
2.25	*	*	*	208(5)	127(3)	88(2)	77(2)	68(2)	61(2)	30(1)	22(1)
2.50	*	*	*	*	150(4)	109(3)	77(2)	68(2)	61(2)	30(1)	22(1)
2.75	*	*	*	*	173(5)	109(3)	95(3)	68(2)	61(2)	30(1)	22(1)
3.00	*	*	*	*	195(6)	129(4)	95(3)	84(3)	61(2)	30(1)	22(1)
3.25	*	*	*	*	*	148(5)	112(4)	84(3)	61(2)	30(1)	22(1)
3.50	*	*	*	*	*	167(6)	112(4)	84(3)	76(3)	40(2)	22(1)
3.75	*	*	*	*	*	185(7)	129(5)	100(4)	76(3)	40(2)	22(1)
4.00	*	*	*	*	*	*	146(6)	100(4)	89(4)	40(2)	22(1)
5.00	*	*	*	*	*	*	*	158(8)	116(6)	40(2)	30(2)
6.00	*	*	*	*	*	*	*	*	179(11)	50(3)	30(2)
7.00	*	*	*	*	*	*	*	*	*	68(5)	37(3)

* Sample size is too large to be cost-effective for most audit applications.

NOTE: This table assumes a large population.

EXAMPLE 2 ♦ USE OF TABLE 1 TO DETERMINE SAMPLE SIZE

> The auditor would like to assess control risk at below the maximum level. In this case, in order to do this, the auditor must have 95% confidence that the actual population deviation rate (i.e., the percentage of vouchers that are paid without being approved) is not greater than 6%. Therefore, the tolerable rate is 6%; i.e., the auditor will be able to assess control risk at below the maximum level as long as the auditor can conclude with 95% confidence that not more than 6% of the unpaid vouchers lack approval. Based on the error rate observed in last year's sample, the auditor expects a population deviation rate of only 1.50% this year. Using Table 1, 103 vouchers should be examined to yield the desired confidence about the population error rate.

8. **SELECT AND AUDIT THE SAMPLE ITEMS** Audit procedures should be applied to the items in the sample to determine deviations from the prescribed control procedures previously identified. Deviations should be grouped according to whether they are occurring with some regularity or are isolated events. In cases where selected items cannot be examined, they should be counted as deviations from control procedures. This occurs, for example, when documentation used to test for the procedures has been misplaced, lost, or destroyed. Voided items would generally be replaced by another randomly selected item, if it was properly voided.

9. **EVALUATE THE SAMPLE RESULTS** The results of the sample must be analyzed in order to make an inference about the population error rate. This can be done by formula, but is most often accomplished by tables or computer programs.

TABLE 2 ♦ ACTUAL NUMBER OF DEVIATIONS FOUND

Statistical Sample Results Evaluation
Upper Limit at 5% of Assessing Control Risk Too Low

Sample Size	0	1	2	3	4	5	6	7	8	9	10
25	11.3	17.6	*	*	*	*	*	*	*	*	*
30	9.5	14.9	19.6	*	*	*	*	*	*	*	*
35	8.3	12.9	17.0	*	*	*	*	*	*	*	*
40	7.3	11.4	15.0	18.3	*	*	*	*	*	*	*
45	6.5	10.2	13.4	16.4	19.2	*	*	*	*	*	*
50	5.9	9.2	12.1	14.8	17.4	19.9	*	*	*	*	*
55	5.4	8.4	11.1	13.5	15.9	18.2	*	*	*	*	*
60	4.9	7.7	10.2	12.5	14.7	16.8	18.8	*	*	*	*
65	4.6	7.1	9.4	11.5	13.6	15.5	17.4	19.3	*	*	*
70	4.2	6.6	8.8	10.8	12.6	14.5	16.3	18.0	19.7	*	*
75	4.0	6.2	8.2	10.1	11.8	13.6	15.2	16.9	18.5	20.0	*
80	3.7	5.8	7.7	9.5	11.1	12.7	14.3	15.9	17.4	18.9	*
90	3.3	5.2	6.9	8.4	9.9	11.4	12.8	14.2	15.5	16.8	18.2
100	3.0	4.7	6.2	7.6	9.0	10.3	11.5	12.8	14.0	15.2	16.4
125	2.4	3.8	5.0	6.1	7.2	8.3	9.3	10.3	11.3	12.3	13.2
150	2.0	3.2	4.2	5.1	6.0	6.9	7.8	8.6	9.5	10.3	11.1
200	1.5	2.4	3.2	3.9	4.6	5.2	5.9	6.5	7.2	7.8	8.4

* Over 20 percent

NOTE: This table presents upper limits as percentages. This table assumes a large population.

a. The first step in the evaluation of the results is tabulating the number of deviations found and comparing this to the number of deviations expected to occur using the sample size determined from the above table. The expected number of deviations is the parenthetical number found next to each sample size. In cases where the deviations found are less than the number that would be expected (the parenthetical number), it can be assumed that the risk of assessing control risk too low and the allowance for sampling risk is not more than the tolerable rate.

b. When the actual deviations are more than those that would be expected according to the parenthetical number in Table 1, the auditor can calculate the maximum deviation rate in the population using a table similar to Table 2. Table 2 is for evaluating sample results for a 5 percent risk of assessing control risk too low or a 95 percent confidence level.

c. No one table can accommodate an evaluation of every possible size and number of deviations, and the auditor will often need to use other references to find appropriate tables. In cases where a particular sample size does not appear in a table, it is a good idea to be conservative by using the next smaller sample size shown.

EXAMPLE 3 ♦ USE OF TABLE 2

Only one error is discovered from the 103 sample items selected in Example 2. Use of Table 2, reveals that there is no corresponding sample size for 103 items, so the next lowest (100 sample size) is used. The intersection of the sample size and the number of deviations found reveals the maximum population deviation rate in this case is 4.7%. Since this maximum population deviation rate is less than the tolerable rate of 6%, it can be concluded that within a 95% reliability level, the control is functioning as required.

10. REACH AN OVERALL CONCLUSION The auditor uses professional judgment to reach an overall conclusion about the effect of the evaluation of the test of controls on the nature, timing, and extent of planned substantive tests. If the sample results, along with other relevant evidential matter, support the assessed level of control risk, the auditor generally does not need to modify planned substantive tests. If the sample results do not support the assessed level of control risk, the auditor would ordinarily either perform tests of controls on other relevant internal controls for which control risk can be assessed at below the maximum level, or assess control risk at a higher, or the maximum, level and modify the nature, timing, and/or extent of substantive testing. In addition to the evaluation of the frequency and amounts of monetary misstatements, consideration should be given to the qualitative aspects of the misstatements. These would include the nature and cause of the misstatements. For example, were there differences in principle or applications or differences due to misunderstanding of instructions or carelessness? Also, consideration should be given to the possible relationship of the misstatements to other phases of the audit.

11. DOCUMENT THE SAMPLING PROCEDURE Documentation might include such items as follows:

a. A description of the prescribed control procedure being tested

b. The objectives of the test, including the relationship to planned substantive testing

c. The definition of the population and sampling unit

d. The definition of the deviation condition (i.e., what is considered a deviation from prescribed internal control policies and procedures)

e. The rationale for the confidence level, the tolerable rate, and the expected population deviation rate used in the application

f. The method of sample size determination

g. The method of sample selection

h. A description of the sampling procedure performed and a listing of compliance deviations identified in the sample

i. The evaluation of the sample and a summary of the overall conclusion

V. Classical Variables Sampling

A. Substantive Tests of Details

Substantive tests are performed by the auditor to either detect misstatements or obtain evidence about the validity and propriety of the accounting treatment of transactions and balances. In substantive testing, the auditor is primarily interested in **dollar amounts**. An example of a substantive test is the use of a sample from the accounts receivable subsidiary ledger to estimate the balance in the control account. The traditional method of performing substantive tests of details is by variables sampling.

Substantive Tests → Variables Sampling → Dollar Amount

B. Methods

1. **Simple Extension (Mean-per-unit Approach)** A method of estimating variables in which the auditor finds the *average audited value* for the items in the sample and then estimates the population value by multiplying the average sample value by the size of the population. For example, if the mean of a sample of 50 accounts is calculated to be $100 and there are 1,000 accounts in the population, the total value of the 1,000 accounts would be estimated at $100,000 [i.e., ($100 per account) x (1,000 accounts)] plus or minus an allowance for sampling error that is statistically determined. Note that the auditor needs to know the audited values of the items in the sample but does not need to know their book values.

2. **Difference Estimation** The auditor first finds the *average difference* between the audited value and the book value of the items in the sample. This average difference is then multiplied by the size of the population in order to estimate the difference between the book value of the population and its actual value. For example, if the average difference between the book value and audited value for each account in a sample of 100 accounts is $10 and if there are 10,000 accounts in the population, the auditor will estimate that there is a $100,000 difference between the book value of the population and the actual value (i.e., $10 x 10,000 accounts) plus or minus an allowance for sampling risk that is statistically determined. The interval, so determined, is then compared against the precision required (i.e., against the amount of acceptable difference) in order to decide if the account appears to be reasonably stated.

3. **Ratio Method** The auditor uses sample results to estimate the ratio of audited value to book value. This ratio is then applied to the population to estimate the actual value. Ratio estimation should be used when each population item has a book value, an audited value may be ascertained for each sample item, and differences occur frequently. For example, if the auditor finds that the average ratio of audited value to book value for the sample is 1.05 and if the book value for the population is $100,000, the actual value for the population can be estimated to be $105,000 (i.e., 1.05 x $100,000) plus or minus an allowance for sampling risk.

C. Steps

The following general steps are appropriate in substantive tests of details.

1. **Determine the Objectives** It is important for the auditor to specify the purpose of the test because this will determine the population of the test. For example, the purpose may be to prove the existence of an account balance or to show that the account is complete.

2. **Define the Population** The auditor must match the objectives of the test to the appropriate population. The population is made up of the account balances or class of transactions of

interest to the auditor. Defining the population involves consideration of the individual sampling units of the entire population, whether or not the entire population is available to be picked, and the identification of those items that are individually significant. Those items that are individually significant may be accounts that are large enough to exceed the level of tolerable deviation by themselves. These would not be included in the population available for sampling, but should be tested separately.

3. **Determine the Confidence Level** The confidence level for the auditor's substantive tests will generally vary inversely with the assessed level of control risk (i.e., the stronger the internal control is judged to be, the lower the assessed level of control risk, thereby affecting the extent of substantive tests). The confidence level for a particular substantive test is a matter of judgment, but the auditor should consider the overall confidence level in making the determination. This confidence level is related to the auditor's assessment of sampling risk.

4. **Determine the Expected Standard Deviation of the Population, or the Expected Amount of Misstatement Directly in Dollar Value** This is also a matter of judgment, frequently based on the prior year's audit or on the results of a small pilot sample. As expected misstatement increases, a larger sample size is required.

5. **Determine the Tolerable Misstatement** The tolerable misstatement is the maximum monetary misstatement that may exist without causing the financial statements to be materially misstated. This is a judgmental value which should closely relate to the auditor's preliminary estimates of materiality levels. As tolerable misstatement increases, sample size decreases.

6. **Select a Method of Audit Sampling** These can be either statistical or nonstatistical. If statistical sampling is used, either PPS or classical variables techniques would be used.

7. **Determine Sample Size** Compute the sample size by using a sample size table, formula, or computer software. The sample size formula for substantive testing is as follows:

$$n = \frac{c^2 \times s^2 \times N^2}{A^2} = \frac{c^2 \times s^2}{a^2}$$

Where:

n	=	Size of the sample.
c	=	Confidence (reliability) coefficient. This is the number of standard deviations that corresponds to the selected confidence level.
s	=	Standard deviation of the population (usually the standard deviation of a small pilot sample or the standard deviation found in previous years).
N	=	Size of the population.
A	=	Population allowance for sampling error (tolerable misstatement less expected amount of misstatement).
a	=	Allowance for sampling error per population item.

EXAMPLE 4 ♦ SAMPLE SIZE

An auditor wishes to apply statistical sampling as part of substantive testing of the accounts receivable control account. The account has a book value of $500,000 and is composed of 5,000 individual accounts. The auditor determines that 90% confidence is necessary in the results of substantive testing for this account. The auditor sets total allowance for sampling error (precision) at $40,000. Next, the auditor takes a small pilot sample in order to estimate the standard deviation of the population. The pilot sample has a standard deviation of $40. The number of standard deviations corresponding to 90% for a normal distribution is 1.64.

N	=	5,000	A	=	$40,000
c	=	1.64	s	=	$40
a	=	$40,000/5,000 = $8			

REQUIRED: Calculate the sample size.

SOLUTION: Substituting the information into the sample size formula and solving the equation gives the following:

$$n = \frac{(1.64)^2\ (\$40)^2}{(\$8)^2} = 67.24 \approx 68 \text{ accounts}$$

The auditor should take a random sample of 68 accounts from the population of 5,000 accounts receivable in order to have 90% confidence that the inference based on the sample results will be within $40,000 of the true (actual) value of accounts receivable. That is, if a population of 5,000 accounts actually has a standard deviation of $40, 90% of the possible samples of 68 accounts will yield estimates that are within $40,000 of the actual value of accounts receivable.

EXHIBIT 5 ♦ SUMMARY OF SAMPLING FACTOR RELATIONSHIPS

Decrease in	Effect on Sample Size
Confidence (reliability) coefficient	Decrease
Tolerable misstatement	Increase
Expected standard deviation of the population	Decrease

Sample Size	Decrease in
Increase	Risk-Incorrect Acceptance
Increase	Risk-Incorrect Rejection

8. **INSPECTION** Select and audit the sample items.

9. **EVALUATE THE SAMPLE RESULTS** The auditor computes the actual sampling error (precision) and confidence level attained by the sample.

   a. Estimate the population value (multiply the sample mean by the population size).

   b. Compute the actual sampling error (i.e., precision) by solving the sample size formula for A.

$$A = \frac{c \times s \times N}{\sqrt{n}}$$

c. Compute the actual confidence level by solving the sample size formula for c.

$$c = \frac{A \times \sqrt{n}}{s \times N}$$

EXAMPLE 5 ♦ COMPUTATION OF SAMPLING ERROR

The auditor selects a sample of 68 accounts as described in Example 4. The auditor would audit these accounts to determine the actual value of each account, then compute the average audited balance. Assume that the average audited balance is \$95 per account. The estimated population value is \$475,000 (\$95 x 5,000 accounts). If the standard deviation of the sample is assumed to be \$40, we can compute the actual sampling error (precision) as follows:

$$A = \frac{c \times s \times N}{\sqrt{n}} = \frac{(1.64)\ (\$40)\ (5{,}000)}{\sqrt{68}} = \$39{,}775 \approx \$40{,}000$$

And the confidence level coefficient as follows:

$$c = \frac{A \times \sqrt{n}}{s \times N} = \frac{\$40{,}000 \times \sqrt{68}}{(\$40)\ (5{,}000)} = 1.649 \approx 1.65$$

The auditor can rely on the results of the test, with 90% confidence, yielding an estimated value for accounts receivable that differs from the true value by no more than \$40,000.

10. **REACH AN OVERALL CONCLUSION** The auditor should project the results of the sample to the population from which the sample was taken before evaluating the results of the sample. The client may adjust the book value of the account to correct the misstatements actually found in the sample and any misstatements discovered in any 100 percent-examined items. The total projected misstatement after the book value has been adjusted should be compared with the tolerable misstatement. If the auditor considers the projected misstatement unacceptable, the auditor should take appropriate action (for example, performing other substantive tests on the account). Note that the auditor also considers the qualitative aspects of misstatements (i.e., misstatements in amount vs. misapplication of accounting principle, or errors vs. fraud) in reaching an overall conclusion.

11. **DOCUMENT THE SAMPLING PROCEDURE** Documentation might include the following:

a. The objectives of the test and a description of other audit procedures related to those objectives

b. The definition of the population and the sampling unit, including how the auditor considered completeness of the population

c. The definition of a misstatement

d. The rationale for the risk of incorrect acceptance, the risk of incorrect rejection, the tolerable misstatement, and the expected population deviation amount used in the application

e. The audit sampling technique used

f. The method of sample selection

g. A description of the performance of the sampling procedure and a listing of misstatements identified in the sample

h. The evaluation of the sample and a summary of the overall conclusion

VI. Probability-Proportional-to-Size Sampling

A. Distinguishing Features

PPS is a form of variables sampling that uses attribute sampling theory and is used for substantive testing. The sampling unit is not an individual account or transaction, but an individual dollar in an account balance (or another logical unit). PPS sampling has two unique properties.

1. **Stratification** The audit population is automatically stratified by monetary value.

2. **Overstatements** Larger dollar amounts have a higher probability of being selected. Therefore, overstatements are more likely to be detected than understatements. Hence, PPS sampling is most appropriate when an auditor desires testing for material overstatements. PPS sampling is ineffective in searching for unrecorded items. (The probability of an item being selected is directly proportional to its dollar value.)

Example 6 ♦ Probability-Proportional-To-Size Sampling

X Co.'s account receivable balance is $2,000,000	The population is 2,000,000
Customer Y has a balance of $120,000	The sampling unit is 1

Required: Figure the probability that Customer Y has of being selected.

Solution: Customer Y has a 6% chance of being selected (120,000 / 2,000,000 = 6%).

B. Advantages

Sample sizes in low-error environments tend to be relatively small because their approach does not use standard deviations (which tend to be large in most credit environments) in determining sample size. This method also reduces audit work because several dollars selected will appear in the same sample item (for example, a customer's account balance) and, therefore, the same audit procedures often determine the audited value of more than one sample item. Also, this approach does not require a high number of errors to be observed in the sample for the results to be statistically valid, as is the case with Difference Estimation and Ratio Estimation.

C. Disadvantages

An understatement is less likely to be discovered than an overstatement, since those accounts receivable with higher dollar values have a greater chance of being selected. Therefore, PPS sampling is generally considered inappropriate for liability accounts. Also, special consideration must be given to zero and negative balance accounts which are usually excluded from the PPS sample. A third disadvantage occurs when the population has a high expected misstatement rate; the auditor may obtain sample sizes larger than those required by classical variables sampling.

D. Determining Sample Size

Requires that the auditor determine a reliability factor for overstatement errors, a tolerable rate, and an expected error rate.

1. **Reliability Factor for Overstatement Errors** Can be determined from tables after specifying the expected number of overstatement errors and the risk of incorrect acceptance. The auditor controls the risk of incorrect acceptance by specifying the risk level for the sampling plan.

   a. PPS sampling is most appropriate when no errors are expected. Therefore, zero is the appropriate estimate for the number of overstatement errors.

b. The risk of incorrect acceptance is a matter of professional judgment. With PPS sampling, it represents an auditor's risk that book value is not materially overstated when material monetary overstatements exist.

TABLE 3 ♦ RELIABILITY FACTORS FOR ERRORS OF OVERSTATEMENT

Number of Overstatement Errors	Risk of Incorrect Acceptance								
	1%	5%	10%	15%	20%	25%	30%	37%	50%
0	4.61	3.00	2.31	1.90	1.61	1.39	1.21	1.00	.70
1	6.64	4.75	3.89	3.38	3.00	2.70	2.44	2.14	1.68
2	8.41	6.30	5.33	4.72	4.28	3.93	3.62	3.25	2.68
3	10.05	7.76	6.69	6.02	5.52	5.11	4.77	4.34	3.68
4	11.61	9.16	8.00	7.27	6.73	6.28	5.90	5.43	4.68
5	13.11	10.52	9.28	8.50	7.91	7.43	7.01	6.49	5.68
6	14.57	11.85	10.54	9.71	9.08	8.56	8.12	7.56	6.67
7	16.00	13.15	11.78	10.90	10.24	9.69	9.21	8.63	7.67
8	17.41	14.44	13.00	12.08	11.38	10.81	10.31	9.68	8.67
9	18.79	15.71	14.21	13.25	12.52	11.92	11.39	10.74	9.67
10	20.15	16.97	15.41	14.42	13.66	13.02	12.47	11.79	10.67
11	21.49	18.21	16.60	15.57	14.78	14.13	13.55	12.84	11.67
12	22.83	19.45	17.79	16.72	15.90	15.22	14.63	13.89	12.67
13	24.14	20.67	18.96	17.86	17.02	16.32	15.70	14.93	13.67
14	25.45	21.89	20.13	19.00	18.13	17.40	16.77	15.97	14.67
15	26.75	23.10	21.30	20.13	19.24	18.49	17.84	17.02	15.67
16	28.03	24.31	22.46	21.26	20.34	19.58	18.90	18.06	16.67
17	29.31	25.50	23.61	22.39	21.44	20.66	19.97	19.10	17.67
18	30.59	26.70	24.76	23.51	22.54	21.74	21.03	20.14	18.67
19	31.85	27.88	25.91	24.63	23.64	22.81	22.09	21.18	19.67
20	33.11	29.07	27.05	25.74	24.73	23.89	23.15	22.22	20.67

EXAMPLE 7 ♦ USING TABLE 3

The auditor's risk of incorrect acceptance for Co. X is 5% and the number of overstatement errors is 0. The reliability factor for errors of overstatement is 3.00.

2. TOLERABLE RATE The tolerable rate (or tolerable error) is the maximum monetary error that may exist in an account balance without causing the financial statements to be materially misstated. Thus, tolerable error in PPS sampling is closely related to the auditor's planned level of materiality. The sampling interval and the sample size can be determined using the following formulas:

$$\textit{Sampling Interval} = \frac{\textit{Tolerable Misstatement}}{\textit{Reliability Factor for the Error of Overstatement}}$$

$$\textit{Sampling Size} = \frac{\textit{Population}}{\textit{Sampling Interval}}$$

EXAMPLE 8 ♦ SAMPLING INTERVAL AND SAMPLE SIZE

Using the same assumptions as Example 7, the population is 2,000,000 and the tolerable misstatement is $60,000.

REQUIRED: Figure the sampling interval and the sample size.

SOLUTION: The sampling interval is $20,000. (60,000 / 3.00 = 20,000)

The sample size is 100. (2,000,000 / 20,000 = 100)

3. **EXPECTED ERROR RATE** If some errors are expected, the sample interval can be computed by determining the expected error rate.

a. $$\textit{Expected Error Rate} = \frac{\textit{Expected Misstatements}}{\textit{Population}}$$

EXAMPLE 9 ♦ SAMPLING INTERVAL AND SAMPLE SIZE

> Using the same assumptions as Example 7, we determine that the expected misstatement for Co. X is $10,000 based on our prior experience with the client. The population is 2,000,000. Our expected error rate is .005 (10,000 / 2,000,000 = .005). Remember that our tolerable rate is 3%. (This example is unrelated to Example 8.)
>
> **REQUIRED:** Figure the sampling interval and the sample size.
>
> **SOLUTION:** Using Table 1, our sample size is 157.
>
> The sampling interval is then computed by dividing the population by the sample size. (2,000,000 / 157 = 12,739)

b. In cases where the expected error rate is not shown on the table, the auditor would use the sample size for the next higher percentage. If the tolerable rate percentage is not found it would be appropriate to select the sample size for the next smaller percentage shown. This follows the accounting convention of conservatism.

E. **SELECT AND AUDIT THE SAMPLE ITEM**
Systematic sampling selection is most often used. Audit procedures are then employed to determine the value of each sample item.

F. **EVALUATE THE SAMPLE RESULTS**
Misstatements from the sample should be **projected** to the population to calculate an allowance for sampling risk. This allowance for sampling risk is a calculation with an incremental allowance for projected errors (misstatements). If the sample contains less than 100 percent errors, the formula for determining the upper limits is as follows:

$$\begin{array}{c}\textit{Upper limit}\\ \textit{for errors}\\ \textit{(misstatements)}\end{array} = \begin{array}{c}\textit{Projected}\\ \textit{errors}\\ \textit{(misstatements)}\end{array} + \begin{array}{c}\textit{Basic}\\ \textit{precision}\end{array} + \begin{array}{c}\textit{Incremental allowance}\\ \textit{for projected errors}\\ \textit{(misstatements)}\end{array}$$

1. The upper limit on misstatement is calculated by adding the projected misstatement, the basic precision, and the incremental allowance.

   a. Projected misstatements are calculated for each sample item depending on whether the recorded book value is less than or greater than the sampling interval. If less than, the difference between the recorded value and the audited value is divided by the recorded value to arrive at a percentage error known as "tainting." The projected misstatement is the "tainting" percentage multiplied by the sampling interval.

   b. Basic precision is calculated by multiplying the reliability factor by the sampling interval.

   c. An incremental allowance for projected misstatement is calculated using only those errors in logical units less than the sampling interval. These are ranked from highest to lowest (in terms of tainting %), considering the incremental changes in reliability factors for the actual number of errors found.

2. Finishing the evaluation procedure involves comparing the upper limit on errors to the previously estimated tolerable error. If the upper limit on misstatements is less than the tolerable misstatement, such as above, it can be concluded that the total population is not

misstated by an amount greater than the originally estimated tolerable misstatement, at the specified risk of incorrect acceptance.

3. If the upper limit on misstatements is greater than the tolerable misstatement, then the sample result does not support the conclusion that the population is not misstated by more than the tolerable misstatement. This may occur if the population was not represented by the sample, the sample was too small due to an excessively low expectation of misstatement, or if the population itself was misstated.

4. In cases where the recorded book value is greater than the sampling interval, the projected misstatement is equal to the actual error.

5. If no errors are found, both the projected errors and the incremental allowance for projected errors would be zero. Therefore, the auditor could conclude that the recorded amount of accounts is not overstated by more than the tolerable error estimated earlier because the only factor with a value other than zero would be the basic precision.

EXAMPLE 10 ♦ EVALUATING SAMPLE RESULTS

Audit procedures reveal four errors. The projected misstatement total is calculated first, followed by the other two components of the upper limits, precision, and the incremental allowance for projected misstatement.

a. Projected Misstatement:

(1) Book value	(2) Audited value	(3) Tainting % (1) – (2) ÷ (1)	(4) Sampling interval	(5) Projected error (3) x (4)
$ 500	$ 450	.10	$12,739	$1,274
11,000	10,340	.06	12,739	764
5,700	5,625	.013	12,739	166
25,350	23,350	--	--	2,000
				$4,204

b. Basic precision: 3 x $12,739 = $38,217

c. Incremental allowance:

(1) Projected error	(2) Reliability factor (from table)	(3) Incremental change in reliability factor (from table) (increment–1)	(4) Incremental allowance (3) x (1)
$1,274	4.75	.75 [1]	$ 956
764	6.30	.55 [2]	420
166	7.76	.46 [3]	76
			$1,452

[1] 4.75 – 3.00 – 1.00 = .75 [2] 6.30 – 4.75 – 1.00 = .55 [3] 7.76 – 6.30 – 1.00 = .46

d. Overall conclusion:

Projected misstatement	$ 4,204
Precision	38,217
Incremental allowance	1,452
Upper limit	$43,873

In this example, it can be concluded that the audited sample supports the conclusion that the population is not misstated by more than the tolerable misstatement.

APPENDIX: SAMPLING TERMS

1. **allowance for sampling error (precision; sampling error)** A measure of the closeness of a sample estimate to the corresponding population characteristic for a specified sampling risk.
2. **alpha risk** See risk of incorrect rejection and risk of assessing control risk too high.
3. **attribute** Any characteristic that is either present or absent. In tests of controls directed toward operating effectiveness, the presence or absence of evidence of the application of a specified internal control policy or procedure is sometimes referred to as an attribute.
4. **attributes sampling** A statistical procedure based on estimating whether the rate of occurrence of a particular attribute in a population exceeds a tolerable rate.
5. **audit sampling** The application of an audit procedure to less than 100 percent of the items within an account balance or class of transactions for the purpose of evaluating some characteristic of the balance or class.
6. **beta risk** See risk of incorrect acceptance and risk of assessing control risk too low.
7. **block sample (cluster sample)** A sample consisting of contiguous transactions.
8. **classical variables sampling** A sampling approach that measures sampling risk using the variation of the underlying characteristic of interest. This approach includes methods such as mean-per-unit, ratio estimation, and difference estimation.
9. **confidence level (reliability level)** The complement of the applicable sampling risk (see risk of incorrect acceptance, risk of assessing control risk too low, risk of incorrect rejection, and risk of assessing control risk too high). In practice, the confidence level is often set equal to the complement of the risk of incorrect rejection (i.e., to the complement of the alpha risk).
10. **difference estimation** A classical variables sampling technique that uses the total difference between audited values and individual book values to estimate the total dollar error in a population and an allowance for sampling error.
11. **dollar-unit sampling** See probability-proportional-to-size sampling.
12. **expected population deviation rate** An anticipation of the deviation rate in the entire population. It is used in determining an appropriate sample size for an attributes sample.
13. **haphazard sample** A sample consisting of sampling units selected by the auditor without any special reason for including or omitting particular items.
14. **mean-per-unit method** A classical variables sampling technique that uses the sample average to project the total population dollar value by multiplying the sample average by the number of items in the population.
15. **nonsampling risk** All aspects of audit risk not due to sampling.
16. **nonstatistical sampling** A sampling technique for which the auditor considers sampling risk in evaluating an audit sample without using statistical theory to measure that risk.
17. **population (field; universe)** The items comprising the account balance or class of transactions, or a portion of that balance or class of interest. The population excludes individually significant items of which the auditor has decided to examine 100 percent or other items that will be tested separately.
18. **precision** See allowance for sampling errors.

19. **probability-proportional-to-size (PPS) sampling** (**Dollar-unit sampling; CMA sampling**) A variables sampling procedure that uses attributes theory to express a projection of the error in a population in dollar amounts.

20. **random sample** A sample drawn so that every combination of the same number of items in the population has an equal probability of selection.

21. **ratio estimation** A classical variables sampling technique that uses the ratio of audited values to book values in the sample to estimate the total dollar value of the population and an allowance for sampling error.

22. **reliability level** See confidence level.

23. **risk of assessing control risk too high** The risk that the assessed level of control risk based on the sample is greater than the true operating effectiveness of the internal control policies or procedures.

24. **risk of assessing control risk too low** The risk that the assessed level of control risk based on the sample is less than the true operating effectiveness of the internal control policies or procedures.

25. **risk of incorrect acceptance** (**beta risk; type II misstatement**) The risk that the sample supports the conclusion that the recorded account balance is not materially misstated when it is, in fact, materially misstated.

26. **risk of incorrect rejection** (**alpha risk; type I misstatement**) The risk that the sample supports the conclusion that the recorded account balance is materially misstated when, in fact, it is not.

27. **sample** Items selected from a population to reach a conclusion about the population.

28. **sampling risk** The risk that the auditor's conclusion based on a sample may be different from the conclusion the auditor would reach if the test were applied in the same way to the entire population. For tests of controls, sampling risk is the risk of assessing control risk too high or too low. For substantive testing, sampling risk is the risk of incorrect acceptance or rejection.

29. **sequential sampling** A sampling plan for which the sample is selected in several steps, with each step conditional on the results of the previous steps.

30. **standard deviation** A measure of the dispersion among the respective values of a particular characteristic as measured for all items in the population for which a sample estimate is developed.

31. **statistical sampling** Audit sampling that uses the laws of probability for selecting and evaluating a sample from a population for the purpose of reaching a conclusion about the population.

32. **stratification** Division of the population into relatively homogeneous groups.

33. **systematic sampling** A method of drawing a sample in which every nth item is drawn from one or more random starts.

34. **tolerable misstatement** An estimate of the maximum monetary misstatement that may exist in an account balance or class of transactions without causing the financial statements to be materially misstated.

35. **tolerable rate** The maximum population rate of deviations from a prescribed control procedure that the auditor will tolerate without modifying the nature, timing, or extent of substantive testing.

36. **variables sampling** Statistical sampling that reaches a conclusion on the monetary amounts of a population.

CHAPTER 37—AUDIT SAMPLING

PROBLEM 37-1 MULTIPLE CHOICE QUESTIONS (60 to 75 minutes)

1. Which of the following courses of action would an auditor most likely follow in planning a sample of cash disbursements if the auditor is aware of several unusually large cash disbursements?

a. Set the tolerable rate of deviation at a lower level than originally planned.
b. Stratify the cash disbursements population so that the unusually large disbursements are selected.
c. Increase the sample size to reduce the effect of the unusually large disbursements.
d. Continue to draw new samples until all the unusually large disbursements appear in the sample. (11/94, Aud., #55, 5128)

2. In confirming a client's accounts receivable in prior years, an auditor found that there were many differences between the recorded account balances and the confirmation replies. These differences, which were not misstatements, required substantial time to resolve. In defining the sampling unit for the current year's audit, the auditor most likely would choose

a. Individual overdue balances.
b. Individual invoices.
c. Small account balances.
d. Large account balances. (5/95, Aud., #49, 5667)

3. An auditor is determining the sample size for an inventory observation using mean-per-unit estimation, which is a variables sampling plan. To calculate the required sample size, the auditor usually determines the

	Variability in the dollar *amounts of inventory items*	Risk of incorrect *acceptance*
a.	Yes	Yes
b.	Yes	No
c.	No	Yes
d.	No	No

(R/99, Aud., #20, 6836)

4. The risk of incorrect acceptance and the likelihood of assessing control risk too low relate to the

a. Allowable risk of tolerable misstatement.
b. Preliminary estimates of materiality levels.
c. Efficiency of the audit.
d. Effectiveness of the audit. (11/95, Aud., #19, 5966)

5. An auditor may decide to increase the risk of incorrect rejection when

a. Increased reliability from the sample is desired.
b. Many differences (audit value minus recorded value) are expected.
c. Initial sample results do **not** support the planned level of control risk.
d. The cost and effort of selecting additional sample items is low. (11/92, Aud., #38, 2972)

6. The diagram below depicts an auditor's estimated maximum deviation rate compared with the tolerable rate, and also depicts the true population deviation rate compared with the tolerable rate.

Auditor's estimate based on sample results	*True state of population* Deviation rate is less than tolerable rate	 Deviation rate exceeds tolerable rate
Maximum deviation rate is less than tolerable rate	I.	III.
Maximum deviation rate exceeds tolerable rate	II.	IV.

As a result of tests of controls, the auditor assesses control risk too low and thereby decreases substantive testing. This is illustrated by situation

a. I.
b. II.
c. III.
d. IV. (11/95, Aud., #17, 5964)

7. As a result of tests of controls, an auditor assessed control risk too low and decreased substantive testing. This assessment occurred because the true deviation rate in the population was

a. Less than the risk of assessing control risk too low, based on the auditor's sample.
b. Less than the deviation rate in the auditor's sample.
c. More than the risk of assessing control risk too low, based on the auditor's sample.
d. More than the deviation rate in the auditor's sample. (5/95, Aud., #28, 5646)

8. An advantage of statistical sampling over nonstatistical sampling is that statistical sampling helps an auditor to

a. Eliminate the risk of nonsampling errors.
b. Reduce the level of audit risk and materiality to a relatively low amount.
c. Measure the sufficiency of the evidential matter obtained.
d. Minimize the failure to detect errors and fraud.

(11/95, Aud., #44, amended, 5991)

9. In statistical sampling methods used in substantive testing, an auditor most likely would stratify a population into meaningful groups if

a. Probability proportional to size (PPS) sampling is used.
b. The population has highly variable recorded amounts.
c. The auditor's estimated tolerable misstatement is extremely small.
d. The standard deviation of recorded amounts is relatively small.

(5/95, Aud., #50, 5668)

10. Using statistical sampling to assist in verifying the year-end accounts payable balance, an auditor has accumulated the following data:

	Number of accounts	Book balance	Balance determined by the auditor
Population	4,100	$5,000,000	?
Sample	200	$ 125,000	$150,000

Using the ratio estimation technique, the auditor's estimate of year-end accounts payable balance would be

a. $6,150,000.
b. $6,000,000.
c. $5,125,000.
d. $5,050,000.

(Editors, 9414)

11. What is an auditor's evaluation of a statistical sample for attributes when a test of 50 documents results in 3 deviations if tolerable rate is 7%, the expected population deviation rate is 5%, and the allowance for sampling risk is 2%?

a. Modify the planned assessed level of control risk because the tolerable rate plus the allowance for sampling risk exceeds the expected population deviation rate.
b. Accept the sample results as support for the planned assessed level of control risk because the sample deviation rate plus the allowance for sampling risk exceeds the tolerable rate.
c. Accept the sample results as support for the planned assessed level of control risk because the tolerable rate less the allowance for sampling risk equals the expected population deviation rate.
d. Modify the planned assessed level of control risk because the sample deviation rate plus the allowance for sampling risk exceeds the tolerable rate.

(5/92, Aud., #54, 2807)

ITEMS 12 AND 13 are based on the following:

An auditor desired to test credit approval on 10,000 sales invoices processed during the year. The auditor designed a statistical sample that would provide 1% risk of assessing control risk too low (99% confidence) that not more than 7% of the sales invoices lacked approval. The auditor estimated from previous experience that about 2½% of the sales invoices lacked approval. A sample of 200 invoices was examined and 7 of them were lacking approval. The auditor then determined the achieved upper precision limit to be 8%.

12. In the evaluation of this sample, the auditor decided to increase the level of the preliminary assessment of control risk because the

a. Tolerable rate (7%) was less than the achieved upper precision limit (8%).
b. Expected deviation rate (7%) was more than the percentage of errors in the sample (3½%).
c. Expected deviation rate (2½%) was less than the tolerable rate (7%).
d. Achieved upper precision limit (8%) was more than the percentage of errors in the sample (3½%).

(11/90, Aud., #59, amended, 0250)

13. The allowance for sampling risk was

a. 5½%.
b. 4½%.
c. 3½%.
d. 1%.

(11/90, Aud., #60, 0251)

14. An auditor who uses statistical sampling for attributes in testing internal controls should reduce the planned reliance on a prescribed control when the

a. Sample rate of deviation plus the allowance for sampling risk equals the tolerable rate.
b. Sample rate of deviation is less than the expected rate of deviation used in planning the sample.
c. Tolerable rate less the allowance for sampling risk exceeds the sample rate of deviation.
d. Sample rate of deviation plus the allowance for sampling risk exceeds the tolerable rate.

(11/95, Aud., #25, 5972)

15. The expected population deviation rate of client billing misstatements is 2%. The auditor has established a tolerable rate of 3%. In the review of client invoices the auditor should use

a. Stratified sampling.
b. Discovery sampling.
c. Variable sampling.
d. Attribute sampling. (Editors, 0266)

16. Which of the following sampling methods would be used to estimate a numerical measurement of a population, such as a dollar value?

a. Attributes sampling
b. Stop-or-go sampling
c. Variables sampling
d. Random-number sampling

(11/94, Aud., #54, 5127)

17. An auditor should consider the tolerable rate of deviation when determining the number of check requests to select for a test to obtain assurance that all check requests have been properly authorized. The auditor should also consider

	The average dollar value of the check requests	*The allowable risk of assessing control risk too low*
a.	Yes	Yes
b.	Yes	No
c.	No	Yes
d.	No	No

(R/99, Aud., #17, 6833)

18. An auditor established a $60,000 tolerable misstatement for an asset with an account balance of $1,000,000. The auditor selected a sample of every twentieth item from the population that represented the asset account balance and discovered overstatements of $3,700 and understatements of $200. Under these circumstances, the auditor most likely would conclude that

a. There is an unacceptably high risk that the actual misstatements in the population exceed the tolerable misstatement because the total projected misstatement is more than the tolerable misstatement.
b. There is an unacceptably high risk that the tolerable misstatement exceeds the sum of actual overstatements and understatements.
c. The asset account is fairly stated because the total projected misstatement is less than the tolerable misstatement.
d. The asset account is fairly stated because the tolerable misstatement exceeds the net of projected actual overstatements and understatements. (R/00, Aud., #13, 6938)

19. For which of the following audit tests would an auditor most likely use attribute sampling?

a. Selecting accounts receivable for confirmation of account balances
b. Inspecting employee time cards for proper approval by supervisors
c. Making an independent estimate of the amount of a LIFO inventory
d. Examining invoices in support of the valuation of fixed asset additions (5/96, Aud., #4, 6236)

20. The likelihood of assessing control risk too high is the risk that the sample selected to test controls

a. Does **not** support the auditor's planned assessed level of control risk when the true operating effectiveness of internal control justifies such an assessment.
b. Contains misstatements that could be material to the financial statements when aggregated with misstatements in other account balances or transactions classes.
c. Contains proportionately fewer monetary errors or deviations from prescribed internal control structure policies or procedures than exist in the balance or class as a whole.
d. Does **not** support the tolerable error for some or all of management's assertions.

(11/94, Aud., #33, amended, 5106)

21. An auditor is testing internal control procedures that are evidenced on an entity's vouchers by matching random numbers with voucher numbers. If a random number matches the number of a voided voucher, that voucher ordinarily should be replaced by another voucher in the random sample if the voucher

a. Constitutes a deviation.
b. Has been properly voided.
c. Cannot be located.
d. Represents an immaterial dollar amount.

(5/90, Aud., #43, 0253)

22. Samples to test internal control procedures are intended to provide a basis for an auditor to conclude whether

a. The control procedures are operating effectively.
b. The financial statements are materially misstated.
c. The risk of incorrect acceptance is too high.
d. Materiality for planning purposes is at a sufficiently low level.

(5/91, Aud., #40, amended, 0246)

23. Which of the following statements is correct concerning statistical sampling in tests of controls?
a. As the population size increases, the sample size should increase proportionately.
b. Deviations from specific internal control procedures at a given rate ordinarily result in misstatements at a lower rate.
c. There is an inverse relationship between the expected population deviation rate and the sample size.
d. In determining tolerable rate, an auditor considers detection risk and the sample size.
(11/94, Aud., #27, 5100)

24. Which of the following most likely would be an advantage in using classical variables sampling rather than probability-proportional-to-size (PPS) sampling?
a. An estimate of the standard deviation of the population's recorded amounts is **not** required.
b. The auditor rarely needs the assistance of a computer program to design an efficient sample.
c. Inclusion of zero and negative balances generally does **not** require special design considerations.
d. Any amount that is individually significant is automatically identified and selected.
(5/93, Aud., #43, 3939)

25. When using classical variables sampling for estimation, an auditor normally evaluates the sampling results by calculating the possible error in either direction. This statistical concept is known as
a. Precision.
b. Reliability.
c. Projected error.
d. Standard deviation. (5/91, Aud., #18, 0244)

26. The use of the ratio estimation sampling technique is most effective when
a. The calculated audit amounts are approximately proportional to the client's book amounts.
b. A relatively small number of differences exist in the population.
c. Estimating populations whose records consist of quantities, but **not** book values.
d. Large overstatement differences and large understatement differences exist in the population.
(5/95, Aud., #51, 5669)

27. When planning a sample for a substantive test of details, an auditor should consider tolerable misstatement for the sample. This consideration should
a. Be related to the auditor's business risk.
b. Not be adjusted for qualitative factors.
c. Be related to preliminary judgments about materiality levels.
d. Not be changed during the audit process.
(5/90, Aud., #51, 0255)

28. Hill has decided to use probability-proportional-to-size (PPS) sampling, sometimes called dollar-unit sampling, in the audit of a client's accounts receivable balances. Hill plans to use the following PPS sampling table:

TABLE
Reliability Factors for Errors of Overstatement

Number of overstatement misstatements	Risk of incorrect acceptance 1%	5%	10%	15%	20%
0	4.61	3.00	2.31	1.90	1.61
1	6.64	4.75	3.89	3.38	3.00
2	8.41	6.30	5.33	4.72	4.28
3	10.05	7.76	6.69	6.02	5.52
4	11.61	9.16	8.00	7.27	6.73

Additional Information:

Tolerable misstatement (net of effect of expected misstatement)	$ 48,000
Risk of incorrect acceptance	20%
Number of misstatements allowed	1
Recorded amount of accounts receivable	$480,000
Number of accounts	360

What sample size should Hill use?
a. 120
b. 108
c. 60
d. 30 (Editors, 9416)

29. In a probability-proportional-to-size sample with a sampling interval of $10,000, an auditor discovered that a selected account receivable with a recorded amount of $5,000 had an audited amount of $4,000. If this were the only misstatement discovered by the auditor, the projected misstatement of this sample would be
a. $ 1,000
b. $ 2,000
c. $ 5,000
d. $10,000 (R/00, Aud., #10, 6935)

30. Which of the following statements is correct concerning probability-proportional-to-size (PPS) sampling, also known as dollar-unit sampling?
a. The sampling distribution should approximate the normal distribution.
b. Overstated units have a lower probability of sample selection than units that are understated.
c. The auditor controls the risk of incorrect acceptance by specifying that risk level for the sampling plan.
d. The sampling interval is calculated by dividing the number of physical units in the population by the sample size. (5/91, Aud., #17, 0243)

PROBLEM 37-2 ADDITIONAL MULTIPLE CHOICE QUESTIONS (18 to 23 minutes)

31. Given random selection, the same sample size, and the same precision requirement for the testing of two unequal populations, the risk of assessing control risk too low on the smaller population is

a. Higher than assessing control risk too low for the larger population.
b. Indeterminate relative to assessing control risk too low for the larger population.
c. Lower than assessing control risk too low for the larger population.
d. The same as assessing control risk too low for the larger population. (Editors, 9413)

32. Which of the following factors is(are) considered in determining the sample size for a test of controls?

	Expected deviation rate	*Tolerable deviation rate*
a.	Yes	Yes
b.	No	No
c.	No	Yes
d.	Yes	No

(11/95, Aud., #33, 5980)

33. How would increases in tolerable misstatement and assessed level of control risk affect the sample size in a substantive test of details?

	Increase in tolerable misstatement	*Increase in assessed level of control risk*
a.	Increase sample size	Increase sample size
b.	Increase sample size	Decrease sample size
c.	Decrease sample size	Increase sample size
d.	Decrease sample size	Decrease sample size

(11/95, Aud., #43, 5990)

34. An auditor may use a systematic sampling technique with a start at any randomly selected item when performing a test of controls with respect to control over cash receipts. The biggest disadvantage of this type of sampling is that the items in the population

a. Must be systematically replaced in the population after sampling.
b. May occur in a systematic pattern, thus destroying the sample randomness.
c. Must be recorded in a systematic pattern before the sample can be drawn.
d. May systematically occur more than once in the sample. (Editors, 0267)

35. While performing a test of details during an audit, an auditor determined that the sample results supported the conclusion that the recorded account balance was materially misstated. It was, in fact, not materially misstated. This situation illustrates the risk of

a. Assessing control risk too high.
b. Assessing control risk too low.
c. Incorrect rejection.
d. Incorrect acceptance. (5/94, Aud., #43, 4708)

36. A principal advantage of statistical methods of attribute sampling over nonstatistical methods is that they provide a scientific basis for planning the

a. Risk of assessing control risk too low.
b. Expected population deviation rate.
c. Tolerable rate.
d. Sample size. (Editors, 0260)

37. Which of the following statements is correct concerning the auditor's use of statistical sampling?

a. An auditor needs to estimate the dollar amount of the standard deviation of the population to use classical variables sampling.
b. The selection of zero balances usually does **not** require special sample design considerations when using PPS sampling.
c. A classical variables sample needs to be designed with special considerations to include negative balances in the sample.
d. An assumption of PPS sampling is that the underlying accounting population is normally distributed. (Editors, 0265)

38. In performing tests of controls over authorization of cash disbursements, which of the following statistical sampling methods would be most appropriate?

a. Variables
b. Stratified
c. Ratio
d. Attributes (5/93, Aud., #25, 3921)

39. In determining the number of documents to select for a test to obtain assurance that all sales returns have been properly authorized, an auditor should consider the tolerable rate of deviation from the control activity. The auditor should also consider the

I. Likely rate of deviations.
II. Allowable risk of assessing control risk too high.

a. I only.
b. II only.
c. Both I and II
d. Either I or II (11/97, Aud., #16, 6579)

ESSAY QUESTIONS

ESSAY 37-3 (15 to 25 minutes)

Mead, CPA, was engaged to audit Jiffy Co.'s financial statements for the year ended August 31. Mead is applying sampling procedures.

During the prior years' audits, Mead used classical variables sampling in performing tests of controls on Jiffy's accounts receivable. For the current year Mead decided to use probability-proportional-to-size (PPS) sampling (also known as dollar-unit sampling) in confirming accounts receivable because PPS sampling uses each account in the population as a separate sampling unit. Mead expected to discover many overstatements, but presumed that the PPS sample still would be smaller than the corresponding size for classical variables sampling.

Mead reasoned that the PPS sample would automatically result in a stratified sample because each account would have an equal chance of being selected for confirmation. Additionally, the selection of negative (credit) balances would be facilitated without special considerations.

Mead computed the sample size using the risk of incorrect acceptance, the total recorded book amount of the receivables, and the number of misstated accounts allowed. Mead divided the total recorded book amount of the receivables by the sample size to determine the sampling interval. Mead then calculated the standard deviation of the dollar amounts of the accounts selected for evaluation of the receivables.

Mead's calculated sample size was 60 and the sampling interval was determined to be $10,000. However, only 58 different accounts were selected because two accounts were so large that the sampling interval caused each of them to be selected twice. Mead proceeded to send confirmation requests to 55 of the 58 customers. Three selected accounts each had insignificant recorded balances under $20. Mead ignored these three small accounts and substituted the three largest accounts that had not been selected in the sample. Each of these accounts had balances in excess of $7,000, so Mead sent confirmation requests to those customers.

The confirmation process revealed two differences. One account with an audited amount of $3,000 had been recorded at $4,000. Mead projected this to be a $1,000 misstatement. Another account with an audited amount of $2,000 had been recorded at $1,900. Mead did not count the $100 difference because the purpose of the test was to detect overstatements.

In evaluating the sample results, Mead determined that the accounts receivable balance was not overstated because the projected misstatement was less than the allowance for sampling risk.

REQUIRED:

Describe each incorrect assumption, statement, and inappropriate application of sampling in Mead's procedures. (11/93, Aud., amended, #5)

ESSAY 37-4 (15 to 25 minutes)

Baker, CPA, was engaged to audit Mill Company's financial statements. After obtaining an understanding of Mill's internal control structure, Baker decided to obtain evidential matter about the effectiveness of both the design and operation of the policies and procedures that may support a low assessed level of control risk concerning Mill's shipping and billing functions. During the prior years' audits Baker used nonstatistical sampling but for the current year Baker used a statistical sample in the tests of controls to eliminate the need for judgment.

Baker wanted to assess control risk at a low level, so a tolerable rate of deviation or acceptable upper precision limit (UPL) of 20% was established. To estimate the population deviation rate and the achieved UPL, Baker decided to apply a discovery sampling technique of attribute sampling that would use a population expected error rate of 3% for the 8,000 shipping documents, and decided to defer consideration of allowable risk of assessing control risk too low (risk of overreliance) until evaluating the sample results. Baker used the tolerable rate, the population size, and the expected population error rate to determine that a sample size of 80 would be sufficient. When it was subsequently determined that the actual population was about 10,000 shipping documents, Baker increased the sample size to 100.

Baker's objective was to ascertain whether Mill's shipments had been properly billed. Baker took a sample of 100 invoices by selecting the first 25 invoices from the first month of each quarter. Baker then compared the invoices to the corresponding prenumbered shipping documents.

When Baker tested the sample, eight errors were discovered. Additionally, one shipment that should have been billed at $10,443 was actually billed at

$10,434. Baker considered this $9 to be immaterial and did not count it as an error.

In evaluating the sample results Baker made the initial determination that a reliability level of 95% (risk of assessing control risk too low 5%) was desired and, using the appropriate statistical sampling table, determined that for eight observed deviations from a sample size of 100, the achieved UPL was 14%. Baker then calculated the allowance for sampling risk to be 5%, the difference between the actual sample deviation rate (8%) and the expected error rate (3%). Baker reasoned that the actual sample deviation rate (8%) plus the allowance for sampling risk (5%) was less than the achieved UPL (14%); therefore, the sample supported a low level of control risk.

REQUIRED:

Describe each incorrect assumption, statement, and inappropriate application of attribute sampling in Baker's procedures.

(11/91, Aud., #5, amended, 3041)

ESSAY 37-5 (15 to 25 minutes)

Sampling for attributes is often used to allow an auditor to reach a conclusion concerning a rate of occurrence in a population. A common use in auditing is to test the rate of deviation from a prescribed internal control policy or procedure to determine whether planned assessed level of control risk is appropriate.

REQUIRED:

a. When an auditor samples for attributes, identify the factors that should influence the auditor's judgment concerning the determination of

1. Acceptable level of risk of assessing control risk too low,
2. Tolerable deviation rate, and
3. Expected population deviation rate.

b. State the effect on sample size of an increase in each of the following factors, assuming all other factors are held constant:

1. Acceptable level of risk of assessing control risk too low,
2. Tolerable deviation rate, and
3. Expected population deviation rate.

c. Evaluate the sample results of a test for attributes if authorizations are found to be missing on 7 check requests out of a sample of 100 tested. The population consists of 2500 check requests, the tolerable deviation rate is 8%, and the acceptable level of risk of assessing control risk too low is low.

d. How may the use of statistical sampling assist the auditor in evaluating the sample results described in c., above? (11/88, Aud., #3)

ESSAY 37-6 (15 to 25 minutes)

Edwards has decided to use probability-proportional-to-size (PPS) sampling, sometimes called dollar-unit sampling, in the audit of a client's accounts receivable balance. Few, if any, misstatements of account balance overstatement are expected. Edwards plans to use the following PPS sampling table:

TABLE
Reliability Factors for Errors of Overstatement

Number of overstatement misstatements	Risk of incorrect acceptance 1%	5%	10%	15%	20%
0	4.61	3.00	2.31	1.90	1.61
1	6.64	4.75	3.89	3.38	3.00
2	8.41	6.30	5.33	4.72	4.28
3	10.05	7.76	6.69	6.02	5.52
4	11.61	9.16	8.00	7.27	6.73

REQUIRED:

a. Identify the advantages of using PPS sampling over classical variables sampling.

NOTE: Requirements b. and c. are **not** related.

b. Calculate the sampling interval and the sample size Edwards should use given the following information:

Tolerable misstatement	$ 15,000
Risk of incorrect acceptance	5%
Number of misstatements allowed	0
Recorded amount of accounts receivable	$300,000

c. Calculate the total projected misstatement if the following three misstatements were discovered in a PPS sample:

	Recorded amount	Audit amount	Sampling interval
1st misstatement	$ 400	$ 320	$1,000
2nd misstatement	500	0	1,000
3rd misstatement	3,000	2,500	1,000

(5/87, Aud., #3)

ESSAY 37-7 (15 to 25 minutes)

Smith, CPA, has decided to assess control risk at below the maximum level for an audit client's internal controls affecting receivables. Smith plans to use sampling to obtain substantive evidence concerning the reasonableness of the client's accounts receivable balances. Smith has identified the first few steps in an outline of the sampling plan as follows:

1. Determine the audit objectives of the test.
2. Define the population.
3. Define the sampling unit.
4. Consider the completeness of the population.
5. Identify individually significant items.

REQUIRED:

Identify the remaining steps which Smith should include in the outline of the sampling plan. Illustrations and examples need not be provided.

(5/86, Aud., #5)

SOLUTION 37-1 MULTIPLE CHOICE ANSWERS

AUDIT SAMPLING

1. (b) In planning a sample of cash disbursements, if the auditor is aware of several unusually large cash disbursements, the auditor will most likely stratify the sample to include the unusually large disbursements. By stratifying the sample, the auditor will decrease the effect of the variances in the total population, and, therefore, be able to reduce the number of items in the sample.

2. (b) It is easiest to reconcile differences and for customers to research the auditor's questions on an individual invoice level. The designation of a sampling unit depends on the type of applied auditing procedures. The auditor considers which sampling unit leads to the most efficient and effective application, given the circumstances. In the case of a high number of expected differences in amounts for accounts receivable confirmations, if the auditor selects the customer balance as a sampling unit, the auditor may need to test each individual transaction supporting that balance in the event of a contradictory report from the customer.

3. (a) With the mean-per-unit method, stratification of a highly variable population into segments allows an auditor to use a smaller sample size. Thus, variability in the dollar amounts of inventory items is considered. The risk of incorrect assessment has an inverse relationship with sample size.

4. (d) AU 350.14 states, "The risk of incorrect acceptance and the risk of assessing control risk too low relate to the effectiveness of an audit in detecting an existing material misstatement." If the auditor incorrectly accepts an account as being materially accurate or incorrectly concludes that control risk is below the maximum, additional procedures that may detect this incorrect conclusion are either eliminated or reduced and the audit would prove ineffective in detecting misstatements. Answers (a) and (b) are incorrect because of an inappropriate combination of terms. In (a), risk should relate to exceeding tolerable misstatement levels. In (b), materiality is judged, not estimated, and related to tolerable misstatement (AU 350.18). Audit efficiency is related to the risk of incorrect rejection or the risk of assessing control risk as too high. (AU 350.13)

5. (d) The risk of incorrect rejection is the risk that the auditor will conclude that an account balance is materially misstated when, in fact, it is not. When this error occurs, the auditor will generally extend his/her audit procedures and would eventually discover that the original conclusion of a material misstatement was incorrect. The cost of this mistake is the cost of the additional procedures that were necessary to discover that the original conclusion was erroneous. If, however, the cost and effort of those additional procedures is low, the auditor may well decide to use a high risk of incorrect rejection because doing so will reduce original sample size. If the desired results are achieved with the original small sample, overall audit cost will be lowered. If an incorrect rejection occurs, however, the incremental cost incurred would not be excessive. An increase in the desired reliability would likely result in a decrease (not increase) in the risk of incorrect rejection. The number of differences expected should have no bearing on the risk of incorrect rejection specified. The "risk of incorrect rejection" is not a concept associated with tests of controls. "Risk of underreliance" would be the corresponding risk that is associated with control testing.

6. (c) Per AU 350.12-.14, when the auditor's estimate based on the sample results indicates that the maximum deviation rate is less than the tolerable rate and the true state of the population shows that the deviation rate exceeds the tolerable rate, the auditor assesses control risk too low and does not plan sufficient substantive testing. Answer (b) is an example of the auditor accessing control risk higher than necessary and, thereby increasing substantive testing. Answer (a) and (d) represent correct audit decisions regarding controls and planned substantive evidence.

7. (d) If the sample deviation rate is lower than the true deviation rate in the population, the auditor mistakenly assesses control risk too low.

The result is that detection risk is allowed to rise too high and substantive testing is decreased.

STATISTICAL SAMPLING

8. (c) AU 350.04 indicates that both statistical and nonstatistical sampling plans can provide sufficient evidential matter if properly applied. Statistical sampling, as well as nonstatistical sampling, is subject to nonsampling errors (procedural mistakes or human error). Both methods of sampling may be used to reduce audit risk, but neither would affect the level of materiality. Both can be used to reduce the risk of failing to detect errors and fraud, which is the risk of incorrect acceptance.

9. (b) Stratified sampling can be particularly useful in reducing the overall sample size on populations that have a wide range of dollar values (or highly variable recorded amounts). The primary objective is to decrease the effect of variance in the total population, thereby reducing sample size. PPS sampling insures items with large amounts all make it into the sample, but not by stratifying the population. The estimated tolerable misstatement and standard deviation are irrelevant to a decision to stratify.

10. (b) Under the ratio estimation technique, the auditor uses sample results to estimate the ratio of audited value to book value. The ratio is then applied to the population book value to estimate the audited value of the population. The sample "audited value/book value" ratio equals 1.2:1 ($150,000 ÷ $125,000). When this ratio is applied to the population book balance of $5,000,000, an estimated $6,000,000 audited value results.

11. (d) The auditor should modify his or her planned assessed level of control risk when the sample deviation rate plus the allowance for sampling risk exceeds the tolerable rate. In this question, the deviation rate of 6% (3 deviations among 50 documents) plus the allowance for sampling risk of 2% is greater than the given tolerable rate of 7%.

12. (a) The auditor would increase the preliminary assessment of control risk because the achieved upper precision limit of 8% (sample error rate plus an allowance for sampling risk) exceeded the tolerable error rate of 7% (determined by professional judgment). Therefore, the results of the test did not allow the auditor to conclude with 99% confidence that the error rate in the population did not exceed 7%. All other answers describe comparisons that are meaningless.

13. (b) The allowance for sampling risk is the difference between the observed sample rate and the achieved upper precision limit. The observed sample rate was 3.5% (7/200). Therefore, the allowance for sampling risk would be 4.5% (8% – 3.5%).

14. (d) When the sample rate of deviation plus the allowance for sampling risk, which is the upper deviation limit, exceeds the tolerable rate, the sample results do not support the assessed level of control risk and the auditor should reduce the planned reliance on a prescribed control. Answers (a), (b), and (c) represent results that support planned reliance.

15. (d) Attribute sampling provides evidence of the rate of occurrence of a specified characteristic in a population at auditor-specified levels of precision and reliability. Variable sampling is used by the auditor to estimate the total dollar amount of a population at auditor-specified levels of precision and reliability. Discovery sampling is a form of attribute sampling that is designed to locate at least one exception if the rate of occurrence in the population is at or above a specified rate. This method is used to search for critical occurrences that may indicate the existence of an irregularity, and is appropriate when the expected occurrence rate is quite low (usually near zero) and the auditor wants a sample that will provide a specified chance to observe one occurrence. Answer (a) is incorrect, as the population is not divided into groups according to a common characteristic.

16. (c) Substantive tests of details are performed by the auditor to either detect misstatements or obtain evidence about the validity and propriety of the accounting treatment of transactions and balances. In substantive testing, the auditor is primarily interested in dollar amounts, and the traditional method of performing substantive tests is by variables sampling.

ATTRIBUTES SAMPLING

17. (c) Check authorization is an internal control. In tests of internal controls, the auditor is determining the rate of occurrence of a deviation from the control procedure, not testing the dollar amounts reported in the financial statements. The allowable risk of assessing control risk too low affects the degree of assurance desired by the auditor. If a high degree of assurance is sought, sampling risk must be low. Sample size and risk are inversely related.

18. (a) The net of projected actual misstatements [($3,700 – $200) x 20 =] is $70,000, which is larger than the tolerable misstatement of $60,000. If the tolerable misstatement exceeds the sum of actual overstatements and understatements, the auditor may consider the account fairly stated.

19. (b) In performing tests of controls, the auditor is frequently interested in determining the rate of deviation from prescribed internal control policies and procedures. The sampling plan generally used in this situation is attribute sampling.

20. (a) AU 350.12 states, "The risk of assessing control risk *too high* is the risk that the assessed level of control risk based on the sample is greater than the true operating effectiveness of the control structure policy or procedure." Answer (b) is incorrect because fewer errors or deviations would be discovered; therefore, the auditor would not identify those misstatements. Answer (c) is incorrect because the true operating effectiveness of internal control would not support such an assessment; the auditor would find fewer errors or deviations. Answer (d) is incorrect because the sample would support the tolerable error for misstatements because the sample would reveal fewer errors or deviations than exist in the balance or class of transactions.

21. (b) In an auditor's test of transactions, if a random number matches the number of a voided voucher, that voucher ordinarily should be replaced by another voucher in the random sample if the voucher has been properly voided. The voucher would be counted as an error and would not be replaced if it constituted a deviation or could not be located. The materiality of the dollar amount is irrelevant because the focus in a test of controls is whether or not procedures are properly performed, not the dollar value of the transaction being tested.

22. (a) "Rather than using the sample to estimate an unknown, the auditor's objective is generally to corroborate the accuracy of certain client data, such as data about account balances or classes of transactions, or to evaluate the internal accounting controls over the processing of data" (AICPA Audit Sampling Guide, p. 12). Thus, the auditor is concerned with whether the control procedures are operating effectively. Answers (b) and (c) relate to substantive tests rather than to tests of controls. Materiality is based on the auditor's judgment, not on sampling procedures.

23. (b) AU 350.35 states, "Deviations from pertinent control procedures at a given rate ordinarily would be expected to result in misstatements at a lower rate." The sufficiency of audit sample sizes is determined by factors such as the assessments of control risk, inherent risk, and risk for other substantive tests related to a given assertion, and other factors as listed in AU 350.19. Population size is not a determining factor. The relationship between the expected population deviation rate and sample size is direct, not inverse. In determining tolerable rate, an auditor should consider control risk and the degree of assurance desired by the evidential matter, per AU 350.34.

Variables Sampling

24. (c) A disadvantage of PPS sampling to classical variables sampling is that special consideration must be given to zero and negative balance accounts because they are usually excluded from the PPS sample. Answers (a), (b), and (d) are advantages of PPS sampling.

25. (a) In classical variables sampling for estimation, precision represents the range within which the sample result is expected to be accurate. Hence, it provides a calculation of the maximum acceptable error in either direction. Reliability varies inversely with the assessed level of control risk and is a measure of the probability the sample result will fall within the precision range as mentioned above. Projected error is the anticipated deviation rate, based on the sample, in the entire population. The standard deviation is a measure of the dispersion among the relative values of a particular characteristic.

26. (a) The use of the ratio estimation sampling technique is most effective when the calculated audit amounts are approximately proportional to the client's book amounts. The auditor uses sample results to estimate the ratio of audited value to book value, which is then applied to the population to estimate the actual value. Ratio estimation should be used when each population item *has a book value*, an audited value may be ascertained for each sample item, and *differences occur frequently*. Large overstatement or understatement differences would reduce the effectiveness of this technique.

27. (c) AU 350.18 states, "Tolerable misstatement is a planning concept and is related to the auditor's preliminary judgments about materiality levels in such a way that tolerable misstatement, combined for the entire audit plan, does not exceed those estimates." Materiality judgments (tolerable misstatements) are not affected by the auditor's business risk. Judgments about materiality (tolerable misstatements) are subjective and do involve consideration of qualitative as well as quantitative factors (AU 312.27) and ordinarily will change during

the process of conducting an audit as the auditor develops new evidence (AU 312.15).

PPS SAMPLING

28. (d) This is one of several approaches that can be used to determine sample size when errors are expected, but it is the only approach possible with the information given.

$$\textit{Sampling Interval} = \frac{\textit{Tolerable Misstatement}}{\textit{Reliability Factor for Misstatement of Overstatement}}$$

$$\textit{Sample Size} = \frac{\$48{,}000}{3.00}$$

$$= \frac{\textit{Recorded Amount}}{\textit{Sample Interval}} = \mathbf{\$16{,}000}$$

$$= \frac{\$480{,}000}{\$\ 16{,}000} = 30$$

29. (b) Book value less audit value divided by book value is the tainting percentage. [($5,000 – $4,000) / $5,000 = .2] The tainting percentage times the sampling interval is the projected error. .2 x $10,000 = $2,000 The sum of all the projected errors is the projected misstatement; there was only one error in this sample.

30. (c) In PPS sampling, the auditor achieves control over the risk of incorrect acceptance by specifying the level of risk he or she is willing to assume. PPS sampling does not require direct consideration of the standard deviation of dollar amounts to determine the appropriate sample. The book value of the unit determines how probable it is that it will be included in the sample, not whether it is over or understated. The sampling interval is calculated by dividing the book value of the population by the sample size.

SOLUTION 37-2 ADDITIONAL MULTIPLE CHOICE ANSWERS

AUDIT SAMPLING

31. (c) AU 350.12 states, "The risk of assessing control risk too low is the risk that the assessed level of control risk based on the sample is less than the true operating effectiveness of the control structure policy or procedure." All things being equal, a sample taken from a smaller population will be more representative of the population than a sample of the same size taken from a larger population. Thus, the risk that the sample taken from the smaller population will yield a result different from the result obtained had the entire population been examined, is *lower* than such a risk inherent in sampling from a larger population.

32. (a) According to AU 350.38, both the expected deviation rate and the tolerable deviation rate are considerations in determining the sample size for a test of controls.

33. (c) According to AU 350.48, increasing the tolerable misstatement would lead to a decrease in the sample size. Increasing the assessed level of control risk would lead to an increase in the sample size.

34. (b) When using the systematic sampling technique, the auditor determines a uniform interval by dividing the number of physical units in the population by the sample size. A random number is selected as a starting point for the first interval, and one item is selected throughout the population at each of the uniform intervals from the starting point. The randomness of the sample can be destroyed if the items in the population occur in a systematic pattern. *For example,* a population of employees on a payroll for a construction company might be organized by teams; each team consists of a crew leader and nine other workers. A selection of every tenth employee will list either every crew leader or no crew leaders, depending on the random start. No combination would include both crew leaders and other employees.

35. (c) AU 350.12 states, "the risk of incorrect rejection is the risk that the sample supports the conclusion that the recorded account balance is materially misstated when it is not materially misstated. The risk of assessing control risk too high is the risk that the assessed level of control risk based on the sample is greater than the true operating effectiveness of the control structure policy or procedure." The risk of assessing control risk too low is just the opposite. "The risk of incorrect acceptance is the risk that the sample supports the conclusion that the recorded account balance is not materially misstated when it is materially misstated."

STATISTICAL SAMPLING

36. (d) The principal advantage of statistical over nonstatistical sampling can be expressed in several ways. One such expression is that statistical

sampling provides a scientific (mathematical) basis for determining sample size while nonstatistical sampling does not. Answers (a), (b), and (c) are factors used in determining sample sizes for tests of controls but are determined on the basis of auditor judgment rather than scientifically.

37. (a) The factors affecting sample size when using classical variables sampling are (1) desired precision, (2) desired sample reliability, (3) variability among item values in the population (the estimate of the population's standard deviation) and (4) population size. PPS is a non-parametric method that does not assume a normal distribution. PPS plans require special design to deal with negative balances and zero balances because sample selection is based on the *cumulative sum* of dollars of the population. Negative figures distort the cumulative sum and zero balances would not be considered without special adjustments in a PPS plan. Classical variables techniques are unaffected by either zero balances or negative balances.

38. (d) When performing tests of controls, the auditor is looking for the deviation rate from established control procedures set by the client. Thus, the auditor performs attributes sampling procedures. Answers (a) and (c) represent substantive sampling procedures. Answer (b) describes a selection method that is not relevant to attribute sampling.

39. (a) When determining sample size, the auditor gives consideration to assessing control risk too low and the tolerable deviation rate. The "allowable risk of assessing control risk too high" is a distracter.

PERFORMANCE BY SUBTOPICS

Each category below parallels a subtopic covered in Chapter 37. Record the number and percentage of questions you correctly answered in each subtopic area.

Audit Sampling

Question #	Correct √
1	
2	
3	
4	
5	
6	
7	
# Questions	7
# Correct	
% Correct	

Statistical Sampling

Question #	Correct √
8	
9	
10	
11	
12	
13	
14	
15	
16	
# Questions	9
# Correct	
% Correct	

Attributes Sampling

Question #	Correct √
17	
18	
19	
20	
21	
22	
23	
# Questions	7
# Correct	
% Correct	

Variables Sampling

Question #	Correct √
24	
25	
26	
27	
# Questions	4
# Correct	
% Correct	

PPS Sampling

Question #	Correct √
28	
29	
30	
# Questions	3
# Correct	
% Correct	

ESSAY SOLUTIONS

SOLUTION 37-3 PPS AND CLASSICAL SAMPLING

The incorrect assumptions, statements, and inappropriate applications of sampling are as follows:

1. Classical variables sampling is **not designed for tests of controls**.

2. PPS sampling uses **each dollar** in the population, not each account, as a **separate sampling unit**.

3. PPS sampling is **not efficient if many misstatements** are **expected** because the sample size can become larger than the corresponding sample size for classical variables sampling as the expected amount of misstatement increases.

4. Each account does not have an equal chance of being selected; the probability of selection of the accounts is **proportional** to the **accounts' dollar amounts**.

5. PPS sampling requires **special consideration for negative (credit) balances.**

6. **Tolerable misstatement** was **not considered** in calculating the sample size.

7. **Expected** (anticipated) **misstatement** was **not considered** in calculating the sample size.

8. The **standard deviation** of the dollar amounts is **not required** for PPS sampling.

9. The three selected accounts with **insignificant balances should not have been ignored or replaced** with other accounts.

10. The account with the $1,000 difference (recorded amount of $4,000 and audited amount of $3,000) was **incorrectly projected** as a **$1,000 misstatement**; projected misstatement for this difference was actually **$2,500 ($1,000 ÷ $4,000 × $10,000 interval).**

11. The **difference** in the understated account (recorded amount of $1,900 and audited amount of $2,000) **should not have been omitted** from the calculation of projected misstatement.

12. The **reasoning** (the comparison of projected misstatement with the allowance for sampling risk) concerning the decision that the receivable balance was not overstated was **erroneous.**

SOLUTION 37-4 ATTRIBUTE SAMPLING

1. Statistical sampling **does not eliminate** the **need for professional judgment.**

2. The **tolerable rate of deviation** or acceptable upper precision limit (UPL) is **too high (20%)** if Baker plans to assess control risk at a **low level (substantial reliance).**

3. **Discovery sampling** is **not an appropriate sampling technique** in this attribute sampling application.

4. The sampling technique employed is **not discovery sampling.**

5. The **increase** in the **population size** has **little or no effect** on determining sample size.

6. Baker failed to consider the **allowable risk** of assessing control risk too low (**risk of overreliance**) in **determining the sample size.**

7. The population from which the sample was chosen (invoices) was an **incorrect population.**

8. The sample selected was **not randomly selected.**

9. Baker failed to consider the difference of an immaterial amount to be an **error**.

10. The **allowance for sampling risk** was **incorrectly calculated.**

11. Baker's reasoning concerning the decision that the sample **supported a low assessed level of control risk** was **erroneous.**

SOLUTION 37-5 ATTRIBUTE SAMPLING EVALUATION

a. 1. In determining an **acceptable level of risk of assessing control risk too low**, an auditor should consider the **importance** of the control to be tested in determining the **extent** to which substantive tests will be **restricted** and the **planned assessed level of control risk.**

2. In determining the **tolerable deviation rate**, an auditor should consider the planned assessed level of control risk for the controls to be tested and how **materially** the financial statements would be affected if the control does not function properly. For example, **how likely** is the control to **prevent** or **detect material misstatements.**

3. In determining the **expected population deviation rate**, an auditor should consider the results of **prior years' tests**, the **overall control environment**, or **utilize a preliminary sample.**

b. 1. There is a **decrease** in sample size if the **acceptable level of risk of assessing control risk too low** is **increased.**

2. There is a **decrease** in sample size if the **tolerable deviation rate is increased.**

3. There is an **increase** in sample size if the **population deviation rate is increased.**

c. For a **low risk of assessing control risk too low** it is generally appropriate to reconsider the planned assessed level of control risk as the **calculated estimate of the population deviation rate** identified in the sample (7%) **approaches the tolerable deviation rate** (8%). This is because there may be an **unacceptably high sampling risk** that these sample results could have occurred with an **actual population deviation rate higher than the tolerable deviation rate.**

d. If statistical sampling is used, an allowance for sampling risk can be calculated. If the **calculated**

estimate of the population deviation rate plus the allowance for sampling risk is **greater than the tolerable deviation rate**, the sample results should be interpreted as **not supporting** the assessed level of control risk for the control.

SOLUTION 37-6 PPS SAMPLING

a. The advantages of PPS sampling over classical variables sampling are as follows:

- PPS sampling is generally **easier to use** than classical variables sampling.
- **Size** of a PPS sample is **not based on the estimated variation** of audited amounts.
- PPS sampling automatically results in a **stratified sample.**
- Individually significant items are automatically identified.
- If no misstatements are expected, PPS sampling will usually result in a **smaller sample** size than classical variables sampling.
- A PPS sample can be easily designed and sample selection can begin before the complete population is available.

b.

$$\textit{Sampling Interval} = \frac{\textit{Tolerable Misstatement}}{\textit{Reliability Factor for Misstatement of Overstatement}}$$

$$= \frac{\$15{,}000}{3.00} = \$5{,}000$$

$$\textit{Sample Size} = \frac{\textit{Recorded Amount}}{\textit{Sample Interval}}$$

$$= \frac{\$300{,}000}{\$\ \ 5{,}000} = 30$$

c.

	Recorded amount	Audit amount	Tainting	Sampling interval	Projected misstatement
1st misstatement	$ 400	$ 320	20%	$1,000	$ 200
2nd misstatement	500	0	100%	1,000	1,000
3rd misstatement	3,000	2,500	*	1,000	500
Total projected misstatement					$ 1,700

* The recorded amount is greater than the sampling interval; therefore, the **projected misstatement equals the actual misstatement.**

SOLUTION 37-7 STEPS IN A SAMPLING PLAN

The remaining steps are as follows:

6. Treat the individually significant items as a **separate population.**
7. **Choose** an audit **sampling technique.**
8. **Determine** the **sample size**, giving consideration for—
   a. **Variations** within the population.
   b. **Acceptable level of risk.**
   c. **Tolerable misstatement.**
   d. Expected amount of misstatement.
   e. Population size.
9. Determine the **method** of selecting a representative sample.
10. **Select** the sample items.
11. **Apply** appropriate **audit procedures** to the sample items.
12. **Evaluate** the sample **results.**
    a. Project the misstatement to the population and consider sampling risk.
    b. Consider the qualitative aspects of misstatements and reach an overall conclusion.
13. **Document** the sampling procedure.

Wondering how to allocate your study time?

In your excitement to answer multiple choice questions, don't forget that the examiners ask questions in other formats!

The first pass through a chapter:

1. Strive to answer **all** the multiple choice and other objective format questions.
2. Choose one or more of the essay questions to answer.

When you review the chapter later:

1. Answer **at least** those objective questions that you did not understand the first time. (If you had a lucky guess, did you really understand?)
2. Select a new essay question to answer.

When you review the chapter for the final time (for some chapters, the second time may **be** the final time):

1. Only review the notes you would review just before the exam. For a whole exam section, this should take less than five minutes. Answer the questions "cold turkey" (without reviewing the text materials just before answering questions).
2. Answer **at least** those objective questions that you did not understand the first time.
3. Select a new essay question to answer.

Remember, with the techniques and information in your material,

A passing score is well within reach!

CHANGE ALERT

SAS 94, THE EFFECT OF INFORMATION TECHNOLOGY ON THE AUDITOR'S CONSIDERATION OF INTERNAL CONTROL IN A FINANCIAL STATEMENT AUDIT In May 2001, the Auditing Standards Board of the AICPA issued Statement on Audit Standards (SAS) 94, *The Effect of Information Technology on the Auditor's Consideration of Internal Control in a Financial Statement Audit*. SAS 94 amends the guidance in SAS 55, as previously amended by SAS 78. SAS 94 is effective for audits of financial statements for periods beginning on or after June 1, 2001.

EXAM COVERAGE: The Obtain and Document Information portion of the Auditing section of the CPA exam is designated by the examiners to be 35 percent of the section's point value. Historically, exam coverage of the topics in this chapter hovers at 3 to 5 percent of the Auditing section. More information about the point value of various topics is included in the **Practical Advice** section of this volume.

CHAPTER 38

AUDITING EDP SYSTEMS

CHAPTER 38

AUDITING EDP SYSTEMS

I. EDP-BASED SYSTEMS

A. ELECTRONIC DATA PROCESSING (EDP)

An EDP-based system includes (1) hardware, (2) software, (3) documentation, (4) personnel, (5) data, and (6) controls. There can be significant differences between EDP activities and non-EDP activities.

1. **DOCUMENTATION** Many control procedures in EDP systems do not leave documentary evidence of performance.

2. **ELECTRONIC INFORMATION** Files and records are usually in machine-readable form and cannot be read without using a computer.

3. **REDUCED HUMAN INVOLVEMENT** Computers may obscure errors that a human would notice while handling the transaction.

4. **RELIABILITY** EDP systems are more reliable than manual systems because all of the data is subjected to the same controls. Manual systems are subject to human error on a random basis. Computer processing virtually eliminates computational errors associated with manual processing.

5. **KNOWLEDGE** An auditor may need specialized EDP knowledge to perform an audit.

6. **DIFFICULTY OF CHANGE** It is harder to change an EDP system once it is implemented than it is to change a manual system. Therefore, the auditor will want to become familiar with a new EDP system at an early stage of the development process so that the auditor can anticipate possible future audit problems.

EXHIBIT 1 ♦ COMPUTER HARDWARE CONFIGURATION

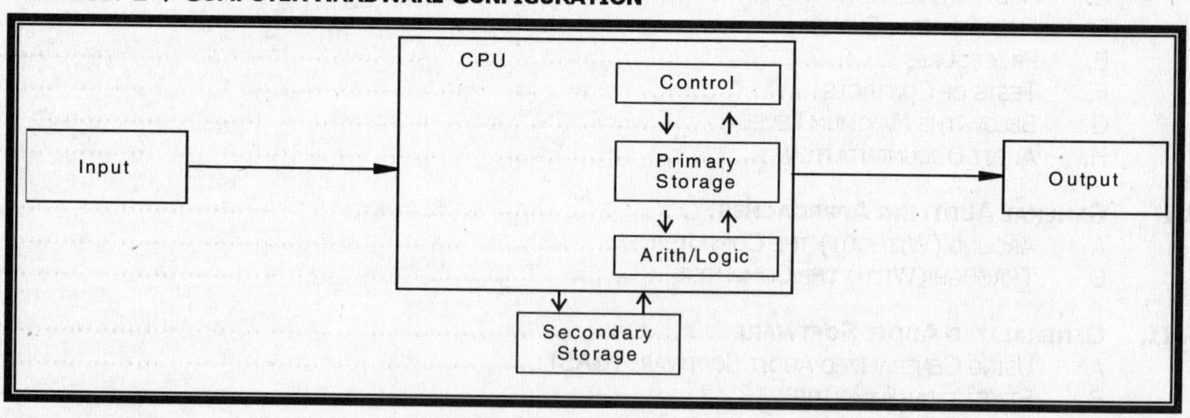

B. DATA PROCESSING

1. **TRANSACTION PROCESSING MODES** Transactions may be processed either in batches or on-line.

   a. **BATCH PROCESSING** Transactions to be processed are accumulated in groups (batches) before processing and are then processed as a batch. Batch processing frequently involves sequential access to the data files. For example, a company may accumulate a day's charge sales before processing them against the master file during the night. Before they are processed, the transactions would be sorted into the order of the records on the master file. One disadvantage of batch processing is that, because of the time delays, errors may not be detected immediately.

b. **On-Line Processing** Transactions are processed and the file is updated as the transactions occur. On-line processing usually involves files that can be directly accessed. For example, a cash register terminal may automatically update the inventory file when a sale is made.

(1) **Real-Time Processing** An on-line system is operating in real-time if the data is processed fast enough to get the response back in time to influence the process. For example, an airline reservation system is an on-line, real-time (OLRT) system since the customer receives reservations after waiting only a few moments.

(2) **Integrated System** All files affected by a transaction are up-dated in one transaction-processing run, rather than having a separate run for each file. The files are usually stored on magnetic disks. For example, in an integrated system, a sales transaction may update the sales summary file, the accounts receivable master file, and the inventory file during one processing run.

2. **File Updating** The updating process is most efficient when the transaction file has been sorted into the same order as the master file. There are four basic steps in the process of updating a batch of records in a master file that is kept on a magnetic disk. First, a transaction enters the CPU. Second, the record to be updated is read from its location on the disk into the CPU. Third, the record is updated in the CPU. Fourth, the updated record is written onto the disk in the same location as the original record. The result is that the original record is replaced by the updated record. This results in the original record being erased. This can be contrasted with the updating of a tape file (Exhibit 2) in which the original record still exists on the original tape after the updating process.

Exhibit 2 ♦ Updating a Master File Kept on Tape

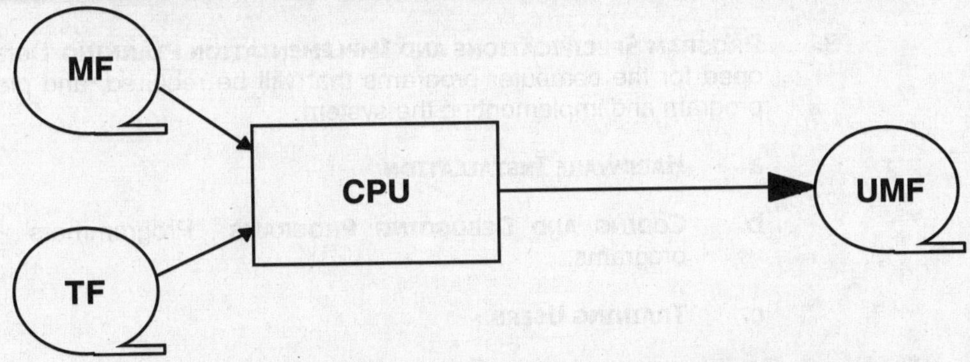

Three reels of tape are required: the **master file** (MF), the **transaction file** (TF), and the reel that becomes the **updated master file** (UMF). There are three basic steps in the updating process. **First**, records are read into the CPU from the master file (MF) and the transaction file (TF). **Second**, the records from the master file are updated in the CPU. **Third**, the updated records are written onto the output reel to form the updated master file (UMF). It is important to note that **after** updating is complete, **all** three tapes will still be intact.

3. **PROCESSING OUTSIDE OF THE CLIENT** While many companies have their own equipment to do their processing within the company (i.e., in-house), others utilize outside processors. Several common arrangements are as follows:

   a. **BLOCK TIME** Client rents a certain block of computer time from an outside party. For example, a company may rent time from a bank that does not utilize its computer system 24 hours per day.

   b. **TIME-SHARING** A number of users share a computer system. Each may have a terminal that it can use to access a CPU located outside of the client. Each user can access the system whenever it wishes.

   c. **SERVICE BUREAU** An outside organization that provides a wide range of data processing services for a fee.

C. DEVELOPMENT AND IMPLEMENTATION

The CPA sometimes becomes involved in the development and implementation of a computer-based application system. The CPA may do the work or may work with client personnel (systems analysts, programmers, etc.). The development and implementation process involves the following phases:

1. **SYSTEMS ANALYSIS (FEASIBILITY STUDY)** The system's overall objectives and requirements are clearly determined. The existing system is then studied to see if it is adequately meeting them. Broad alternative approaches are also considered.

2. **SYSTEMS DESIGN**

   a. **GENERAL SYSTEMS DESIGN** The alternative approaches are evaluated in more detail and a specific proposal is developed for implementing the alternative that is felt to be best.

   b. **DETAILED SYSTEM DESIGN** The recommended system is designed in detail. This includes designing files, determining resource requirements, and developing plans for the following phases.

3. **PROGRAM SPECIFICATIONS AND IMPLEMENTATION PLANNING** Detailed specifications are developed for the computer programs that will be required, and plans are made for testing the program and implementing the system.

   a. **HARDWARE INSTALLATION**

   b. **CODING AND DEBUGGING PROGRAMS** Programmers write and test the required programs.

   c. **TRAINING USERS**

   d. **SYSTEMS TESTING** The system is tested thoroughly. The results of the tests are compared with the specifications and requirements of the system to determine whether it does what it is supposed to do.

   e. **CONVERSION AND VOLUME TESTING** Conversion is done from the old system to the new system. This involves such things as converting and verifying files and data. Frequently, conversion involves parallel processing (i.e., parallel operations) in which the old system and the new system are run at the same time with the actual data for the period and the results compared. This checks the new system and avoids disaster if the new system fails the first time it is used.

4. **IMPLEMENTATION** The system is released to the user.

5. **MONITORING** Once the system is operating routinely, it is reviewed to be sure it is attaining the original objectives set for it, and to correct any problems.

D. CLIENT DOCUMENTATION

Documentation is an important aspect of control as well as of communication. It generally provides (1) an understanding of the system's objectives, concepts, and output, (2) a source of information for systems analysts and programmers when involved in program maintenance and revision, (3) information that is needed for a supervisory review, (4) a basis for training new personnel, (5) a means of communicating common information, (6) a source of information about accounting controls, and (7) a source of information that will aid in providing continuity in the event experienced personnel leave. If reliable documentation is not available, the auditor must find other sources of information. There are several types of documentation.

DOCUMENTATION OF AN EDP SYSTEM	
O	**Operations Documentation**
P	**Problem Definition Documentation**
S	**Systems Documentation**
O	**Operator Documentation**
U	**User Documentation**
P	**Program Documentation**

1. **PROBLEM DEFINITION DOCUMENTATION** Permits the auditor to gain a general understanding of the system without having to become involved in the details of the programs. Contents include the following:

   a. Description of the reasons for implementing the system.

   b. Description of the operations performed by the system.

   c. Project proposals.

   d. Evidence of approval of the system and subsequent changes (for example, a particular individual may have to sign a form to indicate these).

   e. A listing of the assignment of project responsibilities.

2. **SYSTEMS DOCUMENTATION** Provides sufficient information to trace accounting data from its original entry to system output. Contents include the following:

   a. A description of the system.

   b. A systems flowchart shows the flow of data through the system and the interrelationships between the processing steps and computer runs.

   c. Input descriptions.

   d. Output descriptions.

   e. File descriptions.

   f. Descriptions of controls.

g. Copies of authorizations and their effective dates for systems changes that have been implemented.

3. **PROGRAM DOCUMENTATION** Primarily used by systems analysts and programmers to provide a control over program corrections and revisions. However, it may be useful to the auditor to determine the current status of a program. Contents include the following:

   a. Brief narrative description of the program.

   b. Program flowchart, decision table, or detailed logic narrative.

      (1) **PROGRAM FLOWCHART** Shows the steps followed by the program in processing the data.

      (2) **DECISION TABLE** Describes a portion of the logic used in the program. Although it is not always used, it can replace or supplement the program flowchart.

      (3) **DETAILED LOGIC NARRATIVE** Narrative description of the logic followed by a program.

   c. Source statements (i.e., a listing of the program instructions) or parameter listings.

   d. List of control features.

   e. Detailed description of file formats and record layouts.

   f. Table of code values used to indicate processing requirements.

   g. Record of program changes, authorizations, and effective dates.

   h. Input and output formats.

   i. Operating instructions.

   j. Descriptions of any special features.

4. **OPERATIONS DOCUMENTATION** Information provided to the computer operator. It can be used by the auditor to obtain an understanding of the functions performed by the operator and to determine how data is processed. Contents include the following:

   a. A brief description of the program.

   b. Description of the inputs and outputs that are required (e.g., the forms used).

   c. Sequence of cards, tapes, disks, and other files.

   d. Set-up instructions and operating system requirements.

   e. Operating notes listing program messages, halts, and action necessary to signal the end of jobs.

   f. Control procedures to be performed by operations.

   g. Recovery and restart procedures (to be used for hardware or software malfunctions).

   h. Estimated normal and maximum run time.

   i. Instructions to the operator in the event of an emergency.

5. **USER DOCUMENTATION** Description of the input required for processing and an output listing. The auditor may use it to gain an understanding of the functions performed by the user and the general flow of information. Contents include a description of the system, description of the input and output, list of control procedures and an indication of the position of the person performing the procedures, error correction procedures, cutoff procedures for submitting the data to the EDP department, and a description of how the user department should check reports for accuracy.

6. **OPERATOR DOCUMENTATION** Documentation should be prepared that will indicate the jobs run and any operator interaction.

   a. **DAILY COMPUTER LOG** May be manually prepared by the computer operator. It indicates the jobs run, the time required, who ran them, etc.

   b. **CONSOLE LOG** A listing of all interactions between the console and the CPU. Prepared by the computer as messages are entered from the console, it can be a valuable control for detecting unauthorized intervention of the computer operator during the running of a program. It also shows how the operator responded to processing problems.

II. THE EFFECTS OF EDP-BASED SYSTEMS ON AUDITS

A. PLANNING THE ENGAGEMENT

An auditor's objectives do not change when auditing the financial statements of a company using an EDP system. The *ultimate objective is still to express an opinion* on the fairness of presentation of the financial statements. The auditor must still (1) become familiar with the client, (2) plan the engagement, (3) consider internal control, (4) perform tests of controls, (5) perform substantive tests, (6) evaluate the evidence, and (7) express an opinion. While the audit objectives do not change, the audit procedures used to accomplish them may change. The auditor should consider the following matters.

1. **EXTENT** The extent to which the computer is used in each significant accounting application.

2. **COMPLEXITY** The complexity of the entity's computer operations, including the use of an outside service center.

3. **ORGANIZATION** The organizational structure of the computer processing activities.

4. **AVAILABILITY OF DATA** Some data may only be available for a limited time.

5. **ANALYTICAL PROCEDURES** An additional factor in the use of analytical procedures is the increased availability of data that is used by management. Such computer-prepared data and analyses, although not necessarily a part of the basic accounting records, may be valuable sources of information (e.g., budget and variance information).

6. **CAAT** The use of computer-assisted audit techniques (CAAT) to increase the efficiency of performing audit procedures. If specific skills are needed, and a specialist is used, the auditor should have sufficient computer-related knowledge to (a) communicate the objectives of the other professional's work; (b) evaluate whether the specified procedures will meet the auditor's objectives; and (c) evaluate the results of the procedures applied as they relate to the nature, timing, and extent of other planned audit procedures. The auditor's responsibilities with respect to using such a professional are equivalent to those for other assistants.

B. CONSIDERATION OF INTERNAL CONTROL

1. **BASIC CONCEPTS** The characteristics that distinguish computer processing from manual processing include the following:

a. **TRANSACTION TRAILS** Some computer systems are designed so that a complete transaction trail that is useful for audit purposes might exist for only a short period of time or only in computer-readable form. This trail is used to monitor the system, answer queries, and deter fraud.

b. **UNIFORM PROCESSING OF TRANSACTIONS** Computer processing uniformly subjects like transactions to the same processing instructions. Consequently, computer processing virtually eliminates the occurrence of clerical error normally associated with manual processing. Conversely, errors will result in all like transactions being processed incorrectly.

c. **SEGREGATION OF FUNCTIONS** Many internal control procedures once performed by separate individuals in manual systems may be concentrated in systems that use computer processing. Therefore, an individual who has access to the computer may be in a position to perform incompatible functions. As a result, other control procedures may be necessary in computer systems to achieve the control objectives ordinarily accomplished by segregation of functions in manual systems.

d. **POTENTIAL FOR ERRORS AND FRAUD** Decreased human involvement in handling transactions processed by computers can reduce the potential for observing errors and fraud. Errors or fraud occurring during the design or changing of application programs can remain undetected for long periods of time.

e. **POTENTIAL FOR INCREASED MANAGEMENT SUPERVISION** Computer systems offer management a wide variety of analytical tools that may be used to review and supervise the operations of the company. The availability of these additional controls may serve to enhance the entire internal control structure on which the auditor may wish to assess control risk at below the maximum level. For example, comparisons by management of budget to actual results and the response by management to unusual fluctuations indicate management's monitoring of the ongoing operations as a prevention of unfavorable crisis situations.

f. **INITIATION OR SUBSEQUENT EXECUTION OF TRANSACTIONS BY COMPUTER** The authorization of "automatic" transactions or procedures may not be documented in the same way as those initiated in a manual accounting system, and management's authorization of those transactions may be implicit in its acceptance of the design of the computer system.

g. **DEPENDENCE OF OTHER CONTROLS ON CONTROLS OVER COMPUTER PROCESSING** Computer processing may produce reports and other output that are used in performing manual control procedures. The effectiveness of these manual control procedures can be dependent on the effectiveness of controls over the completeness and accuracy of computer processing.

2. **ACCOUNTING CONTROL PROCEDURES** Internal accounting control procedures are sometimes defined by classifying control procedures into two types: general and application control procedures.

a. **GENERAL CONTROLS** Those controls that relate to all or many computerized accounting applications and often include control over the development, modification, and maintenance of computer programs and control over the use of and changes to data maintained on computer files. When an auditor anticipates assessing control risk at a low level, the auditor would initially focus on these general controls.

b. **APPLICATION CONTROLS** Those controls that relate to specific computerized accounting applications, i.e., input, processing, and output controls for an accounts payable application.

3. **REVIEW OF INTERNAL CONTROL** Due to the increased concentration of functions within the computer processing operation, the auditor's concern over the interdependence of control procedures is generally greater than it is in a manual system. In fact, application controls are often dependent upon general controls. Accordingly, it may be more efficient to review the design of general controls before reviewing the specific application controls.

4. **TESTS OF CONTROL** Some internal control procedures consist of the approval or independent review of documents that evidence transactions. If an accounting application is processed by computer, those procedures performed by an application program frequently do not provide visible evidence indicating the control procedures performed. Furthermore, the application program may not perform *any* procedures subsequent to the original processing of the transactions.

   a. Tests of controls on the procedures performed by a computer may be made, provided the computer produces *visible evidence* to (1) verify that the procedures were in operation and (2) evaluate the propriety of their performance.

   b. With respect to incompatible functions, a computer processing system should include (1) adequate segregation of incompatible functions within the data processing department, (2) segregation between data processing and user department personnel who perform review procedures, and (3) adequate control over access to data and computer programs.

5. **ASSESSING CONTROL RISK** After obtaining an understanding of the client's EDP controls, the auditor must assess control risk for the EDP portion of the client's internal control. The procedures that the auditor would use are the same as for a manual system and would include inquiries, observations, and inspections.

C. EVIDENTIAL MATTER

The auditor can use either manual audit procedures, computer-assisted audit techniques, or a combination of both to obtain sufficient, competent evidential matter. However, SAS 80, *Amendment to SAS No. 31, Evidential Matter,* notes, "Because of the growth in the use of computers and other information technology, many entities process [transmit, maintain, or access] significant information electronically."

1. **SUBSTANTIVE TESTS IMPRACTICAL** In entities that handle significant information electronically, the auditor may conclude, for one or more financial statement assertions, that it is impractical to reduce detection risk to a acceptable level through substantive tests only. For example, the potential for improper information alternation or initiation to occur undetected may increase if information is handled only in electronic form. In these situations, auditors should gather evidential matter (by performing tests of controls) to use in assessing control risk and should consider the effect on reports.

2. **INFORMATION AVAILABILITY** Sometimes information and corroborating evidential matter are available in electronic form only. Source documents (purchase orders, bills of lading, invoices, and checks) may be in the form of electronic messages. Certain electronic evidence may not be accessible after a specified period of time if files are changed, unless backup files are created. The auditor should consider the time when information is available in determining the nature, timing, and extent of substantive tests and tests of controls.

   a. **ELECTRONIC DATA INTERCHANGE (EDI)** With EDI, an entity and its customers or vendors transact business electronically. (Purchasing, shipping, billing, cash receipt, and cash disbursement functions are achieved through electronic exchanges, ordinarily without paper documents.)

   b. **IMAGE PROCESSING** With image processing systems, paper documents are scanned into electronic images for electronic storage and retrieval. The entity might only keep paper documents for a limited time after this conversion.

3. **INTERNAL CONSISTENCY** Auditors test accounting information by analysis and review, retracing, recalculation, and reconciliation. By performing these procedures, auditors may evaluate the internal consistency of information. Normally, internally consistent information provides evidence about the fairness of financial statement presentations.

4. **DATA MINING** Data mining (also known as relationship mapping, data interrogation, or knowledge discovery) is the distillation of previously unknown information from raw data. The largest strength of data mining is identification of unexpected relationships. Manual review may be inefficient for entities with a high number of transactions. Data mining is used for many purposes (streamlining operations, marketing analysis), although this discussion focuses on auditing. Data mining tools can assist auditors to perceive patterns in mountainous databases in a timely manner. By quickly discovering a fraudulent scheme, auditors can prevent future fraud and facilitate asset recovery.

   a. A data mining tool is like a sieve, allowing an auditor to sift through large amounts of data quickly, providing an overview of an entity. These preliminary procedures can be performed on entire populations, instead of relatively small samples. Auditors analyze identified questionable relationships, allowing them to devote more time to examining relationships that appear characteristic of error or fraud.

   b. For example, a bank may have the same employees who authorized a loan to a debtor named Jones being named on checks drawn on the account that Jones opened with the loan proceeds. This coincidence might escape manual detection and yet warrant extra auditor scrutiny.

   c. Analysis tools can also highlight individual transactions that fit a fraud profile. A fraud profile is a summary of expected data characteristics that an auditor expects to find in a particular type of fraudulent transaction, based on an understanding of a given entity's internal control weaknesses. Not all transactions fitting a fraud profile are fraudulent, but an auditor may increase audit efficiency by selecting transactions to examine based on a fraud profile.

EXHIBIT 3 ♦ FRAUD PROFILE EXAMPLES FOR ACCOUNTS PAYABLE

Vendor records that list more than one payment address. (Vendors may have multiple branches, or payments to a legitimate vendor may have been fraudulently redirected.)

Vendor records showing only post office box addresses. (While payments are frequently sent to lock boxes, usually there is one address—for instance, shipping or purchasing—that is a street address.)

In a large organization, records for one vendor showing the same authorized signer on every check and/or the same receiving clerk accepting every delivery connected with that vendor. (In an organization with several possible signers and receiving clerks for any given transaction, this circumstance is an unlikely coincidence.)

Matching employee and vendor addresses. (It is rare that an employee's home-based business is a legitimate vendor.)

Mailing addresses that are shared by vendors. (Several false vendors may share the same address or payments may be fraudulently redirected to the same address for a perpetrator's convenience.)

Payments close to payment-review thresholds. (Management review is not necessary up to the threshold. Employees may aim to commit fraud for the largest amount possible per transaction.)

Invoice numbers from the same vendor that are close in sequence. (Legitimate vendors typically have many customers.)

III. General Controls (GC)

A. Organization and Operation Controls

1. **GC 1:** Segregation of functions between the EDP department and users.

2. **GC 2:** Provision for general authorization over the execution of transactions (prohibiting the EDP department from initiating or authorizing transactions).

3. **GC 3:** Part of proper internal control is the segregation of functions within the EDP department. Among the various functions that should be segregated are the following:

SEGREGATION OF FUNCTIONS WITHIN THE EDP DEPARTMENT

C	CONTROL GROUP	Responsible for internal control within EDP department.
O	OPERATORS	Convert data into machine readable form.
P	PROGRAMMER	Develops and writes the computer programs. Responsible for debugging of programs. Writes the run manual.
A	ANALYST	Designs the overall system and prepares the system flowchart.
L	LIBRARIAN	Keeps track of program and file use. Maintains storage of all data and backups. Controls access to programs.

a. **Input Preparation** Process of converting the input data into machine-readable form. Input methods include key-to-tape (i.e., keying the information directly onto the magnetic tape), key-to-disk, and OCR.

b. **Computer Operations** Computer operators physically run the equipment. This includes loading (i.e., entering) the program and data into the computer at the correct time, mounting tapes and disks on the appropriate tape and disk drives, and dealing with problems that occur during processing.

c. **Programming**

(1) Applications programmers write, test, and debug the application programs from the specifications provided by the systems analyst.

(2) Systems programmers implement, modify, and debug the software necessary to make the hardware operate.

d. **Systems Analysis** Systems analysts investigate a business system and decide how the computer can be applied. This includes designing the system, deciding what the programs will do, and determining how the outputs should appear.

e. **Librarians** Provide control over the various programs, data tapes, disks, and documentation (manuals, etc.) when they are not in use; also, librarians are responsible for restricting access to EDP materials to authorized personnel only. Library-control software may be used in some systems to keep control over programs, data, etc., that is kept on-line.

f. **Data Integrity** Data must be safeguarded for maximum control. To this end, users are given passwords or IDs to ensure that only authorized persons can access selected data. These passwords and IDs are frequently changed to further ensure the integrity of the system and its data. Passwords can be used to limit access to the entire system and to limit what the individual can access and/or change once in the system.

g. **DATA BASE ADMINISTRATOR** The data base administrator is responsible for maintaining the data base and restricting its access to authorized personnel.

- **AUDIT EFFECT OF A SMALL EDP ENVIRONMENT** In a small EDP environment, many of the computer personnel functions are combined for a small number of employees. In these situations, two key functions that should be segregated are the applications programmer and the operator. When these functions are not segregated, fraud can be perpetrated and concealed because the programmer knows exactly what the EDP system is capable of performing.

B. SYSTEMS DEVELOPMENT AND DOCUMENTATION CONTROLS

1. **GC 4:** The procedures for system design, including the acquisition of software packages, should require active participation by representatives of the users and, as appropriate, the accounting department and internal auditors.

2. **GC 5:** Each system should have written specifications that are reviewed and approved by an appropriate level of management and users in applicable departments.

3. **GC 6:** Systems testing should be a joint effort of users and EDP personnel and should include both the manual and computerized phases of the system.

4. **GC 7:** Final approval should be obtained prior to placing a new system into operation.

5. **GC 8:** All master file and transaction file conversions should be controlled to prevent unauthorized changes and to provide accurate and complete results.

6. **GC 9:** After a new system has been placed in operation, all program changes should be approved before implementation to determine whether they have been authorized, tested, and documented.

7. **GC 10:** Management should require various levels of documentation and establish formal procedures to define the system at appropriate levels of detail.

- **AUDIT EFFECT OF A WEAKNESS IN SYSTEMS DEVELOPMENT AND DOCUMENTATION CONTROLS**—Auditor will usually have to spend more time in order to understand the system and evaluate the controls. Because application controls are often dependent on the quality of general controls, the absence of effective system development controls may weaken the accounting application controls.

C. HARDWARE AND SYSTEMS SOFTWARE CONTROLS

Hardware controls are controls that are built into the computer.

1. **PARITY BIT (REDUNDANT CHARACTER CHECK)** In odd parity, an odd number of magnetized dots (on tape, disk, etc.) should always represent each character. When recording data, the computer automatically checks this. Then, when reading the data, the computer checks to see if there is still an odd number. In even parity, an even number of magnetized dots is used to represent each character. For example, the use of a parity bit would probably discover a distortion caused by dust on a tape or a distortion caused by sending data over telephone lines.

2. **ECHO CHECK** CPU sends a signal to activate an input or output device in a certain manner. The device then sends a signal back to verify activation. The CPU then compares the signals.

3. **HARDWARE CHECK** Computer checks to make sure the equipment is functioning properly. For example, periodically the computer may search for circuits that are going bad.

4. **BOUNDARY PROTECTION** Keeps several files or programs separate when they share a common storage. For example, in time-sharing, several users may share primary storage. Boundary protection would prevent their data and/or programs from becoming mixed and from accessing each other's data.

5. **GC 11:** The control features inherent in the computer hardware, operating system, and other supporting software should be utilized to the maximum possible extent to provide control over operations and to detect and report hardware malfunctions.

6. **GC 12:** Systems software should be subjected to the same control procedures as those applied to the installation of, and changes to, application programs.

- **AUDIT EFFECT OF A WEAKNESS IN HARDWARE AND SYSTEMS SOFTWARE CONTROLS** May seriously affect the auditor's assessed level of control risk.

D. **ACCESS CONTROLS**

1. **PHYSICAL ACCESS CONTROLS** Only authorized personnel should have access to the facilities housing EDP equipment, files and documentation.

2. **ELECTRONIC ACCESS CONTROLS** Access control software and other sophisticated devices are available to limit system access.

3. **GC 13:** Access to program documentation should be limited to those persons who require it in the performance of their duties.

4. **GC 14:** Access to data files and programs should be limited to those individuals authorized to process or maintain particular systems.

5. **GC 15:** Access to computer hardware should be limited to authorized individuals.

- **AUDIT EFFECT OF A WEAKNESS IN ACCESS CONTROLS** Weakness increases the opportunity for unauthorized modifications of files and programs and misuse of the system; thereby decreasing the integrity of the system.

E. **DATA AND PROCEDURAL CONTROLS**

1. **FILE LABELS**

a. **EXTERNAL LABELS** Human-readable labels attached to the outside of a secondary storage device, indicating the name of the file, expiration date, etc.

b. **INTERNAL LABELS** Labels in machine-readable form.

(1) **HEADER LABEL** Appears at the *beginning* of the file and contains such information as the file name, identification number, and the tape reel number.

(2) **TRAILER LABEL** Appears at the *end* of the file and contains such information as a count of the number of the records in the file and an end-of-file code.

2. **FILE PROTECTION RING** A plastic ring that must be attached to a reel of magnetic tape before the tape drive will write on the tape. Since writing on magnetic tape automatically erases the data already there, the file protection ring guards against the inadvertent erasure of the information on the tape.

3. **FILE PROTECTION PLANS**

a. **DUPLICATE FILES** The most important data files are duplicated and the duplicates are stored away from the computer center.

EXHIBIT 4 ♦ GRANDPARENT-PARENT-CHILD RETENTION CONCEPT

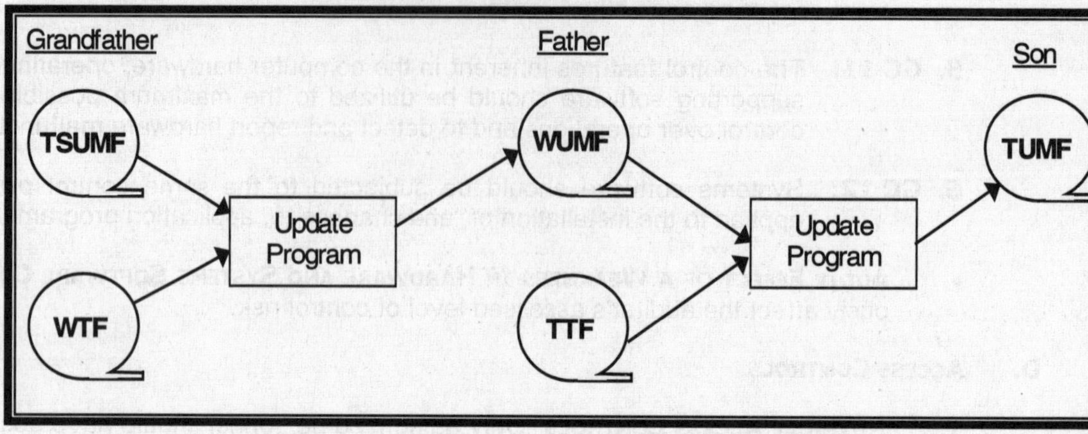

b. **GRANDPARENT-PARENT-CHILD (OR VICE VERSA) RETENTION CONCEPT** This is also known as Grandfather-Father-Son Retention. The master file is updated at the end of each day by the day's transaction file, illustrated in Exhibit 3. After updating on Thursday, the Thursday updated master file (TUMF) is the child, the Wednesday updated master file (WUMF) is the parent, and the Tuesday updated master file (TSUMF) is the grandparent. These three files plus Wednesday's and Thursday's transaction files (WTF and TTF, respectively) are retained. If there is a problem during Friday's update run, the TUMF can be regenerated by running the copy of the WUMF with Thursday's transaction file. If necessary the WUMF could be reconstructed by processing TSUMF with Wednesday's transaction file. Once updating is completed on Friday, Friday's updated master file (FUMF) becomes the child, TUMF becomes the parent and WUMF becomes the grandparent. Therefore, at that time, TSUMF and Wednesday's transaction file can be erased.

c. **DISK RECONSTRUCTION PLAN** In updating a record in a disk file, the record is read from the disk into the CPU, altered, and then written back to its previous location on the disk, thereby erasing the preupdated record. Therefore, a "disk dump" is used in which a copy of the contents of the disk is made on magnetic tape periodically, say each morning. Then, as the day's transactions are processed against the disk file, copies of the transactions are recorded on another tape. If it becomes necessary to reconstruct the disk file at any time during the day, the old file can be read from the tape to the disk and reupdated with the transactions from the transaction tape.

4. **PHYSICAL SAFEGUARDS**

a. **PROPER PHYSICAL ENVIRONMENT** Consider extreme temperature, humidity, dust, etc.

b. **ENVIRONMENT FREE FROM POSSIBILITY OF NATURAL DISASTERS** Includes proper fire-proofing and locating the computer in a safe place (for example, not in the basement if there is a danger of flooding).

c. **BACKUP FACILITIES** Arrangements should be made to use other equipment in the case of serious problems. Backup arrangements are frequently made with service bureaus or with computer installations of subsidiaries. Backup facilities are referred to as "hot" or "cold" sites, depending on their state of readiness.

d. **CONTROL ACCESS TO THE COMPUTER ROOM** Only authorized personnel should have access. For example, computer operators would be authorized to be in the computer room, but programmers would not be. Further, there should always be at least two people in the computer room at all times. A weakness in internal control exists when a client uses microcomputers, because these computers are rarely isolated in a limited-access location and operators may more readily remove hardware and software components and modify them at home.

5. **GC 16:** A control function should be responsible for receiving all data to be processed, for ensuring that all data are recorded, for following up on errors detected during processing to see that the transactions are corrected and resubmitted by the proper party, and for verifying the proper distribution of output.

6. **GC 17:** A written manual of systems and procedures should be prepared for all computer operations and should provide for management's general or specific authorizations to process transactions.

7. **GC 18:** Internal auditors or an other independent group within an organization should review and evaluate proposed systems at critical stages of development.

8. **GC 19:** On a continuing basis, internal auditors, or an other independent group within an organization should review and test computer processing activities.

- **AUDIT EFFECT OF WEAKNESSES IN DATA AND PROCEDURAL CONTROLS** Serious weaknesses can affect the auditor's assessment of control risk when establishing the scope of the substantive testing.

IV. APPLICATION CONTROLS (AC)

A. INPUT CONTROLS

Input controls are designed to provide reasonable assurance that data received by EDP have been properly authorized, converted into machine sensible form, and identified, and that data have not been lost, suppressed, added, duplicated, or otherwise improperly changed. Basic categories of input to be controlled are (1) transaction entry, (2) file maintenance transactions (e.g., changing sales prices on a product master file), (3) inquiry transactions (e.g., how many units of a particular inventory item are on hand), and (4) error correction transactions.

1. **AC 1:** Only properly authorized and approved input, prepared in accordance with management's general or specific authorization, should be accepted for processing by EDP.

2. **AC 2:** The system should verify all significant codes used to record data.

3. **AC 3:** Conversion of data into machine-sensible form should be controlled.

4. **COMMON ERRORS IN CONVERSION** Keying errors and the losing or dropping of records.

5. **INPUT CONTROL TECHNIQUES**

a. **CONTROL TOTALS** A total is computed and then recomputed at a later time. The totals are compared and should be the same. Control totals can be used as *input*, processing, and output controls.

(1) **FINANCIAL TOTAL** Has financial meaning in addition to being a control. For example, the dollar amount of accounts receivable to be updated can be compared with a computer-generated total of the dollar amount of updates read from the tape.

(2) HASH TOTAL Has meaning only as a control. For example, a total of the account numbers of those accounts that should have been updated can be compared with a computer-generated total of those account numbers actually entered.

(3) RECORD COUNT (DOCUMENT COUNT) A count of the number of transactions processed. For example, the computer can be programmed to print the total number of A/R records actually inputted.

b. COMPUTER EDITING Computers can be programmed to perform a wide range of edit tests (i.e., edit checks) on records as they are being entered into the system. If a particular record does not meet the test, it is not processed. Edit tests include the following:

(1) LIMIT (REASONABLENESS) TEST A particular field of an input transaction record is checked to be sure it is not greater (or smaller) than a prespecified amount, or that it is within a prespecified range of acceptable values. For example, "hours worked" on a payroll record may be checked to be sure it does not exceed 50 hours.

(2) VALID FIELD AND/OR CHARACTER TEST The particular field is examined to be sure it is of the proper size and composition. For example, if a customer account number should be seven numeric digits appearing in the first 7 spaces of the record, the first 7 spaces can be examined to be sure there are 7 numerals there.

(3) VALID NUMBER OR CODE TEST Verifies that a particular number or code is one of those that is recognized by the system. For example, if a company has 5 retail outlets and records sales by using a location code of 1-5, the computer can check to be sure the code digit on the transaction record is a 1, 2, 3, 4, or 5.

(4) SEQUENCE CHECK If the input records should be in some particular sequence, the computer can be programmed to verify the sequence. For example, after sorting, the day's transaction file that is being entered should be in ascending order by customer account number.

(5) MISSING DATA TEST Verifies that all of the data fields actually contain data. For example, a point-of-sale terminal may be programmed not to accept a transaction unless the clerk has entered 10 pieces of required data.

(6) VALID TRANSACTION TEST Since there are only a certain number of transaction types that would be expected for most files, the computer can be programmed to verify that a particular transaction is an appropriate type for a particular file. For example, in the case of inventory, the only valid transaction may be to debit the inventory account when inventory is added and credit the account when inventory is taken away.

(7) VALID COMBINATION OF FIELDS Checks to be sure a certain combination of fields is reasonable. For example, a large retail outlet may program its computer to check the reasonableness of the product code field and the quantity-sold field. This would disclose a clerical error that resulted in a sale being entered for 10 television sets when only 1 was sold; i.e., it is not reasonable that one retail customer would purchase 10 television sets.

(8) CHECK DIGIT (SELF-CHECKING DIGIT) Digit (determined according to a prespecified mathematical routine) that is added to the end of a piece of numeric data to permit the numeric data to be checked for accuracy during input, processing, or output. For example, a customer account number may be 1234. A check digit could be formed by adding the first and third digits and using the sum. Since the sum of the two digits is 4 (i.e., 1 + 3), the check digit is 4. It is added to the end of the number that is assigned to the customer. The new customer account number becomes 12344. The computer can be programmed to verify the check digit at appropriate times. For instance, if the number is accidentally entered as 13244, the check digit would not match and the transaction would not be accepted. In practice, the mathematical routine is more complex than the one illustrated here.

(9) **VALID SIGN TEST** A particular field can be checked to be sure it has the proper sign. For example, the quantity received in an inventory record should not be negative.

6. **AC 4:** Movement of data between one processing step and another, or between departments, should be controlled.

7. **AC 5:** The correction of all errors detected by the application system and the resubmission of corrected transactions should be reviewed and controlled.

- **ERROR LOG (ERROR LISTING)** A computer-prepared list of those transactions that were not processed because of some error condition (e.g., an invalid customer account number). When an error is encountered, the usual procedure is for the computer to not process the erroneous transaction but to skip it and continue processing the valid transactions rather than to halt processing altogether. A control function should be responsible for following up on errors detected during processing to see that the transactions are corrected and resubmitted by the proper party. This control function should ideally be delegated to a special EDP control group that is independent from system analysis, programming, and operation.

B. PROCESSING CONTROLS

(**NOTE**: Many of the input controls are also valid processing controls.)

1. **AC 6:** Control totals should be produced and reconciled with input control totals.
2. **AC 7:** Controls should prevent processing the wrong file, detect errors in file manipulation, and highlight operator-caused errors.
3. **AC 8:** Limit and reasonableness checks should be incorporated within programs.
4. **AC 9:** Run-to-run controls should be verified at appropriate points in the processing cycle.

C. OUTPUT CONTROLS

Primarily balancing, visual scanning or verification, and distribution.

1. **AC 10:** Output control totals should be reconciled with input and processing controls.
2. **AC 11:** Output should be scanned and tested by comparison to original source documents.
3. **AC 12:** Systems output should be distributed only to authorized users.

D. AUDIT EFFECT OF A WEAKNESS IN APPLICATION CONTROLS

Must be considered in relation to the particular application and to the total audit. Controls in the categories of input, processing, and output must be considered in relation to each other; i.e., a strong control in processing may compensate for a weakness in input.

V. INFORMATION TECHNOLOGY IMPACT ON CONSIDERATION OF INTERNAL CONTROL

A. OBJECTIVES

The objectives of SAS 94 include to:

1. Emphasize that in circumstances where a significant amount of information supporting financial statement assertions is electronically initiated, recorded, processed, and reported, the auditor may be compelled to obtain evidential matter about the effectiveness of both the design and operation of controls to reduce the assessed level of control risk.

2. Clarify that in obtaining an understanding of the entity's financial reporting process, the auditor should understand how both standard, recurring entries and nonstandard, non-recurring entries are initiated and recorded, and the auditor should understand the controls that have been placed in operation to ensure that such entries are authorized, complete, and correctly recorded.

B. OVERVIEW

Because technology is becoming increasing integral to business processes, it is becoming more difficult for auditors to rely on traditional (paper) audit evidence in obtaining sufficient competent evidential matter. SAS 94 incorporates and expands on the concepts delineated in SAS 80 related to an auditor's consideration of internal controls when it is not practical or possible to restrict overall audit risk to an acceptably low level by performing only substantive tests in a financial statement audit. An audit involves both an assessment of control risk and the design, performance, and evaluation of substantive tests to reduce audit risk to an acceptably low level.

1. **SUBSTANTIVE TESTS ONLY** SAS 94 does **not** mandate that the auditor must be able to assess control risk below the maximum level in all IT environments. To the extent that the auditor believes that assessing control risk at the maximum level and performing a substantive audit would be an effective approach, the auditor can do so. Auditor must be aware that in many IT environments, because audit evidence does not exist outside the IT environment, such an approach might not result in an effective audit.

2. **SUBSTANTIVE TESTS REQUIRED** Even when the auditor has obtained evidential matter which allows for an assessment of control risk below the maximum level, there will still be a need to perform substantive tests on significant amounts.

3. **COMPELLED IN SOME AUDITS** The auditor is required in all audits to obtain an understanding of internal control sufficient to plan the audit. To obtain this understanding, the auditor will need to consider how the entity uses IT, manual procedures, and other processes and how those processes affect the controls which are relevant to the audit. In an IT environment, it may not be practical or even possible to reduce audit risk to an acceptably low level through the use of substantive testing only. That is, in many IT situations, it will be an absolute necessity that the auditor obtain evidence which allows for control risk to be assessed at a level below the maximum level.

4. **ONLY REASONABLE ASSURANCE** All internal control systems, regardless of how well designed, face certain inherent limitation which make the achievement of absolute assurance an impossibility. In an IT system, errors can occur in designing, maintaining, or monitoring automated controls. For example, IT personnel may not understand how an IT system processes sales transactions which could result in incorrect changes to the system which process sales for a new product line. Additionally, errors can occur in the use of the information produced by the IT system.

C. AUDIT EVIDENCE

The term **electronic evidence** relates to information that is transmitted, processed, maintained, and/or accessed by electronic means (e.g., using a computer, scanner, sensor, and/or magnetic media). Many of the issues related to electronic evidence also are applicable to evidence in the form of computer-printed documents and reports, particularly if there is no way to independently review or validate the printed information. The attributes of audit evidence (paper versus electronic) are:

1. **DIFFICULTY OF ALTERATION** Easily-altered evidence lacks credibility and has reduced value to the auditor. Paper evidence is difficult to alter without detection. An auditor has a reasonable likelihood of detecting significant alterations that have been made to paper documents. This quality provides auditors with some assurance that the evidence represents original information. Alterations due to the operation of a EDP system may not be detected, unless specifically-designed tests are performed.

2. **PRIMA FACIE CREDIBILITY** SAS No. 80 establishes a hierarchy of credibility for evidence. Credibility is enhanced when the source of the evidence is independent in relation to the client and the auditor has the ability to corroborate that evidence. Paper documents (e.g., incoming purchase orders) usually have a high degree of credibility. However, a purchase order transmitted electronically from a customer derives its credibility primarily from the controls within the electronic environment. A fraudulent or altered electronic purchase order exhibits no apparent difference, compared to a valid purchase order, when extracted from the electronic environment of the entity.

3. **COMPLETENESS OF DOCUMENTS** Competent evidence includes the essential terms of a transaction so that an auditor can verify the validity of the transaction. Paper evidence typically includes all of the essential terms of a transaction. Paper evidence also includes information regarding other parties to the transaction (e.g., customer name and address, or preferred shipping methods), on the face of the document. Work on the completeness assertion for paper documents often includes review of acknowledgments of data entry and postings. An electronic environment may mask this evidence with codes or by cross-references to other data files that may not be visible to the users of the data.

4. **EVIDENCE OF APPROVALS** Approvals integrated into the evidence add to the completeness of the evidence. Paper documents typically show approvals on their face. For example, incoming purchase orders may have marketing department price approvals and credit department approvals written on the face of each original document. The same treatment may apply to electronic approvals by integrating approvals into the electronic record. Electronic elements may require additional interpretation.

5. **EASE OF USE** This factor relates to evaluating and understanding evidence. Auditors use traditional paper evidence without additional tools or expert analysis. Electronic evidence often requires extraction of the desired data by an auditor knowledgeable in electronic data extraction techniques or through use of a specialist.

6. **CLARITY** Competent evidence should allow the same conclusions to be drawn by different auditors performing the same tasks. The nature of electronic evidence is not always clear.

D. FUNDAMENTAL CHANGE

Auditors may need to consider the implications of IT in evaluating any of the five components of internal control as they relate to the achievement of the entity's objectives. For example, in today's business world, it is not uncommon to find entities which have complex, highly integrated IT systems that share data and that are used to support all aspects of the entity's financial reporting, operations, and compliance objectives. As **enterprise resource planning** (ERP) systems become more comprehensive and more widely in use, this issue becomes more prevalent—even for small and mid-sized entities. The use of IT often changes the fundamental manner in which transactions are initiated, recorded, processed, and reported from paper-based systems that rely primarily on manual controls to electronic systems using a combination of manual and automated controls.

1. **MANUAL** In a manual system, an entity uses manual procedures and records in paper format (e.g., to enter sales orders, authorize credit, prepare shipping reports and invoices, and maintain accounts receivable records). Controls in a "traditional" system also are manual,

and may include procedures such as approvals and reviews of activities, and reconciliations and follow-up of reconciling items.

2. **AUTOMATIC** Alternatively, an entity may have complex IT systems that use automated procedures to initiate, record, process, and report transactions, in which case records in electronic format replace paper documents such as purchase orders, invoices, and shipping documents. Controls in systems that use IT consist of a combination of automated controls (e.g., controls embedded in computer programs) and manual controls. Further, manual controls may be independent of the IT system and may use information produced by the IT system, or may be limited to monitoring the effective functioning of the system and the automated controls and handling exceptions. An entity's mix of manual and automated controls varies with the nature and complexity of the entity's use of IT.

3. **BENEFITS** An IT environment provides benefits to the auditor related to effectiveness and efficiency because it enables the entity to:

   a. Consistently apply predefined business rules and perform complex calculations in processing large volumes of transactions or data.

   b. Enhance the timeliness, availability, and accuracy of information.

   c. Facilitate the additional analysis of information.

   d. Enhance the ability to monitor the performance of the entity's activities and its policies and procedures.

   e. Reduce the risk that controls will be circumvented, especially if controls over changes to the IT system are effective.

4. **RISKS** Some of the risks that an auditor faces when working within an IT environment:

   a. Overreliance on information provided by the IT system that could be incorrectly processing data or consistently processing inaccurate data.

   b. Unauthorized access to data that may result in destruction of data or improper changes to data including the recording of unauthorized or nonexistent transactions or inaccurate recording of transactions.

   c. Unauthorized changes to computer programs.

   d. Failure to make necessary changes to computer programs.

   e. Inappropriate manual intervention.

   f. Potential loss of data.

E. PROCEDURES

In understanding a reporting entity's financial reporting process, SAS 94 specifically stipulates that the auditor must understand procedures utilized for entering transaction totals into the general ledger, procedures utilized for initiating, recording, and processing journal entries in the general ledger (both standard and non-standard journal entries), and procedures utilized for recording recurring and nonrecurring adjustments to financial statements that are not reflected in formal journal entries (e.g., consolidating adjustments, report combinations, and reclassifications).

F. TESTS OF CONTROLS

In some situations, SAS 94 requires that the auditor perform tests of controls regarding both the design and operations of controls in order to reduce the assessed level of control risk. The inability to do so would likely result in a scope limitation which would preclude the auditor from issuing an opinion on the financial statements in these situations.

1. When the auditor is not performing tests of controls, the auditor needs to be satisfied that performing substantive tests alone would be effective in restricting detection risk to an acceptable level. For example, the auditor may determine that performing substantive tests alone would be effective and more efficient than performing tests of controls for assertions related to fixed assets and to long-term debt in an entity where a limited number of transactions are related to those financial statement elements and when the auditor can readily obtain corroborating evidence in the form of documents and confirmations.

2. In complex situations—especially where there is a large volume of transactions processed within the complex IT environment—the auditor may determine that performing tests of controls to assess control risk below the maximum level for certain assertions would be effective and more efficient than performing only substantive tests. Alternatively, the auditor may determine that it is not practical or even possible to restrict detection risk to an acceptable level by performing only substantive tests.

3. In making the determination as to whether tests of controls are mandatory, factors an auditor considers include:

   a. The nature of the financial statement assertion.

   b. The volume of transactions or data related to the financial statement assertion.

   c. The nature and complexity of the systems, including the use of IT, by which the entity processes and controls information supporting the financial statement assertions.

   d. The nature of the available evidential matter, including audit evidence that is available only in electronic form.

4. Examples of situations where the auditor may determine that tests of controls are necessary are:

   a. An entity that conducts business using a system in which the computer initiates orders for goods based on predetermined rules and pays the related payables based on electronic information in transactions regarding receipt of goods. No other documentation of orders or goods received is produced or maintained.

   b. An entity that provides electronic services to customers (e.g., an Internet service provider or a telephone company) and uses computer applications to log services provided to users, initiate bills for the services, process the billing transactions, and automatically record such amounts in electronic accounting records that are used to produce the financial statements.

G. Below the Maximum Level

Assessing control risk below the maximum level involves the same broad steps in an IT environment as it does in any other audit. The knowledge that the auditor gains from obtaining an understanding about internal controls should be used to identify the types of potential misstatements that could occur in financial statement assertions. Additionally, the auditor will need to consider factors that affect the risk of material misstatements. In assessing control risk, the auditor should identify the controls that are likely to prevent or detect material misstatements in specific assertions.

1. In making this determination, certain IT application controls may relate directly to one or more financial statement assertions, but their continued effective operation usually depends on general controls that are indirectly related to the assertions. Indirect general controls usually include program change controls and access controls that restrict access to

programs and related data. The auditor should consider the need to identify not only IT applications controls directly related to the assertions, but also other indirect general controls on which they depend.

2. To test automated controls, the auditor may need to use techniques that are different from those used to test manual controls. For example, computer-assisted audit techniques may be used to test automated controls or data related to assertions. Also, the auditor may use other automated tools or reports produced by the computer system to test the operating effectiveness of indirect controls, such as program change controls and access controls. The auditor should consider whether specialized skills are needed to design and perform the tests of controls.

H. Audit Documentation

Consistent with the previous guidance, the auditor should document the understanding of the entity's internal control components obtained to plan the audit. In addition, the auditor needs to document the basis for his or her conclusions about the assessed level of control risk. Conclusions about the assessed level of control risk may differ as they relate to various account balances or classes of transactions. The form and extent of this documentation is influenced by the nature and complexity of the entity's controls. Generally, the more complex internal control and the more extensive the procedures performed, the more extensive the auditor's work papers would need to be.

1. **Maximum Level** Where control risk is assessed at the maximum level, the auditor should document the conclusion that control risk is at the maximum level but need not document the basis for that conclusion.

2. **Below Maximum Level** Where the assessed level of control risk is below the maximum level, the auditor would need to document the basis for this conclusion that the effectiveness of the design and operation of controls supports that assessed level. The nature and extent of the auditor's documentation are affected by the assessed level of control risk used, the nature of the entity's internal control, and the nature of the entity's documentation of internal control.

VI. General Auditing Approaches

A. Around (Without) the Computer

The computer is treated as a "black box" that is ignored for all practical purposes. The auditor concentrates on input and output; i.e., if the inputs are correct and the outputs are correct, what went on within the computer must also be correct. The auditor does **not** test or directly examine the computer program, nor use the computer to perform the tests. Rather, the auditor relies on computer-prepared documents and printouts, which provide a visible audit trail that can be used in performing the audit procedures.

1. **Type of System** Auditing around the computer is appropriate for simple systems that provide extensive printouts of processing, i.e., systems that provide a good audit trail.

2. **Testing of Controls** Extensive use is made of the **error listing** (error log) to verify the existence and functioning of the control procedures. For example, if the error listing shows that a payroll transaction was not processed because the "hours-worked" field exceeded the limit allowed, the auditor has evidence that the limit test exists and is functioning. The auditor will also trace transactions from the source documents (for example, a sales slip) through processing to their final place in the accounts and reports. Note that while computer-generated output is being used, the computer is not being used as an audit tool.

3. **Substantive Testing** The computer-prepared output is used as a basis for substantive testing. For example, the auditor may select a sample of accounts receivable to be confirmed from a computer-prepared listing of all the individual accounts receivable.

B. THROUGH (WITH) THE COMPUTER

The computer is used to perform tests of controls and substantive testing. The auditor places emphasis on the **input** data and the **processing** of the data. While output is not ignored, the auditor reasons that if the input is correct and the processing is correct, then the output must be correct. As a system becomes more complex, more processing is done within the computer and more data files are kept only in machine-readable form. This causes the audit trail to disappear. When this happens, auditing through the computer is really the only alternative open to the auditor. The following techniques are available to the auditor.

AUDITING THROUGH THE COMPUTER

W Writing own program
E Embedded audit modules
T Tagging

C Client-prepared program
U Utility programs (utility routines)
P Program comparison

T Test data (test deck)
R Review of program logic
I Integrated test facility (ITF, minicompany approach)
P Parallel simulation
P Program tracing

1. **WRITING OWN PROGRAM** Auditor writes a program for the specific substantive test to be performed. The major drawback is the time and effort required to get the program operational.

2. **EMBEDDED AUDIT MODULES** Sections of program code included in the client's application program to collect audit data for the auditor. For example, at the auditor's direction, a file may be created of all sales transactions that are for more than $100. This monitors the client's system as transactions are actually processed. It can be hard to install once the application program is operational. Thus, it may be most efficiently included during system design.

3. **TAGGING** Selected transactions are "tagged" (i.e., are specially marked) at the auditor's direction. Then, as they are processed, additional documentation is generated so that the auditor can see how the transactions are handled as they are processed, i.e., it allows the auditor to examine the transactions at the intermediate steps in processing that are normally done within the computer but not displayed.

4. **CLIENT-PREPARED PROGRAM** Often the internal audit staff has programs to do the same things the auditor would like to do. Therefore, the auditor may be able to use the programs. However, first the auditor must test them to make sure that they do what they are supposed to do and that their integrity can be relied on.

5. **UTILITY PROGRAMS (UTILITY ROUTINES)** Standard programs furnished by the computer manufacturer for performing common data processing functions such as (1) changing the media a file is stored on (e.g., tape-to-disk, disk-to-tape, tape-to-paper), (2) modifying the data by changing or deleting records within a file, (3) creating or destroying a file, (4) changing the name or password of a file, (5) printing the contents of a file so it may be

inspected visually, (6) sorting a file, and (7) merging two or more files. Utility programs may be more technical than GAS (discussed below). Therefore, the auditor may have to be more technically proficient with EDP to use them efficiently. The auditor must also be sure the utility program has not been altered. Consideration should be given as to whether the use of a utility routine will decrease the audit time or if GAS may be more appropriate.

6. **PROGRAM COMPARISON** The auditor-controlled copy of the program is compared with the program the client is currently using (usually done on a surprise basis). The idea behind this technique is that the comparison will disclose unauthorized changes made in the program. While the auditor may do this manually, there is software available to do it. A major drawback is the problem of the auditor maintaining a current copy of the program. Routine maintenance (updating) by programmers may mean that the auditor's copy does not agree with the copy being used, and it is the auditor's copy that is wrong.

7. **TEST DATA (TEST DECK)** Auditor prepares a series of fictitious transactions (test data), some of which are valid and some of which contain errors that should be detected by the controls the auditor wants to test. The auditor uses the client's programs to process the test data and then examines the output to check processing, including the computer-prepared error listing.

   a. For example, if the payroll program is not supposed to process payroll data for employees whose employee time cards indicates they have worked more than 60 hours per week, the auditor's test data would contain at least one time card with more than 60 hours worked on it. If the control is working, the particular transaction should not be processed but should appear on the computer-prepared error listing.

   b. There are at least three potential problems with using test data: (1) Care must be exercised to prevent the fictitious data from becoming part of the client's real data files. (2) Time and care are required to prepare the test data so that it will test for the things that could really go wrong and that are of interest to the auditor. (3) The auditor must take steps to make sure that the program being tested (i.e., the program testing the fictitious data) is the one that is actually used in routine processing.

8. **REVIEW OF PROGRAM LOGIC** Auditor reviews the application program's documentation including the flowcharts and possibly the program listing, to obtain a sufficient understanding of the logic of the program in order to evaluate it. This may be time consuming. Unless the auditor specifically believes there is a logic error in the program, other audit techniques will probably be more efficient.

9. **INTEGRATED TEST FACILITY (ITF, MINICOMPANY APPROACH)** Auditor creates a fictitious entity within the client's actual data files. The fictitious data is then processed for the entity as part of the client's regular data processing. For example, if the auditor wants to test the accounts receivable update program, the auditor could create a fictitious customer's account receivable in the client's actual accounts receivable master file. During the period under audit, the auditor would occasionally introduce transactions for the fictitious customer. For instance, the "customer" would make credit purchases, would overpay the account, would not pay the account, would make purchase returns, etc. These transactions would be processed as part of the client's normal processing. Since the auditor knows what effect the various transactions should have on the accounts receivable, the auditor can check the status of the account at any time to verify that transactions are being processed correctly, i.e., that the application programs are working as they should.

   a. **ADVANTAGE OVER TEST DATA** Two of the main advantages of ITF over the use of test data are that the auditor introduces fictitious data throughout the period (approaches continuous auditing) and it is processed along with the client's other "live" (i.e., actual) data.

   b. **PROBLEMS** Several potential problems relating to the use of ITF are as follows:

(1) Since the data is part of the client's data files, it may *accidentally be included* in the financial statements and reports that are prepared. To avoid this, the auditor may wish to introduce reversing entries to reverse the effects of the fictitious transactions (for example, to remove the "sales" made to the fictitious customer from the sales account) or the auditor may have the statement preparation program modified to skip the fictitious account when preparing the financial statements. Or, the auditor may decide to use small dollar amounts so that even if they are not removed, they will not have a material effect.

(2) Time, effort, and skill are required to make the fictitious entity operational and make sure the transactions processed against it will test the conditions and controls of interest to the auditor.

(3) There is also the problem of secrecy, since the auditor's confidence in the technique will decrease if the client's data preparation and computer operations personnel know that the entity is fictitious and that the transactions for it are being introduced by the auditor in order to audit compliance.

10. **Parallel Simulation** Once the auditor has checked a program, the auditor must determine that the client continues to use it. Parallel simulation involves processing actual client data through an auditor's software program, possibly using the client's computer. After processing the data, the auditor compares the output with output obtained from the client. Two techniques that can be used to help the auditor verify that the program being used for routine processing is the one that has been checked are as follows:

a. **Controlled Processing** The auditor observes (i.e., controls) an actual processing run and compares the results against those expected.

b. **Controlled Reprocessing** The auditor tests a program and keeps a copy of the program. At some future point in time, the auditor has the client use the auditor's control copy of the program to process some actual transactions. The results are compared with those from the client's *routine* processing run. For example, the auditor may have a control copy of the payroll program. The auditor would select the time cards and payroll data for several employees and have them processed using the control copy. The auditor would then compare the results of gross pay, net pay, withholding, etc., from the program with those that were attained by the payroll program the client had just used. A major problem is for the auditor to keep the control copy of the program current.

11. **Tracing (Program Tracing, Tracing Software)** Prints a listing of the program instructions (steps) that were executed in processing a transaction. The auditor must be familiar with the programming language in which the client's application program is written. Even then, it may be time consuming to follow through the program listing.

VII. Generalized Audit Software

(Primary Source: AICPA Audit Guide; *Computer Assisted Audit Techniques*)

A. Using Generalized Audit Software (GAS)

A set of programs or routines (i.e., a software package) *specifically* designed to perform certain data processing functions that are useful to the auditor. The auditor can use GAS on the data files of a variety of clients. The auditor need only briefly describe the organization of each client's files to GAS, rather than write computer programs. Also known as General Purpose Audit Software or General Purpose Computer Audit Software, this is the most prevalently used computer-assisted audit technique.

1. **REASONS**

   a. **USE OF A LARGE VARIETY OF DATA** Much of a client's data is retained only in *machine-readable* form. GAS makes it possible for the auditor to access the data, analyze it, and present the results in a meaningful and convenient form.

   b. **EFFECTIVELY DEAL WITH LARGE QUANTITIES OF DATA** GAS lets the auditor examine *more data* in *more detail*. For example, given an insurance company that has a policy file maintained on disk, the auditor can use GAS to perform mathematical tests on each of the policy records in the file. If auditing the file manually, the auditor could examine only a sample of the policies.

   c. **LESSENS DEPENDENCE ON CLIENT EDP PERSONNEL** The auditor can do much of the computerized testing; i.e., the auditor does not need to rely on client EDP personnel.

   d. **ECONOMY** Produces economies in the audit while increasing audit quality.

   e. **ACCESS TO DATA** Enables the auditor to gain access and test information stored in the client's files without having to acquire a complete understanding of the client's EDP system.

2. **AUDIT TASKS PERFORMED BY GAS** While the exact procedures performed will vary among software packages, audit software is used to accomplish six basic types of audit tasks.

   a. **EXAMINING RECORDS FOR QUALITY, COMPLETENESS, CONSISTENCY, AND CORRECTNESS** GAS can be instructed to scan the records in a file and print those that are exceptions to auditor-specified criteria. Examples include (1) reviewing accounts receivable balances for amounts that are *over* the credit limit, (2) reviewing inventory quantities for *negative* or *unreasonably large* balances, (3) reviewing payroll files for *terminated* employees, and (4) reviewing bank demand deposit files for *unusually large* deposits or withdrawals.

   b. **TESTING CALCULATIONS AND MAKING COMPUTATIONS** GAS can test the *accuracy* of mathematical computations and can perform quantitative analyses to evaluate the *reasonableness* of client representations. Examples include (1) *recalculating* the extensions of inventory items, depreciation amounts, the accuracy of sales discounts, and interest, and (2) determining the *accuracy* of the net pay computations for employees.

   c. **COMPARING DATA ON SEPARATE FILES** GAS can be used to determine if *identical* information on *separate* files agrees. Examples include (1) comparing changes in accounts receivable balances between two dates with details of sales and cash receipts on transaction files, (2) comparing payroll details with personnel records, and (3) comparing current and prior-period inventory files to assist in locating obsolete or slow-moving items.

   d. **SELECTING, PRINTING, AND ANALYZING AUDIT SAMPLES** GAS can *select* statistical samples (random, stratified, etc.), *print* the items for the auditor's working papers or on special confirmation forms, and then, when the results are known (for example, when the confirmations are returned), *analyze* the data statistically. Examples include (1) select and print accounts receivable confirmations, (2) select inventory items for observation, and (3) select fixed asset additions for vouching.

   e. **SUMMARIZING OR RESEQUENCING DATA AND PERFORMING ANALYSES** GAS can *reformat* and *aggregate* data in a variety of ways. Examples include (1) *refooting* account files, (2) *testing* accounts receivable aging, (3) *preparing* general ledger trial balances, (4) *summarizing* inventory turnover statistics for obsolescence analysis, and (5) *resequencing* inventory items by location to facilitate physical observations.

f. **COMPARING DATA OBTAINED THROUGH OTHER AUDIT PROCEDURES WITH COMPANY RECORDS** Manually-gathered audit evidence can be converted to machine-readable form and then GAS can compare it to other machine-readable data. Examples include (1) comparison of inventory test counts with perpetual records and (2) comparison of creditor statements with accounts payable files.

EXAMPLE 1 ♦ POTENTIAL APPLICATIONS OF GAS IN THE AUDIT OF INVENTORY

1. Determine the inventory items that should be reduced for quick sale, according to company policy.
2. Merge last year's inventory file with this year's and list those items that have unit costs of more than $100 that have increased by more than 10 percent.
3. Test for quantities on hand in excess of units sold during a period and list possible obsolete inventory items.
4. Select a sample of inventory items for a physical count and reconcile to the perpetual records.
5. Scan the sequence of inventory tag numbers and print a list of any missing numbers.
6. Select a random sample of inventory items for price testing and test the price.
7. Perform a net-realizable value test on year-end inventory quantities, using unit selling price data, and list any items where inventory cost exceeds net realizable value.

EXAMPLE 2 ♦ POTENTIAL APPLICATIONS OF GAS IN THE AUDIT OF ACCOUNTS RECEIVABLE

1. Select and list accounts according to auditor-defined past-due conditions (e.g., over $5,000 and more than 90 days past-due).
2. List a random sample of past-due accounts to use in determining if follow-up procedures conform to company policy.
3. Select a sample of customer accounts for confirmation and have the computer print the confirmation requests.
4. Determine if the accounts receivable master file balance agrees with the general ledger and independently prove a company-prepared aging of accounts.
5. Match subsequent cash collections with accounts receivable records and independently age receivables not yet paid several weeks after the trial balance date.
6. Compare amounts due from individual customers with their approved credit limits and print a list of customers with balances in excess of their authorized amounts.
7. Print, for review and follow-up, a list of accounts for which collection efforts have been temporarily suspended.

3. **FEASIBILITY** When deciding whether to use GAS, the auditor should consider the following.

   a. **NATURE OF THE AUDIT AREA AND AUDIT APPROACH** In some cases, the use of GAS may be the *only* feasible approach to attain the audit objective, *for example,* in complex systems with invisible audit trails. Does the client support or oppose the use of GAS?

   b. **SIGNIFICANCE OF AUDIT EFFORT AND TIMING** GAS may permit the auditor to complete an audit procedure quicker than any other alternative.

c. **Availability of Data** Some data is only in machine-readable form. Other data is not in machine-readable form and would, therefore, have to be converted before GAS could be applied to it.

d. **Availability of Qualified Staff Personnel** Does the auditor or staff possess the necessary technical expertise to use GAS on the system being audited? For example, an auditor may be experienced in using GAS on relatively simple systems, but not on complex systems.

e. **Economic Considerations** While GAS can accomplish many things for the auditor, it has *costs* associated with its use such as staff hours, technical review hours, mechanical assistance hours, confirmations and other forms, keypunch and verification expense, and computer time.

4. **Planning GAS Applications** The following steps should be followed in planning.

a. Set the objectives of the GAS application.

b. Determine the reports and other output requirements.

c. Review the content, accessibility, etc., of client data files.

d. Identify client personnel who may provide administrative or technical assistance.

e. Determine the need for equipment and supplies.

f. Determine the degree of audit control needed so that the auditor will have confidence that the GAS is processed correctly.

g. Prepare application budgets and timetables.

5. **Steps in Using GAS** The auditor goes through a series of steps in applying GAS.

a. **Determine Routines** Determine the *specific* GAS routines to be used and the particular *order* in which to use them for the particular application. The auditor does not have to use all of the routines available. Any routine can be used as many times as the auditor wishes.

b. **Complete Coding Sheets** The auditor describes the routines to use, the order in which to use them, the client's system, and data files to GAS.

c. **Processing** The GAS, the auditor's instructions, and the client's data files are entered into a computer and processed. The auditor should maintain physical control over the GAS (i.e., it should be kept in the auditor's possession) and should be present when it is run. The auditor should also be present to receive the output directly from the computer.

d. **Use Output** The auditor uses the GAS output in the audit.

B. **Statistical Sampling**

This section is adapted from the AICPA audit guide, *Audit Sampling*. (See also Chapter 37.)

1. **Advantages** Computer programs have been developed to assist the auditor in planning and evaluating sampling procedures. These programs overcome the limitations of tables and perform calculations, such as a standard deviation computation, that are difficult and time-consuming to perform manually.

a. Computer programs are flexible. For example, they can calculate sample sizes for different sampling techniques. They can help the auditor select a random sample. They can evaluate samples covering single or multiple locations and can offer many more options for the auditor's planning considerations. These programs generally have built-in controls over human errors. For example, programs can be designed to include controls to identify unreasonable input.

b. The printed output is generally written in nontechnical language that can be easily understood by an auditor. The printout can be included in the auditor's working papers as documentation of the sampling procedure.

2. **Time-Sharing Programs** Programs offered by time-sharing vendors generally are developed by the vendors, by third parties for the vendor, or by CPA firms.

a. **Appropriateness of Program** In selecting a time-sharing program, the auditor should obtain reasonable assurance that the program is suitable. Vendors have significant differences in philosophies about their responsibility to the user of their programs. The extent to which the vendor is willing to assume responsibility for the programs may indicate the degree to which the vendor believes the programs are suitable for an auditor's purpose.

(1) In most circumstances, more than one statistical theory may be acceptable for use in developing programs. The auditor should inquire which theory was used in order to determine whether that theory is appropriate for the auditor's specific purpose.

(2) It is important for the auditor to determine the extent of a vendor's testing of its programs before using the programs. For example, the auditor should inquire whether the programs were tested with data that an auditor may encounter both in usual and in rare, but possible, circumstances.

b. **Program Controls** Statistical sampling software should contain basic control features that, for example, reject negative numbers where inapplicable or alert the auditor to inappropriately high risk levels or tolerable rates. The auditor should also inquire whether documentation of the controls is available for review. The software also should contain prompts to lead an auditor who is new to statistical sampling through the various input requirements and alternatives.

c. **Vendor Services** A clear and comprehensive user manual should accompany each program. The auditor also should consider if the availability of programs will meet the needs based on work hours and the location of the auditor's offices. For example, some vendors make their programs available twenty-four hours a day. The auditor should consider the amount of technical support available from the vendor during program use.

d. **Convenience** Many time-sharing vendors provide simple operating instructions designed to meet the needs of the auditor. The program instructions should indicate the program's capabilities. The amount of required input should be minimal and free of complex, special codes. The printout reports should be concise and readily understandable to the auditor.

3. **Batch Programs** Batch programs are especially useful where the company's records are in computer-readable form and the auditor wishes to perform other procedures along with the statistical procedures. For example, the auditor may wish to print confirmation requests at the same time the auditor selects a sample of items to be confirmed using a random selection technique. Many batch processing computer-assisted auditing packages contain routines for statistical sampling to allow this flexibility. Batch processing normally leaves an audit trail

that is relatively easy to follow. Many of the criteria used in the selection of a time-sharing program also apply to selection of a batch program.

VIII. Auditing Special Systems

A. On-line, Real Time (OLRT) Systems

These are also called quick response systems. Transactions are *processed* and files *updated* as transactions occur. The data is processed fast enough to get the response back in time to influence the process. Common examples include airline reservations systems in which the customer receives the reservations after waiting only a few moments and point-of-sale (POS) terminals in retail stores where a customer's credit limit is checked while the customer waits.

1. **Common Characteristics**

   a. On-line terminals are usually used.

   b. Data files are usually disk files.

   c. A supervisory program (software) is used to manage the OLRT system.

2. **General Controls** Hardware controls that control the transmittal of the transactions from the terminal to the CPU and back are important (for example, a parity bit). Documentation of the transaction is often produced as a by-product of processing. For example, in point-of-sale terminals, a multicopy sales receipt is usually prepared when the transaction is processed. Further, many terminals automatically prepare an input log (input listing) that includes the code number of the employees who entered the data as well as information about the transactions.

3. **Application Controls** Because of the nature of OLRT systems, these are very important. They include the following:

   a. **Passwords** In some systems, only certain passwords can input certain kinds of transactions or access certain data files. For example, a salesman could input sales orders under a password but the salesman could not change the payroll records.

   b. **Input Edit Tests** Limit and reasonableness tests, valid customer number tests, missing data tests, etc. Transactions that are found to contain an error will not be accepted for processing and the clerk will be notified immediately. Normal error correction is through correction and resubmission.

   c. **Control Totals** Control totals can be prepared by the terminal and later checked against totals prepared by the CPU, e.g., the number of transactions processed or the dollar value of sales processed for a day. Either of these totals could also be checked against the copies of the sales slips.

4. **Audit Impact** Because of the technical complexity of OLRT systems, the auditor will need more technical expertise to consider internal control. Care must also be exercised not to disrupt the system. Techniques such as test data, ITF, and tagging may be used. GAS may be used to perform substantive tests on the data files.

B. Mini- and Microcomputer Systems

The basic control and audit considerations in a small computer environment are the same as those in a larger and more complex EDP system. However, the specific procedures the auditor uses needs to be adapted to fit the minicomputer environment.

1. **Planning** Since the number of records that can be stored in a minicomputer system is limited, audit trails are often retained for a limited period of time. Therefore, the auditor must plan the audit steps to take place when sufficient supporting information is available.

2. General Controls

a. Segregation of Functions Often, segregation of functions within the EDP department and between the EDP department and user departments does not exist to a significant extent in a small business system. Users may even perform EDP functions. The most desirable segregation controls in this environment would include (1) segregation between data entry and processing or (2) segregation between EDP and user transaction authorization. The auditor should assist management in identifying and implementing alternative or compensating controls where separation of functions does not exist. When the auditor finds weaknesses in segregation, the audit program should include more substantive tests.

b. System Design and Documentation Since the choice of software in small systems is influenced by the hardware, users should be involved in the selection of both hardware and software. Although access to program documentation should be limited, it is difficult to enforce in many small computer environments where the data processing group is small. Regardless, there may be times when the auditor may not be able to rely upon the documentation in such an environment.

c. File Conversion and System Testing Frequently, an organization's initial EDP applications include the use of a small business computer system. File conversion and system testing are particularly important in these initial applications and, therefore, should influence the auditor in the audit. Before relying on the contents of converted files, the auditor should evaluate the controls used to ensure against lost or distorted data during conversion. If the auditor determines that sufficient user system testing has not been performed by the client, the auditor should perform procedures that will allow for sufficient testing of the system.

d. Hardware Control Limiting access to computer hardware is difficult in the small computer environment. Often, these systems lack controls that would prevent access to the actual hardware. Such a situation may cause the auditor to reduce reliance on stored data records. However, good application controls can usually compensate for problems caused by the absence or ineffectiveness of hardware controls.

e. Software Control All program changes should be authorized, tested, and documented. However, in some small data processing environments, the auditor will not be able to rely on program change controls. Thus, the auditor may find it appropriate to obtain a copy of the original software directly from the manufacturer. It is also important to control disks with stored data when not in use. Files should be copied or backed up to ensure against loss of data. The use of hard disk drives calls for access protection with the use of passwords, IDs, and the like.

3. Application Controls Most application controls have the same relevance in the minicomputer environment as they do in large EDP systems. The following are problems characteristic of small computer environments:

a. Many of the protection controls available in large systems to prohibit file manipulation or processing errors are not available in minicomputer systems.

b. Limit (reasonableness) checks are not generally adapted to specific situations since most small system software is purchased off the shelf.

c. The auditor should look for the existence of external labels on software. Review of the client's storage and use procedures is also appropriate.

d. Most data is **not** converted into machine-readable form before input into the mini- or microcomputer system. This should cause the auditor to be more concerned with data input controls and less concerned with data conversion controls.

e. In small organizations or situations that generally characterize these environments, there is usually less movement of data between departments. Also, data processing personnel are familiar with system output users. Therefore, the auditor may be less concerned with controls over movement of data between departments and the distribution of output to authorized users than if the auditor was in a large EDP environment.

4. **Distributed Systems** Distributed systems are a network of remote computer sites where small computers are connected to the main computer system.

a. **Advantages** A reduced work load on the main computer results, since edit and processing functions can be performed at the small computer station, as well as increased efficiency from faster turnaround of information.

b. **Audit Considerations** Access at each location should be well controlled and audited separately to verify the integrity of the data processed. Also, because users may have both authorization and recording duties, compensating controls should exist for this lack of segregation of duties.

C. **Client Uses an EDP Service Center (Service Bureau)** A service center provides EDP services to its clients for a fee. Processing of client data occurs **at** the service center and the client's computerized master files are usually maintained **at** the center.

EDP SERVICE CENTER CONTROLS

T Transmission
E Error correction
A Audit trail
M Master file changes
O Output
S Security

1. Certain controls are particularly important because of the *nature* of the client-EDP service center relationship.

a. **Transmission** Document counts, hash totals, financial totals, etc., may be used to control the transmission of data to and from the client's office.

b. **Error Correction** Client should receive an error listing that identifies all of the errors that occurred in the system. Correction, review, and approval procedures should be established and used.

c. **Audit Trail** An audit trail must be maintained. This may be done through proper filing and sequencing of original transaction documents, and also through periodic printouts of journal and ledger balances.

d. **Master File Changes** Printout of all master file changes should be sent to the client. Control counts of master file records and control totals of items within master file records may be used.

e. **Output** Output must be *restricted* to the client. An output distribution list (indicating who should receive the output) and control tests on samples of output may be used.

f. **Security** Service center must have adequate controls to protect the client's data (while being stored and during processing). Further, there must be adequate *reconstruction* procedures so that the client's data files can be reconstructed (i.e., recreated) if all or part of them are destroyed.

2. **Audit Procedures**

a. **Review the client's controls.**

b. **Review Some Processed Transactions** To evaluate control and processing.

C. **EVALUATE THE CONTROLS AND SECURITY OF THE SERVICE CENTER** A service center sometimes hires a CPA to issue a report on its internal control and security. An auditor whose client uses the service center may rely on this report, or if the auditor feels it is inadequate, the auditor may visit the service center to observe the operations.

D. TIME-SHARING SYSTEMS

A time-sharing center *rents* time on its central computer to a number of users, with each user having one or more remote input and output devices. The user usually accesses the central computer over telephone lines. To each user, it seems as if they are the only one using the system. User files and programs are maintained at the time-sharing center.

1. Controls are needed (a) to prevent *alteration* and *destruction* of the client's programs and data files, (b) to prevent the *unauthorized* use of the client's programs and data files, (c) to *reconstruct* the data files and other data in the event of a catastrophe or computer breakdown, and (d) to guard against *inaccurate transmission* of data between the client's terminal and the time-sharing center, and vice versa.

2. Common controls include programmed application controls (as discussed earlier); control totals for data transmission; control totals for processing; boundary protection features (to prevent programs from entering storage, both primary and secondary, that they are not authorized to enter); and the use of passwords or codes that must be furnished by the user to access programs and files.

3. Audit considerations are primarily the same as previously discussed for on-line, real-time systems. Additionally, the auditor may decide to *visit* the time-sharing center to review its controls if the auditor (a) feels that a *large amount* of the client's important financial data is processed there and (b) is not able to determine from other sources (such as the review of another auditor) the quality of the center's control and compliance procedures.

APPENDIX: EDP TERMS

ad hoc report Non-standardized report composed when the need arises. Frequently developed by users, rather than programmers with extensive training, for limited use.

application program Designed to perform the processing of a specific application. For example, an accounts receivable update program is an application program that processes accounts receivable data to update the accounts receivable master file.

bit A binary digit (0 or 1, on or off, etc.), representing the smallest unit of data possible.

byte A group of bits that represents a single character, whether alphabetic or numeric.

characters Letters, numbers, and special symbols (e.g., periods, commas, and hyphens).

central processing unit (CPU, mainframe) Primary hardware component. The actual **processing** of data occurs in the CPU. It contains primary storage, a control unit, and an arithmetic/logic unit.

primary storage (main memory) Portion of the CPU that holds the program, data, and results (intermediate and final) **during** processing; therefore, this includes only temporary storage. The primary storage contains the data and program steps that are being processed by the CPU and is divided into RAM (random access memory) and ROM (read only memory).

control unit Portion of the CPU that **controls** and **directs** the operations of the computer. It interprets the instructions from the program and directs the computer system to carry them out.

arithmetic/logic unit Portion of the CPU that has special circuitry for performing arithmetic calculations and logical operations. This may be combined with the control unit.

cold site Location where equipment and power is available in the event of disaster at the primary location, but requiring considerable effort to get an operational system functioning. (Compare to hot site.)

collaborative computing applications (groupware, shareware) A program that allows several people to have access to the same information and attempts to track the authors of changes.

CPA WebTrust A symbol appearing on a web site that indicates that the organization meets joint Canadian Institute of Chartered Accountants and AICPA business practice disclosures, transaction integrity, and information protection criteria.

data base A structured set of interrelated files combined to eliminate redundancy of data items within the files and to establish logical connections between data items. For example, within personnel and payroll files, some of the data in the two records will be the same; in a data base system, these files would be combined to eliminate the redundant data.

data base management system (DBMS) A set of programs (software) that manages the data base (i.e., creates, accesses, and maintains the data base).

decision tables Decision tables emphasize the relationships among conditions and actions, and present decision choices. Decision tables often supplement systems flowcharts.

document management Electronic document storage and retrieval.

downtime Time when the computer is not functioning. This may be scheduled or unscheduled.

edit Refers to the addition, deletion, and/or rearrangement of data. **Input editing** refers to editing before processing and **output editing** refers to editing after processing.

electronic commerce (eCommerce) Business via the Internet, including EDI.

electronic document submission Submission of documents such as federal tax returns and securities reports in electronic form, usually over the Internet. (Also see EDGAR.)

electronic data interchange (EDI) Electronic communication among entities such as financial institutions and customer-vendor partners (typically involving order placement, invoicing, and payment and may involve inventory monitoring and automatic restocking). ANSI X12 is a domestic EDI format. EDIFACT is an international EDI format.

email, eMail Electronic messages, typically delivered through the Internet. The messages may have attached files, including documents and programs.

enterprise resource planning software Large multi-module applications that manage a business' different aspects, from traditional accounting to inventory management and advanced planning and forecasting.

extranet A password-protected internet, usually for established vendors and customers. (Compare to internet.)

field Group of related characters. For example, a customer name.

file Group of related records. For example, a customer file. (Also see master file and transaction file.)

firewall Software designed to prevent unauthorized access to data by separating one segment from another.

gateway Software or hardware that links two or more computer networks.

groupware A program designed to allow several people to work on a single project. While this allows for greater flexibility, there is a loss of accountability. (Also see collaborative computing applications.)

hardware maintenance Involves equipment service. Routine service is scheduled. Unscheduled maintenance arises when there are unanticipated problems.

hot site Location where a functioning system is planned for use with minimal preparation in the event of a disaster at the primary work location. (Compare to cold site.)

heuristic In computing, the adjective *heuristic* signifies *able to change*; it is used to describe a computer program that can modify itself in response to the user, for example, a spell check program. Routers (switches that transfer incoming messages to outgoing links via the most efficient route possible, for example, over the Internet).

input/output devices Devices for transferring data in and out of the CPU. Examples include:

bar code reader An input device to scan bar codes, such as universal product codes on merchandise.

keyboard Typewriter-like device to allow the user to type information into the computer.

magnetic ink character recognition (MICR) Sensing information recorded in special magnetized ink. MICR is commonly used by the banking industry for check processing.

magnetic tape reader A device to sense information recorded as magnetized spots on magnetic tape (e.g., the magnetic strips used on credit cards and ATM cards).

modem A device to allow users to transfer files over telephone lines to distant computers.

monitor, screen A television-like screen to display information, providing feedback to the user.

mouse, trackball A pointing device to manipulate representations displayed on a screen.

optical character recognition (OCR) scanner A device to sense printed information through the use of light-sensitive devices.

printer A device to produce output on paper, including invoices and checks.

internet A network of networks. The **Internet** is a public network of many networks. (Compare to intranet.)

intranet A network generally restricted to employee access. LANs are typically intranets. (Compare to internet and extranet.)

inventory control system A system that tracks the quantity of inventory bought and sold.

library program (library routine) Programs that are frequently used by other programs. They are kept within the system and "called up" whenever necessary. One example is generating random numbers.

local area network (LAN) A network of computers within a small area (i.e., a building) to transmit information electronically and share files and peripheral equipment among members (compare to wide area network).

management information system (MIS) An information system within an organization that provides management with the information needed for planning and control. This involves an integration of the functions of gathering and analyzing data, and reporting (i.e., communicating) the results to management in a meaningful form.

master file Contains relatively permanent data. For example, an accounts receivable master file would contain a record for each customer and each record would include fields for customer number, name, address, credit limit, amount owed, etc. (Compare to transaction file.)

network An arrangement of computers to allow users access to common data, hardware, and/or software.

operating system (O/S) Manages the coordinating and scheduling of various application programs and computer functions. Examples include the following:

multiprocessing Allows the execution of two or more programs at the same time and requires the utilization of more than one CPU.

multiprogramming A program is processed until some type of input or output is needed. The O/S then delegates the process to a piece of peripheral equipment, and the CPU begins executing other programs. Processing speed is enhanced considerably, making it appear as if more than one program is being processed concurrently, while utilizing only one CPU.

virtual storage The O/S divides a program into segments (called pages) and brings only sections of the program into memory as needed to execute the instructions. This saves memory and processing cost because the majority of the program remains in less expensive secondary storage.

pass (run) A complete cycle of input, processing, and output in the execution of a computer program.

patch Addition of a new part to a program. It may be added to correct or update a program. For example, if a new government regulation affecting withholding tax becomes effective, a patch may be added to the payroll program to provide for this. A patch may also be added for a fraudulent purpose. For example, an employee might insert a patch into a payroll program to print an extra check.

peripheral equipment Equipment that is **not** part of the CPU but that may be placed under the control of the CPU, i.e., which may be accessed directly by the CPU. Input/output devices and secondary storage devices are peripheral equipment.

point-of-sale (POS) system A system that records goods sold and figures the amount due at the cash register, frequently also verifying credit cards or checks.

program Set of instructions that the computer follows to accomplish a specified task (e.g., accounts receivable update program, inventory management program, and payroll program).

program maintenance Refers to making changes in the program in order to keep it current and functioning properly. For example, maintenance of the payroll program may involve modifying it because of changes in the social security law or to provide for a greater number of employees.

record Group of related fields. For example, a customer record would include ID number, name, address, etc.

router Switches that transfer incoming messages to outgoing links via the most efficient route possible, for example, over the Internet.

secondary storage Devices external to the CPU that store data.

disk, diskette Randomly accessible data is represented in concentric circles called "tracks." A magnetic disk is a platter coated on both sides with a material on which data can be represented as magnetized dots according to a predetermined code. Diskettes are more common than disks, as they hold more data. Still more data can be stored on CDs (also called laser disks). A disk drive is used to read data from the disk into the CPU and to write data from the CPU onto the disk. A hard drive is more permanently fixed than a disk or diskette, with faster retrieval. Disks are usually more easily moved than a hard drive.

magnetic tape Plastic tape that is coated with a material on which data can be represented as magnetized dots according to a predetermined code. It resembles audio tape.

off-line storage Not in direct communication with the CPU. Human intervention is needed for the data to be processed. For example, a disk must be inserted in a disk drive before it can be accessed.

on-line storage In direct communication with the CPU without human intervention. For example, a hard drive ordinarily is accessed by the CPU without human intervention.

randomly accessible (direct access) Data records can be accessed directly. Disks are an example. For example, if the customer records are stored in a file on a disk, the disk drive could go directly to Joe Zablonski's record without having to read any of the other customer records.

sequentially accessible Requires the reading of all data between the starting point and the information sought. Magnetic tape is sequentially accessible. For example, if alphabetized records are on magnetic tape and none are read, most of the tape must be read to get to the Joe Zablonski data.

self-service applications Software that allows customers to provide much of their own customer service.

software Programs, routines, documentation, manuals, etc., that make it possible for the computer system to operate and process data. (Compare to hardware.)

systems programs (supervisory programs) Perform the functions of coordinating and controlling the overall operation of the computer system.

telecommuting Working outside of a traditional office, remaining connected by the Internet, phone, et cetera. Usually implies a office in the employee's home, although a sales agent or insurance adjuster might also work from a vehicle and/or customer sites.

transaction (detail) file Contains current, temporary data. A transaction file is used to update a master file. For example, the day's charge sales would be accumulated on a transaction file that would be used to update the accounts receivable master file during an update run.

universal inbox A system to collect email and voice mail in one "place", accessible by either regular phone or computer.

utility program (utility routine) Standard program for performing routine functions, e.g., sorting and merging.

value-added network (VAN) A network service that provides additional services beyond mere connections to the Internet, particularly services enabling EDI.

video conference Real-time meeting over the Internet.

virus A program that replicates and attaches itself to other programs. The effects of a virus can be a merely annoying message or malicious activity, such as reformatting a hard drive or flooding an email system.

voice mail A system that records, directs, stores, and re-plays telephone messages.

wide area network (WAN) A computer network encompassing a large area (i.e., city-wide or globally) to transmit information electronically and share files among members (typically company-wide only). (Compare to local area network).

State Boards of Accountancy

Certified Public Accountants are licensed to practice by individual State Boards of Accountancy. Application forms and requirements to sit for the CPA Exam should be requested from your individual State Board. IT IS EXTREMELY IMPORTANT THAT YOU COMPLETE THE APPLICATION FORM CORRECTLY AND RETURN IT TO YOUR STATE BOARD BEFORE THE SPECIFIED DEADLINE. Errors and/or delays may result in the rejection of your application. Be extremely careful in filling out the application and be sure to enclose all required materials. In many states, applications must be received by the State Board at least **ninety** days before the examination date. Requirements as to education, experience, internship, and other matters vary. If you have not already done so, take a moment to call the appropriate State Board for specific and current requirements. Complete the application in a timely manner.

It may be possible to sit for the exam in another state as an out-of-state candidate. Candidates wishing to do so should contact the State Board of Accountancy in their home state.

Approximately one month before the exam, check to see that your application to sit for the exam has been processed. DON'T ASSUME THAT YOU ARE PROPERLY REGISTERED UNLESS YOU HAVE RECEIVED YOUR CANDIDATE ID NUMBER.

The AICPA publishes a booklet entitled <u>Information for CPA Candidates</u>, usually distributed by State Boards of Accountancy to candidates upon receipt of their applications. To request a complimentary copy, write your <u>State Board</u> or the <u>AICPA</u>, Examination Division, 1211 Avenue of the Americas, New York, NY 10036. Addresses of State Boards of Accountancy are provided in the **Practical Advice** section of this volume and on the site of the National Association of the State Boards of Accountancy (http://www.nasba.org).

CHAPTER 38—AUDITING EDP SYSTEMS

PROBLEM 38-1 MULTIPLE CHOICE QUESTIONS (80 to 100 minutes)

1. Computer systems are typically supported by a variety of utility software packages that are important to an auditor because they
a. May enable unauthorized changes to data files if **not** properly controlled.
b. May be significant components of a client's application programs.
c. Are very versatile programs that can be used on hardware of many manufacturers.
d. Are written specifically to enable auditors to extract and sort data. (Editors, 0281)

2. Which of the following is an example of how specific internal controls in a database environment may differ from controls in a nondatabase environment?
a. Controls should exist to ensure that users have access to and can update only the data elements that they have been authorized to access.
b. Controls over data sharing by diverse users within an entity should be the same for every user.
c. The employee who manages the computer hardware should also develop and debug the computer programs.
d. Controls can provide assurance that all processed transactions are authorized, but cannot verify that all authorized transactions are processed. (R/00, Aud., #8, 6933)

3. Which of the following represents an additional cost of transmitting business transactions by means of electronic data interchange (EDI) rather than in a traditional paper environment?
a. Redundant data checks are needed to verify that individual EDI transactions are **not** recorded twice.
b. Internal audit work is needed because the potential for random data entry errors is increased.
c. Translation software is needed to convert transactions from the entity's internal format to a standard EDI format.
d. More supervisory personnel are needed because the amount of data entry is greater in an EDI system. (5/98, Aud., #9, 6626)

4. Many entities use the Internet as a network to transmit electronic data interchange (EDI) transactions. An advantage of using the Internet for electronic commerce rather than a traditional value-added network (VAN) is that the Internet
a. Permits EDI transactions to be sent to trading partners as transactions occur.
b. Automatically batches EDI transactions to multiple trading partners.
c. Possesses superior characteristics regarding disaster recovery.
d. Converts EDI transactions to a standard format without translation software. (5/98, Aud., #10, 6627)

5. Which of the following is usually a benefit of using electronic funds transfer for international cash transactions?
a. Improvement of the audit trail for cash receipts and disbursements.
b. Creation of self-monitoring access controls.
c. Reduction of the frequency of data entry errors.
d. Off-site storage of source documents for cash transactions. (R/99, Aud., #8, 6824)

6. Which of the following statements is correct concerning the security of messages in an electronic data interchange (EDI) system?
a. When the confidentiality of data is the primary risk, message authentication is the preferred control rather than encryption.
b. Encryption performed by physically secure hardware devices is more secure than encryption performed by software.
c. Message authentication in EDI systems performs the same function as segregation of duties in other information systems.
d. Security at the transaction phase in EDI systems is **not** necessary because problems at that level will usually be identified by the service provider. (R/99, Aud., #12, 6828)

7. Which of the following would an auditor ordinarily consider the greatest risk regarding an entity's use of electronic data interchange (EDI)?
a. Authorization of EDI transactions
b. Duplication of EDI transmissions
c. Improper distribution of EDI transactions
d. Elimination of paper documents (6/99, Aud., #3, 6850)

8. Which of the following characteristics distinguishes electronic data interchange (EDI) from other forms of electronic commerce?
a. The cost of sending EDI transactions using a value-added network (VAN) is less than the cost of using the Internet.
b. Software maintenance contracts are unnecessary because translation software for EDI transactions need not be updated.
c. EDI commerce is ordinarily conducted without establishing legally binding contracts between trading partners.
d. EDI transactions are formatted using strict standards that have been agreed to worldwide (6/99, Aud., #4, 6851)

9. A retail entity uses electronic data interchange (EDI) in executing and recording most of its purchase transactions. The entity's auditor recognizes that the documentation of the transactions will be retained for only a short period of time. To compensate for this limitation, the auditor most likely would
a. Increase the sample of EDI transactions to be selected for cutoff tests
b. Perform tests several times during the year, rather than only at year end
c. Plan to make a 100% count of the entity's inventory at or near the year end
d. Decrease the assessed level of control risk for the existence or occurrence assertion (R/00, Aud., #9, 6934)

10. When evaluating internal control of an entity that processes sales transactions on the Internet, an auditor would be most concerned about the
a. Lack of sales invoice documents as an audit trail.
b. Potential for computer disruptions in recording sales.
c. Inability to establish an integrated test facility.
d. Frequency of archiving and data retention. (R/99, Aud., #10, 6826)

11. Which of the following statements is correct concerning internal control in an electronic data interchange (EDI) system?
a. Preventive controls generally are more important than detective controls in EDI systems.
b. Control objectives for EDI systems generally are different from the objectives for other information systems.
c. Internal controls in EDI systems rarely permit control risk to be assessed at below the maximum.
d. Internal controls related to the segregation of duties generally are the most important controls in EDI systems. (R/99, Aud., #11, 6827)

12. Which of the following most likely represents a significant deficiency in internal control?
a. The systems programmer designs systems for computerized applications and maintains output controls.
b. The systems analyst reviews applications of data processing and maintains systems documentation.
c. The control clerk establishes control over data received by the EDP department and reconciles control totals after processing.
d. The accounts payable clerk prepares data for computer processing and enters the data into the computer. (Editors, 2304)

13. Which of the following is an essential element of the audit trail in an electronic data interchange (EDI) system?
a. Disaster recovery plans that ensure proper back-up of files.
b. Encrypted hash totals that authenticate messages.
c. Activity logs that indicate failed transactions.
d. Hardware security modules that store sensitive data. (R/99, Aud., #13, 6829)

14. Which of the following activities most likely would detect whether payroll data were altered during processing?
a. Monitor authorized distribution of data control sheets
b. Use test data to verify the performance of edit routines
c. Examine source documents for approval by supervisors
d. Segregate duties between approval of hardware and software specifications (R/00, Aud., #14, 6939)

15. Which of the following computer documentations would an auditor most likely utilize in obtaining an understanding of internal control?
a. Systems flowcharts
b. Record counts
c. Program listings
d. Record layouts (5/90, Aud., #27, amended, 0278)

16. Which of the following is **not** a major reason for maintaining an audit trail for a computer system?
a. Deterrent to fraud
b. Monitoring purposes
c. Analytical procedures
d. Query answering (11/91, Aud., #24, 2292)

17. An auditor anticipates assessing control risk at a low level in a computerized environment. Under these circumstances, on which of the following procedures would the auditor initially focus?
a. Programmed control procedures
b. Application control procedures
c. Output control procedures
d. General control procedures
(5/92, Aud., #36, 2789)

18. Misstatements in a batch computer system caused by incorrect programs or data may **not** be detected immediately because
a. Errors in some transactions may cause rejection of other transactions in the batch.
b. The identification of errors in input data typically is **not** part of the program.
c. There are time delays in processing transactions in a batch system.
d. The processing of transactions in a batch system is **not** uniform. (11/94, Aud., #37, 5110)

19. Which of the following procedures would an entity most likely include in its computer disaster recovery plan?
a. Develop an auxiliary power supply to provide uninterrupted electricity.
b. Store duplicate copies of critical files in a location away from the computer center.
c. Maintain a listing of all entity passwords with the network manager.
d. Translate data for storage purposes with a cryptographic secret code. (6/99, Aud., #2, 6849)

20. An auditor would most likely be concerned with which of the following controls in a distributed data processing system?
a. Hardware controls
b. Systems documentation controls
c. Access controls
d. Disaster recovery controls
(5/91, Aud., #16, 0273)

21. To obtain evidence that on-line access controls are properly functioning, an auditor most likely would
a. Create checkpoints at periodic intervals after live data processing to test for unauthorized use of the system.
b. Examine the transaction log to discover whether any transactions were lost or entered twice due to a system malfunction.
c. Enter invalid identification numbers or passwords to ascertain whether the system rejects them.
d. Vouch a random sample of processed transactions to assure proper authorization.
(5/93, Aud., #41, 3937)

22. Which of the following is a general control that would most likely assist an entity whose systems analyst left the entity in the middle of a major project?
a. Grandfather-father-son record retention
b. Input and output validation routines
c. Systems documentation
d. Check digit verification (11/91, Aud., #32, 2300)

23. Which of the following controls is a processing control designed to ensure the reliability and accuracy of data processing?

	Limit test	*Validity check test*
a.	Yes	Yes
b.	No	No
c.	No	Yes
d.	Yes	No

(11/94, Aud., #38, 5111)

24. The completeness of EDP-generated sales figures can be tested by comparing the number of items listed on the daily sales report with the number of items billed on the actual invoices. This process uses
a. Check digits.
b. Control totals.
c. Process tracing data.
d. Validity tests.
(Editors, 0292)

Items 25 and 26 are based on the following:

Invoice #	Product	Quantity	Unit price
201	F10	150	$ 5.00
202	G15	200	$10.00
203	H20	250	$25.00
204	K35	300	$30.00

25. Which of the following numbers represents the record count?
a. 1
b. 4
c. 810
d. 900
(5/98, Aud., #3, 6620)

26. Which of the following most likely represents a hash total?
a. FGHK80
b. 4
c. 204
d. 810
(5/98, Aud., #4, 6621)

27. An EDP input control is designed to ensure that
a. Only authorized personnel have access to the computer area.
b. Machine processing is accurate.
c. Data received for processing are properly authorized and converted to machine readable form.
d. Electronic data processing has been performed as intended for the particular application.
(Editors, 0306)

28. A customer intended to order 100 units of product Z96014, but incorrectly ordered nonexistent product Z96015. Which of the following controls most likely would detect this error?
a. Check digit verification.
b. Record count.
c. Hash total.
d. Redundant data check. (5/98, Aud., #5, 6622)

29. Which of the following input controls is a numeric value computed to provide assurance that the original value has **not** been altered in construction or transmission?
a. Hash total.
b. Parity check.
c. Encryption.
d. Check digit. (5/98, Aud., #8, 6625)

30. One of the major problems in an EDP system is that incompatible functions may be performed by the same individual. One compensating control for this is the use of
a. Echo checks.
b. A self-checking digit system.
c. Computer-generated hash totals.
d. A computer log. (Editors, 0297)

31. Decision tables differ from program flowcharts in that decision tables emphasize
a. Ease of manageability for complex programs.
b. Logical relationships among conditions and actions.
c. Cost benefit factors justifying the program.
d. The sequence in which operations are performed. (5/92, Aud., #55, 2808)

32. When an auditor tests a computerized accounting system, which of the following is true of the test data approach?
a. Several transactions of each type must be tested.
b. Test data are processed by the client's computer programs under the auditor's control.
c. Test data must consist of all possible valid and invalid conditions.
d. The program tested is different from the program used throughout the year by the client.
(5/95, Aud., #72, 5690)

ITEM 33 is based on the following flowchart:

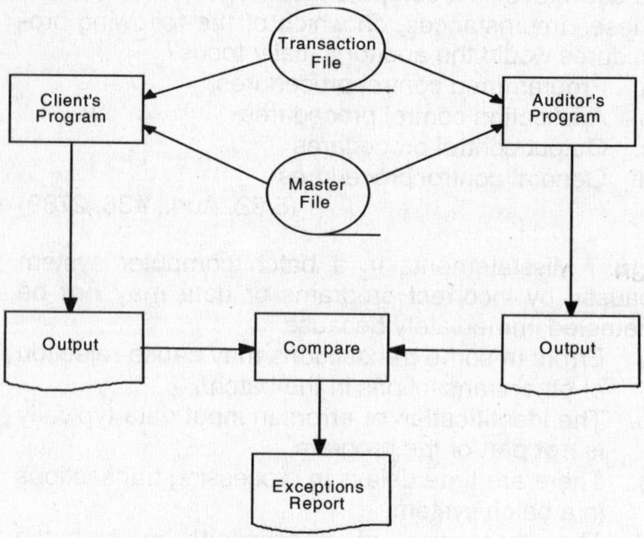

33. The preceding flowchart depicts
a. Program code checking.
b. Parallel simulation.
c. Controlled reprocessing.
d. Integrated test facility. (Editors, 0308)

34. An auditor most likely would introduce test data into a computerized payroll system to test internal controls related to the
a. Existence of unclaimed payroll checks held by supervisors.
b. Early cashing of payroll checks by employees.
c. Discovery of invalid employee I.D. numbers.
d. Proper approval of overtime by supervisors.
(5/94, Aud., #31, 4696)

35. An auditor most likely would test for the presence of unauthorized EDP program changes by running a
a. Program with test data.
b. Check digit verification program.
c. Source code comparison program.
d. Program that computes control totals.
(11/92, Aud., #37, 2971)

36. Processing data through the use of simulated files provides an auditor with information about the operating effectiveness of control policies and procedures. One of the techniques involved in this approach makes use of
a. Controlled reprocessing.
b. An integrated test facility.
c. Input validation.
d. Program code checking.
(11/92, Aud., #36, 2970)

Questions 38-42

37. Which of the following computer-assisted auditing techniques allows fictitious and real transactions to be processed together without client operating personnel being aware of the testing process?
a. Integrated test facility
b. Input controls matrix
c. Parallel simulation
d. Data entry monitor (11/94, Aud., #70, 5143)

38. A primary advantage of using generalized audit software packages to audit the financial statements of a client that uses an EDP system is that the auditor may
a. Access information stored on computer files while having a limited understanding of the client's hardware and software features.
b. Consider increasing the use of substantive tests of transactions in place of analytical procedures.
c. Substantiate the accuracy of data through self-checking digits and hash totals.
d. Reduce the level of required tests of controls to a relatively small amount.
(11/95, Aud., #52, 5999)

39. An auditor would **least** likely use computer software to
a. Construct parallel simulations.
b. Access client data files.
c. Prepare spreadsheets.
d. Assess EDP control risk. (5/93, Aud., #40, 3936)

40. Using microcomputers in auditing may affect the methods used to review the work of staff assistants because
a. Supervisory personnel may not have an understanding of the capabilities and limitations of microcomputers.
b. Working paper documentation may **not** contain readily observable details of calculations.
c. Documenting the supervisory review may require assistance of management services personnel.
d. The audit field work standards for supervision may differ. (Editors, 0196)

PROBLEM 38-2 ADDITIONAL MULTIPLE CHOICE QUESTIONS (42 to 53 minutes)

41. Able Co. uses an online sales order processing system to process its sales transactions. Able's sales data are electronically sorted and subjected to edit checks. A direct output of the edit checks most likely would be a
a. Report of all missing sales invoices.
b. File of all rejected sales transactions.
c. List of all voided shipping documents.
d. Printout of all user code numbers and passwords. (11/95, Aud., #3, amended, 5952)

42. Which of the following is usually a benefit of transmitting transactions in an electronic data interchange (EDI) environment?
a. A compressed business cycle with lower year-end receivables balances.
b. A reduced need to test computer controls related to sales and collections transactions.
c. An increased opportunity to apply statistical sampling techniques to account balances.
d. No need to rely on third-party service providers to ensure security. (R/99, Aud., #9, 6825)

43. Which of the following would most likely be a weakness in internal control of a client that utilizes microcomputers rather than a larger computer system?
a. Employee collusion possibilities are increased because microcomputers from one vendor can process the programs of a system from a different vendor.
b. The microcomputer operators may be able to remove hardware and software components and modify them at home.
c. Programming errors result in all similar transactions being processed incorrectly when those transactions are processed under the same conditions.
d. Certain transactions may be automatically initiated by the microcomputers and management's authorization of these transactions may be implicit in its acceptance of the system design. (Editors, 9418)

44. Which of the following characteristics distinguishes computer processing from manual processing?
a. Computer processing virtually eliminates the occurrence of computational error normally associated with manual processing.
b. The potential for systematic error is ordinarily greater in manual processing than in computerized processing.
c. Errors or fraud in computer processing will be detected soon after their occurrences.
d. Most computer systems are designed so that transaction trails useful for audit purposes do not exist. (Editors, 0289)

45. Which of the following are essential elements of the audit trail in an electronic data interchange (EDI) system?
a. Network and sender/recipient acknowledgments.
b. Message directories and header segments.
c. Contingency and disaster recovery plans.
d. Trading partner security and mailbox codes. (R/99, Aud., #14, 6830)

46. Which of the following is an engagement attribute for an audit of an entity that processes most of its financial data in electronic form without any paper documentation?
a. Discrete phases of planning, interim, and year-end fieldwork.
b. Increased effort to search for evidence of management fraud.
c. Performance of audit tests on a continuous basis.
d. Increased emphasis on the completeness assertion. (R/99, Aud., #22, 6838)

47. Which of the following strategies would a CPA most likely consider in auditing an entity that processes most of its financial data only in electronic form, such as a paperless system?
a. Continuous monitoring and analysis of transaction processing with an embedded audit module.
b. Increased reliance on internal control activities that emphasize the segregation of duties.
c. Verification of encrypted digital certificates used to monitor the authorization of transactions.
d. Extensive testing of firewall boundaries that restrict the recording of outside network traffic. (R/99, Aud., #23, 6839)

48. Which of the following statements most likely represents a disadvantage for an entity that keeps microcomputer-prepared data files rather than manually prepared files?
a. Attention is focused on the accuracy of the programming process rather than errors in individual transactions.
b. It is usually easier for unauthorized persons to access and alter the files.
c. Random error associated with processing similar transactions in different ways is usually greater.
d. It is usually more difficult to compare recorded accountability with physical count of assets. (5/94, Aud., #16, 4681)

49. Which of the following control procedures most likely could prevent EDP personnel from modifying programs to bypass programmed controls?
a. Periodic management review of computer utilization reports and systems documentation.
b. Segregation of duties within EDP for computer programming and computer operations.
c. Participation of user department personnel in designing and approving new systems.
d. Physical security of EDP facilities in limiting access to EDP equipment. (11/95, Aud., #14, 5961)

50. When an accounting application is processed by computer, an auditor **cannot** verify the reliable operation of programmed control procedures by
a. Constructing a processing system for accounting applications and processing actual data from throughout the period through both the client's program and the auditor's program.
b. Manually comparing detail transaction files used by an edit program to the program's generated error listings to determine that errors were properly identified by the edit program.
c. Manually reperforming, as of a point in time, the processing of input data and comparing the simulated results to the actual results.
d. Periodically submitting auditor-prepared test data to the same computer process and evaluating the results. (Editors, 0279)

51. Matthews Corp. has changed from a system of recording time worked on clock cards to a computerized payroll system in which employees record time in and out with magnetic cards. The EDP system automatically updates all payroll records. Because of this change
a. A generalized computer audit program must be used.
b. Part of the audit trail is altered.
c. Transactions must be processed in batches.
d. The potential for payroll-related fraud is diminished. (Editors, 0296)

52. Which of the following is an example of a validity check?
a. The computer ensures that a numerical amount in a record does **not** exceed some predetermined amount.
b. As the computer corrects errors and data are successfully resubmitted to the system, the causes of the errors are printed out.
c. The computer flags any transmission for which the control field value did **not** match that of an existing file record.
d. After data for a transaction are entered, the computer sends certain data back to the terminal for comparison with data originally sent.
(11/95, Aud., #10, 5957)

53. If a control total were computed on each of the following data items, which would best be identified as a hash total for a payroll EDP application?
a. Total debits and total credits
b. Net pay
c. Department numbers
d. Hours worked (11/92, Aud., #20, 2954)

54. An auditor who is testing EDP controls in a payroll system would most likely use test data that contain conditions such as
a. Deductions **not** authorized by employees.
b. Overtime **not** approved by supervisors.
c. Payroll checks with unauthorized signatures.
d. Time tickets with invalid job numbers.
(Editors, 0286)

55. An auditor using audit software probably would be **least** interested in which of the following fields in a computerized perpetual inventory file?
a. Economic order quantity
b. Warehouse location
c. Date of last purchase
d. Quantity sold (5/91, Aud., #15, 0272)

56. In a computerized payroll system environment, an auditor would be **least** likely to use test data to test controls related to
a. Missing employee numbers.
b. Proper approval of overtime by supervisors.
c. Time tickets with invalid job numbers.
d. Agreement of hours per clock cards with hours on time tickets. (5/91, Aud., #31, 0049)

57. The two requirements crucial to achieving audit efficiency and effectiveness with a microcomputer are selecting
a. The appropriate audit tasks for microcomputer applications and the appropriate software to perform the selected audit tasks.
b. The appropriate software to perform the selected audit tasks and client data that can be accessed by the auditor's microcomputer.
c. Audit procedures that are generally applicable to several clients in a specific industry and the appropriate audit tasks for microcomputer applications.
d. Client data that can be accessed by the auditor's microcomputer and audit procedures that are generally applicable to several clients in a specific industry. (Editors, 9419)

58. A client is concerned that a power outage or disaster could impair the computer hardware's ability to function as designed. The client desires off-site backup hardware facilities that are fully configured and ready to operate within several hours. The client most likely should consider a
a. Cold site.
b. Cool site.
c. Warm site.
d. Hot site. (5/98, Aud., #6, 6623)

59. Which of the following is considered a component of a local area network?
a. Program flowchart.
b. Loop verification.
c. Transmission media.
d. Input routine. (5/98, Aud., #7, 6624)

60. Which of the following is a term for an attest engagement in which a CPA assesses a client's commercial Internet site for predefined criteria that are designed to measure transaction integrity, information protection, and disclosure of business practices?
a. ElectroNet
b. EDIFACT
c. TechSafe
d. WebTrust (R/99, Aud., #2. 6818)

61. Which of the following is a network node that is used to improve network traffic and to set up as a boundary that prevents traffic from one segment to cross over to another?
a. Router
b. Gateway
c. Firewall
d. Heuristic (R/00, Aud., #7, 6932)

OTHER OBJECTIVE FORMAT QUESTIONS

FLOWCHART 38-3

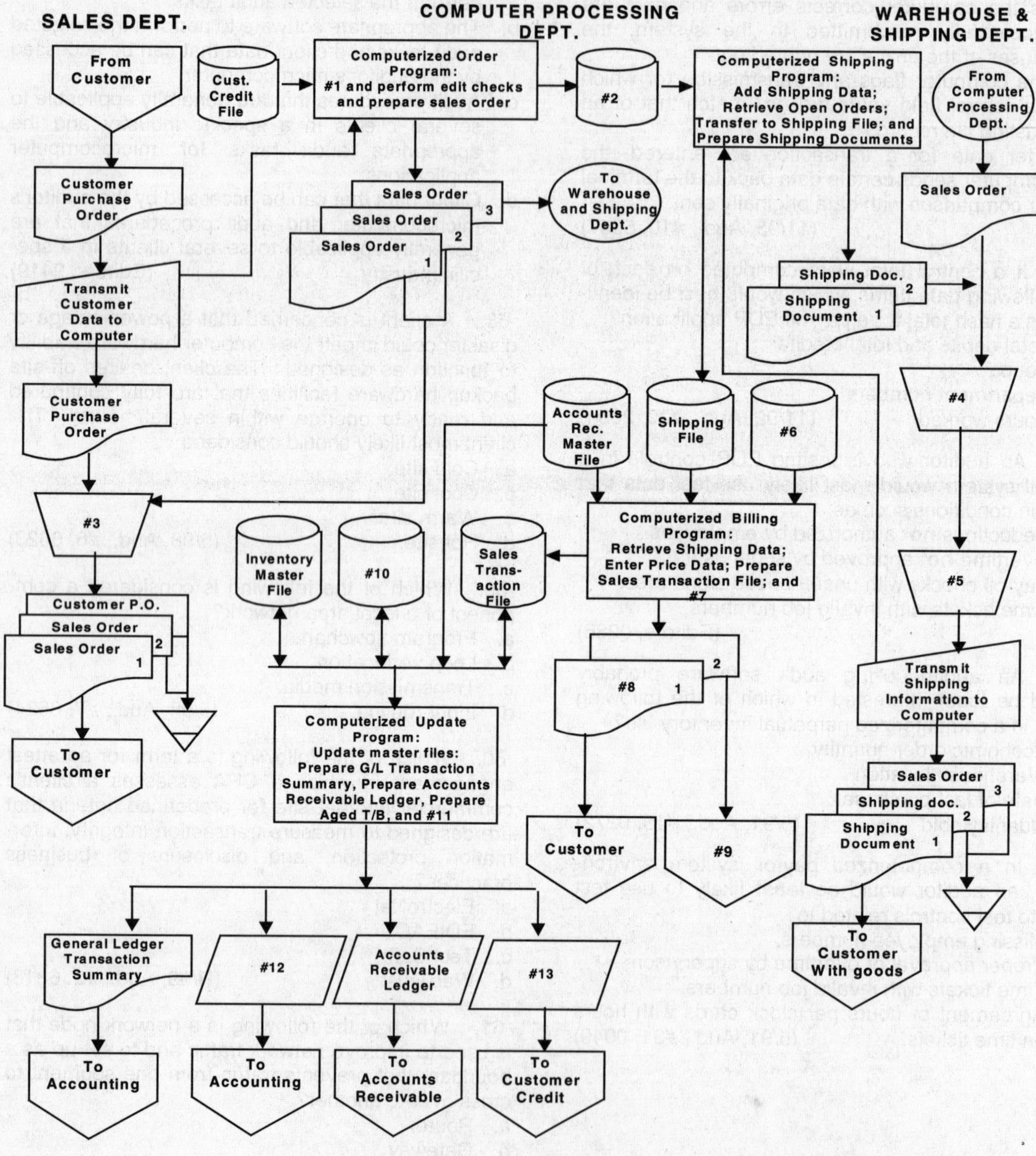

PROBLEM 38-3 (15 to 25 minutes)

Flowchart 38-3 depicts part of a client's revenue cycle. Some of the flowchart symbols are labeled to indicate control procedures and records. **For each symbol 1 through 13**, select one response from the answer lists below. Each response in the lists may be selected once or **not** at all.

Answer Lists

Operations and control procedures

A. Enter shipping data
B. Verify agreement of sales order and shipping document
C. Write off accounts receivable
D. To warehouse and shipping department
E. Authorize account receivable write-off
F. Prepare aged trial balance
G. To sales department
H. Release goods for shipment
I. To accounts receivable department
J. Enter price data
K. Determine that customer exists
L. Match customer purchase order with sales order
M. Perform customer credit check
N. Prepare sales journal
O. Prepare sales invoice

Documents, journals, ledgers, and files

P. Shipping document
Q. General ledger master file
R. General journal
S. Master price file
T. Sales journal
U. Sales invoice
V. Cash receipts journal
W. Uncollectible accounts file
X. Shipping file
Y. Aged trial balance
Z. Open order file

(11/93, Aud., #2)

PROBLEM 38-4 (3 to 5 minutes)
Based on Flowchart 38-4 of a client's revenue cycle, what do the following most likely represent?

1. Symbol A
2. Symbol B

Answer List

A. Accounts receivable master file.
B. Cash disbursements transaction file.
C. Customer checks.
D. Customer orders.
E. Receiving reports.
F. Receiving report file.
G. Remittance advice file.
H. Sales invoices.

(11/95, Aud., #7 and #8, amended, 9434)

FLOWCHART 38-4

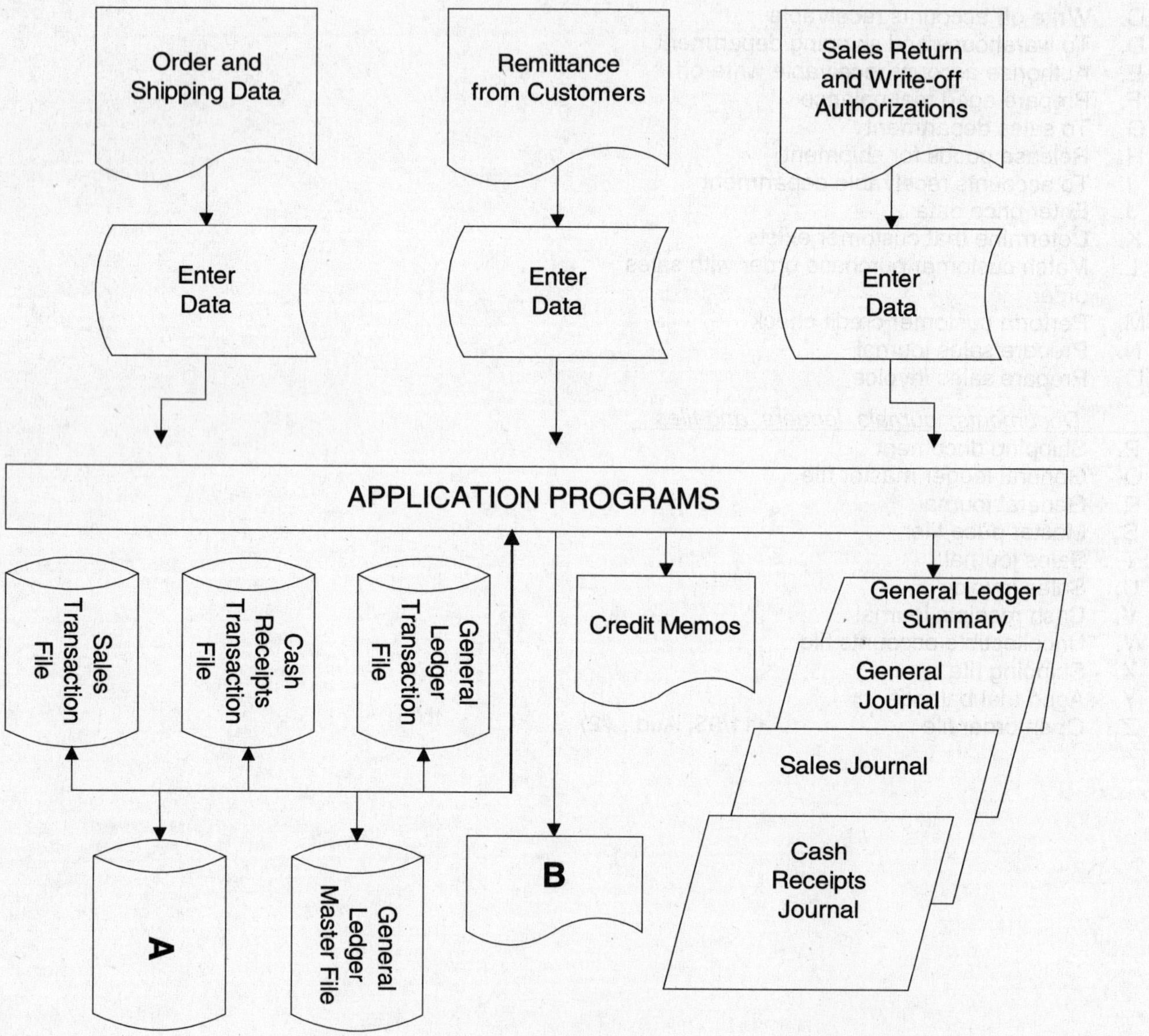

ESSAY QUESTIONS

ESSAY 38-5 (15 to 25 minutes)

Microcomputer software has been developed to improve the efficiency and effectiveness of the audit. Electronic spreadsheets and other software packages are available to aid in the performance of audit procedures otherwise performed manually.

REQUIRED:

Describe the potential benefits to an auditor of using microcomputer software in an audit as compared to performing an audit without the use of a computer.

(11/87, Aud., #4)

ESSAY 38-6 (15 to 25 minutes)

Brown, CPA, is auditing the financial statements of Big Z Wholesaling, Inc., a continuing audit client, for the year ended January 31, 20X1. Brown issued an unqualified opinion on the prior year's financial statements. On January 5, 20X1, Brown observed the tagging and counting of Big Z's physical inventory and made appropriate test counts. All inventory is purchased for resale and located in a single warehouse. These test counts have been recorded on a computer file. As in prior years, Big Z gave Brown two computer files. One file represents the perpetual inventory (FIFO) records for the year ended January 31, 20X1. The other file represents the January 5 physical inventory count. Brown has appropriate computerized audit software.

The perpetual inventory file contains the following information in item number sequence:

(1) Beginning balances at February 1, 20X0; item number, item description, total quantity, and prices.

(2) For each item purchased during the year: date received, receiving report number, vendor, item number, item description, quantity, and total dollar amount.

(3) For each item sold during the year: date shipped, invoice number, item number, item description, quantity shipped, and dollar amount of the cost removed from inventory.

(4) For each item adjusted for physical inventory count differences: date, item number, item descriptions, quantity, and dollar amount.

The physical inventory file contains the following information in item number sequence: tag number, item number, item description, and count quantity.

REQUIRED:

Describe the substantive auditing procedures Brown may consider performing with computerized audit software using Big Z's two computer files and Brown's computer file of test counts. The substantive auditing procedures described may indicate the reports to be printed out for Brown's follow-up by subsequent application of manual procedures. Do **not** describe subsequent manual auditing procedures. Group the procedures by those using (1) the perpetual inventory file and (2) the physical inventory and test count files.

(5/92, Aud., #4, amended, 6297)

SOLUTION 38-1 MULTIPLE CHOICE ANSWERS

EDP-BASED SYSTEMS

1. (a) Utility programs are used to perform tasks such as copying, sorting, merging, and printing. This type of software is usually easily accessible and can lead to unauthorized changes if not properly controlled. Answers (b) and (c) do not have any special importance to the auditor. Utility software is not written specifically for auditors.

2. (a) Controls in a database environment can be very specific as to which elements of a record can be accessed or changed, resulting in a more detailed set of authorizations. [Note: The examiners' say to select the best answer.] Controls over data sharing should be appropriate for each user, usually resulting in diverse controls. Preferably, hardware management and software development are segregated. The relationship between authorization and processing usually is the same within a database and a non-database environment.

EDI

3. (c) EDI involves electronic communication among two or more entities. These entities need a common standard transmission format. Individual EDI transactions are no more likely to be recorded twice than transactions performed in a paper environment. One primary advantage of EDI is the reduction of data entry and a corresponding reduction of associated errors. Random data entry errors are generally reduced in an EDI system, because information is entered once (allowing one opportunity

for errors), instead of entered, printed, and reentered (allowing multiple opportunities for errors).

4. (a) The Internet is a no-frills option, but it does offer immediacy. VANs can offer services to customers such as batching EDI transactions, providing disaster recovery services, and converting EDI transactions to and from a standard format.

5. (c) With EDI, information is entered into a system once and transmitted to other parities. These other parties to not have to re-enter the information into their systems, eliminating an opportunity for errors to occur. Using EDI, audit trails typically are less clear, if anything. Creation of self-monitoring access controls and off-site storage of source documents for cash transactions could occur with or without EDI.

6. (b) Physically secure hardware devices are less likely to be compromised than software. Message authentication provides assurance about messages' sources. Encryption provides assurance about privacy. Message authentication performs similarly to control duties in non-EDP systems, but not the segregation of duties aspect. Service providers usually do **not** provide security at the transaction level.

7. (c) Improper transactions, regardless of the media, are usually the greatest risk. Appropriate authorization of EDI transactions doesn't present a risk. Duplication of EDI transactions would likely be found by one of the involved parties upon reconciliation. Elimination of paper documents is a goal of EDI.

8. (d) EDI is possible only through the use of strict protocols and legally binding contracts between trading partners. EDI software must be updated in synchronization with protocol changes. VANs and EDI provide more capabilities than the Internet. Typically, a greater amount of service costs more.

COMPUTER PROCESSING EFFECTS

9. (b) SAS 80 notes that the auditor should consider the time when information is available in determining the timing of tests. Increasing the extent of cut-off tests would provide additional information about only year-end transactions. The nature of the business may make a 100% count of inventory at year end impractical or insufficient. Increasing the assessed level of control risk for the existence / occurrence assertion because records are unavailable is unduly harsh, but decreasing it is unjustified.

10. (b) Computer disruptions could destroy the only record of an online transaction. By their nature, sales transactions processed on the Internet don't involve sales invoice documents. Integrated test facilities, archiving, and data retention are issues that arise whether sales are on the Internet or entered into a computer system by the entity.

11. (a) Preventive controls are generally more important than detective controls in EDI systems because of the speed with which goods and services are delivered. Objectives remain the same as for other information systems. Internal controls in EDI systems must be strong to minimize losses. Segregation of duties is not as important as protection of assets in an EDI system.

12. (a) A weakness in internal control exists where an individual is in a position to both perpetrate and conceal an error or fraud. Hence, a systems programmer should not be given any control over the review or distribution of the output of the EDP system.

13. (c) Logs with failed transactions are examined to determine whether the corrected transactions were eventually executed and to detect attempts of unauthorized system use. Proper file backup is a recovery issue. Message authentication and hardware security modules are security issues.

14. (b) With test data, the auditor can readily compare actual results to anticipated results. Monitoring distribution wouldn't detect data alteration. Source documents could be correctly approved and data could be later altered in processing without impact on the source documents. Segregation of duties discourages fraud, but not unintentional mistakes. Further, approval of hardware and software specifications are not necessarily the most critical functions to segregate in the IT area.

15. (a) An auditor is likely to use systems flowcharts in obtaining an understanding of internal control. Systems flowcharts show the flow of data through the system and the interrelationships between the processing steps and computer runs. A record count is an input control technique. Program listings are the source statements or language of the client's programs. Record layouts are the input and output formats.

16. (c) Analytical procedures involve the analysis of the plausible relationship among both financial and nonfinancial data. A lack of an accounting audit trail for a computer system would not preclude the auditor from performing analytical

procedures. The purpose of an audit trail would be to monitor the system, answer queries, and deter fraud.

17. (d) When an auditor anticipates assessing control risk at a low level in a computerized environment, generally, the auditor would initially focus on general control procedures, which are those controls that relate to all or many computerized accounting activities and often include control over the development, modification, and maintenance of computer programs and control over the use of and changes to data maintained on computer files.

18. (c) There are time delays when data is processed in batches, so errors may not be detected immediately. The time delays in processing cause a delay in error detection. The identification of errors in input data would be identified through various means such as the use of batch totals and would generally be made part of the program. The processing of transactions in a batch system is uniform; for example, all sales invoices would be part of a group of transactions entered together in a batch system.

General Controls

19. (b) Having duplicate off-site copies of critical files is a relatively inexpensive and highly effective disaster recovery measure. An auxiliary power supply is a secondary concern in a contingency plan. Passwords and storing data in code are more closely related to security than disaster recovery.

20. (c) A distributed data processing system is one in which many different users have access to the main computer through various computer locations. Thus, access controls, which restrict access to the main computer, are necessary to maintain a strong internal control structure, since those with access to the computer are in a position to perform incompatible functions. Hardware controls, systems documentation controls, and disaster recovery controls would not be as important in assessing control risk and would not likely present unusual problems in a distributed system.

21. (c) Password controls, used in restricting access to computers, are designed to preclude access capabilities of those employees whose regular functions are incompatible with computer use. To obtain evidence that user identification and password controls are functioning as designed, an auditor would most likely examine a sample of invalid passwords or numbers to determine whether the computer is recognizing the invalid passwords and rejecting access. Answer (a) checks the level of authorization an employee has once within the system rather than access to the online system. Answer (b) is a procedure for determining the completeness of transaction processing. Answer (d) does not address whether the online access is being limited or circumvented.

22. (c) When an entity's systems analyst leaves the entity in the middle of a major project, the greatest assistance in continuing the project could be obtained from systems documentation that adequately describes the systems operations and procedures up to that point in time. Given good documentation, a new systems analyst could immediately begin to understand the systems operations.

Application Controls

23. (a) Computers can be programmed to perform a wide range of edit tasks on records as they are being inputted into the system. If a particular record does not meet the test, it would not be processed. Edit tests include limit tests, validity check tests, check digit tests, etc.

24. (b) The use of control totals is an example of a processing control which is designed to provide reasonable assurances that EDP has been performed as intended for the particular application, i.e., that all transactions are processed as authorized, that no authorized transactions were omitted, and that no unauthorized transactions were added. A *check digit* is a number that is added at the end of a numerical entry to check its accuracy. A *validity test*, is designed to ensure that only data meeting specific criteria are allowed. Answer (c) apparently refers to "tagging" of data, a technique used by auditors to follow a transaction through the processing cycle.

25. (b) A record count is a count of the number of records in a batch or file or similar group.

26. (d) A hash total is a numeric total with meaning only as a control. Because of the alpha characters in the product codes, a hash total cannot be derived from product codes without a conversion of letters into numeric amounts. Totals of quantities have meaning beyond a control.

27. (c) Input controls are designed to provide reasonable assurance that data received by EDP have been properly authorized, converted into machine sensible form and identified and that data have not been lost, added, duplicated, or otherwise improperly changed. Answer (a) describes an access control. Answer (b) describes an output control. Answer (d) describes a processing control.

28. (a) A check digit is a digit that is appended to a piece of numeric data following a pre-specified routine. A record count is a count of the number of

records in a batch or file or similar group. A hash total is a numeric total with meaning only as a control. A redundant data check would check one piece of data against another, not the elements of a product code label against each other.

29. (d) A check digit is a digit that is appended to a piece of numeric data following a pre-specified routine. A hash total is a numeric total with meaning only as a control. A parity check is an extra bit attached to the end of a string of bits to detect errors resulting from electronic interference when transmitting the string. Encryption is the conversion of a message into a coded message.

DOCUMENTATION

30. (d) A computer log provides evidence as to which employees used the computer system and the operations performed by them. As a result, the computer log will protect against unauthorized use of the EDP system, and it will provide an audit trail with respect to incompatible operations performed by the same individual. Incompatible functions are the concern of general controls, i.e., controls that relate to all EDP activities. A self-checking digit system and computer-generated hash totals are input controls, i.e., they relate to application controls. An echo check is a hardware control aimed at determining whether the computer is operating properly. It has no effect on the control over incompatible functions.

31. (b) A systems flowchart shows the flow of data through the system and the interrelationships between the processing steps and computer runs. A decision table describes a portion of the logic used in the program.

CAATs

32. (b) In the test data approach to testing a computerized accounting system, test data are processed by the client's computer programs under the auditor's control. The auditor will determine how many transactions and what types of transactions to test which may or may not include several transactions of each type. The auditor need not include test data for all possible valid and invalid conditions. The object is to test the client's program that is used throughout the year and the auditor must take steps to make sure that the program being tested is the one that is actually used in routine processing; thus, a different program would not be tested.

33. (b) In parallel simulation, the auditor compares the results of the client's processing with results obtained by using the client's input and files and the auditor's own program. In program code checking, the auditor reviews the client's program documentation, including a narrative description and the source code. An integrated test facility includes processing of dummy records with the client's records using the client's program. In controlled reprocessing, the auditor maintains control over the reprocessing of previously processed results using a version of the program the auditor has tested and compares the computer output of the original processing and reprocessing.

34. (c) An auditor testing computer controls in a payroll system would most likely use test data containing invalid employee I.D. numbers. The computer should be programmed to compare employee I.D. numbers with a list of valid, authorized employee numbers. Answer (d) relates to preparation of data before it enters the computer system. Answers (a) and (b) relate to controls after data processing has taken place.

35. (c) A source code comparison program could be used to compare the original code written for a specific program to the current code in use for that program. Thus, it would make note of any differences in the program from the time it was originally written. Test data would generally be used to test the output of the program but would provide no evidence as to whether the program code had been changed. A check digit program involves the use of a digit that is added to the end of a piece of numeric data to permit the data to be checked for accuracy during input, processing, or output. Control totals are totals computed at different times in the computer process and are used as input, processing, and output controls. They would not provide evidence as to whether any changes were made to the original program code.

36. (b) Processing data through the use of simulated files makes use of an integrated test facility. Using this method, the auditor creates a fictitious entity within the client's actual data files. He or she then processes fictitious data for the entity as part of the client's regular data processing. Controlled reprocessing involves the processing of the client's actual data through the auditor's controlled copy of the client's program. Input validation is concerned only that the inputted data is accurate. Program code checking involves analysis of the client's actual program.

37. (a) An integrated test facility (ITF) processes fictitious data with real data in order to test computer controls; client personnel are unaware of the testing. An input control matrix documents controls and their presence. Parallel simulation processes client input data on an auditor-controlled program to test controls; test data is not utilized. The term "data entry monitor" is not commonly used.

GENERALIZED AUDIT SOFTWARE

38. (a) In the AICPA Audit Guide entitled "Computer Assisted Audit Techniques," one of the reasons for using generalized audit software (GAS) is that it enables the auditor to gain access and test information stored in the client's files without having to acquire a complete understanding of the client's EDP system. Although the use of GAS enables the auditor to deal more effectively with large quantities of data and produces economies in the audit while increasing the quality of the audit, it cannot replace analytical procedures. Self-checking digits and hash totals are controls in the client system. Reducing the level of required tests of controls to a relatively small amount is the result of assessing control risk and applying preliminary tests of controls, not a result of using a GAS package.

39. (d) After obtaining an understanding of the client's EDP controls, the auditor must assess control risk for the EDP portion of the client's internal control. Assessing control risk is the process of evaluating the effectiveness of an entity's internal control policies and procedures in preventing or detecting material misstatements in the financial statements. Procedures to judge the effectiveness of internal control design would include inquiries, observations, and inspections. One would not need computer software to accomplish this task. Gaining access to client data files, preparing spreadsheets, and constructing parallel simulations would all make use of computer software.

40. (b) Working paper documentation may not contain readily observable details of calculations because these calculations would be performed by the computer. If supervisory personnel do not have an understanding of the capabilities and limitations of microcomputers, the auditor should seek the assistance of a professional possessing such skills, who may be either on the auditor's staff or an outside professional. The auditor's responsibilities with respect to using such a professional are equivalent to those for other assistants. The audit field work standards for supervision do not differ when microcomputers are used in an audit.

SOLUTION 38-2 ADDITIONAL MULTIPLE CHOICE ANSWERS

EDI

41. (b) The most likely output from an online sales order processing system is a file of all rejected sales transactions. For answer (a), sales invoices would be generated by the system. Answers (c) and (d) are not relevant outputs from the online sales order processing system, but would be outputs of other system applications.

42. (a) EDI generally results in a compressed cycle of orders, purchases, deliveries, and payments. EDI generally increases the need to test computer controls and the need for security. EDI has no impact on the application of sampling techniques for account balances.

COMPUTER PROCESSING EFFECTS

43. (b) Both large computer systems and microcomputers are vulnerable to employee collusion and programming errors. Microcomputer hardware and software could more readily be removed from a place of business than large computer systems.

44. (a) An advantage of computer processing is that it virtually eliminates computational errors. Errors or fraud are not detected more quickly when computer processing is used. The potential for systematic errors is greater in computer processing than in manual processing. Transaction trails useful for audit purposes are created but the data may be available for only a short period of time.

45. (a) Acknowledgements are a logical opposite of failed transaction logs—they denote complete activity. Message directories and header segments are part of message administration. Contingency and recovery plans are recovery issues. Trading partner security and mailbox codes are security issues.

46. (c) When a client processes financial data in electronic form without paper documentation, the auditor may audit on a more continuous basis than a traditional system, as a convenience, and may be required to audit on a more continuous basis to obtain sufficient, competent evidence as documentation for some transactions may only be available for a limited time. This is the opposite of

discrete phases of planning, interim, and year-end fieldwork. The level of effort to search for management fraud and emphasis on the completeness assertion would likely not be significantly affected.

47. (a) When a client processes financial data in electronic form without paper documentation, the auditor may audit on a more continuous basis than a traditional system, as a convenience, and may be required to audit on a more continuous basis to obtain sufficient, competent evidence as documentation for some transactions may only be available for a limited time. An embedded audit module can facilitate this "continuous" auditing. If anything, an auditor may rely less on internal control activities that emphasize the segregation of duties. Digital certificate verification and testing of firewall boundaries are more concerned with security than internal control.

48. (b) Many internal control procedures once performed by separate individuals in manual systems may be concentrated in systems that use computer processing. Therefore, an individual who has access to the computer may be in a position to perform incompatible functions. Answers (a) and (c) are false statements. Detailed ledger accounts may be maintained as easily with microcomputer data files as with manually prepared files.

49. (b) A control procedure for preventing employees from modifying programs to bypass programmed controls is to segregate the functions of programming and computer operations. Answers (a), (c), and (d) are all appropriate EDP controls but in themselves would not prevent employees from modifying programs.

50. (c) The auditor would not be able to verify the reliable operation of programmed control procedures by the reperformance of the processing of the *client's* input data through the *client's* computer program as it would produce the same output as that created by the client. The auditor would be able to verify the reliable operation of control procedures when he or she is submitting auditor-prepared test data to the client's computer process, submitting actual data to the auditor's computer program, or utilizing an edit program, as these would allow the auditor to make comparisons between the client's expected output, using the client's data and computer program, and the auditor's expected results using auditor-prepared data, the auditor's computer program, and the auditor's edit program.

51. (b) When time clock cards are used, they constitute a form of physical evidence that can be examined in determining the proper amount of wage expense. By changing to an EDP system, part of the audit trail is altered—although not necessarily destroyed. The EDP system can be audited in numerous ways that don't require the use of a generalized audit program. The potential for payroll fraud may or may not change depending on the internal controls incorporated into the new payroll system. The system automatically updates the payroll records whenever anyone punches in or out. Batch processing is eliminated in this system.

Application Controls

52. (c) A validity check ensures that only authorized data codes will be entered into and accepted by the system. Answer (a) is an example of a limit (reasonableness) check. Answer (b) is an example of an error report being generated. There is no comparison performed as in answer (d).

53. (c) Control totals may be used to detect errors in processing when information is batched before entry. One type of control total is a *hash total* which is a total of field amounts for all the records in a batch that are computed for control purposes only. For example, the total of the department numbers would have no intrinsic value. Conversely, the total of hours worked, debits and credits, and net pay are normally computed in the payroll process and have intrinsic meaning in the engagement.

CAATs

54. (d) An auditor testing EDP controls in a payroll system would most likely use test data containing time tickets with invalid job numbers. The computer should be programmed to compare job numbers on the time tickets with a list of valid, authorized job numbers. Answers (a) and (b) relate to preparation of data before it enters the EDP system. Answer (c) relates to controls after data processing has taken place.

Generalized Audit Software

55. (a) Audit software for a perpetual inventory file would include fields such as warehouse location, date of last purchase, and quantity sold since these fields would have a bearing on the audit of the inventory balance as recorded in the computerized perpetual inventory file. On the other hand, the economic order quantity would be less likely to provide information as to the actual quantity of inventory to be reported in the financial statements, since it is simply a useful guideline which can be used in ordering inventory. The client's *actual* orders of inventory would be much more useful.

56. (b) Proper approval of overtime would most likely be made by inspection of the related documents and reports to assess whether the authorization policy was applied. The computerized system would be unable to make such a judgment. The computerized payroll system could be utilized to test controls related to missing employee numbers, time tickets with invalid job numbers, and agreement of hours per clock cards with hours on time tickets.

57. (a) Microcomputers may be used to prepare trial balances, to perform analytical procedures, for automated working papers, word processing, and graphics, among other uses. With the appropriate software, applied to the appropriate audit tasks, microcomputers can improve audit efficiency and effectiveness.

DEFINITIONS

58. (d) A cold site is space where furnishings and power is available in the event of a disaster at a primary location, but a computer system is not installed. A hot site is one that is ready for use with minimal preparation—for example, with hardware and software installed, links established, and backups of information available. The terms *warm site* and *cool site* are not generally used.

59. (c) A local area network is a network of computers within a small area to transmit information among network members. By its nature, it requires a means of transmission. Program flowcharts relate to software. An input routine generally is a program that relates to the acceptance of information (data entry). Loop verification is not a commonly used term.

60. (d) The CPA WebTrust symbol on a web site indicates that the organization meets AICPA business practice disclosures, transaction integrity, and information protection criteria. A specially trained and licensed CPA reviews compliance with these criteria every 90 days. EDIFACT is an international EDI format. (ANSI X12 is a domestic EDI format.) ElectroNet and TechSafe are not widely used terms.

61. (c) A firewall is designed to prevent unauthorized access to data by separating one segment from another. Routers (switches that transfer incoming messages to outgoing links via the most efficient route possible, for example, over the Internet) and gateways (software or hardware that link two computer networks) allow traffic. In computing, heuristic signifies *able to change*; it is used to describe a computer program that can modify itself in response to the user, for example, a spell check program.

PERFORMANCE BY SUBTOPICS

Each category below parallels a subtopic covered in Chapter 38. Record the number and percentage of questions you correctly answered in each subtopic area.

EDP-based Systems

Question #	Correct √
1	
2	
# Questions	2
# Correct	
% Correct	

EDI

Question #	Correct √
3	
4	
5	
6	
7	
8	
# Questions	6
# Correct	
% Correct	

Computer Processing Effects

Question #	Correct √
9	
10	
11	
12	
13	
14	
15	
16	
17	
18	
# Questions	10
# Correct	
% Correct	

General Controls

Question #	Correct √
19	
20	
21	
22	
# Questions	4
# Correct	
% Correct	

Application Controls

Question #	Correct √
23	
24	
25	
26	
27	
28	
29	
# Questions	7
# Correct	
% Correct	

Documentation

Question #	Correct √
30	
31	
# Questions	2
# Correct	
% Correct	

CAATs

Question #	Correct √
32	
33	
34	
35	
36	
37	
# Questions	6
# Correct	
% Correct	

Generalized Audit Software

Question #	Correct √
38	
39	
40	
# Questions	3
# Correct	
% Correct	

OTHER OBJECTIVE FORMAT QUESTION SOLUTIONS

SOLUTION 38-3 FLOWCHARTS

1. M Before preparing a sales order, the computer processing department should perform a credit check to determine that the sale will be made to a creditworthy customer. This information may be obtained from the customer credit file or from outside sources.

2. Z Once the sales order has been prepared, it will be recorded and placed in the open order file.

3. L This manual operation represents the process of matching customer purchase orders with sales orders for agreement.

4. B This manual operation represents matching the shipping document with the sales order for agreement.

5. H Once the shipping document and sales order have been matched, the goods will be released for shipment.

6. S In order to prepare the customer bill, the computerized billing program will retrieve the shipping data from the shipping file and enter the price data from the master price file.

7. O Once the shipping data and price data have been retrieved and the sale to the customer generated, the sales invoice will be prepared.

8. U This document represents the duplicate copy sales invoice generated by the computerized billing program.

9. I One copy of the sales invoice will be sent to the customer, and one will be sent to the accounts receivable department as support for the entry to the accounts receivable ledger—to be held until remittance is made by the customer.

10. Q The computer processing department will (daily, weekly, or monthly) update the master files, such as the accounts receivable ledger, the inventory master file, the sales transaction file, and the general ledger master file.

11. N The computer processing department will prepare, based upon the update program, an accounts receivable ledger, an aged trial balance, a general ledger transaction summary, and a sales journal.

12. T This output function represents the sales journal which was generated by the computerized update program for either the day, week, or month, depending upon the frequency of report generation established by management.

13. Y This output report represents the aged trial balance generated by the computerized update program, which combined information from the general ledger master file, the sales transaction file, and the inventory master file.

SOLUTION 38-4 FLOWCHARTS

1. A This symbol represents a file. In the revenue cycle application process, the most likely output among the choices given is an accounts receivable master file, especially since there is a cash receipts transaction file. A remittance file (G) is not typically a separately constructed file. Answers F and B are not part of the revenue cycle.

2. H This symbol represents some sort of printed output. Sales invoices are the most likely output from the system at this point. The customer orders would most likely be at the beginning of the revenue cycle. Receiving reports are not part of the revenue cycle. Customer checks are not created by the system but are received from the customer.

ESSAY SOLUTIONS

SOLUTION 38-5 ADVANTAGES OF USING CAATs

The potential benefits to an auditor of using micro-computer software in an audit as compared to performing an audit without the use of a computer include the following:

1. **Time** may be **saved** by eliminating manual footing, cross-footing, and other routine calculations.

2. **Calculations,** comparisons, and other data manipulations are **more accurately performed.**

3. **Analytical procedures** calculations may be **more efficiently performed.**

4. The **scope** of analytical procedures may be **broadened.**

5. Audit **sampling** may be **facilitated.**

6. Potential **weaknesses** in a client's internal control structure may be more readily **identified**.

7. Preparation and **revision of flowcharts** depicting the flow of financial transactions in a client's structure may be **facilitated.**

8. **Working papers** may be easily **stored** and accessed.

9. **Graphics capabilities** may allow the auditor to generate, display, and evaluate various financial and nonfinancial relationships graphically.

10. Engagement-management information such as **time budgets** and the monitoring of **actual time vs. budgeted amounts** may be more easily generated and analyzed.

11. **Customized working papers** may be developed with greater ease.

12. **Standardized audit correspondence,** such as engagement letters, client representation letters, and attorney letters **may be stored and easily modified.**

13. **Supervisory-review time** may be **reduced**.

14. Staff morale and productivity may be improved by reducing the time spent on clerical tasks.

15. **Client's personnel may not need to manually prepare** as many **schedules** and otherwise spend as much time assisting the auditor.

16. Computer-generated working papers are generally more **legible** and consistent.

SOLUTION 38-6 AUDITING PROCEDURES

The **substantive auditing procedures** Brown may consider performing include the following:

Using the **perpetual** inventory file,

- **Recalculate the beginning and ending balances** (prices x quantities), foot, and print out a report to be used to reconcile the totals with the general ledger (or agree beginning balance with the prior year's working papers).
- **Calculate the quantity balances** as of the physical inventory date **for comparison to** the **physical inventory file**. (Alternatively, update the physical inventory file for purchases and sales from January 6 to January 31, 20X1, for comparison to the perpetual inventory at January 31, 20X1.)
- Select and print out a **sample of items received and shipped** for the periods (a) before and after January 5 and 31, 20X1, **for cut-off testing**, (b) between January 5 and January 31, 20X1, **for vouching or analytical procedures,** and (c) prior to January 5, 20X1, **for tests of details** or analytical procedures.
- Compare quantities sold during the year to quantities on hand at year end. Print out a **report of items for which turnover is less than expected**. (Alternatively, calculate the number of days' sales in inventory for selected items.)
- **Select items** noted as possibly **unsalable** or **obsolete** during the physical inventory observation and print out information about purchases and sales for further consideration.
- **Recalculate** the prices used to value the year-end FIFO inventory by matching prices and quantities to the most recent purchases.
- Select a **sample** of **items for comparison** to **current sales prices**.
- **Identify** and print out **unusual transactions.** (These are transactions other than purchases or sales for the year, or physical inventory adjustments as of January 5, 20X1.)
- **Recalculate the ending inventory** (or selected items) by taking the beginning balances plus purchases, less sales, (quantities and/or amounts) and print out the differences.
- **Recalculate the cost of sales** for selected items sold during the year.

Using the **physical inventory** and test count files,

- **Account for all inventory tag numbers** used and print out a report of missing or duplicate numbers for follow-up.
- **Search for tag numbers** noted during the physical inventory observation as being **voided or not used.**
- **Compare the physical inventory file to the file of test counts** and print out a report of differences for auditor follow-up.
- Combine the quantities for each item appearing on more than one inventory tag number for comparison to the perpetual file.
- **Compare** the **quantities** on the file to the calculated quantity balances on the perpetual inventory file as of January 5, 20X1. (Alternatively, compare the physical inventory file updated to year end to the perpetual inventory file.)
- **Calculate the quantities and dollar amounts of the book-to-physical adjustments** for each item and the total adjustment. Print out a report to reconcile the total adjustment to the adjustment recorded in the general ledger before the year end.
- Using the calculated book-to-physical adjustments for each item, **compare the quantities and dollar amounts of each adjustment to the perpetual inventory file** as of January 5, 20X1, and print out a report of differences for follow-up.

AUDITING HOT•SPOT™ VIDEO DESCRIPTIONS

(subject to change without notice)

CPA 2604 Audit Standards & Planning

This discussion concentrates on the ten generally accepted auditing standards, quality control, governmental auditing standards, and audit planning. This lecture includes the steps in the audit process, types of audits, peer reviews, predecessor auditors, client background information, risk, materiality, errors, fraud, and illegal client acts. Approximate time is 3:00.

CPA 2100 Internal Control

Learn how to reason through a flowchart of a company's operations and prepare internal control questionnaires and narratives. Topics include audit risk, the five components of internal control, and the assessment of control risk. Bob Monette discusses mnemonics and question-answering techniques. Approximate time is 2:10.

CPA 2110 Audit Evidence

This program will help prepare you for both objective and essay questions on audit evidence, including step-by-step instructions on how to build an audit program. Bob Monette provides invaluable mnemonics for substantive tests, management assertions, and subsequent events. Levels of evidence persuasiveness, workpapers, types of A/R confirmations, and analytics are also discussed. One 15-item OOAF question, 36 multiple choice questions, and three essay questions highlight recurring topics and hone exam skills. Approximate time is 2:45.

CPA 2548 EDP Auditing & Statistical Sampling

Robert Monette explains how a computer system impacts an audit and audit sampling procedures. Learn the general and application controls necessary for auditing EDP systems, techniques of auditing through the computer, and what you should know about generalized audit software. Clear up the confusion surrounding attribute and variable sampling including risk, variability, mean per unit estimation, tolerable misstatement, precision, ratio estimation, difference estimation, sample size, PPS sampling, discovery sampling—and more. Recurring exam topics are highlighted in the 40 multiple choice questions. Approximate time is 2:50.

CPA 2000 Standard Audit Reports

This discussion concentrates on the unqualified, qualified, and adverse opinions and disclaimers of opinion applicable to engagements to audit financial statements. The program includes the impact that GAAS have on reports, conditions necessary to issue various types of opinions, the details of standard audit reports likely to be tested, the use of other auditors, required supplementary information, comparative financial statements, subsequent events, and re-issuance of a report. Approximate time is 3:00.

CPA 3230 Other Reports, Reviews & Compilations

This program concentrates on the reports applicable to engagements other than typical audit engagements including reports on OCBOA financial statements, specified elements, and contractual agreement compliance. The invaluable mnemonics will help you recall review and compilation report elements under exam conditions. Bob Monette discusses an OOAF question with 17 items, 21 multiple choice questions, and an essay question while highlighting recurring topics and honing your exam skills. Approximate time is 1:50.

STUDY TIP: STANDARD AUDIT REPORTS

Since audit report questions frequently appear on the CPA exam, the editors recommend that candidates memorize the standard report **verbatim**. Learning the modifications for various situations is considerably easier than learning dozens of reports. These modifications are summarized in Exhibit 25, *Conditions Requiring Modification of Report.*

CHANGE ALERT

SAS 93, *Omnibus Statement on Auditing Standards—2000,* is discussed in Chapters 32 and 39.

SAS 93 amends SAS 58, *Reports on Audited Financial Statements*, to require that a practitioner identify the country of GAAS and GAAP referred to in a practitioner's report. Two different acceptable sets of phrases are illustrated in the standard: "U.S. generally accepted accounting principles" and "U.S. generally accepted auditing standards" as well as "accounting principles generally accepted in the United States of America" and "auditing standards generally accepted in the United States of America."

SAS 93 amends SAS 84, *Communications Between Predecessor and Successor Auditors*, to explicitly include, within the definition of *predecessor auditor*, any auditor who is engaged to perform, but does not complete, an audit.

SAS 93 retracts SAS 75, *Engagements to Apply Agreed-Upon Procedures to Specified Elements, Accounts, or Items of a Financial Statement.* The withdrawal of SAS 75 is concurrent with the effective date of SSAE 10, *Attestation Standards: Revision and Recodification.* SSAE 10, among other provisions, removes the requirement for a written assertion in connection with agreed-upon procedures engagements.

CHAPTER 39

REPORTS ON AUDITED FINANCIAL STATEMENTS

CHAPTER 39

REPORTS ON AUDITED FINANCIAL STATEMENTS

I. Reporting Standards

A. Adherence to GAAP

Auditor judgment determines which accounting principles should be used in any situation. This standard requires an **opinion** by the auditor, not a statement of absolute fact.

Exhibit 1 ♦ The First Standard of Reporting

> "The report shall state whether the financial statements are presented in conformity with U.S. generally accepted accounting principles."

1. **GAAP** GAAP is described in Meaning of *Present Fairly in Conformity With Generally Accepted Accounting Principles* in the Independent Auditor's Report (AU 411, SAS 69). Independent auditors agree on the existence of a body of accounting principles, and they are experts in those accounting principles and the determination of their general acceptance. Nevertheless, the determination that a particular accounting principle is generally accepted may be difficult because no single reference source exists for all principles.

   a. A technical accounting term encompassing the *conventions*, *rules*, and *procedures* that define accepted accounting practice at a particular time.

   b. GAAP includes *broad* guidelines and *detailed* practices and procedures.

2. **GAAP Hierarchy** The sources of established accounting principles for entities other than governmental entities that are generally accepted in the United States are as follows:

   a. **Category (a)** This includes unsuperseded FASB Statements and Interpretations, APB Opinions, and AICPA Accounting Research Bulletins.

      (1) Rule 203 provides that an unqualified opinion should not be expressed if the financial statements contain a material departure from such pronouncements unless, due to unusual circumstances, adherence to the pronouncements would make the statements misleading.

      (2) Therefore, Rule 203 implies that application of officially established accounting principles results in the fair presentation of financial position, results of operations, and cash flows in conformity with GAAP.

   b. **Category (b)** This category is composed of FASB Technical Bulletins, and, if cleared by the FASB, AICPA Industry Audit and Accounting Guides and AICPA Statements of Position (SOP).

   c. **Category (c)** This category is composed of AICPA Practice Bulletins that have been cleared by the FASB and consensus positions of the FASB Emerging Issues Task Force (EITF).

   d. **Category (d)** These include AICPA accounting interpretations and implementation guides published by the FASB staff, and practices that are widely recognized and prevalent either generally or in the industry.

EXHIBIT 2 ♦ GAAP HIERARCHY

Nongovernmental Entities	State and Local Governments	Federal Governmental Agencies
	CATEGORY A (LEVEL ONE)	
FASB Statements (SFAS)	GASB Statements	FASAB Statements
FASB Interpretations	GASB Interpretations	FASAB Interpretations
APB Opinions	AICPA and FASB Pronouncements if made applicable to state and local governments by GASB Statements or Interpretations	AICPA and FASB pronouncements made applicable to federal governmental entities by FASAB Statements or Interpretations
AICPA Accounting Research Bulletins (ARB)		
	CATEGORY B (LEVEL TWO)	
FASB Technical Bulletins	GASB Technical Bulletins	FASAB Technical Bulletins
AICPA Industry Audit and Accounting Guides and Statements of Position	AICPA Industry Audit and Accounting Guides and Statements of Position*	AICPA Industry Audit and Accounting Guides and AICPA SOP**
	CATEGORY C (LEVEL THREE)	
EITF Consensuses	GASB EITF Consensuses (not yet organized by GASB)	AICPA Practice Bulletins**
AICPA Practice Bulletins	AICPA Practice Bulletins*	Technical Releases of the Accounting and Auditing Policy Committee of the FASAB
	CATEGORY D (LEVEL FOUR)	
AICPA Accounting Interpretations	"Qs and As" published by GASB staff	Implementation guides published by the FASAB staff
"Qs and As" published by FASB staff	Prevalent practice	Practices that are widely recognized and prevalent in the federal government
Prevalent practice	* If made applicable to state and local governments by AICPA	**If specifically made applicable to federal governmental entities and cleared by the FASAB.

3. **UNSPECIFIED TREATMENT** In cases where the accounting treatment of a transaction or event is not specified by a pronouncement under Rule 203, the auditor should consider whether the accounting treatment is specified by another source of established accounting principles. In cases where a conflict arises between accounting principles from categories, the auditor should follow the treatment specified by the source in the **higher** category. For example, category (b) should be followed before categories (c) or (d).

   a. Due to the evolution of new businesses transactions, there will not be an established accounting principle for reporting a specific transaction or event. When this occurs, an accounting principle similar to an established principle to an analogous transaction or event should be selected.

b. Other accounting literature may also be considered in the absence of pronouncements or other established accounting principles. The appropriateness of other accounting literature depends on its relevance to particular circumstances, the specificity of the guidance, and the general recognition of the issuer or author as an authority.

4. **State & Local Governments (SLG)** A separate, parallel, hierarchy exists for SLG composed of four categories, or levels of authority, similar to those for nongovernmental entities.

   a. **Category (a)** Consists of GASB Statements and Interpretations, as well as AICPA and FASB pronouncements made applicable to state and local governmental entities by GASB Statements or Interpretations.

   b. **Category (b)** Consists of GASB Technical Bulletins and when **cleared** by the GASB, AICPA Statements of Position and Industry Auditing and Accounting Guides, to the extent the AICPA makes these latter documents applicable to SLG.

   c. **Category (c)** Consists of AICPA Practice Bulletins to the extent these bulletins are made applicable to state and local governmental entities and cleared by the GASB. Also included are consensus positions of a group of accountants organized by the GASB that attempt to reach consensus positions on accounting issues applicable to state and local governmental entities.

   d. **Category (d)** Consists of questions and answers published by the GASB staff, as well as practices that are widely recognized and prevalent in SLG.

5. **Federal Government** SAS 91 outlines a parallel hierarchy for federal governmental units composed of four categories, or levels of authority.

   a. **Category (a)** Consists of Federal Accounting Standards Advisory Board (FASAB) Statements and Interpretations, as well as AICPA and FASB pronouncements made applicable to federal governmental entities by FASAB Statements or Interpretations.

   b. **Category (b)** Consists of FASAB Technical Bulletins and, if specifically made applicable to federal entities by the AICPA and cleared by the FASAB, AICPA Industry Audit and Accounting Guides and AICPA SOP.

   c. **Category (c)** Consists of AICPA Practice Bulletins, if specifically made applicable to federal governmental entities and cleared by the FASAB, as well as Technical Releases of the Accounting and Auditing Policy Committee of the FASAB.

   d. **Category (d)** Includes implementation guides published by the FASAB staff, as well as practices that are widely recognized and prevalent in the federal government.

B. Consistency of Application of GAAP

The objective of the second standard is to provide assurance that (1) comparability has not been materially affected by changes in accounting principles, and (2) if comparability has been materially affected, that the auditor appropriately discloses the changes and their effects. The following are accounting changes affecting consistency.

Exhibit 3 ♦ The Second Standard of Reporting

> "The report shall identify those circumstances in which such principles have not been consistently observed in the current period in relation to the preceding period."

1. **Change in Accounting Principle** Per APB Opinion No. 20, a change in accounting principle arises (a) from the use of a generally accepted accounting principle that is different from

the one previously used (e.g., changing from the straight-line method of computing depreciation to the units-of-production method) or (b) from the use of a different method of applying a generally accepted accounting principle (e.g., changing the method of allocating manufacturing overhead to inventory from direct labor hours to machine hours). The auditor must recognize the change in the report if it has a material effect on the financial statements (i.e., the auditor will add an explanatory paragraph to an unqualified opinion). This is not a qualification of the audit opinion.

a. **Unjustified** If management has not provided reasonable justification for a change in accounting principle, the auditor's opinion should express an exception to the change having been made without reasonable justification. This would result in a qualified opinion. In addition, the auditor should continue to express the exception with respect to the financial statements for as long as they are presented and reported on.

b. **Changes in Presentation of Cash Flows** An enterprise should disclose its policy for determining which items are treated as cash equivalents. Any change to that policy is a change in accounting principle that is reported by restating financial statements for earlier years presented for comparative purposes.

2. **Change in the Reporting Entity** Recognition is required in the auditor's report, as an explanatory paragraph with an unqualified opinion, because of lack of consistency. The following situations represent changes in the reporting entity:

   a. The presentation of **consolidated** or **combined** statements in place of the statements of individual companies.

   b. A change in specific subsidiaries that comprise the group of companies for which the consolidated statements are presented. [This doesn't include a change resulting from a transaction or event, (e.g., a pooling of interests), nor the creation, cessation, partial or complete purchase, or disposition of a subsidiary or other business unit.]

   c. A change in the companies that are included in **combined** financial statements.

   d. A change among the cost, equity, and consolidation methods of accounting for subsidiaries or other investments in common stock.

   e. A business combination accounted for by the pooling of interest method that also results in a different reporting entity, in accordance with APB Opinion No. 20.

3. **Correction of an Error in Principle** This involves changing from an accounting principle that is **not** generally accepted to one that is (including correcting a mistake in the application of a principle). This type of change is accounted for as a correction of an error. Also, it will necessitate a changed audit opinion.

4. **Inseparable Change in Principle and Estimate** When the effect of a change in accounting principle cannot be separated from a change in estimate, the accounting for the change is handled as a *change in estimate*, but still requires **recognition** in the audit report for consistency.

5. **Changes Not Affecting Consistency** The following changes do not affect the consistency of application of accounting principles and, therefore, do **not** require recognition in the auditor's report as to a lack of consistency. However, if material, they may require disclosure in the financial statements.

   a. **Changes in Accounting Estimates** Even though accounting estimates will be changed as circumstances change, estimates such as expected salvage values and service lives of fixed assets are a normal part of doing business.

b. **Error Correction That Does Not Involve an Accounting Principle** The correction of an error in previously issued financial statements that resulted from mathematical mistakes, oversight, or misunderstanding of facts is considered an error correction that does not involve an accounting principle.

c. **Changes in Classification and Reclassification** The classification of items in previously issued financial statements should be adapted to increase comparability with current financial statements.

d. **Substantially Different Transactions or Events** A consistency problem does not arise when the use of a different accounting principle is required because the transactions and events being processed are clearly different from those in the previous period.

e. **Changes Expected to Have a Material Future Effect** When an accounting change does not affect the current year's financial statements but is expected to have a substantial effect in later years, it should be **disclosed** in the notes to the financial statements of the year of change.

f. **Qualification** While the changes above do not require the addition of an explanatory paragraph in the auditor's report because of lack of consistency, the opinion must be **qualified** if *adequate disclosure* in the financial statements is **not** made.

6. **Current Year** When reporting only on the current period's financial statements, the auditor should obtain sufficient, competent, evidential matter about the consistency of accounting principles with the previous period even though the prior-period financial statements are not presented. When the auditor has not audited the financial statements of the preceding year, the auditor should adopt procedures that are practicable and reasonable in the circumstances to be assured that the accounting principles are consistent between the current and the preceding year.

- SAS 88 eliminates the requirement to qualify the auditor's report and consider adding an explanatory paragraph on consistency to the report if single-year financial statements that report a pooling of interests do not disclose combined information for the prior year.

7. **Multiple Years** When reporting on the financial statements of two or more years that are presented for comparative purposes, the auditor should report on a lack of consistency **between** the years. The auditor should also report on a lack of consistency between the years and the year prior to the earliest year presented. The auditor is not required to report on a lack of consistency if the change is at the beginning of the earliest year presented and the change was accounted for by retroactive restatement.

- SAS 88 eliminates the requirement for an explanatory paragraph on consistency in the auditor's report if a pooling of interests is not accounted for retroactively in comparative financial statements. (In these circumstances, the auditor would be required to express a qualified or adverse opinion because of the departure from GAAP.)

C. **Adequacy of Disclosure in Financial Statements**

Exhibit 4 ♦ The Third Standard of Reporting

> "Informative disclosures in the financial statements are to be regarded as reasonably adequate unless otherwise stated in the report."

1. **DISCLOSURE OF MATERIAL MATTERS**

   a. Financial statements presented in conformity with GAAP must contain adequate disclosure of material matters. Adequate disclosure includes the form, arrangement, and content of the statements and notes, including the terminology used, amount of detail, classification of items, and the bases of amounts set forth. In determining whether a particular matter should be disclosed, the auditor should consider the **circumstances** and **facts** that the auditor is aware of at the time.

   b. Failure by management to include information required by GAAP in the financial statements will result in the auditor expressing a **qualified** or **adverse** opinion on the statements. If practicable, the auditor should provide the information in the report, unless its omission from the report is sanctioned by a specific SAS. "Practicable" means that the information can reasonably be obtained from the client's accounts and records, and that providing it in the report does **not** require the auditor to assume the position of *preparer* of financial information. For instance, an auditor is not expected to provide a basic financial statement or segment information omitted by management.

2. **CONFIDENTIAL INFORMATION** In conducting an audit of financial statements and in other areas of work with the client, the auditor uses confidential information provided by the client. Thus, the auditor should **not** disclose—without management's consent—information not required to be disclosed in financial statements to comply with GAAP.

D. **ASSOCIATION WITH FINANCIAL STATEMENTS**

The objective of the fourth standard is to prevent any misinterpretation of the **degree of responsibility** which the auditor is assuming when his or her name is associated with financial statements. Reference to the financial statements taken as a whole applies **equally** to a *complete set* of financial statements and to an *individual* financial statement, such as a balance sheet, and also applies to the current period as well as any prior periods that are presented on a comparative basis. Thus, an auditor may express one opinion on a balance sheet and another opinion or disclaim an opinion on an income statement, if circumstances warrant. (AU §508.05)

EXHIBIT 5 ♦ THE FOURTH STANDARD OF REPORTING

> "The report shall either contain an expression of opinion regarding the financial statements, taken as a whole, or an assertion to the effect that an opinion cannot be expressed. When an overall opinion cannot be expressed, the reasons therefor should be stated. In all cases where an auditor's name is associated with financial statements, the report should contain a clear-cut indication of the character of the auditor's work and the degree of responsibility, if any, the auditor is taking."

1. **CERTAIN IDENTIFIED ITEMS** An auditor is able to express an opinion on one or more certain identified items of a financial statement, provided that the identified items and the scope of the related audit are not intended to encompass so many elements as to constitute a major portion of the financial statements. (For example, an auditor may express an opinion on an entity's accounts receivable balance even if the auditor disclaimed an opinion on the financial statements taken as a whole.) A report on identified items should be presented separately from the report on the financial statements. (AU §623.14)

2. **PIECEMEAL OPINIONS** Piecemeal opinions are expressions of opinion as to specified elements, accounts, or items (certain identified items) in the financial statements. Piecemeal opinions should **not** be expressed when the auditor has **disclaimed** an opinion or has expressed an *adverse* opinion on the financial statements taken as a whole because piecemeal opinions tend to overshadow or contradict a disclaimer of opinion or an adverse opinion. Therefore, piecemeal opinions are **inappropriate** and should **not** be issued in *any* situation.

II. Types of Opinions

A. Unqualified Opinion, Standard Report

The standard report is issued when the auditor feels the financial statements fairly present, in all material respects, the financial position, results of operations, and cash flows in conformity with U.S. GAAP (including adequate disclosure). The audit must have been conducted in accordance with U.S. GAAS.

Exhibit 6 ♦ Necessary Conditions for an Unqualified Opinion

1. No departures from GAAP.
2. Disclosures in financial statements (footnotes) are adequate and complete.
3. No unusual uncertainties (contingencies) surrounding the financial statements.
4. No scope limitations.
5. GAAP must be consistently followed between periods.
6. Independent auditor.

B. Unqualified Opinion, Explanatory Language Added to the Auditor's Report

Certain circumstances, while not affecting the auditor's unqualified opinion on the financial statements, may require that the auditor add an explanatory paragraph (or other explanatory language) to the report. Explanatory language would be added when part of the audit is performed by other independent auditors; or when change in consistency, material uncertainty, going concern exists; or when the auditor wants to emphasize a matter.

C. Qualified Opinion

States that the financial statements present fairly, in all material respects, the results of operations, financial position, and cash flows in conformity with GAAP "except for" the effects of the matter to which the qualification relates. A qualification may exist due to a scope limitation.

D. Adverse Opinion

Expressed when, in the *auditor's judgment*, the financial statements taken as a whole do **not** fairly present the financial position, results of operations, or cash flows in conformity with GAAP.

E. Disclaimer of Opinion

States that the auditor does not express an opinion on the financial statements, typically due to independence or scope limitations.

III. Unqualified Opinions and the Standard Report

A. Implications of the Standard Report

The auditor's standard report states that the financial statements present fairly, in all material respects, an entity's financial position, results of operations, and cash flows in conformity with U.S. GAAP. The auditor may express this opinion only when an audit conducted according to U.S. GAAS has been completed and the necessary conditions are met. The auditor's standard report identifies the financial statements audited in an opening, introductory paragraph, describes the nature of an audit in a scope paragraph, and expresses the auditor's opinion in a separate opinion paragraph. SAS 93 requires that the country of the origin of the GAAS and GAAP be specified.

B. Components of the Standard Report

The basic elements of the report include the following:

1. **Title** A title that includes the word "independent."

2. **Address** Addressed to the company, to its board of directors, or to its **stockholders** (not to management). If the auditor is retained to audit the financial statements of a company that is

not the auditor's client, the report would be addressed to the client and not to the directors or stockholders of the company being audited.

3. **INTRODUCTORY PARAGRAPH**

   a. A statement that identifies the financial statements that were audited.

   b. A statement that the financial statements are the responsibility of the Company's management and that the auditor's responsibility is to express an opinion on the financial statements based on the audit.

4. **SCOPE PARAGRAPH**

   a. A statement that the audit was conducted in accordance with U.S. GAAS.

   b. A statement that GAAS requires that the auditor plan and perform the audit to obtain reasonable assurance about whether the financial statements are free of material misstatement.

   c. A statement that an audit includes

      (1) Examining, on a test basis, evidence supporting the amounts and disclosures in the financial statements.

      (2) Assessing the accounting principles used and significant estimates made by management.

      (3) Evaluating the overall financial statement presentation.

   d. A statement that the auditor believes that the audit provides a reasonable basis for the auditor's opinion.

5. **OPINION PARAGRAPH** An opinion as to whether the financial statements present fairly, in all material respects, the financial position of the Company as of the balance sheet date and the results of its operations and its cash flows for the period then ended in conformity with U.S. GAAP.

6. **SIGNATURE** The manual or printed signature of the auditor's firm.

7. **DATE** Generally, the date upon which the auditor's field work is completed.

EXHIBIT 7 ♦ THE FORM OF THE AUDITOR'S STANDARD REPORT FOR A SINGLE YEAR

<u>Independent Auditor's Report</u>

Address (The title and address should be included in all letters, but is not reproduced in all subsequent exhibits.)

(Introductory paragraph)

We have audited the accompanying balance sheet of X Company as of December 31, 20XX, and the related statements of income, retained earnings, and cash flows for the year then ended. These financial statements are the responsibility of the Company's management. Our responsibility is to express an opinion on these financial statements based on our audit.

(continued on next page)

(Scope paragraph)

We conducted our audit in accordance with U.S. generally accepted auditing standards. Those standards require that we plan and perform the audit to obtain reasonable assurance about whether the financial statements are free of material misstatement. An audit includes examining, on a test basis, evidence supporting the amounts and disclosures in the financial statements. An audit also includes assessing the accounting principles used and significant estimates made by management, as well as evaluating the overall financial statement presentation. We believe that our audit provides a reasonable basis for our opinion.

(Opinion paragraph)

In our opinion, the financial statements referred to above present fairly, in all material respects, the financial position of X Company as of (at) December 31, 20XX, and the results of its operations and its cash flows for the year then ended in conformity with U.S. generally accepted accounting principles.

Signature & Date (These should be included in all letters, but is not reproduced in all subsequent exhibits.)

C. Explanatory Language Added to the Auditor's Standard Report

There are certain circumstances which, while not affecting the auditor's unqualified opinion, may require that the auditor add explanatory language to the standard report. These circumstances include the following:

1. Part of Audit Performed by Other Independent Auditors (AU 543)

a. **Principal Auditor** Sometimes the auditor will be in a position where other independent auditors have audited the financial statements of subsidiaries, divisions, branches, components, or investments that are included in the financial statements the auditor is auditing. The auditor must first decide whether he or she has participated sufficiently to be the principal auditor (i.e., to report on the financial statements).

b. **Whether to Make Reference to the Other Auditor** As principal auditor, the auditor must decide whether to take responsibility for the work of the other auditor as it relates to the expression of an opinion. If the principal auditor does not assume this responsibility, the principal auditor should make reference to the other auditor's examination and clearly indicate the division of responsibility in the audit report.

(1) **Decision Not to Make Reference** The principal auditor must be satisfied of the other auditor's independence, professional reputation, and the quality and scope of the audit performed. This position is usually appropriate when (a) the other auditor is an associated or correspondent firm, (b) the other auditor was retained by the principal auditor, (c) the principal auditor takes steps necessary to be satisfied with the other auditor's work, or (d) the other auditor audited an immaterial portion of the financial statements.

(2) **Decision to Make Reference** The principal auditor's report should clearly indicate, in the introductory, scope, and opinion paragraphs, the **division of responsibility** between the portion of the financial statements covered by the principal auditor's own audit and that covered by the audit of the other auditor. The portion examined by the other auditor should be indicated (e.g., dollar amounts or percentages of total assets, total revenues, etc.). The other auditor may only be named if (a) the other auditor has given permission, and (b) the other auditor's report is included.

EXHIBIT 8 ♦ REPORT INDICATING A DIVISION OF RESPONSIBILITY

<u>Independent Auditor's Report</u>

(Introductory paragraph)

We have audited the consolidated balance sheets of ABC Company as of December 31, 20X2 and 20X1, and the related consolidated statements of income, retained earnings, and cash flows for the years then ended. These financial statements are the responsibility of the company's management. Our responsibility is to express an opinion on these financial statements based on our audits. We did not audit the financial statements of B Company, a wholly owned subsidiary, which statements reflect total assets of $______ and $______ as of December 31, 20X2 and 20X1, respectively, and total revenues of $______ and $______ for the years then ended. Those statements were audited by other auditors whose report has been furnished to us, and our opinion, insofar as it relates to the amounts included for B Company, is based solely on the report of other auditors.

(Scope paragraph)

We conducted our audits in accordance with U.S. generally accepted auditing standards. Those standards require that we plan and perform the audit to obtain reasonable assurance about whether the financial statements are free of material misstatements. An audit includes examining on a test basis, evidence supporting the amounts and disclosures in the financial statements. An audit also includes assessing the accounting principles used and significant estimates made by management, as well as evaluating the overall financial statements presentation. We believe that our audits and other auditors' reports provide a reasonable basis for our opinion.

(Opinion paragraph)

In our opinion, based on our audits and other auditors' reports, the consolidated financial statements referred to above present fairly, in all material respects, the financial position of ABC Company as of December 31, 20X2 and 20X1, and the results of its operations and its cash flows for the years then ended in conformity with U.S. generally accepted accounting principles.

c. **OTHER PROCEDURES** Regardless of whether or not reference is made, the principal auditor should inquire as to the professional reputation and independence of the other auditors and should attempt to achieve a proper coordination of their activities.

2. **JUSTIFIABLE DEPARTURE FROM A PROMULGATED ACCOUNTING PRINCIPLE (RULE 203)** In the rare circumstance where the auditor can demonstrate that, due to unusual circumstances, the financial statements would be misleading if promulgated GAAP were applied, the auditor must describe the departure, its approximate effects, if practicable, and the reasons why compliance would result in a misleading statement. In this situation, it is appropriate for the auditor to express an unqualified opinion on the financial statements with an explanatory paragraph.

3. **LACK OF CONSISTENCY** The auditor's standard report implies that the accounting principles have been consistently applied between periods. In these cases, the auditor should **not** refer to consistency in the report. If there has been a change affecting consistency, the auditor should refer to the change in an explanatory paragraph of the report. The explanatory paragraph, following the opinion paragraph, should identify the nature of the change and refer the reader to the note in the financial statements that discusses the change in detail. An unqualified opinion would be expressed. The auditor's concurrence with a change is implicit unless the auditor takes exception to the change.

EXHIBIT 9 ♦ CHANGE IN ACCOUNTING PRINCIPLE (FOLLOWING OPINION PARAGRAPH)

> As discussed in Note X to the financial statements, the Company changed its method of computing depreciation in 20X1.

4. **UNCERTAINTIES** A matter involving an uncertainty is one that is expected to be resolved at a future date when sufficient competent evidential matter concerning its outcome should become available. In some instances, the outcome of future events may affect the financial statements.

   a. **EVALUATION** Since management may not always be able to estimate the effect of such events, the auditor must consider the likelihood of a material loss resulting from the resolution of the uncertainty.

      (1) **REMOTE LIKELIHOOD OF A MATERIAL LOSS** In this case, the auditor would not add an explanatory paragraph to the report because of the matter.

      (2) **PROBABLE CHANCE OF MATERIAL LOSS** If management is unable to provide a reasonable estimate of the amount or range of a material probable loss, the auditor should consider adding an explanatory paragraph to the report. This is not, however, a substitute for accrual if a reasonable estimate is available. If management makes a reasonable accrual for the potential loss, the auditor would decide whether an explanatory paragraph would be appropriate depending upon the materiality of the loss and the likelihood of its occurrence.

      (3) **REASONABLE POSSIBILITY OF MATERIAL LOSS** When the chance of material loss is more than remote but less than probable, in deciding whether to add an explanatory paragraph, the auditor would consider the magnitude by which the amount of the potential loss exceeds the auditor's judgment about materiality and the likelihood of its occurrence.

   b. **NEED FOR EXPLANATORY PARAGRAPH** As long as any matter is sufficiently disclosed in the financial statement footnotes, an auditor **may** add an explanatory paragraph to the auditor's report. SAS 79 removes the requirement for an uncertainties explanatory paragraph to the auditor's report when certain criteria are met. The revised SAS 58 now reads, "emphasis paragraphs are never required; they may be added solely at the auditor's discretion." If a material uncertainty affects the financial statements, an auditor can disclaim an opinion.

   c. **LOCATION** If the auditor concludes that an explanatory paragraph is warranted, it should be included following the opinion paragraph. The explanatory paragraph should include a description of the matter giving rise to the uncertainty and should indicate that its outcome cannot be determined. The separate paragraph may be shortened by making reference to financial statement notes. No reference should be made to the uncertainty in the introductory, scope, or opinion paragraphs. If, however, the uncertainty is **not** properly accounted for or disclosed, the auditor should issue a qualified or adverse opinion.

EXHIBIT 10 ♦ UNCERTAINTY: EXPLANATORY PARAGRAPH (AFTER THE OPINION PARAGRAPH)

> As discussed in Note X to the financial statements, the Company is a defendant in a lawsuit alleging infringement of certain patent rights and claiming royalties and punitive damages. The Company has filed a counteraction, and preliminary hearings and discovery proceedings on both actions are in progress. The ultimate outcome of the litigation cannot presently be determined. Accordingly, no provision for any liability that may result upon adjudication has been made in the accompanying financial statements.

5. **GOING CONCERN QUESTIONS** The audit report should include an explanatory paragraph following the opinion paragraph if the auditor concludes that substantial doubt about the entity's ability to continue as a going concern does exist. If the auditor concludes that the entity's disclosures regarding its ability to continue as a going concern for a reasonable time are inadequate, misleading, or a departure from GAAP, a qualified or an adverse opinion should be issued. This paragraph should **not** include any conditional language, per SAS 79.

EXHIBIT 11 ♦ GOING CONCERN UNCERTAINTY: EXPLANATORY PARAGRAPH

> The accompanying financial statements have been prepared assuming that the Company will continue as a going concern. As discussed in Note X to the financial statements, the Company has suffered recurring losses from operations and has a net capital deficiency, raising substantial doubt about its ability to continue as a going concern. Management's plans in regard to these matters are also described in Note X. The financial statements do not include any adjustments that might result from the outcome of this uncertainty.

6. **EMPHASIS OF A MATTER** The auditor may wish to emphasize a matter regarding the financial statements even though the auditor intends to express an unqualified opinion. For example, the auditor may wish to emphasize that the entity is a component of a larger business enterprise or that it has had significant transactions with related parties. The auditor may wish to mention an important subsequent event. This should be presented in a separate paragraph in the auditor's report with an unqualified opinion.

IV. DEPARTURES FROM UNQUALIFIED OPINIONS

A. QUALIFIED OPINIONS

When the auditor expresses a qualified opinion, the auditor should disclose all of the substantive reasons in one or more separate explanatory paragraph(s) **preceding** the opinion paragraph of the report. A qualified opinion should include the word *except* or *exception* in a phrase such as *except for* or *with the exception of*. Phrases such as *subject to* and *with the foregoing explanation* are not clear or forceful enough and should **not** be used.

1. **SCOPE LIMITATIONS** Restrictions on the scope of an audit, whether imposed by the client or by circumstances, may require the auditor to express a qualified opinion. The decision depends upon the auditor's assessment of the importance of the omitted procedure(s) in relation to the financial statements. When a significant scope limitation is imposed by the client, the auditor would normally disclaim an opinion on the financial statements.

   a. **QUALIFIED OPINION** If a qualified opinion is expressed, the reasons should be explained in the audit report in an explanatory paragraph (preceding the opinion paragraph) and referred to in both the scope and opinion paragraphs. The wording in the opinion paragraph should indicate that the qualification pertains to the possible effects on the financial statements and **not** to the scope limitation itself.

   b. **EXAMPLES OF SCOPE LIMITATIONS**

      (1) The auditor is unable to observe physical inventories or apply alternative procedures to verify their balances.

      (2) The client refuses to permit its attorney to furnish information requested in a letter of audit inquiry.

   c. **LIMITED REPORTING ENGAGEMENTS** The auditor is not precluded from reporting on only one of the basic financial statements and not the others. A scope limitation would not exist if the auditor is able to apply all the procedures to the one financial statement the auditor considers necessary. Such engagements involve limited **reporting** objectives.

EXHIBIT 12 ♦ SCOPE LIMITATIONS

> Independent Auditor's Report
>
> (Same first paragraph as the standard report)
>
> Except as discussed in the following paragraph, we conducted our audits in accordance with U.S. generally accepted auditing standards. Those standards require that we plan and perform the audit to obtain reasonable assurance about whether the financial statements are free of material misstatement. An audit includes examining, on a test basis, evidence supporting the amounts and disclosures in the financial statements. An audit also includes assessing the accounting principles used and significant estimates made by management, as well as evaluating the overall financial statement presentation. We believe that our audits provide a reasonable basis for our opinion.
>
> We were unable to obtain audited financial statements supporting the Company's investment in a foreign affiliate stated at $_____ and $_____ at December 31, 20X2 and 20X1, respectively, or its equity in earnings of that affiliate of $______ and $______, which is included in net income for the years then ended as described in Note X to the financial statements; nor were we able to satisfy ourselves as to the carrying value of the investment in the foreign affiliate or the equity in its earnings by other auditing procedures.
>
> In our opinion, except for the effects of such adjustments, if any, as might have been determined to be necessary had we been able to examine evidence regarding the foreign affiliate investment and earnings, the financial statements referred to in the first paragraph above present fairly, in all material respects, the financial position of X Company as of December 31, 20X2 and 20X1, and the results of its operations and its cash flows for the years then ended in conformity with U.S. generally accepted accounting principles.

2. DEPARTURE FROM GAAP

a. When financial statements are materially affected by a departure from GAAP, the auditor should express a qualified or an adverse opinion. Materiality, significance of an item to the entity, pervasiveness of the misstatement, and the effect of the misstatement on the financial statements as a whole, must be considered in deciding whether to express a qualified or an adverse opinion.

b. When the auditor expresses a qualified opinion, the auditor should disclose, in a separate explanatory paragraph(s) preceding the opinion paragraph, the substantive reasons that have led the auditor to conclude that there is a departure from GAAP. The opinion paragraph should include appropriate qualifying language and should refer to the explanatory paragraph(s). The explanatory paragraph(s) should also disclose the principal effects of the matter on the financial position, results of operations and cash flows, if practicable. If the effects cannot be determined, the report should so state.

EXHIBIT 13 ♦ DEPARTURE FROM GAAP

> Independent Auditor's Report
>
> (Same first and second paragraphs as the standard report)
>
> The company has excluded, from property and debt in the accompanying balance sheets, certain lease obligations that, in our opinion, should be capitalized in order to conform with generally accepted accounting principles. If these lease obligations were capitalized, property would be increased by $_____ and $_____, long-term debt by $_____ and $_____, and retained earnings by $_____ and $_____ as of December 31, 20X2 and 20X1, respectively. Additionally, net income would be increased (decreased) by $_____ and $_____, and earnings per share would be increased (decreased) by $_____ and $_____, respectively, for the years then ended.
>
> In our opinion, except for the effects of not capitalizing certain lease obligations as discussed in the preceding paragraph, the financial statements referred to above present fairly, in all material respects, the financial position of X Company as of December 31, 20X2 and 20X1, and the results of its operations and its cash flows for the years then ended in conformity with U.S. generally accepted accounting principles.

3. INADEQUATE DISCLOSURE

a. If information, which is essential for a fair presentation of financial statements in conformity with GAAP, is not disclosed in the financial statements or accompanying notes, the auditor should express a qualified or an adverse opinion, and should provide the information in the report if practicable, unless its omission from the auditor's report is recognized as appropriate by a specific SAS.

EXHIBIT 14 ♦ REPORT QUALIFIED FOR INADEQUATE DISCLOSURE

> Independent Auditor's Report
>
> (Same first and second paragraphs as the standard report)
>
> The Company's financial statements do not disclose (describe the nature of the omitted disclosures). In our opinion, disclosure of this information is required by U.S. generally accepted accounting principles.
>
> In our opinion, except for the omission of the information discussed in the preceding paragraph,...

b. The auditor is not required to prepare a basic financial statement and include it in the report if the company's management declines to present the statement. In the case of, for example, the omission of a cash flow statement, a qualified opinion would be appropriate, with an explanatory paragraph added preceding the opinion paragraph.

EXHIBIT 15 ♦ REPORT QUALIFIED: LACKING A BASIC FINANCIAL STATEMENT

> Independent Auditor's Report
>
> We have audited the accompanying balance sheets of X Company as of December 31, 20X2 and 20X1, and the related statements of income and retained earnings for the years then ended. These financial statements are the responsibility of the Company's management. Our responsibility is to express an opinion on these financial statements based on our audit.
>
> (continued on next page)

(Same second paragraph as the standard report)

The Company declined to present a statement of cash flows for the years ended December 31, 20X2 and 20X1. Presentation of such statement summarizing the Company's operating, investing, and financing activities is required by U.S. generally accepted accounting principles.

In our opinion, except that the omission of a statement of cash flows results in an incomplete presentation as explained in the preceding paragraph, the financial statements referred to above present fairly, in all material respects, the financial position of X Company as of December 31, 20X2 and 20X1, and the results of its operations for the years then ended in conformity with U.S. generally accepted accounting principles.

4. **Accounting Changes** The auditor should evaluate a change in accounting principle to be satisfied that (a) the newly adopted accounting principle is a generally accepted accounting principle, (b) the method of accounting for the effect of the change is in conformity with GAAP, and (c) management's justification for the change is reasonable. If a change in accounting principle does **not** meet these conditions, the auditor should express a qualified opinion, or if the effect of the change is sufficiently material, an adverse opinion should be expressed.

Exhibit 16 ♦ Report Qualified: Accounting Change Not Justified by Management

Independent Auditor's Report

(Same first and second paragraphs as the standard report)

As disclosed in Note X to the financial statements, the Company adopted, in 20X2, the first-in, first-out method of accounting for its inventories, whereas it previously used the last-in, first-out method. Although use of the first-in, first-out method is in conformity with generally accepted accounting principles, in our opinion, the Company has not provided reasonable justification for making this change as required by generally accepted accounting principles.

In our opinion, except for the change in accounting principle discussed in the preceding paragraph, the financial statements referred to above present fairly, in all material respects, the financial position of X Company as of December 31, 20X2 and 20X1, and the results of its operations and its cash flows for the years then ended in conformity with U.S. generally accepted accounting principles.

B. **Adverse Opinions**
State that financial statements do not present fairly the financial position, the results of operations, or cash flows in conformity with GAAP.

1. The auditor should disclose in a separate explanatory paragraph(s) preceding the opinion paragraph of the report (a) all the substantive reasons for the adverse opinion, and (b) the principal effects of the subject matter of the adverse opinion on financial position, results of operations, and cash flows, if practicable. If the effects are not reasonably determinable, the report should so state.

2. The opinion paragraph should include a direct reference to a separate paragraph that discloses the basis for the adverse opinion.

EXHIBIT 17 ♦ ADVERSE OPINION

> Independent Auditor's Report
>
> (Same first and second paragraphs as the standard report)
>
> As discussed in Note X to the financial statements, the Company carries its property, plant and equipment accounts at appraisal values, and provides depreciation on the basis of such values. Further, the Company does not provide for income taxes with respect to differences between financial income and taxable income arising because of the use, for income tax purposes, of the installment method of reporting gross profit from certain types of sales. Generally accepted accounting principles require that property, plant, and equipment be stated at an amount not in excess of cost, reduced by depreciation based on such amount, and that deferred income taxes be provided.
>
> Because of the departures from generally accepted accounting principles identified above, as of December 31, 20X2 and 20X1, inventories have been increased $_____ and $_____ by inclusion in manufacturing overhead of depreciation in excess of that based on cost; property, plant, and equipment, less accumulated depreciation, is carried at $_____ and $_____ in excess of an amount based on the cost to the Company; and deferred income taxes of $_____ and $_____ have not been recorded, resulting in an increase of $_____ and $_____ in retained earnings and in appraisal surplus of $_____ and $_____, respectively. For the years ended December 31, 20X2 and 20X1, cost of goods sold has been increased $_____ and $_____, respectively, because of the effects of the depreciation accounting referred to above and deferred income taxes of $_____ and $_____ have not been provided, resulting in an increase in net income of $_____ and $_____, respectively.
>
> In our opinion, because of the effects of the matters discussed in the preceding paragraphs, the financial statements referred to above do not present fairly, in conformity with U.S. generally accepted accounting principles, the financial position of X Company as of December 31, 20X2 and 20X1, or the results of its operations or its cash flows for the years then ended.

C. DISCLAIMER OF OPINION

States that the auditor does not express an opinion on the financial statements. It is appropriate when the auditor has not performed an audit sufficient in scope to enable the auditor to form an opinion on the financial statements.

1. **SCOPE LIMITATION** If a scope limitation is the reason for the disclaimer, the auditor should indicate in a separate paragraph the reasons for the scope limitation. The auditor should state that the scope of the audit was not sufficient to warrant the expression of an opinion, but the auditor should **not** identify the procedures that were performed nor include the paragraph describing the characteristics of an audit (that is, the scope paragraph).

2. **MATERIAL DEPARTURES** A disclaimer of opinion should **not** be expressed when the auditor believes, on the basis of the audit, that there are material departures from GAAP.

EXHIBIT 18 ♦ DISCLAIMER OF OPINION DUE TO SCOPE LIMITATION

> Independent Auditor's Report
>
> We were engaged to audit the accompanying balance sheets of X Company as of December 31, 20X2 and 20X1, and the related statements of income, retained earnings, and cash flows for the years then ended. These financial statements are the responsibility of the Company's management.
>
> (continued on next page)

> [Second (scope) paragraph of standard report should be omitted.]
>
> The Company did not make a count of its physical inventory in 20X2 or 20X1, stated in the accompanying financial statements at $_____ as of December 31, 20X2, and at $_____ as of December 31, 20X1. Further, evidence supporting the cost of property and equipment acquired prior to December 31, 20X1, is no longer available. The Company's records do not permit the application of other auditing procedures to inventories or property and equipment.
>
> Since the Company did not take physical inventories and we were not able to apply other auditing procedures to satisfy ourselves as to inventory quantities and the cost of property and equipment, the scope of our work was not sufficient to enable us to express, and we do not express, an opinion on these financial statements.

V. Reports on Comparative Financial Statements

A. Standard Report

An auditor's standard report covers statements of the current period **and** those of one or more prior periods that are **presented** on a comparative basis. Therefore, a continuing auditor, an auditor who has audited the current period's financial statements and those of one or more immediately preceding periods, will update the report (re-express an opinion) on the individual financial statements of those prior periods. The updated opinion may differ from that previously given if circumstances warrant a change. During the audit of the current period financial statements, the auditor should be alert for circumstances or events that affect the prior-period financial statements.

Exhibit 19 ♦ Auditor's Standard Report: Comparative Financial Statements

> Independent Auditor's Report
>
> We have audited the accompanying balance sheets of X Company as of December 31, 20X2 and 20X1, and the related statements of income, retained earnings, and cash flows for the years then ended. These financial statements are the responsibility of the Company's management. Our responsibility is to express an opinion on these financial statements based on our audits.
>
> We conducted our audits in accordance with U.S. generally accepted auditing standards. Those standards require that we plan and perform the audit to obtain reasonable assurance about whether the financial statements are free of material misstatement. An audit includes examining, on a test basis, evidence supporting the amounts and disclosures in the financial statements. An audit also includes assessing the accounting principles used and significant estimates made by management, as well as evaluating the overall financial statement presentation. We believe that our audits provide a reasonable basis for our opinion.
>
> In our opinion, the financial statements referred to above present fairly, in all material respects, the financial position of X Company as of December 31, 20X2 and 20X1, and the results of its operations and its cash flows for the years then ended in conformity with U.S. generally accepted accounting principles.

B. Differing Opinions

The auditor's report on the comparative statements applies to the **individual** financial statements that are presented. Therefore, the same type of opinion is **not** required (qualified, unqualified, etc.) on all of the statements. When it is not the same, the auditor should (1) disclose all of the substantive reasons for the modified opinion (or for disclaiming an opinion) in a separate explanatory paragraph of the report, and (2) in the opinion paragraph, include an appropriate modification (or disclaimer of opinion) along with a reference to the explanation.

EXHIBIT 20 ♦ DIFFERING OPINIONS

Independent Auditor's Report

(Same first and second paragraphs as the standard report)

The Company has excluded, from property and debt in the accompanying 20X2 balance sheet, certain lease obligations that were entered into in 20X2 which, in our opinion, should be capitalized in order to conform with U.S. generally accepted accounting principles. If these lease obligations were capitalized, property would be increased by $_____, long-term debt by $_____, and retained earnings by $_____ as of December 31, 20X2, and net income and earnings per share would be increased (decreased) by $_____ and $_____, respectively, for the year then ended.

In our opinion, except for the effects on the 20X2 financial statements of not capitalizing certain lease obligations as described in the preceding paragraph, the financial statements referred to above present fairly, in all material respects, the financial position of ABC Company as of December 31, 20X2 and 20X1, and the results of its operations and its cash flows for the years then ended in conformity with U.S. generally accepted accounting principles.

C. SUBSEQUENT RESTATEMENT OF PRIOR PERIOD STATEMENTS TO CONFORM WITH GAAP

If the auditor, during the current audit, becomes aware of circumstances or events that affect the financial statements of a prior period, the auditor should consider such matters when updating the report.

EXHIBIT 21 ♦ CHANGED OPINION

Independent Auditor's Report

(Same first and second paragraphs as the standard report)

In our report dated March 1, 20X2, we expressed an opinion that the 20X1 financial statements did not fairly present financial position, results of operations, and cash flows in conformity with generally accepted accounting principles because of two departures from such principles: (1) the Company carried its property, plant and equipment at appraisal values, and provided for depreciation on the basis of such values, and (2) the Company did not provide for deferred income taxes with respect to differences between income for financial reporting purposes and taxable income. As described in Note X, the Company has changed its method of accounting for these items and restated its 20X1 financial statements to conform with generally accepted accounting principles. Accordingly, our present opinion on the 20X1 financial statements, as presented herein, is different from that expressed in our previous report.

In our opinion, the financial statements referred to above present fairly, in all material respects, the financial position of X Company as of December 31, 20X2 and 20X1, and the results of its operations and its cash flows for the years then ended in conformity with U.S. generally accepted accounting principles.

1. **UNQUALIFIED OPINION** If an auditor has previously qualified the opinion on the financial statements of a prior period because of a departure from GAAP, and the prior period financial statements are restated in the current period to conform with GAAP, the updated report of the prior period should indicate that the statements have been restated and should express an unqualified opinion with respect to the restated financial statements.

2. **DIFFERENT OPINION THAN PREVIOUS** If the auditor decides to express a different opinion than that previously expressed, the auditor should disclose all the substantive reasons for the different opinion in a separate explanatory paragraph(s) preceding the opinion paragraph of the report. The explanatory paragraph should disclose (a) the date of the auditor's previous report, (b) the type of opinion previously expressed, (c) the circumstances or events

that caused the auditor to express a different opinion, and (d) that the auditor's updated opinion on the financial statements of the prior period is different from the auditor's previous opinion on those statements.

D. REPORT OF THE PREDECESSOR AUDITOR

1. **REISSUED** The predecessor auditor should consider whether the opinion previously issued on the financial statements of the prior period is still appropriate. This should include (a) reading the financial statements of the current period, (b) comparing the statements reported on with those that are being presented for comparative purposes, (c) obtaining a letter of representation from the successor auditor as to whether the successor's audit found anything that might have a material effect on (or require disclosure in) the prior period's statements, and (d) obtaining an updating representation letter from management.

   a. **PROCEDURES** If the predecessor becomes aware of circumstances that may affect the predecessor's own previous opinion, the predecessor should inquire about the event and may want to perform tests such as reviewing the working papers of the successor auditor in regard to the matter. The predecessor must then decide whether to revise the opinion.

   b. **REPORT** When the predecessor reissues the report, the predecessor should use the same date as that of the predecessor's own previous report to avoid any implication that the predecessor examined any records, transactions, or events after that date. The predecessor should **not** refer to the work or report of the successor auditor. If the predecessor revises the report or if the financial statements are restated, the report should be dual-dated.

2. **NOT PRESENTED** If the financial statements of a prior period are presented for comparative purposes but the report of the predecessor auditor is not presented, the successor auditor should modify the introductory paragraph of the report to indicate (a) that another auditor audited the prior-period financial statements, (b) the date of the predecessor's report, (c) the type of report issued by the predecessor auditor, and (d) if the report was other than standard, and the substantive reasons therefor.

EXHIBIT 22 ♦ REPORT WHEN THE PREDECESSOR'S REPORT IS NOT PRESENTED

> We have audited the balance sheet of ABC Company as of December 31, 20X2, and the related statements of income, retained earnings, and cash flows for the year then ended. These financial statements are the responsibility of the Company's management. Our responsibility is to express an opinion on these financial statements based on our audit. The financial statements of ABC Company as of December 31, 20X1, were audited by other auditors whose report dated March 31, 20X2, expressed an unqualified opinion on those statements.
>
> (Same second paragraph as the standard report)
>
> In our opinion, the 20X2 financial statements referred to above present fairly, in all material respects, the financial position of ABC Company as of December 31, 20X2, and the results of its operations and its cash flows for the year then ended in conformity with U.S. generally accepted accounting principles.

   a. If the predecessor auditor's opinion was other than a standard report, the successor auditor should describe the nature of and the reasons for the explanatory paragraph added to the predecessor's report of the opinion qualification.

EXHIBIT 23 ♦ PREDECESSOR AUDITOR'S REPORT NOT STANDARD

> ...were audited by other auditors whose report, dated March 1, 20X2, on those statements included an explanatory paragraph that described the litigation discussed in Note X to the financial statements.

b. If the financial statements of the prior period have been restated, the introductory paragraph should indicate that a predecessor auditor reported on the financial statements of the prior period before restatement. In addition, if the successor auditor is engaged to audit and applies sufficient procedures to satisfy the appropriateness of the restatement adjustments, the successor may also state this in the report.

EXHIBIT 24 ♦ PRIOR PERIOD IS RESTATED

> We also audited the adjustments described in Note X that were applied to restate the 20X1 financial statements. In our opinion, such adjustments are appropriate and have been properly applied.

VI. SUMMARY OF VARIOUS AUDIT OPINIONS AND CORRESPONDING REPORTS

A. UNQUALIFIED

1. **ALL NECESSARY CONDITIONS FOR AN UNQUALIFIED OPINION** Standard report issued.

2. **PART OF AUDIT PERFORMED BY OTHER AUDITOR**

   a. **PRINCIPAL AUDITOR TAKES RESPONSIBILITY FOR OTHER AUDITOR'S WORK** Standard report issued.

   b. **PRINCIPAL AUDITOR DOES NOT TAKE RESPONSIBILITY FOR OTHER AUDITOR'S WORK** Make reference to other auditor and clearly indicate division of responsibility (do not name unless other gives permission and other's report is included). Introductory, scope, and opinion paragraphs should all be changed to reflect this. (No explanatory paragraph.)

3. **JUSTIFIABLE DEPARTURE FROM GAAP (RARE)** Add explanatory paragraph. Describe departure, approximate effects, and reasons why compliance would result in a misleading statement.

4. **UNCERTAINTIES**

   a. **REMOTE** Standard report issued.

   b. **PROBABLE** Explanatory paragraph if not estimable; if estimable, management should accrue, or this would be a departure from GAAP (resulting in a qualified or adverse opinion).

5. **DOUBT ABOUT ABILITY TO CONTINUE AS A GOING CONCERN** Explanatory paragraph.

6. **LACK OF CONSISTENCY**

   a. **IF MATERIAL EFFECT** Explanatory paragraph added.

   b. **IF IMMATERIAL** Standard report issued.

7. **EMPHASIS OF A MATTER** Explanatory paragraph added. When an explanatory paragraph is necessary and it doesn't impact the opinion, it should be placed **after** the opinion paragraph.

EXHIBIT 25 ♦ CONDITIONS REQUIRING MODIFICATION OF REPORT

Reasons for Modification*	Opinion Expressed	Explanatory Paragraph	Opinion Paragraph
GAAP Departure	Qualified or Adverse	**Before** opinion paragraph to explain the departure and amount(s)	**Modified** to provide qualifying language and refer to explanatory paragraph(s)
Inadequate Disclosure	Qualified or Adverse	**Before** opinion paragraph to explain missing disclosure	**Modified** to provide qualifying language and refer to explanatory paragraph(s)
Scope Limitation	Qualified or Disclaimer	**Before** opinion paragraph to explain scope limitation and potential monetary effects	**Modified** to provide qualifying language or to provide disclaimer**
Uncertainty	Unqualified (disclaimer is allowed)	**After** opinion paragraph to describe uncertainty and refer reader to the financial statement footnote***	**Not** modified
Going Concern Uncertainty	Unqualified (disclaimer is allowed)	**After** opinion paragraph to describe going concern using wording "substantial doubt" about entity's ability to continue as a going concern and refer reader to the financial statement footnote	**Not** modified
Consistency Violation (if properly accounted for and disclosed, if not, treat as GAAP departure)	Unqualified	**After** opinion paragraph describing accounting GAAP departure change and referring reader to financial statement footnote	**Not** modified
Emphasis of a Matter	Unqualified	**After** opinion paragraph describing matter and referring reader to financial statement footnote	**Not** modified
Reliance on Another Auditor	Unqualified	Division of responsibility indicated in introductory paragraph including significance of portion of entity done by other auditor	**Modified** to refer to other auditor
Changed Opinion on Prior Period Information	Unqualified	**After** opinion paragraph to describe reason for different opinion	**Not** modified

NOTE: When not qualifying an opinion, an explanatory paragraph comes after the opinion paragraph (which is not modified). When the opinion is other than unqualified and an explanatory paragraph is included, it comes before the opinion.

* Assuming item is material

** Qualified opinion requires modification of second paragraph (using "except for" language). Disclaimer requires modification of introductory paragraph and the second (scope) paragraph is NOT included.

*** This explanatory paragraph is optional per SAS 79.

B. QUALIFIED

An explanatory paragraph is added preceding the opinion paragraph; words such as except for or with the exception of are used.

1. **SCOPE LIMITATION** If significant, disclaim; otherwise, explanatory paragraph preceding opinion paragraph added and referred to in scope and opinion paragraphs. This does not refer the reader to footnotes for details.

2. **MATERIAL DEPARTURE FROM GAAP** Qualified or adverse depending on materiality, significance of item to entity, pervasiveness of misstatement, and effect of misstatement on statements taken as a whole. If qualified, explanatory paragraph added preceding opinion paragraph and referred to in opinion.

3. **INADEQUATE DISCLOSURE—QUALIFIED OR ADVERSE** Explanatory paragraph added and referred to in opinion.

4. **INAPPROPRIATE ACCOUNTING CHANGES—QUALIFIED OR ADVERSE** Explanatory paragraph preceding opinion paragraph added and referred to in opinion.

C. ADVERSE

Explanatory paragraph **preceding** opinion paragraph. Explanatory paragraph added and referred to in adverse opinion.

D. DISCLAIMER

Explanatory paragraph **preceding** "opinion" paragraph. If a scope limitation, scope paragraph omitted, explanatory paragraph added and referred to in the disclaimer of opinion paragraph.

E. COMPARATIVE

1. **QUALIFIED PRIOR YEAR, STANDARD IN CURRENT YEAR** Explanatory paragraph preceding opinion, referred to in opinion paragraph: "except for..."

2. **QUALIFIED PRIOR YEAR, CHANGE MADE IN CURRENT YEAR TO CONFORM TO GAAP** Explanatory paragraph preceding opinion, standard opinion paragraph.

F. PREDECESSOR AUDITOR

If predecessor report is not presented with comparative statements, modify introductory paragraph, no change to scope paragraph, and only express opinion on audited (current year, by successor) statements.

VII. TIMING ISSUES

A. DATING THE AUDITOR'S REPORT

1. **GENERAL RULE** The date of the report is the date the auditor completes the field work. The auditor does **not** have responsibility to make any inquiries or to conduct any audit procedures after this date (with the exception of filings under the Securities Act of 1933).

2. **SUBSEQUENT EVENTS**

   a. **ADJUSTMENT** If the auditor becomes aware of an event requiring **adjustment** (Type I subsequent event) of the financial statements that occurred after the date of the report but before it is issued, the statements should be adjusted or the opinion should be qualified. If the adjustment is made without any disclosure in the financial statements, the report is still dated as of the last day of field work. If the adjustment is made and is disclosed in the financial statements or if the audit report is qualified because of a lack of adjustment, the auditor may **dual-date** the report by dating the report as of the last day of field work except for the subsequent event which is dated later.

   b. **DISCLOSURE** The auditor may become aware of a new event requiring **disclosure** (Type II subsequent event) (such as a lawsuit filed after the balance sheet date but before the financial statements are issued.) If disclosure is not made, the audit opinion would be qualified. If disclosure is made, the auditor may dual-date the report. If dual-dating is used, the responsibility for any events that occurred after the auditor completed the field work is **limited** to the particular subsequent event that is dual-dated. If the auditor chooses, the later date may be used for the entire report.

However, the auditor's responsibility for events occurring after the completion of field work will then extend to the later date.

3. **Reissuance** When an auditor reissues a report, the **original** report date should be used. This implies that there has been no audit past this date. When events that occurred subsequent to the date of the report require modification of the statements or the opinion, a **dual-date** is appropriate. If events that occurred subsequent to the date of the report only require disclosure in the financial statements, the events may be disclosed in a note to the statements and the date of the original report may be used.

B. **Subsequent Events**

These are events or transactions having a **material effect** on the financial statements that occur **after** the balance sheet date, but **before** the financial statements and the auditor's report are issued.

1. **Types**

a. **Require Adjustment** Subsequent events that provide additional evidence about conditions that **existed** at the date of the balance sheet and affect the estimates used in preparing the financial statements require adjustment of the financial statements. Examples include a loss on an uncollectible trade account because a customer went bankrupt shortly after the end of the period (this indicates that the customer's financial position at the balance sheet date was not adequate to meet obligations), and the settlement of litigation for an amount different from the amount recorded in the accounts (as long as the reason for the litigation occurred prior to the balance sheet date).

b. **Do Not Require Adjustment** Subsequent events that provide evidence about conditions that did **not** exist at the balance sheet date but arose after that date, do not require adjustment of the financial statements. The conditions should be **disclosed** if their disclosure is required to keep the financial statements from being misleading. In some cases, pro forma statements may be prepared. Occasionally, the auditor may decide to include an explanatory paragraph in the report to draw the attention of the reader to the event. Examples of events requiring disclosure (but not adjustment) include (a) sale of a bond or capital stock issue, (b) purchase of a business, (c) settlement of litigation arising from events that occurred subsequent to the balance sheet date, (d) loss of plant or inventories as a result of a fire or flood, and (e) losses on receivables resulting from conditions that arose after the balance sheet date (such as a customer's major casualty loss).

2. **Reissuance of Financial Statements** Events that occur **between** the time of the original issuance of the statements and the time of reissuance of the statements (for example, in reports filed with a regulatory agency) should **not** result in an adjustment of the financial statements unless the adjustment would meet the criteria for the correction of an error or the criteria for prior-period adjustments.

3. **Auditing Procedures in the Subsequent Period** The subsequent period extends from the balance sheet date to the date of the auditor's report.

a. Certain audit procedures should be performed after the balance sheet date to assure a proper cutoff and to evaluate the balances of certain asset and liability accounts.

b. Additional auditing procedures should be applied to the period after the balance sheet date to identify subsequent events that may require adjustment or disclosure. These generally include (1) reading the latest interim financial statements and comparing them with the financial statements being reported on, (2) discussing with management the existence of substantial contingent liabilities, any significant change in stockholders' equity items, the current status of financial statement items that were accounted for on a tentative basis, and the existence of any unusual adjustments made after the balance sheet date, (3) reading the minutes of the board of directors' and stockholders' meetings, (4) inquiring of the client's legal counsel about litigation, claims, and assessments, (5) obtaining a letter of representation from management, dated as of the date of the auditor's report, as to whether any subsequent events occurred that would require adjustment to or disclosure in the statements, and (6) making any additional inquiries and performing any procedures that are considered necessary by the auditor.

C. **Subsequent Discovery of Facts Existing at the Date of the Auditor's Report**
The auditor may, after the date of the report, become aware of facts that existed at that date and that might have affected the report had the auditor been aware of them.

1. **Responsibility** The auditor does not have any obligation to perform auditing procedures or make inquiries after the report date **unless** the auditor becomes aware of this type of information. When the auditor becomes aware of information that relates to financial statements previously reported on by the auditor, but that was **not** known at the date of the report, and that is of such a nature and from such a source that the auditor would have investigated it had the auditor been aware of it during the audit, the auditor should, as soon as practicable, determine whether the information is reliable and whether the facts existed at the date of the report.

   a. The auditor should discuss the matter with the appropriate level of the client's management, and request cooperation in the investigation into the matter.

   b. The auditor should consult an attorney when encountering these circumstances because of legal implications that may be involved, including the confidentiality of auditor-client communications.

2. **Preventing Future Reliance on the Report** When the subsequently discovered information is found both to be reliable and to have existed at the report date, the auditor should take action if the nature and effect of the matter are such that the report would have been affected by the information had it been known, and such that the auditor believes there are persons currently relying on, or likely to rely on, the financial statements. To prevent future reliance on the report, the auditor should advise the client to make appropriate disclosure of the newly discovered information, and the effect of the facts to the persons relying on, or likely to rely on, the statements.

   a. **Client Cooperates** If the client cooperates, the method used will depend on the circumstances.

      (1) **Revise and Reissue** The statements should be revised and reissued if the effect of the subsequently discovered information can be determined **promptly**. The reasons for the revision will usually be described in a note to the statements and referred to in the auditor's report.

      (2) **Statements of a Subsequent Period** If the issuance of financial statements and the auditor's report for a subsequent period is imminent, appropriate revision can be made in such statements.

      (3) **Notification by Client** If the effect on the statements cannot be promptly determined but it appears the statements will be revised after investigation, the client should notify persons who are relying (or are likely to rely) on the statements and report that they should not do so, and that revised statements and the report will be issued when the investigation is complete.

   b. **Client Does Not Cooperate** If the client does not cooperate, the auditor should notify the board of directors that unless the client cooperates, the auditor will (a) notify the client that the auditor's report cannot be associated with the financial statements,

(b) notify regulatory agencies that the auditor's report should not be relied upon, and (c) notify each person that the auditor knows is relying on the statements and report that they should no longer do so.

3. Guidelines for Disclosure to Other Parties

a. When the auditor must make a disclosure and the auditor has been able to make a satisfactory investigation and determine that the information is reliable, the disclosure should include a description of the nature of the subsequently acquired information and describe the **effect** of the information on the financial statements and the report. The disclosure should be as factual and precise as possible, but it should not contain any comment on the conduct or motive of any person.

b. When the auditor has been prevented from making a satisfactory investigation, the auditor need not provide detailed information but can indicate that additional information, that the client has not helped substantiate, has come to the auditor's attention, and if true, the auditor believes the report should no longer be relied upon. No such disclosure should be made unless the auditor believes that the financial statements are likely to be misleading.

D. Consideration of Omitted Procedures After the Report Date

1. Responsibility The auditor may conclude, after the date of the report, that one or more auditing procedures considered necessary at that date were omitted from the audit, even though there is no indication that the financial statements are not fairly presented in conformity with GAAP or another comprehensive basis of accounting. Although the auditor does not have any responsibility to perform a retrospective review of the work performed, the omission of a necessary auditing procedure may be disclosed when the reports and working papers relating to the engagement are subjected to post-issuance review (e.g., a firm's internal inspection program or peer review).

2. Assessment Upon concluding that a necessary auditing procedure has been omitted, the auditor should assess the importance of the omitted procedure to the auditor's present ability to support a previously expressed opinion regarding the financial statements in question. This assessment can be aided by (1) reviewing the working papers, (2) discussing the audit circumstances with engagement personnel and others, and (3) reevaluating the overall scope of the audit. The results of other procedures that were applied may tend to compensate for or make less important the omitted procedure.

3. Course of Action If the auditor concludes that the omission of the necessary procedure impairs the present ability to support the previously expressed opinion, and the auditor believes that there are persons currently relying, or likely to rely, on the report, the auditor should proceed as follows:

a. Previously Omitted Procedures Can Be Applied The auditor should promptly apply the omitted procedure(s) or alternative procedures that would provide a satisfactory basis for the auditor's opinion. If, as a result, the auditor becomes aware of facts existing at the date of the report that would have affected that report had the auditor been aware of them, then the auditor should take steps to prevent future reliance on the report.

b. Previously Omitted Procedures Can Not Be Applied The auditor should consult an attorney to determine an appropriate course of action concerning responsibilities to the client, regulatory authorities, if any, having jurisdiction over the client, and persons relying, or likely to rely, on the report.

VIII. Association With Financial Statements (AU 504, SAS 26)

A. Objective

The Fourth Standard of Reporting seeks to avoid any misunderstanding as to the responsibility the accountant is assuming when his or her name is associated with financial statements. The objective is to provide reporting guidance to a CPA who is associated with the audited or unaudited financial statements of a public entity or with the audited financial statements of a nonpublic entity. [Statements on Standards for Accounting and Review Services (SSARS) apply to the unaudited financial statements of a nonpublic entity.]

Exhibit 26 ♦ The Fourth Standard of Reporting

> "...In all cases where an auditor's name is associated with financial statements, the report should contain a clear-cut indication of the character of the auditor's work, and the degree of responsibility the auditor is taking."

B. Association

The CPA is associated with an entity's financial statements when the CPA (1) has agreed to the use of his or her name in a report, document, or written communication that contains the financial statements and/or (2) submits financial statements that the CPA has prepared (or assisted in preparing) to the client or to others (even if the CPA does not append his or her name to the financial statements). Association does **not** occur when the CPA prepares data, such as tax returns, solely for submission to taxing authorities since these do not constitute financial statements.

C. Disclaimer of Opinion on Unaudited Financial Statements

When associated with a **public** entity's financial statements that the CPA has **not** audited **or** reviewed, the CPA should issue the disclaimer shown in Exhibit 27. Note that this disclaimer is different from a disclaimer of opinion due to a scope limitation discussed earlier.

Exhibit 27 ♦ Disclaimer

> The accompanying balance sheet of X Company as of December 31, 20X1, and the related statements of income, retained earnings, and cash flows for the year then ended were not audited by us and, accordingly, we do not express an opinion on them.

1. **Location** Disclaimer may accompany, or may be placed directly on, the unaudited financial statements.
2. **Markings** Each page of the statement should be marked as *unaudited.*
3. **Responsibility** CPA's only responsibility is to read the financial statements for obvious material misstatements.
4. **Procedures** The CPA should **not** describe any procedures that may have been applied, since to do so might give the impression that the CPA audited or reviewed the financial statements.
5. **Inclusion of Name** When a CPA learns that a client who is a public entity plans to include the CPA's name in a client-prepared written communication that will contain financial statements that the CPA has not audited or reviewed, the CPA should ask (a) that his or her name **not** be used or (b) that the client clearly **mark** the financial statements as *unaudited* and that a notation be made that the auditor does not express an opinion on them. If the client refuses, the CPA may need to consult legal counsel as to appropriate actions.

D. Disclaimer of Opinion on Unaudited OCBOA Financial Statements

1. **Modification of Disclaimer** The unaudited disclaimer applies except that the identification of the financial statements should be modified to conform to SAS 62, *Special Reports.*

Exhibit 28 ♦ OCBOA Financial Statements

> The accompanying statement of assets and liabilities resulting from cash transactions of XYZ Corporation as of December 31, 20X1, and the related statement of revenues collected and expenses paid during the year then ended were not audited by us and, accordingly, we do not express an opinion on them.

2. **Note to Financial Statements** Should describe the difference between the basis of presentation and GAAP. The monetary effect of such differences does not need to be stated.

E. Disclaimer of Opinion When the CPA Is Not Independent

The Second General Standard requires independence in mental attitude. Since the CPA cannot be in accordance with GAAS if the CPA is not independent, the CPA should disclaim an opinion and clearly state that he or she is not independent (the CPA should **not** give the reasons for this lack of independence).

Exhibit 29 ♦ Lack of Independence

> We are not independent with respect to XYZ Company, and the accompanying balance sheet as of December 31, 20X1, and the related statements of income, retained earnings, and cash flows for the year then ended were not audited by us and, accordingly, we do not express an opinion on them.

1. **Nonpublic Entity** The CPA should follow SSARS when the financial statements are those of a nonpublic entity.

2. **Public Entity** Paragraphs 1. through 4. of C., above, should be followed except that the disclaimer should be modified so that it clearly indicates the CPA is not independent. The reasons for lack of independence should **not** be described.

F. Circumstances Requiring a Modified Disclaimer

If the CPA feels the unaudited financial statements do not conform to GAAP (which includes adequate disclosure), the CPA should ask the client to revise the statements. If the client refuses, the CPA should describe the departure in a disclaimer by (1) specifically referring to the nature of the departure and (2) if practicable, stating the effects of the departure on the financial statements or including the information that is needed in order to provide adequate disclosure.

1. If the effects of the departure cannot be reasonably determined, the CPA should state this in the disclaimer. In the case of inadequate disclosure, it may not be practicable for the CPA to include the omitted disclosures in the disclaimer.

2. If the client refuses to revise the statements or accept the disclaimer describing the departure, the CPA should refuse to be associated with the statements. The CPA may find it necessary to withdraw from the engagement.

G. Audited and Unaudited Financial Statements Presented in Comparative Form

1. **Documents Filed With the SEC** Unaudited financial statements presented in comparative form with audited financial statements should be clearly marked "unaudited." The auditor's report should not refer to the unaudited statements.

2. **Documents Other Than Those Filed With the SEC** The unaudited financial statements should be clearly marked to indicate they have not been audited and either (a) the report on the prior period should be reissued or (b) the current period's report should contain a separate paragraph that describes the responsibility assumed for the financial statements of the prior period. In either case, the CPA should consider any information that has come to his or her attention during the CPA's current engagement that would help in evaluating the current form and presentation of the prior-period information.

   a. **Current Period Financial Statements Unaudited, Prior Period Financial Statements Audited** If a separate paragraph is to be used, it should state (1) the prior-period's statements were previously audited, (2) the date of the previous report, (3) the type of opinion that was previously expressed, (4) if it was not unqualified, the substantive reasons for this, and (5) that no auditing procedures have been performed after the date of the previous report.

   Exhibit 30 ♦ Prior Audited, Current Unaudited

   > The financial statements for the year ended December 31, 20X1, were audited by us (other accountants) and we (they) expressed an unqualified opinion on them in our (their) report dated March 1, 20X2, but we (they) have not performed any auditing procedures since that date.

   b. **Prior Period Financial Statements Were Not Audited** If a separate paragraph is to be used, it should (1) state the service that was performed in the prior period, (2) state the date of the report on that service, (3) describe any material modifications noted in that report, and (4) state that the scope of the service was **less** than that of an audit and, therefore, does not provide a basis for the expression of an opinion on the financial statements taken as a whole. When the financial statements are those of a public entity, the separate paragraph should include a disclaimer of opinion or a description of a review. When the prior period statements are for a nonpublic entity and were compiled or reviewed, the separate paragraph should contain an appropriate description of the compilation or review. The unaudited financial statements should be clearly marked to indicate their status.

   Exhibit 31 ♦ Review Performed on Financial Statements of the Prior Period and Current Year's Statements Audited

   > The 20X1 financial statements were reviewed by us (other accountants) and our (their) report thereon, dated March 1, 20X2, stated we (they) were not aware of any material modifications that should be made to those statements for them to be in conformity with generally accepted accounting principles. However, a review is substantially less in scope than an audit and does not provide a basis for the expression of an opinion on the financial statements taken as a whole.

   Exhibit 32 ♦ Compiled Prior Period Financial Statements

   > The 20X1 financial statements were compiled by us (other accountants) and our (their) report thereon, dated March 1, 20X2, stated we (they) did not audit or review those financial statements and, accordingly, express no opinion or other form of assurance on them.

H. Negative Assurance

The CPA should **not** include statements in the disclaimer that would give negative assurance **except** as specifically permitted by the AICPA. (One permissible area is letters for underwriters.)

IX. Consideration of an Entity's Ability to Continue as a Going Concern (AU 341, SAS 59)

A. Responsibility

Continuation of an entity as a going concern is assumed in financial reporting in the absence of significant information to the contrary. The auditor is responsible for evaluating information gathered during the audit to determine whether there is substantial doubt about the entity's ability to continue as a going concern for a reasonable period of time. (A reasonable period of time is defined as a period not to exceed one year from the date of the financial statements.)

1. The auditor's evaluation is based on knowledge of events and relevant conditions preceding or existing at the time of the field work.

2. Key information to be considered includes the entity's inability to meet its obligations in a timely manner without substantial disposal of assets outside the normal course of business, restructuring of debt, externally forced revisions of operations, or similar actions. Some examples of nonfinancial factors include the possible loss of key personnel, suppliers, and/or major customers.

B. Audit Procedures

Audit procedures do not need to be designed specifically to identify conditions and events that, when considered in the aggregate, may indicate substantial doubt about the entity's ability to continue as a going concern. The results of auditing procedures designed and performed to achieve other audit objectives should be sufficient for that purpose. The following are examples of procedures that may identify such conditions and events:

1. Analytical procedures.

2. Review of subsequent events.

3. Review of compliance with the terms of debt and loan agreements.

4. Reading of minutes of meetings of stockholders, board of directors, and major committees of the board.

5. Inquiry of an entity's legal counsel about litigation, claims, and assessments.

6. Confirmation with related and third parties of the details of arrangements to provide or maintain financial support.

C. Indications

Procedures such as those listed above may identify conditions and events that, when considered in the aggregate, indicate that substantial doubt may exist. Such conditions and events include the following:

1. **Negative Trends** For example, working capital deficiencies, recurring operating losses, negative cash flows from operating activities, or adverse key financial ratios.

2. **Other Indications of Possible Financial Difficulties** For example, default on loan or similar agreements, arrearages in dividends, denial of usual trade credit from suppliers, restructuring of debt, noncompliance with statutory capital requirements, need to seek new sources or methods of financing, or to dispose of substantial assets.

3. **Internal Matters** For example, work stoppages or other labor difficulties, substantial dependence on the success of a particular project, uneconomic long-term commitments, or need to significantly revise operations.

4. **External Matters That Have Occurred** For example, legal proceedings, legislation, or similar matters that might jeopardize an entity's ability to operate; loss of a key franchise,

license, or patent; loss of a principal customer or supplier; or uninsured or underinsured catastrophe such as a drought, earthquake, or flood.

D. **CONCLUSIONS**

If, after completing the audit, the auditor finds that conditions and events exist that, when considered in the aggregate, indicate that there could be substantial doubt about the entity's ability to continue as a going concern for a reasonable period of time, the following steps should be taken:

1. The auditor should obtain any additional information available about the conditions and events or about mitigating factors including management's plans.

2. The auditor must consider management's plans in order to evaluate the likelihood of successful implementation.

3. The auditor should consider the adequacy of the disclosure of the doubt about the entity's ability to continue and include an explanatory paragraph following the opinion paragraph in the audit report.

4. If the auditor concludes that substantial doubt does **not** exist, the auditor should consider the disclosure of the information that triggered concern about the entity's ability to continue as a going concern for a reasonable period of time and outline mitigating circumstances including management's plans.

E. **MANAGEMENT'S PLANS**

Management's plans for dealing with the adverse effects of the conditions and events must be considered when there is substantial doubt regarding the entity's ability to continue. The auditor should obtain information about the plans and decide whether it is likely the adverse effects will be mitigated for a reasonable period of time and that such plans can be effectively implemented. The auditor's consideration relating to management's plans may include the following.

1. **DISPOSE OF ASSETS**

   a. Restrictions on disposal of assets, such as covenants limiting such transactions in loan or similar agreements or encumbrances against assets.

   b. Apparent marketability of assets that management plans to sell.

   c. Possible direct or indirect effects of disposal of assets.

2. **BORROW MONEY OR RESTRUCTURE DEBT**

   a. Availability of debt financing, including existing or committed credit arrangements, such as lines of credit or arrangements for factoring receivables or sale-leaseback of assets.

   b. Existing or committed arrangements to restructure or subordinate debt or to guarantee loans to the entity.

   c. Existing restrictions on additional borrowing or the sufficiency of available collateral.

3. **REDUCE OR DELAY EXPENDITURES**

   a. Apparent feasibility of plans to reduce overhead or administrative expenditures, to postpone maintenance or research and development projects, or to lease rather than purchase assets.

   b. Possible direct or indirect effects of reduced or delayed expenditures.

4. Increase Ownership Equity

a. Apparent feasibility of plans to increase ownership equity, including existing or committed arrangements to raise additional capital.

b. Existing or committed arrangements to reduce current dividend requirements or to accelerate cash distributions from affiliates or other investors.

F. Prospective Financial Information
When prospective financial information is significant to management's plans, the auditor should request management to provide that information and should consider the adequacy of support for significant assumptions underlying that information. The auditor should give particular attention to assumptions that are (1) material to the prospective financial statements, (2) especially sensitive or susceptible to change, or (3) inconsistent with historical trends. The auditor's consideration should include reading the information and the underlying assumptions, comparing the prospective information in prior periods with actual results, and comparing prospective information for the current period with actual results to date.

G. Disclosure
If the auditor concludes that substantial doubt about the entity's ability to continue as a going concern exists, the auditor must consider disclosure of the conditions or events in the financial statements. Information that might be disclosed include the following:

1. Pertinent conditions and events giving rise to the assessment of substantial doubt about the entity's ability to continue as a going concern for a reasonable period of time.

2. The possible effects of such conditions and events.

3. Management's evaluation of the significance of those conditions and events and any mitigating factors.

4. Possible discontinuance of operations.

5. Management's plans (including relevant prospective financial information).

6. Information about the recoverability or classification of recorded asset amounts or the amounts or classification of liabilities.

H. Audit Report
The audit report should include an explanatory paragraph following the opinion paragraph if the auditor concludes that substantial doubt about the entity's ability to continue as a going concern does exist. If the auditor concludes that the entity's disclosures regarding its ability to continue as a going concern for a reasonable time are inadequate, misleading, or a departure from GAAP, a qualified or an adverse opinion should be issued. SAS 77 prohibits the use of conditional language regarding the entity's ability to continue as a going concern.

1. **Inappropriate Statement** "If XYZ Company is unable to renegotiate the labor contract, there may be substantial doubt about XYZ Company's ability to continue as a going concern."

2. **Appropriate Statement** SAS 77 presents the following example of an appropriate statement: "The accompanying financial statements have been prepared assuming that the Company will continue as a going concern. As discussed in Note X to the financial statements, the Company has suffered recurring losses from operations and has a net capital deficiency that raise substantial doubt about its ability to continue as a going concern. Management's plans in regard to these matters are also described in Note X. The financial statements do not include any adjustments that might result from the outcome of this uncertainty."

I. COMPARISON WITH PRIOR FINANCIAL STATEMENTS
Substantial doubt about an entity's ability to continue as a going concern that arose in the current period should not affect the auditor's report on the financial statements of prior periods used for comparison with current financial statements. If substantial doubt existed in the prior period, but has been alleviated in the current period, the explanatory paragraph following the opinion paragraph in the auditor's report should not be repeated.

J. FUTURE OCCURRENCES
The auditor is not expected to predict future conditions or events. If an entity ceases to exist within a year of receiving an audit report which does not refer to substantial doubt about the entity's ability to continue as a going concern, it does not necessarily indicate an inadequate performance by the auditor. The absence of a reference to substantial doubt should not be interpreted as an assurance of the entity's ability to continue as a going concern.

X. OTHER INFORMATION IN DOCUMENTS CONTAINING AUDITED FINANCIAL STATEMENTS (AU 550)

A. APPLICABILITY
Applies to (1) annual reports for owners of the company, annual reports of charitable organizations that are distributed to the public, and annual reports filed with regulatory authorities under the Securities Exchange Act of 1934 or (2) other documents the auditor devotes attention to at the client's request. This section does not apply to reports filed under the Securities Act of 1933 or to other information on which the auditor is engaged to express an opinion.

B. RESPONSIBILITIES
Auditors' responsibility does **not** extend beyond the financial information that has been identified in the report. The auditor has **no** obligation to perform any procedures to corroborate other information that is contained in documents (e.g., annual report) that contain the financial statements the auditor is reporting on. However, the auditor should read the information and consider whether there appear to be any material inconsistencies between the other data (or its presentation) and the financial statements.

1. **INCONSISTENCY** When the auditor concludes that a material inconsistency exists, the auditor must decide whether the financial statements, the report, or both require revision. If the auditor decides that they do not, but that the other information does require revision, the client should be requested to revise the other information. If the client refuses, the auditor should consider revising the report to describe the material inconsistency, withholding the use of the report in the document, and, possibly, withdrawing from the engagement.

2. **MISSTATEMENT** While reading the other information, the auditor may become aware of information the auditor believes is a material misstatement of fact although it is not a material inconsistency. The matter should be discussed with the client. If the auditor continues to feel there is a material misstatement, the auditor should propose that the client consult with some other party such as its legal counsel. If the auditor still is not satisfied, consideration should be given to notifying the client of these views in writing and consulting with legal counsel.

C. PUBLIC COMPUTER NETWORKS
Electronic sites on public computer networks (for instance, the SEC's EDGAR system or the World Wide Web area of the Internet) are a means of information distribution and are **not** documents under AU §550 criteria. Entities may include annual reports and general company information (press releases, promotional material, et cetera). The auditor is not required to read other information on these sites or to consider its consistency with the audited financial statements.

XI. REQUIRED SUPPLEMENTARY INFORMATION (AU 558, SAS 52)

A. APPLICABILITY
Some FASB and GASB requirements call for supplementary information outside of the basic financial statements. SAS 52 applies to an audit conducted according to GAAS of financial statements

that are included in a document that should contain such information. It does **not** apply if the auditor has been engaged to audit the supplementary information.

1. **Procedures Applied** Although not required to do so, a company may voluntarily decide to include supplementary information the FASB or the GASB requires of others in a document of its own that contains audited financial statements. In this situation, SAS 52 applies unless (a) the client clearly indicates that the auditor has not applied the procedures that are contained in this Statement or (b) the auditor includes a disclaimer on the information in the report on the audited financial statements.

2. **Procedures Not Applied** *Other Information in Documents Containing Audited Financial Statements* (AU 550, SAS 8), applies when the information is included voluntarily, but the auditor does not apply the procedures described in SAS 52.

B. Information Outside of the Financial Statements

While GAAS does not require the auditor to audit information that is outside the basic financial statements, the auditor's responsibility with respect to this information depends on the information and the documents in which they appear. For example, SAS 8 applies to other information that is included in annual reports but not required by the FASB.

C. Required by the FASB or GASB

This information is unique from other types of information presented outside of the basic financial statements because (1) the FASB or the GASB consider the information to be an essential part of financial reporting and (2) guidelines for measuring and presenting the information are established. Therefore, the auditor should apply certain limited procedures to the supplementary information. Any deficiencies in, or omission of, such information should be reported.

1. **Procedures** The auditor should first consider whether the FASB or the GASB requires supplementary information in the circumstances. If so, the auditor should ordinarily

   a. Inquire of management about the methods used in preparing the information. This includes (1) whether FASB or GASB prescribed guidelines were followed in measuring and presenting the information, (2) whether there has been a change (from the prior period) in the methods used in measuring and presenting the information (and if so, the reasons why), and (3) any significant assumptions or interpretations that underlie the measurement or presentation.

   b. Compare the information for consistency with (1) the responses management gives to inquiries, (2) the audited financial statements, and (3) other knowledge that was obtained during the audit engagement.

   c. Consider whether representations in the supplementary information required by the FASB or the GASB should be included in specific written representations from management gathered per SAS 85 (AU 333), *Management Representations*.

   d. Apply additional procedures if prescribed by other Statements for specific types of supplementary information required by the FASB or GASB.

   e. Make additional inquiries if the auditor feels the information gathered through the foregoing procedures may not meet the guidelines.

2. **Circumstances That Require Reporting** The auditor usually will **not** refer to the supplementary information or to the auditor's limited procedures in the audit report, since the auditor has not audited the information and it is not a required part of the basic financial statements. Additional paragraphs that might be included in the auditor's report are presented below.

a. **Explanatory Paragraph** An explanatory paragraph should be added to the report if (1) supplementary information required by the FASB or GASB is omitted (the auditor does not need to present the information), (2) the auditor feels that the measurement or presentation is materially different from that prescribed by the FASB or GASB, (3) the auditor cannot complete the prescribed procedures, or (4) the auditor is unable to remove substantial doubts about whether the supplementary information conforms to prescribed guidelines.

Exhibit 33 ♦ Omission of Required Supplementary Information

> The (Company or Government Unit) has not presented (describe the supplementary information required by the FASB or GASB in the circumstances) that the (Financial or Governmental) Accounting Standards Board has determined is necessary to supplement, although not required to be part of, the basic financial statements.

Exhibit 34 ♦ Material Departures From Guidelines

> The (specifically identify the supplementary information) on page XX is not a required part of the basic financial statements, and we did not audit and do not express an opinion on such information. However, we have applied certain limited procedures, which consisted principally of inquiries of management regarding the methods of measurement and presentation of the supplementary information. As a result of such limited procedures, we believe that the (specifically identify the supplementary information) is not in conformity with guidelines established by the Financial (or Governmental) Accounting Standards Board because (describe the material departure[s] from the FASB or GASB guidelines).

Exhibit 35 ♦ Prescribed Procedures Not Completed

> The (specifically identify the supplementary information) on page XX is not a required part of the basic financial statements, and we did not audit and do not express an opinion on such information. Further, we were unable to apply to the information certain procedures prescribed by professional standards because (state the reasons).

b. **Effect on Opinion** The occurrence of any of these four circumstances will not affect the auditor's opinion on the basic financial statements since the supplementary information does not affect the standards that apply to the basic statements.

c. **Facts Known to the Auditor** Even if the auditor cannot complete the prescribed procedures, the auditor may feel that the supplementary information has not been properly measured and/or presented. In this case, the auditor should suggest appropriate revision and, if not revised, the auditor should describe the nature of any material departure(s) in the audit report.

d. **Client Disclosure** The auditor should expand the report to include a disclaimer on the supplementary information if the client includes statements with the supplementary information that the auditor performed some procedures on the information, but fails to state that an opinion is not expressed by the auditor on the information.

e. **Presentation of Supplementary Information** Generally, supplementary information required by the FASB or GASB should be presented distinct from the audited financial statements and should be separately identified from other information outside of the financial statements (and which is not required by the FASB or GASB).

- If management chooses to include the supplementary information in the basic financial statements, the information should be clearly marked as unaudited. If it is not so marked, the audit report should be expanded to include a disclaimer on the supplementary information.

XII. Segment Information (AU 435)

A. Financial Reporting

SFAS 131 requires public business entities (and encourages nonpublic and nonprofit entities) to use a decision-maker focus to identify operating segments and to assess financial information regarding those segments. SFAS 131 also requires disclosure of information about these entities' goods and services, geographic locations, and major customers.

B. Impact on Auditing Procedures

The auditor performing a financial statement audit in accordance with GAAS considers segment information, as other informative disclosures, in relation to the financial statements taken as a whole, and is not required to apply auditing procedures that would be necessary to express a separate opinion on the segment information.

1. **Materiality** The dollar magnitude of segment information is related to the financial statements taken as a whole, along with qualitative judgments. For instance, a distortion of trends among segments, although quantitatively immaterial, could be qualitatively material.

2. **Procedures** During planning, the auditor identifies the functional chief operating decision maker (CODM) as well as obtains an understanding of the entity's method of determining segments for internal reports and any differences between systems used to generate internal reports (used to budget and measure results of operating segments) and external reports. Beyond procedures normally applied in a financial statement audit, the auditor considers applying the following procedures to segment information.

   a. Ask management about its methods of determining segment information, and assess the reasonableness of those methods.

   b. Examine corroborating evidence for consistency with other statement disclosures.

   c. Consider if management's determination of operating segments is appropriate, if the CODM uses multiple sets of segment information in making decisions.

   d. Evaluate whether the entity applied applicable aggregation criteria and quantitative thresholds to identify reportable operating segments.

   e. Obtain management's written representation that operating segments are identified and disclosed in conformity with SFAS 131.

   f. Use analytical procedures to determine and asses unusual relationships and individual items that may indicate misstatements.

   g. Assess the adequacy of disclosures regarding general information, segment information, and reconciliations of segment and total amounts.

   h. Evaluate whether significant items in the reconciliations are appropriately disclosed.

   i. Evaluate whether segment information for prior periods is restated appropriately, if changes in components of the entity's reportable segments have occurred.

C. Impact on the Auditor's Report

Prepared in conformity with GAAP implicitly applies to segment information included in those statements in the same manner that it applies to other informative disclosures that are not clearly marked as "unaudited." The auditor's standard report would not refer to segment information unless the audit revealed a misstatement or omission, or a change in accounting principle, relating to the segment information that is material in relation to the financial statements taken as a whole, or the auditor was unable to apply the auditing procedures that are considered necessary in the circumstances.

1. **MISSTATEMENT** If the audit reveals a misstatement and that misstatement is not corrected, the auditor modifies his or her opinion (qualified or adverse) on the financial statements because of a departure from GAAP.

2. **OMISSION** If the entity declines to include in the financial statements part or all of the segment information that the auditor believes is required to be disclosed, the auditor modifies the opinion on the financial statements because of inadequate disclosure and describes the type of information omitted. The auditor is not required to provide the omitted information.

EXHIBIT 36 ♦ OMISSION OF REQUIRED SEGMENT INFORMATION

(Same first and second paragraphs as the standard report)

(Explanatory paragraph)

The Company declined to present segment information for the year ended December 31, 20XX. In our opinion, presentation of segment information concerning the Company's operations in different goods and services, its geographic areas, and its major customers, is required by generally accepted accounting principles. The omission of segment information results in an incomplete presentation of the Company's financial statements.

(Opinion paragraph)

In our opinion, except for the omission of segment information, as discussed in the preceding paragraph, the financial statements referred to above present fairly...

3. **POSSIBLE OMISSION** An entity may represent that it does not have segments required to be disclosed by SFAS 131. If the auditor is unable to reach a conclusion as to whether the entity has such segments and the entity declines to develop the information that the auditor considers necessary to reach a conclusion, the auditor indicates (in the scope paragraph of the report) the scope limitation and qualifies the opinion.

EXHIBIT 37 ♦ POSSIBLE OMISSION OF REQUIRED SEGMENT INFORMATION

(Same first paragraph as the standard report)

(Scope paragraph)

...Except as discussed in the following paragraph, we conducted our audit in accordance with...

(Explanatory paragraph)

The Company has not developed the information we consider necessary to reach a conclusion as to whether the presentation of segment information concerning the Company's operations in different goods and services, its geographic areas, and its major customers, is necessary to conform to generally accepted accounting principles.

(Opinion paragraph)

In our opinion, except for the possible omission of segment information, the financial statements referred to above present fairly...

4. **Scope Limitation** The auditor qualifies the opinion if the auditor is unable to apply to reported segment information the auditing procedures that the auditor considers necessary.

Exhibit 38 ♦ Scope Limitation

(Scope paragraph)

...Except as discussed in the following paragraph, we conducted our audit in accordance with...

(Explanatory paragraph)

In accordance with the Company's request, our audit of the financial statements did not include the segment information presented in Note X concerning the Company's operations in different goods and services, its geographic areas, and its major customers.

(Opinion paragraph)

In our opinion, except for the effects of such adjustments or disclosures, if any, as might have been determined to be necessary had we applied to the segment information the procedures we considered necessary in the circumstances, the financial statements referred to above...

D. Reporting Separately on Segment Information

An audit of segment information for the purpose of reporting on it separately is more extensive than if it were considered in conjunction with a financial statement audit. In a separate report on segment information, the measurement of materiality is related to the segment information itself rather than the financial statements taken as a whole.

TIME MANAGEMENT

Approximately 10 percent of the multiple choice questions in every section of every exam given after November 1995 are questions that are being pre-tested. These questions are **not** included in candidates' final grades; they are presented only so that the Board of Examiners may evaluate them for effectiveness and possible ambiguity.

The Scholastic Achievement Test and the Graduate Record Exam both employ similar but not identical strategies. Those tests include an extra section, which is being pre-tested, and test-takers do not know which section is the one that will not be graded. On the Uniform CPA Examination, however, the extra questions are mixed in among the graded questions.

This makes time management crucial. Candidates who are deciding how much time to spend on a difficult multiple choice question must keep in mind that there is a 10 percent chance that the answer to the question will not affect them either way. Also, candidates should not allow a question that seems particularly difficult or confusing to shake their confidence or affect their attitude towards the rest of the test; it may not even count.

This experimental 10 percent works against candidates who are not sure whether they have answered enough questions to earn 75 percent. Candidates should try for a safety margin, so that they will have accumulated enough correct answers to pass, even though some of their correctly answered questions will not be scored.

See the **Practical Advice** appendix for more information regarding the exam.

CHAPTER 39—REPORTS ON AUDITED FINANCIAL STATEMENTS

PROBLEM 39-1 MULTIPLE CHOICE QUESTIONS (180 to 225 minutes)

1. When issuing an unqualified opinion, the auditor who evaluates the audit findings should be satisfied that the
a. Amount of known misstatement is documented in the management representation letter.
b. Estimate of the total likely misstatement is less than a material amount.
c. Amount of known misstatement is acknowledged and recorded by the client.
d. Estimate of the total likely misstatement includes the adjusting entries already recorded by the client. (11/98, Aud., #21, 6712)

2. Several sources of GAAP consulted by an auditor are in conflict as to the application of an accounting principle. Which of the following should the auditor consider the most authoritative?
a. FASB Technical Bulletins
b. AICPA Accounting Interpretations
c. FASB Statements of Financial Accounting Concepts
d. AICPA Technical Practice Aids (11/93, Aud., #52, 4289)

3. The fourth standard of reporting requires the auditor's report to contain either an expression of opinion regarding the financial statements taken as a whole or an assertion to the effect that an opinion cannot be expressed. The objective of the fourth standard is to prevent
a. An auditor from expressing different opinions on each of the basic financial statements.
b. Restrictions on the scope of the audit, whether imposed by the client or by the inability to obtain evidence.
c. Misinterpretations regarding the degree of responsibility the auditor is assuming.
d. An auditor from reporting on one basic financial statement and not the others. (11/95, Aud., #68, 6015)

4. Field is an employee of Gold Enterprises. Hardy, CPA, is asked to express an opinion on Field's profit participation in Gold's net income. Hardy may accept this engagement only if
a. Hardy also audits Gold's complete financial statements.
b. Gold's financial statements are prepared in conformity with GAAP.
c. Hardy's report is available for distribution to Gold's other employees.
d. Field owns controlling interest in Gold. (11/95, Aud., #83, 6030)

5. When single-year financial statements are presented, an auditor ordinarily would express an unqualified opinion in an unmodified report if the
a. Auditor is unable to obtain audited financial statements supporting the entity's investment in a foreign affiliate.
b. Entity declines to present a statement of cash flows with its balance sheet and related statements of income and retained earnings.
c. Auditor wishes to emphasize an accounting matter affecting the comparability of the financial statements with those of the prior year.
d. Prior year's financial statements were audited by another CPA whose report, which expressed an unqualified opinion, is not presented. (5/94, Aud., #74, 4739)

6. If a publicly held company issues financial statements that purport to present its financial position and results of operations but omits the statement of cash flows, the auditor ordinarily will express a(an)
a. Disclaimer of opinion.
b. Qualified opinion.
c. Review report.
d. Unqualified opinion with a separate explanatory paragraph. (5/93, Aud., #46, 3942)

7. Restrictions imposed by a client prohibit the observation of physical inventories, which account for 35% of all assets. Alternative audit procedures cannot be applied, although the auditor was able to examine satisfactory evidence for all other items in the financial statements. The auditor should issue a(an)
a. "Except for" qualified opinion.
b. Unqualified opinion with an explanation in the scope paragraph.
c. Unqualified opinion with a separate explanatory paragraph.
d. Disclaimer of opinion. (Editors, 9421)

8. In which of the following circumstances would an auditor not express an unqualified opinion?
a. There has been a material change between periods in accounting principles.
b. Quarterly financial data required by the SEC has been omitted.
c. The auditor wishes to emphasize an unusually important subsequent event.
d. The auditor is unable to obtain audited financial statements of a consolidated investee. (11/95, Aud., #69, 6016)

9. An explanatory paragraph following the opinion paragraph of an auditor's report describes an uncertainty as follows:

As discussed in Note X to the financial statements, the Company is a defendant in a lawsuit alleging infringement of certain patent rights and claiming damages. Discovery proceedings are in progress. The ultimate outcome of the litigation cannot presently be determined. Accordingly, no provision for any liability that may result upon adjudication has been made in the accompanying financial statements.

What type of opinion should the auditor express under these circumstances?

a. Adverse
b. Qualified due to a scope limitation
c. Qualified due to a GAAP violation
d. Unqualified (11/95, Aud., #70, 6017)

10. An auditor most likely would express an unqualified opinion and would **not** add explanatory language to the report if the auditor

a. Wishes to emphasize that the entity had significant transactions with related parties.
b. Concurs with the entity's change in its method of computing depreciation.
c. Discovers that supplementary information required by FASB has been omitted.
d. Believes that there is a remote likelihood of a material loss resulting from an uncertainty.

(11/95, Aud., #64, 6011)

11. If a client makes a change in accounting principle that is inseparable from the effect of a change in estimate, this material event should be accounted for as a change in

a. Estimate and the auditor would report a consistency exception.
b. Estimate and the auditor would not modify the report.
c. Principle and the auditor would report a consistency exception.
d. Principle and the auditor would **not** modify the report. (Editors, 9422)

12. Park, CPA, was engaged to audit the financial statements of Tech Co., a new client, for the year ended December 31, 20X1. Park obtained sufficient audit evidence for all of Tech's financial statement items except Tech's opening inventory. Due to inadequate financial records, Park could not verify Tech's January 1, 20X1, inventory balances. Park's opinion on Tech's 20X1 financial statements most likely will be

	Balance sheet	Income statement
a.	Disclaimer	Disclaimer
b.	Unqualified	Disclaimer
c.	Disclaimer	Adverse
d.	Unqualified	Adverse

(5/94, Aud., #76, amended, 4741)

13. In which of the following situations would an auditor ordinarily choose between expressing a qualified opinion or an adverse opinion?

a. The auditor did **not** observe the entity's physical inventory and is unable to become satisfied about its balance by other auditing procedures.
b. Conditions that cause the auditor to have substantial doubt about the entity's ability to continue as a going concern are inadequately disclosed.
c. There has been a change in accounting principles that has a material effect on the comparability of the entity's financial statements.
d. The auditor is unable to apply necessary procedures concerning an investor's share of an investee's earnings recognized on the equity method. (R/00, Aud., #17, 6942)

14. Which of the following statements is a basic element of the auditor's standard report?

a. The disclosures provide reasonable assurance that the financial statements are free of material misstatement.
b. The financial statements are consistent with those of the prior period.
c. An audit includes assessing significant estimates made by management.
d. The auditor evaluated the overall internal control. (11/95, Aud., #62, amended, 6009)

15. March, CPA, is engaged by Monday Corp., a client, to audit the financial statements of Wall Corp., a company that is not March's client. Monday expects to present Wall's audited financial statements with March's auditor's report to 1st Federal Bank to obtain financing in Monday's attempt to purchase Wall. In these circumstances, March's auditor's report would usually be addressed to

a. Monday Corp., the client that engaged March.
b. Wall Corp., the entity audited by March.
c. 1st Federal Bank.
d. Both Monday Corp. and 1st Federal Bank.

(11/95, Aud., #78, 6025)

16. An auditor's responsibility to express an opinion on the financial statements is

a. Explicitly represented in the opinion paragraph of the auditor's standard report.
b. Explicitly represented in the opening paragraph of the auditor's standard report.
c. Explicitly represented in the scope paragraph of the auditor's standard report.
d. Implicitly represented in the auditor's standard report. (5/92, Aud., #11, amended, 9423)

17. For an entity that does **not** receive governmental financial assistance, an auditor's standard report on financial statements generally would **not** refer to

a. Significant estimates made by management.
b. The entity's internal control.
c. Management's responsibility for the financial statements.
d. An assessment of the entity's accounting principles. (5/94, Aud., #71, amended, 4736)

18. Which paragraphs of an auditor's standard report on financial statements should refer to generally accepted auditing standards (GAAS) and generally accepted accounting principles (GAAP) in which paragraphs?

	GAAS	GAAP
a.	Opening	Scope
b.	Scope	Scope
c.	Scope	Opinion
d.	Opening	Opinion

(5/94, Aud., #77, 4742)

19. The existence of audit risk is recognized by the statement in the auditor's standard report that the

a. Auditor is responsible for expressing an opinion on the financial statements, which are the responsibility of management.
b. Financial statements are presented fairly, in all material respects, in conformity with GAAP.
c. Audit includes examining, on a test basis, evidence supporting the amounts and disclosures in the financial statements.
d. Auditor obtains reasonable assurance about whether the financial statements are free of material misstatement. (11/94, Aud., #9, 5082)

20. In which of the following circumstances would an auditor most likely add an explanatory paragraph to the standard report while **not** affecting the auditor's unqualified opinion?

a. The auditor is asked to report on the balance sheet, but **not** on the other basic financial statements.
b. There is substantial doubt about the entity's ability to continue as a going concern.
c. Management's estimates of the effects of future events are unreasonable.
d. Certain transactions **cannot** be tested because of management's records retention policy. (5/93, Aud., #47, 3943)

21. An auditor would express an unqualified opinion with an explanatory paragraph added to the auditor's report for

	An unjustified accounting change	*A material weakness in internal control*
a.	Yes	Yes
b.	Yes	No
c.	No	Yes
d.	No	No

(11/95, Aud., #65, amended, 6012)

22. In which of the following situations would an auditor ordinarily issue an unqualified audit opinion without an explanatory paragraph?

a. The auditor wishes to emphasize that the entity had significant related party transactions.
b. The auditor decides to make reference to the report of another auditor as a basis, in part, for the auditor's opinion.
c. The entity issues financial statements that present financial position and results of operations, but omits the statement of cash flows.
d. The auditor has substantial doubt about the entity's ability to continue as a going concern, but the circumstances are fully disclosed in the financial statements. (11/90, Aud., #6, 0324)

23. Which of the following procedures would the principal auditor most likely perform after deciding to make reference to another CPA who audited a subsidiary of the entity?

a. Review the working papers and the audit programs of the other CPA.
b. Visit the other CPA and discuss the results of the other CPA's audit procedures.
c. Make inquiries about the professional reputation and independence of the other CPA.
d. Determine that the other CPA has a sufficient understanding of the subsidiary's internal control. (R/99, Aud., #15, 6831)

24. The introductory paragraph of an auditor's report contains the following sentences:

We did not audit the financial statements of EZ Inc., a wholly-owned subsidiary, which statements reflect total assets and revenues constituting 27 percent and 29 percent, respectively, of the related consolidated totals. Those statements were audited by other auditors whose report has been furnished to us, and our opinion, insofar as it relates to the amounts included for EZ Inc., is based solely on the report of the other auditors.

These sentences

a. Indicate a division of responsibility.
b. Assume responsibility for the other auditor.
c. Are an improper form of reporting.
d. Require a departure from an unqualified opinion. (11/95, Aud., #77, amended, 6024)

25. Pell, CPA, decides to serve as principal auditor in the audit of the financial statements of Tech Consolidated, Inc. Smith, CPA, audits one of Tech's subsidiaries. In which situation(s) should Pell make reference to Smith's audit?

I. Pell reviews Smith's working papers and assumes responsibility for Smith's work, but expresses a qualified opinion on Tech's financial statements.
II. Pell is unable to review Smith's working papers; however, Pell's inquiries indicate that Smith has an excellent reputation for professional competence and integrity.

a. I only
b. II only
c. Both I and II
d. Neither I nor II (5/97, Aud., #5, 6394)

26. When financial statements contain a departure from GAAP because, due to unusual circumstances, the statements would otherwise be misleading, the auditor should explain the unusual circumstances in a separate paragraph and express an opinion that is

a. Unqualified.
b. Qualified.
c. Qualified or adverse, depending on materiality.
d. Adverse. (5/94, Aud., #75, amended, 4740)

27. Delta Life Insurance Co. prepares its financial statements on an accounting basis insurance companies use pursuant to the rules of a state insurance commission. If Wall, CPA, Delta's auditor, discovers that the statements are **not** suitably titled, Wall should

a. Disclose any reservations in an explanatory paragraph and qualify the opinion.
b. Apply to the state insurance commission for an advisory opinion.
c. Issue a special statutory basis report that clearly disclaims any opinion.
d. Explain in the notes to the financial statements the terminology used. (5/93, Aud., #57, 3953)

28. The following explanatory paragraph was included in an auditor's report to indicate a lack of consistency:

"As discussed in note T to the financial statements, the company changed its method of computing depreciation in 20X1."

How should the auditor report on this matter if the auditor concurred with the change?

	Type of opinion	*Location of explanatory paragraph*
a.	Unqualified	Before opinion paragraph
b.	Unqualified	After opinion paragraph
c.	Qualified	Before opinion paragraph
d.	Qualified	After opinion paragraph

(11/91, Aud., #18, amended, 2286)

29. When an entity changes its method of accounting for income taxes, which has a material effect on comparability, the auditor should refer to the change in an explanatory paragraph added to the auditor's report. This paragraph should identify the nature of the change and

a. Explain why the change is justified under generally accepted accounting principles.
b. Describe the cumulative effect of the change on the audited financial statements.
c. State the auditor's explicit concurrence with or opposition to the change.
d. Refer to the financial statement note that discusses the change in detail. (5/93, Aud., #49, 3945)

30. In the first audit of a client, an auditor was not able to gather sufficient evidence about the consistent application of accounting principles between the current and the prior year, as well as the amounts of assets or liabilities at the beginning of the current year. This was due to the client's record retention policies. If the amounts in question could materially affect current operating results, the auditor would

a. Be unable to express an opinion on the current year's results of operations and cash flows.
b. Express a qualified opinion on the financial statements because of a client-imposed scope limitation.

c. Withdraw from the engagement and refuse to be associated with the financial statements.
d. Specifically state that the financial statements are **not** comparable to the prior year due to an uncertainty. (5/98, Aud., #15, 6632)

31. For which of the following events would an auditor issue a report that omits any reference to consistency?
a. A change in the method of accounting for inventories
b. A change from an accounting principle that is not generally accepted to one that is generally accepted
c. A change in the useful life used to calculate the provision for depreciation expense
d. Management's lack of reasonable justification for a change in accounting principle
(11/96, Aud., #15, 6367)

32. When there has been a change in accounting principles, but the effect of the change on the comparability of the financial statements is not material, the auditor should
a. Refer to the change in an explanatory paragraph.
b. Explicitly concur that the change is preferred.
c. Not refer to consistency in the auditor's report.
d. Refer to the change in the opinion paragraph.
(5/94, Aud., #73, 4738)

33. If an auditor is satisfied that there is only a remote likelihood of a loss resulting from the resolution of a matter involving an uncertainty, the auditor should express a(an)
a. Unqualified opinion.
b. Unqualified opinion with a separate explanatory paragraph.
c. Qualified opinion or disclaimer of opinion, depending upon the materiality of the loss.
d. Qualified opinion or disclaimer of opinion, depending on whether the uncertainty is adequately disclosed. (5/91, Aud., #44, 0315)

34. Management believes and the auditor is satisfied that the chance of a material loss resulting from the resolution of a lawsuit is more than remote but less than probable. Which of the following matters should the auditor consider in deciding whether to add an explanatory paragraph?

	Likelihood that the loss is closer to probable than remote	*Magnitude by which the loss exceeds the auditor's materiality*
a.	Yes	Yes
b.	Yes	No
c.	No	Yes
d.	No	No

(11/93, Aud., #47, 4284)

35. Management believes and the auditor is satisfied that a material loss probably will occur when pending litigation is resolved. Management is unable to make a reasonable estimate of the amount or range of the potential loss, but fully discloses the situation in the notes to the financial statements. If management does not make an accrual in the financial statements, the auditor
a. May express a qualified opinion due to a scope limitation.
b. Must express a qualified opinion due to a scope limitation.
c. May express an unqualified opinion with an explanatory paragraph.
d. Must express an unqualified opinion with an explanatory paragraph.
(5/94, Aud., #86, amended, 4751)

36. Tech Company has disclosed an uncertainty due to pending litigation. The auditor's decision to issue a qualified opinion rather than an unqualified opinion with an explanatory paragraph most likely would be determined by the
a. Lack of sufficient evidence.
b. Inability to estimate the amount of loss.
c. Entity's lack of experience with such litigation.
d. Lack of insurance coverage for possible losses from such litigation. (11/90, Aud., #5, 0323)

37. An auditor includes a separate paragraph in an otherwise unmodified report to emphasize that the entity being reported on had significant transactions with related parties. The inclusion of this separate paragraph
a. Is considered an "except for" qualification of the opinion.
b. Violates generally accepted auditing standards if this information is already disclosed in footnotes to the financial statements.
c. Necessitates a revision of the opinion paragraph to include the phrase "with the foregoing explanation."
d. Is appropriate and would not negate the unqualified opinion. (5/94, Aud., #69, 4734)

38. Which of the following phrases should be included in the opinion paragraph when an auditor expresses a qualified opinion?

	When read in connection with Note X	*With the foregoing explanation*
a.	Yes	No
b.	No	Yes
c.	Yes	Yes
d.	No	No

(11/92, Aud., #46, 2980)

39. An auditor may **not** issue a qualified opinion when
a. An accounting principle at variance with GAAP is used.
b. The auditor lacks independence with respect to the audited entity.
c. A scope limitation prevents the auditor from completing an important audit procedure.
d. The auditor's report refers to the work of a specialist. (11/95, Aud., #63, 6010)

40. When qualifying an opinion because of an insufficiency of audit evidence, an auditor should refer to the situation in the

	Opening (introductory) paragraph	*Scope paragraph*
a.	No	No
b.	Yes	No
c.	Yes	Yes
d.	No	Yes

(5/94, Aud., #88, 4753)

41. An auditor may reasonably issue an "except for" qualified opinion for a(an)

	Scope limitation	*Unjustified accounting change*
a.	Yes	No
b.	No	Yes
c.	Yes	Yes
d.	No	No

(11/91, Aud., #16, 2284)

42. An auditor decides to issue a qualified opinion on an entity's financial statements because a major inadequacy in its computerized accounting records prevents the auditor from applying necessary procedures. The opinion paragraph of the auditor's report should state that the qualification pertains to
a. A client-imposed scope limitation.
b. A departure from generally accepted auditing standards.
c. The possible effects on the financial statements.
d. Inadequate disclosure of necessary information. (11/93, Aud., #49, 4286)

43. A limitation on the scope of an audit sufficient to preclude an unqualified opinion will usually result when management
a. Is unable to obtain audited financial statements supporting the entity's investment in a foreign subsidiary.
b. Refuses to disclose in the notes to the financial statements related party transactions authorized by the Board of Directors.
c. Does not sign an engagement letter specifying the responsibilities of both the entity and the auditor.
d. Fails to correct a reportable condition communicated to the audit committee after the prior year's audit. (5/93, Aud., #56, 3952)

44. Due to a scope limitation, an auditor disclaimed an opinion on the financial statements taken as a whole, but the auditor's report included a statement that the current asset portion of the entity's balance sheet was fairly stated. The inclusion of this statement is
a. Not appropriate because it may tend to overshadow the auditor's disclaimer of opinion.
b. Not appropriate because the auditor is prohibited from reporting on only one basic financial statement.
c. Appropriate provided the auditor's scope paragraph adequately describes the scope limitation.
d. Appropriate provided the statement is in a separate paragraph preceding the disclaimer of opinion paragraph. (5/94, Aud., #72, 4737)

45. Harris, CPA, has been asked to audit and report on the balance sheet of Fox Co. but not on the statements of income, retained earnings, or cash flows. Harris will have access to all information underlying the basic financial statements. Under these circumstances, Harris may
a. Not accept the engagement because it would constitute a violation of the profession's ethical standards.
b. Not accept the engagement because it would be tantamount to rendering a piecemeal opinion.
c. Accept the engagement because such engagements merely involve limited reporting objectives.
d. Accept the engagement but should disclaim an opinion because of an inability to apply the procedures considered necessary. (11/95, Aud., #61, 6008)

46. When disclaiming an opinion due to a client-imposed scope limitation, an auditor should indicate in a separate paragraph why the audit did not comply with generally accepted auditing standards. The auditor should also omit the

	Scope paragraph	*Opinion paragraph*
a.	No	Yes
b.	Yes	Yes
c.	No	No
d.	Yes	No

(11/93, Aud., #46, 4283)

47. When a qualified opinion results from a limitation on the scope of the audit, the situation should be described in an explanatory paragraph

a. Preceding the opinion paragraph and referred to only in the scope paragraph of the auditor's report.
b. Following the opinion paragraph and referred to in both the scope and opinion paragraphs of the auditor's report.
c. Following the opinion paragraph and referred to only in the scope paragraph of the auditor's report.
d. Preceding the opinion paragraph and referred to in both the scope and opinion paragraphs of the auditor's report. (5/90, Aud., #22, 0340)

48. Which of the following phrases would an auditor most likely include in the auditor's report when expressing a qualified opinion because of inadequate disclosure?

a. Subject to the departure from generally accepted accounting principles, as described above
b. With the foregoing explanation of these omitted disclosures
c. Except for the omission of the information discussed in the preceding paragraph
d. Does not present fairly in all material respects (11/95, Aud., #71, 6018)

49. When an auditor qualifies an opinion because of inadequate disclosure, the auditor should describe the nature of the omission in a separate explanatory paragraph and modify the

	Introductory paragraph	*Scope paragraph*	*Opinion paragraph*
a.	Yes	No	No
b.	Yes	Yes	No
c.	No	Yes	Yes
d.	No	No	Yes

(5/91, Aud., #46, 0317)

50. In which of the following circumstances would an auditor be most likely to express an adverse opinion?

a. The chief executive officer refuses the auditor access to minutes of board of directors' meetings.
b. Tests of controls show that the entity's internal control structure is so poor that it **cannot** be relied upon.
c. The financial statements are **not** in conformity with the FASB Statements regarding the capitalization of leases.
d. Information comes to the auditor's attention that raises substantial doubt about the entity's ability to continue as a going concern. (5/94, Aud., #87, 4752)

51. An auditor most likely would issue a disclaimer of opinion because of

a. Inadequate disclosure of material information.
b. The omission of the statement of cash flows.
c. A material departure from generally accepted accounting principles.
d. Management's refusal to furnish written representations. (5/91, Aud., #53, 0319)

52. When comparative financial statements are presented, the fourth standard of reporting, which refers to financial statements "taken as a whole," should be considered to apply to the financial statements of the

a. Periods presented plus one preceding period.
b. Current and immediately preceding period only.
c. Current period and those of the other periods presented.
d. Current period only. (Editors, 9426)

53. A registration statement filed with the SEC contains the reports of two independent auditors on their audits of financial statements for different periods. The predecessor auditor who audited the prior-period financial statements generally should obtain a letter of representation from the

a. Successor independent auditor.
b. Client's audit committee.
c. Principal underwriter.
d. Securities and Exchange Commission. (11/95, Aud., #86, 6033)

54. The predecessor auditor, who is satisfied after properly communicating with the successor auditor, has reissued a report because the audit client desires comparative financial statements. The predecessor auditor's report should make

a. Reference to the report of the successor auditor only in the scope paragraph.
b. Reference to the work of the successor auditor in the scope and opinion paragraphs.
c. Reference to both the work and the report of the successor auditor only in the opinion paragraph.
d. No reference to the report or the work of the successor auditor. (5/90, Aud., #13, 0334)

55. A former client requests a predecessor auditor to reissue an audit report on a prior period's financial statements. The financial statements are not restated and the report is not revised. What date(s) should the predecessor auditor use in the reissued report?

a. The date of the prior-period report
b. The date of the client's request
c. The dual-dates
d. The date of reissue (Editors, 0352)

56. When a predecessor auditor reissues the report on the prior period's financial statements at the request of the former client, the predecessor auditor should

a. Indicate in the introductory paragraph of the reissued report that the financial statements of the subsequent period were audited by another CPA.
b. Obtain an updated management representation letter and compare it to that obtained during the prior period audit.
c. Compare the prior period's financial statements that the predecessor reported on with the financial statements to be presented for comparative purposes.
d. Add an explanatory paragraph to the reissued report stating that the predecessor has not performed additional auditing procedures concerning the prior period's financial statements.

(5/92, Aud., #3, 2756)

57. When reporting on comparative financial statements, an auditor ordinarily should change the previously issued opinion on the prior-year's financial statements if the

a. Prior year's financial statements are restated to conform with generally accepted accounting principles.
b. Auditor is a predecessor auditor who has been requested by a former client to reissue the previously issued report.
c. Prior year's opinion was unqualified and the opinion on the current year's financial statements is modified due to a lack of consistency.
d. Prior year's financial statements are restated following a pooling of interests in the current year.

(11/95, Aud., #75, 6022)

58. Jewel, CPA, audited Infinite Co.'s prior-year financial statements. These statements are presented with those of the current year for comparative purposes without Jewel's auditor's report, which expressed a qualified opinion. In drafting the current year's auditor's report, Crain, CPA, the successor auditor, should

I. Not name Jewel as the predecessor auditor.
II. Indicate the type of report issued by Jewel.
III. Indicate the substantive reasons for Jewel's qualification.

a. I only
b. I and II only
c. II and III only
d. I, II, and III (11/95, Aud., #76, 6023)

59. An auditor issued an audit report that was dual dated for a subsequent event occurring after the completion of field work but before issuance of the auditor's report. The auditor's responsibility for events occurring subsequent to the completion of field work was

a. Limited to include only events occurring up to the date of the last subsequent event referenced.
b. Limited to the specific event referenced.
c. Extended to subsequent events occurring through the date of issuance of the report.
d. Extended to include all events occurring since the completion of field work.

(11/94, Aud., #67, 5140)

60. In May 20X3, an auditor reissues the auditor's report on the 20X1 financial statements at a continuing client's request. The 20X1 financial statements are not restated and the auditor does not revise the wording of the report. The auditor should

a. Dual date the reissued report.
b. Use the release date of the reissued report.
c. Use the current-period auditor's report date on the reissued report.
d. Use the original report date on the reissued report. (5/94, Aud., #66, amended, 4731)

61. Samson, CPA, completed the field work of the audit of Coco's December 31, 20X1, financial statements on March 6, 20X2. A subsequent event requiring adjustment to the 20X2 financial statements occurred on April 10, 20X2, and came to Samson's attention on April 24, 20X2. If the adjustment is made without disclosure of the event, Samson's report ordinarily should be dated

a. March 6, 20X2.
b. April 10, 20X2.
c. April 24, 20X2.
d. Using dual dating. (Editors, 2765)

62. On February 25, a CPA issued an auditor's report expressing an unqualified opinion on financial statements for the year ended January 31. On March 2, the CPA learned that on February 11 the entity incurred a material loss on an uncollectible trade receivable as a result of the deteriorating financial condition of the entity's principal customer that led to the customer's bankruptcy. Management then refused to adjust the financial statements for this subsequent event. The CPA determined that the information is reliable and that there are creditors currently relying on the financial statements. The CPA's next course of action most likely would be to

a. Notify the entity's creditors that the financial statements and the related auditor's report should **no** longer be relied on.
b. Notify each member of the entity's board of directors about management's refusal to adjust the financial statements.
c. Issue revised financial statements and distribute them to each creditor known to be relying on the financial statements.
d. Issue a revised auditor's report and distribute it to each creditor known to be relying on the financial statements. (R/99, Aud., #32, 6848)

63. Which of the following procedures would an auditor most likely perform to obtain evidence about the occurrence of subsequent events?
a. Confirming a sample of material accounts receivable established after year end
b. Comparing the financial statements being reported on with those of the prior period
c. Investigating personnel changes in the accounting department occurring after year end
d. Inquiring as to whether any unusual adjustments were made after year end

(11/95, Aud., #56, 6003)

64. Zero Corp. suffered a loss that would have a material effect on its financial statements on an uncollectible trade account receivable due to a customer's bankruptcy. This occurred suddenly due to a natural disaster ten days after Zero's balance sheet date, but one month before the issuance of the financial statements and the auditor's report. Under these circumstances,

	The financial statements should be adjusted	*The event requires financial statement disclosure, but no adjustment*	*The auditor's report should be modified for a lack of consistency*
a.	Yes	No	No
b.	Yes	No	Yes
c.	No	Yes	Yes
d.	No	Yes	No

(5/94, Aud., #53, 4718)

65. A client acquired 25% of its outstanding capital stock after year-end and prior to completion of the auditor's field work. The auditor should
a. Advise management to adjust the balance sheet to reflect the acquisition.
b. Disclose the acquisition in the opinion paragraph of the auditor's report.
c. Advise management to disclose the acquisition in the notes to the financial statements.
d. Issue pro forma financial statements giving effect to the acquisition as if it had occurred at year-end. (Editors, 0372)

66. An auditor is concerned with completing various phases of the audit after the balance-sheet date. This "subsequent period" extends to the date of the
a. Final review of the audit working papers.
b. Delivery of the auditor's report to the client.
c. Public issuance of the financial statements.
d. Auditor's report. (Editors, 0381)

67. Which of the following events occurring after the issuance of an auditor's report most likely would cause the auditor to make further inquiries about the previously issued financial statements?
a. An uninsured natural disaster occurs that may affect the entity's ability to continue as a going concern.
b. A contingency is resolved that had been disclosed in the audited financial statements.
c. New information is discovered concerning undisclosed lease transactions of the audited period.
d. A subsidiary is sold that accounts for 25% of the entity's consolidated net income.

(11/95, Aud., #85, 6032)

68. After issuing a report, an auditor has **no** obligation to make continuing inquiries or perform other procedures concerning the audited financial statements, unless
a. Information, which existed at the report date and may affect the report, comes to the auditor's attention.
b. Management of the entity requests the auditor to reissue the auditor's report.
c. Information about an event that occurred after the end of field work comes to the auditor's attention.
d. Final determinations or resolutions are made of contingencies that had been disclosed in the financial statements. (11/91, Aud., #20, 2288)

69. Subsequent to the issuance of an auditor's report, the auditor became aware of facts existing at the report date that would have affected the report had the auditor then been aware of such facts. After determining that the information is reliable, the auditor should next
a. Determine whether there are persons relying or likely to rely on the financial statements who would attach importance to the information.
b. Request that management disclose the newly discovered information by issuing revised financial statements.
c. Give public notice that the auditor is **no** longer associated with financial statements.
d. Issue revised pro forma financial statements taking into consideration the newly discovered information. (11/94, Aud., #89, amended, 5162)

70. On March 15, 20X2, Kent, CPA, issued an unqualified opinion on a client's audited financial statements for the year ended December 31, 20X1. On May 4, 20X2, Kent's internal inspection program disclosed that engagement personnel failed to observe the client's physical inventory. Omission of this procedure impairs Kent's present ability to support the unqualified opinion. If the stockholders are currently relying on the opinion, Kent should first

a. Advise management to disclose to the stockholders that Kent's unqualified opinion should **not** be relied on.
b. Undertake to apply alternative procedures that would provide a satisfactory basis for the unqualified opinion.
c. Compensate for the omitted procedure by performing tests of controls to reduce audit risk to a sufficiently low level.
d. Reissue the auditor's report and add an explanatory paragraph describing the departure from generally accepted auditing standards.

(5/94, Aud., #70, amended, 4735)

71. An auditor concludes that an audit procedure considered necessary at the time of the audit had been omitted. The auditor should assess the importance of the omitted procedure to the ability to support the previously expressed opinion. Which of the following would be **least** helpful in making that assessment?

a. A discussion with the client about whether there are persons relying on the auditor's report
b. A discussion of the circumstances with engagement personnel
c. A reevaluation of the overall scope of the audit
d. A review of the other audit procedures that were applied that might compensate for the one omitted (Editors, 0371)

72. An auditor is considering whether the omission of a substantive procedure considered necessary at the time of an audit may impair the auditor's present ability to support the previously expressed opinion. The auditor need **not** apply the omitted procedure if the

a. Financial statements and auditor's report were **not** distributed beyond management and the board of directors.
b. Auditor's previously expressed opinion was qualified because of a departure from GAAP.
c. Results of other procedures that were applied tend to compensate for the procedure omitted.
d. Omission is due to unreasonable delays by client personnel in providing data on a timely basis.

(5/95, Aud., #85, 5703)

73. An auditor concludes that a substantive auditing procedure considered necessary during the prior period's audit was omitted. Which of the following factors would most likely cause the auditor promptly to apply the omitted procedure?

a. There are **no** alternative procedures available to provide the same evidence as the omitted procedure.
b. The omission of the procedure impairs the auditor's present ability to support the previously expressed opinion.
c. The source documents needed to perform the omitted procedure are still available.
d. The auditor's opinion on the prior period's financial statements was unqualified.

(5/92, Aud., #33, 2786)

74. When an independent CPA is associated with the financial statements of a publicly held entity but has **not** audited or reviewed such statements, the appropriate form of report to be issued must include a (an)

a. Regulation S-X exemption.
b. Report on pro forma financial statements.
c. Unaudited association report.
d. Disclaimer of opinion. (11/94, Aud., #76, 5149)

75. When unaudited financial statements of a nonpublic entity are presented in comparative form with audited financial statements in the subsequent year, the unaudited financial statements should be clearly marked to indicate their status and

I. The report on the unaudited financial statements should be reissued.
II. The report on the audited financial statements should include a separate paragraph describing the responsibility assumed for the unaudited financial statements.

a. I only
b. II only
c. Both I and II
d. Either I or II (5/94, Aud., #89, 4754)

76. When an independent CPA assists in preparing the financial statements of a publicly held entity, but has **not** audited or reviewed them, the CPA should issue a disclaimer of opinion. In such situations, the CPA has **no** responsibility to apply any procedures beyond

a. Ascertaining whether the financial statements are in conformity with generally accepted accounting principles.
b. Determining whether management has elected to omit substantially all required disclosures.

c. Documenting that the client's internal control is **not** being relied on.
d. Reading the financial statements for obvious material misstatements. (5/92, Aud., #2, amended, 2755)

77. If an accountant concludes that unaudited financial statements on which the accountant is disclaiming an opinion also lack adequate disclosure, the accountant should suggest appropriate revision. If the client does **not** accept the accountant's suggestion, the accountant should
a. Issue an adverse opinion and describe the appropriate revision in the report.
b. Accept the client's inaction because the statements are unaudited and the accountant has disclaimed an opinion.
c. Describe the appropriate revision to the financial statements in the accountant's disclaimer of opinion.
d. Make reference to the appropriate revision and issue a modified report expressing limited assurance. (Editors, 9428)

78. Cooper, CPA, believes there is substantial doubt about the ability of Zero Corp. to continue as a going concern for a reasonable period of time. In evaluating Zero's plans for dealing with the adverse effects of future conditions and events, Cooper most likely would consider, as a mitigating factor, Zero's plans to
a. Discuss with the lenders the terms of all debt and loan agreements.
b. Strengthen internal controls over cash disbursements.
c. Purchase production facilities currently being leased from a related party.
d. Postpone expenditures for research and development projects. (11/95, Aud., #59, 6006)

79. Which of the following conditions or events most likely would cause an auditor to have substantial doubt about an entity's ability to continue as a going concern?
a. Significant related party transactions are pervasive.
b. Usual trade credit from suppliers is denied.
c. Arrearages in preferred stock dividends are paid.
d. Restrictions on the disposal of principal assets are present. (5/98, Aud., #13, 6630)

80. An auditor concludes that there is substantial doubt about an entity's ability to continue as a going concern for a reasonable period of time. If the entity's financial statements adequately disclose its financial difficulties, the auditor's report is required to include an explanatory paragraph that specifically uses the phrase(s)

	"Reasonable period of time, not to exceed one year"	*"Going concern"*
a.	Yes	Yes
b.	Yes	No
c.	No	Yes
d.	No	No

(5/98, Aud., #14, 6631)

81. Mead, CPA, had substantial doubt about Tech Co.'s ability to continue as a going concern when reporting on Tech's audited financial statements for the year ended June 30, 20X1. That doubt has been removed in 20X2. What is Mead's reporting responsibility if Tech is representing its financial statements for the year ended June 30, 20X2, on a comparative basis with those of 20X1?
a. The explanatory paragraph included in the 20X1 auditor's report should **not** be repeated.
b. The explanatory paragraph included in the 20X1 auditor's report should be repeated in its entirety.
c. A different explanatory paragraph describing Mead's reasons for the removal of doubt should be included.
d. A different explanatory paragraph describing Tech's plans for financial recovery should be included. (11/95, Aud., #73, amended, 6020)

82. An auditor concludes that there is substantial doubt about an entity's ability to continue as a going concern for a reasonable period of time. If the entity's disclosures concerning this matter are adequate, the audit report may include a(an)

	Disclaimer of opinion	*"Except for" qualified opinion*
a.	No	Yes
b.	No	No
c.	Yes	Yes
d.	Yes	No

(Editors, 0346)

83. Which of the following auditing procedures most likely would assist an auditor in identifying conditions and events that may indicate substantial doubt about an entity's ability to continue as a going concern?
a. Inspecting title documents to verify whether any assets are pledged as collateral
b. Confirming with third parties the details of arrangements to maintain financial support
c. Reconciling the cash balance per books with the cut-off bank statement and the bank confirmation
d. Comparing the entity's depreciation and asset capitalization policies to other entities in the industry (5/94, Aud., #55, 4720)

84. Which of the following statements is correct with respect to the auditor's consideration of an entity's ability to continue as a going concern?

a. The auditor's workpapers must include evidential matter which provides assurance that the entity will continue as a going concern.
b. If there is absence of reference to substantial doubt in the auditor's report, this should be viewed as assurance as to an entity's ability to continue as a going concern.
c. It is not necessary for the auditor to design audit procedures solely to identify conditions and events that, when considered in the aggregate, indicate there could be substantial doubt about the entity's ability to continue as a going concern for a reasonable period of time.
d. The auditor has a responsibility to evaluate whether there is substantial doubt about the entity's ability to continue as a going concern for a reasonable period of time, not to exceed the date of the financial statements being audited.

(Editors, 9430)

85. When an auditor concludes there is substantial doubt about a continuing audit client's ability to continue as a going concern for a reasonable period of time, the auditor's responsibility is to

a. Issue a qualified or adverse opinion, depending upon materiality, due to the possible effects on the financial statements.
b. Consider the adequacy of disclosure about the client's possible inability to continue as a going concern.
c. Report to the client's audit committee that management's accounting estimates may need to be adjusted.
d. Reissue the prior year's auditor's report and add an explanatory paragraph that specifically refers to "substantial doubt" and "going concern."

(5/94, Aud., #62, 4727)

86. When audited financial statements are presented in a client's document containing other information, the auditor should

a. Perform inquiry and analytical procedures to ascertain whether the other information is reasonable.
b. Add an explanatory paragraph to the auditor's report without changing the opinion on the financial statements.
c. Perform the appropriate substantive auditing procedures to corroborate the other information.
d. Read the other information to determine that it is consistent with the audited financial statements.

(11/92, Aud., #57, 2991)

87. Investment and property schedules are presented for purposes of additional analysis in an auditor-submitted document. The schedules are not required parts of the basic financial statements, but accompany the basic financial statements. When reporting on such additional information, the measurement of materiality is the

a. Same as that used in forming an opinion on the basic financial statements taken as a whole.
b. Lesser of the individual schedule of investments or schedule of property taken by itself.
c. Greater of the individual schedule of investments or schedule of property taken by itself.
d. Combined total of both the individual schedules of investments and property taken as a whole.

(5/94, Aud., #63, 4728)

88. An auditor concludes that there is a material inconsistency in the other information in an annual report to shareholders containing audited financial statements. If the auditor concludes that the financial statements do **not** require revision, but the client refuses to revise or eliminate the material inconsistency, the auditor may

a. Revise the auditor's report to include a separate explanatory paragraph describing the material inconsistency.
b. Issue an "except for" qualified opinion after discussing the matter with the client's board of directors.
c. Consider the matter closed, since the other information is **not** in the audited financial statements.
d. Disclaim an opinion on the financial statements after explaining the material inconsistency in a separate explanatory paragraph.

(11/94, Aud., #86, 5159)

89. What is an auditor's responsibility for supplementary information, such as segment information, which is outside the basic financial statements, but required by the FASB?

a. The auditor has **no** responsibility for required supplementary information as long as it is outside the basic financial statements.
b. The auditor's only responsibility for required supplementary information is to determine that such information has **not** been omitted.
c. The auditor should apply certain limited procedures to the required supplementary information, and report deficiencies in, or omissions of, such information.
d. The auditor should apply tests of details of transactions and balances to the required supplementary information and report any material misstatements in such information.

(5/94, Aud., #82, 4747)

90. If management declines to present supplementary information required by the Governmental Accounting Standards Board (GASB), the auditor should issue a(an)
a. Adverse opinion.
b. Qualified opinion with an explanatory paragraph.
c. Unqualified opinion.
d. Unqualified opinion with an additional explanatory paragraph. (5/90, Aud., #25, 0399)

PROBLEM 39-2 ADDITIONAL MULTIPLE CHOICE QUESTIONS (30 to 38 minutes)

91. The first standard of reporting requires that "the report shall state whether the financial statements are presented in conformity with generally accepted accounting principles." This should be construed to require
a. A statement of fact by the auditor.
b. An implied measure of fairness.
c. An objective measure of compliance.
d. An opinion by the auditor. (Editors, 9420)

92. Digit Co. uses the FIFO method of costing for its international subsidiary's inventory and LIFO for its domestic inventory. Under these circumstances, the auditor's report on Digit's financial statements should express an
a. Unqualified opinion.
b. Opinion qualified because of a lack of consistency.
c. Opinion qualified because of a departure from GAAP.
d. Adverse opinion. (11/95, Aud., #67, 6014)

93. In which of the following situations would an auditor ordinarily choose between expressing an "except for" qualified opinion or an adverse opinion?
a. The auditor did **not** observe the entity's physical inventory and is unable to become satisfied as to its balance by other auditing procedures.
b. The financial statements fail to disclose information that is required by generally accepted accounting principles.
c. The auditor is asked to report only on the entity's balance sheet and **not** on the other basic financial statements.
d. Events disclosed in the financial statements cause the auditor to have substantial doubt about the entity's ability to continue as a going concern. (5/93, Aud., #58, 3954)

94. An auditor concludes that a client's illegal act, which has a material effect on the financial statements, has not been properly accounted for or disclosed. Depending on the materiality of the effect on the financial statements, the auditor should express either a(an)
a. Adverse opinion or a disclaimer of opinion.
b. Qualified opinion or an adverse opinion.
c. Disclaimer of opinion or an unqualified opinion with a separate explanatory paragraph.
d. Unqualified opinion with a separate explanatory paragraph or a qualified opinion. (5/95, Aud., #13, 5631)

95. Which of the following representations does an auditor make explicitly and which implicitly when issuing an unqualified opinion?

	Conformity with GAAP	*Adequacy of disclosure*
a.	Implicitly	Implicitly
b.	Explicitly	Explicitly
c.	Implicitly	Explicitly
d.	Explicitly	Implicitly (Editors, 0363)

96. Eagle Company's financial statements contain a departure from generally accepted accounting principles because, due to unusual circumstances, the statements would otherwise be misleading. The auditor should express an opinion that is
a. Unqualified but **not** mention the departure in the auditor's report.
b. Unqualified and describe the departure in a separate paragraph.
c. Qualified and describe the departure in a separate paragraph.
d. Qualified or adverse, depending on materiality, and describe the departure in a separate paragraph. (11/90, Aud., #12, 0329)

97. In the first audit of a new client, an auditor was able to extend auditing procedures to gather sufficient evidence about consistency. Under these circumstances, the auditor should
a. Not report on the client's income statement.
b. Not refer to consistency in the auditor's report.
c. State that the consistency standard does **not** apply.
d. State that the accounting principles have been applied consistently. (11/95, Aud., #74, 6021)

98. A limitation on the scope of an audit sufficient to preclude an unqualified opinion will usually result when management
a. States that the financial statements are **not** intended to be presented in conformity with generally accepted accounting principles.
b. Presents financial statements that are prepared in accordance with the cash receipts and disbursements basis of accounting.
c. Does **not** make the minutes of the Board of Directors' meetings available to the auditor.
d. Asks the auditor to report on the balance sheet and **not** on the other basic financial statements. (Editors, 0345)

99. When an auditor qualifies an opinion because of a scope limitation, which paragraph(s) of the auditor's report should indicate that the qualification pertains to the possible effects on the financial statements and **not** to the scope limitation itself?
a. The scope paragraph and the separate explanatory paragraph
b. The scope paragraph only
c. The opinion paragraph and the separate explanatory paragraph
d. The opinion paragraph only (Editors, 0373)

100. Under which of the following circumstances would a disclaimer of opinion **not** be appropriate?
a. The auditor is unable to determine the amounts associated with an employee fraud scheme.
b. Management does **not** provide reasonable justification for a change in accounting principles.
c. The client refuses to permit the auditor to confirm certain accounts receivable or apply alternative procedures to verify their balances.
d. The chief executive officer is unwilling to sign the management representation letter. (11/95, Aud., #66, 6013)

101. The auditor's report should be dated as of the date on which the
a. Report is delivered to the client.
b. Review of the working papers is completed.
c. Fiscal period under audit ends.
d. Field work is completed. (Editors, 0386)

102. Six months after issuing an unqualified opinion on audited financial statements, an auditor discovered that the engagement personnel failed to confirm several of the client's material accounts receivable balances. The auditor should first
a. Request the permission of the client to undertake the confirmation of accounts receivable.
b. Perform alternative procedures to provide a satisfactory basis for the unqualified opinion.
c. Assess the importance of the omitted procedures to the auditor's ability to support the previously expressed opinion.
d. Inquire whether there are persons currently relying, or likely to rely, on the unqualified opinion. (11/90, Aud., #35, 0332)

103. Kane, CPA, concludes that there is substantial doubt about Lima Co.'s ability to continue as a going concern for a reasonable period of time. If Lima's financial statements adequately disclose its financial difficulties, Kane's auditor's report is required to include an explanatory paragraph that specifically uses the phrase(s)

	"Possible discontinuance of operations"	*"Reasonable period of time, **not** to exceed one year"*
a.	Yes	Yes
b.	Yes	No
c.	No	Yes
d.	No	No

(11/95, Aud., #72, 6019)

104. If the auditor concludes that the entity's disclosures with respect to the entity's ability to continue as a going concern for a reasonable period of time are inadequate, the independent auditor should issue a(n)
a. Adverse opinion or a disclaimer of opinion.
b. Qualified opinion or a disclaimer of opinion.
c. Qualified opinion or an adverse opinion.
d. Unqualified opinion with a consistency modification. (Editors, 9429)

105. Which of the following conditions or events most likely would cause an auditor to have substantial doubt about an entity's ability to continue as a going concern?
a. Cash flows from operating activities are negative.
b. Research and development projects are postponed.
c. Significant related party transactions are pervasive.
d. Stock dividends replace annual cash dividends. (11/94, Aud., #71, 5144)

OTHER OBJECTIVE FORMAT QUESTIONS

PROBLEM 39-3 (15 to 25 minutes)

REQUIRED:

ITEMS 1 THROUGH 7 present various independent factual situations an auditor might encounter in conducting an audit. List A represents the types of opinions the auditor ordinarily would issue and List B represents the report modifications (if any) that would be necessary. For each situation, select one response from List A and one from List B. Select as the **best** answer for each item, the action the auditor normally would take. The types of opinions in List A and the report modifications in List B may be selected once, more than once, or not at all.

ASSUME:

- The auditor is independent.
- The auditor previously expressed an unqualified opinion on the prior year's financial statements.
- Only single-year (not comparative) statements are presented for the current year.
- The conditions for an unqualified opinion exist unless contradicted in the factual situations.
- The conditions stated in the factual situations are material.
- No report modifications are to be made except in response to the factual situation.

ITEMS TO BE ANSWERED:

1. In auditing the long-term investments account, an auditor is unable to obtain audited financial statements for an investee located in a foreign country. The auditor concludes that sufficient competent evidential matter regarding this investment cannot be obtained.
2. Due to recurring operating losses and working capital deficiencies, an auditor has substantial doubt about an entity's ability to continue as a going concern for a reasonable period of time. However, the financial statement disclosures concerning these matters are adequate.
3. A principal auditor decides to take responsibility for the work of another CPA who audited a wholly owned subsidiary of the entity and issued an unqualified opinion. The total assets and revenues of the subsidiary represent 17% and 18%, respectively, of the total assets and revenues of the entity being audited.
4. An entity issues financial statements that present financial position and results of operations but omits the related statement of cash flows. Management discloses in the notes to the financial statements that it does not believe the statement of cash flows to be a useful financial statement.
5. An entity changes its depreciation method for production equipment from the straight-line to a units-of-production method based on hours of utilization. The auditor concurs with the change although it has a material effect on the comparability of the entity's financial statements.
6. An entity is a defendant in a lawsuit alleging infringement of certain patent rights. However, the ultimate outcome of the litigation cannot be reasonably estimated by management. The auditor believes there is a reasonable possibility of a significant material loss, but the lawsuit is adequately disclosed in the notes to the financial statements.
7. An entity discloses in the notes to the financial statements certain lease obligations. The auditor believes that the failure to capitalize these leases is a departure from generally accepted accounting principles.

List A: Types of Opinions

A. An "except for" qualified opinion.

B. An unqualified opinion.

C. An adverse opinion.

D. A disclaimer of opinion.

E. Either an "except for" qualified opinion or an adverse opinion.

F. Either a disclaimer of opinion or an "except for" qualified opinion.

G. Either an adverse opinion or a disclaimer of opinion.

List B: Report Modifications

H. Describe the circumstances in an explanatory paragraph **preceding** the opinion paragraph **without modifying** the three standard paragraphs.

I. Describe the circumstances in an explanatory paragraph **following** the opinion paragraph **without modifying** the three standard paragraphs.

J. Describe the circumstances in an explanatory paragraph **preceding** the opinion paragraph and **modify** the **opinion** paragraph.

K. Describe the circumstances in an explanatory paragraph **following** the opinion paragraph and **modify** the **opinion** paragraph.

L. Describe the circumstances in an explanatory paragraph **preceding** the opinion paragraph and **modify** the **scope** and **opinion** paragraphs.

M. Describe the circumstances in an explanatory paragraph **following** the opinion paragraph and **modify** the **scope** and **opinion** paragraphs.

N. Describe the circumstances within the **scope** paragraph without adding an explanatory paragraph.

O. Describe the circumstances within the **opinion** paragraph without adding an explanatory paragraph.

P. Describe the circumstances within the **scope** and **opinion** paragraphs without adding an explanatory paragraph.

Q. Issue the **standard** auditor's report **without modification.** (5/92, Aud., #61-67)

PROBLEM 39-4 (15 to 25 minutes)

Webb & Weber, CPAs, audited the consolidated financial statements of Quest Co. and all but one of its subsidiaries for the year ended September 30, 20X1, and expressed a qualified opinion because Quest capitalized certain research and development expenditures that should have been expensed.

Webb & Weber also audited Quest's consolidated financial statements and all but one of its subsidiaries for the year ended September 30, 20X2. These consolidated financial statements are being presented on a comparative basis with those of the prior year and an unqualified opinion is being expressed.

Webb, the engagement partner, instructed Perry, an assistant on the engagement, to draft the auditor's report on November 4, 20X2, the date of completion of the field work. In drafting the report on page 15, Perry considered the following:

- In preparing its 20X2 financial statements, Quest changed its method of accounting for research and development costs and properly expensed these amounts. Quest also restated its 20X1 financial statements to conform with GAAP. Consequently, Webb & Weber's present opinion on the 20X1 financial statements is different (unqualified) from the opinion expressed on November 5, 20X1.

- Hill & Hall, CPAs, audited the financial statements of Biotherm, Inc., a consolidated subsidiary of Quest, for the years ended September 30, 20X2 and 20X1. The subsidiary's financial statements reflect total assets constituting 23% and 22% at September 30, 20X2 and 20X1, respectively, and total revenues constituting 21% and 20% in 20X2 and 20X1, respectively, of the consolidated totals. Hill & Hall expressed an unqualified opinion each year and furnished Webb & Weber with a copy of each year's auditor's report. Webb & Weber have decided not to assume responsibility for the work of Hill & Hall insofar as it relates to the expression of an opinion on the consolidated financial statements taken as a whole because of the materiality of Biotherm's financial statements to the consolidated financial statements. Hill & Hall's report will not be presented together with that of Webb & Weber.

- Quest is the subject of a grand jury investigation into possible violations of federal antitrust laws and possible related crimes. Related civil class actions are pending. This is adequately disclosed in Note 12 to Quest's consolidated financial statements. Because of the early stage of the investigation, the ultimate outcome of these matters cannot presently be determined. Therefore, no provision for any liability that may result has been recorded.

- Quest experienced a net loss in 20X2 and is currently in default under substantially all of its debt agreements. Management's plans in regard to these matters are adequately disclosed in Note 14 to Quest's consolidated financial statements, although the financial statements do not include any adjustments that might result from the outcome of this uncertainty. These matters raise substantial doubt about Quest's ability to continue as a going concern.

Webb reviewed Perry's draft and indicated (in *Webb's Review Notes*) that there were many deficiencies in Perry's draft.

Independent Auditor's Report

We have audited the consolidated financial statements of Quest Co. and subsidiaries as of September 30, 20X2 and 20X1, and the related consolidated statements of income, changes in stockholders' equity, and cash flows for the years then ended. These financial statements are the responsibility of the Company's management. Our responsibility is to express an opinion on these financial statements based on our audits. We did not audit the financial statements of Biotherm, Inc., a wholly-owned subsidiary, which statements reflect total assets constituting 23% and 22% at September 30, 20X2 and 20X1, respectively, and total revenues constituting 21% and 20% in 20X2 and 20X1, respectively, of the consolidated totals. Those statements were audited by Hill & Hall, CPAs, whose reports have been furnished to us, and our opinion, insofar as it relates to the amounts included for Biotherm, Inc., is based solely on their reports.

We conducted our audits in accordance with generally accepted auditing standards. Those standards require that we plan and perform the audit to obtain reasonable assurance about whether the financial statements are free of material misstatement. An audit includes examining, on a test basis, evidence supporting the amounts and disclosures in the financial statement. An audit also includes assessing the accounting principles used, as well as assessing control risk. We believe that our audits provide a reasonable basis for our opinion.

In our previous report dated November 5, 20X1, we expressed a qualified opinion that, except for the effects on the 20X1 financial statements of not expensing certain research and development costs, the 20X1 financial statements present fairly, in all material respects, the financial position of Quest Co. and subsidiaries as of September 30, 20X1, and the results of its operations and its cash flows for the year then ended in conformity with generally accepted accounting principles. As described in Note 10, the Company has changed its method of accounting for these items and restated its 20X1 financial statements to conform with generally accepted accounting principles. Accordingly, our present opinion on the 20X1 financial statements, as presented herein, is different from that expressed in our previous report.

In our opinion, based on our audits and the reports of the other auditors, the consolidated financial statements referred to above present fairly, in all material respects, the financial position of Quest Co. as of September 30, 20X2 and 20X1, in conformity with generally accepted accounting principles, except for the uncertainty, which is discussed in Note 12 to the consolidated financial statements.

The accompanying consolidated financial statements have been prepared assuming that the Company will continue in existence for a reasonable period of time. As discussed in Note 14 to the consolidated financial statements, the Company suffered a net loss in 20X2 and is currently in default under substantially all of its debt agreements. Management's plans in regard to these matters are also described in Note 14. The consolidated financial statements do not include any adjustments that might result from the outcome of this uncertainty.

Webb & Weber, CPAs
November 4, 20X2

REQUIRED:

ITEMS 1 THROUGH 16 represent the deficiencies noted by Webb. For each deficiency, indicate whether

W. Webb's review note is correct.
P. Perry's draft is correct
B. Both Webb's review note and Perry's draft are incorrect.

Webb's Review Notes

1. The reference to the subsidiary, Biotherm, and the magnitude of its financial statements should be in the scope paragraph rather than in the opening (introductory) paragraph.

2. The other independent auditors, Hill & Hall, should be named in the scope paragraph rather than in the opening (introductory) paragraph.

3. The reference in the scope paragraph to "the financial statements are free of material misstatement" should be followed by the phrase "whether caused by error or fraud."

4. The required reference in the scope paragraph to assessing "significant estimates made by management" has been omitted.

5. The reference in the scope paragraph to "assessing control risk" is inappropriate and should be omitted from the report.

6. The required reference in the scope paragraph to "evaluating the overall financial statement presentation" has been omitted.

7. A separate explanatory paragraph describing the grand jury investigation into possible violations

of federal antitrust laws is required to be placed between the scope and opinion paragraphs.

8. The reference in the first explanatory paragraph (between the scope and opinion paragraphs) to the qualified opinion on the 20X1 financial statements is not properly placed. It should be placed in the opinion paragraph.

9. The reference in the first explanatory paragraph (between the scope and opinion paragraphs) to Note 10 does not express our concurrence with Quest's change in accounting principle. Our concurrence should be specifically expressed in this paragraph.

10. The reference to the other auditors in the opinion paragraph is incomplete. It should specifically include the words "unqualified opinion" to describe the type of opinion expressed by Hill & Hall.

11. The opinion paragraph should extend the auditor's opinion beyond financial position to include the results of Quest's operations and its changes in stockholders' equity.

12. The reference to the uncertainty in the opinion paragraph is incomplete. It should describe the nature of the uncertainty as pertaining to the grand jury investigation into possible violations of federal antitrust laws.

13. The explanatory paragraph following the opinion paragraph does not include the term "substantial doubt." This term is required to be used in this paragraph under these circumstances.

14. The explanatory paragraph following the opinion paragraph does not include the term "going concern." This term is required to be used in this paragraph under these circumstances.

15. The explanatory paragraph following the opinion paragraph includes an inappropriate statement that "the consolidated financial statements do not include any adjustments that might result from the outcome of this uncertainty." This statement is misleading and should be omitted.

16. The auditor's report is not correctly dated. It should be dual dated because of Note 12, the grand jury investigation, and also because of Note 14, the going concern uncertainty.

(11/98, Aud., #2, amended, 6716-6731)

ESSAY QUESTIONS

ESSAY 39-5 (15 to 25 minutes)

The auditor's report below was drafted by Miller, a staff accountant of Pell & Pell, CPAs, at the completion of the audit of the consolidated financial statements of Bond Co. for the year ended July 31, 20X2. The report was submitted to the engagement partner who reviewed the audit working papers and properly concluded that an unqualified opinion should be issued. In drafting the report, Miller considered the following:

- Bond's consolidated financial statements for the year ended July 31, 20X1, are to be presented for comparative purposes. Pell previously audited these statements and appropriately rendered an unmodified report.
- Bond has suffered recurring losses from operations and has adequately disclosed these losses and management's plans concerning the losses in a note to the consolidated financial statements. Although Bond has prepared the financial statements assuming it will continue as a going concern, Miller has substantial doubt about Bond's ability to continue as a going concern.
- Smith & Smith, CPAs, audited the financial statements of BC Services, Inc., a consolidated subsidiary of Bond, for the year ended July 31, 20X2. The subsidiary's financial statements reflected total assets and revenues of 15% and 18%, respectively, of the consolidated totals. Smith expressed an unqualified opinion and furnished Miller with a copy of the auditor's report. Smith also granted permission to present the report together with the principal auditor's report. Miller decided not to present Smith's report with that of Pell, but instead to make reference to Smith.

Independent Auditor's Report

We have audited the consolidated balance sheets of Bond Co. and subsidiaries as of July 31, 20X2, and 20X1, and the related consolidated statements of income and retained earnings for the years then ended. Our responsibility is to express an opinion on these financial statements based on our audits. We did not audit the financial statements of BC Services, Inc., a wholly-owned subsidiary. Those statements were audited by Smith & Smith, CPAs, whose report has been furnished to us, and our opinion, insofar as it relates to the amounts included for BC Services, Inc., is based solely on the report of Smith & Smith.

We conducted our audits in accordance with generally accepted auditing standards. Those standards require that we plan and perform the audit to obtain reasonable assurance about whether the financial statements are free of material misstatement. An audit includes assessing control risk, the accounting principles used, and significant estimates made by management, as well as evaluating the overall financial statement presentation. We believe that our audits provide a reasonable basis for our opinion.

In our opinion, based on our audits and the report of Smith & Smith, CPAs, the consolidated financial statements referred to above present fairly, in all material respects except for the matter discussed below, the financial position of Bond Co. as of July 31, 20X2, and 20X1, and the results of its operations for the years then ended.

The accompanying consolidated financial statements have been prepared with the disclosure in Note 13 that the company has suffered recurring losses from operations. Management's plans in regard to those matters are also discussed in Note 13. The financial statements do not include any adjustments that might result from the outcome of this uncertainty.

Pell & Pell, CPAs
November 4, 20X2

REQUIRED:

Identify the deficiencies in the auditor's report as drafted by Miller. Group the deficiencies by paragraph and in the order in which the deficiencies appear. Do **not** redraft the report.

(11/93, Aud., #3, amended, 6298)

ESSAY 39-6 (15 to 25 minutes)

Post, CPA, accepted an engagement to audit the financial statements of General Co., a new client. General is a publicly held retailing entity that recently replaced its operating management. In the course of applying auditing procedures, Post discovered that General's financial statements may be materially misstated due to the existence of fraud.

REQUIRED:

a. Describe Post's responsibilities on the circumstances described above.

b. Describe Post's responsibilities for reporting on General's financial statements and other communications if Post is precluded from applying necessary procedures in searching for fraud.

c. Describe Post's responsibilities for reporting on General's financial statements and other communications if Post concludes that General's financial statements are materially affected by fraud.

d. Describe the circumstances in which Post may have a duty to disclose fraud to third parties outside General's management and its audit committee.

(5/93, Aud., #4)

ESSAY 39-7 (15 to 25 minutes)

The auditors' report below was drafted by Moore, a staff accountant of Tyler & Tyler, CPAs, at the completion of the audit of the financial statements of Park Publishing Co., Inc., for the year ended September 30, 20X2. The report was submitted to the engagement partner who reviewed the audit working papers and properly concluded that an unqualified opinion should be issued. In drafting the report, Moore considered the following:

- During fiscal year 20X2, Park changed its depreciation method. The engagement partner concurred with this change in accounting principle and its justification and Moore included an explanatory paragraph in the auditor's report.
- The 20X2 financial statements are affected by an uncertainty concerning a lawsuit, the outcome of which cannot presently be estimated. Moore has included an explanatory paragraph in the auditors' report.
- The financial statements for the year ended September 30, 20X1, are to be presented for comparative purposes. Tyler & Tyler previously audited these statements and expressed an unqualified opinion.

<u>Independent Auditors' Report</u>

To the Board of Directors of Park Publishing Co., Inc.:

We have audited the accompanying balance sheets of Park Publishing Co., Inc. as of September 30, 20X2, and 20X1, and the related statements of income and cash flows for the years then ended. These financial statements are the responsibility of the company's management.

We conducted our audits in accordance with generally accepted auditing standards. Those standards require that we plan and perform the audit to obtain reasonable assurance about whether the financial statements are fairly presented. An audit includes examining, on a test basis, evidence supporting the amounts and disclosures in the financial statements. An audit also includes assessing significant estimates made by management, as well as evaluating the overall financial statement presentation. We believe that our audits provide a basis for determining whether any material modifications should be made to the accompanying financial statements.

As discussed in Note X to the financial statements, the company changed its method of computing depreciation in fiscal 20X2.

In our opinion, except for the accounting change, with which we concur, the financial statements referred to above present fairly, in all material respects, the financial position of Park Publishing Co., Inc. as of September 30, 20X2, and the results of its operations and its cash flows for the year then ended in conformity with generally accepted accounting principles.

As discussed in Note Y to the financial statements, the company is a defendant in a lawsuit alleging infringement of certain copyrights. The company has filed a counteraction, and preliminary hearings on both actions are in progress. Accordingly, any provision for liability is subject to adjudication of this matter.

Tyler & Tyler, CPAs
November 5, 20X2

REQUIRED:

Identify the deficiencies in the auditors' report as drafted by Moore. Group the deficiencies by paragraph and in the order in which the deficiencies appear. Do **not** redraft the report.

(11/92, Aud., #3, amended)

ESSAY 39-8 (15 to 25 minutes)

Green, CPA, is auditing the financial statements of Taylor Corporation for the year ended December 31, 20X1. Green plans to complete the field work and sign the auditor's report about May 10, 20X2. Green is concerned about events and transactions occurring after December 31, 20X1 that may affect the 20X1 financial statements.

REQUIRED:

a. What are the general types of subsequent events that require Green's consideration and evaluation?

b. What are the auditing procedures Green should consider performing to gather evidence concerning subsequent events? (5/90, Aud., #4, amended, 3057)

ESSAY 39-9 (15 to 25 minutes)

On September 30, 20X1, White & Co., CPAs, was engaged to audit the consolidated financial statements of National Motors, Inc. for the year ended December 31, 20X1. The consolidated financial statements of National had not been audited the prior year. National's inadequate inventory records precluded White from forming an opinion as to the proper or consistent application of generally accepted accounting principles to inventory balances on January 1, 20X1. Therefore, White decided not to express an opinion on the results of operations for the year ended December 31, 20X1. National elected not to present comparative financial statements.

Rapid Parts Company, a consolidated subsidiary of National, was audited for the year ended December 31, 20X1, by Green & Co., CPAs. Green completed its field work on February 28, 20X2, and submitted an unqualified opinion on Rapid's financial statements on March 7, 20X2. Rapid's statements reflect total assets and revenues constituting 22% and 25%, respectively, of the consolidated totals of National. White decided not to assume responsibility for the work of Green. Green's report on Rapid does not accompany National's consolidated statements.

White completed its field work on March 28, 20X2, and submitted its auditor's report to National on April 4, 20X2.

REQUIRED:

Prepare White and Company's auditor's report on the consolidated financial statements of National Motors, Inc. (11/86, Aud., #5, amended)

ESSAY 39-10 (15 to 25 minutes)

The CPA firm of May & Marty has audited the consolidated financial statements of BGI Corporation. May & Marty performed the audit of the parent company and all subsidiaries except for BGI-Western Corporation, which was audited by the CPA firm of Dey & Dee. BGI-Western constituted approximately 10% of the consolidated assets and 6% of the consolidated revenue.

Dey & Dee issued an unqualified opinion on the financial statements of BGI-Western. May & Marty will be issuing an unqualified opinion on the consolidated financial statements of BGI.

REQUIRED:

a. What procedures should May & Marty consider performing with respect to Dey & Dee's audit of BGI-Western's financial statements that will be appropriate whether or not reference is to be made to the other auditors?

b. Describe the various circumstances under which May & Marty could take responsibility for the work of Dey & Dee and make no reference to Dey & Dee's audit of BGI-Western in May & Marty's auditor's report on the consolidated financial statements of BGI. (11/85, Aud., #2)

ESSAY 39-11 (25 to 35 minutes)

On November 19, 20X1, Wall, CPA, was engaged to audit the financial statements of Trendy Auto Imports, Inc. for the year ended December 31, 20X1. Wall is considering Trendy's ability to continue as a going concern.

REQUIRED:

a. Describe Wall's basic responsibility in considering Trendy's ability to continue as a going concern.

b. Describe the audit procedures Wall most likely would perform to identify conditions and events that may indicate that Trendy has a going concern problem.

c. Describe the management plans that Wall should consider that could mitigate the adverse effects of Trendy's financial difficulties if Wall identified conditions and events that indicated a potential going concern problem.

(5/95, Aud., #5, amended, 6161)

SOLUTION 39-1 MULTIPLE CHOICE ANSWERS

REPORTING STANDARDS

1. (b) An unqualified opinion should be issued only when the auditor is satisfied that the financial statements present fairly, in all material respects, the financial position of the entity as of the balance sheet date and the results of its operations and its cash flows in conformity with GAAP. Documentation, acknowledgment, or recording of the amount of known misstatements are insufficient to accomplish this goal. Adjusting entries already recorded by the client would correct misstatements, not be a part of the total misstatement.

2. (a) AU 411.10 lists the new GAAP hierarchy which indicates that FASB Technical Bulletins are in the second category. Answer (b) is included in the fourth category. AU 411.11 states that in the absence of a pronouncement covered by Rule 203 or another source of established accounting principles, the auditor may consider other accounting literature, depending on its relevance in the circumstances. Other accounting literature includes FASB Statements of Financial Accounting Concepts and AICPA Technical Practice Aids.

3. (c) AU 508.05 states, "The objective of the fourth reporting standard is to prevent misinterpretation of the degree of responsibility the accountant is assuming when his [or her] name is associated with financial statements." The auditor may express different opinions on the statements presented. Material scope restrictions result in a qualification or disclaimer of opinion. Per AU 508.33, an auditor is not precluded from reporting on only one of the basic financial statements and not the others.

4. (a) According to AU 623.16, "If the specified...item...is based upon an entity's net income...the auditor should have audited the complete financial statements to express an opinion on the specified...item." Hardy could express an opinion even if Gold's financial statements are not prepared in conformity with GAAP or if Field does not own controlling interest in Gold. A requirement that Hardy's report be available for distribution to Gold's other employees is nonexistent; such disclosure might actually conflict with client confidentiality requirements. Also see the text discussion of piecemeal opinions.

TYPES OF OPINIONS

5. (d) Since single-year financial statements are presented, an auditor need not modify his or her report to indicate that the prior year statements were audited by other auditors. The inability to obtain audited financial statements supporting an entity's investment in a foreign affiliate represents a scope limitation resulting in a qualified opinion or a disclaimer of opinion. The entity's omission of the statement of cash flows would result in a qualified opinion. While emphasis of a matter does not preclude the issuance of an unqualified opinion, the report must be modified to include a separate paragraph discussing the matter.

6. (b) AU 508.36 and .43 state that the omission of a basic financial statement, such as the statement of cash flows, is a departure from GAAP and requires the auditor to express a qualified or an adverse opinion, depending on materiality, the significance of the item to the entity, the pervasiveness of the misstatement, and the effect of the misstatement on the financial statements as a whole. Disclaimer opinions are issued for scope limitations. Separate explanatory paragraphs are added to an unqualified opinion for the emphasis of a matter, uncertainties, and changes in accounting principles. A review report opinion would be changed for the omission of a required basic financial statement.

7. (d) AU 508.24 states, "When restrictions that significantly limit the scope of the audit are *imposed by the client*, ordinarily the auditor should disclaim an opinion on the financial statements."

8. (d) Per AU 508.24, the inability to obtain audited financial statements of a consolidated investee represents a scope limitation resulting in a qualified opinion or a disclaimer of opinion. Per AU 508.11, the circumstances in answers (a), (b), and (c) may require an explanatory paragraph, but they do not preclude an unqualified opinion.

9. (d) AU 508.30 states, "If, after considering the existing conditions and available evidence, the auditor concludes that sufficient evidential matter supports management's assertions about the nature of a matter involving an uncertainty...an unqualified opinion is ordinarily appropriate." When an explanatory paragraph does not affect an opinion, it comes after the opinion paragraph.

10. (d) AU 508.30 states, "If, after considering the existing conditions and available evidence, the auditor concludes that sufficient evidential matter supports management's assertions about the nature of a matter involving an uncertainty...an unqualified opinion is ordinarily appropriate." Per AU 508.11, answers (a), (b), and (c) would be appropriate for mention in explanatory language to an auditor's standard report.

11. (a) AU 420.12 states, "The effect of a change in accounting principle may be inseparable from the effect of a change in estimate. Although the accounting for such a change is the *same as that accorded a change only in estimate*, a change in principle is involved. Accordingly, this type of change requires recognition in the auditor's report through the addition of an explanatory paragraph."

12. (b) AU 508.05 and .67 allow the auditor to express differing opinions on the balance sheet and income statement. The opinion on the balance sheet is unqualified because the ending inventory is fairly stated. The opinion on the income statement is a disclaimer because of an inability to obtain sufficient audit evidence (a scope limitation) regarding cost of goods sold (because beginning inventory has a significant impact on cost of goods sold).

13. (b) When inadequately disclosed conditions exist that cause an auditor to have substantial doubt about the entity's ability to continue as a going concern, the statements are not in accordance with GAAP. An adverse opinion generally is not an option when a scope limitation is present. An inability to apply procedures (including not observing physical inventory) is a scope limitation. A change in accounting principles, if adequately disclosed, would not result in an adverse opinion.

STANDARD REPORT

14. (c) Per AU 508.08, the fourth sentence of the scope paragraph of an auditor's standard report states, "An audit also includes assessing the accounting principles used and significant estimates made by management, as well as evaluating the overall financial statement presentation." Answers (a) and (d) are not mentioned in the report. Per AU 508.16, consistency is only mentioned when it is absent, and requires explanatory language be added to the standard report after the opinion paragraph.

15. (a) AU 508.09 states that if the auditor is engaged to audit the financial statements of a company that is not the auditor's client, the report should be addressed to the client and **not** to the directors or stockholders of the company being audited.

16. (b) The basic elements of the introductory paragraph of the auditor's standard report are a statement that financial statements identified in the report were audited and a statement that the financial statements are the responsibility of the Company's management and that the auditor's responsibility is to express an opinion on the financial statements based on the audit (AU 508.08).

17. (b) AU 508.08 identifies the basic elements of the audit report; item f.(2) includes, "assessing the accounting principles used and significant estimates made by management," item c. indicates, "a statement that the financial statements are the responsibility of the Company's management," and item h. includes, "an opinion as to whether the financial statements present fairly, in all material respects,...in conformity with generally accepted accounting principles." Answers (a), (c), and (d) are included in the report.

18. (c) AU 508.08 presents the standard form of the auditor's report. GAAS is referred to in the scope paragraph; GAAP is referred to in the opinion paragraph.

19. (d) The statement that the auditor obtains *reasonable* assurance about whether the financial statements are free of material misstatement recognizes the existence of audit risk. Answers (a), (b), and (c) do not recognize the existence of audit risk.

EXPLANATORY LANGUAGE

20. (b) AU 341.12 provides guidance on the auditor's considerations in deciding whether an explanatory paragraph needs to be added to his or her report because of a matter involving the uncertainty as to an entity's ability to continue as a going concern. Answers (a), (c), and (d) are examples of when a qualified, adverse, or disclaimer opinion should be issued.

21. (d) Per AU 508.50 through 57, a material unjustified accounting change would require that the auditor express a qualified or adverse opinion. Both require an explanatory paragraph. A material weakness in internal control is generally not mentioned in the auditor's report.

22. (b) If reference is made to the report of another auditor as a basis, in part, for the opinion, this divided responsibility is indicated in the introductory, scope, and opinion paragraphs of the report (AU 508.12 and .13).

ANOTHER AUDITOR

23. (c) When the principal auditor makes reference to another auditor, the principal auditor doesn't assume responsibility for the other auditor's work. At a minimum, the principal auditor should inquire about the professional reputation and independence of the other CPA. Reviewing the other CPA's working papers, discussing the results of the other CPA's procedures, and determining that the other CPA has a sufficient understanding of the subsidiary's internal control are beyond the principal auditor's minimum duties.

24. (a) AU 508.12 states, "When the auditor decides to make reference to the report of another auditor as a basis, in part, for his [or her] opinion, he [or she] should disclose this fact in the introductory paragraph of his [or her] report and should refer to the report of the other auditor in expressing his [or her] opinion. These references indicate division of responsibility for performance of the audit." AU 508.13 gives an example of such a report that is similar to the illustrated paragraph.

25. (b) AU §543.04 states that if the principal auditor is able to satisfy him- or herself as to the independence and professional reputation of the other auditor, he or she may be able to express an opinion on the financial statements taken as a whole without making reference in the report to the audit of the other auditor. Issuing a standard report with an unqualified opinion would be the result of deciding not to make reference to the other CPA, not the reason for not making reference.

DEPARTURE FROM GAAP

26. (a) AU 508.14 and .15 state that if the statements or data contain a departure from the reporting requirements of Rule 203 and the member can demonstrate that due to unusual circumstances the financial statements would otherwise have been misleading, the member can comply with the rule by describing the departure, its approximate effects, and the reasons why compliance with the principle would result in a misleading statement. The auditor's report should include, in a separate paragraph, the information required by the rule and it would still be appropriate for him or her to express an unqualified opinion with respect to the conformity of the financial statements with GAAP.

27. (a) AU 623.07 states that the auditor should consider whether the financial statements are suitably titled. If the auditor believes that the financial statements are not suitably titled, the auditor should disclose these reservations in an explanatory paragraph of the report and qualify the opinion. The auditor should not rely on someone else for his or her opinion. The opinion should be qualified; a disclaimer opinion is issued when there has been a scope limitation. Terms such as balance sheet, statement of financial position, statement of income, statement of operations, and statement of cash flows or similar titles are generally understood to be applicable only to financial statements that are intended to present financial position, results of operations, or cash flows in conformity with GAAP. Therefore, explanatory language in the notes to the financial statements is insufficient.

CONSISTENCY

28. (b) AU 508.16 states, "If there has been a change in accounting principles or in the method of their application that has a material effect on the comparability of the company's financial statements, the auditor should refer to the change in an explanatory paragraph of his [or her] report. Such

explanatory paragraph (following the opinion paragraph) should identify the nature of the change and refer the reader to the note in the financial statements that discusses the change in detail."

29. (d) AU 508.16 states that if there has been a change in accounting principles or in the method of their application that has a material effect on the comparability of the company's financial statements, the auditor should refer to the change in an explanatory paragraph, identify the nature of the change, and refer the reader to the note in the financial statements that discussed the change in detail. The justification of the change should not be given, the justification is implied by the statement in the auditor's report that the financial statements are presented fairly. The auditor would not describe the effect of the change in the audit report nor his or her concurrence because this is also implied in the auditor's opinion.

30. (a) An auditor must disclaim an opinion if unable to gather sufficient evidence.

31. (c) Consistency is only mentioned when it is absent in the financial statements. A change in the useful life used to calculate the provision for depreciation expense is merely a change in estimate and does not require comment by the auditor. The other three answer options would require a comment that the financial statements were not consistent with the prior period.

32. (c) AU 508.34 states that the auditor should not refer to consistency in his or her report when there has been no change in accounting principles or there has been a change in an accounting principle whose effect on the comparability of the financial statements is *not* material. A change in accounting principles that has a *material* effect on the comparability of the company's financial statements is referred to in an explanatory paragraph of the audit report. The auditor's concurrence with a change is implicit unless he or she takes exception to the change in expressing his or her opinion as to fair presentation of the financial statements in conformity with GAAP. The change in accounting principle is only referred to in the opinion paragraph if the auditor does not concur with the change.

UNCERTAINTY

33. (a) AU 508.30 states, "If, after considering the existing conditions and available evidence, the auditor concludes that sufficient evidential matter supports management's assertions about the nature of a matter involving an uncertainty…an unqualified opinion is ordinarily appropriate." Thus, an unqualified opinion would be appropriate in this situation, and an explanatory paragraph or qualification of the opinion would be unnecessary.

34. (a) AU 508.47 states, "The auditor's consideration is influenced by his [or her] perception of the needs of a reasonable person who will rely on the financial statements. Materiality judgments involving risks or uncertainties are made in light of the surrounding circumstances."

35. (c) AU 508.11 states, "Certain circumstances, while not affecting the auditor's unqualified opinion, may require that the auditor add an explanatory paragraph to his [or her] standard report. The auditor may add an explanatory paragraph to emphasize a matter…" AU 508.11 does not list an uncertainty as a circumstance requiring an explanatory paragraph. AU 508.30 states, "If…the auditor concludes that sufficient evidential matter supports management's assertions about the nature of a matter involving an uncertainty…an unqualified opinion is ordinarily appropriate." An **emphasis** paragraph [containing explanatory information] is never required (AU 508.19).

36. (a) The auditor's decision to qualify his or her opinion rather than issue an unqualified opinion with an explanatory paragraph indicates that sufficient evidential matter was not obtained which would resolve the uncertainty, its presentation, or disclosure in the financial statements, or which would indicate that the financial statements are not in conformity with GAAP (AU 508.30). Answers (b), (c), and (d) are measurements of the uncertainty, which would be disclosed in footnotes and possibly in an emphasis paragraph of the auditor's report.

EMPHASIS

37. (d) AU 508.19 states, "The auditor may emphasize a matter regarding the financial statements [but intends to express an unqualified opinion.] Examples [include situations where the auditor may wish to emphasize] that the entity is a component of a larger business enterprise, [or that it] has had significant transactions with related parties…." These circumstances would not require "except for" wording in the auditor's report. The information may be included in both places. Typically, more detail regarding the matter is provided in the footnotes. AU 508.19 states specifically that phrases such as "with the foregoing explanation" should not be used in the opinion paragraph in a situation of this type.

QUALIFIED OPINIONS

38. (d) Neither phrase should be used when the auditor is expressing a qualified opinion. AU 508.21 states, "Phrases such as *subject to* and *with the foregoing explanation* are not clear or forceful enough and should not be used. Since accompanying notes are part of the financial statements, wording such as *fairly presented, in all material respects, when read in conjunction with Note 1* is likely to be misunderstood and should not be used."

39. (b) Since the CPA cannot be in accordance with GAAS if the CPA is not independent, the nonindependent CPA must disclaim an opinion (AU 504.08 - .10). AU 508.35 provides for a qualified opinion when there is a material departure from GAAP. When there are scope limitations, AU 508.22 indicates that the auditor should qualify or disclaim an opinion. AU 336.16 allows reference be made to the work of a specialist when there is a departure from an unqualified opinion and such reference will help to clarify the reason for the qualification.

40. (d) AU 508.26 notes that in a qualified opinion resulting from a scope limitation, the scope and opinion paragraphs are modified and an explanatory paragraph is added.

41. (c) AU 508.22 states, "Restrictions on the scope of [the auditor's] audit, whether imposed by the client or by circumstances, such as the timing of his [or her] work, the inability to obtain sufficient competent evidential matter, or an inadequacy in the accounting records, may require him [or her] to qualify his [or her] opinion or to disclaim an opinion." If management has not provided reasonable justification for a change in accounting principle, the auditor should express a qualified opinion or, if the effect of the change is sufficiently material, the auditor should express an adverse opinion on the financial statements (AU 508.50).

42. (c) AU 508.26 states that when an auditor qualifies an opinion because of a scope limitation, the opinion paragraph should indicate that the qualification pertains to the possible effects on the financial statements and not to the scope limitation itself. There are no reporting requirements for departures from GAAS; however, there are separate reporting requirements for departures from GAAP.

SCOPE LIMITATION

43. (a) AU 508.07 states that the auditor can determine that he or she is able to express an unqualified opinion only if the audit has been conducted in accordance with GAAS and if he or she has, therefore, been able to apply all the procedures he or she considers necessary in the circumstances. Restrictions on the scope of work, the inability to obtain sufficient competent evidential matter, or an inadequacy in the accounting records may require him or her to qualify or disclaim an opinion. An unqualified opinion may be issued in the circumstances in answer (b), but an explanatory paragraph and language would be added to the report stating that disclosures required by GAAP have not been presented. An engagement letter is not a required procedure to be performed in order for the financial statements to be in conformity with GAAP, but it is a recommended procedure. Reportable conditions and management's decisions concerning costs to be incurred and related benefits are the responsibility of management. Provided the audit committee has acknowledged its understanding and consideration of deficiencies and associated risks, the auditor may decide a matter does not need to be repeated.

44. (a) AU 508.64 states that piecemeal opinions (expressions of opinion as to certain identified items in financial statements) should not be expressed when the auditor has disclaimed an opinion because piecemeal opinions tend to overshadow a disclaimer of opinion. The auditor may issue an audit report on only one basic financial statement. When disclaiming an opinion due to a scope limitation, the scope paragraph is omitted from the audit report. The inclusion of the statement is inappropriate in any paragraph of an audit report that disclaims an opinion.

45. (c) According to AU 508.33, an auditor is not precluded from reporting on only one of the basic financial statements and not the others. A scope limitation would not exist if the auditor is able to apply all the procedures the auditor considers necessary. Such engagements involve limited reporting objectives. Acceptance of the engagement is not a violation of the profession's ethical standards, as the work can be expected to be accomplished. Per AU 508.64, a "piecemeal opinion" is an opinion on specific elements of the financial statements when the auditor has disclaimed an opinion on the statements as a whole and is unacceptable. A disclaimer of opinion would be unnecessary because Harris will have access to all information underlying the basic financial statements and, thus, could apply all the procedures he or she considers necessary.

46. (d) AU 508.62 states, "When disclaiming an opinion because of a scope limitation,...the

auditor should not identify the procedures that were performed nor include the paragraph describing the characteristics of an audit [i.e., the scope paragraph]; to do so may tend to overshadow the disclaimer." The disclaimer of opinion paragraph replaces the opinion paragraph.

47. (d) AU 508.25 states, "When a qualified opinion results from a limitation on the scope of the audit or an insufficiency of evidential matter, the situation should be described in an explanatory paragraph preceding the opinion paragraph and referred to in both the scope and opinion paragraphs of the auditor's report."

INADEQUATE DISCLOSURE

48. (c) According to AU 508.42, the language generally used in this circumstance is "except for the omission of the information discussed in the preceding paragraph" "Subject to" and "With the foregoing explanation" is unacceptable language. The language in answer (d) is for an adverse opinion.

49. (d) AU 508.42 illustrates the proper treatment of an opinion qualified due to inadequate disclosure and the resulting modification of the opinion paragraph. The scope and introductory paragraphs are not affected.

ADVERSE OPINIONS

50. (c) This is a departure from GAAP; if the departure has a material, pervasive effect, an adverse opinion is appropriate (AU 508.58). Answer (a) is a scope limitation problem and could result in a disclaimer (AU 508.61). The situation in (b) will result in expanding substantive tests or determining that the entity is not auditable. AU 341.12 notes that the situation in (d) will result in the addition of an explanatory paragraph.

DISCLAIMER OF OPINION

51. (d) AU 508.61 states, "A disclaimer of opinion states that the auditor does not express an opinion on the financial statements." AU 508.62 states, "[It] is appropriate when the auditor has not performed an audit sufficient in scope to enable him [or her] to form an opinion on the financial statements." In addition, AU 508.24 states, "When restrictions that significantly limit the scope of the audit are imposed by the client, ordinarily the auditor should disclaim an opinion on the financial statements." Answers (a), (b), and (c) are all departures from GAAP and should be accounted for with a qualified or an adverse opinion.

COMPARATIVE FINANCIAL STATEMENTS

52. (c) AU 508.65 states, "Reference in the fourth reporting standard to the financial statements taken as a whole applies not only to the financial statements of the current period, but also to those of one or more prior periods that are presented on a comparative basis with those of the current period." The expression relates only to the statements of the periods presented. Answers (b) and (d) limit the application of the expression to the current period or current and immediately preceding periods, respectively.

53. (a) AU 508.71 indicates that the predecessor auditor should, before reissuing a auditor report, obtain a letter of representations from the *successor auditor*.

54. (d) A predecessor auditor who reissues a report because the audit client desires comparative statements should not refer in the reissued report to the report or work of the successor auditor (AU 508.71).

55. (a) AU 508.73 states, "A predecessor auditor's knowledge of the current affairs of his or her former client is obviously limited in the absence of a continuing relationship. Consequently, when reissuing a report on prior-period financial statements, a predecessor auditor should use the date of the previous report to avoid any implication that he [or she] has examined any records, transactions, or events after that date. If the predecessor auditor revises his [or her] report or if the financial statements are restated, he [or she] should dual-date the report."

56. (c) AU 508.71 states, "Before reissuing (or consenting to the reuse of) a report previously issued on the financial statements of a prior period, a predecessor auditor should consider whether his [or her] previous report on those statements is still appropriate. Either the current form or manner of presentations of the financial statements of the prior period or one or more subsequent events might make a predecessor auditor's previous report inappropriate. Consequently, a predecessor auditor should (1) read the financial statements of the current period, (2) compare the prior-period financial statements that he [or she] reported on with the financial statements to be presented for comparative purposes, and (3) obtain a letter of representations from the successor auditor." Answer (b) could be perceived as performing additional audit procedures and would be insufficient for the performance of an audit in accordance with GAAS. The predecessor auditor should not refer in his or her reissued report

to the report or the work of the successor auditor (AU 508.71). Answer (d) is incorrect because no explanatory paragraph of this nature would be added to the report.

57. (a) AU 508.68 states that if an auditor's previous opinion on financial statements was qualified or adverse due to a GAAP departure and those statements are restated to comply with GAAP, the auditor should, in a reissued report, note that the statements are restated and express an unqualified opinion. Per AU 508.74, a successor auditor cannot change a predecessor auditor's opinion, but should inform the predecessor of the restatement and make note of it in the audit report. The prior year report is not affected. The current and updated report should refer to the prior year financial statements as restated.

58. (d) AU 508.74 states, "If the financial statements of a prior period have been audited by a predecessor auditor whose report is not presented, the successor auditor should indicate in the introductory paragraph of his [or her] report (a) that the financial statements of the prior period were audited by another auditor, (b) the date of his [or her] report, (c) the type of report issued by the predecessor auditor, and (d) if the report was other than a standard report, the substantive reasons therefore." AU 508.74 provides an example of such a report, in which the predecessor auditor is **not** referred to by name.

DATING

59. (b) AU 530.05 notes than when using dual dating, the auditor's responsibility for events occurring subsequent to the completion of field work is limited to the specific event disclosed. Under no circumstances does the auditor's responsibility extend to all of the events up to the date of the last subsequent event. Responsibility for subsequent events does not extend through the date of report issuance and does not extend past the completion of field work.

60. (d) AU 530.06 states, "An independent auditor may...be requested by his or her client to furnish additional copies of a previously issued report. Use of the original report date in a reissued report removes any implication that records, transactions, or events after that date have been examined or reviewed." Dual dating is used when the auditor makes reference to a subsequent event disclosed in the financial statements which occurs after completion of the fieldwork, but before issuance of the report (AU 530.03). The release date is never used in dating the report on financial statements. The current period report date would only be used for comparative financial statement dating.

61. (a) AU 530.03 states, "In case a subsequent event of the type requiring adjustment of the financial statements...occurs after the date of the independent auditor's report but before its issuance, and the event comes to the attention of the auditor, the financial statements should be adjusted or the auditor should qualify his [or her] opinion. When the adjustment is made without disclosure of the event, the report should ordinarily be dated [as of the date of the completion of the field work]." Answers (b), (c), and (d) are incorrect because other methods, including dual dating, would be considered when disclosure of the event is made, either in a note or in the auditor's report.

SUBSEQUENT EVENTS

62. (b) Informing third parties is appropriate only when the audit committee (a committee of the board of directors) fails to take appropriate action.

63. (d) Subsequent events occur between the period ending date and the issuance of the financial statements. AU 560.12 states that one of the auditor's procedures about the occurrence of subsequent events is inquiry of management concerning unusual adjustments after year end. Confirming a sample of accounts receivable established after year end would be a secondary step in obtaining evidence about subsequent events, if it were done at all. Comparison between the current and the prior year financial statements is an analytical procedure unlikely to uncover evidence about the occurrence of subsequent events. Investigating personnel changes in the accounting department occurring after year end would be more likely when possible misconduct, rather than a subsequent event, is being considered.

64. (d) AU 560.05 states, "The second type of [subsequent]...event [which includes losses on receivables resulting from conditions arising subsequent to the balance sheet date] provide[s] evidence with respect to conditions that did not exist at the date of the balance sheet being reported on but arose subsequent to that date. These events should not result in adjustment of the financial statements. Some,...however, may be of such a nature that disclosure of them is required to keep the financial statements from being misleading." Consistency is implied in the auditor's report, and a subsequent event does not give rise to a report modification for consistency.

65. (c) Section 560 of the AICPA Auditing Standards identifies two types of events occurring subsequent to the balance sheet date but before the statements are issued ("subsequent events"): *Type 1* events provide additional evidence with respect to conditions that *existed at the balance sheet date; Type 2* events concern conditions that *did not exist at the balance sheet date* but arose subsequent to that date. Type 2 events should not result in adjustment to the financial statements, but may be of such nature that disclosure of them is required to keep the financial statements from being misleading (AU 560.05). Management, not the auditor, is responsible for presenting the financial statements, including appropriate disclosures.

66. (d) AU 560.10 states, "There is a period after the balance sheet date with which the auditor must be concerned in completing various phases of his [or her] audit. This period is known as the *subsequent period* and is considered to extend to the date of the auditor's report. Its duration will depend upon the practical requirements of each audit and may vary from a relatively short period to one of several months."

Subsequent Discovery of Facts

67. (c) AU 561.04, "When the auditor becomes aware of information which relates to financial statements previously reported on...not known at the date of his [or her] report,...he [or she] should [follow up on the information]." Answers (a), (b), and (d) do not fit this requirement.

68. (a) AU 561.03 states, "After he [or she] has issued his [or her] report, the auditor has no obligation to make any further or continuing inquiry or perform any other auditing procedures with respect to the audited financial statements covered by that report, unless new information which may affect his [or her] report comes to his [or her] attention."

69. (a) According to AU 561.05, after determining that information regarding subsequent discovery of facts is reliable, the auditor next determines if people are relying on the information who would believe the information is important.

Consideration of Omitted Procedures

70. (b) AU 390.05 states that if the auditor concludes that the omission of a procedure considered necessary at the time of the audit in the circumstances then existing impairs his or her present ability to support the previously expressed opinion regarding the financial statements, and the auditor believes there are persons currently relying on the report, he or she should promptly undertake to apply the omitted procedure or alternative procedures that would provide a satisfactory basis for the opinion. Answer (a) is a procedure to be followed when the auditor determines, after attempting to perform procedures, that an unqualified opinion is inappropriate. Answer (c) would not be feasible and would not eliminate the need to perform some auditing procedures beyond tests of controls. Answer (d) would not be an alternative in any situation.

71. (a) When an auditor concludes that an audit procedure considered necessary has been omitted, the first concern should be to determine whether the previously issued opinion can still be supported. A review of the working papers, discussion of the circumstances with engagement personnel and others, and a reevaluation of the overall scope of the audit may be helpful in making this assessment. If the opinion can still be supported, no further action is necessary. Otherwise, if the auditor believes there are persons relying on the report, then the auditor must promptly undertake the omitted procedures or alternative procedures (AU 390.04). A determination of whether or not there are persons relying on the report would provide no evidence to the auditor in assessing the importance of the omitted procedure.

72. (c) AU 390.04 states that the results of other procedures that were applied during the audit may tend to compensate for the one omitted or make its omission less important. Other compensating procedures may compensate for the one omitted, regardless of whether the financial statements had been released or not. Qualification of the report does not reduce the auditor's responsibility to perform required procedures or those the auditor considers necessary. Client delays do not justify omitting audit procedures considered necessary to perform the audit.

73. (b) AU 390.05 states, "If the auditor concludes that the omission of a procedure considered necessary at the time of the audit in the circumstances then existing impairs his [or her] present ability to support his [or her] previously expressed opinion regarding the financial statements taken as a whole, and he [or she] believes there are persons currently relying, or likely to rely, on his [or her] report, he [or she] should promptly undertake to apply the omitted procedure or alternative procedures that would provide a satisfactory basis for his [or her] opinion."

Association With Financial Statements

74. (d) A disclaimer of opinion is the appropriate report in this situation, per AU 504.05. The other reports noted are not appropriate.

75. (d) AU 504.15 allows either alternative.

76. (d) When an accountant is associated with the financial statements of a public entity, but has not audited or reviewed such statements, the form of report to be issued is a disclaimer of opinion. The disclaimer of opinion is the means by which the accountant complies with the fourth standard of reporting when associated with unaudited financial statements in those circumstances. When an accountant disclaims an opinion, he or she has no responsibility to apply any procedures beyond reading the financial statements for obvious material misstatements (AU 504.05).

77. (c) AU 504.11 states, "If the accountant concludes on the basis of facts known to him [or her] that the unaudited financial statements on which he [or she] is disclaiming an opinion are not in conformity with [GAAP], which include adequate disclosure, he [or she] should suggest appropriate revision; failing that, he [or she] should describe the departure in his [or her] disclaimer of opinion." When an auditor disclaims an opinion, he or she cannot, by definition, issue an adverse opinion or a modified opinion.

Going Concern

78. (d) According to AU 341.07, an entity's plans to reduce or delay expenditures would be one of the primary considerations in reviewing management's plans. Plans to discuss the terms of debt and loan agreements with lenders would not be given much weight. The availability of financing or existing or committed arrangements to restructure or subordinate debt would be more important. Strong internal control will not keep an entity from bankruptcy. Purchasing instead of leasing assets during an unstable period would generally work against plans to delay expenditures.

79. (b) Denial of usual trade credit from suppliers may drive a business into bankruptcy, even if it wasn't floundering previously. As suppliers have the conflicting goals of selling as much as possible, but extending credit only to creditworthy customers, they remain cognizant of the recent payment history of their debtors. Related party transactions and restrictions on the disposal of assets are commonly encountered in healthy businesses. The payment of arrearages in preferred stock dividends are generally made only when "surplus" money is available.

80. (c) The phrases *substantial doubt* and *ability to continue as a going concern* are required.

81. (a) AU 341.16 states, "If substantial doubt about the entity's ability to continue as a going concern existed at the date of prior period financial statements that are presented on a comparative basis, and that doubt has been removed in the current period, the explanatory paragraph included in the auditor's report...should not be repeated."

82. (d) AU 341.12 states, "If, after considering identified conditions and events and management's plans, the auditor concludes that substantial doubt about the entity's ability to continue as a going concern for a reasonable period of time remains, the audit report should include an explanatory paragraph (following the opinion paragraph) to reflect that conclusion." The inclusion of the explanatory paragraph should serve adequately to inform the users of the statements. However, the auditor is not precluded from declining to express an opinion in cases involving uncertainties.

83. (b) AU 341.05 lists examples of auditing procedures which may "identify conditions and events that, when considered in the aggregate, indicate there could be substantial doubt about the entity's ability to continue as a going concern for a reasonable period of time," including analytical procedures and confirmation with related and third parties of the details of arrangements to provide or maintain financial support. Pledging assets as collateral does not indicate an inability to continue as a going concern. The auditor may, however, discover by confirming related loans outstanding that the payments have become overdue. Answers (c) and (d) would not uncover any evidence about an entity's ability to continue as a going concern.

84. (c) "A reasonable period of time" is considered to extend up to one year beyond the date of the financial statements (AU 340.02). The absence of reference to substantial doubt in an auditor's report should **not** be viewed as providing assurance as to an entity's ability to continue as a going concern (AU 340.04). Continuation of an entity as a going concern is assumed in financial reporting in the absence of significant information to the contrary (AU 340.01).

85. (b) AU 341.10 states, "When...the auditor concludes there is substantial doubt about the entity's ability to continue as a going concern for a reasonable period of time, the auditor should consider the

possible effects on the financial statements and the adequacy of the related disclosure." AU 341.14 states the auditor would issue a qualified or adverse opinion if the auditor concludes that the entity's disclosure with respect to the ability to continue as a going concern is inadequate. The auditor may report such adjustments to the audit committee, however, further action is required to deal specifically with the going concern issue, regardless of the changes to any unrelated or related accounting estimates. AU 341.15 states that substantial doubt about the entity's ability to continue as a going concern for a reasonable period of time that arose in the current period does not imply that a basis for such doubt existed in the prior period and should not affect the auditor's report on the financial statements of the prior period presented on a comparative basis.

Other Information in Documents Containing Audited Financial Statements

86. (d) AU 550.04 states, "The auditor's responsibility with respect to information in a document does not extend beyond the financial information identified in his [or her] report, and the auditor has no obligation to perform any procedures to corroborate other information contained in a document. However, he [or she] should read the other information and consider whether such information, or the manner of its presentation, is materially inconsistent with information, or the manner of its presentation, appearing in the financial statements." The auditor has no obligation to perform inquiry, analytical procedures, or other substantive auditing procedures to corroborate other information in a document. An explanatory paragraph would only be considered if the auditor concludes that there is a material inconsistency in the other information, and the other information is not revised to eliminate the material inconsistency.

87. (a) AU 551.08 states that when reporting on additional information included in auditor-submitted documents, "The measurement of materiality is the same as that used in forming an opinion on the basic financial statements taken as a whole." Answers (b) and (c) are irrelevant and neither would be used as a basis for determining materiality. The total of both statements would most likely be too high a materiality level to set, creating the possibility that no individual items would be tested.

88. (a) AU 550.04 states, "If the other information is not revised to eliminate the material inconsistency, he [or she] should consider other actions such as revising [the] report to include an explanatory paragraph describing the material inconsistency, withholding the use of…[the] report in the document, and withdrawing from the engagement." Answers (b), (c), and (d) are not appropriate ways to address the situation.

Required Supplementary Information

89. (c) AU 551.15 presents the auditor's responsibilities for supplementary information. The responsibilities extend beyond determining that the supplementary information has not been omitted. The procedures noted in answer (d) are those used to audit the financial statements, not the supplementary information.

90. (d) AU 558.08 states, "Since the required supplementary information does not change the standards of financial accounting and reporting used for the preparation of the entity's basic financial statements,…the auditor's opinion on the fairness of presentation of such financial statements in conformity with [GAAP is not affected]." AU 558.08 adds that the auditor should issue an unqualified opinion with an additional explanatory paragraph.

Solution 39-2 ADDITIONAL MULTIPLE CHOICE ANSWERS

Reporting Standards

91. (d) AU 410.02 states, "The first reporting standard is construed not to require a statement of fact by the auditor, but an opinion as to whether the financial statements are presented in conformity with [GAAP]." The auditor must also judge whether the financial statements are presented fairly within the framework of GAAP (AU 411.03), not some implied measure of fairness. The audit report contains the auditor's *subjective* opinion concerning the financial statement presentation.

Types of Opinions

92. (a) The auditor's standard report implies that the auditor is satisfied that the statements are consistent with respect to GAAP, and such principles have been consistently applied *between periods* (AU 508.16). Use of different cost principles for different inventories is not inherently inconsistent.

93. (b) AU 508.50 states, "When financial statements are materially affected by a departure from GAAP and the auditor has audited the statements in accordance with generally accepted auditing

standards, he [or she] should express a qualified opinion." In deciding whether the effects of a departure from GAAP are sufficiently material to require either a qualified or adverse opinion, one factor to be considered is the dollar magnitude of such effects. Answer (a) represents a scope limitation which would result in a disclaimer of opinion. Answer (c) is an example of an "except for" qualified opinion, but not an adverse opinion. Answer (d) is an example of a situation where an explanatory paragraph would be added to an unqualified opinion.

94. (b) Whenever an auditor concludes that the financial statements do not represent the activities and position of an entity in conformity with GAAP, the auditor must either issue an adverse or qualified opinion, depending on the materiality of the discrepancy. Disclaimers of opinions are reserved for scope limitations, lack of independence, and nonperformance of an audit. An unqualified opinion, with or without explanation, should never be given on financial statements containing a material departure from GAAP. Unqualified opinions with explanations are reserved for situations when part of the audit is performed by other independent auditors, when the statements would be misleading if a particular GAAP were followed, when uncertainties exist, when there is a lack of consistency, and when the auditor wants to emphasize a matter.

Standard Report

95. (d) AU 508.10 states, "An unqualified opinion states that the financial statements present fairly, in all material respects, financial position, results of operations, and cash flows in conformity with generally accepted accounting principles [which include adequate disclosure]."

Departure From GAAP

96. (b) Rule 203 of the Code of Professional Conduct requires members to follow GAAP whenever possible. However, if by following GAAP the financial statements would be misleading, the member can comply with the rule by, "describing the departure, its approximate effects, if practicable, and the reasons why compliance with the principle would result in a misleading statement." This should be done in a separate paragraph, or paragraphs, of the auditor's report, and an unqualified opinion issued (AU 508.14 and .15). The departure from GAAP should be mentioned. Answers (c) and (d) are situations in which an unqualified opinion is appropriate.

Consistency

97. (b) AU 420.23 states, "When the independent auditor has not audited the financial statements of a company for the preceding year, he [or she] should adopt procedures that are practicable to assure him- [or her-] self that the accounting principles employed are consistent. Where adequate records have been maintained by the client, it is usually practicable to gather sufficient competent evidential matter about consistency." Thus an auditor would issue an unqualified opinion in a standard report. According to AU 420.24, the auditor would not report on the income statement only if precluded from obtaining appropriate evidence as to consistency. The consistency standard <u>does</u> apply in first year audits. The standard report doesn't explicitly mention consistency.

Scope Limitation

98. (c) AU 508.24 states, "When restrictions that significantly limit the scope of the audit are *imposed by the client*, ordinarily the auditor should disclaim an opinion on the financial statements." The auditor is not precluded from reporting on financial statements prepared in accordance with the cash receipts and disbursements basis of accounting. Answer (b) is simply an example of an other comprehensive basis of accounting and would require a special report (AU 623.01). Answer (a) contemplates a departure from GAAP, not a scope limitation. The auditor is not precluded from reporting on one basic financial statement and not on the others. These engagements do not involve scope limitations if the auditor's access to information underlying the basic financial statements is not limited and if he or she is able to apply all necessary procedures (AU 508.33).

99. (d) Only the opinion paragraph should indicate that the qualification pertains to the possible effects on the financial statements and *not* to the scope limitation itself. The qualifying language generally used reads, "In our opinion, except for the above mentioned limitation on the scope of the audit..." (AU 508.26).

Disclaimer of Opinion

100. (b) Per AU 508.51, an unjustified accounting change would require that the auditor express a qualified or adverse opinion. Answers (a), (b), and (c) represent various restrictions of the scope of the audit. A restriction of the scope of the audit, whether imposed by the client or circumstances, may require the auditor to express a qualified opinion (AU 508.22).

DATING

101. (d) AU 530.01 states, "Generally, the date of completion of field work should be used as the date of the auditor's report." The auditor cannot be certain of the date on which the report is delivered to the client. Most of the audit work, for which the auditor is responsible, occurs after the end of the fiscal period under audit. The auditor may have to perform more audit work after the working papers are reviewed. The auditor must take responsibility for such additional audit work.

CONSIDERATION OF OMITTED PROCEDURES

102. (c) AU 390.04 states, "When the auditor concludes that an auditing procedure considered necessary at the time of the audit in the circumstances then existing was omitted from his [or her] audit of financial statements, he [or she] should assess the importance of the omitted procedure to his [or her] present ability to support his [or her] previously expressed opinion regarding those financial statements taken as a whole." Answers (a), (b), and (d) are steps that can be performed after the required assessment.

GOING CONCERN

103. (d) AU 341.12 specifically requires the words "substantial doubt" and "going concern" be used and also requires a phrase similar to "substantial doubt about its ability to continue as a going concern" be used. "Possible discontinuance of operations" and "Reasonable period of time, not to exceed one year" are not mentioned.

104. (c) AU 340.14 states, "If the auditor concludes that the entity's disclosures with respect to the entity's ability to continue as a going concern for a reasonable period of time are inadequate, a departure from generally accepted accounting principles exists. This may result in either a qualified (except for) or an adverse opinion."

105. (a) AU 341.06 specifically mentions negative cash flows from operating activities as an example of a condition that, when considered with other events, may indicate there is substantial doubt about an entity's ability to continue as a going concern.

PERFORMANCE BY SUBTOPICS

Each category below parallels a subtopic covered in Chapter 39. Record the number and percentage of questions you correctly answered in each subtopic area.

Reporting Standards

Question #	Correct √
1	
2	
3	
4	
# Questions	4
# Correct	
% Correct	

Types of Opinions

Question #	Correct √
5	
6	
7	
8	
9	
10	
11	
12	
13	
# Questions	9
# Correct	
% Correct	

Standard Report

Question #	Correct √
14	
15	
16	
17	
18	
19	
# Questions	6
# Correct	
% Correct	

Explanatory Language

Question #	Correct √
20	
21	
22	
# Questions	3
# Correct	
% Correct	

Another Auditor

Question #	Correct √
23	
24	
25	
# Questions	3
# Correct	
% Correct	

Departure From GAAP

Question #	Correct √
26	
27	
# Questions	2
# Correct	
% Correct	

Consistency

Question #	Correct √
28	
29	
30	
31	
32	
# Questions	5
# Correct	
% Correct	

Uncertainty

Question #	Correct √
33	
34	
35	
36	
# Questions	4
# Correct	
% Correct	

Emphasis

Question #	Correct √
37	

\# Questions 1

\# Correct ____

% Correct ____

Qualified Opinions

Question #	Correct √
38	
39	
40	
41	
42	

\# Questions 5

\# Correct ____

% Correct ____

Scope Limitation

Question #	Correct √
43	
44	
45	
46	
47	

\# Questions 5

\# Correct ____

% Correct ____

Inadequate Disclosure

Question #	Correct √
48	
49	

\# Questions 2

\# Correct ____

% Correct ____

Adverse Opinions

Question #	Correct √
50	

\# Questions 1

\# Correct ____

% Correct ____

Disclaimer of Opinion

Question #	Correct √
51	

\# Questions 1

\# Correct ____

% Correct ____

Comparative Financial Statements

Question #	Correct √
52	
53	
54	
55	
56	
57	
58	

\# Questions 7

\# Correct ____

% Correct ____

Dating

Question #	Correct √
59	
60	
61	

\# Questions 3

\# Correct ____

% Correct ____

Subsequent Events

Question #	Correct √
62	
63	
64	
65	
66	

\# Questions 5

\# Correct ____

% Correct ____

Subsequent Discovery of Facts

Question #	Correct √
67	
68	
69	

\# Questions 3

\# Correct ____

% Correct ____

Consideration of Omitted Procedures

Question #	Correct √
70	
71	
72	
73	

\# Questions 4

\# Correct ____

% Correct ____

Association With Financial Statements

Question #	Correct √
74	
75	
76	
77	

\# Questions 4

\# Correct ____

% Correct ____

Going Concern

Question #	Correct √
78	
79	
80	
81	
82	
83	
84	
85	

\# Questions 8

\# Correct ____

% Correct ____

Other Information in Documents Containing Audited Financial Statements

Question #	Correct √
86	
87	
88	

\# Questions 3

\# Correct ____

% Correct ____

Required Supplementary Information

Question #	Correct √
89	
90	

\# Questions 2

\# Correct ____

% Correct ____

OTHER OBJECTIVE FORMAT QUESTION SOLUTIONS

SOLUTION 39-3 TYPES OF OPINIONS/REPORT MODIFICATIONS

1. F, L AU 508.22 states, "Restrictions on the scope of [an auditor's] audit, whether imposed by the client or by the circumstances, such as an inability to obtain sufficient competent evidential matter, or an inadequacy in the accounting records, may require the auditor to qualify his [or her] opinion or to disclaim an opinion." Further, AU 508.22 notes that a "common scope restriction involves accounting for long-term investments when the auditor has not been able to obtain audited financial statements of an investee."

AU 508.25 states, "When a qualified opinion results from a limitation on the scope of the audit or an insufficiency of evidential matter, the situation should be described in an explanatory paragraph preceding the opinion paragraph and referred to in both the scope and opinion paragraphs of the auditor's report."

2. B, I A substantial doubt about an entity's ability to continue as a going concern is listed in AU 508.11 as one of the circumstances which does not affect the auditor's unqualified opinion, but may require the addition of an explanatory paragraph.

AU 341.12 states, "If, after considering identified conditions and events and management's plans, the auditor concludes that substantial doubt about the entity's ability to continue as a going concern for a reasonable period of time remains, the audit report should include an explanatory paragraph (following the opinion paragraph) to reflect that conclusion." Inadequate disclosure with respect to an entity's ability to continue as a going concern is a departure from GAAP, resulting in either an "except for" qualified opinion or an adverse opinion (AU 341.14). In this case, however, because it was concluded that financial statement disclosures were adequate, an unqualified opinion with an explanatory paragraph is appropriate.

3. B, Q If the principal auditor is able to satisfy him- or herself as to the independence and professional reputation of the other auditor and takes steps considered appropriate to satisfy him- or herself as to the audit performed by the other auditor, he or she may express an unqualified opinion on the financial statements taken as a whole (AU 543.04).

AU 543.03 states, "If the auditor decides that it is appropriate for him [or her] to serve as the principal auditor, he [or she] must then decide whether to make reference in his [or her] report to the audit performed by another auditor. If the principal auditor decides to assume responsibility for the work of the other auditor insofar as that work relates to the principal auditor's expression of an opinion taken as a whole, no reference should be made to the other auditor's work or report."

4. A, J AU 508.44 states, "The auditor is not required to prepare a basic financial statement and include it in his [or her] report if the company's management declines to present the statement." Accordingly, the auditor should issue an "except for" qualified opinion. The circumstances surrounding the qualification are to be reported in a separate paragraph preceding the opinion paragraph. The opinion paragraph should then be modified using the appropriate "except for" wording, making reference to the separate explanatory paragraph.

5. B, I Since the auditor concurs with the change in accounting principle, he or she does not take exception to the change in expressing his or her opinion as to fair presentation of the financial statements in conformity with generally accepted accounting principles. Therefore, the auditor may express an unqualified opinion.

Changes in accounting principle having a material effect on the financial statements require recognition in the independent auditor's report through the addition of an explanatory paragraph (following the opinion paragraph). Such explanatory paragraph should identify the nature of the change and refer the reader to the note in the financial statements that discusses the change in detail (AU 508.16).

6. B, Q AU 508.30 states, "If, after considering existing conditions and available evidence, the auditor concludes that sufficient evidential matter supports management's assertions about...an uncertainty and its presentation or disclosure...,an unqualified opinion ordinarily is appropriate."

AU 508.11 lists circumstances that may require the auditor to add an explanatory paragraph to a standard report, while not precluding an unqualified opinion. An uncertainty is not among these circumstances. An emphasis paragraph may be added. However, AU 508.19 states, "Emphasis paragraphs are never required; they may be added solely at the auditor's discretion."

7. E, J AU 508.35 states, "When financial statements are materially affected by a departure from generally accepted accounting principles and the auditor has audited the statements in accordance with generally accepted auditing standards, he [or she] should express a qualified or an adverse opinion." AU 508.36 indicates that factors to consider when deciding whether to issue either of these two opinions include: (1) the dollar magnitude of the effect, (2) the qualitative and quantitative aspects of the departure, (3) the pervasiveness of the misstatement, and (4) the effects on the other financial statements.

AU 508.37 indicates that the auditor should disclose, in a separate explanatory paragraph preceding the opinion paragraph, all the substantive reasons for a departure from generally accepted accounting principles and that the opinion paragraph should include appropriate qualifying language.

Solution 39-4 Report Deficiencies

1. P A division of responsibility is indicated in the introductory paragraph including the significance of the portion of the entity audited by another auditor. Either the amount or the percentage of total assets and revenues that are reflected in the subsidiary's statements are adequate.

2. B A division of responsibility is indicated in the introductory paragraph including the significance of the portion of the entity audited by another auditor. The scope and opinion paragraphs are also modified to refer to the other auditor.

3. P The phrase, "whether caused by error or fraud," is not part of the standard auditor's report.

4. W The phrase, "significant estimates made by management," is included in the scope paragraph of the standard report.

5. W Control risk is not mentioned in the standard report. The auditor is reporting on an audit of financial statements, not an examination of internal control.

6. W The phrase, "evaluating the overall financial statement presentation" is included in the scope paragraph of the standard report.

7. P As the investigation is adequately disclosed in the notes to the financial statements, it need not be mentioned in the auditor's report. If the auditor wanted to emphasize this matter and yet still issue an unqualified opinion, the auditor would mention it in an explanatory paragraph following the opinion paragraph.

8. P If an auditor had previously qualified the opinion on the financial statements of a prior period because of a departure from GAAP, and the prior period financial statements are restated in the current period, the updating report should indicate that the statements have been restated in a paragraph preceding the opinion paragraph.

9. P Concurrence with a change in accounting principle is implicit and need not be explicitly stated. If management does not provide reasonable justification for a change, the auditor's opinion would be qualified.

10. P Such a reference is not required.

11. B The opinion paragraph should extend the auditor's opinion beyond the statement of financial position to include the results of operations and cash flows, not changes in stockholders' equity.

12. B SAS 79 removes the requirement for an uncertainties paragraph in an auditor's report. If an uncertainty is mentioned, it should be in a paragraph following the opinion paragraphs and include a description of the matter giving rise to the uncertainty and should indicate that its outcome cannot be determined. No reference should be made to the uncertainty in the introductory, scope, or opinion paragraphs.

13. W If the auditor concludes that substantial doubt about the entity's ability to continue as a going concern exists, the term "substantial doubt" is required to be used in an explanatory paragraph.

14. W If the auditor concludes that substantial doubt about the entity's ability to continue as a going concern exists, the term "going concern" is required to be used in an explanatory paragraph.

15. P This sentence is the last sentence in the standard going concern uncertainty paragraph.

16. P Auditors use dual dates when subsequent events, not going concern uncertainties, are mentioned.

ESSAY SOLUTIONS

SOLUTION 39-5 REPORT DEFICIENCIES—GOING CONCERN UNCERTAINTY/OTHER AUDITORS

Deficiencies in Miller's draft are as follows:

Within the opening (introductory) paragraph

- The **statement of cash flows** is not identified in this paragraph or in the opinion paragraph.
- The financial statements are not stated to be the **responsibility of management**.
- The magnitude of the portion of the consolidated financial statements audited by the **other auditors** is not disclosed.
- Smith **may not be named** in this paragraph or in the opinion paragraph unless Smith's report is presented together with Pell's report.

Within the second (scope) paragraph

- The statement "An audit includes examining, on a test basis, evidence supporting the amounts and disclosures in the financial statements" is omitted.
- It is inappropriate to state that an audit includes "assessing control risk."
- Reference to the audit of the other auditors as part of the basis for the opinion is omitted.
- Within the third (opinion) paragraph
- Use of the phrase "except for the matter discussed below" is inappropriate.
- Reference to "conformity with generally accepted accounting principles" is omitted.

Within the fourth (explanatory) paragraph

- The terms "substantial doubt" and "going concern" are omitted.

SOLUTION 39-6 REPORTING FRAUD

a. If Post discovers that General's financial statements may be materially misstated due to the **existence of fraud**, Post should consider the **implications** for other aspects of the audit and discuss the matter and approach to further investigation with an **appropriate level of management that is at least one level above those involved** with the fraud. Post should also attempt to obtain sufficient competent evidential matter to determine whether, in fact, material fraud exist and, if so, their effect. Post may suggest that General consult with its legal counsel on matters concerning questions of law.

b. If Post is precluded from applying necessary procedures, Post should **disclaim or qualify** the financial statements and communicate these findings to General's audit committee or its board of directors.

c. If Post concludes that General's financial statements **are materially affected** by fraud, Post should insist that the **financial statements be revised** and, if they are not, express a **qualified or** an **adverse** opinion on the financial statements, disclosing all the substantive reasons for such an opinion. Additionally, Post should adequately inform General's audit committee or its board of directors about the fraud.

d. Post may have a duty to disclose fraud to **third parties** outside General's management and its audit committee in the following circumstances:

- When General reports an **auditor change** under the appropriate securities law.
- When a **successor auditor appropriately makes inquiries** of a predecessor auditor.
- When responding to a **subpoena.**
- When **communicating with a funding or other specified agency,** as required for entities that receive financial assistance from a government agency.

SOLUTION 39-7 REPORT DEFICIENCIES: UNCERTAINTY AND ACCOUNTING CHANGE

Deficiencies in the auditors' report are as follows:

First (Introductory) Paragraph

1. The **statement of retained earnings** is not identified.
2. The auditor's **responsibility to express an opinion** is omitted.

Second (Scope) Paragraph

3. The auditor obtains reasonable assurance about whether the financial statements are **"free of material misstatement,"** not **"fairly presented."**
4. The auditors' **assessment of the accounting principles** used is omitted.
5. An audit provides a **"reasonable basis for an opinion,"** not a "basis for determining whether any material modifications should be made."

Third (First Explanatory) Paragraph

6. An explanatory paragraph added to the report to describe a change in accounting principle (lack of consistency) should **follow the opinion paragraph,** not precede it.

Fourth (Opinion) Paragraph

7. The phrase **"except for" should not be used.**
8. The auditor's **concurrence** with the change in accounting principles **is implicit** and should **not be mentioned.**
9. **Reference to the prior year's** (20X1) financial statements is omitted.

Fifth (Second Explanatory) Paragraph

10. The **fact that the outcome** of the lawsuit **cannot presently be estimated is omitted.**
11. It is **inappropriate** to state that "provision for any liability is subject to adjudication" because the report is ambiguous as to whether a liability has been recorded.

SOLUTION 39-8 SUBSEQUENT EVENTS

a. The first type of subsequent event includes those events that provide **additional evidence concerning conditions that existed at the balance sheet date** and affect the estimates inherent in the process of preparing financial statements. This type of subsequent event **requires that the financial statements** be adjusted for any changes in estimates resulting from the use of such additional evidence.

The second type of subsequent event consists of those events that provide evidence concerning **conditions that did not exist** at the balance sheet date but **arose subsequent** to that date. These events should **not result in adjustment** to the financial statements but may be such that **disclosure** is required to keep the financial statements from being misleading.

b. The auditing procedures Green should consider performing to gather evidence concerning subsequent events include the following:

- **Compare** the latest available **interim statements** with the financial statements being audited.
- Ascertain whether the interim statements were prepared on the same basis as the audited financial statements.
- Inquire whether any contingent liabilities or commitments existed at the balance sheet date or the date of inquiry.
- **Inquire** whether there was any significant **change** in the capital stock, long-term debt, or working capital to the date of inquiry.
- **Inquire** about the current status of **items** in the audited financial statements that were accounted for on the basis of **tentative, preliminary, or inconclusive data**.
- Inquire about any unusual adjustments made since the balance sheet date.
- **Read or inquire about** the **minutes** of meetings of stockholders or the board of directors.
- Inquire of the client's **legal counsel** concerning litigation, claims, and assessments.
- Obtain a **management representation letter**, dated as of the date of Green's report, as to whether any subsequent events would require adjustment or disclosure.
- Make such additional inquiries or perform such additional procedures Green considers necessary and appropriate.

SOLUTION 39-9 AUDIT REPORT

To the Board of Directors of National Motors, Inc.:

We have audited the consolidated balance sheet of National Motors, Inc. and subsidiaries as of December 31, 20X1, and the related consolidated statements of income, retained earnings, and cash flows for the year then ended. These financial statements are the responsibility of the Company's management. Our responsibility is to express an opinion on these financial statements based on our audit. **We did not audit** the financial statements of Rapid Parts Company, a consolidated subsidiary, which statements reflect total assets and revenues constituting 22 percent and 25 percent, respectively, of the related consolidated totals. **Those statements were audited by other auditors** whose report has been furnished to us, and **our opinion**, insofar as it relates to the amounts included for Rapid Parts Company, **is based solely upon the report of the other auditors.**

Except as explained in the following paragraph, we conducted our audit in accordance with generally accepted auditing standards. Those standards require that we plan and perform the audit to obtain reasonable assurance about whether the financial statements are free of material misstatement. An audit includes examining, on a test basis, evidence supporting the amounts and disclosures in the financial statements. An audit also includes assessing the accounting principles used and significant estimates made by management, as well as evaluating the overall financial statement presentation. **We believe that our audits and the report of other auditors provide a reasonable basis for our opinion.**

We did not observe the taking of the physical inventory as of December 31, 20X0, since that date was prior to our appointment as auditors for National Motors, Inc. and we were unable to satisfy ourselves regarding inventory quantities by means of other auditing procedures. Inventory amounts as of December 31, 20X0, enter into the determination of net income and cash flows for the year ended December 31, 20X1.

Because of the matter discussed in the **preceding paragraph**, the **scope** of our work was **not sufficient** to enable us to express, and **we do not express**, an opinion on the results of operations and cash flows for the year ended December 31, 20X1.

In our opinion, based on our audit and the report of the other auditors, **the balance sheet referred to above presents fairly**, in all material respects, the financial position of National Motors, Inc. and subsidiaries as of December 31, 20X1, in conformity with generally accepted accounting principles.

White & Co.
March 28, 20X2

SOLUTION 39-10 OTHER AUDITORS

a. In order for May & Marty to satisfy itself about the independence and professional reputation of Dey & Dee and assure itself that there has been coordination of activities between the two auditors in order to achieve a proper review of matters affecting consolidation, May & Marty, whether or not it makes reference to Dey & Dee's audit, should consider performing the following procedures:

Make **inquiries about the professional reputation** and standing of Dey & Dee to one or more of the following:

- AICPA, applicable state society of CPAs, and/or local chapter.
- Other appropriate sources such as other practitioners, bankers, and other credit grantors.

Obtain a representation from Dey & Dee that it is independent under the requirements of the AICPA and, if appropriate, the requirements of the SEC. Ascertain through **communication with Dey & Dee that**

- Dey & Dee is aware that the **BGI-Western financial statements are to be included** in the BGI consolidated financial statements on which May & Marty will report, and that **Dey & Dee's report will be relied upon** by May & Marty.
- Dey & Dee is familiar with GAAP and GAAS and will conduct its audit in accordance therewith.
- Dey & Dee has knowledge of the relevant financial reporting requirements for statements and schedules to be filed with regulatory agencies such as the SEC, if appropriate.
- A review will be made of matters affecting elimination of intercompany transactions and accounts and, if appropriate in the circumstances, the uniformity of accounting practices among components included in the financial statements.

b. May & Marty could adopt the position of not making reference to Dey & Dee's audit of BGI-Western if May & Marty is able to satisfy itself about the independence and professional reputation of Dey & Dee and takes steps it considers appropriate to satisfy itself as to Dey & Dee's audit of BGI-Western. Ordinarily, May & Marty would be able to adopt the position of not making reference to Dey & Dee's audit when any one of the following conditions exists:

- **Dey & Dee is an associate or correspondent firm** and its work is acceptable to May & Marty based on May & Marty's knowledge of the professional standards and competence of Dey & Dee; or
- **Dey & Dee is retained by May & Marty** and the work is performed under May & Marty's guidance and control; or
- **May & Marty takes steps it considers necessary to satisfy itself as to Dey & Dee's audit**. Such steps may include a visit to Dey and Dee to discuss Dey and Dee's audit procedures or a review of Dey and Dee's audit programs and/or working papers. In addition, May and Marty is satisfied about the reasonableness of the statements of BGI-Western for purposes of inclusion in BGI's consolidated financial statements; or
- **BGI-Western's financial statements are not a material part** of BGI's consolidated financial statements.

Solution 39-11 Going Concern

a. Wall has a responsibility to evaluate whether there is substantial doubt about Trendy's ability to continue as a going concern for a **reasonable period of time, not to exceed one year** beyond the date of Trendy's audited financial statements. This evaluation is based on Wall's knowledge of **conditions and events that exist at**, or have **occurred before,** the **completion of field work.**

b. While it is not necessary that Wall design specific audit procedures solely to identify conditions and events that may indicate Trendy's has a going concern problem, Wall most likely would perform analytical procedures to identify ratios and patterns indicative of present and future financial difficulties.

Wall most likely would review any debt and **loan agreements** to ascertain whether Trendy is complying with their terms. Additionally, if there are any **agreements with stockholders or creditors** to provide or maintain financial support, **confirmation of the details** of these arrangements would be appropriate.

Wall's **review of subsequent events** near the completion of field work also would produce evidence about Trendy's financial difficulties. Wall would especially focus on **reading the minutes of the directors' meetings, inquiring** of Trendy's legal **counsel** concerning litigation, and reading the **latest interim financial statements.**

c. Wall should **consider** any **management plans** to increase sales, reduce costs, or dispose of assets that could mitigate the adverse effects of Trendy's financial difficulties. The **marketability** of the assets, any **restrictions** on their disposal and the possible **operational effects** of their disposal should be considered in evaluating whether such plans can be effectively implemented.

If management plans to borrow money or restructure its debts, Wall should consider several factors including the **availability of financing**, the **possibility of restructuring** or subordinating debt, the effects of **existing borrowing restrictions,** and the **sufficiency of collateral**.

Wall should evaluate any management plans to **reduce or delay expenditures**, such as overhead or administrative expenditures. The **postponement** of maintenance and R&D, and the leasing of assets ordinarily purchased also may be feasible.

Wall also should consider any plans to increase ownership equity and raise capital. Arrangements to reduce current dividend requirements or accelerate cash distributions from subsidiaries or cash infusions from investors also may be possible.

What is this I've been hearing about the computerized exam?

The AICPA is in the process of converting the CPA exam into a "computerized" exam. Currently, candidates read questions from a printed page, darken ovals on a machine-readable sheet for the objective answers, and write essay answers on lined paper. To some extent, the exam is already computerized; the objective answers are machine-graded.

The next step in this conversion is likely to be essentially the same exam, with candidates reading questions from, and entering answers into, a personal computer. Before this happens, laws in many jurisdictions must change to allow this format, among other things.

The examination division has targeted November 2003 as the date for this next stage. There may be only pilot groups who sit for the computerized exam in November 2003. Candidates are unlikely to have much say in whether they will be part of a pilot group.

As we go to press, the AICPA has not yet decided most details; even the implementation date is subject to change. There has been some discussion regarding eliminating essay questions from the exam, in order that the entire exam may be computer-graded. When the exam becomes "computerized," Bisk Education will provide necessary details in its updating supplements, just as it provides information regarding new pronouncements, laws, and other related material.

Because the details of the computerized exam are subject to change, we don't recommend that candidates wait to take the exam in order, say, to avoid the essay questions. After waiting, candidates may find that the computerized exam has essay questions after all.

FYI: A further step in the conversion to a computerized exam may involve the computer selecting additional sets of questions based on a candidate's responses to a first set of questions. As opposed to current types of essay questions, candidates instead may complete research tasks (given a CD-ROM library) and express conclusions in written form.

Candidates interested in learning more about the computerized exam should contact the AICPA. As we go to press, the AICPA web-site (www.aicpa.org) has an exposure draft available for downloading. However, do not confuse time spent learning about proposals for the computerized exam with review time. Bisk Education's updating supplements will include a concise summary of need-to-know information for candidates, when it becomes relevant to passing the exam.

CHAPTER 40

OTHER TYPES OF REPORTS

EXAM COVERAGE: The Prepare Communication portion of the Auditing section of the CPA exam (also discussed in Chapters 32 and 33) is designated by the examiners to be 20 percent of the section's point value. Historically, exam coverage of the topics in Chapter 40 and Chapter 41 each is 2 to 13 percent of the Auditing section. (There is considerable fluctuation.) More information about the point value of various topics is included in the **Practical Advice** section of this volume.

CHAPTER 40

OTHER TYPES OF REPORTS

I. Information Accompanying Basic Financial Statements in Auditor-Submitted Documents

A. Overview

AU 551 provides guidance on reporting when the auditor submits to a client, or others, a document containing information in addition to the basic financial statements and the audit report.

	GUIDELINES FOR AUDITOR'S REPORT
A	**Audit** made to form opinion on financial statements taken as whole
S	**State** (or disclaim) opinion as to whether accompanying information is fairly stated in all material respects in relation to basic financial statements taken as a whole
A	**Accompanying** information not a required part of financial statements
I	**Identify** accompanying information
R	**Report** on accompanying information may be added to standard audit report or may appear in separate auditor-submitted document

1. Such information (**not** required by GAAP) includes additional details or explanations of items in or related to the basic financial statements, consolidating information, historical summaries of items extracted from the basic financial statements, statistical data, and other material, some of which may be from sources outside the accounting system or the entity.

2. AU 551 does **not** apply when the client merely includes other information (that the auditor has not been engaged to report upon) in a document containing the basic financial statements and the auditor's standard report. In this instance, the auditor must read the information to ensure that it is consistent with the audited financial statements (SAS 8). Only if there is an inconsistency will the auditor report on other information (exception reporting).

B. Objectives

The objectives of the auditor's report on information accompanying the basic financial statements are the same as the report on the basic financial statements (i.e., to describe the character of the work and the degree of responsibility, if any, the auditor is taking).

1. **Guidelines**

   a. The report should state that the audit has been made for the purpose of forming an opinion on the basic financial statements taken as a whole.

   b. The report should identify the accompanying information. (Identification may be by descriptive title or page number of the document.)

   c. The report should state that the accompanying information is presented for purposes of additional analysis and is not a required part of the basic financial statements.

   d. The report should include either an opinion on whether the accompanying information is fairly stated in all material respects in relation to the basic financial statements taken as a whole or a disclaimer of opinion, depending on whether the information was subject to the auditing procedures applied in the audit of the basic financial statements. The auditor may express an opinion on a portion of the accompanying information and disclaim an opinion on the remainder.

e. The report on the accompanying information may be added to the auditor's standard report on the basic financial statements or may appear separately in the auditor-submitted document.

2. **MATERIALITY** The purpose of an audit is to provide an opinion on the fairness of the basic financial statements **taken as a whole**. If the auditor expresses an opinion on the additional accompanying information, the same materiality level used for the financial statements is used. Accordingly, the auditor does not need to apply additional procedures on the additional information taken by itself.

3. **MISSTATEMENTS** If the auditor believes that the additional information is materially misstated, in relation to the financial statements, the auditor should discuss it with management and propose a revision. If the client does not agree, the auditor should either:

   a. Modify the report on the accompanying information and describe the misstatement.

   b. Refuse to include the information in the document.

EXHIBIT 1 ♦ AUDITING PROCEDURES PERFORMED ON ACCOMPANYING INFORMATION

Our audit was conducted for the purpose of forming an opinion on the basic financial statements taken as a whole. The (identify accompanying information) is presented for purposes of additional analysis and is not a required part of the basic financial statements. Such information has been subjected to the auditing procedures applied in the audit of the basic financial statements and, in our opinion, is fairly stated in all material respects in relation to the basic financial statements taken as a whole.

EXHIBIT 2 ♦ DISCLAIMER ON ACCOMPANYING INFORMATION

Our audit was conducted for the purpose of forming an opinion on the basic financial statements taken as a whole. The (identify accompanying information) is presented for purposes of additional analysis and is not a required part of the basic financial statements. Such information has not been subjected to the auditing procedures applied in the audit of the basic financial statements, and, accordingly, we express no opinion on it.

C. **EFFECTS OF REPORT**

If the auditor modifies the report on the basic financial statements, the auditor should consider the effects on any related accompanying information (see Exhibit 3). When the auditor expresses an adverse opinion or disclaims an opinion on the basic financial statements, the auditor should disclaim an opinion on all accompanying information.

EXHIBIT 3 ♦ REPORTING ON ACCOMPANYING INFORMATION TO WHICH A QUALIFICATION IN THE AUDITOR'S REPORT ON THE BASIC FINANCIAL STATEMENTS APPLIES

Our audit was made for the purpose of forming an opinion on the basic financial statements taken as a whole. The schedules of investments (page 7), property (page 8) and other assets (page 9) as of December 31, 20X1, are presented for purposes of additional analysis and are not a required part of the basic financial statements. The information in such schedules has been subjected to the auditing procedures applied in the audit of the basic financial statements, and, in our opinion, except for the effects on the schedule of investments of not accounting for the investments in certain companies by the equity method as explained in the third paragraph of this report, such information is fairly stated in all material respects in relation to the basic financial statements taken as a whole.

D. REQUIRED SUPPLEMENTARY INFORMATION (RSI)

When supplementary information required by the FASB or GASB is presented outside the basic financial statements in an auditor-submitted document, the auditor should disclaim an opinion on the information unless he or she has been engaged to audit and express an opinion on it.

EXHIBIT 4 ♦ DISCLAIMER ON RSI PRESENTED OUTSIDE THE BASIC STATEMENTS

> The (identify the supplementary information) on page XX is not a required part of the basic financial statements but is supplementary information required by the (Financial or Governmental) Accounting Standards Board. We have applied certain limited procedures, which consisted principally of inquiries of management regarding the methods of measurement and presentation of the supplementary information. However, we did not audit the information, and express no opinion on it.

- The auditor's report should be expanded if RSI is omitted, the auditor has concluded that the measurement or presentation of RSI departs materially from guidelines prescribed by the FASB or GASB, the auditor is unable to remove substantial doubts about whether the RSI conforms to prescribed guidelines, or the auditor is unable to complete the procedures prescribed by SAS 52.

E. CONSOLIDATING INFORMATION

1. An auditor may be engaged to provide an opinion on consolidated financial statements on which consolidating information is also provided (e.g., the individual amounts making up the consolidated totals). The auditor must be satisfied that the consolidating information is suitably identified.

EXHIBIT 5 ♦ CONSOLIDATING INFORMATION NOT SEPARATELY AUDITED

> Our audit was conducted for the purpose of forming an opinion on the consolidated financial statements taken as a whole. The consolidating information is presented for purposes of additional analysis of the consolidated financial statements rather than to present the financial position, results of operations, and cash flows of the individual companies. The consolidating information has been subjected to the auditing procedures applied in the audit of the consolidated financial statements, and, in our opinion, is fairly stated in all material respects in relation to the consolidated financial statements taken as a whole.

2. An auditor may be engaged to form an opinion on **both** the consolidated statements and the separate statements of the components of a consolidated group. In this case, the auditor's responsibility with respect to the separate financial statements is the same as the responsibility for the consolidated statements.

II. SPECIAL REPORTS (AU 623, SAS 62)

A. SPECIAL PURPOSE REPORTS

Auditor's reports that apply only to (1) financial statements prepared in conformity with OCBOA; (2) specified elements, accounts, or items of a financial statement; (3) compliance with aspects of contractual agreements or regulatory requirements related to audited financial statements; (4) incomplete presentation; or (5) financial information presented in prescribed forms or schedules that require a prescribed form of auditor's report.

B. REPORTS ON FINANCIAL STATEMENTS PREPARED IN CONFORMITY WITH OCBOA

GAAS apply whenever an auditor conducts an audit of and reports on any financial statement.

1. **OCBOA** A comprehensive basis other than GAAP is (a) a basis that is used to comply with the requirements or financial provisions of a government regulatory agency, but only for filing

with that agency (e.g., state insurance commission rules for insurance companies); (b) a basis used (or expected to be used) for filing the client's income tax return for the period covered by the financial statements; (c) the cash receipts and disbursements basis (including modifications to cash basis that have substantial support); and (d) a definite set of criteria having substantial support that is applied to all material financial statement items, (e.g., price-level basis of accounting).

2. **Statement Titles** "Balance sheet," "statement of financial position," "statement of income," "statement of operations," "statement of cash flows," etc., apply only to statements prepared in conformity with GAAP. Suitable titles should be given to financial statements prepared in conformity with a comprehensive basis of accounting other than GAAP. For example, an appropriate title for a cash-basis financial statement might be "statement of assets and liabilities arising from cash transactions," and an appropriate title for a financial statement prepared on a statutory basis might be "statement of income—statutory basis."

3. **Auditor's Report** The auditor's report includes the following.

Exhibit 6 ♦ Auditor's Report on Cash Basis Financial Statements

Independent Auditor's Report*

We have audited the accompanying statements of assets and liabilities arising from cash transactions of XYZ Company as of December 31, 20X2 and 20X1, and the related statements of revenue collected and expenses paid for the years then ended. These financial statements are the responsibility of the company's management. Our responsibility is to express an opinion on these financial statements based on our audits.

We conducted our audits in accordance with U.S. generally accepted auditing standards. Those standards require that we plan and perform the audit to obtain reasonable assurance about whether the financial statements are free of material misstatement. An audit includes examining, on a test basis, evidence supporting the amounts and disclosures in the financial statements. An audit also includes assessing the accounting principles used and significant estimates made by management, as well as evaluating the overall financial statement presentation. We believe that our audits provide a reasonable basis for our opinion.

As described in Note X, these financial statements were prepared on the basis of cash receipts and disbursements, which is a comprehensive basis of accounting other than generally accepted accounting principles.

In our opinion, the financial statements referred to above present fairly, in all material respects, the assets and liabilities arising from cash transactions of XYZ Company as of December 31, 20X2 and 20X1, and the revenue collected and expenses paid during the years then ended, on the basis of accounting described in Note X.

* This report should be addressed, signed, and dated as previously discussed. For the sake of brevity, these elements are omitted from this and most other exhibits of reports in this chapter.

a. **Same** Elements the same as the standard auditor's report are: (1) a title that includes the word "independent", (2) paragraph one is an introductory paragraph, (3) paragraph two is a scope paragraph, (4) the signature of the auditor's firm, (5) a date.

b. **Paragraph Three** States: (1) the basis of presentation, and refers to the note that describes the basis, and (2) that the basis of presentation is a comprehensive basis of accounting other than GAAP.

c. **Paragraph Four** Expresses the auditor's opinion on the financial statements in accordance with the OCBOA basis.

d. **Restrictive Paragraph** This paragraph is used when the financial statements are prepared in conformity with the requirements of a government regulatory agency. It states that the distribution of the report is restricted to those within the entity and for filing with the regulatory agency.

e. **Financial Statement Titles** The auditor should disclose reservations in an explanatory paragraph of the report and qualify the opinion in cases where the auditor believes the financial statements are not appropriately titled.

C. Reports on Specified Elements, Accounts, or Items of a Financial Statement

Examples include rentals, royalties, a profit participation, or a provision for income taxes.

Exhibit 7 ♦ Report Relating to Royalties

Independent Auditor's Report

We have audited the accompanying schedule of royalties applicable to engine production of the Q Division of XYZ Corporation for the year ended December 31, 20X2, under the terms of a license agreement dated May 14, 20X0, between ABC Company and XYZ Corporation. This schedule is the responsibility of XYZ Corporation's management. Our responsibility is to express an opinion on this schedule based on our audit.

We conducted our audit in accordance with U.S. generally accepted auditing standards. Those standards require that we plan and perform the audit to obtain reasonable assurance about whether the schedule of royalties is free of material misstatement. An audit includes examining, on a test basis, evidence supporting the amounts and disclosures in the schedule. An audit also includes assessing the accounting principles used and significant estimates made by management, as well as evaluating the overall schedule presentation. We believe that our audit provides a reasonable basis for our opinion.

We have been informed that, under XYZ Corporation's interpretation of the agreement referred to in the first paragraph, royalties were based on the number of engines produced after giving effect to a reduction for production retirements that were scrapped, but without a reduction for field returns that were scrapped, even though the field returns were replaced with new engines without charge to customers.

In our opinion, the schedule of royalties referred to above presents fairly, in all material respects, the number of engines produced by the Q Division of XYZ Corporation during the year ended December 31, 20X2, and the amount of royalties applicable thereto, under the license agreement referred to above.

This report is intended solely for the information and use of the boards of directors and management of XYZ Corporation and ABC Company and should not be used for any other purpose.

1. **GAAS** The ten GAAS are applicable with the exception of the first standard of reporting which is applicable only when the specified elements, accounts, or items are intended to be presented in conformity with GAAP.

2. **Materiality** An engagement to express an opinion on one or more specified elements, accounts, or items may be undertaken as a separate engagement or in conjunction with an audit of the financial statements. Since an opinion is being expressed on each of the specified elements, accounts, or items encompassed by the auditor's report, materiality must be related to each of the specified elements, accounts, or items. Therefore, the audit will usually be more extensive in regard to the element, account, or item than it would be if the only objective were to express an opinion on the financial statements taken as a whole. The

auditor must consider any interrelationships among the specified elements, accounts, or items being reported on and other items in the financial statements.

3. **PIECEMEAL OPINION** When the auditor has expressed an adverse opinion or disclaimed an opinion on the financial statements taken as a whole, the auditor should **not** report on specified elements, accounts, or items that are included in those statements if the effect is to express a piecemeal opinion. The auditor is able to report on one or more specified elements, accounts, or items provided that a major portion of the financial statements is not involved. In this case, the report should **not** accompany the financial statements.

D. REPORTS ON COMPLIANCE WITH ASPECTS OF CONTRACTUAL AGREEMENTS OR REGULATORY REQUIREMENTS RELATED TO AUDITED FINANCIAL STATEMENTS

Contractual agreements sometimes require entities to furnish compliance reports prepared by independent auditors (e.g., a loan agreement may contain provisions relating to payments made into a sinking fund and the maintenance of a specified current ratio).

EXHIBIT 8 ♦ COMPLIANCE WITH CONTRACTUAL PROVISIONS GIVEN IN A SEPARATE REPORT

> We have examined the balance sheet of XYZ Company as of December 31, 20X2, and the related statements of income, retained earnings, and cash flows for the year then ended, and have issued our report thereon dated February 16, 20X3. Our examination was made in accordance with U.S. generally accepted auditing standards and, accordingly, included such tests of the accounting records and such other auditing procedures as we considered necessary in the circumstances.
>
> In connection with our examination, nothing came to our attention that caused us to believe that the company failed to comply with the terms, covenants, provisions or conditions of Sections XX to XX, inclusive, of the Indenture dated July 21, 20X0, with ABC Bank. However, it should be noted that our examination was not directed primarily toward obtaining knowledge of such noncompliance.

1. **NEGATIVE ASSURANCE** The auditor normally gives negative assurance regarding compliance with agreements. This may be done by using a separate report or it may be added to the report accompanying the financial statements. Negative assurance should be given only when the auditor has **audited** the financial statements to which the agreements or requirements relate and the report's use will be **restricted** to the named parties.

2. **REPORT** The auditor's report includes the following.

   a. **TITLE** A title that includes the word "independent."

   b. **PARAGRAPH ONE** The financial statements were audited in accordance with GAAS and includes the date of the auditor's report on those financial statements. Any departure from the standard report should also be disclosed.

   c. **PARAGRAPH TWO** A reference to the specific covenants or paragraphs of the agreement, provides negative assurance relative to the compliance with the applicable covenants insofar as they relate to accounting matters, and specifies that the negative assurance is being given in connection with the audit of the financial statements.

   d. **PARAGRAPH THREE** A description and source of significant interpretations, if any, made by the company's management relating to the provisions of a relevant agreement.

   e. **PARAGRAPH FOUR** Restricts the use of the report to those within the entity and the parties to the contract or agreement or for filing with the regulatory agency.

   f. **SIGNATURE AND DATE**

E. **Incomplete Presentation Otherwise in Conformity With GAAP or OCBOA**
This might include a situation where a buy-sell agreement requires that assets and liabilities be presented in accordance with GAAP, but it only includes those items that will be sold and transferred under the agreement rather than all the entity's assets and liabilities. This does constitute a financial statement in the limited circumstances addressed by SAS 62.

1. **Presentation** The presentation should be appropriately titled so that no confusion exists (terms such as balance sheet, income statement, statement of cash flows should **not** be used). Disclosures should be made similar to those provided in a complete set of financial statements.

2. **Materiality** Materiality is in relation to the presentation taken as a whole.

3. **Report** The audit report includes the following.

   a. An introductory paragraph that identifies the financial information being reported on and states the responsibilities of management and the auditor.

   b. A scope paragraph.

   c. An explanatory paragraph that (1) explains what the financial presentation is intended to present and refers the reader to a note that describes the basis of the financial presentation, and (2) states that the financial presentation is not intended to be a complete set of financial information in accordance with GAAP.

   d. An opinion paragraph.

   e. A paragraph restricting the use of the report.

F. **Statements Prepared on a Prescribed Basis Not in Conformity With GAAP or OCBOA**
An auditor can be associated with financial statements using specified reporting requirements. For example, a loan application may call for financial statements, with the inventory to be valued at sales price; or in an acquisition agreement, the financial statements may request that fixed assets and inventories be measured at their liquidation values.

1. **Materiality** The auditor considers the adequacy of the disclosures associated with the financial statements. Materiality is considered at the financial statement level.

2. **Report** The auditor's report includes the following.

   a. A responsibility paragraph

   b. A scope paragraph

   c. An explanatory paragraph similar to an incomplete presentation otherwise in conformity with GAAP

   d. A paragraph that includes a description and the source of significant interpretations made by management

   e. An opinion paragraph

   f. A paragraph restricting the distribution of the report

G. **Financial Information Presented in Prescribed Forms or Schedules**
Regulatory bodies, government agencies, and others sometimes use printed forms or schedules that prescribe the form of the auditor's report. A problem arises if the prescribed report does not conform to the applicable professional reporting standards of the public accounting profession (e.g., calling for assertions that are not consistent with the auditor's function).

1. **Procedures** Insertion of additional wording can make some report forms acceptable; other report forms require complete revision.
2. **Assertions** If a printed report calls for an assertion the auditor believes is not justified, the auditor should either reword the form or attach a separate report.

III. Letters for Underwriters

A. **Filings Under Federal Securities Statutes (AU 711, SAS 37)**
The financial representations contained in documents filed with the SEC are the responsibility and representations of management. However, the Securities Act of 1933 imposes responsibility on an auditor for false or misleading financial statements (or for omissions that make them misleading) in an effective registration statement prepared or certified by the CPA.

1. **Auditor's Defense** The auditor must prove that (a) there were reasonable grounds to believe (and the auditor did believe) that the statements in the registration statement were true and that there was no omission of a material fact at the date of the registration statement **or** (b) that the part of the registration statement that is in question did not fairly represent the auditor's statement as an expert or was not fairly copied or extracted from the report or valuation.

    - **Reasonableness Standard** The standard of reasonableness is that standard which would be used by a prudent person in the management of his or her own property.

2. **Date** The auditor's responsibility extends to the effective date of the registration statement.
3. **Use of Name** The auditor should be sure his or her name is not used in a way that may indicate that the auditor's responsibility is greater than it really is.

4. **Subsequent Events Procedures in 1933 Act Filings** The auditor should **extend** subsequent event procedures from the date of the report to the effective date of the registration statement. The auditor can rely, for the most part, on inquiries of responsible officials and employees. The auditor should perform the auditing procedures used to assess the existence of subsequent events (e.g., inquiry of management, reading of minutes, etc.) and, in addition, should (a) read the entire prospectus and other pertinent portions of the registration statement, and (b) obtain written confirmation from officers and other executives regarding subsequent events that have a material effect on the audited financial statements included in the registration statement or which require disclosure in order to keep the statements from being misleading.

5. **Response to Subsequent Events and Subsequently Discovered Facts** If the auditor discovers (a) subsequent events requiring adjustment or disclosure or (b) facts existing at the time of the report which might have affected the report had the auditor known about them, the auditor should do the following:

    a. Ask management to revise the statements and/or add the required disclosures.

    b. If management refuses, the auditor should modify the report accordingly and consider obtaining advice from legal counsel.

6. **Reports Based on a Review of Interim Financial Information** The SEC requires that when a report based on a review of interim financial information is presented or incorporated

in a registration statement by reference, a clarification should be made that the review report is not a "report" or "part" of the registration statement within the meaning of Sections 7 and 11 of the Securities Act of 1933.

7. **Two or More Auditors** A registration statement filed with the SEC may contain the reports of two or more auditors for different periods. An auditor who has not audited the financial statements for the most recent period has a responsibility for events that have a material effect on the financial statements the auditor reported on that occurred during the period running from the date of the report until the effective date of the registration statement. The auditor generally should (a) read the pertinent portions of the prospectus and registration statement and (b) obtain a letter of representation from the successor auditor about subsequent events about which the successor has become aware.

B. Letters for Underwriters and Certain Other Requesting Parties (AU 634)

SAS 72, 76, and 86 provide guidance to accountants for reporting on the results of and performing engagements to issue letters for underwriters and certain other requesting parties, commonly referred to as comfort letters, in connection with financial statements and financial statement schedules contained in registration statements filed with the SEC under the Securities Act of 1933. Comfort letters are not required under the Act, and copies are not filed with the SEC. It is nonetheless a common condition of an underwriting agreement in connection with the offering for sale of securities registered with the SEC under the Act that the accountants are to furnish a comfort letter.

1. **Purpose** Section 11 of the Act provides that underwriters, among others, could be liable if any part of a registration statement contains material omissions or misstatements. The Act also provides for an affirmative defense for underwriters if it can be demonstrated that, after an investigation, the underwriter has reasonable grounds to believe that there were no material omissions or misstatements. An accountant's issuance of a comfort letter is one procedure used to establish that an underwriter has conducted a reasonable investigation.

2. **Representations** Using a statutory due diligence defense under Section 11 of the Act, a comfort letter may be addressed to parties other than a named underwriter, only when a law firm or attorney for the requesting party issues a written opinion to the accountants that states that such party has a due diligence defense under Section 11 of the Act. SAS 76 precludes the accountant from providing a comfort letter if an appropriate representation letter is not provided. An attorney's letter indicating that a party "may" be deemed to be an underwriter, or has liability substantially equivalent to that of an underwriter under the securities laws, would not meet this requirement. If the requesting party, in a securities offering registered pursuant to the Act, other than a named underwriter, cannot provide such a letter, he or she must provide a representation letter for the accountant to provide him or her with a comfort letter. The letter should be addressed to the accountants, signed by the requesting party, and contain a due diligence process paragraph.

Exhibit 9 ♦ Representation Letter Excerpt

> This review process, applied to the information relating to the issuer, is substantially consistent with the due diligence review process that we would perform if this placement of securities were being registered pursuant to the Securities Act of 1933. We are knowledgeable with respect to the due diligence review process that would be performed if this placement of securities were being registered pursuant to the Act.

3. **Limitations** In requesting comfort letters, underwriters are generally seeking assistance on matters of importance to them. They wish to perform a "reasonable investigation" of financial and accounting data not "expertized" as a defense against possible claims under Section 11 of the Act. Accountants normally are willing to assist underwriters, but the assistance accountants can provide by way of comfort letters is subject to limitations. One limitation is that independent accountants can properly comment in their professional capacity only on matters to which their professional expertise is substantially relevant. Another

limitation is that procedures short of an audit, such as those contemplated in a comfort letter, provide the accountants with a basis for expressing, at the most, negative assurance.

4. **Draft** Because the underwriter will expect the accountants to furnish a comfort letter of a scope to be specified in the underwriting agreement, a draft of that agreement should be furnished to the accountants so that they can indicate whether they will be able to furnish a letter in acceptable form. It is a desirable practice for the accountants, promptly after they have received the draft of the agreement, to prepare a draft of the form of the letter they expect to furnish. The draft should deal with all matters to be covered in the final letter.

5. **Prohibited** Accountants should not comment on matters merely because they are capable of reading, counting, measuring, or performing other functions that might be applicable. Examples of matters that, unless subjected to the controls over financial reporting, should not be commented on by accountants include the square footage of facilities and backlog information. Accountants should not comment on tables, statistics, and other financial information relating to an unaudited period, unless they have obtained knowledge of the client's internal control over financial reporting (comparable to that obtained during an audit). In addition, accountants should not comment on information subject to legal interpretation.

6. **Additional Letters** Accountants may not issue any additional letters or reports to the underwriter or the other requesting parties, in connection with the offering or placement of securities, in which the accountants comment on items for which commenting is otherwise precluded by SAS 72, as amended, such as square footage of facilities.

7. **Format and Content**

   a. **Permissible Topics** Generally, accountants may comment only with respect to information (1) obtained from accounting records that are subject to the entity's controls over financial reporting and that is expressed in dollars (or percentages derived from such dollar amounts), or (2) derived directly from accounting records by analysis or computation. Accountants also may comment on quantitative information that has been obtained from an accounting record, if the information is subject to the same controls over financial reporting as the dollar amounts.

      (1) The independence of the accountants.

      (2) Whether the audited financial statements and financial statement schedules included in the registration statement comply as to form in all material respects with the applicable accounting requirements of the Act and the related published rules and regulations.

      (3) Unaudited financial statements, condensed interim financial information, capsule financial information, pro forma financial information, financial forecasts, and changes in selected financial statement items during a period subsequent to the date and period of the latest registration statement.

      (4) Tables, statistics, and other financial information included in the registration statement.

      (5) Negative assurance as to whether certain non-financial statement information complies as to form with Regulation S-K, if the information is (a) derived from the accounting records subject to the entity's controls over financial reporting and (b) capable of evaluation against SEC criteria. Accountants may perform procedures and report findings with respect to conformity with Regulation S-K.

   b. **Date** The letter ordinarily is dated on or shortly before the date on which the registration statement becomes effective.

c. **Addressee** The letter should not be addressed or given to any parties other than the client and the named underwriter, broker-dealer, financial intermediary, or buyer or seller. The appropriate addressee is the intermediary who has negotiated the agreement with the client, and with whom the accountants will deal in discussions regarding the scope and sufficiency of the letter.

d. **Explanatory Paragraph** When the report on the audited financial statements and financial statement schedules included in the registration statement departs from the standard report, the accountants should refer to that fact in the comfort letter and discuss the subject matter of the paragraph.

e. **Reiterate Audit Opinion** The underwriter occasionally requests the accountants to repeat in the comfort letter their report on the audited financial statements included in the registration statement. Because of the special significance of the date of the accountants' report, the accountants should **not** repeat their opinion. The underwriter sometimes requests negative assurance regarding the accountants' report. Because accountants have a statutory responsibility with respect to their opinion as of the effective date of a registration statement, and because the additional significance, if any, of negative assurance is unclear and such assurance may therefore give rise to misunderstanding, accountants should **not** give **negative** assurance.

f. **Optional** Accountants may refer (in the introductory paragraphs of the comfort letter) to the fact that they have issued reports on (1) condensed financial statements that are derived from audited financial statements; (2) selected financial data; (3) interim financial information; (4) pro forma financial information; (5) a financial forecast; and (6) management's discussion and analysis. Any optional references should be to previously-issued accountants' reports. If the reports were not included (or incorporated by reference) in the registration statement, they may be attached to the comfort letter. The accountants should not repeat previously-issued reports, otherwise imply that they are reporting as of the date of the comfort letter, or imply that they assume responsibility for the sufficiency of the procedures for the underwriter's purposes. For certain information on which they have reported, accountants may agree to comment regarding compliance with SEC criteria. Accountants should not mention reports issued in accordance with SAS 60 or any restricted-use reports issued in connection with procedures performed on the client's internal control in accordance with SSAE 2 (as amended).

g. **Pro Forma Information** Accountants should **not** comment in a comfort letter on pro forma financial information unless they have an appropriate level of knowledge of the accounting and financial reporting practices of the entity. This would ordinarily have been obtained by the accountant's audit or review of historical financial statements of the entity for the most recent annual or interim period for which the pro forma financial information is presented.

h. **Compliance** Accountants may be requested to express an opinion on whether the financial statements covered by their report comply as to form with the pertinent SEC accounting requirements. Accountants may provide positive assurance on compliance as to form with SEC requirements only with respect to those rules and regulations applicable to the form and content of financial statements and financial statement schedules that they have audited. Accountants are limited to providing negative assurance on compliance as to form on unaudited statements or schedules. If there is a material departure from SEC criteria, it must be disclosed.

EXHIBIT 10 ♦ SAMPLE PARAGRAPH REGARDING COMPLIANCE WITH SEC CRITERIA

In our opinion (include phrase *except as disclosed in the registration statement*, if applicable) the (*identify the financial statements and financial statement schedules*) audited by us and included (incorporated by reference) in the registration statement comply as to form in all material respects with the applicable accounting requirements of the Act and the related rules and regulations adopted by the SEC.

8. **SUBSEQUENTLY DISCOVERED MATTERS** Accountants who discover matters that may require mention in the final comfort letter but that are not mentioned in the **draft** letter that has been furnished to the underwriter, such as changes, increases, or decreases in specified items not disclosed in the registration statement will naturally want to discuss them with their client so that consideration can be given to whether disclosure should be made in the registration statement. If disclosure is not to be made, the accountants should inform the client that the matters will be mentioned in the comfort letter and should suggest that the underwriter be informed promptly.

IV. SERVICE ORGANIZATIONS (SAS 70, 78, 88)

A. OVERVIEW

SAS 70, 78, and 88 provide guidance on the factors an independent auditor considers when auditing the financial statements of an entity that uses a service organization to process transactions. They also provide guidance for independent auditors who issue reports on the processing of transactions by a service organization for use by other auditors.

1. **USER ORGANIZATION** The entity that has engaged a service organization and whose financial statements are being audited.

2. **USER AUDITOR** The auditor who reports on the financial statements of the user organization.

3. **SERVICE ORGANIZATION** The entity (or a segment of that entity) that provides services to the user organization. Services could include the processing of payroll information by a service organization for other companies or the processing of checks and daily paperwork for banks by a service organization.

4. **SERVICE AUDITOR** The auditor who reports on the processing of transactions by a service organization.

B. RESPONSIBILITIES OF SERVICE AUDITORS FOR SPECIAL-PURPOSE REPORTS

1. The service auditor is responsible for the representations in his or her report and for exercising due care in the application of procedures that support those representations. The service auditor's work should be performed in accordance with the general standards and relevant field work and reporting standards. The service auditor should be independent from the service organization. However, the service auditor is **not** required to be independent with regard to each client organization.

2. The type of engagement to be performed and report to be prepared should be established by the service organization. A service auditor's report on a service organization's description of the controls that may be relevant to a user organization's internal control. The service auditor may issue either of the following types of reports.

   a. **REPORTS ON CONTROLS PLACED IN OPERATION** The auditor reports on whether the controls were (1) suitably designed to achieve specified objectives and (2) placed in operation as of a specific date.

b. Reports on Controls Placed in Operation and Tests of Operating Effectiveness Like the report previously discussed, the auditor reports on whether such controls were (1) suitably designed to achieve specified objectives and (2) placed in operation as of a specific date. The auditor also reports on whether the controls that were tested were operating with sufficient effectiveness to provide reasonable, but not absolute, assurance that the related objectives were achieved during the period specified.

C. Format and Content of Special-Purpose Reports

A report expressing an opinion on a description of controls placed in operation at a service organization should contain the following:

Exhibit 11 ♦ Report on the Internal Controls at a Service Organization

> To XYZ Service Organization:
>
> We have examined the accompanying description of the ______ application of XYZ Service Organization. Our examination included procedures to obtain reasonable assurance about whether (1) the accompanying description presents fairly, in all material respects, the aspects of XYZ Service Organization's controls that may be relevant to a user organization's internal control, (2) the internal controls included in the description were suitably designed to achieve the objectives specified in the description, if those controls were complied with satisfactorily, and (3) such controls had been placed in operation as of ______. The objectives were specified by ______. Our examination was performed in accordance with standards established by the American Institute of Certified Public Accountants and included those procedures we considered necessary in the circumstances to obtain a reasonable basis for rendering our opinion.
>
> We did not perform procedures to determine the operating effectiveness of controls for any period. Accordingly, we express no opinion on the operating effectiveness of any aspects of XYZ Service Organization's controls, individually or in the aggregate.
>
> In our opinion, the accompanying description of the aforementioned application presents fairly, in all material respects, the relevant aspects of XYZ Service Organization's controls that had been placed in operation as of ______. Also, in our opinion, the controls, as described, are suitably designed to provide reasonable assurance that the specified objectives would be achieved if the described controls were complied with satisfactorily.
>
> The description of controls at XYZ Service Organization is as of ______ and any projection of such information to the future is subject to the risk that, because of change, the description may no longer portray the system in existence. The potential effectiveness of specific controls at the Service Organization is subject to inherent limitations and, accordingly, errors or fraud may occur and not be detected. Furthermore, the projection of any conclusions, based on our findings, to future periods is subject to the risk that changes may alter the validity of such conclusions.
>
> This report is intended solely for use by the management of XYZ Service Organization, its customers, and the independent auditors of its customers.

1. A specific reference to the applications, services, products or other aspects of the service organization covered.

2. A description of the scope and nature of the service auditor's procedures.

3. Identification of the party specifying the objectives.

4. An indication that the purpose of the service auditor's engagement was to obtain reasonable assurance about whether the service organization's description presents fairly, in all material

respects, the aspects of the service organization's controls that may be relevant to a user organization's internal control; that the controls were suitably designed to achieve specified control objectives; and that such controls had been placed in operation as of a specific date.

5. A disclaimer of opinion on the operating effectiveness of the controls.

6. The service auditor's opinion on whether the description presents fairly, in all material respects, the relevant aspects of the service organization's policies and procedures that had been placed in operation as of a specific date and whether, in the service auditor's opinion, the policies and procedures were suitably designed to provide reasonable assurance that the specified objectives would be achieved if those controls were complied with satisfactorily.

7. A statement of the inherent limitations of the potential effectiveness of the policies and procedures at the service organization and of the risk of projecting to future periods any evaluation of the description.

8. Identification of the parties for whom the report is intended.

D. Considerations of the User Auditor in Using a Service Auditor's Report

1. In considering whether the service auditor's report is satisfactory for his or her purposes, the user auditor should make inquiries concerning the service auditor's professional reputation.

2. If the user auditor believes that the service auditor's report may not be sufficient to meet his or her objectives, the user auditor may supplement his or her understanding of the service auditor's procedures and conclusions by discussing with the service auditor the scope and results of the service auditor's work. If the user auditor believes it is necessary, he or she may contact the service organization, through the user organization, to request that the service auditor perform agreed-upon procedures at the service organization, or the user auditor may perform such procedures.

3. The user auditor should not make reference to the service auditor's report as a basis for his or her own opinion on the user organization's financial statements.

4. Under SAS 88, a service organization's services are part of an entity's information system if they affect any of the following: (a) how the entity's transactions are initiated; (b) the accounting records, supporting information, and specific accounts in the financial statements involved in the processing and reporting of the entity's transactions; (c) the accounting processing involved from the initiation of the transactions to their inclusion in the financial statements, including electronic means used to transmit, process, maintain, and access information; and (d) the financial reporting process used to prepare the entity's financial statements, including significant accounting estimates and disclosures.

5. SAS 88 notes that the significance of the service organization's controls to those of the user organization depends on the nature of the services provided by the service organization in two primary areas: (a) the nature and materiality of the transactions it processes for the user organization, and (b) the degree of interaction between its activities and those of the user organization.

6. The explicit addition of service organizations to the **audit planning** requirement clarifies the auditor's responsibility to understand all controls relevant to a financial statement audit. The auditor should obtain an understanding of each of the five components of an entity's internal control (control environment, etc.) sufficient to plan the audit. SAS 88 states that this understanding may encompass controls placed in operation by the entity and by service organizations whose services are part of the entity's information system.

V. Review of Interim Financial Information (SAS 71, 90)

A. Applicability

SAS 71 and 90 provide guidance as to the nature, timing, and extent of procedures to be applied for a **review** of interim financial information (i.e., financial information or statements for less than a full year or for a twelve-month period ending on a date other than the entity's fiscal year end) and on the resulting report. It also establishes certain communication requirements.

1. Reviews of interim financial information presented alone (including interim financial statements and summarized interim financial data) that purports to comply with APB Opinion No. 28.

2. Reviews of interim financial information that accompanies, or is included in a note to audited financial statements.

3. SAS 71 also provides guidance on reporting when certain quarterly data required by Regulation S-K are not presented or are presented but have not been reviewed.

B. Objective

To provide the CPA with a basis for reporting whether **material modifications** are needed to make the information conform with GAAP. This differs substantially from the objective of an audit.

- The CPA may be asked to review interim financial information so that the client can make that representation in documents issued to stockholders or to third parties or in Form 10-Q (a quarterly report filed with the SEC). When the client represents that the CPA made such a review, the CPA should request that the CPA's report be included.

C. Procedures

Because interim financial information is made available more quickly than annual information, many costs and expenses are **estimated** to a greater extent than for annual financial statements. Also, the interim information is related to the annual financial information (e.g., accruals at the end of an interim period are affected by the estimate of the results of operations for the remainder of the annual period).

1. **Nature** Primarily inquiries and analytical procedures.

   a. **Inquiry About Internal Control** Inquiry concerning (1) how the system works, and (2) any significant changes in internal control.

   b. **Analytical Procedures** Applied to interim financial information to provide a basis for inquiring about unusual items. These procedures consist of (1) comparing the financial information with the immediately preceding interim period and with the corresponding previous period(s), (2) comparing actual results with anticipated results, and (3) studying the relationships of those elements that can be expected to conform to predictable patterns. The CPA should consider the types of matters that required accounting adjustments in the preceding year or quarters.

   c. **Reading Minutes** Reading the minutes of meetings of the stockholders, board of directors, and committees of the board of directors.

   d. **Reading the Interim Financial Information** To determine whether it conforms to GAAP.

   e. **Obtaining Reports From Other Accountants** If any have reviewed the interim financial information of significant components of the reporting entity, its subsidiaries, or other investees.

f. **Inquiring of Officers and Other Executives** To determine (1) whether the interim financial information conforms to GAAP consistently applied, (2) any changes in the company's business activities or accounting practices, (3) questions that have arisen during the review procedures, and (4) subsequent events (subsequent to the date of the interim financial information).

g. **Obtaining Written Representations** From management, concerning management's responsibility for the financial information, completeness of the minutes, subsequent events, etc.

2. **Timing** Performing some of the work before the end of the interim period (a) usually permits the work to be carried out more efficiently, and (b) permits early consideration of accounting matters that affect the interim financial information.

3. **Extent** The extent to which the CPA applies procedures depends on the accountant's knowledge of changes in accounting practices or in the nature or volume of business activity; inquiry concerning litigation, claims, and assessments; questions raised in performing other procedures; and modification of review procedures.

4. **Understanding With the Client** The CPA must reach an understanding as to the nature of the procedures to be performed should be established, usually in the form of an engagement letter that includes: a general description of the procedures; a statement that the procedures are substantially less in scope than an audit performed in accordance with GAAS; an explanation that the financial information is the responsibility of the company's management; and a description of the form of the report, if any.

5. **Knowledge of Internal Control** SAS 71 requires that, for an accountant to perform a review of interim financial information, there must exist a sufficient knowledge of the client's internal control policies and procedures as they relate to the preparation of both annual and interim financial information to

a. Identify types of potential material misstatements in the interim financial information and consider the likelihood of their occurrence.

b. Select the inquiries and analytical procedures that will provide the accountant with a basis for reporting whether material modifications should be made for such information to conform with GAAP.

6. **Subsequent Events** Subsequent discovery of facts that existed at the date of the auditor's report should be handled in accordance with AU 561.

D. **Presented Alone**

The report should consist of (1) a statement that the review conformed to the standards for a review of interim financial information, (2) an identification of the information reviewed, (3) a description of the procedures for a review, (4) a statement that the **scope** of a review is substantially less than that of an audit and that an opinion on the financial statements, taken as a whole, is **not** expressed, and (5) a statement as to whether the CPA is aware of any material modifications needed to make the financial information conform with GAAP.

1. **Form of Report**

a. **Addressee** Addressed to the company, its board of directors, or its stockholders.

b. **Date** Date of completion of the review.

c. **"Unaudited"** Each page of the interim financial information should be clearly marked "unaudited."

d. **Other Accountants** May use and make reference to the report of another accountant. The reference indicates a division of responsibility for performing the review.

EXHIBIT 12 ♦ REPORT ON INTERIM FINANCIAL INFORMATION

> We have reviewed the accompanying (describe the information or statement reviewed) of ABC Company and consolidated subsidiaries as of September 30, 20X1, and for the three-month and nine-month periods then ended. These financial statements (information) are (is) the responsibility of the company's management.
>
> We conducted our review in accordance with standards established by the American Institute of Certified Public Accountants. A review of interim financial information consists principally of applying analytical procedures to financial data, and making inquiries of persons responsible for financial and accounting matters. It is substantially less in scope than an audit conducted in accordance with U.S. generally accepted auditing standards, the objective of which is the expression of an opinion regarding the financial statements taken as a whole. Accordingly, we do not express such an opinion.
>
> Based on our review, we are not aware of any material modifications that should be made to the accompanying financial (information or statements) for them (it) to be in conformity with U.S. generally accepted accounting principles.

2. **MODIFICATION OF THE CPA'S REPORT** Neither an uncertainty **nor** a lack of consistency in applying accounting principles would result in a modified report as long as the matters are **adequately disclosed** in the interim financial information or statements. However, a modification is required if a change in accounting principle is **not** in conformity with GAAP.

   a. **DEPARTURE FROM GAAP** Report should be modified when the interim financial information is materially affected by a departure from GAAP. The nature of the departure and, if practicable, its effects should be disclosed.

> **EXHIBIT 13 ♦ DEPARTURE FROM GAAP**
>
> (Explanatory third paragraph)
>
> Based on information furnished to us by management, we believe that the Company has excluded from property and debt in the accompanying balance sheet certain lease obligations that should be capitalized to conform with generally accepted accounting principles. This information indicates that if these lease obligations were capitalized at September 30, 20X1, property would be increased by $_____, long term debt by $______, and net income and earnings per share would be increased (decreased) by $______, $______, $______, and $______, respectively, for the three-month and nine-month periods then ended.
>
> (Concluding paragraph)
>
> Based on our review, with the exception of the matter(s) described in the preceding paragraph(s), we are not aware of any material modifications that should be made to the accompanying financial (information or statements) for them (it) to be in conformity with U.S. generally accepted accounting principles.

b. **INADEQUATE DISCLOSURE** Report should be modified and, if practicable, the needed information should be included.

EXHIBIT 14 ♦ INADEQUATE DISCLOSURE

> (Explanatory third paragraph)
>
> Management has informed us that the Company is presently contesting deficiencies in federal income taxes proposed by the Internal Revenue Service for the years 20X1 through 20X3 in the aggregate amount of approximately $_____, and that the extent of the company's liability, if any, and the effect on the accompanying (information or statements) are (is) not determinable at this time. The (information or statements) fail to disclose these matters, which we believe are required to be disclosed in conformity with generally accepted accounting principles.
>
> (Concluding paragraph)
>
> Based on our review, with the exception of the matter(s) described in the preceding paragraph(s), we are not aware of any material modifications that should be made to the accompanying financial (information or statements) for them (it) to be in conformity with U.S. generally accepted accounting principles.

E. **PRESENTED IN A NOTE TO AUDITED FINANCIAL STATEMENTS**
SEC Regulation S-K requires some companies to include a note containing selected quarterly financial information in their audited financial statements. In addition, other companies may choose to do so. If the quarterly data is **voluntarily** presented, the auditor should review it or the auditor should expand the report to state the data has not been reviewed. The interim financial information is **not** required by GAAP and has not been audited; therefore, the auditor ordinarily will **not** modify the report on the audited financial statements to refer to the quarterly data.

1. If the CPA has audited the annual financial statements for which the quarterly information **required** by Regulation S-K is presented, the CPA should review the quarterly information. If unable to perform such review, the report on the audited financial statements may need to be modified.

2. If the quarterly data either has been omitted **or** has not been reviewed, the auditor's report on the annual statements should be modified.

3. The auditor's report should also be expanded when the following occurs: the interim financial information is not marked "unaudited;" the interim information is voluntarily presented but has not been reviewed and is not appropriately marked as such; the interim information does not conform to GAAP; or the information, although reviewed, fails to indicate that a review is substantially less in scope than an audit performed per GAAS.

F. **AUDIT COMMITTEE**

1. **MISSTATEMENT** If the accountant becomes aware of matters that cause him or her to believe that interim financial information is probably materially misstated as a result of a departure from GAAP, the accountant should discuss the matter with the appropriate level of management as soon as practicable.

   a. **MANAGEMENT RESPONSE** If, in the accountant's judgment, management does not respond appropriately within a reasonable time period, the accountant should notify the audit committee, or its equivalent, of the matter. The communication can be written or oral. If oral, the communication should be documented in the working papers.

b. **AUDIT COMMITTEE RESPONSE** If, in the accountant's judgment, the audit committee does not respond appropriately within a reasonable time period, the accountant should consider whether to resign from the engagement and whether to remain as the entity's auditor.

2. **QUALITY OF PRINCIPLES AND ESTIMATES** SAS 90 requires an auditor to discuss the quality of accounting principles and accounting estimates (similarly to SAS 61), but limited to the impact of transactions, events, and changes considered in performing review procedures. The auditor should attempt a discussion with the audit committee prior to filing the Form 10-Q. The discussion should occur before the filing or as soon thereafter as practicable.

VI. REPORTING ON CONDENSED FINANCIAL STATEMENTS AND SELECTED FINANCIAL DATA (AU 552)

A. CONDENSED FINANCIAL STATEMENTS

AU 552 (SAS 42) provides guidance on reporting in a **client-prepared** document on condensed financial statements that are derived from audited financial statements of a public entity that are required to be filed with a regulatory agency.

EXHIBIT 15 ♦ CONDENSED FINANCIAL STATEMENTS WITH AUDITED FINANCIAL STATEMENTS

> We have audited, in accordance with U.S. generally accepted auditing standards, the consolidated balance sheet of X Company and subsidiaries as of December 31, 20X0, and the related consolidated statements of income, retained earnings, and cash flows for the year then ended (not presented herein); and in our report dated February 15, 20X1, we expressed an unqualified opinion on those consolidated financial statements.
>
> In our opinion, the information set forth in the accompanying condensed consolidated financial statements is fairly stated, in all material respects, in relation to the consolidated financial statements from which it has been derived.

1. Condensed financial statements are presented in considerably less detail than statements presented in conformity with GAAP. Therefore, they should be read in conjunction with the entity's most recent **complete** financial statements.

2. Because condensed financial statements do not constitute a fair presentation of financial position, results of operations, and cash flows in conformity with GAAP, an auditor engaged to report on such statements should not report in the same manner as an auditor reporting on the complete financial statements from which the condensed statements are derived.

3. The report on condensed financial statements that are derived from financial statements that the auditor has audited should indicate the following.

   a. That the auditor has audited and expressed an opinion on the complete financial statements

   b. The date of the auditor's report on the complete financial statements, thereby removing any implication that records, transactions, or events after that date have been audited

   c. The type of opinion expressed

   d. Whether, in the auditor's opinion, the information set forth in the condensed financial statements is fairly stated in all material respects in relation to the complete financial statements from which it has been derived

4. If a client makes a statement in a client-prepared document that both names the auditor and states that condensed financial statements have been derived from audited financial

statements, the auditor is **not** required to report on the condensed financial statements *provided that* they are included in a document that either contains the audited financial statements or incorporates such statements by reference to information filed with a regulatory agency.

- **a.** If such a statement is included in a client-prepared document of a public entity, and that document neither contains the audited financial statements nor incorporates such statements by reference, the auditor should request the client to either delete the auditor's name from the document or include the auditor's report on the condensed financial statements as described in 3., above.

- **b.** If the client does not comply with the auditor's request, the auditor should consider other appropriate actions, such as consulting legal counsel.

5. Condensed financial statements derived from audited financial statements of a public entity may be presented on a comparative basis with interim financial information as of a subsequent date that is accompanied by the auditor's review report. In such a case, the auditor should report on the condensed financial statements of each period in a manner appropriate for the type of service rendered in each period.

B. SELECTED FINANCIAL DATA

SAS 42 also provides guidance for selected financial data that are derived from audited financial statements and are presented in a document that either includes audited financial statements or incorporates such statements by reference to information filed with a regulatory agency.

1. Selected financial data are not a required part of the basic financial statements, and the entity's management is responsible for determining the specific selected financial data to be presented. However, certain reports must include, for each of the last five fiscal years, selected financial data in accordance with SEC regulation S-K. (There is no SEC requirement for the **auditor** to report on such selected financial data.)

2. If the auditor is engaged to report on the selected financial data, the report should be limited to data that are derived from audited financial statements.

- **a.** If the selected data includes both data derived from audited statements and other information (such as the number of employees or square footage of facilities), the report should specifically identify the data on which the auditor is reporting and should indicate the same items as mentioned in A.3., above.

- **b.** The auditor is not precluded from expressing an opinion on one or more of the specified elements, accounts, or items of a financial statement in accordance with the provisions of SAS 62, *Special Reports*.

3. If the selected financial data are derived from financial statements that were audited by another independent auditor, the report on the selected financial data should state so, and the auditor should not express an opinion on that data.

4. In situations where the client names the independent auditor in a client-prepared document and states that the selected financial data are derived from financial statements audited by the named auditor, the auditor is not required to report on the selected financial data provided that the document either contains audited financial statements or incorporates such statements by reference to information filed with a regulatory agency.

- **a.** If the client document is lacking these characteristics, the auditor should either:
  - **(1)** Request that neither the auditor's name nor reference to the auditor be associated with the information.
  - **(2)** Disclaim an opinion on the selected information and request that the disclaimer be included in the document.

b. If the client does not comply, the client should be advised that there is no consent to either the use of the auditor's name or the reference to the auditor, and the auditor should consider a consultation with legal counsel.

EXHIBIT 16 ♦ SELECTED FINANCIAL DATA WITH AUDITED FINANCIAL STATEMENTS

We have audited the accompanying consolidated balance sheets of ABC Company and subsidiaries as of December 31, 20X2 and 20X1, and the related consolidated statements of income, retained earnings, and cash flows for each of the three years in the period ended December 31, 20X2. These financial statements are the responsibility of the company's management. Our responsibility is to express an opinion on these financial statements based on our audits.

We conducted our audits in accordance with U.S. generally accepted auditing standards. Those standards require that we plan and perform the audit to obtain reasonable assurance about whether the financial statements are free of material misstatement. An audit includes examining, on a test basis, evidence supporting the amounts and disclosures in the financial statements. An audit also includes assessing the accounting principles used and significant estimates made by management, as well as evaluating the overall financial statement presentation. We believe that our audits provided a reasonable basis for our opinion.

In our opinion, the consolidated financial statements referred to above present fairly, in all material respects, the financial position of the ABC Company and subsidiaries as of December 31, 20X2 and 20X1, and the results of its operations and their cash flows for each of the three years in the period ended December 31, 20X2, in conformity with U.S. generally accepted accounting principles.

We have also previously audited, in accordance with U.S. generally accepted auditing standards, the consolidated balance sheets as of December 31, 20X3, 20X2, and 20X1, and the related consolidated statements of income, retained earnings, and cash flows for the years ended December 31, 20X2 and 20X1 (none of which are presented herein); and we expressed unqualified opinions on those consolidated financial statements.

In our opinion, the information set forth in the selected financial data for each of the five years in the period ended December 31, 20X2, appearing on page XX is fairly stated in all material respects in relation to the consolidated financial statements from which it has been derived.

VII. REPORTS ON THE APPLICATION OF ACCOUNTING PRINCIPLES (AU 625, SAS 50)

A. GENERAL

SAS 50 outlines the required procedures for accountants in public practice who report or give either written or oral advice (either to management of an entity or to intermediaries such as lenders, major suppliers, underwriters, or regulatory agencies) on the following.

1. The application of accounting principles to specific completed or uncompleted transactions
2. The type of opinion that may be rendered on an entity's financial statements
3. The application of accounting principles to factual or circumstantial hypothetical transactions

B. EXCEPTIONS

1. Engagements to report on financial statements, assist in litigation involving accounting matters, provide expert testimony in accounting-related litigation, or give advice to another accountant in public practice.

2. Communications such as position papers. Position papers include newsletters, articles, speeches or lectures, and text of speeches or lectures. Position papers do not include communications intended to provide guidance on the application of accounting principles to a **specific** transaction.

C. **PROCEDURES**

The accountant should be capable of making reasonable professional judgments. The general standards of training and due care must be followed. The work must be adequately planned and assistants must be properly supervised. Sufficient information must be gathered to provide a reasonable basis for a professional judgment. Prior to making a judgment, the accountant should (1) obtain an understanding of the form and substance of the transactions involved; (2) review applicable generally accepted accounting principles; (3) perform research to ascertain and consider the existence of creditable precedents or analogies; and (4) consult with other professionals or experts, if necessary.

D. **REPORTING STANDARDS**

1. **TYPE OF OPINION** When preparing the report and the included opinion, the accountant should consider the requester of the report, the circumstances under which the request is made, the purpose of the request, and the intended use of the report.

   a. The **reporting** accountant who has been engaged by the principal or intermediary to give advice has the responsibility to consult with the **continuing** accountant who prepares or audits the financial statements to determine the form and substance of transactions, how the management applied accounting principles to similar transactions, if management disputes the method of accounting recommended by the continuing accountant, and if the continuing accountant has reached a different conclusion on the application of accounting principles or type of opinion.

   b. The responsibilities of the continuing accountant to respond to the reporting accountant are the same as the responsibilities of a predecessor auditor to a successor auditor.

2. The report is addressed to the principals or intermediary.

3. The first part of the report should describe the engagement.

   a. Include a brief description of the nature of the engagement and state that the engagement was performed in accordance with acceptable AICPA standards.

   b. Describe the transactions, relevant facts, circumstances, assumptions, and sources of information. This includes identifying principals to specific transactions, describing hypothetical transactions, describing nonspecific principals such as Company A and Company B.

   c. Describe the appropriate accounting principles or the type of opinion, and the reasons for the reporting accountant's conclusion.

4. The last part of the report should state that (a) responsibility for proper accounting rests with the preparers of the financial statements who should consult with their continuing accountants; and (b) any difference in the facts, circumstances, or assumptions presented may change the report.

EXHIBIT 17 ♦ REPORT ON APPLICATION OF ACCOUNTING PRINCIPLES OR TYPE OF OPINION

(Introduction)

We have been engaged to report on the appropriate application of U.S. generally accepted accounting principles to the specific (hypothetical) transaction described below. This report is being issued to the ABC Company (XYZ Intermediaries) for assistance in evaluating accounting principles for the described specific (hypothetical) transaction. Our engagement has been conducted in accordance with standards established by the American Institute of Certified Public Accountants.

(Description of transaction)

The facts, circumstances, and assumptions relevant to the specific (hypothetical) transaction as provided to us by the management of the ABC Company (XYZ Intermediaries) are as follows:

(Appropriate accounting principles)

[Text discussing principles]

(Concluding comments)

The ultimate responsibility for the decision on the appropriate application of U.S. generally accepted accounting principles for an actual transaction rests with the preparers of financial statements, who should consult with their continuing accountants. Our judgment on the appropriate application of generally accepted accounting principles for the described specific (hypothetical) transaction is based solely on the facts provided to us as described above. Should these facts and circumstances differ, our conclusion may change.

VIII. REPORTING ON FINANCIAL STATEMENTS PREPARED FOR USE IN OTHER COUNTRIES (AU 534)

A. APPLICABILITY

SAS 51 provides guidelines for an independent auditor engaged to report on financial statements of a U.S. entity for use outside the United States, given the following conditions.

1. Financial statements are prepared in conformity with GAAP of another country.
2. The entity is organized or domiciled in the U.S.
3. The auditor practices in the United States.

B. PURPOSE OF STATEMENTS

Such financial statements may be prepared, for example, when: (1) The statements will be included in the financial statements of a non-U.S. parent; (2) The entity has substantial non-U.S. investors; and (3) Capital is to be raised in another country.

C. GENERAL AND FIELDWORK STANDARDS

The auditor should comply with the general and field work standards of U.S. generally accepted auditing standards. The U.S. procedures may need to be modified, however, to apply when there are differences in accounting principles generally accepted in another country and U.S. GAAP. Examples of this include:

1. Accounting principles generally accepted in another country may require that certain assets be revalued to adjust for the effects of inflation—in which case, the auditor should perform procedures to test the revaluation adjustments.

2. Another country's accounting principles may not require or permit recognition of deferred taxes—consequently, procedures for testing deferred tax balances would not be applicable.

D. AUDITOR'S UNDERSTANDING AND KNOWLEDGE

The auditor should understand the accounting principles and auditing standards generally accepted in the other country and the legal responsibilities involved.

1. The auditor may obtain such knowledge by reading the applicable statutes, professional literature, and codification of accounting principles and auditing standards generally accepted in that country.

2. If the accounting principles of another country are not established with sufficient authority or by general acceptance, the auditor may report on the financial statements if

   a. The auditor judges the client's principles and practices to be appropriate, and

   b. The client's principles and practices are disclosed in a clear and comprehensive manner.

3. The auditor should consider consulting with persons having expertise in the accounting principles and auditing standards of the other country.

4. The International Accounting Standards established by the International Accounting Standards Committee may be used.

E. REPORTING STANDARDS

The auditor may prepare either a U.S.-style or foreign-style report, or both.

EXHIBIT 18 ♦ FINANCIAL STATEMENTS PREPARED IN CONFORMITY WITH ACCOUNTING PRINCIPLES GENERALLY ACCEPTED IN ANOTHER COUNTRY IN A U.S.-STYLE REPORT

We have audited the balance sheet of the International Company as of December 31, 20X1, and the related statements of income, retained earnings, and cash flows for the year then ended, which, as described in Note X, have been prepared on the basis of accounting principles generally accepted in (name of country). These financial statements are the responsibility of the Company's management. Our responsibility is to express an opinion on these financial statements based on our audit.

We conducted our audit in accordance with auditing standards generally accepted in the United States (and in [name of country]). U.S. standards require that we plan and perform the audit to obtain reasonable assurance about whether the financial statements are free of material misstatement. An audit includes examining, on a test basis, evidence supporting the amounts and disclosures in the financial statements. An audit also includes assessing the accounting principles used and significant estimates made by management, as well as evaluating the overall financial statement presentation. We believe that our audit provides a reasonable basis for our opinion.

In our opinion, the financial statements referred to above present fairly, in all material respects, the financial position of the International Company at December 31, 20X1, and the results of its operations and cash flows for the year then ended, in conformity with accounting principles generally accepted in (name of country).

1. A U.S.-style report that is modified to the accounting principles is preferred. Recall that the standard U.S.-style report includes that the U.S. GAAP is used.

    a. The report should include, in addition to standard required items:

        (1) A note to the financial statements that describes the basis of preparation including the nationality of the accounting principles.

        (2) A note that says the audit was made in accordance with GAAS and the auditing standards of the other country, if appropriate.

    b. Although the report is intended for use only outside the U.S., this is not intended to preclude limited use of the financial statements to parties (such as banks) within the U.S. that deal directly with the entity.

2. The standard report of another country may be used, provided that the following is evident:

    a. The standard report is used by auditors in the other country, given similar circumstances.

    b. The auditor understands the meaning and implications of the report with respect to different customs and different word interpretations.

    c. The auditor is in the position to make the attestations contained in the report.

    d. When using a standard report of a foreign country that is similar to the one used in the U.S., the country name should be added to the report to avoid erroneous interpretation due to a different custom or culture.

3. Use of both a U.S.-style and a foreign-style report is also allowed. The auditor should include a note such as the one in Exhibit 21.

EXHIBIT 19 ♦ NOTE DESCRIBING DIFFERENCES BETWEEN U.S. AND FOREIGN GAAP

> We also have reported separately on the financial statements of International Company for the same period presented in conformity with accounting principles generally accepted in (name of country). (The significant differences between the accounting principles accepted in [name of country] and those generally accepted in the United States are summarized in Note X.)

IX. RESTRICTING THE USE OF AN AUDITOR'S REPORT (SAS 87)

A. APPLICABILITY

SAS 87 provides guidance in determining whether an engagement necessitates a *restricted-use* report, and the components to include in restricted-use reports. SAS 87 is not applicable to reports issued under the provisions of SAS 70 or 72. SAS 87 amends SAS 51, 60, 61, 62, and 75. SAS 87 replaces the former terms *general distribution* and *restricted distribution* with the terms *general use* and *restricted-use*.

B. GUIDANCE

General use signifies that the report is not restricted to specified parties. *Restricted use* signifies that reports are intended only for specified parties. Practitioners are not responsible for the distribution of their reports.

1. **RESTRICTIONS** Auditors should restrict the use of a report when: (1) the subject matter of the report is based on criteria contained in agreements of regulatory provisions not in accordance with GAAS or OCBOA; (2) the accountants are reporting when specified parties accept responsibility for the sufficiency of the procedures performed; (3) the report is a

by-product of an audit of financial statements (SAS 60, 61, and 62). Auditors should not add other parties (other than the entity's audit committee, management, other internal users, specified regulatory agencies, or contractual parties) as specified parties when issuing a restricted-use report.

2. **COMBINED REPORT** If an auditor issues a combined report where one part would require a restriction on use and one part does not, the combined report is a *restricted-use* report.

CHAPTER 40—OTHER TYPES OF REPORTS

PROBLEM 40-1 MULTIPLE CHOICE QUESTIONS (50 to 63 minutes)

1. What is an auditor's reporting responsibility concerning information accompanying the basic financial statements in an auditor-submitted document?
a. The auditor should report on all the accompanying information included in the document.
b. The auditor should report on the accompanying information only if the auditor participated in its preparation.
c. The auditor should report on the accompanying information only if the auditor did **not** participate in its preparation.
d. The auditor should report on the accompanying information only if it contains obvious material misstatements. (5/98, Aud., #16, 6633)

2. Information accompanying the basic financial statements in an auditor-submitted document should **not** include
a. An analysis of inventory by location.
b. A statement that the allowance for doubtful accounts is adequate.
c. An analysis of revenue by product line.
d. A statement that the depreciable life of a new asset is 20 years. (Editors, 9431)

3. If information accompanying the basic financial statements in an auditor-submitted document has been subjected to auditing procedures, the auditor may include in the auditor's report on the financial statements an opinion that the accompanying information is fairly stated in
a. Accordance with generally accepted auditing standards.
b. Conformity with generally accepted accounting principles.
c. All material respects in relation to the basic financial statements taken as a whole.
d. Accordance with attestation standards expressing a conclusion about management's assertions. (5/95, Aud., #87, 5705)

4. Helpful Co., a nonprofit entity, prepared its financial statements on an accounting basis prescribed by a regulatory agency solely for filing with that agency. Green audited the financial statements in accordance with generally accepted auditing standards and concluded that the financial statements were fairly presented on the prescribed basis. Green should issue a
a. Qualified opinion.
b. Standard three paragraph report with reference to footnote disclosure.
c. Disclaimer of opinion.
d. Special report. (11/91, Aud., #17, 2285)

5. An accountant who is **not** independent of a client is precluded from issuing a
a. Report on consulting services.
b. Compilation report on historical financial statements.
c. Compilation report on prospective financial statements.
d. Special report on compliance with contractual agreements. (11/90, Aud., #37, 0393)

6. An accountant may accept an engagement to apply agreed-upon procedures that are not sufficient to express an opinion on one or more specified accounts or items of a financial statement provided that
a. The accountant's report does **not** enumerate the procedures performed.
b. The accountant is also the entity's continuing auditor.
c. Use of the accountant's report is restricted.
d. The financial statements are prepared in conformity with a comprehensive basis of accounting other than generally accepted accounting principles. (Editors, 2933)

7. An auditor is engaged to report on selected financial data that are included in a client-prepared document containing audited financial statements. Under these circumstances, the report on the selected data should
a. Be limited to data derived from the audited financial statements.
b. Be distributed only to senior management and the board of directors.
c. State that the presentation is a comprehensive basis of accounting other than GAAP.
d. Indicate that the data are **not** fairly stated in all material respects. (11/95, Aud., #87, 6034)

8. When an auditor reports on financial statements prepared on an entity's income tax basis, the auditor's report should
a. Disclaim an opinion on whether the statements were examined in accordance with generally accepted auditing standards.
b. Not express an opinion on whether the statements are presented in conformity with the comprehensive basis of accounting used.
c. Include an explanation of how the results of operations differ from the cash receipts and disbursements basis of accounting.
d. State that the basis of presentation is a comprehensive basis of accounting other than GAAP. (5/94, Aud., #83, 4748)

9. An auditor's report on financial statements prepared on the cash receipts and disbursements basis of accounting should include all of the following **except**

a. A reference to the note to the financial statements that describes the cash receipts and disbursements basis of accounting.
b. A statement that the cash receipts and disbursements basis of accounting is **not** a comprehensive basis of accounting.
c. An opinion as to whether the financial statements are presented fairly in conformity with the cash receipts and disbursements basis of accounting.
d. A statement that the audit was conducted in accordance with generally accepted auditing standards. (5/95, Aud., #82, 5700)

10. Which of the following statements is correct concerning letters for underwriters, commonly referred to as comfort letters?

a. Letters for underwriters are required by the Securities Act of 1933 for the initial public sale of registered securities.
b. Letters for underwriters typically give negative assurance on unaudited interim financial information.
c. Letters for underwriters usually are included in the registration statement accompanying a prospectus.
d. Letters for underwriters ordinarily update auditors' opinions on the prior year's financial statements. (5/95, Aud., #86, 5704)

11. Comfort letters ordinarily are signed by the client's

a. Independent auditor.
b. Underwriter of securities.
c. Audit committee.
d. Senior management. (11/92, Aud., #58, 2992)

12. When an independent accountant's report based on a review of interim financial information is presented in a registration statement, a prospectus should include a statement about the accountant's involvement. This statement should clarify that the

a. Accountant is **not** an "expert" within the meaning of the Securities Act of 1933.
b. Accountant's review report is **not** a "part" of the registration statement within the meaning of the Securities Act of 1933.
c. Accountant performed only limited auditing procedures on the interim financial statements.
d. Accountant's review was performed in accordance with standards established by the American Institute of CPAs. (5/90, Aud., #24, 0398)

13. The Securities and Exchange Commission has authority to

a. Require a change of auditors of governmental entities after a given period of years as a means of ensuring auditor independence.
b. Deny lack of privity as a defense in third-party actions for gross negligence against the auditors of public companies.
c. Determine accounting principles for the purpose of financial reporting by companies offering securities to the public.
d. Prescribe specific auditing procedures to detect fraud concerning inventories and accounts receivable of companies engaged in interstate commerce. (Editors, 9432)

14. When an accountant issues to an underwriter a comfort letter containing comments on data that have **not** been audited, the underwriter most likely will receive

a. Negative assurance on capsule information.
b. Positive assurance on supplementary disclosures.
c. A limited opinion on "pro forma" financial statements.
d. A disclaimer on prospective financial statements. (5/92, Aud., #8, 2761)

15. The objective of a review of interim financial information of a public entity is to provide an accountant with a basis for reporting whether

a. Material modifications should be made to conform with generally accepted accounting principles.
b. A reasonable basis exists for expressing an updated opinion regarding the financial statements that were previously audited.
c. Condensed financial statements or pro forma financial information should be included in a registration statement.
d. The financial statements are presented fairly in accordance with generally accepted accounting principles. (5/95, Aud., #83, 5701)

16. An independent accountant's report is based on a review of interim financial information. If this report is presented in a registration statement, a prospectus should include a statement clarifying that the

a. Accountant's review report is **not** a part of the registration statement within the meaning of the Securities Act of 1933.
b. Accountant assumes **no** responsibility to update the report for events and circumstances occurring after the date of the report.
c. Accountant's review was performed in accordance with standards established by the Securities and Exchange Commission.
d. Accountant obtained corroborating evidence to determine whether material modifications are needed for such information to conform with GAAP. (5/94, Aud., #64, 4729)

17. Which of the following procedures ordinarily should be applied when an independent accountant conducts a review of interim financial information of a publicly held entity?

a. Verify changes in key account balances.
b. Read the minutes of the board of directors' meeting.
c. Inspect the open purchase order file.
d. Perform cut-off tests for cash receipts and disbursements. (11/92, Aud., #51, 2985)

18. Which of the following circumstances requires modification of the accountant's report on a review of interim financial information of a publicly held entity?

	An uncertainty	Inadequate disclosure
a.	No	No
b.	Yes	Yes
c.	Yes	No
d.	No	Yes

(Editors, 0410)

19. An auditor may report on condensed financial statements that are derived from complete financial statements if the

a. Condensed financial statements are distributed to stockholders along with the complete financial statements.
b. Auditor describes the additional procedures performed on the condensed financial statements.
c. Condensed financial statements are presented in comparative form with the prior year's condensed financial statements.
d. Auditor indicates whether the information in the condensed financial statements is fairly stated in all material respects in relation to the complete financial statements from which it has been derived. (5/98, Aud., #17, amended, 6634)

20. In the standard report on condensed financial statements that are derived from a public entity's audited financial statements, a CPA should indicate that the

a. Condensed financial statements are prepared in conformity with another comprehensive basis of accounting.
b. CPA has audited and expressed an opinion on the complete financial statements.
c. Condensed financial statements are **not** fairly presented in all material respects.
d. CPA expresses limited assurance that the financial statements conform with GAAP. (11/94, Aud., #87, 5160)

21. A CPA is permitted to accept a separate engagement (**not** in conjunction with an audit of financial statements) to audit an entity's schedule of

	Accounts receivable	Royalties
a.	Yes	Yes
b.	Yes	No
c.	No	Yes
d.	No	No

(11/93, Aud., #56, 4293)

22. An auditor may express an opinion on an entity's accounts receivable balance even if the auditor has disclaimed an opinion on the financial statements taken as a whole provided the

a. Report on the accounts receivable discloses the reason for the disclaimer of opinion on the financial statements.
b. Distribution of the report on the accounts receivable is restricted to internal use only.
c. Auditor also reports on the current asset portion of the entity's balance sheet.
d. Report on the accounts receivable is presented separately from the disclaimer of opinion on the financial statements. (5/96, Aud., #8, 6240)

23. In connection with a proposal to obtain a new audit client, a CPA in public practice is asked to prepare a report on the application of accounting principles to a specific transaction. The CPA's report should include a statement that

a. The engagement was performed in accordance with Statements on Standards for Accounting and Review Services.
b. Responsibility for the proper accounting treatment rests with the preparers of the financial statements.
c. The evaluation of the application of accounting principles is hypothetical and may not be used for opinion-shopping.
d. The guidance is provided for management's use only and may not be communicated to the prior or continuing auditor. (R/00, Aud., #20, 6945)

24. The financial statements of KCP America, a U.S. entity, are prepared for inclusion in the consolidated financial statements of its non-U.S. parent. These financial statements are prepared in conformity with the accounting principles generally accepted in the parent's country and are for use only in that country. How may KCP America's auditor report on these financial statements?

I. A U.S.-style report (unmodified)
II. A U.S.-style report modified to report on the accounting principles of the parent's country
III. The report form of the parent's country

	I	II	III
a.	Yes	No	No
b.	No	Yes	No
c.	Yes	No	Yes
d.	No	Yes	Yes

(5/91, Aud., #49, 0389)

25. Before reporting on the financial statements of a U.S. entity that have been prepared in conformity with another country's accounting principles, an auditor practicing in the U.S. should

a. Understand the accounting principles generally accepted in the other country.
b. Be certified by the appropriate auditing or accountancy board of the other country.
c. Notify management that the auditor is required to disclaim an opinion on the financial statements.
d. Receive a waiver from the auditor's state board of accountancy to perform the engagement.

(11/94, Aud., #88, 5161)

ESSAY QUESTION

ESSAY 40-2 (15 to 25 minutes)

The auditor's report below was drafted by a staff accountant of Baker and Baker, CPAs, at the completion of the audit of the comparative financial statements of Ocean Shore Partnership for the years ended December 31, 20X2 and 20X1. Ocean Shores prepares its financial statements on the income tax basis of accounting. The report was submitted to the engagement partner who reviewed matters thoroughly and properly concluded that an unqualified opinion should be expressed.

Auditor's Report

We have audited the accompanying statements of assets, liabilities, and capital—income tax basis of Ocean Shore Partnership as of December 31, 20X2 and 20X1, and the related statements of revenue and expenses—income tax basis and changes in partners' capital accounts—income tax basis for the years then ended.

We conducted our audits in accordance with standards established by the American Institute of Certified Public Accountants. Those standards require that we plan and perform the audit to obtain reasonable assurance about whether the financial statements are free of material misstatement. An audit includes examining, on a test basis, evidence supporting the amounts and disclosures in the financial statements. An audit also includes assessing the accounting principles used as well as evaluating the overall financial statement presentation.

As described in Note A, these financial statements were prepared on the basis of accounting the Partnership uses for income tax purposes. Accordingly, these financial statements are not designed for those who do not have access to the Partnership's tax returns.

In our opinion, the financial statements referred to above present fairly, in all material respects, the assets, liabilities, and capital of Ocean Shore Partnership as of December 31, 20X2 and 20X1, and its revenue and expenses and changes in partners' capital accounts for the years then ended, in conformity with generally accepted accounting principles applied on a consistent basis.

Baker and Baker, CPAs
April 3, 20X3

REQUIRED:

Identify the deficiencies contained in the auditors' report as drafted by the staff accountant. Group the deficiencies by paragraph, where applicable. Do **not** redraft the report. (5/91, Aud., #2, amended)

SOLUTION 40-1 MULTIPLE CHOICE ANSWERS

ACCOMPANYING INFORMATION

1. (a) Note that this question concerns an *auditor*-submitted document. The auditor's report on information accompanying the basic financial statements describes the character of the work and the degree of responsibility that the auditor is taking.

2. (b) Information accompanying the basic financial statements in an auditor-submitted document is presented outside the basic financial statements and is not considered necessary for presentation of financial position, results of operations, or cash flows in conformity with GAAP. Such information includes additional details or explanations of items in or related to the basic financial statements [see answers (a), (c), and (d) for examples] (AU 551.03). The adequacy of the allowance for doubtful accounts is implied in the financial statements and would not be necessary as additional information.

3. (c) AU 551.06 presents guidelines that apply to an auditor's report on information accompanying the basic financial statements and states, "The report should include either an opinion on whether the accompanying information is fairly stated in all material respects in relation to the basic financial statements taken as a whole, or a disclaimer of opinion..." The auditor's opinion is on whether the statements are fairly stated in conformity with GAAP, not GAAS. The auditor's opinion on fair presentation in conformity with GAAP relates to the basic financial statements and does not extend to the accompanying information. The auditor does not express a conclusion on management's assertions in his or her report. The attestation standards relate to a separate reporting engagement.

SPECIAL REPORTS

4. (d) Special reports include those that are related to financial statements prepared on an accounting basis prescribed by a regulatory agency solely for filing with that agency.

5. (d) AU 623.19 states, "Entities may be required by contractual agreements, such as certain bond indentures and loan agreements, or by regulatory agencies to furnish compliance reports by independent auditors." A lack of independence would not preclude an accountant from issuing compilation reports (AR 100.22) or a report on consulting services.

6. (c) AU 622.33 requires the accountant's report in this circumstance to include, "a statement of restrictions on the use of the report because it is intended to be used solely by the specified users." If the report is a matter of public record, the report should state so and also state, "its distribution is not limited."

7. (a) According to AU 552.09, an auditor's report on information accompanying the basic financial statements should include either an opinion on whether the accompanying information is fairly stated in all material respects in relation to the basic financial statements taken as a whole or as a disclaimer of opinion. The report should be limited to data that are derived from financial statements audited by that auditor. There is no restriction on the distribution. The basis of accounting is not necessarily other than GAAP. The data are generally indicated as fairly stated in all material respects.

8. (d) AU 623.05 presents this requirement. (Also see the explanation to question #9.) The auditor utilized GAAS in the examination; thus, there is no need for a disclaimer. Answer (b) is incorrect because an opinion is presented. The auditor is not required to include the explanation described in answer (c).

9. (b) The cash receipts and disbursements schedule is merely a comprehensive basis of accounting other than GAAP (OCBOA). AU 623.05(d) states that the auditor's report should include a paragraph that refers to the note to the financial statements that describes the basis of accounting. AU 623.05(e) states that the report should include a paragraph that expresses the auditor's opinion on whether the financial statements are presented fairly. AU 623.05(c) states that the report should include a paragraph that states that the audit was conducted in accordance with GAAS.

LETTERS FOR UNDERWRITERS

10. (b) Per AU 634.64, Example A, a typical comfort letter includes a statement regarding the accountant's independence, an opinion regarding whether the audited financial information included or incorporated by reference complies to the Securities Act of 1933, *negative assurance on unaudited condensed interim financial information* included or incorporated by reference, and negative assurance on whether there has been any later changes in specified accounts in the financial statement items included in the registration statement. Per AU 634.14, "Comfort letters are not required under the Act [Securities Act of 1933, par. .01], and copies are not filed with the SEC." Comfort letters ordinarily express an opinion regarding the audited financial

statements' compliance with the Act, which is not an "update" of the audit opinion.

11. (a) In connection with audited financial statements and schedules included in a registration statement to be filed with the SEC, a client may request the services of an independent auditor. One of these services is the issuance of comfort letters for underwriters (AU 634.01). The underwriter of securities receives the comfort letter. The client and senior management do not sign the comfort letter.

12. (b) AU 711.09 states, "The Securities and Exchange Commission requires that, when an independent accountant's report based on a review of interim financial information is presented or incorporated by reference in a registration statement, a prospectus that includes a statement about the independent accountant's involvement should clarify that his or her review report is not a 'report' or 'part' of the registration statement within the meaning of Sections 7 and 11 of the Securities Act of 1933."

13. (c) The SEC has the authority to prescribe the accounting and reporting requirements for companies under its jurisdiction. However, the SEC has looked to the private sector for leadership in establishing and improving accounting principles and standards through the FASB. The SEC does not have the authority to prescribe specific auditing procedures, deny lack of privity as a defense in third-party actions, or require a change of auditors of governmental entities.

14. (a) When an accountant issues to an underwriter a comfort letter containing comments on data that have not been audited, the underwriter most likely will receive negative assurance on capsule information [AU 634.22(c)]. AU 634.22 does not mention supplementary disclosures or "pro forma" or prospective financial statements. However, negative assurance should not be given, with respect to capsule information, unless the accountants have obtained knowledge of the client's internal control policies and procedures relating to the preparation of financial statements (AU 634.36). This problem gave no indication that such knowledge was not obtained.

Interim Financial Information

15. (a) AU 722.09 states that the objective of a review of interim financial information is to provide the accountant with a basis for reporting whether material modifications should be made for such information to conform with GAAP. Only the statements under current review should be reported on. The objective of the review is to provide the accountant with a basis for reporting whether material modifications should be made, not whether condensed statements or pro forma information should be included. In a review, the accountant supplies only limited assurance and would not provide an opinion stating the financial statements are presented fairly.

16. (a) AU 711.09 states that when an independent accountant's report based on a review of interim financial information is presented in a registration statement, a prospectus that includes a statement about the accountant's involvement should clarify that his or her review report is not a 'report' or 'part' of the registration statement within the meaning of the Securities Act of 1933. The accountant does have a responsibility to follow the guidance in AU 560 and 561 regarding subsequent events and the disclosure or adjustment requirements included therein. There are no standards established by the SEC which the auditor must comply with. The accountant does not obtain corroborating evidence in a review engagement.

17. (b) Among the procedures set forth in AU 722.13 for a review of interim financial information is to "read the minutes of meetings of stockholders, board of directors, and committees of the board of directors to identify actions that may affect the interim financial information." Answers (a), (c), and (d) are not among the procedures normally applied in a review of interim financial information.

18. (d) AU 722.30 states, "The accountant's report on a review of interim financial information should be modified for departures from generally accepted accounting principles, which include *adequate disclosure*... The existence of an *uncertainty*...or a lack of consistency in the application of accounting principles affecting interim financial information would not require the accountant to include an additional paragraph in the report, provided that the interim financial information appropriately discloses such matters."

Condensed Statements & Selected Data

19. (d) The auditor's report on condensed financial statements that are derived from financial statements that he or she has audited should indicate (1) that the auditor has audited and expressed an opinion on the complete financial statements, (2) the date of the auditor's report on the complete financial statements, (3) the type of opinion expressed, and (4) whether, in the auditor's opinion, the information set forth in the condensed financial statements is fairly stated in all material respects in relation to the complete financial statements from

which it has been derived (AU 552.05). The statements need not be distributed to stockholders merely because an auditor reports on them. The auditor generally does not describe procedures performed on the condensed statements. Condensed financial statements need not be presented in comparison to another year's statements.

20. (b) AU 552.06 provides a sample report on condensed financial statements when the auditor issued a standard report on the audited financial statements.

21. (a) AU 623.13 states that an engagement to express an opinion on one or more specified elements, accounts, or items of a financial statement may be undertaken either as a separate engagement or in conjunction with an audit of financial statements.

22. (d) AU 623.14 states, "The auditor should not express an opinion on specified elements, accounts, or items included in financial statements on which he or she has expressed an adverse opinion or disclaimed an opinion based on an audit, if such reporting would be tantamount to expressing a piecemeal opinion on the financial statements. However, an auditor would be able to express an opinion on one or more specified elements... provided that the matters...were not intended to and did not encompass so many elements...as to constitute a major portion of the financial statements. However, the report on the specified element... should be presented separately from the report on the financial statements of the entity."

ACCOUNTING PRINCIPLES

23. (b) The final paragraph of a report on application of accounting principles states, "The ultimate responsibility for the decision on the appropriate application of [GAAP]...rests with the preparers of the financial statements...." The report states that the engagement is performed "in accordance with standards established by the AICPA" and doesn't refer to opinion-shopping. There is no restriction on the use of the report.

FOR USE IN OTHER COUNTRIES

24. (d) AU 534.07 states, "If financial statements prepared in conformity with accounting principles generally accepted in another country are prepared for use *only* outside the United States, the auditor may report using either (1) a U.S.-style report modified to report on the accounting principles of another country or (2) if appropriate, the report form of the other country." An unmodified U.S.-style report would be inappropriate in this situation.

25. (a) Per AU 534.05, the auditor must understand the accounting principles of the other country. The auditor does not have to be certified in the other country, disclaim an opinion, or receive a waiver from the State Board of Accountancy.

PERFORMANCE BY SUBTOPICS

Each category below parallels a subtopic covered in Chapter 40. Record the number and percentage of questions you correctly answered in each subtopic area.

Accompanying Information

Question #	Correct √
1	
2	
3	
# Questions	3
# Correct	
% Correct	

Special Reports

Question #	Correct √
4	
5	
6	
7	
8	
9	
# Questions	6
# Correct	
% Correct	

Letters for Underwriters

Question #	Correct √
10	
11	
12	
13	
14	
# Questions	5
# Correct	
% Correct	

Interim Financial Information

Question #	Correct √
15	
16	
17	
18	
# Questions	4
# Correct	
% Correct	

Condensed Statements & Selected Data

Question #	Correct √
19	
20	
21	
22	
# Questions	4
# Correct	
% Correct	

Accounting Principles

Question #	Correct √
23	
# Questions	1
# Correct	
% Correct	

For Use in Other Countries

Question #	Correct √
24	
25	
# Questions	2
# Correct	
% Correct	

ESSAY SOLUTIONS

SOLUTION 40-2 INCOME TAX BASIS AUDIT REPORT

The auditors' report contains the following deficiencies:

1. **"Independent"** is omitted from the title of the auditors' report.

Introductory paragraph

2. **Management's responsibility** for the financial statements is omitted.

3. The auditors' **responsibility** to **express** an **opinion** on the financial statements is omitted.

Scope paragraph

4. **"Generally accepted auditing standards"** should be referred to, not standards established by the AICPA.

5. Reference to assessing "significant estimates made by management" is omitted.

6. The concluding statement that the auditors "believe that our audits provide a reasonable basis for our opinion" is omitted.

Explanatory paragraph

7. Reference to the income tax basis of accounting as **"a comprehensive basis of accounting other than generally accepted accounting principles"** is omitted.

8. The statement that the financial statements are **"not designed for those who do not have access to the Partnership tax returns"** is inappropriate.

Opinion paragraph

9. **"The income tax basis of accounting described in Note A"** should be referred to, not "generally accepted accounting principles."

10. There should be **no reference to consistency unless** the accounting principles **have not been applied consistently**.

CHANGE ALERT

SSARS 8, Amendment to Statement on Standards for Accounting and Review Services No. 1, *Compilation and Review of Financial Statements*, provides communication and performance requirements for unaudited financial statements submitted to a client in three circumstances, when an accountant: (1) is engaged to report on compiled financial statements; (2) submits financial statements to a client that are, or reasonably might be expected to be, used by a third party; or (3) submits financial statements to a client where there is no expectation that the statements will be used by third parties. The requirements for the first and second situations basically are the same as under SSARS 1.

SSAE 10, *Attestation Standards: Revision and Recodification*, supersedes the previous nine SSAEs and related interpretations. While there are a variety of changes made to the attestation literature by SSAE 10, the most significant revisions relate to the performance and reporting standards for examination and review engagements and the authoritative guidance associated with agreed-upon procedures engagements. A major change made by SSAE 10 is that a CPA may report on either a written assertion or directly on the subject matter. SSAE 10 is discussed in Chapter 41.

CHAPTER 41

OTHER PROFESSIONAL SERVICES

CHAPTER 41

OTHER PROFESSIONAL SERVICES

I. Compilation and Review of Financial Statements (SSARS 1)

A. Overview

Statements on Standards for Accounting and Review Services (SSARS) are issued by the Accounting and Review Services Committee of the AICPA. SSARS apply when a CPA is associated with the unaudited financial statements of a **nonpublic** entity. (SAS 71 applies to reviews of public companies.) A CPA must issue either a compilation report or a review report whenever a compilation or review of a nonpublic entity's financial statements is performed. The CPA cannot issue any unaudited financial statements to a client or others unless the CPA has at least complied with the provisions that apply to a compilation.

1. **Nonpublic Entity** An entity other than one (a) whose securities are traded in a public market (i.e., on a stock exchange or in the over-the-counter market, including those quoted only locally or regionally); (b) that has filed with a regulatory agency in preparation for the sale, in a public market, of any class of its securities; or (c) that is a subsidiary, corporate joint venture, or other entity controlled by an entity described in (a) or (b).

2. **Financial Statements** Balance sheet, statement of income, statement of cash flows, etc. Financial forecasts, projections, and financial presentations included in tax returns are not considered financial statements for SSARS 1. The method by which the statement was prepared (e.g., manual, computer, etc.) is irrelevant in defining a financial statement.

3. **Compilation of Financial Statements** Presenting information that is the representation of management in the form of financial statements without undertaking to express any assurance on the statements. The CPA may perform other accounting services (e.g., preparing a working trial balance) to enable the CPA to compile the financial statements.

4. **Review of Financial Statements** Performing inquiry and analytical procedures to provide a reasonable basis for the CPA to express limited assurance that there are no material modifications that need to be made to the financial statements in order for them to be in conformity with GAAP or, if applicable, with some other comprehensive basis of accounting. The CPA may need to perform a compilation and/or other accounting services to review the financial statements.

    a. **Review vs. Compilation** The objective of a review is to express limited assurance. A compilation does not involve any assurance.

    b. **Review vs. Audit** An audit provides the basis for expression of an opinion on the financial statements taken as a whole. A review aims for limited assurance. A review does not involve obtaining an understanding of internal control or assessing control risk.

5. **More Than One Service** Whenever the CPA performs more than one level of service (e.g., a compilation and a review or a review and an audit), the CPA should issue the report for the highest level of service rendered.

6. **Use of Name** The CPA's name should not appear in documents or written communications containing the unaudited statements unless the CPA has compiled or reviewed them and the report is included, or there is a clear indication in the documents that the CPA has **not** compiled or reviewed the statements and the CPA assumes no responsibility for them. If a CPA becomes aware that his or her name has been used improperly, the client should be

advised that the use of the CPA's name is inappropriate, and the CPA should consider consulting an attorney.

7. **Typing and Reproducing** The CPA must, at a minimum, comply with the provisions applicable to a compilation when submitting unaudited financial statements of a nonpublic entity to his or her client or others. Submission of financial statements is defined as presenting to a client or others financial statements that the CPA has

   a. Generated, either manually or through the use of computer software, or

   b. Modified by materially changing account classification, amounts, or disclosures directly on client-prepared financial statements.

8. **Exempt Services** The following do not constitute a submission of financial statements:

   a. Reading client-prepared financial statements.

   b. Typing or reproducing client-prepared financial statements, without modification, as an accommodation to a client.

   c. Proposing correcting journal entries or disclosures to the financial statements, either orally or in written form, that materially change client-prepared financial statements, as long as the CPA does not directly modify the client-prepared financial statements.

   d. Preparing standard monthly journal entries (e.g., standard entries for depreciation and expiration of prepaid expenses).

   e. Providing a client with a financial statement format that does not include dollar amounts, to be used by the client to prepare financial statements.

   f. Advising a client about the selection or use of computer software that the client will use to generate financial statements.

   g. Providing the client with the use of or access to computer hardware or software that the client will use to generate financial statements.

9. **Accounting Services** SSARS 1 does not apply to such accounting services as (a) preparing a working trial balance, (b) assisting in adjusting the books, (c) consulting on accounting and tax matters, (d) preparing tax returns, (e) providing manual or automated bookkeeping or data processing services (unless the output is in the form of financial statements), or (f) processing financial data for the clients of other accounting firms.

10. **Engagement Letter** The CPA must reach an understanding, preferably in writing, with the client as to the services to be performed. An engagement letter is recommended. It should include (1) a description of the nature and limitations of the compilation or review, (2) a description of the report that the CPA expects to render, and (3) a statement that the engagement cannot be relied upon to disclose errors, fraud or illegal acts, and that the CPA will inform the appropriate level of management of any material errors of which the CPA becomes aware, and any fraud or illegal acts that come to his or her attention, unless they are inconsequential.

B. Compilation of Financial Statements

The following guidelines apply to a compilation engagement.

1. **Knowledge of the Accounting Principles and Practices of the Industry** To compile financial statements that are appropriate in form for a particular industry, the CPA must understand the accounting principles and practices of the client's industry. The CPA need not possess this knowledge when accepting the engagement as long as the CPA can

acquire it through AICPA industry guides, industry publications, talking with other practitioners, etc.

2. **KNOWLEDGE ABOUT THE CLIENT** The CPA must possess a general understanding of the nature of the client's business transactions, the form of its accounting records, the stated qualifications of its accounting personnel, the accounting basis used for the financial statements, and the form and content of the financial statements. This knowledge is usually acquired through experience with the client or inquiry of the client's personnel. It provides a basis for the CPA to assess the need to perform any accounting services of the type described in A. 9, above, when compiling the financial statements.

3. **NOT REQUIRED TO VERIFY, CORROBORATE, OR REVIEW INFORMATION SUPPLIED** The CPA is not required to make additional inquiries or to perform any other procedures designed to verify, corroborate, or review the information that the client supplies for a compilation. However, if the information furnished appears to be incorrect, incomplete, or otherwise unsatisfactory, the CPA should request additional or revised information. If the client refuses to provide it, the CPA should withdraw from the compilation engagement.

4. **READING THE COMPILED FINANCIAL STATEMENTS** Before issuing the compilation report, the CPA should read the compiled financial statements to be sure they appear to be appropriate in form and free from obvious material errors (such as math mistakes and mistakes in applying accounting principles, including inadequate disclosure).

EXHIBIT 1 ♦ STANDARD REPORT FOR A COMPILATION*

> I (We) have compiled the accompanying balance sheet of XYZ Company as of December 31, 20X0, and the related statements of income, retained earnings, and cash flows for the year then ended, in accordance with Statements on Standards for Accounting and Review Services issued by the American Institute of Certified Public Accountants.
>
> A compilation is limited to presenting, in the form of financial statements, information that is the representation of management (owners). I (We) have not audited or reviewed the accompanying financial statements and, accordingly, do not express an opinion or any other form of assurance on them.
>
> *This report should be properly titled, addressed, signed, and dated. For the sake of brevity, these elements are omitted from this and most other reports in this chapter.

5. **REPORTING ON COMPILED FINANCIAL STATEMENTS**

   a. **DATE** The report should be dated as of the date of completion of the compilation.

   b. **REFERENCE** Each page of the financial statement should contain a reference such as "See Accountant's Compilation Report."

   c. **REPORT** Statements compiled by the CPA should be accompanied by a report stating

      (1) A compilation has been performed in accordance with Statements on Standards for Accounting and Review Services issued by the AICPA, (similar to a scope paragraph).

      (2) A compilation is limited to presenting, in the form of financial statements, information that is the representation of management, (similar to an introductory paragraph).

(3) The statements have not been audited or reviewed and, therefore, no opinion or other form of assurance is expressed on them (similar to a disclaimer paragraph).

d. Modifications The report should **not** mention any other procedures the CPA may have performed.

e. Limited Reporting Engagement The CPA is **not** precluded from issuing a compilation report on one financial statement (e.g., balance sheet) and not on the others.

6. Substantially All Disclosures Omitted The CPA may be asked to compile financial statements that omit substantially all the disclosures required by GAAP or OCBOA. The CPA can do so as long as the CPA feels the omissions are not designed to mislead the users of the statements and the CPA clearly indicates in the report that the disclosures are omitted.

Exhibit 2 ♦ Substantially All Disclosures Omitted

> Management has elected to omit substantially all the disclosures required by U.S. generally accepted accounting principles. If the omitted disclosures were included in the financial statements, they might influence the user's conclusions about the company's financial position, results of operations, and cash flows. Accordingly, these financial statements are not designed for those who are not informed about such matters.

a. Include Selected Disclosures If the client omits most disclosures but does disclose a few matters in the form of notes to the financial statements, the disclosures should be labeled "Selected Information—Substantially All Disclosures Required by Generally Accepted Accounting Principles Are Not Included."

b. OCBOA When the financial statements are prepared on a comprehensive basis of accounting other than GAAP (OCBOA) and the basis is not disclosed in the statements (including the notes), the basis must be disclosed in the CPA's report.

7. Independence The CPA may compile financial statements when the CPA is not independent. While the reason for this lack of independence should not be disclosed, the last paragraph of the report should specifically disclose the lack of independence: I am (we are) not independent with respect to XYZ Company.

C. Review of Financial Statements

The CPA uses inquiry and analytical procedures to provide a basis for expressing limited assurance that the financial statements do not contain material deviations from GAAP (or, where applicable, from OCBOA). The CPA must be independent when engaged to perform a review of financial statements. The following guidelines apply to a review engagement.

1. Knowledge of the Accounting Principles and Practices of the Industry Required so that the CPA can determine and apply proper inquiry and analytical procedures. This does not prevent a CPA from accepting a review engagement for an entity in an industry in which the CPA has no previous experience. The CPA has a responsibility to obtain the required level of knowledge.

2. Knowledge of the Client's Business The CPA needs a general understanding of the client's business including organization, operating characteristics, nature of assets, liabilities, revenues, and expenses; production, distribution, and compensation methods; types of products and services; operating locations, and material transactions with related parties. This is normally obtained through experience with the client (or its industry) and inquiry of client personnel.

3. **Representation Letter** The CPA must obtain a representation letter from the client to complete a review.

4. **Procedures**

   a. **Inquiries as to Accounting Principles and Practices** Inquiries should be made concerning the client's accounting principles and practices, including methods used in applying them. Inquiries should be made concerning the client's procedures for recording, classifying, and summarizing transactions, and for accumulating information to be disclosed in the financial statements.

   b. **Analytical Procedures** Designed to identify relationships and individual items that appear to be unusual. They consist of (1) comparison of the current financial statements with those of comparable prior periods, (2) comparison of the financial statements with anticipated results such as budgets and forecasts, and (3) examination of those elements of the financial statements that can reasonably be expected to conform to a predictable pattern over time (e.g., changes in sales and accounts receivable, and changes in depreciation and property, plant, and equipment).

   c. **Inquiries About Important Meetings** Inquiries should be made as to actions taken at meetings of such groups as stockholders, board of directors, and committees of the board of directors that may have an effect on the financial statements.

   d. **Reading the Financial Statements** The CPA should read the financial statements to see if they appear to be in conformity with GAAP.

   e. **Obtain Reports From Other Accountants** The financial statements of the client should include an accounting for all significant components (unconsolidated subsidiaries, investees, etc.). If other CPAs have audited or reviewed the financial statements, the CPA should obtain their reports. The CPA may decide to refer to the other CPAs' work in the report and, if so, should indicate the magnitude of the portion of the financial statements the other CPAs audited or reviewed.

   f. **Additional Inquiries** Inquiries should be made of individuals who have responsibility for financial accounting matters concerning (1) whether the financial statements have been prepared in conformity with GAAP consistently applied, (2) changes in the client's business activities or accounting principles and practices, (3) matters about which questions have arisen from applying the foregoing procedures, and (4) events subsequent to the date of the financial statements that would have a material effect on the financial statements.

5. **One Statement Only** A CPA may be asked to issue a review report on one financial statement such as a balance sheet and not on other related financial statements (i.e., statements of income, retained earnings, and cash flows). The CPA may do so if the scope of his or her inquiry and analytical procedures has not been restricted.

6. **Review Is Not an Audit** In performing a review, it is not intended that the CPA will (a) obtain an understanding of internal control or assess control risk, (b) test accounting records and responses to inquiries through obtaining corroborating evidential matter, or (c) perform certain other procedures normally performed during an audit. Because of this, the CPA may not become aware of all the significant matters an audit would disclose. Yet, if the CPA becomes aware that information is incorrect, incomplete, or otherwise unsatisfactory, the CPA should perform whatever additional procedures are necessary to permit the CPA to achieve limited assurance that the financial statements do not contain material deviations from GAAP (or, where applicable, from OCBOA).

7. **Working Papers** The workpapers should describe the matters covered by the inquiry and analytical procedures, and any unusual matters considered during the review (including how they were resolved).

8. **Reporting on Reviewed Financial Statements**

   a. **Date** The report should be dated as of the completion of the inquiry and analytical procedures.

   b. **Reference** Each page of the financial statements should contain a reference, such as "See Accountant's Review Report."

   c. **Content** The reviewed financial statements should be accompanied by a report that states that (1) the review was performed in accordance with Statements on Standards for Accounting and Review Services issued by the AICPA; (2) all of the information included in the financial statements is the representation of management; (3) a review consists primarily of inquiries of company personnel and analytical procedures applied to the financial data; (4) the scope of a review is substantially less than an audit, the objective of which is to express an opinion on the financial statements taken as a whole and, therefore, no such opinion is expressed; and (5) except for those modifications indicated in the report, the CPA is not aware of any material modifications needed in order for the financial statements to conform to GAAP (or, if applicable, to another comprehensive basis of accounting).

   d. **Modifications** Any other procedures the CPA may have performed (including those performed in connection with a compilation of the financial statements) should not be described in the report.

   e. **Scope Limitations** In those cases where the CPA cannot perform the inquiry and analytical procedures the CPA considers necessary or the client does not provide the CPA with a representation letter, a review report cannot be issued.

9. **Independence** The CPA cannot issue a review report if the CPA is **not** independent. However, the CPA may be able to issue a compilation report.

10. **Omitted Disclosures** A CPA can **not** issue a review report on financial statements that omit substantially all disclosures required by GAAP.

Exhibit 3 ♦ Standard Report for a Review

I (We) have reviewed the accompanying balance sheet of XYZ Company as of December 31, 20X0, and the related statements of income, retained earnings, and cash flows for the year then ended, in accordance with Statements on Standards for Accounting and Review Services issued by the American Institute of Certified Public Accountants. All information included in these financial statements is the representation of the management (owners) of XYZ Company.

A review consists principally of inquiries of company personnel and analytical procedures applied to financial data. It is substantially less in scope than an audit in accordance with U.S. generally accepted auditing standards, the objective of which is the expression of an opinion regarding the financial statements taken as a whole. Accordingly, I (we) do not express such an opinion.

Based on my (our) review, I am (we are) not aware of any material modifications that should be made to the accompanying financial statements in order for them to be in conformity with U.S. generally accepted accounting principles.

D. Reporting Issues

Applicable to both compilations and reviews.

1. **Departures From GAAP** The CPA may become aware of a departure from GAAP that is material to the financial statements. The CPA should always **first** ask the client to revise the financial statements so that they conform with GAAP. If the statements are not revised and if the departure is not the omission of substantially all disclosures from financial statements that have been compiled (see B.6., above), the CPA should consider whether the departure can be adequately disclosed by modifying the standard report. If it can, a separate paragraph should be used to disclose the departure and its effects (if they have been determined by management or are known through the CPA's procedures).

   a. **Determination** If management has not determined the effects of the departure, the CPA is **not** required to determine them if the CPA does not already know the effects, as long as the CPA states in the report that no such determination was made.

   b. **Modification** The CPA would not usually modify the report because of an uncertainty including an uncertainty about an entity's ability to continue as a going concern, or an inconsistency in the application of accounting principles if the financial statements provide adequate disclosure. However, the CPA is not precluded from emphasizing such a matter in a separate paragraph of the report.

   c. **Withdrawal** In cases where the CPA believes the deficiencies cannot be adequately disclosed by modifying the report, the CPA should withdraw from the compilation or review engagement and not provide any further services regarding those financial statements. The CPA may want to consult with legal counsel.

Exhibit 4 ♦ Compilation Report That Discloses Departures From GAAP

<same title and introductory paragraph as the standard compilation report>

A compilation is limited to presenting, in the form of financial statements, information that is the representation of management (owners). I (We) have not audited or reviewed the accompanying financial statements and, accordingly, do not express an opinion or any other form of assurance on them. However, I (we) did become aware of a departure (certain departures) from U.S. generally accepted accounting principles that is (are) described in the following paragraph(s).

(Separate paragraph)

As disclosed in note X to the financial statements, generally accepted accounting principles require that land be stated at cost. Management has informed me (us) that the company has stated its land at appraised value and that, if generally accepted accounting principles had been followed, the land account and stockholders' equity would have been decreased by $500,000.

or

A statement of cash flows for the year ended December 31, 20X0, has not been presented. Generally accepted accounting principles require that such a statement be presented when financial statements purport to present financial position and results of operations. (**NOTE**: The first paragraph should be modified accordingly when a statement of cash flows is not presented.)

EXHIBIT 5 ♦ REVIEW REPORT THAT DISCLOSES DEPARTURES FROM GAAP

<same title and introductory paragraph as the standard review report>

<same scope paragraph as the standard review report>

Based on my (our) review, with the exception of the matter(s) described in the following paragraph(s), I am (we are) not aware of any material modifications that should be made to the accompanying financial statements in order for them to be in conformity with U.S. generally accepted accounting principles.

(Separate paragraph)

As disclosed in note X to the financial statements, generally accepted accounting principles require that inventory cost consists of material, labor, and overhead. Management has informed me (us) that the inventory of finished goods and work in process is stated in the accompanying financial statements at material and labor cost only, and that the effects of this departure from generally accepted accounting principles on financial position, results of operations, and cash flows have not been determined.

or

As disclosed in note X to the financial statements, the company has adopted (description of newly adopted method), whereas it previously used (description of previous method). Although the (description of newly adopted method) is in conformity with generally accepted accounting principles, the company does not appear to have reasonable justification for making a change as required by Opinion No. 20 of the Accounting Principles Board.

2. **SUBSEQUENT DISCOVERY OF FACTS EXISTING AT DATE OF REPORT** After the date of the compilation or review report, the CPA may become aware that facts may have existed at that date that, had the CPA been aware of them, might have caused the CPA to believe that the information the client supplied was incorrect, incomplete, or otherwise unsatisfactory. The CPA should consult SAS 1 to help determine the course of action (allowing for differences between the CPA's engagement and an audit). The CPA also should consider consulting with an attorney.

3. **SUPPLEMENTARY INFORMATION** In cases where the basic financial statements are accompanied by information that is presented for purposes of supplementary analysis, the CPA should clearly indicate the responsibility, if any, that the CPA is taking with respect to the information.

   a. **REVIEW** In the review report (or in a separate report), the CPA may indicate that the supplementary information was subjected to the same review procedures as the financial statements and the CPA is not aware of any material modifications that should be made to it, or the CPA may indicate that the data is presented only for supplementary purposes and has not been subjected to the review procedures applied to the financial statements, but was compiled from information that is the representation of management (and no opinion or any other form of assurance is given).

   b. **COMPILATION** The compilation report should include the supplementary data when the CPA has compiled the supplementary information to be presented with the basic financial statements.

E. CHANGE IN ENGAGEMENT TYPE

Before an audit (or review) engagement has been completed, the client may ask the CPA to change the engagement to a review or a compilation. In reaching a decision, the CPA should consider (1) the client's reason for making the request (especially if either the client or circumstances have imposed a restriction on the scope of the audit or review), (2) the amount of audit (review) effort needed to complete the audit (review), and (3) the estimated additional cost to complete the audit (review).

1. **Reasonable Basis for Changing** A change in the circumstances that caused the client to require an audit (or review), or a misunderstanding concerning the nature of an audit, review, or compilation would usually be considered acceptable reasons for changing. For example, the client's bank may have decided to accept reviewed financial statements in place of audited financial statements.

2. **Restriction on Engagement Scope** The CPA should consider whether the information affected by the scope restriction may be incorrect, incomplete, or otherwise unsatisfactory. When the CPA has been engaged to audit an entity's financial statements, the CPA would ordinarily be precluded from issuing a review or a compilation report when the client has prohibited correspondence with the client's legal counsel. If in an audit or a review engagement a client does not provide the CPA with a signed representation letter, the CPA would be precluded from issuing a review report on the financial statements and ordinarily would be precluded from issuing a compilation report on the financial statements.

3. **Procedures Are Substantially Complete or the Cost to Complete Is Relatively Insignificant** In these circumstances, the CPA should consider carefully the propriety of changing the engagement.

4. **Report** When the CPA decides that a change in engagement is appropriate and the requirements for a compilation or a review have been met, the CPA should issue an appropriate compilation or review report. It should not include any reference to the original engagement, any auditing or review procedures that may have been performed, or any scope limitations that resulted in the changed engagement.

II. Compilation and Review of Comparative Financial Statements (SSARS 2)

A. Overview

SSARS 2 applies when reporting on comparative financial statements of a **nonpublic** entity when the financial statements of one or more periods presented have been compiled or reviewed per SSARS 1. The CPA should issue an appropriate report that covers each of the periods presented in the comparative financial statements.

1. **Comparative Financial Statements** Financial statements of two or more periods which are presented in a columnar format.

2. **Continuing Accountant** An accountant engaged to audit, review, or compile the current period's financial statements and has audited, reviewed, or compiled those of one or more consecutive periods immediately prior to the current period.

3. **Updated Report** Issued by the continuing accountant. It takes into account information the continuing accountant becomes aware of during the current engagement. In it, the continuing accountant will either re-express the previous conclusion on the prior-period statements or, in some cases, express a different conclusion on the prior-period statements as of the date of the continuing CPA's current report.

4. **Reissued Report** Issued after the date of the original report, but bearing the same date as the original report. If it must be revised because of the effects of specific events, it should be dual-dated, using the original date and a separate date that applies to the effects of such events.

5. **Separate Pages** It is permissible for the client to include client-prepared financial statements of some periods that have not been audited, reviewed, or compiled by the CPA on

separate pages of a document containing financial statements on which the CPA has issued an audit, review, or compilation report, provided that they are accompanied by an indication from the client that the CPA has not audited, reviewed, or compiled those statements and, therefore, the CPA does not assume any responsibility for them.

6. **Columnar Form** If the CPA becomes aware that, within the comparative financial statements, the client has included in a columnar format some information that the CPA has not audited, reviewed, or compiled and some that the CPA has, and the report on the latter or the CPA's name is included in the documents containing the comparative statements, the CPA should advise the client that this is inappropriate. The CPA should consider appropriate action, including consultation with legal counsel.

7. **Modified Report** When financial statements are presented for comparative purposes in columnar form, the CPA may issue an unmodified report on some statements and a modified report on others.

8. **Omission of Disclosures** Statements that omit substantially all disclosures are not comparable to financial statements that include such disclosures. Therefore, the CPA should not issue a report on comparative statements when statements for some, but not all, of the periods presented omit substantially all required disclosures.

9. **Reference** A reference such as "See Accountant's Report" should be included on each page of the comparative financial statements.

10. **Change of Status (Public/Nonpublic Entity)** A question arises as to whether SAS or SSARS applies when the status of an entity changes. For example, a company is a public entity in the current period, but was a nonpublic entity in the prior period.

    a. **Current Status** The current status of the entity governs when the CPA is reporting on comparative financial statements for either interim or annual periods. If a previously issued report is not appropriate for the current status of the entity, it should **not** be reissued or referred to in the report on the current-period statements.

    b. **Public** It is not appropriate to reissue or refer to the compilation or review report on the prior-period financial statements if the entity is a public entity in the current period but was a nonpublic entity in the prior period (SAS should be followed).

    c. **Nonpublic** If an entity is currently nonpublic and an unaudited disclaimer was issued for the prior period, the disclaimer should not be reissued or referred to in the report on the current statements.

B. **Continuing Accountant's Standard Report**
Form depends on the level of service (compilation or review) provided with respect to the financial statements presented.

1. **Same or Higher Level of Service in the Current Period** The continuing CPA should update the report on the financial statements of a prior period that are presented with those of the current period when the CPA (a) compiled the prior-period statements and the current-period statements, (b) compiled the prior-period statements and reviewed the current statements, or (c) reviewed the prior-period statements and the current-period statements.

EXHIBIT 6 ♦ COMPILATION EACH PERIOD

I (We) have compiled the accompanying balance sheets of XYZ Company as of December 31, 20X2 and 20X1 and the related statements of income, retained earnings, and cash flows for the years then ended, in accordance with Statements on Standards for Accounting and Review Services issued by the American Institute of Certified Public Accountants.

A compilation is limited to presenting, in the form of financial statements, information that is the representation of management (owners). I (We) have not audited or reviewed the accompanying financial statements and, accordingly, do not express an opinion or any other form of assurance on them.

EXHIBIT 7 ♦ REVIEW EACH PERIOD

I (We) have reviewed the accompanying balance sheets of XYZ Company as of December 31, 20X2 and 20X1, and the related statements of income, retained earnings, and cash flows for the years then ended, in accordance with Statements on Standards for Accounting and Review Services issued by the American Institute of Certified Public Accountants. All information included in these financial statements is the representation of the management (owners) of XYZ Company.

A review consists principally of inquiries of company personnel and analytical procedures applied to financial data. It is substantially less in scope than an audit in accordance with U.S. generally accepted auditing standards, the objective of which is the expression of an opinion regarding the financial statements taken as a whole. Accordingly, I (we) do not express such an opinion.

Based on my (our) reviews, I am (we are) not aware of any material modifications that should be made to the accompanying financial statements in order for them to be in conformity with U.S. generally accepted accounting principles.

EXHIBIT 8 ♦ REVIEW IN THE CURRENT PERIOD AND COMPILATION IN THE PRIOR PERIOD

I (We) have reviewed the accompanying balance sheet of XYZ Company as of December 31, 20X2, and the related statements of income, retained earnings, and cash flows for the year then ended, in accordance with Statements on Standards for Accounting and Review Services issued by the American Institute of Certified Public Accountants. All information included in these financial statements is the representation of the management (owners) of XYZ Company.

A review consists principally of inquiries of company personnel and analytical procedures applied to financial data. It is substantially less in scope than an audit in accordance with U.S. generally accepted auditing standards, the objective of which is the expression of an opinion regarding the financial statements taken as a whole. Accordingly, I (we) do not express such an opinion.

Based on my (our) review, I am (we are) not aware of any material modifications that should be made to the 20X2 financial statements in order for them to be in conformity with U.S. generally accepted accounting principles.

The accompanying 20X1 financial statements of XYZ Company were compiled by me (us). A compilation is limited to presenting, in the form of financial statements, information that is the representation of management (owners). I (We) have not audited or reviewed the 20X1 financial statements and, accordingly, do not express an opinion or any other form of assurance on them.

2. **Lower Level of Service in the Current Period** A continuing CPA who has compiled the current-period financial statements and previously reviewed those of the prior period(s) presented for comparative purposes should either issue a compilation report or a combined report. Alternatively, the CPA may separately present the compilation report on the current statements and the review report on the prior period.

   a. **Compilation Report** The auditor includes, in the compilation report on the current-period financial statements, a paragraph that describes the responsibility the auditor is assuming for the prior-period statements. The description should include the date of the original report and a statement that the auditor has not performed any procedures pertaining to the review engagement after that date.

   Exhibit 9 ♦ Descriptive Paragraph for a Compilation Report When Prior-Period Financial Statements Were Reviewed

   > The accompanying 20X1 financial statements of XYZ Company were previously reviewed by me (us) and my (our) report dated March 1, 20X2, stated that I was (we were) not aware of any material modifications that should be made to those statements in order for them to be in conformity with U.S. generally accepted accounting principles. I (We) have not performed any procedures in connection with that review engagement after the date of my (our) report on the 20X1 financial statements.

   b. **Combined Report** The auditor may combine the compilation report on the current-period financial statements with the reissued review report on the prior-period financial statements. The combined report should contain a statement that the auditor has not performed any procedures pertaining to the review after the date of the review report.

C. **Continuing Accountant's Changed Reference to a Departure From GAAP**
Circumstances or events may come to the CPA's attention during the current engagement which affect the prior-period financial statements that are presented (including the adequacy of their disclosure). If the CPA's report on the comparative statements includes a changed reference to a departure from GAAP, a separate explanatory paragraph is included in the report indicating the date of the CPA's previous report, the circumstances or events that caused the CPA to refer to the change and, when applicable, that the prior-period financial statements have been changed.

- **Changed Reference** Includes a reference that is different from the one made in the previous report, the removal of a prior reference, or the inclusion of a new reference.

Exhibit 10 ♦ Explanatory Paragraph For a Changed Reference to a GAAP Departure

> In my (our) previous (compilation) (review) report dated March 1, 20X2, on the 20X1 financial statements, I (we) referred to a departure from generally accepted accounting principles because the company carried its land at appraised values. However, as disclosed in note X, the company has restated its 20X1 financial statements to reflect its land at cost in conformity with U.S. generally accepted accounting principles.

D. **Predecessor's Compilation or Review Report**
At the client's request, a predecessor CPA may reissue the compilation or review report on the prior-period financial statements. (The CPA does not have to do so.)

1. **Predecessor's Report Not Presented** When a predecessor CPA has compiled or reviewed the financial statements of a prior period (that are presented for comparative purposes) but does not reissue the compilation or review report, the successor CPA should either

a. Perform a compilation, review, or audit of the prior-period financial statements and issue an appropriate report, or

b. Include an additional paragraph(s) in the report on the current-period financial statements that makes reference to the predecessor's report on the prior-period financial statements.

- **MAKING REFERENCE TO PREDECESSOR'S REPORT** The additional paragraph(s) should include (1) a statement that another accountant compiled or reviewed the prior-period financial statements (the predecessor should not be named); (2) the date of the predecessor's report; (3) a description of the standard form of disclaimer or limited assurance that appeared in the report; and (4) a description of any modifications that were made to the standard report and of any paragraphs that were included to emphasize a matter(s) in the financial statements.

EXHIBIT 11 ♦ ADDITIONAL PARAGRAPH FOR A PREDECESSOR COMPILATION

> The 20X1 financial statements of XYZ Company were compiled by other accountants whose report, dated February 1, 20X2, stated that they did not express an opinion or any other form of assurance on those statements.

EXHIBIT 12 ♦ ADDITIONAL (LAST) PARAGRAPH FOR A PREDECESSOR REVIEW

> The 20X1 financial statements of XYZ Company were reviewed by other accountants whose report, dated March 1, 20X2, stated that they were not aware of any material modifications that should be made to those statements in order for them to be in conformity with U.S. generally accepted accounting principles.

2. PREDECESSOR'S REPORT REISSUED A predecessor considers whether the report on the prior-period financial statements is still appropriate before the predecessor reissues it. In this regard, the predecessor should consider (a) the current form and manner of presentation of the prior-period financial statements, (b) subsequent events that the predecessor was not aware of at the time of the original report, and (c) if there are any changes in the financial statements that would require the predecessor to either add or delete modifications to the standard report.

a. **MINIMAL PROCEDURES** Before reissuance of the compilation or review report of a prior period, the predecessor should (1) read the current-period financial statements and the report of the successor CPA; (2) compare the prior-period financial statements with those that were previously issued and with those of the current period; and (3) obtain a letter from the successor indicating whether any matters came to his or her attention which, in the successor's opinion, might have a material effect on the prior-period statements, including disclosures. The predecessor should not refer to the successor's letter or report in the reissued report.

b. **ADDITIONAL PROCEDURES** If the predecessor becomes aware of information that may affect the financial statements of the prior period and/or the report on them, the predecessor should make inquiries or perform analytical procedures similar to the ones the predecessor would have performed at the date of the report on the prior-period statements had the predecessor been aware of the information, and perform any other necessary procedures. Examples include discussion with the successor and/or review of the successor's working papers on the matter.

c. **Date** The date of the previous report should be used when reissuing a report. This avoids any connotation that the predecessor performed any procedures (other than those in a. and b., above) after that date. Dual-dating is appropriate if the predecessor revised the report or if the financial statements are restated (e.g., "March 15, 20X1 except for note X, as to which the date is March 31, 20X2").

- **Written Statement From Former Client** The predecessor should obtain a written statement from the former client that states the information currently acquired and its effect on the prior-period financial statements and, if applicable, includes an expression of the former client's understanding of the information's effect on the predecessor's reissued report.

d. **Limitation** The predecessor should not reissue the report if the predecessor is unable to complete the procedures described in a., b., and c., above. The predecessor may want to consult legal counsel in deciding the appropriate course of action.

3. **Changed Prior-Period Financial Statements** Either the predecessor or the successor should report on prior-period financial statements that have been changed.

a. **Predecessor** When reporting, the predecessor should adhere to D.2., above.

b. **Successor** When reporting, the successor should comply with SSARS 1 (or perform an audit). The successor should not refer to the predecessor's previously issued report in the successor's report.

c. **Restatement Not Involving a Change in Accounting Principle** It is possible that the restatement may be for reasons other than a change in accounting principles or their application, e.g., a revision to correct an error. In this case, as long as the financial statements adequately disclose the matter, the CPA may decide to include an explanatory paragraph in the report, concerning the restatement. However, the CPA should not modify the report beyond this.

E. Reporting When One Period Is Audited

1. **Current-Period Financial Statements Audited** SASs apply when reporting on comparative financial statements in which the current-period statements have been audited and those for one or more prior periods have been compiled or reviewed. AU 504.15 states that when unaudited financial statements are presented in comparative form with audited financial statements, the financial statements that have not been audited should be clearly marked to indicate their status and either (a) the report on the prior period should be reissued or (b) the report on the current period should include as a separate paragraph an appropriate description of the responsibility assumed for the unaudited financial statements.

2. **Prior-Period Financial Statements Audited** When a nonpublic entity's current-period financial statements have been compiled or reviewed and the prior-period statements (presented for comparative purposes) have been audited, an appropriate compilation or review report should be issued on the current-period statements. In addition, either the prior-period report should be reissued or a separate paragraph should be added to the current-period's report.

- **Separate Paragraph** If a separate paragraph is used, it should describe the responsibility the CPA is assuming for the financial statements of the prior period. Specifically, it should indicate (1) that the prior-period's financial statements were audited previously; (2) the date of the previous report; (3) the type of opinion that was previously expressed; (4) if the previous opinion was not unqualified, the substantive reasons for this; and (5) that no auditing procedures have been performed since the date of the previous report.

EXHIBIT 13 ♦ SEPARATE PARAGRAPH

> The financial statements for the year ended December 31, 20X1, were audited by us (other accountants) and we (they) expressed an unqualified opinion on them in our (their) report dated March 1, 20X2, but we (they) have not performed any auditing procedures since that date.

F. REPORTING ON FINANCIAL STATEMENTS THAT PREVIOUSLY DID NOT OMIT DISCLOSURES

Even though a CPA may have compiled, reviewed, or audited financial statements that did not omit substantially all required disclosures, the CPA may later be asked to compile financial statements for the same period that **do** omit substantially all the disclosures required by GAAP so that the statements can be presented in comparative financial statements. In this case, the CPA may report on these statements as long as an additional paragraph is included in the report that indicates the nature of the previous service and the date of the previous report.

EXHIBIT 14 ♦ PRIOR-PERIOD STATEMENTS OMITTING SUBSTANTIALLY ALL DISCLOSURES COMPILED FROM PREVIOUSLY REVIEWED STATEMENTS

> I (We) have compiled the accompanying balance sheet of XYZ Company as of December 31, 20X2, and the related statements of income, retained earnings, and cash flows for the year then ended, in accordance with Statements on Standards for Accounting and Review Services issued by the American Institute of Certified Public Accountants.
>
> A compilation is limited to presenting, in the form of financial statements, information that is the representation of management (owners). I (We) have not audited or reviewed the accompanying financial statements and, accordingly, do not express an opinion or any other form of assurance on them.
>
> Management has elected to omit substantially all the disclosures required by U.S. generally accepted accounting principles. If the omitted disclosures were included in the financial statements, they might influence the user's conclusions about the company's financial position, results of operations, and cash flows. Accordingly, these financial statements are not designed for those who are not informed about such matters.
>
> The accompanying 20X1 financial statements were compiled by me (us) from financial statements that did not omit substantially all the disclosures required by U.S. generally accepted accounting principles and that I (we) previously reviewed as indicated in my (our) report dated March 1, 20X2.

III. PRESCRIBED FORMS (SSARS 3)

A. OVERVIEW

There is a presumption that the information required by a **prescribed form** is sufficient to meet the needs of the body that designed or adopted the form and that there is no need for that body to be advised of departures from GAAP required by the prescribed form or related instructions. Therefore, without a requirement or a request for a review report on the financial statements included in a prescribed form, the following form of standard compilation report may be used when the unaudited financial statements of a **nonpublic** entity are included in a prescribed form that calls for a departure from GAAP.

1. **APPLICABILITY** SSARS 1 and SSARS 2 are applicable when the unaudited financial statements of a nonpublic entity are included in a prescribed form. SSARS 3 amends SSARS 1 and SSARS 2 to provide for an alternative form of standard compilation report when the prescribed form or related instructions call for departure from GAAP by specifying a measurement principle not in conformity with GAAP or by failing to request the disclosures

required by GAAP. This statement also provides additional guidance applicable to reports on financial statements included in a prescribed form.

2. **Definition** A prescribed form is any standard preprinted form designed or adopted by the body to which it is to be submitted, for example, forms used by industry trade associations, credit agencies, banks, and governmental and regulatory bodies other than those concerned with the sale or trading of securities. A form designed or adopted by the entity whose financial statements are to be compiled is **not** considered to be a prescribed form.

3. **Departures From Other Requirements** If the CPA becomes aware of a departure from the requirements of the prescribed form or related instructions, the CPA considers that departure as the equivalent of a departure from GAAP in determining its effect on the CPA's report.

Exhibit 15 ♦ Compilation Report For Prescribed Form

> I (We) have compiled the [identification of financial statements, including period covered and name of entity] included in the accompanying prescribed form in accordance with Statements on Standards for Accounting and Review Services issued by the American Institute of Certified Public Accountants.
>
> My (Our) compilation was limited to presenting in the form prescribed by (name of body) information that is the representation of management (owners). I (We) have not audited or reviewed the financial statements referred to above and, accordingly, do not express an opinion or any other form of assurance on them.
>
> These financial statements (including related disclosures) are presented in accordance with the requirements of [name of body], which differ from U.S. generally accepted accounting principles. Accordingly, these financial statements are not designed for those who are not informed about such differences.

B. Departures From GAAP

If the CPA becomes aware of a departure from GAAP other than departures that may be called for by the prescribed form or related instructions, the CPA should follow the guidance in SSARS 1 regarding such departures. The sentence introducing the separate paragraph of the report disclosing the departure might read as follows: "However, I did become aware of a departure from generally accepted accounting principles that is not called for by the prescribed form or related instructions, as described in the following paragraph."

C. Preprinted Form Not Conforming With SSARS

The CPA should **not** sign a preprinted report form that does not conform with the guidance in SSARS 3 or SSARS 1 (as amended) whichever is applicable. In such circumstances, the CPA should append an appropriate report to the prescribed form.

IV. Communications Between Predecessor and Successor Accountants (SSARS 4)

A. Inquiries Regarding Acceptance of an Engagement

SSARS 4 provides guidance to a successor accountant who decides to communicate with a predecessor accountant regarding an engagement to compile or review the financial statements of a **nonpublic** entity.

1. **Successor Accountant** An accountant who has been invited to make a proposal for an engagement to compile or review financial statements or who has accepted such an engagement.

2. **Predecessor Accountant** An accountant who has resigned or who has been notified that his or her services have been terminated.

3. **OPTIONAL** A successor is not required to communicate with a predecessor in connection with a compilation or review engagement, but a successor may decide to do so, for example, when circumstances such as the following exist: the information obtained about the prospective client and its management and principals is limited or appears to require special attention, the change in accountants takes place substantially after the end of the accounting period, or there have been frequent changes in accountants.

4. **CLIENT CONSENT** Except as permitted by the AICPA Rules of Conduct, a CPA is precluded from disclosing any confidential information obtained during a professional engagement without the consent of the client.

   a. Accordingly, when the successor decides to communicate with the predecessor, the successor should request the client to permit the successor to make inquiries of the predecessor, and authorize the predecessor to respond fully to those inquiries.

   b. If the client refuses to comply fully with this request, the successor should consider the reasons for, and implications of, that refusal in connection with acceptance of the engagement.

5. **CONTENT** When the successor decides to communicate with the predecessor, inquiries may be oral or written and ordinarily includes inquiries concerning the following.

   a. Information that might bear on the integrity of management.

   b. Disagreements with management about accounting principles or the necessity for the performance of certain procedures and the cooperation of management in providing additional or revised information, if necessary.

   c. The predecessor's understanding of the reason for the change of accountants.

6. **RESPONSE** The predecessor should respond promptly and fully, on the basis of known facts, when the predecessor receives inquiries described above, as distinguished from other inquiries. However, if the predecessor decides, due to unusual circumstances such as impending litigation, not to respond fully, the predecessor should indicate that his or her response is limited. The successor should consider the reasons for, and implications of, such a response in connection with acceptance of the engagement.

B. **OTHER INQUIRIES**
The successor may wish to make other inquiries of the predecessor to facilitate the conduct of the compilation or review engagement.

1. Examples of such inquiries include questions about prior periods regarding the following:

   a. Inadequacies noted in the entity's underlying financial data.

   b. The necessity to perform other accounting services.

   c. Areas that have required an inordinate amount of time in prior periods.

2. A successor also may wish to obtain access to the predecessor's working papers. In these circumstances, the successor should request the client to authorize the predecessor to allow such access. Ordinarily, the predecessor should provide the successor access to working papers relating to matters of continuing accounting significance and those related to contingencies. Valid business reasons (including, but not limited to, unpaid fees) may lead the predecessor to decide not to allow access to the working papers.

3. The successor should not refer to the report or work of a predecessor in his or her own report, except as specifically permitted by SSARS 2 or SAS 26 regarding the financial statements of a prior period.

C. Prior Financial Statements Require Revision
If during the engagement the successor becomes aware of information that leads to a belief that financial statements reported on by the predecessor may require **revision**, the successor should request the client to communicate this information to the predecessor. If the client refuses to communicate with the predecessor or if the successor is not satisfied with the predecessor's course of action, the successor should consult with an attorney.

V. Exceptions to SSARS 1 Requirements

A. Personal Financial Statements (SSARS 6)
SSARS 6 allows a CPA to submit a written personal financial plan containing unaudited personal financial statements to a client without complying with the amended requirements of SSARS 1 when certain conditions exist.

1. **Requirements**

   a. **Understanding** The CPA must establish an understanding with the client that the financial statements will be used solely to assist the client and the client's advisers to develop the client's personal financial goals and objectives, and will not be used to obtain credit or for any purposes other than developing these goals and objectives.

   b. **Conflicting Information Absent** Nothing comes to the CPA's attention during the engagement that contradicts this understanding.

2. **Report** A CPA using the exemption provided by SSARS 6 should issue a written report.

Exhibit 16 ♦ Personal Financial Statement Report Excerpt

> The accompanying Statement of Financial Condition of X, as of December 31, 20X0, was prepared solely to help you develop your personal financial plan. Accordingly, it may be incomplete or contain other departures from generally accepted accounting principles and should not be used to obtain credit or for any purposes other than developing your financial plan. We have not audited, reviewed, or compiled the statement.

B. Plain Paper Financial Statements (SSARS 8)
SSARS 8 provides communication and performance requirements for unaudited financial statements submitted to a client in three circumstances, when the accountant: (1) is engaged to report on compiled financial statements; (2) submits financial statements to a client that are, or reasonably might be expected to be, used by a third party; or (3) submits financial statements to a client where there is no expectation that the statements will be used by third parties. The requirements for the first and second situations basically are the same as under SSARS 1. SSARS 8 gives practitioners **reporting** alternatives, not **performance** alternatives. In any financial statement compilation, practitioners must meet the same performance standards as before SSARS 8 was issued. SSARS 8 has a report alternative (which basically follows SSARS 1) and it has a no-report alternative. Practitioners may reach an agreement with the client that the statements are only for the client's internal use (the statements will not be distributed to other parties) and document that agreement in an engagement letter. In this case, practitioners may elect the no-report alternative.

1. **Without Report** SSARS 8 (¶ 20) states, "When an accountant submits unaudited financial statements to his or her client that are not expected to be used by a third party, he or she should either issue a compilation report in accordance with the reporting requirements...[or] document an understanding with the entity through the use of an engagement letter,

preferably signed by management, regarding the services to be performed and the limitations on the use of those financial statements." A written communication is required, if the engagement is to compile financial statements under this alternative.

2. **Reliance** A CPA may rely on management's representation that the statements will only be used internally, without further inquiry, unless information comes to his or her attention that contradicts management's representation.

3. **Combination** A CPA may adopt the no-report alternative for interim financial statements and use the report alternative for annual financial statements.

4. **Improper Distribution** Upon becoming aware that financial statements were distributed to third parties, the CPA should request that the client have the statements returned. If the client does not do so within a reasonable time period, the CPA should notify known third parties that the statements are not intended for their use, in consultation with an attorney.

VI. Overview of Attest Standards (AT 100, SSAE 10)

A. Attest Engagements

SSAE 10 defines an attest engagement as one in which a CPA in public practice (or practitioner) is engaged to, or does, issue an **examination, review,** or **agreed-upon procedures** report on subject matter or an assertion about subject matter that is the responsibility of another party. The eleven attest standards are a natural extension of the ten generally accepted auditing standards; however, they are broader in scope and apply to an array of engagements. (The attest standards do not supersede auditing standards.) In our coverage, guidelines for AT 100 (the first section of SSAE 10) are applicable to all attest engagements, unless otherwise stated; specific guidelines in other sections are applicable only to the subject matter in that particular section, unless otherwise stated. This coverage uses the terms "CPA" and "practitioner" to signify an independent CPA in public practice, unless otherwise noted.

1. **Other Engagements** When the practitioner performs an attest engagement for a government and agrees to follow specified governmental standards, the practitioner must follow those standards in addition to SSAE standards. An attest engagement may be part of a larger engagement, for example, a feasibility study or business acquisition study that includes an examination of prospective financial information. In such circumstances, these standards apply only to the attest portion of the engagement. Any report issued by a practitioner under other professional standards should be clearly distinguishable from attest reports; similar reports may be inferred to be attest reports.

2. **Inapplicable Engagements** A CPA may perform several services outside the scope of the attestation standards, including engagements: (a) Performed in accordance with SAS, (b) Performed in accordance with SSARS, (c) Performed in accordance with SSCS, (d) Client advocacy engagements (e.g., as before the IRS), and (e) Tax advice and return preparation services.

3. **Subject Matter** The subject matter of an attest engagement may take many forms, including: (a) Historical or prospective performance or condition (e.g., historical or prospective financial information, performance measurements, and backlog data); (b) Physical characteristics (e.g., narrative descriptions, square footage of facilities); (c) Historical events (e.g., the market price of products or services at a specific point in time); (d) Analyses (e.g., break-even analyses or target profit levels); Systems and processes (e.g., internal control); (e) Behavior (e.g., corporate governance, compliance with laws and regulations, and human resource practices).

4. **Written Assertion** An assertion is any declaration(s) about whether subject matter is based on, or in conformity with, selected criteria. A practitioner may attest to a written assertion or directly on the subject matter. In either situation, the CPA typically obtains a written assertion in an examination or a review engagement. A written assertion may be

presented to the CPA in several ways, including: a narrative description, a schedule, or as part of a representation letter which clearly identifies what is being presented and the point in time or period of time covered. Without a written assertion, the CPA may still report on the subject matter; however, the CPA needs to exercise caution and ensure that interested parties clearly understand the subject matter in question, including restricting use of the report, when appropriate.

5. **Practitioner** Throughout this discussion of attest standards, unless otherwise stated, the terms "CPA" and "practitioner" signify an independent CPA in public practice.

B. Responsible Party

The CPA attests to either a written assertion or subject matter that is the representation of a responsible party. The responsible party is the person or persons who are responsible for the subject matter. The responsible party may be management of the client entity or it may be another party (such as management of an entity seeking to sell a property to the client).

1. **No Responsible Party** Due to the nature of the subject matter, there may be no obvious responsible party. In that situation, a party who has a reasonable basis for making a written assertion about the subject matter becomes the responsible party. Practitioners may be engaged to gather information to enable the responsible party to evaluate the subject matter in connection with providing a written assertion. Regardless of the procedures performed by the CPA, the responsible party must accept responsibility for the assertion and the subject matter and must not base that assertion solely on procedures performed by the CPA. Because the CPA's attest role, the CPA may **not** assume the role of the responsible party in an attest engagement.

2. **Prerequisite** The identification of a responsible party is a prerequisite for an attest engagement. A CPA may accept an engagement to perform an examination, a review, or an agreed-upon procedures engagement on subject matter or a written assertion provided that **one** of the following conditions is met:

   a. The party wishing to engage the CPA is responsible for the subject matter, or has a reasonable basis for providing a written assertion about the subject matter if the nature of the subject matter is such that a responsible party does not otherwise exist.

   b. The party wishing to engage the CPA is not responsible for the subject matter but is able to (or have a third party who is responsible for the subject matter) provide the CPA with evidence of the third party's responsibility for the subject matter.

3. **Acknowledgment** The CPA should obtain written acknowledgment or other evidence of the responsible party's responsibility for the subject matter, or the written assertion, as it relates to the engagement. The responsible party can acknowledge that responsibility in a number of ways including in an engagement letter, a representation letter, the presentation of the subject matter, or a written assertion. If the CPA is not able to obtain direct written acknowledgment, the CPA should obtain other evidence of the responsible party's responsibility for the subject matter (e.g., by reference to legislation, regulation, or contract).

C. Quality Control Standards

Attest standards relate to the conduct of individual engagements; quality control standards relate to the conduct of a firm's attest practice as a whole. Attestation standards and quality control standards are related and the quality control policies and procedures that a firm adopts may affect both the conduct of individual attest engagements and the conduct of a firm's attest practice.

D. General Standards

Note that three of these five standards parallel the three auditing general standards.

1. **Training** CPAs performing attest engagements should have adequate technical training and proficiency in the attest function.

2. **KNOWLEDGE** Attest engagements should be performed by CPAs having adequate knowledge in the subject matter. The CPA may use specialists, provided that the CPA has enough knowledge of the subject matter (1) to communicate to the specialist the objectives of the work, and (2) to evaluate the specialist's work to determine if the objectives were achieved.

3. **CRITERIA** CPAs should perform attest engagements only when there is an assertion capable of evaluation against criteria that are suitable and available to users. Suitable criteria are objective, measurable, complete, and relevant.

    a. Criteria promulgated by a body designated by Council under the AICPA Code of Professional Conduct is considered suitable criteria by definition. Criteria issued by regulatory agencies and other bodies of experts that follow due-process procedures are also considered suitable. Criteria issued by industry associations or other groups should be critically examined for suitability. Such criteria should be clearly described in the presentation.

    b. Competent persons using the same or similar criteria ordinarily should be able to obtain materially similar estimates or measurements. However, competent persons will not always reach the same conclusions because: (a) Measurements often require exercise of considerable professional judgment, and (b) A slightly different evaluation of the facts could yield a significant difference.

    c. Criteria may be available to users in several ways. If criteria availability is limited, the practitioner's report must be restricted to those who have access.

4. **INDEPENDENCE** CPAs must be independent to perform attest engagements.

5. **DUE PROFESSIONAL CARE** CPAs must exercise due professional care in the performance of the engagement.

E. **FIELDWORK STANDARDS**

Note that these two standards are similar to two of the three auditing fieldwork standards; however, there is no attest standard that parallels the auditing internal control standard.

1. **PLANNING AND SUPERVISION** The work shall be adequately planned and assistants, if any, shall be properly supervised. An understanding with the client as to the services to be preformed must be reached.

2. **EVIDENCE** Sufficient evidence shall be obtained to provide a reasonable basis for the conclusion that is expressed in the report.

    a. **AUDIT DOCUMENTATION** The quantity, type, and content of work papers will vary with the situation. (An examination will require more evidence than a review.) A CPA prepares and retains work papers during attest engagements that are appropriate to the situation and the CPA's needs. (The guidance regarding attest work papers is similar to that for audit work papers.) Work papers should be sufficient to document that: (1) Work was adequately planned and supervised; and (2) The CPA obtained evidential matter providing a reasonable basis for the conclusion expressed in the CPA's report.

    b. **REPRESENTATIONS** If the client or responsible party refuses to furnish appropriate written representations, the CPA should consider the effects of this refusal on his or her ability to rely on other representations. If the representation letter is necessary evidence for reporting, this refusal constitutes a scope limitation on the examination sufficient to require a qualified opinion, a disclaimer of an opinion, or withdrawal from the engagement.

F. REPORTING STANDARDS

SSAE 10 provides for three types of attestation engagements: examinations, reviews, and applications of agreed-upon procedures. Reports on examination or review engagements may be used by the general public. Use of reports on agreed-upon procedures are restricted to the use of parties who have agreed to the specified procedures.

1. **IDENTIFICATION** The report identifies the subject matter or assertion and states the engagement character. If the attestation is on the assertion, the assertion must accompany, or be restated within, the CPA's report. The statement of the character of an attest engagement designed to result in a general-use report (i.e., an examination or a review) includes two elements: (a) A description of the nature and scope of the work performed, and (b) A reference to the professional (AICPA) standards governing the engagement.

2. **CONCLUSION** The report states the CPA's conclusion about whether the subject matter or assertion is presented in conformity with the established or stated criteria against which it was evaluated.

   a. **MISSTATEMENTS** If deviations from the criteria or material misstatements exist, the practitioner should modify the report, directly expressing an opinion on the subject matter, rather than the assertion.

   b. **MATERIALITY** The CPA should consider the idea of materiality in applying this standard. Materiality is determined by the relative size of a misstated or omitted fact, rather than by its absolute amount. Materiality would consider whether a reasonable person relying on the presentation of assertions would be influenced by the inclusion or correction of an individual assertion.

   c. **USE** General-use attest reports are limited to two levels of assurance: one based on a reduction of attestation risk to an appropriately low level (an "examination") and the other based on a reduction of attestation risk to a moderate level (a "review").

      (1) **EXAMINATIONS** A practitioner selects, from all available procedures, any combination that restricts attest risk to an appropriately low level. A conclusion is expressed in the form of a **positive** opinion.

      (2) **REVIEWS** Procedures typically are limited to inquiries and analytical procedures. The conclusion is expressed in the form of **limited** assurance.

3. **RESERVATIONS** The report states all of the CPA's significant reservations about the subject matter, assertion, and engagement.

   a. **UNRESOLVED PROBLEM** "Reservations about the engagement" refers to any unresolved problem the CPA had in complying with the standards and guidance applicable to attestation services. An unqualified conclusion should not be expressed if the CPA has been unable to apply all the procedures considered necessary or, if applicable, those procedures agreed-upon with the user(s).

   b. **SCOPE RESTRICTIONS** Restrictions on the scope of the engagement, whether imposed by the client or by other circumstances, may require the CPA to qualify the report, to disclaim any assurance, or to withdraw from the engagement. The decision as to the appropriate course of action depends on the effect of the omitted procedure(s) on the CPA's ability to express assurance on the presentation of assertions. When restrictions that significantly limit the scope of the engagement are imposed by the client, the CPA generally should either withdraw from the engagement or disclaim any assurance on the subject matter, assertions, or presentation. An incomplete **review** engagement requires the CPA to withdraw.

4. **RESTRICTIONS** AT 100 does **not** prohibit a practitioner from restricting the use of any report. When a report is restricted as to use, it contains a separate final paragraph that includes the statements that:

   a. Indicate the report is intended solely for the use of the specified parties.

   b. Identify the specified parties.

   c. Indicate the report is not intended to be, and should not be, used by anyone other than the specified parties.

5. **OTHER INFORMATION IN A CLIENT-PREPARED DOCUMENT** The client may publish documents containing information in addition to the practitioner's attest report and the related assertion. This guidance is inapplicable if the practitioner or another practitioner is engaged to issue an opinion on the other information or when the other information appears in a registration statement filed under the Securities Act of 1933.

   a. The practitioner's responsibility doesn't extend beyond the information identified in the practitioner's report or by the report of another practitioner. The practitioner should read the other information in the document and consider whether it, or the manner of its presentation, is materially inconsistent with the information appearing in the practitioner's report.

   b. If the practitioner is aware of inconsistencies with the other information, either the practitioner's report or the other information is revised. If the practitioner believes the other information must be changed, and it is not, the practitioner considers other actions: adding an explanatory paragraph to the practitioner's report, withholding the use of the report in the document, or withdrawal.

   c. If the practitioner is aware of an apparent material misstatement of fact in the other information, the practitioner discusses such concerns with the client. If a valid basis for concern remains, the practitioner should propose the client consult with another party whose advice may be useful (for example, legal counsel). If a valid basis for concern remains after discussion, the practitioner should consider consulting legal counsel and notifying the client's management and audit committee of the practitioner's views.

G. EXAMINATIONS

Examinations represent the highest level of assurance.

1. **SUBJECT MATTER OR ASSERTION** When CPAs are engaged to express an opinion as the result of an attestation engagement, they clearly should state whether (a) management's assertion is presented (or fairly stated), in all material respects, based on (or in conformity with) the established/stated criteria, or (b) the subject matter of the assertion is based on (or in conformity with) the established or stated criteria in all material respects. SSAE 10 doesn't prohibit a practitioner from examining the assertion and opining on the subject matter.

2. **MODIFICATIONS** Reports expressing a positive opinion on the reliability of an assertion may be qualified or modified for an aspect of the subject matter, assertion, or the engagement. In addition, examination reports may emphasize certain matters relating to the attest engagement, subject matter, or assertion. Remember, if deviations from the criteria or material misstatements exist, the practitioner should modify the report, directly expressing an opinion on the **subject matter**, rather than the **assertion**.

3. **REPORT COMPONENTS** The practitioner reports on either the subject matter or the assertion. The practitioner's examination report includes the following.

a. **Title** The title includes the word *independent*.

b. **Identification** An identification of the *subject matter* [or, assertion] and the responsible party. When reporting on the assertion, if the assertion doesn't accompany the practitioner's report, the first paragraph of the report also contains a statement of the assertion.

c. **Responsible Party's Responsibility** A statement that the *subject matter* [or, assertion] is the responsible party's responsibility.

d. **Practitioner's Responsibility** A statement that the practitioner's responsibility is to express an opinion on the *subject matter* [or, assertion] based on his or her examination.

e. **Standards** A statement that the examination was performed in accordance with standards established by the AICPA, and, accordingly, included procedures that the practitioner considered necessary in the situation.

f. **Basis** A statement that the practitioner believes the examination provides a reasonable basis for his or her opinion.

g. **Conclusion** The practitioner's opinion on whether the *subject matter is based on (or in conformity with)* [or, assertion is presented (or fairly stated) based on] the criteria in all material respects.

h. **Restriction** A statement restricting the report use to specified parties under the following situations:

   (1) **Suitability** When the practitioner determines the criteria used to evaluate the subject matter are appropriate only for a limited number of parties who either participated in criteria development or can be inferred to have an adequate understanding of the criteria.

   (2) **Availability** When the criteria used to evaluate the subject matter are available only to specified parties.

   (3) **Written Assertion** When a written assertion was not provided by the responsible party.

i. **Signature** The practitioner's manual or printed signature.

j. **Date**

Exhibit 17 ♦ Examination Report on Subject Matter

We have examined the [identify the subject matter—for example, the accompanying schedule of investment returns of X Company for the year ended December 31, 20X1]. X Company's management is responsible for the schedule of investment returns. Our responsibility is to express an opinion based on our examination.

Our examination was made in accordance with attestation standards established by the American Institute of Certified Public Accountants and, accordingly, included examining, on a test basis, evidence supporting [identify the subject matter—for example, X Company's schedule of investment returns] and performing such other procedures as we considered necessary in the circumstances. We believe our examination provides a reasonable basis for our opinion.

(continued on next page)

> [Additional paragraph(s) may be added to emphasize certain matters relating to the attest engagement or the subject matter.]
>
> In our opinion, the schedule referred to above presents, in all material respects, [identify the subject matter—for example, the schedule of investment returns of X Company for the year ended December 31, 20X1] in conformity with [identify established or stated criteria—for example, the ABC criteria set forth in Note 1].

H. REVIEWS

A review report provides **limited** assurance.

1. **GENERAL** The CPA's report states whether any information came to the CPA's attention on the basis of the work performed that indicates that the subject matter is materially misstated or divergent from criteria or assertions are **not** presented in all material respects in conformity with criteria. The report: (a) indicates that the work performed was less in scope than an examination, (b) disclaims a positive opinion on the assertions, and (c) contains a statement of limitations on the use of the report when it has been prepared in conformity with specified criteria that have been agreed upon by the specified parties because it is intended solely for specified parties.

2. **REPORT COMPONENTS** The practitioner reports on either the subject matter or the assertion. The practitioner's review report includes the following.

   a. **TITLE** The title includes the word *independent*.

   b. **IDENTIFICATION** An identification of the *subject matter* [or, assertion] and the responsible party. When reporting on the assertion, if the assertion doesn't accompany the practitioner's report, the first paragraph of the report also contains a statement of the assertion.

   c. **RESPONSIBLE PARTY'S RESPONSIBILITY** A statement that the *subject matter* [or, assertion] is the responsible party's responsibility.

   d. **STANDARDS** A statement that the review was performed in accordance with standards established by the AICPA.

   e. **DISCLAIMER** A statement that a review is substantially less in scope than an examination, the objective of which is an expression of an opinion on the subject matter [or, assertion], and accordingly, no such opinion is expressed.

   f. **CONCLUSION** A statement about whether the practitioner is aware of any material modifications that should be made to the *subject matter in order for it to be based on (or in conformity with), in all material respects,* [or, assertion in order for it to be presented (or fairly stated) in all material respects, based on (or in conformity with)] the criteria, other than those modifications, if any, indicated in the practitioner's report.

   g. **RESTRICTION** A statement restricting the report use to specified parties in the same situations as in examination engagements (suitability, availability, or written assertion).

   h. **SIGNATURE** The practitioner's manual or printed signature.

   i. **DATE**

EXHIBIT 18 ♦ RESTRICTED REVIEW REPORT

> We have reviewed management's assertion that [identify the assertion—for example, the accompanying schedule of investment returns of XYZ Company for the year ended December 31, 20X1, is presented in accordance with the ABC criteria referred to in Note 1]. XYZ Company's management is responsible for the schedule of investment returns.
>
> Our review was conducted in accordance with attestation standards established by the American Institute of Certified Public Accountants. A review is substantially less in scope than an examination, the objective of which is the expression of an opinion on management's assertion. Accordingly, we do not express such an opinion.
>
> [Additional paragraph(s) may be added to emphasize certain matters.]
>
> Based on our review, nothing came to our attention that caused us to believe that management's assertion referred to above is not fairly stated, in all material respects, based on [identify the criteria—for example, the ABC criteria referred to in the investment management agreement between XYZ Company and DEF Investment Managers, dated November 15, 20X1].
>
> This report is intended solely for the information and use of XYZ Company and [identify other specified parties—for example, DEF Investment Managers] and is not intended to be and should not be used by anyone other than these specified parties.

I. SUBSEQUENT EVENTS

Subsequent events are defined by AT 100 in the same manner as for audits.

1. **RESPONSIBILITY** While the practitioner has no responsibility to detect subsequent events, the practitioner should **inquire** of the responsible party (and the client, if different) as to whether they are aware of any subsequent events through the date of the practitioner's report.

2. **REPRESENTATION LETTER** The representation letter ordinarily contains a representation about subsequent events.

3. **POST-REPORT** The practitioner has no responsibility to detect events subsequent to the date of the practitioner's report, but may later become aware of conditions that existed at that date that might have affected the report had the practitioner been aware of them. In this situation, the practitioner considers the guidance in the auditing standards (AU 561).

VII. GUIDANCE FOR PARTICULAR ATTEST ENGAGEMENTS (SSAE 10)

A. AGREED-UPON PROCEDURES (AT 200)

An agreed-upon procedures engagement is one in which a practitioner is engaged to issue a report of findings based on specific procedures performed on subject matter. A client engages the practitioner to assist specified parties in evaluating subject matter or an assertion as a result of needs of specified parties. The specified parties and the practitioner agree upon procedures to be performed by the practitioner that the specified parties believe are appropriate. The nature, timing and extent of procedures may vary widely. The specified parties assume responsibility for the sufficiency of the procedures since they best understand their own needs. The practitioner does not provide an opinion or negative assurance. Instead, the practitioner's report on agreed-upon procedures should be in the form of procedures and findings. A practitioner's report on such engagements should clearly indicate that is use is **restricted** to those specified parties. A written assertion is **not** required for engagements covered by AT 200, unless another attest standard section also applies.

1. **REQUIRED CONDITIONS FOR ENGAGEMENTS** To satisfy the agreement and responsibility requirements enumerated here, the practitioner ordinarily communicates directly with, and

obtains affirming acknowledgments from, each specified party. If there is no such communication, the practitioner may find other procedures adequate, such as: (1) Comparing proposed procedures to written requirements from specified parties; (2) Discussing procedures with appropriate representatives of specified parties; or (3) Reviewing relevant contracts with, or correspondence from, specified parties.

a. **RESPONSIBILITY** The specified parties take responsibility for the adequacy of the procedures for their purpose, plus a party responsible for the subject matter (either the client or third party, see AT 100 coverage) exists.

b. **AGREEMENT** The specified parties and the practitioner agree upon procedures to be performed and the criteria to be used in the determination of findings.

c. **SUITABILITY** (1) The specific subject matter is subject to reasonably consistent measurement. (2) The procedures are expected to result in reasonably consistent findings using the criteria. (3) Evidential matter related to the specific subject matter is expected to exist to provide a reasonable basis for expressing findings in the practitioner's report.

d. **MATERIALITY** Where applicable, the practitioner and the specified parties agree on any materiality limits; these are described in the practitioner's report.

e. **USE** Use of the report is restricted to the specified parties.

f. **DISCLOSURE** For engagements involving prospective financial information, prospective financial statements include a summary of significant assumptions.

2. **NATURE, EXTENT, AND TIMING OF PROCEDURES**

a. **ATTEST STANDARDS** The requirements of the attest standards, except the second reporting standard, are applicable. A management representation letter is optional.

b. **SPECIALIST** The specified parties and the practitioner must explicitly agree on the involvement of a specialist. The practitioner's report should describe the nature of the assistance provided by the specialist.

c. **INTERNAL AUDITORS AND OTHER PERSONNEL** The agreed-upon procedures are to preformed entirely by the practitioner and any assisting specialists; however, internal auditors or other client personnel may prepare schedules or provide other information for the practitioner's use in performing the procedures.

3. **FINDINGS** The practitioner reports all findings from applying the agreed-upon procedures. The concept of materiality is inapplicable unless the specified parties and the practitioner have established a definition of materiality.

4. **REPORT COMPONENTS** The practitioner's report contains the following.

a. **TITLE** A title that includes the word *independent*.

b. **IDENTIFICATION** An identification of the subject matter (or the written assertion related thereto), the character of the engagement, and the responsible party.

c. **RESPONSIBILITY** A statement that the subject matter is the responsible party's responsibility. A statement that the sufficiency of the procedures is solely the specified parties' responsibility. A disclaimer of responsibility on the part of the practitioner for the sufficiency of the procedures.

d. **STANDARDS** A statement that the engagement was performed in accordance with attest standards established by the AICPA.

e. **DESCRIPTION** A list of, or reference to, the procedures performed and related findings.

f. **MATERIALITY** Where applicable, a description of any agree-upon materiality limits.

g. **DISCLAIMER** A statement that the practitioner did not conduct an examination of the subject matter, the objective of which would be the expression of an opinion on the subject matter, and a statement that if the practitioner had performed additional procedures, other matters might have come to his or her attention that would have been reported.

h. **RESTRICTION** A statement restricting the report use because it is intended solely for the use of specified parties (see the fourth reporting standard).

i. **LIMITATIONS** Where applicable, reservations or restrictions concerning procedures or findings.

j. **PROSPECTIVE FINANCIAL INFORMATION** Where applicable, items required by AT 300.

k. **SPECIALIST** Where applicable, a description of the nature of the assistance provided by a specialist.

l. **SIGNATURE** The practitioner's manual or printed signature.

m. **DATE** The date of completion of the procedures.

5. **EXPLANATORY LANGUAGE** The practitioner may include explanations about issues such as the following: (a) Disclosures of stipulated facts, assumptions, or interpretations used in applying procedures; (b) Condition of records, controls, or data; (c) A statement that the practitioner has no responsibility to update the report.

6. **SCOPE LIMITATIONS** When the situation imposes restrictions on the performance of procedures the practitioner should obtain agreement from the specified parties to modify the agreed-upon procedures, describe any restrictions in the report, or withdraw from the engagement.

7. **ADDITIONAL SPECIFIED PARTIES** After completing an engagement, a practitioner may add another party as a specified party, considering such factors as used in determining the original specified parties. If the report is re-issued, the practitioner does not change the date.

8. **OUTSIDE KNOWLEDGE** The practitioner need not perform additional procedures, but if a matter comes to the practitioner's attention that significantly contradicts the subject matter, the practitioner should include this matter in the report.

9. **REQUEST TO CHANGE ENGAGEMENT TYPE** If the practitioner concludes, based on professional judgment, that there is reasonable justification to change the engagement, and provided the practitioner complies with the standards applicable to that engagement, the practitioner issues the report appropriate to the new engagement type. This report should not include reference to either the original engagement or performance limitations that resulted in a different engagement. If the original engagement procedures are substantially complete or the effort to do so is relatively insignificant, the practitioner evaluates the propriety of an engagement change.

10. **COMBINED REPORTS** The reports on applying agreed-upon procedures may be combined with reports on other services, provided the types of services can be clearly distinguished and applicable guidance for each service is followed.

EXHIBIT 19 ♦ REPORT ON AGREED-UPON PROCEDURES

To the Board of Directors and Management of ABC Inc.

We have performed the procedures enumerated below, which were agreed to by the board of directors and management of ABC Inc., solely to assist you in connection with the proposed acquisition of XYZ Company as of December 31, 20X1. XYZ Company is responsible for its cash and accounts receivable records. This agreed-upon procedures engagement was performed in accordance with standards established by the American Institute of Certified Public Accountants. The sufficiency of these procedures is solely the responsibility of the parties specified in this report. Consequently, we make no representation regarding the sufficiency of the procedures described below either for the purpose for which the is report has been requested or for any other purpose.

The procedures and associated findings are as follows:

(1) We reconciled cash on deposit with the following banks to the balances in the respective general ledger accounts and obtained confirmation of the related balances from the banks.

Bank	Balance Per General Ledger
First National Bank	$ 5,000
DEF State Bank	13,776
Sun Trust Company—regular account	86,912
Sun Trust Company—payroll account	5,000

(2) We obtained an aged trial balance of the accounts receivable subsidiary records, traced the age and amounts of approximately 10 percent of the accounts to the accounts receivable ledger, and added the trial balance and compared the total with the balance in the general ledger control account. We mailed requests for positive confirmation of balances to 150 customers. The differences disclosed in confirmation replies were minor in amount and nature, and we reconciled them to our satisfaction. The results are summarized as follows:

	Account Balance	Accounts Receivable Aging and Confirmation Results: Requested	Received
Current:	$156,000	$ 76,000	$ 65,000
Past due:			
Less than one month	60,000	30,000	19,000
One to three months	36,000	18,000	10,000
Over three months	48,000	48,000	8,000
	$300,000	$172,000	$102,000

We were not engaged to, and did not, perform an audit, the objective of which would be the expression of an opinion on the cash and accounts receivable of XYZ Company. Accordingly, we do not express such an opinion. Had we performed additional procedures, other matters might have come to our attention that would have been reported to you.

This report is intended solely for the use of the board of directors and management of ABC Inc., and is not intended to be, and should not be, used by anyone other than these specified parties.

B. FINANCIAL FORECASTS & PROJECTIONS (AT 300)

AT 300 establishes guidance concerning performance and reporting for engagements to examine, compile, or apply agreed-upon procedures to prospective financial statements (PFS).

1. **APPLICABILITY** The guidance applies to a CPA who submits (to the client or others) PFS that the CPA has assembled or assisted in assembling, or reports on PFS, if such statements are (or reasonably might be) expected to be used by a third party. In deciding whether the PFS are (or reasonably might be) expected to be used by a third party, the CPA may rely on either the written or oral representation of the responsible party, unless contradictory information comes to his or her attention. An exception to this guidance exists for litigation support services, because the practitioner's work is subject to detailed analysis and challenge by parties to the dispute. This exception is inapplicable when either all third parties do not have opportunity for analysis and challenge or if the practitioner is specifically engaged to issue a report on PFS.

2. **PREPARATION** The practitioner's work may not be described as including *preparation* of the PFS. The practitioner may assist the responsible party in identifying assumptions, gathering information, or assembling the statements. The responsible party still has sole responsibility for the preparation and presentation of the PFS, because the PFS are dependent on the responsible party's actions, plans, and assumptions. A practitioner may prepare a financial analysis, including collecting information, forming assumptions, and assembling a presentation. Such an analysis is inappropriate for general use and is not a forecast or projection. If the responsible party reviews and adopts the assumptions and presentation, or bases assumptions and a presentation on the analysis, the practitioner may perform an AT 300 engagement and issue a report appropriate for general use.

3. **DEFINITIONS**

   a. **PROSPECTIVE FINANCIAL STATEMENTS (PFS)** Either financial forecasts or financial projections that include summaries of significant assumptions and accounting policies (does not include pro forma financial statements or partial presentations).

   b. **PARTIAL PRESENTATION** A presentation of prospective financial information excluding required elements of PFS.

   c. **FINANCIAL FORECAST** PFS that present, to the best of the responsible party's knowledge and belief, an entity's expected financial position, results of operations, and cash flows. A financial forecast may be expressed in specific monetary amounts as a single-point estimate of forecasted results or as a range, where the responsible party selects key assumptions to form a range within which it reasonably expects, to the best of its knowledge and belief, the item or items subject to the assumptions to actually fall.

   d. **FINANCIAL PROJECTION** PFS that present, to the best of the responsible party's knowledge and belief, given one or more hypothetical assumptions, an entity's expected financial position, results of operations, and cash flows. A financial projection is sometimes prepared to present one or more hypothetical courses of action for evaluation. It answers the question, "What would happen if...?" A financial projection is based on the responsible party's assumptions reflecting conditions it expects would exist and the course of action it expects would be taken, given one or more hypothetical assumptions. It may also contain a range.

   e. **ENTITY** Any unit, existing or to be formed, for which financial statements could be prepared in conformity with GAAP or OCBOA.

   f. **HYPOTHETICAL ASSUMPTION** An assumption used in a financial projection to present a condition or course of action that is not necessarily expected to occur, but is consistent with the purpose of the projection.

   g. **RESPONSIBLE PARTY** The person or persons who are responsible for the assumptions underlying the prospective financial statements, usually management. It can be persons outside the entity who do not currently have authority to direct operations.

h. **ASSEMBLY** Processing related to the presentation of prospective financial statements.

i. **KEY FACTORS** The significant matters on which an entity's future results are expected to depend. Key factors are the bases for assumptions.

j. **MATERIALITY** Materiality is a concept that is judged in the light of the expected range of reasonableness of the information. Users should not expect prospective information to be as precise as historical information.

4. **USES OF PFS**

a. **GENERAL USE** Refers to the use of PFS by persons with whom the responsible party is not negotiating directly. Since users are unable to ask questions of the responsible party, the presentation most useful to them is one that portrays, to the best of the responsible party's knowledge and belief, the expected results. Only a financial forecast is appropriate for general use.

b. **LIMITED USE** Refers to the use of PFS by the responsible party alone or by the responsible party and third parties with whom the responsible party is **negotiating directly**. Third-party recipients of PFS intended for limited use can ask questions of the responsible party and directly negotiate terms with it. Any type of PFS that would be useful in the circumstances normally is appropriate for limited use. The presentation may be a financial forecast **or** a financial projection.

5. **COMPILATION OF PFS** A compilation of PFS involves (a) assembling, to the extent necessary, the PFS based on the responsible party's assumptions, (b) performing the required compilation procedures, including reading the statements and considering whether they are appropriate and are presented in conformity with AICPA presentation guidelines, and (c) issuing a compilation report.

a. **LIMITED PROCEDURES** A compilation is not intended to provide assurance on the PFS or the assumptions underlying such statements. Because of the limited nature of the CPA's procedures, a compilation does not provide assurance that the CPA will become aware of significant matters that might be disclosed by more extensive procedures.

b. **SUMMARY OF SIGNIFICANT ASSUMPTIONS** Since this summary is essential to the reader's understanding of PFS, the CPA should not compile PFS that exclude disclosure of the summary of significant assumptions. Also, the CPA should not compile a financial projection that excludes (1) an identification of the hypothetical assumptions or (2) a description of the limitations on the usefulness of the presentation.

c. **GENERAL STANDARDS** Independence is **not** necessary.

d. **OBVIOUSLY INAPPROPRIATE** The practitioner should consider when representations or other information appear to be obviously inappropriate, incomplete, etc., and if so, should attempt to clarify the matter. If the matter is not clarified, the practitioner ordinarily withdraws from the engagement.

6. **COMPILATION REPORTS**

a. **STANDARD REPORT** The standard report includes: (1) Identification of the PFS presented by the responsible party; (2) A statement that the CPA has compiled the PFS in accordance with standards established by the AICPA; (3) A statement that a compilation is limited in scope and does not enable the CPA to express an opinion or any other form of assurance on the PFS or the assumptions; (4) A caveat that the prospective results may **not** be achieved; (5) A statement that the CPA assumes no responsibility to update the report for events and circumstances occurring after the date of the report; (6) The manual or printed signature of the practitioner; and (7) The date of the completion of the CPA's compilation procedures.

b. **PROJECTION PRESENTATION** The practitioner's report should include a separate paragraph that describes the limitations on the usefulness of the presentation.

EXHIBIT 20 ♦ COMPILATION REPORT ON A FORECAST [PROJECTION]

> We have compiled the accompanying *forecasted* [projected] balance sheet, statements of income, retained earnings, and cash flows of XYZ Company as of December 31, 20X1, and for the year then ending, in accordance with standards established by the American Institute of Certified Public Accountants. [The accompanying projection and this report were prepared for the information and use of (state special purpose, for example, "the DEF National Bank for the purpose of negotiating a loan to expand XYZ Company's plant").]
>
> A compilation is limited to presenting in the form of a *forecast* [projection] information that is the representation of management and does not include evaluation of the support for the assumptions underlying the projection. We have not examined the *forecast* [projection] and, accordingly, do not express an opinion or any other form of assurance on the accompanying statements or assumptions. Furthermore, [even if (describe hypothetical assumption, for example, "the loan is granted and the plant is expanded,")] there will usually be differences between the *forecasted* [projected] and actual results, because events and circumstances frequently do not occur as expected, and those differences may be material. We have no responsibility to update this report for events and circumstances occurring after the date of this report.
>
> <Additional paragraph for a projection report>
>
> The accompanying projection and this report are intended solely for the information and use of (identify specified parties, for example, "XYZ Company and DEF National Bank") and is not intended to be and should not be used by anyone other than these specified parties.

c. **RANGE** The practitioner's report should also include a separate paragraph that states that the responsible party has elected to portray the expected results of one or more assumptions as a range.

EXHIBIT 21 ♦ PARAGRAPH FOR A COMPILED FORECAST CONTAINING A RANGE

> As described in the summary of significant assumptions, management of XYZ company has elected to portray forecasted [describe financial statement element or elements for which the expected results of one or more assumptions fall within a range, and identify the assumptions expected to fall within a range, for example, "revenue at the amounts $X,XXX and $Y,YYY, which is predicated upon occupancy rates of XX percent and YY percent of available apartments,"] rather than as a single point estimate. Accordingly, the accompanying forecast presents forecasted financial position, results of operations, and cash flows [describe one or more assumptions expected to fall within a range, for example, "at such occupancy rates"]. However, there is no assurance that the actual results will fall within the range [describe one or more assumptions expected to fall within a range, for example, "occupancy rates"] presented.

d. **INDEPENDENCE** A CPA may compile PFS for an entity with respect to which a CPA is not independent. In such circumstances, the CPA should specifically disclose this lack; however, the reason for the lack is not described. When the CPA is not independent, the CPA may issue the standard compilation report, but should include the following after the last paragraph, "We are not independent with respect to XYZ Company."

e. **EMPHASIS OF A MATTER** In some circumstances, a CPA may wish to expand the report to emphasize a matter regarding the PFSs. Such information may be presented in a separate paragraph of the CPA's report. However, the CPA should exercise care that emphasizing such a matter does not give the impression that the CPA is expressing assurance or expanding the degree of responsibility the CPA is taking regarding such information.

f. **HISTORICAL FINANCIAL STATEMENTS** PFS may be included in a document that also includes historical financial statements (HFS) with a related practitioner's report. Additionally, HFS may be summarized and presented with PFS for comparative purposes.

EXHIBIT 22 ♦ PARAGRAPH FOR A FORECAST PRESENTED WITH HISTORICAL INFORMATION

> The historical financial statements for the year ended December 31, 20X1, and our report thereon are set forth on pages XX-YY of this document.

g. **OMITTED INFORMATION** An entity may request a CPA to compile PFS that contain presentation deficiencies or omit disclosures other than those relating to significant assumptions. The CPA may compile such PFS provided the deficiency or omission is clearly indicated in the report and is not, to the CPA's knowledge, undertaken with the intention of misleading those who might reasonably be expected to use such statements. In particular, if the compiled PFS are presented in conformity with OCBOA and do not disclose the basis of accounting, the basis should be disclosed in the CPA's report.

EXHIBIT 23 ♦ PARAGRAPH FOR A FORECAST WITH OMITTED INFORMATION

> Management has elected to omit the summary of significant accounting policies required by the guidelines for presentation of a forecast established by the American Institute of Certified Public Accountants. If the omitted disclosures were included in the forecast, they might influence the user's conclusions about the Company's financial position, results of operations, and cash flows for the forecast period. Accordingly, this forecast is not designed for those who are not informed about such matters.

7. **EXAMINATION OF PFS** An examination of PFS is a professional service that involves (a) evaluating the preparation of the PFS, (b) evaluating the support underlying the assumptions, (c) evaluating the presentation of the PFS for conformity with AICPA presentation guidelines, and (d) issuing an examination report. The practitioner follows the general, fieldwork, and reporting standards outlined in AT 100 as applicable to examination engagements.

8. **EXAMINATION REPORTS** As a result of the examination, the CPA has a basis for reporting on whether, in the CPA's opinion, (a) The assumptions provide a reasonable basis for the responsible party's forecast or projection, given the hypothetical assumptions, and (b) Whether the PFS are presented in accordance with AICPA guidelines.

a. **STANDARD REPORT** The CPA's standard report on an examination of PFS includes the following: (1) A title that includes the word *independent*; (2) An identification of the PFS presented; (3) An identification of the responsible party and a statement that the PFS are the responsibility of the responsible party; (4) A statement that the practitioner's responsibility is to express an opinion on the PFS based on an examination; (5) A statement that the examination of the PFS was made in accordance with AICPA standards, and a brief description of the nature of such an examination; (6) The CPA's opinion that the PFS are presented in accordance with AICPA presentation guidelines and that the underlying assumptions provide a reasonable basis for the forecast (or projection given the hypothetical assumptions); (7) A caveat that the prospective results may not be achieved; (8) A statement that the CPA assumes no responsibility to update the report for events and circumstances occurring after the date of the report; (9) The practitioner's manual or printed signature; and (10) The date of completion of the examination procedures as the report date.

b. Projection When a CPA examines a projection, the CPA's opinion regarding the assumptions should be conditioned on the hypothetical assumptions; that is, the CPA should express an opinion on whether the assumptions provide a reasonable basis for the projection given the hypothetical assumptions. Also, the report should include a separate paragraph that limits the use to specified parties.

Exhibit 24 ♦ Standard Report on an Examination of a Forecast [Projection]

We have examined the accompanying *forecasted* [projected] balance sheet, statements of income, retained earnings, and cash flows of XYZ Company as of December 31, 20X1, and for the year then ending. XYZ Company is responsible for the *forecast* [projection]. Our responsibility is to express an opinion on the *forecast* [projection] based on our examination.

Our examination was made in accordance with attestation standards established by the American Institute of Certified Public Accountants and, accordingly, included such procedures as we considered necessary to evaluate both the assumptions used by management and the preparation and presentation of the *forecast* [projection]. We believe our examination provides a reasonable basis for our opinion.

<Opinion paragraph for a forecast report>

In our opinion, the accompanying forecast is presented in conformity with guidelines for presentation of a forecast established by the American Institute of Certified Public Accountants, and the underlying assumptions provide a reasonable basis for management's forecast. However, there will usually be differences between the forecasted and actual results, because events and circumstances frequently do not occur as expected, and those differences may be material. We have no responsibility to update this report for events and circumstances occurring after the date of this report.

< Opinion paragraph for a projection report>

In our opinion, the accompanying projection is presented in conformity with guidelines for presentation of a projection established by the American Institute of Certified Public Accountants, and the underlying assumptions provide a reasonable basis for management's projection [describe the hypothetical assumption, for example, "assuming the granting of the requested loan to expand XYZ Company's plant as described in the summary of significant assumptions."]. However, even if [describe hypothetical assumption, for example, "the loan is granted and the plant is expanded,"] there will usually be differences between the projected and actual results, because events and circumstances frequently do not occur as expected, and those differences may be material. We have no responsibility to update this report for events and circumstances occurring after the date of this report.

<Additional paragraph for a projection report>

The accompanying projection and this report were prepared for [identify specified parties, for example, "XYZ Company and DEF National Bank"] and are not intended to be and should not be used by anyone other than these specified parties.

c. **Range** When the PFS contain a range, the practitioner's report also should include a separate paragraph that states that the responsible party has elected to portray the expected results of one or more assumptions as a range.

Exhibit 25 ♦ Paragraph for a Forecast With a Range

> As described in the summary of significant assumptions, management of XYZ Company has elected to portray forecasted [describe financial statement element or elements for which the expected results of one or more assumptions fall within a range, and identify assumptions expected to fall within a range, for example, "revenue at the amounts of $X,XXX and $Y,YYY, which is predicated upon occupancy rates of XX percent and YY percent of available apartments"], rather than as a single point estimate. Accordingly, the accompanying forecast presents forecasted financial position, results of operations and cash flows [describe one or more assumptions expected to fall within a range, for example, "at such occupancy rates."]. However, there is no assurance that the actual results will fall within the range of [describe one or more assumptions expected to fall within a range; for example, "occupancy rates"] presented.

d. **Emphasis of a Matter** The practitioner may wish to emphasize a matter regarding the PFS, but issue an unqualified opinion. The practitioner may present other information and comments, such as explanatory comments or other informative material, in a separate paragraph of the report.

e. **Evaluation Based in Part on a Report of Another Accountant** When the principal practitioner decides to refer to the report of another CPA as a basis, in part, for the principal's own opinion, the principal practitioner should disclose that fact in stating the scope of the examination and refer to the report of the other CPA in expressing the opinion. Such a reference indicates the division of responsibility for the performance of the examination.

f. **Comparative Historical Financial Information** Historical financial information is handled as discussed for a compilation.

g. **Part of a Larger Engagement** When the practitioner's examination of PFS is part of a larger engagement, for example, a financial feasibility study or business acquisition study, it is appropriate to expand the report on the examination of the PFS to describe the entire engagement.

h. **Qualified Opinion** In a qualified report, the CPA states, in a separate paragraph, all the substantive reasons for modifying the opinion and describe the departure from AICPA presentation guidelines. The opinion includes the words "except" or "exception" as the qualifying language and refer to the separate explanatory paragraph.

Exhibit 26 ♦ Qualifying Language for a Forecast

> The forecast does not disclose the significant accounting policies. Disclosure of such policies is required by guidelines for presentation of a forecast established by the American Institute of Certified Public Accountants.
>
> In our opinion, except for the omission of the disclosure of the significant accounting policies as discussed in the preceding paragraph, the accompanying forecast is presented in conformity with…

i. **Adverse Opinion** In an adverse opinion, the CPA states, in a separate paragraph, all the substantive reasons for the adverse opinion. The opinion should state that the presentation is not in conformity with presentation guidelines and should refer to the explanatory paragraph. When applicable, the opinion paragraph should also state that, in the accountant's opinion, the assumptions do not provide a reasonable basis for the prospective financial statements.

(1) If the presentation, including the summary of significant assumptions, fails to disclose assumptions that, at the time, appear to be significant, the CPA should describe the assumptions in the report and issue an adverse opinion.

(2) The CPA should not examine a presentation that omits all disclosures of assumptions. Also, the CPA should not examine a financial projection that omits (a) An identification of the hypothetical assumptions or (b) A description of the limitations on the usefulness of the presentation.

EXHIBIT 27 ♦ ADVERSE OPINION FOR A FORECAST

> We have examined the accompanying forecasted balance sheet, statements of income, retained earnings, and cash flows of XYZ Company as of December 31, 20X1, and for the year then ending. XYZ Company is responsible for the forecast. Our responsibility is to express an opinion on the forecast based on our examination.
>
> Our examination was made in accordance with attestation standards established by the American Institute of Certified Public Accountants and, accordingly, included such procedures as we considered necessary to evaluate both the assumptions used by management and the preparation and presentation of the forecast. We believe our examination provides a reasonable basis for our opinion.
>
> As discussed under the caption "Sales" in the summary of significant forecast assumptions, the forecasted sales include, among other things, revenue from the Company's federal defense contracts continuing at the current level. The Company's present federal defense contracts will expire in March 20X1. No new contracts have been signed and no negotiations are under way for new federal defense contracts. Furthermore, the federal government has entered into contracts with another company to supply the items being manufactured under the Company's present contracts.
>
> In our opinion, the accompanying forecast is not presented in conformity with guidelines for presentation of a financial forecast established by the American Institute of Certified Public Accountants because management's assumptions, as discussed in the preceding paragraph, do not provide a reasonable basis for management's forecast. We have no responsibility to update this report for events or circumstances occurring after the date of this report.

j. DISCLAIMER OF OPINION In a disclaimer of opinion, the CPA's report should indicate, in a separate paragraph, the respects in which the examination did not comply with standards for an examination. The CPA should state that the scope of the examination was not sufficient to enable an opinion to be expressed concerning the presentation or the underlying assumptions, and the CPA's disclaimer of opinion should include a direct reference to the explanatory paragraph. When there is a scope limitation and the CPA also believes there are material departures from the presentation guidelines, those departures should be described in the CPA's report.

EXHIBIT 28 ♦ DISCLAIMER OF OPINION

> We were engaged to examine the accompanying forecasted balance sheet, statements of income, retained earnings, and cash flows of XYZ Company as of December 31, 20X1, and for the year then ending. XYZ Company is responsible for the forecast.
>
> (continued on next page)

> As discussed under the caption "Income From Investee" in the summary of significant forecast assumptions, the forecast includes income from an equity investee constituting 23 percent of forecasted net income, which is management's estimate of the Company's share of the investee's income to be accrued for 20X1. The investee has not prepared a forecast for the year ending December 31, 20X1, and we were therefore unable to obtain suitable support for this assumption.
>
> Because, as described in the preceding paragraph, we are unable to evaluate management's assumption regarding income from an equity investee and other assumptions that depend thereon, we express no opinion concerning the presentation of or the assumptions underlying the accompanying forecast. We have no responsibility to update this report for events and circumstances occurring after the date of this report.

9. Agreed-Upon Procedures

a. **Standards** The guidance in AT 100 (including general, fieldwork, and reporting standards) and AT 200 applies to engagements to apply agreed-upon procedures to PFS. This includes the extent of procedures and agreement among the parties regarding the procedures.

b. **Conditions** A practitioner may accept an engagement to apply agreed-upon procedures to PFS provided that: (1) The practitioner is independent, (2) The practitioner and the specified users agree upon the procedures and criteria; (3) The specified users take responsibility for the sufficiency of the agreed-upon procedures for their purposes; (4) The PFS include a summary of significant assumptions; (5) The PFS are subject to reasonably consistent evaluation against criteria that are suitable and available to the specified parties; (6) The procedures are expected to result in reasonably consistent finding using the criteria; (7) Evidential matter related to the PFS is expect to exist to provide a reasonable basis for expressing the findings in the practitioner's report; (8) Where applicable, the practitioner and the specified user agree on any materiality limits for reporting purposes.; and (9) Use of the report is restricted to the specified parties.

10. Reports on the Results of Applying Agreed-Upon Procedures

a. **Required Elements** The practitioner's report includes: (1) A title that includes the word *independent*; (2) Identification of the specified parties; (3) Reference to the PFS by the report and the character of the engagement; (4) A statement that the procedures performed were those agreed to by the specified parties identified in the report; (5) Identification of the responsible party and a statement that the PFS are the responsible party's responsibility; (6) A statement that the engagement was conducted in accordance with attestation standards established by the AICPA; (7) A statement that the sufficiency of the procedures is solely the responsibility of the specified parties and a disclaimer of responsibility for the sufficiency of those procedures; (8) A list of (or reference to) procedures preformed and related findings; (9) Where applicable, a description of any agreed-upon materiality limits; (10) A statement that the practitioner was not engaged to and did not conduct an examination of PFS, a disclaimer of opinion on whether the presentation of the PFS is in conformity with AICPA presentation guidelines and on whether the underlying assumptions provide a reasonable basis for the forecast or a reasonable basis for the projection given the hypothetical assumptions, and a statement that if the practitioner had performed additional procedures, other matters might have come to his or attention that would have been reported; (11) A restriction on the use of the report, because it is intended to be used solely by the specified parties, and should not be used by others; (12) Where applicable, reservations or restrictions concerning procedures or findings; (13) A caveat that the prospective results may not be achieved; (14) A statement that the CPA assumes no responsibility to update the report for events and circumstances occurring after the report date; (15) Where applicable, a description of assistance provided by a specialist; (16) The practitioner's manual or printed signature; and (17) The date.

b. NEGATIVE ASSURANCE When the CPA reports on the results of applying agreed-upon procedures, the CPA should **not** express any form of negative assurance on the PFS.

11. PARTIAL PRESENTATIONS The practitioner's procedures in an engagement connected with a partial presentation is affected by the nature of the information presented. The scope for an examination or compilation of some partial presentations may be similar to that for the examination or compilation of a presentation of PFS. Reports on partial presentations of both forecasted and projected information should include a description of any limitations of the usefulness of the presentation.

C. PRO FORMA FINANCIAL INFORMATION (AT 400)

Pro forma financial information is used to show what the significant effects on historical financial information *might have been* if a consummated or proposed transaction or event had occurred at an earlier date. Pro forma financial information is generally used to show the effects of transactions such as a business combination, a change in capitalization, the disposition of a significant portion of a business, a change in the form of business organization, or the proposed sale of securities and the application of proceeds. Engagements to report on an examination or review of pro forma financial information are covered by AT 100 and AT 400. When pro forma financial information is presented outside the basic financial statements but within the same document, and the CPA is not engaged to report on the pro forma financial information, the CPA's responsibilities are described in SAS 8, *Other Information in Documents Containing Audited Financial Statements* (AU 550), and in SAS 37, *Filings Under Federal Securities Statutes* (AU 711).

1. REQUIREMENTS A CPA may agree to report on an examination or a review of pro forma financial information if the following conditions are met:

a. Pro forma adjustments should be based on management's assumptions and should consider all significant effects directly attributable to the transaction or event. The transaction or event reflected in the pro forma information should be described, as well as the source of the historical information upon which it is based, the significant assumptions used, and any significant uncertainties about those assumptions. The presentation should indicate that the pro forma information should be read in conjunction with the historical data. The presentation should also state that the pro forma financial information does not necessarily indicate the results that would have been attained had the transaction actually taken place earlier.

b. The document containing pro forma information includes (or incorporates by reference), complete historical financial statements (HFS) of the entity for the most recent year, or for the preceding year if financial statements for the most recent year are not yet available. Interim pro forma financial information must include (or incorporate by reference), historical interim financial information, which may be condensed, for that period. In the case of a business combination, the document must include (or incorporate by reference) the appropriate historical financial information for the significant constituent parts of the combined entity.

c. The HFS of the entity (or, of each significant constituent part of the combined entity) on which the pro forma financial information is based must have been audited or reviewed. The practitioner's attestation risk relating to the pro forma financial information is affected by the scope of the engagement providing the practitioner with assurance about the underlying historical financial information to which the pro forma adjustments are applied.

(1) The level of assurance given by the CPA on the pro forma financial information is limited to the lowest level of assurance provided on the underlying HFS of any significant constituent part of the combined entity. For example, if the underlying HFS of each significant constituent part of the combined entity have been audited at year-end **and** reviewed at an interim date, the CPA may perform an examination or a review of the pro forma financial information at year-end, **but** is limited to performing a review of the pro forma financial information at the interim date.

(2) The practitioner must have an appropriate level of knowledge of the accounting and financial reporting practices of each significant constituent part of the combined entity.

2. **Examination Objective** Examination procedures applied to pro forma financial information are to provide reasonable assurance as to whether the following exists: (a) Management's assumptions provide a reasonable basis for presenting the significant effects directly attributable to the underlying transaction or event; (b) The related pro forma adjustments give appropriate effect to those assumptions; (c) The pro forma column reflects the proper application of those adjustments to the HFS.

3. **Review Objective** Review procedures are to provide negative assurance as to whether any information came to the CPA's attention to cause a belief that: (a) Management's assumptions do **not** provide a reasonable basis for presenting the significant effects directly attributable to the transaction or event; (b) The related pro forma adjustments do **not** give appropriate effect to those assumptions; (c) The related pro forma column does **not** reflect the proper application of those adjustments to the HFS.

4. **Procedures** The procedures the CPA applies to the assumptions and pro forma adjustments for either an examination or a review engagement, other than those applied to the HFS, are as follows:

   a. Obtain an understanding of the underlying transaction or event, for example, by reading relevant contracts and minutes of meetings of the board of directors, and by making inquiries of appropriate officials.

   b. Obtain a level of knowledge of each significant constituent part of the combined entity in a business combination. Matters to consider include accounting principles and financial reporting practices followed, transactions between the entities, and material contingencies.

   c. Discuss with management its assumptions regarding the effects of the transaction or event.

   d. Evaluate whether pro forma adjustments are included for all significant effects directly attributable to the transaction or event.

   e. Obtain sufficient evidence in support of adjustments. The evidence required to support the level of assurance given is a matter of professional judgment. The CPA typically would obtain more evidence in an examination engagement than in a review engagement. Examples of evidence are purchase, merger, or exchange agreements; appraisal reports; debt agreements; employment agreements; actions of the board of directors; and existing or proposed legislation or regulatory actions.

   f. Evaluate whether management's assumptions that underlie the pro forma adjustments are presented in a sufficiently clear and comprehensive manner. Also, evaluate whether the pro forma adjustments are consistent with each other and with the data used to develop them.

g. Determine that computations of pro forma adjustments are mathematically correct, and that the pro forma column reflects the proper application of those adjustments to the HFS.

h. Obtain written representations from management acknowledging responsibility for the assumptions used in determining the pro forma adjustments and concerning management's belief that: (1) The assumptions provide a reasonable basis for presenting all the significant effects directly attributable to the transaction or event; (2) The related pro forma adjustments give appropriate effect to those assumptions; (3) The pro forma column reflects the proper application of those adjustments to the historical financial statements; and (4) The significant effects directly attributable to the transaction or event are appropriately disclosed in the pro forma financial information.

i. Read the pro forma financial information and evaluate whether (1) The underlying transaction or event, the pro forma adjustments, the significant assumptions, and the significant uncertainties, if any, about those assumptions have been appropriately described; and (2) The source of the historical financial information on which the pro forma financial information is based has been appropriately identified.

5. **Report** The report on pro forma financial information may be added to the CPA's report on historical financial information, or it may appear separately.

a. **Contents** A report on pro forma financial information includes the following.

(1) **Title** A title that includes the word *independent*.

(2) **Identification** An identification of the pro forma financial information.

(3) **Responsible Party** An identification of the responsible party and a statement that the responsible party is responsible for the pro forma financial information.

(4) **Limitation** A separate paragraph explaining the objective of pro forma financial information and its limitations.

(5) **Signature** The practitioner's manual or printed signature.

(6) **Date** The CPA's report on pro forma financial information should be dated as of the completion of the appropriate procedures. If the reports are combined and the date of completion of the procedures for the examination or review of the pro forma financial information is **after** the date of completion of the field work for the audit or review of the historical financial information, the combined report should be dual-dated.

b. **Examination** An examination report also includes the following.

(1) **Reference** A reference to the financial statements from which the historical financial information is derived and a statement that such financial statements were audited, and any modification in the practitioner's report on the historical financial information.

(2) **Responsibility** A statement that the practitioner's responsibility is to express an opinion on the pro forma financial information based on his or her examination.

(3) **Standards** A statement that the examination was made in accordance with attestation standards established by the AICPA, and accordingly, included such procedures as the practitioner considered necessary in the circumstances.

(4) **Basis** A statement that the practitioner believes that the examination provides a reasonable basis for his or her opinion.

(5) **Opinion** The practitioner's opinion as to whether management's assumptions provide a reasonable basis for presenting the significant effects directly attributable to the transaction or event, whether the related pro forma adjustments give appropriate effect to those assumptions, and whether the pro forma column reflects the proper application of those adjustments to the historical financial statements.

c. **Review** An review report also includes the following.

(1) **Reference** A reference to the financial statements from which the historical financial information is derived and a statement as to whether such financial statements were audited or reviewed, and any modification in the practitioner's report on the historical financial information.

(2) **Standards** A statement that the review was conducted in accordance with attestation standards established by the AICPA.

(3) **Disclaimer** A statement that a review is substantially less in scope than an examination, the objective of which is the expression of an opinion on the pro forma financial information, and accordingly, the practitioner does not express such an opinion.

(4) **Conclusion** The practitioner's conclusion as to whether any information came to the CPA's attention to cause a belief that management's assumptions do not provide a reasonable basis for presenting the significant effects directly attributable to the transaction or event, or that the related pro forma adjustments do not give appropriate effect to those assumptions, or that the pro forma column does not reflect the proper application of those adjustments to the historical financial statements.

d. **Business Combinations** A report on a proposed pooling transaction need not address management's assumptions unless the pro forma financial information includes adjustments to conform the accounting principles of the combining entities.

e. **Modifications** Restrictions on the scope of the engagement, significant uncertainties about the assumptions that could materially affect the transaction or event, reservations about the propriety of the assumptions and the conformity of the presentation with those assumptions (including inadequate disclosure of significant matters), or other reservations may require the CPA to qualify the opinion, render an adverse opinion, disclaim an opinion or withdraw from the engagement. The CPA should disclose **all** substantive reasons for **any** report modifications. Uncertainty as to whether the transaction or event will be consummated would not ordinarily require a report modification.

Exhibit 29 ♦ Report on Examination of Pro Forma Financial Information

We have examined the pro forma adjustments reflecting the transaction [or event] described in Note 1 and the application of those adjustments to the historical amounts in [the assembly of] the accompanying pro forma condensed balance sheet of X Company as of December 31, 20X1, and the pro forma condensed statement of income for the year then ended. The historical condensed financial statements are derived from the historical financial statements of X Company, which were audited by us, and of Y Company, which were audited by other accountants, appearing elsewhere herein [or incorporated by reference]. Such pro forma adjustments are based upon management's assumptions described in Note 2. X Company's management is responsible for the pro forma financial statements. Our responsibility is to express an opinion on the pro forma financial information based on our examination.

(continued on next page)

> Our examination was made in accordance with attestation standards established by the American Institute of Certified Public Accountants and, accordingly, included such procedures as we considered necessary under the circumstances. We believe our examination provides a reasonable basis for our opinion.
>
> The objective of this pro forma financial information is to show what the significant effects on the historical financial information might have been had the transaction [or event] occurred at an earlier date. However, the pro forma condensed financial statements are not necessarily indicative of the results of operations or related effects on financial position that would have been attained had the above-mentioned transaction [or event] occurred earlier.
>
> [Additional paragraph(s) may be added to emphasize certain matters relating to the engagement.]
>
> In our opinion, management's assumptions provide a reasonable basis for presenting the significant efforts directly attributable to the above-mentioned transaction [or event] described in Note 1, the related pro forma adjustments give appropriate effect to those assumptions, and the pro forma column reflects the proper application of those adjustments to the historical financial statement amounts in the pro forma condensed balance sheet as of December 31, 20X1, and the pro forma condensed statement of income for the year then ended.

EXHIBIT 30 ♦ REPORT ON REVIEW OF PRO FORMA FINANCIAL INFORMATION

> We have reviewed the pro forma adjustments reflecting the transaction [or event] described in Note 1 and the application of those adjustments to the historical amounts in [the assembly of] the accompanying pro forma condensed balance sheet of X Company as of March 31, 20X2, and the pro forma condensed statement of income for the three months then ended. These historical condensed financial statements are derived from the historical unaudited financial statements of X Company, which were reviewed by us, and of Y Company, which were reviewed by other accountants, appearing elsewhere herein [or incorporated by reference]. Such pro forma adjustments are based on management's assumptions as described in Note 2. X Company's management is responsible for the pro forma financial statements.
>
> Our review was conducted in accordance with attestation standards established by the American Institute of Certified Public Accountants. A review is substantially less in scope than an examination, the objective of which is the expression of an opinion on management's assumptions, the pro forma adjustments, and the application of those adjustments to historical financial information. Accordingly, we do not express such an opinion.
>
> <Same third paragraph as in an examination report.>
>
> [Additional paragraph(s) may be added to emphasize certain matters relating to the engagement.]
>
> Based on our review, nothing came to our attention that caused us to believe that management's assumptions do not provide a reasonable basis for presenting the significant effects directly attributable to the above-mentioned transaction [or event] described in Note 1, that the related pro forma adjustments do not give appropriate effect to those assumptions, or that the pro forma column does not reflect the proper application of those adjustments to the historical financial statement amounts in the pro forma condensed balance sheet as of March 31, 20X2, and the pro forma condensed statement of income for the three months then ended.

D. INTERNAL CONTROL OVER FINANCIAL REPORTING (AT 500)

An entity's internal control over financial reporting includes policies and procedures pertaining to its ability to record, process, summarize, and report financial information. A practitioner may examine or perform agreed-upon procedures relating to (but not review) the effectiveness of the entity's internal control. A practitioner engaged to **examine** the effectiveness of an entity's internal control

(IC) should comply with the general, fieldwork, and reporting standards in AT 100 and the specific requirements in AT 500.

1. **Applicability** AT 500 doesn't apply to the following engagements: (a) Agreed-upon procedures (AT 200 applies instead); (b) Examining controls over operations or compliance with laws and regulations; (c) Certain other internal control services (SEC reports) covered by other authoritative guidance; (d) Consulting; and (e) Gathering information for management.

2. **Required Conditions for Engagement Performance**

   a. The entity's management accepts responsibility for IC effectiveness.

   b. The responsible party (the management personnel who accept responsibility for the entity's IC effectiveness) evaluates the entity's IC effectiveness using suitable criteria (also referred to as control criteria).

   c. Sufficient evidential matter exists or can be developed to support the responsible party's evaluation.

   d. Management may present its **written assertion** about the effectiveness of the entity's internal control in either (a) A separate report that will accompany the practitioner's report; or (b) A representation letter to the practitioner. The assertion may take many forms such as (a) "W Company maintained effective internal control over financial reporting as of [date]" or (b) "W Company internal control over financial reporting as of [date] are sufficient to meet the stated objectives." Assertions that are so subjective that competent people using the same criteria would not ordinarily be able to arrive at similar conclusions (for example, "W Company maintained very effective internal control") should not be used. Without a written assertion, the practitioner must withdraw from the engagement unless an examination of internal control is required by law or regulation. In that situation, the practitioner may either disclaim an opinion or express an adverse opinion.

3. **Objective** The practitioner's objective is to express an opinion on (a) the effectiveness of an entity's IC, in all material respects, based on control criteria, or (b) whether the responsible party's written assertion about the effectiveness of IC is fairly stated, in all material respects, based on control criteria. The practitioner's opinion relates to the effectiveness of IC taken as a whole, and not to the effectiveness of each individual component. Therefore, the practitioner considers the interrelationship of the IC components in achieving control criteria objectives.

4. **Procedures** The practitioner accumulates sufficient evidence about the design and operating effectiveness of IC, thereby limiting attestation risk to an acceptably low level. Controls and control objectives should be appropriately documented to serve as a basis for the responsible party's assertion and the practitioner's report; the practitioner may assist in preparing or gathering such documentation, which may take various forms. When evaluating design effectiveness, the practitioner considers whether controls suitably are designed to prevent or detect material misstatements on a timely basis. When evaluating operating effectiveness, the practitioner considers how controls are applied, the consistency of application, and by whom the controls are applied.

5. **Evaluating the Design Effectiveness of Controls** The practitioner focuses on the significance of controls in achieving control criteria objectives rather than on specific controls in isolation. The inadequacy of a specific control may not be a deficiency if other controls specifically address the same criterion.

6. **Testing and Evaluating the Operating Effectiveness of Controls** Performing an examination of the effectiveness of an entity's internal control involves the following: (a) Planning the engagement; (b) Obtaining an understanding of internal control; (c) Evaluating

the design effectiveness of IC policies and procedures; (d) Testing and evaluating the operating effectiveness of IC policies and procedures; (e) Forming an opinion on management's assertion about the effectiveness of the entity's IC, based on the control criteria, or the responsible party's assertion thereon. The practitioner considers such matters as the: (a) Nature of the control; (b) Significance of the control in achieving the control criteria objectives; (c) Nature and extent of texts of the entity's tests of the operating effectiveness of the controls; and (d) Risk of noncompliance with the control.

7. **Communications** If the practitioner becomes aware of significant deficiencies in the entity's internal control, the practitioner should communicate reportable conditions to the client's audit committee and identify which conditions are also considered to be material weaknesses, preferably in writing. The practitioner may **not** issue a written report stating that no reportable conditions were noted during the engagement. The practitioner may communicate reportable conditions during the course of the examination rather than after the examination is finished. The practitioner need not communicate reportable conditions to the responsible party if it is not the client, but the practitioner is not prohibited from doing so.

8. **Written Representations** The responsible party's refusal to furnish the appropriate written representations constitutes a scope limitation on the examination sufficient to require a qualified opinion, disclaimer of an opinion, or withdrawal. (Further, the practitioner should consider the effects of the responsible party's refusal on his or her ability to rely on other representations.) Practitioners generally obtain written representations from the responsible party including statements that:

    a. Acknowledge the responsible party's responsibility for establishing and maintaining internal controls.

    b. The responsible party has performed an evaluation of the effectiveness of internal controls and specifies the control criteria.

    c. States the responsible party's assertion about the effectiveness of internal controls (based on the control criteria) as of a specified date.

    d. The responsible party has disclosed to the practitioner all significant deficiencies in the design or operation of internal control which could adversely affect the entity's ability to record, process, summarize, and report financial information consistent with the assertions of management in the financial statements and has identified those that it believes to be material weaknesses in internal control.

    e. Describes any material fraud and any other fraud that (although not material) involves management or other employees who have a significant role in internal control.

    f. States whether there were, subsequent to the specified date any changes in IC or other factors that might significantly affect internal controls, including any corrective actions taken by management with regard to significant deficiencies and material weaknesses.

9. **Reporting** The practitioner may examine and report directly either on the effectiveness of an entity's internal control or on the responsible party's written assertion, unless there are one or more material weaknesses; in that case, the practitioner reports directly on the effectiveness of an entity's internal control.

    - **Modifications** The practitioner may issue qualified, adverse, and disclaimers of opinion by making appropriate revisions to the standard report. Situations requiring modification to the standard report include cases where the following conditions exist: (1) There is a material weakness in the entity's IC; (2) There is a restriction on the scope of the engagement; (3) The practitioner decides to refer to the report of another practitioner as the basis, in part, for the practitioner's own report; (4) A significant subsequent event occurred since the effective date of the assertion; (5) The engagement relates to only a segment of the entity; (6) The engagement relates only to the suitability of design of the entity's IC; or (7) The criteria are unsuitable for general use.

EXHIBIT 31 ♦ STANDARD REPORT ON INTERNAL CONTROL EFFECTIVENESS

> Independent Accountant's Report
>
> We have examined the effectiveness of W Company's internal control over financial reporting as of December 31, 20X1, based upon [identify criteria]. W Company's management is responsible for maintaining effective internal control over financial reporting. Our responsibility is to express an opinion on the effectiveness of internal control based on our examination.
>
> Our examination was conducted in accordance with attestation standards established by the American Institute of Certified Public Accountants and, accordingly, included obtaining an understanding of internal controls over financial reporting, testing, and evaluating the design and operating effectiveness of internal controls, and performing such other procedures as we considered necessary in the circumstances. We believe that our examination provides a reasonable basis for our opinion.
>
> (Inherent limitations paragraph)
>
> Because of inherent limitations in any internal control, misstatements due to error or fraud may occur and not be detected. Also, projections of any evaluation of the internal controls over financial reporting to future periods are subject to the risk that internal controls may become inadequate because of changes in conditions, or that the degree of compliance with policies or procedures may deteriorate.
>
> In our opinion, W Company's management maintained an effective internal control over financial reporting as of December 31, 20X1, based upon [identify criteria].

10. **RELATIONSHIP TO AUDIT OPINION** An auditor's consideration of IC in a financial statement audit is more **limited** than that of a practitioner engaged to examine the effectiveness of the entity's IC. However, knowledge the practitioner obtains about the entity's IC as part of the examination engagement may serve as the basis for his or her understanding of IC in a financial statement audit. Also, the practitioner may consider the results of tests of controls performed in connection with an examination engagement, as well as any material weaknesses identified, when assessing control risk in the audit of the entity's financial statements. Different practitioners may perform the audit and examination; the practitioner performing an examination may which to consider any material weaknesses and reportable conditions identified by the auditor and any disagreement between the responsible party and the auditor regarding such matters.

E. COMPLIANCE ATTESTATION (AT 600)

AT 600 provides guidance for engagements related to (a) an entity's compliance with requirements of specified laws, regulations, rules, contracts, or grants, or (b) the effectiveness of an entity's internal control (IC) over compliance with specified requirements. The subject matter may be financial or nonfinancial compliance requirements. An attest engagement must comply with the general, fieldwork, and reporting standards delineated in AT 100 as well as specific standards established in AT 600. Internal controls over compliance may include parts of (but are not the same as) IC over financial reporting.

1. **APPROPRIATE ENGAGEMENTS** CPAs may be engaged to perform agreed-upon procedures to assist users in evaluating compliance with specified requirements (or related assertions) and/or the effectiveness of an entity's IC over compliance. These engagements are also subject to the requirements of AT 200. CPAs also may be engaged to **examine**, but **not**

review, an entity's compliance with specified requirements, or related written assertions. CPAs may provide non-attest services connected with compliance; these services adhere to professional consulting standards, rather than SSAE 10.

2. **CONDITIONS FOR ENGAGEMENT PERFORMANCE** The responsible party must:

   a. **BOTH TYPES OF ENGAGEMENTS** Accepts responsibility for the entity's compliance with specified requirements and the effectiveness of the entity's IC over compliance and provides a written assertion about compliance with specified requirements or IC over compliance in either: (a) A separate report to accompany the practitioner's report; or (b) A representation letter to the practitioner.

   b. **AGREED-UPON PROCEDURES** Evaluates compliance with specified requirements or the effectiveness of the entity's IC over compliance.

   c. **EXAMINATIONS** The responsible party evaluates compliance with specified requirements and sufficient evidential matter exists, or could be developed, to support that evaluation.

3. **WRITTEN ASSERTION** In an examination, the responsible party's refusal to provide a written assertion requires the practitioner to withdraw unless the engagement is legally mandated. In that case, the practitioner must either express an adverse opinion in a restricted-use report or disclaim an opinion. In an agreed-upon procedures engagement where the client is the responsible party, absence of a written assertion requires the practitioner to withdraw, unless the engagement is legally mandated. In an agreed-upon procedures engagement where the client is not the responsible party, absence of a written assertion does not force the practitioner to withdraw, but the practitioner should consider the effects of the refusal on the engagement and report.

4. **REPRESENTATIONS** When the practitioner's client is not the responsible party, the practitioner may also obtain written representations from the client. A responsible party's refusal to provide a written representation letter is a limitation on the scope of an examination or agreed-upon procedures engagement sufficient to preclude an unqualified opinion. Based on the nature of the representations not received or the refusal, the practitioner may determine that a qualified opinion is appropriate. When the practitioner's client is the responsible party, the refusal constitutes a limitation on the engagement scope sufficient to require the practitioner to withdraw. When the practitioner's client is not the responsible party, the practitioner is not required to withdraw. The practitioner should consider the effects of the responsible party's refusal on his or her ability to relay on other representations by the responsible party.

5. **RESPONSIBILITIES** The responsible party is responsible for ensuring that the entity complies with the requirements applicable to its activities.

6. **AGREED-UPON PROCEDURES ENGAGEMENT** The objective of this engagement is to present specific findings to assist users in evaluating an entity's assertion with compliance with specified requirements or about the effectiveness of an entity's IC over compliance based on procedures agreed-upon by the report users. The CPA's procedures generally may be as limited or as extensive as the specified parties desire as long as the specified users: (a) Participate in establishing the procedures to be performed; and (b) Take responsibility for the adequacy of such procedures for their purposes. Prior to performing procedures, the practitioner should obtain an understanding of the specified compliance requirements.

   a. When a situation imposes restrictions on the engagement scope, the practitioner attempts to obtain agreement to modify the procedures. If such agreement is not obtained, the practitioner should describe the restrictions in the report or withdraw from the engagement.

b. If noncompliance is found by other means or in the subsequent period, it typically is reported. The practitioner has no obligation to perform beyond the agreed-upon procedures and no responsibility to perform procedures to detect noncompliance in the subsequent period, beyond obtaining the responsible party's representation about noncompliance in the subsequent period (the period starting at the end of the period addressed by the practitioner's report and ending on the date of completion of the procedures, also the report date).

c. If the practitioner is engaged to report on both compliance with specified requirements and the effectiveness of IC over compliance, the practitioner may issue one report.

d. The practitioner's report should **not** provide negative assurance about whether management's assertion is fairly stated.

EXHIBIT 32 ♦ STANDARD REPORT ON AGREED-UPON COMPLIANCE PROCEDURES

Independent Accountant's Report

We have performed the procedures enumerated below, which were agreed to by [list specified parties], solely to assist the specified parties in evaluating W Company's internal control over compliance with [list specified compliance requirements] during the three months ending December 31, 20X1. Management is responsible for W Company's compliance with those requirements. This agreed-upon procedures engagement was conducted in accordance with attestation standards established by the American Institute of Certified Public Accountants. The sufficiency of the procedures is solely the responsibility of those parties specified in this report. Consequently, we make no representation regarding the sufficiency of the procedures described below either for the purpose for which this report has been requested for fro any other purpose.

[List the procedures performed and related findings.]

We were not engaged to and did not conduct an examination, the objective of which would be the expression of an opinion on compliance. Accordingly, we do not express such an opinion. Had we performed additional procedures, other matters might have come to the our attention that would have been reported to you.

This report is intended solely for the information and use of [list or refer to specified parties] and is not intended to be and should not be used by anyone other than these specified parties.

7. **EXAMINATION ENGAGEMENT** The objective of an examination is to express an opinion on an entity's compliance with specified requirements (or related assertion) based on specified criteria. To express such an opinion, the practitioner accumulate sufficient evidence regarding the entity's compliance with specified requirements, thereby limiting attestation risk to an appropriately low level. Among other procedures, the practitioner considers subsequent events. The practitioner considers issues that parallel those in a financial statement audit, but the perspective may be different. (Some of these issues are risk, materiality, planning, professional skepticism, relevant internal controls and internal audit functions, use of specialists, and obtaining sufficient evidence.)

EXHIBIT 33 ♦ STANDARD REPORT ON EXAMINATION OF COMPLIANCE

Independent Accountant's Report

We have examined W Company's internal control over compliance with [list specified compliance requirements] during the three months ending December 31, 20X1. W Company's management is responsible for W Company's compliance with those requirements. Our responsibility is to express an opinion on W Company's compliance based on our examination.

Our examination was conducted in accordance with attestation standards established by the American Institute of Certified Public Accountants and, accordingly, included examining, on a test basis, evidence about W Company's compliance with those requirements and performing such other procedures as we considered necessary in the circumstances. We believe that our examination provides a reasonable basis for our opinion. Our examination does not provide a legal determination on W Company's compliance with specified requirements.

In our opinion, W Company's complied, in all material respects, with the aforementioned requirements for the three months ended December 31, 20X1.

8. **MODIFICATIONS** The practitioner modifies the report if: (a) Material noncompliance with specified requirements exists; (b) A restriction on the engagement scope exists; or (c) The practitioner refers to another practitioner's report as the basis, in part, for the report.

F. MANAGEMENT'S DISCUSSION & ANALYSIS (AT 700)

AT 700 provides specific guidance to CPAs related to the performance of an attest engagement with respect to MD&A prepared pursuant to Securities and Exchange Commission (SEC) regulations. This guidance does not change an auditor's responsibility in an financial statement audit or apply to situations where CPAs provide recommendations rather than assurance. (SAS 8 requires an auditor to read the MD&A and consider whether it is materially inconsistent with information appearing in the financial statements.) A practitioner engaged to examine or review MD&A complies with AT 100 and the specific standards in AT 700. A practitioner engaged to perform agreed-upon procedures on MD&A follows the guidance in AT 200.

1. **OBJECTIVES** The objective is to report on MD&A taken as a whole. An **examination** of MD&A provides users with an independent opinion regarding whether (a) the presentation meets SEC criteria, (b) the historical financial information is accurately derived from the financial statements, and (c) the underlying information and assumptions provide a reasonable basis for the disclosures contained therein. A **review** of MD&A provides users and preparers with negative assurance concerning such matters.

2. **ENGAGEMENT ACCEPTANCE** A CPA may perform an examination or review of MD&A for an annual period, an interim period, or a combined annual and interim period. A base knowledge of the entity gained through a financial statement audit is necessary to provide the CPA with sufficient knowledge to evaluate the results of procedures. For nonpublic entities, the CPA also must receive a written assertion from management that MD&A was prepared using SEC criteria.

   a. **ANNUAL PERIOD** A CPA may accept an engagement to examine or review MD&A of an entity for an annual period, provided the practitioner audits the financial statements for at least the latest period to which MD&A relates and the financial statements for the other periods covered by MD&A have been audited.

   b. **REVIEW OF INTERIM PERIOD** A CPA may accept an engagement to review MD&A for an interim period provided that MD&A for the most recent fiscal year has been (or will be) examined or reviewed (by either the CPA or a predecessor) and the CPA performs either an audit of the interim financial statements or performs

(1) **FOR A PUBLIC ENTITY** A review of the financial statements for the related comparative interim periods and issues a review report in accordance with SAS 71.

(2) **FOR A NONPUBLIC ENTITY** A review of either (a) The financial statements for the related interim periods under SSARSs and issues a review report, or (b) The related condensed interim financial information in accordance with SAS 71 and issues a review report, and such information is accompanied by complete financial statements for the most recent audited fiscal year.

c. **PREDECESSOR** If a predecessor audited prior-period financial statements, the successor CPA must acquire sufficient knowledge of the entity and apply appropriate procedures relating to prior years included in the MD&A presentation.

d. **MANAGEMENT** A practitioner considers whether management (and any assistants) has appropriate knowledge of rules and regulations of the SEC to prepare MD&A..

3. **RESPONSIBILITIES** Management is responsible for MD&A preparation.

4. **SCOPE** The practitioner considers the following as well as historical financial information.

a. **PRO FORMA INFORMATION** The guidance in AT 400 when performing procedures with respect to any pro forma information, even if MD&A indicates that certain information is derived from unaudited financial statements.

b. **EXTERNAL INFORMATION** (for example, debt ratings of a rating agency) also is subject to the CPA's procedures.

c. **FORWARD-LOOKING INFORMATION** is tested only for the purpose of expressing an opinion or providing limited assurance on MD&A taken as a whole. The CPA considers whether cautionary language concerning achievability is included.

d. **VOLUNTARY INFORMATION** When the entity includes other information in MD&A required by other SEC regulations, the CPA also considers those other SEC criteria in subjecting such information to procedures.

5. **ENGAGEMENT PROCEDURES** The CPA obtains an understanding of the SEC criteria for MD&A and management's MD&A preparation method; plans the engagement; considers materiality; considers relevant portions of the entity's internal control; considers subsequent events; and obtains appropriate written representations from management. The misstatement of an individual assertion is material if the magnitude of the misstatement (individually or aggregated) is such that a reasonable person would be influenced by its correction.

a. **EXAMINATION** The CPA obtains sufficient evidence, including testing completeness, and forms an opinion consistent with examination objectives. The CPA considers the results of financial statement audits for the periods covered by MD&A, including the possible impact on the examination engagement scope of a modified auditor's report.

b. **REVIEW** Procedures generally are limited to inquiries and analytical procedures concerning factors that have a material effect on financial condition, results of operations, and cash flows. The CPA also forms a conclusion consistent with review objectives.

6. **EXAMINATION PERFORMANCE** The CPA applies procedures to obtain reasonable assurance of detecting material misstatements. Determining these procedures and evaluating the sufficiency of the evidence are matters of professional judgment. In a financial statement audit, the auditor applies procedures to some information included in MD&A. Because the objective of an audit is different than an examination of MD&A, additional procedures typically are performed in an examination.

7. **Review Performance** The CPA develops an overall strategy for analytical procedures and inquiries. The CPA considers factors such as matters affecting the entity's industry; matters relating to the entity's business; the types of relevant information that management reports to external analysts; the extent of management's knowledge of, and experience with, SEC criteria for MD&A; if the entity is a nonpublic entity, the intended use of MD&A; matters identified during other engagements; and, the nature of complex or subjective matters that may require special skill or knowledge.

8. **Reports** A report on a examination or review of MD&A includes: (a) A title that includes the word independent; (b) The manual or printed signature of the CPA's firm; (c) The date of the completion of the CPA's procedures, which should not precede the date of the audit (or review) report on the latest historical financial statements covered by the MD&A. If the entity is a nonpublic entity, the following sentence is added to the beginning of the explanatory paragraph, "Although W Company is not subject to the rules and regulations of the Securities and Exchange Commission, the accompanying Management's Discussion and Analysis is intended to be a presentation in accordance with the rules and regulations adopted by the Securities and Exchange Commission."

9. **Review Presentation** In order for a CPA to issue a report on a review of MD&A, the financial statements for the periods covered by MD&A and the related auditor's or practitioner's report(s) should accompany MD&A (or be incorporated by reference to information filed with a regulatory agency). There are additional requirements in the following circumstances.

   a. **Interim Periods** The comparative financial statements for the most recent annual period and the related MD&A should accompany the interim MD&A (or be incorporated by reference). Generally, this requirement is satisfied by a public entity that has filed its annual financial statements and MD&A in its annual Form 10-K.

   b. **Nonpublic Entity** The MD&A should include a statement that it was prepared using SEC criteria or a separate written assertion should accompany MD&A.

Exhibit 34 ♦ Standard Report on Examination of MD&A

<u>Independent Accountant's Report</u>

We have examined W Company's Management's Discussion and Analysis taken as a whole, included [incorporated by reference] in the company's [insert description of registration statement or document]. Management is responsible for the preparation of the company's Management's Discussion and Analysis, pursuant to rules and regulations adopted by the Securities and Exchange Commission. Our responsibility is to express an opinion on the presentation based on our examination. We have audited, in accordance with auditing standards generally accepted in the United States of America, the financial statements of W Company as of December 31, 20X2 and 20X1, and for each of the years in the three-year periods ended December 31, 20X2, and in our report dated March 31, 20X3, we expressed an unqualified opinion on those financial statements.

The preparation of Management's Discussion and Analysis requires management to interpret the criteria, make determinations as to the relevancy of information to be included, and make estimates and assumptions that affect reported information. Management's Discussion and Analysis includes information regarding the estimated future impact of transactions and events that have occurred or are expected to occur, expected sources of liquidity and capital resources, operating trends, commitments, and uncertainties. Actual results in the future may differ materially from management's present assessment of this information because events and circumstances frequently do not occur as expected.

(continued on next page)

Our examination of Management's Discussion and Analysis was conducted in accordance with attestation standards established by the American Institute of Certified Public Accountants and, accordingly, included examining, on a test basis, evidence supporting the historical amounts and disclosures in the presentation. An examination also includes assessing the significant determinations made by management as to the relevancy of information to be included and the estimates and assumptions that affect reported information. We believe that our examination provides a reasonable basis for our opinion.

In our opinion, the company's presentation of Management's Discussion and Analysis includes, in all material respects, the required elements of the rules and regulations adopted by the Securities and Exchange Commission; the historical financial amounts included therein have been accurately derived, in all material respects, from the company's financial statements; and the underlying information, determinations, estimates, and assumptions of the company provide a reasonable basis for the disclosers contained therein.

EXHIBIT 35 ♦ STANDARD REPORT ON REVIEW OF MD&A

Independent Accountant's Report

We have reviewed W Company's Management's Discussion and Analysis taken as a whole, included [incorporated by reference] in the company's [insert description of registration statement or document]. Management is responsible for the preparation of the company's Management's Discussion and Analysis, pursuant to rules and regulations adopted by the Securities and Exchange Commission. We have audited, in accordance with auditing standards generally accepted in the United States of America, the financial statements of W Company as of December 31, 20X2 and 20X1, and for each of the years in the three-year periods ended December 31, 20X2, and in our report dated March 31, 20X3, we expressed an unqualified opinion on those financial statements.

We conducted our review of Management's Discussion and Analysis in accordance with attestation standards established by the American Institute of Certified Public Accountants. An review of Management's Discussion and Analysis consists principally of applying analytical procedures and making inquires of persons responsible for financial, accounting, and operational matters. It is substantially less in scope than an examination, the objective of which is the express of an opinion on the presentation. Accordingly, we do not express such an opinion.

<Same explanatory paragraph as in an examination report>

Based on our review, nothing came to our attention that caused us to believe that the company's presentation of Management's Discussion and Analysis does not include, in all material respects, the required elements of the rules and regulations adopted by the Securities and Exchange Commission; that the historical financial amounts included therein have not been accurately derived, in all material respects, from the company's financial statements; or that the underlying information, determinations, estimates, and assumptions of the company do not provide a reasonable basis for the disclosures contained therein.

This report is intended solely for the information and use of [list or refer to specified parties] and is not intended to be and should not be used by anyone other than the specified parties.

CHAPTER 41—OTHER PROFESSIONAL SERVICES

PROBLEM 41-1 MULTIPLE CHOICE QUESTIONS (100 to 125 minutes)

1. North Co., a privately held entity, asked its tax accountant, King, a CPA in public practice, to generate North's interim financial statements on King's microcomputer when King prepared North's quarterly tax return. King should **not** submit these financial statements to North unless, as a minimum, King complies with the provisions of
a. Statements on Standards for Accounting and Review Services.
b. Statements on Standards for Unaudited Financial Services.
c. Statements on Standards for Consulting Services.
d. Statements on Standards for Attestation Engagements. (5/94, Aud., #9, 4674)

2. An accountant should perform analytical procedures during an engagement to

	Compile a nonpublic entity's financial statements	*Review a nonpublic entity's financial statements*
a.	No	No
b.	Yes	Yes
c.	Yes	No
d.	No	Yes

(5/94, Aud., #59, 4724)

3. When an accountant performs more than one level of service (for example, a compilation and a review, or a compilation and an audit) concerning the financial statements of a nonpublic entity, the accountant generally should issue the report that is appropriate for
a. The lowest level of service rendered.
b. The highest level of service rendered.
c. A review engagement.
d. A compilation engagement. (Editors, 0427)

4. May an accountant accept an engagement to compile or review the financial statements of a not-for-profit entity if the accountant is unfamiliar with the specialized industry accounting principles, but plans to obtain the required level of knowledge before compiling or reviewing the financial statements?

	Compilation	*Review*
a.	No	No
b.	Yes	No
c.	No	Yes
d.	Yes	Yes

(5/94, Aud., #46, 4711)

5. If requested to perform a review engagement for a nonpublic entity in which an accountant has an immaterial direct financial interest, the accountant is
a. Not independent and, therefore, may **not** be associated with the financial statements.
b. Not independent and, therefore, may **not** issue a review report.
c. Not independent and, therefore, may issue a review report, but may **not** issue an auditor's opinion.
d. Independent because the financial interest is immaterial and, therefore, may issue a review report. (5/95, Aud., #20, 5638)

6. An accountant who had begun an audit of the financial statements of a nonpublic entity was asked to change the engagement to a review because of a restriction on the scope of the audit. If there is reasonable justification for the change, the accountant's review report should include reference to the

	Scope limitation that caused the changed engagement	*Original engagement that was agreed to*
a.	Yes	No
b.	No	Yes
c.	No	No
d.	Yes	Yes

(11/94, Aud., #78, 5151)

7. A CPA is required to comply with the provisions of *Statements on Standards for Accounting and Review Services* when

	Processing financial data for clients of other CPA firms	*Consulting on accounting matters*
a.	Yes	Yes
b.	Yes	No
c.	No	Yes
d.	No	No

(11/93, Aud., #12, 4249)

8. An accountant is required to comply with the provisions of *Statements on Standards for Accounting and Review Services* when

I. Reproducing client-prepared financial statements, without modification, as an accommodation to a client.
II. Preparing standard monthly journal entries for depreciation and expiration of prepaid expenses.

a. I only
b. II only
c. Both I and II
d. Neither I nor II (5/96, Aud., #1, 6233)

9. When engaged to compile the financial statements of a nonpublic entity, an accountant is required to possess a level of knowledge of the entity's accounting principles and practices. This requirement most likely will include obtaining a general understanding of the

a. Stated qualifications of the entity's accounting personnel.
b. Design of the entity's internal controls placed in operation.
c. Risk factors relating to misstatements arising from illegal acts.
d. Internal control awareness of the entity's senior management. (R/99, Aud., #7, 6823)

10. Miller, CPA, is engaged to compile the financial statements of Web Co., a nonpublic entity, in conformity with the income tax basis of accounting. If Web's financial statements do **not** disclose the basis of accounting used, Miller should

a. Disclose the basis of accounting in the accountant's compilation report.
b. Clearly label each page "Distribution Restricted—Material Modifications Required."
c. Issue a special report describing the effect of the incomplete presentation.
d. Withdraw from the engagement and provide **no** further services to Web. (11/94, Aud., #81, 5154)

11. An accountant may compile a nonpublic entity's financial statements that omit all of the disclosures required by GAAP only if the omission is

I. Clearly indicated in the accountant's report.
II. Not undertaken with the intention of misleading the financial statement users.

a. I only
b. II only
c. Both I and II
d. Either I or II (5/94, Aud., #79, 4744)

12. Compiled financial statements should be accompanied by a report stating that

a. A compilation is substantially less in scope than a review or an audit in accordance with generally accepted auditing standards.
b. The accountant does **not** express an opinion but expresses only limited assurance on the compiled financial statements.
c. A compilation is limited to presenting in the form of financial statements information that is the representation of management.
d. The accountant has compiled the financial statements in accordance with standards established by the Auditing Standards Board. (5/94, Aud., #78, 4743)

13. Financial statements of a nonpublic entity compiled without audit or review by an accountant should be accompanied by a report stating that

a. The scope of the accountant's procedures has **not** been restricted in testing the financial information that is the representation of management.
b. The accountant assessed the accounting principles used and significant estimates made by management.
c. The accountant does **not** express an opinion or any other form of assurance on the financial statements.
d. A compilation consists principally of inquiries of entity personnel and analytical procedures applied to financial data. (11/95, Aud., #80, 6027)

14. Compiled financial statements should be accompanied by an accountant's report stating that

a. A compilation includes assessing the accounting principles used and significant management estimates, as well as evaluating the overall financial statement presentation.
b. The accountant compiled the financial statements in accordance with *Statements on Standards for Accounting and Review Services.*
c. A compilation is substantially less in scope than an audit in accordance with GAAS, the objective of which is the expression of an opinion.
d. The accountant is **not** aware of any material modifications that should be made to the financial statements to conform with GAAP. (5/95, Aud., #78, 5696)

15. An accountant has compiled the financial statements of a nonpublic entity in accordance with Statements on Standards for Accounting and Review Services (SSARS). Does SSARS require that the compilation report be printed on the accountant's letterhead and that the report be manually signed by the accountant?

	Printed on the accountant's letterhead	Manually signed by the accountant
a.	Yes	Yes
b.	Yes	No
c.	No	Yes
d.	No	No

(R/99, Aud., #1, 6817)

16. Which of the following representations does an accountant make implicitly when issuing the standard report for the compilation of a nonpublic entity's financial statements?
a. The accountant is independent with respect to the entity.
b. The financial statements have **not** been audited.
c. A compilation consists principally of inquiries and analytical procedures.
d. The accountant does **not** express any assurance on the financial statements.
(11/93, Aud., #54, 4291)

17. Clark, CPA, compiled and properly reported on the financial statements of Green Co., a nonpublic entity, for the year ended March 31, 20X1. These financial statements omitted substantially all disclosures required by generally accepted accounting principles (GAAP). Green asked Clark to compile the statements for the year ended March 31, 20X2, and to include all GAAP disclosures for the 20X2 statements only, but otherwise present both years' financial statements in comparative form. What is Clark's responsibility concerning the proposed engagement?
a. Clark may **not** report on the comparative financial statements because the 20X1 statements are **not** comparable to the 20X2 statements that include the GAAP disclosures.
b. Clark may report on the comparative financial statements provided Clark updates the report on the 20X1 statements that do **not** include the GAAP disclosures.
c. Clark may report on the comparative financial statements provided an explanatory paragraph is added to Clark's report on the comparative financial statements.
d. Clark may report on the comparative financial statements provided the 20X1 statements do **not** contain any obvious material misstatements.
(5/92, Aud., #4, amended, 2757)

18. What type of analytical procedure would an auditor most likely use in developing relationships among balance sheet accounts when reviewing the financial statements of a nonpublic entity?
a. Trend analysis
b. Regression analysis
c. Ratio analysis
d. Risk analysis (5/95, Aud., #74, 5692)

19. Which of the following procedures should an accountant perform during an engagement to review the financial statements of a nonpublic entity?
a. Communicating reportable conditions discovered during the assessment of control risk
b. Obtaining a representation letter from members of management
c. Sending bank confirmation letters to the entity's financial institutions
d. Examining cash disbursements in the subsequent period for unrecorded liabilities
(11/94, Aud., #75, amended, 5148)

20. Each page of a nonpublic entity's financial statements reviewed by an accountant should include the following reference:
a. See Accompanying Accountant's Footnotes.
b. Reviewed, **No** Material Modifications Required.
c. See Accountant's Review Report.
d. Reviewed, No Accountant's Assurance Expressed. (5/95, Aud., #81, 5699)

21. Baker, CPA, was engaged to review the financial statements of Hall Co., a nonpublic entity. During the engagement Baker uncovered a complex scheme involving client illegal acts and fraud that materially affect Hall's financial statements. If Baker believes that modification of the standard review report is **not** adequate to indicate the deficiencies in the financial statements, Baker should
a. Disclaim an opinion.
b. Issue an adverse opinion.
c. Withdraw from the engagement.
d. Issue a qualified opinion.
(5/95, Aud., #80, amended, 5698)

22. During an engagement to review the financial statements of a nonpublic entity, an accountant becomes aware that several leases that should be capitalized are not capitalized. The accountant considers these leases to be material to the financial statements. The accountant decides to modify the standard review report because management will not capitalize the leases. Under these circumstances, the accountant should
a. Issue an adverse opinion because of the departure from GAAP.
b. Express **no** assurance of any kind on the entity's financial statements.
c. Emphasize that the financial statements are for limited use only.
d. Disclose the departure from GAAP in a separate paragraph of the accountant's report.
(5/96, Aud., #7, 6239)

23. Financial statements of a nonpublic entity that have been reviewed by an accountant should be accompanied by a report stating that a review
a. Provides only limited assurance that the financial statements are fairly presented.
b. Includes examining, on a test basis, information that is the representation of management.
c. Consists principally of inquiries of company personnel and analytical procedures applied to financial data.
d. Does **not** contemplate obtaining corroborating evidential matter or applying certain other procedures ordinarily performed during an audit.
(11/95, Aud., #79, 6026)

24. The standard report issued by an accountant after reviewing the financial statements of a nonpublic entity states that
a. A review includes assessing the accounting principles used and significant estimates made by management.
b. A review includes examining, on a test basis, evidence supporting the amounts and disclosures in the financial statements.
c. The accountant is **not** aware of any material modifications that should be made to the financial statements.
d. The accountant does **not** express an opinion or any other form of assurance on the financial statements. (11/92, Aud., #53, 2987)

25. Gole, CPA, is engaged to review the 20X2 financial statements of North Co., a nonpublic entity. Previously, Gole audited North's 20X1 financial statements and expressed an unqualified opinion. Gole decides to include a separate paragraph in the 20X2 review report because North plans to present comparative financial statements for 20X2 and 20X1. This separate paragraph should indicate that
a. The 20X2 review report is intended solely for the information of management and the board of directors.
b. There are justifiable reasons for changing the level of service from an audit to a review.
c. No auditing procedures were performed after the date of the 20X1 auditor's report.
d. The 20X1 auditor's report may **no** longer be relied on. (11/94, Aud., #79, amended, 5152)

26. Moore, CPA, has been asked to issue a review report on the balance sheet of Dover Co., a nonpublic entity. Moore will not be reporting on Dover's statements of income, retained earnings, and cash flows. Moore may issue the review report provided the
a. Balance sheet is presented in a prescribed form of an industry trade association.
b. Scope of the inquiry and analytical procedures has **not** been restricted.
c. Balance sheet is **not** to be used to obtain credit or distributed to creditors.
d. Specialized accounting principles and practices of Dover's industry are disclosed.
(5/95, Aud., #79, 5697)

27. Financial information is presented in a printed form that prescribes the wording of the independent auditor's report. The form is not acceptable to the auditor because the form calls for statements that are inconsistent with the auditor's responsibility. Under these circumstances, the auditor most likely would
a. Withdraw from the engagement.
b. Reword the form or attach a separate report.
c. Express a qualified opinion with an explanation.
d. Limit distribution of the report to the party who designed the form. (11/96, Aud., #16, 6368)

28. Must a CPA in public practice be independent in fact and appearance when providing the following services?

	Compilation of personal financial statements	*Preparation of a tax return*	*Compilation of a financial forecast*
a.	No	No	No
b.	No	No	Yes
c.	Yes	No	No
d.	No	Yes	No

(5/92, Aud., #56, 2809)

29. Kell engaged March, CPA, to submit to Kell a written personal financial plan containing unaudited personal financial statements. March anticipates omitting certain disclosures required by GAAP because the engagement's sole purpose is to assist Kell in developing a personal financial plan. For March to be exempt from complying with the requirements of SSARS 1, *Compilation and Review of Financial Statements*, Kell is required to agree that the

a. Financial statements will **not** be presented in comparative form with those of the prior period.
b. Omitted disclosures required by GAAP are **not** material.
c. Financial statements will **not** be disclosed to a non-CPA financial planner.
d. Financial statements will **not** be used to obtain credit. (5/95, Aud., #21, 5639)

30. An entity engaged a CPA to determine whether the client's web sites meet defined criteria for standard business practices and controls over transaction integrity and information protection. In performing this engagement, the CPA should comply with the provisions of

a. Statements on Assurance Standards.
b. Statements on Standards for Attestation Engagements.
c. Statements on Standards for Management Consulting Services.
d. Statements on Auditing Standards (R/99, Aud., #3, 6819)

31. In performing an attestation engagement, a CPA typically

a. Supplies litigation support services.
b. Assesses control risk at a low level.
c. Expresses a conclusion about an assertion.
d. Provides management consulting advice. (11/93, Aud., #9, 4246)

32. Which of the following is a conceptual difference between the attestation standards and generally accepted auditing standards?

a. The attestation standards provide a framework for the attest function beyond historical financial statements.
b. The requirement that the practitioner be independent in mental attitude is omitted from the attestation standards.
c. The attestation standards do **not** permit an attest engagement to be part of a business acquisition study or a feasibility study.
d. **None** of the standards of field work in generally accepted auditing standards are included in the attestation standards. (5/94, Aud., #10, 4675)

33. Negative assurance may be expressed when an accountant is requested to report on the

I. Results of applying agreed-upon procedures to an account within unaudited financial statements.
II. Compilation of prospective financial statements.

a. I only.
b. II only.
c. Both I and II.
d. Neither I or II. (Editors, 0430)

34. Which of the following is **not** an attestation standard?

a. Sufficient evidence shall be obtained to provide a reasonable basis for the conclusion that is expressed in the report.
b. The report shall identify the assertion being reported on and state the character of the engagement.
c. The work shall be adequately planned and assistants, if any, shall be properly supervised.
d. A sufficient understanding of internal control shall be obtained to plan the engagement. (5/93, Aud., #4, amended, 3900)

35. An accountant's standard report on a compilation of a projection should **not** include a

a. Statement that a compilation of a projection is limited in scope.
b. Disclaimer of responsibility to update the report for events occurring after the report's date.
c. Statement that the accountant expresses only limited assurance that the results may be achieved.
d. Separate paragraph that describes the limitations on the presentation's usefulness. (11/93, Aud., #57, 4294)

36. An accountant may accept an engagement to apply agreed-upon procedures to prospective financial statements provided that

a. Use of the report is restricted to the specified users.
b. The prospective financial statements are also examined.
c. Responsibility for the adequacy of the procedures performed is taken by the accountant.
d. Negative assurance is expressed on the prospective financial statements taken as a whole. (11/94, Aud., #23, amended, 5096)

37. When an accountant examines a financial forecast that fails to disclose several significant assumptions used to prepare the forecast, the accountant should describe the assumptions in the accountant's report and issue a(an)
a. Unqualified opinion with a separate explanatory paragraph.
b. "Subject to" qualified opinion.
c. "Except for" qualified opinion.
d. Adverse opinion. (Editors, 0432)

38. When an accountant examines projected financial statements, the accountant's report should include a separate paragraph that
a. Describes the limitations on the usefulness of the presentation.
b. Provides an explanation of the differences between an examination and an audit.
c. States that the accountant is responsible for events and circumstances up to one year after the report's date.
d. Disclaims an opinion on whether the assumptions provide a reasonable basis for the projection. (11/95, Aud., #82, 6029)

39. Which of the following conditions is necessary for a practitioner to accept an attest engagement to examine and report on an entity's internal control over financial reporting?
a. The practitioner anticipates relying on the entity's internal control in a financial statement audit.
b. Management presents its written assertion about the effectiveness of internal control.
c. The practitioner is a continuing auditor who previously has audited the entity's financial statements.
d. Management agrees **not** to present the practitioner's report in a general-use document to stockholders.
(11/94, Aud., #18, amended, 5091)

40. In reporting on an entity's internal control over financial reporting, a practitioner should include a paragraph that describes the
a. Documentary evidence regarding the control environment factors.
b. Changes in internal control since the prior report.
c. Potential benefits from the practitioner's suggested improvements.
d. Inherent limitations of any internal control structure. (5/95, Aud., #84, amended, 5702)

41. Brown, CPA, has accepted an engagement to examine and report on Crow Company's written assertion about the effectiveness of Crow's internal control. In what form may Crow present its written assertion?

I. In a separate report that will accompany Brown's report
II. In a representation letter to Brown

a. Neither I nor II
b. Either I or II
c. I only
d. II only (11/95, Aud., #36, amended, 5983)

42. Payroll Data Co. (PDC) processes payroll transactions for a retailer. Cook, CPA, is engaged to express an opinion on a description of PDC's internal controls placed in operation as of a specific date. These controls are relevant to the retailer's internal control, so Cook's report may be useful in providing the retailer's independent auditor with information necessary to plan a financial statement audit. Cook's report should
a. Contain a warning that misstatements may occur and not be detected.
b. State whether PDC's controls were suitably designed to achieve the retailer's objectives.
c. Identify PDC's controls relevant to specific financial statement assertions.
d. Disclose Cook's assessed level of control risk for PDC. (R/99, Aud., #30, amended 6846)

43. Lake, CPA, is auditing the financial statements of Gill Co. Gill uses the EDP Service Center, Inc. to process its payroll transactions. EDP's financial statements are audited by Cope, CPA, who recently issued a report on EDP's internal control. Lake is considering Cope's report on EDP's internal control in assessing control risk on the Gill engagement. What is Lake's responsibility concerning making reference to Cope as a basis, in part, for Lake's own opinion?
a. Lake may refer to Cope only if Lake is satisfied as to Cope's professional reputation and independence.
b. Lake may refer to Cope only if Lake relies on Cope's report in restricting the extent of substantive tests.
c. Lake may refer to Cope only if Lake's report indicates the division of responsibility.
d. Lake may not refer to Cope under the circumstances above.
(5/94, Aud., #36, amended, 4701)

44. A CPA's report on agreed-upon procedures related to management's assertion about an entity's compliance with specified requirements should contain

a. A statement of limitations on the use of the report.
b. An opinion about whether management's assertion is fairly stated.
c. Negative assurance that control risk has **not** been assessed.
d. An acknowledgment of responsibility for the sufficiency of the procedures.

(11/95, Aud., #81, 6028)

45. An accountant's report on a review of pro forma financial information should include a

a. Statement that the entity's internal control was **not** relied on in the review.
b. Disclaimer of opinion on the financial statements from which the pro forma financial information is derived.
c. Caveat that it is uncertain whether the transaction or event reflected in the pro forma financial information will ever occur.
d. Reference to the financial statements from which the historical financial information is derived.

(5/94, Aud., #68, amended, 4733)

PROBLEM 41-2 ADDITIONAL MULTIPLE CHOICE QUESTIONS (50 to 63 minutes)

46. The authoritative body designated to promulgate standards concerning an accountant's association with unaudited financial statements of an entity that is **not** required to file financial statements with an agency regulating the issuance of the entity's securities is the

a. Financial Accounting Standards Board.
b. General Accounting Office.
c. Accounting and Review Services Committee.
d. Auditing Standards Board.

(11/90, Aud., #40, 0006)

47. When unaudited financial statements are presented in comparative form with audited financial statements in a document filed with the Securities and Exchange Commission, such statements should be

	Marked as "unaudited"	*Withheld until audited*	*Referred to in the auditor's report*
a.	Yes	No	No
b.	Yes	No	Yes
c.	No	Yes	Yes
d.	No	Yes	No

(11/93, Aud., #50, 4287)

48. Which of the following statements is correct concerning both an engagement to compile and an engagement to review a nonpublic entity's financial statements?

a. The accountant should obtain a written management representation letter.
b. The accountant must be independent in fact and appearance.
c. The accountant expresses **no** assurance on the financial statements.
d. The accountant does **not** contemplate obtaining an understanding of internal control.

(11/91, Aud., #59, amended, 2327)

49. When providing limited assurance that the financial statements of a nonpublic entity require **no** material modifications to be in accordance with generally accepted accounting principles, the accountant should

a. Assess the risk that a material misstatement could occur in a financial statement assertion.
b. Confirm with the entity's lawyer that material loss contingencies are disclosed.
c. Understand the accounting principles of the industry in which the entity operates.
d. Develop audit programs to determine whether the entity's financial statements are fairly presented.

(5/95, Aud., #58, 5676)

50. *Statements on Standards for Accounting and Review Services* (SSARS) require an accountant to report when the accountant has

a. Typed client-prepared financial statements, without modification, as an accommodation to the client.
b. Provided a client with a financial statement format that does **not** include dollar amounts, to be used by the client in preparing financial statements.
c. Proposed correcting journal entries to be recorded by the client that change client-prepared financial statements.
d. Generated, through the use of computer software, financial statements prepared in accordance with a comprehensive basis of accounting other than GAAP.

(11/94, Aud., #22, 5095)

51. *Statements on Standards for Accounting and Review Services* establish standards and procedures for which of the following engagements?
a. Assisting in adjusting the books of account for a partnership
b. Reviewing interim financial data required to be filed with the SEC
c. Processing financial data for clients of other accounting firms
d. Compiling an individual's personal financial statement to be used to obtain a mortgage
(11/91, Aud., #13, 2281)

52. Which of the following procedures is ordinarily performed by an accountant in a compilation engagement of a nonpublic entity?
a. Reading the financial statements to consider whether they are free of obvious mistakes in the application of accounting principles.
b. Obtaining written representations from management indicating that the compiled financial statements will **not** be used to obtain credit.
c. Making inquiries of management concerning actions taken at meetings of the stockholders and the board of directors.
d. Applying analytical procedures designed to corroborate management's assertions that are embodied in the financial statement components.
(5/95, Aud., #75, 5693)

53. When compiling the financial statements of a nonpublic entity, an accountant should
a. Review agreements with financial institutions for restrictions on cash balances.
b. Understand the accounting principles and practices of the entity's industry.
c. Inquire of key personnel concerning related parties and subsequent events.
d. Perform ratio analyses of the financial data of comparable prior periods.
(11/92, Aud., #44, 2978)

54. How does an accountant make the following representations when issuing the standard report for the compilation of a nonpublic entity's financial statements?

	*The financial statements have **not** been audited*	*The accountant has compiled the financial statements*
a.	Implicitly	Implicitly
b.	Explicitly	Explicitly
c.	Implicitly	Explicitly
d.	Explicitly	Implicitly

(11/91, Aud., #26, 2294)

55. When an accountant is engaged to compile a nonpublic entity's financial statements that omit substantially all disclosures required by GAAP, the accountant should indicate in the compilation report that the financial statements are
a. Not designed for those who are uninformed about the omitted disclosures.
b. Prepared in conformity with a comprehensive basis of accounting other than GAAP.
c. Not compiled in accordance with Statements on Standards for Accounting and Review Services.
d. Special-purpose financial statements that are **not** comparable to those of prior periods.
(11/94, Aud., #82, 5155)

56. Which of the following procedures is usually performed by the accountant in a review engagement of a nonpublic entity?
a. Sending a letter of inquiry to the entity's lawyer
b. Comparing the financial statements with statements for comparable prior periods
c. Confirming a significant percentage of receivables by direct communication with debtors
d. Communicating reportable conditions discovered during the study of internal control
(5/92, Aud., #34, amended, 2787)

57. Which of the following inquiry or analytical procedures ordinarily is performed in an engagement to review a nonpublic entity's financial statements?
a. Analytical procedures designed to test the accounting records by obtaining corroborating evidential matter
b. Inquiries concerning the entity's procedures for recording and summarizing transactions
c. Analytical procedures designed to test management's assertions regarding continued existence
d. Inquiries of the entity's attorney concerning contingent liabilities (11/92, Aud., #43, 2977)

58. Which of the following procedures would an accountant **least** likely perform during an engagement to review the financial statements of a nonpublic entity?
a. Observing the safeguards over access to and use of assets and records
b. Comparing the financial statements with anticipated results in budgets and forecasts
c. Inquiring of management about actions taken at the board of directors' meetings
d. Studying the relationships of financial statement elements expected to conform to predictable patterns (11/94, Aud., #74, 5147)

59. An accountant has been engaged to review a nonpublic entity's financial statements that contain several departures from GAAP. If the financial statements are **not** revised and modification of the standard review report is **not** adequate to indicate the deficiencies, the accountant should

a. Withdraw from the engagement and provide **no** further services concerning these financial statements.
b. Inform management that the engagement can proceed only if distribution of the accountant's report is restricted to internal users.
c. Determine the effects of the departures from GAAP and issue a special report on the financial statements.
d. Issue a modified review report provided the entity agrees that the financial statements will **not** be used to obtain credit.

(11/94, Aud., #20, amended, 5093)

60. Which of the following procedures is **not** usually performed by the accountant during a review engagement of a nonpublic entity?

a. Inquiring about actions taken at meetings of the board of directors that may affect the financial statements.
b. Issuing a report stating that the review was performed in accordance with standards established by the AICPA.
c. Reading the financial statements to consider whether they conform with generally accepted accounting principles.
d. Communicating any material weaknesses discovered during the consideration of internal control. (11/92, Aud., #45, amended, 2979)

61. Which of the following is a prospective financial statement for general use upon which an accountant may appropriately report?

a. Pro forma financial statement
b. Partial presentation
c. Financial projection
d. Financial forecast (Editors, 9435)

62. Which of the following statements concerning prospective financial statements is correct?

a. Only a financial forecast would normally be appropriate for limited use.
b. Only a financial projection would normally be appropriate for general use.
c. Any type of prospective financial statement would normally be appropriate for limited use.
d. Any type of prospective financial statement would normally be appropriate for general use.

(5/90, Aud., #23, 0424)

63. An accountant's compilation report on a financial forecast should include a statement that

a. The forecast should be read only in conjunction with the audited historical financial statements.
b. The accountant expresses only limited assurance on the forecasted statements and their assumptions.
c. There will usually be differences between the forecasted and actual results.
d. The hypothetical assumptions used in the forecast are reasonable in the circumstances.

(11/94, Aud., #83, 5156)

64. Accepting an engagement to examine an entity's financial projection most likely would be appropriate if the projection were to be used by

a. All employees who work for the entity.
b. Potential stockholders who request a prospectus or a registration statement.
c. All stockholders of record as of the report date.
d. A bank with which the entity is negotiating for a loan. (5/94, Aud., #14, amended, 4679)

65. An examination of a financial forecast is a professional service that involves

a. Compiling or assembling a financial forecast that is based on management's assumptions.
b. Evaluating the preparation of a financial forecast and the support underlying management's assumptions.
c. Assuming responsibility to update management on key events for one year after the report's date.
d. Limiting the distribution of the accountant's report to management and the board of directors. (5/95, Aud., #22, amended, 5640)

66. An accountant has been engaged to report on an entity's internal controls without performing an audit of the financial statements. What restrictions, if any, should the accountant place on the use of this report?

a. The accountant does **not** need to place any restrictions on the use of this report.
b. This report should be restricted for use by the audit committee.
c. This report should be restricted for use by a specified regulatory agency.
d. This report should be restricted for use by management. (Editors, 0407)

67. How do the scope, procedures, and purpose of an engagement to express an opinion on an entity's system of internal accounting control compare to those for obtaining an understanding of internal control and assessing control risk as part of an audit?

	Scope	Procedures	Purpose
a.	Similar	Different	Similar
b.	Different	Similar	Similar
c.	Different	Different	Different
d.	Different	Similar	Different

(5/90, Aud., #40, amended, 0400)

68. An accountant's report expressing an opinion on an entity's internal controls should state that

a. Only those controls on which the accountant intends to rely were reviewed, tested, and evaluated.
b. The examination was made in accordance with standards established by the AICPA.
c. The study and evaluation of the internal controls was conducted in accordance with generally accepted auditing standards.
d. Distribution of the report is restricted for use only by management and the board of directors.

(Editors, 9433)

69. Computer Services Company (CSC) processes payroll transactions for schools. Drake, CPA, is engaged to report on CSC's policies and procedures placed in operation as of a specific date. These policies and procedures are relevant to the schools' internal control, so Drake's report will be useful in providing the schools' independent auditors with information necessary to plan their audits. Drake's report expressing an opinion on CSC's policies and procedures placed in operation as of a specific date should contain a(an)

a. Description of the scope and nature of Drake's procedures.
b. Statement that CSC's management has disclosed to Drake all design deficiencies of which it is aware.
c. Opinion on the operating effectiveness of CSC's policies and procedures.
d. Paragraph indicating the basis for Drake's assessment of control risk.

(11/95, Aud., #37, amended, 5984)

70. An accountant's report expressing an unqualified opinion on an entity's system of internal accounting control should state that the

a. Accountant did **not** apply procedures in the engagement that duplicate those procedures previously applied in assessing control risk as part of an audit.
b. Accountant's opinion does **not** necessarily increase the reliability of the entity's financial statements unless they are audited.
c. Practitioner believes the examination provided a reasonable basis for his or her opinion.
d. Engagement is different in purpose and scope from obtaining an understanding of internal control and assessing control risk as part of an audit. (Editors, 0394)

OTHER OBJECTIVE FORMAT QUESTIONS

PROBLEM 41-3 (15 to 25 minutes)

This question consists of 17 items pertaining to possible deficiencies in an accountant's report on comparative financial statements. Select the **best** answer for each item.

Wallace & Wallace, CPAs, audited the financial statements of West Co., a nonpublic entity, for the year ended September 30, 20X1, and expressed an unqualified opinion. For the year ended September 30, 20X2, West issued comparative financial statements. Wallace & Wallace reviewed West's 20X2 financial statements and Gordon, an assistant on the engagement, drafted the accountant's review report below. Martin, the engagement supervisor, decided not to reissue the prior year's auditor's report, but instructed Gordon to include a separate paragraph in the current year's review report describing the responsibility assumed for the prior year's audited financial statements.

Martin reviewed Gordon's draft and indicated in *Martin's Review Notes* that there were many deficiencies in Gordon's draft.

ACCOUNTANT'S REVIEW REPORT

We have reviewed the accompanying balance sheet of West Company as of September 30, 20X2, and the related statements of income and cash flows for the year then ended, in accordance with standards issued by the American Institute of Certified Public Accountants. All information included in these financial statements is the representation of the management of West Company. Our responsibility is to express limited assurance on these financial statements based on our review.

A review consists principally of inquiries of company personnel and analytical procedures applied to financial data. A review also includes assessing the accounting principles used and significant estimates made by management, as well as evaluating the overall financial statement presentation.

Based on our review, we are not aware of any material modifications that should be made to the accompanying financial statements. Accordingly, the accompanying financial statements have been prepared assuming that the company will continue as a going concern. Furthermore, we have no responsibility to update this report for events and circumstances occurring after the date of this report.

The financial statements for the year ended September 30, 20X1, were audited by us and we expressed an unqualified opinion on them in our report dated November 7, 20X1, but we have not performed any auditing procedures since that date. In our opinion, the financial statements referred to above are presented fairly, in all material respects, for the year then ended in conformity with generally accepted accounting principles.

Wallace & Wallace, CPAs
November 6, 20X2

REQUIRED:

ITEMS 1 THROUGH 17 represent the deficiencies noted by Martin. For each deficiency, indicate whether Martin is correct and Gordon is incorrect (M); Gordon is correct and Martin is incorrect (G); or both Martin and Gordon are incorrect (B).

Martin's Review Notes

1. There should be a reference to the prior year's audited financial statements in the first (introductory) paragraph.
2. All of the current year's basic financial statements are **not** properly identified in the first (introductory) paragraph.
3. The standards referred to in the first (introductory) paragraph should **not** be standards issued by the American Institute of Certified Public Accountants, but should be standards for the compilation and review of financial statements.
4. The accountant's responsibility to express limited assurance on the financial statements, mentioned in the first (introductory) paragraph, should be in the second (scope) paragraph.
5. There should be a reference to the prior year's audited financial statements in the second (scope) paragraph.
6. There should be a comparison of the scope of a review to an audit in the second (scope) paragraph.
7. There should be **no** reference to "assessing the accounting principles used," "significant estimates made by management," and "evaluating the overall financial statement presentation" in the second (scope) paragraph.
8. There should be a statement that **no** opinion is expressed on the current year's financial statements in the second (scope) paragraph.
9. There should be a reference to "conformity with generally accepted accounting principles" in the third paragraph.
10. There should be a reference to consistency in the third paragraph.
11. There should be a restriction on the distribution of the accountant's review report in the third paragraph.
12. The reference to "going concern" in the third paragraph should be in the second (scope) paragraph.
13. The accountant's lack of responsibility to update the report in the third paragraph should be in the second (scope) paragraph.
14. There should be **no** mention of the type of opinion expressed on the prior year's audited financial statements in the fourth (separate) paragraph.
15. All of the prior year's basic financial statements are **not** properly identified in the fourth (separate) paragraph.
16. The reference in the fourth (separate) paragraph to the fair presentation of the prior year's audited financial statements in accordance with generally accepted accounting principles should be omitted.
17. The report should be dual dated to indicate the date of the prior year's auditor's report.

(11/96, Aud., #2, amended, 6369-6385)

PROBLEM 41-4 (15 to 25 minutes)

ITEMS 1 THROUGH 15 represent a series of unrelated procedures that an accountant may consider performing in separate engagements to review the financial statements of a nonpublic entity (a review) and to compile the financial statements of a nonpublic entity (a compilation). Select, as the best answer for each item, whether the procedure is required (R) or not required (N) for both review and compilation engagements. Select the **best** answer for each item. Make two selections for each procedure.

1. The accountant should establish an understanding with the entity regarding the nature and limitations of the services to be performed.

2. The accountant should make inquiries concerning actions taken at the board of directors' meetings.

3. The accountant, as the entity's successor accountant, should communicate with the predecessor accountant to obtain access to the predecessor's working papers.

4. The accountant should obtain a level of knowledge of the accounting principles and practices of the entity's industry.

5. The accountant should obtain an understanding of the entity's internal control structure.

6. The accountant should perform analytical procedures designed to identify relationships that appear to be unusual.

7. The accountant should make an assessment of the control risk.

8. The accountant should send a letter of inquiry to the entity's attorney to corroborate the information furnished by management concerning litigation.

9. The accountant should obtain a management representation letter from the entity.

10. The accountant should study the relationships of the financial statement elements that would be expected to conform to a predictable pattern.

11. The accountant should communicate to the entity's senior management illegal employee acts discovered by the accountant that are clearly inconsequential.

12. The accountant should make inquiries about events subsequent to the date of the financial statements that would have a material effect on the financial statements.

13. The accountant should modify the accountant's report if there is a change in accounting principles that is adequately disclosed.

14. The accountant should submit a hard copy of the financial statements and accountant's report when the financial statements and accountant's report are submitted on a computer disk.

15. The accountant should perform specific procedures to evaluate whether there is substantial doubt about the entity's ability to continue as a going concern. (11/95, Aud., #91-105, 6053-6082)

ESSAY QUESTIONS

ESSAY 41-5 (15 to 25 minutes)

The following report was drafted on October 25, 20X1, by Major, CPA, at the completion of the engagement to compile the financial statements of Ajax Company for the year ended September 30, 20X1. Ajax is a nonpublic entity in which Major's child has a material direct financial interest. Ajax decided to omit substantially all of the disclosures required by generally accepted accounting principles because the financial statements will be for management's use only. The statement of cash flows was also omitted because management does not believe it to be a useful financial statement.

To the Board of Directors of Ajax Company:

I have compiled the accompanying financial statements of Ajax Company as of September 30, 20X1, and for the year then ended. I planned and performed the compilation to obtain limited assurance about whether the financial statements are free of material misstatements.

A compilation is limited to presenting information in the form of financial statements. It is substantially less in scope than an audit in accordance with generally accepted auditing standards, the objective of which is the expression of an opinion regarding the financial statements taken as a whole. I have not audited the accompanying financial statements and, accordingly, do not express any opinion on them.

Management has elected to omit substantially all of the disclosures required by generally accepted accounting principles. If the omitted disclosures were included in the financial statements, they might influence the user's conclusions about the Company's financial position, results of operations, and changes in financial position.

I am not independent with respect to Ajax Company. This lack of independence is due to my child's ownership of a material direct financial interest in Ajax Company.

This report is intended solely for the information and use of the Board of Directors and management of Ajax Company and should not be used for any other purpose.

Major, CPA

REQUIRED:

Identify the deficiencies contained in Major's report on the compiled financial statements. Group the deficiencies by paragraph where applicable. Do **not** redraft the report. (11/90, Aud., #5, amended, 3069)

ESSAY 41-6 (15 to 25 minutes)

An accountant is sometimes called on by clients to report on or assemble prospective financial statements for use by third parties.

REQUIRED:

a. 1. Identify the types of engagements that an accountant may perform under these circumstances.

2. Explain the difference between "general use" of and "limited use" of prospective financial statements.

3. Explain what types of prospective financial statements are appropriate for "general use" and what types are appropriate for "limited use."

b. Describe the contents of the accountant's standard report on a compilation of a financial projection. (5/88, Aud., #2, 3074)

ESSAY 41-7 (25 to 35 minutes)

Hart, CPA, has been approached by Unidyne Co. to accept an attest engagement to examine and report on management's written assertion about the effectiveness of Unidyne's internal control over financial reporting as of June 30, 20X1, the end of its fiscal year.

REQUIRED:

a. Describe the required conditions that must be met for Hart to accept an attest engagement to examine and report on management's assertion about the effectiveness of Unidyne's internal control.

b. Describe the broad engagement activities that would be involved in Hart's performing an examination of management's assertion about the effectiveness of Unidyne's internal control.

c. Describe the other types of attest services that Hart may provide and those specifically **not** permitted in connection with Unidyne's internal control. (5/95, Aud., #4, amended, 6160)

SOLUTION 41-1 MULTIPLE CHOICE ANSWERS

COMPILATIONS & REVIEWS

1. (a) AR 100.01 states, "The accountant should not issue any report on the unaudited financial statements of a nonpublic entity or submit such financial statements to his [or her] client or others unless he [or she] complies with the provisions of SSARS." Answer (b) does not exist. Answers (c) and (d) apply to other specific types of engagements.

2. (d) AR 100.12 states that for a compilation of financial statements, "The accountant is not required to make inquiries or perform other procedures to verify, corroborate, or review information supplied by the entity." AR 100.04 states that a review of financial statements involves performing inquiry and analytical procedures that provide the accountant with a reasonable basis for expressing limited assurance that there are no material modifications that should be made to the statements in order for them to be in conformity with GAAP.

3. (b) AR 100.05 states, "...whenever an accountant compiles or reviews financial statements of a nonpublic entity, he [or she] should issue a report prepared in accordance with the applicable standards....However, when the accountant performs more than one service (for example, a compilation and an audit), he [or she] should issue the report that is appropriate for the highest level of service rendered."

4. (d) AR 100.10 states that for a compilation, and AR 100.25 states that for a review, the requirement that the accountant possess a level of knowledge of the accounting principles and practices of the industry in which the entity operates does not prevent an accountant from accepting a compilation or review engagement for an entity. However, it does place upon the accountant a responsibility to obtain the required level of knowledge.

5. (b) AR 100.38 states, "An accountant is precluded from issuing a review report on the financial statement of an entity with respect to which he [or she] is not independent." Judgments about independence should be guided by the AICPA Code of Professional Conduct. Rule 101 states that independence is considered impaired if there is *any* direct or material indirect financial interest.

6. (c) AR 100.49 notes that when there is reasonable justification to change the engagement because of scope restriction, the report should not include reference to the original engagement, any auditing procedures that were performed, or the scope limitation.

SSARS

7. (d) AR 100.02 states that the SSARS do not establish standards or procedures for other accounting services such as consulting on accounting, tax, and similar matters, or processing financial data for clients of other accounting firms.

8. (d) AR 100.07 states, "The following services do not constitute a submission of financial statements:...typing or reproducing client-prepared financial statements, without modification, as an accommodation to a client...[and] preparing standard monthly journal entries (e.g., standard entries for depreciation and expiration of prepaid expenses)."

Compilation Engagements

9. (a) AR 110.11 states, "To compile financial statements, the accountant should possess a general understanding of the nature of the entity's business transactions, the form of its accounting records, the stated qualifications of its accounting personnel...." Generally, a compilation of financial statements is limited to presenting information that is the representation of management in the form of financial statements without undertaking to express any assurance on the statements. Generally, internal control is not considered in a compilation.

10. (a) AR 100.20 notes that if financial statements which are compiled in conformity with a comprehensive basis of accounting other than GAAP do not include disclosure of the basis, the accountant must disclose the basis. Answers (b), (c), and (d) are not options mentioned in the Standards.

11. (c) AR 100.19 presents both requirements.

Compilation Reports

12. (c) AR 100.14 prescribes the components of a compilation report; including the requirements noted in answer (c). (Also see the explanation to question #20.) Answer (a) is incorrect because it refers to GAAS. By using the term "limited assurance," answer (b) is referring to a review. The AICPA establishes the standards.

13. (c) According to AR 100.14, "Financial statements compiled without audit or review should be accompanied by a report stating that...the accountant does not express an opinion or any other form of assurance on the financial statements." One of the elements of a compilation report is that the "statements have not been audited or reviewed and, therefore, no opinion or other form of assurance is expressed on them." No reference to testing the financial information or to assessing the principles and estimates used is made in the report. Testing the information supplied is not required in a compilation. A *review* consists primarily of inquiries of entity personnel and analytical procedures applied to financial data.

14. (b) According to AR 100.14, the compilation report should state, "A compilation has been performed in accordance with Statements on Standards for Accounting and Review Services issued by the [AICPA]." A compilation does not include the assessments and evaluations in answer (a) and thus this would not be appropriate in a compilation report. Answers (c) and (d) are both items that should be in a report accompanying a review, but not in a compilation report.

15. (d) Just as working papers need not be stored on paper, there is no requirement that a compilation report be printed on paper (including letterhead) or that it be manually signed.

16. (a) An accountant would only explicitly discuss independence in the compilation report when he or she *lacks* independence. Thus, when the accountant is independent, it is not specifically stated in the report. AR 100.14 states that financial statements compiled by an accountant should be

accompanied by a report stating that the financial statements have not been audited or reviewed and, accordingly, the accountant does not express an opinion or any other form of assurance on them; thus answers (b) and (d) are *explicitly* stated. Inquiry and analytical procedures are performed during a review engagement, not in a compilation.

17. (a) AR 200.05 states, "Compiled financial statements that omit substantially all of the disclosures required by [GAAP] are not comparable to financial statements that include such disclosures. Accordingly, the accountant should not issue a report on the comparative financial statements when statements for one or more, but not all, of the periods presented omit substantially all of the disclosures required by [GAAP]."

Review Engagements

18. (c) In reviewing the financial statements of a nonpublic entity, the auditor would most likely use ratio analysis as the analytical procedure for developing relationships among balance sheet accounts. Ratios are useful in evaluating an entity's solvency. Ratio analysis that includes relationships between income statement and balance sheet accounts are useful in evaluating operational efficiency and profitability. Ratio analysis provides an indication of the firm's financial strengths and weaknesses.

19. (b) Obtaining a management representation letter is required by AR 100.28. The procedures in (a), (c), and (d) are not mentioned.

20. (c) AR 100.16 states, "Each page of the financial statements reviewed by the accountant should include a reference, such as 'See Accountant's Review Report.'"

21. (c) AR 100.41 states that when the accountant believes that modification of the standard report is not adequate to indicate the deficiencies in the financial statements as a whole, the accountant should withdraw from the compilation or review engagement.

Review Reports

22. (d) AR 100.39 states, that when a departure from GAAP is in the financial statements, "....If the financial statements are not revised, the accountant should consider whether modification of his [or her] standard report is adequate to disclose the departure." AR 100.40 states "If the accountant concludes that modification of the standard report is appropriate, the departure should be disclosed in a separate paragraph...." The other answers are irrelevant to this circumstance. Answer (a) is appropriate to an audit.

23. (c) AR 100.32 states, "Financial statements reviewed by an accountant should be accompanied by a report stating that a review consists primarily of inquiries of company personnel and analytical procedures applied to the financial data." A review report *disclaims* an opinion on the fair presentation of the financial statements. An *audit* report mentions "examining, on a test basis, information that is the representation of management." A review report does not mention the items in answer (d).

24. (c) Among the statements set forth in AR 100.32 for inclusion in the standard report for a financial statement review is, "The accountant is not aware of any material modifications that should be made to the financial statements in order for them to be in conformity with generally accepted accounting principles, other than those modifications, if any, indicated in his [or her] report." "A review consists principally of inquiries of company personnel and analytical procedures applied to financial data." A review report does not express an opinion, but it does indicate *limited assurance.*

25. (c) AR 200.28 notes that if the accountant issues a report on the current period with a separate paragraph covering the prior period, the separate paragraph should include a statement that no auditing procedures were performed since the date of the previous report. Answers (a), (b), and (d) are not noted in AR 200.28.

26. (b) According to AR 100.37, the CPA may issue the review report on just the balance sheet "if the scope of his [or her] inquiry and analytical procedures has not been restricted." This is the only restriction provided for in the Code.

Prescribed Forms

27. (b) AU §323.33 states, "When a printed report form calls upon an independent auditor to make a statement that he of she is not justified in making, the auditor should reword the form or attach a separate report."

Personal Financial Statements

28. (a) The CPA need not be independent to perform compilation services; nor must he or she be independent to prepare a tax return for a client.

29. (d) AR 600.03 includes an understanding with the client that the financial statements will not

be used to obtain credit as one condition of exemption from SSARS 1. The statements may be presented in comparative form and may be in conformity with GAAP or another comprehensive basis of accounting. The certification of the user financial planner is irrelevant to the issuance of the report.

ATTESTATION STANDARDS

30. (b) Attestation engagements involve the expression of a written report on an assertion by another party. Statements on Auditing Standards apply to interim reviews of public companies' financial statements and financial statement audits.

31. (c) AT 100.01 states, "An attest engagement is one in which a practitioner is engaged to issue or does issue a written communication that expresses a conclusion about the reliability of a written assertion that is the responsibility of another party." Answers (a) and (d) are specifically identified in AT 100.02 as examples of services not considered to be attest engagements. The CPA would not necessarily assess control risk during every attestation engagement.

32. (a) AT 100.05 states that an attest engagement may be part of a larger engagement, such as a feasibility study, that includes an examination of prospective financial information. Answer (b) represents the fourth general standard for attestations. The two attestation field work standards are the same as the first and third standards of field work for audits, or GAAS.

33. (d) AU 622.26 states, "An accountant should present the results of applying agreed-upon procedures to specific subject matter in the form of findings. The accountant should not provide negative assurance about whether the specified elements, accounts, or items of a financial statement are fairly stated in accordance with established or stated criteria...." AT 200.11 states, "A compilation is not intended to provide assurance on the prospective financial statements or the assumptions underlying such statements."

34. (d) A sufficient understanding of internal control for planning an engagement is not a requirement of the general, fieldwork, or reporting standards for an attestation engagement. AT 100.82 provides a comparison of the Attestation Standards with GAAS. Answer (a) represents the second standard of fieldwork, answer (b) represents the first standard of reporting, and answer (c) represents the first standard of fieldwork for an attestation engagement.

FINANCIAL FORECASTS & PROJECTIONS

35. (c) AT 200.16 states, "The accountant's standard report on a compilation of prospective financial statements should include...a statement that a compilation is limited in scope and does not enable the accountant to express an opinion or any other form of assurance on the prospective financial statements or the assumptions...[and] a statement that the accountant assumes no responsibility to update the report for events and circumstances occurring after the date of the report." AT 200.18 states, "The accountant's report should include a separate paragraph that describes the limitations on the usefulness of the presentation."

36. (a) AT 200.50 states, "An accountant may perform an agreed-upon procedures attestation engagement to prospective financial statements provided that,...use of the report is to be restricted to the specified users." SSAE 4 merely requires the subject matter to be subject to reasonably consistent estimation or measurement. Responsibility for adequacy for the procedures performed is taken by the specified users, not the accountant (AT 200.50). AT 600.26 states, "The practitioner should not provide negative assurance...."

37. (d) When a CPA examines a financial forecast that fails to disclose several assumptions that, at the time, appear to be significant, the CPA should describe the assumptions in the report and issue an adverse opinion (AT 200.40).

38. (a) According to AT 200.33, the report contains a paragraph describing the limitations on the use of the presentation. The report does not provide an explanation of the differences between an examination and an audit. The accountant is not responsible for events occurring after the date of the report. The standard report contains the phrase, "In our opinion, the underlying assumptions provide a reasonable basis for management's projection."

REPORTING ON INTERNAL CONTROL

39. (b) AT 400.10 states, "A practitioner may examine and report on management's assertion about the effectiveness of an entity's internal control structure if...(d.) management presents its written assertion...about the effectiveness of the entity's internal control." Answer (a) is not a requirement for accepting the engagement. Answer (c) is not a requirement; this engagement can be performed for new clients and may be a revenue-generating source of new business. Answer (d) is not required for acceptance of the engagement, but would be part of the reporting requirements if management's

assertion is presented only in a representation letter to the practitioner.

40. (d) AT 400.45 states that the practitioner's report should include a paragraph describing the inherent limitations of any internal control structure. AT 400.45 states that the practitioner's report should include a statement that the engagement included testing and evaluating the design and effectiveness of internal control. Evidence obtained would not be reported. Answer (b) is incorrect; the practitioner is reporting on the current year controls only. The practitioner would not include suggested improvements in his or her report.

41. (b) In accordance with AT 400.03, management may present its written assertion about the effectiveness of the entity's internal control in **either** of two forms—in a separate report that will accompany the practitioner's report, or in a representation letter to the practitioner.

42. (a) Cook was engaged to express an opinion on a description of internal controls, not on the operating effectiveness of those controls. Evaluating whether the controls are suitably designed to achieve PDC's client's objectives, identifying control relevant to PDC's client's assertions, or assessing a level of control risk are beyond the scope of this engagement.

43. (d) AU 324.21 states, "The user auditor should not make reference to the report of the service auditor as a basis,...for his or her own opinion."

Other Attestation Engagements

44. (a) According to AT 500.23, a report on an engagement consisting of applying agreed-upon procedures related to management's assertion about compliance with specific requirements should include a statement of limitations on the use of the report. A practitioner's report on the application of agreed-upon procedures ordinarily should also indicate that the work performed was less in scope than an examination and disclaim an opinion on the assertions. Negative assurance as to fair statement of the assertion is not allowed. Negative assurance concerning the assessment of control risk is not expressed. The CPA does not take responsibility for the sufficiency of the procedures.

45. (d) AT 300.12 states, "The accountant's report on pro forma financial information should include...reference to the financial statements from which the historical financial information is derived...." The statement in answer (a) should not be made in any review engagement. Answer (b) is incorrect because the report on pro forma information is a different engagement from reporting on the financial statements from which the pro forma information was derived. A review report would not require a disclaimer because the accountant is not issuing an opinion. No reference to uncertainty should be made as that is assumed, based upon the nature of the engagement, and the accountant need only provide a conclusion as to whether any information came to his or her attention to cause him or her to believe management's assumptions do not provide a reasonable basis for the effects directly attributable to the transaction or event or that the pro forma column does not reflect the proper application of those adjustments to the historical financial statements.

Solution 41-2 ADDITIONAL MULTIPLE CHOICE ANSWERS

Compilations & Reviews

46. (c) SSARS are issued by the AICPA Accounting and Review Services Committee, the senior technical committee of the institute designated to issue pronouncements in connection with the unaudited financial statements or other unaudited financial information of a *nonpublic* entity.

47. (a) AU 504.14 states, "When unaudited financial statements are presented in comparative form with audited financial statements in documents filed with the Securities and Exchange Commission, such statements should be clearly marked as 'unaudited' but not referred to in the auditor's report."

48. (d) AR 100.04 states that neither a review nor a compilation engagement contemplates "obtaining an understanding of internal control...or assessing control risk, testing of accounting records and of responses to inquiries by obtaining corroborating evidential matter,...and certain other procedures ordinarily performed during an audit."

49. (c) In a review of financial statements, where the CPA expresses limited assurance that the financial statements do not contain material

deviations from GAAP, the accountant is required to obtain a knowledge of the accounting principles and practices of the industry in which the entity operates. This is required so that the CPA can determine and apply proper inquiry and analytical procedures. It is not intended that the CPA will apply the procedures listed in the other answers for a review.

SSARS

50. (d) SSARS 1 indicates that the CPA must, at a minimum, comply with the provisions applicable to a compilation when submitting unaudited financial statements of a nonpublic entity. Submission of financial statement is defined as presenting to the client financial statements the accountant has generated, either manually or through the use of computer software. Answers (a), (b), and (c) are examples, per AR 100.02, of services that do **not** constitute the submission of financial statements.

51. (d) A written personal financial plan containing unaudited personal financial statements may be submitted to a client without complying with the requirements of SSARS 1 if they will not be used to obtain credit. However, when the personal financial statement is compiled and used for any other purposes than developing financial goals, the accountant must follow SSARS standards and procedures (AR 600.03).

Compilations

52. (a) AR 100.13 states, "Before issuing his [or her] report, the accountant should read the compiled financial statements and consider whether such financial statements appear to be appropriate in form and free from obvious material errors. In this context, the term *error* refers to mistakes in the compilation of financial statements, including arithmetical or clerical mistakes, and mistakes in the application of accounting principles, including inadequate disclosure." A representation letter from members of management is not usually obtained in a compilation engagement. Inquiries of management concerning actions taken at meetings of the stockholders and the board of directors is an analytical procedure normally used in a review engagement [AR 100.27(d)] but not necessary in a compilation engagement. AR 100.12 states, "The accountant is not required to make inquiries or perform other procedures to verify, corroborate, or review information supplied by the entity."

53. (b) AR 100.10 states, "The accountant should possess a level of knowledge of the accounting principles and practices of the industry in which the entity operates that will enable him [or her] to compile financial statements that are appropriate in form for an entity operating in that industry." Answers (a), (c), and (d) represent procedures beyond the scope of a compilation.

54. (b) AR 100.14 states, "Financial statements compiled without audit or review by an accountant should be accompanied by a report stating that—(1) A compilation has been performed in accordance with Statements on Standards for Accounting and Review Services issued by the American Institute of Certified Public Accountants. (2) A compilation is limited to presenting in the form of financial statements information that is the representation of management (owners). (3) The financial statements have not been audited or reviewed and, accordingly, the accountant does not express an opinion or any other form of assurance on them."

55. (a) AR 100.21 presents an example report of this situation. Further, AR 100.19 notes that when compiled financial statements omit substantially all disclosures, the accountant should indicate that substantially all disclosures are omitted. Answers (b), (c), and (d) are not options allowed by the Standards.

Reviews

56. (b) An accountant's review procedures will include inquiry and analytical procedures. Analytical procedures are designed to identify relationships and individual items that appear to be unusual, and consist of (1) comparison of the financial statements with statements for comparable prior period(s), (2) comparison of the statements with anticipated results, if available, and (3) study of the relationships of the elements of the statements that would be expected to conform with a predictable pattern based on the entity's experience [AR 100.27(c)]. Answers (a), (c), and (d) are procedures that should be performed in an audit engagement.

57. (b) Inquiries and analytical procedures ordinarily performed during a review of a nonpublic entity's financial statements include inquiries concerning the entity's procedures for recording and summarizing transactions (AR 100.27). They would not be concerned with corroborating evidential matter, management's assertions concerning continued existence, or the entity's attorney's opinion concerning contingent liabilities.

58. (a) The procedures in answers (b) and (d) are noted in AR 100.27c, and the procedures in answer (c) are noted in AR 100.27d as appropriate in a review.

59. (a) Per AR 100.41, if the accountant believes that modification of his or her standard report is not adequate to indicate the deficiencies in the financial statements taken as a whole, he or she should withdraw from the compilation or review engagement and not provide any further services regarding those financial statements. Answer (b) is incorrect because the accountant cannot be assured the financial statements would not be delivered to external users. The accountant would follow the procedures in answer (c) if modification of the report was considered adequate.

60. (d) AR 100.30 states, "A review does *not* contemplate obtaining an understanding of the internal control or assessing control risk, tests of accounting records and of responses to inquiries by obtaining corroborating evidential matter, and certain other procedures ordinarily performed during an audit." Answers (a), (b), and (c) are usually performed by the accountant in a review engagement of a nonpublic entity.

FINANCIAL FORECASTS & PROJECTIONS

61. (d) AT 200.07 states, "Prospective financial statements are either *general use* or *limited use*. *General use* of prospective financial statements refers to use of the statements by persons with whom the responsible party is not negotiating directly, for example, in an offering statement of an entity's debt or equity interests. Because recipients of prospective financial statements distributed for general use are unable to ask the responsible party directly about the presentation, the presentation most useful to them is one that portrays, to the best of the responsible party's knowledge and belief, the expected results. Thus, only a *financial forecast* is appropriate for general use."

62. (c) AT 200.08 states, "Any type of prospective financial statements that would be useful in the circumstances would normally be appropriate for limited use. Thus, the presentation may be a financial forecast or a financial projection." Only the financial forecast is appropriate for general use (AT 200.07). (Also see the explanation to question #61.)

63. (c) The standard report in AT 200.17 includes a statement that there will usually be differences between the forecasted and actual results. The items in answers (a), (b), and (d) are not in the standard report.

64. (d) AT 200.07 states that a projection, since it is not meant for general use, would be inappropriate for all stockholders of record and employees, as it would be unreasonable to expect these groups to be familiar with the basis of the projection or to be closely involved with those preparing it.

65. (b) AT 200.27 states, "An examination of a financial forecast...involves evaluating the preparation of the prospective financial statements, evaluating the support underlying the assumptions, evaluating the presentation of the prospective financial statements for conformity with AICPA presentation guidelines, and issuing an examination report." This service does not include compiling the forecast, or assuming responsibility to update management on key events afterwards. The report may be for general use, in which case the distribution need not be limited.

REPORTING ON INTERNAL CONTROL

66. (a) When an accountant has been engaged to report on an entity's internal controls without performing a financial statement audit, he or she does not need to place any restrictions on the use of the report unless management does not present its written assertion in a separate report to accompany the practitioner's report. (AT 400.03)

67. (d) An engagement to express an opinion on an entity's system of internal accounting control and a consideration of internal control made as part of an audit differ in purpose (AT 400.79) and generally differ in scope (AT 400.81). However, the procedures are similar in nature (AT 400.26, .80).

68. (b) AT 400.45 states, "The practitioner's report [expressing an opinion on an entity's system of internal control] should include...a statement that the examination was made in accordance with the standards established by the AICPA...."

69. (a) According to AU 324.29, one of the items that should be included in a service auditor's report expressing an opinion on a description of policies and procedures placed in operation at a service organization is a description of the scope and nature of the service auditor's procedures. A statement that management had disclosed all design deficiencies of which it is aware is not appropriate in the report. The report should also contain, per AU 324.29, a disclaimer of opinion on the operating effectiveness of the policies and procedures. A paragraph indicating the basis for assessment of control risk is not appropriate in the report.

70. (c) AT 400.46 provides an example of a report that includes, "We believe that our examination provides a reasonable basis for our opinion."

PERFORMANCE BY SUBTOPICS

Each category below parallels a subtopic covered in Chapter 41. Record the number and percentage of questions you correctly answered in each subtopic area.

Compilations & Reviews

Question #	Correct √
1	
2	
3	
4	
5	
6	

\# Questions 6

\# Correct ____
% Correct ____

SSARS

Question #	Correct √
7	
8	

\# Questions 2

\# Correct ____
% Correct ____

Compilation Engagements

Question #	Correct √
9	
10	
11	

\# Questions 3

\# Correct ____
% Correct ____

Compilation Reports

Question #	Correct √
12	
13	
14	
15	
16	
17	

\# Questions 6

\# Correct ____
% Correct ____

Review Engagements

Question #	Correct √
18	
19	
20	
21	

\# Questions 4

\# Correct ____
% Correct ____

Review Reports

Question #	Correct √
22	
23	
24	
25	
26	

\# Questions 5

\# Correct ____
% Correct ____

Prescribed Forms

Question #	Correct √
27	

\# Questions 1

\# Correct ____
% Correct ____

Personal Financial Statements

Question #	Correct √
28	
29	

\# Questions 2

\# Correct ____
% Correct ____

Attestation Standards

Question #	Correct √
30	
31	
32	
33	
34	

\# Questions 5

\# Correct ____
% Correct ____

Financial Forecasts & Projections

Question #	Correct √
35	
36	
37	
38	

\# Questions 4

\# Correct ____
% Correct ____

Reporting on Internal Control

Question #	Correct √
39	
40	
41	
42	
43	

\# Questions 5

\# Correct ____
% Correct ____

Other Attestation Engagements

Question #	Correct √
44	
45	

\# Questions 2

\# Correct ____
% Correct ____

OTHER OBJECTIVE FORMAT QUESTION SOLUTIONS

SOLUTION 41-3 REVIEW REPORT

1. G Gordon is correct. The first paragraph of the report should not include a reference to the prior year's audited financial statements. The standard review report should be issued on the current-period statements and the prior-period report should be reissued or a separate paragraph should be added to the current-period report.

2. M Martin is correct. The statement of retained earnings should be listed in the first paragraph.

3. B Both are incorrect. The review should be conducted in accordance with Statements on Standards for Accounting and Review Services which are issued by the AICPA.

4. B Both are incorrect. The statement, "Our responsibility is to express limited assurance on these financial statements based on our review" should be omitted. The standard review report does not express an opinion on the financial statements.

5. G Gordon is correct. The prior year's audited financial statements should not be referred to in the second paragraph of the review report. Either the prior-period report should be reissued or a separate paragraph should be added to the current-period report.

6. M Martin is correct. The second paragraph of the review report should include the following comparison of the scope of a review to an audit, "It is substantially less in scope than an audit in accordance with generally accepted auditing standards, the objective of which is the expression

of an opinion regarding the financial statements taken as a whole."

7. M Martin is correct. There should be no reference to "assessing the accounting principles used," "significant estimates made by management," or "evaluating the overall financial statement presentation," since these statements are not part of the standard review report.

8. M Martin is correct. The scope paragraph should include the statement, "Accordingly, we do not express such an opinion.'

9. M Martin is correct. The third paragraph should include a reference to "conformity with generally accepted accounting principles."

10. G Gordon is correct. The standard review report does not refer to consistency.

11. G Gordon is correct. The standard review report does not contain a restriction on distribution.

12. B Both are incorrect. The standard review report does not contain a reference to a "going concern."

13. B Both are incorrect. The statement regarding responsibility to update the report should be omitted.

14. G Gordon is correct. The fourth paragraph should describe the responsibility the CPA is assuming for the financial statements of the prior period. Specifically, it should indicate (1) that the prior-period's financial statements were audited previously; (2) the date of the previous report; (3) the type of opinion that was previously expressed and (4) that no auditing procedures have been performed since the date of the previous report.

15. G Gordon is correct. A list of the basic financial statements is not required in the fourth paragraph.

16. M Martin is correct. The reference in the fourth paragraph to the fair presentation of the prior year's audited financial statements in accordance with generally accepted accounting principles should be omitted.

17. G Gordon is correct. The report should be dated as of the completion of the inquiry and analytical procedures; the report should not be dual dated. The fourth paragraph correctly indicates the date of the audit report for the prior year's financial statements.

Solution 41-4 Engagement Requirements

1. R,R AR 100.08 states, "The accountant should establish an understanding with the entity, preferably in writing, regarding the services to be performed." AR 100.08 applies to both reviews and compilations.

2. R,N AR 100.27, applicable to reviews, lists several procedures that ordinarily are performed in a review, including "Inquiries concerning actions taken at meetings of stockholders, board of directors, committees of the board of directors, or comparable meetings that may affect the financial statements." AR 100.12, applicable to compilations, indicates that the accountant is not required to make inquiries about information supplied by the client.

3. N,N AR 400.08 states, "A successor accountant may wish to obtain access to the predecessor's working papers." This step is **not** required in either a review or a compilation.

4. R,R AR 100.10, applicable to compilations, states, "The accountant should possess a level of knowledge of the accounting principles and practices of the industry in which the entity operates that will enable him [or her] to compile financial statements that are appropriate in form for an entity operating in that industry." AR 100.24, applicable to reviews, states a similar, but more comprehensive, requirement than for a compilation.

5. N,N AR 100.30 states, "A review does not contemplate obtaining an understanding of the internal control structure or assessing control risk, tests of accounting records and of responses to inquiries by obtaining corroborating evidential matter, and certain other procedures ordinarily performed during an audit." A compilation engagement is even more narrow in scope than a review.

6. R,N AR 100.27(c) describes such analytics for a review. AR 100.12 indicates that, for compilations, the accountant is not required to perform such procedures.

7. N,N According to AR 100.30, a review does not contemplate obtaining an understanding of internal control or assessing control risk. A compilation is even more narrow in scope than a review.

8. N,N AR 100.27 indicates various inquiries appropriate to a review, all of which are of client's personnel. Inquiries of a client's lawyer would be considered corroborative evidence and is beyond the scope of a review. A compilation engagement is even more narrow in scope than a review.

9. R,N AR 100.28 states that the accountant is required to obtain a written representation from members of management in a review engagement. AR 100.12 indicates verifying evidence is not required in a compilation. A representation letter would not usually be obtained in a compilation engagement.

10. R,N AR 100.27(c) identifies types of analytical procedures in a review. A study of the relationships of the elements of the statements that would be expected to conform with a predictable pattern based on the entity's experience is item (3). A compilation does not require analytical procedures.

11. N,N AR 100.08 states, "The understanding [with the client] should also provide (a) that the engagement cannot be relied upon to disclose errors, irregularities, or illegal acts and (b) that the accountant will inform the appropriate level of management of any material errors and any irregularities or illegal acts that come to his or her attention, unless they are clearly inconsequential." This guidance is applicable to both a review and a compilation.

12. R,N AR 100.27(g), applicable to a review, states, "Inquires of persons having responsibility for financial and accounting matters concerning events subsequent to the date of the financial statements that would have a material effect on the financial statements." A compilation does not require inquiries about subsequent events. (AR 100.12)

13. N,N According to AR 100.39 - .40 (footnote 18), as long as the change is appropriate and is appropriately disclosed in the financial statements, there is no requirement to alter the report. A compilation is more narrow in scope than a review.

14. N,N There is no professional requirement that the accountant submit a hard copy of financial statements or the accountant's report for a review or a compilation.

15. N,N AR 100.27 states that, for a review, only inquires and analytical procedures are required. AR 100.12, for a compilation, indicates that no verifying procedures are required.

ESSAY SOLUTIONS

SOLUTION 41-5 COMPILATION REPORT

Deficiencies in the report on the compiled financial statements are as follows:

Within the first paragraph:

- The financial statements are **not properly identified**.
- **Statements on Standards for Accounting and Review Services** issued by the AICPA should be referred to.
- The expression **"to obtain limited assurance"** should not be used.

Within the second paragraph:

- The information is not stated to be the **representation of management**.
- The phrase **"less in scope than an audit"** is **inappropriate**.
- Reference to the **financial statements not being reviewed** is omitted.
- Reference to **"any other form of assurance"** is omitted.

Within the third paragraph:

- Reference to the **omission of the statement of cash flows** is omitted.
- There should be a statement that the financial statements are **not designed for those uninformed about the omitted disclosures**.
- It is inappropriate to refer to **changes in financial position.**

Within the fourth paragraph:

- The reason for the accountant's lack of independence should not be described.

Inclusion of the **fifth paragraph is inappropriate**.

The accountant's compilation report is **not dated** October 25, 20X1.

SOLUTION 41-6 FINANCIAL PROJECTIONS

a. 1. An accountant who reports on or assembles **prospective financial statements for use by third parties** should perform any one of three engagements. The accountant may **compile**, **examine**, or **apply agreed-upon procedures** to the prospective financial statements.

2. **"General use"** of prospective financial statements refers to use of the statements by persons (creditors, stockholders, etc.) with whom the **responsible party** (management) is **not negotiating directly. "Limited use"** of prospective financial statements refers to the use of prospective financial statements by the **responsible party and third parties** with whom the responsible party is **negotiating directly.**

3. Only a **financial forecast is appropriate for general use,** but any type of prospective financial statements (either a financial forecast or a financial projection) would normally be appropriate for **limited use.**

b. The accountant's standard report on a compilation of a financial projection should include

- An **identification** of the **projection** presented by the responsible party.
- A statement that the accountant has **compiled** the **projection in accordance with standards established by the AICPA.**
- A separate paragraph that describes the **limitations** on the **use of the presentation.**
- A statement that a compilation is **limited in scope** and **does not enable** the accountant to **express an opinion** or any other **form of assurance** on the **projection** or the **assumptions.**
- A caveat that the **prospective results may not be achieved.**
- A statement that the **accountant assumes no responsibility to update** the report for events and circumstances occurring after the date of the report.

SOLUTION 41-7 INTERNAL CONTROL

a. Hart may accept the attest engagement to examine and report on management's assertion about the effectiveness of Unidyne's internal control over financial reporting only if Unidyne's **management accepts responsibility** for internal control effectiveness. Management then would evaluate internal control effectiveness using **reasonable benchmarks** or criteria established by a **recognized body** such as the AICPA, COSO, or a **regulatory agency**.

b. Performing an examination of management's assertion about the effectiveness of Unidyne's internal control initially would involve **planning** the engagement, which includes developing an **overall strategy** for the scope and performance of the engagement. Hart then would **obtain an understanding** of Unidyne's internal control by making **inquiries** of management and employees, by **inspecting** documents, and by **observing** Unidyne's activities and operations.

Next, Hart would test and evaluate the design effectiveness of internal control policies and procedures within each element (control activities, risk assessment, information & communication, monitoring, and control environment) of internal control, and then test and evaluate the operating effectiveness of the policies and procedures. Hart would perform tests of relevant controls to obtain evidence that supports the report's opinion by focusing on how the policies and procedure are applied, the consistency with which they are applied, and by whom they are applied.

Finally, Hart would **consider all the evidence** obtained, including the results of tests of controls and any control deficiencies identified, in forming an opinion on management's assertion about the effectiveness of Unidyne's internal control.

c. In addition to the proposed engagement to **examine and report** on management's written assertion about the effectiveness of Unidyne's internal control over financial reporting, Hart may also be engaged to perform **agreed-upon procedures** relating to management's assertion about the effectiveness of Unidyne's internal control. Hart's report on agreed-upon procedures would be in the form of procedures and findings.

Hart should not accept an engagement to **review and report** on management's assertion about the effectiveness of Unidyne's internal control or provide **negative assurance** about whether management's assertion is fairly stated in an agreed-upon procedures engagement.

CPA Exam Week Checklist

WHAT TO PACK FOR EXAM WEEK:

1. CPA exam registration material.
2. Hotel confirmation.
3. Cash and/or a major credit card.
4. Alarm clock—Don't rely on a hotel wake-up call.
5. Comfortable clothing that can be layered to suit varying temperatures.
6. A watch.
7. Appropriate review materials, pencils, erasers, and pencil sharpener.
8. Healthy snack foods.

EVENINGS BEFORE EXAM SECTIONS:

1. Read through your Bisk Education chapter outlines for the next day's section(s).
2. Eat lightly and monitor your intake of alcohol and caffeine. Get a good night's rest.
3. Do **not** try to cram. A brief review of your notes will help to focus your attention on important points and remind you that you are well prepared, but too much cramming can shatter your self-confidence. If you have reviewed conscientiously, you are already well-prepared for the CPA exam.

THE MORNING OF EACH EXAM SECTION:

1. Eat a satisfying breakfast. It will be several hours before your next meal. Eat enough to ward off hunger, but not so much that you feel uncomfortable.
2. Dress appropriately. Wear layers you can take off to suit varying temperatures in the room.
3. Take ample supplies of permissible materials (may vary by jurisdiction).
4. Arrive at the exam center thirty minutes early. Check in as soon as you are allowed to do so.

More helpful exam information is included in the **Practical Advice** appendix in this volume.

APPENDIX A
FINAL EXAMINATION

PROBLEM 1 MULTIPLE CHOICE QUESTIONS (120 to 150 minutes)

1. To exercise due professional care an auditor should
a. Attain the proper balance of professional experience and formal education.
b. Design the audit to detect all instances of illegal acts.
c. Critically review the judgment exercised by those assisting in the audit.
d. Examine all available corroborating evidence supporting management's assertions.

2. A CPA establishes quality control policies and procedures for deciding whether to accept a new client or continue to perform services for a current client. The primary purpose for establishing such policies and procedures is
a. To enable the auditor to attest to the integrity or reliability of a client.
b. To comply with the quality control standards established by regulatory bodies.
c. To lessen the exposure to litigation resulting from failure to detect fraud in client financial statements.
d. To minimize the likelihood of association with clients whose management lacks integrity.

3. When auditing an entity's financial statements in accordance with *Government Auditing Standards*, an auditor should prepare a written report on the auditor's
a. Identification of the causes of performance problems and recommendations for actions to improve operations.
b. Understanding of internal control and assessment of control risk.
c. Field work and procedures that substantiated the auditor's specific findings and conclusions.
d. Opinion on the entity's attainment of the goals and objectives specified by applicable laws and regulations.

4. Prior to the acceptance of an audit engagement with a client who has terminated the services of the predecessor auditor, the CPA should
a. Contact the predecessor auditor without advising the prospective client and request a complete report of the circumstances leading to the termination, with the understanding that all information disclosed will be kept confidential.
b. Accept the engagement without contacting the predecessor auditor since the CPA can include audit procedures to verify the reason given by the client for the termination.
c. Not communicate with the predecessor auditor because this would violate the confidential relationship between auditor and client.
d. Advise the client of the intention to contact the predecessor auditor and request permission for the contact.

5. Before accepting an audit engagement, a successor auditor should make specific inquiries of the predecessor auditor regarding the predecessor's
a. Awareness of the consistency in the application of generally accepted accounting principles between periods.
b. Evaluation of all matters of continuing accounting significance.
c. Opinion of any subsequent events occurring since the predecessor's audit report was issued.
d. Understanding as to the reasons for the change of auditors.

6. If specific information comes to an auditor's attention that implies the existence of possible illegal acts that could have a material, but indirect effect on the financial statements, the auditor should next
a. Apply audit procedures specifically directed to ascertaining whether an illegal act has occurred.
b. Seek the advice of an informed expert qualified to practice law as to possible contingent liabilities.
c. Report the matter to an appropriate level of management at least one level above those involved.
d. Discuss the evidence with the client's audit committee, or others with equivalent authority and responsibility.

7. On the basis of audit evidence gathered and evaluated, an auditor decides to increase the assessed level of control risk from that originally planned. To achieve an overall audit risk level that is substantially the same as the planned audit risk level, the auditor would

a. Increase inherent risk.
b. Increase materiality levels.
c. Decrease substantive testing.
d. Decrease detection risk.

8. A difference of opinion regarding the results of a sample cannot be resolved between the assistant who performed the auditing procedures and the in-charge auditor. The assistant should

a. Refuse to perform any further work on the engagement.
b. Accept the judgment of the more experienced in-charge auditor.
c. Document the disagreement and ask to be disassociated from the resolution of the matter.
d. Notify the client that a serious audit problem exists.

9. Which of the following statements best describes the auditor's responsibility regarding the detection of material errors and fraud?

a. The auditor is responsible for the failure to detect material errors and fraud only when such failure results from the nonapplication of generally accepted accounting principles.
b. Extended auditing procedures are required to detect material errors and fraud if the audit indicates that they may exist.
c. The auditor is responsible for the failure to detect material errors and fraud only when the auditor fails to confirm receivables or observe inventories.
d. Extended auditing procedures are required to detect unrecorded transactions even if there is no evidence that material errors and fraud may exist.

10. In planning an audit, the auditor's knowledge about the design of relevant internal control policies and procedures should be used to

a. Identify the types of potential misstatements that could occur.
b. Assess the operational efficiency of the internal control structure.
c. Determine whether controls have been circumvented by collusion.
d. Document the assessed level of control risk.

11. Which of the following is **not** a component of an entity's internal control?

a. Control risk
b. Control activities
c. The information and communication
d. The control environment

12. After his or her consideration of an entity's internal control, the auditor decides to assess control risk at the maximum level for all financial statement assertions. Documentation may be limited to the auditor's

a. Understanding of internal control.
b. Understanding of internal control and the auditor's conclusion that control risk is at the maximum level.
c. Understanding of internal control, the auditor's conclusion that control risk is at the maximum level, and the basis for that conclusion.
d. Completed internal control questionnaire.

13. Which of the following statements is correct concerning the auditor's required communication of material weaknesses in internal control?

a. If the auditor does not become aware of any material weaknesses during the audit, that fact must be communicated.
b. Weaknesses reported at interim dates should be tested for correction before completion of the engagement.
c. Although written communication is preferable, the auditor may communicate the findings orally.
d. Weaknesses reported at interim dates must be repeated in the communication at the completion of the engagement.

14. Which one of the following would the auditor consider to be an incompatible operation if the cashier receives remittances from the mailroom?

a. The cashier posts the receipts to the accounts receivable subsidiary ledger cards.
b. The cashier makes the daily deposit at a local bank.
c. The cashier prepares the daily deposit.
d. The cashier endorses the checks.

15. Sound internal control policies and procedures dictate that defective merchandise returned by customers should be presented to the

a. Inventory control clerk.
b. Sales clerk.
c. Purchasing clerk.
d. Receiving clerk.

16. A client erroneously recorded a large purchase twice. Which of the following internal control measures would be most likely to detect this error in a timely and efficient manner?
a. Footing the purchases journal
b. Reconciling vendors' monthly statements with subsidiary payable ledger accounts
c. Tracing totals from the purchases journal to the ledger accounts
d. Sending written quarterly confirmations to all vendors

17. To improve accountability for fixed asset retirements, management most likely would implement a system of internal control that includes
a. Continuous analysis of the repairs and maintenance account.
b. Periodic inquiry of plant executives by internal auditors as to whether any plant assets have been retired.
c. Continuous utilization of serially numbered retirement work orders.
d. Periodic inspection of insurance policies by the internal auditors.

18. An internal control questionnaire indicates that an approved receiving report is required to accompany every check request for payment of merchandise. Which of the following procedures provides the greatest assurance that this control is operating effectively?
a. Select and examine canceled checks and ascertain that the related receiving reports are dated **no** earlier than the checks.
b. Select and examine canceled checks and ascertain that the related receiving reports are dated **no** later than the checks.
c. Select and examine receiving reports and ascertain that the related canceled checks are dated **no** earlier than the receiving reports.
d. Select and examine receiving reports and ascertain that the related canceled checks are dated **no** later than the receiving reports.

19. Which of the following is intended to detect deviations from prescribed Accounting Department procedures?
a. Substantive tests specified by a standardized audit program.
b. Tests of controls designed specifically for the client.
c. Analytical procedures as designed in the industry audit guide.
d. Computerized analytical procedures tailored for the configuration of EDP equipment in use.

20. The auditor would be **least** likely to be concerned about internal control as it relates to
a. Land and buildings.
b. Common stock.
c. Shareholder meetings.
d. Minutes of board of directors meetings.

21. While substantive tests may support the accuracy of underlying records, these tests frequently provide no affirmative evidence of segregation of duties because
a. Substantive tests rarely guarantee the accuracy of the records if only a sample of the transactions has been tested.
b. The records may be accurate even though they are maintained by persons having incompatible functions.
c. Substantive tests relate to the entire period under audit, but tests of control ordinarily are confined to the period during which the auditor is on the client's premises.
d. Many computerized procedures leave no audit trail of who performed them, so substantive tests may necessarily be limited to inquiries and observation of office personnel.

22. Which of the following types of audit evidence is the most persuasive?
a. Prenumbered client purchase order forms
b. Client work sheets supporting cost allocations
c. Bank statements obtained from the client
d. Management representation letter

23. In assessing the objectivity of internal auditors, an independent auditor should
a. Evaluate the quality control program in effect for the internal auditors.
b. Examine documentary evidence of the work performed by the internal auditors.
c. Test a sample of the transactions and balances that the internal auditors examined.
d. Determine the organizational level to which the internal auditors report.

24. The auditor notices significant fluctuations in key elements of the company's financial statements. If management is unable to provide an acceptable explanation, the auditor should
a. Consider the matter a scope limitation.
b. Perform additional audit procedures to investigate the matter further.
c. Intensify the audit with the expectation of detecting management fraud.
d. Withdraw from the engagement.

25. A written representation from a client's management which, among other matters, acknowledges responsibility for the fair presentation of financial statements, should normally be signed by the

a. Chief executive officer and the chief financial officer.
b. Chief financial officer and the chairman of the board of directors.
c. Chairman of the audit committee of the board of directors.
d. Chief executive officer, the chairman of the board of directors, and the client's lawyer.

26. The auditor is most likely to seek information from the plant manager with respect to the

a. Adequacy of the provision for uncollectible accounts.
b. Appropriateness of physical inventory observation procedures.
c. Existence of obsolete machinery.
d. Deferral of procurement of certain necessary insurance coverage.

27. For audits of financial statements made in accordance with generally accepted auditing standards, the use of analytical procedures is required to some extent

	As a substantive test	In the final review stage
a.	Yes	Yes
b.	Yes	No
c.	No	Yes
d.	No	No

28. Two months before year-end, the bookkeeper erroneously recorded the receipt of a long-term bank loan by a debit to cash and a credit to sales. Which of the following is the most effective procedure for detecting this type of error?

a. Analyze the notes payable journal
b. Analyze bank confirmation information
c. Prepare a year-end bank reconciliation
d. Prepare a year-end bank transfer schedule

29. The auditor's primary means of obtaining corroboration of management's information concerning litigation is a

a. Letter of audit inquiry to the client's lawyer.
b. Letter of corroboration from the auditor's lawyer upon review of the legal documentation.
c. Confirmation of claims and assessments from the other parties to the litigation.
d. Confirmation of claims and assessments from an officer of the court presiding over the litigation.

30. Which of the following documentation is **not** required for an audit in accordance with generally accepted auditing standards?

a. A written audit program setting forth the procedures necessary to accomplish the audit's objectives
b. An indication that the accounting records agree or reconcile with the financial statements
c. A client engagement letter that summarizes the timing and details of the auditor's planned field work
d. The basis for the auditor's conclusions when the assessed level of control risk is below the maximum level

31. The permanent file section of the working papers that is kept for each audit client most likely contains

a. Review notes pertaining to questions and comments regarding the audit work performed.
b. A schedule of time spent on the engagement by each individual auditor.
c. Correspondence with the client's legal counsel concerning pending litigation.
d. Narrative descriptions of the client's accounting procedures and internal control structure.

32. The auditor will most likely perform extensive tests for possible understatement of

a. Revenues.
b. Assets.
c. Liabilities.
d. Capital.

33. In the confirmation of accounts receivable, the auditor would most likely

a. Request confirmation of a sample of the inactive accounts.
b. Seek to obtain positive confirmations for at least 50% of the total dollar amount of the receivables.
c. Require confirmation of all receivables from agencies of the federal government.
d. Require that confirmation requests be sent within one month of the fiscal year-end.

34. Which of the following might be detected by an auditor's review of the client's sales cut-off?

a. Excessive goods returned for credit
b. Unrecorded sales discounts
c. Lapping of year-end accounts receivable
d. Inflated sales for the year

35. Which of the following is **not** one of the independent auditor's objectives regarding the examination of inventories?
a. Verifying that inventory counted is owned by the client
b. Verifying that the client has used proper inventory pricing
c. Ascertaining the physical quantities of inventory on hand
d. Verifying that all inventory owned by the client is on hand at the time of the count

36. When an auditor is unable to inspect and count a client's investment securities until after the balance-sheet date, the bank where the securities are held in a safe deposit box should be asked to
a. Verify any differences between the contents of the box and the balances in the client's subsidiary ledger.
b. Provide a list of securities added and removed from the box between the balance sheet date and the security-count date.
c. Confirm that there has been **no** access to the box between the balance sheet date and the security-count date.
d. Count the securities in the box so the auditor will have an independent direct verification.

37. The accounts payable department receives the purchase order form to accomplish all of the following **except**
a. Compare invoice price to purchase order price.
b. Ensure the purchase had been properly authorized.
c. Ensure the goods had been received by the party requesting the goods.
d. Compare quantity ordered to quantity purchased.

38. In auditing intangible assets, an auditor most likely would review or recompute amortization and determine whether the amortization period is reasonable in support of management's financial statement assertion of
a. Valuation or allocation.
b. Existence or occurrence.
c. Completeness.
d. Rights and obligations.

39. Which of the following statements is correct concerning statistical sampling in testing of controls?
a. The population size has little or no effect on determining sample size except for very small populations.
b. The expected population deviation rate has little or **no** effect on determining sample size except for very small populations.
c. As the population size doubles, the sample size also should double.
d. For a given tolerable rate, a larger sample size should be selected as the expected population deviation rate decreases.

40. The theoretical distribution of means from all possible samples of a given size is a normal distribution and this distribution is the basis for statistical sampling. Which of the following statements is **not** true with respect to the sampling distribution of sample means?
a. Approximately 68% of the sample means will be within one standard deviation of the mean for the normal distribution.
b. The distribution is defined in terms of its mean and its standard error of the mean.
c. An auditor can be approximately 95% confident that the mean for a sample is within two standard deviations of the population mean.
d. The items drawn in an auditor's sample will have a normal distribution.

41. The tolerable rate of deviations for a test of controls is generally
a. Lower than the expected rate of misstatements in the related accounting records.
b. Higher than the expected rate of misstatements in the related accounting records.
c. Identical to the expected rate of misstatements in the related accounting records.
d. Unrelated to the expected rate of misstatements in the related accounting records.

42. When evaluating internal control of an entity that processes sales transactions on the Internet, an auditor would be most concerned about the
a. Lack of sales invoice documents as an audit trail.
b. Potential for computer disruptions in recording sales.
c. Inability to establish an integrated test facility.
d. Frequency of archiving and data retention.

43. Camela Department Stores has a fully integrated EDP accounting system and is planning to issue credit cards to creditworthy customers. To strengthen internal control by making it difficult for one to create a valid customer account number, the company's independent auditor has suggested the inclusion of a check digit which should be placed

a. At the beginning of a valid account number, only.
b. In the middle of a valid account number, only.
c. At the end of a valid account number, only.
d. Consistently in any position.

44. Which of the following strategies would a CPA most likely consider in auditing an entity that processes most of its financial data only in electronic form, such as a paperless system?

a. Continuous monitoring and analysis of transaction processing with an embedded audit module.
b. Increased reliance on internal control activities that emphasize the segregation of duties.
c. Verification of encrypted digital certificates used to monitor the authorization of transactions.
d. Extensive testing of firewall boundaries that restrict the recording of outside network traffic.

45. Which of the following subsequent events will be **least** likely to result in an adjustment to the financial statements?

a. Culmination of events affecting the realization of accounts receivable owned as of the balance sheet date.
b. Culmination of events affecting the realization of inventories owned as of the balance sheet date.
c. Material changes in the settlement of liabilities which were estimated as of the balance sheet date.
d. Material changes in the quoted market prices of listed investment securities since the balance sheet date.

46. The principal auditor is satisfied with the independence and professional reputation of the other auditor who has audited a subsidiary but wants to indicate the division of responsibility. The principal auditor should

a. Modify only the scope paragraph of the report.
b. Modify both the scope and opinion paragraph of the report.
c. Modify the introductory, scope and opinion paragraphs of the report.
d. **Not** modify the report except for inclusion of a separate explanatory paragraph.

47. Which of the following will **not** result in modification of the auditor's report due to a scope limitation?

a. Restrictions imposed by the client
b. Reliance placed on the report of another auditor
c. Inability to obtain sufficient competent evidential matter
d. Inadequacy in the accounting records

48. When comparative financial statements are presented but the predecessor auditor's report is **not** presented, the current auditor should do which of the following in the audit report?

a. Disclaim an opinion on the prior year's financial statements.
b. Identify the predecessor auditor who audited the financial statements of the prior year.
c. Make **no** comment with respect to the predecessor audit.
d. Indicate the type of opinion expressed by the predecessor auditor.

49. When using the work of a specialist, the auditor may make reference to and identification of the specialist in the auditor's report if the

a. Auditor decides to express a qualified opinion.
b. Specialist's reputation or professional certification is being emphasized.
c. Auditor wishes to indicate a division of responsibility.
d. Specialist's work provides the auditor greater assurance of reliability.

50. An auditor would be most likely to consider expressing a qualified opinion if the client's financial statements include a footnote on related party transactions that

a. Lists the amounts due from related parties including the terms and manner of settlement.
b. Discloses compensating balance arrangements maintained for the benefit of related parties.
c. Represents that certain transactions with related parties were consummated on terms equally as favorable as would have been obtained in transactions with unrelated parties.
d. Presents the dollar volume of related party transactions and the effects of any change in the method of establishing terms from that of the prior period.

51. Jones, CPA, audited the 20X3 financial statements of Ray Corp. and issued an unqualified opinion on March 10, 20X4. On April 2, 20X4, Jones became aware of a 20X3 transaction that may materially affect the 20X3 financial statements. This transaction would have been investigated had it come to Jones' attention during the course of the audit. Jones should
a. Take **no** action because an auditor is **not** responsible for events subsequent to the issuance of the auditor's report.
b. Contact Ray's management and request their cooperation in investigating the matter.
c. Request that Ray's management disclose the possible effects of the newly discovered transaction by adding an unaudited footnote to the 20X3 financial statements.
d. Contact all parties who might rely upon the financial statements and advise them that the financial statements are misleading.

52. The management of Blue Company has decided not to account for a material transaction in accordance with the provisions of a FASB Standard. In setting forth its reasons in a note to the financial statements, management has clearly demonstrated that due to unusual circumstances the financial statements presented in accordance with the FASB Standard would be misleading. The auditor's report should include an explanatory separate paragraph and contain a(an)
a. Adverse opinion.
b. Unqualified opinion.
c. "Except for" qualified opinion.
d. "Subject to" qualified opinion.

53. The auditor concludes that there is a material inconsistency in the other information in an annual report to shareholders containing audited financial statements. If the client refuses to revise or eliminate the material inconsistency, the auditor should
a. Revise the auditor's report to include a separate explanatory paragraph describing the material inconsistency.
b. Consult with a party whose advice might influence the client, such as the client's legal counsel.
c. Issue a qualified opinion after discussing the matter with the client's board of directors.
d. Consider the matter closed since the other information is **not** in the audited financial statements.

54. After issuing a report an auditor concludes that an auditing procedure considered necessary at the time of the audit was omitted from the audit. The auditor should first
a. Undertake to apply the omitted procedure or alternative procedures that would provide a satisfactory basis for the auditor's opinion.
b. Assess the importance of the omitted procedure to the auditor's ability to support the opinion expressed on the financial statements taken as a whole.
c. Notify the audit committee or the board of director's that the auditor's opinion can **no** longer be relied upon.
d. Review the results of other procedures that were applied to compensate for the one omitted or to make its omission less important.

55. An auditor's report issued in connection with which of the following is generally not considered to be a special report?
a. Compliance with aspects of contractual agreements unrelated to audited financial statements.
b. Specified elements, accounts, or items of a financial statement presented in a document.
c. Financial statements prepared in accordance with an entity's income tax basis.
d. Financial information presented in a prescribed schedule that requires a prescribed form of auditor's report.

56. The objective of a review of interim financial information is to provide the accountant with a basis for reporting whether
a. A reasonable basis exists for expressing an updated opinion regarding the financial statements that were previously audited.
b. Material modifications should be made to conform with generally accepted accounting principles.
c. The financial statements are presented fairly in accordance with standards of interim reporting.
d. The financial statements are presented fairly in conformity with generally accepted accounting principles.

57. When an accountant compiles projected financial statements, the accountant's report should include a separate paragraph that
a. Describes the differences between a projection and a forecast.
b. Identifies the accounting principles used by management.
c. Expresses limited assurance that the actual results may be within the projection's range.
d. Describes the limitations on the projection's usefulness.

58. When an accountant examines projected financial statements, the accountant's report should include a separate paragraph that
a. Describes the limitations on the usefulness of the presentation.
b. Provides an explanation of the differences between an examination and an audit.
c. States that the accountant is responsible for events and circumstances up to one year after the report's date.
d. Disclaims an opinion on whether the assumptions provide a reasonable basis for the projection.

59. Which one of the following is generally more important in a review than in a compilation?
a. Determining the accounting basis on which the financial statements are to be presented.
b. Gaining familiarity with industry accounting principles and practices.
c. Obtaining a signed engagement letter.
d. Obtaining a signed representation letter.

60. An auditor's report on the internal controls of a publicly held company would ordinarily be of least use to
a. Shareholders.
b. Officers.
c. Directors.
d. Regulatory agencies.

OTHER OBJECTIVE FORMAT QUESTIONS

Problem 2 (15 to 25 minutes)

Perry & Price, CPAs, audited the consolidated financial statements of Bond Company for the year ended December 31, 20X1, and expressed an adverse opinion because Bond carried its plant and equipment at appraisal values, and provided for depreciation on the basis of such values.

Perry & Price also audited Bond's financial statements for the year ended December 31, 20X1. These consolidated financial statements are being presented on a comparative basis with those of the prior year and an unqualified opinion is being expressed.

Smith, the engagement supervisor, instructed Adler, an assistant on the engagement, to draft the auditor's report on May 3, 20X3, the date of completion of the field work. In drafting the report below, Adler considered the following:

- Bond recently changed its method of accounting for plant and equipment and restated its 20X1 consolidated financial statements to conform with GAAP. Consequently, the CPA firm's present opinion on those statements is different (unqualified) from the opinion expressed on May 12, 20X2.
- Larkin & Lake, CPAs, audited the financial statements of BX, Inc., a consolidated subsidiary of Bond, for the year ended December 31, 20X2. The subsidiary's financial statements reflected total assets and revenues of 2% and 3%, respectively, of the consolidated totals. Larkin & Lake expressed an unqualified opinion and furnished Perry & Price with a copy of the auditor's report. Perry & Price has decided to assume responsibility for the work of Larkin & Lake insofar as it relates to the expression of an opinion on the consolidated financial statements taken as a whole.
- Bond is a defendant in a lawsuit alleging patent infringement. This is adequately disclosed in the notes to Bond's financial statements, but no provision for liability has been recorded because the ultimate outcome of the litigation cannot presently be determined.

Auditor's Report

We have audited the accompanying consolidated balance sheets of Bond Company and subsidiaries as of December 31, 20X2 and 20X1, and the related consolidated statements of income, retained earnings, and cash flows for the years then ended. These financial statements are the responsibility of the Company's management. Our responsibility is to express an opinion on these financial statements based on our audits.

We conducted our audits in accordance with generally accepted auditing standards. Those standards require that we plan and perform the audit to obtain reasonable assurance about whether the financial statements are free of material misstatement. An audit includes examining, on a test basis, evidence supporting the amounts and disclosures in the financial statements. An audit also includes assessing the accounting principles used, as well as evaluating the overall financial statement presentation. We believe that our audits provide a reasonable basis for our opinion.

In our previous report, we expressed an opinion that the 20X1 financial statements did not fairly present financial position, results of operations, and cash flows in conformity with generally accepted accounting principles because the Company carried its plant and equipment at appraisal values and provided for depreciation on the basis of such values. As described in Note 12, the Company has changed its method of accounting for these items and restated its 20X1 financial statements to conform with generally accepted accounting principles. Accordingly, our present opinion on the 20X1 financial statements, as presented herein, is different from that expressed in our previous report.

In our opinion, the consolidated financial statements referred to above present fairly, in all material respects, the financial position of Bond Company and subsidiaries as of December 31, 20X2 and 20X1, and the results of its operations and its cash flows for the years then ended in conformity with generally accepted accounting principles except for the change in accounting principles with which we concur and the uncertainty, which is discussed in the following explanatory paragraph.

The Company is a defendant in a lawsuit alleging infringement of certain patent rights. The Company has filed a counteraction, and preliminary hearings and discovery proceedings are in progress. The ultimate outcome of the litigation cannot presently be determined. Accordingly, no provision for any liability that may result upon adjudication has been made in the accompanying financial statements.

Perry & Price, CPAs
May 3, 20X3

REQUIRED:

Smith reviewed Adler's draft and indicated in the *Supervisor's Review Notes* below that there were deficiencies in Adler's draft. **ITEMS 61 THROUGH 75** represent the deficiencies noted by Smith. For each deficiency, indicate whether Smith is correct or incorrect in the criticism of Adler's draft.

Supervisor's Review Notes

61. The report is improperly titled.
62. All the basic financial statements are **not** properly identified in the introductory paragraph.
63. There is **no** reference to the American Institute of Certified Public Accountants in the introductory paragraph.
64. Larkin & Lake are **not** identified in the introductory and opinion paragraphs.
65. The subsidiary, BX Inc., is **not** identified and the magnitude of BX's financial statements is **not** disclosed in the introductory paragraph.
66. The report does **not** state in the scope paragraph that generally accepted auditing standards require analytical procedures to be performed in planning an audit.
67. The report does **not** state in the scope paragraph that an audit includes assessing the internal control structure.
68. The report does **not** state in the scope paragraph that an audit includes assessing significant estimates made by management.
69. The date of the previous report (May 12, 20X2) is **not** disclosed in the first explanatory paragraph.
70. It is inappropriate to disclose in the first explanatory paragraph the circumstances that caused Perry & Price to express a different opinion on the 20X1 financial statements.
71. The concurrence with the accounting change is inappropriate in the opinion paragraph.
72. Reference to the (litigation) uncertainty should **not** be made in the opinion paragraph.
73. Bond's disclosure of the (litigation) uncertainty in the notes to the financial statements is **not** referred to in the second explanatory paragraph.
74. The letter of inquiry to Bond's lawyer concerning litigation, claims, and assessments is **not** referred to in the second explanatory paragraph.
75. The report is **not** dual dated, but it should be because of the change of opinion on the 20X1 financial statements.

PROBLEM 3 (15 to 25 minutes)

ITEMS 76 THROUGH 87 represent audit objectives for the investments, accounts receivable, and property and equipment accounts. To the right of each set of audit objectives is a listing of possible audit procedures for that account. For each audit objective, select the audit procedure that would primarily respond to the objective. Select only one procedure for each audit objective. A procedure may be selected only once or not at all.

Audit Objectives for Investments

76. Investments are properly described and classified in the financial statements.

77. Recorded investments represent investments actually owned at the balance sheet date.

78. Available-for-sale investments are properly valued at the market value at the balance sheet date.

Audit Procedures for Investments

A. Trace opening balances in the subsidiary ledger to prior year's audit working papers.

B. Determine that employees who are authorized to sell investments do not have access to cash.

C. Examine supporting documents for a sample of investment transactions to verify that prenumbered documents are used.

D. Determine that any impairments in the price of investments have been properly recorded.

E. Verify that transfers from the current to the noncurrent investment portfolio have been properly recorded.

F. Obtain positive confirmations as of the balance sheet date of investments held by independent custodians.

G. Trace investment transactions to minutes of the Board of Directors' meetings to determine that transactions were properly authorized.

Audit Objectives for Accounts Receivable

79. Accounts receivable represent all amounts owed to the entity at the balance sheet date.

80. The entity has legal right to all accounts receivable at the balance sheet date.

81. Accounts receivable are stated at net realizable value.

82. Accounts receivable are properly described and presented in the financial statements

Audit Procedures for Accounts Receivable

A. Analyze the relationship of accounts receivable and sales and compare it with relationships for preceding periods.

B. Perform sales cut-off tests to obtain assurance that sales transactions and corresponding entries for inventories and cost of goods sold are recorded in the same and proper period.

C. Review the aged trial balance for significant past due accounts.

D. Obtain an understanding of the business purpose of transactions that resulted in accounts receivable balances.

E. Review loan agreements for indications of whether accounts receivable have been factored or pledged.

F. Review the accounts receivable trial balance for amounts due from officers and employees.

G. Analyze unusual relationships between monthly accounts receivable balances and monthly accounts payable balances.

Audit Objectives for Property & Equipment

83. The entity has legal right to property and equipment acquired during the year.

84. Recorded property and equipment represent assets that actually exist at the balance sheet date.

85. Net property and equipment are properly valued at the balance sheet date.

Audit Procedures for Property & Equipment

A. Trace opening balances in the summary schedules to the prior year's audit working papers.

B. Review the provision for depreciation expense and determine that depreciable lives and methods used in the current year are consistent with those used in the prior year.

C. Determine that the responsibility for maintaining the property and equipment records is segregated from the responsibility for custody of property and equipment.

D. Examine deeds and title insurance certificates.

E. Perform cut-off tests to verify that property and equipment additions are recorded in the proper period.

F. Determine that property and equipment is adequately insured.

G. Physically examine all major property and equipment additions.

ESSAY QUESTIONS

PROBLEM 4 (15 to 25 minutes)

A CPA has been asked to audit the financial statements of a publicly-held company for the first time. All preliminary verbal discussions and inquiries have been completed between the CPA, the company, the predecessor auditor, and all other necessary parties. The CPA is now preparing an engagement letter.

REQUIRED:

List the items that should be included in the typical engagement letter in these circumstances and describe the benefits derived from preparing an engagement letter.

PROBLEM 5 (20 to 25 minutes)

Various types of "accounting changes" can affect the second reporting standard of the generally accepted auditing standards. This standard reads: "The report shall identify those circumstances in which such principles have not been consistently observed in the current period in relation to the preceding period."

REQUIRED:

Identify the type of change that is described in each item below, state whether any modification is required in the auditor's report as it relates to the second standard of reporting, and state whether the prior year's financial statements should be restated when presented in comparative form with the current year's statements. Organize your answer sheet as shown below.

For example, a change from the LIFO method of inventory pricing to the FIFO method of inventory pricing would appear as shown.

Item No.	Type of Change	Should Auditor's Report Be Modified?	Should Prior Year's Statement Be Restated?
Example	An accounting change from one generally accepted accounting principle to another generally accepted accounting principle.	Yes	Yes

The following list describes changes that have a material effect on a client's financial statements for the current year.

1. A change from the completed-contract method to the percentage-of-completion method of accounting for long-term construction-type contracts.

2. A change in the estimated useful life of previously recorded fixed assets based on newly acquired information.

3. Correction of a mathematical error in inventory pricing made in a prior period.

4. A change from prime costing to full absorption costing for inventory valuation.

5. A change from presentation of statements of individual companies to presentation of consolidated statements.

6. A change from deferring and amortizing preproduction costs to recording such costs as an expense when incurred because future benefits of the costs have become doubtful. The new accounting method was adopted in recognition of the change in estimated future benefits.

7. A change to including the employer share of FICA taxes as "Retirement benefits" on the income statement from including it as "Other taxes."

8. A change from the FIFO method of inventory pricing to the LIFO method of inventory pricing.

MULTIPLE CHOICE QUESTION SOLUTIONS

CHAPTER 31: STANDARDS & RELATED TOPICS

1. (c) AU 230.02 states, "Exercise of due care requires critical review at every level of supervision of the work done and the judgment exercised by those assisting in the audit." Answers (a), (b), and (d) do not relate to the third general standard regarding due care.

2. (d) SQCS 2 states, "Policies and procedures should be established for deciding whether to accept or continue a client relationship [in order to minimize] the likelihood of association with a client whose management lacks integrity." SQCS 2 states, "Establishing such procedures does not imply that a firm vouches for the integrity or reliability of a client, nor does it imply that a firm has a duty to anyone but itself." The failure to detect fraud in client financial statements will result in exposure to litigation regardless of whether the CPA has quality control policies and procedures. However, the existence of quality control procedures would reduce the likelihood of not detecting such fraud.

3. (b) In the *Government Auditing Standards* for financial audits, the third supplemental reporting standard states that the auditor should prepare a written report on his or her understanding of the entity's internal control and the assessment of control risk made as part of a financial statement audit or a financial related audit. Answer (a) represents procedures to be reported in a performance audit, not a financial statement audit. Specific procedures performed are not included in the auditor's report. The auditor does not provide an opinion on the entity's attainment of the goals and objectives as specified by laws and regulations; rather, the auditor provides an opinion on the fairness of the presentation of the financial statements taken as a whole.

CHAPTER 32: PLANNING

4. (d) AU 315.05 states, "The successor auditor should explain to his [or her] prospective client the need to make an inquiry of the predecessor and should request permission to do so." The arrangement in answer (a) would cause the predecessor to violate the confidential relationship between the client and the predecessor. The

predecessor should be contacted prior to acceptance of the engagement. The predecessor may communicate with the successor provided that the client grants permission for the contact. Such communication does not violate the auditor-client confidentiality.

5. (d) AU 315.06 states, "The successor auditor should make specific and reasonable inquiries of the predecessor regarding matters that the successor believes will assist him [or her] in determining whether to accept the engagement. His [or her] inquiries should include specific questions regarding, among other things, facts that might bear on the integrity of management; on disagreements with management as to accounting principles, auditing procedures, or other similarly significant matters; and on the predecessor's understanding as to the reasons for the change of auditors."

6. (a) AU 317.07 states, "If specific information comes to the auditor's attention that provides evidence concerning the existence of possible illegal acts that could have a material indirect effect on the financial statements, the auditor should apply audit procedures specifically directed to ascertaining whether an illegal act has occurred." Only after determining that an illegal act has occurred would the auditor contemplate the steps in the alternatives.

7. (d) AU 319.80 states, "After considering the level to which he or she seeks to restrict the risk of a material misstatement in the financial statements and the assessed levels of inherent risk and control risk, the auditor performs substantive tests to restrict detection risk to an acceptable level. As the assessed level of control risk decreases [or increases], the acceptable level of detection risk increases [or decreases]. To increase control risk while maintaining the same audit risk level, the auditor could also reduce inherent risk. If the auditor were to increase materiality levels, that would reduce the overall audit risk. When the auditor increases control risk and thus decreases detection risk, substantive testing would need to be increased.

8. (c) AU 9311.37 states, "...each assistant has a professional responsibility to bring to the attention of the appropriate individuals in the firm, disagreements or concerns the assistant might have....In addition, each assistant should have a right to document his [or her] disagreement if he [or she] believes it is necessary to disassociate himself [or herself] from the resolution of the matter."

9. (b) AU 110.02 states, "The auditor has a responsibility to plan and perform the audit to obtain reasonable assurance about whether the financial statements are free of material misstatements, whether caused by error or fraud." The auditor usually satisfies this responsibility by exercising due skill and care in the performance of the audit procedures considered appropriate under the circumstances. If procedures indicate that material errors or fraud may exist, the auditor should extend the audit procedures.

CHAPTER 33: INTERNAL CONTROL: GENERAL

10. (a) AU 319.16 states, "The auditor's knowledge obtained in planning the audit should be used to identify types of potential misstatements, consider factors that affect the risk of material misstatements, and design substantive tests." AU 319.17 refers to the auditor's consideration of operating effectiveness, not efficiency. Answer (c) refers to an inherent limitation (AU 319.15). Answer (d) is not a reason for obtaining knowledge (AU 319.26).

11. (a) AU 319.07 states that an entity's internal control consists of five components: the control environment, the control activities, risk assessment, information and communication, and monitoring. Control risk is one of the three components of audit risk (AU 312.20).

12. (b) AU 319.57 states, "In addition to the documentation of the understanding of internal control..., the auditor should document the basis for...conclusions about the assessed level of control risk. However, for those financial statement assertions where control risk is assessed at the *maximum level*, the auditor should document his or her conclusion that control risk is at the maximum level but need not document the basis for that conclusion."

13. (c) AU 325.09 states, "Conditions noted by the auditor that are considered reportable...should be reported, preferably in writing. If information is communicated orally, the auditor should document the communication by appropriate...notations in the working papers." If the auditor does not become aware of any material weaknesses in internal control during the audit of the financial statements, the auditor may, but is not required to, communicate that fact. However, he or she should not issue a written report stating that "no material weaknesses were noted" (AU 325.17). There is no requirement for follow-up reporting of conditions reported at interim dates. AU 325.18 states, "Because timely communication may be important, the auditor may choose to communicate significant matters during the course of the audit *rather* than after the audit is concluded."

CHAPTER 34: INTERNAL CONTROL: TRANSACTION CYCLES

14. (a) Incompatible functions are those that place any person in a position to both perpetrate and conceal errors or fraud in the normal course of his or her duties. An employee who has access to assets as well as the accounting records related to those assets performs incompatible functions. The cashier performs incompatible functions if he or she can both receive remittances and post the receipts to the accounts receivable subsidiary ledger. Answers (b), (c), and (d) are all functions normally performed by the cashier.

15. (d) Sound internal control procedures dictate that an employee should be responsible for performing a given function, and that the same employee should not perform an incompatible function. Thus, all incoming shipments, including returns by customers, should be processed by personnel in the receiving department. A receiving clerk should inspect the merchandise and prepare a receiving report. This employee should not have control over the inventory records because that would enable him or her to divert merchandise without recording it.

16. (b) By reconciling the vendors' monthly statements with the subsidiary payable ledger accounts, the error would be corrected in at most a month's time. Footing the purchases journal only verifies the mathematical accuracy of the journal. Answer (c) is incorrect because the erroneous purchase amount in the purchases journal was originally carried through from the client's ledger accounts. Answer (d) is incorrect because the vendor may not confirm the fact that the client is overstating its liability for the purchases.

17. (c) Continuous utilization of serially numbered retirement work orders will provide assurance that the authorized retirements were in fact reflected in the accounting records. Continuous analysis of the repair and maintenance account [answer (a)] will provide assurance that capitalizable expenditures are not expensed. Periodic inquiry of plant executives [answer (b)] is not an effective procedure because such executives are not in a position to be aware of fixed asset retirements. Periodic inspection of insurance policies by internal auditors [answer (d)] will improve accountability of insurance expense, but some fixed assets may not be insured. Nor would the retirement of such assets be indicated in the insurance policies.

18. (b) The question requirement is to determine the best test of controls for an internal control procedure that calls for an approved receiving report to accompany every check. This control can be tested by selecting canceled checks and ascertaining that the related receiving reports are dated no later than the check. (In addition, the auditor would probably want to ascertain that the amount of the checks corresponds to the price of the goods received.) If the auditor selects receiving reports (rather than checks) to test the control in answer (c), he or she will not become aware of instances of checks being written with no accompanying receiving report.

19. (b) AU 319.52 states, "Tests of controls directed toward the effectiveness of the design of a control are concerned with whether that control is *suitably designed* to prevent or detect material misstatements in specific financial statement assertions." Answers (a), (c), and (d) consist of substantive tests which are tests of details and analytical procedures performed *to detect* material misstatements in the account balance, transaction class, and disclosure components of financial statements.

20. (c) The independent auditor is primarily concerned with those internal control policies and procedures that are relevant to the audit. AU 319.10 states, "Generally, controls that are relevant to the audit pertain to an entity's objective of preparing financial statements for external purposes that are fairly presented in conformity with [GAAP]." Internal controls over land and buildings and common stock are of primary concern to the auditor because they relate directly to financial statement assertions. Internal control over meetings of shareholders and the minutes of board of directors meetings are in the nature of administrative controls. Although these controls are of secondary concern to the auditor, the controls over the minutes of board of directors meetings are more important than those over shareholder meetings because they relate **directly** to management's authorization of transactions. Shareholder meetings can only have an indirect impact on such authorization.

CHAPTER 35: EVIDENCE & PROCEDURES

21. (b) The primary purpose of substantive tests is to determine the validity or propriety of the accounting treatment of transactions, or, conversely, monetary errors or fraud therein. Substantive tests may support the accuracy of underlying records, but these tests frequently provide no affirmative evidence of segregation of duties because the records may be accurate even though they are maintained by persons having incompatible functions. *Tests of controls* directed toward

operation are used to provide evidence of segregation of duties since the primary purpose of these tests is to determine how the policies or procedures are applied, the consistency with which they were applied, and by whom they were applied (AU 319.53).

22. (c) Despite the bank statements being handled by the client, they originate outside the entity and are, therefore, the most persuasive of the choices. Both purchase orders and work sheets originate within the client. The management representation letter merely documents oral representations the client has made.

23. (d) AU 322.10 states, "When assessing the internal auditor's objectivity, the auditor should obtain…information…about…the organizational status of the internal auditor…including the organizational level to which the internal auditor reports." Answers (a), (b), and (c) would give an indication as to competency, not objectivity.

24. (b) If management is unable to provide an acceptable explanation of significant fluctuations, the auditor should perform additional procedures to investigate those fluctuations further (AU 329.21). A scope limitation would only result if, after applying all the procedures considered necessary, the auditor is not able to explain the significant fluctuations. The existence of fluctuations is not necessarily indicative of management fraud. The auditor should consider withdrawal from the engagement if his or her audit indicates fraud or illegal acts by clients. The discovery of significant fluctuations in the financial statements does not provide the auditor with enough evidence to indicate these types of problems.

25. (a) AU 332.09 states that the written representation letter, "…should be signed by members of management who the auditor believes are responsible for and knowledgeable, directly or through others in the organization, about the matters covered by the representations. Normally, the chief executive officer and chief financial officer should sign the letter." Answers (b), (c), and (d) all suggest that the representation letter be signed by those who are not members of management, such as the chairman of the board of directors, the chairman of the board's audit committee, and the client's lawyer.

26. (c) The plant manager has a thorough knowledge of the operation of the factory. This knowledge comprehends an awareness of the productive capability of all the machinery in the plant, as well as new machinery on the market. As a result, he or she would know whether a particular machine is obsolete. The plant manager has no contact with accounts receivable and, thus, is not in a position to know about the adequacy of the provision for uncollectible accounts. The auditor must determine the appropriateness of the inventory observation procedures. The plant manager, on the other hand, would be helpful in identifying the location of all the inventory. The plant manager is not responsible for procuring necessary insurance coverage and, therefore, would not be aware that such procurement was deferred.

27. (c) AU 329.04 states that analytical procedures should be applied to some extent to assist the auditor in planning the nature, timing, and extent of the auditing procedures to be performed and as an overall review of the financial information in the final review stage of all audits.

28. (b) An analysis of bank confirmation information will reveal that the long-term liability accounts of the client are understated. The notes payable journal would not appear to be in error until the notes payable were confirmed. A year-end bank reconciliation and a year-end bank transfer schedule are used to verify the accuracy of the cash account which are not affected, in this case, by the bookkeeper's error.

29. (a) AU 337.08 states, "A letter of audit inquiry to the client's lawyer is the auditor's primary means of obtaining corroboration of the information furnished by management concerning litigations, claims, and assessments." Note that auditors are not presumed to be experts on legal matters and so are not required to review legal documentation.

30. (c) Client engagement letters are a matter of sound business practice, rather than a professional requirement. AU 311.05 states that a written audit program establishing auditing procedures to accomplish the audit's objectives is necessary. AU 326.15 states that the basic accounting data and all corroborating information support the financial statements. Without an indication that the accounting records agree or reconcile with the financial statements, the auditor cannot express an opinion upon them. AU 319.57 states the basis for the auditor's conclusions is required to be documented when the assessed level of control risk is below the maximum level.

31. (d) The permanent file (as indicated by its name) contains information on the client which is **not** likely to change from year to year. This information should be periodically updated and it is often used as a basis for the preliminary design of the current year's engagement. Descriptions of the client's accounting procedures and internal control are the

types of information found in this file. The types of information listed in answers (a), (b), and (c) mainly affect only the current year's engagement and so they are likely to be found in the current file, not the permanent file.

32. (c) The financial statements are the representations of management, who would like the financial position of the entity to appear as sound as possible. Thus, the auditor is concerned with possible *overstatements* of revenues, income, assets, and capital. Conversely, the auditor is concerned with the possible *understatement* of any losses, expenses, and liabilities.

CHAPTER 36: AUDIT PROGRAMS

33. (a) By requesting confirmation of a sample of the inactive accounts, the auditor is seeking to determine the accuracy of the financial records with regard to the accounts. Due to their inactive nature, defalcations could occur in these accounts, e.g., through lapping or an improper writing-off of the account balance. The cost of obtaining positive confirmations for at least 50% of the total dollar amount of the receivables would generally far outweigh the benefits derived from such confirmations. The auditor does not treat receivables from agencies of the federal government any differently than other receivables, i.e., they are also subject to selective testing. Receivable confirmations can be sent as of any date.

34. (d) The main objective of the sales cut-off test is to determine that sales were recorded in the proper period. The auditor would test for excessive sales returns and discounts from a sample encompassing the entire period, not just the year-end work. Lapping of accounts receivable would be detected by tracing payments received to postings in the appropriate receivable subsidiary ledger.

35. (d) It is common practice for inventory to be sold on consignment. When this is the case, it is not necessary for the consigned inventory to be on hand at the time of the count. However, the auditor should perform audit procedures to verify the existence and amount of consigned inventory. Answers (a), (b), and (c) are all audit objectives regarding the examination of inventory.

36. (c) The bank should be asked to confirm that there has been no access to the box between the balance sheet date and the security-count date. If the client has had access to the box between those dates, the auditor should obtain from the client a list of securities added or removed, so as to reconcile the securities on hand on the count date to the securities listed in the subsidiary ledger on the balance-sheet date. Furthermore, the auditor should test the list of securities added or removed by tracing them to brokers' documents indicating sale or purchase of the securities. The procedures in answers (a) and (d) should be performed by the auditor, not by the bank's staff. In general, evidential matter is more persuasive when directly obtained by the auditor than when obtained from third parties. Banks normally don't keep lists of contents of safe deposit boxes.

37. (c) The accounts payable department receives the vendor's invoice which contains the quantities, descriptions, and prices of the items subject to the bill. A copy of the purchase order will enable the accounts payable department to (1) compare the invoice price with the purchase order price [answer (a)], (2) ensure that the purchase was properly authorized [answer (b)], and (3) compare the quantity ordered to the quantity purchased [answer (d)]. The accounts payable copy of the purchase order will not ensure that the goods had been received by the party requesting the goods.

38. (a) Amortization allocates the cost of the intangible to the periods in which the benefit is received and yields an appropriate valuation of the intangible in those periods. Amortization is not relevant to the existence or occurrence, completeness, or rights and obligations assertions.

CHAPTER 37: AUDIT SAMPLING

39. (a) When a sample is small in relation to the population, the population size has little or no effect on the determination of an appropriate sample size. However, in the rare case when the sample size is greater than 10% of the population size, a finite population correction factor may be used, which tends to decrease the required sample size. The required sample size varies with the expected deviation rate. As the population increases in size, the sample size necessary to represent the population with specified precision and reliability will increase, but not in proportion to the increase in population size. The tolerable rate is the maximum population rate of deviations from a prescribed control procedure that the auditor will tolerate without modifying the nature, timing, or extent of substantive testing. For a given tolerable rate, a smaller sample size should be selected as the expected population deviation rate decreases.

40. (d) Upon repeated random samples of a given size from a population, the distribution of the means of those samples will be a normal distribution. The mean of the distribution is equal to the

population mean and the standard error of the mean of the distribution equals the population standard deviation divided by the square root of the sample size [answer (b)]. Approximately 68% and 95% of the sample means will be within one and two standard deviations, respectively, of the mean of the distribution [answers (a) and (c)]. All of these characteristics relate to the distribution of sample means that results from repeated samples of a given size from a population. However, the distribution of the items drawn by the auditor in a particular sample may take on any form. Such a sample distribution is not necessarily a normal distribution, and therefore, the statement in answer (d) is not true.

41. (b) The tolerable rate of deviations is the maximum rate of deviations from a prescribed control procedure that the auditor is willing to accept without altering his or her assessed level of control risk. Deviations from pertinent control procedures do not necessarily result in misstatements because the transactions may still be recorded properly. Therefore, deviations from pertinent control procedures at a given rate ordinarily would be expected to result in misstatements at a lower rate (AU 350.33-.34).

Chapter 38: Auditing EDP Systems

42. (b) Computer disruptions could destroy the only record of an online transaction. By their nature, sales transactions processed on the Internet don't involve sales invoice documents. Integrated test facilities, archiving, and data retention are issues that arise whether sales are on the Internet or entered into a computer system by the entity.

43. (d) A check digit is a redundant digit added to a code or identification number for validation purposes. It can be inserted into any position as long as it is inserted consistently. In this respect, the auditor is able to recompute the check digit to determine whether an invalid number has been created.

44. (a) When a client processes financial data in electronic form without paper documentation, the auditor may audit on a more continuous basis than a traditional system, as a convenience, and may be required to audit on a more continuous basis to obtain sufficient, competent evidence as documentation for some transactions may only be available for a limited time. An embedded audit module can facilitate this "continuous" auditing. If anything, an auditor may rely less on internal control activities that emphasize the segregation of duties. Digital certificate verification and testing of firewall boundaries are more concerned with security than internal control.

Chapter 39: Reports on Audited Financial Statements

45. (d) AU 560.07 states, "Subsequent events such as changes in the quoted market prices of securities ordinarily should not result in adjustment of the financial statements because such changes typically reflect a concurrent evaluation of new conditions." The financial statements are typically adjusted for subsequent events that (1) provide additional evidence with respect to conditions that existed at the balance sheet date and (2) affect the estimates inherent in the process of preparing financial statements. Answers (a), (b), and (c) are all examples of the type of subsequent events that typically result in adjustments to the financial statements, because they are examples of conditions which existed at the balance sheet date.

46. (c) When the principal auditor decides that he or she will make reference to the audit of the other auditor, the report should clearly indicate, in the introductory, scope, and opinion paragraphs, the division of responsibility as between that portion of the financial statements covered by his or her own audit and that covered by the audit of the other auditor (AU 543.07).

47. (b) When reliance is placed on the report of another auditor, the report should disclose the division of responsibility between the two auditors but would not necessarily modify the opinion (AU 543.08). Answers (a), (c), and (d) are all examples of restrictions on the scope of the audit which will result in modification of the report (AU 508.20 and .41).

48. (d) AU 508.74 states, "The [current] auditor should indicate in the introductory paragraph of his [or her] report (1) that the financial statements of the prior period were audited by another auditor, (2) the date of [the prior] report, (3) the type of report issued by the predecessor auditor, and (4) [the reasons for any report] other than a standard report." The current auditor expresses an opinion in the opinion paragraph only on the period which he or she audited. The current auditor does not disclaim or express an opinion on the prior period statements. The successor auditor should not name the predecessor auditor in his or her report unless the predecessor's practice was acquired by, or merged with, that of the successor auditor (AU 508, footnote 27).

49. (a) AU 336.16 provides that "If the auditor decides to depart from an unqualified opinion…as a result of the report or findings of a specialist, reference to an identification of the specialist may be

made in the auditor's report if the auditor believes such reference will facilitate an understanding of the reason for the departure." Reference to a specialist should be made only if the reference will clarify an explanatory paragraph or other than unqualified opinion (AU 336.16).

50. (c) It is difficult to substantiate representations that a transaction was consummated on terms equivalent to those that prevail in arm's-length transactions. Thus, if a footnote includes such a representation, the auditor should express a qualified or adverse opinion because of a departure from GAAP (AU 334.12). Answers (a), (b), and (d) are all proper disclosures with respect to related party transactions.

51. (b) AU 561.04 provides that an auditor should, in this situation, discuss the matter with the client at whatever management levels he or she deems appropriate, including the board of directors, and request cooperation in whatever investigation may be necessary. The transaction arose before the balance sheet date (and so is not a subsequent event) and the auditor is responsible for reporting on such an event. An *unaudited* footnote should not be added to the 19X3 financial statements. The client (not the auditor) is the party responsible for notifying those who might rely on the financial statements.

52. (b) An independent auditor generally cannot express an unqualified opinion stating that financial statements are presented in conformity with GAAP if such statements contain a departure from accounting principles promulgated by the designated body, and the departure has a material effect on the financial statements taken as a whole. However, an independent auditor can express an unqualified opinion on such statements if he or she can demonstrate that due to unusual circumstances, the financial statements would otherwise be misleading (AU 508.14 and .15).

53. (a) AU 550.04 states, "If the other information is not revised to eliminate the material inconsistency, [the auditor] should consider other actions such as revising his [or her] report to include an explanatory paragraph describing the material inconsistency." The auditor should never consult with the client's legal counsel without first obtaining permission from the client. The issuance of a qualified opinion would be misleading since the financial statements themselves are presented fairly in conformity with GAAP.

54. (b) The omission of an auditing procedure that was considered necessary at the time of the audit does not necessarily imply that the opinion originally rendered is faulty, or that not enough auditing procedures were performed. Thus, the auditor should first assess the importance of the omitted procedure to his or her present ability to support the previously expressed opinion (AU 390.04). The results of other procedures originally applied or the results of subsequent audits may provide audit evidence of the audit opinion originally rendered. If at this point the auditor concludes that the omitted procedure is indeed necessary to support the opinion, then he or she should undertake to apply the omitted or an alternative procedure (AU 390.05).

Chapter 40: Other Types of Reports

55. (a) AU 623.01 states that special reports include "...auditors' reports issued in connection with... (1) financial statements that are prepared in conformity with a comprehensive basis of accounting other than [GAAP], (2) specified elements, accounts, or items of a financial statement, (3) compliance with aspects of contractual agreements or regulatory requirements related to audited financial statements, (4) financial presentations to comply with contractual agreements or regulatory provisions, and (5) financial information presented in prescribed forms or schedules that require a prescribed form of auditor's report." An auditor's report issued in connection with compliance with aspects of contractual agreements *unrelated* to audited financial statements is not considered to be a special report.

56. (b) AU 722.09 states, "The objective of a review of interim financial information is to provide the accountant, based on objectively applying his or her knowledge of financial reporting practices to significant accounting matters of which he or she becomes aware through inquiries and analytical review procedures, with a basis for reporting whether material modifications should be made for such information to conform with generally accepted accounting principles."

Chapter 41: Other Professional Services

57. (d) When an accountant compiles projected financial statements, the accountant's report should include a separate paragraph that describes the limitations on the usefulness of the presentation.

58. (a) AT 200.33 states that the report contains a separate paragraph describing the limitations on the use of the presentation. The report does not provide an explanation of the differences between an examination and an audit. The accountant is not responsible for events occurring after the date of the

report. The standard report contains the phrase, "In our opinion, the underlying assumptions provide a reasonable basis for management's projection."

59. (d) In a compilation, the accountant presents, in the form of financial statements, information that is the representation of management. No expression of assurance is contemplated in a compilation. In a review, however, the accountant makes inquiries and performs analytical procedures which should provide a reasonable basis for expressing limited assurance that there are no material modifications that should be made to the financial statements. Because of this increased level of responsibility in a review, the accountant is required to obtain a management representation letter. Answers (a), (b), and (c) each list one of the prerequisites for performing either a compilation or a review.

60. (a) AT 400.02 states, "An entity's internal control structure over financial reporting includes those policies and procedures that pertain to an entity's ability to record...and report financial data consistent with the assertions...in...financial statements." Of the categories of people listed, shareholders have the least to do with establishing and maintaining internal control or financial reporting.

PERFORMANCE BY TOPICS

The final examination questions corresponding to each chapter of the Auditing text are listed below. To assess your preparedness for the CPA exam, record the number and percentage of questions you correctly answered in each topic area. The point distribution of the multiple choice questions (not counting the other objective format or essay questions) approximates that of the CPA exam.

Chapter 31: Standards & Related Topics

Question #	Correct √
1	
2	
3	

Questions 3

Correct ______
% Correct ______

Chapter 32: Planning

Question #	Correct √
4	
5	
6	
7	
8	
9	

Questions 6

Correct ______
% Correct ______

Chapter 33: Internal Control: General

Question #	Correct √
10	
11	
12	
13	

Questions 4

Correct ______
% Correct ______

Chapter 34: Internal Control: Transaction Cycles

Question #	Correct √
14	
15	
16	
17	
18	
19	
20	

Questions 7

Correct ______
% Correct ______

Chapter 35: Evidence & Procedures

Question #	Correct √
21	
22	
23	
24	
25	
26	
27	
28	
29	
30	
31	
32	

Questions 12

Correct ______
% Correct ______

Chapter 36: Audit Programs

Question #	Correct √
33	
34	
35	
36	
37	
38	

Questions 6

Correct ______
% Correct ______

Chapter 37: Audit Sampling

Question #	Correct √
39	
40	
41	

Questions 3

Correct ______
% Correct ______

Chapter 38: Auditing EDP Systems

Question #	Correct √
42	
43	
44	

Questions 3

Correct ______
% Correct ______

Chapter 39: Reports on Audited Financial Statements

Question #	Correct √
45	
46	
47	
48	
49	
50	
51	
52	
53	
54	

Questions 10

Correct ______
% Correct ______

Chapter 40: Other Types of Reports

Question #	Correct √
55	
56	

Questions 2

Correct ______
% Correct ______

Chapter 41: Other Professional Services

Question #	Correct √
57	
58	
59	
60	

Questions 4

Correct ______
% Correct ______

OTHER OBJECTIVE FORMAT QUESTION SOLUTIONS

Solution 2 Standard Audit Report

61. C A proper title contains the words *independent auditors' report.*

62. I The introductory paragraph contains all the necessary references to the audited financial statements.

63. I Reference to the American Institute of Certified Public Accountants does not belong anywhere in the report.

64. I Perry & Price have decided to assume responsibility for the work of Larkin & Lake as it relates to the expression of an opinion on the consolidated financial statements taken as a whole. In this circumstance it is inappropriate for Perry & Price to refer to Larkin & Lake anywhere in the report.

65. I The subsidiary and its magnitude need not be referred to anywhere in the auditor's report.

66. I The auditor's report need not state anywhere the requirements of GAAS.

67. I The auditor's report need not state anywhere the evaluation of the internal control structure is part of an audit.

68. C The auditor's report should state in the scope paragraph that an audit includes assessing significant estimates made by management.

69. C When a client subsequently restates prior period financial statements to conform with GAAP, and the auditor decides to express a different opinion than that previously expressed, the auditor should disclose all the substantive reasons for the different opinion in a separate explanatory paragraph preceding the opinion paragraph of the report, that should include: (1) the date of the auditor's previous report; (2) the type of opinion previously expressed; (3) the circumstances or events that caused the auditor to express a different opinion; and (4) that the auditor's updated opinion on the financial statements is different from the auditor's previous opinion on those financial statements.

70. I See the explanation to #69.

71. C The opinion paragraph should contain only the opinion. Concurrence is assumed if the restated opinion is favorable, and therefore no such explicit statement is necessary in other paragraphs.

72. C No reference to any uncertainties should be made in the introductory, scope, or opinion paragraphs. Reference to the uncertainty should be made in a separate explanatory paragraph following the opinion paragraph.

73. I AU 508.11 states, "Certain circumstances, while not affecting the auditor's unqualified opinion, may require that the auditor add an explanatory paragraph to his [or her] standard report. The auditor may add an explanatory paragraph to emphasize a matter..." AU 508.11 does not list an uncertainty as a circumstance requiring an explanatory paragraph. AU 508.30 states, "If...the auditor concludes that sufficient evidential matter...[exists], an unqualified opinion ordinarily is appropriate."

74. I Letters of inquiry to a client's lawyer concerning litigation, claims, and assessments are covered by AU 337. No reference should be made in the auditor's report to such a letter. SAS 73 allows mention of a specialist, such as a lawyer, in an auditor's report only when the reference to the specialist will increase the reader's understanding of the qualification or explanatory paragraph, such as in the interpretation of a contractual agreement. SAS 73 does not cover letters of inquiry to a client's lawyer.

75. I Reports are dual dated in response to a change in opinion when there has been a subsequent event. Changing the financial statements to conform to GAAP is not considered a subsequent event in this context.

Solution 3 Audit Objectives

76. E Of the choices given, the best audit procedure to ensure that investments are properly described and classified in the financial statements is to verify that transfers from the current to the noncurrent investment portfolio have been properly recorded.

77. F Of the choices given, the best audit procedure to ensure that recorded investments represent investments actually owned at the balance sheet date is to obtain positive confirmations as of the balance sheet date of investments held by independent custodians.

78. D Of the choices given, the best audit procedure to ensure that investments are properly valued at market at the balance sheet date is to

determine that any impairments in the price of investments have been properly recorded.

79. B Of the choices given, the best audit procedure to ensure that accounts receivable represent all amounts owed to the entity at the balance sheet date is to perform sales cut-off tests to obtain assurance that sales transactions and corresponding entries for inventories and costs of goods sold are recorded in the same and proper period.

80. E Of the choices given, the best audit procedure to ensure that the entity has legal right to all accounts receivable at the balance sheet date is to review loan agreements for indications of whether accounts receivable have been factored or pledged.

81. C Of the choices given, the best audit procedure to ensure that accounts receivable are stated at net realizable value is to review the aged trial balance for significant past due accounts.

82. F Of the choices given, the best audit procedure to ensure that accounts receivable are properly described and presented in the financial statements is to review the accounts receivable trial balance for amounts due from officers and employees.

83. D Of the choices given, the best audit procedure to ensure that the entity has legal right to property and equipment acquired during the year is to examine deeds and title insurance certificates.

84. G Of the choices given, the best audit procedure to ensure that recorded property and equipment represent assets that actually exist at the balance sheet date is to physically examine all major property and equipment additions.

85. B Of the choices given, the best audit procedure to ensure that net property and equipment are properly valued at the balance sheet date is to review the provision for depreciation expense and determine that depreciable lives and methods used in the current year are consistent with those used in the prior year.

ESSAY SOLUTIONS

SOLUTION 4 ENGAGEMENT LETTER

The typical engagement letter generally includes the following:

(1) The **name** and address of the person or **persons who retained the auditor** to perform the auditing services.
(2) An opening paragraph that confirms the **understandings** of the auditor and the client.
(3) A summary of **significant events** that led to the retention of the services of the auditor.
(4) A **general description** of the CPA firm that will conduct the audit.
(5) A **statement that the audit will be performed in accordance with generally accepted auditing standards.**
(6) A **description of the scope** of the services to be rendered, which should establish the nature of the engagement.
(7) Any **scope restriction** or **special limitations** and their effect on the auditor's report.
(8) A statement regarding the **auditor's responsibility for the detection of fraud.**
(9) An indication of the possible **use of client personnel** in connection with the audit to be performed.
(10) A statement that the **auditor will provide a management letter** if required in the circumstances.
(11) The **method and timing of billings** as well as billing rates and fee arrangements.
(12) Space for the **client representative's signature**, which indicates "acceptance" of the letter and the understandings therein.

The benefits of preparing an engagement letter include the **avoidance of possible problems** between the CPA and the client concerning (1) the **scope** of the work, (2) the **service** to be rendered, and (3) the audit **fee**. In addition, the "in-charge" auditor conducting the audit can avoid misunderstanding the nature and scope of the engagement if the engagement letter is included in the permanent section of the audit working papers. The **letter should eliminate misunderstandings and confusion** about the type of financial statements to be audited, the estimated report date, and the type of opinion expected. In this respect, the letter lessens any problems associated with the first standard of field work, which requires the work to be adequately planned and assistants to be properly supervised. In addition to avoiding possible misunderstandings, any legal problems relating to the auditor's failure to perform certain procedures can be reviewed with reference to the contractual commitment assumed. (For example, if scope limitations prevent the auditor from performing normal audit procedures, the auditor cannot be legally responsible if an irregularity is not detected when clearly it would have been detected if such procedures were performed.)

The engagement letter is also useful as a **reference document** when preparing for future engagements.

SOLUTION 5 STANDARD AUDIT REPORT

Item No.	Type of Change	Should Auditor's Report Be Modified?	Should Prior Year's Statement Be Restated?
1.	An accounting change involving a change from one generally accepted accounting principle to another generally accepted accounting principle.	**Yes**	**Yes**
2.	An accounting change involving a **change in an accounting estimate.**	**No**	**No**
3.	An **error correction** not involving an accounting principle.	**No**	**Yes**
4.	An accounting change involving a **correction of an error in principle** which is **accounted for as a correction of an error.**	**Yes**	**Yes**
5.	An accounting change involving a **change in the reporting entity** which is a special type of change in accounting principle.	**Yes**	**Yes**
6.	An accounting change involving **both a change in accounting principle and a change in accounting estimate.** Although the effect of the change in each may be inseparable and the accounting for such a change is the same as that accorded a change in estimate only, an accounting principle is involved.	**Yes**	**No**
7.	Not an accounting change but rather a **change in classification.**	**No**	**Yes**
8.	An accounting change **from one generally accepted accounting principle to another** generally accepted accounting principle.	**Yes**	**No**

APPENDIX B
PRACTICAL ADVICE

Your first step toward an effective CPA Review program is to **study** the material in this appendix. It has been carefully developed to provide you with essential information that will help you succeed on the CPA exam. This material will assist you in organizing an efficient study plan and will demonstrate effective techniques and strategies for taking the CPA exam.

SECTION ONE: GENERAL COMMENTS ON THE CPA EXAM

The difficulty and comprehensiveness of the CPA exam is a well-known fact to all candidates. However, success on the CPA exam is a **reasonable**, **attainable** goal. You should keep this point in mind as you study this appendix and develop your study plan. A positive attitude toward the examination, combined with determination and discipline, will enhance your opportunity to pass.

PURPOSE OF THE CPA EXAM

The CPA exam is designed as a licensing requirement to measure the technical competence of CPA candidates. Although licensing occurs at the State Board level, it is a uniform exam with national acceptance. Generally, passing the CPA exam in one jurisdiction allows a candidate to obtain a reciprocal certificate or license if they meet all the requirements imposed by the jurisdiction from which reciprocity is being sought.

State Boards also rely upon other means to ensure that candidates possess the necessary technical and character attributes, including interviews, letters of reference, affidavits of employment, ethics examinations, and educational requirements. Addresses of state boards are listed in this section of the **Practical Advice** appendix or (along with applicable links) on the web site of the National Association of the State Boards of Accountancy (http://www.nasba.org).

Generally speaking, the CPA exam is essentially an academic examination that tests the breadth of material covered by good accounting curricula. It also emphasizes the body of knowledge required for the practice of public accounting. It is to your advantage to take the exam as soon as possible after completing the formal education requirements. We also recommend that you study for the entire examination the first time you take it, since there is a **synergistic** learning effect to be derived through preparing for all four parts. That is, all sections of the exam share some common subjects (particularly Financial Accounting & Reporting, Accounting & Reporting, and Auditing); so as you study for one section, you are also studying for the others.

EXAMINATION SCHEDULE AND FORMAT

The CPA exam is given twice a year, on Wednesday and Thursday of the first week of May and November. AICPA-scheduled exam dates are May 8 and 9, 2002, and November 6 and 7, 2002. Unofficial projections for 2003 are May 7 and 8 as well as November 5 and 6. As the exam is becoming further computerized, projections past November 2002 are subject to greater uncertainty than in the past.

The four sections of the exam cover the following:

1. **Business Law & Professional Responsibilities**—This section covers the legal implications of business transactions generally confronted by CPAs, and the CPA's professional responsibility to the public and the profession (formerly covered in the Auditing section). This section's name is frequently abbreviated as BLPR. (3 hours)

2. **Auditing**—This section covers the generally accepted auditing standards, procedures, and related topics. The CPA's professional responsibility is no longer tested in this area. This section's name is frequently abbreviated as AUD. (4½ hours)

3. **Accounting & Reporting-Taxation, Managerial, and Governmental and Not-for-Profit Organizations**—This section covers federal taxation, managerial accounting, and accounting for governmental and nonprofit organizations. This section consists of multiple choice and other objective format questions only. This section has no essay questions or problems. This section's name is frequently abbreviated as ARE. (3½ hours)

4. **Financial Accounting & Reporting**—This section covers generally accepted accounting principles for business enterprises. This section's name is frequently abbreviated as FARE. (4½ hours)

The examination has the following formats and times:

Section	Format: Multiple Choice	Format: Other Objective Answer Formats	Format: Essays or Problems	Day and Time	Duration
BLPR	50-60%	20-30%	20-30%	Wed. 9:00 -12:00	3 hours
Auditing	50-60%	20-30%	20-30%	Wed. 1:30 - 6:00	4 1/2 hours
ARE	50-60%	40-50%	---	Thur. 8:30 -12:00	3 1/2 hours
FARE	50-60%	20-30%	20-30%	Thur. 1:30 - 6:00	4 1/2 hours
					15 1/2 hours

CONDITIONAL STATUS

You will receive four scores. A passing score for each section is 75. Individual Boards of Accountancy may grant conditional status to those candidates who receive a passing grade in some, but not all, sections. Some Boards of Accountancy grant conditional status to candidates who pass only one section, while other Boards require that at least two sections be passed before conditional status is awarded. Many Boards require a minimum grade in the sections failed to receive conditional credit for the sections passed. Candidates should check with their State Board of Accountancy concerning details on conditional status.

ATTORNEYS' WAIVER

Some Boards of Accountancy may waive the Business Law section for members of the state bar. Once again, candidates should check with their particular state Board of Accountancy concerning this matter.

WRITING SKILLS CONTENT

Answers to selected essay responses from Business Law & Professional Responsibilities, Auditing, and Financial Accounting & Reporting sections will be used to assess candidates' writing skills. Additional information regarding writing skills is included in the **Accounting for 5%** section of those volumes. Five percent of the points available on each of these sections will be allocated to writing skills. Effective writing skills include the following six characteristics:

1. Coherent organization
2. Conciseness
3. Clarity
4. Use of standard English
5. Responsiveness to the requirements of the question
6. Appropriateness for the reader

REFERENCE MATERIALS

All the material you need to review to pass the CPA exam is in your Bisk Education *CPA Comprehensive Review* texts! However, should you desire more detailed coverage in any area, you should consult the actual promulgations. Individual copies of recent pronouncements are available from the FASB or AICPA. To order materials from the **FASB** or **AICPA** contact:

FASB Order Department
P.O. Box 5116
Norwalk, CT 06856-5116
Telephone (203) 847-0700

AICPA Order Department
P.O. Box 1003
New York, NY 10108-1003
Telephone (800) 334-6961

The FASB offers a student discount that varies depending on the publication. The AICPA offers a 30% educational discount, which students may claim by submitting proof of their eligibility (e.g., copy of ID card or teacher's letter). AICPA members get a 20% discount and delivery time is speedier because members may order by phone.

THE NONDISCLOSED EXAM

The Uniform CPA Examination is nondisclosed. This means that candidates are not allowed to keep (or receive) their examination booklets after the test. Candidates are also required to sign a statement of confidentiality in which they promise not to reveal questions or answers. After the exam, only the Institute will have access to the tests themselves. (The AICPA releases a small number of questions with unofficial answers from each nondisclosed exam.) Bisk Education's editors will continue to update our diagnostic tests for your convenience, with questions based upon the representative items, items from previously disclosed tests, and the teaching expertise of our editors.

BACKGROUND

The AICPA made this change (beginning May 1996), in order to increase consistency, facilitate possible future computer administration of the test, and improve examination quality by pretesting questions. Because the examination is no longer completely changed every year, statistical equating methods will be more relevant, and the usefulness of specific questions as indicators of candidates' knowledge can be tested.

EFFECTS ON TIME MANAGEMENT

Approximately 10% of the multiple choice questions in every section of every nondisclosed exam are questions that are being pretested. These questions are not included in candidates' final grades; they are presented only so that the Board of Examiners may evaluate them for effectiveness and possible ambiguity. The Scholastic Achievement Test and the Graduate Record Exam both employ similar but not identical strategies: those tests include an extra section that is being pretested, and test-takers do not know which section is the one which will not be graded. On the Uniform CPA Examination, however, the extra questions are mixed in among the graded questions. This makes time management even more crucial. Candidates who are deciding how much time to spend on a difficult multiple choice question must keep in mind that there is a 10% chance that the answer to the question will not affect them either way. Also, candidates should not allow a question that seems particularly difficult or confusing to shake their confidence or affect their attitude towards the rest of the test; it may not even count. This experimental 10% works against candidates who are not sure whether they have answered enough questions to earn 75%. Candidates should try for a safety margin, so that they will have accumulated enough correct answers to pass, even though some of their correctly answered questions will not be scored.

POST-EXAM DIAGNOSTICS

The AICPA Board of Examiners' Advisory Grading Service provides boards of accountancy with individual diagnostic reports for all candidates along with the candidates' grades. The accountancy boards may mail the diagnostic reports to candidates along with their grades. Candidates should contact the state board in their jurisdiction to find out its policy on this issue. A sample of a diagnostic report is in Section Five of this appendix. As before, grades are mailed approximately 90 days after the examination.

DISCUSSING THE EXAM

Remember that candidates are required to sign a statement of confidentiality in which they promise not to reveal questions or answers. Due to the nondisclosure requirements, Bisk Education's editors are no longer able to address questions about specific examination questions, although we continue to supply help with similar study problems and questions in our texts.

QUESTION RE-EVALUATION

Candidates who believe that an examination question contains errors that will affect the grading should fax their complaint to the AICPA Examinations Division, at (201) 938-3443, within 4 days after taking the examination. Only this method of communication will satisfy the requirements of the AICPA. The Advisory Grading Service asks candidates to be as precise as possible about the question and their reason for believing that it should be re-evaluated, and, if possible, to supply references to support their position. Since candidates are no longer able to keep or discuss the examination questions, it is important to remember as much detail as possible about a disputed question.

AICPA NONDISCLOSED EXAMINATION COVERAGE SUMMARY

The following chart provides an analysis of the AICPA Content Specification Outline coverage for the Auditing section of the November 1998 through November 2000 Uniform CPA Examinations, all "nondisclosed" exams. This summary, provided by the AICPA, is intended only as a study aid and should not be used to predict the content of future examinations. More detail on the content specification outline is available in Section 5 of this appendix.

The percentages indicate the format and subject of questions on the November 1998 through November 2000 CPA exams. For instance, on the Auditing section of the November 2000 exam, 50 percent of the questions were multiple choice and 30 percent of the questions were other objective format (OOAF). Different details were released from the AICPA for different exams; some columns have more detail than others.

The actual number of some of the multiple choice questions asked for each area and group of the Content Specification Outline is also provided, when available. For example, under the *Plan, Evaluate, Agreement* area on the November 1999 exam, there were 30 multiple choice questions: of those, 3 dealt with the *Assess Risk* group. The May and November 2000 information doesn't have the number or percentage of questions at the group level.

	Multiple Choice					OOAFs					Essays				
	N00	M00	N99	M99	N98	N00	M00	N99	M99	N98	N00	M00	N99	M99	N98
	75 (50%)	75 (50%)	75 (50%)	75 (50%)	75 (50%)	51 30%	50 30%	30%	30%	30%	20%	20%	20%	20%	20%
I. Plan, Evaluate, Agreement (40%)	37* (25%)	30* (20%)	30 (20%)	30 (20%)	23 (15%)	9* 5%	17* 10%	10%	10%	5%	* 10%	* 10%	10%	10%	20%
A. Scope			3	6	5										
B. Assess Risk			3	5	3										
C. Predecessor			1	2	1			2%							
D. Accept/Continue			2	2	1										
E. Terms			1	1	1			2%							
F. Client & Industry			1	1	1										
G. Analytics			0	3	0			5%		5%					
H. Preliminary Materiality			2	2	2										
I. Inherent Risk			5	0	5				10%						
J. Internal Control			5	1	0								8%	10%	20%
K. Other Matters			4	4	2								2%		
L. Assertions/Objectives			2	2	1										
M. Nature, Extent, Timing			1	1	1			1%							
II. Obtain, Document Information (35%)	26* (17%)	23* (15%)	27 (18%)	23 (15%)	34 (23%)	18* 10%	17* 10%	17%	20%	12%	* 8%	* 10%	0%	0%	0%
A. Perform Procedures			20	18	25			12%	10%	12%					
B. Contingencies			1	0	1			1%	2%						
C. Lawyers' Letters			1	0	1			1%	8%						
D. Subsequent Events			2	1	2										
E. Representations			0	2	2			2%							
F. Reportable Conditions			2	1	2										
G. Audit Committee			1	1	1			1%							
III. Review the Engagement (5%)	0%	7* (5%)	3 (2%)	7 (5%)	3 (2%)	8* 5%	0%	3%	0%	3%	0%	0%	0%	0%	0%
A. Analytics			0	2	0			3%		3%					
B. Evaluate Evidence			2	3	2										
C. Review			1	2	1										
IV. Prepare Communications (20%)	12* (8%)	15* (10%)	15 (10%)	15 (10%)	15 (10%)	16* 10%	16* 10%	0%	0%	10%	* 2%	0%	10%	10%	0%
A. Prepare Reports			15	10	11					10%			10%	10%	
B. Prepare Letters			0	3	4										
C. Other Matters			0	2	0										

AICPA
Uniform CPA Examination
Candidate Diagnostic Report

Jurisdiction SAMPLE **Candidate Number** 0-00-0000 **Examination Date** May 2001

SECTION	GRADE	CONTENT AREA AND SECTION COVERAGE		PERCENTAGE OF AREA EARNED ≤ 50	51-60	61-70	71-80	81-90	> 90
LPR	**64**	I PROFESSIONAL AND LEGAL RESPONSIBILITIES	15%			◆			
		II BUSINESS ORGANIZATIONS	20%				◆		
		III CONTRACTS	10%		◆				
		IV DEBTOR-CREDITOR RELATIONSHIPS	10%	◆					
		V GOVERNMENT REGULATION OF BUSINESS	15%				◆		
		VI UNIFORM COMMERCIAL CODE	20%	◆					
		VII PROPERTY	10%						◆
			100%						
AUDIT	**68**	I EVALUATE CLIENT AND PLAN ENGAGEMENT	40%				◆		
		II OBTAIN AND DOCUMENT INFORMATION	35%			◆			
		III REVIEW ENGAGEMENT	5%				◆		
		IV PREPARE COMMUNICATION	20%		◆				
			100%						
ARE	**78**	I FEDERAL TAXATION—INDIVIDUALS	20%			◆			
		II FEDERAL TAXATION—CORPORATIONS	20%						◆
		III FEDERAL TAXATION—PARTNERSHIPS	10%			◆			
		IV FEDERAL TAXATION—OTHER	10%				◆		
		V GOVERNMENTAL AND NOT-FOR-PROFIT ORGANIZATIONS	30%			◆			
		VI MANAGERIAL ACCOUNTING	10%				◆		
			100%						
FARE	**80**	I CONCEPTS AND STANDARDS FOR FINANCIAL STATEMENTS	20%					◆	
		II TYPICAL ITEMS IN FINANCIAL STATEMENTS	40%			◆			
		III SPECIFIC TRANSACTIONS AND EVENTS IN FINANCIAL STATEMENTS	40%					◆	
			100%						

STATE BOARDS OF ACCOUNTANCY

Certified Public Accountants are licensed to practice by individual State Boards of Accountancy. Application forms and requirements to sit for the CPA exam should be requested from your individual State Board. IT IS EXTREMELY IMPORTANT THAT YOU COMPLETE THE APPLICATION FORM CORRECTLY AND RETURN IT TO YOUR STATE BOARD BEFORE THE SPECIFIED DEADLINE. Errors and/or delays may result in the rejection of your application. Be extremely careful in filling out the application and be sure to enclose all required materials. In many states, applications must be received by the State Board at least ninety days before the examination date. Requirements as to education, experience, internship, and other matters vary. If you have not already done so, take a moment to call the appropriate State Board for specific and current requirements. Complete the application in a timely manner. Some states arrange for an examination administrator, such CPA Examination Services [a division of the National Association of State Boards of Accountancy (NASBA), (800) CPA-EXAM (272-3926)] or Continental Examination Services [(800) 717-1201], to handle candidate registration, examination administration, etc.

It may be possible to sit for the exam in another state as an out-of-state candidate. Candidates wishing to do so should also contact the State Board of Accountancy in the state where they plan to be certified. NASBA has links (**http://www.nasba.org**) to most state board sites.

Approximately one month before the exam, check to see that your application to sit for the exam has been processed. DON'T ASSUME THAT YOU ARE PROPERLY REGISTERED UNLESS YOU HAVE RECEIVED YOUR CANDIDATE ID NUMBER.

The AICPA publishes a booklet entitled *Information for CPA Candidates*, usually distributed by State Boards of Accountancy to candidates upon receipt or acceptance of their applications. To request a complimentary copy, write your **State Board** or the **AICPA**, Examination Division, 1211 Avenue of the Americas, New York, NY 10036.

EXAMINATION SERVICES

CPA Examination Services, a division of the National Association of State Boards of Accountancy (NASBA), administers the examination for 25 states. Contact CPA Examination Services at (800) CPA-EXAM (272-3926), (615) 880-4250, or www.nasba.org.

CO	CT	DE	GA	HI	IA	IN	KS	LA	MA	ME	MI	
MO	NJ	NM	NY	OH	PA	PR	RI	SC	TN	VA	VT	WA

Continental Testing Services at (800) 717-1201 administers the examination for WI.

The following are the telephone numbers and addresses of the boards in states that administer the exam themselves.

STATE	ADDRESS	PHONE NUMBER
AK	P.O. Box 110806, Juneau 99811-0806	907/465-2580
AL	P.O. Box 300375, Montgomery 36130-0375	334/242-5700
AR	101 E. Capitol Avenue, Ste. 430, Little Rock 72201	501/682-1520
AZ	3877 North Seventh Street, Ste. 106, Phoenix 85014	602/255-3648
CA	2000 Evergreen St., Ste. 250, Sacramento 95815-3832	916/263-3680
DC	614 H Street, N.W., Room 910, P.O. Box 37200, Washington, DC 20013-7200	202/442-4461
FL	2610 N.W. 43rd St., Ste. 1A, Gainesville 32606-4599	352/333-2500
GU	P.O. Box P, Agana, GU 96910	671/477-1050
ID	P.O. Box 83720, Boise 83720-0002	208/334-2490
IL	505 E. Green, Room 216, Champaign 61820-5723	217/333-1565
KY	332 W. Broadway, Ste. 310, Louisville 40202-2115	502/595-3037
MD	501 St. Paul Place, 9th Floor, Baltimore 21202-2272	410/333-6322
MN	85 East 7th Place, Ste. 125, St. Paul 55101	651/296-7937
MS	653 North State Street, Jackson 39202-3304	601/354-7320
MT	111 N. Jackson, P.O. Box 200513, Helena 59620-0513	406/841-2388
NC	P.O. Box 12827, Raleigh 27605-2827	919/733-4222
ND	2701 S. Columbia Road, Grand Forks 58201	800/532-5904
NE	P.O. Box 94725, Lincoln 68509-4725	402/471-3595
NH	57 Regional Dr., Concord 03301	603/271-3286
NV	200 South Virginia Street, Ste. 670, Reno 89501-2408	775/786-0231
OK	4545 N. Lincoln Blvd., Ste. 165, Oklahoma City 73105-3413	405/521-2397
OR	3218 Pringle Rd. S.E., Ste. 110, Salem 97302-6307	503/378-4181
SD	301 E. 14th St., Ste. 200, Sioux Falls 57104	605/367-5770
TX	333 Guadalupe Tower III, Suite 900, Austin 78701-3900	512/305-7850
UT	P.O. Box 146741, Salt Lake City 84114-6741	801/359-4417
VI	P.O. Box Y, Christiansted, St. Croix VI, 00822	340/773-2226
WI	P.O. Box 8935, Madison 53708-8935 [Call 800/717-1201]	608/266-5511
WV	201 L&S Bldg., 812 Quarrier Street, Charleston 25301-2695	304/558-3557
WY	2020 Carey Avenue Ste. 100, Cheyenne 82002-0610	307/777-7551

These addresses and phone numbers are subject to change without notice. Bisk Education assumes no responsibility with regard to their accuracy.

TEN ATTRIBUTES OF EXAMINATION SUCCESS

1.	**Positive Mental Attitude**	6.	**Examination Grading**
2.	**Development of a Plan**	7.	**Solutions Approach™**
3.	**Adherence to the Plan**	8.	**Examination Strategies**
4.	**Time Management**	9.	**Focus on Ultimate Objective—Passing!**
5.	**Knowledge**	10.	**Examination Confidence**

We believe that successful CPA candidates possess these ten characteristics that contribute to their ability to pass the exam. Because of their importance, we will consider each attribute individually.

1. Positive Mental Attitude

Preparation for the CPA exam is a long, intense process. A positive mental attitude, above all else, can be the difference between passing and failing.

2. Development of a Plan

The significant commitment involved in preparing for the exam requires a plan. We have prepared a Study Plan in the preceding "Getting Started" section. Take time to read this plan. Whether you use our "Study Plan" or create your own, the importance of this attribute can't be overlooked.

3. Adherence to the Plan

You cannot expect to accomplish a successful and comprehensive review without adherence to your study plan.

4. Time Management

We all lead busy lives, and the ability to budget study time is a key to success. We have outlined steps to budgeting time in the **Personalized Training Plan** found in the "Getting Started" section.

5. Knowledge

There is a distinct difference between understanding the material and knowing the material. A superficial understanding of accounting, auditing, and business law is not enough. You must know the material likely to be tested on the exam. Your Bisk Education text is designed to help you acquire the working knowledge that is essential to exam success.

6. Examination Grading

An understanding of the CPA exam grading procedure will help you to maximize grading points on the exam. Remember that your objective is to score 75 points on each section. Points are assigned to individual questions by the grader who reads your exam. In essence, your job is to satisfy the grader by writing answers that closely conform to the grading guide. In Section Two, we explain AICPA grading procedures and show you how to tailor your answer to the grading guide and thus earn more points on the exam.

7. Solutions Approach™

The Solutions Approach™ is an efficient, systematic method of organizing and solving questions found on the CPA exam. This Approach will permit you to organize your thinking and your written answers in a logical manner that will maximize your exam score. Candidates who do not use a systematic answering method often neglect to show all their work on difficult problems or essays—work that could earn partial credit if it were presented to the grader in an orderly fashion. The Solutions Approach™ will help you avoid drawing "blanks" on the exam; with it, you always know where to begin.

Many candidates have never developed an effective problem-solving methodology in their undergraduate studies. The "cookbook" approach, in which students work problems by following examples, is widespread among accounting schools. Unfortunately, it is not an effective problem-solving method for the CPA exam or for problems you will encounter in your professional career. Our Solutions Approach™ teaches you to derive solutions independently, without an example to guide you.

Our **Solutions Approach™** and grader orientation skills, when properly developed, can be worth at least 10 to 15 points for most candidates. These 10 to 15 points can often make the difference between passing and failing.

The **Solutions Approach™** for objective questions, problems, and essays is outlined in Section Three. Examples are worked and explained.

8. Examination Strategies

You should be familiar with the format of the CPA exam and know exactly what you will do when you enter the examination room. In Section Four, we discuss the steps you should take from the time you receive the test booklet, until you hand in your answer sheet. Planning in advance how you will spend your examination time will save you time and confusion on exam day.

9. Focus on Ultimate Objective—Passing!

Your primary goal in preparing for the CPA exam is to attain a grade of 75 or better on all sections and, thus, **pass the examination**. Your review should be focused on this goal. Other objectives, such as learning new material or reviewing old material, are important only insofar as they assist you in passing the exam.

10. Examination Confidence

Examination confidence is actually a function of the other nine attributes. If you have acquired a good working knowledge of the material, an understanding of the grading system, a tactic for answering the problems or essays, and a plan for taking the exam, you can go into the examination room **confident** that you are in control.

SECTION TWO: EXAMINATION GRADING ORIENTATION

The CPA exam is prepared and graded by the AICPA Examinations Division. It is administered by the various State Boards of Accountancy.

An understanding of the grading procedure will help you maximize grading points on the CPA exam. Remember that your objective is to pass the exam. You cannot afford to spend time on activities that will not affect your grade, or to ignore opportunities to increase your points. The following material abstracted from the *Information for CPA Candidates* booklet summarizes the important substantive aspects of the Uniform CPA Examination itself and the grading procedures used by the AICPA.

SECURITY

The examination is prepared and administered under tight security measures. The candidates' anonymity is preserved throughout the examination and grading process. Unusual similarities in answers among candidates are reported to the appropriate State Boards.

OBJECTIVE QUESTIONS

Objective questions consist of four-option, multiple-choice questions and other objective answer formats, which include: yes-no, true-false, matching, and questions requiring a numerical response. Objective questions are machine graded. Thus, you will accomplish nothing (and only waste time) by writing explanations beside your answers—only the blackened response is considered by the optical scanner. It is also important to understand that there is **no grade reduction** for incorrect responses to objective questions—your total objective question grade is determined solely by the number of correct answers. Thus, you **should answer every question**. If you do not know the answer, make an intelligent guess.

There are two or three formats for questions on each section of the CPA exam. In the past, difficulty points were assigned to these parts as a means of curving the entire section. This no longer occurs. Instead, difficulty points are assigned to the exam as a whole, not to each individual question. The point to remember is to avoid getting "bogged down" on one answer. Move along and answer **all** the questions. This helps you avoid leaving questions unanswered or panic-answering questions due to poor budgeting of test time.

ESSAY QUESTIONS

Essay questions are graded by CPAs and AICPA staff members, using the following procedures as described in the *Information for CPA Candidates* booklet:

FIRST GRADING

The first grading is done by graders assigned to individual questions. For example, each essay in the Auditing section will be graded by a different grader. A grader assigned to a single question, that will be graded during the full grading session of six or seven weeks, becomes an expert in the subject matter of the question and in the evaluation of the candidates' answers. Thus, grading is objective and uniform.

The purpose of the first grading is to separate the candidates' papers into three groups: obvious passes, marginal, and obvious failures.

SECOND GRADING

Upon completion of the first grading, a second grading is done by reviewers. Obvious passes and failures are subjected to cursory reviews as part of the grading controls. Marginal papers, however, receive an extensive review.

The graders who make the extensive reviews have had years of experience grading the CPA Examination. They have also participated in the development of the grading bases and have access to item analysis for objective questions, identifying concepts as discriminating (those included by most candidates passing the exam) or as rudimentary (those included by candidates both passing and failing the exam). An important indicator of the competence of the candidate is whether grade points were earned chiefly from discriminating concepts or from rudimentary concepts.

THIRD GRADING

After the papers have been through the second grading for all parts of the examination, the resultant grades are listed by candidate number and compared for consistency among subjects. For example, if a candidate passes two subjects and receives a marginal grade in a third, the marginal paper will receive a third grading in the hope that the candidate, now identified as possessing considerable competence, can have the paper raised to a passing grade by finding additional points for which to grant positive credit. This third grading is done by the section head or a reviewer who did not do the second grading of the paper.

FOURTH GRADING

The Director of Examinations applies a fourth grading to papers that have received the third grading but have grades that are inconsistent. The Director knows that the papers have already been subjected to three gradings, and that it would be difficult to find additional points for which the candidates should be given credit. Obviously, very few candidates are passed in this manner, but this fourth grading assures that marginal candidates receive every possible consideration.

ESSAY QUESTION EXAMPLE—GRADING GUIDE

Points are assigned to essay questions on the basis of **key concepts**. A key concept is an idea, thought, or option that can be clearly defined and identified. Through a grading of sample papers, a list of key concepts related to each question is accumulated. These key concepts become the **grading bases** for the question. That is, your answer will be scored according to the number of key concepts it contains. Note that you need not include **all** possible key concepts to receive full credit on a question. The total number of grading bases exceeds the point value of the question. For example, a 10-point question may have 15 or more grading bases. Thus, a candidate would not have to provide all the key concepts to get the maximum available points. Conversely, a candidate cannot receive more points even if he or she provides more than 10 key concepts.

To illustrate the grading procedure and the importance of using key concepts in your answers, we will develop a hypothetical grading guide for a question adapted from a past Auditing exam. We will assume that the entire question is worth 10 points.

EXAMPLE 1—SAMPLE ESSAY

Microcomputer software has been developed to improve the efficiency and effectiveness of the audit. Electronic spreadsheets and other software packages are available to aid in the performance of audit procedures otherwise performed manually.

REQUIRED:

Describe the potential benefits to an auditor of using microcomputer software in an audit as compared to performing an audit without the use of a computer.

Now let's look at the unofficial answer. Notice that we have boldfaced the key concepts in the answer. Later, as we develop a grading guide for the answer, you will see the importance of using key concepts to tailor your answer to parallel the grading guide.

SOLUTION: ADVANTAGES OF USING A COMPUTER IN AN AUDIT

The potential benefits to an auditor of using microcomputer software in an audit as compared to performing an audit without the use of a computer include the following:

1. **Time** may be **saved by eliminating manual** footing, cross-footing, and other routine **calculations.**
2. Calculations, comparisons, and other data manipulations are more **accurately** performed.
3. **Analytical procedures** calculations may be **more efficiently** performed.
4. The **scope of analytical procedures** may be **broadened.**
5. **Audit sampling** may be **facilitated.**
6. **Potential weaknesses** in a client's **internal control** may be **more readily identified.**
7. **Preparation and revision** of **flowcharts** depicting the flow of financial transactions in a client's internal control may be **facilitated.**
8. **Working papers** may be **easily stored and accessed.**
9. **Graphics capabilities** may allow the auditor to **generate, display, and evaluate** various **financial and nonfinancial relationships graphically.**
10. **Engagement-management information** such as time budgets and the monitoring of actual time vs. budgeted amounts may be **more easily generated and analyzed.**
11. **Customized working papers** may be **developed with greater ease.**
12. **Standardized audit correspondence** such as engagement letters, client representation letters, and attorney letters may be **stored and easily modified.**
13. **Supervisory-review time** may be **reduced.**
14. **Staff morale** and **productivity** may be improved by **reducing** the **time spent on clerical tasks.**
15. **Client's personnel** may **not need to manually prepare as many schedules** and otherwise spend as much time assisting the auditor.
16. **Computer-generated working papers** are generally **more legible and consistent.**

The grading guide consists of a list of the key concepts relevant to the question, both in key word form and in detailed phrases. Each concept is assigned a point (more than one point if it is particularly important or fundamental). A point is also given on many questions for neatness and clarity of answer (including the use of proper formats, schedules, etc.). A hypothetical grading guide for our sample question follows.

EXAMPLE 2—GRADING GUIDE FOR ESSAY

STATE ____________________

CANDIDATE NO. ____________________

POINTS		KEY WORD CONCEPTS
2	1.	Time saved by eliminating manual calculations.
2	2.	Accuracy.
2	3.	Analytical procedures more efficient.
2	4.	Scope of analytical procedures broadened.
1	5.	Audit sampling facilitated.
1	6.	Potential weaknesses in internal control more readily identified.
1	7.	Preparation and revision of flowcharts facilitated.
1	8.	Working papers easily stored and accessed.
1	9.	Graphics capabilities to generate, display, and evaluate financial and nonfinancial relationships graphically.
1	10.	Engagement-management information more easily generated and analyzed.
1	11.	Customized working papers developed with greater ease.
1	12.	Standardized audit correspondence stored and easily modified.
1	13.	Supervisory-review time reduced.
1	14.	Staff morale and productivity improved by reducing time spent on clerical tasks.
1	15.	Client's personnel time assisting auditor decreased.
1	16.	Computer-generated working papers more legible and consistent.
20		

GRADE CONVERSION CHART: POINTS TO GRADE

POINTS	1 2	3 4	5 6	7 8	9 10	11 12	13 14	15 16	17 18	19 20
GRADE	1	2	3	4	5	6	7	8	9	10

IMPORTANCE OF KEY CONCEPTS

A grading guide similar to the one in Example 2 is attached to every candidate's paper, with the key concepts or grading bases for each question. On the first grading, answers may be scanned first for key words, then read carefully to ascertain that no key concepts were overlooked. Each key concept in the answer increases the candidate's grade. The candidate's total grade for the question is easily determined by converting raw points, using a conversion chart. For example, a candidate who provides 17 of the 20 key concepts for this question would earn a grade of 9 for the answer. The process is repeated by the second grader and subsequent graders if necessary (i.e., borderline papers).

The point you should notice is that **key concepts earn points**. The unofficial answer closely conforms to the grading guide, making the grader's task simple. In turn, the unofficial answer also conforms to the format of the question. That is, each answer is numbered and lettered to correspond to the requirements. This should be your standard format.

There are two more points you should observe as you study the unofficial answer for our example. First, the answer is written in standard English, with clear, concise sentences and short paragraphs. A simple listing of key words is **unacceptable**; the concepts and their interrelationships must be logically presented. Secondly, remember that the unofficial answer represents the most acceptable solution to a question. This is not to say, however, that alternative answers are not considered. During the accumulation of grading bases, many concepts are added to the original "correct answer." Additionally, a paper that is near the passing mark receives a third (and perhaps fourth) grading, at which time individual consideration is given to the merits of each answer.

Parenthetically, we should mention that all the Bisk Education *CPA Review* essays and problems are solved using the unofficial AICPA answers. Thus, you have ample opportunity to accustom yourself to the favored answer format.

Importance of Writing Skills

At least two essay responses will be graded for writing skills. A response is defined as a part of an essay. Therefore, if an essay question has a **Part a** and a **Part b,** it has two responses. The two responses graded for writing skills may be from the same question or from different questions. Either way, they will be totally independent topics requiring different technical knowledge. Five percent of the candidate's grade for the essay portion of the exam will be allocated to writing skills. For more coverage of this area, refer to the section of your book entitled **Accounting for 5%.**

Grading Implications for CPA Candidates

To summarize this review of the AICPA's grading procedure, we can offer the following conclusions that will help you to **satisfy the grader** and maximize your score:

1. Attempt an answer on every question.
2. Do not explain answers to multiple choice questions or other objective answer formats.
3. Respond directly to the requirements of the questions.
4. Use of a well-chosen example is an easy way of expressing an understanding of the subject or supporting a conclusion.
5. Use schedules and formats favored by the AICPA examiners.
6. Answer all requirements.
7. Develop a **Solutions Approach™** to each question type.
8. Essay questions:

   Label your solutions parallel to the requirements.

   Offer reasons for your conclusions.

   Emphasize key words by underlining them.

   Separate grading concepts into individual sentences or paragraphs.

   Do **not** present your answer in outline format.
9. Allocate your examination time based on AICPA point value.
10. Write neatly and legibly to avoid demerits.

SECTION THREE: THE SOLUTIONS APPROACH™

The **Bisk Education Solutions Approach™** is an efficient, systematic method of organizing and solving questions found on the CPA exam. Remember that all the knowledge in the world is worthless unless you can get it down on paper. Conversely, a little knowledge can go a long way if you use a proper approach. The **Solutions Approach™** was developed by our Editorial Board in 1971; all subsequently developed stereotypes trace their roots from the original "Approach" that we formulated. Our **Solutions Approach™** and grader orientation skills, when properly developed, can be worth at least 10 to 15 points for most candidates. These 10 to 15 points often make the difference between passing and failing.

We will suggest a number of steps for deriving a solution that will help maximize your grade on the exam. Although you should remember the important steps in our suggested approach, don't be afraid to adapt these steps to your own taste and requirements. When you work the questions at the conclusion of each chapter, make sure you use your variation of the **Solutions Approach™**. It is also important for you to attempt to pattern the organization and format of your written solution to the unofficial answer reprinted after the text of the questions. However, DO NOT CONSULT THE UNOFFICIAL ANSWER UNTIL YOU FINISH THE QUESTION. The worst thing you can do is look at old questions and then turn to the answer without working the problem. This will build false confidence and provide **no** skills in developing a **Solutions Approach™**. Therefore, in order to derive the maximum number of points from an essay solution, you should **first** apply the **Solutions Approach™** to reading and answering the question, and **secondly**, write an essay answer using an organization and format identical to that which would be used by the AICPA in writing the unofficial answer to that essay question.

SOLUTIONS APPROACH™ FOR ESSAY QUESTIONS

Our **six steps** are as follows:

1. Scan the text of the question for an overview of the subject area and content of the question.
2. Study the question requirements slowly and thoroughly. Underline portions of the requirements as needed.
3. Visualize the unofficial answer format based on the requirements of the question.
4. Carefully study the text of the question. Underline important data.
5. Outline the solution in key words and phrases. Be sure to respond to the requirements, telling the grader only what he or she needs to know. You must explain the reasons for your conclusions.
6. Write the solution in the proper format based upon your key word outline. Write legibly in concise, complete sentences. Do not forget to proofread and edit your solution.

ESSAY QUESTION EXAMPLE

To illustrate the **Solutions Approach™** for essay questions, we consider a question from a past examination.

EXAMPLE 3—SAMPLE ESSAY

Cook, CPA, has been engaged to audit the financial statements of General Department Stores, Inc., a continuing audit client, which is a chain of medium-sized retail stores. General's fiscal year will end on June 30, 20X1, and General's management has asked Cook to issue the auditor's report by August 1, 20X1. Cook will not have sufficient time to perform all of the necessary field work in July 20X1, but will have time to perform most of the field work as of an interim date, April 30, 20X1.

For the accounts to be tested at the interim date, Cook will also perform substantive tests covering the transactions of the final two months of the year. This will be necessary to extend Cook's conclusions to the balance sheet date.

REQUIRED:

a. Describe the factors Cook should consider before applying principal substantive tests to General's balance sheet accounts at April 30, 20X1.
b. For accounts tested at April 30, 20X1, describe how Cook should design the substantive tests covering the balances as of June 30, 20X1, and the transactions of the final two months of the year.

Let's look at the steps you go through to arrive at your solution:

In **Step 1**, you scan the question. Do not read thoroughly, simply get an overview of the subject area and content of the question. You notice the question deals with substantive testing.

In **Step 2**, you study the question requirements thoroughly. **Part a** asks about factors important to the reliance of substantive testing of the balance sheet accounts, while **Part b** refers to the period between the date of testing and year end. Underline key phrases and words.

In **Step 3**, you visualize the format of your solution. The solution will be in paragraph form. **Part a** will discuss the factors considered in the decision to rely on substantive testing. **Part b** will discuss the design of substantive tests to be used and the risks inherent to this area.

In **Step 4**, you carefully study the text of the question, given the requirements you want to satisfy, i.e., read the question carefully. You should mark important information.

In **Step 5**, you outline your answer in keyword form. In your exam preparation, as you work Auditing essays, notice that sometimes you are not asked to make a decision or reach a conclusion, but rather you are asked to identify and discuss all important factors in the situation.

OUTLINE ANSWER

a. Assess difficulty in controlling incremental audit risk
consider:
reliability of accounting records
management integrity
business environment
predictability of year-end balances
internal control for cutoffs
availability of information for final two months
cost of substantive tests necessary to provide level of assurance
(control risk assessed at < maximum) not required to extend audit conclusions to final two months
(if control risk = maximum) - during final two months - will effectiveness be impaired?

b. Design of tests
level of assurance meets audit objectives
comparison of year-end information to comparable interim
to identify and investigate unusual amounts
Other analytical procedures
to extend conclusions based on interim date to balance sheet date

In **Step 6**, you write your solution in a format similar to the unofficial answer. Notice how clear and concise the AICPA unofficial answers are. There is no doubt as to their decision or the reasoning supporting the decision. Notice also how they answer each requirement separately and in the same order as in the question. Be sure to proofread and edit your solution.

EXAMPLE 4—UNOFFICIAL ANSWER

a. Before applying principal substantive tests to balance sheet accounts at April 30, 20X1, the interim date, Cook should assess the difficulty in controlling incremental audit risk. Cook should consider whether

- Cook's experience with the reliability of the accounting records and management's integrity has been good;
- Rapidly changing business conditions or circumstances may predispose General's management to misstate the financial statements in the remaining period;
- The year-end balances of accounts selected for interim testing will be predictable;
- General's procedures for analyzing and adjusting its interim balances and for reestablishing proper accounting cutoffs will be appropriate;
- General's accounting system will provide sufficient information about year-end balances and transactions in the final two months of the year to permit investigation of unusual transactions, significant fluctuations, and changes in balance compositions that may occur between the interim and balance sheet dates;
- The cost of the substantive tests necessary to cover the final two months of the year and provide the appropriate audit assurance at year end is substantial.

Assessing control risk at below the maximum would not be required to extend the audit conclusions from the interim date to the year end; however, if Cook assesses control risk at the maximum during the final two months, Cook should consider whether the effectiveness of the substantive tests to cover that period will be impaired.

b. Cook should design the substantive tests so that the assurance from those tests and the tests to be applied as of the interim date, and any assurance provided from the assessed level of control risk, achieve the audit objectives at year end. Such tests should include the comparison of year-end information with comparable interim information to identify and investigate unusual amounts. Other analytical procedures and/or substantive test should be performed to extend Cook's conclusions relative to the assertions tested at the interim date to the balance sheet date.

SOLUTIONS APPROACH™ FOR OBJECTIVE QUESTIONS

The **Solutions Approach™** is also adaptable to objective questions. We recommend the following framework:

1. Read the "Instructions to Candidates" section on your particular exam to determine if the AICPA's standard is the same. Generally, your objective portion will be determined by the number of correct answers with no penalty for incorrect answers.

2. Read the question carefully, noting exactly what the question is asking. Negative requirements are easily missed. Underline key words and note when the requirement is an exception (e.g., "except for...," or "which of the following does **not**..."). Perform any intermediate calculations necessary to the determination of the correct answer.

3. Anticipate the answer by covering the possible answers and seeing if you **know** the correct answer.

4. Read the answers given.

5. Select the best alternative. Very often, one or two possible answers will be clearly incorrect. Of the other alternatives, be sure to select the alternative that **best answers the question asked**.

6. Mark the correct answer on the examination booklet itself. After completing all of the individual questions in an overall question, transfer the answers to the machine readable answer sheet with extreme care. Before you hand in your answer sheet, **go back** and double check your answers—make sure the answer is correct and make sure the sequence is correct. The AICPA uses answer sheets with varying formats; it is extremely important to follow the correct sequence (across the sheet vs. down or vice versa). READ THE INSTRUCTIONS CAREFULLY.

7. Answer the questions in order. This is a proven, systematic approach to objective test taking. You will generally be limited to a maximum of 2 minutes per multiple choice question. Under no circumstances should you allow yourself to fall behind schedule. If a question is too difficult, too long, or is a multiple question fact situation, be sure you remain cognizant of the time you are using. If after a minute or so you feel that it is too costly to continue on with a particular question, select the letter answer you tentatively feel is the best answer and go on. Return to these questions at a later time and attempt to finally answer them when you have time for more consideration. If you cannot find a better answer when you return to the question, use your preliminary answer because your first impressions are often correct. However, as

you read other question(s), if something about these subsequent questions or answers jogs your memory, return to the previous tentatively answered question(s) and make a note of the idea for later consideration (time permitting).

A particularly challenging format is a group of objective questions based on one hypothetical situation. In this case, you should skim all the related questions (but not answer possibilities) before you begin answering, since an overall view of the problem will guide you in the work you do.

Note also that many incorrect answer choices are based on the erroneous application of one or more items in the text of the question. Thus, it is extremely important to **anticipate** the answer before you read the alternatives. Otherwise, you may be easily persuaded by an answer choice that is formulated through the incorrect use of the given data.

Let's consider a multiple choice question adapted from a past examination.

EXAMPLE 5—SAMPLE OBJECTIVE QUESTION

Which of the following is an element of a CPA firm's quality control system that should be considered in establishing its quality control policies and procedures?

a. Complying with laws and regulations
b. Using statistical sampling techniques
c. Assigning personnel to engagements
d. Considering audit risk and materiality (5/94, Aud., #15, 4680)

APPLYING THE SOLUTIONS APPROACH

Let's look at the steps you should go through to arrive at your objective question solution.

In **Step 1**, you must carefully read the "**Instructions**" that precede your particular objective CPA exam portion.

In **Step 2**, you must read the question and its requirements carefully. Look out for questions that require you to provide those options **not** applicable, **not** true, etc...

In **Step 3**, you must anticipate the correct answer **after** reading the question **but before** reading the possible answers.

In **Step 4**, you must read the answer carefully and select the alternative that best answers the question asked. Ideally, the best alternative will immediately present itself because it roughly or exactly corresponds with the answer you anticipated before looking at the other possible choices.

In **Step 5**, you select the best alternative. If there are two close possibilities, make sure you select the **best** one in light of the **facts** and **requirements** of the question.

In **Step 6**, you must make sure you accurately mark the **correct answer** in the proper sequence. If **anything** seems wrong, stop, go back and double check your answer sheet. As a fail safe mechanism, circle the correct letter on the exam sheet first, before you move it to the answer sheet.

In **Step 7**, you must make sure you answer the questions on the answer sheet in order, with due regard to time constraints.

EXAMPLE 6—UNOFFICIAL ANSWER

Solution: The answer is (c). SQCS 2 states, "The quality control policies and procedures…should encompass…personal management…." Answer (a) is irrelevant. Answers (b) and (d) would be associated with auditing procedures and requirements.

BENEFITS OF THE SOLUTIONS APPROACH™

The **Solutions Approach™** may seem cumbersome the first time you attempt it; candidates frequently have a tendency to write as they think. It should be obvious to you that such a haphazard approach will result in a disorganized answer. The Solutions Approach™ will help you write a solution that parallels the question requirements. It will also help you recall information under the pressure of the exam. The technique assists you in directing your thoughts toward the information required for the answer. Without a Solutions Approach™, you are apt to become distracted or confused by details that are irrelevant to the answer. Finally, the Solutions Approach™ is a **faster** way to answer exam questions. You will not waste time on false starts or rewrites. The approach may seem time-consuming at first, but as you become comfortable using it, you will see that it actually saves time and results in a better answer.

We urge you to give the **Solutions Approach™** a good try by using it throughout your CPA review. As you practice, you may adapt or modify it to your own preferences and requirements. The important thing is to develop a system so that you do not approach exam questions with a storehouse of knowledge that you can not put down on paper.

SECTION FOUR: EXAMINATION STRATEGIES

The CPA exam is more than a test of your knowledge and technical competence. It is also a test of your ability to function under psychological pressure. You could easily be thrown off balance by an unexpected turn of events during the days of the exam. Your objective is to avoid surprises and eliminate hassles and distractions that might shake your confidence. You want to be in complete control so that you can concentrate on the exam material, rather than the exam situation. By taking charge of the exam, you will be able to handle pressure in a constructive manner. The keys to control are adequate preparation and an effective examination strategy.

Overall Preparation

Advance preparation will arm you with the confidence you need to overcome the psychological pressure of the exam. As you complete your comprehensive review, you will cover most of the material that will be tested on the exam; it is unlikely that an essay, problem, or series of objective questions will deal with a topic you have not studied. But if an unfamiliar topic **is** tested, you will not be dismayed because you have learned to use the **Solutions Approach™** to derive the best possible answer from the knowledge you possess. Similarly, you will not feel pressured to write "perfect" answers, because you understand the grading process. You recognize that there is a limit to the points you can earn for each answer, no matter how much you write.

The components of your advance preparation program have previously been discussed in this appendix. Briefly summarizing, they include:

1. Comprehensive review materials such as your Bisk Education CPA Review Program.

2. A method for pre-review and ongoing self-evaluation of your level of proficiency.

3. A study plan that enables you to review each subject area methodically and thoroughly.

4. A **Solutions Approach™** for each type of examination question.

5. An understanding of the grading process and grader orientation skills.

CPA Exam Strategies

The second key to controlling the exam is to develop effective strategies for the days during which the exam is given. Your objective is to avoid surprises and frustrations so that you can focus your full concentration on the questions and your answers.

You should be familiar with the format of the CPA exam and know exactly what you will do when you enter the examination room. Remember to carefully read the instructions on the cover page of the exam booklet AND for each problem. Disregarding the instructions may mean loss of points.

On the following pages, we discuss the steps you should take from the time you receive the test booklet until the time you hand in your booklet. Planning in advance how you will spend your examination time will save you time and confusion on exam day.

INVENTORY OF THE EXAMINATION

You should spend the first few minutes of the exam surveying the exam booklet and planning your work. **Do not** plunge head-first into answering the questions without a plan of action. You do not want to risk running out of time, becoming frustrated by a difficult question, or losing the opportunity to answer a question that you could have answered well. Your inventory should take no longer than five minutes. The time you spend will help you "settle in" to the examination and develop a feel for your ability to answer the questions.

1. Carefully read the "Instructions to Candidates" on the cover page.

2. Note the number of questions/problems on the cover page.

3. Once permission is given, go through the booklet and see what topics each question covers. Jot down the topics and devise a time schedule on the front cover, forming a table of contents.

ORDER OF ANSWERING QUESTIONS

Once you have completed your inventory of the exam, the next step is to develop an order for answering the objective questions and problems/essays. We recommend that you begin with the objective questions and then proceed to the problems/essays, beginning with the problem/essay that you feel is the least difficult.

Objective questions comprise a majority of the point value of each section. Because of their objective nature, the correct solution is listed as one of the answer choices. By solving these questions, not only do you gain confidence, but they often involve the same or a related topic to that covered in one of the problems or essays.

A very effective and efficient manner of answering the objective questions is to make **two passes** through the questions. On the first pass, you should answer those questions that you find the easiest. If you come across a question that you find difficult to solve, mark it and proceed to the next one. This will allow you to avoid wasting precious time and will enable your mind to clear and start anew on your **second pass**. On the second pass, you should go back and solve those questions you left unanswered on the first pass. Some of these questions you may have skipped over without an attempt, while in others you may have been able to eliminate one or two of the answer choices. Either way, you should come up with an answer on the second pass, even if you have to guess! After completing all of the individual questions in an overall question, transfer the answers to the machine readable answer sheet with extreme care. Simply make note of those questions that gave you difficulty and then proceed to the problems or essays.

Essay questions should be worked only through the key word outlines on the first pass. Then return to write your essay solution with a fresh look at the question.

EXAMINATION TIME BUDGETING

You must **plan** how you will use your examination time and adhere faithfully to your schedule. If you budget your time carefully, you should be able to answer all parts of all questions. To demonstrate a realistic time budget, refer again to the time parameters in the examination booklet.

The time limitation on the exam is 4½ hours for the Auditing section. You should subtract five minutes for your initial inventory on each section. Assuming you will use the **Solutions Approach™** and there will be two problem/essay type questions, your time budget may be similar to the one below. The actual exam may differ from this scenario so be sure to adjust your time budget to accommodate the number and type of questions asked.

	Minutes			
	FAR	ARE	Auditing	BLPR
Inventory examination	5	5	5	5
Answer objective questions	120	190	180	120
Write problem solutions (45-50 min. for each)	90			
Key word outline essays (10 min. for each)	20		20	20
Write essay solutions (10-30 min. for each)	20		50	20
Review answers	15	15	15	15
	270	210	270	180

Your objective in time budgeting is to avoid running out of time to answer a question. Work quickly but efficiently (i.e., use the **Solutions Approach™**). Remember that when you are answering an essay question, a partial answer is better than no answer at all. If you don't write anything, how can a grader justify giving you any points?

Page Numbering

Follow all instructions on the front of each exam section. Remember to arrange your answers in numerical order and number pages consecutively. The multiple choice answer sheet should be numbered page 1 and the numbering of your other pages should start with page 2. Start every essay question on a new sheet of paper and write on one side. For problem type questions, identify and include scratch pages. Write "continued" on the bottom of sheets when another answer sheet for the same problem or essay follows.

Psychology of Examination Success

As stated previously, the CPA exam is in itself a physical and mental strain. You can minimize this strain by avoiding all unnecessary distractions and inconveniences during exam week. For example:

- **Make reservations for lodging well in advance.** It's best to reserve a room for Tuesday night so that you can check in, get a good night's sleep, and locate the exam site early the next morning.
- **Stick to your normal eating, sleeping, and exercise habits.** Eat lightly before the exam, and take small candies with you for quick energy. Watch your caffeine and alcohol intake. If you are accustomed to regular exercise, continue a regular routine during exam week.
- **Visit the examination facilities before the examination** and familiarize yourself with the surroundings.
- **Arrive early for the exam.** Allow plenty of time for unexpected delays. Nothing is more demoralizing than getting caught in a traffic jam ten minutes before the exam is scheduled to begin.
- **Avoid possible distractions**, such as friends and pre-exam conversation, immediately before the exam.
- In general, **you should not attempt to study on the nights before exam sessions**. It's better to relax—go to a movie, read a novel, or watch television. If you feel you must study, spend half an hour or so going over the chapter outlines in the text.
- **Don't discuss exam answers with other candidates**. Not only have you signed a statement of confidentiality, but someone is sure to disagree with your answer, and if you are easily influenced by his or her reasoning, you can become doubtful of your own ability. Wait and analyze the entire exam yourself after you have finished all sections.

AICPA General Rules Governing Examination

1. Read carefully the identification card assigned to you; sign it; make note of your number for future reference; when it is requested, return the card to the examiner. Only the examination number on your card shall be used on your papers for the purpose of identification. The importance of remembering this number and recording it on your examination paper correctly cannot be overemphasized. If a question calls for an answer involving a signature, **do not** sign your own name or initials.

2. Seating during the exam is assigned according to your ID number in most states.

3. Answers must be submitted on paper furnished by the Board and must be completed in the total time allotted for each subject stated on the printed examinations. Begin your answer to each question on a separate page.

4. Answers should be written in pencil using No. 2 lead. **Neatness and orderly presentation of work are important**. Credit cannot be given for answers that are illegible.

5. Use a soft No. 2 lead pencil to blacken the spaces on the answer sheets for the objective-type questions.

6. Supplies furnished by the Board shall remain its property and must be returned whether used or not. You must hand in your printed examination booklet before leaving the examination room or your examination will not be graded.

7. Any reference during the examination to books or other matters or the exchange of information with other persons shall be considered misconduct sufficient to bar you from further participation in the examination.

8. The only aids candidates are permitted to have in the examination room are pens, pencils, and erasers. Calculators will be provided. Handbags and purses must be placed on the floor at candidates' locations during the entire time they are taking the exam. Briefcases, files, books, and other material brought to the examination site by candidates must be placed in a designated area before the start of the examination.

9. The fixed time for each session must be observed by all candidates. Each period will start and end promptly. It is the candidate's responsibility to be present and ready at the start of the period and to stop writing when told to do so.

10. Candidates arriving late should not be permitted any extension of time, but may be allowed to take the examination with proctor approval.

11. Smoking is allowed only in designated areas away from the general examination area.

12. No telephone calls are permitted during the examination session.

13. Only two time warnings are given: (1) thirty minutes prior to the end of session, and (2) five minutes prior to the end of session. (Additional warnings are not considered necessary.)

CPA Exam Week Checklist

WHAT TO PACK FOR EXAM WEEK:

1. CPA exam registration material.

2. Hotel confirmation.

3. Cash and/or a major credit card.

4. Alarm clock—Don't rely on a hotel wake-up call.

5. Comfortable clothing that can be layered to suit varying temperatures.

6. A watch.

7. Appropriate review materials, pencils, erasers, and pencil sharpener.

8. Healthy snack foods.

EVENINGS BEFORE EXAM SECTIONS:

1. Read through your Bisk Education chapter outlines for the next day's section(s).

2. Eat lightly and monitor your intake of alcohol and caffeine. Get a good night's rest.

3. Do **not** try to cram. A brief review of your notes will help to focus your attention on important points and remind you that you are well prepared, but too much cramming can shatter your self-confidence. If you have reviewed conscientiously, you are already well-prepared for the CPA exam.

THE MORNING OF EACH EXAM SECTION:

1. Eat a satisfying breakfast. It will be several hours before your next meal. Eat enough to ward off hunger, but not so much that you feel uncomfortable.

2. Dress appropriately. Wear layers you can take off to suit varying temperatures in the room.

3. Take ample supplies.

4. Arrive at the exam center thirty minutes early. Check in as soon as you are allowed to do so.

WHAT TO BRING TO THE EXAM:

1. ID card—This is your official entrance permit to the exam.

2. Several sharpened No. 2 pencils, erasers, and a small pencil sharpener. Some states provide pencils and do not allow candidates to bring their own.

3. A watch.

4. Tissues, small candies, gum, and aspirin.

5. Do **not** take articles that will not be allowed in the exam room. Highlighters are not allowed.

DURING THE EXAM:

1. Always read all instructions and follow the directions of the exam administrator. If you don't understand any written or verbal instructions, or if something doesn't seem right, ASK QUESTIONS. Remember that an error in following directions could invalidate your **entire** exam.

2. Budget your time. Always keep track of the time and avoid getting too involved with one question.

3. **Satisfy the grader**. Remember that the grader cannot read your mind. You must explain every point. Focus on key words and concepts. Tell the grader what you know, don't **worry** about any points you don't know.

4. Answer every question, even if you must guess.

5. Use **all** the allotted time. If you finish a section early, go back and reconsider the more difficult questions.

6. Check the answer sheet frequently to see that the number of each answer corresponds to the number of the question you intended. Many examinees get out of sequence on the answer sheet.

7. Stop working **immediately** when time is called. You do not want to risk being disqualified just to get one last answer recorded.

8. Get up and stretch if you feel sluggish. Walk around if you are allowed. Breathe deeply; focus your eyes on distant objects to avoid eye strain. Do some exercises to relax muscles in the face, neck, fingers, and back.

9. Take enough time to write neatly and organize your answer. Legible, well-organized answers will impress the grader.

10. Remember that you are well-prepared for the CPA exam, and that you can **expect to pass**! A confident attitude will help you overcome examination anxiety.

SECTION FIVE: CONTENT SPECIFICATION OUTLINES AND FREQUENTLY TESTED AREAS

The AICPA Board of Examiners has developed a **Content Specification Outline** of each section of the exam to be tested. These outlines list the areas, groups, and topics to be tested and indicate the approximate percentage of the total test score devoted to each area. The content of the examination is based primarily on results of national studies of public accounting practice and the evaluation of CPA practitioners and educators.

I. Plan the Engagement, Evaluate the Prospective Client and Engagement, Decide Whether to Accept or Continue the Client and the Engagement, and Enter Into an Agreement With the Client (40%)

A. Determine Nature and Scope of Engagement

1. Generally Accepted Auditing Standards
2. Standards for Accounting and Review Services
3. Standards for Attestation Engagements
4. Compliance Auditing Applicable to Governmental Entities and Other Recipients of Governmental Financial Assistance
5. Other Assurance Services
6. Appropriateness of Engagement to meet Client's Needs

B. Assess Engagement Risk and the CPA Firm's Ability to Perform the Engagement

1. Engagement Responsibilities
2. Staffing and Supervision Requirements
3. Quality Control Considerations
4. Management Integrity
5. Researching Information Sources for Planning and Performing the Engagement

C. Communicate With the Predecessor Accountant/Auditor

D. Decide Whether to Accept or Continue the Client and Engagement

E. Enter Into an Agreement With the Client as to the Terms of the Engagement

F. Obtain an Understanding of the Client's Operations, Business, and Industry

G. Perform Analytical Procedures

H. Consider Preliminary Engagement Materiality

I. Assess Inherent Risk and Risk of Misstatements

1. Errors
2. Fraud
3. Illegal Acts by Clients

J. Consider Internal Control

1. Obtain and Document an Understanding of Internal Control—Automated and Manual
2. Assess Control Risk
3. Consider Limitations of Internal Control
4. Consider the Effects of Information Technology on Internal Control
5. Consider the Effects of Service Organizations on Internal Control

K. Consider Other Planning Matters

1. Using the Work of Other Independent Auditors
2. Using the Work of a Specialist
3. Internal Audit Function
4. Related Parties and Related Party Transactions
5. Electronic Evidence

L. Identify Financial Statement Assertions and Formulate Audit Objectives

1. Accounting Estimates
2. Routine Financial Statement Balances, Classes of Transactions, and Disclosures
3. Unusual Financial Statement Balances, Classes of Transactions, and Disclosures

M. Determine and Prepare the Work Program Defining the Nature, Timing, and Extent of the Auditor's Procedures

II. Obtain and Document Information to Form a Basis for Conclusions (35%)

A. Perform Planned Procedures Including Planned Applications of Audit Sampling

1. Tests of Controls
2. Analytical Procedures
3. Confirmation of Balances and/or Transactions With Third Parties
4. Physical Examination of Inventories and Other Assets
5. Other Tests of Details
6. Computer Assisted Audit Techniques
7. Substantive Tests Prior to the Balance Sheet Date
8. Tests of Unusual Year-End Transactions

B. Evaluate Contingencies
C. Obtain and Evaluate Lawyers' Letters
D. Review Subsequent Events
E. Obtain Representations From Management
F. Identify Reportable Conditions and Other Control Deficiencies
G. Identify Matters for Communication With Audit Committees

III. Review the Engagement to Provide Reasonable Assurance That Objectives are Achieved, and Evaluate Information Obtained to Reach and to Document Engagement Conclusions (5%)

A. Perform Analytical Procedures

B. Evaluate the Sufficiency and Competence of Audit Evidence and Document Engagement Conclusions

1. Consider Substantial Doubt About an Entity's Ability to Continue as a Going Concern
2. Evaluate Whether Financial Statements Are Free of Material Misstatements
3. Consider Other Information in Documents Containing Audited Financial Statements

C. Review the Work Performed to Provide Reasonable Assurance That Objectives Are Achieved

IV. Prepare Communications to Satisfy Engagement Objectives (20%)

A. Prepare Reports

1. Reports on Audited Financial Statements
2. Reports on Reviewed and Compiled Financial Statements
3. Reports Required by Government Auditing Standards
4. Reports on Compliance With Laws and Regulation
5. Reports on Internal Control
6. Reports on Prospective Financial Information
7. Reports on Agreed-upon Procedures
8. Reports on Other Assurance Services
9. Reports on the Processing of Transactions by Service Organizations
10. Reports on Supplementary Financial Information
11. Other Special Reports
12. Reissuance of Auditors' Reports

B. Prepare Letters and Other Required Communications

1. Errors and Fraud
2. Illegal Acts
3. Special Reports
4. Communication With Audit Committees
5. Other Reporting Considerations Covered by Statements on Auditing Standards and Statements on Standards for Attestation Engagements

C. Other Matters

1. Subsequent Discovery of Facts Existing at the Date of the Auditor's Report
2. Consideration of Omitted Procedures After the Report Date

Although recent changes in describing content coverage make it difficult to know with certainty what the AICPA will now ask, we can use exam history to highlight those areas that have been emphasized. Based on analysis of past exams, we have identified the areas most heavily tested in the past. Keep in mind that lightly tested areas may be heavily tested on any one exam and there is the potential for **any area** to be tested.

Candidates frequently review this information and then ask, "Yes, but how do the Bisk Education chapters correspond to these specifications?" In order to present information in the most easily-assimilated manner possible, the text is not aligned exactly with the divisions in the content specifications. The first chapters are concerned mostly with typical audit engagements and the last two chapters deal with other types of engagements. Therefore, Chapters 40 and 41 include all four parts of the content specifications. Part I of the content specifications is also covered by Chapters 31-34; Part II by Chapters 35-38; Part III by Chapters 35 and 39; and Part VI by Chapter 39.

Frequently Tested Areas

Heavy		Light	
Ch. 33	Internal Control: General	Ch. 31	Standards & Related Topics
Ch. 34	Internal Control: Transaction Cycles	Ch. 37	Audit Sampling
Ch. 35	Evidence & Procedures	Ch. 38	Auditing EDP Systems
Ch. 36	Audit Programs		
Ch. 39	Reports on Audited Financial Statements		

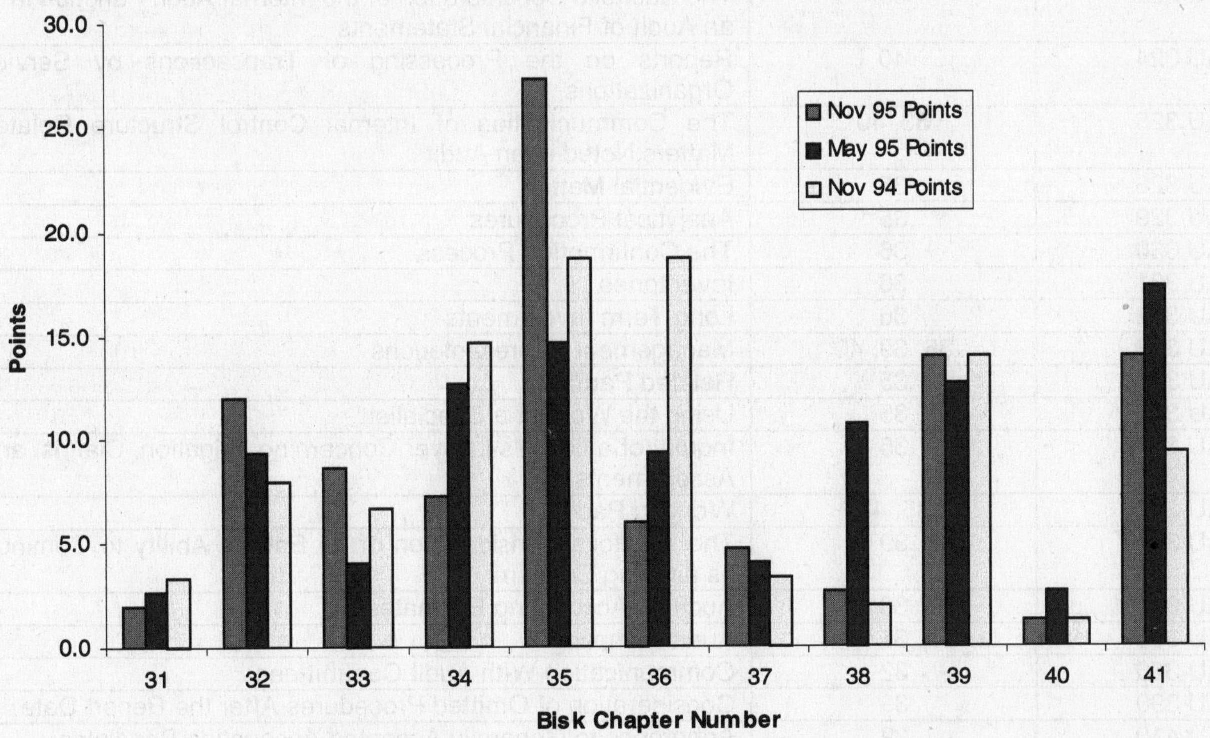

November 1995 was the last fully disclosed examination.
(Please bear in mind that the content specifications changed slightly since the November 1995 exam.)

SECTION SIX:
AUTHORITATIVE PRONOUNCEMENTS CROSS-REFERENCE

Section No.	Bisk Education Chapter Number(s)	Statements on Auditing Standards
AU 110	31	Responsibilities and Functions of the Independent Auditor
AU 150	31	Generally Accepted Auditing Standards
AU 161	31	The Relationship of Generally Accepted Auditing Standards to Quality Control Standards
AU 201	31	Nature of the General Standards
AU 210	31	Training and Proficiency of the Independent Auditor
AU 220	31	Independence
AU 230	31	Due Care in the Performance of Work
AU 310	32	Relationship Between the Auditor's Appointment and Planning
AU 311	32	Planning and Supervision
AU 312	32	Audit Risk and Materiality in Conducting an Audit
AU 313	32	Substantive Tests Prior to the Balance Sheet Date
AU 315	32	Communications Between Predecessor and Successor Auditors
AU 316	32, 40	Consideration of Fraud in a Financial Statement Audit
AU 317	32, 40	Illegal Acts by Clients
AU 319	31, 40	Consideration of Internal Control in a Financial Statement Audit
AU 322	35	The Auditor's Consideration of the Internal Audit Function in an Audit of Financial Statements
AU 324	40	Reports on the Processing of Transactions by Service Organizations
AU 325	33, 40	The Communication of Internal Control Structure Related Matters Noted in an Audit
AU 326	35	Evidential Matter
AU 329	35	Analytical Procedures
AU 330	36	The Confirmation Process
AU 331	36	Inventories
AU 332	36	Long-Term Investments
AU 333	35, 39, 40	Management Representations
AU 334	35	Related Parties
AU 336	35	Using the Work of a Specialist
AU 337	35	Inquiry of a Client's Lawyer Concerning Litigation, Claims, and Assessments
AU 339	35, 40	Working Papers
AU 341	39	The Auditor's Consideration of an Entity's Ability to Continue as a Going Concern
AU 342	36	Auditing Accounting Estimates
AU 350	37	Audit Sampling
AU 380	32	Communication With Audit Committees
AU 390	39	Consideration of Omitted Procedures After the Report Date
AU 410	39	Adherence to Generally Accepted Accounting Principles

Section No.	Bisk Education Chapter Number(s)	Statements on Auditing Standards
AU 411	39	The Meaning of *Present Fairly in Conformity With Generally Accepted Accounting Principles* in the Independent Auditor's Report
AU 420	39	Consistency of Application of Generally Accepted Accounting Principles
AU 431	39	Adequacy of Disclosure in Financial Statements
AU 435	39	Segment Information
AU 504	39	Association With Financial Statements
AU 508	39	Reports on Audited Financial Statements
AU 530	39	Dating of the Independent Auditor's Report
AU 534	40	Reporting on Financial Statements Prepared for Use in Other Countries
AU 543	39	Part of Audit Performed by Other Independent Auditors
AU 544	39	Lack of Conformity With Generally Accepted Accounting Principles
AU 550	39, 41	Other Information in Documents Containing Audited Financial Statements
AU 551	40	Reporting on Information Accompanying the Basic Financial Statements in Auditor-Submitted Documents
AU 552	40	Reporting on Condensed Financial Statements and Selected Financial Data
AU 558	39	Required Supplementary Information
AU 560	39	Subsequent Events
AU 561	39, 40	Subsequent Discovery of Facts Existing at the Date of the Auditor's Report
AU 622	39, 40	Special Reports—Applying Agreed-Upon Procedures to Specified Elements, Accounts, or Items of a Financial Statement
AU 623	40	Special Reports
AU 625	40	Reports on the Application of Accounting Principles
AU 634	40	Letters for Underwriters and Certain Other Requesting Parties
AU 711	40, 41	Filings Under Federal Securities Statutes
AU 722	40	Interim Financial Information
AU 801	40	Compliance Auditing Applicable to Governmental Entities and Other Recipients of Governmental Financial Assistance
AU 901	36	Public Warehouses—Internal Control Policies and Procedures and Auditing Procedures for Goods Held

Section No.	Bisk Education Chapter Number(s)	Statements on Standards for Accounting and Review Services
AR 100	41	Compilation and Review of Financial Statements
AR 200	41	Reporting on Comparative Financial Statements
AR 300	41	Compilation Reports on Financial Statements Included in Certain Prescribed Forms
AR 400	41	Communications Between Predecessor and Successor Accountants
AR 600	41	Reporting on Personal Financial Statements Included in Written Personal Financial Plans
	41	Plain Paper Financial Statements

Section No.	Bisk Education Chapter Number(s)	Statements on Standards for Attestation Engagements
AT 100–700	41	Attestation Standards: Revision and Recodification

Reference	Bisk Education Chapter Number(s)	Statements on Quality Control Standards
SQCS No. 2	31	System of Quality Control for a CPA Firm's Accounting and Auditing Practice
SQCS No. 3	31	Monitoring a CPA Firm's Accounting and Auditing Practice
SQCS No. 4	31	System of Quality Control for a CPA Firm's Accounting and Auditing Practice (SEC)
SQCS No. 5	31	Competencies Required by a PIC
Reference	**Bisk Education Chapter Number(s)**	**Other Standards**
QR 100	31	Standards for Performing and Reporting on Quality Reviews
	31	Government Auditing Standards (Yellow Book)

From the AICPA's *Information for CPA Candidates*:

"Candidates are responsible for knowing accounting and auditing pronouncements, including the pronouncements in the governmental and not-for-profit organizations area, six months after a pronouncement's *effective* date, unless early application is permitted. When early application is permitted, candidates are responsible for knowing the new pronouncement six months after the *issuance* date. In this case, candidates are responsible for knowing both the old and new pronouncements until the old pronouncement is superseded."

APPENDIX C
ACCOUNTING FOR 5%

CONTENTS

INTRODUCTION

Before skipping this appendix, review at least the following writing samples and the "Writing an Answer to an Exam Question" starting on page C-5. Be sure to take the Diagnostic Quiz on C-8.

To assess candidates' writing skills, answers to selected essay responses from Business Law & Professional Responsibilities, Auditing, and Financial Accounting & Reporting sections will be used. Five percent of the points available on each of these sections will be allocated to writing skills. If you are not convinced that the five points in a section will make a significant difference, consider this: of the passing grades in each section, the vast majority are scored at 75, the minimum. For many candidates, therefore, writing skills may determine whether or not they pass a section.

If an essay question is divided into parts a, b, and c, for example, each of these parts is considered a separate response. It is possible that only one of these three parts will be graded for writing skills. However, at least two responses from each section will be used for this assessment. These responses may or may not be from the same question, but they will cover different technical areas. If a question is graded differently for writing skills, then the number of points allocated to the technical concepts of the essay is reduced so that the total number of points per question does not change.

The AICPA considers the following six characteristics to constitute effective writing and will make its evaluations of candidates' writing skills based on these criteria:

1. **Coherent organization.** Does each paragraph begin with a topic sentence? Are ideas arranged logically, and do they flow smoothly?

2. **Conciseness.** Are complete thoughts presented in the fewest possible words?

3. **Clarity.** Are sentences constructed properly? Are meanings and reasons clear? Are proper technical terminology and key words and phrases used?

4. **Standard English.** Is your work free of nonstandard usage; that is, does it demonstrate proper spelling, punctuation, capitalization, diction, and knowledgeable usage choices?

5. **Responsiveness to the requirements of the question.** Make sure your answers respond directly to the question and are not broad discourses on the general subject.

6. **Appropriateness for the reader.** If not otherwise mentioned in the question, you should assume that the reader is a CPA. Questions asking that you write something for a client or anyone else with less technical knowledge should be answered with that particular audience in mind.

When writing your exam answers, write on **every other line only**. This will give you space for editing.

Accounting for 5% has been designed primarily to help CPA candidates polish their writing skills. Beyond this purpose, we hope that it will continue to serve as a useful reference in the future.

WRITING SKILLS SAMPLES

The following problems taken from past exams are answered in various ways to illustrate good, fair, and poor writing skills.

Essex Company has a compensation plan for future vacations for its employees. What conditions must be met for Essex to accrue compensation for future vacations? FAR Problem—From Chapter 7—Liabilities

GOOD: Essex must accrue compensation for future vacations if all of the following criteria are met. Essex's obligation relating to employees' rights to receive compensation for future vacations is attributable to employees' services already rendered. The obligation relates to rights that vest or accumulate. Payment of the vacation benefits is probable. The amount can be reasonably estimated.

EXPLANATION: This essay is coherent, concise, and well organized. The first sentence uses the wording of the question to introduce the elements of the answer. Each point is then made clearly and concisely. There are no unnecessary words or elements. The language and vocabulary are appropriate, and there are no mistakes in grammar or spelling.

FAIR: In order for Essex to accrue compensation for future vacations, they must attribute their obligation to employees services already rendered, recognize that the obligation relates to vested and accumulated rights, and that payment is probable and the amount can be reasonably estimated.

EXPLANATION: This passage is also coherent and concise; however, it lacks the clarity and detail of the previous answer. The language is appropriate, but the grammatical construction is somewhat weak.

POOR: It is based on accrual. The employees must have vested or accumulated rights. They must be able to estimate amounts of compensation and their payment. Vested rights means that the employer must pay the employees even if he is fired or quits.

EXPLANATION: This answer is so poorly worded and disorganized as to be virtually incoherent. There are also some grammar mistakes. The final sentence is additional information but not necessary to answer the question.

PARAGRAPHS

The kind of writing you do for the CPA exam is called **expository writing** (writing in which something is explained in straightforward terms). Expository writing uses the basic techniques we will be discussing here. Other kinds of writing (i.e., narration, description, argument, and persuasion) will sometimes require different techniques.

Consider a paragraph as a division of an essay that consists of one or more sentences, deals with one point, and begins on a new, indented line. Paragraphs provide a way to write about a subject one point or one thought at a time.

Usually, a paragraph begins with a **topic sentence**. The topic sentence communicates the main idea of the paragraph, and the remainder of the paragraph explains or illuminates that central idea. The paragraph sometimes finishes with a restatement of the topic sentence. This strategy is easily read by the exam graders.

Often the topic sentence of the first paragraph is the central idea of the entire composition. Each succeeding paragraph then breaks down this idea into subtopics with each of the new topic sentences being the central thought of that subtopic.

Let's take a look at a simple paragraph to see how it's put together.

> The deductibility of home mortgage interest has been under recent review by Congress as a way to raise revenue. There have been two major reasons for this scrutiny. First, now that consumer interest is nondeductible and investment interest is limited to net investment income, taxpayers have been motivated to rearrange their finances to maximize their tax deductions. Second, most voters do not own homes costing more than $500,000 and, therefore, putting a cap on mortgage loans does not affect the mass of voters. Given the pressure to raise revenue, two major changes have occurred in this area.

The first sentence of the example is the **topic sentence**. The second sentence introduces the supporting examples which appear in the next two sentences beginning with *first* and *second*. The final sentence of the paragraph acts as a preview to the contents of the next paragraph.

Now, let's examine the makeup of a single paragraph answer to a Business Law Exam essay question.

> Question: Dunhill fraudulently obtained a negotiable promissory note from Beeler by misrepresentation of a material fact. Dunhill subsequently negotiated the note to Gordon, a holder in due course. Pine, a business associate of Dunhill, was aware of the fraud perpetrated by Dunhill. Pine purchased the note for value from Gordon. Upon presentment, Beeler has defaulted on the note.
>
> Required: Answer the following, setting forth reasons for any conclusions stated.
>
> 1. What are the rights of Pine against Beeler?
> 2. What are the rights of Pine against Dunhill?

Examples of possible answers:

> 1. The rights of Pine against Beeler arise from Pine's having acquired the note from Gordon, who was a holder in due course. Pine himself is not a holder in due course because he had knowledge of a defense against the note. The rule wherein a transferee, not a holder in due course, acquires the rights of one by taking from a holder in due course is known as the "shelter rule." Through these rights, Pine is entitled to recover the proceeds of the note from Beeler. The defense of fraud in the inducement is a personal defense and not valid against a holder in due course.

The first sentence of the paragraph is the topic sentence in which the basic answer to the question is given. The third and fourth sentence explains the rule governing Pine's rights. (The *shelter rule* would be considered a *key phrase* in this answer.) The final sentence of the paragraph is not really necessary to answer the question but was added as an explanation of what some might mistakenly believe to be the key to the answer.

> 2. As one with the rights of a holder in due course, Pine is entitled to proceed against any person whose signature appears on the note, provided he gives notice of dishonor. When Dunhill negotiated the note to Gordon, Dunhill's signature on the note made him secondarily liable. As a result, if Pine brings suit against Dunhill, Pine will prevail because of Dunhill's secondary liability.

The first sentence of this paragraph restates the fact that Pine has the rights of a holder in due course and what these rights mean. The second sentence explains what happened when Dunhill negotiated the note, and the third sentence states the probable outcome of these results.

Note that in both answers 1. and 2., the sentences hang together in a logical fashion and lead the reader easily from one thought to the next. This is called *coherence*, a primary factor in considerations of conciseness and clarity.

TRANSITIONS

To demonstrate how to use **transitions** in a paragraph to carry the reader easily from one thought or example to another, let's consider a slightly longer and more detailed paragraph. The transitions are indicated in italics.

> A concerted effort to reduce book income in response to AMT could have a significant impact on corporations. *For example,* the auditor-client relationship may change. *Currently,* it isn't unusual for corporate management to argue for higher rather than lower book earnings, *while* the auditor would argue for conservative reported numbers. Such a corporate reporting posture may change as a consequence of the BURP adjustment. *Furthermore,* stock market analysts often rely on a price/earnings ratio. Lower earnings for essentially the same level of activity may have a significant effect on security prices.

The first sentence of the paragraph is the topic sentence. The next sentence, beginning with the transition *for example,* introduces the example with a broad statement. The following sentence, beginning with *currently,* gives a specific example to support the basic premise. The sentence beginning *furthermore* leads us into a final example. Without these transitions, the paragraph would be choppy and lack coherence.

What follows is a list of some transitions divided by usage. We suggest you commit some of these to memory so that you will never be at a loss as to how to tie your ideas together.

TRANSITIONAL WORDS AND PHRASES

One idea plus one idea:

again	equally important	in addition	likewise	similarly
also	finally	in the same fashion	moreover	third
and	first	in the same respect	next	thirdly
and then	further	last	second	too
besides	furthermore	lastly	secondly	

To show time or place:

after a time	at that time	immediately	presently	thereafter
after a while	at the same time	in due time	second	thereupon
afterwards	before	in the meantime	shortly	to the left
as long as	earlier	lately	since	until
as soon as	eventually	later	soon	when
at last	finally	meanwhile	temporarily	while
at length	first	next	then	
	further	of late		

To contrast or qualify:

after all	at the same time	however	nevertheless	on the other hand
although true	but	in any case	nonetheless	otherwise
and yet	despite this fact	in contrast	notwithstanding	still
anyway	for all that	in spite of	on the contrary	yet

To introduce an illustration

for example	in particular	incidentally	specifically	to illustrate
for instance	in other words	indeed	that is	
in fact	in summary	namely	thus	

To indicate concession		To indicate comparison:
after all	I admit	in a likewise manner
although this may be	naturally	likewise
at the same time	of course	similarly
even though		

WRITING AN ANSWER TO AN EXAM QUESTION

Now that we have examined the makeup of an answer to an exam question, let's take an actual question from a past Business Law Exam and see how to go about writing a clear, comprehensive answer, step by step, sentence by sentence. A question similar to the one that follows would very likely be one the examiners would choose to grade writing skills.

QUESTION:

Bar Manufacturing and Cole Enterprises were arch rivals in the high technology industry, and both were feverishly working on a new product that would give the first to develop it a significant competitive advantage. Bar engaged Abel Consultants on April 1, 1983, for one year, commencing immediately, at $7,500 a month to aid the company in the development of the new product. The contract was oral and was consummated by a handshake. Cole approached Abel and offered them a $10,000 bonus for signing, $10,000 a month for nine months, and a $40,000 bonus if Cole was the first to successfully market the new product. In this connection, Cole stated that the oral contract Abel made with Bar was unenforceable and that Abel could walk away from it without liability. In addition, Cole made certain misrepresentations regarding the dollar amount of its commitment to the project, the state of its development, and the expertise of its research staff. Abel accepted the offer.

Four months later, Bar successfully introduced the new product. Cole immediately dismissed Abel and has paid nothing beyond the first four $10,000 payments plus the initial bonus. Three lawsuits ensued: Bar sued Cole, Bar sued Abel, and Abel sued Cole.

REQUIRED: Answer the following, setting forth reasons for any conclusions stated.

Discuss the various theories on which each of the three lawsuits is based, the defenses that will be asserted, the measure of possible recovery, and the probable outcome of the litigation.

COMPOSING AN ANSWER:

Analyze requirements.

Plan on one paragraph for each lawsuit. Each paragraph will contain four elements: theory, defenses, recovery, and outcome.

PARAGRAPH ONE:

STEP 1: Begin with the first lawsuit mentioned, Bar vs. Cole. Write a topic sentence that will sum up the theory of the suit.

Topic sentence: Bar's lawsuit against Cole will be based upon the intentional tort of wrongful interference with a contractual relationship.

STEP 2: Back up this statement with law and facts from the question scenario.

The primary requirement for this cause of action is a valid contractual relationship with which the defendant knowingly interferes. This requirement is met in the case of Cole.

STEP 3: State defenses.

The contract is not required to be in writing since it is for exactly one year from the time of its making. It is, therefore, valid even though oral.

STEP 4: Introduce subject of recovery (damages).

Cole's knowledge of the contract is obvious.

STEP 5: Explain possible problems to recovery.

The principal problem, however, is damages. Since Bar was the first to market the product successfully, it would seem that damages are not present. It is possible there were actual damages incurred by Bar (for example, it hired another consulting firm at an increased price).

STEP 6: Discuss possible outcome.

It also might be possible that some courts would permit the recovery of punitive damages since this is an intentional tort.

PARAGRAPH ONE COMPLETED:

Bar's lawsuit against Cole will be based upon the intentional tort of wrongful interference with a contractual relationship. The primary requirement for this cause of action is a valid contractual relationship with which the defendant knowingly interferes. The requirement is met in the case of Cole. The contract is not required to be in writing since it is for exactly one year from the time of its making. It is, therefore, valid even though oral. Cole's knowledge of the contract is obvious. The principal problem, however, is damages. Since Bar was the first to market the product successfully, it would seem that damages are not present. It is possible there were actual damages incurred by Bar (for example, it hired another consulting firm at an increased price). It also might be possible that some courts would permit the recovery of punitive damages since this is an intentional tort.

PARAGRAPH TWO:

STEP 1: Discuss second lawsuit mentioned, Bar vs. Abel. Write a topic sentence that will sum up the theory of the suit.

Topic sentence: Bar's cause of action against Abel would be for breach of contract.

STEP 2: State defenses. [Same as for first paragraph; this could be left out.]

The contract is not required to be in writing since it is for exactly one year from the time of its making. It is, therefore, valid even though oral.

STEP 3: Introduce subject of recovery (damages).

Once again, [*indicating similarity and tying second paragraph to first*] damages would seem to be a serious problem.

STEP 4: Explain possible problems to recovery.

Furthermore, punitive damages would rarely be available in a contract action. Finally, Bar cannot recover the same damages twice.

STEP 5: Discuss possible outcome.

Hence, if it proceeds against Cole and recovers damages caused by Abel's breach of contract, it will not be able to recover a second time.

PARAGRAPH TWO COMPLETED:

Bar's cause of action against Abel would be for breach of contract. [The contract is not required to be in writing since it is for exactly one year from the time of its making. It is, therefore, valid even though oral.] Once again, damages would seem to be a serious problem. Furthermore, punitive damages would rarely be available in a contract action. Finally, Bar cannot recover the same damages twice. Hence, if it proceeds against Cole and recovers damages caused by Abel's breach of contract, it will not be able to recover a second time.

PARAGRAPH THREE:

STEP 1: Discuss third lawsuit mentioned, Abel vs. Cole. Write a topic sentence that will sum up the theory of the suit.

Topic sentence: Abel's lawsuit against Cole will be based upon fraud and breach of contract.

STEP 2: State defenses.

There were fraudulent statements made by Cole with the requisite intent and that were possibly to Abel's detriment. The breach of contract by Cole is obvious.

STEP 3: Back up these statements with law and facts from the question scenario.

However, the contract that Cole induced Abel to enter into and which it subsequently breached was an illegal contract, that is, one calling for the commission of a tort.

STEP 4: Explain possible problems to recovery and possible outcome.

Therefore, both parties are likely to be treated as wrongdoers, and Abel will be denied recovery.

PARAGRAPH THREE COMPLETED:

Abel's lawsuit against Cole will be based upon fraud and breach of contract. There were fraudulent statements made by Cole with the requisite intent and that were possibly to Abel's detriment. The breach of contract by Cole is obvious. However, the contract that Cole induced Abel to enter into and which it subsequently breached was an illegal contract, that is, one calling for the commission of a tort. Therefore, both parties are likely to be treated as wrongdoers, and Abel will be denied recovery.

PARAGRAPH EDITING:

After you have written your essay, go back over your work to check for the six characteristics that the AICPA will be looking for; coherent organization, conciseness, clarity, use of standard English, responsiveness to the requirements of the question, and appropriateness to the reader.

DIAGNOSTIC QUIZ

The following quiz is designed to test your knowledge of standard English. The correct answers follow the quiz, along with references to the sections that cover that particular area. By identifying the sections that are troublesome for you, you will be able to assess your weaknesses and concentrate on reviewing these areas. If you simply made a lucky guess, you'd better do a review anyway.

CIRCLE THE CORRECT CHOICE IN THE BRACKETS FOR ITEMS 1 THROUGH 17.

1. The company can assert any defenses against third party beneficiaries that [they have/it has] against the promisee.

2. Among those securities [which/that] are exempt from registration under the 1933 Act [are/is] a class of stock given in exchange for another class by the issuer to its existing stockholders without the [issuer's/issuer] paying a commission.

3. This type of promise will not bind the promisor [as/because/since] there is no mutuality of obligation.

4. Under the cost method, treasury stock is presented on the balance sheet as an unallocated reduction of total [stockholders'/stockholders/stockholder's] equity.

5. Jones wished that he [was/were] not bound by the offer he made Smith, while Smith celebrated [his/him] having accepted the offer.

6. [Non-cash/Noncash] investing and financing transactions are not reported in the statement of cash flows because the statement reports only the [affects/effects] of operating, investing, and financing activities that directly [affect/effect] cash flows.

7. Since [its/it's] impossible to predict the future and because prospective financial statements can be [effected/affected] by numerous factors, the accountant must use [judgment/judgement] to estimate when and how conditions are [likely/liable] to change.

8. A common format of bank reconciliation statements [is/are] to reconcile both book and bank balances to a common amount known as the "true balance."

9. Corporations, clubs, churches, and other entities may be beneficiaries so long as they are sufficiently identifiable to permit a determination of [who/whom] is empowered to enforce the terms of the trust.

10. None of the beneficiaries [was/were] specifically referred to in the will.

11. Either Dr. Kline or Dr. Monroe [have/has] been elected to the board of directors.

12. The letter should be signed by Bill and [me/myself].

13. Any trust [which/that] is created for an illegal purpose is invalid.

14. When the nature of relevant information is such that it cannot appear in the accounts, this [principal/principle] dictates that such relevant information be included in the accompanying notes to the financial statements. Financial reporting is the [principal/principle] means of communicating financial information to those outside an entity.

15. The inheritance was divided [between/among] several beneficiaries.

16. Termination of an offer ends the offeree's power to [accept/except] it.

17. The consideration given by the participating creditors is [their/there] mutual promises to [accept/except] less than the full amount of [their/there] claims. Because [their/there] must be such mutual promises [between/among] all the participating creditors, a composition or extension agreement requires the participation of at least two or more creditors.

FOLLOW INSTRUCTIONS FOR ITEMS 18 THROUGH 20.

18. The duties assigned to the interns were to accompany the seniors on field work assignments and the organization and filing of the work papers.

Fix this sentence so that it will read more smoothly. ______________________________

____

____

19. Circle the correct spelling of the following pairs of words.

liaison laison	privilege priviledge	paralleled paraleled
achieve acheive	occasion occassion	accommodate accomodate

20. Each set of brackets in the following example represents a possible location for punctuation. If you believe a location needs no punctuation, leave it blank; if you think a location needs punctuation, enter a comma, a colon, or a semicolon.

If the promises supply the consideration [ ] there must be a mutuality of obligation [ ] in other words [ ] both parties must be bound.

ANSWERS TO DIAGNOSTIC QUIZ

Each answer includes a reference to the section that covers what you need to review.

1.	it has	Pronouns—Antecedents, p. C-27.
2.	that; is; issuer's	Subordinating Conjunctions, p. C-30; Verbs—Agreement, p. C-23; Nouns—Gerunds, p. C-26.
3.	because	Subordinating Conjunctions, p. C-30.
4.	stockholders'	Possessive Nouns, p. C-25.
5.	were; his	Verbs, Mood, p. C-22; Nouns—Gerunds, p. C-26.
6.	Noncash; effects; affect	Hyphen, p. C-20; Syntax: Troublesome Words, p. C-13.
7.	it's; affected; judgment, likely	Syntax: Troublesome Words, p. C-13; Spelling: Troublesome Words, p. C-22; Diction: List of Words, p. C-11.
8.	is	Verbs—Agreement, p. C-23.
9.	who	Pronouns, Who/Whom, p. C-26.
10.	were	Verbs—Agreement with Each/None, p. C-24.
11.	has	Verbs—Agreement, p. C-23.
12.	me	Pronouns, that follow prepositions, p. C-27.
13.	that	Subordinating Conjunctions, p. C-30.
14.	principle; principal	Syntax: Troublesome Words, p. C-12.
15.	among	Diction: List of Words, p. C-10.
16.	accept	Syntax: Troublesome Words, C-12

17. their; accept; their; there; among; Syntax: Troublesome Words, p. C-12; Diction: List of Words, p. C-10.

18. Two possible answers: Parallelism: p. C-15.

 The duties assigned to the interns were *accompanying* the seniors on field work assignments and *organizing* and filing the work papers.
 or
 The duties assigned to the interns were to accompany the seniors on field work assignments and *to organize* and *file* the work papers.

19. In every case, the **first choice** is the correct spelling.
 Refer to Spelling: Troublesome Words, p. C-21.

20. If the promises supply the consideration [,] there must be a mutuality of obligation [;] in other words [,] both parties must be bound. Refer to Punctuation, p. C-16.

Scoring

Count one point for each item (some numbers contain more than one item) and one point for question number 18 if your sentence came close to the parallelism demonstrated by the answer choices. There are a total of 40 points.

If you scored 37-40, you did very well. A brief review of the items you missed should be sufficient to make you feel fairly confident about your grammar skills.

If you scored 33-36, you did fairly well—better than average—but you should do a thorough review of the items you missed.

If you scored 29-32, your score was average. Since "average" will probably not make it on the CPA exam, you might want to consider a thorough grammar review, in addition to the items you missed.

If you scored below average (28 or less), you **definitely** should make grammar review a high priority when budgeting your exam study time. You should consider using resources beyond those provided here.

SENTENCE STRUCTURE

A sentence is a statement or question, consisting of a subject and a predicate. A subject, at a minimum is a noun, usually accompanied by one or more modifiers (for example, "The Trial Balance"). A predicate consists, at a minimum, of a verb. Cultivate the habit of a quick verification for a subject, predicate, capitalized first word, and ending punctuation in each sentence of an essay. A study of sentence structure is essentially a study of grammar but also moves just beyond grammar to diction, syntax, and parallelism. As we discuss how sentences are structured, there will naturally be some overlapping with grammar.

DICTION

Diction is appropriate word choice. There is no substitute for a diversified vocabulary. If you have a diversified vocabulary or "a way with words," you are already a step ahead. A good general vocabulary, as well as a good accounting vocabulary, is a prerequisite of the CPA exam. Develop your vocabulary as you review for the Exam.

An important aspect of choosing the right words is knowing the audience for whom you are choosing those "perfect words." A perfect word for accountants is not necessarily the perfect word for mechanics or lawyers or English professors. If a CPA exam question asks you to write a specific document for a reader other than another accountant or CPA, you need to be very specific but less technical than you would be otherwise.

Accounting, auditing, and related areas have a certain diction and syntax peculiar unto themselves. Promulgations, for instance, are written very carefully so as to avoid possible misinterpretations or misunderstandings. Of course, you are not expected to write like this—for the CPA exam or in other situations. Find the best word possible to explain clearly and concisely what it is you are trying to say. Often the "right word" is simply just not the "wrong word," so be certain you know the exact meaning of a word before you use it. As an accountant writing for accountants, what is most important is knowing the technical terms and the "key words" and placing them in your sentences properly and effectively. Defining or explaining key words demonstrates to graders that you understand the words you are using and not merely parroting the jargon.

The following is a list of words that frequently either are mistaken for one another or incorrectly assumed to be more or less synonymous.

Among—preposition, refers to more than two
Between—preposition, refers to two; is used for three or more if the items are considered severally and individually

> If only part of the seller's capacity to perform is affected, the seller must allocate deliveries *among* the customers, and he or she must give each one reasonable notice of the quota available to him or her.
> *Between* merchants, the additional terms become part of the contract unless one of the following applies. (This sentence is correct whether there are two merchants or many merchants.)

Amount—noun, an aggregate; total number or quantity
Number—noun, a sum of units; a countable number
Quantity—noun, an indefinite amount or number

> The checks must be charged to the account in the order of lowest *amount* to highest *amount* to minimize the *number* of dishonored checks.
> The contract is not enforceable under this paragraph beyond the *quantity* of goods shown in such writing.

Allude—verb, to state indirectly
Refer—verb, to state clearly and directly

> She *alluded* to the fact that the company's management was unscrupulous.
> She *referred* to his poor management in her report.

Bimonthly—adjective or adverb; every two months
Semimonthly—adjective or adverb; twice a month

> Our company has *bimonthly* meetings.
> We get paid *semimonthly*.

Continual—adjective, that which is repeatedly renewed after each interruption or intermission
Continuous—adjective, that which is uninterrupted in time, space, or sequence

> The *continuous* ramblings of the managing partner caused the other partners to *continually* check the time.

Cost—noun, the amount paid for an item
Price—noun, the amount set for an item
Value—noun, the relative worth, utility, or importance of an item
Worth—noun, value of an item measured by its qualities or by the esteem in which it is held

> The *cost* of that stock is too much.
> The *price* of that stock is $100 a share.
> I place no *value* on that stock.
> That stock's *worth* is overestimated.

Decide—verb, to arrive at a solution
Conclude—verb, to reach a final determination; to exercise judgment

Barbara *decided* to listen to what the accountant was saying; she then *concluded* that what he was saying was true.

Fewer—adjective, not as many; consisting or amounting to a smaller number (used of numbers; comparative of few)
Less—adjective, lower rank, degree, or importance; a more limited amount (used of quantity—for the most part)

My clients require *fewer* consultations than yours do.
My clients are *less* demanding than yours are.

Good—adjective, of a favorable character or tendency; noun, something that is good
Well—adverb, good or proper manner; satisfactorily with respect to conduct or action; adjective, being in satisfactory condition or circumstances

It was *good* [adjective] of you to help me study for the CPA exam.
The decision was for the *good* [noun] of the firm.
He performed that task *well* [adverb].
His work was *well* [adjective] respected by the other accountants.

Imply—verb, to suggest
Infer—verb, to assume; deduce

Her report seems to *imply* that my work was not up to par.
From reading her report, the manager *inferred* that my work was not up to par.

Oral—adjective, by the mouth, spoken; not written
Verbal—adjective, relating to or consisting of words
Vocal—adjective, uttered by the voice, spoken; persistence and volume of speech

Hawkins, Inc. made an *oral* agreement to the contract.
One partner gave his *verbal* consent while the other partner was very *vocal* with his objections.

State—verb, to set forth in detail; completely
Assert—verb, to claim positively, sometimes aggressively or controversially
Affirm—verb, to validate, confirm, state positively

The attorney *stated* the facts of the case.
The plaintiff asserted that his rights had been violated.
The judge *affirmed* the jury's decision.

SYNTAX

Syntax is the order of words in a sentence. Errors in syntax occur in a number of ways; the number one way is through hasty composition. The only way to catch errors in word order is to read each of your sentences carefully to make sure that the words you meant to write or type are the words that actually appear on the page and that those words are in the best possible order. The following list should help you avoid errors in both diction and syntax and gives examples where necessary.

TROUBLESOME WORDS

Accept—verb, to receive or to agree to willingly
Except—verb, to take out or leave out from a number or a whole; conjunction, on any other condition but that condition

Except for the items we have mentioned, we will *accept* the conditions of the contract.

Advice—noun, information or recommendation
Advise—verb, to recommend, give advice

The *accountant advised* us to take his *advice.*

Affect—verb, to influence or change (**Note:** affect is occasionally used as a noun in technical writing only.)
Effect—noun, result or cause; verb, to cause

The effect [noun] of Ward, Inc.'s decision to cease operations affected many people.
He quickly *effected* [verb] policy changes for office procedures.

All Ready—adjectival phrase, completely prepared
Already—adverb, before now; previously

Although the tax return was *all ready* to be filed, the deadline had *already* passed.

All Right; Alright—adjective or adverb, beyond doubt; very well; satisfactory; agreeable, pleasing. (Although many grammarians insist that **alright** is not a proper form, it is widely accepted.)

Appraise—verb, set a value on
Apprise—verb, inform

Dane Corp. *apprised* him of the equipment's age, so that he could *appraise* it more accurately.

Assure—verb, to give confidence to positively
Ensure—verb, to make sure, certain, or safe
Insure—verb, to obtain or provide insurance on or for; to make certain by taking necessary measures and precautions

The accountant assured his client that he would file his return in a timely manner.
He added the figures more than once to *ensure* their accuracy.
She was advised to *insure* her diamond property.

Decedent—noun, a deceased person
Descendant—noun, proceeding from an ancestor or source

The decedent left her vast fortune to her *descendants.*

Eminent—adjective, to stand out; important
Imminent—adjective, impending

Although he was an *eminent* businessman, foreclosure on his house was *imminent.*

Its—possessive
It's—contraction, **it is**

The company held *its* board of directors meeting on Saturday. *It's* the second meeting this month.

Lay—verb, to place or set
Lie—verb, to recline

He *lies* down to rest.
He *lays* down the book.

Percent—used with numbers only
Percentage—used with words or phrases

Each employee received 2 *percent* of the profits.
They all agreed this was a small *percentage.*

Precedence—noun, the fact of preceding in time, priority of importance
Precedent—noun, established authority; adjective, prior in time, order, or significance

The board of directors meeting took *precedence* over his going away.
The president set a *precedent* when making that decision.

Principal—noun, a capital sum placed at interest; a leading figure; the corpus of an estate; adjective, first, most important
Principle—noun, a basic truth or rule

Paying interest on the loan's *principal* [noun] was explained to the company's *principals* [noun].
The principal [adjective] part of...
She refused to compromise her *principles.*

Than—conjunction, function word to indicate difference in kind, manner, or identity; preposition, in comparison with (indicates comparison)
Then—adverb, at that time; soon after that (indicates time)

BFE Corp. has more shareholders *than* Hills Corp.
First, we must write the report, and *then* we will meet with the clients.

Their—adjective, of or relating to them or themselves
There—adverb, in or at that place

There were fifty shareholders at the meeting to cast *their* votes.

Modifier Placement

Pay close attention to where modifiers are placed, especially adverbs such as **only** and **even**. In speech, inflection aids meaning but, in writing, placing modifiers improperly can be confusing and often changes the meaning. The modifier should usually be placed before the word(s) it modifies.

She *almost* finished the whole report.
She finished *almost* the whole report.

Only she finished the report.
She *only* finished the report.
She finished *only* the report.

Phrases also must be placed properly, usually, but not always, following the word or phrase they modify. Often, **reading the sentence aloud** will help you decide where the modifier belongs.

Fleming introduced a client to John with a counter-offer. (*With a counter-offer* modifies *client*, not *John*, and should be placed after *client.)*
The accountant recommended a bankruptcy petition to the client under Chapter 7. (*Under Chapter 7* modifies *bankruptcy petition*, not *the client*, and should be placed after *bankruptcy petition.)*

Split Infinitives

Infinitives are the root verb form (e.g., to be, to consider, to walk). Generally speaking, infinitives should not be split except when to do so makes the meaning clearer.

Awkward:	Management's responsibility is to clearly represent its financial position.
Better:	Management's responsibility is to represent its financial position clearly.
Exception:	Management's responsibility in the future is to better represent its financial position.

Sentence Fragments

To avoid sentence fragments, read over your work carefully. Each sentence needs at least (1) a subject and (2) a predicate.

> Unlike the case of a forged endorsement, a drawee bank charged with the recognition of its drawer-customer's signature. (The verb *is*, before the word *charged*, has been left out.)

PARALLELISM

Parallelism refers to a similarity in structure and meaning of all parts of a sentence or a paragraph. In parallelism, parts of a sentence (or a paragraph) that are parallel in meaning are also parallel in structure. Sentences that violate rules of parallelism will be difficult to read and may obscure meaning. The following are some examples of different **violations** of parallelism.

(1) A security interest can be effected through a financing statement or the creditor's taking possession of it. (The two prepositional phrases separated by **or** should be parallel.)

Corrected: A security interest can be effected through a financing statement or through possession by the creditor.

(2) The independent auditor should consider whether the scope is appropriate, adequate audit programs and working papers, appropriate conclusions, and reports prepared are consistent with results of the work performed. (The clause beginning with **whether** (which acts as the direct object of the verb **should consider**) is faulty. The items mentioned must be similarly constructed to each other.)

Corrected: The independent auditor should consider whether the scope is appropriate, audit programs and working papers are adequate, conclusions are appropriate, and reports prepared are consistent with results of the work performed.

(3) The CPA was responsible for performing the inquiry and analytical procedures and that the review report was completed in a timely manner. (The prepositional phrase beginning with **for** is faulty.)

Corrected: The CPA was responsible for performing the inquiry and analytical procedures and ensuring that the review report was completed in a timely manner.

(4) Procedures that should be applied in examining the stock accounts are as follows:
(1) Review the corporate charter...
(2) Obtain or preparing an analysis of...
(3) Determination of authorization for... (All items in a list must be in parallel structure.)

Corrected:

1. Review the corporate charter...
2. Obtain or prepare an analysis of...
3. Determine the authorization for...

There are many other types of faulty constructions that can creep into sentences—too many to detail here. Furthermore, if any of the above is not clear, syntax may be a problem for you and you might want to consider a more thorough review of this subject.

NUMBERS

1. The basic rule for writing numbers is to write out the numbers ten and under and use numerals for all the others. More formal writing may dictate writing out all round numbers and numbers under 101. Let style, context of the sentence and of the work, and common sense be your guide.

The partnership was formed 18 years ago.
Jim Bryant joined the firm four years ago.
Baker purchased 200 shares of stock.

2. When there are two numbers next to each other, alternate the styles.

three 4-year certificates of deposit 5 two-party instruments

3. Never begin a sentence with numerals, such as:

1989 was the last year that Zinc Co. filed a tax return.

This example can be corrected as follows:

Nineteen hundred and eighty-nine was the last year that Zinc Co. filed a tax return. (For use only in very formal writing)
or
Zinc Co. has not filed a tax return since 1989.

CAPITALIZATION

This section mentions only areas that seem to cause particular difficulties.

1. The first word **after a colon** is capped only when it is the beginning of a complete sentence.

We discussed several possibilities at the meeting: Among them were liquidation, reorganization, and rehabilitation.
We discussed several possibilities at the meeting: liquidation, reorganization, and rehabilitation.

2. The capitalization of titles and headings is especially tricky. In general, the first word and all other important words, no matter what length they are, should be capped. Beyond this general rule, there are several variations relating to the capitalization of pronouns. The important thing here is to pick a style and use it consistently within a single document, article, etc.

For example, the following pair of headings would both be acceptable depending on the style and consistency of style:

Securities to which SFAS 115 Applies **or** Securities to Which SFAS 115 Applies
Issues for Property other than Cash **or** Issues For Property Other Than Cash

PUNCTUATION

PERIOD

Probably the two most common errors involving periods occur when incorporating quotation marks and/or parentheses with periods.

1. When a period is used with closing quotation marks, the period is always placed **inside**, regardless of whether the entire sentence is a quote or only the end of the sentence.
2. When a period is used with parentheses, the period goes **inside** the closing parenthesis if the entire sentence is enclosed in parentheses. When only the last word or words is enclosed in parentheses, the period goes **outside** the closing parenthesis.

(See Chapter 38, Contracts.)
The answer to that question is in the section on contracts (Chapter 38).

EXCLAMATION POINT

An exclamation point is used for emphasis and when issuing a command. In many cases, this is determined by the author when he or she wants to convey urgency, irony, or stronger emotion than ordinarily would be inferred.

COLON

A colon is used to introduce something in the sentence—a list of related words, phrases, or items directly related to the first part of the sentence; a quotation; a **direct** question; or an example of what was stated in the first part of the sentence. The colon takes the place of **that is** or **such as** and should never be used **with** such phrases.

> The accountant discussed two possibilities with the clients: first, a joint voluntary bankruptcy petition under Chapter 7, and second,...
>
> The following will be discussed: life insurance proceeds; inheritance; and property.
>
> My CPA accounting review book states the following: "All leases that do not meet any of the four criteria for capital leases are operating leases."

Colons are used in formal correspondence after the salutation.

> Dear Mr. Bennett:
> To Whom it May Concern:

Note: When **that is** or **such as** is followed by a numeric list, it may be followed by a colon.

When writing a sentence, if you're not sure whether or not a colon is appropriate, it probably isn't. When in doubt, change the sentence so that you're sure it doesn't need a colon.

SEMICOLON

A semicolon is used in a number of ways:

1. Use a **semicolon in place of a conjunction** when there are two or more closely related thoughts and each is expressed in a coordinate clause (a clause that could stand as a complete sentence).

   > A marketable title is one that is free from plausible or reasonable objections**;** it need not be perfect.

2. Use a **semicolon** as in the above example **with a conjunction** when the sentence is very long and complex. This promotes **clarity** by making the sentence easier to read.

   > Should the lease be prematurely terminated, the deposit may be retained only to cover the landlord's actual expenses or damages; ***and*** any excess must be returned to the tenant.
   >
   > An assignment establishes privity of estate between the lessor and assignee; ***[and]*** therefore, the assignee becomes personally liable for the rent.

3. When there are commas in a series of items, use a **semicolon** to separate the main items.

   > Addison, Inc. has distribution centers in Camden, Maine; Portsmouth, New Hampshire; and Rock Island, Rhode Island.

COMMA

Informal English allows much freedom in the placement or the omission of commas, and the overall trend is away from commas. However, standard, formal English provides rules for its usage. Accounting "language" can be so complex that using commas and using them correctly and appropriately is a necessity to avoid obscurity and promote clarity. Accordingly, we encourage you to learn the basics about comma placement.

What follows is not a complete set of rules for commas but should be everything you need to know about commas to make your sentences clear and concise. Because the primary purpose of the comma is to clarify meaning, it is the opinion of the authors that in the case of a complex subject such as accounting, it is better to overpunctuate than to underpunctuate. If you are concerned about overpunctuation, try to reduce an unwieldly sentence to two or more sentences.

1. Use a comma to **separate a compound sentence** (one with two or more independent coordinate clauses joined by a conjunction).

   Gil Corp. has current assets of $90,000, but the corporation has current liabilities of $180,000.
   Jim borrowed $60,000, and he used the proceeds to purchase outstanding common shares of stock.

   Note: In these examples, a comma would **not** be necessary if the **and** or the **but** were not followed by a noun or pronoun (the subject of the second clause). In other words, if by removing the conjunction, the sentence could be separated into two complete sentences, it needs a comma.

2. Use a comma after an **introductory word or phrase**.

   During 1992, Rand Co. purchased $960,000 of inventory.
   On April 1, 1993, Wall's inventory had a fair value of $150,000.

   Note: Writers often choose to omit this comma when the introductory phrase is very short. Again, we recommend using the comma. It will never be incorrect in this position.

3. Use a comma after an **introductory adverbial clause**.

   Although insurance contracts are not required by the Statute of Frauds to be in writing, most states have enacted statutes that now require such.

4. Use commas to separate **items, phrases, or clauses in a series.**

   To be negotiable, an instrument must be in writing, signed by the maker or drawer, contain an unconditional promise or order to pay a sum certain in money on demand or at a specific time, and be payable to order or to bearer.

   Note: Modern practice often omits the last comma in the series (in the above example, the one before **and**). Again, for the sake of clarity, we recommend using this comma.

5. In most cases, use a comma or commas to separate **a series of adjectives**.

   Silt Co. kept their inventory in an old, decrepit, brick building.
   He purchased several outstanding shares of common stock. (*No* commas are needed.)

When in doubt as to whether or not to use a comma after a particular adjective, try inserting the word **and** between the adjectives. If it makes sense, use a comma. (In the second example, above, **several and outstanding**, or **outstanding and several** don't make sense.)

6. Use a comma or commas to set off any **word or words, phrase, or clause that interrupts the sentence** but does not change its essential meaning.

   SLD Industries, as drawer of the instrument, is only secondarily liable.

7. Use commas to set off **geographical names** and **dates**.

Feeney Co. moved its headquarters to Miami, Florida, on August 16, 1992.

QUOTATION MARKS

Quotation marks are used with **direct quotations; direct discourse and direct questions**; and **definitions or explanations of words**. Other uses of quotation marks are used rarely in the accounting profession and, therefore, are not discussed in this review.

HYPHEN

1. Use a hyphen to separate words into syllables. It is best to check a dictionary, because some words do not split where you might imagine.

2. Modern practice does not normally hyphenate prefixes and their root words, even when both the prefix and the root word begin with vowels. A common exception is when the root word begins with a capital letter or a date or number.

prenuptial	nonexempt	semiannual
pre-1987	nonnegotiable	non-American

3. Although modern practice is moving away from using hyphens for **compound adjectives** (a noun and an adjective in combination to make a single adjective), clarity dictates that hyphens still be used in many cases.

long-term investments	two-party instrument
a noninterest-bearing note	short-term capital losses

4. Use a hyphen **only** when the compound adjective or compound adjective-adverb **precedes the noun**.

The well-known company is going bankrupt.
The company is well known for its quality products.

Note: There are certain word combinations that are always hyphenated, always one word, or always two words. Use the dictionary.

5. **Suspended hyphens** are used to avoid repetition in compound adjectives. For example, instead of having to write **himself or herself**, especially when these forms are being used repeatedly as they often must be in our newly nongender-biased world, use **him- or herself**.

10-, 15-, and 18-year depreciation	first-, second-, and third-class

SPELLING

Just as many of us believe that arithmetic can always be done by our calculators, we also believe that spelling will be done by our word processors and, therefore, we needn't worry too much about it. There is no doubt that these devices are tremendous boons to writers and others. However, although you soon will be able to use a calculator during the CPA exam, you will not be able to use a word processor. And like it or not, you will encounter many other situations where a spell-checker will not be available to you, so you'd better be able to **spell!** Also, a spell-checker cannot tell the difference between words that you have misspelled which are nonetheless real words, such as **there** and **their**. (See the list in this section of words often confused.)

Let's hit some highlights here of troublesome spellings with some brief tips that should help you become a better speller.

1. **IE** or **EI**? If you are still confused by words containing the **ie** or **ei** combinations, you'd better relearn those old rhymes we ridiculed in grade school.

"**i** before **e** except after **c**." (This works only for words where the ie-ei combination sounds like **ee**.)

ach**ie**ve	bel**ie**ve	ch**ie**f
ceiling	re**cei**ve	re**cei**pt

Of course there are always **exceptions** such as:

either neither seize financier

When **ie** or **ei** have a different sound than **ee**, the above rule does not apply. For example:

fr**ie**nd	s**ie**ve	effic**ie**nt
for**ei**gn	sover**ei**gn	surf**ei**t

2. **Doubling final consonants.** When an ending **(suffix)** beginning with a vowel is added to a root word that ends in a single consonant, that final consonant is **usually doubled.**

lag—lagging bid—bidding top—topped

The exceptions generally fall under three rules.

First, double only after a short vowel and **not** after a double vowel.

big—bigger	tug—tugging	get—getting
need—needing	keep—keeping	pool—pooled

Second, a **long** vowel (one that "says its own name"), which is almost always followed by a silent **e** that must be dropped to add the suffix, is **not** doubled.

hope—hoping tape—taped rule—ruled

Note: Sometimes, **as** in the first two examples above, doubling the consonants would create entirely new words.

Third, with root words of two or more syllables ending in a single consonant, double the consonant **only** when the last syllable is the **stressed syllable.**

Double:	be**gin**—beginning, beginner	pre**fer**—preferred, preferring
	regret—regretted, regrettable	ad**mit**—admitted, admittance
Don't Double:	pro**hi**bit—prohibited, prohibitive	**ben**efit—benefited, benefiting
	de**vel**op—developing	**pref**erence—preferable

3. **Drop** the silent **e** before adding a suffix **beginning with a vowel.**

store—storing take—taking value—valuing

Keep the **e** before adding a suffix **beginning with a consonant**, such as:

move—movement achieve—achievement

Again, there are **exceptions.**

e: mile—mileage dye—dyeing

No e: argue—argument due—duly true—ruly

4. Change **y** to **ie** before adding **s** when it is the single final vowel.

country—countries study—studies quantity—quantities

Change **y** to **i** before adding other endings **except s**.

busy—business dry—drier copy—copier

Exceptions: Keep **y** for the following:

copying studying trying

Y is also usually preserved when it follows another vowel.

delays joys played

Exceptions:

day—daily lay—laid pay—paid say—said

5. **Forming Plurals.** The formation of some plurals does not follow the general rule of adding **s** or **es** to the singular. What follows are some of the more troublesome forms.
Some singular nouns that end in **o** form their plurals by adding **s**; some by adding **es**.

ratio**s** zeros hero**es** potato**es**

Many nouns taken directly from **foreign languages** retain their original plural. Below are a few of the more common ones.

alumnus—alumni basis—bases crisis—crises
criterion—criteria datum—data matrix—matrices

Other nouns taken directly from foreign languages have **two acceptable plural forms**: the foreign language plural and the anglicized plural. Here are some of the more common:

medium—media, mediums appendix—appendices, appendixes
formula—formulae, formulas memorandum—memoranda, memorandums

Finally, in this foreign language category are some commonly used Latin nouns that form their plurals by adding **es**.

census—censuses consensus—consensuses
hiatus—hiatuses prospectus—prospectuses

Troublesome Words: Spelling

Spelling errors occur for different reasons; probably the most common reason is confusion with the spelling of similar words. The following is a list of commonly misspelled words. You will find those you may have misspelled in taking the Diagnostic Quiz, and you may recognize others you have problems with. Memorize them. (Note: some of these words may have acceptable alternative spellings; however, the spellings listed below are the preferred form.)

accommodate bankruptcy irrelevant paralleled skillful
achieve deferred judgment privilege supersede
acknowledgment existence liaison receivable surety
balance fulfill occasion resistance trial

GRAMMAR

This section on grammar is intended to be a brief overview only. Consequently, the authors have chosen to focus on items that seem to cause the most problems. If you did not do well on the Diagnostic Quiz, you would be well advised to go over all the material in this section and consider a more thorough grammar study than provided here.

VERBS

The verb is the driving force of the sentence: it is the word or words to which all other parts of the sentence relate. When trying to analyze a sentence to identify its grammatical parts or its meaning, or when attempting to amend a sentence, you should always identify the verb or verbs first. A verb expresses action or being.

Action: The accountant *visits* his clients regularly.
Being: Kyle *is* an accountant.

VOICE

1. The **active voice** indicates that the subject of the sentence (the person or thing) does something. The **passive voice** indicates that the subject is acted upon.

   Active: *The accountant worked* on the client's financial statements.
   Passive: The client's financial statements *were worked on by the accountant.*

2. The most important thing to understand about voice is that it should be consistent; that is, you should avoid shifts from one voice to another, especially within the same sentence as below.

   Taylor Corporation *hired* an independent computer programmer to develop a simplified payroll application for its new computer, and an on-line, data-based microcomputer system *was developed.*

   Use the active voice for the entire sentence:

   Taylor Corporation *hired* an independent computer programmer to develop a simplified payroll application for its new computer, and he *developed* an on-line, data-based microcomputer system.

MOOD

1. Common errors in syntax are made when **more than one mood** is used in a single sentence. The first example that follows begins with the **imperative** and shifts to the **indicative.** The second example corrects the sentence by using the imperative in both clauses, and the third example corrects the sentence by using the indicative in both clauses. The fourth example avoids the problem by forming two sentences.

   Pick up (imperative) that work program for me at the printer, and then we will go (indicative) to the client.
   Pick up that work program for me at the printer, and then go to the client with me.
   After you pick up that work program for me at the printer, we will go to the client.
   Pick up that work program for me at the printer. Then we will go to the client.

2. There are three moods: the indicative, the imperative, and the subjunctive. We do not examine the subjunctive. Most sentences are **indicative**:

   The percentage-of-completion method is justified. Declarative indicative.
   Is the percentage-of-completion method justified? Interrogative indicative.

3. Sentences that give a command are called **imperative** sentences:

   Pick up your books!
   Be sure to use the correct method of accounting for income taxes.

Tense

1. Tense is all about *time.* If the proper sequence of tenses is not used, confusion can arise as to what happened when. Consider:

   Not getting the raise he was expecting, John was unhappy about the additional work load. [???]
   Having not gotten the raise he was expecting, John was unhappy about the additional work load. [Much clearer]

2. The **present tense** is used to express action or a state of being that is taking place in the present. The present tense is also used to express an action or a state of being that is habitual and when a definite time in the future is stated.

   Dan *is taking* his CPA exam.
   Robin *goes* to the printer once a week.
   The new computer *arrives* on Monday.

3. The **present perfect tense** is used to indicate action that began in the past and has continued to the present.

   From the time of its founder, the CPA firm *has celebrated* April 16 with a fabulous dinner party.

4. The **future tense** is used to indicate action that takes place in the indefinite future.

   A plan of reorganization *will determine* the amount and the manner in which the creditors *will be paid*, in what form the business *will continue*, and any other necessary details.

5. The **future perfect tense** is used to indicate action that has not taken place yet but will take place before a specific future time.

   Before Susan arrives at the client's office, the client *will have prepared* the documents she needs.

6. The **past tense** is used to indicate an action that took place in the past. The **past tense** is also used to indicate a condition or state occurring at a specific time in the past.

   The predecessor auditor *resigned* last week.
   The company *contacted* its auditor the first of every new year.

7. The **past perfect tense** is used to indicate an action that is completed before another action that also took place in the past.

   The work load *had been* so heavy that she was required to work overtime. (Not *was*)

Agreement

1. The first element of agreement to examine is **verb** and **subject**. These two components must agree **in number**. Number is just one of several things to consider when examining the agreement of the components of a sentence.

2. The subject of the sentence is the noun or pronoun (person, place, or thing) doing the action stated by the verb (in the case of the active voice) or being acted upon by the verb (in the case of the passive voice). Although the subject normally precedes the verb, this is not always the case. Thus, you must be able to identify sentence elements no matter where they happen to fall. This is not a difficult matter, at least most of the time. Consider:

   (1) Lewis, Bradford, Johnson & Co. [is or are] the client with the best pay record.

   (2) For me, one of the most difficult questions on the exam [was or were] concerned with correcting weaknesses in internal controls.

In both examples, the first choice, the singular verb form, is correct. In sentence (1), Lewis, Bradford, Johnson & Co. is considered singular in number because we are talking about the company, not Lewis, Bradford, and Johnson per se. In sentence (2), the verb is also singular because **one** is the subject of the sentence, not **questions**. **Questions** is the object of the preposition **of**. If this seems confusing, rearrange the sentence so that the prepositional phrase appears first, and the agreement of subject and verb will be clearer. Thus:

> Of the most difficult questions, one *was concerned* with correcting weaknesses in internal controls.

We will address special problems associated with prepositional phrases in other sections.

3. Beware of the word **number**. When it is preceded by the word **the**, it is always singular, and when it is preceded by the word **a**, it is always plural.

> *The number* of listings generated by the new EDP system *was* astounding.
> *A number* of listings *were generated* by the new EDP system.

4. A **compound subject**, even when made up of nouns singular in number, always takes a plural verb.

> The balance sheet, the independent auditor's report, and the quarterly report *are lying* on the desk. (Not *is lying)*

5. Continuing now with **compound subjects**, let's address the problem of when there are two or more subjects—one (or more) singular and one (or more) plural. When the sentence contains subjects connected by **or** or **nor**, or **not only...but also**, the verb should agree with the subject nearer to the verb.

> Either the auditors or the partner *is going* to the client.
> Not only the partner but also the auditors *are going* to the client.

In the case of the first example above, which sounds awkward, simply switch the order of the subjects **(the partner; the auditors)** and use the verb **are going** to make it read better.

6. When one subject is **positive** and one is **negative**, the verb always agrees with the positive.

> The partner, and not the auditors, *is going* to the client.
> Not the partner but the auditors frequently go to the client.

7. You should use **singular verbs** with the following: **each, every, everyone, everybody, anyone, anybody, either, neither, someone, somebody, no one, nobody,** and **one**.

> Anybody who wants to go *is* welcome.
> Neither the accountant nor the bookkeeper ever *arrives* on time.
> One never *knows* what to expect.

Watch out for the words **each** and **none**. They can trip up even careful writers.

8. Improper placement of **each** in the sentence will confuse the verb agreement.

> The balance sheet, the income statement, and the statement of cash flows each [*has/have*] several errors.

In this example, we know that the verb must be **has** (to agree with **each**), but then again, maybe it should be **have** to agree with the subjects. The problem is that we have a sentence with a compound subject that must take a plural verb, but here it is connected with a singular pronoun (each). This is a very common error. This particular example may be fixed in one of two ways. First, if the word **each** is not really necessary in the sentence, simply drop it. Second, simply place the word **each** in a better position in the sentence. In the example below, placing the word **each** at the end of the sentence properly connects it to **errors**; also it no longer confuses verb agreement.

The balance sheet, the income statement, and the statement of cash flows *have* several errors *each*.

9. The word **none** has special problems all its own. Not too many years ago, it was the accepted rule that every time **none** was the subject of the sentence, it should take a **singular verb**. Most modern grammarians now agree that the plural may be used when followed by a prepositional phrase with a plural object (noun) or with an object whose meaning in the sentence is plural.

   None of the statements *were* correct.

   When **none** stands alone, some purists believe it should take the singular and others believe that the plural is the proper form when the meaning conveys plurality. Consequently, in the following example, either the singular or plural is generally acceptable.

   All the financial statements had been compiled, but none *was* **or** *were* correct.

> When in doubt, use **not one** in place of **none** (with a singular verb, of course).

NOUNS

Nouns are people, places, and things and can occur anywhere in the sentence. Make sure that, when necessary, the nouns are the same in number.

Do the exercises at the end of each chapter by answering the *questions* true or false. (Not singular *question*)
At the end of the engagement, everyone must turn in their *time sheets.* (Not singular *time sheet*)

Possessive Nouns

1. The basic rule for making a **singular noun** possessive is to add an **apostrophe and an s.** If a singular noun ends in s, **add apostrophe and an s**. To make a **plural noun** possessive, add an **apostrophe alone** when the plural ends in **s** or an **apostrophe and an s** when the plural does not end in an **s**.

Singular:	client*'s*	system*'s*	beneficiary*'s*	*Chris'*
Plural:	clients*'*	systems*'*	beneficiaries*'*	

2. A common area of difficulty has to do with **ownership**, that is, when two or more individuals or groups are mentioned as owning something. If the ownership is **not common** to all, apostrophes appear after each individual or group. If the ownership **is common** to all, only the last individual or group in the series takes an apostrophe.

   Not common to all: The accountant's and the attorney's offices...
   Common to all: Robert, his brother, and their sons' company...

> Most of the confusion associated with possessives seems to be with the plural possessive. Remember to make the noun **plural** first and **possessive** second.

3. Modern usage tends to make possessive forms into adjectives where appropriate. Thus:

   Company's (possessive) management becomes *company* (adjective) management.
   A *two weeks'* (possessive) vacation becomes a *two weeks* or *two-week* (both adjectives) vacation.

> In most instances, either the possessive form or the adjectival form is acceptable. Go with the form that seems most appropriate for that particular sentence.

GERUNDS

1. A gerund is a verb changed to a noun by adding **ing**. A noun preceding a gerund must be possessive so that it may be construed as **modifying the noun.**

   Caroline's telecommuting was approved by the partner.

   In this example, the subject of the sentence is **telecommuting**, not Caroline or Caroline's. Since we know that nouns cannot modify nouns, Caroline must become **Caroline's** to create a possessive form that can modify the noun **telecommuting**.

2. The same holds true for **gerunds** used as **objects of prepositions**:

   The partner objected to *Caroline's telecommuting.*

   In this example, **telecommuting** is the object of the preposition **to**. Caroline's is an appositive (or possessive) form modifying **telecommuting.**

PRONOUNS

Like Latin where most words have "cases" according to their function in the sentence, English **pronouns** also have cases. Sometimes you may be aware that you are using a case when determining the proper form of the pronoun and sometimes you may not.

He met *his* partner at *their* office.

1. Let's begin by tackling everybody's favorite: **who and whom**. We're going to take some time reviewing this one since it seems to be a major area of confusion. There is little or no confusion when **who** is clearly the **subject** of the sentence:

   Who is going with us?

   And little or no confusion when **whom** is clearly (1) the **object** of the sentence or (2) the **object** of the preposition.

   (1) Jenny audited *whom*? *Whom* did Jenny audit?

   (2) Jenny is working for *whom*? For *whom* is Jenny working?

> If you are having difficulty with **questions**, try changing them into declarative sentences (statements) and substituting another pronoun. Thus: Jenny audits **them** (objective), obviously not **they** (subjective), or Jenny is working for **her**, obviously not **she**.

2. **Who** or **whoever** is the subjective case, and **whom** or **whomever** is the objective case. Common errors occur frequently in two instances: (1) when **who or whoever** is interrupted by a parenthetical phrase and (2) when an entire clause is the subject of a preposition.

   (1) *Whoever* she decides is working with her should meet her at six o'clock.

   In this example, **she decides** is a parenthetical phrase (one that could be left out of the sentence and the sentence would still be a complete thought). When you disregard **she decides**, you can see that **whoever** is the subject of the sentence, not **she**. The error occurs when **she** is believed to be the subject and **whomever**, the object of **decides**.

   (2) Jenny will work with *whoever* shows up first.

   This example represents what seems the most problematic of all the areas relating to who or whom. We have been taught to use the objective case after the preposition (in this case **with**). So why isn't **whomever** the correct form in this example? The answer is that it would be the correct form if the sentence ended with the word **whomever**. (**Whomever** would be the object of the preposition **with**.) In this case, it is not the last word but, rather, it is the **subject** of the clause **whoever shows up first**.

Again, make the substitution of another pronoun as a test of whether to use the subjective or objective case.

Let's look at a few more examples. See if you are better able to recognize the correct form.

(1) I'm sure I will be comfortable with [*whoever/whomever*] the manager decides to assign.

(2) To [*who/whom*] should she speak regarding that matter?

(3) He always chooses [*whoever/whomever*] in his opinion is the best auditor.

(4) She usually enjoys working with [*whoever/whomever*] the partner assigns.

(5) [*Who/Whom*] should I ask to accompany me?

Let's see how well you did.

(1) **Whomever** is correct. The whole clause after the preposition **with** is the object of the preposition, and **whomever** is the object of the verb **to assign.** Turn the clause around and substitute another pronoun. Thus, **the manager decides to assign *him*** .

(2) **Whom** is correct. **Whom** is the object of the preposition **to**. Make the question into a declarative sentence and substitute another pronoun. Thus, **She should speak to *him* regarding that matter**.

(3) **Whoever** is correct. The entire clause **whoever is the best auditor** is the object of the main verb **chooses**. **Whoever** is the subject of that clause. **In his opinion** is a parenthetical phrase and doesn't affect the rest of the sentence.

(4) **Whomever** is correct. The entire clause **whomever the partner assigns** is the object of the preposition **with**, and **whomever** is the object of the verb **assigns**. Again, turn the clause around and substitute another pronoun. Thus, **the partner assigns *him*.**

(5) **Whom** is correct. **Whom** is the object of the main verb **ask**. Turn the question into a regular declarative sentence and substitute another pronoun. Thus, **I should ask *her* to accompany me**.

3. Pronouns that follow prepositions are always in the **objective case**, except when serving as the subject of a clause, as discussed above. The most popular misuse occurs when using a pronoun after the preposition **between**. **(I, he, she, they,** are never used after **between**, no matter where the prepositional phrase falls in the sentence.)

   Between you and me, I don't believe our client will be able to continue as a going concern.
   That matter is strictly between her and them.

ANTECEDENTS

1. An antecedent is the word or words for which a pronoun stands. Any time a pronoun is used, its antecedent must be clear and agree with the word or words for which it stands.

   The accountant placed *his* work in the file.

   In this example, **his** is the pronoun with **the accountant** as its antecedent. **His** agrees with **the accountant** in person and number. **His** is used so as not to repeat **the accountant**.

2. Confusion most often occurs when using indefinite pronouns such as **it**, **that**, **this**, and **which**.

   The company for *which* he works always mails *its* paychecks on Friday.

In this example, the pronouns **which** and **its** both clearly refer to **the company**. Consider the next example. Since it is not clear what the antecedent for **it** is, we can't tell for sure whether the company or the paycheck is small.

The company always mails my paycheck on Friday and *it* is a small one.

3. So far in our discussion of antecedents, we have talked about agreement in person. We have not addressed agreement in **number**. The following examples demonstrate pronouns that **do not agree** in number with their antecedents.

   The company issued quarterly financial reports to *their* shareholders. (*Its* is the correct antecedent to agree in number with *company.*)

   Each of the methods is introduced on a separate page, so that the student is made aware of *their* importance. (*Its* is the correct antecedent to agree in number with *each.*) **Note: Importance** refers to **each**, the subject of the sentence, not to **methods,** which is the object of the preposition **of.**

4. When a pronoun refers to singular antecedents that are connected by **or** or **nor**, the pronoun should be **singular**.

   Joe or Buddy has misplaced *his* workpapers.
   Neither Joe nor Buddy has misplaced *his* workpapers.

5. When a pronoun refers to a singular and a plural antecedent connected by **or** or **nor**, the pronoun should be **plural**.

   Neither Joe nor his associates can locate *their* workpapers.

6. Pronouns must also agree with their antecedents in **gender**. Because English language has no way of expressing gender-neutral in pronoun agreement, it has been the custom to use **his** as a convenience when referring to both sexes. To avoid this "gender bias" in writing, there is a growing use of a more cumbersome construction in order to be more politically correct.

   Old: When a new partner's identifiable asset contribution is less than the ownership interest *he* is to receive, the excess capital allowed *him* is considered as goodwill attributable to *him.*

   New: When a new partner's identifiable asset contribution is less than the ownership interest *he or she* is to receive, the excess capital allowed *the new partner* is considered as goodwill attributable to *him or her.*

   You will note in the above example that **he or she (he/she)** and **him or her (him/her)** have been used only once each and the antecedent **new partner** has been repeated once.

> The idea is to not overload a single sentence with too many repetitions of each construction. When it seems that **he/she** constructions are overwhelming the sentence, repeat the noun antecedent where possible, even if it sounds a bit labored.

7. **Reflexive pronouns** are pronouns that are used for **emphasizing their antecedents** and should **not be used as substitutes** for regular pronouns. The reflexive pronouns are **myself, yourself, himself, herself, itself, ourselves, yourselves, and themselves.**

   The financing is being handled by the principals *themselves.* (Demonstrates emphasis)
   The partner *himself* will take care of that matter. (Demonstrates emphasis)
   My associate and *I* accept the engagement. (Not my associate and *myself...*)
   I am fine; how about *you*? (Not how about *yourself?)*

ADJECTIVES AND ADVERBS

1. Most of us understand that adjectives and adverbs are **modifiers**, but many of us can't tell them apart. In fact, there are many words that can be used as either depending on their use. Consequently, differentiating adjectives from adverbs is really not very important as long as you know how to use them. Understanding, however, that **adjectives modify nouns or pronouns**, and **adverbs modify verbs** and adjectives will help you choose the correct form.

    Falcone Co. purchased *two* computers from Wizard Corp., a very *small* manufacturer. (*two* is an adjective describing the noun *computers, very* is an adverb modifying the adjective *small*, and *small* is an adjective describing the noun *manufacturer.*)

    Acme advised Mason that it would deliver the appliances on July 2 as *originally* agreed. (*originally* is an adverb describing the verb *agreed.*)

2. In writing for the CPA exam, avoid colloquial uses of the adjectives **real** and **sure.** In the following examples, adverbs are called for.

    I am *very* (not *real*) sorry that you didn't pass the exam.
    He will *surely* (not *sure*) be glad if he passes the exam.

3. **Comparisons** using adjectives frequently present problems. Remember that when comparing two things, the **comparative** (often **er**) form is used, and when comparing more than two, the **superlative** (often **est**) form is used.

    This report is *larger* than the other one.
    This report is the *largest* of them all.
    This report is *more* detailed than the others.
    This report is the *most* detailed of them all.

4. **Articles** are adjectives. **An** precedes most vowels, but when the vowel begins with a **consonant sound**, we should use **a.**

    a usual adjustment...
    a one in a million deal...

    Similarly, when **a** or **an** precedes abbreviations or initials, it is the next **sound** that we should consider, not the next letter. In other words, if the next sound is a vowel sound, **an** should be used. Usually, your reader will be reading the abbreviations or initials and not the whole term, title, etc.

    An S.A. will be used to head up the field work on this engagement.
    An F.O.B. contract is a *contract* indicating that the seller will bear that degree of risk and expense that is appropriate to the F.O.B. terms.

CONJUNCTIONS

There are three types of conjunctions: coordinating, subordinating, and correlative.

Coordinating Conjunctions

Coordinating conjunctions are conjunctions that connect equal elements in a sentence. These conjunctions include **and, but, for, yet, so, or,** and **nor**. Examples of common problems involving coordinating conjunctions:

1. Leaving out the **and**, leading to difficulties with comprehension and clarity.

    The accountant studied some of management's representations, marked what she wanted to discuss in the meeting. (The word *and* should be in the place of the comma.)

Mike's summer job entails opening the mail, stamps it with a dater, routing it to the proper person. (Should be: ...opening the mail from other offices, *stamping* it with a dater, *and* routing it to the proper person. **This example also demonstrates a lack of parallelism,** which is addressed in an earlier section.)

2. Omission of **and** is correct when the sentence is a compound sentence (meaning that it contains two independent clauses), in which case a semicolon takes the place of **and**. When the semicolon is used, the ideas of each independent clause should be closely related.

   The security is genuine; it has not been materially altered.

3. Although the rules for **or** and **nor** have become less strict over time, you should understand proper usage for the sake of comprehension and clarity. Most of us are familiar with **either...or** and **neither... nor**:

   Either the creditor must take possession *or* the debtor must sign a security agreement that describes the collateral.

   The company would neither accept delivery of the water coolers, nor pay for them, because Peterson did not have the authority to enter into the contract.

Subordinating Conjunctions

Subordinating conjunctions are conjunctions that introduce subordinate elements of the sentence. The most common and the ones we want to concentrate on here are **as, since, because, that, which, when, where,** and **while.**

1. As; Since; Because

Because is the only word of the three that **always** indicates cause. **Since** usually indicates **time** and, when introducing adverbial clauses, may mean either **when** or **because**. **As** should be avoided altogether in these constructions and used only for comparisons. We strongly recommend using the exact word to avoid any confusion, especially when clarity is essential.

Attachment of the security interest did not occur because Pix failed to file a financing statement. (Specifically indicates *cause.*)
Green has not paid any creditor since January 1, 1992. (Specifically indicates *time.*)

The following example is a typical misuse of the conjunction **as** and demonstrates why **as** should not be used as a substitute for **because**:

As the partners are contributing more capital to the company, the stock prices are going up.

The meaning of this sentence is ambiguous. Are the stock prices going up **while** the partners are contributing capital or are the stock prices going up **because** the partners are contributing more capital?

2. That; Which

Many people complain about not understanding when to use **that** and when to use **which** more than just about anything else. The rule to follow requires that you know the difference between a restrictive and a nonrestrictive clause. A **restrictive clause** is one that must remain in the sentence for the sentence to make sense. A **nonrestrictive** clause is one that may be removed from a sentence and the sentence will still make sense.

That is used with restrictive clauses; *which* is used with nonrestrictive clauses.

(1) An accountant who breaches his or her contract with a client may be subject to liability for damages and losses *which* the client suffers as a direct result of the breach.

(2) As a result, the accountant is responsible for errors resulting from changes *that* occurred between the time he or she prepared the statement and its effective date.

(3) A reply *that* purports to accept an offer but which adds material qualifications or conditions is not an acceptance; rather, it is a rejection and a counter-offer.

In example (1) above, the clause beginning with **which** is nonrestrictive (sentence would make sense without it). In examples (2) and (3), the clauses that follow **that** are restrictive (necessary for the meaning of the sentence).

> If you can put commas around the clause in question, it is usually nonrestrictive and thus takes **which**. Occasionally, there will be a fine line between what one might consider restrictive or nonrestrictive. In these cases, make your choice based on which sounds better and, if there is another **which** or **that** nearby, let that help your decision. (Unless truly necessary, don't have two or three uses of **which** or two or three uses of **that** in the same sentence.)

3. **WHEN; WHERE**

The most common incorrect usage associated with these words occurs when they are used to define something.

(1) Exoneration is *where* the surety takes action against the debtor, which seeks to force the debtor to pay his or her debts.

(2) A fiduciary relationship is *where* the agent acts for the benefit of the principal.

(3) Joint liability is *when* all partners in a partnership are jointly liable for any contract actions against the partnership.

The above three examples are **faulty constructions**. The verb **to be** (**is**, in this case) must be followed by a predicate adjective (an adjective modifying the subject) or a predicate nominative (a noun meaning the same as the subject), **not** an adverbial phrase or clause. These sentences should be rewritten as follows:

(1) Exoneration is *an action* by the surety against the debtor, which seeks to force the debtor to pay his or her debts.

(2) A fiduciary relationship is *the association* of the agent and the principal whereby the agent acts for the benefit of the principal.

(3) Joint liability is *the liability* of all partners in a partnership for any contract actions against the partnership.

4. **WHILE**

Formerly, **while** was acceptable only to denote time. Modern practice accepts **while** and **although** as nearly synonymous. In example (1), either while or although is acceptable. In example (2), **while** is **not** a proper substitution for **although**.

(1) *While/Although* Acme contends that its agreement with Mason was not binding, it is willing to deliver the goods to Mason.

(2) Under a sale or return contract, the sale is considered as completed *although* it is voidable at the buyer's election.

CORRELATIVE CONJUNCTION

The third type of conjunction is the **correlative conjunction**. We have briefly mentioned and presented examples of **either ... or** and **neither ... nor** earlier in connection with nouns, verbs, and agreement. Now we want to discuss these correlatives in connection with **parallelism.**

1. **Not only** should be followed by **but (also).**

   In determining whether a mere invitation or an offer exists, the courts generally will look *not only* to the specific language *but also* to the surrounding circumstances, the custom within the industry, and the prior practice between the parties.

2. Watch out for **placement of correlatives**. Faulty placement leads to faulty construction and obstructs clarity.

   The lawyer *either* is asked to furnish specific information *or* comment as to where the lawyer's views differ from those of management.

Below is the same sentence in much clearer form. Note that the phrases introduced by *either* and *or* are now in parallel construction: *either to furnish ... or to comment.*

> The lawyer is asked *either* to furnish specific information *or to* comment as to where the lawyer's views differ from those of management.

APPENDIX D
FINANCIAL STATEMENT RATIOS

Analytics (or analytical procedures) concern the test of plausible relationships. In the absence of changes in conditions, it is reasonable to expect relationships among the elements of financial statements to remain similar from one period to the next. Several common financial statement ratios are reproduced here for your information. For more coverage of ratio analysis, consult your FAR volume.

When computing a ratio, remember to consider the following:

1. Net or gross amounts (e.g., receivables).
2. Average for the period or year-end (e.g., receivables, inventories, common shares outstanding).
3. Adjustments to income (e.g., interest, income taxes, preferred dividends).

We suggest that you concern yourself with knowing how to arrive at the less common ratios, rather than rote memorization of ratios. For instance, when *margin* is in the ratio name, it usually is a reference to sales. Thus *gross margin percentage* is the gross margin divided by sales, expressed as a percentage, and *net operating margin percentage* is operating income divided by sales, expressed as a percentage. *Turnover* refers to the number of cycles in a fiscal period. Thus *total asset turnover* is sales divided by total assets.

1. Working Capital — Current Assets - Current Liabilities
2. Current Ratio — $\frac{\text{Current Assets}}{\text{Current Liabilities}}$
3. Acid-Test or Quick Ratio — $\frac{\text{Cash + Marketable Securities + Net Receivables}}{\text{Current Liabilities}}$
4. Defensive-Interval Ratio — $\frac{\text{Cash + Marketable Securities + Net Receivables}}{\text{Average Daily Cash Expenditures}}$
5. Debt to Equity — $\frac{\text{Total Liabilities}}{\text{Owners' Equity}}$
6. Times Interest Earned — $\frac{\text{Income Before Income Taxes and Interest Charges}}{\text{Interest Charges}}$
7. Times Preferred Dividends Earned — $\frac{\text{Net Income}}{\text{Annual Preferred Dividend Requirement}}$
8. Accounts Receivable Turnover — $\frac{\text{Net Credit Sales}}{\text{Average Net Receivables}}$
9. Number of Days' Sales in Average Receivables — $\frac{360}{\text{Receivables Turnover}}$
10. Inventory Turnover — $\frac{\text{Cost of Goods Sold}}{\text{Average Inventory}}$
11. Return on Total Assets — $\frac{\text{Net Income + Interest Expense (Net of Tax)}}{\text{Average Total Assets}}$
12. Number of Days' Supply in Average Inventory — $\frac{360}{\text{Inventory Turnover}}$

- The number of days' supply in average (ending) inventory can also be computed in the following manner:

$$\frac{\text{Average (Ending) Inventory}}{\text{Average Daily Cost of Goods Sold}}$$

- Average daily cost of goods sold is determined by dividing cost of goods sold by the number of business days in the year (e.g., 365, 360, 300, or 250).

13. Length of Operating Cycle — *Number of days' sales in average receivables* + *Number of days' supply in average inventory*

14. Book Value Per Common Share

$$\frac{\text{Common Stockholders' Equity}}{\text{Number of Common Shares Outstanding}}$$

- To determine common stockholders' equity, preferred stock is subtracted from total stockholders' equity at the greater of its liquidation, par or stated value. Cumulative preferred stock dividends in arrears are also similarly subtracted. Treasury stock affects the denominator as the number of common shares outstanding is reduced.

15. Book Value Per Preferred Share

$$\frac{\text{Preferred Stockholders' Equity}}{\text{Number of Preferred Shares Outstanding}}$$

- Preferred stockholders' equity is comprised of (a) preferred stock at the greater of its liquidation, par or stated value and (b) cumulative preferred stock dividends in arrears.

16. Return on Common Stockholders' Equity

$$\frac{\text{Net Income - Preferred Dividends}}{\text{Average Common Stockholders' Equity}}$$

17. Return on Stockholders' Equity

$$\frac{\text{Net Income}}{\text{Average Stockholders' Equity}}$$

18. Earnings Per Share

$$\frac{\text{Net Income - Preferred Dividends}}{\text{Average Number of Common Shares Outstanding}}$$

19. Price-Earnings Ratio

$$\frac{\text{Market Price Per Common Share}}{\text{Earnings Per Common Share}}$$

20. Dividend Payout Ratio

$$\frac{\text{Cash Dividend Per Common Share}}{\text{Earnings Per Common Share}}$$

21. Yield on Common Stock

$$\frac{\text{Dividend Per Common Share}}{\text{Market Price Per Common Share}}$$

INDEX

A

S

T

U

V

W

Y

Writing Skills Content

Answers to selected essay responses from Business Law & Professional Responsibilities, Auditing, and Financial Accounting & Reporting sections are used to assess candidates' writing skills. **Five percent** of the points available on each of these sections are allocated to writing skills. Effective writing skills include the following six characteristics:

1. Coherent organization.
2. Conciseness.
3. Clarity.
4. Use of standard English.
5. Responsiveness to the requirements of the question.
6. Appropriateness for the reader.

Due to the importance of writing skills, we discuss these six characteristics in the **Practical Advice** and the **Accounting for 5%** sections of this volume.